September 11-15, 2016
Haifa, Israel

Association for
Computing Machinery

Advancing Computing as a Science & Profession

PACT'16

Proceedings of the 2016 International Conference on Parallel Architectures and Compilation

Sponsored by:

ACM SIGARCH, IEEE, & IFIP

Supported by:

Intel, TCE, National Science Foundation,
Israel Science Foundation,
Minestry of Science, Technology & Space,
Technion – Israel Institute of Technology, IBM, Microsoft,
Mellanox Technologies, NVidia, Google, ARM, WeGreened.com,
and Israel-Europe R&D Directorate

Association for
Computing Machinery

Advancing Computing as a Science & Profession

The Association for Computing Machinery
2 Penn Plaza, Suite 701
New York, New York 10121-0701

Notice to Past Authors of ACM-Published Articles
ACM intends to create a complete electronic archive of all articles and/or other material previously published by ACM. If you have written a work that has been previously published by ACM in any journal or conference proceedings prior to 1978, or any SIG Newsletter at any time, and you do NOT want this work to appear in the ACM Digital Library, please inform permissions@acm.org, stating the title of the work, the author(s), and where and when published.

ISBN: 978-1-4503-4121-9 (Digital)

ISBN: 978-1-4503-4678-8 (Print)

Additional copies may be ordered prepaid from:

ACM Order Department
PO Box 30777
New York, NY 10087-0777, USA

Phone: 1-800-342-6626 (USA and Canada)
+1-212-626-0500 (Global)
Fax: +1-212-944-1318
E-mail: acmhelp@acm.org
Hours of Operation: 8:30 am – 4:30 pm ET

Printed in the USA

General Chairs' Welcome

We are very happy to welcome you to the 25th anniversary of *PACT* and host you in Haifa, Israel for the *2016 International Conference on Parallel Architectures and Compilation Techniques*. This is a unique closure – *PACT* started as a Data Flow Workshop in conjunction with ISCA 1989 in Israel and quickly evolved into a unique venue at the intersection of "classical" parallel architectures and compilers. The event will take place at the Dan Carmel Hotel, which hosted Micro 1999.

Putting together *PACT'16* was truly a team effort. We first thank the authors and presenters for providing the content of the program. We are grateful to the PC Chairs, members of the Program Committee and external reviewers who worked very hard in reviewing papers and providing feedback for authors. Sadly, Nacho Navarro passed away suddenly on February 28th; a great personal loss, to our PC, and to the community at large.

PACT'16 features an Artifact Evaluation process where an independent committee assesses the artifacts submitted by interested authors. Successfully evaluated papers receive a seal, and authors of the highest ranked artifact will also receive a special prize! The conference also features an ACM Student Research Competition (SRC) and a poster session.

We thank all the organizers who took part in building this event, including AE Chairs and committee members, SRC Chair and committee members, Workshop and Tutorial Chairs and organizers, Publicity Chairs, Submission and Publication Chairs, Financial Chair, Student Travel and Grants Chair, Steering Committee members, and volunteers for their diligent work to make PACT 2016 successful. Our special thanks to Lawrence Rauchwerger for his industrious efforts and assistance throughout the process of organizing this event. We thank the local organization led by Ruth Boneh together with Liraz Menchell Blumenkrantz; our technical sponsors ACM, IEEE, IFIP, NSF and in particular Ashley Cozzi from ACM for her help; our generous industrial sponsors Mellanox, IBM, Microsoft, NVidia, ARM, Google, HIPR and especially Intel; and our local supporters: The Technion and in particular Technion Computer Engineering center, The Haifa Municipality, The Israeli Ministry of Science, Space and Technology, Israel-Europe R&D Directorate and The Israel Science Foundation.

We specially thank the participants for making their way to Haifa to take part in PACT'16. We hope you have a great experience at the event and enjoy your stay in Israel.

Ayal Zaks **Bilha Mendelson**

PACT'16 General Chairs
Haifa, Israel

Message from the Program Co-Chairs

The International Conference on Parallel Architectures and Compilation Techniques (PACT) started as a Data Flow Workshop in conjunction with the ISCA 1989 in Israel but has quickly evolved into a unique venue at the intersection of parallel architecture and compilers.

This year we celebrate PACT's 25th anniversary as a mature multi-disciplinary conference that brings together researchers from modern hardware and software areas to present original research related to the parallel computing systems and their applications. PACT covers topics ranging from instruction-level and thread-level parallelism to low power wearable multicore systems and heterogeneous CPU-GPU computing systems.

This September, PACT returns to Israel, which represents a timely recognition of the contributions to the field made by researchers from this country. Haifa, our conference venue on the shores of the Mediterranean Sea, is home to a large and diverse set of high-tech companies and top universities.

PACT 2016 received 180 initial paper abstracts that materialized in 119 actual submissions from countries all over the world. The submitted papers have undergone a rigorous two phase review process. To maintain fairness and uniform standards, we have used a double blind review process throughout. Each of the 119 submissions has been reviewed in the first phase by at least three members of the Program Committee (PC) and External Review Committee (ERC). After the first rebuttal phase and one week of online discussions, reviewers reached a consensus to relegate about half of the submissions. Their authors were subsequently notified. In the second phase the remaining papers have received at least two additional reviews representing. After a second rebuttal period PC and ERC members continued their online discussions to either reach an early consensus or establish the need for further discussion at the PC meeting. Finally the PC members met on June 27 on the campus of the University of Chicago and accepted 31 of the 58 papers that advanced to the second stage. To improve the quality of the program almost half the papers were shepherded by a PC member.

Because there were many quality papers which could not be accommodated as regular contributions, the PC decided to invite several papers which had been reviewed during the second phase to be presented as posters at the conference. As a result 14 papers are be published as 2 page abstracts. The posters were presented during a special two hour late afternoon session. We found that the two phase review and two rebuttal periods resulted in a manageable average load of 9 papers for each PC member and offered authors timely opportunities to respond to all reviews.

This year we also had an Artifact Evaluation Committee which evaluated five submitted papers and gave all of them the AE stamp of approval. Many thanks go to Hugh Leather and his team for their hard work.

We would like to take the opportunity to thank all reviewers and the program committee for their reviews and fruitful online discussions. Special thanks go to the PC members who flew in from all over the world to the meeting in Chicago and deliberated for an entire day to produce the PACT 2016 program. We would also like to thank Professor Andrew Chien for hosting the PC meeting in his department at the University of Chicago.

Last but not least we would like to thank our General Co-Chairs, Bilha Mendelson and Ayal Zaks and their entire team for their excellent organization.

We hope you will enjoy the program and Israel, our host country.

Lawrence Rauchwerger **Wen-mei Hwu**

PACT'16 Program Chairs

Table of Contents

Session 7: Keynote

Session 8A: System Acceleration

Session 8B: System Optimization II

Poster Presentations

Student Research Poster Presentations

PACT 2016 Conference Organization

General Chairs: Ayal Zaks *(Intel, Israel)*
Bilha Mendelson *(Optitura, Israel)*

Program Chairs: Lawrence Rauchwerger *(Texas A&M University, USA)*
Wen-mei W. Hwu *(University of Illinois at Urbana-Champaign, USA)*

Workshops Chair: Yoav Etsion *(Technion, Israel)*

Tutorials Chair: Christian Fensch *(Heriot-Watt University, UK)*

ACM Student Research Competition Chair: Erik Altman *(IBM, USA)*

Finance Chair: Christophe Dubach *(University of Edinburgh, UK)*

Student Travel & Awards Chair: David Kaeli *(Northeastern University, USA)*

Artifact Evaluation Chairs: Hugh Leather *(University of Edinburgh, UK)*
Zheng Wang *(Lancaster University, UK)*

Publication Chair: EJ (Eun Jung) Park *(Los Alamos National Laboratory, USA)*

Submission Chairs: Nathan Thomas *(Texas A&M University, USA)*
Timmie Smith *(Texas A&M University, USA)*

Publicity Committee: Albert Cohen *(INRIA, France)*
Dibyendu Das *(AMD, India)*
Kei Hiraki *(University of Tokyo, Japan)*
Michael Gschwind *(IBM, USA)*

Local Organization: Ruth Boneh *(Technion, Israel)*
Liraz Menchell Blumenkrantz *(Technion, Israel)*

Program Committee: Pavan Balaji *(Argonne National Laboratory, USA)*
Calin Cascaval *(Qualcomm, USA)*
Albert Cohen *(INRIA, France)*
Jason Cong *(University of California at Los Angeles, USA)*
Dan Connors *(University of Colorado, Denver, USA)*
Bronis R. de Supinski *(Lawrence Livermore National Laboratory, USA)*
Chen Ding *(University of Rochester, USA)*
Michel Dubois *(University of Southern California, USA)*
Mattan Erez *(University of Texas at Austin, USA)*
Maria Garzaran *(Intel, USA)*
Bill Gropp *(University of Illinois at Urbana Champaign, USA)*
Thomas Gross *(ETH, Switzerland)*
Mike Gschwind *(IBM, USA)*
Yuxiong He *(Microsoft, USA)*
Maurice Herlihy *(Brown University, USA)*
Kei Hiraki *(Tokyo University, Japan)*
Jeff Huang *(Texas A&M University, USA)*
Robert Hundt *(Google, USA)*
Ravi Iyer *(Intel, USA)*
Daniel Jimenez *(Texas A&M University, USA)*
Hyesoon Kim *(Georgia Tech, USA)*
Angelina Lee *(Washington University St. Louis, USA)*
Jaejin Lee *(Seoul National University, Korea)*
Andrew Lumsdaine *(Indiana University, USA)*
Scott Mahlke *(University of Michigan, USA)*
Avi Mendelson *(Technion, Israel)*
Jose Moreira *(IBM, USA)*
Miquel Moreto *(UPC Barcelona, Spain)*
Nacho Navarro (1958-2016) *(UPC Barcelona, Spain)*
Michael O'Boyle *(University of Edinburgh, UK)*
Cosmin Oancea *(University of Copenhagen, Denmark)*
Keshav Pingali *(University of Texas at Austin, USA)*
Arch Robison *(Intel, USA)*
Larry Rudolph *(MIT, USA)*
Valentina Salapura *(IBM, USA)*
Xipeng Shen *(NC State University, USA)*
Mark Silberstein *(Technion, Israel)*
Marc Snir *(Argonne National Laboratory, USA)*
Yan Solihin *(NC State University, USA)*
Josep Torrellas *(University of Illinois at Urbana Champaign, USA)*
Pedro Trancoso *(University of Cyprus, Cyprus)*
Jennifer Welch *(Texas A&M University, USA)*
Yuan Xie *(University of California at Santa Barbara, USA)*
Pen Yew *(University of Minnesota, USA)*
Antonia Zhai *(University of Minnesota, USA)*

Steering Committee Chair: Kemal Ebcioglu *(Global Supercomputing, USA)*

Steering Committee:

Erik Altman *(IBM, USA)*
J. Nelson Amaral *(University of Alberta, Canada)*
Michel Cosnard *(INRIA, France)*
Skevos Evripidou *(University of Cyprus, Cyprus)*
Guang Gao *(University of Delaware, USA)*
Jean Luc Gaudiot *(University of California, USA)*
Costin Iancu *(Lawrence Berkeley National Laboratory, USA)*
Bilha Mendelson *(Consultant, Israel)*
Yale Patt *(University of Texas at Austin, USA)*
Lawrence Rauchweger *(Texas A&M University, USA)*
Valentina Salapura *(IBM, USA)*
Vivek Sarkar *(Rice University, USA)*
Gabriel Silberman *(Dell Research, USA)*
Marc Snir *(University of Illinois at Urbana-Champaign, USA)*
Josep Torrellas *(University of Illinois at Urbana-Champaign, USA)*
Mateo Valero *(UPC Barcelona, Spain)*
Kathy Yelick *(Lawrence Berkeley National Laboratory, USA)*

External Review Committee:

Aditya Agrawal
David Callahan
Aparna Chandramowlishwaran
Eiman Ebrahimi
Mootaz Elnozahy
Michelle Goodstein
Paul Gratz
Gagan Gupta
Francois Irigoin
Melanie Kambadur
Eun Kim
Tushar Krishna
Eren Kursun
Yun (Eric) Liang
Lei Liu
Li Lu
Brandon Lucia
Mikel Lujan
Sam Midkiff
Timothy Miller
Kunle Olukotun
Moinuddin Qureshi
Narasimha Reddy
TB Schardl
Martin Schulz
Roy Soumyaroop
Zehra Sura
Peng Tu
Najjar Walid
Lei Wang
Michael Wolfe
Carole Wu
Zhibin Yu
Huiyang Zhou

PACT 2016 Sponsors & Supporters

Big Data Analytics on Flash Storage with Accelerators

Arvind
Computer Science and Artificial Intelligence Laboratory
Massachusetts Institute of Technology
Cambridge, MA, USA
arvind@mit.edu

ABSTRACT

Complex analytics of the vast amount of data collected via social media, cell phones, ubiquitous smart sensors, and satellites is likely to be the biggest economic driver for the IT industry over the next decade. For many "Big Data" applications, the limiting factor in performance is often the transportation of large amount of data from hard disks to where it can be processed, i.e. DRAM. We will present BlueDBM, an architecture for a scalable distributed flash store which overcomes this limitation by providing a high-performance, high-capacity, scalable random-access flash storage, and by allowing computation near the data via a FPGA-based programmable flash controller. We will present the preliminary results for two applications, (1) *key-value store* (KVS) and (2) *sparse-matrix accelerator* for graph processing, on BlueDBM consisting of 20 nodes and 20TB of flash.

Keywords

NAND flash storage; In-storage computing; Big Data Analytics; Hardware Accelerators

Biography

Arvind is the Johnson Professor of Computer Science and Engineering at MIT. Arvind's group, in collaboration with Motorola, built the Monsoon dataflow machines and its associated software in the late eighties. In 2000, Arvind started Sandburst which was sold to Broadcom in 2006. In 2003, Arvind co-founded Bluespec Inc., an EDA company to produce a set of tools for high-level synthesis. In 2001, Dr. R. S. Nikhil and Arvind published the book "Implicit parallel programming in pH." Arvind's current research focus is on enabling rapid development of embedded systems. Arvind is a Fellow of IEEE and ACM, and a member of the National Academy of Engineering and the American Academy of Arts and Sciences.

PACT '16, September 11-15, 2016, Haifa, Israel
ACM 978-1-4503-4121-9/16/09.
http://dx.doi.org/10.1145/2967938.2970374

Combating the Reliability Challenge of GPU Register File at Low Supply Voltage

Jingweijia Tan
ECE Department
University of Houston
Houston, TX 77004
jtan12@uh.edu

Shuaiwen Leon Song
HPC Group
Pacific Northwest National Lab
Richland, WA 99354
Shuaiwen.Song@pnnl.gov

Kaige Yan
ECE Department
University of Houston
Houston, TX 77004
kyan@uh.edu

Xin Fu
ECE Department
University of Houston
Houston, TX 77004
xfu8@central.uh.edu

Andres Marquez
HPC Group
Pacific Northwest National Lab
Richland, WA 99354
Andres.Marquez@pnnl.gov

Darren Kerbyson
HPC Group
Pacific Northwest National Lab
Richland, WA 99354
Darren.Kerbyson@pnnl.gov

ABSTRACT

Supply voltage reduction is an effective approach to significantly reduce GPU energy consumption. As the largest on-chip storage structure, the GPU register file becomes the reliability hotspot that prevents further supply voltage reduction below the safe limit (V_{min}) due to process variation effects. This work addresses the reliability challenge of the GPU register file at low supply voltages, which is an essential first step for aggressive supply voltage reduction of the entire GPU chip. To better understand the reliability issues posed by undervolting and its energy-saving potential, we first rigorously model and analyze the process variation impact on the GPU register file at different voltages. By further analyzing the GPU architecture, we make a key observation that the time GPU registers contain useless data (i.e., dead time) is long, providing a unique opportunity to enhance register reliability. We then propose GR-Guard, an architectural solution that leverages long register dead time to enable reliable operations from unreliable register file at low voltages. GR-Guard is both effective and low-cost, and does not affect normal (i.e., non-faulty) register accesses. Experimental results show that for a 28nm baseline GPU under aggressive voltage reduction, GR-Guard can maintain the register file reliability with less than 2% overall performance degradation, while achieving an average of 31% energy reduction across various applications.

Keywords

GPU Register File, Process Variation, Fault Patching, Low-Voltage Design, Energy Efficiency

PACT '16, September 11-15, 2016, Haifa, Israel

© 2016 ACM. ISBN 978-1-4503-4121-9/16/09...$15.00

DOI: http://dx.doi.org/10.1145/2967938.2967951

1. INTRODUCTION

Energy efficiency has become a growing concern for modern GPU architecture design. Current GPUs conservatively operate at high supply voltages to tolerate worst-case scenarios due to static (e.g., process variation) and dynamic (e.g., voltage noise and aging) variations. As a consequence, a large amount of energy is wasted as power scales quadratically with supply voltage (V_{dd}). Supply voltage reduction at the chip level has emerged as a highly effective and promising approach to significantly improve GPU energy efficiency. Recent studies [28, 22] reduce the dynamic portion of the supply voltage guardband by smoothing the voltage noise on GPUs, and the effectiveness of these techniques heavily depend on program characteristics. However, no existing work has tried to lower GPU's V_{dd} below the safe supply voltage limit (V_{min}) by reducing the static portion of the voltage guardband (e.g., to tolerate process variation) determined at the chip-fabrication time, which is program-independent and can be used to further improve the energy efficiency beyond voltage noise smoothing [28, 22] and other traditional energy saving techniques (e.g., dynamic voltage and frequency scaling and power/clock gating). In this work, we explore the possibilities of further pushing V_{dd} beyond the V_{min} limit through combating the reliability challenges without hurting the overall performance.

Due to the process variation (PV) effects, the largest on-chip storage structure often determines a chip's V_{min} [40, 13, 14]. PV effects cause variations in transistor parameters due to the imprecise control capability at small feature sizes [37, 23, 39, 25]. Such impact from PV is especially exacerbated on large on-chip storage structures which usually constitute a large portion of the die area and contain numerous transistors, making the minimum supply voltage required by each cell to function correctly (i.e., $V_{min,cell}$) vary significantly. In order to ensure that all the storage cells operate reliably, V_{min} is determined by the cell with the highest $V_{min,cell}$. This unnecessarily increases the supply voltage of the other cells and reduces energy efficiency.

Unlike CPUs, the register file in GPUs is usually the largest on-chip data storage structure [3, 4, 2]. In order to support massive thread-level parallelism (TLP) and fast context switch among threads, GPUs are designed to have huge register files to hold the contexts of thousands of active threads [3, 4, 2]. For example, in NVIDIA Kepler GPUs [4] the register file is 3.75MB, and the register file size of the recent GPU products is larger than the size of their L1 and L2 cache combined [4, 3, 2]. Consequently, it occupies a large fraction of the die area and consumes a large amount of chip power [17, 21, 7, 26, 39].

Under a low supply voltage, the GPU register file becomes a major reliability hopspot due to its large size and susceptibility to process variations. Moreover, it is frequently accessed by thousands of concurrent threads and is very critical to the GPU performance. Thus techniques that can efficiently handle faulty register entries at low V_{dd} without hurting the overall performance are highly desired. They may enable substantial energy savings and serve as an essential first step to relax the limitation of the minimum V_{dd} requirement for the entire GPU chip. To the best of our knowledge, no such solutions currently exist. Although a variety of circuit- and architecture-level techniques [40, 31, 42, 10, 11, 33, 24] have been previously proposed to tolerate faulty entries at the cache and memory level, they are either incapable or too expensive to tolerate faulty GPU register entries at low voltages, which will be discussed in detail in a later section.

In this work, we address the reliability challenge of the GPU register file at low supply voltage in order to facilitate future aggressive chip-level V_{dd} reduction. First, to understand the reliability issues posed by undervolting, we rigorously model and analyze the process variation impact on GPU register file at different voltages. Based on the model, we observe that only a small percentage of the SRAM cells exhibit large $V_{min,cell}$, which indicates that substantial energy savings can be gained through proper voltage reduction if these small number of outliers can be tolerated. However, these outliers are spread across the entire register file due to PV effects, which may translate to a high percentage of the faulty register entries.

To tolerate these faulty register entries at low voltages, we make a key observation by analyzing the modern GPU architectures: due to the massive thread interleaving and the static register resource allocation that naturally exist in GPUs, the time duration that GPU registers contain useless data (i.e., *dead time*) is long, even comparable to the time they contain useful data (i.e., *live time*) in the majority of cases. More importantly, there are often many dead register entries at each cycle, and are rarely affected by different scheduling policies and software-level optimizations. This interesting observation offers great potential to redirect a large number of faulty register accesses to the dead register entries (we refer to these operations as "patching"), granting the capability of aggressive voltage reduction on GPU register file.

Finally, we propose *GR-Guard*, an architectural solution to tolerate faulty GPU register entries at low supply voltage, for achieving significant energy savings without hurting reliability. GR-Guard enables a simple yet effective *Warp Register Group (WRG)* level patching scheme to maintain GPU's efficient SIMT execution pattern, while hiding the patching overhead by leveraging the massive thread-level parallelism. It also does not affect normal (i.e., non-faulty) register accesses. Furthermore, we exploit the unique features of the GPU architecture to minimize its storage, area, and design overhead. For a 28nm baseline GPU, experimental results show that GR-Guard can enable reliable operations of the register file with less than 2% performance degradation under an aggressive voltage reduction, while achieving an average of 31% energy reduction. GR-Guard is also orthogonal to other energy saving techniques [28, 22, 17, 21, 7, 26, 34, 43, 18, 8, 20] enabling additional energy reduction. To summarize, this paper makes the following contributions:

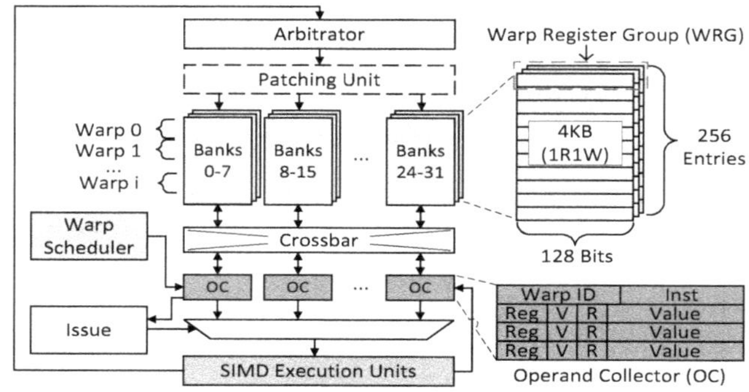

Figure 1: The structure of GPU register file in an SM (V: Valid bit, R: Ready bit).

- This work addresses a major GPU reliability hotspot under low-voltage operations, which servers as an essential step for enabling future GPU chip-wide low-voltage design. To the best of our knowledge, this is the first work exploring the opportunities and reliability challenges of reducing the supply voltage of GPU under process variation effects.
- By leveraging GPU's inherent long register dead-time, we propose an architectural-level low-cost and effective fault-patching design to achieve reliable operations from an unreliable register file at low supply voltages.
- After exploring various design spaces including processing technologies, scheduling policies, process variation ratios, and energy scalability, we demonstrate that our design can enable substantial supply voltage reduction while maintaining reliability with negligible performance overhead.

The rest of this paper is organized as follows. We discuss the background of this work in Section 2. In Section 3, through modeling and analysis, we explore reliability challenges of supply voltage reduction on GPU register file under process variation effects. We present our discovery of the fault-patching opportunities in Section 4. Section 5 details the design of GR-Guard and its overhead analysis. Section 6 presents the experimental methodology and Section 7 evaluates our proposed design. Finally, we discuss the related work and conclude the paper.

2. BACKGROUND: GPU REGISTER FILE

A modern GPU is composed of a number of in-order processors, also known as streaming multiprocessors (SMs) in NVIDIA GPUs [32][1] or Computing Units in AMD GPUs [9]. Each SM consists of hundreds of execution units that can support thousands of concurrent threads in flight. The register file in an SM is a statically allocated resource and each thread has its own physical register portion [21, 7, 39]. To enable low-overhead context switch, a large register file is provided by GPUs to hold all active thread contexts. For instance, typical NVIDIA Kepler GPUs [4] have 65536 32-bit

[1]In this paper, we use the NVIDIA CUDA terminology to describe the GPU architecture. However our work is independent of the terminology itself.

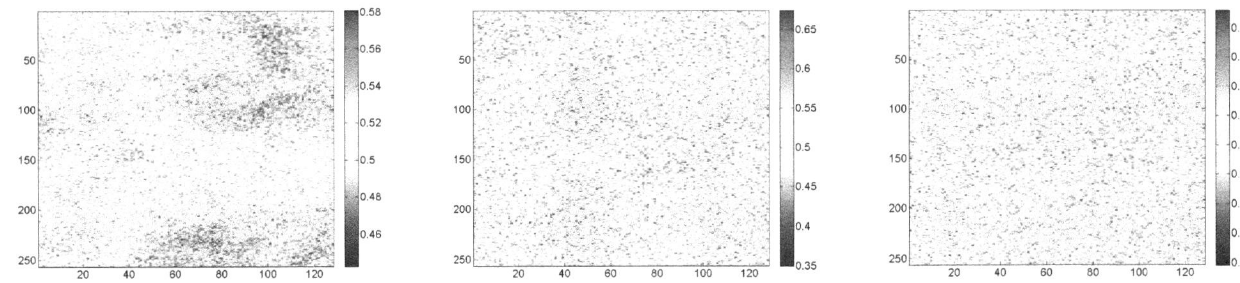

Figure 2: $V_{min,cell}$ variation map for a register bank (128 bits $\times$ 256 entries) of 3 different 28nm chips, (left) $\sigma_{rand} : \sigma_{sys} = 1 : 4$; (middle) $\sigma_{rand} : \sigma_{sys} = 1 : 1$; (right) $\sigma_{rand} : \sigma_{sys} = 4 : 1$. Individual dot represents $V_{min,cell}$ of each cell.

registers per SM, which is much larger than the register file sizes for commercial CPUs (e.g., only 336 physical registers per core on a Intel Haswell CPU [19]).

Each SM in GPU follows the Single Instruction Multiple Thread (SIMT) execution model by executing the same instruction with different operand values together from a group of threads (e.g., 32), called a warp. Before a warp executes an instruction, the operand values for all 32 threads are read from the register file. In the NVIDIA PTX standard, an instruction can read up to 4 registers and write 1 register [21, 39]. Thus a large bandwidth of 32 threads $\times$ 4 operand value is required. In order to avoid the high complexity by using multiple read ports, GPU register file is constructed with multiple SRAM banks to provide high bandwidth [17, 21, 26].

Figure 1 shows the structure of the baseline GPU register file used in this work, which is similar to the ones used previously [17, 7, 26].[2] Note that the patching unit is not part of the baseline and will be described later. A 128KB baseline register file in an SM is composed of 32 dual-ported (i.e., 1 read and 1 write port) 4KB banks [17, 26]. There are 256 register entries in a bank, each of which is 128-bit wide and contains four 32-bit registers. All the 32 same-named registers required by a warp (e.g., R0s of all threads within warp 1) are allocated to the same register entries of the 8 consecutive banks [26]. We refer to these same-named registers as a *warp register group (WRG)*. In every cycle, register access requests to different banks can proceed simultaneously, while concurrent requests to the same bank have to be serialized, causing bank conflicts. In order to handle the additional access latency caused by bank conflicts, operand collectors are used to buffer the operands without stalling the pipeline. When all the operands are ready in an operand collector, the instruction in it can proceed to the next pipeline stage.

3. RELIABILITY CHALLENGE ANALYSIS

In this section, we explore the reliability challenge of supply voltage reduction on the GPU register file under process variation effects through modeling and analysis. The observations and conclusions gained from this process enhance our understanding of the reliability issues and energy-saving potentials of voltage reduction on GPU register file.

[2]In this figure, we show a global crossbar similar to the baseline design introduced in [26]. However, our proposed design is also compatible with local crossbar design [17].

3.1 Modeling Process Variation Effects

Process variation is a combination of random effects (i.e., due to random dopant fluctuations) and systematic effects (i.e., due to lithographic lens aberrations) that occur during manufacturing. Random variations randomly differ the transistor parameters across the chip, while systematic variations cause nearby transistors to share the similar parameters. The transistor threshold voltage (V_{th}) and effective channel length (L_{eff}) are the two key parameters that are subject to variations [37, 23, 39]. Generally speaking, the variation of these two parameters can be represented as Equation (1) and (2) [37]:

$$\Delta V_{th} = \Delta V_{th,rand} + \Delta V_{th,sys} \quad (1)$$

$$\Delta L_{eff} = \Delta L_{eff,rand} + \Delta L_{eff,sys} \quad (2)$$

To better describe the cell-level reliability impact from voltage reduction, we model each SRAM cell's minimum supply voltage ($V_{min,cell}$) that enables reliable operations. We first model the V_{th} and L_{eff} values of all the transistors in a register file under process variation following the VARIUS model [37]. Based on these parameters, we then model the $V_{min,cell}$ value of all the cells by calculating the minimum supply voltage required by each cell to avoid the hold failure and write-stability failure based on the equations used in VARIUS-NTV [23].[3] Figure 2 shows the $V_{min,cell}$ distribution of 3 register banks from 3 chips under different random and systematic impact ratios (i.e., $\sigma_{rand} : \sigma_{sys}$) using 28nm technology (see Section 6 for the detailed experimental methodology). Note that 1:1 is a commonly used ratio for process variations in the previous literature [37, 23]. To better cover the design space, we further evaluate the other two relatively extreme scenarios, i.e., 1:4 and 4:1. Three of them together can adequately reflect the trend of the impact of different random and systematic effects on a chip. As shown, $V_{min,cell}$ exhibits large variations under various random and systematic impacts.

3.2 Reliability Challenge of Voltage Reduction

The minimum supply voltage required by the entire register file (referred as $V_{min,RF}$) is determined by the highest $V_{min,cell}$ value among all the cells, in order to ensure all the

[3]Note that we model the more robust 8T SRAM cell in this work instead of the traditional 6T SRAM cell [23, 33]. Read failures do not occur in the 8T SRAM, since the read access uses a different port and cannot flip the cell. Our proposed design though is independent of the SRAM cell structure itself.

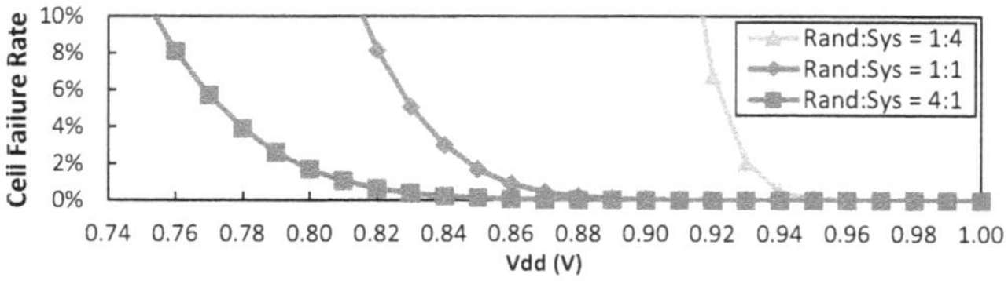

Figure 3: The average cell failure rate of the entire register file under different supply voltages (V_{dd}) for 100 chips using 28nm technology.

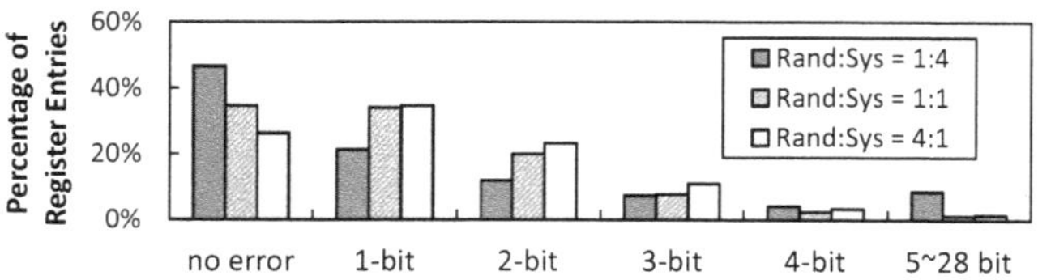

Figure 4: Distribution of register entries with different number of faulty bits (i.e., number of faulty cells in an entry) under 1% cell failure rate (corresponding to Figure 3).

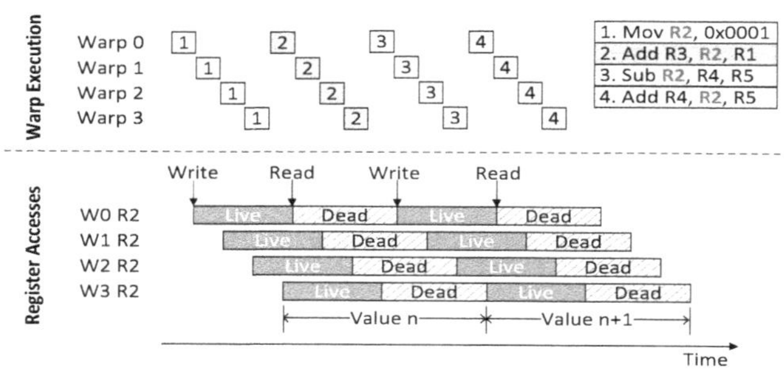

Figure 5: An example of warp execution and its register access sequence under RR.

registers function reliably. If V_{dd} of the register file is reduced below $V_{min,RF}$, some cells begin to fail. We define a cell as *faulty* if the V_{dd} is lower than its $V_{min,cell}$. We also define the *cell failure rate* as the number of faulty cells within the entire register file under a given V_{dd}. In this subsection, we analyze the impact of supply voltage reduction on cell failure rate.

Figure 3 shows the average cell failure rate for 100 28nm chips under three different $\sigma_{rand} : \sigma_{sys}$ ratios. The highest $V_{min,cell}$ under these three ratios are normalized to 1V to make the comparison clearer. As shown, under the same cell failure rate, the reduction range of V_{dd} becomes larger as the random impact increases. For instance, under a 1% cell failure rate, V_{dd} can only be reduced by 62mV under $\sigma_{rand} : \sigma_{sys} = 1 : 4$, while it can be reduced by 188mV under $\sigma_{rand} : \sigma_{sys} = 4 : 1$. This shows process variation impact ratio largely affects the value distribution of $V_{min,cell}$. The larger the random impact, the wider range of $V_{min,cell}$ values are distributed. In contrast, when the systematic impact dominates, cells show a more "clustering" effect, and tend to have similar $V_{min,cell}$. Figure 3 also shows that only a small percentage of the cells (e.g., <1%) have relatively large $V_{min,cell}$ values, called *outliers*. This indicates that significant power reduction can be achieved through proper voltage reduction if these outliers are tolerated.

We further model the location distribution of the outliers by calculating the number of error bits (or faulty cells) within a *register entry* (i.e., a row in Figure 2 consists of four 32-bit registers) under a given cell failure rate. Figure 4 shows the distribution of the register entries with different number of faulty bits under 1% cell failure rate. We present the distribution results under three $\sigma_{rand} : \sigma_{sys}$ ratios. For space reasons, we group the entries that contain error bits greater than or equal to 5 together. Note that since the register files of recent GPU products [4, 3, 2] are equipped with SECDED (Single-Error Correction, Double-Error Detection) ECC, single-bit errors can be corrected without causing program crash. Thus in this paper, we consider the register entries with no or one faulty bit as *reliable*, and the ones with multi-bit errors, which cannot be protected by SECDED ECC, as *faulty*.

Based on Figure 4, we can make two observations. (1) To gain significant power saving by allowing a small percentage (e.g., 1%) cells to fail (i.e., 188mV voltage reduction under $\sigma_{rand} : \sigma_{sys} = 4 : 1$ in Figure 3), GPUs need to tolerate a large number of faulty register entries (i.e., 31%-39%). (2) When the systematic effect dominates, the distribution of faulty cells tend to become more clustered, causing the number of faulty bits in some register entries to be very high, e.g., 28-bit. We use these observations to motivate our proposed design next.

4. FAULT-TOLERANCE OPPORTUNITY

To enable a reliable GPU register file under low supply voltage, efficiently tolerating faulty register entries becomes essential. We will start the discussion on why traditional techniques are impractical to tolerate a large number of GPU faulty register entries at low voltage. Then we introduce a unique GPU fault-tolerance opportunity that can effectively handle high percentage of faulty register entries.

4.1 Discussion on Traditional Techniques

A common solution to handle faulty memory cells is to apply row or column redundancy, which are used in industry for storage structure design [40]. However, these schemes are impractical when dealing with a large number of faulty register entries with multi-bit errors at low voltages. For example, 28 redundant columns are needed for each bank to handle the faulty register entries for the case shown in Figure 4, which translates to an additional 28KB storage overhead for a 128KB baseline register file, not to mention the decoder and remapping costs. This overhead can be even higher considering that the redundant columns may also contain faulty cells.

Stronger ECCs can be adopted [40, 24, 30] to better tolerate a high percentage of faulty entries with multi-bit errors. However, such ECCs require not only larger storage for correction codes but also complex and slow encoders/decoders to identify errors [40, 24]. For instance, under a rough estimation [30], 9 ECC bits are required for a 128-bit wide GPU register entry to correct single-bit errors, but as many as 16 ECC bits are required to correct double-bit errors. Thus the two common techniques above are not suitable fault-tolerance techniques for enabling low-voltage operations on GPU register file.

4.2 GPU Unique Fault-Tolerance Opportunity

We discovered that the GPU register file itself has a unique feature that can provide opportunities for "**patching**" faulty register entries effectively. "**Patching**" means redirecting

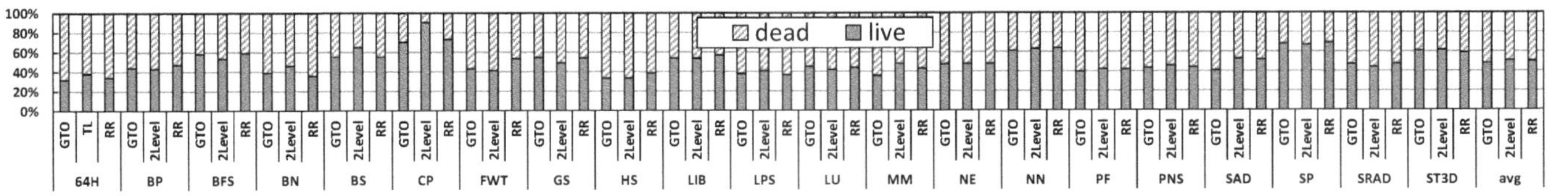

Figure 6: Average live and dead time portions for all register values within each benchmark under different warp scheduling policies. GTO [36]: *Greedy Then Oldest*; 2Level [17]: *Two-Level*; RR: *Round Robin*.

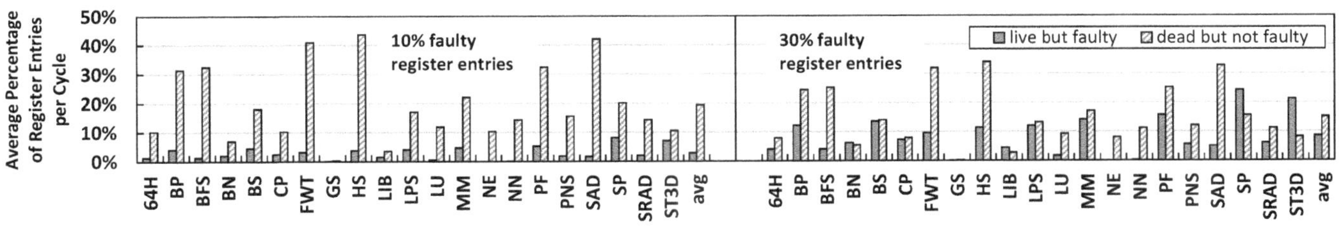

Figure 7: Average live register entries that are faulty and dead register entries that are not faulty per cycle for each benchmark, under 10% and 30% faulty rate of register entries using GTO scheduling.

the access to one register entry to another. First, when GPU interleaves the execution of thousands of concurrent threads within a simple in-order SM, the time interval between the execution of two consecutive instructions in the same thread is relatively long. Additionally, based on our observation, since each thread has its own register slot in the GPU register file, the access interval to the same physical register is also long. When a register value is dead (i.e., after the value's last read), the physical register contains useless data and will not become live again until the instruction that writes another value to the same register from the same thread is executed. *Live time* represents the cycles between a value's write and its last read. *Dead time* represents the cycles between a value's last read and the next value's write. Figure 5 illustrates an example of a register access sequence of four warps executing four consecutive instructions under Round Robin scheduling. Its lower half shows the read and write accesses to the Warp Register Groups (Section 2) for 'R2s'. Note that this instruction sequence makes sure that R2 is accessed in all four consecutive instructions and is reused immediately after it is dead, which is the best scenario that a compiler-level optimization can achieve for R2 to minimize its access interval and maximize its utilization. Due to thread interleaving and static register resource allocation, the access interval for each warp's R2 is greatly extended, leading to its long dead-time. Thus the GPU registers' long dead-time is a result of the GPU unique features and cannot be eliminated by the compiler.

Figure 6 further illustrates the average live and dead portions of the residency time (i.e., cycles between a value's write and the next value's write) for all the register values for various representative benchmarks under different warp scheduling policies. Despite the differences among the scheduling policies, the average dead time is comparable to the live time for the majority of benchmarks. The only exception is CP application under Two-Level scheduling [17], where the average dead time is only 10% of the residency time. This is because the majority of execution time in CP executes a computation intensive loop, which is dominated by back to back instructions. Since the two-level scheduler keeps scheduling the active warps until they are stalled by long latency operations, the register dead time during this loop is greatly reduced. Across all the benchmarks, the average dead time for each register value is between 48% and 51% for different warp schedulers.

To further explore if these dead-time opportunities can be used to patch a large amount of faulty register entries at low voltages, we obtain the average number of live and dead register entries per cycle during the execution of each benchmark. Under a given rate of faulty register entries $N\%$, we then estimate the average number of *live register entries that are faulty* (i.e., number of live register entries $\times$ $N\%$) per cycle, and the average number of *dead register entries that are not faulty* (i.e., number of dead register entries $\times$ (1-$N\%$)) per cycle. Figure 7 shows the results under GTO (Greedy-Then-Oldest) scheduling policy [36] for 10% and 30% faulty register entries respectively. Here we only show the results under GTO as an example since the observations for the other schedulers are very similar. Across all the benchmarks under 10% faulty rate, approximately 20% of the entries on average can be used to patch (i.e., dead but not faulty) in each cycle, while only 3% of the entries need to be patched (i.e., live but faulty). Similarly, under 30% faulty rate, 15% of the entries on average can be used to patch per cycle, while only 8% of the entries on average require patching. The majority of studied benchmarks have shown that adequate resources from register dead-time are available for fault-patching per cycle, except for SP and ST3D under 30% faulty rate of register entries. Overall, the register dead-time provides promising patching opportunities per cycle, even under a high percentage of faulty register entries.

Other possible patching opportunities come from the unallocated registers. In [7], authors observe that a large portion of the register file is not allocated to any thread during program execution for some GPU applications. However, such scenarios are application and optimization dependent. For instance, based on our experiments, the unallocated register portions of some applications such as SP and ST3D are very small (6% and 3% respectively). Note that all the benchmarks we use are default versions without aggressive optimizations for higher register usage. Take SP as an example, there are only 6% unallocated register entries, but there are on average of 8% and 24% live register entries that require patching *per cycle* under 10% and 30% faulty rate respectively, shown in Figure 7. Thus the limited unallocated registers may often be inadequate for patching (Section 7). Additionally, the unallocated entries may also contain multi-bit errors, which further limits this opportunity. Moreover, GPU on-chip resources are designed to support high thread-level parallelism and to be maximally utilized by programmers to achieve the peak performance. Since the opportunities provided by the unallocated registers heavily rely on applications and optimizations, they are not suitable to be used as the sole patching resources.

5. FAULT OCCLUSION WITH GR-GUARD

In this section, we present our proposed design named *GR-Guard*, which leverages the opportunities that naturally exist in GPUs (i.e., register dead-time) to occlude a high rate of faulty register entries at low voltages. Before explaining the GR-Guard's design, we want to clarify the following terms. A *faulty entry* is a register entry (128-bit wide) that contains multi-bit errors (Section 3.2). A *patching entry* is a *dead but not faulty entry* (Section 4.2) that is used to patch either a faulty entry or another reliable entry that is currently occupied for patching a previous faulty entry (named *occupied entry*). A *Warp Register Group (WRG)* (Figure 1) consists of 8 register entries from the same locations of 8 consecutive banks, and contains 32 same-named registers required by a warp (Section 2). A WRG may include a mix of reliable and faulty entries.

5.1 Identifying Register Dead Time

As shown in Figure 5, hardware cannot know if the register's read operation is its last read until another register value is written to the same physical register slot. Therefore, hardware is unable to detect the register dead time in advance. To address this, we leverage the compiler to identify the register dead time opportunities.

We first connect the basic blocks in backward order and perform the live variable analysis [12] at the instruction level. In this way, live register operands can be detected before and after the execution of each instruction. If a register is dead after an instruction execution, this instruction is the register operand's last read and it can be leveraged to patch a faulty entry. As introduced in Section 2, each instruction has at most four input operands based on the NVIDIA PTX standard [21, 39]. To indicate if the corresponding registers of an instruction are dead after its execution, one option is to add one bit for each source operand (four bits per instruction), which could cause nontrivial overhead. Since we are only interested in finding the dead registers, the exact live information for all the operands is not necessary. Based on our experiments, most instructions have at most two input operands for almost all the benchmarks. To reduce the overhead without losing patching opportunities, only two bits are added to each instruction to indicate whether the first two input register operands are dead. In this way, the first two input register operands can still be utilized for patching even for instructions with three or four input operands.

As discussed in Section 2, all the active threads within a warp access their same-named registers simultaneously. Thus after obtaining the register operand dead information of each instruction in the compiler, the hardware performs the register dead time identification at the *warp register group* (WRG) level. Control flow divergence may occur during the program execution, which causes different threads within a warp to execute distinct paths. In order to ensure the correctness of register dead time identification (i.e., the active threads in a warp will not mistakenly mark the live registers for the other inactive threads as dead during branch divergence), we only mark the dead registers for non-divergent warp instructions (i.e., all threads in a warp execute the same instruction). Detailed justification for this design is shown in Section 7.2.

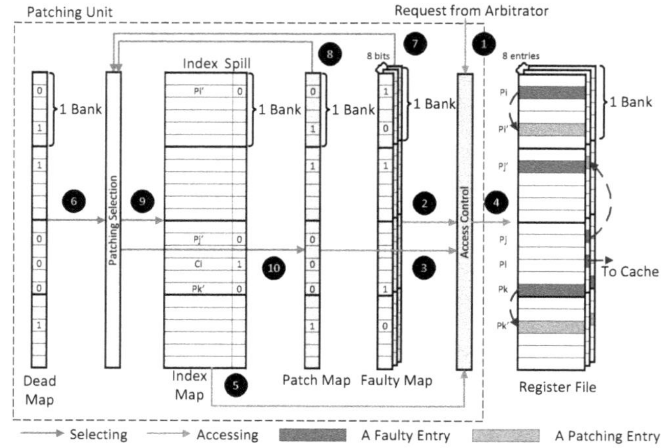

Figure 8: The detailed microarchitecture of GR-Guard.

5.2 GR-Guard: Structure of the Patching Unit

After obtaining the dead register information, patching can be performed for the faulty entries. We add a *Patching Unit* between the arbitrator and register banks in the GPU architecture as shown in Figure 1. Figure 8 shows the detailed architecture of the Patching Unit, which includes a *Dead Map*, a *Faulty Map*, an *Index Map*, a *Patch Map*, an *Access Control* logic and a *Patching Selection* logic.

The **Dead Map** contains one *dead bit* for each *WRG* to indicate if its corresponding register entries are dead. Before kernel execution, all register entries are treated as dead. During the register read stage, the operands' dead information in a non-divergent warp instruction is checked and its physical WRG's dead bit is set accordingly.

The **Faulty Map** contains one *faulty bit* for each *register entry* to indicate if the corresponding entry is faulty at a given supply voltage. In reality, this map can be obtained by following the basic faulty memory cell detection mechanism introduced in [39, 33]: During the post-fabrication testing, at a specific supply voltage all register cells are tested to see if they can correctly store a bit by comparing the read value bit and written value bit. If a cell fails the test, the cell is considered as faulty. Also, in this work, we assume the worst case scenarios under the other source of variations (e.g., dynamic factors such as voltage noise and wearout effects) in faulty register identification. Thus, our technique does not change V_{dd} dynamically, and the faulty map information is set only once for a given chip and is fixed at runtime. This method is often conducted in practice. Alternatively, a more complex method using self-testing mechanism and writable faulty map can also be applied but it is beyond the scope of this paper.

The **Index Map** contains one entry for each WRG. Each of these entries consists of a *patch index* to indicate the location index of the patching WRG, and a *spill bit* to indicate if the patching is a normal or spill patching (Section 5.4).

The **Patch Map** contains one *patched bit* for each WRG to indicate if the corresponding WRG is currently occupied for patching another WRG with faulty entries.

We use the RAM scheme instead of the CAM scheme to implement these four maps in order to reduce the comparison and latency overheads. Additionally, we design these maps to be banked and each bank contains the same number of entries as register file banks, in order to support concurrent requests from different register file banks.

The **Access Control** logic is used to differentiate between the normal and patching access, while the *Patching Selection* logic is used to find dead register entries for patching. Next subsection details the operations of these two logic blocks.

Since the size of the patching unit is very small compared to the register file (Section 5.6), the PV impact on it is comparatively trivial. If protection is required, techniques such as redundancy or cell redesign can be adopted to effectively enhance its reliability with negligible overhead.

5.3 GR-Guard: Operations

Access Control. Figure 8 shows the operations of our proposed GR-Guard. When a register access request is sent from the arbitrator (❶), the corresponding *faulty bits* in the Faulty Map (❷) and the *patched bit* in the Patch Map (❸) are read. Based on this information, the Access Control logic checks if the register entries to be accessed are faulty or occupied entries. If not, these normal accesses are performed the same as in the baseline GPU register file (❹). Accessing these two maps is extremely fast due to their very small sizes, and introduces almost no latency overhead to the normal (i.e., non-faulty and non-occupied) register accesses (Section 5.6). On the other hand, a request to the faulty or occupied entries uses the *patch index* and *spill bit* in the Index Map (❺) to obtain the address of the *patching entries* and accesses accordingly (❹).

A patching access within the same register bank (e.g., Pi to Pi' in Figure 8) can be completed in the following cycle. A patching access to a different bank (e.g., Pj to Pj' and Pk to Pk') requires to send another register access request to the arbitrator, which may encounter a small delay waiting for other pending requests to that bank to be completed. We leverage the operand collectors of the baseline architecture (shown in Figure 1) to buffer the pending operand accesses to avoid pipeline stall. Although the execution of a single warp may be slightly delayed due to patching, this overhead can be well hidden by leveraging the massive thread-level parallelism in the GPU architecture. Note that GR-Guard treats the occupied entries the same as the faulty entries upon accessing, to avoid complicated re-patching. In other words, occupied entries will not be released for their own normal register accesses until completing the current patching.

Patching Selection. When a faulty or occupied entry from a WRG is written, a *patching entry* will be selected. To select an available WRG that contains required patching entries (patching is performed at WRG level, which will be explained later), the Patching Selection logic reads the Dead Map (❻), the Faulty Map (❼) and the Patch Map (❽) to make the decision. GR-Guard gives the patching entries from the same bank higher priority during patching selection. After the decision is made, the corresponding *index* field in the Index Map for the WRG that needs to be patched, will be updated with the location of the selected patching WRG (each WRG has its distinct index) (❾). The corresponding *patched bit* in the Patch Map for this selected WRG is also set (❿). Once a WRG is dead or written again during execution, its corresponding patching entry or entries (if exists) will be released. During patching, the WRGs for the divergent warp instructions are treated the same as the non-divergent instructions.

5.4 Design and Optimizations

WRG-Level Patching. To simplify the design without compromising patching opportunities, GR-Guard performs fault patching at WRG level. Although patching at register entry level seems to provide the most patching opportunities, it incurs some design issues. First, it breaks the GPU specific feature that register entries within the same WRG are accessed simultaneously by the same warp, which results in increased design complexity and alters GPUs' SIMT execution pattern. For example, if available register entries within the same physical WRG are used to patch the register entries from different WRGs, this WRG will be prevented from being released for its own normal register accesses. Second, the storage overhead of the current Patch Map and Index Map in Figure 8 will be dramatically increased since each register entry will require its own designated slots.

Additionally, only the faulty entries of a WRG are patched, and the faulty entries in one WRG can only be patched to the mapping entries in the other available patching WRG. As shown in Figure 8, two entries (the first and the last) from WRG Pk are faulty, and they are patched to their mapping entries (also the first and the last) from WRG Pk'. Note that a WRG that contains faulty entries can also be selected for patching, as long as the required mapping entries are not faulty. For example, in Figure 8, even though one entry in Pj' is faulty, its corresponding non-faulty entry can still be used to patch that faulty entry in Pj.

Spill Patching. For the cases that the patching selection logic cannot find any available WRG for patching, the faulty entries will be patched to the L1 data cache as a *spill patching* (e.g., Pl in Figure 8). Each way in our baseline GPU L1 data cache contains 32 cache lines and the cache line size equals to the size of a WRG (128B). Based on the experiments on a wide range of applications, the spill patching only requires at most 23 cache lines concurrently under a very high percentage of the faulty register entries. Thus we reserve one way in the L1 data cache for spill patching. If there is no spill patching, the L1 data cache functions normally. Otherwise, the cache capacity is slightly reduced by one way during spill patching, and the cache lines in the reserved way are not used for cache accesses. An extra bit is used to indicate if the reserved cache way is used as spill patching, and one bit per cache line in the reserved way is used to indicate if the given cache line is currently used for patching. During spill patching, an available cache line is selected and the address of this cache line is written to the *patch index* of the Index Map (e.g., Ci in Figure 8). Meanwhile, the corresponding *spill bit* in the Index Map is set to "1" and the selected cache line is marked as used. The reserved cache way will return to normal function again when all the cache lines used for patching are released.

5.5 Discussions

Comparison with Pure Compiler-Based Patching. The compiler itself cannot effectively use the detected dead-register information to patch the faulty register entries, since it treats all the threads the same in GPU. Once a register of a single thread requires patching, the same-named registers in all the threads of the entire program kernel will also be patched, which significantly limits patching opportunities.

DVFS Support. As mentioned in Section 5.2, in our current design the faulty map is only set once at the chip-testing time. In other words, we further reduce the lower bound of the safe V_{dd} range, and accordingly disable the unreliable entries at such lower bound. Regular DVFS schemes can benefit from this voltage-range expansion and function normally as long as the voltage is not reduced below this V_{dd} lower bound to ensure correctness. This lower bound can be changed if other sources of variations (e.g., voltage droop) are addressed. Since our current design is conservative in faulty register identification, some faulty entries classified by our approach may actually function correctly under DVFS but will not be used.

5.6 Overhead Analysis

Storage Overhead. For a 128KB register file (per SM), Dead Map and Patch Map are both 128B (RF_size/WRG_size = 128KB / (128 × 8)), the size of the Index Map is 1.375KB ($RF\_size/WRG\_size \times (log_2(num\_of\_WRGs) + 1)$ = 128KB / (128 × 8) × (10 + 1)), while the Faulty Map size is 1KB ($RF\_size/register\_entry\_size$= 128KB/128). For a baseline L1 data cache with 32 sets, only 32 extra bits are required by the reserved way for spill patching. To sum them all together, the total storage overhead is 2.629KB, which is only around 2% of a 128KB register file. We want to emphasize that this storage overhead will remain the same under different cell failure rates and scale well as register file size increases (i.e., almost a fixed percentage of the register file size).

Area Overhead. We use CACTI 6.5 [41] to estimate the area overhead of the added storage structures in the patching unit under 28nm process technology. For the patching selection and access control logic, we apply a similar method used in [35] to aggressively estimate their area overhead as four times of the added storage structures. As a result, area overhead of the patching unit is 0.063 mm^2. For a 28nm-based GPU with 15 SMs, the total area overhead is 0.94 mm^2, which is approximately 0.36% of the GPU chip area.

Access Latencies. We model the access latencies to the Faulty Map and Patch Map using CACTI, since they directly affect the latency of the *normal register access* (Section 5.3). Due to their small sizes, accessing these two structures only increases the normal register file access latency by 0.0027ns (for a baseline GPU running at 700 MHz, the cycle time is 1.42ns), which is negligible. Thus we consider the access latencies to the normal registers the same as those in the baseline GPU. We also model the patching selection logic as a tree of 4-input arbiters with priority encoder under 28nm technology in HSPICE. For an input size of 1K, the selection delay is approximately 0.105ns. Additionally, updating the Index Map and Patch Map only takes 0.018ns. Therefore, we aggressively model the latency of the patching selection as one cycle. Note that if some entries in a WRG require patching, the patching selection process will happen in parallel with the accesses to the normal entries in this WRG.

6. EXPERIMENTAL METHODOLOGY

Table 1 shows the parameters we use to model the $V_{min,cell}$ under the process variation effects for a modern 28nm baseline GPU, as discussed in Section 3.1. The basic formulas used in our model are consistent with the previous work [37, 23, 39]. The model is implemented in R [6]. In Section 7, we perform sensitivity analysis of our design on three different technology nodes, including 11nm, 28nm and 45nm.

Process Variation Parameters	
Sample size	100 chips
Technology node	28nm
V_{thNOM}	0.35V
Correlation Range (ϕ)	0.5
V_{th}'s total σ/μ	12%
L_{eff}'s total σ/μ	6%
$\sigma_{rand} : \sigma_{sys}$	1:1
GPU Parameters	
Core (SM) frequency	700 MHz
Number of SMs	15
Warp size	32
Number of Warp Schedulers	2
SIMT pipeline width	32
Warp scheduling policy	Greedy-Then-Oldest (GTO)
Register file size	128KB/SM (32 banks, 256 entries/bank)
Shared memory size	48KB/SM
L1 data cache size	16KB/SM (4-way/128B)
L2 cache size	128KB/memory channel (8-way/128B)
Memory channels	6

Table 1: Evaluation configurations for the baseline GPU.

We use GPGPU-Sim V3.2.2 [15] to evaluate our proposed technique. The configuration parameters of the baseline GPU architecture are shown in Table 1. In order to faithfully evaluate our proposed technique, we collect a large set of representative benchmarks from the NVIDIA CUDA SDK [1], Rodinia benchmark suite [16] and Parboil benchmark suite [5]. We use PTXPlus instruction set simulation in our experiments, which is a one-to-one mapping to the native hardware instruction set, in order to provide a more accurate register lifetime analysis. GPGPU-Sim provides a detailed parser framework for PTXPlus, which includes the control flow graph at the basic block level. We implement our simple register live/dead time detection scheme described in Section 5.1 in GPGPU-Sim. Note that we modeled two warp schedulers in this paper, but our design still works for a larger number of warp schedulers, which may reduce both live and dead time duration together but the proportion between them remains largely unchanged.

We use a modified GPUWattch [27] to evaluate the dynamic and leakage energy consumption of GR-Guard under different voltages and frequencies. The frequency scaling factor under V_{dd} reduction is modeled by calculating the frequency of a 50-stage FO4 inverter chain [38] under 28nm technology and different V_{dd} values in HSPICE. Additionally, the energy consumption of the patching unit and cache accesses due to spill patching are also included in our evaluation.

In order to solely evaluate the effectiveness of GR-Guard, only the GPU register file is evaluated with the reduced voltage, and all the other on-chip components in GPU operate under the baseline supply voltage without any reliability degradation in our evaluation. We also assume the worst case scenarios under the other source of variations (e.g., voltage noise, thermal, and aging effects) in faulty-register identification. Our approach is conservative to ensure execution correctness, which means at runtime, some registers classified as faulty by our approach may still function correctly depending on the actual dynamic variations, but they are not used. Our technique is orthogonal to the other variation-tolerance techniques, such as voltage noise smoothing [28, 22].

Based on Figure 3, V_{dd} for the register file on a given chip is statically set to a value causing 1% cell failure rate in our evaluation and is independent of runtime characteristics

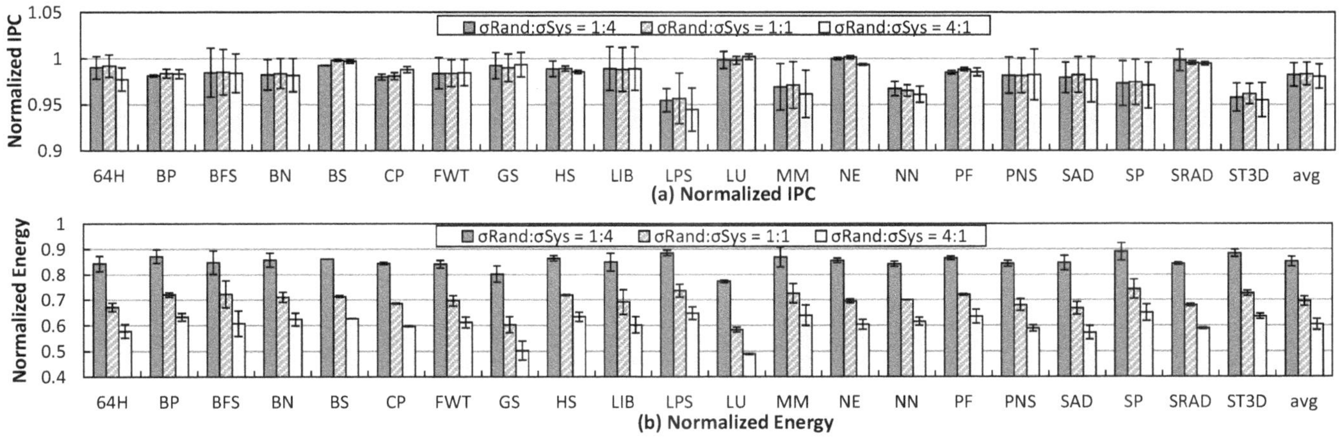

Figure 9: The average (a) IPC and (b) energy of the GPU register file with GR-Guard under a 1% register cell failure rate and different $\sigma_{rand} : \sigma_{sys}$ ratios across 100 chips. IPC and energy are normalized to the baseline case at normal voltage (no faulty cells). The +/-3 standard deviations across all chips are also shown for each benchmark.

of applications. 1% is approximated as the highest failure rate at which GR-Guard may achieve the maximum energy savings without significantly affecting performance, demonstrating the error-handling capability of our design. This is also a reasonable value to achieve the desired yield for manufacturing.

7. EXPERIMENTAL RESULTS

This section details experimental results and analysis for our proposed design. First, we explore the overall performance and energy impact of GR-Guard. Then, we quantify different patching opportunities through analyzing the breakdown of register accesses. After that, we explore if the spill patching in GR-Guard affects the L1 data cache performance. Finally, we conduct several sensitivity studiesto explore various design choices for GR-Guard. Without specific mention, *all the results are averaged across 100 chips under 1% cell failure rate and 28nm technology.* The results are also normalized to the baseline scenario without register file voltage reduction.

7.1 Performance and Energy Impact

Overall Performance (IPC). Figure 9(a) shows the average IPC of the GPU with GR-Guard enabled under different $\sigma_{rand} : \sigma_{sys}$ ratios. The +/-3 standard deviations (3σ) are also shown in the figure, which comprises 99.7% of all values. Figure 9(a) shows that overall GR-Guard achieves good performance across all the benchmarks under 1% cell failure rate and three process variation ratios. On average, it only incurs negligible IPC degradation (less than 2%) for all three scenarios. Several factors contribute to this low performance overhead of GR-Guard when combating a high percentage of faulty register entries: (1) the patching opportunities provided by the register dead time are quite adequate; (2) the high TLP of GPU effectively hides the patching overhead during execution; and (3) the WRG-level patching mechanism in GR-Guard maintains GPU's highly-parallel SIMT execution pattern. On average, performance is slightly worse under a larger random impact (σ_{rand}). This is because although the register cell failure rate (1%) is consistent among all three scenarios, the number of faulty register entries could be larger under a higher random impact due to a less clustered faulty cell distribution.

Additionally, under a higher random impact ($\sigma_{rand} : \sigma_{sys} = 4 : 1$), computation intensive benchmarks, including `LPS` and `MM`, have experienced a small IPC degradation under GR-Guard: 5% and 4% respectively. This small performance degradation is due to the overhead incurred from patching a single warp. Although such overhead can normally be hidden quite well in GR-Guard, it becomes more visible for computation intensive cases due to their high pipeline occupancy. The other case with a small IPC loss (4%) is `NN`. Since most of its kernels contain only one warp, there is not enough warp-level parallelism to hide the patching overhead. Moreover, since `SP` and `ST3D` show less adequate patching opportunities under a high percentage of faulty entries (Section 4.2), GR-Guard incurs 3% and 4% IPC degradation for them respectively due to spill patching, which will be analyzed in detail later.

Energy Reduction for GPU Register File. Figure 9(b) shows the average register file energy with GR-Guard enabled under different $\sigma_{rand} : \sigma_{sys}$ ratios. As shown, GR-Guard can effectively tolerate a high failure rate of register entries caused by aggressive voltage reduction, resulting in substantial energy savings. On average, with the support of GR-Guard, the energy consumption of the GPU register file is reduced by 15% under $\sigma_{rand} : \sigma_{sys} = 1 : 4$, 31% under $\sigma_{rand} : \sigma_{sys} = 1 : 1$, and 40% under $\sigma_{rand} : \sigma_{sys} = 4 : 1$. The figure also shows that a larger random impact can result in higher energy savings when undervolting. This is because $V_{min,cell}$ has a larger variation under a higher random impact, which results in a bigger V_{dd} *reduction range* compared to the other two cases that are under the same cell failure rate (e.g., Figure 3 in Section 3.2).

Chip-Level Energy Saving. The average energy saving for the entire chip through GR-Guard is around 6%. Note that the primary goal of this work is to address a major GPU reliability hotspot under low voltage operations, which is a necessary first step for enabling future GPU chip-level V_{dd} reduction. Additionally, recent design trend has clearly indicated that the size of the GPU register file has doubled every generation from Kepler to Pascal (i.e., from 3.75 MB to 14MB), making its energy consumption increas-

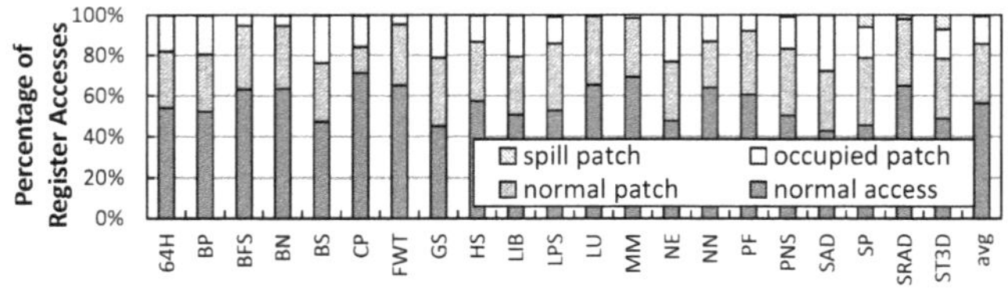

Figure 10: The breakdown of the register accesses under GR-Guard for a 1% register cell failure rate.

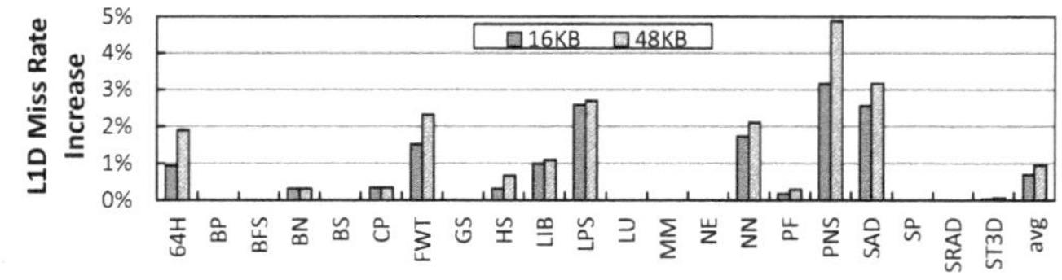

Figure 11: The increase of L1 data cache miss rate under GR-Guard for a 1% register cell failure rate.

ingly significant. Moreover, if techniques enable other less reliability-critical on-chip structures (e.g., caches) to run at lower voltages in the future, our technique can be combined with them to enable aggressive chip-level supply-voltage reduction, resulting in even greater energy conservation. Finally, GR-Guard is orthogonal to the previous GPU energy saving techniques, such as power gating and DVFS.

7.2 Evaluation of the Patching Opportunities

Figure 10 shows the breakdown of the register accesses under GR-Guard for a 1% cell failure rate. On average, 56% of the register accesses under GR-Guard are *normal accesses*, which means that GR-Guard does not incur overhead for more than half of the register accesses. 30% of the accesses are *normal patching accesses*, which are used to patch most of the faulty register entries. There are also 13% of the accesses used for patching the occupied entries, indicating that the dead time of the occupied entries is not long enough for the requested patching duration. GR-Guard has to patch the normal accesses to these entries somewhere else if they are not released on time. Finally, on average, only around 1% of the accesses are for *spill patching*. This indicates that the register dead-time opportunities are adequate to patch almost all the faulty register entries in most benchmarks under a high cell failure rate. Among the 21 applications, only `SP` and `ST3D` show a small percentage of the register accesses for spill patching (6% and 7% respectively) due to the large number of live registers. However, compared to the other accesses, this number is still small and has negligible impact on the application performance, demonstrated in Figure 9(a).

Recall Section 5.1, for simplifying the design and ensuring the correctness of register dead-time identification, at hardware-level GR-Guard excludes the divergent warp instructions from the selection pool. Figure 9(a) shows that for benchmarks with high divergence, including `BFS`, `GS`, `HS`, `LPS`, `LU`, and `SAD`, no significant performance degradation is observed. Additionally, Figure 10 demonstrates that no significant spill patching occurs for these benchmarks either. Take `HS` as an example. Although 46% of warp instructions are divergent, there is no spill patching in the register accesses. This proves that the register dead-time opportunities in the non-divergent warp instructions are adequate for patching a high percentage of faulty register entries at low voltage, without the need of further increasing the design complexity and overhead to identify the additional opportunities from the divergent warp instructions.

7.3 The Impact on Cache Miss Rate

Discussed in Section 5.4, as a backup strategy, GR-Guard reserves cache lines in one way of the L1 data cache (L1D) for spill patching when it cannot gain any patching opportunity from the dead registers. Here we evaluate the impact of GR-Guard design on the miss rate of the baseline 16KB and a larger 48KB L1D. For a fair comparison, we keep the number of sets the same for the two configurations, while only increasing the number of ways by 3 times in the 48KB L1D. Figure 11 shows that the average L1D miss rate across all the applications only increases by less than 1% for both configurations. The L1D miss rate increase is slightly higher for the 48KB configuration, since the reduction in miss rate from a larger cache size slightly increases the impact of GR-Guard on the cache performance. However, GR-Guard does not noticeably affect the performance for both configurations due to the small difference in the L1D miss rates. As a relatively cache-friendly benchmark, `PNS` has the highest cache miss rate increase, which is only around 3% in 16KB L1D and 5% in 48KB L1D, respectively. The minor increase in cache misses can be attributed to the small amount of spill patches shown in Figure 10. Also, in GR-Guard, the L1D capacity is only reduced by one way during spill patching, so for the majority of the time, L1D is used as a normal cache. As shown in Figure 10, despite `SP` and `ST3D` having a relatively larger amount of spill patches, they incur almost no increase in cache miss rate. This is because both `SP` and `ST3D` exhibit little data locality and almost all the cache accesses are misses. On the contrary, `BFS` and `LIB` are cache sensitive and have relatively good data locality. However, they have no and only 1% cache miss rate increase under GR-Guard, respectively. This is because they have no or very small amount of spill patches. So for the L1D miss rate to increase significantly under GR-Guard, applications need to have both *good data locality* and *a large amount of spill patches*. So far we have not found any GPU application that has both of these features.

7.4 Sensitivity Analysis

Scheduling Policies. Figure 12(a) shows the impact of different warp scheduling policies (i.e., GTO, 2Level, and RR) on register file IPC, Energy and EDP (energy-delay product) through GR-Guard. The results are averaged across all the benchmarks for 100 chips. Although different warp scheduling policies slightly change the average live/dead time portions of register values, their overall impact on performance and energy is almost the same.

Process Technologies. Figure 12(b) shows the effectiveness of GR-Guard under 1% register cell failure rate and three different process technologies (i.e., 45nm, 28nm, and 11nm). Under the same cell failure rate, the IPC degradation across different process technologies is very similar, which is around 2%. Since the process variation impact becomes larger under smaller feature sizes, GR-Guard achieves the highest energy savings for the register file under 11nm due to its larger supply voltage (V_{dd}) reduction range, while still maintaining the reliability. On average, GR-Guard reduces the energy consumption of GPU register file by 24%, 31%, and 35% under 45nm, 28nm, and 11nm, respectively.

Energy Scalability under Voltage Reduction. Figure 13 shows the energy scaling curves of the GPU register

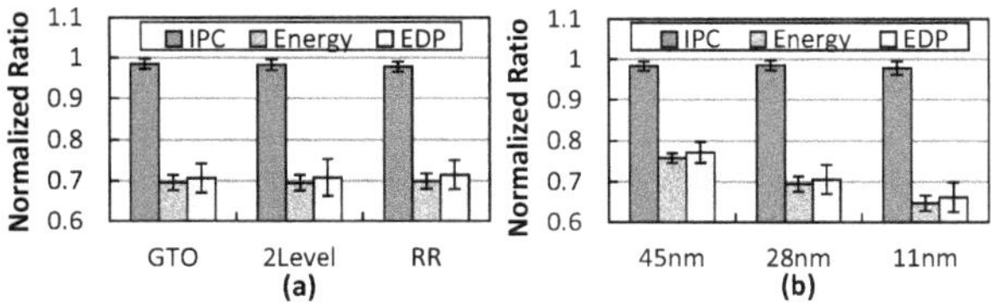

Figure 12: The normalized IPC, energy, and EDP of GPU register file with GR-Guard enabled under (a) GTO, 2Level, and RR scheduling policies, and (b) 45nm, 28nm, and 11nm. The +/-3 standard deviations are also shown in the figure.

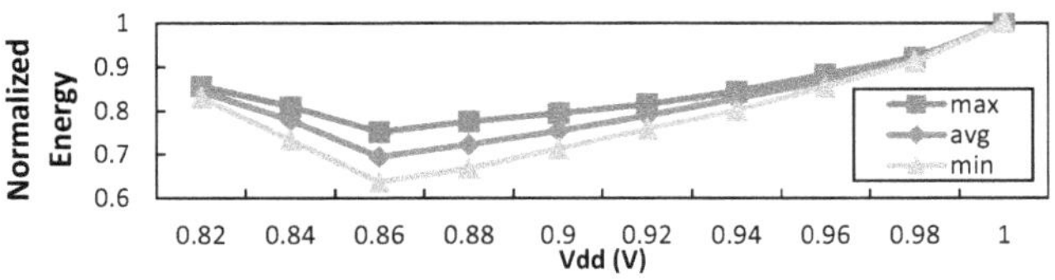

Figure 13: Energy scaling curves under V_{dd} scaling.

file under voltage reduction. The average, maximum, and minimum results are selected across all the benchmarks for 100 chips under 28nm technology. This figure helps us identify the optimal scaling point for register file V_{dd} in order to achieve the maximum energy savings. Since the cell failure rate increases when V_{dd} is reduced, we can observe that at 0.86V ($\sim$ 1% cell failure rate) GPU register file has the minimal energy consumption through GR-Guard. Further reducing V_{dd} beyond this point will cause the extra power reduction from the lower voltages to be offset by the overhead of tolerating a higher percentage of faulty register entries (e.g., >40%).

8. RELATED WORK

GPU Energy Saving Approaches: Recent work has been proposed to reduce GPU energy consumption [28, 22, 17, 21, 7, 26, 34, 43, 18, 8, 20]. Leng et al. proposed two voltage noise smoothing techniques for GPU to reduce its dynamic portion (i.e., voltage noise) of the supply voltage guardband [28, 22]. In contrast, our work explores the opportunities and challenges of reducing the static portion (i.e., process variation) of the guardband at design testing time. Although [22] suggested that the die-to-die (D2D) process variation effects may not be as significant as the voltage droop, based on our experiments, the within-die (WID) variation can be very significant, which is as high as 0.32V. Maximally reducing this static portion of the supply voltage guardband at chip testing time while still maintaining the reliability is our primary focus.

Several other techniques have been proposed to reduce the energy consumption of a portion of the GPU. For example, Rhu et al. [34] proposed to dynamically adjust the memory access granularity to save memory energy. Majeed et al. [7] proposed to reduce the register file energy by power gating the unallocated registers and turn a register into drowsy state after it is accessed. These techniques aim to temporarily or spatially reduce a portion of the GPU energy (e.g., power gating only reduces the leakage energy consumption). In addition, the effectiveness of these techniques is highly application-dependent. For example, the effectiveness of power gating the unallocated registers [7] highly relies on application register utilization. In contrast, our work explores a different kind of opportunity that reduces the minimum supply voltage requirement while maintaining the reliability at chip testing time, which is independent of application characteristics and software optimizations. Recently, Jeon et al [20] explored a technique to reduce the register utilization by compacting the live registers to smaller physical register file. Although this paper also explores the register liveness, it is different from our approach as it only considers the amount of live registers. In contrast, we consider both the amount of dead registers and length of dead time. Our approach is orthogonal to all the techniques above, and more importantly, it addresses the GPU reliability hotspot under low-voltage operations.

Enhancing the Reliability of Storage Cells: Several architecture and circuit level solutions have been proposed to improve the reliability of storage cells in cache and memory. For instance, the faulty entries in cache and memory can be handled via disabling their faulty cells at different granularities [40, 31, 42, 10, 11, 33]. However, these methods may result in significant capacity reduction. Since the GPU register file is a statically allocated resource and is critical to the computational throughput, reducing its capacity could cause concurrency reduction, which directly affects performance. And it may even fail to execute applications that require high register usage. One recently proposed technique [33] leverages the redundant data copies in other hardware structures (e.g., MSHRs and store queue) to patch the faulty subblocks in cache. When the required redundant data copies are not found, the cache accesses are treated as misses to the lower memory hierarchy. However, this opportunistic fault-patching technique is not applicable to the GPU register file. If the correct data copies from the other hardware components do not exist upon request, treating accesses to the faulty register entries as misses could result in program crash. Finally, some circuit-level solutions were proposed to design more robust cell structures. For example, a more PV-tolerant 3T1D DRAM cell structure was designed to build cache [29]. Although it has several benefits over the traditional 6T SRAM cell, it is still susceptible to process variation effects in the form of retention time. In addition, the 3T1D cell suffers from periodic refresh due to its DRAM nature. Thus applying it for GPU register design may cause nontrivial performance overhead as the register file is frequently accessed by thousands of threads.

9. CONCLUSIONS

As the largest on-chip storage structure, the GPU register file becomes a major reliability hotspot at low voltages. This work addresses the reliability challenge of GPU register file under aggressive voltage reduction, which aims to achieve further energy reduction beyond the existing energy-saving techniques. We propose an effective architectural solution named GR-Guard that leverages the inherent long register dead-time on GPU to enable reliable operations at low voltages with negligible performance overhead. More importantly, this work serves as a first step for realizing chip-wide supply voltage reduction for future GPU design.

10. ACKNOWLEDGMENTS

This research is supported by the U.S. Department of Energy's (DOE) Office of Science, Office of Advanced Scientific Computing Research, under award 66150: "CENATE - Center for Advanced Architecture Evaluation". PNNL is operated by Battelle for the U.S. Department of Energy under contract DE-AC05-76RL01830.

11. REFERENCES

[1] Nvidia cuda sdk. https://developer.nvidia.com/cuda-downloads.

[2] NVIDIA GeForce GTX 980: Featuring Maxwell, The Most Advanced GPU Ever Made. http://international.download.nvidia.com/geforce-com/international/pdfs/GeForce_GTX_980_Whitepaper_FINAL.PDF.

[3] NVIDIA's Next Generation CUDA Computer Architecture: Fermi. http://www.nvidia.com/content/pdf/fermi_white_papers/nvidia_fermi_compute_architecture_whitepaper.pdf.

[4] NVIDIA's Next Generation CUDA Computer Architecture: Kepler. http://www.nvidia.com/content/PDF/kepler/NVIDIA-Kepler-GK110-Architecture-Whitepaper.pdf.

[5] Parboil benchmark suite. https://github.com/abduld/Parboil.

[6] R: The r project for statistical computing. https://www.r-project.org/.

[7] M. Abdel-Majeed and M. Annavaram. Warped register file: A power efficient register file for gpgpus. In *Proceedings of the 2013 IEEE 19th International Symposium on High Performance Computer Architecture (HPCA)*, HPCA '13, pages 412–423, Washington, DC, USA, 2013. IEEE Computer Society.

[8] M. Abdel-Majeed, D. Wong, and M. Annavaram. Warped gates: Gating aware scheduling and power gating for gpgpus. In *Proceedings of the 46th Annual IEEE/ACM International Symposium on Microarchitecture*, MICRO-46, pages 111–122, New York, NY, USA, 2013. ACM.

[9] AMD. AMD Accelerated Parallel Processing: OpenCL Programming Guide. http://developer.amd.com/wordpress/media/2013/07/AMD_Accelerated_Parallel_Processing_OpenCL_Programming_Guide-rev-2.7.pdf.

[10] A. Ansari, S. Feng, S. Gupta, and S. Mahlke. Archipelago: A polymorphic cache design for enabling robust near-threshold operation. In *High Performance Computer Architecture (HPCA), 2011 IEEE 17th International Symposium on*, pages 539–550, Feb 2011.

[11] A. Ansari, S. Gupta, S. Feng, and S. Mahlke. Zerehcache: Armoring cache architectures in high defect density technologies. In *Microarchitecture, 2009. MICRO-42. 42nd Annual IEEE/ACM International Symposium on*, pages 100–110, Dec 2009.

[12] A. W. Appel. *Modern Compiler Implementation in C: Basic Techniques*. Cambridge University Press, New York, NY, USA, 1997.

[13] A. Bacha and R. Teodorescu. Dynamic reduction of voltage margins by leveraging on-chip ecc in itanium ii processors. In *Proceedings of the 40th Annual International Symposium on Computer Architecture*, ISCA '13, pages 297–307, New York, NY, USA, 2013. ACM.

[14] A. Bacha and R. Teodorescu. Using ecc feedback to guide voltage speculation in low-voltage processors. In *Microarchitecture (MICRO), 2014 47th Annual IEEE/ACM International Symposium on*, pages 306–318, Dec 2014.

[15] A. Bakhoda, G. Yuan, W. Fung, H. Wong, and T. Aamodt. Analyzing cuda workloads using a detailed gpu simulator. In *Performance Analysis of Systems and Software, 2009. ISPASS 2009. IEEE International Symposium on*, pages 163–174, April 2009.

[16] S. Che, M. Boyer, J. Meng, D. Tarjan, J. Sheaffer, S.-H. Lee, and K. Skadron. Rodinia: A benchmark suite for heterogeneous computing. In *Workload Characterization, 2009. IISWC 2009. IEEE International Symposium on*, pages 44–54, Oct 2009.

[17] M. Gebhart, D. R. Johnson, D. Tarjan, S. W. Keckler, W. J. Dally, E. Lindholm, and K. Skadron. Energy-efficient mechanisms for managing thread context in throughput processors. In *Proceedings of the 38th Annual International Symposium on Computer Architecture*, ISCA '11, pages 235–246, New York, NY, USA, 2011. ACM.

[18] N. Goswami, B. Cao, and T. Li. Power-performance co-optimization of throughput core architecture using resistive memory. In *High Performance Computer Architecture (HPCA2013), 2013 IEEE 19th International Symposium on*, pages 342–353, Feb 2013.

[19] P. Hammarlund, A. Martinez, A. Bajwa, D. Hill, E. Hallnor, H. Jiang, M. Dixon, M. Derr, M. Hunsaker, R. Kumar, R. Osborne, R. Rajwar, R. Singhal, R. D'Sa, R. Chappell, S. Kaushik, S. Chennupaty, S. Jourdan, S. Gunther, T. Piazza, and T. Burton. Haswell: The fourth-generation intel core processor. *Micro, IEEE*, 34(2):6–20, Mar 2014.

[20] H. Jeon, G. S. Ravi, N. S. Kim, and M. Annavaram. Gpu register file virtualization. In *Proceedings of the 48th International Symposium on Microarchitecture*, MICRO-48, pages 420–432, New York, NY, USA, 2015. ACM.

[21] N. Jing, Y. Shen, Y. Lu, S. Ganapathy, Z. Mao, M. Guo, R. Canal, and X. Liang. An energy-efficient and scalable edram-based register file architecture for gpgpu. In *Proceedings of the 40th Annual International Symposium on Computer Architecture*, ISCA '13, pages 344–355, New York, NY, USA, 2013. ACM.

[22] R. B. P. B. V. J. R. Jingwen Leng, Alper Buyuktosunoglu. Safe limits on voltage reduction efficiency in gpus: a direct measurement approach. In *in Proceedings of the IEEE International Symposium On Microarchitecture (MICRO)*, Dec 2015.

[23] U. R. Karpuzcu, K. B. Kolluru, N. S. Kim, and J. Torrellas. Varius-ntv: A microarchitectural model to capture the increased sensitivity of manycores to process variations at near-threshold voltages. In *Proceedings of the 2012 42Nd Annual IEEE/IFIP International Conference on Dependable Systems and Networks (DSN)*, DSN '12, pages 1–11, Washington, DC, USA, 2012. IEEE Computer Society.

[24] J. Kim, N. Hardavellas, K. Mai, B. Falsafi, and J. Hoe. Multi-bit error tolerant caches using two-dimensional error coding. In *Microarchitecture, 2007. MICRO 2007. 40th Annual IEEE/ACM International Symposium on*, pages 197–209, Dec 2007.

[25] E. Krimer, P. Chiang, and M. Erez. Lane decoupling for improving the timing-error resiliency of wide-simd architectures. In *Computer Architecture (ISCA), 2012 39th Annual International Symposium on*, pages 237–248, June 2012.

[26] S. Lee, K. Kim, G. Koo, H. Jeon, W. W. Ro, and M. Annavaram. Warped-compression: Enabling power efficient gpus through register compression. In *Proceedings of the 42Nd Annual International*

Symposium on Computer Architecture, ISCA '15, pages 502–514, New York, NY, USA, 2015. ACM.

[27] J. Leng, T. Hetherington, A. ElTantawy, S. Gilani, N. S. Kim, T. M. Aamodt, and V. J. Reddi. Gpuwattch: Enabling energy optimizations in gpgpus. In *Proceedings of the 40th Annual International Symposium on Computer Architecture*, ISCA '13, pages 487–498, New York, NY, USA, 2013. ACM.

[28] J. Leng, Y. Zu, and V. Reddi. Gpu voltage noise: Characterization and hierarchical smoothing of spatial and temporal voltage noise interference in gpu architectures. In *High Performance Computer Architecture (HPCA), 2015 IEEE 21st International Symposium on*, pages 161–173, Feb 2015.

[29] X. Liang, R. Canal, G.-Y. Wei, and D. Brooks. Process variation tolerant 3t1d-based cache architectures. In *Proceedings of the 40th Annual IEEE/ACM International Symposium on Microarchitecture*, MICRO 40, pages 15–26, Washington, DC, USA, 2007. IEEE Computer Society.

[30] S. Lin and D. J. Costello. *Error Control Coding, Second Edition*. Prentice-Hall, Inc., Upper Saddle River, NJ, USA, 2004.

[31] P. J. Nair, D.-H. Kim, and M. K. Qureshi. Archshield: Architectural framework for assisting dram scaling by tolerating high error rates. In *Proceedings of the 40th Annual International Symposium on Computer Architecture*, ISCA '13, pages 72–83, New York, NY, USA, 2013. ACM.

[32] NVIDIA. CUDA C Programming Guide. http://docs.nvidia.com/cuda/cuda-c-programming-guide/.

[33] D. Palframan, N. S. Kim, and M. Lipasti. ipatch: Intelligent fault patching to improve energy efficiency. In *High Performance Computer Architecture (HPCA), 2015 IEEE 21st International Symposium on*, pages 428–438, Feb 2015.

[34] M. Rhu, M. Sullivan, J. Leng, and M. Erez. A locality-aware memory hierarchy for energy-efficient gpu architectures. In *Proceedings of the 46th Annual IEEE/ACM International Symposium on Microarchitecture*, MICRO-46, pages 86–98, New York, NY, USA, 2013. ACM.

[35] T. G. Rogers, D. R. Johnson, M. O'Connor, and S. W. Keckler. A variable warp size architecture. In *Proceedings of the 42Nd Annual International Symposium on Computer Architecture*, ISCA '15, pages 489–501, New York, NY, USA, 2015. ACM.

[36] T. G. Rogers, M. O'Connor, and T. M. Aamodt. Cache-conscious wavefront scheduling. In *Proceedings of the 2012 45th Annual IEEE/ACM International Symposium on Microarchitecture*, MICRO-45, pages 72–83, Washington, DC, USA, 2012. IEEE Computer Society.

[37] S. Sarangi, B. Greskamp, R. Teodorescu, J. Nakano, A. Tiwari, and J. Torrellas. Varius: A model of process variation and resulting timing errors for microarchitects. *Semiconductor Manufacturing, IEEE Transactions on*, 21(1):3–13, Feb 2008.

[38] S. Seo, R. Dreslinski, M. Woh, Y. Park, C. Charkrabari, S. Mahlke, D. Blaauw, and T. Mudge. Process variation in near-threshold wide simd architectures. In *Design Automation Conference (DAC), 2012 49th ACM/EDAC/IEEE*, pages 980–987, June 2012.

[39] J. Tan and X. Fu. Mitigating the susceptibility of gpgpus register file to process variations. In *Parallel and Distributed Processing Symposium (IPDPS), 2015 IEEE International*, pages 969–978, May 2015.

[40] C. Wilkerson, H. Gao, A. R. Alameldeen, Z. Chishti, M. Khellah, and S.-L. Lu. Trading off cache capacity for reliability to enable low voltage operation. In *Proceedings of the 35th Annual International Symposium on Computer Architecture*, ISCA '08, pages 203–214, Washington, DC, USA, 2008. IEEE Computer Society.

[41] S. Wilton and N. Jouppi. Cacti: an enhanced cache access and cycle time model. *Solid-State Circuits, IEEE Journal of*, 31(5):677–688, May 1996.

[42] D. H. Yoon, N. Muralimanohar, J. Chang, P. Ranganathan, N. Jouppi, and M. Erez. Free-p: Protecting non-volatile memory against both hard and soft errors. In *High Performance Computer Architecture (HPCA), 2011 IEEE 17th International Symposium on*, pages 466–477, Feb 2011.

[43] W.-k. S. Yu, R. Huang, S. Q. Xu, S.-E. Wang, E. Kan, and G. E. Suh. Sram-dram hybrid memory with applications to efficient register files in fine-grained multi-threading. In *Proceedings of the 38th Annual International Symposium on Computer Architecture*, ISCA '11, pages 247–258, New York, NY, USA, 2011. ACM.

μC-States: Fine-grained GPU Datapath Power Management

Onur Kayıran[1] Adwait Jog[2] Ashutosh Pattnaik[3] Rachata Ausavarungnirun[4] Xulong Tang[3]
Mahmut T. Kandemir[3] Gabriel H. Loh[1] Onur Mutlu[5,4] Chita R. Das[3]

[1]Advanced Micro Devices, Inc. [2]College of William and Mary
[3]Pennsylvania State University [4]Carnegie Mellon University [5]ETH Zürich

ABSTRACT

To improve the performance of Graphics Processing Units (GPUs) beyond simply increasing core count, architects are recently adopting a *scale-up* approach: the peak throughput and individual capabilities of the GPU cores are increasing rapidly. This *big-core* trend in GPUs leads to various challenges, including higher static power consumption and lower and imbalanced utilization of the datapath components of a *big core*. As we show in this paper, two key problems ensue: (1) the lower and imbalanced datapath utilization can waste power as an application does not always utilize all portions of the big core datapath, and (2) the use of big cores can lead to application performance degradation in some cases due to the higher memory system contention caused by the more memory requests generated by each big core.

This paper introduces a new analysis of datapath component utilization in big-core GPUs based on queuing theory principles. Building on this analysis, we introduce a fine-grained dynamic power- and clock-gating mechanism for the entire datapath, called μC-States, which aims to minimize power consumption by turning off or tuning-down datapath components that are not bottlenecks for the performance of the running application. Our experimental evaluation demonstrates that μC-States significantly reduces both static and dynamic power consumption in a big-core GPU, while also significantly improving the performance of applications affected by high memory system contention. We also show that our analysis of datapath component utilization can guide scheduling and design decisions in a GPU architecture that contains heterogeneous cores.

1. INTRODUCTION

Graphics Processing Units (GPUs) have been used extensively to efficiently execute modern data-parallel applications. To improve GPU performance, architects have traditionally increased the number of GPU cores while keeping each core simple. More recently, in addition to increasing the processing core count, architects are adopting a *scale-up* approach to GPUs: the peak throughput and individual capabilities of each core are increasing rapidly (i.e., each core is getting bigger). For example, the AMD GCN [5] and TeraScale [32] architectures, and the NVIDIA Kepler architecture [69] have enhanced their core micro-architectures with more fetch/decode units, wavefront/warp schedulers, and functional units, compared to their predecessors. This *big core trend* in GPU design increases each GPU core's peak throughput and capabilities in successive generations, and can potentially enable significant performance boosts for many classes of applications.

PACT '16, September 11–15, 2016, Haifa, Israel.

DOI: http://dx.doi.org/10.1145/2967938.2967941

Unfortunately, the *big core design approach* also leads to challenges in power consumption and performance. First, a big core dissipates more static power than a small one due to the larger and wider components in the datapath. Even if application performance increases with big cores, the additional performance benefit might not compensate for the increase in power consumption, which can reduce the overall energy efficiency of the system. Second, some applications do *not* gain performance from the enhanced features of big cores, which leads to extra power consumption without any benefit. Third, some applications whose performance is limited by the memory system[1] can lose performance with big cores, due to the higher memory contention created by big cores (as we demonstrate in this paper), which results in both lower performance and higher power consumption.

To illustrate the effect of the big core designs on performance, Figure 1 shows the performance (in instructions per cycle) of six representative applications running on a GPU with 16 big cores, normalized to each application's performance on a GPU with 16 small cores.[2] The system with big cores dissipates 44% more static power than the system with small cores. We observe that using the big-core system (1) significantly improves the performance of two applications (SLA, MM), (2) does not affect the performance of two others (SCAN and SSSP), and (3) degrades the performance of yet two others (BLK, SCP). The applications that lose performance with big cores stress the memory system significantly, and also generate a high number of memory requests per wavefront. In our big-core system, these characteristics lead to (1) more requests to be generated per core, (2) more requests from different wavefronts to contend with each other for memory service, leading to more wavefront stalls (because each wavefront can continue execution only when *all* of its memory requests are serviced and memory contention increases the likelihood of at least one of each wavefront's requests taking longer), and (3) more cache line reservation (i.e., allocation) failures due to small L1 caches in GPUs and longer queuing latencies at the caches due to cache and memory contention. Overall, these experiments with representative applications show that a GPU architecture with big cores is *not* always the best design choice.

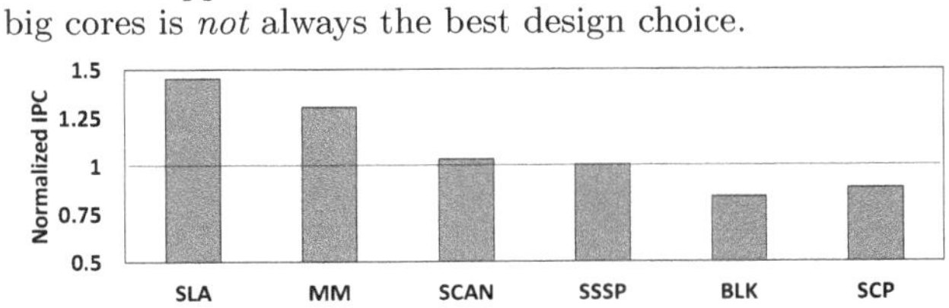

Figure 1: Performance of a GPU consisting of 16 big cores, normalized to a GPU with 16 small cores.

[1]We use the term *memory system* for the combination of caches, interconnect, and DRAM.

[2]Section 2 provides details of our small-core and big-core systems.

As we have shown, both the small-core and the big-core GPU designs have pros and cons. **Our goal** is to design a GPU architecture that enables the big-core GPU designs to be practical and efficient in terms of both performance and power consumption. We achieve this by keeping the power consumption under control while reaping the performance benefits of big cores whenever possible, and preventing the big-core design from degrading application performance when memory becomes the performance bottleneck.

To this end, we first conduct a new, queuing theory-based analysis of the pipeline of a big-core GPU. From our detailed study, we observe that (1) *most* of the pipeline components are heavily under-utilized, (2) the utilization levels of different pipeline components vary significantly *across different applications*, and *within the same application*, and (3) the utilization level of a particular component varies significantly *across different phases of the execution*. Based on this component-level analysis, we identify the pipeline components that are critical for performance for different applications. We introduce a dynamic power- and clock-gating mechanism for the entire datapath, called μC-States, which aims to minimize power consumption by turning off or tuning-down datapath components that are not bottlenecks for the performance of the running application. We name our mechanism building on *C-States* [34], which is a *core-level* power-management technique employed in current general-purpose microprocessors under the direction of the system software. In contrast to this CPU mechanism, our proposal, μC-States, is (1) fine-grained, because it manages power consumption at the *datapath component level*, and (2) invisible to software.

The basic idea of μC-States is simple: power-gate or clock-gate datapath components (1) that are underutilized or (2) that, if operated at their full bandwidth, would lead to performance loss by causing higher memory contention (as described above). μC-States employs an algorithm that starts power/clock-gating from the pipeline back-end (i.e., execution units) and gradually ripples the power/clock-gating to the front-end (e.g, fetch/decode stages) in three different phases, in order to ensure minimal performance loss. μC-States employs clock-gating for certain pipeline components that would lose data or execution state when power-gated (see Section 2.3 and Section 4), which ensures that no state that affects correctness is lost.

Our comprehensive evaluations of μC-States show that it reduces average static chip power by 16% and dynamic chip power by 7%, compared to a baseline big-core design across 34 GPU applications. μC-States also improves the performance of applications that would otherwise lose performance with big cores by 9%, without significantly degrading the performance of any other applications. Our results demonstrate that μC-States is not specific to any wavefront scheduler and can work effectively with different schedulers. We also show that its benefits are not sensitive to power-gating related timing and energy overheads.

This paper also illustrates how our analysis of datapath component utilization of applications can be used to exploit (and perhaps design) a *heterogeneous GPU architecture* that contains both small and big GPU cores. We provide a case study that, based on our application bottleneck analysis, categorizes applications according to their affinity to small or big cores and maps each application appropriately to the core type it executes most efficiently on, in a multi-programmed environment where applications execute concurrently on the GPU system. Our study shows that such a heterogeneous GPU architecture reduces power and area cost over a big-core design, without hurting performance, and improves performance over a small-core design, due to the effective mapping of the core type to application needs.

To our knowledge, this is the first work that provides (1) a detailed and rigorous characterization of application sensitivity to datapath components in a GPU that contains big cores, and (2) a comprehensive fine-grained power- and clock-gating mechanism across the entire GPU datapath that builds upon observations from this characterization. We make the following **contributions**:

- We conduct a new, queuing-theory-based analysis of the GPU pipeline datapath components of a big-core GPU architecture across 34 applications. This study is the first to demonstrate (1) the utilization levels of all major GPU datapath components and (2) varying utilization of the components across and within applications. We believe this study and its methodology can help architects to explore the big-core and heterogeneous-core design spaces for GPUs.
- We propose μC-States, a comprehensive fine-grained dynamic power- and clock-gating technique for GPU datapath components in a big-core GPU design. We show μC-States works effectively for 14 different datapath components across 34 workloads, reducing both static and dynamic power consumption and improving performance.
- We demonstrate the advantages of a heterogeneous GPU design consisting of both big and small GPU cores on the same chip, for efficient concurrent execution of multiple applications. Our analysis shows that application-to-core mapping guided by our bottleneck datapath component analysis provides significant power and chip area savings over a big-core design, without hurting system performance.

2. BACKGROUND

2.1 GPU Architecture and Core Pipeline

A GPU compute pipeline consists of multiple components: fetch/decode units (IFID), wavefront schedulers (SCH), pipeline registers, operand collectors (OC), streaming processors (SP), special function units (SFU), and load store (LDST) units. The SP unit is composed of an integer and a floating point unit. Our small core configuration is similar to an Nvidia GTX480 GPU [9], which is based on the Fermi architecture [68]. Our big core configuration, shown in Figure 2, has twice the number of SP, SFU, LDST, and SCH units as our small core-based system. This configuration is similar to an NVIDIA GTX 660, which is based on the Kepler architecture [69], with slightly higher DRAM bandwidth. In our big core, there are 4 wavefront schedulers, and 2 SP, SFU, and LDST groups, where each group consists of 32 SP, 4 SFU, and 16 LDST units, respectively. The big core also has twice the number of IFID and OC units, and the pipeline register size as the small core. Table 3 shows the details of our big core configuration. We show in Section 6.4 that our proposal works effectively with a larger register file and a larger number of Cooperative Thread Arrays (CTAs) per-core.

Figure 3 shows the high-level diagram of a GPU core pipeline. The IFID block fetches/decodes instructions, and handles all types of instructions, including integer and floating (SP), special function (SFU), and memory (LDST) instructions. SCH schedules the instructions from the IFID stage and sends them to the appropriate pipeline. Depending on its type, an instruction is inserted into its corresponding pipeline register ($IDOC_{SP}$, $IDOC_{SFU}$, or $IDOC_{LDST}$). Each pipeline register is connected to a specialized operand collector (OC_{SP}, OC_{SFU}, or OC_{LDST}) that keeps track of the register accesses by the instructions. After the operand

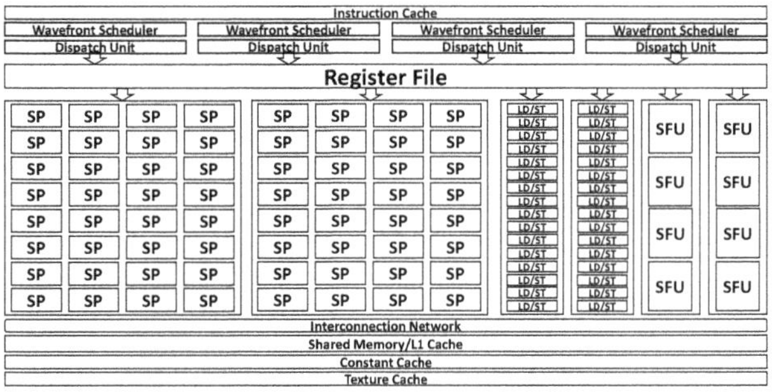

Figure 2: GPU core microarchitecture.

collectors, the control and data signals of the instruction are inserted into the corresponding pipeline register ($OCEX_{SP}$, $OCEX_{SFU}$, or $OCEX_{LDST}$) before they get sent into the execution unit (EX_{SP}, EX_{SFU}, or EX_{LDST}).

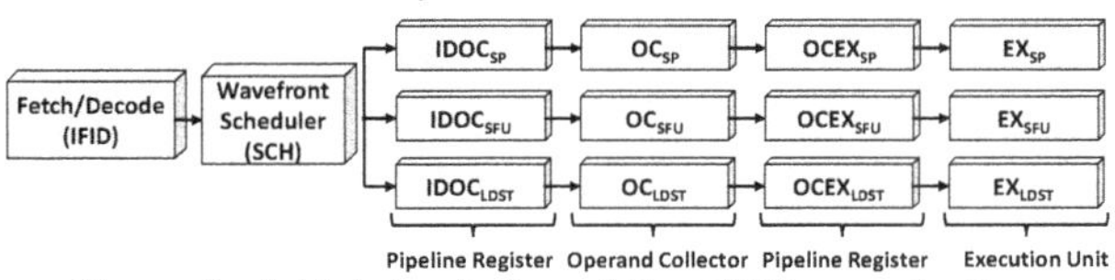

Figure 3: A high-level view of the GPU core pipeline.

2.2 Methods for Analyzing Core Bottlenecks

To identify performance bottlenecks and to gauge opportunities for turning off individual GPU datapath components, we borrow ideas from queuing theory. We make use of two key concepts. The *Utilization Law* states that the component with the highest utilization is the performance bottleneck [36]. To determine whether the performance bottleneck for memory instructions is the memory pipeline (LDST unit) or the rest of the memory system, we estimate memory latencies using *Little's Law* [56].

First, we investigate the utilization of each pipeline component. The utilization of the IFID block is calculated as the ratio of the cycles the IFID block is busy over total cycles, averaged across the width of the block. For example, in a single cycle, if IFID is 2-wide (i.e., IFID can fetch and decode two instructions per cycle), and fetches and decodes one instruction, its utilization is 0.5. The SCH utilization is given as the ratio of the cycles SCH is busy over total cycles, averaged across the SCH width. Similarly, we calculate the utilization of each pipeline register ($IDOC_{SP}$, $IDOC_{SFU}$, $IDOC_{LDST}$, $OCEX_{SP}$, $OCEX_{SFU}$, $OCEX_{LDST}$), operand collector (OC_{SP}, OC_{SFU}, OC_{LDST}), and execution unit, as the ratio of busy time of each over total cycles.

Utilization of a component is defined as the product of its throughput (X) and its average service time (S); $U = XS$. Throughput is defined as the number of completions per unit time. Service time is defined as the time for a completion. Based on the utilization levels of the pipeline components in Figure 3, we can detect the bottleneck (i.e., the component with the highest utilization). This analysis can be used for power/clock-gating of relatively less utilized (i.e., non-bottleneck) components without degrading performance.

We use the above utilization-based analysis for SP and SFU pipelines. The execution units for these two stages have deterministic service times, and from our simulations we observe little queueing delay for these units. By measuring the throughput of the SP and SFU unit each and multiplying it with the known service time of each, the utilization value calculated with Utilization Law closely matches the actual utilization value we measure for each of these two units.

However, this calculation is not so accurate in the memory pipeline, where the service time is variable and depends on memory system performance. We observe that the queuing delay in the memory pipeline is neither low nor predictable. The inability of the service time metric to capture queuing delay leads to an incomplete picture of the total delays in the unit. Therefore, for the memory pipeline, we use the *Response Time* metric, which is defined as the time between when a memory instruction is sent from the pipeline register $OCEX_{LDST}$ to the EX_{LDST} unit and when the memory instruction is committed. Response time captures both the service time as well as the queuing delay of the unit. Due to the difficulty in measuring response time in hardware, we estimate its value using *Little's Law. Little's Law* states that the average number of jobs (J) in the queue of a system is equal to the average arrival rate of the jobs to the system (λ) multiplied by the average response time for a job in the system (W): $J = \lambda W$.[3]

Utilization Law and Little's Law allow us to determine the performance bottlenecks of GPUs using a theoretical framework, which we then use to develop our power/clock-gating mechanism. This theory-based background provides robustness to our proposal, making it less sensitive to effects of the wavefront scheduler (Section 6.4) and dynamic changes in application behavior.

2.3 Power- and Clock-Gating

We power/clock-gate components at the granularity of a group (as defined in Section 2.1). We do not gate all of the groups of the same type. For example, when power-gating SP, we power-gate only *one* of the two groups.[4] All of the integer and floating point units in the power-gated SP group are turned off. Similarly, we clock-gate only half of the LDST units. We call a component as ***tuned-down*** if one of the groups (i.e., half of the units) in that component is power/clock-gated. Tuning-down a component halves its peak throughput.

While power-gating (PG) reduces static power, clock-gating (CG) reduces dynamic power. The potential power savings with PG is more than that with CG, and this difference will be even more significant as static power becomes more important with technology scaling [78]. However, PG is more difficult to employ because it has higher timing overheads, requires more idle time to be employed, and needs to be employed for long enough (i.e., at least for *break-even time*) to compensate for its energy overhead. Moreover, PG results in loss of data for the gated component. Thus, we use PG to tune-down components that do *not* store data (instruction decoder, wavefront scheduler, integer and floating-point units, and special functional units), and CG to tune-down components that store data (instruction buffer, pipeline registers, operand collectors, and load/store queue). For example, tuning-down for IFID means clock-gating half of the IFID. A tuned-down IFID can fetch and decode at most 2 instructions per cycle, which is half the peak number of instructions per cycle in our baseline. Tuning-down for EX_{SP} means power-gating half of the SP. While the baseline system can execute 64 integer instructions per cycle, this number is 32 for a tuned-down EX_{SP}.

Overheads. A component should be power-gated for at least a time period, called *break-even time*, in order to compensate for the incurred energy overhead of entering and

[3] We use the memory response time calculated based on Little's Law to determine whether or not the memory system is congested.

[4] We do not explore having more groups, because having more than two power domains per core might not be practical to implement.

exiting the PG mode . The time that is needed to turn the component back on is known as the *wake-up delay*. We assume a break-even time of 19 cycles and wake-up delay of 9 cycles [33]. Section 6.4 provides a sensitivity study of these parameters. CG is employed by disabling the clock signal to a pipeline component. It effectively reduces the component's activity factor, has no break-even overhead, and the clock-gated component can wake up in the next clock cycle by enabling the clock signal.

2.4 Existing Component Gating Mechanisms

Traditional CPUs. Prior works that employ pipeline-component-level gating mechanisms focused on CG [8, 55, 58]. However, such mechanisms are employed at a very fine granularity, and thus are not suitable for PG due to the wake-up and break-even overheads. As static power becomes a major contributor to the total chip power with CMOS technology scaling [78], PG will be increasingly important for power management. Furthermore, some of these works [8,55] do not consider gating the issue stage. However, as we will show in Section 3.2, reducing the peak throughput of the issue stage via a gating mechanism does not only reduce power consumption, but can also improve application performance in a GPU.

GPUs. Warped Gates [2] is the only work that proposes a pipeline-level PG mechanism for GPUs. However, it leads to significant performance losses in some applications because it can power-gate performance-critical components. It is also employed at a fine granularity, and is dependent on the wavefront scheduling algorithm to create idle cycles for the components that will be power-gated. We will show (in Section 3.2) that a rigorous analysis of component utilization in the whole GPU pipeline can guide us in determining the performance-critical components. This enables us to tune-down components without significant performance loss even if they have non-idle cycles. GpuWattch [54] employs CG for SIMD lanes in the presence of branch divergence, and does not consider any of the possible component-level power-saving opportunities that occur due to underutilization (as we analyze in Section 3.2).

3. MOTIVATION AND ANALYSIS

Through detailed workload analysis, we first show that GPU pipeline resources are heavily under-utilized. We then conduct a utilization analysis of the entire GPU pipeline to identify performance-limiting components, which motivates our bottleneck-aware power/clock-gating mechanism.

3.1 The Problem: Under-utilized GPU Core

To demonstrate the under-utilization of the GPU pipeline, we profiled our 34 GPU applications (Table 1) on an NVIDIA K20 card using the CUDA profiler. Because K20 has higher peak throughput and DRAM bandwidth than our baseline (shown in Table 3), we also profiled 27 different kernels from CUDA SDK 6.5 on an NVIDIA GTX 660 card, which is similar to our baseline. Figure 4 shows the ALU and LDST utilization of each application/kernel on a scale from 0 to 10, where 10 denotes 100% utilization of the component, on the two systems. We show only 10 representative applications with their names in Figure 4a for comparison with our simulation results in Table 1. Overall, the real system results in Figure 4 demonstrate that ALUs are heavily under-utilized in most of the applications, and several applications make heavy use of the LDST pipelines. Thus, the pipeline under-utilization problem we address in this paper is a problem clearly visible in existing GPU hardware executing real GPU workloads (and it is not an artifact of simulation or that of an over-provisioned baseline).

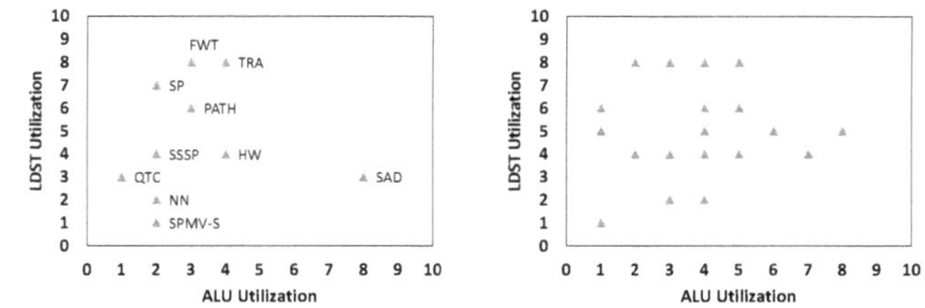

(a) NVIDIA K20 (b) NVIDIA GTX 660

Figure 4: ALU and LDST pipeline utilization in real GPUs.

The GPU profiler does not provide utilization statistics for pipeline components except ALU and LDST. To get a better understanding of the under-utilization problem, we tabulate the utilization of 14 different components in Table 1 across 34 benchmarks, obtained using GPGPU-Sim [9]. The y-axis lists the benchmarks, and the x-axis shows the utilization (between 0% and 100%) of each component. We break down IFID and SCH utilization into the type of instruction (SP, SFU or MEM) that is decoded and issued.

Five key observations are in order. First, we observe that the real experiment and the simulation results follow the same trends: there is significant ALU under-utilization, and the LDST pipeline is stressed in several applications. We observe the same trends for other benchmarks that are not shown in Figure 4a. Second, each application stresses *different* components *differently*. For example, compute-intensive applications (e.g., `SAD`, `MM`, `HW`) utilize IFID, SCH, and EX_{SP} significantly, and do not utilize EX_{LDST} to the same extent. Conversely, memory-intensive applications (e.g., `QTC`, `BFS`, `BLK`) do not utilize IFID, SCH, and EX_{SP}, but heavily utilize EX_{LDST}. Third, in the applications that have high EX_{SP} or EX_{SFU} utilization, the OCEX register, SCH and IFID units also have similar utilization as the execute stage, but the IDOC register and the operand collectors usually have lower utilization. This leads us to conclude that the bottleneck for SP or SFU instructions in such applications is one of IFID, SCH, OCEX, or EX units. Fourth, in the applications that have high EX_{LDST} utilization, units other than $IDOC_{LDST}$, OC_{LDST}, $OCEX_{LDST}$, and EX_{LDST} have very low utilization. Memory instructions in such applications are bottlenecked by either the LDST unit, or the memory system. Due to the heavy utilization of these units, the SCH units stall for long periods either waiting for data to come back from memory, or not finding independent instructions to execute, leading to low IFID and SCH utilization. Fifth, we observe very low utilization in SFU-related components (0.8% in OC_{SFU}) as well as OC_{SP} (1.8%) units across all applications. We also note that, across the 34 applications, the average utilization of memory instruction-related components is around 50%-60%, and average IFID, SCH, and EX_{SP} utilization is 24%, 21%, and 17%, respectively.

3.2 Application Performance Sensitivity to Pipeline Resources

3.2.1 Representative Applications

We now evaluate the impact of tuning-down GPU core components on application performance. The intuition is that tuning-down components that are not highly utilized, or less utilized compared to other components would not degrade performance, but would lead to power savings. We evaluate 8 different core configurations listed in Table 2, where each entry is a different type of tuned-down core. For

Table 1: Component-wise utilization breakdown for 34 CUDA applications. A more shaded bar indicates higher utilization. IFID and SCH utilization is further broken down into SP, SFU, and LDST instruction utilizations, from left to right with different shades of gray.

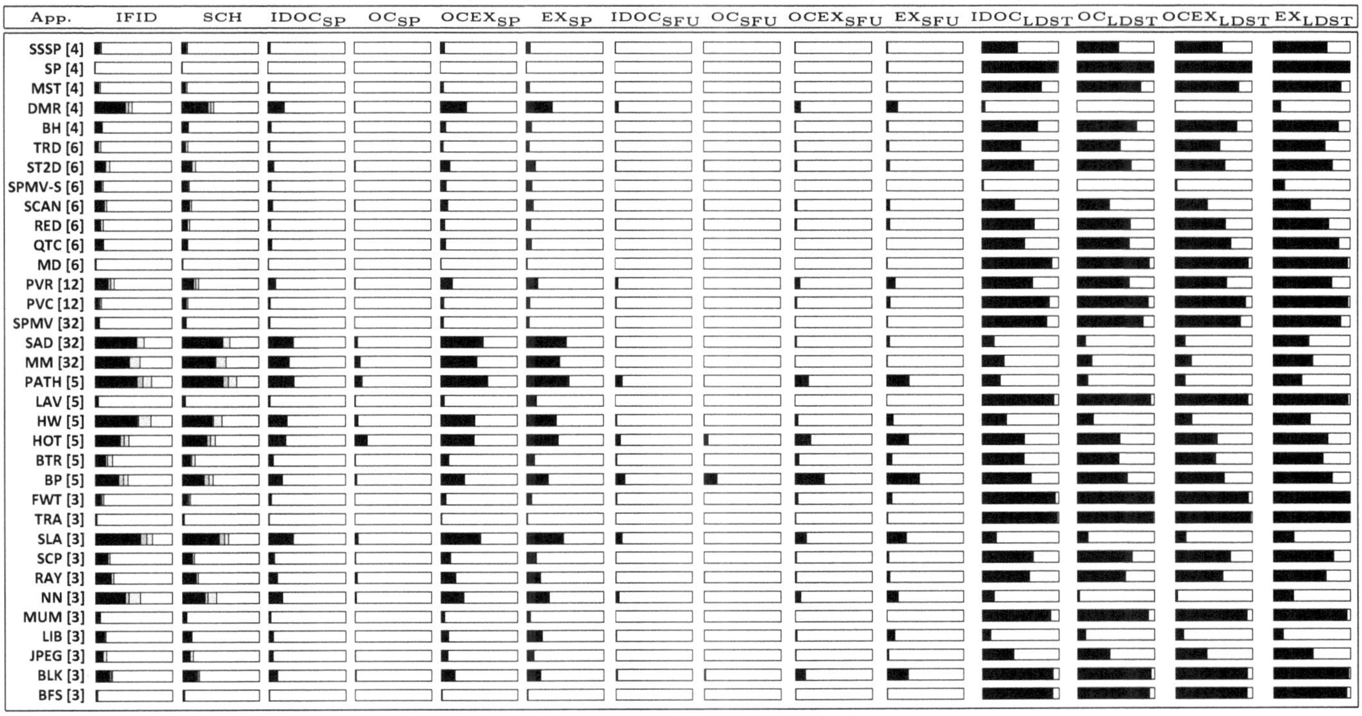

example, in C_{HALF}, all 14 components are tuned down (i.e., operate at half their peak baseline throughput). In C_{IFID}, all components except IFID are tuned-down. Similarly, in C_{SP}, all components except EX_{SP} are tuned-down. In C_{COMP}, all components except components related to the compute path (including IFID and SCH) are tuned-down. In C_{MEM}, all components except components related to the memory path (including IFID and SCH) are tuned-down. Note that tuning-down a component means power-gating/clock-gating only half of that component.

Table 2: Different Tuned Down Configurations

Config.	Tuned-down components	Config.	Tuned-down components
C_{HALF}	ALL	C_{COMP}	ALL except IFID, SCH, and Compute Related Components
C_{IFID}	ALL except IFID		
C_{SCH}	ALL except SCH		
C_{SP}	ALL except EX_{SP}	C_{MEM}	ALL except IFID, SCH, and Memory Related Components
C_{SFU}	ALL except EX_{SFU}		
C_{LDST}	ALL except EX_{LDST}		

Figure 5 shows the effect of these 8 tuned-down configurations on the performance of 5 representative applications. `HW`, a compute-intensive application, demonstrates a case where IFID, SCH, and EX_{SP} are all critical for performance. `SPMV-S`, `QTC`, and `BLK` show three different cases in which we analyze memory related performance bottlenecks. Finally, we study `NN`, which is sensitive to most of the components in the pipeline.

We observe in `HW` that C_{COMP} has almost no performance impact. This is expected, as all components related to memory ($IDOC_{LDST}$, OC_{LDST}, $OCEX_{LDST}$, EX_{LDST}) have low utilization (Table 1) and tuning them down would not lead to performance loss. We also observe that C_{HALF} degrades performance to 69% of that of the baseline. C_{IFID} (76%) performs significantly better than C_{SCH} (68%), because the utilization of IFID is higher than that of SCH and the other components that are used by SP and SFU instructions (Table 1). Thus, for SP and SFU instructions, IFID is the bottleneck component. Therefore, tuning down IFID causes more performance loss than tuning-down the other components. In C_{IFID}, the bottleneck moves to the execution units, and increasing these bottleneck resources in C_{COMP} leads to higher performance compared to C_{IFID}. `HW` *exemplifies a compute-intensive application. Because many compute components such as IFID, SCH, and the execution units have similar utilization values, all of these resources are critical for performance in such an application.*

The next three applications, `SPMV-S`, `QTC`, and `BLK` are sensitive to memory pipeline resources. As shown in Table 1, all of the components in `SPMV-S` are under-utilized. This means that the bottleneck is not the memory system. However, EX_{LDST} is the unit with the highest utilization, thus EX_{LDST} is the bottleneck component for this application. Therefore, C_{LDST} performs close to the baseline. Also, similar to `HW`, since IFID utilization is slightly higher than SCH utilization, C_{IFID} performs slightly better than C_{SCH}. Thus, C_{MEM}, which combines the benefits of C_{IFID} and C_{LDST}, performs as well as the baseline. `SPMV-S` *exemplifies a case where performance is highly dependent on EX_{LDST} even when the LDST pipeline utilization is low.*

Both `QTC` and `BLK` demonstrate high memory pipeline utilization. However, they show contrasting sensitivities to different configurations. `QTC` is similar to `SPMV-S`, because the utilization of EX_{LDST} is significantly higher than that of all the other components (making EX_{LDST} the bottleneck component), and contributes significantly to performance. However, in `BLK`, the bottleneck is the memory system,[1] not EX_{LDST}, because we observe very high DRAM bandwidth utilization and very long memory latencies. In this application, a higher issue width degrades performance significantly because it leads to more contention in the already-oversubscribed memory system. Thus, configurations that tune-down components in a way that reduces memory contention (C_{HALF}, C_{IFID}, C_{SP}, C_{SFU}, C_{LDST}) significantly improve performance over the baseline.

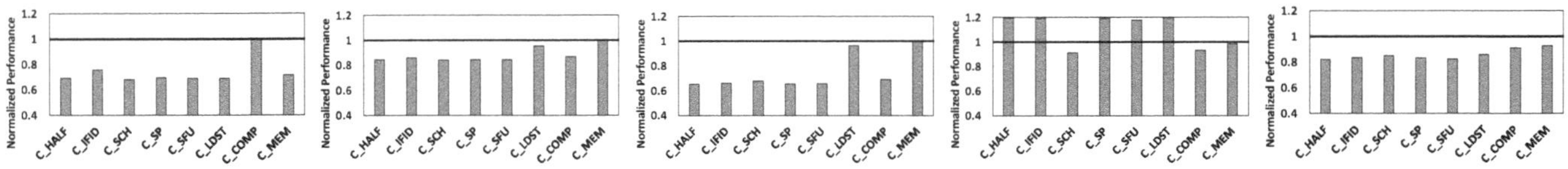

(a) HW (b) SPMV-S (c) QTC (d) BLK (e) NN

Figure 5: Effect of tuned-down configurations on performance. All results are normalized to the baseline (Section 2).

In applications bottlenecked by memory bandwidth (e.g., BLK), we observe high memory access latencies. This is in contrast to QTC, where latency is relatively low, and the performance bottleneck is EX_{LDST}. In applications bottlenecked by the memory system,[1] we see a high number of stalls *after* the memory instructions leave EX_{LDST} (this can be due to contention anywhere in the memory system). From a theoretical point of view, the average memory latency is similar to the response time of EX_{LDST}, described in Section 2.2. We observe that both the average memory latency and the average response time of EX_{LDST} in QTC is approximately half of those in BLK. In summary, QTC *demonstrates a case where the memory pipeline (EX_{LDST}) is the bottleneck, and more memory pipeline resources improve memory-level parallelism, leading to better performance. On the other hand,* BLK *(similar to* SCP, TRA, FWT, SPMV, RAY, *and* RED*) demonstrates a case where the memory system (i.e., caches, network, DRAM) is the bottleneck, and increasing the instruction throughput aggravates the problem of memory contention, leading to lower performance.*

In NN, almost all components affect performance. Thus, tuning-down most of the components reduces performance, and the baseline outperforms all other configurations.

3.2.2 Memory-Bottlenecked Applications

In applications such as BLK (Figure 5d), SCP, TRA, FWT, SPMV, RAY, and RED, the performance bottleneck is the contended memory system. These applications have very high memory bandwidth utilization, and injecting more requests to the system by doubling the instruction throughput (e.g., C_{SCH} compared to C_{HALF}) leads to significant performance degradation. To understand the reason for this, we investigate the stalls incurred at L1 caches. The stalls happen due to three main reasons. First, due to the high number of memory requests, Miss Status Handling Registers are filled, and further incoming requests stall. Second, miss queue buffers are filled, and this prevents new packets from being injected into the network. Third, if the L1 data cache uses an Allocate-on-Miss policy, misses cannot reserve cache lines before they can be serviced. If the policy is Allocate-on-Fill, our simulations show that the problem manifests itself at L2 and DRAM, and the memory system bottleneck still causes performance issues. Figure 6 shows the performance and the *L1 stall cycles per L1 miss* of C_{SCH}, normalized to those of C_{HALF}, for representative applications. We observe that the increase in L1 stall cycles per miss correlates well with the performance loss due to doubling the instruction throughput in C_{SCH} compared to C_{HALF}. The applications with higher memory bandwidth consumption suffer higher performance losses compared to the others. We find these main trends to be similar in other applications as well.

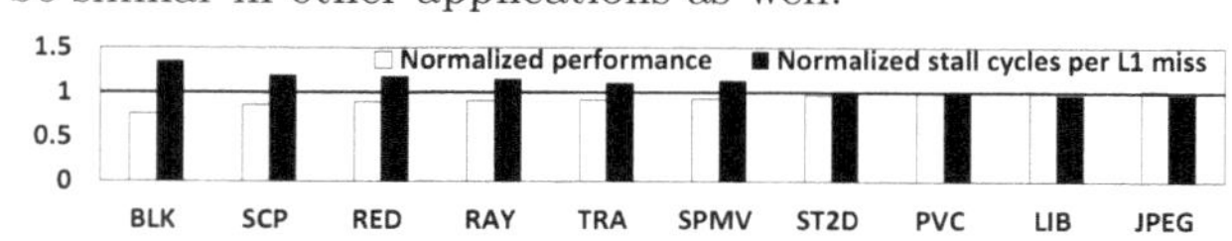

Figure 6: Performance and the number of L1 stall cycles per L1 miss with C_{SCH}, normalized to C_{HALF}.

In order to provide insight into the increase in stalls due to doubled issue width, Figure 7 provides an illustration by showing how the execution latency of a memory instruction in a wavefront (Figure 7a) can more than double if another wavefront's (Wavefront 2) memory instruction contends with this wavefront's (Wavefront 1) instruction when the issue width is doubled (Figure 7b).

In Figure 7a, the scheduler issues an instruction from only a *single* wavefront due to the small issue width. This wavefront issues two memory requests (R1 and R2), and it stalls until *all* of these requests are serviced and their data returns to the core. Assume that the memory bandwidth is close to saturation and allows only two requests to be serviced per unit time and that the wavefront's two requests return to the core after a single time unit. Once they arrive, the wavefront can continue its execution with the next instruction. Thus, *the latency of the wavefront's instruction is only a single time unit* since both of the instruction's memory requests arrive after a single time unit. Assuming all instructions in the wavefront are similar, performance is sustained at one instruction per time unit.

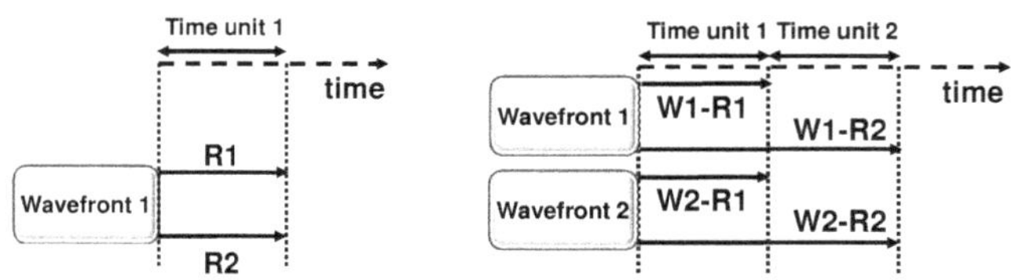

(a) Single issue width (b) Doubled issue width

Figure 7: Effect of increasing issue width on performance.

In Figure 7b, the issue width is doubled, and the scheduler can issue one instruction each from *two* wavefronts at the same time. Similar to (a), assume that due to limited memory bandwidth, only two requests can be serviced per time unit. Also assume that, due to contention in the memory system, the memory system services R1 from each wavefront concurrently and these two (W1-R1 and W2-R1) return in one time unit. Thus, neither of the instructions in different wavefronts is complete at the end of the first time unit because R2 is not even sent to the memory system. Once R1 from each wavefront is complete, R2 from each wavefront is sent to the memory system. Only at the end of the second time unit, R2 from each wavefront is also complete, and hence each wavefront can now move to issue its next instruction. Thus, *the latency of each instruction is two time units* since both of the instructions' memory requests arrive after two time units. Assuming all instructions in a wavefront are similar, performance is sustained at one instruction per *two* time units. Thus, the performance of each wavefront halves compared to the case where issue width is half (Figure 7a). The actual performance of the system in (b) is actually even worse than depicted: due to the larger number of outstanding memory requests in the system, contention and queueing delays and buffering conflicts in various parts of the memory system (caches, interconnect, and DRAM banks, buses, row buffers) increase [7,17–19,21,42,47–49,51,62,64–66,82,84], and, hence, the latency of servicing each request becomes larger than a single time unit. Thus, *either wavefront in (b) can complete one instruction long after two time units, leading to overall system performance degradation compared to when the issue width is half.*[5]

We observe this scenario especially in applications with high memory divergence [7, 14, 59] and those where some requests are much more critical than others [7, 42] for application performance. Such applications are more prone to longer latencies for an instruction because one or few memory requests can easily dominate the performance of an instruction if they get delayed due to increased memory contention. This problem becomes more severe in cases where a wavefront instruction issues a high number of requests. For example, Figure 6 shows that `PVC` is not very sensitive to issue width although it has high bandwidth consumption. This is because, a wavefront in `PVC` generates 2.36 memory requests, on average, whereas this number is much higher in more sensitive applications (e.g., 4.60 in `BLK`).

Several works [7,14,59] identified that, if multiple requests from the same wavefront are serviced at different levels in the memory hierarchy (e.g., one request is an L1 hit, while the other is served by the DRAM), long latency operations such as DRAM accesses become critical for performance, and cause significant wavefront stalls. The problem we observe is evident *even when all the requests are served at the same level in the memory hierarchy.* The increase in outstanding requests puts pressure on the memory system. Specifically, as L1 caches are small in GPUs, applications with high miss rates cause a majority of the cache lines to be reserved (waiting for misses to return), preventing other misses to be served. This causes cache stalls to increase. A miss that cannot be served increases the probability of its corresponding wavefront to stall longer, and becomes critical for performance. In a big core configuration, because there are more requests in the system, the number of critical requests increases, causing performance degradation. Overall, we find that *memory-divergent applications that are bottlenecked by memory bandwidth benefit from reduced issue width.*[6]

Summary. We conclude that applications utilize various datapath components differently and are bottlenecked by different parts of the datapath or the memory system. Hence, a PG/CG mechanism that is aware of the performance bottlenecks of each application is promising to achieve both power reduction and performance improvement in a GPU system with big cores.

4. μC-States: A DYNAMIC POWER- AND CLOCK-GATING MECHANISM

We describe μC-States, our approach for tuning-down components that are *not* critical for performance. In contrast to the core-level CPU power-management technique, C-States [34], μC-States works at the datapath component level and is invisible to software. The objective is to 1) reduce the static and dynamic power of the GPU pipeline by employing PG and CG in appropriate pipeline resources, and 2) maintain and, when possible, improve GPU performance by employing PG/CG in a bottleneck-aware fashion, based on our analysis in Section 3.2.

Power Benefits. We employ μC-States to reduce both static and dynamic power consumption. As opposed to the prior pipeline-level PG mechanism that creates idle times to power-gate components [2] via a smart wavefront scheduling mechanism, our mechanism relies on our analysis to determine the components that are *not critical* for application performance. Gating such components, even if they are not idle, does not have a significant effect on performance. Since we do not need to create idle times for gating, our mechanism (1) can be employed at a *coarser time granularity,* (2) has benefits that are unlikely to be dependent on the energy overheads of entering/exiting the power-gating state, (3) is independent of the underlying wavefront scheduler.

Performance Benefits. Our strategy aims to improve the performance of applications that are bottlenecked by the memory system. Section 3.2 already showed that such applications benefit from reduced instruction throughput. The performance benefits of our technique mainly come from clock-gating the wavefront scheduler and reducing the issue width. This is fundamentally different from prior works that focus on reducing GPU cache thrashing [7,41,43,44,67,76] (see Section 6.2), and pipeline-level CG techniques for traditional CPUs [8,55] that do not focus on limiting issue width. Note that we power-gate or clock-gate only one group in a component. Because the peak throughput of the tuned-down component is halved, the progress of instructions inside the datapath is not entirely blocked.

Maintaining Execution State. μC-States employs power-gating for components that do *not* store data and clock-gating for components that do (see Section 2.3). When μC-States decides to power-gate a component, it stops pushing more work into the component. Once the component finishes all its outstanding work, the component is power-gated. Thus, no data or execution state is lost.

μC-States Gating Algorithm. In order to dynamically tune the pipeline components, each core requires a *Gating Control Unit.* As shown in Figure 8, the controller periodically decides whether or not a group of components should be tuned-down. Because tuning-down a component might impact the utilization of that component and other components, tuning *all* components at the same time is sub-optimal. μC-States gates components in three *phases.* As the performance of the system is determined by the throughput of the functional units and the LDST units, and because the throughput of these components do not *directly* affect the instruction count incoming to any other component, the algorithm starts with gating these components. In the first phase (after an interval of 2048 cycles), the controller tunes only the EX_{SP}, EX_{SFU} and EX_{LDST} units. In the second phase (2048 cycles after the decision for the first phase), the remaining components belonging to SP, SFU, and LDST pipelines (i.e., IDOC registers, OCEX registers, OC units, and register file banks) are tuned. In the third phase, the components that affect all types of instructions (i.e., IFID and SCH units) are tuned. Then, the controller moves back to the first phase. Each type of resource in our architecture comprises of two groups. We tune only one group during run-time (Section 2.3). Thus, at a given time, there is always at least one group active from each type of resource to ensure forward progress. Algorithm 1 provides the pseudocode of μC-States.

The First Phase. The first phase of our algorithm tunes EX_{SP}, EX_{SFU}, and EX_{LDST}. It makes two main decisions. The first decision is related to EX_{SP} and EX_{SFU}. As dis-

[5] A better memory system design that tries to service each wavefront's requests in parallel (e.g., using *ranking* principles similar to those in [7,13,18,22,48,49,63,66,71,73,83,84,91]), can provide better performance than existing GPU memory systems, but they cannot eliminate the memory contention problem. Thus, we leave the exploration of such memory systems to future work.

[6] Note that the problem we have described is different from the one observed by prior work [43,67,76], where limiting the number of wavefronts/CTAs reduces cache line reuse distances and improves locality. In this paper, we reduce the *issue width,* which does *not* have a significant effect on cache line reuse. In fact, reducing the issue width can actually benefit applications that do *not* benefit from caching, whereas the aforementioned prior works obtain performance benefits mainly via improved cache performance.

Algorithm 1 μC-States

Phase 1
for i = SP, SFU **do**
  if $U[EX_i] < th_U$ **then**
    if EX_i not tuned down **then**
      $tune-down[EX_i]$.
  else
    $tune-up[EX_i]$.
if $ResponseTime[EX_{LDST}] > th_{RT}$ **then**
  if LDST not tuned down **then**
    $tune-down[EX_{LDST}]$.
else
  $tune-up[EX_{LDST}]$.

Phase 2
for i = OCEX, OC, IDOC **do**
  for j = SP, SFU, LDST **do**
    if $U[i_j] < U[EX_j]$ **then**
      if i_j not tuned down **then**
        $tune-down[i_j]$.
    else
      $tune-up[i_j]$.

*U[i] = Utilization of component i
*$tune-up[i]$ = Turn ON all groups of component i

Phase 3
if $(U[SCH] < (th_U \times 2))$ && $(U[SCH_i] < U[EX_i])$ $\forall$ i = SP, SFU, LDST **then**
  if SCH not tuned down **then**
    $tune-down[SCH]$.
  if $U[IFID] < U[SCH]$ **then**
    if IFID not tuned down **then**
      $tune-down[IFID]$.
  else
    $tune-up[IFID]$.
else
  $tune-up[SCH]$; $tune-up[IFID]$.

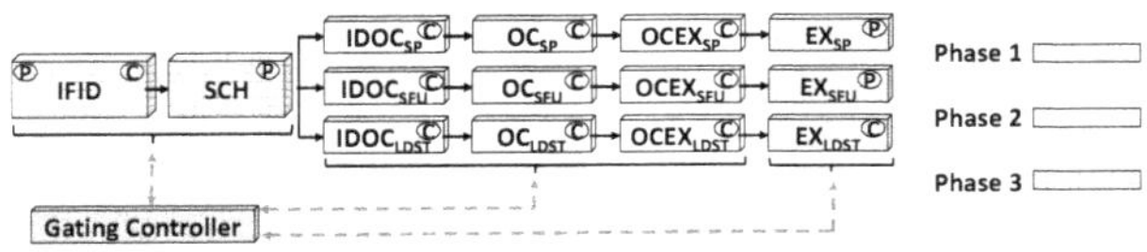

Figure 8: Phases of μC-States. Components marked with P and C are power-gated, and clock-gated respectively. In IFID, the instruction decoder is power-gated, and the instruction-buffer is clock-gated.

cussed in Section 3.1, the performance of the applications that have high EX_{SP} or EX_{SFU} utilization are sensitive to those resources. Thus, the controller tracks the utilization of EX_{SP} and EX_{SFU} during an interval. At the end of the interval, it tunes-down the components with low utilization levels. In order to track component utilization, the controller tracks the busy cycles of each component during the interval. EX_{SP} busy cycles in an interval is between 0 and the number of powered-on SPs, multiplied by the interval length. Dividing this number by the total number of SPs, and then by the interval length yields EX_{SP} utilization. If this value is lower than a threshold (th_U), the component is tuned-down. If it is above the threshold, all groups are turned on. Note that, if a component is tuned-down, its utilization will double assuming its throughput remains unchanged. Thus, a threshold greater than 0.5 is likely to cause performance loss.

The second decision is related to EX_{LDST}. Applications do not benefit from more LDST units if the performance bottleneck of the application is the memory system rather than the memory pipeline (Section 3.2). Applications that are bottlenecked by the memory system observe high memory access latency. Thus, tracking memory access latency can be one way to find which applications are bottlenecked by the memory system. However, since tracking the average memory access latency in hardware is costly due to the need of tagging each request with a time-stamp and measuring the latency of each returned request, we approximate it by calculating the response time of EX_{LDST} using Little's Law (see Section 2.2). The controller calculates the average response time of EX_{LDST}, and tunes-down the unit if the response time is higher than the Response Time threshold (th_{RT}). Response time is calculated by keeping track of the number of wavefronts that have outstanding memory accesses (J) and the number of wavefronts that have entered EX_{LDST} during the last interval (λ). Note that the first phase does not require EX_{LDST} tracking utilization, but requires calculating EX_{LDST} response time.

The Second Phase. This phase tunes IDOC and OCEX pipeline registers, OC units, and register file banks. It makes use of the fact that the bottleneck component is the component with the highest utilization. Based on this, the controller calculates the ratio of the utilization of each component to the utilization of its corresponding execute stage unit (e.g., $IDOC_{SP}$ is compared against EX_{SP}; or $OCEX_{LDST}$ is compared against EX_{LDST}). If this ratio is lower than 1 (i.e., the component is not the bottleneck), the component is tuned-down. The ratio must be less than 0.5 to ensure that the bottleneck does not move from the execute stage to the tuned-down component. However, we find that the pipeline registers, OC units, and the register file banks are rarely bottleneck components, therefore, we employ an aggressive approach for tuning-down these components. In case these components become the bottleneck after this phase, the decision is reverted back in the next execution of this phase. This phase requires the utilization values for all IDOC, OC, OCEX, and EX stage components.

The Third Phase. This phase tunes IFID and SCH. Tuning these components is different from tuning others, because IFID and SCH serve *all* types of instructions, whereas other components are dedicated for a specific type of instruction. In this phase, we break the utilization of SCH into three: SP, SFU, and MEM type instructions. The controller compares SCH utilization for each type of instruction to the utilization of the corresponding execute stage unit. If SCH utilization is higher for at least one of the instruction types, SCH is considered to be the bottleneck, and is not tuned-down. Also, if SCH utilization is greater than a threshold ($2\times$ th_U), it is not tuned-down.[7] Otherwise, SCH is tuned-down. If the overall IFID utilization is lower than SCH utilization, IFID is *not* the bottleneck component, and it is also tuned-down whenever SCH is tuned-down.

Component Interactions. Tuning-down a component affects the other components that share the same instruction path. For example, if EX_{SP} is tuned-down, its utilization increases, which creates opportunities for tuning-down other non-bottleneck components. Following this, if SCH is also tuned-down, its utilization increases. If this moves the bottleneck to SCH, SCH will not be tuned-down anymore, as the limited SCH throughput would reduce system throughput. Thus, μC-States tries to achieve a system with balanced component utilization levels across its iterations.

5. EXPERIMENTAL METHODOLOGY

Simulated System. We simulate the baseline architecture described in Table 3 using a modified version of GPGPU-Sim v3.2.2 [9]. The modifications allow GPGPU-Sim to run multiple applications concurrently and support heterogeneous core configurations.

Application Suites for GPUs. We evaluated 34 GPU applications from various suites such as the CUDA SDK [9], Rodinia [15], Parboil [81], Mars [30], SHOC [16], and LonestarGPU [11], listed in Table 1.

[7]We pick this threshold, because we observe that SCH is utilized mainly due to SP and SFU components, not LDST (see Table 1). The threshold for keeping all SCH groups on should be greater than th_U, because SCH serves both classes of instructions, each using th_U in their respective Phase-1 tuning decisions. Thus, we use $2\times$ th_U to tune SCH.

Table 3: Baseline GPGPU configuration.

Core Config.	16 Shader Cores, SIMT Width = 32 × 4
Resources/Core	Max. 1536 Threads, 32 threads/wavefront, 48 wavefronts, 36864 Registers
Caches/Core	16KB 4-way L1 Data Cache, 12KB 24-way Texture, 8KB 2-way Constant Cache, 2KB 4-way I-cache, 48KB Shared Memory, 128B Line Size
LLC Cache	768 KB/Memory Partition, 128B Line, 16-way
Wavefront Sch.	Greedy-then-oldest [76]
Features	Memory Coalescing, Inter-wavefront Merging
Interconnect	16×6 Crossbar, 32B Channel Width
Memory Model	6 Shared GDDR5 MCs (×2 sub-partitions), 924 MHz, FR-FCFS [75, 92], 16 DRAM-banks/MC

Performance Metrics. We report Instructions Per Cycle (IPC). For heterogeneous GPU simulations, we report Weighted speedup (WS) [23, 24, 80], defined as $WS = \sum_{i=1}^{N} SD_i$, where SD_i is the slowdown of the ith application given by $SD_i = \frac{IPC_i}{IPC_i^{alone}}$, where IPC_i^{alone} is IPC of the ith application running alone on the entire GPU.

Power Metrics. We use GPUWattch [54] to obtain the dynamic power consumption. To estimate static power, we configure GPUWattch [54] to model our baseline, and use its area estimates to obtain the area of individual core components. We assume the static power of each core component is directly proportional to its area [79]. We conservatively assume that non-core components, such as the memory subsystem and DRAM, contribute to 40% of static power (using a smaller ratio would increase our power benefits). We assume no static power for a component group when it is power-gated. We report dynamic and static power separately from each other.

Mechanism Thresholds. Our scheme uses 2 thresholds: th_U and th_{RT}. We determine th_U to be 0.15, based on the data given in Table 1 and the sensitivity of each application to EX_{SP} and EX_{SFU}. Phase-3 of our scheme uses 2× th_U for tuning SCH. We observe that our scheme works efficiently when th_U is between 0.1 and 0.2. Phase-1 uses 100 cycles as th_{RT}, and our scheme is effective when this value is between 80 and 150. All thresholds are empirically determined.

Hardware Overhead. To implement μC-States, each core requires a storage overhead of 32B. For the computation of the response time and the utilization of the pipeline components, each core requires a 14-bit division unit, a 7-bit adder, and a 14-bit comparator.

6. EXPERIMENTAL RESULTS

6.1 Dynamic Adaptation

We analyze the dynamic behavior of μC-States. We show how it tunes down components during execution in two different applications with different dynamic behavior, RED and PATH, in Figures 9a and 9b, respectively.[8] Note that SCH and EX_{SP} are power-gated, whereas EX_{LDST} is clock-gated. RED is one of the applications that experiences significant tuning-down/up at run-time. Since this application has low EX_{SP} utilization (Table 1), μC-States tunes down the SP units after the first interval, and keeps it tuned down during the whole execution. Following this, the scheduler becomes under-utilized compared to the execution units, and is also tuned-down throughout the execution. Although SCH and EX_{SP} show a stable behavior over time, one group of EX_{LDST} units is frequently turned on and off. This happens due to the sudden changes in response time observed by EX_{LDST}. The most frequent re-tuning of EX_{LDST} is done at an interval of 6144 (2048 × 3) cycles. Overall, we observe that a group of EX_{LDST} units is tuned down 80% of the time. Our analysis shows that RED performs as good as the baseline with C_{HALF} (Table 2), and tuning down the components most of the time does not hurt performance. In contrast to RED, PATH shows stable behavior throughout execution. In PATH, most of the components have high utilization and EX_{LDST} observes low response time. Therefore, SCH, EX_{SP}, and EX_{LDST} are *not* tuned-down throughout execution, except for a short period of time where EX_{SP} is tuned down. Thus, our proposal tunes each component only a few times during execution, and does so at a coarse granularity. This provides robustness, and reduces the impact of PG-related timing overheads on performance and potential power savings.

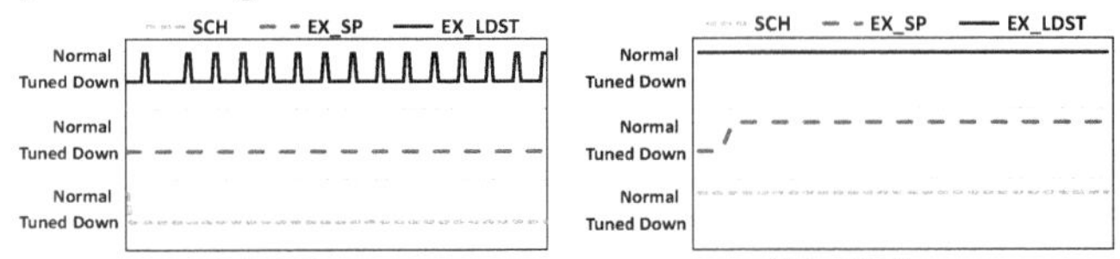

(a) RED (b) PATH

Figure 9: Dynamic behavior of applications showing the tuning down of three components: SCH, EX_{SP}, EX_{LDST}. "Normal" denotes the case where all groups are turned on.

To demonstrate the effect of μC-States on the utilization of each datapath component, Figure 10 shows the average utilization of each component with our baseline and with μC-States, for two applications with different behavior. We make three observations. First, the utilization levels of the components in compute-intensive PATH do not change significantly with μC-States, because, as shown in Figure 9b, μC-States rarely tunes-down the pipeline components. Second, in SCP, IFID and SCH utilization increases. This is because: (1) since we tune-down IFID and SCH during most of the execution, component utilization increases as the same amount of work is done with fewer resources; and (2) because our definition of SCH utilization is directly related to wavefront IPC,[9] and because μC-States improves performance in SCP (14%), we see an increase in SCH utilization. Third, in SCP, the reduced scheduler throughput reduces queuing in the memory pipeline, leading to lower memory pipeline utilization. μC-States also reduces the average response time of the EX_{LDST} unit by 9%, across 34 applications.

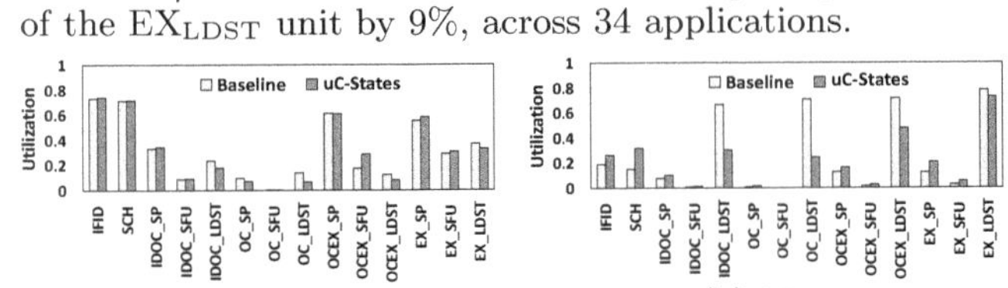

(a) PATH (b) SCP

Figure 10: Component utilization with baseline and μC-States.

In Figure 11, we show the average fraction of time that IFID, SCH, EX_{SP}, EX_{SFU}, and EX_{LDST} units are on. Note that this value changes between 0.5 and 1, because when we tune-down a component, we power-gate or clock-gate only half of its units. A component with a value of 0.5 means that the component is tuned-down throughout the entire execution. The figure demonstrates that IFID is usually critical for performance, and it is tuned-down moderately. SCH is less critical for performance, and it is tuned-down in most of the applications except the ones that can achieve high throughput and are compute-intensive. The execute-stage

[8]For clarity, we analyze only SCH, EX_{SP}, and EX_{LDST}, because they are the most critical components for performance. We plot a representative period starting from the kernel launch.

[9]Wavefront IPC is defined as the number of wavefront instructions issued per cycle. It does not consider control divergence.

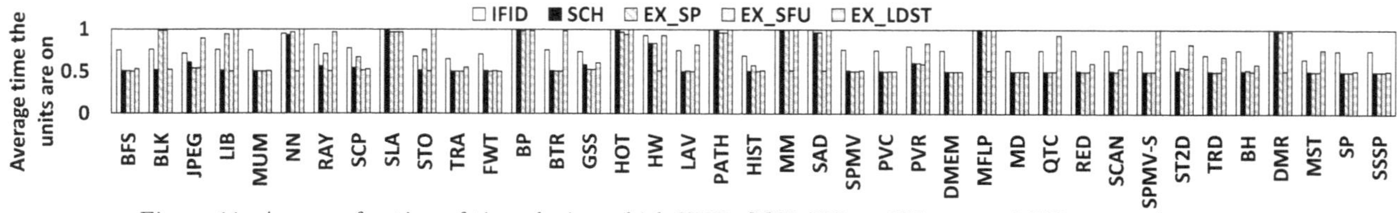

Figure 11: Average fraction of time during which IFID, SCH, EX_{SP}, EX_{SFU}, and EX_{LDST} units are on.

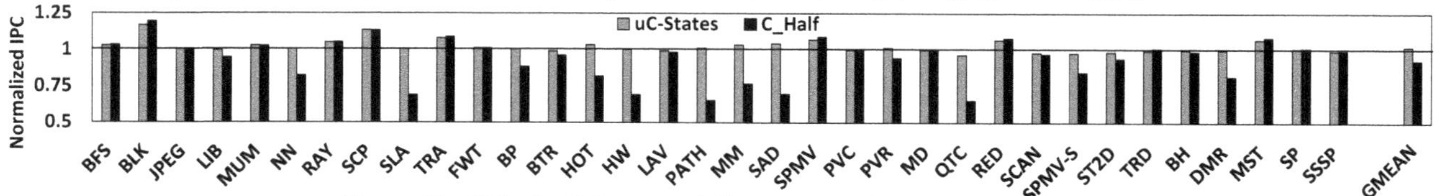

Figure 12: IPC of μC-States and C_{HALF} normalized to the baseline.

units are tuned-down according to the application's compute requirements. EX_{LDST} is often tuned-down in applications that observe high memory access latency. Overall, μC-States is effective at determining the components that are not critical for performance and tuning them down.

6.2 Application Performance

Figure 12 shows the impact of μC-States on performance (IPC), normalized to that of the baseline. We also compare our mechanism to C_{HALF}. We make four major observations. First, overall, μC-States performs 2% and 10% better than the baseline and C_{HALF}, respectively, on average. Second, μC-States does not degrade any application's performance significantly, compared to the baseline. The worst performing application is QTC, with only 3% performance loss. In comparison, Abdel-Majeed *et al.* [2] demonstrate in their work that their proposal causes up to 10% performance loss. Third, μC-States improves the performance of applications that benefit from C_{HALF}. In applications such as BLK, SCP, RAY, TRA, SPMV, RED and MST, μC-States performs better than the baseline, and as good as C_{HALF}, due to the positive effect of halving the scheduler width (as discussed in Section 3.2 for Figure 5d). These seven applications experience 9% average performance improvement with μC-States over the baseline. Fourth, μC-States performs as good as the baseline in applications that significantly benefit from more pipeline resources (i.e., the applications that perform poorly with C_{HALF}). These applications either require more compute resources (SLA, HW, PATH, MM, and SAD), more memory pipeline resources (QTC and SPMV-S), or both (NN and DMR). We conclude that μC-States enables a big-core GPU to become higher performance than both a small-core GPU and an unmanaged big-core GPU.

Comparison to CCWS. Our approach for improving performance is significantly different from previously proposed wavefront throttling techniques such as CCWS [76]. CCWS *reduces the number of wavefronts* that can issue requests if the first level data cache is detected to be thrashed due to high TLP, and is thus *useful for cache-sensitive applications.* In contrast, our approach does *not* consider cache thrashing. Instead, it *reduces the issue width* if we detect that the *memory system* is the bottleneck resource in the system, and is thus *useful for memory-bottlenecked applications that suffer from memory divergence.* We evaluated CCWS using two cache-insensitive applications that benefit from our technique (BLK and TRA), and observed that the application performance degrades by 4% and 2%, respectively, compared to the baseline. Our technique and CCWS aim to solve different problems, and thus can be combined to provide further benefits.

6.3 Power Consumption

Static Power. Figure 13 shows the impact of μC-States on static power consumption, normalized to that of the baseline. The figure also shows the static power of C_{HALF} as a straight line. We show the component-wise breakdown in Figure 14. We observe that μC-States reduces **static power** to the levels of that of C_{HALF} in applications that do not need all the pipeline resources for higher performance. In such applications, the majority of the benefits come from tuning down the EX_{SP} units. The only exception is BLK, in which EX_{SP} can be tuned down without affecting performance, but its utilization is greater than the respective threshold to be tuned down. Since performance of BLK improves due to the reduced issue width, we also observe significant SCH static power savings. Overall, 81% of μC-States' static power savings come from EX_{SP}, and 9% from IFID and SCH. μC-States provides 16% average static power savings.

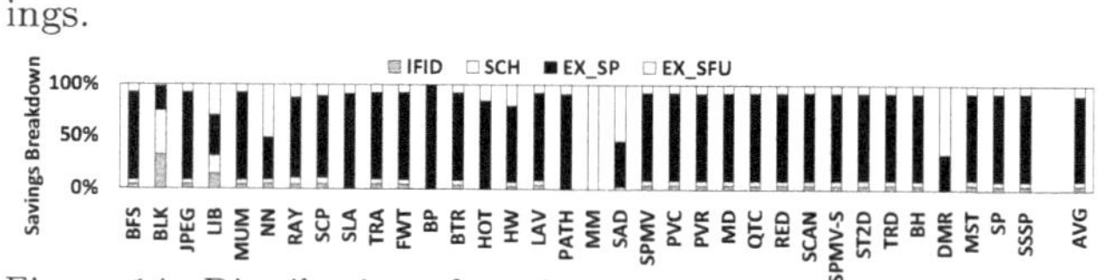

Figure 14: Distribution of static power savings with μC-States, for different pipeline components.

Dynamic Power. μC-States also reduces the average **dynamic power** consumption by 7% (not graphed). The dynamic power savings mainly come from clock-gating the pipeline registers, EX_{LDST}, operand collectors, and the register file banks. The savings from the instruction buffers is negligible. MM, an application that rarely utilizes EX_{LDST}, is the application that experiences the highest dynamic power

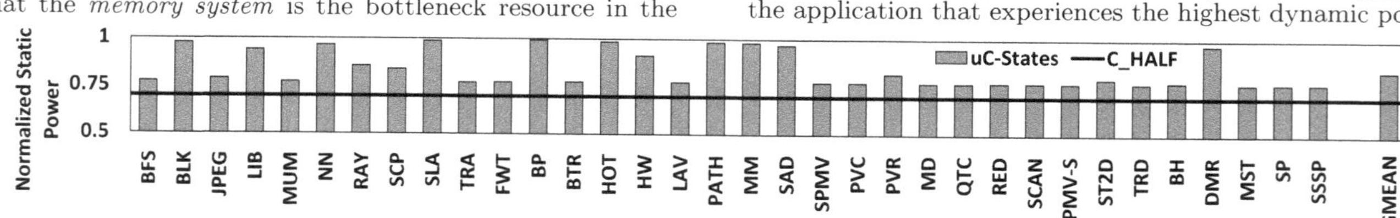

Figure 13: Static power of μC-States and C_{HALF} normalized to the baseline.

savings (14%). Assuming that static/dynamic power contributes to 40%/60% of the total chip power in a similar architecture [57], μC-States reduces average chip power by around 11%.

Comparison to GPUWattch. We compare μC-States to the per-lane CG strategy proposed in GPUWattch [54]. GPUWattch clock gates the individual SIMD lanes that are not used in the presence of branch divergence. Thus, it reduces power consumption only when *some of the SIMD lanes of an active component* are idle. In contrast, μC-States clock-gates a component group when it predicts that not using that group negligibly impacts application performance. We find that these two approaches are complementary. GPUWattch alone saves 5% dynamic power, and when combined with μC-States (with 7% dynamic power savings alone), the total dynamic power savings become 10%. μC-States provides static power savings on top of this, which the GPUWattch strategy cannot provide.

6.4 Sensitivity Studies

Sensitivity to register file size and the number of CTAs/core. In our baseline, we used a register file size and CTAs/core limit similar to NVIDIA Fermi [68], because prior work shows that the register file is underutilized [50, 88] and high CTA load can cause performance degradation [43]. We conduct a sensitivity study to show that μC-States works with a larger register file (64KB) and a higher CTAs/core limit (16), as in the NVIDIA Kepler architecture. Figures 15a and 15b show the performance and static power of μC-States normalized to the baseline with more register file and CTA resources, respectively. Similar to our previous results with the baseline configuration, we observe 2% performance improvement and 16% static power savings. Most of the applications that have low component utilization levels do not experience higher utilization by executing more CTAs. These applications are usually the ones that experience power savings when components are tuned-down. Because the component utilization levels are low even with more CTAs, there is still ample scope for tuning-down cores. Thus, the power benefits with μC-States do not reduce with more CTAs. On the other hand, the applications that have high component utilization levels do not provide significant power savings in our baseline, and thus the power savings they obtain with μC-States do not change significantly. We also observe that μC-States maintains the performance of these applications. We conclude that μC-States works effectively when employed in a system that has a larger register file and a higher CTAs/core limit.

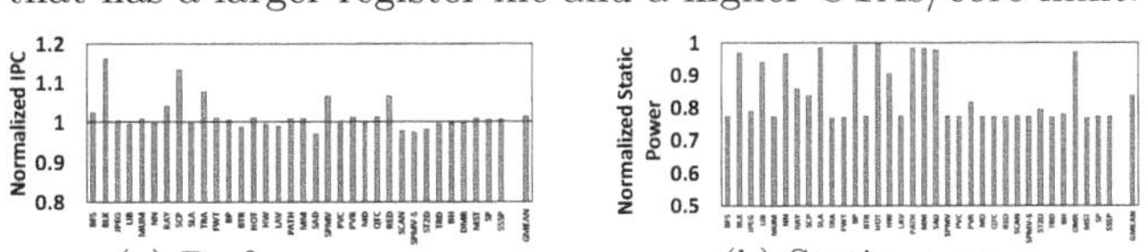

(a) Performance (b) Static power

Figure 15: Performance and static power of μC-States using a larger register file and CTAs/core limit, normalized to the baseline with a larger register file and CTAs/core limit.

Sensitivity to wavefront scheduling mechanisms. We conduct a study to show that μC-States can be employed with different wavefront schedulers [26, 40, 41, 53, 67, 76, 77]. We change our baseline GTO wavefront scheduler [76] to a round-robin (RR) scheduler [26]. Figure 16a and Figure 16b show the performance and static power of μC-States normalized to the baseline with RR, respectively. Overall, we observe that the performance benefits of μC-States increase to 5%, and static power savings remain at 16% with the RR scheduler.[10] Thus, our mechanism can work with any scheduler, but its power and performance benefits may vary with different schedulers. This is in contrast to recent work (e.g., Abdel-Majeed *et al.* [2]) where the power saving mechanisms are scheduler specific. Because the major goal of a warp scheduler is to improve performance, and not to make the utilization of pipeline components similar, we expect PG/CG opportunities to remain similar with different schedulers. Thus, our mechanism can identify any not-so-performance-critical components for power savings regardless of the choice of the wavefront scheduler.

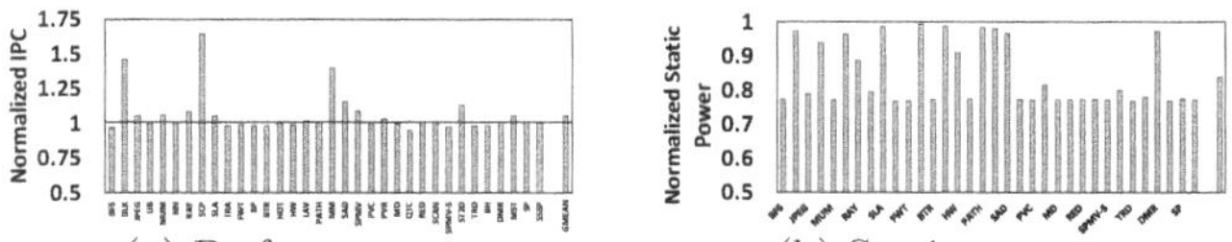

(a) Performance (b) Static power

Figure 16: Performance and static power of μC-States with the RR scheduler normalized to the baseline with RR scheduler.

Sensitivity to timing overhead parameters. We evaluated μC-States with different break-even and wake-up time parameters (Section 2.3) to show that our mechanism is not sensitive to these overheads. Taking a more conservative approach compared to Warped Gates [2], which uses break-even times of 9, 14, and 19 cycles, and wake-up times of 3, 6, and 9 cycles, we experimented with higher break-even times of 19, 29, and 39 cycles, and higher wake-up times of 9, 15, and 21 cycles. Since μC-States works at a much coarser granularity, and since it does not re-tune components frequently, we did not observe any significant impact on its power and performance benefits.

Sensitivity to the time interval between phases. In μC-States, the interval between two phases is 2048 cycles. Setting this parameter to 4K, 8K, and 16K cycles reduces performance benefits to 1.7%, 1.6%, and 1.1%, and static power benefits to 14%, 13.5%, and 12%, respectively. This reduction is because the responsiveness of μC-States to dynamic changes in the application behavior reduces with a longer interval.

7. HETEROGENEOUS-CORE GPU

Although we used our detailed GPU datapath component characterization to propose a new PG/CG technique, it can also be used for other purposes. One example is scheduling and design decisions in a GPU that contains heterogeneous (both small and big) cores. We provide a case study that shows having heterogeneous GPU cores is beneficial from power, performance and area aspects in a multiple application environment, when combined with a simple application mapping mechanism driven by our bottleneck analysis.

We simulate a heterogeneous GPU system consisting of 8 big cores used in our baseline, and 8 C_{HALF} cores. We compare this system to two different homogeneous configurations: our baseline (16 *big cores*) and C_{HALF} (16 *small cores*). We use nine workloads formed by mixing three applications that prefer C_{HALF} (`BLK`, `SCP`, and `FWT`) with three applications that prefer baseline cores (`MM`, `SAD`, and `NN`). The applications that prefer C_{HALF} are mapped to small cores. The other applications are mapped to the large cores. Figure 17 shows the performance of our heterogeneous-core GPU and C_{HALF} normalized to our baseline. We observe that 1) C_{HALF} causes 12% average performance loss over

[10] RR has been shown to perform poorly compared to GTO [76]. μC-States provides higher performance benefits for applications that prefer lower issue width with RR, compared to GTO.

the baseline, mainly because of the performance loss experienced by the applications that prefer more pipeline resources than C_{HALF} provides, and 2) the heterogeneous-core GPU performs as good as the baseline with fewer resources. Thus, having a heterogeneous-core GPU for executing multiple applications can provide the same performance as the baseline with 15% lower static power and lower area, when applications are intelligently mapped to the heterogeneous cores. We defer a detailed study of design issues to a future work.

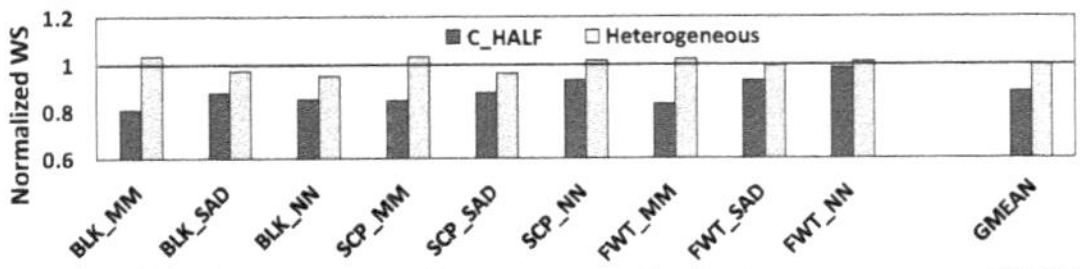

Figure 17: Performance of an example heterogeneous GPU and C_{HALF}, normalized to the baseline.

8. RELATED WORK

To our knowledge, this is the first work that performs a study on the sensitivity of the entire GPU datapath on performance, proposes a comprehensive power gating and clock gating mechanism for GPUs, and shows a proof-of-concept case study for *heterogeneous cores* within GPUs.

Power Saving Techniques. Abdel-Majeed *et al.* [2] propose a wavefront scheduler that clusters the same type of instructions and issues them to the execution units closeby in time before switching to other instruction type(s). This increases the idle time of specific execution units, and, thus, the PG opportunities. Our mechanism is different in four major ways: 1) instead of only execution units, we target the *whole* pipeline, and also the interactions between different pipeline components, based on well-established ideas from queuing theory to identify performance bottlenecks in GPU cores, 2) our scheme does *not* rely on long idle periods and is independent of the wavefront scheduler choice, 3) our strategy is *not* sensitive to timing and energy overhead parameters because it works at a coarser granularity, and 4) our mechanism does *not* cause significant performance loss for any of our applications, and improves performance of applications where the memory system is the bottleneck.

There are white papers on power saving mechanisms by AMD [4] and NVIDIA [70]. Our approach of using CG for some components instead of PG, to maintain execution state, is similar to AMD's approach. In AMD's design [4], some blocks are always-on (AON), and some are on-and-off (ONO), whereas we employ CG for the blocks that we do not power-gate. ONO blocks are 3D-graphics blocks, and they can be power-gated during runtime, whereas we focus on compute-related datapath components. NVIDIA Tegra 4 [70] employs CG and DVFS techniques for compute and graphics units when executing graphics and compute applications, respectively. Our mechanism works at a finer time and component granularity, building on our detailed analyses of fine-grained component utilization in Section 3.2.

Prior works in the context of CPUs clock-gate pipeline components based on resource usage [8, 55, 58], use reduced-size issue buffers for higher energy efficiency [25], dynamically tune resources for higher energy efficiency [3, 10, 74], and use a combination of fetch gating and issue queue adaptation [12]. None of these works improve performance. Hong *et al.* [31] propose core PG mechanisms to allow only a set of GPU cores to be active. Lee *et al.* [52] statically analyze the best GPU configuration under a fixed power budget. Ausavarungnirun *et al.* [6] propose a memory controller design that improves energy efficiency for a heterogeneous CPU-GPU architecture. Other prior works [1, 27, 28, 37, 54, 88–90] propose power efficiency techniques for memory, caches, register files and pipeline components in the context of GPUs. None of these works develop a comprehensive power and clock gating mechanism like this paper does for the entire GPU pipeline.

Configurable and Heterogeneous Architectures. Many works design more configurable and heterogeneous architectures for better power consumption and/or performance. Park *et al.* [72] adaptively customize the SIMD lanes in a multi-threaded architecture to improve energy-efficiency. Several works [35, 45, 46] propose mechanisms to morph larger cores into multiple smaller cores, or combine smaller cores to make larger ones. Van Craeynest *et al.* [87] propose a techniques to estimate an application's performance while executing the application on a larger core. Several works from Suleman *et al.* [85, 86], Joao *et al.* [38, 39] and Du Bois *et al.* [20] propose techniques that accelerate the bottleneck portions of multi-threaded applications on large cores of a heterogeneous multi-core processor. Guevara *et al.* [29] explore various design points for a heterogeneous architecture consisting of Xeon and Atom processors within a certain power budget. Mishra *et al.* [60, 61] design heterogeneous interconnects to maximize performance and power efficiency. None of these works consider fine-grained power or clock gating of GPU pipeline components or having heterogeneous cores in GPUs.

9. CONCLUSION

We introduce μC-States, a new, comprehensive power- and clock-gating framework for GPUs that improves both power consumption and performance. μC-States minimizes power consumption by turning off, or tuning-down, datapath components that are not bottlenecks for the performance of the running application. Our mechanism is based on a new, rigorous, queuing-theory-based analysis of datapath component utilization of various applications in big-core GPUs, which demonstrates that: (1) many GPU datapath components are heavily underutilized, and this underutilization varies across components and within and across applications, and (2) having more resources in a GPU core can sometimes degrade application performance by increasing contention in the memory system. We show that our analysis could also be useful in guiding scheduling and design decisions in a heterogeneous-core GPU with both small and big cores. Our case study demonstrates that a heterogeneous-core GPU can provide lower power consumption and smaller chip area at the same performance as a conventional big-core GPU design. We believe and hope that the analysis and mechanisms provided in this paper can be useful for developing other new analyses and optimization techniques for more efficient GPU and heterogeneous architectures.

ACKNOWLEDGMENTS

The authors would like to thank the reviewers for their feedback. This research is supported in part by NSF grants #1205618, #1213052, #1212962, #1302225, #1302557, #1317560, #1320478, #1320531, #1409095, #1409723, #1439021, #1439057, and #1526750. Adwait Jog acknowledges the start-up grant from the College of William and Mary. AMD, the AMD Arrow logo, and combinations thereof are trademarks of Advanced Micro Devices, Inc. Other product names used in this publication are for identification purposes only and may be trademarks of their respective companies.

REFERENCES

[1] M. Abdel-Majeed and M. Annavaram, "Warped Register File: A Power Efficient Register File for GPGPUs," in *HPCA*, 2013.

[2] M. Abdel-Majeed *et al.*, "Warped Gates: Gating Aware Scheduling and Power Gating for GPGPUs," in *MICRO*, 2013.

[3] D. H. Albonesi *et al.*, "Dynamically Tuning Processor Resources with Adaptive Processing," *IEEE Computer*, 2003.

[4] AMD, "AMD: Power-gating in a High-Performance GPU," 2009. Available: http://www.powerforward.org/media/p/125.aspx

[5] AMD, "AMD Graphics Cores Next (GCN) Architecture," 2012. Available: https://www.amd.com/Documents/GCN_Architecture_whitepaper.pdf

[6] R. Ausavarungnirun *et al.*, "Staged Memory Scheduling: Achieving High Performance and Scalability in Heterogeneous Systems," in *ISCA*, 2012.

[7] R. Ausavarungnirun *et al.*, "Exploiting Inter-Warp Heterogeneity to Improve GPGPU Performance," in *PACT*, 2015.

[8] R. I. Bahar and S. Manne, "Power and Energy Reduction via Pipeline Balancing," in *ISCA*, 2001.

[9] A. Bakhoda *et al.*, "Analyzing CUDA Workloads Using a Detailed GPU Simulator," in *ISPASS*, 2009.

[10] R. Balasubramonian *et al.*, "Memory Hierarchy Reconfiguration for Energy and Performance in General-purpose Processor Architectures," in *MICRO*, 2000.

[11] M. Burtscher *et al.*, "A Quantitative Study of Irregular Programs on GPUs," in *IISWC*, 2012.

[12] A. Buyuktosunoglu *et al.*, "Energy Efficient Co-adaptive Instruction Fetch and Issue," in *ISCA*, 2003.

[13] K. K.-W. Chang *et al.*, "HAT: Heterogeneous Adaptive Throttling for On-Chip Networks," in *SBAC-PAD*, 2012.

[14] N. Chatterjee *et al.*, "Managing DRAM Latency Divergence in Irregular GPGPU Applications," in *SC*, 2014.

[15] S. Che *et al.*, "Rodinia: A Benchmark Suite for Heterogeneous Computing," in *IISWC*, 2009.

[16] A. Danalis *et al.*, "The Scalable Heterogeneous Computing (SHOC) Benchmark Suite," in *GPGPU*, 2010.

[17] R. Das *et al.*, "Application-to-Core Mapping Policies to Reduce Memory System Interference in Multi-Core Systems," in *HPCA*, 2013.

[18] R. Das *et al.*, "Application-aware Prioritization Mechanisms for On-chip Networks," in *MICRO*, 2009.

[19] R. Das *et al.*, "AERGIA: Exploiting Packet Latency Slack in On-chip Networks," in *ISCA*, 2010.

[20] K. Du Bois *et al.*, "Criticality Stacks: Identifying Critical Threads in Parallel Programs Using Synchronization Behavior," in *ISCA*, 2013.

[21] E. Ebrahimi *et al.*, "Fairness via Source Throttling: a Configurable and High-performance Fairness Substrate for Multi-core Memory Systems," in *ASPLOS*, 2010.

[22] E. Ebrahimi *et al.*, "Parallel Application Memory Scheduling," in *MICRO*, 2011.

[23] S. Eyerman and L. Eeckhout, "System-level Performance Metrics for Multiprogram Workloads," *IEEE Micro*, 2008.

[24] S. Eyerman and L. Eeckhout, "Restating the Case for Weighted-IPC Metrics to Evaluate Multiprogram Workload Performance," *IEEE Comput. Arch. Letter*, vol. 13, no. 2, pp. 93–96, Jul. 2014.

[25] D. Folegnani and A. González, "Energy-effective Issue Logic," in *ISCA*, 2001.

[26] W. Fung *et al.*, "Dynamic Warp Formation and Scheduling for Efficient GPU Control Flow," in *MICRO*, 2007.

[27] M. Gebhart *et al.*, "Energy-efficient Mechanisms for Managing Thread Context in Throughput Processors," in *ISCA*, 2011.

[28] S. Z. Gilani *et al.*, "Exploiting GPU Peak-power and Performance Tradeoffs through Reduced Effective Pipeline Latency," in *MICRO*, 2013.

[29] M. Guevara *et al.*, "Navigating Heterogeneous Processors with Market Mechanisms," in *HPCA*, 2013.

[30] B. He *et al.*, "Mars: A MapReduce Framework on Graphics Processors," in *PACT*, 2008.

[31] S. Hong and H. Kim, "An Integrated GPU Power and Performance Model," in *ISCA*, 2010.

[32] M. Houston, "Anatomy of AMD's TeraScale Graphics Engine," 2008. Available: http://s08.idav.ucdavis.edu/houston-amd-terascale.pdf

[33] Z. Hu *et al.*, "Microarchitectural Techniques for Power Gating of Execution Units," in *ISLPED*, 2004.

[34] Intel, "Energy-Efficient Platforms - Considerations for Application Software and Services," 2011. Available: http://www.intel.com/content/dam/doc/white-paper/energy-efficient-platforms-2011-white-paper.pdf

[35] E. Ipek *et al.*, "Core Fusion: Accommodating Software Diversity in Chip Multiprocessors," in *ISCA*, 2007.

[36] R. Jain, "The Art of Computer System Performance Analysis: Techniques for Experimental Design, Measurement, Simulation and Modeling," *New York: John Willey*, 1991.

[37] N. Jing *et al.*, "An Energy-efficient and Scalable eDRAM-based Register File Architecture for GPGPU," in *ISCA*, 2013.

[38] J. A. Joao *et al.*, "Bottleneck Identification and Scheduling in Multithreaded Applications," in *ASPLOS*, 2012.

[39] J. A. Joao *et al.*, "Utility-based Acceleration of Multithreaded Applications on Asymmetric CMPs," in *ISCA*, 2013.

[40] A. Jog *et al.*, "Orchestrated Scheduling and Prefetching for GPGPUs," in *ISCA*, 2013.

[41] A. Jog *et al.*, "OWL: Cooperative Thread Array Aware Scheduling Techniques for Improving GPGPU Performance," in *ASPLOS*, 2013.

[42] A. Jog *et al.*, "Exploiting Core Criticality for Enhanced Performance in GPUs," in *SIGMETRICS*, 2016.

[43] O. Kayiran *et al.*, "Neither More Nor Less: Optimizing Thread-level Parallelism for GPGPUs," in *PACT*, 2013.

[44] O. Kayiran *et al.*, "Managing GPU Concurrency in Heterogeneous Architectures," in *MICRO*, 2014.

[45] Khubaib *et al.*, "MorphCore: An Energy-Efficient Microarchitecture for High Performance ILP and High Throughput TLP," in *MICRO*, 2012.

[46] C. Kim *et al.*, "Composable Lightweight Processors," in *MICRO*, 2007.

[47] H. Kim *et al.*, "Bounding Memory Interference Delay in COTS-based Multi-Core Systems," in *RTAS*, 2014.

[48] Y. Kim *et al.*, "ATLAS: A Scalable and High-performance Scheduling Algorithm for Multiple Memory Controllers," in *HPCA*, 2010.
[49] Y. Kim *et al.*, "Thread Cluster Memory Scheduling: Exploiting Differences in Memory Access Behavior," in *MICRO*, 2010.
[50] N. Lakshminarayana and H. Kim, "Spare Register Aware Prefetching for Graph Algorithms on GPUs," in *HPCA*, 2014.
[51] C. J. Lee *et al.*, "Improving Memory Bank-level Parallelism in the Presence of Prefetching," in *MICRO*, 2009.
[52] J. Lee *et al.*, "Improving Throughput of Power-constrained GPUs Using Dynamic Voltage/Frequency and Core Scaling," in *PACT*, 2011.
[53] S.-Y. Lee and C.-J. Wu, "CAWS: Criticality-aware Warp Scheduling for GPGPU Workloads," in *PACT*, 2014.
[54] J. Leng *et al.*, "GPUWattch: Enabling Energy Optimizations in GPGPUs," in *ISCA*, 2013.
[55] H. Li *et al.*, "Deterministic Clock Gating for Microprocessor Power Reduction," in *HPCA*, 2003.
[56] J. D. Little, "A Proof for the Queuing Formula," *Operations Research*, vol. 9, no. 3, pp. 383–387, 1961.
[57] J. Lucas *et al.*, "How a Single Chip Causes Massive Power Bills GPUSimPow: A GPGPU Power Simulator," in *ISPASS*, 2013.
[58] S. Manne *et al.*, "Pipeline Gating: Speculation Control for Energy Reduction," in *ISCA*, 1998.
[59] J. Meng *et al.*, "Dynamic Warp Subdivision for Integrated Branch and Memory Divergence Tolerance," in *ISCA*, 2010.
[60] A. K. Mishra *et al.*, "A Heterogeneous Multiple Network-on-Chip Design: An Application-Aware Approach," in *DAC*, 2013.
[61] A. K. Mishra *et al.*, "A case for heterogeneous on-chip interconnects for CMPs," in *ISCA*, 2011.
[62] T. Moscibroda and O. Mutlu, "Memory Performance Attacks: Denial of Memory Service in Multi-Core Systems," in *USENIX Security*, 2007.
[63] T. Moscibroda and O. Mutlu, "Distributed Order Scheduling and Its Application to Multi-core DRAM Controllers," in *PODC*, 2008.
[64] S. P. Muralidhara *et al.*, "Reducing Memory Interference in Multicore Systems via Application-Aware Memory Channel Partitioning," in *MICRO*, 2011.
[65] O. Mutlu and T. Moscibroda, "Stall-Time Fair Memory Access Scheduling for Chip Multiprocessors," in *MICRO*, 2007.
[66] O. Mutlu and T. Moscibroda, "Parallelism-Aware Batch Scheduling: Enhancing Both Performance and Fairness of Shared DRAM Systems," in *ISCA*, 2008.
[67] V. Narasiman *et al.*, "Improving GPU Performance via Large Warps and Two-level Warp Scheduling," in *MICRO*, 2011.
[68] NVIDIA, "Fermi: NVIDIA's Next Generation CUDA Compute Architecture," 2011.
[69] NVIDIA, "NVIDIA's Next Generation CUDA Compute Architecture: Kepler GK110," 2012.
[70] NVIDIA, "Tegra 4 Family GPU Architecture," 2013. Available: http://www.nvidia.com/docs/IO/116757/Tegra_4_GPU_Whitepaper_FINALv2.pdf
[71] G. P. Nychis *et al.*, "On-chip networks from a networking perspective: congestion and scalability in many-core interconnects," in *SIGCOMM*, 2012.
[72] Y. Park *et al.*, "Libra: Tailoring SIMD Execution Using Heterogeneous Hardware and Dynamic Configurability," in *MICRO*, 2012.
[73] M. K. Qureshi *et al.*, "A Case for MLP-Aware Cache Replacement," in *ISCA*, 2006.
[74] P. Ranganathan *et al.*, "Reconfigurable Caches and Their Application to Media Processing," in *ISCA*, 2000.
[75] S. Rixner *et al.*, "Memory Access Scheduling," in *ISCA*, 2000.
[76] T. G. Rogers *et al.*, "Cache-Conscious Wavefront Scheduling," in *MICRO*, 2012.
[77] T. G. Rogers *et al.*, "Divergence-Aware Warp Scheduling," in *MICRO*, 2013.
[78] K. Roy *et al.*, "Leakage Current Mechanisms and Leakage Reduction Techniques in Deep-submicrometer CMOS Circuits," *Proceedings of the IEEE*, 2003.
[79] K. Roy *et al.*, "Leakage Current Mechanisms and Leakage Reduction Techniques in Deep-submicrometer CMOS Circuits," *Proceedings of the IEEE*, vol. 91, no. 2, pp. 305–327, 2003.
[80] A. Snavely and D. M. Tullsen, "Symbiotic Jobscheduling for a Simultaneous Multithreaded Processor," in *ASPLOS*, 2000.
[81] J. A. Stratton *et al.*, "Parboil: A Revised Benchmark Suite for Scientific and Commercial Throughput Computing," University of Illinois, at Urbana-Champaign, Tech. Rep. IMPACT-12-01, March 2012.
[82] L. Subramanian *et al.*, "The Blacklisting Memory Scheduler: Achieving High Performance and Fairness at Low Cost," in *ICCD*, 2014.
[83] L. Subramanian *et al.*, "The Application Slowdown Model: Quantifying and Controlling the Impact of Inter-Application Interference at Shared Caches and Main Memory," in *MICRO*, 2015.
[84] L. Subramanian *et al.*, "MISE: Providing performance predictability and improving fairness in shared main memory systems," in *HPCA*, 2013.
[85] M. A. Suleman *et al.*, "Data Marshaling for Multi-core Architectures," in *ISCA*, 2010.
[86] M. A. Suleman *et al.*, "Accelerating Critical Section Execution with Asymmetric Multi-core Architectures," in *ASPLOS*, 2009.
[87] K. Van Craeynest *et al.*, "Scheduling Heterogeneous Multi-cores Through Performance Impact Estimation (PIE)," in *ISCA*, 2012.
[88] N. Vijaykumar *et al.*, "A Case for Core-Assisted Bottleneck Acceleration in GPUs: Enabling Flexible Data Compression with Assist Warps," in *ISCA*, 2015.
[89] B. Wang *et al.*, "Exploring Hybrid Memory for GPU Energy Efficiency Through Software-hardware Co-design," in *PACT*, 2013.
[90] W.-k. S. Yu *et al.*, "SRAM-DRAM Hybrid Memory with Applications to Efficient Register Files in Fine-grained Multi-threading," in *ISCA*, 2011.
[91] J. Zhao *et al.*, "FIRM: Fair and High-Performance Memory Control for Persistent Memory Systems," in *MICRO*, 2014.
[92] W. K. Zuravleff and T. Robinson, "Controller for a Synchronous DRAM that Maximizes Throughput by Allowing Memory Requests and Commands to be Issued Out of Order," no. U.S. Patent Number 5,630,096, Sep. 1997.

Scheduling Techniques for GPU Architectures with Processing-In-Memory Capabilities

Ashutosh Pattnaik[1] Xulong Tang[1] Adwait Jog[2] Onur Kayıran[3]
Asit K. Mishra[4] Mahmut T. Kandemir[1] Onur Mutlu[5,6] Chita R. Das[1]
[1]Pennsylvania State University [2]College of William and Mary
[3]Advanced Micro Devices, Inc. [4]Intel Labs [5]ETH Zürich [6]Carnegie Mellon University

ABSTRACT

Processing data in or near memory (PIM), as opposed to in conventional computational units in a processor, can greatly alleviate the performance and energy penalties of data transfers from/to main memory. Graphics Processing Unit (GPU) architectures and applications, where main memory bandwidth is a critical bottleneck, can benefit from the use of PIM. To this end, an application should be properly partitioned and scheduled to execute on either the main, powerful GPU cores that are far away from memory or the auxiliary, simple GPU cores that are close to memory (e.g., in the logic layer of 3D-stacked DRAM).

This paper investigates two key code scheduling issues in such a GPU architecture that has PIM capabilities, to maximize performance and energy-efficiency: (1) how to automatically identify the code segments, or kernels, to be offloaded to the cores in memory, and (2) how to concurrently schedule multiple kernels on the main GPU cores and the auxiliary GPU cores in memory. We develop two new runtime techniques: (1) a *regression-based affinity prediction model and mechanism* that accurately identifies which kernels would benefit from PIM and offloads them to GPU cores in memory, and (2) a *concurrent kernel management* mechanism that uses the affinity prediction model, a new kernel execution time prediction model, and kernel dependency information to decide which kernels to schedule concurrently on main GPU cores and the GPU cores in memory. Our experimental evaluations across 25 GPU applications demonstrate that these two techniques can significantly improve both application performance (by 25% and 42%, respectively, on average) and energy efficiency (by 28% and 27%).

1. INTRODUCTION

Graphics Processing Units (GPUs) provide very high computational bandwidth at a competitive power budget. These characteristics have led to their deployment in a wide range of platforms, including in many machines that appear in the Top500 and Green500 lists [1,2]. Although GPUs are likely to play a promising role in the design of exascale systems, continuous scaling of their performance and energy efficiency will not be an easy task. One of the biggest impediments to this continuous scaling is the memory system energy consumption due to data transfer overhead [58]. A typical 64-bit DRAM access consumes about 100-1000X the energy consumed by a double-precision floating point operation [24,58], and this gap could increase with technology scaling [77]. Even with optimistic assumptions about improvements in memory technology, reducing the total DRAM access energy from approximately 18-22 pJ/b (in modern GDDR5) to 4 pJ/b and sustaining it for over 100,000 nodes, memory can still consume a significant fraction (e.g., 70%) of the total system's power budget [112].

Figure 1 illustrates the data movement and energy consumption overheads of transferring data between memory and computational units across 25 applications in a modern GPU system,[1] by showing: (1) the fraction of all data movement in the system that is due to off-chip transactions between memory and the GPU, and (2) the fraction of total system energy consumption that is due to this off-chip data movement. We observe that memory accesses result in 49% of all data movement and are responsible for 41% of the energy consumption of the system.

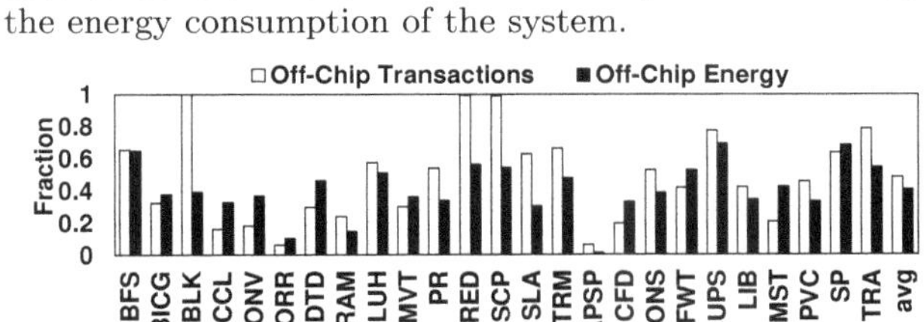

Figure 1: Data movement and system energy consumption caused by off-chip memory accesses.

Figure 2 shows the performance loss due to the overhead of transferring data from/to main memory, by plotting the normalized performance of our applications compared to an *idealized* system where all off-chip memory requests in our baseline are *magically* eliminated, i.e., forced to hit in the last-level cache.[2] Averaged across 25 applications, main memory accesses lead to 45% performance degradation.

A promising approach to minimize data movement, energy and performance overheads of main memory accesses is to move memory-intensive computations closer to memory, i.e., Processing-In Memory (PIM) [3,4,27,33], also known as Processing-Near Memory (PNM) or Near-Data Computing (NDC) [13]. The core of the PIM concept is to have computational units that are closely integrated with memory

PACT '16, September 11-15, 2016, Haifa, Israel

DOI: http://dx.doi.org/10.1145/2967938.2967940

[1]Section 6 provides our experimental methodology.

[2]The minimum DRAM latency after the last-level cache is 100 cycles (see Section 6 for details). The average latency is higher due to significant contention observed in the DRAM system [10, 26,54,57,59–61,63,75,76,78,79,100–102,107,108].

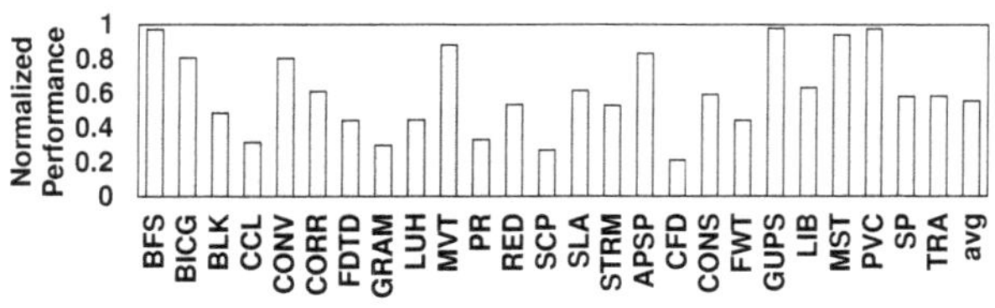

Figure 2: Performance normalized to a hypothetical GPU where all the off-chip accesses hit in the last-level cache.

such that data can be moved from memory to those units at much higher bandwidth, lower latency and lower energy than doable from memory to the main processor. While the PIM concept goes back to late 1960s [99] and it had gathered some momentum through several projects in 1990s (e.g. [33, 40, 55, 62, 67, 85]), its main technological limitation has been the difficulty of integrating computational units very close to memory. With the significant advances in adoption of 3D-stacked memory technology that tightly combines a logic layer and DRAM layers [3, 4, 48, 64, 71, 86, 109], this limitation has been overcome and PIM has become a likely-viable approach to improve system design.

The PIM approach has recently been explored (e.g., [44, 112]) for reducing memory bandwidth and minimizing the data transfer overheads between GPU cores and off-chip DRAM. A promising way to integrate PIM to a GPU-based system is what we call a *PIM-Assisted GPU architecture*, where at least one 3D-stacked memory chip is placed adjacent to the GPU chip, and both chips are interconnected via a memory link on an interposer (as depicted in Figure 3).[3] The 3D-stacked memory contains a base logic layer, housing GPU cores. This architecture has two types of compute engines: (1) large and powerful primary GPU cores, called GPU-PIC, i.e., processing-in-core, which are similar to modern GPU cores, and (2) smaller and less powerful GPU cores, called GPU-PIM, which are placed in the logic layer under main memory and assist in performing computation. No prior work explored how to fully exploit this architecture such that appropriate parts of an application are identified and scheduled to utilize *both* the main GPU cores (GPU-PIC) and cores in memory (GPU-PIM) to maximize the performance and energy-efficiency of the entire system.

Our goal in this paper is to develop mechanisms to fully and automatically exploit the performance and energy-efficiency potential of PIM-Assisted GPU architectures. To this end, we investigate **two key code scheduling problems**. First, *how to automatically identify the code segments to be offloaded to the GPU cores in memory*. Second, *how to concurrently schedule multiple kernels on the main GPU and the cores in memory*. To address these problems, one must consider several questions such as (1) what the granularity of the code segment that is offloaded to GPU-PIM should be, (2) how to determine which code segments benefit from being executed on GPU-PIM, (3) how to efficiently distribute work between the main GPU and the PIM engine to maximize system performance, (4) while executing each code segment on its preferred cores as much as possible.

To this end, we first characterize the execution behavior of different applications at the **kernel granularity** to estimate the performance and energy benefits when each individual kernel is placed in the main GPU or GPU-PIM. Because the CPU offloads computation to the GPU at the kernel-granularity, maintaining the same granularity for PIM execution enables low-overhead computation offloading from the CPU to both GPU-PIC and GPU-PIM. Based on this insight, we propose **two new runtime techniques**, the primary contributions of this paper, that address the two scheduling problems.

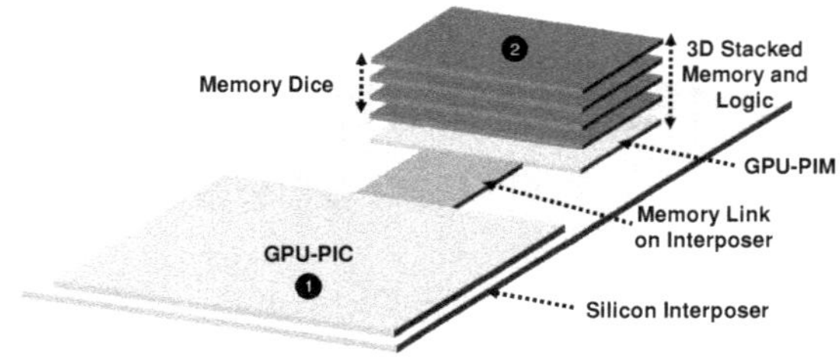

Figure 3: PIM-assisted GPU Architecture.

Kernel Offloading. As an application exhibits varying computation and memory demands during different phases of execution, some kernels (e.g., those that fit in the main GPU scratchpad) benefit more from executing on the main GPU, GPU-PIC, and others (e.g., those that overwhelm the memory bandwidth to the main GPU) on the GPU in memory, GPU-PIM. Thus, identifying the affinity of the kernels correctly and scheduling each on the appropriate computational engine would improve performance. To solve this problem, we develop a *regression-based affinity prediction model and mechanism* that accurately identifies, at runtime, which kernels would benefit from executing on PIM cores and offloads them to the GPU cores in memory. Our regression model, which is built on an in-depth kernel level analysis, considers three broad kernel-level metrics (memory intensity, kernel parallelism, and shared memory (software managed scratchpad) intensity) and is trained using applications randomly picked from our pool of 25 applications (i.e., the training set). Our detailed experimental evaluations on the remaining applications (i.e., the test set) show that the proposed mechanism improves average performance by 25% and energy efficiency by 28% compared to a baseline conventional GPU architecture that contains the same number of GPU cores as that of the combined number of GPU cores present in both GPU-PIC and GPU-PIM.

Concurrent Kernel Management. We find that even a highly accurate prediction mechanism for kernel offloading can leave many resources (e.g., GPU-PIC) underutilized. During the execution of a kernel on either the main GPU or GPU-PIM, the other device is left unutilized, which limits achievable system performance. Thus, identifying *independent kernels* that can be scheduled concurrently and scheduling them on GPU-PIC and GPU-PIM at the same time, in a manner that minimizes overall application execution time, can significantly improve system performance and efficiency. To solve this problem, we develop a *concurrent kernel management* mechanism that uses the affinity prediction model, a new regression-based kernel execution time prediction model, and dependency information across kernels to decide which kernels to schedule concurrently on the main GPU cores and the GPU cores in memory. Our detailed experimental evaluations indicate that our technique improves average performance by 42% and energy-efficiency by 27%, compared to the same baseline described above.

This paper makes the following major **contributions**:

1. It provides an in-depth kernel-level analysis of GPU application behavior with respect to suitability for Processing in Memory. It makes an experimentally-supported case for the use of *kernel granularity* to identify and schedule GPU

[3] Section 2.2 discusses details and advantages of this architecture.

program code segments to execute on either the main GPU cores or the GPU cores in memory.

2. It develops a new regression-based affinity prediction model to estimate the best compute engine to execute a kernel in a PIM-assisted GPU architecture. We show how to use this model to guide a new *kernel offloading* mechanism to GPU cores in memory.

3. It develops a new execution time prediction model for kernel execution in a PIM-assisted GPU architecture. We show how to use this model to guide a new *concurrent kernel management* mechanism that executes multiple kernels concurrently in the main GPU and the in-memory GPU cores in a PIM-assisted GPU architecture.

4. It comprehensively evaluates the *kernel offloading* and *concurrent kernel management* mechanisms and shows that both improve performance and energy efficiency significantly while requiring no support from the programmer.

2. BACKGROUND

This section provides a brief background on GPUs and the PIM-assisted GPU architecture.

2.1 Conventional GPU Architectures

Our baseline conventional GPU consists of multiple cores, also called streaming-multiprocessors (SMs)[4] in NVIDIA terminology [82]. Each SM has a private L1 data cache, a texture cache and a constant cache, along with a software-managed scratchpad memory (called *shared memory*). The SMs are connected to memory channels (partitions) via an interconnection network. Each memory partition is directly connected to a partition of the L2 cache, which is shared by all the cores, and a memory controller. The memory requests are buffered and scheduled by the memory controllers [9, 54, 106]. There are multiple memory controllers, each controlling a memory partition. Data is interleaved at the chunk granularity across the controllers. The parallel parts of a CUDA/OpenCL application, which are offloaded to the GPU, are called *kernels*. The execution of an application starts with the launch of a kernel on the GPU. The kernel launch involves copying the kernel code and the data from the CPU memory to the GPU memory. Once the kernel finishes execution on the GPU, its results are copied back to the CPU memory from the GPU memory.

2.2 PIM-Assisted GPU Architectures

As we discussed in Section 1, 3D-stacked memory technology enables the ability to place computational units in the base logic layer that is underneath the memory stacks [3, 4, 48, 64, 71, 86, 109]. There can be multiple strategies to exploit such a PIM technology in a GPU system.

One strategy is to stack the memory directly on top of a conventional GPU architecture, by placing a conventional GPU in the logic layer [114]. Although such an organization provides the benefits of tight GPU and memory coupling such as high bandwidth and low access latency, it has two primary issues. First, heat from the processor might significantly degrade the retention time of the 3D-stacked memory [68]. Consequently, the refresh rate of the DRAM might need to be increased, leading to reduced peak performance and higher energy consumption [20, 53, 68, 69, 88]. Second, such an organization limits the total memory capacity that could be stacked within the area of the processor.

[4]In this paper, we use the terms *core* and *SM* interchangeably.

Another strategy [44, 112] to exploit PIM in a GPU system is to keep the main GPU same as in conventional systems but connect to it, via memory links on a silicon interposer, one or more 3D-stacked memory units that are capable of doing computation, as depicted in Figure 3 with one 3D-stacked memory. The base logic layer of each 3D-stacked memory houses an auxiliary GPU that is simpler and more power-efficient than the main GPU. Such an organization has considerably lower thermal constraints than the previous strategy and is more scalable in terms of memory capacity. However, if computations are not scheduled appropriately across the main GPU and the computational units in the 3D-stacked memories, the energy consumption, latency and bandwidth overheads of the interposer may limit performance due to excessive communication between the main GPU and the 3D-memory stacks.

In this paper, we call the latter organization (of Figure 3) the *PIM-Assisted GPU architecture*, and aim to maximize its benefits by scheduling computations intelligently across the main GPU and PIM units. This architecture is a heterogeneous system. The main GPU chip, which we call the processing-in-core architecture (GPU-PIC ❶ in Figure 3), provides high throughput to compute-intensive GPGPU applications, but it has limited memory bandwidth due to its horizontal integration with the memory stack (bottlenecked by the memory links). On the other hand, the PIM cores on the base logic layer of the 3D memory stack, which we call the processing-in-memory architecture (GPU-PIM ❷ in Figure 3), achieves the full bandwidth and energy efficiency of 3D stacking of memory and logic, but provides a peak instruction throughput lower than that of GPU-PIC due to the smaller number of the execution engines in the logic layer. Therefore, placing computation correctly on these two different types of GPU units, GPU-PIC and GPU-PIM, is critical for performance and energy efficiency. For example, computations that are memory-intensive and can tolerate the lower parallelism present in the logic layer of GPUs are likely better executed on GPU-PIM instead of GPU-PIC.

Unlike GPU-PIC, GPU-PIM has a direct interface to 3D-stacked DRAM. Therefore, GPU-PIM is able to sustain much higher memory bandwidth (in our configuration, 4×) and it experiences much lower memory latency than GPU-PIC. Because of this, we observe that GPU-PIM does *not* significantly benefit from having an L2 cache and we evaluate a GPU-PIC design without an L2 cache. Table 4 provides the details of our GPU-PIC and GPU-PIM configuration, which is similar to the TOP-PIM configuration [112]. We also perform a sensitivity analysis in Section 8 on the number of cores and cache in GPU-PIM. Note that the cores in GPU-PIC and GPU-PIM use the same ISA, and thus, have the same programmability features.

Thermal Feasibility. Eckert et al. [29] provide extensive models to demonstrate the thermal feasibility of PIM-based GPU architectures. They argue that the power consumed by the logic layer at the GPU-PIM at an ambient temperature of 30°C can be as much as 50W and describe that this is thermally feasible. Considering their study and configuration parameters from [112], our GPU-PIM has four times fewer SIMD compute units, similar to [44]. We estimate the maximum chip power usage of GPU-PIM when running MaxFlops [25][5] to be approximately 45W, using GPUWattch [65]. GPUWattch models NVIDIA Fermi [82]

[5]MaxFlops is compute-intensive benchmark that exhibits high dynamic core power consumption.

SMs, which are obsolete and not power-efficient compared to current generation GPU cores [83]. Therefore, we believe GPU-PIM will be even more power efficient when fabricated for state-of-the-art and future power-efficient designs.

3. MOTIVATION

The PIM-assisted GPU architecture is a scalable and heterogeneous substrate. It provides the flexibility of adding more computational units on the GPU-PIC, and more memory capacity and bandwidth by incorporating additional 3D memory stacks containing GPU-PIM. At the same time, GPU-PIC and GPU-PIM architectures are quite different in terms of their ability to cater to applications with varying computation and memory demands. Given such heterogeneity in the PIM-assisted GPU architecture, it might be desirable for the CPU to offload a compute-bound GPGPU application onto GPU-PIC and a memory-bound GPGPU application onto GPU-PIM. However, this is not optimal, as we demonstrate in this section since it does not fully utilize both the GPU-PIC and GPU-PIM. There are many challenges in designing an offloading strategy to *maximize overall application performance and energy efficiency* by appropriately partitioning and scheduling an application across GPU-PIC and GPU-PIM. This section motivates the potential opportunities and limitations of *application offloading* to motivate our approach of *kernel offloading*.

3.1 Benefits of Application Offloading

Figure 4 shows the normalized performance (in terms of IPC) and energy efficiency (in terms of Instructions/Joules), compared to our baseline conventional GPU architecture with equivalent number of computation units (40 cores), when each application from our workload suite are offloaded by the CPU on either the GPU-PIM (8 cores) or the GPU-PIC (32 cores) in our PIM-Assisted GPU Architecture. *Best Application Offloading* shows the average performance and energy efficiency when each application is, with ideal knowledge, offloaded to the computation unit that provides the *best performance* for that application. We make three major observations.

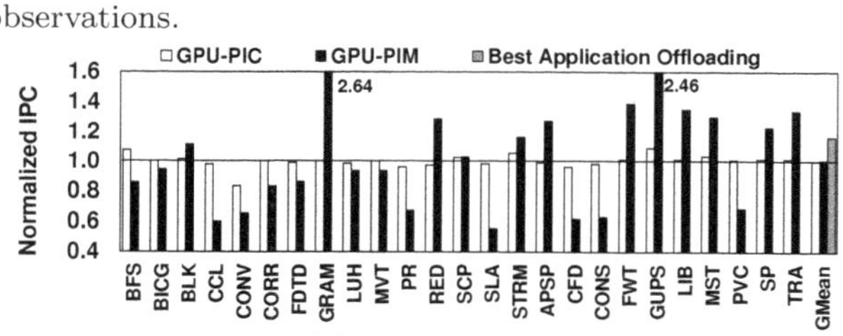

(a) Performance.

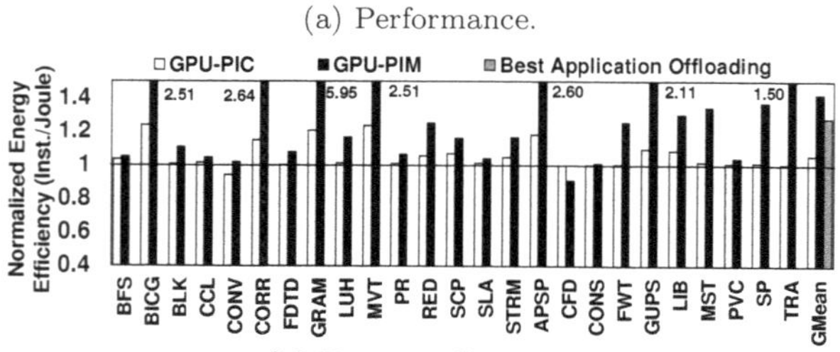

(b) Energy Efficiency.

Figure 4: Effect of application offloading.[6]

[6]The results are normalized to a conventional GPU which has the combined peak instruction throughput of GPU-PIC and GPU-PIM (i.e., 40 cores). The entire application is offloaded to either GPU-PIC (32 cores) or GPU-PIM (8 cores).

First, offloading all applications to either GPU-PIC or GPU-PIM yields similar average performance because some applications prefer GPU-PIC and others GPU-PIM. We find that many applications significantly gain from the high memory bandwidth and low memory latency benefits of GPU-PIM. Some applications, e.g., GRAM and APSP, benefit from GPU-PIM due to low memory access latencies. These two applications (GRAM and APSP) have limited parallelism (as shown later in Table 2), leading to poor latency tolerance. Neither of these applications stress the memory bandwidth and they have a small fraction of accesses going to off-chip memory (Figure 1). In contrast, many applications, such as CCL, PR, and CFD, experience performance degradation when executed on GPU-PIM, because they 1) are bottlenecked by the limited computational power of the PIM cores, 2) do not effectively utilize the high bandwidth of GPU-PIM because they generate a small number of memory requests.

Second, offloading all applications to GPU-PIM provides the highest average energy efficiency (Instructions/Joule), even higher than the *Best Application Offloading* mechanism which chooses the unit that provides the best *performance* on a per-application basis. This is because GPU-PIM leads to a much more energy-efficient memory system, on average. Applications such as GUPS, GRAM, and APSP benefit significantly from GPU-PIM in terms of energy efficiency, primarily because of the reduced execution time due to the performance improvements.

Third, an optimal application offloading scheme that can detect the best platform to execute an application on, based on performance, can provide both performance and energy improvements than offloading always to either GPU-PIC or GPU-PIM. On average, GPU-PIM improves energy efficiency by 42% over GPU-PIC while having the same performance of GPU-PIC. The optimal application offloading scheme (in terms of performance) improves performance by 16% and energy efficiency by 28% over the baseline. Note that the optimal scheme is optimized for performance, not energy efficiency, and therefore its energy efficiency is less than that of offloading all applications to GPU-PIM.

We also note that an optimal offloading scheme could be different based on the metric to optimize for. For example, for MVT, GPU-PIM is much more energy-efficient but lower performance than GPU-PIC. There is no clear winner as one could optimize for either performance or energy-efficiency, depending on the use-case. In this paper, we focus on optimizing performance. However, we also demonstrate the positive impact of our schemes on energy efficiency.

3.2 Limitations of Application Offloading

We demonstrate the limitations of application offloading. Even for an optimal *application* offloading strategy, we find two major limitations that need to be addressed to make offloading more efficient in terms of performance.

Limitation I: Lack of Fine-Grained Offloading. We observe that offloading at the granularity of each application is too coarse-grained to take advantage of the different characteristics of code present within an application that can favor either GPU-PIC or GPU-PIM. To motivate this, Figure 5 shows a *kernel-level*, i.e., finer-grained, execution time breakdown of four representative GPGPU applications on GPU-PIC and GPU-PIM, normalized to the execution time on GPU-PIC. We show only the kernels that dominate each application's execution time. Three observations are in order. First, CONS has two representative kernels and execution times of both kernels increase on GPU-PIM. Therefore, GPU-PIM is not an appropriate computation unit for any of CONS's kernels. Second, FWT has four representative kernels and execution times of all kernels decrease on GPU-PIM. Therefore, GPU-PIM is an appropriate configuration for all its kernels. Third, LUH and FDTD have kernels that demonstrate different behavior. Although both applications as a whole have higher execution times on GPU-PIM, some of their kernels actually benefit from GPU-PIM. For example, in LUH and FDTD, Kernel-K1 has lower execution time on GPU-PIM compared to GPU-PIC.

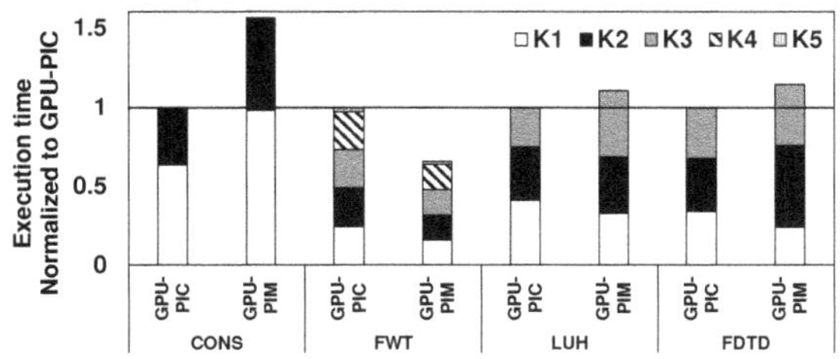

Figure 5: Breakdown of the execution time across different kernels for four representative GPGPU applications.

Thus, a careful *kernel-level* offloading strategy can perform even better than the application offloading strategy we evaluated (Section 3.1). Figure 6 illustrates the potential of kernel offloading for FDTD. Scenario-I and Scenario-II are the two possible application offloading strategies adopted to execute the entire FDTD on GPU-PIM or GPU-PIC, respectively. In the kernel offloading strategy (Scenario-III), each *kernel* of FDTD is offloaded to the computation engine where its execution time is lower (i.e., each kernel is offloaded to the unit it has *affinity* towards). Therefore, Kernel-K1 is offloaded to GPU-PIM and the other two kernels are offloaded to GPU-PIC. Kernel offloading saves many execution cycles (A) even over the best application offloading strategy. However, the key challenge of kernel offloading is in identifying the *affinity* of each kernel, which we provide a new solution for in this paper (Section 4).

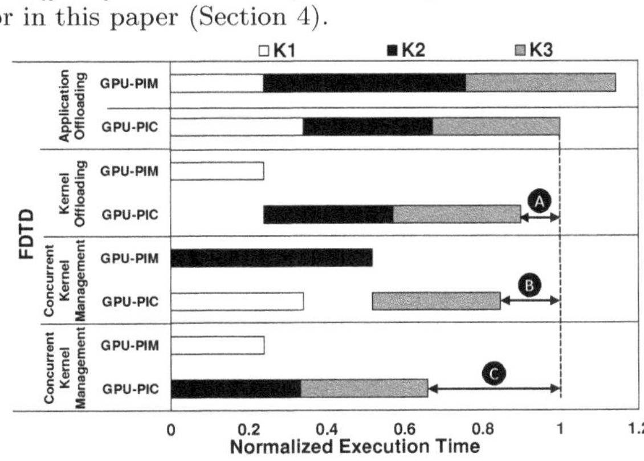

Figure 6: Performance advantages of kernel offloading (III) and concurrent kernel management (IV and V) mechanisms using the FDTD application as an example.

Limitation II: Lack of Concurrent Utilization of GPU-PIM and GPU-PIC. An application offloading mechanism loses out on the opportunity of using *both* the GPU-PIM and GPU-PIC at the same time, because it is too coarse-grained. In contrast, if offloading is performed at the kernel level, as described before, both GPU-PIM and GPU-PIC can be utilized by *concurrently* executing *independent* kernels on them. Figure 6 illustrates an example of this in Scenarios IV and V. In FDTD, Kernel-K3 can start executing only when both Kernel-K1 and Kernel-K2 finish their executions. However, Kernel-K1 and Kernel-K2 can execute in parallel. Because of the concurrent execution of kernels, overall application execution time is reduced (B) over the best application-offloading scenario, in scenario-IV. Scenario-V in Figure 6 demonstrates that kernel affinity, i.e., scheduling each kernel on the execution engine that is best for the kernel's performance matters: Kernels K1 and K2 respectively have affinity for GPU-PIM and GPU-PIC, and executing them concurrently on these engines leads to even higher overall application execution time savings (C) than in Scenario-IV where the same kernels are scheduled onto the opposite engines.

Our Goal. As we illustrated, while an application-level offloading strategy can improve performance and energy efficiency, a finer, kernel-level offloading strategy can provide more opportunity. Therefore, our goal is to develop mechanisms for (1) automatically identifying the architectural affinity (GPU-PIM or GPU-PIC) of each kernel in an application, and (2) scheduling kernels that can concurrently execute on different parts of the PIM-assisted GPU architecture (GPU-PIM or GPU-PIC), while balancing the execution times across architectures and maintaining a kernel's architecture affinity as much as possible.

4. KERNEL OFFLOADING MECHANISM

This section presents an architecture affinity prediction model to enable a runtime mechanism for kernel offloading in PIM-Assisted GPU architectures.

Need for a Prediction Model. If *all* the kernels of an application prefer the same compute engine (either GPU-PIM or GPU-PIC), kernel offloading becomes equivalent to application offloading. However, if different kernels have different affinities, kernel-level offloading can yield higher performance than application offloading (Section 3.2). Because the CPU offloads computation to the GPU at the kernel granularity, maintaining the same granularity for PIM execution enables low-overhead computation offloading from the CPU to either GPU-PIC and GPU-PIM. To avoid the overhead of first sampling the performance of each kernel on both platforms and then deciding the appropriate platform for execution, we would like to *predict* the affinity of the kernel *before* it starts execution. To this end, we make use of a *regression model* that is composed of *predictive variables.*

Metrics. To build our regression model, we need to identify appropriate metrics (i.e., predictive variables) that can characterize the kernel affinity to GPU-PIC or GPU-PIM. We classify kernel characteristics into three primary categories: 1) memory intensity, 2) parallelism, and 3) shared memory (i.e., scratchpad) intensity. Table 1 lists these categories along with their predictive metrics/variables.

Table 1: Metrics used to predict compute engine affinity and GPU-PIC and GPU-PIM execution time.

Primary Category	Predictive Metric	Static/Dynamic
I: Memory intensity of Kernel	Memory to Compute Ratio	Static
	Number of Compute Inst.	Static
	Number of Memory Inst.	Static
II: Available Parallelism in the Kernel	Number of CTAs	Dynamic
	Total Number of Threads	Dynamic
	Number of Thread Inst.	Dynamic
III: Shared Memory Intensity of Kernel	Total Number of Shared Memory Inst.	Static

To measure the effect of *kernel memory intensity* on performance, we consider the memory-to-compute-ratio of the instruction mix executed by that particular kernel. Memory-to-compute ratio gives insight into the level of performance the kernel can achieve with higher memory bandwidth, as the computation requires data from the memory, indicating whether the higher bandwidth available on GPU-PIM is beneficial for performance. We use the *number of cooperative thread arrays (CTAs)* (also called work groups or thread blocks) as a measure of the parallelism in the kernel. This allows us to take into account the difference in the peak instruction throughput between GPU-PIC and GPU-PIM for each kernel. For a kernel with a high number of CTAs, GPU-PIC's performance might be higher than that of GPU-PIM due to the higher number of cores in GPU-PIC. To approximate a kernel's *shared memory intensity*, we measure the total number of shared memory instructions in the kernel. A shared-memory-intensive application might not require high DRAM bandwidth, making it more suitable for GPU-PIC. Predictive metrics/variables (listed in Table 1 middle column) are used to help build a robust model by complementing the primary metrics of the kernel. For example, in applications such as `RED, CONV, STRM`, the number of CTAs along with the number of threads provides a notion about the CTA sizes. Usually a larger CTA has higher resource requirements, which might lead to fewer of such CTAs to be scheduled onto an SM at any given time, even in the presence of available SM resources (but *not enough resources* to schedule another complete CTA). Therefore, having more SMs, as in GPU-PIC, might lead to better performance for such a large CTA. We classify the metrics as static or dynamic, as shown in Table 1. Static metrics are obtained by simply parsing the source code, while dynamic metrics are input-set-based and can be known only at/after kernel launch or during runtime.

Why These Metrics? We choose only the most influential metrics to build our regression model, i.e., those metrics that contribute the most to the model's accuracy. We define accuracy for our regression model for a kernel as either 100%, if the model predicts the kernel's affinity correctly, or 0%, if it predicts incorrectly. We experimented with building the regression model using the number of thread instructions as the only metric, and found that this model has an accuracy of 79% on the *training kernels*. Using all the metrics shown in Table 1 leads to an overall accuracy of 87%. The use of other characterization metrics described in Goswami et al. [34] does not further improve accuracy.

Table 2 provides the detailed characteristics of various application kernels, obtained via offline profiling. It also shows the primary category metrics (memory-to-compute-ratio, the number of CTAs, and shared memory intensity) and architecture affinity of each kernel (GPU-PIM (Y) or GPU-PIC (N)). The affinity of a kernel can be reasoned for most of the kernels by understanding the level of each metric category. For example, kernels such as `convolutionRows` and `prescan` have high shared memory intensity, and prefer to run on GPU-PIC because of the lower DRAM bandwidth demand and the higher instruction throughput available in GPU-PIC compared to GPU-PIM. Kernels of `GRAM` prefer GPU-PIM because of their lower parallelism and high memory intensity. Kernels such as `fdtd_step1_kernel`, which have high memory intensity coupled with high parallelism, prefer GPU-PIM, as they benefit from the higher available memory bandwidth.

Regression Model for Affinity Prediction. We build a logistic regression model [30, 43], shown in Equation 1, which provides a prediction for the affinity of a given kernel. A logistic regression model is a classifier and it generates a discrete output $\sigma(t)$: **1 for GPU-PIM** and **0 for GPU-PIC**. The model uses the metrics in Table 1 as inputs.

$$\sigma(t) = \frac{e^t}{e^t + 1} \quad (1)$$

where:

$$\begin{aligned}
\sigma(t) &= \text{model output } (\sigma(t) < 0.5 => 0,\ \sigma(t) \geq 0.5 => 1)\\
t &= \alpha_0 + \alpha_1 x_1 + \alpha_2 x_2 + \alpha_3 x_3 + \alpha_4 x_4 + \alpha_5 x_5 + \alpha_6 x_6 + \alpha_7 x_7\\
\alpha_i &= \text{Coefficients of the Regression Model}\\
x_i &= \text{Predictive Metrics/Variables (Table 1)}
\end{aligned}$$

To train the logistic regression model, we randomly sample 60% (15) of the 25 GPGPU applications considered in the paper. These 15 applications consist of 82 unique kernels that are used as inputs for the *training* of the model. The remaining 40% (10) of the applications, consisting of 42 unique kernels, are part of the *testing* set and are used to validate the model. We perform offline profiling of entire application execution only once to train the regression model and use this built model at runtime for affinity prediction. The model is able to accurately predict the architecture affinity (either GPU-PIC or GPU-PIM) of 83% of the test kernels. Table 2 shows the affinity prediction (in column D) of our model for each kernel along with the true affinity of the kernel (in column B). The major sources of inaccuracy are due to cache effects and branch divergence, which our regression model fails to accurately capture because of their heavily runtime-dependent characteristics. For example, due to the considerable amount of cache hits in kernels such as `drelax (BFS)` and `dfindelemin (MST)`, GPU-PIC outperforms GPU-PIM, even though these kernels have high parallelism and memory intensity. Yet, our model estimates incorrectly that they are better executed on GPU-PIM. We further discuss the effects of random sampling and application input on our model's accuracy in Section 8.

Kernel affinity could also be predicted statically, without using the dynamic metrics in Table 1. Using only the static metrics, the accuracy of the affinity prediction model decreases from 83% to 74%. We find that the inclusion of dynamic (i.e., input-based) metrics in the model is necessary for accurate prediction in applications such as CFD, STRM and PVC. This is because the affinity of these applications' kernels is highly influenced by input-based kernel dimensions (i.e., number of threads, CTA size) as they significantly affect the compute/resource requirements of these kernels.

Implementation. Figure 7 shows our framework to enable kernel offloading to PIM engines. Before runtime, a simple source to source translation is performed ❶. The purpose is to compute the values of the static metrics, such as the number of memory/compute/shared-memory instructions (in terms of PTX instructions), and embed them as arguments to the kernel launch call. We extend the CUDA runtime to implement the architecture affinity prediction model ❷. The prediction model is trained *offline* and does not incur any overhead of training during online prediction of affinity. At runtime, during kernel launch from the CPU, the dynamic metrics required for the prediction model such as the number of CTAs and the number of threads get populated with their values in the kernel launch call. Using both the static and dynamic metrics, the CUDA runtime on the

Table 2: Kernel characteristics, classification, and architecture affinity. Legend: (I) Memory Intensity (Memory to Compute Ratio = $L :\leq 0.2, 0.2 < M \leq 0.3, H :> 0.3$), (II) Parallelism (No. of CTAs = $L :\leq 64, 64 < M \leq 1024, H :> 1024$), (III) Shared Memory Intensity (Total no. of Shared Mem. Inst. = $L :\leq 2.5 \times 10^5, H :> 2.5 \times 10^5$). (B) Architecture affinity (Y: GPU-PIM, N: GPU-PIC), (C) Major reasons for architecture affinity, (D) Affinity prediction by our regression model in Section 4) (Y: GPU-PIM, N: GPU-PIC). Only kernels that dominate application execution time are shown.

Workload	Kernel Name	I	II	III	B	C	D
BFS [17]	initialize	M	H	L	Y	Cache/BW	Y
	drelax	H	H	L	N	Cache	N
BICG [37]	bicg_kernel1	H	L	L	Y	BW	Y
	bicg_kernel2	M	L	L	N	Cache	Y
BLK [81]	BlackScholesGPU	L	M	L	Y	Cache	Y
CCL [42]	MapperCount	H	M	L	Y	BW	Y
	unitBitonicSortKernel	L	H	M	N	Compute	N
	prescan	M	M	H	N	S.Mem.	Y
CONV [37]	convolution3D_kernel	M	M	L	N	Cache	Y
CORR [37]	std_kernel	M	L	L	Y	BW	Y
	reduce_kernel	M	H	L	N	Compute	N
	corr_kernel	L	L	L	N	Cache	Y
FDTD [37]	fdtd_step1_kernel	H	H	L	Y	BW	Y
	fdtd_step2_kernel	M	H	L	N	Cache	N
	fdtd_step3_kernel	H	H	L	N	Cache	N
GRAM [37]	gramschmidt_kernel1	M	L	L	Y	Lat.	Y
	gramschmidt_kernel2	H	L	L	Y	Lat.	Y
	gramschmidt_kernel3	M	L	L	Y	Lat.	Y
LUH [56]	IntegrateStress-ForElems_kernel	L	M	L	Y	BW/Lat.	Y
	CalcHourglassControl-ForElems_kernel	H	M	H	N	S.Mem.	N
	CalcFBHourglassForce-ForElems_kernel	H	M	H	N	S.Mem.	N
MVT [37]	mvt_kernel1	M	L	L	N	Cache	Y
	mvt_kernel2	H	L	L	Y	BW	Y
PR [42]	MapperCount	H	H	L	Y	BW	Y
	prescan	L	H	H	N	S.Mem.	N

Workload	Kernel Name	I	II	III	B	C	D
RED [25]	reduce	H	M	L	Y	BW	N
SCP [81]	scalarProdGPU	L	M	L	Y	—	N
SLA [81]	prescan	L	H	H	N	S.Mem.	N
STRM [21]	kernel_compute_cost	H	M	L	Y	BW	Y
APSP [16]	sgemmNN_MinPlus	L	L	H	Y	Lat.	Y
	matrixMul	H	M	L	Y	Lat.	N
	apsp_seq	M	L	L	Y	Lat.	Y
CFD [21]	cuda_compute_step_factor	M	M	L	Y	BW	Y
	cuda_compute_flux	L	M	L	N	Cache	Y
	cuda_time_step	H	L	L	Y	BW	Y
CONS [81]	convolutionRows	H	H	H	N	S.Mem.	N
	convolutionColumns	H	H	H	N	S.Mem.	N
FWT [81]	fwtBatch1Kernel	H	H	L	Y	BW	Y
GUPS	RandomAccessUpdate	L	M	L	Y	BW	Y
LIB [81]	Pathcalc_Portfolio_KernelGPU	L	L	L	N	Cache	N
	Pathcalc_Portfolio_KernelGPU2	L	L	L	Y	BW	Y
MST [17]	dfindelemin	H	H	L	Y	Cache	Y
	dfindcompmin	H	H	L	N	Cache	N
	init	H	H	L	Y	Cache	Y
PVC [42]	MapperCount	H	H	L	Y	BW	N
	prescan	L	H	H	N	S.Mem.	N
SP [17]	dinit	H	H	L	Y	Cache	Y
	dupdateeta	H	H	L	Y	Cache	N
TRA [81]	transpose_naive	M	H	L	Y	Cache	Y
	transpose	L	H	L	Y	Cache	N

host-side computes[7] the architecture affinity of the kernel using the affinity prediction model, and offloads the kernel to the architecture that is expected to provide the highest performance. Doing so avoids the overhead of kernel migration, which might arise if the kernel were to be offloaded *after* it starts execution on a less preferred architecture.

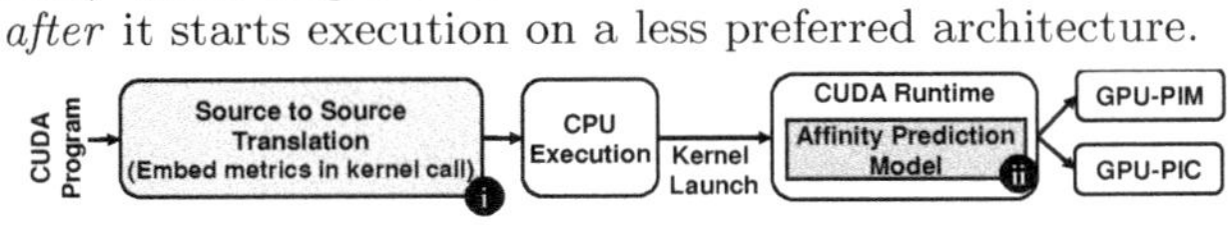

Figure 7: Modified CUDA runtime for kernel offloading

5. CONCURRENT KERNEL MANAGEMENT

This section presents a new runtime kernel management scheme to efficiently execute multiple kernels concurrently in the heterogeneous computational units in a PIM-assisted GPU architecture.

5.1 Analysis

Offloading kernels appropriately to their preferred compute engine (Section 4) leads to performance benefit. However, due to the sequential execution of the kernels, such PIM-assisted GPU architectures are under-utilized as only either the GPU-PIC or the GPU-PIM executes a kernel at a given time, but not both. If there are independent kernels, their concurrent execution on GPU-PIC and GPU-PIM can improve overall system utilization and performance (Section 3.2). We develop a mechanism to achieve such concurrent execution of kernels on both GPU-PIC and GPU-PIM. To efficiently schedule kernels for concurrent execution, we need three key pieces of information: (1) kernel-level dependence information, to identify independent kernels; (2) affinity of each kernel and (3) execution time prediction for each kernel, both to decide what compute engine is the best to execute the kernel on. We first describe how this information is gathered in our runtime system.

(I) Kernel-level Dependence Information. A kernel-level data dependence graph is required to decide which kernels can execute in parallel. For our evaluations, we obtain the dependence graph of an application *for a given input* by profiling the application's execution to determine the correct and complete set of read-after-write (RAW) dependencies across the kernels. Such cross-kernel dependencies can be easily found and marked by a compiler. Most compilers targeting array-based applications already run dependence analysis for each loop nest (kernel). One could extend such an analysis to check dependence's *across* loop nests (kernels) as well.[8]

Note that, our concurrent kernel management mechanism can be directly used for applications that inherently possess concurrent kernels (which could be conveyed by the programmer), without any need for data dependence analysis.

(II) Architecture Affinity Information. We observed in Section 3.2 that kernel affinity information can help improve performance of concurrent kernel execution (Scenario-V, Figure 6). To predict the affinity of a kernel, we use the logistic regression model described in Section 4. This model is used to fill the GPU-PIM and GPU-PIC queues with kernels based on their affinity.

(III) Execution Time Information. Kernel dependence and affinity information is necessary, but not sufficient to balance kernel execution times across GPU-PIC and GPU-PIM. For instance, consider an application consisting of two independent kernels having affinity towards GPU-PIM. If only the affinity information is used, both these kernels are offloaded to GPU-PIM, which leads to the under-

[7]The regression model parameters are kept in CPU memory. During the API call, model-based affinity is predicted by the CPU, which requires only 15 32-bit floating point operations (7 multiplications, 7 additions and 1 comparison).

[8]Note that not all applications have multiple independent kernels and thus can take advantage of concurrent kernel execution. We observe this in SCP and GUPS.

utilization of GPU-PIC (and perhaps a lost opportunity to improve performance). We address such situations by executing kernels in compute engines that do *not* satisfy the kernel affinity, if doing so would reduce overall execution time. Therefore, in this example, we might offload the kernel that has the lower execution time on GPU-PIC, to GPU-PIC. However, this requires the estimation of the kernel execution times on both GPU-PIC and GPU-PIM, for which we develop a model next.

5.2 Execution Time Prediction Model

For predicting a kernel's execution time, we build a linear regression model [74] that uses the same predictive metrics used in our architecture affinity prediction model (Table 1). Equation 2 shows the linear regression model.

$$y = \beta_0 + \beta_1 x_1 + \beta_2 x_2 + \beta_3 x_3 + \beta_4 x_4 + \beta_5 x_5 + \beta_6 x_6 + \beta_7 x_7 \quad (2)$$

where:

y = model output (predicted execution time; classified into bins using Table 3)

β_i = Coefficients of the Regression Model

x_i = Predictive Metrics/Variables (Table 1)

The model is trained using the kernel execution time information obtained from profiling the execution times of applications from the training set that were used in Section 4 to create the affinity prediction model. Earlier work (Dubach et al. [28]) utilizes compile-time parameters to predict the performance of an application, but exactly predicting the absolute execution time of a kernel accurately is a difficult task and exact prediction has significant error. Therefore, rather than utilizing the predicted execution time directly in an absolute manner, we classify the predicted execution time (y) into five different bins, as shown in Table 3. The ranges of the bins were carefully chosen by analyzing the profiled data. With such classification, we can efficiently schedule the kernels on GPU-PIC and GPU-PIM, without having to accurately predict the absolute execution times, albeit perhaps with lower benefit than if we had the correct absolute execution times.

Table 3: Classification of predicted execution time into bins.

Classification Bins	Very Low (1)	Low (2)	Medium (3)	High (4)	Very High (5)
Range (in Cycles)	<10K	10K-500K	500K-5M	5M-50M	>50M

Figure 8 shows the classification error of our regression-based execution time prediction models for GPU-PIC and GPU-PIM. Error is measured by calculating the distance of the predicted bin from the true bin normalized to the total number of bins. For example, a predicted bin of *Low (2)* with a true bin of *Very Low (1)* has an error of $(2-1)/5 = 0.2$, since the total number of bins is 5 and the distance of the predicted bin from the true bin is 1. The results show that the execution time prediction model provides a classification accuracy of 77% and 80% on the test set for GPU-PIC and GPU-PIM, respectively. The inaccuracies are mainly due to the heavily-runtime-dependent cache and branch divergence effects (as discussed in Section 4).

5.3 Algorithmic Details and Implementation

The main incentive to concurrently execute kernels is to maximize system utilization. For this purpose, the execution time on GPU-PIC and GPU-PIM needs to be balanced. However, the problem of balancing execution times across two architectures is equivalent to a known NP-Complete partitioning problem [32]. The partitioning problem is the task

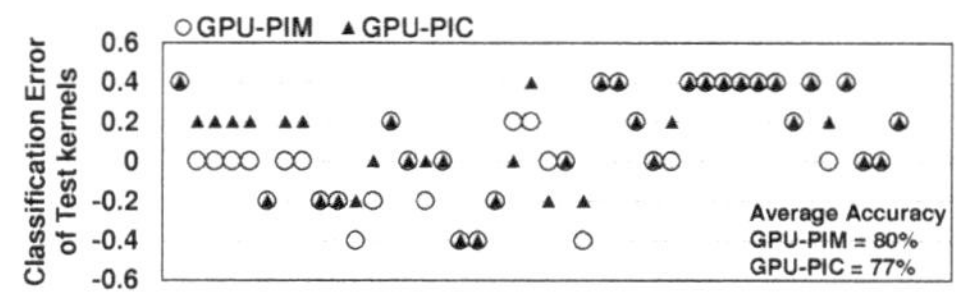

Figure 8: Classification error of test kernel execution times.

of deciding whether a given set of positive integers can be partitioned into two subsets such that the sum of the two subsets are equal. The only difference in our case is that we have a list of pairs (instead of a single number) of positive execution times, where each pair is a tuple of <execution time on GPU-PIC, execution time on GPU-PIM>. We adopt a greedy approach to solve this problem in three steps.

Figure 9 shows the schematic of our concurrent kernel management framework. The CUDA runtime predicts the architecture affinity ⓘⓘ of all kernels launched by the CPU. The kernels are fed into their respective queues in the kernel distribution unit ⓘⓥ and the execution begins. During runtime, there might be a case where all the kernels prefer a single type of compute engine or either the GPU-PIC or GPU-PIM queue is empty but there are still kernels waiting in the other compute engine's queue. To address this, the runtime steals a waiting independent kernel from the non-empty queue to the empty queue based on the kernel's execution time prediction ⓘⓘⓘ on the less preferred architecture. The runtime prefers to steal the *first* independent kernel that has a predicted execution time (on the less preferred architecture) smaller than the remaining execution time of the currently executing kernel. Algorithm 1 describes this greedy process of kernel stealing that enables concurrent kernel management.

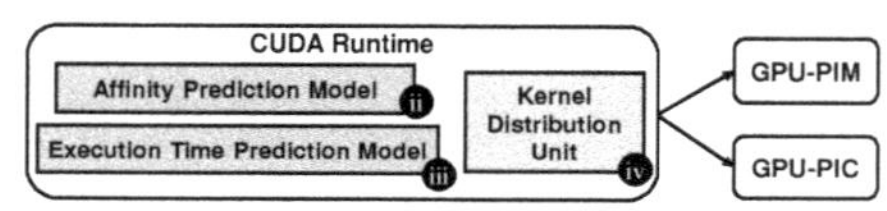

Figure 9: Modified CUDA runtime for concurrent kernel management.

Algorithm 1 Runtime Queue Management

▷ $time(kernel, engine)$ returns the time-bin of the kernel if it is executed on the given engine.
▷ Let X and Y represent the two different engines (GPU-PIC and GPU-PIM).
▷ $independent\_kernels(queue)$ returns the list of the kernels that can run concurrently with the kernels currently executing and have no past dependencies.
▷ $time\_executed(kernel)$ returns the amount of time the kernel has been executing.
if $X = Idle \ \&\& \ X.queue = \emptyset \ \&\& \ Y.queue \neq \emptyset$ **then**
  if $independent\_kernels(Y.queue) \neq \emptyset$ **then**
    for each kernel in $independent\_kernels(Y.queue)$ **do**
      if $time(kernel, X) \leq (time(kernel_{running,y}, Y) - time\_executed(kernel_{running,y}) + time(kernel, Y))$ **then**
        Execute "kernel" on X
        Break
▷ Similarly, repeat the process for Y

6. EVALUATION METHODOLOGY

Infrastructure. We modified the cycle-accurate GPGPU-Sim v3.2.2 [12, 52] to simulate our PIM-Assisted GPU architecture. To enable the execution of two different GPUs, we created two clusters of SMs, one for GPU-PIC and another for GPU-PIM. GPU-PIC and GPU-PIM do *not* concurrently work on the same data. Therefore, to maintain coherence between them, we flush the L2 cache in GPU-PIC after kernel execution. As the L1 caches are write-through, they do not need to be flushed. There is no explicit synchronization needed between GPU-PIC and GPU-PIM as they never share data during concurrent execution. The kernel distribution unit in the CUDA runtime, shown in Figure 9, checks for any inter-kernel dependencies to avoid concurrent scheduling of dependent kernels.

For concurrent kernel execution, we use CUDA Streams, which are supported by GPGPU-Sim. A stream is a series of kernel launches and memory operations between the CPU and GPU that are executed sequentially. Different streams are capable of executing concurrently depending on available resources. In our simulation framework, we create two CUDA Streams: `PIC_CUDAStream` and `PIM_CUDAStream`. GPU-PIM and GPU-PIC are assigned their own streams, thereby making the execution of the streams concurrent. We modified the CUDA runtime support in GPGPU-Sim to overload the API calls with the kernel metrics and added support for the *architecture affinity prediction model* (Section 4), *execution time prediction model* (Section 5.2), and *kernel distribution unit* (Section 5.3). During application execution, our runtime framework is able to read the kernel metrics passed along with the kernel launch call, obtain the runtime metrics, and predict the affinity of the kernel.

Workloads. We chose CUDA applications from various benchmark suites (NVIDIA SDK [81], Rodinia [21], Shoc [25], Polybench [37], Mars [42], LonestarGPU [17]) and several other applications (e.g., LUH [56], APSP [16], GUPS). We collect the results at kernel boundaries to ensure that all comparisons are for the same amount of work completed across different executions. We only simulate the portions of code that are executed on GPU.

Simulated Systems. Table 4 provides the details of the simulated GPU-PIC and GPU-PIM configurations. We assume that GPU-PIC has 32 GPU cores and GPU-PIM has 8 GPU cores underneath a 3D memory stack. We compare this design to a conventional baseline GPU architecture that has 40 GPU cores. These two configurations have the same peak execution throughput. The L2 cache size of the baseline GPU is equal to that of GPU-PIC (768 kB). GPU-PIM does not have an L2 cache Section 2.2). All our simulations on the baseline GPU maintain (if any) inter-kernel data reuse, i.e., the L2 cache is *not* flushed in-between the execution of two kernels, unlike concurrent GPU-PIC and GPU-PIM execution on our proposed architecture.[9]

To simulate the timing of 3D-stacked DRAM, we use the timing parameters provided by Jevdjic et al. [49]. We use GPUWattch [65] for power analysis of GPU-PIC and GPU-PIM cores, caches, and interconnect. For DRAM energy analysis, we augment this model with a simple linear equation adding the wire transfer energy numbers given by Keckler et al. [58] to the DRAM read/write energy for a Hybrid Memory Cube DRAM [86]. We faithfully model the bandwidth, latency, and timing of 3D-stacked DRAM.

Table 4: Parameters of the simulated system.

GPU-PIC Features	1.4GHz, 32 cores, 32 SIMT width, GTO warp scheduler [82]
Shared L2 (GPU-PIC)	16-way 64KB/memory channel, 128B cache block size
GPU-PIM Features	1.4GHz, 8 cores, 32 SIMT width, GTO warp scheduler [82]
Resources per Core [36, 91, 92]	16KB shared memory, 16KB register file, Max. 1536 threads (48 warps, 32 threads/warp)
Private Caches per Core [36, 91, 92]	16KB L1 D-cache, 12KB T-cache, 8KB C-cache, 2KB I-cache, 128B block size
Memory Model	12 Memory Controllers, FR-FCFS, 8 banks/MC, 924 MHz Partition chunk size: 256 bytes [35] $t_{CL} = 11, t_{RP} = 11, t_{RC} = 39, t_{RAS} = 28, t_{CCD} = 2$ $t_{RCD} = 11, t_{RRD} = 5, t_{CDLR} = 5, t_{WR} = 12$
Bandwidth	88.8GB/s (Interposer link per GPU-PIM stack) 355.2GB/s (within GPU-PIM stack)
Interconnect (GPU-PIC) [36]	1 crossbar/direction (32 cores, 12 MCs), flit size=32B, 1.4GHz, islip VC & switch allocators
Interconnect (GPU-PIM) [36]	1 crossbar/direction (8 cores, 12 MCs), flit size=32B, 1.4GHz, islip VC & switch allocators

GPU-PIM has access to the full bandwidth of 3D-stacked DRAM, whereas GPU-PIC has limited bandwidth as it is pin-limited. Table 5 provides the parameters we use for calculating DRAM energy. We assume a crossbar interconnect between the private L1 caches and the shared L2 cache, keeping it consistent with the currently available GPUs [6].

Table 5: Parameters of our DRAM energy model.

Energy per bit [86]	13.7 pJ/bit
Wire Energy (256 bits, 10 mm) [58]	310 pJ
Assumed distance between GPU-PIC and GPU-PIM	20 mm

7. EXPERIMENTAL RESULTS

We compare the performance and energy efficiency of our kernel offloading and concurrent kernel management schemes with their oracle counterparts. The oracle schemes make ideal offloading and concurrent execution decisions by profiling each kernel with its runtime input and obtaining completely accurate execution times for each kernel on GPU-PIC and GPU-PIM (instead of using regression models). Therefore, the oracle schemes provide the best possible performance for each application. The oracle kernel offloading scheme finds the correct kernel affinity for each kernel and schedules it for execution on the best engine. The oracle concurrent kernel management scheme provides the minimal execution time for an application by utilizing both GPU-PIC and GPU-PIM while respecting kernel dependencies. We *normalize* the performance and efficiency results to those of the 40-SM baseline GPU described in Section 6. We report the results separately for the applications used for training and testing, to show the effectiveness of our model.

Effects of Kernel Offloading. Figures 10a and 10b show the performance and energy efficiency benefits of our dynamic kernel offloading scheme, respectively. Our technique increases the performance and energy efficiency of the testing set applications by 25% and 28%, respectively. The oracle kernel offloading scheme provides 34% and 40% average performance and energy efficiency improvement, respectively, on the testing set. The inability of our scheme to perform as good as the oracle scheme is due to the mispredictions of kernel affinity by our regression model.[10]

The inaccuracies of our prediction model (Section 4) usually cause some kernels (e.g., of `CONV` and `CORR`) to be incorrectly offloaded to GPU-PIM, leading to performance losses.

[9] We also considered using a baseline architecture capable of concurrent kernel execution on a *partitioned* set of 32 SMs and 8 SMs, but there are two issues with such a baseline. First, GPGPU applications tend to be highly parallel and fill the entire set of SMs provided, and we take this into account in our 40-SM baseline. Second, we still need a mechanism to decide which partition to launch each of the kernels. Depending on its characteristics, a kernel might prefer lower or higher number of SMs. Our new kernel offloading mechanism may be modified to make such a baseline work, but we leave this as future work. For these reasons, we normalize all results to a baseline with 40 SMs and no concurrent kernel execution.

[10] In some cases where computation parallelism is the main bottleneck, e.g., for `CONV`, even the oracle scheme loses performance compared to the baseline because the baseline can utilize all the 40 GPU cores for each kernel whereas the PIM-assisted GPU architecture can utilize either 32 or 8.

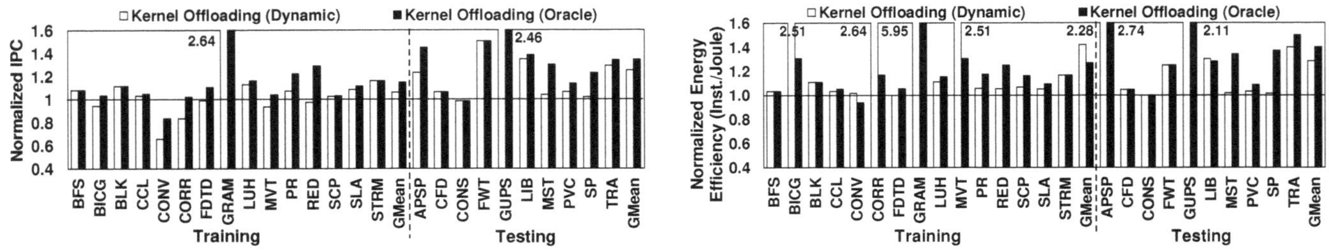

Figure 10: Impact of our Kernel Offloading scheme on (a) Performance, (b) Energy efficiency.

However, because GPU-PIM is significantly more energy efficient than GPU-PIC, in most of the mispredicted kernels (e.g., of APSP and LIB; see Figure 10b), the overall energy efficiency of our scheme is still higher than that of the oracle's, which is optimized for performance, not energy.

Figure 11 shows the percentage of execution time when GPU-PIC and GPU-PIM are executing kernels. Applications such as LUH, PR, and SLA have kernels that exhibit different architecture affinities within the application and thus benefit from kernel offloading over application offloading. Our model is able to capture this variation in affinity and we utilize the opportunity that kernel-level offloading presents us as mentioned in Section 4. In this scheme, GPU-PIC and GPU-PIM *do not execute concurrently*, leading to under-utilization of the system.

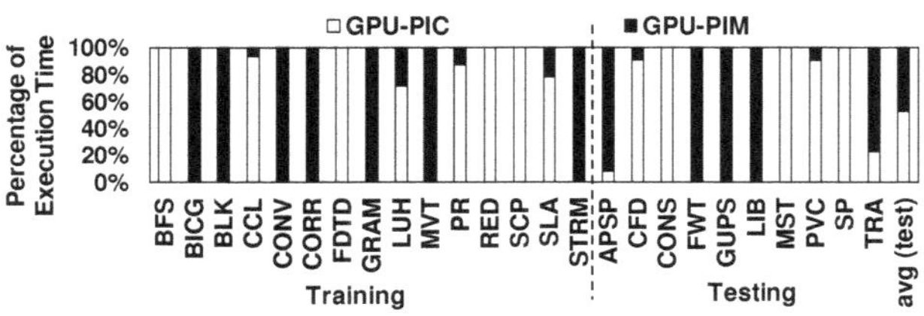

Figure 11: Percentage of execution time GPU-PIM and GPU-PIC execute kernels with our kernel offloading scheme.

We make three observations based on these results. First, kernel offloading gives the same results as the best application offloading (as we showed in Figure 4) for applications such as BFS, BLK, SCP, and GUPS. This is because these applications either consist of a single kernel (BLK, SCP and GUPS), or all the kernels of the application prefer the same engine (BFS). Second, kernel offloading performs better than application offloading in applications such as FDTD, PR, and PVC. This is due to the benefits of fine-grained offloading, discussed in Section 4, which selects the fastest execution engine for each kernel. Third, our scheme performs worse than application offloading for applications such as BICG, CORR, and MST, due to mispredictions in kernel affinity. BICG has two kernels, one of which prefers GPU-PIC and the other GPU-PIM. Due to mispredictions, the kernel that prefers execution on GPU-PIC is executed on GPU-PIM, leading to lower performance compared to application offloading, which offloads the entire application to GPU-PIC. These mispredictions are due to data reuse at the L2 cache, which make GPU-PIC faster than GPU-PIM (lacks an L2 cache).

Effects of Concurrent Kernel Management. Figures 12a and 12b show the performance and energy efficiency benefits of our concurrent kernel management scheme, respectively. On average, our management scheme improves performance and energy efficiency by 42±4% and 27±2%, respectively, over the baseline across the test set.[11] The oracle scheme on the test set provides 53% and 33% improvements in performance and energy efficiency, respectively. Similar to our kernel offloading scheme, affinity mispredictions cause performance penalties, but they improve energy efficiency in general.

Figure 13 shows the percentage of execution time when both GPU-PIC and GPU-PIM are executing kernels concurrently.[12] It can be seen that the applications with high concurrency across the engines are the ones that gain the most in terms of performance.

We make four observations based on these results. First, our scheme performs the same as application offloading in applications such as BLK, GRAM, FWT, and GUPS. There is no kernel-level concurrency in these applications (see Figure 13). BLK and GUPS consist of a single kernel; GRAM and FWT have no independent kernels, leading to sequential execution of kernels in all of these applications.

Second, applications such as FDTD, PR, LIB and MST fail to perform as good as the oracle scheme because their execution times are not predicted accurately (even though their

[11] As a result of the dynamic nature of kernel scheduling and the greediness in our scheme, different concurrent kernel executions might be possible for the same application, which might result in different performance and efficiency. This arises because multiple independent kernels can be predicted to be in the *same execution time bin*. Any one of these kernels could be picked by our concurrent kernel scheduler as they are at equal "priority". The error bounds in Figure 12a and 12b show the variation in performance and energy efficiency due to different choices made by the scheduler at runtime.

[12] The breakdown for the best-case of concurrent kernel execution is shown.

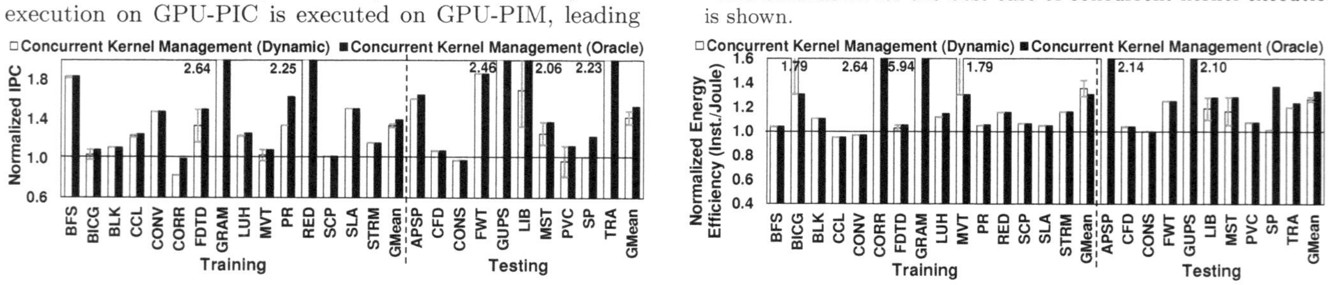

Figure 12: Impact of our Concurrent Kernel Management scheme on (a) Performance, (b) Energy efficiency.

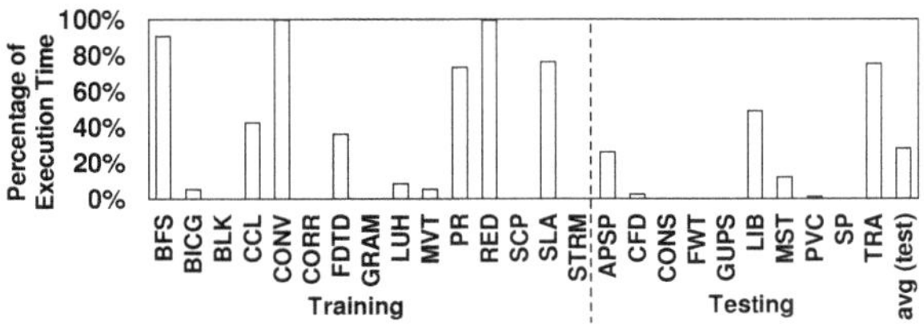

Figure 13: Percentage of execution time when kernels are concurrently running on GPU-PIM and GPU-PIC with our concurrent kernel management scheme.

affinity predictions are correct). Our heuristic checks for the kernel's predicted runtime on the unsuitable platform, and decides whether to wait for its preferred platform to be free, or to execute it concurrently on the less-suitable yet under-utilized platform right away. Our execution time prediction fails to calculate the exact execution time bin, and leads to sub-optimal scheduling decisions in these applications. Third, applications such as `BICG`, `MVT`, `PVC` and `SP` under-perform due to the mispredictions in kernel affinity. In `SP`, one of the two kernels is mispredicted for GPU-PIM, and both of the kernels are executed on GPU-PIM. Following our heuristic of running the kernel with shorter execution time based on the execution time bins does not help because both kernels fall into the same bin. Therefore, the heuristic arbitrarily chooses one kernel for GPU-PIM and the other for GPU-PIC, which negatively affects performance as one of the kernels takes considerably longer on GPU-PIC even though they fall in the same execution time classification bin. Also, due to the lack of many kernels, there is no leeway for mispredictions. The scenario is similar for the other applications as well. `APSP` also suffers from this situation, but because this application has many (200+) kernels that execute, the mispredicted kernels do not dominate the execution time. Thus, we still get significant performance improvement on `APSP`. Finally, for applications such as `CCL`, `RED`, `CFD` and `FWT`, we are able to achieve comparable performance to that of the oracle scheme, which is very significant. In `RED`, even though the affinity is incorrectly predicted, due to kernel stealing, we are able to offload the appropriate kernels to their preferred architecture, which leads to significant performance improvement.

We conclude that our kernel offloading and concurrent kernel management schemes lead to significant average performance and energy efficiency improvements across 25 applications we evaluated for both training and testing.

8. SENSITIVITY STUDIES

We perform multiple sensitivity studies to understand: 1) the impact of architectural decisions for GPU-PIM, 2) sensitivity of the regression model to the testing set and different application inputs, 3) opportunities and challenges of utilizing multiple GPU-PIMs.

8.1 GPU-PIM Design Choices

L2 Cache and Core Count. We analyzed the effect of caches on GPU-PIM's performance. There is 9% slowdown when a 384kB L2 cache is added to GPU-PIM, due to the additional latency the L2 cache introduces to the memory request path, which is heavily used in the presence of memory-intensive kernels. We also varied the number of SMs in GPU-PIM from 4 to 16. With 8 SMs, GPU-PIM achieves within 30% of the performance of 16 SMs. Importantly, 8 SMs is thermally feasible (< 50W), but more SMs likely reduce the feasibility of GPU-PIM.

8.2 Regression Model

Training Set. To evaluate our mechanisms' sensitivity to applications used in the training set, we selected a completely different training set (by picking applications to be included in the training set in a random manner) and rebuilt the regression model. We found the accuracy in predicting the architecture affinity of the test kernels to be 81%. We also performed a semi-random sampling, where 20% of the *most influential* applications (that affect the accuracy of the model) were made a part of the training set and the remaining 40% were chosen randomly to be included in the training set. This leads to an accuracy of 88% for the test kernels. To study the impact of varying the size of the training set on the regression model, we build models using three different training set sizes: 40%, 60% and 80% of the applications. The accuracy of these models on the test set were 70%, 83% and 81%, respectively. As the training set size increases, accuracy improves to a point, but further increase over-fits the model (i.e., when more than 60% of the applications in the training set), after which accuracy starts decreasing.

Sensitivity to Application Input Set. Figure 14 shows the performance of our kernel offloading scheme on 8 GPGPU applications with different input sets. For applications such as `CFD, STRM, PVC`, we are able to predict the affinity accurately. These applications are able to change their parallelism (number of CTAs, number of threads) depending on their inputs, enabling accurate affinity prediction. For `RED Input-2`, we capture affinity accurately, but `RED Input-1` has mispredictions. This is because Input-1 fits inside the cache and has high reuse, unlike Input-2, whose working set is larger than the cache. For applications such as `BFS, MST, SP`, we predict affinity incorrectly, which leads to suboptimal performance. These applications are heavily dependent on their input data and it is difficult for our model to perfectly account for such very irregular cases. In `MST Input-1`, different kernels prefer different affinities, whereas `MST Input-2` contains kernels that always prefer to execute on GPU-PIM.

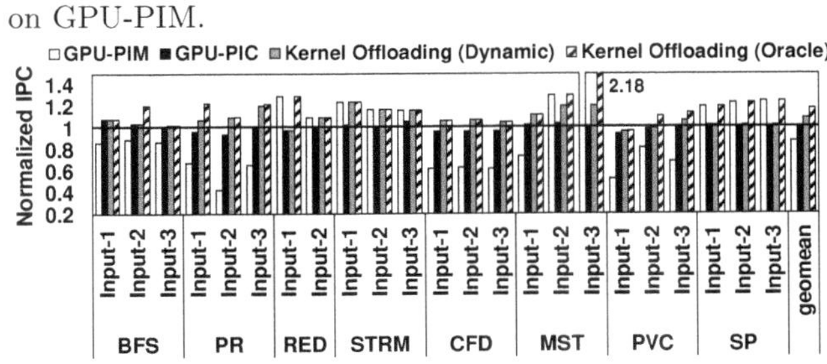

Figure 14: Affinity prediction model's sensitivity to input.

8.3 Systems with Multiple GPU-PIMs

Number of GPU-PIMs. We experimented with two other configurations that have 2 and 4 GPU-PIMs, respectively, while increasing the GPU-PIC memory bandwidth by 2× and 4× (due to multiple memory links between GPU-PIC and GPU-PIMs). Assuming perfect data placement (i.e., data needed by a GPU-PIM is located in its local stacked memory), application offloading onto only GPU-PIMs gives an improvement of 31% and 51% in performance and energy efficiency, respectively. With the *best application offloading* scheme, we see improvements of 53% and 65%, respectively. These trends are similar to the trends discussed in Section 3, and indicate that our schemes are likely to be scalable with number of GPU-PIMs.

Data Placement. Earlier results with multiple GPU-PIMs assumed *perfect* data placement such that each GPU-PIM has the data it needs in its local memory stack. However, this might not always be possible. Therefore, architectures comprising multiple GPU-PIMs might suffer from memory transactions that are requested and served by different (non-local) memory stacks. Moreover, these transactions have to go through the GPU-PIC since there are no direct communication channels between the different GPU-PIMs. With the default CTA scheduler and the default address mapping, we find that approximately 50% of memory transactions are non-local. We changed the striping of data from 256Bytes/bank to 32KBytes/bank, causing non-local accesses to reduce by 8-10% for applications such as `MST`, `STRM` and `LIB`. By modifying the CTA scheduler and/or address mapping intelligently, it is possible to minimize non-local accesses, as shown by a recent work [44].

9. RELATED WORK

To our knowledge, this is the first work that comprehensively investigates kernel-level offloading mechanisms in PIM-Assisted GPU Architectures. It is the first to develop automated models and methods for (1) offloading kernels to PIM units, (2) concurrently executing kernels on different heterogeneous compute engines in a PIM-Assisted GPU Architecture, to maximize system performance and efficiency. We briefly discuss research in related areas.

Processing-in-Memory (PIM) Architectures. There is a substantial body of work on PIM that explores placing computation units within memory (e.g., [18, 33, 40, 55, 62, 67, 85, 89, 90, 93–96, 98, 99]). 3D-stacked memory technology brings new dimensions and better feasibility to PIM-based architectures [3, 4, 14, 15, 27, 39, 41, 44, 70, 71, 73, 87, 109]. Our work is most closely related to the concurrent work of Hsieh et al. [44], which proposes programmer-transparent schemes for offloading code segments to PIM cores and for co-locating code and data together in a 3D-memory stack. They use a compiler-based technique to find the code segments to offload to the PIM compute units based on a cost-benefit analysis. Our work does not require sophisticated compiler support as it performs scheduling at the kernel level and kernels are already well designated in modern GPU applications. Farmahini-Farahani et al. [31] propose an architecture that reduces data transfers by stacking accelerators on top of off-chip DRAM devices. In the context of GPUs, Zhang et al. [112] propose TOP-PIM, a throughput-oriented PIM-Assisted GPU architecture. They show significant energy efficiency improvements by offloading GPU applications closer to memory. However, they evaluate executing the *entire application* on either the host or GPU-PIM. Our work builds upon a similar architecture and proposes mechanisms to more efficiently utilize such an architecture by performing scheduling at the finer-grained kernel level.

Machine Learning-based Prediction Models. Machine learning techniques have been widely deployed for performance and power prediction models (e.g., [7, 11, 45–47, 66, 72, 80, 84, 110, 113]). Wu et al. [110] propose a GPU performance and power model that uses machine learning techniques to predict the behavior of incoming applications from profiled data. Ardalani et al. [7] propose a performance prediction model that takes as input a single-threaded CPU version of an application and predicts the performance for its GPU port. Panwar et al. [84] present an online kernel characterization technique and performance model to estimate the performance of a kernel on different GPU architectures. Ipek et al. [45, 46] develop models for performance prediction of parallel applications and for aiding architectural space exploration. We use a regression-based approach to develop our affinity and execution time prediction models for PIM-Assisted GPU architectures.

Task Scheduling. There has been considerable work done in the domain of task scheduling to improve load balance and performance in both homogeneous and heterogeneous systems (e.g., [8, 19, 23, 26, 38, 50, 51, 97, 103–105, 111]). Aji et al. [5] design an OpenCL runtime called MultiCL, which can effectively map the command queues onto the best device for high performance. Their runtime scheduler involves static device profiling, dynamic kernel profiling, and dynamic device mapping. Chen et al. [22] study a task queue based dynamic load balancing mechanism for a multi-GPU setup. None of these works examine scheduling or load balancing issues in a PIM-Assisted GPU Architecture. In this paper, we develop new affinity and execution time prediction models to efficiently schedule kernels to heterogeneous compute units in such an architecture.

10. CONCLUSION

We developed two new code scheduling techniques that enable effective use of processing-in-memory (PIM) mechanisms in PIM-Assisted GPU architectures, where a conventional GPU is augmented with 3D memory stacks that house simpler GPUs in their logic layers. First, a *kernel offloading* mechanism that accurately decides what code portions to offload to the GPUs in the 3D memory stack, using a new regression-based kernel affinity prediction model. Second, a *concurrent kernel management* mechanism that uses the affinity prediction model, a new kernel execution time prediction model, and kernel dependency information to decide which kernels to schedule concurrently on both the main GPU cores and the GPU cores in memory stacks. These two mechanisms operate at the *kernel-level*, which simplifies scheduling and management, and makes our approach transparent to programmers and compilers, as code is offloaded from the host system to a GPU system at the kernel granularity in modern systems. We have comprehensively evaluated both of our mechanisms and shown that 1) they provide significant performance and energy efficiency improvements across a wide variety of GPU applications and 2) the improvements we obtain are robust to changes in the training set for our regression model and changes in system parameters. We conclude that our kernel-level scheduling mechanisms can be an effective runtime solution for exploiting processing-in-memory in modern GPU-based architectures.

ACKNOWLEDGMENTS

We thank the anonymous reviewers for their feedback. This research is supported in part by NSF grants #1205618, #1213052, #1212962, #1302225, #1302557, #1317560, #1320478, #1320531, #1409095, #1409723, #1439021, #1439057, and #1526750. Adwait Jog also acknowledges the start-up grant from College of William and Mary.

REFERENCES

[1] "The Green500 List - June 2015."

[2] "Top500 Supercomputer Sites - June 2015."

[3] J. Ahn *et al.*, "A Scalable Processing-in-memory Accelerator for Parallel Graph Processing," in *ISCA*, 2015.

[4] J. Ahn *et al.*, "PIM-enabled Instructions: A Low-overhead, Locality-aware Processing-In-Memory Architecture," in *ISCA*, 2015.

[5] A. M. Aji *et al.*, "Automatic Command Queue Scheduling for Task-Parallel Workloads in OpenCL," in *CLUSTER*, 2015.

[6] AMD, "Graphics Cores Next (GCN) Architecture," 2012.

[7] N. Ardalani *et al.*, "Cross-Architecture Performance Prediction (XAPP) Using CPU Code to Predict GPU Performance," in *MICRO*, 2015.

[8] C. Augonnet *et al.*, "Starpu: A unified platform for task scheduling on heterogeneous multicore architectures," *Concurrency and Computation: Practice and Experience*, 2011.

[9] R. Ausavarungnirun *et al.*, "Staged Memory Scheduling: Achieving High Prformance and Scalability in Heterogeneous Systems," in *ISCA*, 2012.

[10] R. Ausavarungnirun *et al.*, "Exploiting Inter-Warp Heterogeneity to Improve GPGPU Performance," in *PACT*, 2015.

[11] P. E. Bailey *et al.*, "Adaptive Configuration Selection for Power-constrained Heterogeneous Systems," in *ICPP*, 2014.

[12] A. Bakhoda *et al.*, "Analyzing CUDA workloads using a detailed GPU simulator," in *ISPASS*, 2009.

[13] R. Balasubramonian *et al.*, "Near-Data Processing: Insights from a MICRO-46 Workshop," in *IEEE Micro*, 2014.

[14] A. Boroumand *et al.*, "LazyPIM: An Efficient Cache Coherence Mechanism for Processing-in-Memory," *IEEE CAL*, 2016.

[15] A. Boroumand *et al.*, "LazyPIM: An Efficient Cache Coherence Mechanism for Processing-in-Memory," *IEEE CAL*, 2014.

[16] A. Buluç *et al.*, "Solving Path Problems on the GPU," *Parallel Computing*, 2010.

[17] M. Burtscher *et al.*, "A Quantitative Study of Irregular Programs on GPUs," in *IISWC*, 2012.

[18] J. Carter *et al.*, "Impulse: Building a Smarter Memory Controller," in *HPCA*, 1999.

[19] R. Chandra *et al.*, "Scheduling and Page Migration for Multiprocessor Compute Servers," in *ASPLOS*, 1994.

[20] K. Chang *et al.*, "Improving DRAM Performance by Parallelizing Refreshes with Accesses," in *HPCA*, 2014.

[21] S. Che *et al.*, "Rodinia: A Benchmark Suite for Heterogeneous Computing," in *IISWC*, 2009.

[22] L. Chen *et al.*, "Dynamic Load Balancing on Single-and Multi-GPU Systems," in *IPDPS*, 2010.

[23] G. Cybenko, "Dynamic load balancing for distributed memory multiprocessors," *JPDC*, 1989.

[24] W. J. Dally, "Challenges for Future Computing Systems," *HiPEAC Keynote*, 2015.

[25] A. Danalis *et al.*, "The Scalable Heterogeneous Computing (SHOC) benchmark suite," in *GPGPU*, 2010.

[26] R. Das *et al.*, "Application-to-core mapping policies to reduce memory system interference in multi-core systems," in *HPCA*, 2013.

[27] J. Draper *et al.*, "The Architecture of the DIVA Processing-in-memory Chip," in *ICS*, 2002.

[28] C. Dubach *et al.*, "Fast Compiler Optimisation Evaluation Using Code-Feature Based Performance Prediction," in *CF*, 2007.

[29] Y. Eckert *et al.*, "Thermal Feasibility of Die-Stacked Processing in Memory," in *WoNDP*, 2014.

[30] R.-E. Fan *et al.*, "LIBLINEAR: A Library for Large Linear Classification," in *JMLR*, 2008.

[31] A. Farmahini-Farahani *et al.*, "DRAMA: An Architecture for Accelerated Processing near Memory," *IEEE CAL*, 2014.

[32] M. R. Garey *et al.*, "Some Simplified NP-complete Problems," in *STOC*, 1974.

[33] M. Gokhale *et al.*, "Processing in Memory: the Terasys Massively Parallel PIM Array," *IEEE Computer*, 1995.

[34] N. Goswami *et al.*, "Exploring GPGPU Workloads: Characterization Methodology, Analysis and Microarchitecture Evaluation Implications," in *IISWC*, 2010.

[35] GPGPU-Sim v3.2.1. Address mapping.

[36] GPGPU-Sim v3.2.1. GTX 480 Configuration.

[37] S. Grauer-Gray *et al.*, "Auto-tuning a High-level Language targeted to GPU Codes," in *InPar*, 2012.

[38] C. Gregg *et al.*, "Dynamic Heterogeneous Scheduling Decisions using Historical Runtime Data," in *A4MMC*, 2011.

[39] Q. Guo *et al.*, "3D-Stacked Memory-Side Acceleration: Accelerator and System Design," in *WoNDP*, 2014.

[40] M. Hall *et al.*, "Mapping Irregular Applications to DIVA, a PIM-based Data-Intensive Architecture," in *SC*, 1999.

[41] M. Hashemi *et al.*, "Accelerating Dependent Cache Misses with an Enhanced Memory Controller," in *ISCA*, 2016.

[42] B. He *et al.*, "Mars: A MapReduce Framework on Graphics Processors," in *PACT*, 2008.

[43] D. W. Hosmer and S. Lemeshow, *Applied Logistic Regression*, 2000.

[44] K. Hsieh *et al.*, "Transparent Offloading and Mapping (TOM): Enabling Programmer-Transparent Near-Data Processing in GPU Systems," in *ISCA*, 2016.

[45] E. Ipek *et al.*, "An Approach to Performance Prediction for Parallel Applications," in *Euro-Par*, 2005.

[46] E. Ipek *et al.*, "Efficiently exploring architectural design spaces via predictive modeling," in *ASPLOS*, 2006.

[47] E. Ipek *et al.*, "Self Optimizing Memory Controllers: A Reinforcement Learning Approach," in *ISCA*, 2008.

[48] JEDEC, *JESD235 High Bandwidth Memory (HBM) DRAM*, Oct. 2013.

[49] D. Jevdjic *et al.*, "Unison Cache: A Scalable and Effective Die-Stacked DRAM Cache," in *MICRO*, 2014.

[50] J. A. Joao *et al.*, "Bottleneck Identification and Scheduling in Multithreaded Applications," in *ASPLOS*, 2012.

[51] J. A. Joao *et al.*, "Utility-based Acceleration of Multithreaded Applications on Asymmetric CMPs," in *ISCA*, 2013.

[52] A. Jog *et al.*, "Anatomy of GPU Memory System for Multi-Application Execution," in *MEMSYS*, 2015.

[53] A. Jog *et al.*, "OWL: Cooperative Thread Array Aware Scheduling Techniques for Improving GPGPU Performance," in *ASPLOS*, 2013.

[54] A. Jog *et al.*, "Exploiting Core Criticality for Enhanced Performance in GPUs," in *SIGMETRICS*, 2016.

[55] Y. Kang *et al.*, "FlexRAM: Toward an Advanced Intelligent Memory System," in *ICCD*, 1999.

[56] I. Karlin *et al.*, "Exploring Traditional and Emerging Parallel Programming Models using a Proxy Application," in *IPDPS*, 2013.

[57] O. Kayiran *et al.*, "Neither More Nor Less: Optimizing Thread-level Parallelism for GPGPUs," in *PACT*, 2013.

[58] S. Keckler *et al.*, "GPUs and the Future of Parallel Computing," in *IEEE Micro*, 2011.

[59] H. Kim *et al.*, "Bounding Memory Interference Delay in COTS-based Multi-Core Systems," in *RTAS*, 2014.

[60] Y. Kim *et al.*, "ATLAS: A Scalable and High-performance Scheduling Algorithm for Multiple Memory Controllers," in *HPCA*, 2010.

[61] Y. Kim *et al.*, "Thread Cluster Memory Scheduling: Exploiting Differences in Memory Access Behavior," in *MICRO*, 2010.

[62] P. Kogge, "EXECUBE-A New Architecture for Scaleable MPPs," in *ICPP*, 1994.
[63] C. J. Lee *et al.*, "Improving Memory Bank-level Parallelism in the Presence of Prefetching," in *MICRO*, 2009.
[64] D. Lee *et al.*, "Simultaneous Multi-Layer Access: Improving 3D-Stacked Memory Bandwidth at Low Cost," in *ACM TACO*, 2016.
[65] J. Leng *et al.*, "GPUWattch: Enabling Energy Optimizations in GPGPUs," in *ISCA*, 2013.
[66] T. Li and L. K. John, "Run-time Modeling and Estimation of Operating System Power Consumption," in *SIGMETRICS*, 2003.
[67] G. Lipovski and C. Yu, "The Dynamic Associative Access Memory Chip and Its Application to SIMD Processing and Full-Text Database Retrieval," in *MTDT*, 1999.
[68] J. Liu *et al.*, "An Experimental Study of Data Retention Behavior in Modern DRAM Devices: Implications for Retention Time Profiling Mechanisms," in *ISCA*, 2013.
[69] J. Liu *et al.*, "RAIDR: Retention-Aware Intelligent DRAM Refresh," in *ISCA*, 2012.
[70] G. H. Loh *et al.*, "A Processing-in-Memory Taxonomy and a Case for Studying Fixed-function PIM," in *WoNDP*, 2013.
[71] G. Loh, "3D-Stacked Memory Architectures for Multi-core Processors," in *ISCA*, 2008.
[72] K. Ma *et al.*, "GreenGPU: A Holistic Approach to Energy Efficiency in GPU-CPU Heterogeneous Architectures," in *ICPP*, 2012.
[73] S. Marko *et al.*, "Processing-in-Memory: Exploring the Design Space," in *ARCS*, 2015.
[74] D. C. Montgomery and E. Peck, *Introduction to Linear Regression Analysis*, 1992.
[75] T. Moscibroda and O. Mutlu, "Memory Performance Attacks: Denial of Memory Service in Multi-Core Systems," in *USENIX Security*, 2007.
[76] S. P. Muralidhara *et al.*, "Reducing Memory Interference in Multicore Systems via Application-Aware Memory Channel Partitioning," in *MICRO*, 2011.
[77] O. Mutlu, "Memory scaling: A systems architecture perspective," in *IMW*, 2013.
[78] O. Mutlu and T. Moscibroda, "Stall-time Fair Memory Access Scheduling for Chip Multiprocessors," in *MICRO*, 2007.
[79] O. Mutlu and T. Moscibroda, "Parallelism-aware Batch Scheduling: Enhancing both Performance and Fairness of Shared DRAM Systems," in *ISCA*, 2008.
[80] H. Nagasaka *et al.*, "Statistical Power Modeling of GPU Kernels using Performance Counters," in *IGCC*, 2010.
[81] NVIDIA, "CUDA C/C++ SDK Code Samples," 2011.
[82] NVIDIA, "Fermi: NVIDIA's Next Generation CUDA Compute Architecture," 2011.
[83] NVIDIA, "NVIDIA's Next Generation CUDA Compute Architecture: Maxwell GM20x," 2015.
[84] L. S. Panwar *et al.*, "Online Performance Projection for Clusters with Heterogeneous GPUs," in *ICPADS*, 2013.
[85] D. Patterson *et al.*, "A Case for Intelligent RAM," in *IEEE Micro*, 1997.
[86] J. T. Pawlowski, "Hybrid Memory Cube," *Hotchips*, 2011.
[87] S. Pugsley *et al.*, "NDC: Analyzing the Impact of 3D-Stacked Memory+Logic Devices on MapReduce Workloads," in *ISPASS*, 2014.
[88] M. Qureshi *et al.*, "AVATAR: A Variable-Retention-Time (VRT) Aware Refresh for DRAM Systems," in *DSN*, 2015.
[89] A. Rahimi *et al.*, "Energy-Efficient GPGPU Architectures via Collaborative Compilation and Memristive Memory-Based Computing," in *DAC*, 2014.
[90] S. F. Reddaway, "DAP - a Distributed Array Processor," in *ISCA*, 1973.
[91] T. G. Rogers *et al.*, "Cache-Conscious Wavefront Scheduling," in *MICRO*, 2012.
[92] T. G. Rogers *et al.*, "Divergence-Aware Warp Scheduling," in *MICRO*, 2013.
[93] G. E. Sayre, "STARAN: An Associative Approach to Multiprocessor Architecture," in *Computer Architecture, Workshop of the Gesellschaft fur Informatik*, 1976.
[94] V. Seshadri *et al.*, "Fast Bulk Bitwise AND and OR in DRAM," *IEEE CAL*, 2015.
[95] V. Seshadri *et al.*, "RowClone: Fast and Energy-efficient in-DRAM Bulk Data Copy and Initialization," in *MICRO*, 2013.
[96] V. Seshadri *et al.*, "Gather-Scatter DRAM: In-DRAM Address Translation to Improve the Spatial Locality of Non-unit Strided Accesses," in *MICRO*, 2015.
[97] B. A. Shirazi *et al.*, *Scheduling and Load Balancing in Parallel and Distributed Systems*, 1995.
[98] D. Smitley and K. Iobst, "Bit-Serial SIMD on the CM-2 and the Cray 2," in *SIAM PP*, 1990.
[99] H. S. Stone, "A Logic-in-Memory Computer," *IEEE TC*, 1970.
[100] L. Subramanian *et al.*, "The Blacklisting Memory Scheduler: Achieving High Performance and Fairness at Low Cost," in *ICCD*, 2014.
[101] L. Subramanian *et al.*, "The Application Slowdown Model: Quantifying and Controlling the Impact of Inter-Application Interference at Shared Caches and Main Memory," in *MICRO*, 2015.
[102] L. Subramanian *et al.*, "MISE: Providing performance predictability and improving fairness in shared main memory systems," in *HPCA*, 2013.
[103] M. A. Suleman *et al.*, "Data marshaling for multi-core architectures," in *ISCA*, 2010.
[104] M. A. Suleman *et al.*, "Accelerating Critical Section Execution with Asymmetric Multi-core Architectures," in *ASPLOS*, 2009.
[105] H. Topcuoglu *et al.*, "Performance-effective and Low-complexity Task Scheduling for Heterogeneous Computing," *IEEE TPDS*, 2002.
[106] H. Usui *et al.*, "DASH: Deadline-Aware High-Performance Memory Scheduler for Heterogeneous Systems with Hardware Accelerators," in *ACM TACO*, 2016.
[107] N. Vijaykumar *et al.*, "A Case for Core-Assisted Bottleneck Acceleration in GPUs: Enabling Flexible Data Compression with Assist Warps," in *ISCA*, 2015.
[108] H. Wang *et al.*, "A-DRM: Architecture-aware Distributed Resource Management of Virtualized Clusters," in *VEE*, 2015.
[109] D. H. Woo *et al.*, "An Optimized 3D-Stacked Memory Architecture by Exploiting Excessive, High-Density TSV Bandwidth," in *HPCA*, 2010.
[110] G. Wu *et al.*, "GPGPU Performance and Power Estimation using Machine Learning," in *HPCA*, 2015.
[111] C. Xu and F. C. Lau, *Load Balancing in Parallel Computers: Theory and Practice*, 1996.
[112] D. Zhang *et al.*, "TOP-PIM: Throughput-oriented Programmable Processing in Memory," in *HPDC*, 2014.
[113] L. Zhang *et al.*, "Accurate Online Power Estimation and Automatic Battery Behavior based Power Model Generation for Smartphones," in *CODES+ISSS*, 2010.
[114] J. Zhao and Y. Xie, "Optimizing Bandwidth and Power of Graphics Memory with Hybrid Memory Technologies and Adaptive Data Migration," in *ICCAD*, 2012.

OAWS: Memory Occlusion Aware Warp Scheduling

Bin Wang
Auburn University
bwang@auburn.edu

Yue Zhu
Florida State University
yzhu@cs.fsu.edu

Weikuan Yu
Florida State University
yuw@cs.fsu.edu

ABSTRACT

We have closely examined GPU resource utilization when executing memory-intensive benchmarks. Our detailed analysis of GPU global memory accesses reveals that divergent loads can lead to the occlusion of Load-Store units, resulting in quick consumption of MSHR entries. Such memory occlusion prevents other ready memory instructions from accessing L1 data cache, eventually stalling warp schedulers and degrading the overall performance. We have designed memory Occlusion Aware Warp Scheduling (OAWS) that can dynamically predict the demand of MSHR entries of divergent memory instructions, and maximize the number of concurrent warps such that their aggregate MSHR consumptions are within the MSHR capacity. Our dynamic OAWS policy can prevent memory occlusions and effectively leverage more MSHR entries for better IPC performance for GPU. Experimental results show that the static and dynamic versions of OAWS achieve 36.7% and 73.1% performance improvement, compared to the baseline GTO scheduling. Particularly, dynamic OAWS outperforms MASCAR, CCWS, and SWL-Best by 70.1%, 57.8%, and 11.4%, respectively.

1 Introduction

GPU applications have a wide range of memory access patterns, many of which are very irregular. Despite the high-bandwidth GPU global memory, irregular patterns can stall the GPU memory and degrade the effectiveness of massive parallelism. GPUs have employed a hierarchy of data caches to reduce memory latency and save the on-chip network and off-chip memory bandwidth when there is locality within the accesses. However, the cache is frequently thrashed by divergent memory accesses. To tackle this problem, GPU L1D bypassing has been well studied to alleviate cache contention [1, 2, 3, 4, 5, 6, 7, 8]. For example, MRPB [1] aggressively bypasses L1D whenever an associativity stall occurs, but the cache is still underutilized. Two recent works [9, 10] reported that throttling the number of concurrent warps reduces the accumulated working set so that the contention on cache capacity is alleviated and locality is preserved.

While the aforementioned efforts improved the memory performance of GPU applications, they overlooked some hazardous situations that are faced by GPU memory instructions. In this paper, we have closely examined execution stalls caused by divergent memory accesses in data-intensive GPU benchmarks. Our detailed analysis of GPU global memory accesses reveals that divergent accesses can lead to the occlusion of Load-Store units and a quick depletion of MSHR (Miss Status Holding Registers) [11] entries. This memory occlusion in turn stalls the execution pipeline, degrading the overall performance. Our analysis shows that memory occlusion can significantly delay both coherent and divergent GPU instructions, propagate into more stalls in the pipeline, and deteriorate the overall utilization of GPU. Furthermore, such memory occlusion cannot be mitigated by a simple provision of more MSHR entries, when there is a lack of appropriate balance between warp parallelism and L1D locality.

Turner [12] investigated instruction replay for mitigating the performance impact of pipeline stalls caused by GPU memory operations, aiming to reduce wasteful replays by predicting resource demands of GPU memory operations. In this paper, we propose memory Occlusion Aware Warp Scheduling (OAWS) to monitor the usage of MSHR entries, predict the MSHR requirement of memory instructions, and schedule the warps that can be satisfied by the available MSHR entries, thereby preventing memory occlusion and increasing the effective parallelism among GPU warps. OAWS is designed with both static and dynamic methods to predict the required MSHR entries from GPU warps. Static OAWS predicts the misses from all warps with a fixed miss rate while dynamic OAWS takes into account the varying access patterns of different warps to predict cache misses on a per-warp basis. Particularly, dynamic OAWS has seamlessly integrated the warp priority and a concurrency estimation model in its prediction policy. It effectively prevents memory occlusion by dynamically predicting an optimal number of concurrent warps, and uses more MSHR entries effectively without thrashing L1D.

We have leveraged a wide variety of memory-intensive benchmarks to evaluate the performance of OAWS and demonstrated that OAWS outperforms three state-of-the-art warp scheduling techniques, i.e., Cache-Conscious Wavefront Scheduling (CCWS) [9], Static Wavefront Scheduling (SWL) [9] and Memory Aware Scheduling and Cache Access Re-execution (MASCAR) [13]. Specifically, our experiments show that our static and dynamic versions of OAWS achieve 36.7% and 73.1% compared to the baseline GTO warp scheduling. In addition, dynamic OAWS helps GPU leverage the benefits of more MSHR entries. Compared to GTO, it improves the IPC performance by 73.1%, 89.1%, 92.6%, and 99.4% when there are 32, 48, 64, and 96 MSHR entries, respectively.

The rest of this paper is organized as follows. Section 2 describes the background on GPU architecture and the execution of memory instructions. Section 3 provides an analysis of memory occlusion. Section 4 details the proposed memory occlusion aware

PACT '16, September 11-15, 2016, Haifa, Israel

DOI: http://dx.doi.org/10.1145/2967938.2967947

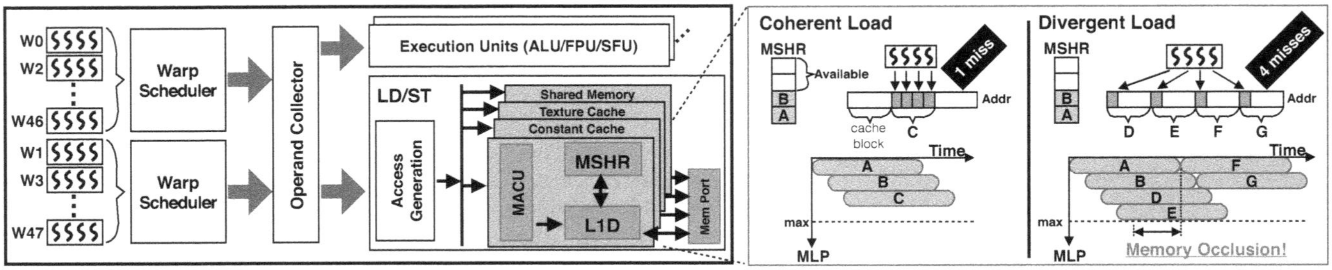

Figure 1: Baseline Streaming Multiprocessor (SM). Other stages of the pipeline are omitted. The MSHR of L1D has 4 entries, two of which have been allocated to track the outstanding memory requests of cache blocks A and B. The remaining MSHR entries are sufficient for a coherent load, but occlude the divergent load so that demand requests of blocks F and G are replayed.

warp scheduling algorithms. The experimental methodology and results are presented in Section 5. Section 6 summarizes the related work, followed by Section 7 that concludes the paper.

2 Background

2.1 GPU and Warp Scheduling

We study a Fermi-like GPU from NVIDIA, which has 32 threads per warp and 32 MSHR entries per Streaming Multiprocessor (SM) as the default configuration. Inside each SM as shown in Figure 1, two warp schedulers independently manage warps with even and odd identifiers [14]. In each cycle, both warp schedulers pick one ready warp and issue its instruction into the SIMD pipeline backend [15, 14, 16], which in our baseline SM mainly consists of *Operand Collector* (i.e., registers), *Execution Units (ALU/FPU/SFU)*, and *Load-Store (LD/ST)* units. To determine the readiness of an instruction, a ready bit is used to track its dependency on other instructions. It is updated in the scoreboard by comparing its source and destination registers with other in-flight instructions [17]. Instructions are ready for scheduling when the ready bits are set, i.e., dependencies are cleared. GPU scheduling logic consists of two stages: qualification and prioritization [18]. In the qualification stage, ready warps are selected based on the ready bit of each instruction. In the prioritization stage, ready warps are prioritized for execution based on a chosen metric, such as cycle-based round-robin [18, 19, 20], warp age [9, 10], instruction age [18, 21], or others that can maximize resource utilization [18]. For example, the Greedy-Then-Oldest (GTO) [9, 10] scheduler maintains the highest priority for an active warp until it is stalled. It then prioritizes the oldest among all ready warps for scheduling.

2.2 GPU Memory Access and Occlusion

According to data destination, GPU memory requests are sent to data cache (L1D), constant cache, texture cache, and shared memory, respectively. Inside GPU LD/ST units, memory accesses are generated by the *Access Generation* unit. A memory instruction is coherent when its memory accesses can be coalesced into 1-2 cache lines; otherwise, it is referred to as a divergent instruction.

For memory instructions to local/global memory, per-thread memory accesses are coalesced into fewer cache lines by the *Memory Access Coalescing Unit (MACU)*. Coalesced accesses are sent to L1D via a single 128-byte port [21]. For a load access, on cache hit, the requested data is loaded to the register file; on cache miss, one demand request is generated to fetch data from the lower memory hierarchy. The Missing Status Holding Register (MSHR) is used to track in-flight memory requests and merge duplicate requests to the same cache line. After MSHR allocation, a memory request is buffered into the *Memory Port* for transfer. An MSHR entry is deallocated after its corresponding memory request is back and all accesses to that block are serviced. L1D does not support coherence, so it evicts cache blocks on stores to global memory. Stores require no MSHR and are directly buffered into the memory port. Memory requests buffered in the memory port are drained by the on-chip network in each cycle when lower memory hierarchy is not saturated.

Memory Occlusion: MSHR is often implemented as a fully-associative structure and thus is limited by capacity. This leads to a structural hazard due to the mismatch between limited memory-level parallelism (MLP) and massive thread-level parallelism (TLP). This hazard can be exacerbated by bursty accesses from divergent loads, causing the propagation of stalls [12] in the execution pipeline. As shown in the right part of Figure 1, the MSHR of L1D has 4 entries. The coherent load with 1 cache miss can be immediately serviced, while the four un-coalesceable accesses of the divergent load suffer from insufficient MSHR entries because only two MSHR entries are available. In this example, the access to block F that misses in L1D is replayed until the memory request of block A is back and its MSHR entry is deallocated. During the access replay, the currently prioritized memory instruction can not make progress, occluding LD/ST units. This occlusion in turn prevents other memory instructions from accessing LD/ST units. We refer to such a scenario as ***Memory Occlusion***. Memory Occlusion degrades memory instruction throughput in LD/ST units and prevents other memory instructions that do not need an MSHR from accessing the L1D.

3 Characterization of Memory Occlusion

We investigate the impacts of memory occlusion by analyzing the breakdown of LD/ST stall cycles, quantifying the global memory access time, and examining the trend of MSHR consumption under the GTO warp scheduling.

3.1 Stalls in LD/ST and Warp Schedulers

When LD/ST units are stalled, a ready memory instruction can not be issued. We refer to such stall cycles as LD/ST stalls. Besides MSHR unavailability and memory port congestion, sequentially processing un-coalesceable memory accesses makes the LD/ST units unavailable to warp schedulers and delays other ready memory instructions accessing L1D. According to these three causes that can stall LD/ST units, we breakdown the LD/ST stall cycles into three categories in Figure 2: 1) coalescing stalls (*LDST_COAL*) — when L1D has successfully serviced one un-coalescable memory access and LD/ST units are stalled by divergent memory accesses; 2) MSHR stalls (*LDST_MSHR*) — when a cache miss can not be processed due to MSHR unavailability; and 3) ICNT stalls (*LDST_ICNT*) — when a cache miss can not be processed due to on-chip network congestion, but MSHR entries are available. Among the memory coherent benchmarks, 2MM, 3MM, SRAD1, SRAD2, and LBM experience a large percentage of *LDST_ICNT*

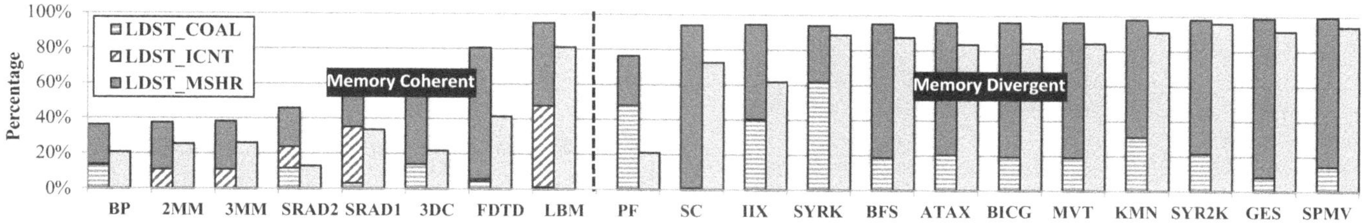

Figure 2: The breakdown of LD/ST stall cycles (the stacked bar on left) and the percentage of cycles for which the warp schedulers are stalled due to LD/ST stalls (the right bar). The dotted line divides all benchmarks into memory coherent (left) and memory divergent (right) ones. Benchmark characteristics and simulator details are summarized in Section 5.

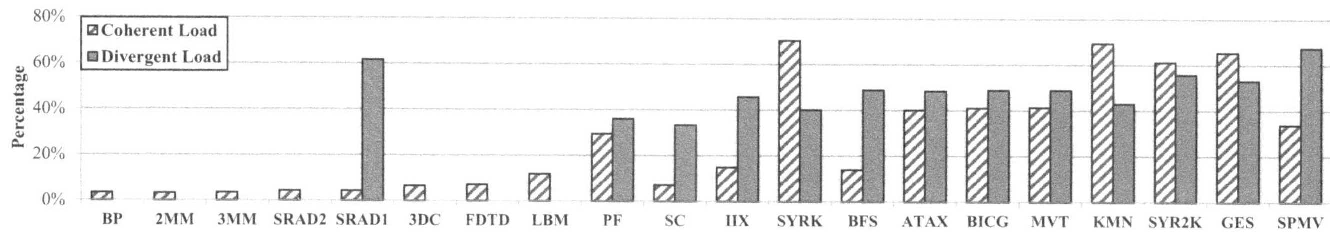

Figure 3: Memory occlusion time in the memory access latency for coherent and divergent loads.

stalls. These five benchmarks write significant amounts of data into global memory, congesting the network from SM to L2 cache. For memory divergent benchmarks, *LDST_MSHR* dominates LD/ST stall cycles, with an average of 66% of total cycles waiting for MSHR entries. The divergent benchmarks are read-intensive. However, read requests impose limited pressure on the network from SM to L2 cache. So *LDST_ICNT* plays a negligible role in these benchmarks.

Although LD/ST units are stalled, warp schedulers can still issue computation instructions into execution units to overlap the stalls in LD/ST units. The capability of overlapping LD/ST stalls explains why warp schedulers (the gray bar) are stalled less than LD/ST units across all of the benchmarks in Figure 2. However, LD/ST stalls eventually deplete ready warps for the schedulers when all warps are waiting to be scheduled to issue memory instructions. For memory coherent benchmarks, on average, warp schedulers waste 28% of the total cycles waiting for the availability of LD/ST units. This percentage increases to 75% for memory divergent benchmarks. Such high stalls in warp schedulers directly lead to severe degradation of instruction throughput.

3.2 Quantifying Memory Occlusion Time

Upon memory occlusion, L1D access latency can be divided into memory occlusion time and L1D hit/miss time. Figure 3 shows the percentage of memory occlusion time in the average L1D access latency for both coherent and divergent load instructions in memory intensive benchmarks. On average, memory occlusion delays account for 4% of L1D access time for all memory coherent benchmarks. SRAD1 has very few divergent loads through its 502 kernel invocations. In memory divergent benchmarks, memory occlusion delays reach 33% and 47% for coherent and divergent loads, respectively. These large delays dramatically prolong memory access time, demanding a higher degree of computation-memory overlap. However, these memory-divergent benchmarks often lack sufficient computation instructions to overlap with memory accesses, causing the warp scheduler stalls shown in Figure 2. It is clear that memory occlusion is a performance destructor for divergent GPGPU workloads, which is the focus in the paper.

Since the lack of MSHR entries is inherently associated with memory occlusion, an intuitive solution is to employ more as a simple solution. We have investigated the impact of more MSHR entries to memory occlusion under different scheduling policies. Our results have shown that, while deeply associated with the number of MSHR entries, memory occlusion cannot be solved by simply adding more MSHR entries (see Section 5.5 for more details).

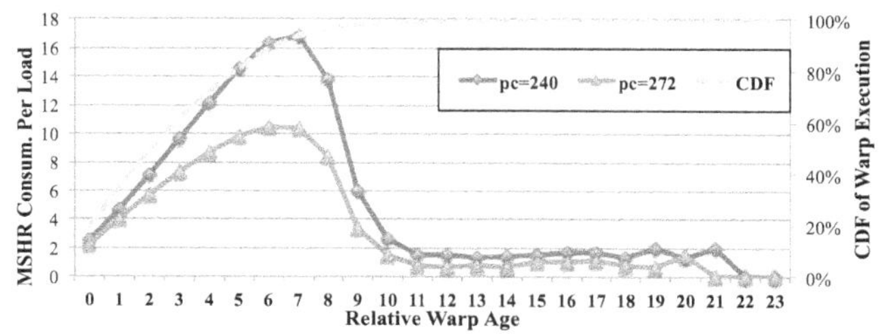

Figure 4: The MSHR consumption of each load instruction in BFS kernel and the CDF of warp execution times when using GTO scheduler. *pc=240* and *pc=272* are the two divergent loads. Age 0 represents the oldest warp.

3.3 Predictability of MSHR consumption

Since the consumption of MSHR entries is a good indicator of potential memory occlusion, we use one kernel from BFS to study MSHR consumption when using a GTO warp scheduler. The two divergent load instructions (pc=240 and pc=272) in this kernel carry high intra-warp locality [9, 10]. Because older warps have higher scheduling priorities under GTO scheduling, older warps are more frequently scheduled and their data blocks have shorter re-reference intervals, leading to lower cache misses and consequently lower MSHR consumption. As shown in Figure 4, the MSHR consumption levels of the two divergent loads are linear to each warp's relative age. The CDF of warp execution times shows that the oldest 8 warps (age=0-7) occupy 94% of total cycles. Note that the warps with even younger ages (age>7) have lower MSHR consumption because they are rarely scheduled, until older warps have very few active threads remained or retired completely. This observation also applies to the other memory divergent benchmarks we have evaluated. Thus, we argue that, because of the existence of a strong linear relationship, the MSHR consumption of a load instruction can be predicted based on its hit/miss history and its warp's GTO scheduling priority.

4 OAWS: Occlusion Aware Warp Scheduling

We propose memory Occlusion Aware Warp Scheduling (OAWS) to monitor the use of MSHR entries and predict memory occlusion, thereby scheduling warps appropriately to alleviate its impact.

4.1 Main Idea of OAWS

Figure 5 provides an example on the benefit of OAWS. For illustration purpose, the number of MSHR entries in Figure 5 is 8. Assume that the example kernel first fetches data from memory and then computes it. There are 3 ready warps, A, B, and C, to be scheduled (Figure 5(a)) . They are ordered by their arrival times. The memory load instructions in warps A, B, and C are divergent and produce 6, 6, and 2 memory load requests to L2 cache, respectively. The varying number of memory requests for warps are caused by either branch divergence or warp locality variation [9, 10]. Unless otherwise noted, we employ by default the GTO [9] warp scheduler.

Figure 5(b) shows how the GTO scheduler works. The load instructions from warps A, B, and C are issued at T_0, T_1, and T_4, respectively, according to their age. At the time T_2, two MSHR entries are allocated to memory requests from warp B. At this point, MSHR entries are used up and memory occlusion occurs. Therefore, the remaining requests of warp B are continuously replayed until the responses for warp A's memory loads arrive at T_3. At T_5, all data required by warp A are returned from L2 and warp A is ready to be issued for computation. While warp A finishes computation at T_6, warps B and C are stalled due to outstanding memory requests. The computation for warps B and C starts at T_7 and T_8, respectively. As shown in Figure 5(b), GTO causes idle cycles between T_6 and T_7.

In contrast, in Figure 5(c), OAWS predicts that available MSHR entries cannot satisfy warp B's demand, so it prevents warp B from issuing its memory instruction at T_1'. OAWS then avoids the memory occlusion that may occur when warp B is scheduled. When warp A's requests return from memory, their MSHR entries are released and warp B is then scheduled. Since the ALU keeps idle, warp A and C are immediately scheduled for computation at T_4' and at T_5', respectively. Finally, warp B is scheduled for computation at T_6'. Since warp C is scheduled ahead of warp B, its computation overlaps with warp B's memory load, reducing the time to complete these warps. Although this example shows only three warps and a miss penalty of 12 cycles for simplicity, the benefit of occlusion-awareness could be more significant because the off-chip memory latency is often between 400 and 500 cycles.

4.1.1 Qualification Metric of OAWS

OAWS aims to prevent memory occlusion with a simple logic, i.e., ensuring that enough MSHR entries are available for a divergent load. To this end, it needs to predict the number of cache misses for an incoming divergent load, and take into account the needs of load instructions that have been issued. Thus, the qualification logic of OAWS is to qualify a memory instruction if its predicted cache misses can satisfy the following condition:

$$Miss_{pred}(pc,w) \leq Avail_{mshr} - Miss_{inflight}, \quad (1)$$

where $Avail_{mshr}$ is the number of available MSHR entries for a L1D, $Miss_{pred}(pc,w)$ is the predicted number of cache misses that warp w is going to incur for the memory instruction at address pc, and $Miss_{\text{inflight}}$ is the number of predicted cache misses from inflight load instructions. At runtime, $Miss_{\text{inflight}}$ is updated as memory instructions are issued or completed by the LD/ST units. Note that stores do not consume MSHR entries because coherent loads rarely consume 2 entries. Coherent loads are predicted to consume one MSHR entry with 1 cache miss. In OAWS, we focus on divergent load instructions which are more likely to cause memory occlusion.

4.1.2 Designing Scheduling Policies for OAWS

To accurately predict the number of cache misses for a divergent load instruction, we have explored both static and dynamic policies for OAWS. Figure 6 presents the microarchitecture for both versions. OAWS is implemented as an extension of the warp scheduler's qualification logic. Conventional qualification logic is used to pick warps that are ready for execution, which is denoted as a N-bit vector *Ready[1:N]* (❶). OAWS relies on the *Divergent Load Classifier (DLC)* to predict $Miss_{\text{pred}}(pc)$ and then re-qualifies ready warps using the logic in Equation 1. The output of OAWS is another N-bit vector *Occlude[1:N]* (❸), in which a bit value 0 denotes a warp predicted to not occlude MSHR entries, 1 otherwise. OAWS then uses the same prioritization logic as GTO to schedule the occlusion-free warps (❹). Therefore, the younger occlusion-free warps still have a chance to share the cycles with the older warps without memory occlusion. The following sections will detail both static and dynamic OAWS.

4.2 Static OAWS

With the static OAWS policy, we adopt a static miss rate (*SMR*) for each divergent load. The number of MSHR entries required for this load ($Miss_{pred}(pc,w)$) is then predicted as $Div_{pred}(pc,w) \times SMR$, where $Div_{pred}(pc,w)$ is the predicted memory divergence of warp w at load instruction pc. $Div_{pred}(pc,w)$ is equal to the number of active threads in w, similar to DAWS [10], because threads often independently fetch data blocks into L1D when memory divergence occurs. With *SMR* being 0%, OAWS is essentially disabled, and all divergent loads are assumed to complete without consuming MSHR entries. When *SMR* is 100%, OAWS assumes each thread will consume one MSHR entry when divergent loads are issued. We tune static OAWS with *SMR* in the range from 0% to 100% for the optimal performance.

In our experiments, we observe that static OAWS with an *SMR* of 50% achieves the optimal performance on the divergent benchmarks evaluated in this study. Given the SIMD width of 32 in our baseline GPU architecture, 50% means that a warp with 32 active threads is predicted to consume 16 MSHR entries. Since there are only 32 MSHR entries per SM, at most two divergent memory loads can be pipelined into LD/ST units. The qualification logic in Equation 1 then serializes divergent load instructions to access the LD/ST units. Because $Miss_{\text{inflight}}$ is decreased only when a load instruction retires from memory pipeline, this serialization conceptually inserts a minimum delay of $Div_{pred}(pc,w)$ cycles before a new divergent load can be qualified. When the miss rate is high, e.g., when the remaining MSHR entries are less than 16, no warp with 32 threads can be scheduled to issue divergent loads and the delay is further extended. Such a serialization delay reduces the frequency of issuing divergent load instructions and also prevents divergent loads from issuing when available MSHR entries are low, thus static OAWS can alleviate the problem of memory occlusion.

To implement static OAWS, we only need to know whether a load is divergent or not. This information is provided by *DLC*. In general, each *DLC* entry records the history of a divergent load, including *PC* address, the number of instruction occurrences (*#inst*), the total number of memory accesses (*#acc*), and cache associativity contention statistics (*#sets*). When a load instruction's memory accesses are coalesced (❺), its *PC* is first checked against *DLC* to make sure that no duplicate records exist in the table. If a new divergent load is detected, a new entry with the current instruction's

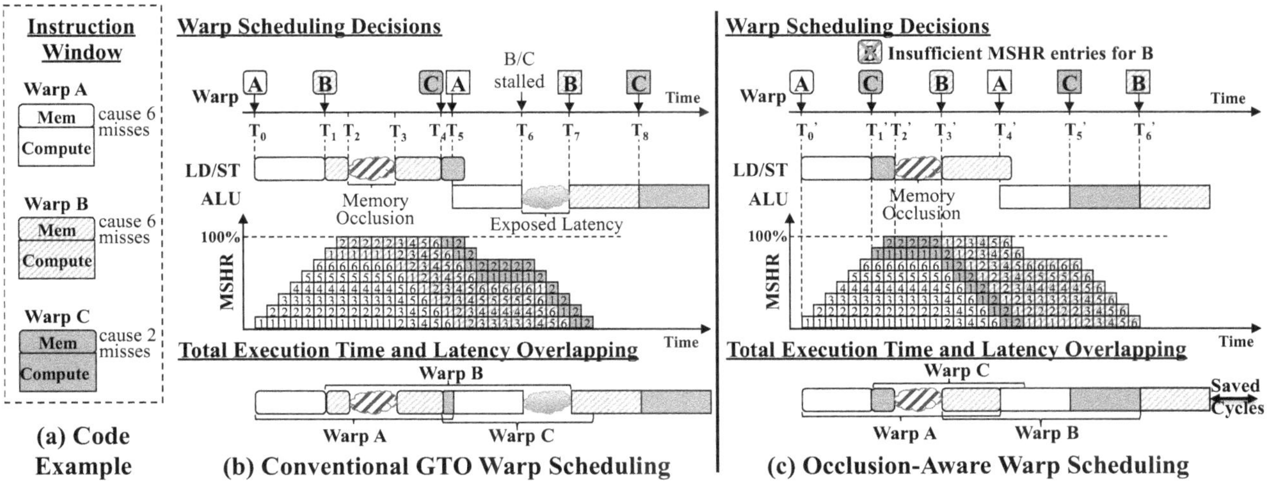

Figure 5: A conceptual example showing the benefit of Occlusion Aware Warp Scheduling

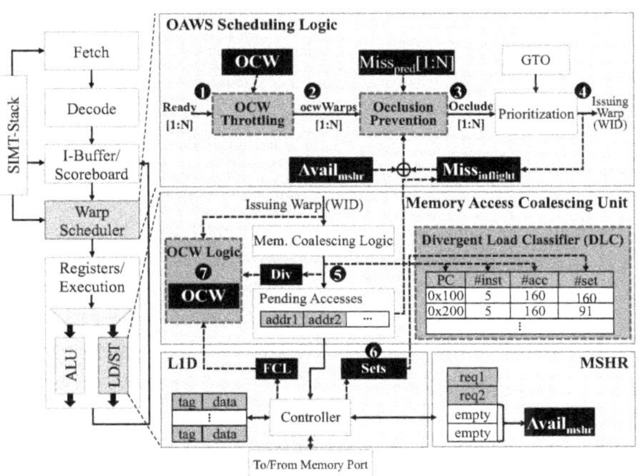

Figure 6: Detailed SM model for our solution. N is the number of warps on each scheduler.

PC, *#inst* (being 1), and *#acc* are inserted into *DLC*; otherwise, the existing entry is updated with this information. *#sets* is updated with the number of cache sets touched by the current load after its requests are processed by L1D(❻). Since OAWS only focuses on divergent loads, coherent loads and their information are not populated into *DLC*. Static OAWS only needs the *PC* field to decide if a load is divergent, while other fields are used by dynamic OAWS.

4.3 Dynamic OAWS

Static OAWS uses a fixed miss rate for all warps, which cannot account for the dynamic nature of divergent accesses across different warps. In addition, memory divergent benchmarks often have high intra-warp locality. Thus, we propose dynamic OAWS to accomplish two objectives: (1) maximizing the number of concurrent warps while preserving L1D cache locality, and (2) maximizing the use of MSHR entries without memory occlusion. This requires a careful selection of appropriate warps that can strike a balance between the maximum resource utilization (cache capacity and MSHR entries) and the best performance (neither memory occlusion nor cache thrashing).

Dynamic OAWS achieves both objectives by enabling a concurrency level at which the aggregate MSHR consumption from all actively scheduled warps is less than MSHR capacity. In order to implement dynamic OAWS, we first propose a light-weight concurrency model to estimate the maximal number of warps that would not occlude the LD/ST units, and then apply this model to predict MSHR consumption on a per-warp basis so that more warps can be opportunistically scheduled.

4.3.1 Estimation of Optimal Warp Concurrency

Divergent benchmarks with high intra-warp locality can benefit from reduced cache contention via concurrency throttling. Meanwhile, under the lock-step execution model, warps that incur cache misses, regardless of the number of missed accesses, will inevitably consume MSHR entries and also thrash other warps' cache blocks. We propose to estimate the optimal number of cached warps based on the consumption of cache blocks by load instructions. Note that being fully cached means that a load's data is completely reserved in L1D and will incur no cache eviction in its re-references. Under GTO prioritization, only a few old warps are actively scheduled, as shown in figure 4, thus monitoring the dynamic changes of fully cached loads gives a close approximation of **Optimal Cached Warps (OCW)**.

We also observe that L1D locality in the memory intensive benchmarks can be associated with both coherent and divergent loads. Since coherent loads often exhibit streaming-like accesses and divergent loads tend to dominate the memory footprint, we only use the locality statistics from divergent loads to estimate OCW.

Figure 7 shows the flow of OCW estimation. In the figure, *OCW* denotes the estimated number of fully cached warps, and *CNT* is a counter used to track the changes in the number of fully cached loads. In our proposal, OCW is no less than 2, because each warp scheduler needs at least one active warp (i.e., the oldest warp in GTO) to reduce the idle cycles in warp schedulers; while *Wmax* is the maximum of OCW, which is the number of physical warps on each SM (48 in our baseline). *Cmax* is the maximum of CNT. We empirically use an 8-bit counter for CNT so that it can record the locality changes in 255 consecutive occurrences of divergent loads, i.e., Cmax=255 in Figure 7. OCW estimation is a component inside MACU, denoted as *OCW Logic* (❼) in Figure 6, and is triggered after the accesses of a divergent load are serviced by L1D. CNT is initialized as 128 while OCW is 2 for each SM. These initial values give OCW estimation the flexibility to gradually learn L1D locality changes at runtime.

At runtime, CNT is increased by 1 for each fully cached divergent load (Ⓐ). When CNT is saturated (CNT==Cmax), if OCW has not reached its maximum value (*Wmax*), OCW is increased by

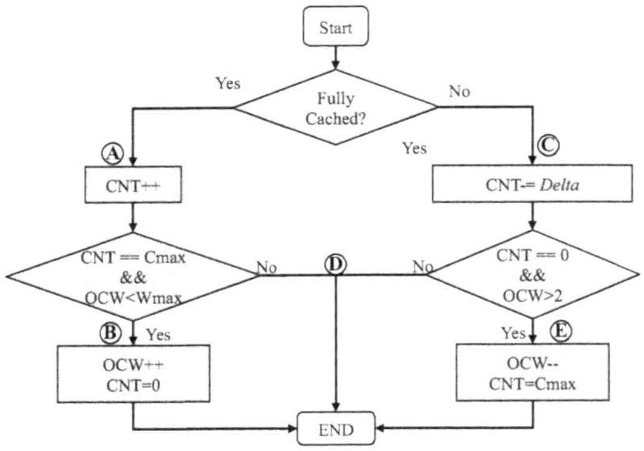

Figure 7: Flow Chart of OCW estimation logic.

1 and accordingly CNT is reset as *0* to track the changes of the fully cached divergent loads under the increased concurrency (Ⓑ). For partially cached loads (Ⓒ), CNT is decreased by *Delta*, where *Delta* is a tuning parameter. When CNT reaches zero, OCW is decreased by 1 so that less warps can be actively scheduled (Ⓔ), and CNT is reset as Cmax. In the corner cases where OCW is equal to 2 or Wmax (Ⓓ), CNT will not be updated if CNT is equal to 0 or Cmax.

To Determine Delta, we have evaluated several heuristics in the tuning process of OCW estimation. Two representative strategies are 1) Delta=1 and 2) Delta=CNT/2. The major difference between the two is that the second strategy can quickly respond to cache contention and bursty MSHR consumption if OCW is overestimated. We observe that cache associativity-sensitive benchmarks, such as these memory-divergent benchmarks from Mars [22] benchmark suite, perform better under the second strategy, but the other memory-divergent benchmarks perform better under the first strategy. For these associativity-sensitive benchmarks, the bursty accesses of each divergent load are concentrated into only a few cache sets [1, 23], severely under-utilizing the L1D capacity. The second strategy then ensures that the estimated OCW can be quickly decreased after a few consecutive occurrences of partially cached divergent loads. We use DLC to track the sensitivity of individual benchmarks to associativity. Ideally, when *#acc* of a divergent instruction is equal to *#sets*, its divergent accesses are uniformly distributed into available cache sets and intra-warp associativity-sensitivity is eliminated. In our implementation, a divergent load is considered as associativity-sensitive if its *#acc* is larger than *#sets*×1.5. Based on this information, we enable strategy 2 for associativity-sensitive loads and strategy 1 for the other loads. Together we can have a robust strategy for Delta.

We use three registers to realize the aforementioned logic of dynamic OAWS. In Figure 6, Register ***Div*** is used to mark whether a load is divergent. Register ***FCL*** is used to track whether a load is fully cached. *FCL* is set when a cache miss happens on it. When all the accesses of the load are serviced, an unset *FCL* indicates a fully cached load. Register ***Sets*** has N-bit, each of which corresponds to one set in the N physical cache sets, and is used to record the number of cache sets touched by the current load. The three registers are reset when a new load instruction is serviced by L1D.

4.3.2 Concurrency-Aware Avoidance of Memory Occlusion

With a scheme from Section 4.3.1 that estimates the optimal cached warps while maintaining L1D cache locality, we can then devise a scheme for our second objective, i.e., maximizing the use of MSHR entries without memory occlusion. We first use the estimated OCW to categorize all warps into two groups: **locality warps** and **thrashing warps**, based on their scheduling priorities. With a descending order for the GTO priorities of warps, a warp is a locality warp if its GTO priority is less than OCW, otherwise a thrashing warp. This classification is based on the observation that older warps are more frequently scheduled in GTO than younger ones so that they are more likely to be fully cached. When a thrashing warp is scheduled, L1D locality is often thrashed.

The estimated OCW can be used to throttle concurrency by only scheduling locality warps, referred to as *OCW Throttling*. However, the training of OCW may take a long time to arrive at the optimal value. This can be a disadvantage for OCW Throttling to quickly respond to program behavior changes during runtime. For example, when L1D locality is well preserved, MSHR consumption from locality warps becomes low; gradually scheduling thrashing warps is then unlikely to immediately incur memory occlusion. Meanwhile, for benchmarks with frequent branch divergences, OCW Throttling may lose the opportunity to schedule thrashing warps with few active threads. Such thrashing warps have small memory footprint, incur little cache thrashing, and consume few MSHR entries. Scheduling them can increase the number of actively scheduled warps. We design dynamic OAWS to opportunistically enable such thrashing warps, when 1) aggregate MSHR consumption of locality warps is low, and 2) some warps have few active threads due to branch divergence.

To prevent memory occlusion while maintaining sufficient concurrency, we integrate the use of OCW in dynamic OAWS for the prediction of cache misses, i.e., the required MSHR entries. For locality warps, we predict their cache misses as 0, i.e., $Miss_{pred}(pc,w) = 0$, because they are fully cached to incur no MSHR consumption. Thus, locality warps will not be excluded from scheduling due to the concern of memory occlusion. Motivated by the little performance fluctuations of per-app SMR with the static OAWS policy, thrashing warps are predicted with a flat miss rate of 50%, i.e., $Miss_{pred}(pc,w) = Div_{pred}(pc,w) \times 50\%$.

A fixed miss rate leads to a uniform prediction for all thrashing warps, unable to capture skewed cache misses from warps with different GTO priorities. As shown in Figure 4, a warp's GTO priority (GTO_{gprio}) is proportional to the number of consumed MSHR entries. In order to enforce the GTO prioritization and provide differentiated predictions for all thrashing warps, we combine both the cache miss rate of a load operation and the GTO_{gprio} of a warp into the predicted misses. Together, we arrive at a formula to predict the required MSHR entries as $Miss_{pred}(pc,w) = Div_{pred}(pc,w) \times 50\% + GTO_{gprio}$.

Combining the estimation of optimal cached warps and the prediction of required MSHR entries, our dynamic OAWS strives to maintain a maximal number of concurrent warps and predict the demands on MSHR entries to prevent memory occlusion. In the integrated scheme for dynamic avoidance of memory occlusion, the OCW Throttling first generates a 2N-bit vector *ocwWarps[1:N]* (❷), in which a value 2 denotes a locality warp, 1 denotes a thrashing warp, and 0 denotes a not-ready warp. Together with the per-warp miss prediction (*$Miss_{pred}$[1:N]*), the *Occlusion Prevention* component finalizes the qualification logic as shown in Equation 1 to inhibit exhausting MSHR resources and then generates the vector Occlude[1:N] (❸) for the *Prioritization* stage.

4.4 Implementation and Overhead

We summarize other implementation details that have not been covered previously. Note that qualification logic is executed at a per-cycle basis. It is impractical to predict the MSHR consumption for thrashing warps at the same frequency. Thus, we store each instruction's predicted cache misses into the instruction buffer, the same way as the ready bit for baseline qualification logic. By doing so,

Table 1: Baseline GPGPU-Sim Configuration

# of SMs	30 (15 clusters of 2)
SM Configuration	1400MHz, Reg #: 32K, Shared Memory: 48KB, SIMD Width: 16, warp: 32 threads, max threads per SM: 1536
Caches / SM	Data: 32KB/128B-line/8-way, Constant: 8KB/64B-line/24-way, Texture: 12KB/128B-line/2-way
Branch Handling	PDOM based method [24]
Warp Scheduling	GTO
Interconnect	Butterfly, 1400MHz, 32B channel width
L2 Unified Cache	768KB, 128B line, 16-way
Min. L2 Latency	120 cycles (compute core clock)
Cache Indexing	Pseudo-Random Hashing Function [25]
Global Memory	6 partitions, min latency: 100 cycles
Memory Controller	Out-of-Order (FR-FCFS), max request queue length: 32
GDDR5 Timing	nbk=16, $t_{CL}=12$, $t_{RP}=12$, $t_{RC}=40$, $t_{RAS}=28$, $t_{RCD}=12$, $t_{RRD}=6$, $t_{CDLR}=5$, $t_{WR}=12$

Table 2: Memory-Intensive CUDA Benchmarks

#	Name	#	Name	#	Name	#	Name
Memory Divergent Benchmarks							
1	ATAX [28]	4	GES [28]	7	PF [27]	10	KMN [27]
2	BICG [28]	5	SYRK [28]	8	BFS [27]	11	SPMV [29]
3	MVT [28]	6	SYR2K [28]	9	SC [27]	12	IIX [22]
Memory Coherent Benchmarks							
13	3DC [28]	15	SRAD1 [27]	17	BP [27]	19	3MM [28]
14	2MM [28]	16	SRAD2 [27]	18	FD [28]	20	LBM [30]

Table 3: Config. for SWL-Best and CCWS

SWL-Best				CCWS	
Bench.	#Warps	Bench.	#Warps	Name	Value
ATAX	2	SYR2K	2	$K_{THROTTLE}$	8
BICG	2	KMN	4	Victim Tag Array	8-way
MVT	2	BFS	3		16 entries/warp
GES	1	SPMV	2		(768 total entries)
SYRK	2	IIX	4	Warp Base Score	100

the process of miss prediction can be executed off the critical path of warp scheduling.

Divergent Load Classifier. The benchmarks we evaluate in this work typically have only one or two divergent loads in each kernel. But IIX from Mars [22] has 26 divergent loads in one of its kernels. Thus we have 32 entries for DLC in both static and dynamic OAWS implementations. Because the fields of DLC are periodically updated, the entries that reach 0 (#inst) could be evicted. DLC could also be managed under the LRU policy for more complicated workloads. In addition, DLC is cleared at each kernel invocation.

Overhead Analysis. To implement the qualification logic in Equation 1, OAWS stores $Avail_{mshr}$ and $Miss_{inflight}$ in two registers. Our baseline GPU has 32 MSHR entries, and both registers need only 5 bits. OCW estimation needs three registers: 1-bit *Div*, 8-bit *FCL*, and 32-bit *Sets*. Our baseline GPU has a SIMD-width of 32. We use 5 bits to store the predicted cache misses for each instruction. Considering that there are 48 warps per SM and each warp can have two instructions, storing the predicted per-instruction cache misses has a total overhead of 480 bits (60 bytes). Each DLC entry needs 9 bytes, i.e., 40 bits for *PC*, 7 bits for *#inst*, 10 bits for *#acc*, and 10 bits for *#set*. Thus, DLC table needs 288 bytes. In total, implementing OAWS needs 348-byte on-chip storage and five registers in each SM.

5 Experimental Evaluation

We use GPGPU-Sim [26] (version 3.2.1), a cycle-accurate simulator, to evaluate our OAWS mechanisms. The baseline GPU architectural parameters are summarized in Table 1. Highly memory-divergent benchmarks from Rodinia [27], PolyBench [28], SHOC [29], Parboil [30], and Mars [22] are used for performance evaluation. These benchmarks are listed in Table 2. We also evaluate the performance of OAWS on memory-coherent benchmarks from PolyBench/GPU [28]. All of the benchmarks are simulated to completion and execute between 70 million and 1.5 billion instructions. The following warp scheduling algorithms are evaluated:

GTO is the baseline warp scheduler. All performance metrics are normalized to GTO.

SWL [9] statically limits the number of warps that can be actively scheduled and needs to be tuned on a per-benchmark basis. Table 3 presents the warp-limiting value with the best performance for some memory divergent benchmarks (*SWL-Best*).

CCWS [9] relies on a dedicated victim cache and a 6-bit Warp ID field in the tag of cache block to detect intra-warp locality and other storage to track per-warp locality changes. The warp that has the largest locality loss is exclusively prioritized. Configuration parameters for CCWS are summarized in Table 3.

MASCAR [13] exclusively prioritizes memory instructions from one "owner" warp when the memory subsystem is saturated; otherwise, memory instructions of all warps are prioritized over any computation instruction. MASCAR uses a re-execution queue to replay L1D accesses that are stalled due to MSHR unavailability or network congestion. Saturation here means that MSHR has only 1 entry or the queue inside memory port has only 1 slot. The re-execution queue has 32 entries.

Static OAWS (*OAWS-Static*) is described in Section 4.2. The default value for *SMR* is 50%. We will present the sensitivity analysis of *SMR* in Section 5.4.

Dynamic OAWS (*OAWS-Dyn*) is described in Section 4.3. *OAWS-Dyn* consists of two components, light-weight estimation of OCW (Optimal Concurrent Warps) and dynamic MSHR prediction.

5.1 Instructions Per Cycle (IPC)

Figure 8 shows IPC comparisons for our scheduling algorithms and three state-of-the-art algorithms. We have the following key observations. First, *OAWS-Static* consistently improves performance for memory divergent benchmarks, and on average achieves 36.7% IPC gains compared to baseline GTO scheduling and outperforms *MASCAR* by 34.4%. The performance improvement of *OAWS-Static* comes with the lowest hardware overhead, which strongly suggests the need of occlusion prevention. Second, by focusing on locality changes at the granularity of individual divergent loads, *OAWS-Dyn* dynamically determines the OCW value, therefore it can outperform *CCWS* and *SWL-Best* by 57.2% and 10.9%, respectively. Lastly, *OAWS-Dyn* effectively increases the performance by opportunistically scheduling thrashing warps. Overall, *OAWS-Dyn* achieves 73.1% IPC improvement and outperforms *MASCAR*, *CCWS*, *SWL-Best* by 70.1%, 57.8%, and 11.4%, respectively.

MASCAR and *CCWS* only improve performance by 1.7% and 9.7% respectively compared to the baseline. This low IPC gains can be explained from the following two aspects. First, we use an allocate-on-fill rather than an allocate-on-miss policy to manage L1D blocks on cache read misses. Given a 32-entry MSHR and 32KB L1D (256 blocks), the allocate-on-miss policy frequently reserves 32 cache blocks for outstanding memory requests in the memory divergent benchmarks, which wastes 12.5% of the L1D

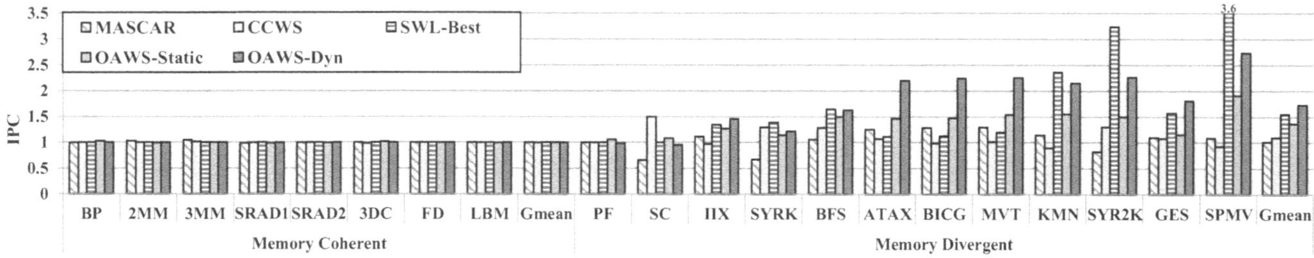

Figure 8: IPCs of various warp scheduling algorithms for memory coherent and memory divergent benchmarks. IPCs are normalized to the GTO scheduling.

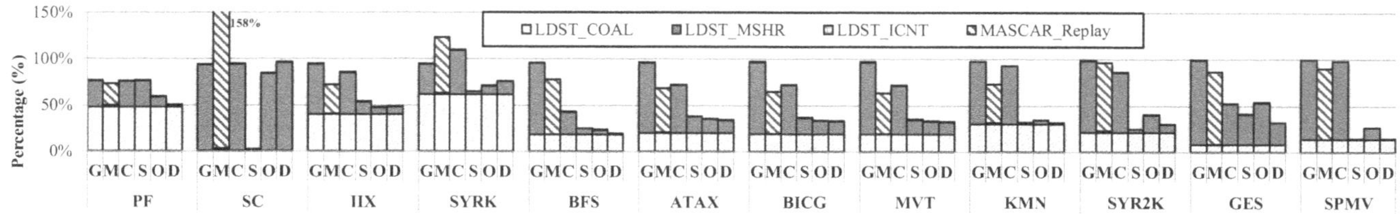

Figure 9: Breakdown of LD/ST stall cycles when the memory divergent benchmarks are scheduled by GTO (G), MASCAR (M), CCWS (C), SWL-Best (S), OAWS-Static (O), and OAWS-Dyn (D). *MASCAR_Replay* only exists in MASCAR and refers to the cycles when the memory access from the re-execution queue cannot be sent out.

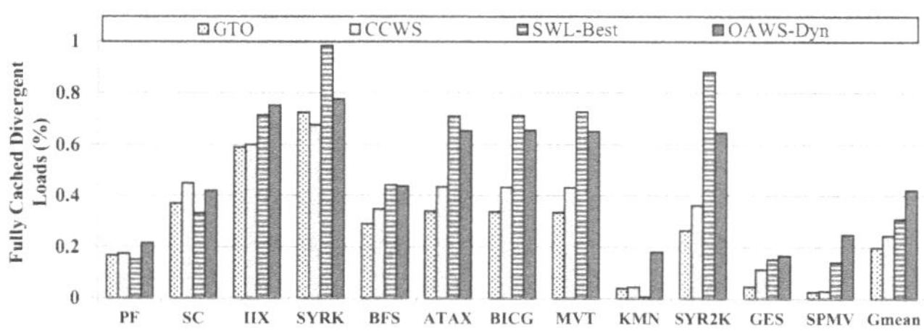

Figure 10: Percentage of fully cached divergent loads in the memory divergent benchmarks.

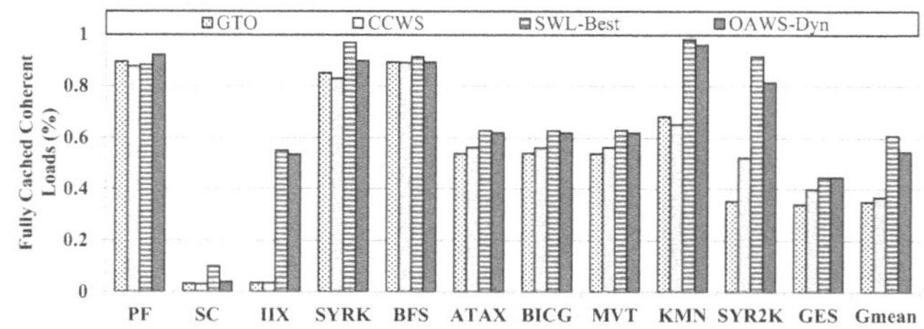

Figure 11: Percentage of fully cached coherent loads in the memory divergent benchmarks. SPMV has no coherent loads and is excluded.

capacity. Second, reserving cache blocks can increase associativity conflicts in L1D. The memory divergent benchmarks from PolyBench/GPU [28] are highly sensitive to cache associativity [1]. Though we have applied the pseudo-random cache indexing function that is used in Fermi architectures [25], associativity conflicts are not well mitigated. For example, each divergent load in ATAX generates 32 requests that are constantly mapped into 8 out of the 32 sets in L1D. Consequently, allocate-on-miss aggravates associativity conflicts. We have evaluated both policies for all benchmarks, as shown in Figure 14, and observe that *MASCAR* performs similarly between the two and *CCWS* favors allocate-on-miss. However, GTO scheduling benefits greatly from allocate-on-fill because of the increased effective L1D capacity and decreased associativity conflicts.

Although *SWL-Best* achieves 55.5% IPC improvement for all memory divergent benchmarks, it is a profile-based static approach that requires tuning experiments for each GPU kernel with every data input. Thus *SWL-Best* is impractical to be implemented in GPU, but it could be a reference to gauge the effectiveness of GPU scheduling algorithms. In our experiments, *OAWS-Dyn* outperforms *SWL-Best* on most of memory divergent benchmarks, except *SYR2K* and *SPMV* benchmarks. This is because of the unique behaviors of *SYR2K* and *SPMV*. *SYR2K* has no branch divergences and very high inter-warp locality, and *SPMV* with little coherent load operations. OAWS first emphasizes a policy to predict and control the use of MSHR entries based on load divergence, then the concurrency level. This causes OAWS to have different decisions than SWL-best, on the set of active warps for SYR2K and SPMV. The performance of *SWL-Best* could have been better if per-kernel tuning had been performed. For example, ATAX, BICG, and MVT have both coherent and divergent kernels. *SWL-Best*'s performance gains in divergent kernels are balanced out by the existence of coherent kernels where *SWL-Best* should not have been enabled. Meanwhile, *IIX* is a highly complicated benchmark with rich branch- and memory-divergence. IIX has 149 kernel invocations with the input size used in this evaluation. Given such complexity, *SWL-Best* has been included for pure performance comparison purposes. For the coherent benchmarks, none of the warp scheduling algorithms achieve significant performance gains. This indicates that our OAWS has no detrimental effects to memory-coherent benchmarks. In the following sections, we will dissect the performance of both *OAWS-Static* and *OAWS-Dyn* using memory divergent benchmarks only.

5.2 LD/ST Unit Stalls

Since the L1D cache misses come from three portions as shown in Figure 2, simply quantifying the accuracy of our MSHR estimation cannot directly determine cache misses. In Figure 9, we break down LD/ST stall cycles when memory divergent benchmarks are scheduled by various scheduling algorithms. All numbers are normalized to LD/ST active cycles in GTO scheduling. Since all the evaluated benchmarks are read-intensive, memory occlusion caused by network congestion (*LDST_ICNT*) is negligible in every scheduling algorithm. Meanwhile, coalescing stalls (*LDST_COAL*) depend on memory divergence characteristics in the benchmarks. Warp scheduling can only impact stall cycles caused by *LDST_MSHR* and, in MASCAR by by re-execution queue delays (*MASCAR_Replay*). At the same time, *LDST_MSHR* stalls are largely reduced by our scheme since the stalls in LD/ST units are overlapped with computations in the execution units. As we can see from Figure 9, *SWL-Best*, *OAWS-Static*, and *OAWS-Dyn* have similar capability in reducing LD/ST stalls, which corresponds to their superior performance shown in Figure 8. Divergent loads in SC are references to arrays of structs and outside of a loop that generates high locality. Without careful concurrency throttling, divergent loads quickly thrash the locality of coherent loads. *OAWS-Dyn* takes time to learn optimal concurrency, while *OAWS-Static* has no direct control over concurrency, thus they perform equally poor in reducing LD/ST stalls for SC. When saturation in the memory subsystem is detected, MASCAR prevents memory accesses of "non-owner" warps from being sent out, i.e., replaying them until saturation is resolved. Such a strict requirement directly reduces LD/ST throughput, leading to the poor performance of MASCAR. *CCWS* prioritizes warps with the highest locality lost, which means that the prioritized warp often has little data reserved in L1D to start with and needs to immediately fetch data from L2. Switching prioritized warps incurs frequent MSHR consumptions, making CCWS less capable of LD/ST stall prevention.

5.3 Fully Cached Load Instructions

Within the SIMD execution, partially cached instructions still suffer from the memory occlusion. More fully cached loads create an opportunity for warp schedulers to better utilize any localities in L1D. Thus we use the number of fully cached loads to quantify effective concurrency in the evaluated concurrency throttling mechanisms, i.e., *CCWS*, *SWL-Best*, and *OAWS-Dyn*. Figure 10 presents the percentages of fully cached divergent loads. The results of GTO are also included as the baseline. *CCWS* has increased fully cached loads for all benchmarks except SYRK. Because SYRK has high inter-warp locality, while *CCWS* is specifically designed for intra-warp locality protection. The exclusively prioritized warp can accelerate progress and evict its own data blocks that could have been utilized by other warps. *SWL-Best* achieves the best results for benchmarks with no branch divergence, such as SYRK, ATAX, BICG, MVT, and SYR2K. Due to high inter-warp locality, *SWL-Best* fully caches 98% and 88% of divergent loads in SYRK and SYR2K, respectively. For memory- and branch-divergent benchmarks, such as IIX and BFS, *OAWS-Dyn* preserves more fully cached divergent loads than *SWL-Best*. On average, GTO, *CCWS*, *SWL-Best*, and *OAWS-Dyn* keep 20%, 25%, 31%, and 45% of the total divergent loads in L1D cache, respectively.

Figure 11 presents the percentages of fully cached coherent loads. Some coherent loads in SC exhibit streaming accesses, achieving very low percentages of fully cached coherent loads in all cases. IIX has observable program behavior changes, i.e., coherent memory operations and large computation strictly follow divergent memory operations. Thus *OAWS-Dyn* preserves more coherent loads in L1D, which explains its performance advantage in IIX as shown in Figure 8. The other benchmarks are relatively simple. Their trend of fully cached loads is similar to that in Figure 10. Results in Figures 10 and 11 are highly correlated to the IPC discrepancy in Figure 8, except that *SWL-Best* does not have the best performance in ATAX, BICG, and MVT. As mentioned earlier, this is due to the fact that the three benchmarks have both memory divergent and memory coherent kernels.

5.4 Sensitivity of Static OAWS

Figure 12 presents the IPC of static OAWS when *SMR* is swept from 0% to 100%, with an increment of 5%. When *SMR* is 0%, static OAWS is equal to GTO. Static OAWS achieves peak performance improvement (geometric mean: 35.3%), when *SMR* is 50%. In addition, when *SMR* ranges from 35% to 90%, the OAWS achieves stable IPC improvement with the standard deviation of 0.014, indicating its insensitivity to *SMR*. This is because with *SMR* larger than 50%, the qualification logic of static OAWS prevents two fully divergent loads from being issued, leading to such similar IPC improvements.

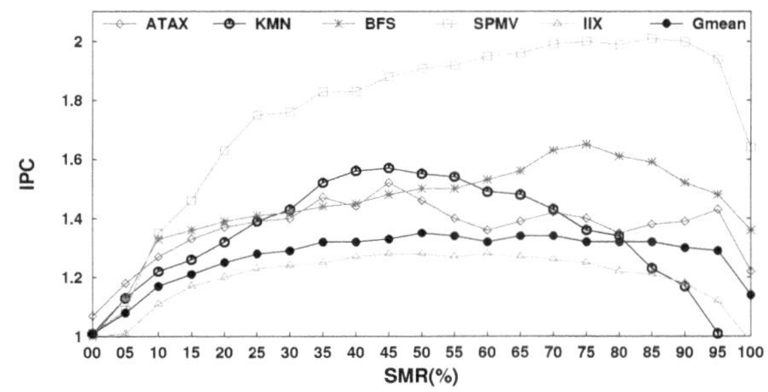

Figure 12: IPC of static OAWS with various *SMR* under five representative benchmarks.

5.5 Sensitivity to MSHR Sizes

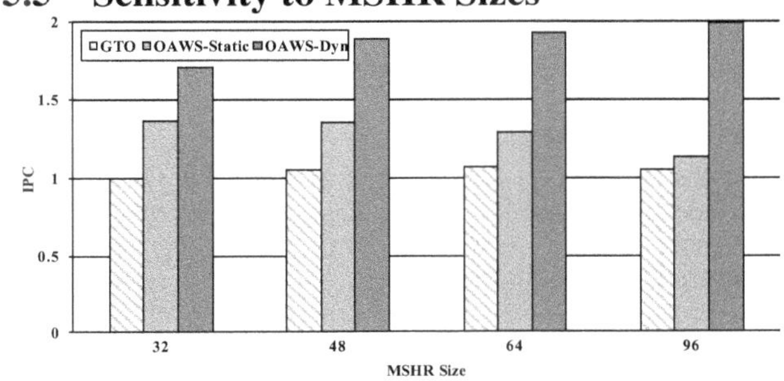

Figure 13: IPC of dynamic OAWS with different MSHR sizes on divergent benchmarks.

Figure 13 shows the IPC improvement (GMean) from three different policies with different MSHR sizes. All results are normalized to GTO with 32 entries and the allocate-on-fill policy. Several interesting trends can be observed. GTO cannot benefit from more MSHR entries, which indicates that the memory occlusion issue cannot be simply addressed by the provision of more resources. Our investigation suggests that on-chip interconnect plays a critical role in this. Adding more MSHRs will increase the volume of bursty in-flight memory requests to the off-chip memory chips, which will congest the on-chip interconnect and prolong memory accesses. In addition, the static scheme *OAWS-Static* with an SMR of 50% cannot benefit from more MSHR entries either. Counter-intuitively, it experiences performance degradation with an increasing number of MSHR entries. This is actually caused by the mismatch between the available MSHR entries and the static prediction. An increasing number of MSHR entries cause the static OAWS policy to schedule more thrashing warps, contending for the limited L1D. In contrast, *OAWS-Dyn* delivers an increasing amount of performance improvement with more MSHR entries. The key for the performance improvement of *OAWS-Dyn* is leveraging additional entries for the load instructions with less divergence and better locality. Therefore, *OAWS-Dyn* alleviates the situation by controlling divergent loads and prioritizing coherent loads for the use of MSHR entries, leading to the better performance and effective concurrency. Thus *OAWS-Dyn* can improve performance by 73.1%, 89.1%, 92.6%, and 99.4% when there are 32, 48, 64, and 96 MSHR entries, respectively. It successfully corrects the problem of memory occlusion by dynamically predicting an optimal number of cached warps and effectively leveraging more MSHR entries without thrashing L1D.

5.6 Sensitivity to L1D Allocate Policy

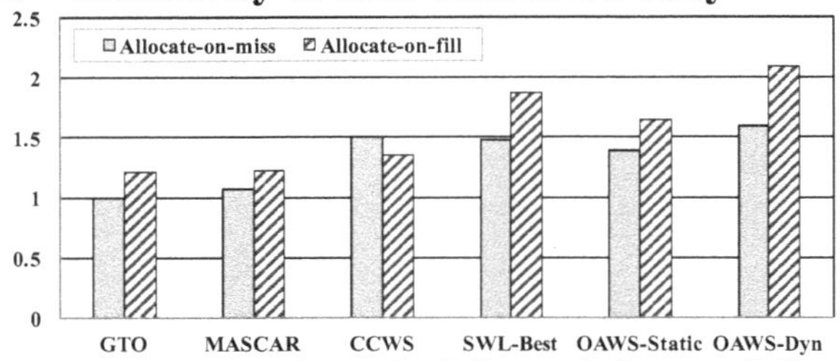

Figure 14: IPC of various scheduling techniques to L1D allocate policies on divergent benchmarks.

Figure 14 provides a comparison of two L1D allocate policies: allocate-on-miss and allocate-on-fill. All results are normalized to allocate-on-miss, the default policy in GPGPU-Sim [26]. GTO achieves 20.9% better performance when the L1D is managed by allocate-on-fill. Among the 7 scheduling techniques, only CCWS favors allocate-on-miss. Although this policy increases cache contention by reserving cache lines for outstanding memory requests, CCWS provides longer prioritization for the warp that has the largest locality loss, leading to 15.5% IPC improvement.

6 Related Work

Warp Scheduling plays a critical role in sustaining GPU performance and various scheduling algorithms have been proposed based on different heuristics. Among concurrency throttling techniques, SWL [9], CCWS [9], and MASCAR [13] were discussed earlier in Section 5 and compared with our proposed scheduling mechanisms. On top of CCWS, DAWS [10] actively schedules warps whose aggregate memory footprint does not exceed L1D capacity. Khairy *et al.* [8] proposed DWT-CS, which use cores sampling to throttle concurrency. When L1D MPKI is above a given threshold, DWT-CS samples all SMs with different number of active warps and applies the best-performing active warp count on all SMs. Different from these concurrency throttling mechanisms, OAWS uses the number of fully cached divergent load instructions to dynamically adjust concurrency at a finer-granularity. CTA scheduling techniques [31, 32, 20] are coarser than warp scheduling at concurrency throttling, thus OAWS is better at locality preservation and LD/ST stall avoidance.

Some other warp scheduling algorithms are designed to improve GPU resource utilization. Fung *et al.* [24, 33] investigated the impact of warp scheduling on techniques aiming at branch divergence reduction, i.e., dynamic warp formation and threadblock compaction. Narasiman *et al.* [19] proposed a two-level round robin scheduler to prevent memory instructions from being issued consecutively. By doing so, memory latency can be better overlapped by computations. Gebhart *et al.* [34] introduced another two-level warp scheduler to manage a hierarchical register file design. None of these warp scheduling directly focuses on the problem of LD/ST stalls. On top of the two-level warp scheduling, Yu *et al.* [35] proposed a Stall-Aware Warp Scheduling (SAWS) to adjust the fetch group size when pipeline stalls are detected. SAWS mainly focuses on pipeline stalls, while OAWS is capable of avoiding LD/ST stalls and preserving L1D locality.

Kayiran et al. [31] proposed a dynamic Cooperative Thread Array (CTA) scheduling mechanism to enable the optimal number of CTAs according to application characteristics. It reduces concurrent CTAs for memory-intensive applications to reduce LD/ST stalls. Lee et al. [32] proposed two alternative CTA scheduling schemes. Lazy CTA scheduling (LCS) utilizes a 3-phase mechanism to determine the optimal number of CTAs per core, while Block CTA scheduling (BCS) launches consecutive CTAs onto the same cores to exploit inter-CTA data locality.

GPU Cache Management has been studied to preserve L1D locality, which can implicitly reduce LD/ST stalls. And L1D bypassing is often adopted to alleviate cache contention [1, 2, 3, 4, 5, 6, 7, 8, 36, 37]. Jia *et al.* [1] designed a memory request buffer to reorder and prioritize L1D accesses, and proposed to bypass L1D accesses that are stalled by cache associativity conflicts. Chen *et al.* [2] used extensions in L2 cache tag to track locality loss in L1D, and bypass is temporarily triggered if a L2 cache block is requested twice by the same SM. Chen *et al.* [3] further proposed coordinated bypassing and warp throttling (CBWT) to orchestrate L1D bypassing and warp scheduling. Based on protection distance prediction [38], CBWT triggers bypassing when all L1D blocks are under protection and throttles concurrency to prevent NOC from being congested by aggressive bypassing. Wang *et al.* [4] proposed a DaCache design to orchestrate GPU cache management and warp scheduling. At runtime, DaCache bypasses divergent loads from warps with low scheduling priorities, and coherent loads with no locality. Dong Li proposed an AgeLRU algorithm [6] to prevent young warps from evicting blocks of old warps. AgeLRU enables bypassing when the replacement score of the replacement candidate is above a given threshold. Based on DAWS, Zheng *et al.* [7] proposed Adaptive Cache and Concurrency (CCA) to bypass streaming memory accesses and accesses from inactive warps. Similarly, Khairy *et al.* [8] also proposed a technique to dynamically detect and bypass streaming memory accesses. Though these cache management schemes can ameliorate the problem of LD/ST stalls via preserved L1D locality, they are all reactive mechanisms. OAWS works from the source to prevent LD/ST stalls from occurring. Besides, cache management schemes are orthogonal to OAWS and can be combined with OAWS to further improve GPU performance.

7 Conclusion

We identified the occlusion of LD/ST units and the depletion of MSHR entries caused by divergent memory accesses in the GPU execution pipeline, which was referred to as memory occlusion. We then characterized and analyzed its impact. To address these issues, we proposed memory occlusion aware warp scheduling that can predict the demand of MSHR entries from GPU instructions and integrate this information into the qualification stage of warp schedulers to prevent memory occlusion. Both static and dynamic prediction methods were designed and implemented to maximize the number of concurrent warps without memory occlusion. We further evaluated OAWS with static and dynamic methods on a wide variety of memory benchmarks. Compared to the default GTO, static and dynamic OAWS policies achieved 36.7% and 73.1% performance gains, respectively. Compared to state-of-the-art warp schedulers, i.e., MASCAR [13], CCWS [9], and SWL-Best [9], dynamic OAWS outperformed them by 70.1%, 57.8%, and 11.4%, respectively. The benefits come from the reduced MSHR stalls as shown in Figure 9 and the increased number of fully cached loads as demonstrated in Figure 10.

Acknowledgment

We are very thankful for the insightful comments from the anonymous reviewers. This work is supported in part by National Science Foundation awards 1059376, 1340947, 1561041, and 1564647.

8 References

[1] W. Jia, K. A. Shaw, and M. Martonosi, "MRPB: Memory Request Prioritization for Massively Parallel Processors," in *HPCA*, 2014.

[2] X. Chen, S. Wu, L.-W. Chang, W.-S. Huang, C. Pearson, Z. Wang, and W. mei W. Hwu, "Adaptive Cache Bypass and Insertion for Many-core Accelerators," in *MES*, 2014.

[3] X. Chen, L.-W. Chang, C. I. Rodrigues, J. Lv, Z. Wang, and W. mei W. Hwu, "Adaptive Cache Management for Energy-Efficient GPU Computing," in *MICRO*, 2014.

[4] B. Wang, W. Yu, X.-H. Sun, and X. Wang, "DaCache: Memory Divergence-Aware GPU Cache Management," in *ICS*, 2015.

[5] C. Li, S. Song, H. Dai, A. Sidelnik, S. K. S. Hari, and H. Zhou, "Locality-Driven Dynamic GPU Cache Bypassing," in *ICS*, 2015.

[6] D. Li, *Orchestrating Thread Scheduling and Cache Management to Improve Memory System Throughput in Throughput Processor*. PhD thesis, University of Texas at Austin, May 2014.

[7] Z. Zheng, Z. Wang, and M. Lipasti, "Adaptive Cache and Concurrency Allocation on GPGPUs," *Computer Architecture Letters*, 2014.

[8] M. Khairy, M. Zahran, and A. G. Wassal, "Efficient Utilization of GPGPU Cache Hierarchy," in *GPGPU*, 2015.

[9] T. G. Rogers, M. O'Connor, and T. M. Aamodt, "Cache-Conscious Wavefront Scheduling," in *MICRO*, 2012.

[10] T. G. Rogers, M. O'Connor, and T. M. Aamodt, "Divergence-aware Warp Scheduling," in *MICRO*, 2013.

[11] D. Kroft, "Lockup-free Instruction Fetch/Prefetch Cache Organization," in *ISCA*, 1981.

[12] A. E. Turner, *On replay and hazards in graphics processing units*. PhD thesis, University of British Columbia, Oct 2012.

[13] A. Sethia, D. A. Jamshidi, and S. A. Mahlke, "Mascar: Speeding up GPU Warps by Reducing Memory Pitstops," in *HPCA*, 2015.

[14] NVIDIA, "NVIDIA's Next Generation CUDA Compute Architecture: Fermi," 2009.

[15] E. Lindholm, J. Nickolls, S. Oberman, and J. Montrym, "NVIDIA Tesla: A Unified Graphics and Computing Architecture," *IEEE Micro*, vol. 28, pp. 39–55, Mar. 2008.

[16] NVIDIA, "NVIDIA's Next Generation CUDA Compute Architecture: Kepler GK110," 2012.

[17] B. Coon, P. Mills, S. Oberman, and M. Siu, "Tracking register usage during multithreaded processing using a scoreboard having separate memory regions and storing sequenti al register size indicators," Oct. 7 2008. US Patent 7,434,032.

[18] P. Mills, J. Lindholm, B. Coon, G. Tarolli, and J. Burgess, "Scheduler in multi-threaded processor prioritizing instructions passing qualification rule," May 24 2011. US Patent 7,949,855.

[19] V. Narasiman, M. Shebanow, C. J. Lee, R. Miftakhutdinov, O. Mutlu, and Y. N. Patt, "Improving GPU Performance via Large Warps and Two-level Warp Scheduling," in *MICRO*, 2011.

[20] A. Jog, O. Kayiran, N. C. Nachiappan, A. K. Mishra, M. T. Kandemir, O. Mutlu, R. Iyer, and C. R. Das, "OWL: Cooperative Thread Array Aware Scheduling Techniques for Improving GPGPU Performance," in *ASPLOS*, 2013.

[21] N. Brunie, S. Collange, and G. F. Diamos, "Simultaneous Branch and Warp Interweaving for Sustained GPU Performance," in *ISCA*, 2012.

[22] B. He, W. Fang, Q. Luo, N. K. Govindaraju, and T. Wang, "Mars: a MapReduce Framework on Graphics Processors," in *PACT*, 2008.

[23] B. Wang, Z. Liu, X. Wang, and W. Yu, "Eliminating intra-warp conflict misses in GPU," in *Proceedings of the 2015 Design, Automation & Test in Europe Conference & Exhibition, DATE 2015, Grenoble, France, March 9-13, 2015*, pp. 689–694, 2015.

[24] W. W. L. Fung, I. Sham, G. Yuan, and T. M. Aamodt, "Dynamic Warp Formation and Scheduling for Efficient GPU Control Flow," in *MICRO*, 2007.

[25] C. Nugteren, G.-J. van den Braak, H. Corporaal, and H. Bal, "A Detailed GPU Cache Model Based on Reuse Distance Theory," in *HPCA*, 2014.

[26] A. Bakhoda, G. L. Yuan, W. W. L. Fung, H. Wong, and T. M. Aamodt, "Analyzing CUDA Workloads Using a Detailed GPU Simulator," in *ISPASS*, 2009.

[27] S. Che, M. Boyer, J. Meng, D. Tarjan, J. W. Sheaffer, S.-H. Lee, and K. Skadron, "Rodinia: A benchmark suite for heterogeneous computing," in *IISWC*, 2009.

[28] S. Grauer-Gray, L. Xu, R. Searles, S. Ayalasomayajula, and J. Cavazos, "Auto-tuning a High-Level Language Targeted to GPU Codes.," in *Innovative Parallel Computing*, 2012.

[29] A. Danalis, G. Marin, C. McCurdy, J. S. Meredith, P. C. Roth, K. Spafford, V. Tipparaju, and J. S. Vetter, "The Scalable Heterogeneous Computing (SHOC) Benchmark Suite," in *GPGPU*, 2010.

[30] J. A. Stratton, C. Rodrigues, I.-J. Sung, N. Obeid, L.-W. Changx, N. Anssari, G. D. Liu, and W. mei W. Hwu, "Parboil: A Revised Benchmark Suite for Scientific and Commercial Throughput Computing," *IMPACT Technical Report, IMPACT-12-01, University of Illinois, at Urbana-Champaign*, 2012.

[31] O. Kayiran, A. Jog, M. T. Kandemir, and C. R. Das, "Neither More nor Less: Optimizing Thread-level Parallelism for GPGPUs," in *PACT*, 2013.

[32] M. Lee, S. Song, J. Moon, J. Kim, W. Seo, Y.-G. Cho, and S. Ryu, "Improving GPGPU Resource Utilization Through Alternative Thread Block Scheduling," in *HPCA*, 2014.

[33] W. W. L. Fung and T. M. Aamodt, "Thread Block Compaction for Efficient SIMT Control flow," in *HPCA*, 2011.

[34] M. Gebhart, D. R. Johnson, D. Tarjan, S. W. Keckler, W. J. Dally, E. Lindholm, and K. Skadron, "Energy-Efficient Mechanisms for Managing Thread Context in Throughput Processors," in *ISCA*, 2011.

[35] Y. Yu, W. Xiao, X. He, H. Guo, Y. Wang, and X. Chen, "A Stall-Aware Warp Scheduling for Dynamically Optimizing Thread-level Parallelism in GPGPUs," in *ICS*, 2015.

[36] W. Jia, K. A. Shaw, and M. Martonosi, "Characterizing and Improving the Use of Demand-fetched Caches in GPUs," in *ICS*, 2012.

[37] X. Xie, Y. Liang, G. Sun, and D. Chen, "An Efficient Compiler Framework for Cache Bypassing on GPUs," in *ICCAD*, 2013.

[38] N. Duong, D. Zhao, T. Kim, R. Cammarota, M. Valero, and A. V. Veidenbaum, "Improving Cache Management Policies Using Dynamic Reuse Distances," in *MICRO*, 2012.

Integrating Algorithmic Parameters into Benchmarking and Design Space Exploration in 3D Scene Understanding

Bruno Bodin
bbodin@inf.ed.ac.uk

Luigi Nardi
l.nardi@imperial.ac.uk

M. Zeeshan Zia
zeeshan.zia@imperial.ac.uk

Harry Wagstaff
h.wagstaff@inf.ed.ac.uk

Govind Sreekar Shenoy
gsreekar@inf.ed.ac.uk

Murali Emani
emani1@llnl.gov

John Mawer
john.mawer@manchester.ac.uk

Christos Kotselidis
christos.kotselidis@manchester.ac.uk

Andy Nisbet
andy.nisbet@manchester.ac.uk

Mikel Lujan
mikel.lujan@manchester.ac.uk

Björn Franke
bfranke@inf.ed.ac.uk

Paul H. J. Kelly
p.kelly@imperial.ac.uk

Michael O'Boyle
mob@inf.ed.ac.uk

ABSTRACT

System designers typically use well-studied benchmarks to evaluate and improve new architectures and compilers. We design tomorrow's systems based on yesterday's applications. In this paper we investigate an emerging application, 3D scene understanding, likely to be significant in the mobile space in the near future. Until now, this application could only run in real-time on desktop GPUs. In this work, we examine how it can be mapped to power constrained embedded systems. Key to our approach is the idea of incremental co-design exploration, where optimization choices that concern the domain layer are incrementally explored together with low-level compiler and architecture choices. The goal of this exploration is to reduce execution time while minimizing power and meeting our quality of result objective. As the design space is too large to exhaustively evaluate, we use active learning based on a random forest predictor to find good designs. We show that our approach can, for the first time, achieve dense 3D mapping and tracking in the real-time range within a 1W power budget on a popular embedded device. This is a 4.8x execution time improvement and a 2.8x power reduction compared to the state-of-the-art.

Keywords

design space exploration; DSE; computer vision; SLAM; embedded systems

PACT '16, September 11 - 15, 2016, Haifa, Israel

ISBN 978-1-4503-4121-9/16/09...$15.00

DOI: http://dx.doi.org/10.1145/2967938.2967963

1. INTRODUCTION

The computing landscape has changed dramatically over the last decade. We have witnessed the decline of desktops and the rise of mobile devices as computing platforms. At the system level, power constraints have caused a fundamental shift to parallel heterogeneous platforms which is particularly important in thermally limited embedded mobile devices.

More recently, the well-known dark silicon challenge suggests that we will not be able to simultaneously power on all the cores (or transistors) on a device [17]. Heterogeneous multi-core systems have emerged as a promising solution to this problem. For example, the ARM big.LITTLE technology [9] puts both a high power, high performance core cluster, and a more efficient but less computationally powerful cluster, on the same die. Software can then partition between these cores, or switch off cores entirely, depending on requirements. By mapping different parts of an application onto the appropriate specialized hardware resource, we can use the available power budget in an optimal manner. For that reason, heterogeneous multi-processor system-on-chips (MPSoCs) have been widely adopted in mobile embedded systems.

In order to design and program heterogeneous MPSoCs, a vertical approach is necessary. Deep knowledge of all levels of the stack, from compilers to the micro-architecture, is needed in order to optimally map the executed code onto such diverse hardware resources. Additionally, deep domain knowledge may be required to tune software parameters to meet multiple conflicting design goals. This paper shows how we can go beyond conventional benchmarking in computer systems research by exposing the algorithmic-level design space.

Traditionally, system designers have evaluated new architecture and compiler features using well-studied and broadly accepted benchmarks such as SPEC2006 [22]. However, since such benchmarks represent a historical snapshot of applications, they are not representative of modern requirements. In contrast, to design tomorrow's systems, we need to consider new emerging applications from diverse domains.

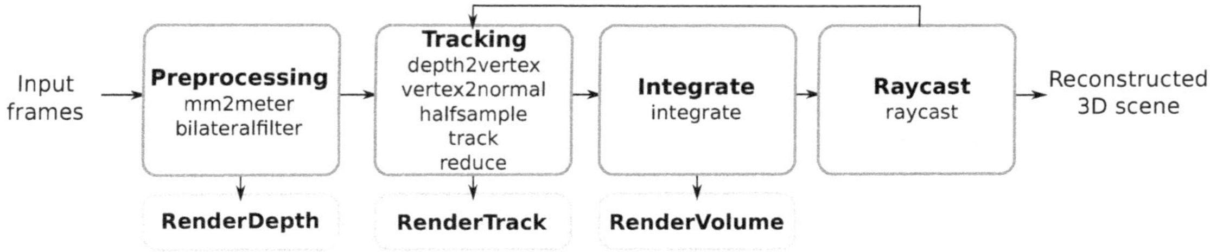

Figure 2: Key computational steps of the KFusion algorithm represented as a task graph. Each task comprises one or more OpenCL kernels as depicted.

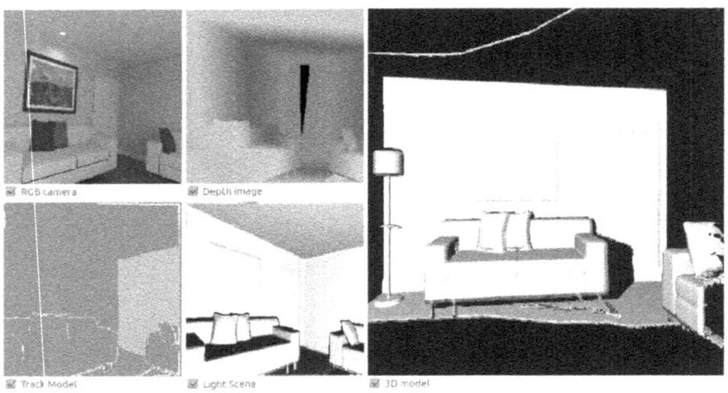

Figure 1: An RGB-D camera provides both RGB and depth information (top left and middle respectively); the depth frame is the input of the KFusion algorithm. Tracking results and reconstruction of the scene as seen from the current camera pose are shown in the bottom left and middle respectively. The reconstructed 3D scene from the initial pose is shown in the right; this is the output of KFusion.

In this paper we focus on one set of emerging applications that is becoming significant in the mobile space: real-time 3D scene understanding in computer vision. In particular, we investigate dense simultaneous localization and mapping (dense SLAM) algorithms which are extremely computationally demanding. One such dense SLAM algorithm is KinectFusion [33] (KFusion) which estimates the pose of a depth camera whilst constructing a highly detailed 3D model of the environment. Since such applications are typically tuned for high-end desktops with high power budget, executing them on power-constrained embedded devices is very challenging and, therefore, represents a realistic future application use case. We use the SLAMBench benchmarking framework [31], which contains a KFusion implementation, as it allows us to capture the performance metrics used to drive our design space exploration.

We explore the mapping of SLAM applications to power constrained heterogeneous platforms. The key element of our approach is the exploration of the mapping problem at multiple levels, vertically integrating the algorithmic domain and the implementation layers. Instead of ignoring levels of the computing stack, we perform co-design space exploration. In other words, we examine how algorithmic, compiler, and architecture configuration choices affect the performance of the underlying system. The rationale behind including the algorithmic parameters in the co-design space exploration is that although these algorithms are tuned for desktop systems, it is unlikely that the same configurations will be optimal in a mobile MPSoC setting.

We define the performance in terms of power consumption (measured in Watts, lower is better), accuracy of the computation (measured in centimeters, lower is better), and runtime (measured as wall clock time per frame in seconds, lower is better). The runtime is sometimes also quantified by the number of frames processed in one second, i.e. frames per second (FPS), higher is better; the current Microsoft Kinect (or equivalent ASUS Xtion Pro) RGB-D sensor runs at 30 FPS, so 30 FPS is needed for real-time processing. These three metrics interact and are considered simultaneously for a holistic evaluation of the system.

Since the co-design space can be extremely large, it is not feasible to try all possible configurations. Instead, we sample the domain space and automatically build a model that predicts the three performance metrics for a given configuration. Using this model, and a methodology from machine learning known as active learning, we predict a three dimensional performance Pareto curve that is then used to feed the lower level layers, driving the compiler and architecture parameter choices. By exploring the resulting Pareto curve we obtain a mapping to an embedded platform that results in a 6.6-fold speedup over the original mobile implementation. More precisely, this new configuration runs at nearly 40 FPS while maintaining an acceptable accuracy (under 5 cm localization error) and keeping power consumption under 2 Watts. The Pareto front contains many more configurations, allowing us to trade between runtime, power consumption, and accuracy, depending on our desired goals. For example, we can also find points which minimize power consumption (e.g., a configuration providing 11.92 FPS at 0.65W) or which optimize for execution time without exceeding a given power budget (29.09 FPS at less than 1W).

This paper demonstrates that our co-design space exploration tailors future applications to future power-constrained systems. The contributions of this paper are as follows:

- We perform a vertical co-design space exploration considering algorithmic, compiler, and hardware layers.
- We show that domain-specific knowledge can be used to trade off multiple optimization goals at an algorithmic level, before considering low-level implementation choices.
- We introduce an effective method to guide the optimization using multi-objective performance prediction based on random forest and active learning.
- In order to explore the potential for this approach we evaluate our methodology on an emerging SLAM

- **Vectorization**: Loop vectorization with various vector widths and directions on kernels that allow this optimization.

- **Coarsening degree**: Thread coarsening is an advanced compiler optimization [29] which merges together multiple parallel threads, reducing the total number of threads instantiated. The factor parameter specifies how many threads have been merged. The stride parameter affects the threads' mapping distribution enabling coalesced access patterns. The dimension parameter specifies the dimension affected by the merge.

The compiler parameters affect both power and performance metrics. In addition, accuracy may be affected by some OpenCL flags which cause relaxed maths to be used, for example cl-fast-relaxed-math.

Architecture Space.
The architectural parameters exposed by each platform differ quite significantly. We considered two platforms the ASUS T200TA and the ODROID-XU3. In the case of the ASUS T200TA we are currently only able to select the CPU frequency governor, which in turn scales the CPU frequency and voltage. In this case we have access to only two governors: 'powersave' and 'performance', which set the CPU frequency to the lowest and highest available settings, respectively.

In the case of the ODROID-XU3 platform, we have access to the parameters listed in Table 1:

- **GPU processor frequency**: By default the GPU dynamic voltage and frequency scaling (DVFS) is active and the GPU dynamically adjusts to a particular frequency depending on the performance/power profile of the application. We disable the DVFS and set the GPU frequency to a specific value.

- **Number of active cores**: The number of CPU cores that are active and running, these include the eight "big" (Cortex-A15) and "LITTLE" (Cortex-A7) cores (Section 5.1). By default all 8 cores are active, and we selectively switch off a number of cores.

CPU DVFS is not available on this platform and, therefore, this dimension in the architecture space cannot be explored. The architectural parameters affect both the performance and the power metrics, but not the accuracy. Future approximate computing techniques which for example involve reducing the voltage of compute units, in order to trade off power against the chance of calculation errors, would produce a situation where architectural exploration would involve optimizing across all three targets (rather than just power and runtime).

3.3 Multi-Objective Optimization Goal

Figure 4 presents a fictitious example depicting samples (in green) over a 2-dimensional optimization space [1]. In order to meet the runtime and accuracy thresholds (in dashed lines), the solutions of our exploration are confined to the bottom left region of the space, the targeted prediction area (in black). In a multi-objective optimization, a single solution that minimizes all performance metrics simultaneously does not exist in general. Therefore, attention is paid to Pareto optimal solutions (in blue); which is, solutions that cannot be improved in any of the objectives without degrading at least one of the other objectives. We aim to find the configurations that are simultaneously in the targeted prediction area and on the Pareto front.

[1]For visualization purposes we are only showing two performance metrics, namely the error and the runtime.

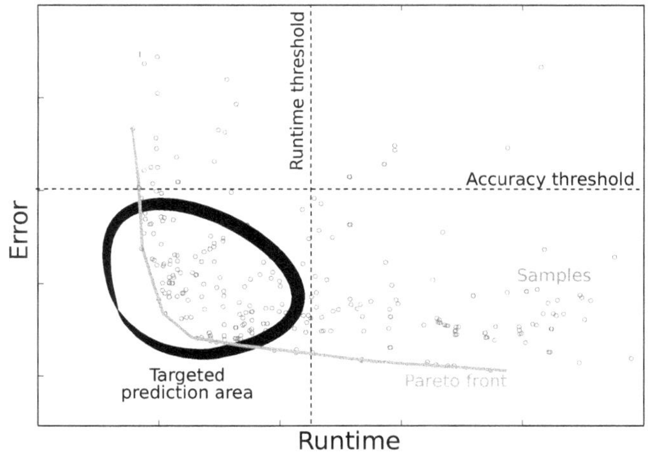

Figure 4: Illustrative example based on fictitious data. This is a two-objective optimization goal in the error and runtime performance metrics. The samples in green are spread all over the space. We are interested in the region highlighted by the black circle, namely the targeted prediction area. The Pareto front is represented in blue.

3.4 Incremental Co-Design Space Exploration

We tackle the co-design space exploration incrementally. We first apply the active learning regressor to the algorithmic parameters. The compiler transformations/optimizations are then applied to the Pareto optimal front points obtained. Since a general tool to drive the compiler exploration is not available for the set of vanilla and advanced compilation parameters that we aim to explore, the compiler space is a mixture of manual and exhaustive search. These are the best performing points of the algorithmic space and are used as an input to the compiler space. The architecture space is then exhaustively evaluated since the size of this space is relatively small (160 points). Our incremental approach enables us to refine the optimal solutions in different steps.

4. SMART SEARCH

The algorithmic parameter space we are investigating is too large to be exhaustively evaluated on the hardware platform. Thus we take the cheaper route of training a predictive machine learning model over a handful of examples (points in the parameter space) evaluated on hardware. We want to use this model to accurately predict the performance over the entire parameter space, while being many orders of magnitude faster as compared to running the application on hardware over a video sequence for millions of parameter settings. Unfortunately since we do not know the performance over the parameter space, we are also unaware of the points for which running a physical experiment will be most informative, in the sense of yielding the greatest increase in

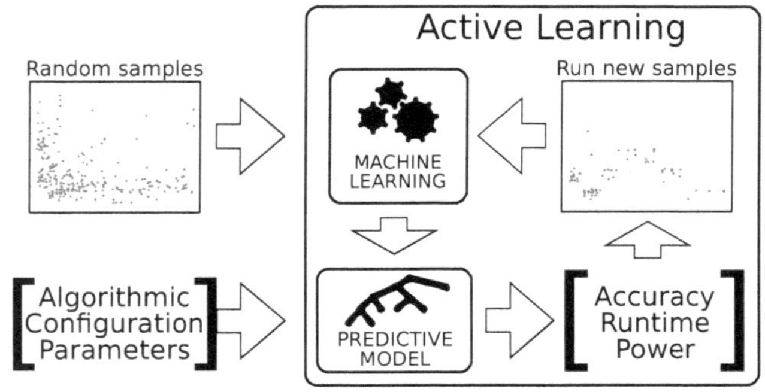

Figure 5: The learning step is based on a tiny subset of the overall algorithmic space; these are the samples that are actually run. Subsequently, the predictive model can predict accuracy, power consumption, and performance of an unseen configuration depending on its parameters.

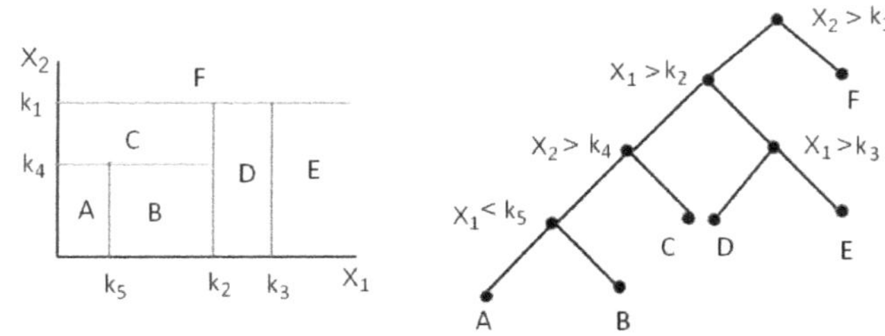

Figure 6: On the left, a 2-dimensional input space with recursive 1-dimensional decision stumps is shown. On the right, a classification decision tree learned over the training data is visualized. Each node represents a portion of the input space.

the prediction accuracy of our model - a classic chicken and egg problem. Thus, we resort to bootstrapping predictive models (three separate randomized decision forests for accuracy, runtime, and power prediction) from a small number of randomly drawn samples in the parameter space. These models are then refined in subsequent iterations by drawing more samples from the parameter space (and retraining over the collective set); the new samples are now drawn to implicitly maximize the prediction accuracy near the respective Pareto optimal fronts. This strategy of letting the predictive model decide which samples will be most beneficial in increasing predictive accuracy over unseen regions of the parameter space is called active learning [16, 41]. Note that we explored a number of base predictive models including artificial neural networks, support vector machines, and nearest neighbors. Our experiments indicated that randomized decision forests outperform these methods, thus we stick to this class of models throughout this paper.

This methodology is depicted in Figure 5 and explained in the next sections.

4.1 Randomized Decision Forest

A decision tree is a tool widely used to formalize decision making processes across a variety of fields. A randomized decision tree is an analogous machine learning model, which "learns" how to classify (or regress) data points based on randomly selected attributes of a set of training examples. The combination of many weak regressors (binary decisions) allows approximating highly non-linear and multimodal functions with great accuracy. Randomized decision forest [12] combines many such decorrelated trees, based on the randomization at the level of training data points and attributes, to yield an even more effective supervised classification and regression model. A decision tree represents a recursive binary partitioning of the input space, and uses a simple decision (a one-dimensional decision threshold) at each non-leaf node that aims at maximizing an "information gain" function. Prediction is performed by "dropping" down the test data point from the root, and letting it traverse a path decided by the node decisions, until it reaches a leaf node. Each leaf node has a corresponding function value (or probability distribution on function values), adjusted according to training data, which is predicted as the function value for the test input. During training, randomization is injected into the procedure to reduce variance and avoid overfitting. This is achieved by training each individual tree on randomly selected subsets of the training samples (also called bagging), as well as by randomly selecting the deciding input variable for each tree node to decorrelate the trees. Figure 6 depicts a decision tree that performs classification over two input dimensions X_1 and X_2, and predicts a class from respective regions.

A regression random forest is built from a set of such decision trees where the leaf nodes output the average of the training data labels, and the output of the whole forest is the average of the predicted results from the different trees. In our experimental setting, we train separate regressors to learn the mapping from our input (parameter) space to each output variable, i.e. the three performance metrics.

4.2 Active Learning

Active learning is a paradigm in supervised machine learning which uses fewer training examples to achieve better prediction accuracy - by iteratively training a predictor, and using the predictor in each iteration to choose the training examples which will increase its accuracy the most. Thus the accuracy of the predictive model is incrementally improved by interleaving exploration and exploitation steps, as shown by the feedback loop in Figure 5. We initialize our base predictors (randomized decision forests) from a very small number of randomly sampled points in the parameter space. For these points the application is evaluated over a video sequence on the hardware platform, yielding accuracy, runtime, and power consumption corresponding to these points (labels in a supervised setting). Since our objective is to accurately estimate the points near the pareto optimal front, we use the current predictor to provide performance values over the entire parameter space and thus estimate the pareto fronts for accuracy, runtime, and power (separately) such as the one in Figure 4. For the next iteration, only parameter points near the predicted pareto front are sampled (and evaluated on hardware), and subsequently used to train new predictors using the entire collection of training points from current and all previous iterations. This process is repeated over a number of iterations. Our experiments (Sect. 5) indicate that this smarter way of searching for highly informative parameter points in fact yields superior predictors as compared to a baseline that uses randomly sampled points alone. Thus by iterating this process several times in the active learning loop, we are able to discover high-quality de-

Machine type	ODROID-XU3	ASUS T200TA
CPU	Samsung Exynos 5422	Intel Atom Z3795
CPU cores	4 (A15) + 4 (A7)	4 Intel Silvermont
CPU GHz	2.0 (A15) 1.4 (A7)	1.6 (2.4 Boost)
GPU	ARM Mali-T628-MP6	Intel HD Graphics
GPU architecture	Midgard 2nd gen.	Bay Trail-T
GPU MHz	600	311 (778 Boost)
OpenCL version	1.1	1.2
Toolkit version	Mali SDK1.1	Beignet v1.1.1
Compiler	gcc 4.8.2	gcc 5.3.1
OS (kernel)	Ubuntu 14.04 (3.10.53)	Fedora 23 (4.2.3)

Table 2: Specification of the platforms selected for experimentation.

sign configurations that lead to good performance outcomes. This approach enables predicting performance metrics over a parameter space comprising of approximately 1,800,000 points in a matter of seconds.

5. EXPERIMENTAL EVALUATION

In this section we describe how we evaluated our novel co-design space exploration techniques. We begin by providing a more detailed description of the target platforms (Section 5.1). We then briefly summarize our key results (Section 5.2), before providing more detail on the results of each stage of our co-design space exploration in Sections 5.3, 5.4, and 5.5.

5.1 Platforms

We use the popular Hardkernel ODROID-XU3 platform, based on the Samsung Exynos 5422, for all of our experiments (refer to Table 2). This board has been previously evaluated for use in UAV applications [34, 24], and is also used in the evaluation of SLAMench [31]. We also considered the ASUS T200TA (refer to Table 2) for comparison during the algorithmic and compilation space. As mentioned earlier, this platform does not provide enough flexibility for a full exploration including the hardware space.

The Exynos 5422 includes a Mali-T628-MP6 GPU alongside ARM's big.LITTLE heterogeneous multiprocessing solution, consisting of four Cortex-A15 "big" performance tuned out-of-order processors, and four Cortex-A7 "LITTLE" energy tuned in-order processors. The Mali-T628-MP6 GPU consists of two separate OpenCL devices: one with four cores and another with two. In our experiments we only use the 4-core OpenCL which excludes partitioning tasks across multiple GPU devices. This is a potential avenue to explore in order to deliver even higher performance within a power budget. The ODROID-XU3 platform has integrated power monitors with on-board voltage/current sensors and split power rails. This allows independent power measurements for the "big" cores, "LITTLE" cores, GPU, and DRAM. The SLAMBench benchmarking framework provides natively an interface to access and log these power sensors.

We also measure performance on an Intel Atom [3] platform in the form of an ASUS Transformer T200 tablet. This contains an Intel Atom Z3795 SoC, which includes a quad-core Intel Atom CPU running at up to 2.4 GHz. An Intel HD Graphics GPU is also present, containing 6 execution units and running at up to 778 MHz. We use the open source Beignet [1] OpenCL runtime which supports version 1.2 of the OpenCL standard and was produced by Intel's Open Technology Center.

Constraint	Speed (FPS)	Max ATE (cm)	Power (Watts)
Default	6.03	4.41	2.77
Best runtime	39.85	4.47	1.47
Best accuracy	1.51	3.30	2.38
Best power	11.92	4.45	0.65
Power < 1W	29.09	4.47	0.98
Power < 2W	39.85	4.47	1.47
FPS > 10	11.92	4.45	0.65
FPS > 20	28.87	4.47	0.91
FPS > 30	32.38	4.47	1.01

Table 3: Best performance on the ODROID-XU3 platform, running KFusion under given constraints.

5.2 Overall Results

We observe that the default configuration provides a frame-rate of 6 FPS for a power budget of 2.77 Watts. Our co-design space exploration results (refer to Table 3) show significantly better frame-rates with reduced power consumption and comparable accuracy. As an example consider a power budget of 1W. Our results show that a configuration exists in the real-time range (29.09 FPS) and with a similar accuracy ATE compared to the default configuration (4.47 cm). The selected best configurations perform well across datasets and in live mode using an actual RGB-D ASUS Xtion Pro camera.

Active learning effectively and consistently pushes the Pareto front towards better solutions. Taking into account the domain layer of the stack unleashes unprecedented performance trade-offs compared to the more usual compiler optimizations. In fact our algorithmic design space exploration provides the greatest improvement on the performance metrics by a large factor (refer to Section 5.3). However, exploration on the hardware parameters shows that important speed/power trade-offs can be obtained in this space. In particular, as we shall see, the greatest improvement in power consumption is provided by exploration of hardware parameters.

5.3 Algorithmic Design Space Exploration

The algorithmic space consists of application parameters summarized in Table 1 and described at the top of Section 3.2. As described in Section 4, we first sample this space at random, and then use active learning in order to push the Pareto front toward better solutions (refer to Figure 5.3).

Sampling.

We draw 3,000 uniformly distributed random samples from the parameter space and evaluate the KFusion pipeline on the video stream; for both platforms the cumulated runtimes take roughly 5 days. By using random sampling, we observe that the Pareto front cannot be improved beyond 2,000 samples. Thus, there is an inflection point beyond which random sampling is unproductive.

Active learning.

In order to further explore optimal points in the design space, we employ active learning in conjunction with random decision forest (Section 4.2). For the ODROID-XU3 this produces 1,142 new samples after 6 iterations, thus increasing the total number of samples to 4,142. Note that the

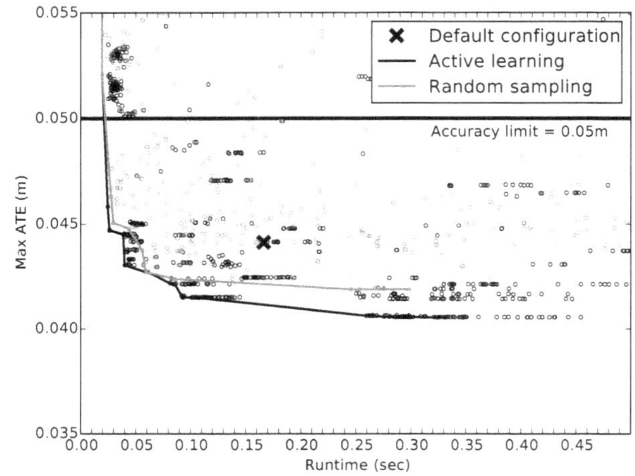

(a) ODROID-XU3

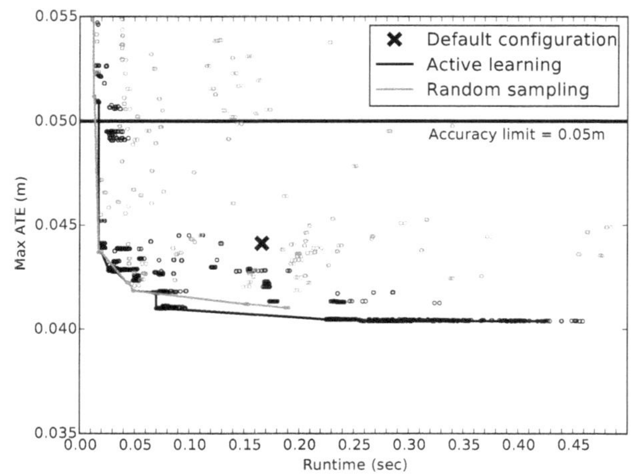

(b) ASUS T200TA

Figure 7: Random sampling (red) and active learning (black). For the sake of visualization we only show two dimensions (max ATE and runtime) of a three dimension plot.

number of samples produced per iteration is not constant as it depends on the predicted points' proximity to the Pareto front. We observe that the number of samples per iteration varies between 100 and 300. The runtime of these new configurations was faster, close to a day, as most of these configurations were good configurations (accurate and fast). The training of the random forest model was fast as well, less than two minutes for every iteration. With the ASUS T200TA platform, 1392 new points has been produced by active learning.

Effectiveness of the active learning method.

Figure 5.3 shows the overall improvement of the Pareto front obtained with active learning (in red) compared to the Pareto obtained with random sampling (in black). For the ODROID-XU3 we observe that random sampling provides a set of 333 valid configurations, i.e. 333 configurations with a max ATE smaller than 5 cm. For the ASUS T200TA, we found 291 valid configurations during the sampling. Furthermore, by using the active learning technique, we observe 642 new possible configurations with an ATE of less than 5 cm on the ODROID-XU3, and 665 on the ASUS T200TA. This means we have produced twice as many valid points as random sampling, for roughly a third of the number of samples. These ratios are an indicator of the effectiveness of our active learning-based prediction model. There is a discrepancy between predicted and measured performance. This is shown by the active learning points in Figure that do not lie on the Pareto front. A performance comparison is also available on Table 4. Note that there are 36 points on the Pareto front for the ODROID-XU3 and 167 points for the ASUS T200TA; these are the configurations forwarded to explore the compiler and architecture parameters in the incremental exploration of section 3.4.

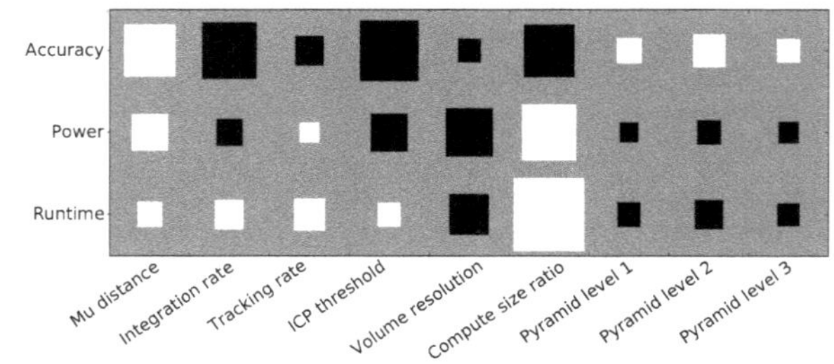

Figure 8: Impact of algorithmic parameters (x-axis) on the performance metrics (y-axis) for the ODROID-XU3 platform (the equivalent diagram for the ASUS T200TA is similar). Bigger squares indicate a higher correlation. A white square denotes a parameter which when increased improves the corresponding metric, whilst a black square shows a worsening.

Relationship between parameters and metrics.

It is particularly interesting to analyze the impact of each algorithmic parameter in isolation. To study the linear relationship of the algorithmic parameters with the performance metrics (frame-rate, accuracy and power) we use the Hinton diagram in Figure 8. In this figure, each square denotes the correlation between a pair (parameter, metric), i.e. the linear relation between a parameter on the x-axis and the performance metric on the y-axis. Note that a bigger square denotes a stronger correlation and vice versa. Furthermore, the square color denotes if a parameter has a positive (white) or negative (black) correlation with the performance metric. For example, an increased *compute size ratio* improves power efficiency and frame-rate but degrades accuracy. This analysis provides a real applicability beyond our design space exploration. It gives an insight into linear relationships between algorithmic parameters and performance goals (frame-rate, accuracy, and power). As shown in the figure there are several parameters that have a non-linear relationship with the performance parameters. It would not be possible for a domain expert to understand these high-dimensional non-linearities, thus emphasizing the importance of automated analysis. For example, *mu*, *integration rate*, *icp threshold*, and the *compute size ratio* are the parameters with strong linear relationship in terms of accuracy, while only *compute size ratio* is strongly linear in execution time.

Constraint		FPS	Error	Power	Volume Resolution	Compute Size Ratio	Pyramid	Integ. Rate	ICP Threshold	μ	Tracking Rate
Default [5]		5.46	4.41	2.1	256	1	10x5x4	2	0.0	0.1	1
Default (measured)		6.03	4.41	2.77	256	1	10x5x4	2	0.0	0.1	1
Best speed	RS	36.11	4.63	2.31	128	4	7x11x7	10	1.0	0.2	1
	AL	**38.28**	**4.47**	**2.16**	128	4	9x3x9	30	1.0	0.2	1
Best accuracy	RS	**3.35**	4.19	2.83	128	1	5x5x11	20	0.0	0.2	1
	AL	3.02	**4.05**	**2.82**	128	1	11x5x5	1	0.0	0.2	1
Best power	RS	19.12	4.73	2.13	128	4	3x11x9	20	0.0	0.1	1
	AL	**38.07**	**4.47**	**2.12**	128	4	9x3x7	30	1.0	0.2	1

Table 4: Comparison of random sampling (RS) best solutions with active learning (AL) search over the algorithmic space for the ODROID-XU3 platform. We list the results for the default configuration given in the original SLAMBench paper [5], and our own results running the same configuration using a newer version of the SLAMBench package. For consistency, in this work our baseline version for performance comparison is the default measured version. The SLAMBench paper provides error as mean ATE over the whole workload, we provide it as the maximum ATE for any frame of the workload.

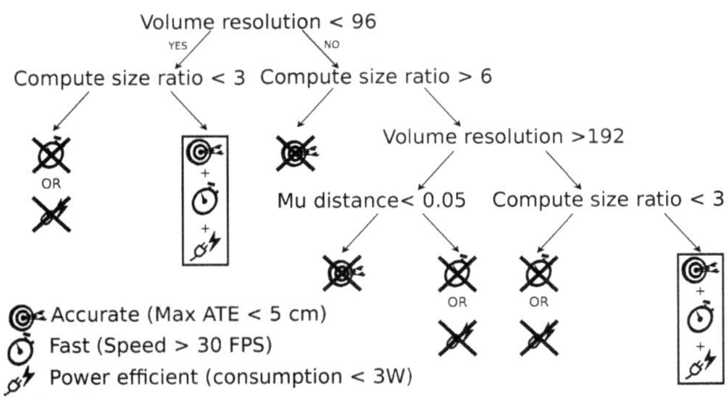

Figure 9: Decision tree showing how algorithmic parameters affect the performance metrics for the ODROID-XU3 platform.

Interpreting the results.

We rank the different algorithmic parameters as a function of their influence on the performance metrics. This is shown as a decision tree (Figure 9) for the ODROID-XU3 platform. The salient advantage of the decision tree is that it can be readily understood. For the sake of presentation we only plot a few levels of the tree.

We observe in our results that the *Volume resolution* is the algorithmic parameter that has the most significant impact on performance. Hence, it is at the root node with a decision threshold of 96. Note that for the *Volume resolution*, 96 is not a valid value but it can be seen as an intermediate of two valid values, i.e. 64 and 128. In addition, note that in Figure 8, the correlation between *Volume resolution* and the performance metrics is relatively small; this further highlights the highly non-linear nature of this parameter. The symbols represent a target performance goal achieved or not achieved, respectively without and with a cross. As we can see, there are two branches that contain configuration points satisfying the three performance metric thresholds depicted in the legend. These branches are *Volume resolution* $<$ 96 and *Compute size ratio* $\geq$ 3, or *Volume resolution* $\leq$ 192 and 3 $\leq$ *Compute size ratio* $\geq$ 6. When in a branch we have a performance metric with a cross, that means that there are no configurations in all that sub-tree able to meet that performance metric requirement.

By using the described techniques to explore the algorithmic space, we have obtained a 6.35x improvement in execution time (best speed), and a 23.5% reduction in power consumption (best power), compared to the default configuration on the ODROID-XU3 board. This means that, even without performing further exploration of the compiler and architectural spaces, we are already able to meet our design requirements. However, as will be seen, some runtime improvements and significant reductions in power consumption can still be obtained.

5.4 Compiler Space

Table 1 summarizes the compiler parameters that are explored in our study. For this study we use the 36 Pareto optimal points of the algorithmic space to conduct a compiler design space study. In other words, we take the best performing configurations of the algorithmic space and use this sub-set of optimal points to further explore the compiler space, as explained in section 3.4

Optimizations.

We consider compiler optimizations that only affect the kernels in isolation. Note that kernel transformations such as vectorization, thread coarsening, and OpenCL local work-group sizes fall in this category. We optimize each kernel independently, which enables us to undertake an exhaustive exploration of the space of our selected optimizations for each kernel. For each vectorizable kernel, we look for every possible loop length vectorization (4 possibilities per axis for a total of 8) and select the best performing configuration. Furthermore, for each kernel we explore 72 different thread coarsening values. Note that a thread coarsening value is a combination of factor, stride, and dimension (see Table 1). To perform this transformation, we use an automatic source to source thread coarsening generation tool [29]. In addition, we also include several LLVM optimizations using the LLVM flags listed in Table 1. In Figure 10, as these optimizations mainly affect the runtime, we only show the impact of exploring the compiler design space on the runtime performance of each kernel of KFusion. These kernels correspond to those summarized in Figure 2 and numerical suffix values differentiate input datasize.

We observe an average runtime speed-up of 23% with the ODROID-XU3, and 16% with the ASUS T200 and a maximum speed-up of 80% for the 'halfSampleRobustIm-

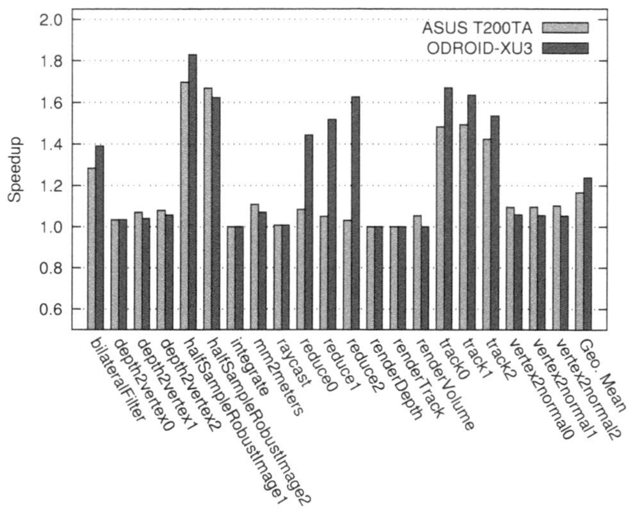

Figure 10: For each Pareto optimal solution in the algorithmic space, we apply some common and advanced compiler optimization techniques. The graph shows the average speed-up obtained for each kernel, for both the ODROID and ASUS platforms.

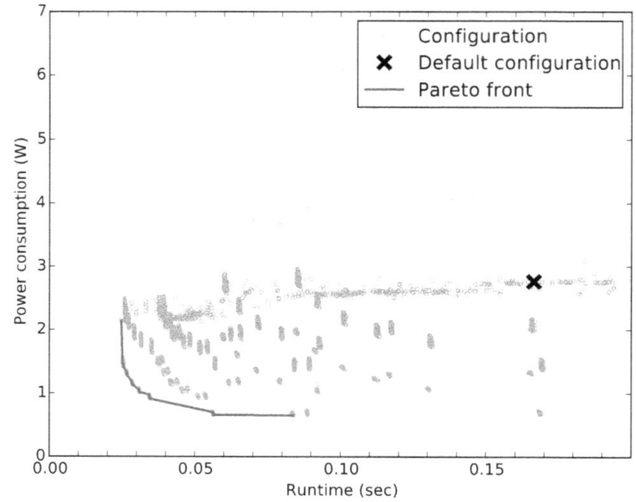

Figure 11: Exhaustive exploration of the architecture design space (grey dots) for the ODROID-XU3 platform. The default configuration (black cross) and the Pareto optimal front (black line) are also depicted.

Constraint		FPS	Error	Power
Best speed	before	38.28	**4.47**	2.16
	after	**39.85**	**4.47**	**1.47**
Best power	before	**38.07**	4.47	2.12
	after	11.92	**4.45**	**0.65**

Table 5: Compiler and architecture space exploration improvements. Our technique has been able to obtain significant improvements in power consumption, without compromising the execution time, and has also found configurations suitable for extremely power constrained environments.

ageKernel1' kernel on ODROID-XU3. Other kernels achieving speedups are the 'bilateralFilter' (which performs image smoothing in the KFusion front end), and kernels associated with the reduction ('reduce') and tracking ('track') portions of the algorithm. However, we observe that these optimizations are effective only on less computationally intensive kernels, and hence they have little significant impact on the overall execution time of KFusion.

Impact of the compilation parameters.

We observe that the compiler parameters explored in our study provide only modest performance improvements. Specifically, we realize that real-time frame rate, i.e. 30 FPS, cannot be obtained by only applying the compiler optimizations. This highlights the need of co-exploring the algorithmic, compiler, and architecture design space.

When running KFusion on the ODROID-XU3 with the optimized kernels, we observe an average of 6% performance improvement and a maximum of 20% performance improvement over the set of Pareto optimal points obtained from the algorithmic space exploration.

5.5 Architecture Space

The last stage in our incremental co-design space exploration is exploring the architecture parameters in Table 1. Note that the architecture parameters only have an impact on the runtime and power, the ATE is not affected by this space exploration. This exploration will be performed across the Pareto optimal points obtained from the compiler design space stage under the constraint that they are accurate enough, i.e. ATE < 5 cm. This constraint is a reasonable assumption in most applications in the SLAM domain.

Exhaustive exploration.

Since the hardware design space size is only 160 configurations on the ODROID-XU3 platform, it can be exhaustively explored. We visualize the power consumption and runtime dimensions in Figure 11. The black cross depicts the default configuration and the black line is the Pareto front. We observe that a configuration exists that provides a frame-rate of 32.38 FPS (runtime 0.03 seconds) while drawing only 1.01 Watts of power. Thus this represents an interesting configuration that supports real-time performance and, at the same time, consuming minimal power. We further observe that there exists a configuration in the Pareto front that provides a frame-rate of nearly 40 FPS while consuming less than 2 Watts of power. There is also an extreme low-power configuration (0.65W) where we are trading power consumption for a lower frame rate. The improvements obtained from the architecture and compilation spaces can be seen in Table 5.

5.6 Discussion

The majority of improvement in runtime came from optimizing at the algorithmic stage. By tuning the various parameters in the co-design space, we were able to achieve significant improvements in both execution time and power consumption (see Table 3). Our optimizations over the compilation and architectural spaces provided minimal improvements in runtime performance, meaning that if we had focused on only the 'lower' two layers of our design space, we would not have been able to reach our design goals with our selected platform. This shows the importance of incorporating domain knowledge into the design space. Although this multi-layered approach may not have converged on an optimal set of solutions, it reduced the size of the design space significantly and allowed us to find good configurations much more quickly.

Importantly, modifying the algorithmic parameters significantly affects the runtime profile of KFusion. As the Hinton plot in Figure 8 shows, each parameter can have varying effects on runtime, accuracy, and power consumption. If we had focused on only the lower tiers of the optimization space, we would have missed this significant opportunity for improvements in runtime and power consumption, and instead obtained only minor improvements.

6. RELATED WORK

The computer vision community primarily focuses on developing accurate algorithms [21, 39], almost always running on high-performance and power hungry systems. As computer vision technology becomes mature, a few benchmarks [40, 15, 38] have attempted to refocus research on runtime constrained contexts. Similarly, new challenges such as the Low-Power Image Recognition Challenge (LPIRC 2016) are emphasizing the importance of low-power embedded implementations of computer vision applications. In this context, recently SLAMBench [31] enabled quantitative, comparable, and validatable experimental research in the form of a benchmark framework for dense 3D scene understanding on a wide range of devices. Adding energy consumption as a metric when evaluating computer vision applications, has enabled energy constrained systems such as battery-powered robots and embedded devices to become evaluation platforms. Zeeshan et al. [42] is a first attempt at exploring SLAM configuration parameters trading off performance for accuracy on embedded systems.

During the last two decades, several design space exploration techniques and frameworks have been used in a variety of different contexts ranging from embedded devices, to compiler research, and system integration [32, 10]. Kang et al. [26] proposed a system which reduces the size of the design space by considering sets of design points to be equivalent. Hu et al. [23] present a user-guided design space exploration framework, allowing the user to identify both good (and bad) design regions, and hence guide the subsequent search. Ansel et al. [8] introduced an extensible and portable framework for empirical performance tuning. It runs an ensemble of search techniques systematically allocating larger budgets to those who perform well, using a multi-armed bandit optimal budget allocation strategy. Norbert et al. tackle the software configurability problem for binary [37] and for both binary and numeric options [36] using a performance-influence model which is based on linear regression. They optimize for execution time on several examples exploring algorithmic and compiler spaces in isolation.

In particular, machine learning (ML) techniques have been recently employed in both architectural and compiler research. Khan et al. [27] employed predictive modeling for cross-program design space exploration in multi-core systems. The techniques developed managed to explore a large design space of chip-multiprocessors running parallel applications with low prediction error. Similarly, Ipek et al. [25] employed an artificial neural network to predict the impact on the performance of hardware parameters, e.g. cache sizes, buffer sizes, of a particular architecture. Furthermore, Lee et al. [28] used polynomial regression to predict power and performance on a multiprocessor design space. Chen et al. [14] suggest that a ML model can be used to produce a relative ranking of design points, rather than predicting their performance precisely.

Regarding compiler optimization research, several efforts to apply ML in this field have been undertaken during the last decade. Cavazos et al. [13] used ML to discover which sequence of compiler optimizations apply better to executed programs. Moreover, the research conducted in [7, 19] employ ML techniques for various compiler optimizations, e.g. loop unrolling, common subexpression elimination, loop hoisting, based on program features.

In contrast to the aforementioned research, to the best of our knowledge, our work is the first to conduct a vertical co-design space exploration, taking into account algorithmic, compiler, and hardware layers in order to solve a three-objective optimization problem. Furthermore, to the best of our knowledge, we show that random forest in conjunction with active learning is effective to focus the search for Pareto optimal configurations in this context.

7. CONCLUSIONS AND FUTURE WORK

We have considered an incremental co-design space exploration on a three-objective optimization goal, optimizing jointly on the runtime, power, and accuracy dimensions. Our incremental co-design is able to combine trade-offs at different levels in the system, refining the Pareto front in subsequent optimization stages. We have been demonstrating our methodology on a popular multi-kernel dense SLAM implementation. As a result, for the first time, this implementation runs in the real-time range on a device with a power budget of 1W. This is a 4.8x improvement in runtime and a 2.8x improvement in power consumption over an hand-tuned implementation by a SLAM domain expert on the same platform for a similar accuracy. This work goes beyond conventional benchmarking in computer systems research by exposing the algorithmic-level design space.

In further work, we will explore how our approach generalizes to different applications, compilers and platforms. We will investigate variable selection methods that reduce the dimension of the space by creating a new feature space and by doing so will enable us to consider larger spaces for bigger mapping problems. There are also a large number of opportunities in transfer learning approaches. In particular, each configuration is likely to give a similar accuracy across a range of devices, and this knowledge might be used to guide exploration toward more interesting points from a power/runtime perspective. Alternatively, we might keep a fixed hardware, and use learned knowledge of the architectural space to more effectively search through design points for different applications running on the same hardware.

8. ACKNOWLEDGMENTS

We acknowledge funding by the EPSRC grant PAMELA EP/K008730/1. M. Luján is funded by a Royal Society University Research Fellowship. We thank the PAMELA Steering Group for the useful discussions.

9. REFERENCES

[1] Beignet. https://www.freedesktop.org/wiki/Software/Beignet/.

[2] Dyson 360 Eye web site. https://www.dyson360eye.com.

[3] Intel Atom Z3795. http://ark.intel.com/products/80267/Intel-Atom-Processor-Z3795-2M-Cache-up-to-2_39-GHz.

[4] Project Tango web site. https://www.google.com/atap/projecttango.

[5] SLAMBench web site. http://apt.cs.manchester.ac.uk/projects/PAMELA/tools/SLAMBench.

[6] *OpenCL 1.1 Specification*, Sept. 2010.

[7] F. Agakov, E. Bonilla, J. Cavazos, B. Franke, G. Fursin, M. F. P. O'Boyle, J. Thomson, M. Toussaint, and C. K. I. Williams. Using machine learning to focus iterative optimization. In *Proceedings of the International Symposium on Code Generation and Optimization*, CGO '06, pages 295–305, Washington, DC, USA, 2006. IEEE Computer Society.

[8] J. Ansel, S. Kamil, K. Veeramachaneni, J. Ragan-Kelley, J. Bosboom, U.-M. O'Reilly, and S. Amarasinghe. Opentuner: an extensible framework for program autotuning. In *Proceedings of the 23rd international conference on Parallel architectures and compilation*, pages 303–316. ACM, 2014.

[9] ARM Ltd. big.little technology.

[10] F. Balarin, Y. Watanabe, H. Hsieh, L. Lavagno, C. Passerone, and A. Sangiovanni-Vincentelli. Metropolis: an integrated electronic system design environment. In *IEEE Computer*, volume 36, pages 45–52, April 2003.

[11] P. J. Besl and N. D. McKay. Method for registration of 3-D shapes. In *Robotics-DL tentative*. Int. Society for Optics and Photonics, 1992.

[12] L. Breiman. *Classification And Regression Trees*. Chapman and Hall, London, UK, 1984.

[13] J. Cavazos, C. Dubach, F. Agakov, E. Bonilla, M. F. P. O'Boyle, G. Fursin, and O. Temam. Automatic performance model construction for the fast software exploration of new hardware designs. In *Proceedings of the 2006 International Conference on Compilers, Architecture and Synthesis for Embedded Systems*, CASES '06, pages 24–34, New York, NY, USA, 2006. ACM.

[14] T. Chen, Q. Guo, K. Tang, O. Temam, Z. Xu, Z.-H. Zhou, and Y. Chen. Archranker: A ranking approach to design space exploration. *SIGARCH Comput. Archit. News*, 42(3):85–96, June 2014.

[15] J. Clemons, H. Zhu, S. Savarese, and T. Austin. MEVBench: A mobile computer vision benchmarking suite. In *IISWC*, 2011.

[16] C. Cohn, L. Atlas, and R. Ladner. Improving generalization with active learning. *Machine Learning*, 15(2):201–221, 1994.

[17] H. Esmaeilzadeh, E. Blem, R. St. Amant, K. Sankaralingam, and D. Burger. Dark silicon and the end of multicore scaling. In *Proceedings of the 38th Annual International Symposium on Computer Architecture*, ISCA '11, pages 365–376, New York, NY, USA, 2011. ACM.

[18] M. Fallon, P. Marion, R. Deits, T. Whelan, M. Antone, J. McDonald, and R. Tedrake. Continuous humanoid locomotion over uneven terrain using stereo fusion. In *ICHR*, 2015.

[19] G. Fursin, Y. Kashnikov, A. Memon, Z. Chamski, O. Temam, M. Namolaru, E. Yom-Tov, B. Mendelson, A. Zaks, E. Courtois, F. Bodin, P. Barnard, E. Ashton, E. Bonilla, J. Thomson, C. K. Williams, and M. O'Boyle. Milepost gcc: Machine learning enabled self-tuning compiler. *International Journal of Parallel Programming*, 39(3):296–327, 2011.

[20] A. Handa, V. Patraucean, V. Badrinarayanan, S. Stent, and R. Cipolla. SceneNet: Understanding Real World Indoor Scenes With Synthetic Data. *ArXiv e-prints 1511.07041*, 2015.

[21] A. Handa, T. Whelan, J. McDonald, and A. Davison. A Benchmark for RGB-D Visual Odometry, 3D Reconstruction and SLAM. In *ICRA*, 2014.

[22] J. L. Henning. SPEC CPU2006 benchmark descriptions. *ACM SIGARCH Computer Architecture News*, 2006.

[23] X. Hu, G. Greenwood, S. Ravichandran, and G. Quan. A framework for user assisted design space exploration. In *Proceedings of 36th Design Automation Conference*, pages 414–419, 1999.

[24] D. Hulens, T. Goedemé, and J. Verbeke. How to choose the best embedded processing platform for on-board UAV image processing? *Proceedings VISAPP 2015*, pages 1–10, 2015.

[25] E. İpek, S. A. McKee, R. Caruana, B. R. de Supinski, and M. Schulz. Efficiently exploring architectural design spaces via predictive modeling. *SIGARCH Comput. Archit. News*, 34(5):195–206, Oct. 2006.

[26] E. Kang, E. Jackson, and W. Schulte. An approach for effective design space exploration. In *Foundations of Computer Software. Modeling, Development, and Verification of Adaptive Systems*, volume 6662 of *Lecture Notes in Computer Science*, pages 33–54. Springer Berlin Heidelberg, 2011.

[27] S. Khan, P. Xekalakis, J. Cavazos, and M. Cintra. Using Predictive Modeling for Cross-Program Design Space Exploration in Multicore Systems. In *Proceedings of the 16th International Conference on Parallel Architecture and Compilation Techniques*, PACT '07, pages 327–338, Washington, DC, USA, 2007. IEEE Computer Society.

[28] B. C. Lee and D. M. Brooks. Accurate and efficient regression modeling for microarchitectural performance and power prediction. *SIGARCH Comput. Archit. News*, 34(5):185–194, Oct. 2006.

[29] A. Magni, C. Dubach, and M. F. O'Boyle. A large-scale cross-architecture evaluation of thread-coarsening. In *Proc. of SC13: Int. Conf. for High Performance Computing, Networking, Storage and Analysis*. ACM, 2013.

[30] S. Moll. Decompilation of LLVM IR. Master's thesis, 2011.

[31] L. Nardi, B. Bodin, M. Z. Zia, J. Mawer, A. Nisbet, P. H. J. Kelly, A. J. Davison, M. Luján, M. F. P. O'Boyle, G. Riley, N. Topham, and S. Furber. Introducing SLAMBench, a performance and accuracy benchmarking methodology for SLAM. In *ICRA*, 2015.

[32] S. Neema, J. Sztipanovits, G. Karsai, and K. Butts. Constraint-based design-space exploration and model synthesis. In *Embedded Software*, volume 2855 of *Lecture Notes in Computer Science*, pages 290–305. Springer Berlin Heidelberg, 2003.

[33] R. A. Newcombe, S. Izadi, O. Hilliges, D. Molyneaux, D. Kim, A. J. Davison, P. Kohli, J. Shotton, S. Hodges, and A. Fitzgibbon. KinectFusion: Real-time dense surface mapping and tracking. In *ISMAR*, 2011.

[34] C. Papachristos, D. Tzoumanikas, and A. Tzes. Aerial robotic tracking of a generalized mobile target employing visual and spatio-temporal dynamic subject perception. In *Intelligent Robots and Systems (IROS), 2015 IEEE/RSJ International Conference on*, pages 4319–4324, Sept 2015.

[35] R. Salas-Moreno, B. Glocker, P. H. J. Kelly, and A. J. Davison. Dense planar SLAM. In *ISMAR*, 2014.

[36] N. Siegmund, A. Grebhahn, S. Apel, and C. Kästner. Performance-influence models for highly configurable systems. In *Proceedings of the 2015 10th Joint Meeting on Foundations of Software Engineering*, pages 284–294. ACM, 2015.

[37] N. Siegmund, S. S. Kolesnikov, C. Kästner, S. Apel, D. Batory, M. Rosenmüller, and G. Saake. Predicting performance via automated feature-interaction detection. In *Proceedings of the 34th International Conference on Software Engineering*, pages 167–177. IEEE Press, 2012.

[38] S. Song, S. P. Lichtenberg, and J. Xiao. Sun rgb-d: A rgb-d scene understanding benchmark suite. In *Computer Vision and Pattern Recognition (CVPR), 2015 IEEE Conference on*, pages 567–576, June 2015.

[39] J. Sturm, N. Engelhard, F. Endres, W. Burgard, and D. Cremers. A benchmark for the evaluation of RGB-D SLAM systems. In *IROS*, 2012.

[40] S. K. Venkata, I. Ahn, D. Jeon, A. Gupta, C. Louie, S. Garcia, S. Belongie, and M. B. Taylor. SD-VBS: The San Diego vision benchmark suite. In *IISWC*, 2009.

[41] M. Warmuth, G. Ratsch, M. Mathieson, J. Liao, and C. Lemmon. Active learning in the drug discovery process. In *Neural Information Processing Systems (NIPS)*, 2001.

[42] M. Z. Zia, L. Nardi, A. Jack, E. Vespa, B. Bodin, P. H. J. Kelly, and A. J. Davison. Comparative Design Space Exploration of Dense and Semi-Dense SLAM. In *ICRA*, 2016.

Fusion of Parallel Array Operations

Mads R. B. Kristensen
Niels Bohr Institute
University of Copenhagen
Denmark
madsbk@nbi.ku.dk

Simon A. F. Lund
Niels Bohr Institute
University of Copenhagen
Denmark
safl@nbi.ku.dk

Troels Blum
Niels Bohr Institute
University of Copenhagen
Denmark
blum@nbi.ku.dk

James Avery
Dept. of Computer Science
University of Copenhagen
Denmark
avery@diku.dk

ABSTRACT

We address the problem of fusing array operations based on criteria such as shape compatibility, data reuse, and minimizing communication. We formulate the problem as a partitioning problem (WSP) that is general enough to handle loop fusion, combinator fusion, and other types of fusion analysis.

Traditionally, when optimizing for data reuse, the fusion problem has been formulated as a static weighted graph partitioning problem (known as the Weighted Loop Fusion problem). We show that this scheme cannot accurately track data reuse between multiple independent loops, since it overestimates total data reuse of certain cases. Our formulation in terms of partitions allows use of realistic cost functions that can track resource usage accurately. We give correctness proofs, and prove that WSP can maximize data reuse in programs exactly, in contrast to prior work.

For the exact optimal solution, which is NP-hard to find, we present a branch-and-bound algorithm together with a polynomial-time preconditioner that reduces the problem size significantly in practice. We further present a polynomial-time greedy approximation that is fast enough to use for JIT-compilation and gives near-optimal results in practice.

All algorithms have been implemented in the automatic parallelization platform Bohrium, run on a set of benchmarks, and compared to existing methods from the literature.

1. INTRODUCTION

Array operation fusion is a program transformation that combines (fuses) multiple array operations into a *kernel* of operations. When it is applicable, the technique can drastically improve cache utilization through temporal data locality and enables other program transformations, such as *scalar replacement* [4, 5] and *array contraction* [2, 10]. In scalar programming languages, such as C, array operation fusion is typically used to combine multiple loops into a single one. The effect is a reduction of array traversals (Fig. 1). Similarly, in functional programming languages it is used to fuse multiple combinators. In array programming languages, such as HPF [20] and ZPL [6], fusing array operations is crucial, since a program written in these languages will consist almost exclusively of array operations. Lewis et al. demonstrate an execution time improvement of up to 400% when optimizing for array contraction at the array rather than the loop level in ZPL [17]. In Single Assignment C, Scholz fuses array operations and utilizes array contractions in order to achieve performance that is competitive with that of hand-optimized Fortran programs [27]. Similarly, Shei et al. have applied loop fusion and array contraction to MATLAB [28].

For automatic parallelization platforms as Bohrium [16], these program transformations can remove memory bottlenecks and facilitate parallel scaling to very high numbers of independent computation cores.

Not all operation fusions are allowed. Consider the two loops in Fig. 1b; since the second loop traverses the result from the first loop in reverse, we must compute the complete result of the first loop before continuing to the second loop, preventing fusion. Clever analysis sometimes allows transforming the program into a form that is amenable to fusion. Methods such as *affine transformations* by Lim and Lam [18] rewrite loop nests into semantically equivalent loop nests through index transformations in order to make parallelization possible. In the following, we assume any such relevant transformations have already been performed.

A legal set of operation fusions corresponds to a partition of the set of operations in which the partition blocks obey the same execution order as the individual operations, and in which no block contains two operations that must not be fused. Out of all such partitions, we want to find one that enables us to save the most memory or computation. It is not an easy problem, in part because fusibility is not transitive. That is, even if it is legal to fuse subroutines x, y and y, z, it may be illegal for all three of x, y, z to be executed together: One local decision can have global consequences for future choices.

The problem can be stated in a quite general way: "*Given a mixed graph and a partition cost function, find a legal partition of vertices that cuts all non-directed edges and mini-*

PACT '16, September 11 - 15, 2016, Haifa, Israel

ISBN 978-1-4503-4121-9/16/09...$15.00

DOI: http://dx.doi.org/10.1145/2967938.2967945

```
#define N 1000
double A[N], B[N], T[N];
for(int i=0; i<N; ++i)
  T[i] = B[i] * A[i];
for(int i=0; i<N; ++i)
  A[i] += T[i];
```

(a) Two forward iterating loops.

```
#define N 1000
double A[N], B[N], T[N];
int j = N;
for(int i=0; i<N; ++i)
  T[i] = B[i] * A[i];
for(int i=0; i<N; ++i)
  A[i] += T[--j];
```

(b) A forward and a reverse iterating loop.

```
for(int i=0; i<N; ++i){
  T[i] = B[i] * A[i];
  A[i] += T[i];
}
```

(c) Loop fusion: the two loops from Fig. 1a fused into one.

```
for(int i=0; i<N; ++i){
  double t = B[i] * A[i];
  A[i] += t;
}
```

(d) Array Contraction: the temporary array T from Fig. 1c is replaced by the scalar t.

Figure 1: Loop fusion and array contraction in C.

mizes the cost of the partition."[1]. We call this problem the *Weighted Subroutine Partition* problem, abbreviated WSP.

The general formulation is applicable to a broad range of optimization objectives. The cost function can penalize any aspect of the partitions, e.g. data accesses, memory use, communication bandwidth, and/or communication latency. The only requirement to the cost function is monotonicity:

- Everything else equal, it must be cost neutral or a cost advantage to merge two blocks.

Similarly, the definition of partition legality is flexible.

- Any aspect of a pair of subroutines can make them illegal to have in the same partition block, such as preventing mixing of sequential and parallel loops, different array shapes, or access patterns.

- Subroutines may have dependencies that impose a partial order. A legal partition must observe this order, i.e. must not introduce cycles.

Notice, in particular, that the cost function assigns a value to partitions; it is not necessary that it can be represented as a static weighted graph. This is important in order to correctly track data locality.

The remainder of the paper is structured as follows:

In Section 2, we discuss related work; in particular we show why the well-known Weighted Loop Fusion (WLF) formulation is incorrect for maximizing data reuse.

In Section 3, we formally define the *Weighted Subroutine Partition problem* (WSP), which unifies the WLF formulation and the series of cost models proposed in the literature as special cases of one general formulation.

Section 4 shows how WSP is used to solve array operation fusion for the *Bohrium* automatic parallelization framework, and gives a correctness proof.

In Section 5, we prove that WSP is NP-hard.

In Section 6, we prove that the exact solution to WSP can be found through a sequence of locally allowed merges and describe a branch-and-bound algorithm that computes exact optimal solutions, as well as polynomial-time approximation algorithms that compute good results rapidly enough to use in JIT-compilation. All the algorithms are implemented in Bohrium, and work for any choice of monotonic cost function, which allows us to compare directly with other fusion schemes from the literature.

Section 7 shows measurements performed on 10 benchmark programs, comparing both the optimal to the approximation schemes, and to three other fusion schemes.

[1]See Sec. 3 for definition of a legal partition and cost.

2. RELATED WORK

The WSP problem presented in this paper generalizes the *Weighted Loop Fusion* (WLF) problem first described by Kennedy in [12] (by the name *Fusion for Reuse*). WLF is designed to maximize data locality through loop fusion, and corresponds to the Reuse cost model in Section 7.2. The WLF problem is a graph-partitioning problem on a *Loop Dependence Graph* with static weights between fusible loops.

Megiddo et al. have shown that it is possible to formulate the WLF problem as integer linear programming (ILP) [24]. Based on the WLF graph, the idea is to transform the edges into linear constraints that implement the dependency and fusibility between the vertices and transform weights into ILP objective variables. The values of the objective variables are either the values of the weights when the associated vertices are in different partitions or zero when in the same partition. The objective of the ILP is then to minimize the value of the objective variables. The problem is NP-hard, but the hope is that with an efficient ILP solver, such as `lp-solve` [3], and a modest problem size it might be practical as a compile time optimization. Darte et al. [8] proved that the WLF problem is NP-hard through a reduction from multiway cut [7]. Furthermore, since maximizing data reuse may not maximize the number of array contractions (Fig. 10), they introduce an ILP formulation with the sole objective of maximizing the number of array contractions (the Contract cost model in Section 7.2).

Robinson et al. [26] describe an ILP scheme that combines the objectives of Megiddo and Darte: both maximizing data reuse and array contractions while giving priority to data reuse (corresponds to our Robinson cost model in Section 7.2).

However, optimization using WLF has a significant limitation: it only allows static edge weights. That is, the edge weights in the WLF graph are assigned once and for all. This limitation is the main reason that pushed us to develop the Weighted Subroutine Partition formalism, because it is inappropriate for accurate calculation of data reuse.

Consider the WLF example in Fig. 2, which consist of six loops and three arrays A, B, C of size 1. The objective is to maximize data reuse, represented by weight edges connecting the loops that access the same arrays. Fig. 2b shows the optimal WLF solution to the example, giving a calculated total weight reduction from 13 to 3. However, the actual number of array accesses is only reduced from 10 to 6. A better strategy is to fuse loop 1-2 (Fig. 2c), which will reduce the actual number of array accesses from 10 to 4.

The problem with the WLF formulation here is that all the loops that read the same data must be pair-wise connected with a weight, leading to over-estimating potential data reuse. To address this problem, Ding and Kennedy [9] introduce a hypergraph formulation[2] where each hyperedge connects array elements accessed by different array opera-

[2]A graph where edges can connect multiple vertices.

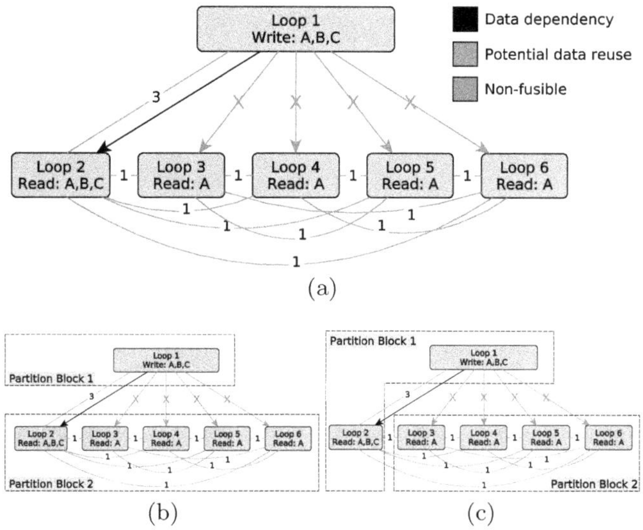

Figure 2: A WLF example where the objective is to maximize data reuse. (a) shows the initial graph. (b) shows a partition where loop 1 is in one block and loops 2-6 are in another block. (c) shows a partition where loops 1-2 are in one block and loops 3-6 are in another block.

tions. This formulation exactly captures data reuse, but only theoretically since it is not feasible to connect billions of individual array elements in practice. When connecting arrays instead of elements, it can solve the data reuse problem exactly in the special case when all views of a particular array are the same size; but when view sizes vary, counterexamples yielding suboptimal solutions can be constructed.

In the Weighted Subroutine Partition formulation (WSP), we work with *partitions* instead of individual edges, and assign a cost to a partition as a whole. The cost-savings of a merge is then the difference in cost between the partitions before and after merging, allowing accurate tracking of the exact data-reuse through the costs function. It can exactly model resource use (and can simulate the theoretical hypergraph formulation of [9]), but contrary to prior work it is both theoretically exact, and works in practice – not just as a heuristic, but also for finding exact solutions.

In addition to those fusion algorithms we directly compare with in this paper, [8, 12, 24, 26], there exist a broad range of existing loop fusion algorithms. The WSP formulation can represent many of these. For instance in [29], Singhai et al. use a very precise cost model that represents the number of cache lines accessed by the innermost loop, which WSP can easily model. Other examples are [1, 10, 17, 22]. However, not everything can be modeled by WSP, due to the requirement that the cost function is monotonic. In [23], McKinley et al. use a cost model that restricts the number of registers a fused loop can use. This can not be modeled using only a monotonic cost function. The closest WSP can get is a cost model that makes loop fusion cost neutral after the maximum number of used registers is reached.

Other work on loop fusion is less directly comparable. For example, the *affine transformations* of Lim et al. in [19] can be seen as both weaker and stronger than the present work: Their algorithms perform loop transformations and partitioning together, allowing simultaneous optimization of array contraction, synchronization, and blocking; but the partitioning is not exact. In [30], strong restrictions on static loop shapes yields a polynomial-time solution to memory reduction through loop fusion. Variations on these schemes, as well as the polyhedral analysis of [25], could yield good results combined with our present work, when used as preprocessing steps before partitioning.

3. THE WEIGHTED SUBROUTINE PARTITION PROBLEM

In this section, we will formally define the Weighted Subroutine Partition (WSP) problem.

Definition 1 (WSP graph).
A WSP graph *is a triplet* $G = (V, E_d, E_f)$ *such that* (V, E_d) *is a directed acyclic graph describing dependency order, and* (V, E_f) *is an undirected graph of forbidden edges.*

Definition 2 (WSP order).
A WSP graph, $G = (V, E_d, E_f)$*, induces a partial order* $\overset{d}{<}$ *on* V *as follows:* $v \overset{d}{<} v'$ *iff there exists a path from* v *to* v' *in* (V, E_d)*. Since* (V, E_d) *is acyclic, this is a strict partial order.*

Definition 3 (Partitions).
A partition *of a set* V *is a set* $P = \{B_1, B_2, \ldots, B_k\}$ *such that* V *is the disjoint union of the* blocks $B_1, \ldots, B_k$*. The set* Π_V *of all partitions of* V *is partially ordered as* $P \leq P'$ *iff* $\forall B \in P \exists B' \in P' \colon B \subseteq B'$*, i.e. if each block in* P *is a subset of a block in* P'*.*

The set of partitions Π_V is a lattice with bottom element $\perp = \{V\}$, where every element is separated, and top element $\top = \{\{V\}\}$, where everything is together in one block. The successors to a partition P in the partition order are those partitions that are identical to P except for merging two of the blocks. Conversely, splitting a block results in a predecessor. We write $P \prec P'$ if P' is a successor to P. This defines a binary *merge operator*:

Definition 4 (Block merge operator).
Given a partition $P = \{B_1, B_2, \ldots\}$*, define* $P/(B_1, B_2) = \{B_1 \cup B_2, \ldots\}$ *to be the successor to* P *in which* B_1 *and* B_2 *are merged and all other blocks are left the same.*

Definition 5 (Legal partition).
Given a WSP graph, $G = (V, E_d, E_f)$*, we say that the partition* $P \in \Pi_V$ *is* legal *when the following holds for every block* $B \in P$*:*

1. $\nexists v_1, v_2 \in B : (v_1, v_2) \in E_f$*, i.e. no block contains both endpoints of a forbidden edge.*
2. *If* $v_1 \overset{d}{<} v_2 \overset{d}{<} v_3$ *and* $v_1, v_3 \in B$ *then* $v_2 \in B$*, i.e. the directed edges between blocks must not form cycles.*

Definition 6 (WSP cost).
A cost function $\mathsf{cost}(P)$ *defines the cost of the partitions and respects the following conditions:*

1. $\mathsf{cost}(P) \geq 0$
2. $P \leq P' \implies \mathsf{cost}(P) \geq \mathsf{cost}(P')$

```
1  import bohrium as bh
2
3  def synthetic():
4      A = bh.zeros(4)
5      B = bh.zeros(4)
6      D = bh.zeros(5)
7      E = bh.zeros(5)
8      A += D[:-1]
9      A[:] = D[:-1]
10     B += E[:-1]
11     B[:] = E[:-1]
12     T = A * B
13     bh.max(T, E[1:], out=D[1:])
14     bh.min(T, D[1:], out=E[1:])
15     return D
16 print synthetic()
```

(a)

```
COPY A, 0
COPY B, 0
COPY D, 0
COPY E, 0
ADD A, A, D[:-1]
COPY A, D[:-1]
ADD B, B, E[:-1]
COPY B, E[:-1]
MUL T, A, B
MAX D[1:], T, E[1:]
MIN E[1:], T, D[1:]
DEL A
DEL B
DEL E
DEL T
SYNC D
DEL D
```

(b)

Figure 3: A Python program that uses the Bohrium runtime system. In order to demonstrate various trade-offs between partitioning schemes, the program is synthetic. (a) shows the Python code and (b) shows the corresponding Bohrium array bytecode.

Definition 7 (WSP problem). *Given a WSP graph, $G = (V, E_d, E_f)$, and a cost function, $\mathsf{cost}(P)$, the WSP problem is the problem of finding a legal partition with minimal cost:*

$$P^* \in \underset{P \in \hat{\Pi}_V}{\text{argmin}} \; \mathsf{cost}(P) \tag{1}$$

where $\hat{\Pi}_V$ denotes the set of legal partitions of V.

4. WSP IN BOHRIUM

Formulating the WSP problem in terms of partitions allows us to define accurate cost functions, since we are not restricted to costs that are representable as static edge weights. The only requirement is that the cost function is monotonic. In this section, we use WSP to solve a concrete real-world optimization problem. The concrete problem is an optimization phase within the Bohrium runtime system [16] in which a set of array operations are partitioned into computation kernels – the *Fusion of Array Operations* (FAO) problem. The following is a brief description of Bohrium, the FAO problem, and a proof that the WSP problem solves the FAO problem (Theorem 1).

Bohrium is an open-source computation backend for array programming languages and libraries[3]. It supports a range of languages, such as Python, C++, and .NET, and a range of computer architectures, such as CPU, GPU, and clusters of these. The idea is to decouple the domain specific frontend language from the hardware specific backend implementation in order to provide a high-productivity and high-performance framework.

A Bohrium array operation operates on a set of inputs and produces a set of outputs [16]. Similar to NumPy [31], both input and output operands are *views* of arrays. An array view is a structured way to access the whole or parts of an underlying *base* array. A base array is always a contiguous flat array, whereas views can have any number of indices, strides, and dimensionality [16]. *In the following, when we refer to an array, we mean an array view; when we refer to identical arrays, we mean identical array views that points to the same base array; and when we refer to overlapping arrays, we mean array views that point to some of the same elements in a common base array.*

[3] Available at http://www.bh107.org and http://www.github.com/bh107/bohrium

Fig. 3a shows a Python program that uses Bohrium as a drop-in replacement for NumPy. The program allocates and initializes four arrays (line 4-7), manipulates those arrays through array operations (line 8-14), and prints the content of one of the arrays (line 16).

Bohrium is language agnostic and translates the Python array operations into bytecode (Fig. 3b), which the Bohrium backend can execute[4]. In the case of Python, the Python array operations and the Bohrium array bytecode are almost in one-to-one correspondence. The first bytecode operand is the output array and the remaining operands are either input arrays or input literals. Since there is no scope in the bytecode, Bohrium uses `DEL` to destroy arrays and `SYNC` to move array data into the address space of the frontend language – in this case triggered by the Python `print` statement (Fig. 3a, line 16). There is no explicit bytecode for constructing arrays; on first encounter, Bohrium constructs them implicitly.

In the next phase, Bohrium partitions the list of array operations into blocks that consist of fusible array operations – the FAO problem. As long as the preceding constraints between the array operations are preserved, Bohrium is free to reorder them as it sees fit, making possible code optimizations based on data locality and array contraction. We define the problem formally as follows:

Definition 8. *Given a set of array operations, A, equipped with the strict partial order from the data dependencies between them, $(A, \overset{d}{<})$, find a partition, P, of A for which:*

1. *All operations within a block in P are fusible (Def. 10)*
2. *For all blocks, $B \in P$, if $a_1 \overset{d}{<} a_2 \overset{d}{<} a_3$ and $a_1, a_3 \in B$ then $a_2 \in B$. (I.e. the partition obeys dependency order).*
3. *The cost of the partition (Def. 12) is minimal.*

In the final phase, the hardware specific backend implementation JIT-compiles each block of array operations and executes them.

Input, Output, and External Arrays

We next introduce some operations that keep track of memory allocation, deallocation, reads, and writes:

Definition 9. *Given an array operation f, the notation $\mathsf{in}[f]$ denotes the set of arrays that f reads; $\mathsf{out}[f]$ is the set of arrays that f writes; $\mathsf{new}[f]$ is the set of new arrays that f allocates; and $\mathsf{del}[f]$ is the set of arrays that f de-allocates. Furthermore, for a block of array operations, B, we define:*

$$\mathsf{out}[B] \equiv \bigcup_{f \in B} \mathsf{out}[f]$$

$$\mathsf{in}[B] \equiv \bigcup_{f \in B} \mathsf{in}[f]$$

$$\mathsf{new}[B] \equiv \bigcup_{f \in B} \mathsf{new}[f]$$

$$\mathsf{del}[B] \equiv \bigcup_{f \in B} \mathsf{del}[f]$$

$$\mathsf{ext}[B] \equiv (\mathsf{in}[B] \setminus \mathsf{new}[B]) \sqcup (\mathsf{out}[B] \setminus \mathsf{del}[B])$$

[4] For a detailed description of this Python-to-bytecode translation we refer to previous work [14, 15].

Here, $\sqcup$ is disjoint union: arrays that are both read and written are counted twice. DEL and SYNC are counted as having no input or output.

Of particular interest in Def. 9 is the set of *external data accesses* $\mathsf{ext}[B]$. This is the set of arrays read from within B, but created outside of B; together with the set of arrays written to by operations in B, but deleted outside of B. This is the data that must be copied to and from a computation kernel implementing B. Conversely, arrays that are not in $\mathsf{ext}[B]$ are *fully internal* to the block, as they are both created and deleted within it. Their memory needs never be allocated, as they can be replaced by per-register computation through *array contraction*, described further down.

Data-parallelism and Fusibility

Performance in array programming languages and libraries depends on *data-parallelism*, which ensures that each output element can be calculated independently with minimal or no communication between threads or processors. In Bohrium, the operations *reduce* and *scan* have logarithmic communication, and all other array operations are fully data parallel with no inter-thread communication. This property should be preserved when fusing operations.

DEFINITION 10. *A block B of Bohrium array operations is data-parallel, i.e., each output element can be calculated independently, when the following holds: If an input and an output or two output arrays overlap, they must be identical. Formally:*

$$\forall i \in \mathsf{in}[B], \forall o, o' \in \mathsf{out}[B]: \quad (i \cap o = \emptyset \vee i = o) \wedge (o \cap o' = \emptyset \vee o = o') \quad (2)$$

Our main criterion for allowing operations to be fused together is that they can be executed together without losing data-parallelism:

DEFINITION 11. *In Bohrium, two array operations, f and f', are said to be fusible when the following holds:*

$$\forall i' \in \mathsf{in}[f'], \quad \forall o \in \mathsf{out}[f]: \quad i' \cap o = \emptyset \vee i' = o \quad (1)$$
$$\forall o' \in \mathsf{out}[f'], \forall o \in \mathsf{out}[f]: \quad o' \cap o = \emptyset \vee o' = o \quad (2)$$
$$\forall o' \in \mathsf{out}[f'], \forall i \in \mathsf{in}[f]: \quad o' \cap i = \emptyset \vee o' = i \quad (3)$$

In addition to the data-parallelism property, the current implementation of Bohrium also requires that the dimensionalities of the arrays fit one other. Presently, Bohrium does not apply any array shape transformations, and thus the array shapes have to match as is.

Cost Model

Our cost model assumes that programs are memory bound and tracks the main cost: memory allocation and access. Fusing enables two program transformations:

Data reuse When a kernel accesses an array multiple times, Bohrium will only read and/or write to that array once, avoiding access to main memory. Consider the two for-loops in Fig. 1a that each traverse `A` and `T`. Fusing the loops avoids one traversal of `A` and one traversal of `T` (Fig. 1c). Furthermore, the compiler can reduce the access to the main memory by $2N$ elements since it can keep the last read element of `A` and `T` in register.

Array contraction When an array is created and destroyed within a single partition block, Bohrium will not allocate the array memory, but calculate the result in-place in one single temporary register variable per parallel computing thread. Consider the program transformation from Fig. 1a to 1d, in which, beside loop fusion, the temporary array T is replaced by the scalar variable t. In this case, the transformation reduces the accessed elements with $3N$ and memory requirement by N elements.

Together, these two program transformations eradicate all allocation and access to memory that is not in the ext-set of a block, replacing it with computation in per-thread register variables. We define the cost of a partition as the total memory reads and writes remaining after these transformations have been performed, i.e. the total number of bytes in the ext-sets:

DEFINITION 12. *In Bohrium, the cost of a partition of array operations, $P = \{B_1, B_2, ..., B_k\}$, is given by:*

$$\mathsf{cost}(P) = \sum_{B \in P} \|\mathsf{ext}[B]\| \quad (3)$$

where the length $\|X\|$ is the total size in bytes of the arrays in X.

The Bohrium cost-savings when merging two partition blocks depends only on the blocks:

PROPOSITION 1 (MERGE-SAVINGS). *Let P be a partition and $P' = P/(B_1, B_2)$ be its successor partition derived by merging B_1 and B_2. Since $P/(B_1, B_2) = P/(B_2, B_1)$, we can assume without loss of generality that $B_1 \not\leadsto B_2$. Then, using the cost function of Def. 12, the difference in cost between the two partitions is:*

$$\begin{aligned}\mathsf{cost}(P) - \mathsf{cost}(P') = \; & \|\mathsf{ext}[B_1] \cap \mathsf{ext}[B_2]\| \\ & + \|\mathsf{new}[B_1] \cap \mathsf{in}[B_2]\| \\ & + \|\mathsf{out}[B_1] \cap \mathsf{del}[B_2]\| \quad (4)\end{aligned}$$

Since this cost reduction depends only on B_1 and B_2, we define a function, $\mathsf{saving}(B_1, B_2)$, that counts the savings from merging B_1 and B_2, which is independent of the rest of the partitions.

PROOF. If $P = \{B_1, B_2, \ldots, \}$ and $P' = \{B_1 \cup B_2, \ldots\}$, then the reduction in cost is

$$\mathsf{cost}(P) - \mathsf{cost}(P') = \|\mathsf{ext}(B_1)\| + \|\mathsf{ext}(B_2)\| - \|\mathsf{ext}(B_1 \cup B_2)\|$$

since all other blocks are the same. Since $B_1 \not\leadsto B_2$, either B_1 executes before B_2, or they are unrelated in the dependency order. In both cases, $\mathsf{in}[B_1] \cap \mathsf{new}[B_2] = \emptyset$ and $\mathsf{del}[B_1] \cap \mathsf{out}[B_2] = \emptyset$; and new's and del's are always disjoint. Direct calculation yields Eq. 4. □

Note that Prop. 1 directly implies that the cost function of Def. 12 is positive and monotonically decreasing, as required by Def. 6. We next show how the problem can be formulated as a WSP instance.

Constructing a WSP-problem from Bohrium bytecode

Given a list A of Bohrium array operations, a WSP problem $G = (V, E_d, E_f)$ is constructed as follows.

1. The data dependencies between array operations define a partial order: $a \overset{d}{<} a'$ iff a' must be executed before a.

2. Each array operation $a \in A$ defines a vertex $v(a) \in V$.

3. The dependency graph E_d has an edge $(v(a), v(a'))$ for each pair $a, a' \in A$ with $a \overset{d}{<} a'$.

4. The fusion-prevention graph E_f has an edge $(v(a), v(a'))$ for each non-fusible pair $a, a' \in A$.

The cost function is as in Def. 12, but note that it can be calculated incrementally using Prop. 1.

The complexity of this transformation is $O(V^2)$ since we may have to check all pairs of array operations for dependecies, fusibility, and cost-saving, all of which is $O(1)$. Fig. 4 shows the trivial partition, $\perp$, of the Python example, where every array operation has its own block. The cost is 94.

WSP solves Fusion of Array Operations

Finally, we can show that WSP also solves the FAO problem.

THEOREM 1. *WSP solves Fusion of Array Operations.*

PROOF. It is clear from Def. 5 and the construction above that the legal partitions $\hat{\Pi}_V$ are exactly all those that fulfill Properties (1) and (2) of Def. 8. Thus, Def. 7 yields a global minimum for all such partitions, fulfilling also Def. 8(3). □

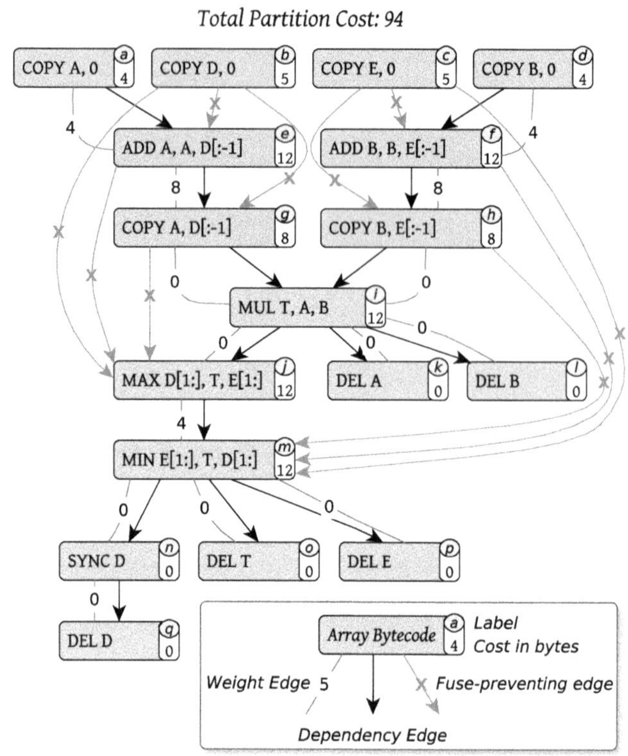

Figure 4: A partition graph of the Python program in Fig. 3 (with array sizes 4 and 5). Notice that the cost of a node/block, B, is the number bytes externally accessed, ext$[B]$, as defined in Def. 9. For illustrative purposes, the array sizes are small, and the graph does not include transitively redundant weight edges.

5. COMPLEXITY OF WSP

We prove NP-hardness of the WSP problem by a reduction from the *Multiway Cut Problem* [7], which Dahlhaus et al. has shown is NP-hard for fixed $k \geq 3$.

DEFINITION 13 (MULTIWAY CUT).
Given a tuple (V, E, S, w) consisting of a graph (V, E), a terminal set $S = \{s_1, \ldots, s_k\}$ *of vertices, and a non-negative weight $w(u, v)$ for each edge $(u, v) \in E$, a* multiway cut *is an edge set E' the removal of which leaves each terminal in separate components. The solutions to the MWC problem are the multiway cuts of minimal total weight.*

THEOREM 2. *The WSP problem is NP-hard for graphs $G = (V, E_d, E_f)$ that have a chain of three or more edges in E_f.*

PROOF. We prove NP-hardness through a reduction from multiway cut. Given an MWC-instance, (V, E, S, w), we build a WSP-instance as follows. Let $G = (V, E_d, E_f)$, $E_f = \{(s_i, s_j) | 1 \leq i < j \leq k\}$, and $E_d = \emptyset$. Define the *cut* of a partition as the set of edges that connect the blocks:

$$\mathsf{cut}(P) = \{(u, v) \in E | \nexists B \in P : (u, v) \in B\}$$

The cuts of the legal WSP partitions $\hat{\Pi}_V$ are exactly the set of multiway cuts:

- The set of directed edges in E_d is empty, which makes Def. 2 and Def. 5(2) trivially satisfied.

- The fuse-preventing edges E_f connect each terminal in S and no other vertices. Hence, by Def. 5(1), $\hat{\Pi}_V$ are exactly those partitions for which no block contains two terminals.

Let now the cost function be the total weight of the cut:

$$\mathsf{cost}(P) = \sum_{(u,v) \in \mathsf{cut}(P)} w(u, v)$$

This is a valid WSP cost function (by Def. 6): it is non-negative, and if $P \leq P'$ in the partition order, then $\mathsf{cut}(P) \supseteq \mathsf{cut}(P')$, whereby $\mathsf{cost}(P) \geq \mathsf{cost}(P')$. Since $\mathsf{cost}(P)$ is the MWC total weight, Eq. (1) gives the multiway cuts of minimal total weight, concluding the proof. □

6. ALGORITHMS

In this section, we present an exact algorithm for finding an optimal solution to WSP (with exponential worst-case execution time), and a fast algorithm that finds an approximate solution. We use the Python program shown in Fig. 3 to demonstrate the results of each partition algorithm.

6.1 Partition graphs and chains of merges

All three algorithms work on data structures called *partition graphs*, defined as follows:

DEFINITION 14 (PARTITION GRAPH).
Given a graph $G = (V, E)$ and a partition P of V, the corresponding partition graph *is the graph $\hat{G}(P) = (P, \hat{E}(P))$ that has an edge (B, B') if there is an edge $(u, v) \in E$ with*

```
function Pick(Ĝ, Ê_w)
  for (v, u) ← Ê_w do
    if not Legal(Ĝ, (u, v)) then
      Remove edge (u, v) from Ê_w
    end if
  end for
  for (v, u) ← Ê_w do
    if degree is less than 2 for either u
    or v when only counting edges in Ê_w
    then
      if θ[u] = θ[v] then
        return (u, v)
      end if
    end if
  end for
  return NIL
end function
```

(a) Help function for Unintrusive

```
function Unintrusive(Ĝ, Ê_w)
  while (u, v) ← Pick(Ĝ, Ê_w) ≠ NIL
  do
    (Ĝ, Ê_w) ← Merge((Ĝ, Ê_w), u, v)
  end while
  return (Ĝ, Ê_w)
end function
```

(b) Unintrusive

```
function Greedy(Ĝ, Ê_w)
  while Ê_w ≠ ∅ do
    (u, v) ← Find-Heaviest(Ê_w)
    if Legal(Ĝ, u, v) then
      (Ĝ, Ê_w) ← Merge((Ĝ, Ê_w), u, v)
    else
      Remove edge (u, v) from Ê_w
    end if
  end while
  return (Ĝ, Ê_w)
end function
```

(c) Greedy

```
function MergeMask(Ĝ, Ê_w, M)
  f ← true                          ▷ Fusibility flag
  for i ← 0 to |Ê_w| − 1 do
    if M_i = 1 then
      (u, v) ← the i'th edge in Ê_w
      if not Legal(Ĝ, (u, v)) then
        f ← false
      end if
      (Ĝ, Ê_w) ← Merge((Ĝ, Ê_w), u, v)
    end if
  end for
  return ((Ĝ, Ê_w), f)
end function
```

(d) Help function for Optimal

```
function Optimal(Ĝ, Ê_w)
  (Ĝ, Ê_w) ← Unintrusive(Ĝ, Ê_w)
  for (v, u) ← |Ê_w| do
    if not Legal(Ĝ, (u, v)) then
      Remove edge (u, v) from E_w
    end if
  end for
  S_min ← Greedy(Ĝ, Ê_w)            ▷ Guess
  M_{0..|Ê_w|} ← 1                  ▷ Fill array M
  o ← 0                             ▷ The mask offset
  Q ← ∅
  Enqueue(Q, (M, o))
  while Q ≠ ∅ do
    (M, o) ← Dequeue(Q)
    (S, f) ← MergeMask(Ĝ, Ê_w, M)
    if cost(S) < cost(S_min) then
      if f then
        S_min ← S                   ▷ New best partition
      end if
      for i ← o to |M| − 1 do
        M' ← M
        M'_i ← 0
        Enqueue(Q, (M', i + 1))
      end for
    end if
  end while
  return S_min
end function
```

(e) Optimal

Figure 5: The partition algorithms. The function $\mathsf{cost}(S)$ returns the partition cost of the WSP state S.

$u \in B$ and $v \in B'$. That is, the vertices are the blocks, connected by the edges that cross block boundaries.

From this we build the state needed in WSP computations:

Definition 15 (WSP state). *Given a WSP-instance $G = (V, E_d, E_f, \mathsf{cost})$ and a partition P, the* WSP state *is $\hat{G}(P) = (P, \hat{E}_d(P), \hat{E}_f(P))$ together with a complete weighted graph $(P, \hat{E}_w(P))$ with weights:*

$$w(B_1, B_2) = \mathsf{cost}(P) - \mathsf{cost}(P/(B_1, B_2)).$$

Notice that $w(B_1, B_2) = \mathsf{saving}(B_1, B_2)$ for the Bohrium cost function, as shown in Prop. 1, and does not require a full cost calculation.

Definition 16 (Merge operator). *We extend the merge operator of Def. 4 to partition graphs as $\hat{G}(P)/(B_1, B_2) = \hat{G}(P/(B_1, B_2))$. This acts exactly as a vertex contraction on the partition graph.*

The merge operator is commutative in the sense that the order in a sequence of successive vertex contractions doesn't affect the result [32]. An auxiliary function, Merge, is used in each algorithm to update the state.

Definition 17. *For a WSP state $S = (\hat{G}, \hat{E}_w)$, we define*

$$\text{Merge}(S, u, v) = (\hat{G}/(u, v), \hat{E_w}')$$

where $\hat{E_w}'$ is the updated weight graph on the edges incident to the new vertex $z = u \cup v$.

The complexity of Merge is dominated by the weight update, which for Bohrium requires a saving computations per edge incident to the merged vertex, and is bounded by $\mathcal{O}(V)$. If one uses an arbitrary cost-function, a full cost-calculation is needed for every edge.

We next need a local condition for when a merge is allowed:

Lemma 1 (Legal merge). *Let $P_{1,2} = P/(B_1, B_2)$ be the successor to a legal partition $P \in \hat{\Pi}_V$, derived by merging blocks B_1 and B_2. Then $P_{1,2} \in \hat{\Pi}_V$ if and only if*

1. *$(B_1, B_2) \notin \hat{E}_f(P)$, and*
2. *there is no path of length ≥ 2 from B_1 to B_2 in the partition graph $(P, \hat{E}_d(P))$.*

Proof. Recall that $\hat{\Pi}_V$ is the subset of partitions in Π_V that satisfy Def. 5. Because P is legal, no block contains an edge in E_f. Hence $P_{1,2}$ obeys Def. 5(1) if and only if no two vertices $u \in B_1$ and $v \in B_2$ are connected in E_f, or equivalently, $(B_1, B_2) \notin \hat{E}_f(P)$.

Similarly, by assumption, there are no cycles in $\hat{E}_d(P)$. Thus, $P_{1,2}$ violates Def. 5(2) if and only if $\hat{E}_d(P)$ contains a path $B_1 \to B' \to \cdots \to B_2$, forming the cycle $B_{1,2} \to B' \to \cdots \to B_{1,2}$ in $\hat{E}_d(P_{1,2})$ (where $B_{1,2} = B_1 \cup B_2$). □

An auxiliary function, Legal(P, B_1, B_2), is used in each algorithm to check if merging the blocks, $B_1, B_2 \in P$, will violate the two conditions in Lemma 1. The complexity of Legal is $\mathcal{O}(V + E)$.

Proposition 2 (Reachability by legal merges). *Given two legal partitions $P < P'$, there exists a successor* *chain $P \prec P_1 \prec P_2 \prec \cdots \prec P'$ entirely contained in $\hat{\Pi}_V$, i.e. corresponding only to legal block merges.*

PROOF. A successor chain $P \prec P_1 \prec \cdots \prec P_{n-1} \prec P'$ always exists in the total set of partitions Π_V, and all such chains are of the same length n. Any such chain contains no partition that violates Def. 5(1): each step is a merge, so if a fuse-preventing edge were placed inside a block, it would be included also in a block from P'. Hence we only need to worry about Def. 5(2).

We now show by induction that a successor chain consisting of only legal partitions exists. First, if $P \prec P'$, it is trivially so. Assume now that the statement is true for all $n \leq N$, and consider $P < P'$ of distance $N+1$.

Pick any successor chain from P to P'. If any step violates Def. 5(2), then let $P_{i+1} = P_i/(B_1, B_2)$ be the first partition in the chain that does so. Then there is a path $B_1 \to B \to \cdots \to B_2$ in the transitive reduction of $\hat{E}_d(P_i)$. Because P' satisfies Def. 5(2), $B_1 \cup B \cup B_2$ is contained in a block from P', whereby $P'_{i+1} \equiv P_i/(B_1, B) < P'$. This merge introduces no cycles, because the path is in the transitive reduction. Now let $P'_{i+1} \prec P'_{i+2} \prec \cdots \prec P'$ be a legal successor chain of length $N-i$, known to exist by hypothesis. Then $P \prec P_1 \prec \cdots \prec P_i \prec P'_{i+1} \prec \cdots \prec P'$ is a length-$(N+1)$ successor chain consisting of only legal partitions, concluding the proof by induction. □

In particular, the optimal solutions can be reached in this way from the bottom partition $\bot = \{\{v_1\}, \{v_2\}, \ldots, \{v_n\}\}$, which we will use in the design of the algorithms.

6.2 Unintrusive Partition Algorithm

In order to reduce the size of the partition graph to be analyzed, we apply an unintrusive preconditioner where we merge vertices that are guaranteed to be part of an optimal solution. Consider the two vertices, a, e, in Fig. 4. The only beneficial merge possibility a has is with e, so if a is merged in the optimal solution, it is with e. Now, since fusing a and e will not impose any restriction to future possible vertex merges in the graph, the two vertices are said to be *unintrusively fusible.* We formalize this property using the *non-fusible sets*:

DEFINITION 18 (θ, NON-FUSIBLE SET).
The non-fusible *set, $\theta[b]$ for a block b is the set of blocks connected with b in $\hat{E}_d$ through a path containing a non-fusible edge.*

THEOREM 3. *Given a partition graph $\hat{G}$, let $z = u \cup v$ be the merged vertex in $\hat{G}/(u, v)$. The vertices u and v are* unintrusively fusible *whenever:*

1. *$\theta[u] = \theta[v] = \theta[z]$, i.e. the non-fusibles are unchanged.*

2. *Either u or v is a pendant vertex in $\hat{E}_d$, i.e. the degree of either u or v must be 1.*

PROOF. If Condition 1 is satisfied, any merge that is disallowed at a further stage due to Def. 5(1) would be disallowed also without the merge. Similarly, merging a pendant vertex with its parent does not affect the possiblity of introducing cycles through future merges (Def. 5(1)). Finally, since the cost function is monotonic, the merge cannot adversely affect a future cost. □

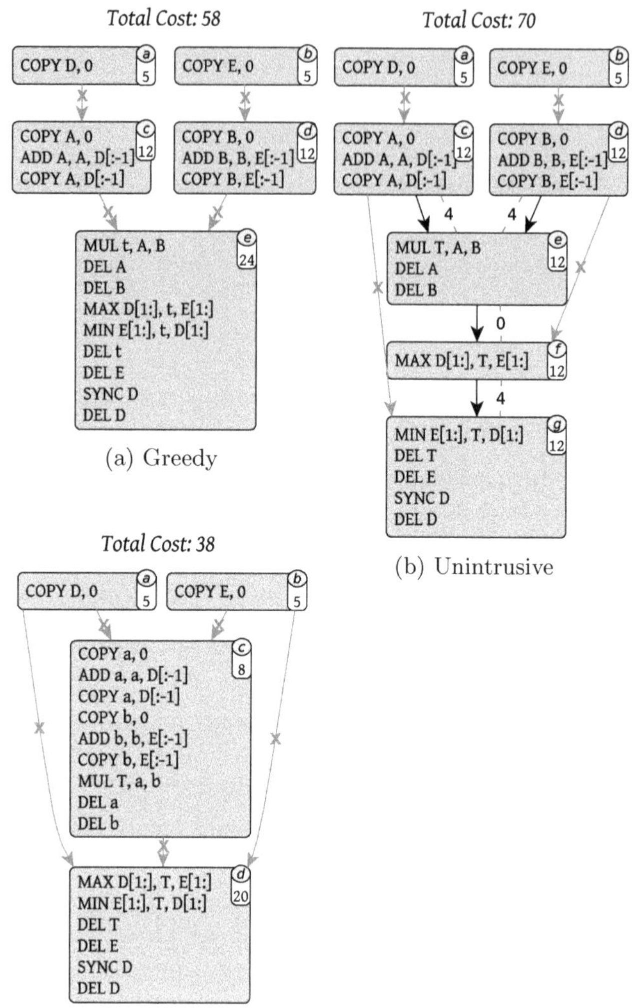

(a) Greedy

(b) Unintrusive

(c) Optimal

Figure 6: Three partition graphs that are the result of running the three partition algorithms with the problem in Fig. 4 as input. Lowercase variable names indicate that they are array contracted.

Fig. 5b shows the unintrusive partitioning algorithm. It uses a helper function, PICK, to find two vertices that are unintrusively fusible. The complexity of PICK is $\mathcal{O}(E(E+V))$, which dominates the while-loop in UNINTRUSIVE, whereby the overall complexity of the unintrusive merge algorithm is $\mathcal{O}(E^2(E+V))$. Note that there is little need to further optimize UNINTRUSIVE since we will only use it as a preconditioner for the optimal solution, which will dominate the computation time.

Fig. 6b shows an unintrusive partition of the Python example with a partition cost of 70. However, the significant improvement is the reduction of the number of weight edges in the graph. As we shall see next, in order to find an optimal graph partition in practical time, the number of weight edges in the graph must be modest.

6.3 Greedy Partition Algorithm

Fig. 5c shows a greedy merge algorithm. It uses the function FIND-HEAVIEST to find the edge in E_w with the greatest weight and either removes it or merges over it. Note that FIND-HEAVIEST must search through E_w in each iteration since MERGE might change the weights.

The number of iterations in the while loop (line 2) is $\mathcal{O}(E)$ since at least one weight edge is removed in each iteration either explicitly (line 7) or implicitly by MERGE (line 5). The complexity of finding the heaviest (line 3) is $\mathcal{O}(E)$, calling LEGAL is $\mathcal{O}(E+V)$, and calling MERGE is $\mathcal{O}(V)$ thus the overall complexity is $\mathcal{O}(VE)$.

In [11], Kennedy describes the problem of introducing transitively redundant edges that circument unfusible edges when merging vertices. Our algorithm solves the same problem, in the same time complexity, without introducing extra bookkeeping data structures. In Fig. 5c, transitively redundant edges are removed as they are encountered on the fly (line 7), rather than by explicity performing a full transitive reduction for each step.

Fig. 6a shows a greedy partition of the Python example. The partition cost is 58, which is a significant improvement over no merge. However, it is not the optimal partitioning, as we shall see later.

6.4 Optimal Partition Algorithm

Because the WSP problem is NP-hard, we cannot in general hope to solve it exactly in polynomial time. However, we may be able to solve the problems within reasonable time in common cases given a carefully chosen search strategy through the 2^E possible partitions. For this purpose, we have implemented a branch-and-bound algorithm, exploiting the monotonicity of the partition cost (Def. 6(2)).

The idea is as follows: We consider both legal and illegal partitions, and begin with the $\top$-partition, where everything is one block, but which in general is illegal. Each recursion step cuts a weight edge that has not been considered before, if it yields a cost that is strictly lower than the currently best legal partition $G_{\min}$ (if the cost is higher than for $G_{\min}$, no further splitting will make it better, and its search subtree can be ignored). If we reach a legal partition, this will be the new best candidate, and no further splitting will yield a better one. When the work queue is empty, $G_{\min}$ holds an optimal solution to WSP.

The feasibility of this scheme relies on two things: Before starting, the largest *unintrusive* partition is found. This is the largest partition that we can ensure is included in any optimal partition. The blocks of the unintrusive partition will be the vertices in our initial partition graph, reducing the problem size without affecting the optimal solutions. Second, a good suboptimal solution is computed before starting the branch and bound, so that we begin with a $G_{\min}$ as close to optimal as possible. We use the greedy algorithm for this purpose, but any scheme will do.

Fig. 5e shows the implementation, Fig. 7 shows an example of a branch-and-bound search tree, and Fig. 6c shows an optimal partition of the Python example with a cost of 38.

6.5 Merge Cache

In order to amortize the execution time of applying the merge algorithms, Bohrium implements a merge cache of previously found partitions of array operation lists. Bohrium generates the stream of bytecode instructions at runtime, whereby many loop iterations will result in the same instruction lists issued many times. The merge cache utilizes this to amortize the overhead of computing the partitions over many iterations.

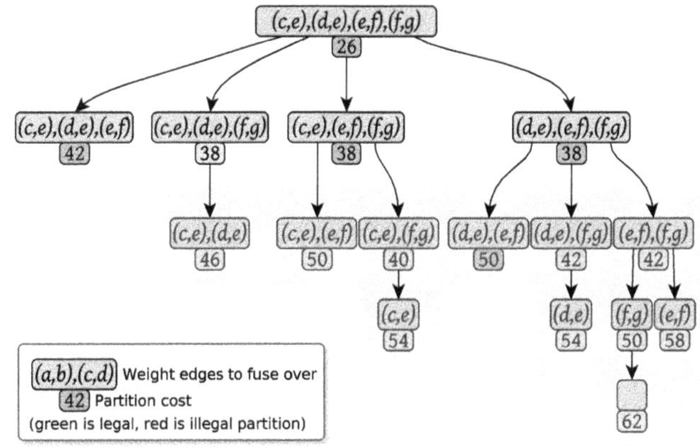

Figure 7: A branch-and-bound search tree of the unintrusively merged partition graph (Fig. 6b). Each vertex lists a sequences of vertex merges that build a specific graph partition. The grayed out area indicates the part of the search tree that a depth-first-search can skip because of the cost bound.

7. EVALUATION

This section consists of two parts. In the first part, we evaluate the performance of the greedy partition algorithm and the partitions it produces; and in the second part, we compare our cost model to alternative cost models used in related literature.

We execute a range of scientific Python benchmarks, which are part of an open-source benchmark tool and suite named Benchpress[5]. We run on an Intel Core i7-3770 machine with 4 CPU-cores and 32GB DDR3 of main memory. It is a standard installation of Ubuntu Linux 14.04.2 with GCC v4.8.4, Python v2.7.6, and NumPy 1.8.2. We run 40 iterations of each benchmark. When reporting execution times, we show the results of the mean of 5 identical executions as well as error bars that show the (very small) standard deviations from the mean.

Table 1 shows the benchmarks, the input sizes (in 64bit floats), and the reduction in the number of weight edges when preconditioning with the unintrusive partition algorithm. As the table shows, this reduction is very important for the exact branch-and-bound algorithm. E.g., for the Jacobi Solver, the number of weight edges is reduced from 69 to 10, which reduces the search tree from size 2^{69} down to 2^{10}. Even if the bound can cut 99.999% of the search tree away, 2^{69} is simply too large to solve in reasonable time, whereas 2^{10} partition combinations are very manageable.

7.1 Greedy Performance

In order to evaluate the greedy partition algorithm, we compare the execute time when Bohrium applies: no fusion, the greedy algorithm, and the optimal algorithm.

As expected the results in Fig. 8 show that fusion drastically improves performance with a best case speedup of 24 in the Rosenbrock benchmark. On the other hand, the

[5]Available at http://benchpress.bh107.org.

Benchmark	Input size	Edge Reduction	Complexity
Black Scholes	1.5×10^7	312 to 170	$\mathcal{O}(n)$
Jacobi Solver	9.000^2	69 to 10	$\mathcal{O}(n^2)$
Game of Life	10.000^2	43 to 11	$\mathcal{O}(n^2)$
Heat Equation	12.000^2	23 to 3	$\mathcal{O}(n^2)$
Leibnitz PI	10^8	49 to 13	$\mathcal{O}(n)$
Gauss Elimination	2800^2	2240 to 0	$\mathcal{O}(n^3)$
LU Factorization	2800^2	2519 to 0	$\mathcal{O}(n^3)$
Monte Carlo PI	10^8	44 to 0	$\mathcal{O}(n)$
27 Point Stencil	350^3	85 to 2	$\mathcal{O}(n^3)$
Rosenbrock	2×10^8	43 to 7	$\mathcal{O}(n)$

Table 1: Benchmark programs.

performance is almost identical for the greedy and optimal partitions. Only the Jacobi Solver and the 27-Point Stencil benchmark differ – optimal is respectively 33% and 10% better than greedy. This indicates that greedy approximates optimal well enough to make the programs computation bound.

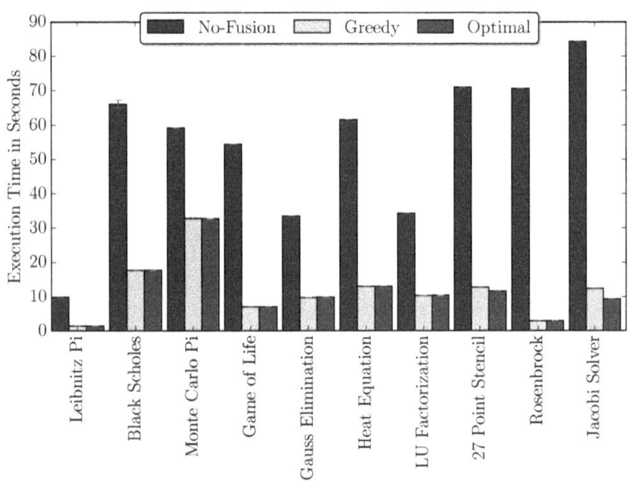

Figure 8: Execution time of the different partition algorithms.

We would like to point out that even though we are using benchmarks implemented in Python/NumPy that use Bohrium, the performance is comparable to traditional high-performance languages such as C and Fortran. This is because Bohrium overloads NumPy array operations [14], JIT compiles and execute them in parallel seamlessly [21]. Table 2 compares Bohrium runtimes with a serial C99 implementation, as well as a regular Python/NumPy execution. For the Heat Equation, the C99 version outperform Bohrium, but in the other four benchmarks, Bohrium is marginally faster than the C99 implementation due to automatic optimization that is difficult to perform by hand. Furthermore, Bohrium achieves good parallel speedup in most benchmarks when utilizing all four CPU-cores. The plain Python/ NumPy execution is a few times slower than both C99 and Bohrium for most benchmarks.

7.2 Alternative Cost Models

With the theoretical and practical framework we are presenting in this paper, it is straightforward to explore the impact of alternative cost models. In this section, we will do exactly that – replace our cost model with alternative cost models and evaluate the effect on the execution time of the generated code.

	C99	Bohrium		NumPy
Threads	1	1	4	1
Leibnitz Pi	1	0.99	0.25	1.79
Black Scholes	1	0.95	0.25	4.76
Monte Carlo Pi	1	0.98	0.25	1.11
Heat Equation	1	1.45	0.87	5.00
Rosenbrock	1	0.96	0.27	7.69

Table 2: Normalized runtime of Bohrium using greedy fusion, compared to a serial C99, and a native NumPy run, using the execution time of C99 as the baseline (lower is better). The timings are for full runs, including overhead from analysis.

Let us define and evaluate three alternative cost models, Contract, Reuse, and Robinson, which are used in related literature [8, 24, 26]:

Definition 19. *The cost model* Contract *defines the cost of a partition, P, of array operations, A, as follows:*

$$\mathsf{Contract}(A, P) = |\mathsf{new}[A]| - \sum_{B \in P} |\mathsf{new}[B] \cap \mathsf{del}[B]| \quad (5)$$

where $|\mathsf{new}[A]|$ is the total number of allocated arrays. Thus, in this cost model, all arrays that are not replaced by scalars add 1 to the cost.

Definition 20. *The cost model* Reuse *defines the cost of a partition, P, of array operations, $A = f_1, \ldots, f_n$, as follows:*

$$\mathsf{Reuse}(A, P) = \sum_{i=1}^{n} \sum_{j=i+1}^{n} \beta_{i,j} \left(|\mathsf{out}[f_i] \cap \mathsf{in}[f_j]| + |\mathsf{in}[f_i] \cap \mathsf{in}[f_j]|\right) \quad (6)$$

where $\beta_{i,j} = 1$ if f_i, f_j belong to different blocks, and 0 otherwise. In other words, each pair of un-fused array accesses contributes a cost of 1. NB: Since this sums over all pairs of identical array accesses, it incorrectly calculates a cost reduction of $n(n-1)/2$ for fusing n accesses to the same array.

Definition 21. *The cost model* Robinson *defines the cost of a partition, P, of array operations, A, as follows:*

$$\mathsf{Robinson}(A, P) = |P| + N \cdot \mathsf{Contract}(A, P) + N^2 \cdot \mathsf{Reuse}(A, P) \quad (7)$$

where N is the total number of accessed arrays. In other words, this cost model combines Reuse, Contract, *and penalizes the number of partition blocks (in that priority). Furthermore, the size of N guaranties that* Reuse *is given more priority over* Contract *which in turn is given priority over the number of partition blocks.*

In Fig. 9, we compare the performance of the different cost models. We show the Game of Life and Jacobi Solver benchmarks because they are affected the most when changing cost model, but in every case the Bohrium cost model

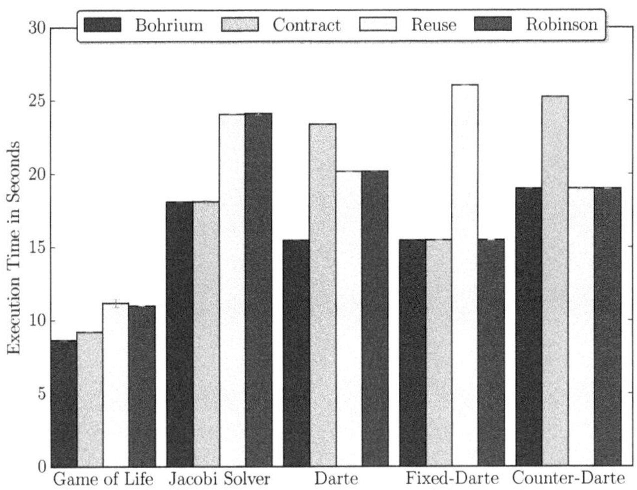

Figure 9: Execution time of the different cost models using the **Optimal** partition algorithm.

performs the best. Additionally, we show two micro benchmarks, Darte and Fixed-Darte, which originate from Darte [8] and our own micro benchmark, Counter-Darte, which is a Darte counterexample.

In Game of Life, the Bohrium cost model performs 7% better than Contract and 28% better than Reuse and Robinson. In Jacobi Solver, the Bohrium and Contract cost model perform 33% better than Reuse and Robinson.

The Darte benchmark is a reimplementation of the Fortran program in Fig. 10(a), which uses assignment statements, such as `+=` and `*=`, in order to avoid introducing anonym arrays not in the Fortran program. In the Darte benchmark, Bohrium is 31%−51% faster than the other cost models. The explanation for this is evident in Fig. 10(b)-(d) that shows how Contract misses the opportunity to fuse the second and third kernel and how Reuse and Robinson overestimate the advantages of reusing the `E[1:N]` access.

Now, consider the different partitions of the Darte benchmark – they all have a Contract partition cost of 67 (Table 3). This means that the performance of an optimal Contract partition can range from being the slowest of all partition algorithms to being on par with Bohrium.

In the Fixed-Darte benchmark, we manually fuse all array operations that lies on the same Fortran code line before running our partition algorithms. We do this to compare with the same partitions that Darte uses in [8]. As in [8], Contract outperforms Reuse significantly because Reuse only replaces three out of five possible arrays by scalars (Fig. 10(e)-(f)).

Finally, we have the Counter-Darte benchmark (Fig. 11) where Bohrium, Reuse, and Robinson fuse the two `gather()` operations, whereas Contract replaces the `A` array with a scalar instead. In this case, prioritizing data reuse over array contraction results in a 33% performance improvement.

Overall, the evaluation shows that our Bohrium cost model outperforms or is on a par with all the alternative cost models.

7.3 Array Streaming on GPUs

In array programming languages, generators (such as random), and reductions (such as sum), will typically produce and consume whole array axes. For example, the `Monte Carlo Pi` program consist of a generator that creates an array with random data, a number of element-wise array operations on this data, and finally a summation of all elements. NumPy-style array operations naively initialize the array in memory, but in fact no memory and only a constant number of registers per-thread are needed. More generally, programs written using only matching array programming primitives can completely eliminate temporary memory overhead. Each output element is calculated independently, and memory is only accessed for reading input and writing the final output, because all calculations are performed in per-thread registers. This technique is known as *streaming* and can significantly improve overall performance and memory use. It is especially important on GPUs due to the limited on-board memory.

In [13], we have applied the methods and programs presented in the present paper to implement array streaming in Bohrium through fusion and array contraction. For benchmarking, we used the Contract cost model to find partitions that maximize the number of array contractions and hence the operation sequences that can be streamed. The kernels were JIT compiled and executed on GPUs through OpenCL.

The results are very promising: we were able to run input three orders of magnitude larger than what was possible to run without streaming, and achieved near-perfect GPU-utilization and parellelization for large input sizes. Even for small examples that fit in GPU memory, we saw a significant speedup: The Monte Carlo Pi benchmark, an x-ray simulator, and a solar magnetic field extrapolation code saw, respectively, a 280%, 430%, and 380% speedup compared to unstreamed Bohrium for the largest calculations that fit in the 3GB onboard memory. These numbers include the overhead of fusion analysis and JIT-compilation. For larger sizes, native NumPy and unstreamed Bohrium simply run out of memory, while streaming-enabled Bohrium had no problem running calculations 1000 times larger.

		Partition Cost			
Benchmark	Partition Algo.	Bohrium	Contract	Reuse	Robinson
Darte	Bohrium	8	67	4	2451
Darte	Contract	10	67	5	3076
Darte	Reuse & Robinson	9	67	3	1899
Fixed-Darte	Bohrium & Contract & Robinson	8	67	4	2451
Fixed-Darte	Reuse	11	69	4	2547
Counter-Darte	Bohrium & Reuse & Robinson	11	61	3	1674
Counter-Darte	Contract	12	60	4	2202

Table 3: The cost of different partitions of the Darte, Fixed-Darte, and Counter-Darte benchmark. The Bohrium cost values has been normalized to the array size.

8. FUTURE WORK

The cost models we present in this paper are abstract – they do not take the memory architecture of the execution hardware into account. Since the WSP formulation makes it easy to change the cost model, we plan to develop cost models that, in detail, model architectures such as NUMA CPU, GPU, Intel Xeon Phi, and distributed shared-memory machines. Furthermore, since the only requirement to the

```
A(1:N)=E(0:N-1)
B = A*2 + 3
C = B + 99
D(1:N) = A(N:1:-1)
      +A(1:N)
E = B + C*D
F = E*4 + 2
G = E*8 - 3
H(1:N)=F(1:N)
      +G(1:N)
      *E(2:N+1)
```

(a)

```
def Darte(A,E):
  N = len(E)-2
  A[1:N] = E[0:N-1]
  b = A[1:N]*2
  b += 3
  c = b + 99
  d=A[N:1:-1]+A[1:N]
  E[1:N] = b
  E[1:N] += c
  E[1:N] *= d
  f = E[1:N]*4
  f += 2
  g = E[1:N]*8
  g -= 3
  H = f + g
  H *= E[2:N+1]
  return H
```

(b) Bohrium

```
def Darte(A,E):
  N = len(E)-2
  A[1:N] = E[0:N-1]
  b = A[1:N]*2
  b += 3
  c = b + 99
  d=A[N:1:-1]+A[1:N]
  E[1:N] = b
  E[1:N] += c
  E[1:N] *= d
  f = E[1:N]*4
  f += 2
  g = E[1:N]*8
  g -= 3
  H = f + g
  H *= E[2:N+1]
  return H
```

(c) Contract

```
def Darte(A,E):
  N = len(E)-2
  A[1:N] = E[0:N-1]
  b = A[1:N]*2
  b += 3
  c = b + 99
  d=A[N:1:-1]+A[1:N]
  E[1:N] = b
  E[1:N] += c
  E[1:N] *= d
  f = E[1:N]*4
  f += 2
  g = E[1:N]*8
  g -= 3
  H = f + g
  H *= E[2:N+1]
  return H
```

(d) Reuse & Robinson

```
def FixedDarte(A,E):
  N = len(E)-2
  A[1:N] = E[0:N-1]
  b = A[1:N]*2
  b += 3
  c = b + 99
  d=A[N:1:-1]+A[1:N]
  E[1:N] = b
  E[1:N] += c
  E[1:N] *= d
  f = E[1:N]*4
  f += 2
  g = E[1:N]*8
  g -= 3
  H = f + g
  H *= E[2:N+1]
  return H
```

(e) Contract & Bohrium & Robinson

```
def FixedDarte(A,E):
  N = len(E)-2
  A[1:N] = E[0:N-1]
  b = A[1:N]*2
  b += 3
  c = b + 99
  d=A[N:1:-1]+A[1:N]
  E[1:N] = b
  E[1:N] += c
  E[1:N] *= d
  F = E[1:N]*4
  F += 2
  G = E[1:N]*8
  G -= 3
  H = F + G
  H *= E[2:N+1]
  return H
```

(f) Reuse

Figure 10: A Fortran program fragment from [8], which is based on [10, 24] (refered to as Darte and Fixed-Darte in Fig. 9) and a reimplementation in Python/NumPy. (a) is the original Fortran version, (b)-(d) are the Darte benchmark, and (e)-(f) are the Fixed-Darte benchmark. The horizontal lines indicate kernels and lowercase variable names indicate arrays replaced by scalars. Table 3 shows the theoretical cost of the different partitions.

```
import bohrium as np
A = np.ones_like(T)
B = np.empty(len(T)+1)
B[1:] = A
C = B[1:]+T+np.gather(S,R)+A
D = B[:-1]+np.gather(S,R)
E = D + T + C
```

(a) Reuse & Bohrium & Robinson

```
import bohrium as np
a = np.ones_like(T)
B = np.empty(len(T)+1)
B[1:] = a
C = B[1:]+T+np.gather(S,R)+a
D = B[:-1]+np.gather(S,R)
E = D + T + C
```

(b) Contract

Figure 11: A Python/NumPy program that is a counterexample to the Darte program (Fig. 10). It shows that maximizing the amount of array contraction is not always best.

cost model is monotonicity, it is perfectly legal to have cost models that reward fusion of specific operation types, e.g. rewarding fusion of multiplication and addition instructions to make use of the FMA instruction set available on recent Intel and AMD microprocessors.

9. CONCLUSION

In this paper, we introduce the *Weighted Subroutine Partition Problem* (WSP), which unifies program transformations for fusion of loops, array operations, and combinators. Contrary to previous formulations of this problem, WSP assigns costs directly to partitions, which makes WSP able to handle many accurate cost models. We show that this is necessary if one wishes to maximize data locality correctly.

We prove that WSP is NP-hard and implement a branch-and-bound algorithm that finds an optimal solution, as well as a preconditioning partial solver that reduces the problem size without preventing the algorithm from finding the optimal solution.

We implement a greedy algorithm that finds a *good* solution to the WSP problem, works with any cost function, and is fast enough for Just-In-Time compilation (40 iterations is enough to amortize overhead).

We have incorporated the algorithms into the open source automatic parallelization framework Bohrium, using as the cost function the exact number of memory accesses remaining after fusion-enabled program transformations, generating Just-In-Time compiled computation kernels.

As expected, our evaluation shows that minimizing data accesses improves performance significantly. The 10 benchmarks we evaluate in this paper saw speedups ranging between 200% and 2400%, compared to no optimization.

However, our evaluation also shows that so long as a decent approximation to WSP is used, real-life performance is generally almost as good as when using the exact WSP solution. Out of 10 benchmarks, only two perform significantly better using the optimal algorithm, with approximately a speedup of 1.3 compared to the greedy approximation. This tells us that approximation algorithms will give us most of the savings, so more is won by making them faster than closer to optimal.

We show that the WSP formulation is general enough to express other optimization objectives from the literature. When optimizing data access reuse, we demonstrate that our WSP formulation outperforms traditional weighted graph formulations, such as the Weighted Loop Fusion Problem, because they must overestimate data reuse in certain cases, where WSP can track data reuse exactly.

Acknowledgements

We thank the reviewers, as well as Chen Ding, for their excellent feedback. This has greatly improved the manuscript.

James Avery was partially supported by the Danish Council for Independent Research *Sapere Aude* grant "Complexity through Logic and Algebra" (COLA).

10. REFERENCES

[1] A. Allam, J. Ramanujam, G. Baumgartner, and P. Sadayappan. Memory minimization for tensor contractions using integer linear programming. In *Proceedings of the 20th International Conference on Parallel and Distributed Processing*, IPDPS'06, pages 382–382, Washington, DC, USA, 2006. IEEE Computer Society.

[2] R. Allen and K. Kennedy. *Optimizing Compilers for Modern Architectures: A Dependence-based Approach.* Morgan Kaufmann Publishers, Oct. 2001.

[3] M. Berkelaar, K. Eikland, and P. Notebaert. *lpsolve : Open source (Mixed-Integer) Linear Programming system.*

[4] D. Callahan, S. Carr, and K. Kennedy. Improving register allocation for subscripted variables. In *Proceedings of the ACM SIGPLAN 1990 Conference on Programming Language Design and Implementation*, PLDI '90, pages 53–65, New York, NY, USA, 1990. ACM.

[5] S. Carr and K. Kennedy. Scalar replacement in the presence of conditional control flow. *Software: Practice and Experience*, 24(1):51–77, 1994.

[6] B. Chamberlain, S.-E. Choi, C. Lewis, C. Lin, L. Snyder, and W. Weathersby. Zpl: a machine independent programming language for parallel computers. *Software Engineering, IEEE Transactions on*, 26(3):197–211, Mar 2000.

[7] E. Dahlhaus, D. S. Johnson, C. H. Papadimitriou, P. D. Seymour, and M. Yannakakis. The complexity of multiway cuts. In *Proceedings of the twenty-fourth annual ACM symposium on Theory of computing*, pages 241–251. ACM, 1992.

[8] A. Darte and G. Huard. New results on array contraction [memory optimization]. In *Application-Specific Systems, Architectures and Processors, 2002. Proceedings. The IEEE International Conference on*, pages 359–370. IEEE, 2002.

[9] C. Ding and K. Kennedy. Improving effective bandwidth through compiler enhancement of global cache reuse. *J. Parallel Distrib. Comput.*, 64(1):108–134, 2004.

[10] G. Gao, R. Olsen, V. Sarkar, and R. Thekkath. Collective loop fusion for array contraction. In U. Banerjee, D. Gelernter, A. Nicolau, and D. Padua, editors, *Languages and Compilers for Parallel Computing*, volume 757 of *Lecture Notes in Computer Science*, pages 281–295. Springer, 1993.

[11] K. Kennedy. Fast greedy weighted fusion. *International Journal of Parallel Programming*, 29(5):463–491, 2001.

[12] K. Kennedy and K. McKinley. Maximizing loop parallelism and improving data locality via loop fusion and distribution. In *Languages and Compilers for Parallel Computing*, volume 768 of *Lecture Notes in Computer Science*, pages 301–320. Springer, 1993.

[13] M. R. B. Kristensen, J. E. Avery, T. Blum, S. A. F. Lund, and B. Vinter. Battling memory requirements of array programming through streaming. In *Proceedings of First International Workshop on Performance Portable Programming Models for Accelerators (P^3MA)*, Lecture Notes in Computer Science. Springer, 2016.

[14] M. R. B. Kristensen, S. A. F. Lund, T. Blum, and K. Skovhede. Separating NumPy API from Implementation. In *5th Workshop on Python for High Performance and Scientific Computing (PyHPC'14)*, 2014.

[15] M. R. B. Kristensen, S. A. F. Lund, T. Blum, K. Skovhede, and B. Vinter. Bohrium: Unmodified NumPy Code on CPU, GPU, and Cluster. In *4th Workshop on Python for High Performance and Scientific Computing (PyHPC'13)*, 2013.

[16] M. R. B. Kristensen, S. A. F. Lund, T. Blum, K. Skovhede, and B. Vinter. Bohrium: a Virtual Machine Approach to Portable Parallelism. In *Parallel & Distributed Processing Symposium Workshops (IPDPSW), 2014 IEEE International*, pages 312–321. IEEE, 2014.

[17] E. C. Lewis, C. Lin, and L. Snyder. The implementation and evaluation of fusion and contraction in array languages. In *Proceedings of the ACM SIGPLAN 1998 Conference on Programming Language Design and Implementation*, PLDI '98, pages 50–59, New York, NY, USA, 1998. ACM.

[18] A. W. Lim and M. S. Lam. Maximizing parallelism and minimizing synchronization with affine partitions. In *Parallel Computing*, pages 201–214. ACM, 1998.

[19] A. W. Lim, S.-W. Liao, and M. S. Lam. Blocking and array contraction across arbitrarily nested loops using affine partitioning. *SIGPLAN Not.*, 36(7):103–112, June 2001.

[20] D. Loveman. High performance fortran. *Parallel & Distributed Technology: Systems & Applications, IEEE*, 1(1):25–42, 1993.

[21] S. A. F. Lund and B. Vinter. Automatic mapping of array operations to specific architectures. *In submission to Elsevier journal on Parallel Computing*, 2015. Ref. PARCO-D-15-00170.

[22] N. Manjikian and T. S. Abdelrahman. Fusion of loops for parallelism and locality. *IEEE Trans. Parallel Distrib. Syst.*, 8(2):193–209, Feb. 1997.

[23] K. S. McKinley, S. Carr, and C.-W. Tseng. Improving data locality with loop transformations. *ACM Trans. Program. Lang. Syst.*, 18(4):424–453, July 1996.

[24] N. Megiddo and V. Sarkar. Optimal weighted loop fusion for parallel programs. In *Proceedings of the ninth annual ACM symposium on Parallel algorithms and architectures*, pages 282–291. ACM, 1997.

[25] S. Mehta, P.-H. Lin, and P.-C. Yew. Revisiting loop fusion in the polyhedral framework. In *ACM SIGPLAN Symposium on Principles and Practice of Parallel Programming, PPoPP '14, Orlando, FL, USA, February 15-19, 2014*, pages 233–246, 2014.

[26] A. Robinson, B. Lippmeier, and G. Keller. Fusing filters with integer linear programming. In *Functional High Performance Computing*, 2014.

[27] S.-B. Scholz. Single Assignment C: Efficient support for high-level array operations in a functional setting. *J. Funct. Program.*, 13(6):1005–1059, Nov. 2003.

[28] C. Y. Shei, A. Yoga, M. Ramesh, and A. Chauhan. Matlab parallelization through scalarization. In *2011 15th Workshop on Interaction between Compilers and Computer Architectures*, pages 44–53, Feb 2011.

[29] S. K. Singhai and K. S. McKinley. A parametrized loop fusion algorithm for improving parallelism and cache locality. *Comput. J.*, 40(6):340–355, 1997.

[30] Y. Song, C. Wang, and Z. Li. A polynomial-time algorithm for memory space reduction. *International Journal of Parallel Programming*, 33(1):1–33, 2005.

[31] S. Van Der Walt, S. Colbert, and G. Varoquaux. The numpy array: a structure for efficient numerical computation. *Computing in Science & Engineering*, 13(2):22–30, 2011.

[32] T. Wolle, H. L. Bodlaender, et al. A note on edge contraction. Technical report, Technical Report UU-CS-2004, 2004.

APPENDIX

A. ARTIFACT DESCRIPTION

A.1 Abstract

Performance evaluation of array operation fusion in Bohrium. In Section 7 of this paper, we perform an evaluation study. The present appendix describes how this can be reproduced. It requires a Linux system, preferably Ubuntu 14.04 or 16.04.

A.2 Description

A.2.1 Check-list (artifact meta information)

- **Algorithm**: loop fusion algorithm using branch-n-bound and greedy heuristics.
- **Program**: Bohrium and Benchpress.
- **Compilation**: GCC v4.8.4
- **Transformations**: Just-In-Time Compilation.
- **Run-time environment**: Ubuntu 14.04 or 16.04 and Bohrium v0.3.
- **Hardware**: CPU
- **Execution**: Sole user
- **Output**: JSON file with performance numbers
- **Experiment workflow**: the Benchpress run-script will run and produce graphs of the performance results
- **Experiment customization**: change number of threads
- **Publicly available?**: yes

A.2.2 How delivered

Both Bohrium and Benchpress is open source and available at github:

- **Bohrium version 0.3**: https://github.com/bh107/bohrium/archive/v0.3.tar.gz
- **Benchpress**: https://github.com/bh107/benchpress

A.2.3 Hardware dependencies

Multi-core x86-64 CPU with 12 GB of main memory

A.2.4 Software dependencies

Bohrium depends on a number of software libraries. See the installation script in the following.

A.3 Installation

An installation guide is also available at www.bh107.org/installation/linux.html. To install Bohrium on Ubuntu (default location `~/.local`), save the following bash script to `install.sh` in a new directory and run it by typing `source install.sh`.

```
#!/usr/bin/env bash
pushd .
sudo apt-get build-dep python-numpy
sudo apt-get install python-numpy python-dev swig python-cheetah cmake unzip cython libhwloc-dev \
libboost-filesystem-dev libboost-serialization-dev libboost-thread-dev libboost-regex-dev \
libboost-system-dev zlib1g-dev
wget https://github.com/bh107/bohrium/archive/v0.3.tar.gz -O bohrium.tgz
tar xzf bohrium.tgz
cd bohrium-0.3
mkdir build
cd build
cmake .. -DCMAKE_BUILD_TYPE=Release -DEXT_FFTW=OFF -DVE_GPU=OFF -DEXT_VISUALIZER=OFF \
-DBRIDGE_NUMCIL=OFF -DBRIDGE_CIL=OFF -DVEM_VISUALIZER=OFF -DVEM_PROXY=OFF -DTEST_CIL=OFF
make
make install
popd
export LD_LIBRARY_PATH=$HOME/.local/lib:$LD_LIBRARY_PATH
python bohrium-0.3/test/python/numpytest.py --file test_primitives.py #Remove the --file argument for a full test
wget https://github.com/bh107/benchpress/archive/master.zip
unzip master.zip
```

This will download Benchpress, Bohrium, and dependent libraries, build Bohrium, and run NumPy tests to check that everythings works.

A.4 Experiment workflow

Make sure that you are in the directory from which you ran install.sh, and set the following environment variables to run Benchpress and Bohrium:

```
export LD_LIBRARY_PATH=$HOME/.local/lib:$LD_LIBRARY_PATH
export PATH=$PWD/benchpress-master/bin:$PATH
export PYTHONPATH=$PWD/benchpress-master/module:$PYTHONPATH
```

Run the greedy performance benchmark suite (Fig. 8). This will take some hours to complete! (Notice that the warming "`[FUSE-CACHE] Couldn't find...`" is expected):

```
bp-run ./bohrium-0.3 ./benchpress-master/suites/pact16_greedy.py --runs 1 --verbose --output warmup_greedy.json
bp-run ./bohrium-0.3 ./benchpress-master/suites/pact16_greedy.py --runs 5 --verbose --output greedy.json
```

Run the cost model benchmark suite (Fig. 9). This will take some hours to complete!:

```
bp-run ./bohrium-0.3 ./benchpress-master/suites/pact16_cost_models.py --runs 1 --verbose --output warmup_cost_model.json
bp-run ./bohrium-0.3 ./benchpress-master/suites/pact16_cost_models.py --runs 5 --verbose --output cost_model.json
```

Compile the C99 implementations:

```
bp-compile --all
```

Run the Bohrium vs C99 vs NumPy benchmark suite (Table 2):

```
bp-run ./bohrium-0.3 ./benchpress-master/suites/pact16_BHvsC.py --runs 5 --verbose --output BHvsC.py.json
```

A.5 Evaluation and expected result

The performance results of the different partition algorithms as raw numbers:

```
bp-times greedy.json
```

The performance results of the different cost models as raw numbers:

```
bp-times cost_model.json
```

The performance results when comparing Bohrium, C99, and regular Python/NumPy:

```
bp-times BHvsC.py.json
```

In order to generate graphs, you need matplotlib:

```
sudo apt-get install python-matplotlib
```

Then run the following script in the directory of the **greedy.json** and **cost_model.json** files:

```
#!/usr/bin/env bash

FONTSIZE=16
SCRIPT_MAP="Leibnitz:,Black Scholes:,Monte:,Game of:,Gauss:,Heat:,kNN:,LU:,Monte:,27:,Shallow:,Rosenbrock:"

#Function to get the --stack-map option
#Arg1 is the price-model name and arg2 is the cache model
function stackmap {
  echo "$1/Singleton/$2/cpu:No-Fusion,$1/Naive/$2/cpu:Linear,$1/Greedy/$2/cpu:Greedy,$1/Optimal/$2/cpu:Optimal"
}

bp-grapher greedy.json --type bar_per_script --fontsize=${FONTSIZE} --format pdf --title unique_memcache \
--stacks-to-display="UniqueViews.*memcache" --stacks-not-to-display="Naive" --data-to-display elapsed --ymin 0 \
--stack-map "$(stackmap UniqueViews memcache)" --scripts-not-to-display="Lattice|Ice|SOR|NBody" \
--script-map "${SCRIPT_MAP}" --ylabel "Execution Time in Seconds"

STACK_MAP="UniqueView:Bohrium,TmpElem:Contract,MaxShare:Reuse,AmosRobinson:Robinson"
SCRIPT_MAP="Game of:,Jacobi:,Alain Example:Darte,Alain Example Fixed:Fixed-Darte,Alain Counterexample:Counter-Darte"

bp-grapher cost_model.json --type bar_per_script --fontsize=${FONTSIZE} --format pdf --title cost_models \
--stacks-to-display="Optimal.*filecache" --data-to-display elapsed --ymin 0 --ymax 30 --script-map "${SCRIPT_MAP}" \
--stack-map "${STACK_MAP}" --ylabel "Execution Time in Seconds" --xticklabel-rotation 0
```

Now, the generated graphs, **greedy.pdf** and **cost_models.pdf**, should be similar to the performance graphs in the paper (Fig. 8 and 9). Furthermore, the raw number of the Bohrium vs C99 should be similar to Table 2.

A.6 Experiment customization

The executions are specified in the Benchpress suite files:

- **benchpress-master/suites/pact16_greedy.py**
- **benchpress-master/suites/pact16_cost_models.py**

We will not provide a full guide of how to customize the suite files. Instead, we refer to: benchpress.readthedocs.io

Reduction Drawing: Language Constructs and Polyhedral Compilation for Reductions on GPUs

Chandan Reddy Michael Kruse Albert Cohen
INRIA and École Normale Supérieure, Paris, France
first.last@inria.fr

ABSTRACT

Reductions are common in scientific and data-crunching codes, and a typical source of bottlenecks on massively parallel architectures such as GPUs. Reductions are memory-bound, and achieving peak performance involves sophisticated optimizations. There exist libraries such as CUB and Thrust providing highly tuned implementations of reductions on GPUs. However, library APIs are not flexible enough to express user-defined reductions on arbitrary data types and array indexing schemes. Languages such as OpenACC provide declarative syntax to express reductions. Such approaches support a limited range of reduction operators and do not facilitate the application of complex program transformations in presence of reductions. We present language constructs that let a programmer express arbitrary reductions on user-defined data types matching the performance of tuned library implementations. We also extend a polyhedral compilation flow to process these user-defined reductions, enabling optimizations such as the fusion of multiple reductions, combining reductions with other loop transformations, and optimizing data transfers and storage in the presence of reductions. We implemented these language constructs and compilation methods in the PPCG framework and conducted experiments on multiple GPU targets. For single reductions the generated code performs on par with highly tuned libraries, and for multiple reductions it significantly outperforms both libraries and OpenACC on all platforms.

1. INTRODUCTION

A reduction is an associative and commutative operator on a collection of data elements that reduces its dimensionality. Reductions can be found in many computational applications such as image processing, linear-algebra, partial differential equations, computational geometry, statistical computing, machine learning, etc. They are often found in convergence tests of iterative algorithms and are executed repeatedly. For example, in Monte Carlo simulations averages and variances of a vast number of random simulations are repeatedly computed. A poorly optimized reduction will become a bottleneck for the whole program's performance. Imperative implementations of reductions apply a binary operator successively to all elements of the input set; this induces dependences between loop iterations and forces them to execute sequentially. Since reduction operators are associative and commutative, it is safe to ignore the sequential dependence, exposing parallelism and enabling more aggressive loop nest optimizations. Since reduction operators are associative, multiple reductions can also be performed in parallel and eventually combined to produce the final output. Furthermore, the reduction operator's commutativity can enable target-specific optimizations on massively parallel architectures such as GPUs.

To optimize reductions, we first need to identify them. Automatic detection of simple reductions with commonly used reduction operators such as addition, multiplication, minimum and maximum is well understood. However, when the reduction is performed on a user-defined data type or with a more complex operator, no existing compiler can do this automatically, even if it remains easy for the programmer to identify the associative and commutative operations and the variables involved in the reduction. Hence our proposal to introduce new language constructs to convey information about reductions to the compiler. For a compiler to optimize reductions, it needs to know the data type and identity element of the binary operation, the set of loop iterations carrying the reduction, and the actual associative and commutative operator. The language constructs we propose allow all this information to be expressed by the programmer with very little modifications to input code. Unlike the declarative syntax of parallel languages like OpenMP or OpenACC, these constructs are embedded into the semantics of the underlying imperative language.

Even after the reduction is identified, it is not trivial to optimize them on massively parallel architectures such as GPUs. Reduction operations typically have very low arithmetic intensity, performing one operation per load. Hence, they are bandwidth-bound and require many optimizations to achieve peak performance. Libraries such as CUB, Thrust provide a highly efficient implementation of reductions. They often achieve more than 90% percent of theoretical peak performance by means of a diverse range of optimizations, including architecture-specific instructions to accelerate reductions and tuning parameters for a given architecture. These libraries let the programmer customize reductions by providing an associative and commutative operator and its identity element; it is indeed easy to embed a single reduction into a library call. But when encountering multiple reductions on the same input data, or if performing the reduction on only a subset of the input elements, or combining the reduction with pre- and post-processing steps, these libraries are inefficient as they require multiple calls involving multiple array traversals. For example, consider a loop computing the minimal and maximal elements of an array simultaneously. A typical library

PACT '16, September 11–15, 2016, Haifa, Israel.
© 2016 ACM. ISBN 978-1-4503-4121-9/16/09...$15.00
DOI: http://dx.doi.org/10.1145/2967938.2967950

approach would need two function calls calls: one to find the minimum and an other one to find the maximum. This is inefficient as one could use a single traversal of the array to find both. In the same spirit, the SLAMBench computer vision application we consider in our experiments has a reduction kernel that performs 32 different reductions [17]. Using library calls in these cases will be highly inefficient. Although library APIs are highly efficient in their optimized use-cases, they are not flexible enough to adapt to all program requirements.

Reductions are usually bound by the maximum available bandwidth of the device. We can improve the arithmetic intensity of reductions by performing certain loop transformations such as loop fusion. Performing two reductions at once can be twice as fast as two separate reductions. In the latter case, input data is scanned twice, whereas in former input data is scanned just once and two reductions are performed per single load. It is also profitable to fuse the parallel map and reduce type of kernels. In order to enable such transformations, we extend the polyhedral framework of compilation to support reductions. In recent times, the polyhedral model has evolved to a powerful, practical and automatic framework to perform loop nest optimizations. We propose a dependence-based abstraction for reductions in the polyhedral model. This abstraction fits well into an existing polyhedral compilation toolchain and also enables loop transformations in the presence of reductions.

We propose a template-based code generator for reductions. It retains the ability to generate code for arbitrary polyhedral program representation, while embedding a reduction template implementing all the optimizations required to achieve peak performance. The code generation algorithm adapts this template to match the reductions defined by the programmer, and to coordinate the scheduling, storage mapping decisions and data transfers across reduction and non-reduction regions of the program. Building on the rich information about the source program's reductions carried by the new language constructs, it is possible to aggressively modify and specialize the template even after loop nest optimizations have been applied. It is also possible to auto-tune the reduction template for a given GPU architecture, to identify the optimal values for parameters such as block size, grid size, and the number reduction elements per thread. Overall, our approach allows generation of highly efficient code for sequences of user-defined reductions embedded into more general array- and loop-intensive computations, and to make that process portable across different architectures.

Building on a start-of-the-art polyhedral compilation flow capable of generating CUDA and OpenCL code from an ISO C program, we extended this framework to handle generalized reduction constructs and to generate efficient code for these. We evaluate our prototype with a selected set of reduction kernels extracted from the SLAMBench, SHOC and Rodinia benchmark suites. We present a performance comparison against highly tuned libraries such as CUB and Thrust, as well as with the PGI OpenACC compiler, targeting three different GPUs to assess the performance portability.

In summary, our main contributions are:

- language constructs embedded into ISO C as builtin functions allowing programmers to express custom reductions on arbitrary data types;
- the support for generalized reductions carried by imperfectly nested loops, and for indirect indexing in reduction arrays (subscripts of subscripts);
- a dependence-based abstraction of user-defined reductions in the polyhedral model to apply loop nest transformations on reductions;
- template-based code generation for custom reductions that are efficient and portable across multiple GPU architectures;
- the evaluation of several single reduction kernels and one complete application with many reductions on multiple GPU architectures.

2. ABOUT PENCIL

Our work builds upon PENCIL [1], a Platform-Neutral Compute Intermediate Language. This section reviews its essential design and syntactic elements.

PENCIL is intended as a target language for DSL compilers and as a high level portable implementation language for programming accelerators. A program domain expert with high-level knowledge about the relevant operations in a given domain knows a lot of information that could be useful to an optimizing compiler. Information regarding aliasing, parallelization, high level data flow and other domain specific information can be exploited by the compiler to perform more accurate static analysis, additional optimizations and to generate more efficient target-specific code. Such information can be difficult to extract by a compiler but might be easily captured from a DSL, or expressed by an expert programmer. PENCIL is a rigorously-defined subset of GNU C99 and provides language constructs that enable communication of this domain-specific information to the PENCIL compiler.

PENCIL was designed with following main objectives:

Sequential Semantics. Its sequential semantics simplifies DSL-to-PENCIL compiler development and flattens the learning curve of an expert directly developing in PENCIL. Note that the sequential semantics does not preclude the expression of information essential to parallelization, such as interprocedural side-effects and (in)dependence properties; but the user is not bound to any particular pattern(s) of parallelism.

Portability. Any standard C99 compiler that supports GNU C attributes is able to compile PENCIL. This ensures portability to platforms without OpenCL/CUDA support and allows existing tools to be used for debugging sequential PENCIL code.

Ease of analysis. The language simplifies static code analysis for a high degree of optimization. The main restriction of this is that the use of pointers is disallowed, except in specific read-only cases.

Support for domain-specific information. PENCIL helps domain experts and high-level DSL compilers to convey, in PENCIL, domain-specific information that can be exploited by the PENCIL compiler during optimization.

Figure 1 shows a high level overview of a PENCIL compiler framework. At the top level a DSL program is translated into PENCIL by a DSL-to-PENCIL compiler, applying domain-specific optimizations in the process.

PPCG is a polyhedral optimizer that performs loop nest transformations, parallelization, data locality optimization and generates efficient OpenCL or CUDA code [34]. PPCG was modified by the authors of PENCIL to handle the language's extensions [1]. It extracts the additional information provided through PENCIL extensions and uses it to apply the aforementioned transformations. This separation of domain-specific optimizations and general loop-level optimizations make PENCIL a lightweight general-purpose language applicable to a wide range of domains, and made it a

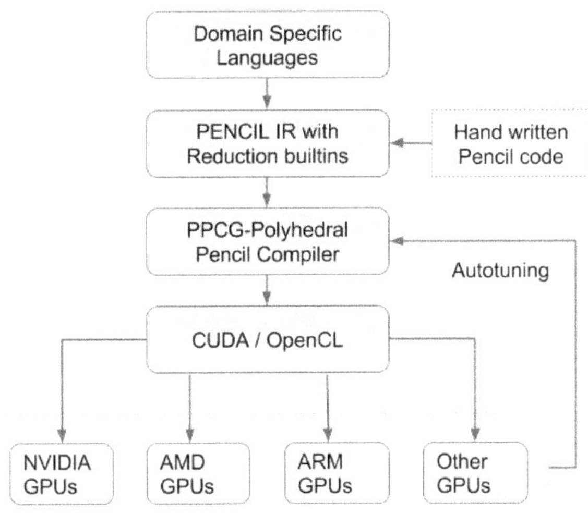

Figure 1: A high level overview of the PENCIL compilation flow

prime candidate for the prototyping of our reduction constructs and compilation methods. Our framework also supports auto-tuning of the generated code to find optimal parameter values for tile sizes, block sizes, grid sizes, etc. for a given target architecture.

We detail the most important restrictions imposed by PENCIL from the point of view of enabling GPU-oriented compiler optimizations. The PENCIL specification [2] contains the rules in full.

Sized, non-overlapping arrays. Arrays must be declared through the C99 variable-length array syntax [11], with the `static const restrict` C99 type qualifiers/keywords. As a shortcut, the `pencil_attributes` macro expands to the latter. Optimizations in the PENCIL compiler know about the length of arrays, and that arrays do not overlap.

Pointer restrictions. Pointer declarations and definitions are allowed in PENCIL, but pointer manipulation (including arithmetic) is not, except that C99 array references are allowed as arguments in function calls. Pointer dereferencing is also not allowed except for accessing C99 arrays. The restricted use of pointers is important for moving data between different address spaces of hardware accelerators, as it essentially eliminates aliasing problems.

No recursion. Recursive calls are not allowed, because they are not supported by accelerator programming languages such as CUDA or OpenCL.

Structured for loops. A PENCIL `for` loop must have a single iterator, a loop-invariant stop value and a constant increment (step).

The main constructs introduced by PENCIL include the `assume` and `kill` builtin functions, the `independent` directive and summary functions. They are described here very briefly, in a form extracted from the more complete description of [2, 1].

2.1 Summary Functions

Summary functions are used to describe the memory access patterns of (1) library functions called from PENCIL code, for which source code is not available for analysis, and (2) non-PENCIL functions called from PENCIL code to enable more precise static analysis. The concept is inspired from stub functions in PIPS [10] and shares the motivations of access specifications in Jade [29] and Access/Execute metadata [9]. As a distinctive feature, the concrete semantics of summary functions captures both may- and must-access information from a single imperative implementation.

```
__attribute__((pencil_access(summary_fft32)))
void fft32(int i, int j, int n,
           float in[pencil_attributes n][n][n]);

int ABF(int n, float in[pencil_attributes n][n][n])
{
  // ...
  for (int i = 0; i < n; i++)
    for (int j = 0; j < n; j++)
      fft32(i, j, n, in);
  // ...
}

void summary_fft32(int i, int j, int n,
           float in[pencil_attributes n][n][n]);
{
  for (int k = 0; k < 32; k++)
    __pencil_use(in[i][j][k]);
  for (int k = 0; k < 32; k++)
    __pencil_def(in[i][j][k]);
}
```

Figure 2: Example code illustrating the use of summary functions

Figure 2 shows an example use of summary functions. The code calls the function `fft32` (Fast Fourier Transform). This function only reads and modifies (in-place) 32 elements of its input array `in`, but does not modify any other parts of the input array. Without a summary function the compiler must conservatively assume that the whole array passed to `fft32` is accessed for reading and writing. Such a conservative assumption prevents parallelization. The effect of a calling `fft32` is given by its summary function `summary_fft32`. The PENCIL compiler derives accurate memory access information (reads and writes of 32 elements) `summary_fft32` enabling parallelization of the loop nest.

Summary functions are a powerful construct enabling polyhedral analysis and transformations for non-affine code. Traditional polyhedral compilers handle control flow with only affine conditionals. When dealing with non-affine parts and data dependent conditionals, one may create a function encapsulating such control flow regions and provide conservative memory accesses information through a summary function. A polyhedral compiler can now perform analyses and transformations based on the memory access information in the summary function. For example, we were able to pencilize the large SLAMBench application, rich in non-affine and data dependent control flow, using summary functions.

2.2 Assume Builtin

`__pencil_assume(e)` is an intrinsic function where e is a logical expression, indicating that e is guaranteed to hold whenever the control flow reaches the intrinsic. This knowledge is taken on trust by the PENCIL compiler, and may enable generation of more efficient code. An assume statement allows a programmer to communicate high level facts to the optimizer.

A *general 2D convolution* in image processing is a a good example that demonstrates the use of `__pencil_assume`. This image processing kernel calculates the weighted sum of the area around each pixel using a kernel matrix for weights. It can be helpful to know that the size of the convolution matrix (the matrix that holds the convolution kernel) is at most 15×15. This can be expressed using the assume builtin as follows:

```
__pencil_assume(kernel_matrix_rows <= 15);
__pencil_assume(kernel_matrix_cols <= 15);
```

This information enables a PENCIL compiler to perform optimizations such as unrolling the inner convolution loops or placing kernel matrix into shared memory.

2.3 Independent Directive

The `independent` directive is used to annotate loops. It indicates that the desired result of the loop execution does not depend in any way upon the execution order of the data accesses from different iterations. In particular, data accesses from different iterations may be executed simultaneously. In practice, the `independent` directive is used to indicate that the marked loop does not have any loop-carried dependences (i.e., it could be run in parallel).

Note that reductions are *not* allowed in a loop annotated with the `independent` directive, as they carry dependences along the successive iterations of the loop. This is a major limitation of PENCIL that we address in this paper.

2.4 Pencil Kill

The **`__pencil_kill`** builtin function allows the user to refine data flow information within and across any control flow region in the program. It is a polymorphic function that signals that its argument (a variable or an array element) is dead at the program point where **`__pencil_kill`** is inserted, meaning that no data flows through the argument from any statement instance executed before the kill to any statement instance executed after. The accurate data flow information avoids unnecessary data transfers between the host and accelerator.

3. REDUCTIONS IN PENCIL

Let us now present the PENCIL extensions to represent user-defined reductions. Figure 3 shows a sample reduction code of complex number multiplications. Automatic techniques for the detection of reductions have been proposed; see [6] for a survey of the polyhedral ones. However, most of these techniques can only detect a simple reduction with standard operators such as sum, max, min, etc. Real-world applications often involve user-defined reductions with custom reduction operators and user-defined data types. Moreover, reductions might be applied only to a range of array indexes. Automatic detection techniques are expensive and fail to detect such complex user-defined reductions. Often the programmer or the code generator for a high-level, domain-specific language, readily knows all information related to reductions. Hence, we provide PENCIL extensions that will allow a programmer to easily express arbitrary reductions.

We analyzed many benchmarks from different suites (SHOC, Rodinia, PolyBench, SLAMBench, etc.) and many DSLs (linear algebra, image processing, signal processing, etc.). Based on these, and considering the semantic constraints of embedding custom reduction information into a statically compiled imperative language with first order functions, we designed the following extensions that are natural and flexible enough to express all the reductions we have encountered. The programmer or DSL compiler needs to convey the following pieces of information regarding reductions to the underlying compiler: *reduction operator*, *identity element* and *reduction domain*. The reduction operator is a commutative and associative function of two arguments that returns one value of the same type. The identity element of the reduction operator is used to initialize the temporary variables that hold the intermediate result. The reduction domain represents the set of iterations for which the reduction operator is called, possibly spanning multiple nested loops.

Figure 4 shows a sample reduction kernel taken from the Srand benchmark of the Rodinia suite. Figure 5 shows the PENCIL version of Figure 4. All the information regarding reductions is expressed using two extensions of PENCIL: **`__pencil_reduction_var_init`** and **`__pencil_reduction`**.

```
typedef struct COMPLEX {
  int a;
  int b;
} Complex;

Complex multiply(Complex x,Complex y) {
  Complex z;
  z.a = x.a*y.a - x.b*y.b;
  z.b = x.a*y.b + x.b*y.a;
  return z;
}

Complex Reduce(const int N, Complex input[N]){
  int i;
  Complex product = {1.0, 0.0};

  for(i=0;i<N;i++)
    product = multiply(product, input[i]);

  return product;
}
```

Figure 3: Complex number multiplication

3.1 Reduction Initialization Builtin

`__pencil_reduction_var_init` is an intrinsic function that is used to express the identity element of the reduction operator. The first argument of this function is the address of the reduction variable. A reduction variable can be a scalar or an array element of a built-in type or a user-defined data type as in the example in Figure 6. The second argument is a function that will take reduction variable as an input and initialize it with the identity element. Having a simple function to initialize reduction variable provides the flexibility to handle initialization of any user-defined data types such as complex numbers. The function provided in **`__pencil_reduction_var_init`** is called by the compiler whenever it wants to initialize the temporary variable required to compute the reductions in parallel. This intrinsic function also marks the beginning of reduction domain.

3.2 Reduction Builtin

`__pencil_reduction` is another intrinsic function that is used to express a single reduction operation. The first argument for this function must be the address of the reduction variable. The second argument must be the current reduction element. The third argument is a function that implements the reduction operator. This function must accept two variables which are of the same type as the reduction variable and return the result of reduction operator. This function is assumed to be both commutative and associative. Every reduction variable must be introduced through an associated **`__pencil_reduction_var_init`** and operated upon through **`__pencil_reduction`**.

The domain of the reduction is the set of all dynaminc instances of **`__pencil_reduction`**.

We believe this intrinsic function approach is flexible enough to express most user-defined reductions.

3.3 Related work

Many programming languages provide high-level abstractions to express user-defined reductions. Google's Map Reduce [4] framework provides parallelization API through which a user can specify custom reduction functions. Intel TBB [28] provides parallel reduction templates that can be specialized through custom reduction methods. Similar to TBB, a user can express reductions in PPL [15]

```
int srand_reduction(int niter, int Nr, int Nc,
                    float image[Nr][Nc]){
  for (int iter=0; iter<niter; iter++) {
    float sum = 0.0; //S1
    float sum2 = 0.0; //S2

    for (int i = 0; i < Nr; i++) {
      for (int j = 0; j < Nc; j++) {
        sum += image[i][j]; //S3
        sum2 += image[i][j] * image[i][j]; //S4
      }
    }

    float meanROI = sum / NeROI; //S5
    float varROI = (sum2 / NeROI) - meanROI*meanROI;
    float q0sqr = varROI / (meanROI*meanROI);

    diffusion( Nr, Nc, q0sqr, image, c);
  }
}
```

Figure 4: Reduction from Rodinia's Srand benchmark

```
void initialize(float *val) {
  *val = 0.0;
}
float reduction_sum(float v1, float v2){
  return v1 + v2;
}

void srand_reduction(int niter, int Nr, int Nc,
                     float image[Nr][Nc]){
  for (int iter=0; iter<niter; iter++) {
    float sum;
    float sum2;
    __pencil_reduction_var_init(&sum2, initialize);
    __pencil_reduction_var_init(&sum, initialize);

    for (int i = 0; i < Nr; i++) {
      for (int j = 0; j < Nc; j++) {
        __pencil_reduction(&sum, image[i][j],
                           reduction_sum);
        __pencil_reduction(&sum2, image[i][j]*image[i][j],
                           reduction_sum);
      }
    }

    float meanROI = sum / NeROI;
    float varROI = (sum2 / NeROI) - meanROI*meanROI;
    float q0sqr = varROI / (meanROI*meanROI);

    diffusion( Nr, Nc, q0sqr, image, c);
  }
}
```

Figure 5: Example from Rodinia's Srand reduction in PENCIL

using parallel reduction templates. In both cases the user needs to pass explicitly the range of values to be reduced. Cilk++ [7] supports a limited number of reduction operators which are used to eliminate the contention of shared reduction variables by performing reductions in a lock-free manner.

MPI [16] includes support for several built-in reduction operators as well as the ability to define custom reduction operators in the context of distributed computing. In MPI, a user needs to create a custom function with fixed syntax which will be called by runtime while reduction is performed across multiple nodes. ZPL [5] relies on overloading for the specification of user defined reductions. The user needs to create two functions with specific signatures, one to return the identity element and another function that implements reduction operator.

OpenMP 3.0 and OpenACC [35] support built-in reduction operators through declarative pragma syntax. OpenMP 4.0 introduced user-defined reductions, specifying the custom associative and commutative function and identity element through a new directive:

```
void initialize(float *val){
  *val = 0.0;
}
float reduction_sum(float v1, float v2){
  return v1 + v2;
}

void kernel_correlation(int M, int N,
                        float data[M][N], float mean[M]){
  for (int j = 0; j < M; j++) {
    __pencil_reduction_var_init(&mean[j], initialize);
    for (int i = 0; i < N; i++)
      __pencil_reduction(&mean[j], data[i][j],
                         reduction_sum, NULL);
    mean[j] /= N;
  }
}
```

Figure 6: Example from PolyBench's correlation benchmark

`#pragma omp declare reduction`. More recently, OpenMP 4.5 introduced pointwise reductions over arrays in C and C++.[1] One may apply user-defined and pointwise array reductions to a specific for loop which forms the domain of the reduction. If multiple, imperfectly nested loops form the reduction domain, it is not directly possible to express it through OpenMP pragmas; the programmer needs to modify the loop structure to handle such cases. In our proposed approach the nesting depth of the reduction and its domain are inferred from reduction builtin locations, and such that the programmer does not need to modify the loop structure. Array reductions that are not pointwise—such as histograms or reductions over unstructured meshes—cannot be expressed in OpenMP or OpenACC.

4. MODELING REDUCTIONS WITHIN A POLYHEDRAL FRAMEWORK

In polyhedral compilation, an abstract mathematical representation is used to model the program and its transformations.

4.1 Polyhedral Framework

Each statement in the program is represented using three pieces of information: an *iteration domain*, an *access relations* and a *schedule*. This representation is first extracted from the program AST, which is then analyzed and transformed (loop optimizations are applied during this step), and finally it is converted back into an AST.

The *iteration domain* of a statement is a set that contains all the execution instances of the statement (a statement in a loop has an execution instance for each iteration where it is executed). Each execution instance of the statement in the loop nest is represented individually by an identifier for the statement and a sequence of integers (typically, the values of the outer loop iterators) that uniquely identifies the execution instance. Instead of listing all the integer tuples in the *iteration domain*, the integer tuples are described using quasi-affine constraints.

A quasi-affine constraint is a constraint over integer values and integer variables involving only the operators `+`, `-`, `*`, `/`, `%`, `&&`, `||`, `<`, `<=`, `>`, `>=`, `==`, `!=` or the ternary `?:` operator. An example of a quasi-affine constraint used in a loop nest is $10 \times i + j + n > 0$ where i and j are the loop iterators and n is a *symbolic constant* (i.e., a variable that has an unknown but fixed value throughout the execution). Examples of non quasi-affine constraints are $i \times i > 0$ and $n \times i > 0$.

In order to be able to extract the polyhedral representation, all loop bounds and conditions need to be quasi-affine with respect to

[1]See http://www.openmp.org for the complete specification.

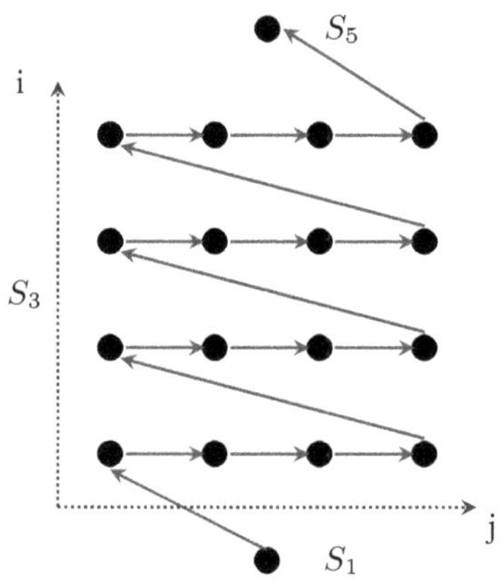

Figure 7: Original reduction domain and dependences

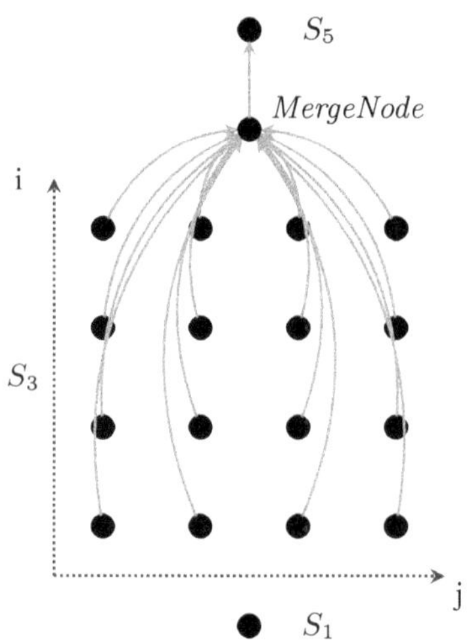

Figure 8: Modified reduction dependences

the loop iterators and a fixed set of symbolic constants. We will abbreviate this condition as *static-affine*.

The *access relations* map statement instances to the array elements that are read or written by those instances, where scalars are treated as zero-dimensional arrays. An accurate representation requires that the index expressions in the input program are static-affine. The *dependence relations* map statement instances to statement instances that depend on them for their execution. These dependence relations are derived from the access relations and the original execution order. In particular, two instances depend on each other if they (may) access the same array element, if at least one of those accesses is a write and if the first is executed before the second. Finally, the *schedule* determines the relative execution order of the statement instances. Program transformations are performed by modifying the schedule.

4.2 Reduction Domain

The reduction domain is defined as the set of all iterations on which the reduction operator is applied. In pragma-based languages such as OpenMP or OpenACC, the reduction domain is simply the loop that is annotated with a reduction pragma. In some benchmarks such as the Rodinia's Srand benchmark shown in Figure 4, the reduction domain is not a single for-loop. The programmer needs to coalesce (flatten) multiple loops into a single one before annotating it with pragmas. Whereas in PENCIL, since the programmer uses builtin functions that are not associated with a specific loop, no modifications of the control flow is required. Note that the reduction domain may not be same as the iteration domain of the `__pencil_reduction` statement. For example, the iteration domain of statement S_3 in Figure 4 is $\{S_3(iter, i, j) : 0 \leq iter \leq niter; 0 \leq i < nr; 0 \leq j < nc\}$ whereas, the reduction domain for the reduction in S_3 is $\{S_3(i, j) : 0 \leq i < nr; 0 \leq j < nc\}$. The reduction operation always starts with the initialization of the reduction variable, using `__pencil_reduction_var_init`. The reduction domain is derived from the iteration domains of the `__pencil_reduction_var_init` and `__pencil_reduction` statements. For each `__pencil_reduction` statement, the reduction variable—the first argument of the function—is looked up to find the dominating `__pencil_reduction_var_init` defining the same reduction variable. The reduction domain is obtained from the iteration domain of `__pencil_reduction` by considering the loop iterators of `__pencil_reduction_var_init` as parameters.

4.3 Reduction Dependences

The Figure 7 depicts the Read-after-Write (RAW) dependences of a single reduction for the program in Figure 4. The arrows between iterations indicate the flow of data, i.e., a value produced by the source iterator is read at the destination iteration. Because the reduction variable is read and written in all iterations of the reduction domain, there is a serial dependence between them. This dependence between iterations of the reduction domain is called a reduction dependence. This dependence usually forces the serial execution of the reduction. Since the reduction operator is associative, we can perform the reductions in parallel and then combine the partial results to obtain a final reduction value. The associativity of the reduction operation is abstracted by relaxing the reduction dependences. We can precisely compute these reduction dependences from the reduction domain. The reduction of partial results and synchronization needed to produce the end result is modeled by introducing an additional node in the dependence graph, called a *merge node*, and adding a new dependence from all iterations in reduction domain to the merge node as shown in Figure 8. These are called *reduction isolation dependences* are necessary to prevent the use of the reduction variable before the reduction operation is complete when the reductions are performed in parallel. The merge node is inserted right after the reduction loops in the input AST. The relaxation of the serial reduction dependences into parallelism-friendly reduction isolation dependences will accurately model the flow of data for the parallel execution of reductions.

4.4 Reduction-Enabled Scheduling

A schedule represents the execution order of statement instances in a program. Various transformations are performed by changing the schedule. Dependences are used to find the valid set of schedules. A schedule is said to be valid if does not violate dependences in the input program, i.e., all the source iterations of dependences are executed before the destination iterations. State-of-the-art polyhedral compilers are seriously limited in the application of affine transformations in the presence of reductions, because of the serial reduction dependence. They do not exploit the associativity of the reduction operator. The explicit dependence manipulation as explained in the previous section enables transformations such as tiling and parallelization of reduction loops. Because the serial reduction dependences are relaxed, the polyhedral scheduler can now safely reorder the reduction iterations.

A practical and automatic scheduling algorithm like Pluto takes a dependence graph as input and recursively constructs schedule. At each level of the recursion, the algorithm first checks for the components that do not depend on each other and hence can be scheduled independently. Within each component, the algorithm uses an ILP solver to construct a sequence of one-dimensional affine functions (hyperplanes), such that each of these functions independently respect all dependences and are optimal based on heuristics such as induced communication. After the construction of a band is completed, the dependence graph is updated to only contain dependences that are mapped to the same values by the current hyperplane, and the process is repeated until the number of hyperplanes found is equal to the dimensionality of the loop. Our dependence based abstraction of reductions fits well with the automatic scheduling algorithms enabling affine transformations for user defined reductions. Because the relaxation of serial reduction dependences, the reduction iterations can now be reordered and parallelized. The new merge dependences represent the required data-flow of combining the partial reduction results to produce the final reduction value. It is essential for the scheduler to know about the cost of performing reductions in parallel and merge dependences accurately represent this cost. For example, consider a loop nest with a parallel loop and a reduction loop. The scheduler should choose the parallel loop with no loop-carried dependences as the outermost loop rather than the reduction loop because of the cost of merge dependences. Hence, with this approach reduction parallelism is exploited and yields communication-free parallelism. Many of the previous approaches that just relax the reduction dependence have the problem of treating both types of parallelism equally which could be lead to poor schedules and additional communication.

4.5 Related work

Modeling reductions was commonly done implicitly, e.g., by ignoring the reduction dependences during a post parallelization step [12, 13, 21, 25, 22, 24, 36, 33]. The first one to introduce reduction dependences, where Pugh and Wonnacott [23]. Similar to most other approaches [26, 31, 27, 8] the detection and modeling of reductions was performed on imperative statements and utilizing a precise but costly access-wise dependence analysis. In the works of Redon and Feautrier [27, 26] the reductions are modeled as Systems of Affine Recurrence Equations (SAREs). Array expansion allow to eliminate the memory-based dependences induced by reductions and facilitate the recognition of induction patterns. They also propose a polyhedral scheduling algorithm that optimally schedules reductions together with other statements, assuming reductions are computable in single time step. Such atomic reduction computation simplifies scheduling choices while preventing schedules that reorder or interleave reduction statement instances with other statement instances. Gupta et al. [8] extended the work of Redon and Feautrier [26] by removing the restriction of an atomic reduction computation. Their scheduling algorithm tries to minimize the latency while scheduling reductions. Compared to these works our dependence based abstraction works on existing practical polyhedral scheduling algorithms such as Pluto [3]. Our approach does not require any preprocessing such as array expansion while dependences accurately model the specific atomicity constraints of reductions.

In contrast to polyhedral optimizations for reductions, Gautam and Rajopadhye [8] propose techniques to exploit the associativity and commutativity of reductions to decrease the complexity of a computation in the context of dynamic programming. Their method reuses intermediate results of reduction computations.

Stock et al. [30] describe how reduction properties can be used to reorder stencil computations, to better exploit register reuse and to eliminate loads and stores. However neither do they describe the detection method nor does their method enable scheduling for generic reductions.

Doerfert et al. [6] propose compiler techniques to automatically detect reductions on LLVM IR. They also propose a model to relax memory-based dependences to enable polyhedral scheduling in the presence of reductions. However, their techniques cannot detect reductions on arbitrary data types such as complex number multiplication and their reduction modeling do not account for the cost of reductions while scheduling them.

5. CODE GENERATION

Parallelizing reductions on GPUs is a challenging task. Reductions typically have low arithmetic intensity performing just one operation per memory load and hence are bound by the device's maximum memory bandwidth. The performance of reductions is often measured by the effective bandwidth achieved by a given implementation. Vendor and highly tuned libraries such as CUB and Thrust provide an optimized implementation of reductions achieving performance above 90% percent of the peak bandwidth.

5.1 Optimizations for Reductions on GPUs

The problem of Optimizing reductions in CUDA is well studied and the list of all the optimizations and their impact on performance for a single reduction is explained in [14]. The important optimizations are listed below.

Kernel Decomposition. The reduction is parallelized at two levels, matching the thread hierarchy of the GPUs. At the first level, each thread block is allocated a portion of the reduction domain. Within each thread block, a tree-based decomposition is used to perform local reductions and to produce partial results. These partial results are stored in global memory. At the second level, another kernel is launched to reduce the partial results and produce the final value.

Shared memory utilization. Within each thread block, multiple threads use shared memory to keep the intermediate reduction values. The tree-based reduction is performed on these values while avoiding divergent branches. Shared memory bank conflicts are avoided by reordering memory loads making use of the reduction operator's commutativity.

Complete unrolling. The kernel is specialized by completely unrolling the reduction tree. This is done using templates to generate a specialized kernel for different block sizes. This eliminates unnecessary control flow and synchronization between the threads in a thread block as the reduction proceeds.

Using shuffle instructions. Shuffle instructions [20] can be used to accelerate fine-grained reductions within a warp. These dedicated instructions control the exchange of data between threads, eliminating data accesses to shared memory and the associated synchronizations.

Multiple reductions per thread. Each thread loads and reduces multiple elements into shared memory before the tree-based reduction in shared memory. More work per thread will help to hide the memory latency. The optimal number of elements per thread depends on the architecture and is determined by tuning this parameter along with the number of blocks and threads per block.

5.2 Template Specialization for User-Defined Reductions

A generic polyhedral optimizer such as PPCG can perform various optimizations such as shared memory allocation and register promotion, memory coalescing, etc. for generic programs [34]. It uses heuristics to determine the profitability of such optimizations. However, it cannot perform all the specialized optimizations required for highly efficient reductions. Some of these optimizations are specific to reductions, and applicable only to specific hardware or device characteristics. Hence it is difficult to come up generic heuristics for these optimizations in order to make them applicable to generic programs. These optimizations are crucial to achieve close-to-peak performance on GPUs. Hence, we follow a template-based approach for generating efficient code for user-defined reductions. We precisely identified the reductions through programmer-provided constructs, hence can generate efficient reduction code capturing all the optimizations above, even on user-defined reductions.

User-defined reduction operator. A reduction is characterized by the reduction operator, its identity element, and the domain of the reduction. The new reduction operator is expressed in a separate PENCIL function. It is easy to adapt the parallel template to user-defined reductions by replacing the reduction operation with the user-defined function, and similarly for the partial value initialization. All these function calls are inlined to eliminate overhead. The reduction domain is equally distributed among multiple thread blocks.

Shared memory allocation. The parallel reduction template allocates temporary storage for each thread, to store partial results in the CUDA shared memory. In the case of a scalar, or pointwise array reduction, each thread only needs one scalar reduction accumulator to be stored in shared memory; generalized reductions may involve larger array segments. Yet the total shared memory available varies from device to device and depends on the optimal number of threads for each device. Therefore, the available shared memory limits certain transformations and thread block sizes. The maximum amount of shared memory on the device is an input to our framework. We then compute the shared memory required to implement the reduction and use it to calculate the maximum thread block size.

Fusing multiple reductions. The template can also be adapted to generate code for multiple fused reductions. Fusion can help increase the arithmetic intensity of the reduction. We use the following heuristic to determine when to fuse. Two reductions are fused if there is an overlap with global data accessed between them. For example, if two separate reductions operate on same input array, then these two reductions are fused and a single reduction template is generated. This optimization is always profitable since by fusion we are enabling data reuse in shared memory. Existing polyhedral techniques can be used to assess the correctness of such a fusion transformation, taking into account all side-effects involved in associated computations involved in the reductions (inductively or not). Code generation for fused reductions is a straightforward extension of the above-mentioned technique: the shared memory required is the sum of shared memory requirement for individual reductions and the two reduction functions are called one after another in the template.

Auto-tuning. The performance of the template depends on the target GPU. The following two parameters are tuned to obtain optimal performance on a given architecture: number of threads, and number of thread blocks. The reduction template supports powers of two only for the number of threads, so there are only few values considered starting from 2 and up to the maximum allowed by the device. The maximum is also limited by the required shared memory for the reduction. The thread block size varies over the 2 to 256 interval.

6. EXPERIMENTAL EVALUATION

We implemented PENCIL reduction support in a developmental branch of PPCG. Our framework takes a C program with PENCIL functions as input, with reduction kernels according to the specification. It generates CUDA code automatically, which is then auto-tuned to a particular GPU architecture. We selected a reduction template for scalar and pointwise array reductions, hence the absence of histogram (subscript of subscript) reductions in the experiments below. Since the auto-tuning search space is relatively small for our reduction template, we could conduct an exhaustive search of the optimization space within minutes on all examples.

We compare the performance of the generated code with highly tuned libraries such as CUB v1.5.1 [18] and Thrust v1.8.1 [19]. Both of these libraries provide APIs for performing reductions. The user can customize them by specifying a reduction operator and an identity value. Note that these libraries are optimized for a particular GPU architecture. CUB, for example, has an internal database of the optimal values for thread block size, number of threads and number of items per thread for all known architectures. We also compare the performance with the OpenACC PGI 2015 compiler [32], which provides high-level directives, including reduction pragmas, to program accelerators. Note that the PGI OpenACC compiler currently only supports a limited set of pre-defined reduction operators.

We evaluate performance on the following three GPU architectures: a desktop NVIDIA GTX 470 with peak memory bandwidth of 133.9 GB/s, the more advanced NVIDIA Quadro K4000 with peak bandwidth of 134.9 GB/s, and the low power embedded GPU NVIDIA Jetson TK1 with peak bandwidth of 14.78 GB/s. We do not present OpenACC numbers on TK1 because the PGI compiler does not support this architecture. All the benchmarks are compiled with the NVIDIA CUDA 7.5 toolkit, with the `-O3` optimization flag. Reduction performance is measured as the effective bandwidth utilized by the benchmark, and is computed using

$$\text{Bandwidth} = \text{InputArraySize}/\text{ReductionTime}.$$

Each benchmark is run 100 times and the average of these times is taken as the reduction time. We also perform a dry-run before benchmarking to hide device configuration and kernel compilation time. In the graphs below, performance numbers are presented as a percentage of peak bandwidth of the device.

6.1 Single Reduction Kernel

The first benchmark is a single sum reduction over an array of 2^{22} elements. This corresponds to a single call in CUB and Thrust, and to a single for-loop marked with a reduction pragma in OpenACC. The performance of the sum benchmark for three different data types is shown in Figures 9, 10 and 11, abbreviated as SumInt, SumFloat and SumDouble. CUB achieves an impressive 92.4% of the peak device bandwidth for int and 81.5% for double on the GTX 470. The performance of Thrust is slightly lower at 73.8% for int and float. OpenACC is only able to achieve 23.7% for int and 45.2 for double, whereas the PENCIL reduction code generated by our framework achieves 90.2% of the peak. This shows the impact of the various optimizations described in the Section 5. There

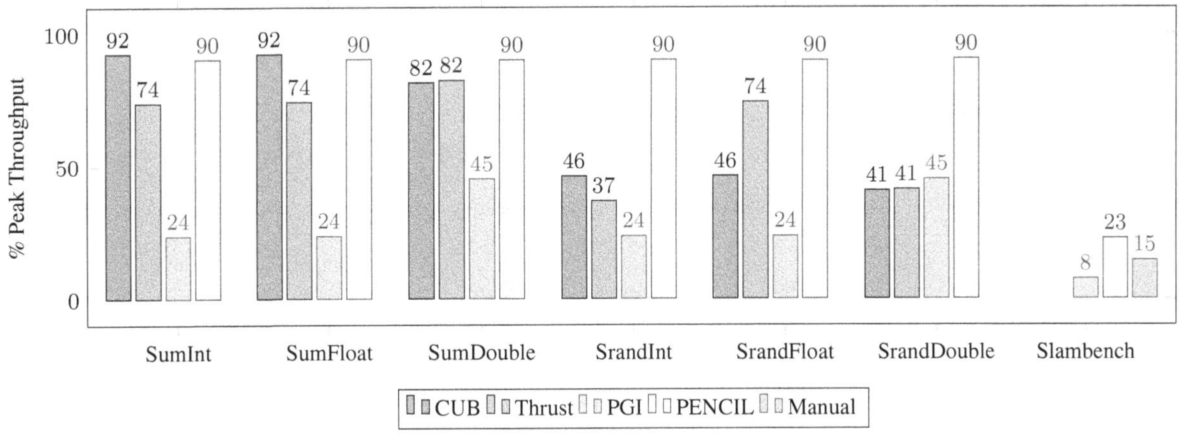

Figure 9: Performance on NVIDIA GeForce GTX 470

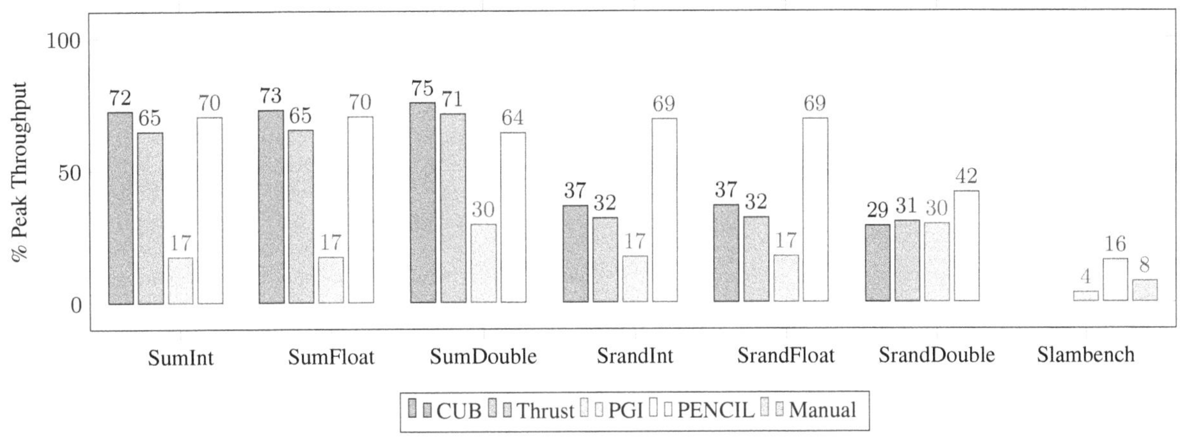

Figure 10: Performance on NVIDIA Quadro K4000

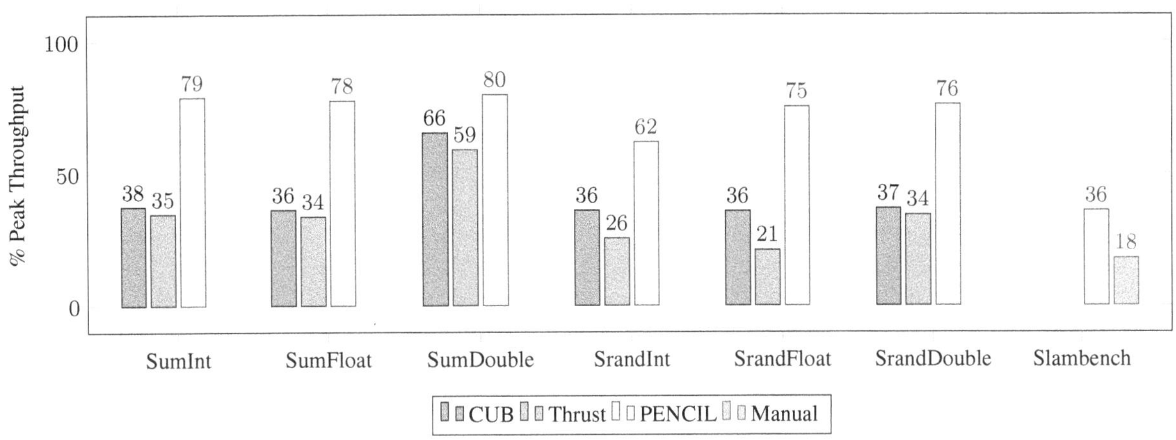

Figure 11: Performance on NVIDIA TK1

was a $0.53\times$ slowdown with and without shared memory access reordering. This optimization is essential to eliminate shared memory bank conflicts and is applicable only if the reduction operator is commutative. Hence we expect the reduction operator to be both associative and commutative.

The performance of CUB on the embedded TK1 is only 37.5% of peak for int and 65.5% for double, whereas the PENCIL version reaches 78.9% and 79.91%, respectively. We suspect that both CUB and Thrust libraries are not tuned for the TK1 platform, whereas our generated code benefited from auto-tuning. This shows the importance and effectiveness of auto-tuning even after all optimizations have been applied and a suitable template is being used. Table 1 collects the optimal values for the number of thread blocks and the number of threads per block. The number of reductions per thread depends on the problem size, grid size and block size. This parameter is tuned implicitly while tuning for the optimal grid and block size parameters. Note that the exhaustive search does not take much time because of the limited search space for reduction templates.

Benchmark	GTX 470	Quadro K4000	TK1
SumInt	$84, 128$	$128, 128$	$222, 128$
SumFloat	$84, 128$	$128, 128$	$103, 512$
SumDouble	$120, 256$	$124, 64$	$253, 256$

Table 1: Optimal parameter values for the number of thread blocks and for the the thread block size

Benchmark	OpenACC	PENCIL
GTX 470	$0.51\times$	$1.53\times$
Quadro K4000	$0.45\times$	$2.00\times$
TK1	–	$1.97\times$

Table 2: Speedup of the SLAMBench reduction kernel relative to the manual implementation

6.2 Srand Reduction kernel

The Srand reduction kernel shown in Figure 4 consists of two reductions on the same array. It is quite straightforward to express such reductions in OpenACC and PENCIL, whereas CUB or Thrust involve two library calls along with some additional processing. One reduction call to compute sum, an intermediate step to compute the square of the input, and then another reduction call to compute the sum of squares. This is clearly inefficient as input array is traversed twice to perform reductions separately. This kernel illustrates the limitations of library-based approaches in real world applications: Figures 9, 10 and 11 show the performance of the Srand kernel abbreviated as SrandInt, SrandFloat and SrandDouble on different GPU architectures. The performance of PENCIL is almost identical to the case of a single reduction kernel. Because the array is scanned only once, reduction time does not vary much. On the other hand, for both CUB and Thrust, the time taken is twice that of a single reduction because of the two array traversals. This kernel illustrates the benefits of fusing multiple reductions, as evaluating multiple reduction operators per memory access made much more effective use of the bandwidth. The OpenACC compiler was also able to fuse the two reductions because both reductions appeared in the same loop. This restriction does not apply to our framework, which supports the fusion of different reduction kernels even if they are two separate loops in the input code.

6.3 SLAMBench reduction kernel

SLAMBench [17] is a computer vision benchmark for 3D modeling and tracking. The benchmark contains a reduction kernel with 32 different reductions. It is straightforward to port these reductions in PENCIL and OpenACC whereas it is tedious and inefficient to do so in CUB and Thrust, as they involve multiple calls to the reduction API. The comparison of our framework with OpenACC and with SLAMBench's manual CUDA implementation is shown in Figures 9, 10 and 11. Because there are 32 reductions performed for a single element, the memory bandwidth is no longer the bottleneck. PENCIL outperforms both OpenACC and the manual implementation. The latter is almost twice as fast as OpenACC. The SLAMBench implementation uses shared memory to store intermediate reduction values while reductions are performed in parallel. In PENCIL, the reduction kernel uses all the optimizations listed in Section 5 for all 32 reductions and auto-tuning results in a $2\times$ improvement on NVIDIA TK1.

7. CONCLUSION

We presented language constructs and compilation methods to express arbitrary reductions on user-defined data types. We also presented dependence-based abstractions of reductions that enable polyhedral loop nest optimizations in the presence of loops carrying reductions. Combining polyhedral and template-based code generation, we are able to perform complex optimizations for user-defined reductions on GPUs, reaching close to peak performance. This approach enables a generic polyhedral compiler to produce highly efficient code for reductions while offering maximum expressiveness to the programmer. We demonstrated the approach on generalized reduction patterns and we believe it may be extended to prefix scans and radix sort algorithms.

Acknowledgments. This work was partly supported by the European Commission and French Ministry of Industry through the ECSEL project COPCAMS id. 332913, and by the French ANR through the European CHIST-ERA project DIVIDEND. We also acknowledge the support of ARM through the Polly Labs initiative. Our experiments with SLAMBench k-fusion benefited from numerous exchanges with Bruno Bodin, Luigi Nardi and Ali Zaidi, with whom we are also working on a PENCIL release of the application. And finally, none of this work would have been possible without the tremendous work of Sven Verdoolaege and Tobias Grosser on isl and PPCG.

8. REFERENCES

[1] R. Baghdadi, U. Beaugnon, A. Cohen, T. Grosser, M. Kruse, C. Reddy, S. Verdoolaege, J. Absar, S. van Haastregt, A. Kravets *et al.*, "PENCIL: A platform-neutral compute intermediate language for accelerator programming," *Proc. Parallel Architectures and Compilation Techniques (PACT)*, 2015.

[2] R. Baghdadi, A. Cohen, T. Grosser, S. Verdoolaege, A. Lokhmotov, J. Absar, S. Van Haastregt, A. Kravets, and A. Donaldson, "PENCIL Language Specification," INRIA, Research Report RR-8706, May 2015. [Online]. Available: https://hal.inria.fr/hal-01154812

[3] U. Bondhugula, A. Hartono, J. Ramanujam, and P. Sadayappan, "A practical automatic polyhedral parallelizer and locality optimizer," in *ACM SIGPLAN conference on Programming Language Design and Implementation*, vol. 43, no. 6. ACM, 2008, pp. 101–113.

[4] J. Dean and S. Ghemawat, "Mapreduce: Simplified data processing on large clusters," *Commun. ACM*, vol. 51, no. 1, pp. 107–113, Jan. 2008.

[5] S. J. Deitz, B. L. Chamberlain, and L. Snyder, "High-level language support for user-defined reductions," *The Journal of Supercomputing*, vol. 23, no. 1, pp. 23–37, 2002.

[6] J. Doerfert, K. Streit, S. Hack, and Z. Benaissa, "Polly's polyhedral scheduling in the presence of reductions," *arXiv preprint arXiv:1505.07716*, 2015.

[7] M. Frigo, P. Halpern, C. E. Leiserson, and S. Lewin-Berlin, "Reducers and other Cilk++ hyperobjects," in *Proceedings of the Twenty-first Annual Symposium on Parallelism in Algorithms and Architectures*, ser. SPAA. New York, NY, USA: ACM, 2009, pp. 79–90. [Online]. Available: http://doi.acm.org/10.1145/1583991.1584017

[8] G. Gupta and S. V. Rajopadhye, "Simplifying reductions." in *ACM Symposium on Principles of Programming Languages (POPL)*, vol. 6, 2006, pp. 30–41.

[9] L. Howes, A. Lokhmotov, A. F. Donaldson, and P. H. J. Kelly, "Towards metaprogramming for parallel systems on a chip," in *Proceedings of the 2009 International Conference on Parallel Processing*, ser. Euro-Par. Berlin, Heidelberg: Springer-Verlag, 2010, pp. 36–45. [Online]. Available: http://dl.acm.org/citation.cfm?id=1884795.1884803

[10] F. Irigoin, P. Jouvelot, and R. Triolet, "Semantical interprocedural parallelization: An overview of the pips project," in *ACM International Conf. on Supercomputing (ICS)*, Cologne, Germany, Jun. 1991.

[11] ISO, "The ANSI C standard (C99)," ISO/IEC, Tech. Rep. WG14 N1124, 1999.

[12] P. Jouvelot, "Parallelization by semantic detection of reductions," in *ESOP 86*. Springer, 1986, pp. 223–236.

[13] P. Jouvelot and B. Dehbonei, "A unified semantic approach for the vectorization and parallelization of generalized reductions," in *Proceedings of the 3rd international conference on Supercomputing*. ACM, 1989, pp. 186–194.

[14] Mark Harris, "Optimizing parallel reduction in CUDA." [Online]. Available: https://docs.nvidia.com/cuda/samples/6_Advanced/reduction/doc/reduction.pdf

[15] Microsoft, "Parallel patterns library." [Online]. Available: https://msdn.microsoft.com/en-us/library/dd470426.aspx#parallel_reduces

[16] MPIF, "MPI-2: Extensions to the message-passing interface," *University of Tennessee, Knoxville*, 1996.

[17] L. Nardi, B. Bodin, M. Z. Zia, J. Mawer, A. Nisbet, P. H. J. Kelly, A. J. Davison, M. Luján, M. F. P. O'Boyle, G. D. Riley, N. Topham, and S. Furber, "Introducing SLAMBench, a performance and accuracy benchmarking methodology for SLAM," *CoRR*, vol. abs/1410.2167, 2014. [Online]. Available: http://arxiv.org/abs/1410.2167

[18] Nvidia, "CUB's collective primitives." [Online]. Available: https://nvlabs.github.io/cub/

[19] Nvidia, "Thrust C++ library." [Online]. Available: https://developer.nvidia.com/thrust/

[20] Nvidia forum, "Faster parallel reductions on Kepler." [Online]. Available: https://devblogs.nvidia.com/parallelforall/faster-parallel-reductions-kepler/

[21] S. S. Pinter and R. Y. Pinter, "Program optimization and parallelization using idioms," *ACM Transactions on Programming Languages and Systems (TOPLAS)*, vol. 16, no. 3, pp. 305–327, 1994.

[22] B. Pottenger and R. Eigenmann, "Idiom recognition in the polaris parallelizing compiler," in *Proceedings of the 9th international conference on Supercomputing*. ACM, 1995, pp. 444–448.

[23] W. Pugh and D. Wonnacott, "Static analysis of upper and lower bounds on dependences and parallelism," *ACM Transactions on Programming Languages and Systems (TOPLAS)*, vol. 16, no. 4, pp. 1248–1278, 1994.

[24] L. Rauchwerger and D. A. Padua, "The lrpd test: Speculative run-time parallelization of loops with privatization and reduction parallelization," *Parallel and Distributed Systems, IEEE Transactions on*, vol. 10, no. 2, pp. 160–180, 1999.

[25] X. Redon and P. Feautrier, "Detection of recurrences in sequential programs with loops," in *Parallel Architectures and Languages Europe (PARLE)*. Springer, 1993, pp. 132–145.

[26] X. Redon and P. Feautrier, "Scheduling reductions," in *Proceedings of the 8th international conference on Supercomputing*. ACM, 1994, pp. 117–125.

[27] X. Redon and P. Feautrier, "Detection of scans," *J. of Parallel Algorithms and Applications*, vol. 15, no. 3-4, pp. 229–263, 2000.

[28] J. Reinders, *Intel Threading Building Blocks*, 1st ed. Sebastopol, CA, USA: O'Reilly & Associates, Inc., 2007.

[29] M. C. Rinard and M. S. Lam, "The design, implementation, and evaluation of Jade," *ACM Trans. Program. Lang. Syst.*, vol. 20, no. 3, pp. 483–545, May 1998. [Online]. Available: http://doi.acm.org/10.1145/291889.291893

[30] K. Stock, M. Kong, T. Grosser, L.-N. Pouchet, F. Rastello, J. Ramanujam, and P. Sadayappan, "A framework for enhancing data reuse via associative reordering," in *ACM SIGPLAN Notices*, vol. 49, no. 6. ACM, 2014, pp. 65–76.

[31] T. Suganuma, H. Komatsu, and T. Nakatani, "Detection and global optimization of reduction operations for distributed parallel machines," in *Proceedings of the 10th international conference on Supercomputing*. ACM, 1996, pp. 18–25.

[32] The Portland Group, "PGI accelerator compilers with OpenACC directives." [Online]. Available: http://www.pgroup.com/resources/accel.htm/

[33] A. Venkat, M. Shantharam, M. Hall, and M. M. Strout, "Non-affine extensions to polyhedral code generation," in *Proceedings of Annual IEEE/ACM International Symposium on Code Generation and Optimization*. ACM, 2014, p. 185.

[34] S. Verdoolaege, J. C. Juega, A. Cohen, J. I. Gómez, C. Tenllado, and F. Catthoor, "Polyhedral parallel code generation for CUDA," *ACM Transactions on Architecture and Code Optimization (TACO)*, Jan. 2013, selected for presentation at the HiPEAC 2013 Conference.

[35] S. Wienke, P. Springer, C. Terboven, and D. an Mey, "OpenACC: first experiences with real-world applications," in *Euro-Par 2012 Parallel Processing*. Springer, 2012, pp. 859–870.

[36] D. N. Xu, S.-C. Khoo, and Z. Hu, "Ptype system: A featherweight parallelizability detector," in *Programming Languages and Systems*. Springer, 2004, pp. 197–212.

Resource Conscious Reuse-Driven Tiling for GPUs

Prashant Singh Rawat, Changwan Hong
Computer Science and Engineering
The Ohio State University
{rawatp,hongc}@cse.ohio-state.edu

Mahesh Ravishankar, Vinod Grover
Nvidia Corporation
Redmond, Washington
{mravishankar,vgrover}@nvidia.com

Louis-Noël Pouchet, Atanas Rountev, P. Sadayappan
Computer Science and Engineering
The Ohio State University
{pouchet,rountev,saday}@cse.ohio-state.edu

ABSTRACT

Computations involving successive application of 3D stencil operators are widely used in many application domains, such as image processing, computational electromagnetics, seismic processing, and climate modeling. Enhancement of temporal and spatial locality via tiling is generally required in order to overcome performance bottlenecks due to limited bandwidth to global memory on GPUs. However, the low shared memory capacity on current GPU architectures makes effective tiling for 3D stencils very challenging – several previous domain-specific compilers for stencils have demonstrated very high performance for 2D stencils, but much lower performance on 3D stencils.

In this paper, we develop an effective resource-constraint-driven approach for automated GPU code generation for stencils. We present a fusion technique that judiciously fuses stencil computations to minimize data movement, while controlling computational redundancy and maximizing resource usage. The fusion model subsumes time tiling of iterated stencils, and can be easily adapted to different GPU architectures. We integrate the fusion model into a code generator that makes effective use of scarce shared memory and registers to achieve high performance. The effectiveness of the automated model-driven code generator is demonstrated through experimental results on a number of benchmarks, comparing against various previously developed GPU code generators.

Keywords

Stencil Computations; GPU; Fusion; Code Generation

1. INTRODUCTION

Stencil computations are central to numerous computational methods, ranging from image processing to the numerical solution of partial differential equations. Many previous efforts for compiler optimization of stencil computations have focused on time-iterated stencils involving repeated application of a stencil operator [23, 4, 5, 8, 9]. In contrast, multi-statement stencils and image processing pipelines apply a sequence of stencil operators on a set of input domains [16, 19]. Such stencil computations can be represented by a directed acyclic graph (DAG) in which nodes represent stencil operators and incoming edges represent inputs to these operators. These stencil pipelines are often bandwidth-bound.

Time-tiling is a key transformation to enhance temporal reuse in bandwidth-bound stencils. In a time-tiled execution, operations from several consecutive time steps of a stencil computation are combined to form a tile, which is executed atomically to exploit data reuse. Previous efforts towards optimizing 2D stencils on GPUs have demonstrated the effectiveness of time-tiling, along with the utilization of shared memory [4, 9]. However, tiling 3D stencils has proved to be a challenge for all previously reported code generators. The difficulty arises from the cubic versus quadratic increase in shared memory requirement for the 3D case, and the very limited (usually under 64 Kbytes) shared memory available per streaming multiprocessor (SM) on GPUs. Consequently, the use of overlapped tiles [9] with 3D stencils results in very rapid increase in redundant computations, even for very small values of the time-tile size.

In this paper, we present a GPU code generator that optimizes a DAG of stencil operators, making effective use of available shared memory and registers. This enables handling of multi-statement stencils and image processing pipelines, as well as time iterated stencils (as arising in multigrid smoothers, etc.) via explicit unrolling of a few time iterations. Thus, a single framework can be used to generate high-performance GPU code, both for time iterated stencils and multi-statement stencil pipelines.

A key issue in optimizing the execution of 3D stencils is the determination of tile shape/size and the amount of fusion across multiple stencils, while making effective use of a combination of shared memory and registers to enable a high degree of reuse. We use a number of strategies to overcome the difficulties faced by previous GPU code generators with 3D stencils:

- Instead of using symmetric 3D tiles, we use a sliding window along one spatial dimension and symmetric overlapped 2D tiling in the other two spatial dimensions to enable significantly greater data reuse than 3D overlapped tiling.
- We exploit the flexibility of associative reordering of stencil contributions to each data element, thereby reducing the demand on the very scarce shared memory via increased use of the more plentiful registers on modern GPUs.
- We develop a model-driven approach to determine which stencil operators to fuse, since excessive fusion leads to increased redundant computation, increased data traffic to/from global memory, and increase in overhead from register spilling.

The paper makes the following contributions:

- It develops a resource-directed model-driven approach to gen-

PACT '16, September 11-15, 2016, Haifa, Israel

DOI: http://dx.doi.org/10.1145/2967938.2967967

erate high-performance GPU code for stencil computations.

- It develops a practically effective stencil fusion algorithm for GPU code generation.
- It presents compiler algorithms for an automated code generator that takes a DAG of stencil computations as input, and generates GPU code which makes effective use of registers, shared memory, and streamed tile execution to achieve high warp occupancy.
- It presents a case study highlighting the factors that can constrain performance, and the impact of effective fusion on a resource-intensive stencil from a partial differential equation solver application.
- It evaluates a set of 3D benchmarks on Kepler and Maxwell devices, demonstrating significantly higher performance than other existing GPU code generators for stencils.

2. OVERVIEW OF APPROACH

2.1 DSL Input to Code Generator

Listing 1 shows a 7-point Jacobi stencil expressed in a domain specific language (DSL). The input language used by our code generator is similar to Forma [19], and is designed to provide a high-level description of the stencil computation. Each function prefixed by *stencil* describes the operations to execute at a point of the computation domain. Array accesses within the stencil function are described in terms of offsets to be used to access an array element. For example, $A[1, 0, -1]$ refers to access to element $A[i+1, j, k-1]$ when executing iteration point (i, j, k).

Even though we can write many operations within a stencil function, each individual operation must be written in a generic form with a view that a separate kernel call may be generated for it. The code generator decides which stencil operations to fuse, how to shift and align the offsets for array accesses when fusing operations with dependences, and how many output stencil functions the input stencil function is split into. To simplify the presentation, in the examples we omit the explicit specification of the domains (array extents) over which the stencils are applied.

The type and size of the arrays used in the computation are explicitly defined (line 10 of Listing 1). Arrays that represent the result of the computation are specified as *return*-ed (line 13). An array listed as *temporary* need not be explicitly stored in memory, freeing the compiler to either store it in temporary scratch memory (such as shared memory buffers on the GPU) or in registers. We note that such information could also be extracted from code in other languages such as C or Fortran, but the required code analyses are outside the scope of this paper.

2.2 Code Generation Challenges for 3D Stencils

For 3D stencils, existing GPU stencil code generators [4, 5, 9, 19, 24] suffer from limitations on one or more of the following issues: (a) effective management of limited GPU resources for tiled execution; (b) optimization of the degree of fusion across multiple stencils (or equivalently, the time-tile size) to achieve reduction in data movement to/from global memory; and (c) exploitation of associativity/commutativity properties of stencil operations to optimize resource usage. Next, we discuss how the approach presented in this paper addresses these issues.

a) Time Tiling and Computational Redundancy.

Time-tiling a stencil computation involves executing operations from multiple time steps of the computation atomically. For example, the stencil of Listing 1 computes two time steps (at lines 2 and 5) of a 7-point Jacobi computation. Tiling the *jacobi-def* stencil on a GPU requires the partitioning of the computational domain into smaller sub-domains, and assigning these sub-domains to thread blocks. However, simple rectangular partitioning of the iteration space into tiles is not feasible, since at time step t, the threads at the boundaries of adjacent tiles each need values at time step $t-1$ from each other. The overlapped boundary region is called the *ghost zone* or *halo region*. Overlapped tiling [9, 12] overcomes this problem of cyclic inter-tile dependences by having the thread blocks redundantly compute values at the halo region, thereby eliminating the mutual dependence between adjacent tiles.

Listing 1: The stencil representation for two time steps of an order-1 7-point Jacobi computation

```
1  stencil jacobi-def (A, B, C, a, b, c) {
2   B[0,0,0] =                  a*(A[1,0,0]) +
3    b*(A[0,-1,0]+A[0,0,-1]+A[0,0,0]+A[0,0,1]+A[0,1,0]) +
4                               c*(A[-1,0,0]);
5   C[0,0,0] =                  a*(B[1,0,0] +
6    b*(B[0,-1,0]+B[0,0,-1]+B[0,0,0]+B[0,0,1]+B[0,1,0]) +
7                               c*(B[-1,0,0]);
8  }
9  parameter L, M, N;
10 float A[L,M,N], B[L,M,N], C[L,M,N], a, b, c;
11 temporary B;
12 jacobi-def (A, B, C, a, b, c);
13 return C;
```

For 2D stencils, the fractional volume of redundant operations with overlapped tiling can be effectively controlled [20]. Let us consider a $B \times B$ thread block size, and a time-tile size of 4. If the intermediate results are stored in shared memory, the amount of memory required is $O(4B^2)$. The total amount of shared memory available on GPUs is typically 48 Kbytes. For time-tile size of 4, it is possible to use a block size of 32×32 while keeping all the intermediates in shared memory. For an order-1 stencil, an overlapped tile will involve reading in a 32×32 block from global memory, and computation of intermediate result blocks of sizes 30×30, 28×28, 26×26, and 24×24, respectively for the 4 time steps in the tile. This represents a total work of $30^2+28^2+26^2+24^2 = 2936$ stencil operations, where the non-redundant work is $4 \times 24^2 = 2304$ stencil operations, resulting in a fractional redundant work volume of $632/2304 = 27\%$.

For a 3D stencil, a thread block size of $10 \times 10 \times 10$ can be used with all the intermediates in shared memory. The work performed for 4 time steps with overlapped tiling would be $8 \times 8 \times 8$, $6 \times 6 \times 6$, $4 \times 4 \times 4$, and $2 \times 2 \times 2$, respectively. The total work is $8^3+6^3+4^3+2^3 = 800$ stencil operations, of which only $4 \times 2^3 = 32$ operations are non-redundant, with a fractional overhead of $768/32 = 2400\%$. Even with a time-tile size of 2, the total work done is $8^3+6^3 = 728$ stencil operations, of which $2 \times 6^3 = 432$ are non-redundant, resulting in a high fractional overhead volume of $294/432 = 68\%$.

This indicates that when using overlapped tiling, going from 2D stencils to 3D stencils significantly increases the computational redundancy. The resulting performance degradation makes overlapped 3D tiling ineffective for 3D stencils.

To overcome this problem, we perform overlapped tiling along two spatial dimensions of the 3D domain, and launch 2D thread blocks that *stream* through the unpartitioned third dimension at each time step [15, 20]. This scheme, referred to as *sliding window* time-tiling, provides full reuse along the unpartitioned dimension. The size of the sliding window at time step t equals the number of input planes read to compute *one* output plane at time step $t+1$. For a 3D order-k single input/output Jacobi stencil, the sliding window size will be $2k+1$ at each time step. For example, since Listing 1 is an order-1 ($k = 1$) stencil, the computation at lines 2–4 needs to

Listing 2: Fusion profitability for multi-statement stencils

```
stencil fusion (A, B, C, D, E, d) {
  s1 : B[0,0,0] = A[1,0,0]+A[0,0,0]+A[-1,0,0];
  s2 : C[0,0,0] = A[1,0,0]+A[0,0,0]+A[-1,0,0]+B[-1,0,0];
  s3 : d += A[0,0,0];
  s4 : D[0,0,0] += E[0,0,0] - E[0,-1,0];
}
parameter L, M, N;
float A[L,M,N], B[L,M,N], C[L,M,N], D[L,M,N], E[L,M,N];
float d;
temporary B;
fusion (A, B, C, D, E, d);
return C, D, d;
```

read only three input planes ($A[1,*,*]$, $A[0,*,*]$, and $A[-1,*,*]$), to compute output plane $B[0,*,*]$ using a 2D grid/thread configuration that spans the extent of the inner dimensions of B. If the planes of A are stored in shared memory, then after computing $B[0,*,*]$, to next compute $B[1,*,*]$ would require loading of just one additional plane of A (i.e., $A[2,*,*]$).

The amount of shared memory also constraints the extent of time-tiling. Consider the case where the shared memory available per SM is 48 Kbytes. If each of the $2k+1$ input planes read by a block is mapped to a distinct shared memory buffer, then for single precision computation with $k=1$ and a maximum of 2048 threads per SM (as is the case for the Nvidia Kepler and Maxwell GPUs used for experiments in this paper), the maximum number of shared memory buffers per thread block is ≤ 6 (i.e., 48 Kbyte/(4×2048)). Since each time step requires 3 shared memory buffers, the time-tile size is constrained to 2 time steps. For $k=2$, we can only perform spatial tiling with a 32×32 thread block. For higher values of k, we must either perform global memory read transactions at each time step, or sacrifice occupancy (and hence thread-level parallelism) to perform time-tiling. Our modeling accounts for such resource constraints in order to generate appropriate code for different GPU devices.

b) Fusion of Stencil Operators.

GPUs have a significant gap between their compute and memory throughput. Many stencil applications are bandwidth-bound, making it extremely difficult to achieve near-peak computational performance. Performance for such stencils can be improved by reducing global memory transactions via caching or use of shared memory and registers. Time-tiling and fusion are two key transformations used to enhance data locality. However, as shown later in Sections 3 and 4, an indiscriminate attempt to time-tile or fuse stencil operators can be counter-productive.

Consider the computation in Listing 2. If s_1 is fused with s_2, array B does not have to be written to global memory since it is marked *temporary*. The output of s_1 can be stored in a register or shared memory buffer before being read by s_2. Thus, global read and write transactions for an entire array can be eliminated after fusion. However, since there is a RAW dependence between s_1 and s_2 due to B, atomic execution of a tile will require computation of a halo region. Fusing s_3 with either s_1 or s_2 will also lead to savings in global read transactions for array A. The savings in global memory transactions are less in this case, but no halo region needs to be computed. Since none of the arrays from s_4 appear in any other statement, fusing s_4 with any other statement will not enhance data reuse.

While fusion can significantly reduce the amount of data moved from/to global memory, it increases demands on shared memory and/or registers. For complex stencils that arise in many applications, the number of possible fusion choices can be large. In this paper, we develop a *fusion profitability* metric and a greedy heuris-

Listing 3: Leveraging associativity to rewrite Listing 1 stencil

```
1  stencil jacobi (A, B, C, a, b, c) {
2    s1  b1: B[1,0,0]   = c*(A[0,0,0]);
3        b2: B[0,0,0]  += b*(A[0,-1,0] + A[0,0,-1] + A[0,0,0]
4                        + A[0, 0,1] + A[0,1, 0]);
5        b3: B[-1,0,0] += a*(A[0,0,0]);
6    s2  b4: C[1,0,0]   = c*(B[0,0,0]);
7        b5: C[0,0,0]  += b*(B[0,-1,0] + B[0,0,-1] + B[0,0,0]
8                        + B[0, 0,1] + B[0,1, 0]);
9        b6: C[-1,0,0] += a*(B[0,0,0]);
10 }
11 parameter L, M, N;
12 float A[L,M,N], B[L,M,N], C[L,M,N], a, b, c;
13 temporary B;
14 jacobi (A, B, C, a, b, c);
15 return C;
```

tic to select good fusion configurations that satisfy all resource constraints.

c) Associative Reordering for Resource Management.

As noted above, complex stencil computations can place excessive demands on shared memory. An approach that has previously been developed to reduce register pressure with high-order stencils, in the context of multi-core processors, is to perform reordering of operations by exploiting the associativity of additive contributions in stencil computations [21]. We use associative reordering to balance resource usage by trading off register use for shared memory. For example, the additive contributions to the statement at lines 2–4 in Listing 1 can be reordered without changing the semantics of the computation. Although floating-point additions are not strictly associative, it is generally acceptable to perform associative reordering of accumulations in stencil computations. DSLs such as Forma [19] and Halide [18] currently do not recognize and exploit associative operations. Our approach uses operator associativity to reduce the shared memory demand by a simple restructuring of the computation. Listing 3 shows the resulting DSL code after restructuring the stencil from Listing 1, which is done automatically by the DSL compiler.

Statement s_1 (s_2) at lines 2–4 (lines 5–7) of Listing 1 is split into sub-statements b_1 through b_3 (b_4 through b_6) at lines 2–5 (lines 6–9) in Listing 3. For the same plane of the input array, these sub-statements update different points of the output domain, i.e., the plane $A[0,*,*]$ is read once to update the values of $B[-1,*,*]$, $B[0,*,*]$, and $B[1,*,*]$. Since the computations per plane are executed in parallel by each thread in a kernel, neighboring threads will access the same element of array A. To reduce the number of global memory accesses, the plane of array A can be loaded into shared memory, with each thread loading a single element of the plane. The threads can then access all the values of $A[0,*,*]$ needed to perform the computation specified in statement s_1 from shared memory.

After executing s_1, the plane corresponding to $B[-1,*,*]$ has received all the updates needed from statement s_1 and can be used to update the value of array C in statement s_2. The plane corresponding to $B[-1,*,*]$ in s_1 is used as the generic plane $B[0,*,*]$ in statement s_2. Again, neighboring threads of the kernel access common elements of the plane $B[0,*,*]$ in statement s_2. It is therefore beneficial to store this plane in shared memory as well for the same reason as above.

Note that the planes corresponding to the writes represented by $B[0,*,*]$, and $B[1,*,*]$ in statement s_1 are not needed in statement s_2 yet. These can be stored in registers. As the sliding window moves across the planes of array A, the values in these registers can be updated. With the execution model described above, only two shared memory buffers are needed, one for the plane corresponding to $A[0,*,*]$ in statement s_1, and the other for the plane corresponding to $B[-1,*,*]$ in statement s_1 (which is the same as the plane corresponding to $B[0,*,*]$ in statement s_2).

In general, for a single statement that executes an order-k stencil, instead of $2k+1$ shared memory buffers per time step, the optimized kernel code uses $2k$ registers and 1 shared memory buffer per time step with reassociation. The advantage of using registers for storage is twofold: (1) in current GPU architectures, registers are more plentiful than shared memory, and (2) the access latency of registers is lower than that of shared memory, and so using them as cache speeds up the computation. We will use the *jacobi* stencil of Listing 3 as a running example throughout the rest of the paper.

3. RESOURCE-CONSTRAINED FUSION

To maximize performance with complex stencil DAGs, we must judiciously use registers and the memory hierarchy of GPUs to reduce expensive data movement. Fusion is a classical loop transformation that can enhance data locality, thereby minimizing data movement. The key idea is to fuse the nodes in the DAG with common predecessors (i.e., stencil operators that access common input arrays), or a chain of nodes in the DAG (i.e., stencil operators that have producer-consumer dependences) so that temporal locality and the per-load data reuse is maximized.

Without violating dependences, different nodes in a DAG can be fused to get different valid schedules. The performance of each schedule can vary depending on the profitability of fusion. The space of all valid execution schedules can be vast. To avoid exploring the entire space to find the best fusion schedule, we use a greedy algorithm which fuses nodes in the DAG with the intent to minimize a chosen objective function. From the initial stencil DAG $D_g = (V, E)$, our aim is to create a resultant *fused* directed graph $D_f = (V_f, E_f)$ such that each $v_f \in V_f$ is a *convex partition* of nodes from V. A convex partition of nodes forms clusters of "macro-nodes' with no dependence chain leaving and re-entering any macro-node. Just as convex-shaped tiles of an iteration space can execute atomically, the fused macro-nodes computed by the fusion algorithm ensure that no dependences are violated upon their atomic execution. The convex partitioning therefore guarantees that D_f is acyclic. Only nodes whose fusion is deemed profitable by the objective function are combined together in v_f. A single GPU kernel is generated for each node in v_f. No global memory transactions are needed for domains whose definition and use do not cross partition boundaries.

Overview of the Greedy Fusion Algorithm.

The rest of this section details a flexible greedy algorithm for fusing nodes in a directed stencil graph, designed for easy incorporation of multiple objective metrics. The fusion algorithm consists of the following steps:

Step 1: Compute the resource usage of each individual statement in the stencil DAG (Section 3.1).

Step 2: Identify pairs of statements that can be legally fused, as well as some profitability metrics that quantify their fusion benefits (Section 3.2).

Step 3: For each statement pair, compute the resource usage of the fused node based on the resource usage of individual statements obtained in Step 1 (Section 3.3).

Step 4: From the resource usage of the fused node, compute the profitability metrics identified in Step 2 (Section 3.4).

Step 5: Define a custom sort to order the profitability metrics of statement pairs, and choose to fuse the most profitable pair that satisfies additional hardware-imposed constraints (discussed in Section 3.6 and Section 4). Update the stencil DAG and the dependence graph, and repeat again from Step 1, until no more statement pairs can be fused (Section 3.5).

Once the fusion algorithm creates the fused stencil DAG D_f, the code generator described in Section 5 generates a CUDA kernel for each node of D_f.

3.1 Modeling Resource Requirements

Efficient management of GPU resources is crucial for performance. In the reordering optimization of Listing 3, each statement uses some registers and shared memory buffers to cache some input and output values. Since fusion of different statements may result in an increase in the resource requirement, it is important to quantify the hardware resources used by each statement. We use the access pattern for each array in the statement for this estimation. The per-statement resource estimates are then used to estimate the resource requirements after fusing any two statements (Section 3.2). Without loss of generality, let us assume that we stream through the outermost dimension of a 3D domain. To determine the resource requirement of a stencil statement that is order-k along the streaming dimension, we need to reason about the storage type of the $2k+1$ accessed planes. We follow a simple chain of reasoning:

(a) If the computation of an output element at (z_0, y_0, x_0) only uses a single input element at (z_r, y_0, x_0) from an input plane z_r, then that input element is stored in an explicit register (i.e., storage type of z_r is register). Otherwise, z_r is cached in shared memory

(b) An output element is written to an explicit register (i.e., its storage type is register) if it is an accumulation statement, or it is not the last assignment to a non-temporary array. For the last assignment to any non-temporary array, the storage is type is global memory.

Here, an *explicit* register refers to a scalar temporary variable created to hold an array element instead of using shared memory. It is expected that the compiler will place such scalars in registers. We distinguish these from other *implicit* registers that are used internally by NVCC, to hold elements of arrays and intermediate results in computing expressions. We note that these terms are used just for the purpose of explanation; in the final code, the explicit registers just appear as thread scalars.

From rule (a), we can infer that statement s_1 of Listing 3 should use a shared memory buffer to store the input plane $A[0,*,*]$. This is because five different values are read from that plane and contribute to different output points. Similarly, from rule (b), it follows that statement s_1 should use three explicit registers to store the output values written to $B[1,0,0]$, $B[0,0,0]$ and $B[-1,0,0]$.

We represent the resource requirement for each statement by a 3-tuple $(N_{reg}, N_{shm}, M_{acc\rightarrow res})$, where N_{reg}, N_{shm} are the number of explicit registers and shared memory buffers used by the statement, and $M_{acc\rightarrow res}$ is a resource map from each accessed plane to a handle that represents the storage used for that plane. For example, the 3-tuple for s_1 is $(3, 1, M_1)$, where $M_1 = \{B[-1,0,0]\rightarrow b_m, B[0,0,0]\rightarrow b_c, B[1,0,0]\rightarrow b_p, A[0,*,*]\rightarrow shm_a\}$; the 3-tuple for s_2 is $(3, 1, M_2)$, where $M_2 = \{C[-1,0,0]\rightarrow c_m, C[0,0,0]\rightarrow c_c, C[1,0,0]\rightarrow c_p, B[0,*,*]\rightarrow shm_b\}$.

3.2 Modeling Fusion Profitability

An objective function is used to choose among multiple valid fusion choices. The impact of fusion on performance is governed by an intricate interplay of many factors, some of which are hardware dependent. Fusion of two nodes can decrease data movement, but may lead to an increase in the shared memory/register requirement. Beyond a certain point, any further increase in resources can result in reduced occupancy and/or excessive register spills, both negating the benefits of fusion. Let us revisit the computation of Listing

2. Clearly, data movement can be significantly reduced by fusion across the first three stencil statements. The data movement savings and total resource requirement after fusing any pair of statements will depend on the data dependences between the statements. Assuming that all the arrays are of the same size, the data movement cost is modeled simply as the number of arrays read from or written into during the computation. Consider the following fusion choices for the code in Listing 2.

- Fusing s_1 and s_2: the data movement cost reduces by 3 (1 load saving for A, and 1 store + 1 load saving for B), but the resources used increase by 2 over s_1 (a register for $B[-1,0,0]$ and $C[0,0,0]$ each).
- Fusing s_1 and s_3: the data movement cost reduces by 1 (1 load saving for A), while the resource requirement increases by 1 over s_1 (a register for d).

If the fusion of any two statements is guaranteed not to exceed resource constraints, then we would prefer to fuse statements s_1 and s_2 if minimizing data movement is the objective, but prefer to fuse s_1 and s_3 if minimizing combined use of resources is the objective. Since there are multiple resources to be managed, and many complex interacting factors that affect overall performance, we do not attempt to develop a single aggregated objective function to guide the choice of fusion. Instead, we use a multi-dimensional vector, whose components quantitatively reflect various considerations of importance, and a lexicographic ordering among the vectors as a basis for choice among valid fusion configurations. Such an approach allows great flexibility in experimenting with different permutations of the "objective-vector" to change the relative priority of the different components in choosing between alternatives.

Components of the Fusion Profitability Metric

The greedy fusion algorithm begins by computing the 3-tuple defined in Section 3.1 for each stencil statement to model its resource requirements. The dependences in the stencil DAG are captured by the dependence graph $G_{dep} = (V, E_{dep})$. From G_{dep}, we compute a transitive dependence graph $G_{trans} = (V, E_{trans})$, such that

$$\begin{aligned} s_i \rightarrow s_j \in E_{trans} \text{ iff } \{\ & \exists s_k \mid s_k \in V \wedge s_k \neq s_i \wedge s_k \neq s_j \wedge \\ & \text{there exists a path from } s_i \text{ to } s_k \text{ (denoted as } s_i \rightsquigarrow s_k \text{)} \wedge \\ & \text{there exists a path from } s_k \text{ to } s_j \text{ i.e., } s_k \rightsquigarrow s_j\ \} \end{aligned} \quad (1)$$

We use G_{trans} to ensure the validity of fusion, i.e., that all partitions generated by fusion are convex. If $s_i \rightarrow s_j \in E_{trans}$, then fusing s_i and s_j will violate convexity unless all the nodes along any path $s_i \rightsquigarrow s_j$ are also included in the fused macro-node. The definition above does not preclude fusion of a statement with its immediate predecessor as long as there are no intervening statements along all paths from s_i to s_j.

Since the benefits from fusing different statement pairs may vary, we construct a *fusion profitability* metric for each distinct stencil statement pair (s_i, s_j). This metric is a 7-tuple $(D_m, S_{reg}, S_{shm}, E_{reg}, E_{shm}, T_{reg}, T_{shm})$, where

- D_m represents the savings in data movement after fusing s_i and s_j
- S_{reg} represents the savings in explicit registers, modeled as the number of common registers between s_i or s_j
- S_{shm} represents the savings in shared memory, modeled as the number of common shared memory buffers between s_i and s_j
- E_{reg} represents the excess of explicit registers, modeled as the minimum extra registers required in the fused node over the amount used by s_i or s_j before fusion.
- E_{shm} represents the excess of shared memory, modeled as the minimum extra shared memory buffers required in the fused node over the amount used by s_i or s_j before fusion.
- T_{reg} represents the total number of explicit registers in the fused node
- T_{shm} represents the total number of shared memory buffers used in the fused node

3.3 Computing the Resource Map

In order to assess the impact of fusing two statements, we need to find the resources that would be needed to execute the fused node. Let M_i and M_j be the maps from accessed array planes to GPU resources ($M_{acc \rightarrow res}$) for the fusion candidates s_i and s_j, respectively. Let M_{fused} be the resource map for the fused node. This map is computed as shown in Algorithm 1. If there is no dependence between s_i and s_j, the resource map of the fused node is a union of the resource map of the individual nodes, where the rules of union are as defined in this section.

If there is a dependence between the two statements, we need first compute the *schedule_id* of the target statement. This id represents the statement's execution schedule. Two statements have the same execution schedule if their instances can be perfectly interleaved. The array accesses in the target statement are shifted by its *schedule_id* along the streaming dimension. The shift is to ensure that the dependences are satisfied within the fused node. For example, in Listing 3, s_2 can read the values of array B at a plane i only after s_1 had read the plane $i+1$ of array A and updated the values of plane i of B. Therefore, the *schedule_id* of s_2 has to be one less than the *schedule_id* of s_1. Function *min_plane_offset()* at line 5 iterates over all the sub-statements of the source statement, and returns the minimum LHS access offset along the streaming dimension. If we stream along the outermost dimension, then the value returned by *min_plane_offset()* for s_1 of Listing 3 will be $min\,(1,0,-1) = -1$. This will be the *schedule_id* for the target statement.

While the *schedule_id* is needed for the correctness of the generated code, it also affects the mapping of resources in the fused node (lines 6–27 of Algorithm 1). Once all array accesses in the target statement have been offset by *schedule_id*, there might a non-empty intersection between the planes accessed by statement s_i and s_j. For example, for s_1 in Listing 3, $B[-1,*,*]$ is mapped to registers (Section 3.1). Since the *schedule_id* for s_2 is -1, $B[0,*,*]$ in s_2 will be shifted to $B[-1,*,*]$ in the fused node. Since this plane is mapped to shared memory in M_2, this plane will be mapped to shared memory in the fused node as well (line 14 of Algorithm 1). There might also be cases where the in-plane accesses of the intersecting plane in statement s_i are different from the in-plane accesses in statement s_j. In these cases as well, the plane is mapped to shared memory in the fused node, in keeping with the approach described in Section 2-c (lines 16–21 of Algorithm 1).

For Listing 3, the fused resource map computed by Algorithm 1 would be $M_{fused} = \{C[-2,0,0] \rightarrow c_m, C[-1,0,0] \rightarrow c_c, C[0,0,0] \rightarrow c_p, B[-1,*,*] \rightarrow shm_b\ B[0,0,0] \rightarrow b_c, B[1,0,0] \rightarrow b_p, A[0,*,*] \rightarrow shm_a\}$.

3.4 Computing the Profitability Metric

Once the resource map of the fused node has been computed using Algorithm 1, we can quantify the profitability of fusing statements s_i and s_j using the 7-tuple described in Section 3.2. We populate the 7-tuple only if $s_i \rightarrow s_j \notin E_{trans}$, to ensure that we do not violate any dependencies. For every $s_i \rightarrow s_j \in E_{raw}$, there is an implicit reduction in data movement for the array carrying the dependence. To capture this, D_m is incremented by 2 for each RAW dependence between the two statements that are carried by arrays marked as *temporary*, once each for the write in s_i and read in s_j. If the RAW dependence is carried by an array that is not

Algorithm 1: Computing the resource map for a fused node

```
Input : s_i, s_j: stencil statements
Input : M_1, M_2: Resource map for s_1 and s_2 respectively
Output: M_fused: Resource map for the fused node
if ¬has_dependence (s_i, s_j) then
  | M_fused ← M_1 ∪ M_2;
end
else
  | schedule_id = min_plane_offset (s_i);
  | M_fused ← M_1;
  | for each entry m ∈ M_2 do
  |   | curr_access_plane ← get_accessed_plane (m);
  |   | new_access_plane ← curr_access_plane + schedule_id;
  |   | accessed_array ← get_accessed_array (m);
  |   | key ← get_map_key (accessed_array, new_access_plane);
  |   | if key ∈ M_fused then
  |   |   | if mapped_to_shared_mem (M_2, key) then
  |   |   |   | M_fused[key] ← new_shared_mem_resources ();
  |   |   | end
  |   |   | else if mapped_to_registers (M_fused, key) then
  |   |   |   | fused_offsets ← in_plane_accesses (s_i,
  |   |   |   |   new_access_plane, accessed_array);
  |   |   |   | curr_offsets ← in_plane_accesses (s_j,
  |   |   |   |   curr_access_plane, accessed_array);
  |   |   |   | if fused_offsets ≠ current_offsets then
  |   |   |   |   | M_fused[key] ← new_shared_mem_resources ();
  |   |   |   | end
  |   |   | end
  |   | end
  |   | else
  |   |   | M_fused.insert (m);
  |   | end
  | end
end
```

marked *temporary*, D_m is incremented by 1 since we do not have to reload the data written to global memory. There is no explicit data movement saving for arrays carrying WAR dependence. If there is WAW dependence between s_i and s_j but no RAW dependence, D_m is incremented by 1 for each WAW dependence to capture the reduction in multiple writes to the same location in global memory. The savings due to RAR dependences can be computed by finding the common arrays accessed among s_i and s_j, and incrementing D_m accordingly.

The other tuple items are computed as follows:

- $S_{reg} = num\_registers(M_i) + num\_registers(M_j) - num\_registers(M_{fused})$
- $S_{shm} = num\_shared(M_i) + num\_shared(M_j) - num\_shared(M_{fused})$
- $E_{reg} = min(num\_registers(M_i), num\_registers(M_j)) - S_{reg}$
- $E_{shm} = min(num\_shared(M_i), num\_shared(M_j)) - S_{shm}$
- $T_{reg} = num\_registers(M_i) + num\_registers(M_j) - S_{reg}$
- $T_{shm} = num\_shared(M_i) + num\_shared(M_j) - S_{shm}$

To illustrate the construction of the profitability metric, we construct the 7-tuple for statements s_1 and s_2 of Listing 3. The 3-tuples for s_1 and s_2 were computed in Section 3.1. Since there is a true dependence from s_1 to s_2, $D_m = 2$. The number of registers used is 3 for M_1, 3 for M_2, and 5 for M_{fused}. Therefore, $S_{reg} = 1$. The number of shared buffers used is 1 for M_1, 1 for M_2, and 2 for M_{fused}. Therefore, $S_{shm} = 0$. Since s_1 requires 3 registers for B and 1 shared memory buffer for A, $E_{reg} = 3 - 1 = 2$ and $E_{shm} = 1 - 0 = 1$. Post fusion, $T_{reg} = 3 + 3 - 1 = 5$, and $T_{shm} = 1 + 1 = 2$. The 7-tuple for s_1 and s_2 is therefore $\{2, 1, 0, 2, 1, 5, 2\}$.

The process described above is codified in Algorithm 2 for computation of the profitability metric for each statement pair.

Algorithm 2: Creating the objective function for fusion

```
   Input : IN: input DAG with n statements
   Output: OUT: A sorted list of 7-tuple, L_tuple
1  L_tuple ← ∅;
2  compute_resource_3-tuple ();
3  {G_raw, G_war, G_waw} ← create_dependence_graphs (IN);
4  G_dep ← G_raw ∪ G_war ∪ G_waw;
5  G_trans ← transitive_closure (G_dep) \G_dep;
6  for each distinct stmt pair (i, j), i, j ≤ n do
7    | D_m ← 0;
8    | if (s_i → s_j ∉ G_trans) then
9    |   | M_i ← resource_usage (s_i);
10   |   | M_j ← resource_usage (s_j);
     |   | // Call Algorithm 1
11   |   | M_fused ← fused_resource_map (s_i, s_j, M_i, M_j);
12   |   | D_m += 2*RAW_dependence_count(s_i, s_j,
     |   |   TEMPORARY_ARRAYS);
13   |   | D_m += RAW_dependence_count (s_i, s_j,
     |   |   NON_TEMPORARY_ARRAYS);
14   |   | D_m += WAW_dependence_count (s_i, s_j);
15   |   | D_m += RAR_dependence_count (s_i, s_j);
16   |   | S_reg ← num_registers (M_i) + num_registers (M_j) -
     |   |   num_registers (M_fused);
17   |   | S_shm ← num_shared (M_i) + num_shared (M_j) - num_shared
     |   |   (M_fused);
18   |   | {E_shm, E_reg, T_shm, T_reg} ← compute (M_i, M_j, S_shm, S_reg);
19   |   | L_tuple.append ((D_m, S_reg, S_shm, E_reg, E_shm, T_reg, T_shm));
20   | end
21 end
22 sort (L_tuple, minimize_data_movement);
```

3.5 Constructing the Objective Function

Once the 7-tuple has been computed for all statement pairs, we need a method to order them based on their fusion profitability. To do so, we define a custom-sort relation $\prec$ as a total order over the list of tuples (L_{tuple}). We first define a set of sorting rules that can be applied to order two 7-tuples $c_i, c_j \in L_{tuple}$.

a. $(D_m)_{c_i} < (D_m)_{c_j} \Rightarrow c_i \prec c_j$
b. $(T_{reg} + T_{shm})_{c_j} < (T_{reg} + T_{shm})_{c_i} \Rightarrow c_i \prec c_j$
c. $(T_{reg})_{c_j} < (T_{reg})_{c_i} \Rightarrow c_i \prec c_j$
d. $(T_{shm})_{c_j} < (T_{shm})_{c_i} \Rightarrow c_i \prec c_j$
e. $(E_{reg} + E_{shm})_{c_j} < (E_{reg} + E_{shm})_{c_i} \Rightarrow c_i \prec c_j$
f. $(E_{reg})_{c_j} < (E_{reg})_{c_i} \Rightarrow c_i \prec c_j$
g. $(E_{shm})_{c_j} < (E_{shm})_{c_i} \Rightarrow c_i \prec c_j$
h. $(S_{reg} + S_{shm})_{c_i} < (S_{reg} + S_{shm})_{c_j} \Rightarrow c_i \prec c_j$
i. $(S_{reg})_{c_i} < (S_{reg})_{c_j} \Rightarrow c_i \prec c_j$
j. $(S_{shm})_{c_i} < (S_{shm})_{c_j} \Rightarrow c_i \prec c_j$
k. $i < j \Rightarrow c_i \prec c_j$

where rule *k* is only used to ensure that a total order can be found in case of tuples with strictly identical metrics.

The order in which the sorting rules are applied to break the tie depends on the minimization objective. If the objective is to minimize the data movement, $\prec$ follows the rule sequence $a \rightarrow b \rightarrow c \rightarrow d \rightarrow e \rightarrow f \rightarrow g \rightarrow h \rightarrow i \rightarrow j \rightarrow k$, where a is the primary sorting rule, and the ties are settled by following the remaining rules in the sequence. If the objective is to minimize the total resource requirement, $\prec$ follows the rule sequence $b \rightarrow c \rightarrow d \rightarrow a \rightarrow e \rightarrow f \rightarrow g \rightarrow h \rightarrow i \rightarrow j \rightarrow k$, where b is the primary sorting rule, and the ties are settled by following the remaining rules. A high priority to minimizing explicit register count (b and c) in both the cases is to ensure that the fused kernel does not generate register spills upon compilation. Line 22 of Algorithm 2 sorts all the 7-tuples with an objective to minimize data movement.

Once sorted, the topmost tuple of L_{tuple} represents the most profitable candidate for fusion. However, the constraints described so far do not account for constraints imposed by hardware, such as the limits on shared memory and registers available per SM, or the trade-off between redundant computation and reduction in global memory accesses due to the use of overlapped tiling. These two constraints are treated differently than the other component metrics in the L_{tuple}. Instead of just being components in a multi-component profitability metric, they are treated as filters. We eliminate any candidate fusion choices that violate either hardware constraints (Section 3.6) or generate too much redundant computation (Section 4). Henceforth, we collectively refer to the hardware constraints and redundancy constraints as *fusibility constraints*. The highest tuple in the list that satisfies the fusibility constraints is chosen, and the nodes corresponding to it are fused. The stencil DAG is updated to include the fused node, and the original statements are removed after updating the dependence graph appropriately. Algorithm 2 is reapplied to this new DAG. This is repeated till no further fusion is feasible.

3.6 Imposing Hardware Constraints

For each node in the stencil DAG, a single kernel is generated to perform the computation represented by that node. We achieve full utilization of the GPU device when the hardware-defined maximum number of concurrent threads supported per SM, say Th_{SM}, are all active. To minimize the volume of redundant computation, we try to maximize the block size on the device, B_{max}, such that the threads are maximally utilized (i.e., maximize B_{max} such that $Th_{SM}\%B_{max}$ is minimum, ideally 0). The number of blocks per SM, say N_B, would be $\lfloor Th_{SM}/B_{max}\rfloor$.

The fusion algorithm described in Algorithm 2 has so far not accounted for the constraints of shared memory available per SM on the device (K_{max}), as well as the number of registers available for each thread (R_{max}). To do so, the sorted list generated at the end of Algorithm 2 is traversed from top to bottom to select the highest tuple that also satisfies the criteria described in the rest of this section.

The amount of shared memory used by each node can be estimated from the resource map ($M_{acc\rightarrow res}$) associated with each node, the size of the thread block used, and the data type of each buffer mapped to shared memory. The tuples in the list where the fused node would require more than the amount of shared memory available per block, i.e., K_{max}/N_B, are ignored.

While the register files on modern GPUs are quite large, a large number of registers per thread can adversely affect the occupancy achieved. We define R_{opt} as the number of registers available to each thread for maximum occupancy. R_{opt} can be computed by dividing the register file size by Th_{sm} ($R_{opt} = \lfloor 65536/2048\rfloor = 32$ for Kepler device). The occupancy decreases from usage of R_{opt} to R_{max}. High occupancy is essential in order to tolerate the access latencies to global memory. To maintain a sufficiently high occupancy, we ignore tuples in L_{tuple} for which the number of explicit registers in the fused node is higher than some threshold. Our current implementation uses a threshold of 12.

It is difficult to model the use of implicit registers as it varies with the compiler version and the optimization level specified during compilation. However, the number of implicit registers used by NVCC usually increases with an increase in the degree of fusion. Our fusion algorithm handles implicit register pressure by ignoring tuples in L_{tuple} which result in register spills upon compilation. The amount of register spills can be determined by using *"-Xptxas -v"* flag during compilation. Setting the threshold of register spills to 0 might seem too conservative. However, determining a perfect balance between spills, occupancy, and performance is beyond the scope of our framework. We currently allow the user to set the threshold on number of spills that can be tolerated.

3.7 Controlling recompilation

Since we need to compile the code generated for each fusion candidate to determine register usage/spills, excessive recompilation can add significant overhead to the code generation time for complex stencils. However, this overhead is mitigated in part due to the choice of a greedy algorithm over one that explores all valid schedules. The number of recompilations is controlled by the following choices:

- Fusion always results in an increase in the resources used by the fused cluster. We only recompile the code of the fused cluster when the fusibility constraints are not already violated by the constraints on shared memory, explicit registers, and redundant computation.
- If fusing any two nodes results in register spills, then we rule out, without recompilation, fusion of any clusters involving either of these two nodes. For example, if fusing nodes A and B results in spills, then we will not consider fusing clusters such as $\{A, C\}$, $\{B, D\}$, etc.
- We provide the user an option to specify a recompilation-bypass size, and only recompile for clusters exceeding that size. For example, if the recompilation-bypass size is 2, then we only recompile when the fusion results in a cluster of size ≥ 3.

With these choices, we prune away a large number of fusion candidates requiring recompilation, thus controlling the total code generation time.

4. MODELING COMPUTATION AND COMMUNICATION REDUNDANCY

We use overlapped tiling to achieve concurrency of tiled execution. Overlapped tiling trades off redundant computation for reduced communication/synchronization overheads. For convenience of description, we make the following assumptions:

- All the stencil operators are order-k, operating on a single N^3 input domain without boundary conditions
- Overlapped tiling applied to any dimension of the input domain tiles it in chunks of size B
- Applying the fusion strategy of Section 3.1 results in the fusion of T stencil operators, where operator O_p has a RAW dependency on operator O_{p-1}

Traditional 3D overlapped tiling partitions the input domain into blocks of size B^3. A stencil operator at fusion depth t will compute an output block of size $(B-2tk)^3$. Since the computable output domain is of size $(N-2Tk)^3$, the total number of thread blocks launched must be $\left(\frac{N-2Tk}{B-2Tk}\right)^3$. If we use sliding window tiling along one dimension and perform overlapped tiling along the other two dimensions, the per-block computation increases, but the total number of blocks launched reduces to $\left(\frac{N-2Tk}{B-2Tk}\right)^2$. Table 1 lists the per-block data transfer and computation volume for both the methods, assuming all global memory transactions are perfectly aligned. Multiplying them by the number of blocks launched gives us the total data transfers and computation volume.

We note that with both forms of overlapped tiling, the fractional redundant computation overhead increases with the time tile size T and stencil order k, and decreases as the block size B is increased. However, the demand on shared memory and registers grows as $O(B^3)$ for 3D overlapped tiling, but only as $O(B^2)$ for sliding-window overlapped tiling. As was illustrated by the exam-

Scheme	Load Inst.	Load Transactions	Store Inst.	Store Transactions	Total Computation	Redundant computation
Traditional 3D Tiling	B^3	$B^2\lceil \frac{B}{W} \rceil$	$(B-2Tk)^3$	$(B-2Tk)^2 \lceil \frac{B-2Tk}{W} \rceil$	$\sum_{i=1}^{T} (B-2ik)^3$	$\sum_{i=1}^{T-1} ((B-2ik)^3 - (B-2Tk)^3)$
Sliding Window with 2D Tiling	NB^2	$NB\lceil \frac{B}{W} \rceil$	$(N-2Tk)$ $(B-2Tk)^2$	$(N-2Tk)(B-2Tk)\lceil \frac{B-2Tk}{W} \rceil$	$\sum_{i=1}^{T} (N-2ik)(B-2ik)^2$	$\sum_{i=1}^{T-1} ((N-2ik)(B-2ik)^2 - (N-2Tk)(B-2Tk)^2)$

Table 1: Per-block data transfers and computational volume for different overlapped tiling schemes. *W* is the warp size.

ple in Section 2, the limited size of shared-memory per SM (under 64 Kbytes) makes it infeasible to use block sizes much larger than 10 for 3D overlapped tiling, while a block size of around 32 is feasible for sliding-window overlapped tiling. Even for k=1, the redundant computation overhead explodes for 3D overlapped tiling, even for fusion over 3 time steps, making it completely ineffective for 3D stencils for the hardware parameters of current GPUs. In contrast, the redundant computation overhead for sliding-window overlapped tiling is much lower, enabling useful fusion over multiple statements or time steps.

We next characterize the redundancy in computation and the global memory transactions for sliding-window overlapped tiling as a function of the input domain and the tiling parameters. Such a characterization is essential for modeling the profitability of fusion for statements with RAW dependence between them.

For a fixed k, the data transfer and redundant computation volume depends on T, which is controlled by the extent of fusion. For illustration, assume that there are four fusion-amenable stencil operators. We can explore several fusion choices – fuse all the four to get a single operator, fuse two to get two resultant operators, or fuse none. For sliding-window tiling, Table 2 explores the profitability of different fusion choices for stencils of various orders.

k	fusion degree	Load Transactions	Store Transactions	Redundant Computation
1	1	18939904	17686800	0
	2	10786022	9364037	39978854
	4	7225344	5334336	144831456
2	1	21572044	18728073	0
	2	14450688	10668672	95227776
	4	15745024	7626496	487849728
4	1	28901376	21337344	0
	2	31490048	15252992	313916416

Table 2: Choosing degree of fusion for varying *k*

We seek to minimize global memory transactions via fusion, while accounting for the increase in redundant computation as more statements are fused together. The hardware constraints used to eliminate tuples of the sorted list L_{tuple} in Section 3.6 usually eliminate high degrees of fusion. The profitability of fusion for the configurations in Table 2 is determined by computing the estimated time for performing global memory transactions (T_{mem}) and the estimated time for performing the computation (T_{comp}). To compute these estimates, we use the peak memory bandwidth and the peak performance achieved by a set of synthetic stencil benchmarks on the underlying device. The comparison metric $T_{max} = max\,(T_{comp}, T_{mem})$, inspired by the roofline model [26], is used to quantify the efficiency of the generated sliding-window overlap-tiled code. If a tuple of the list L_{tuple} has a value of T_{max} for the fused node that is greater than the sum of the values of T_{max} for the unfused nodes, that fusion choice is eliminated from consideration. The configurations with lowest T_{max} for different values of k are highlighted in Table 2. For experimental validation, we plot the performance for 12 time steps of a 13-point order-2 3D Jacobi stencil sequence with varying degree of fusion. The results are shown in Figure 1. The best performance is achieved when the degree of fusion is 2, as predicted by the model.

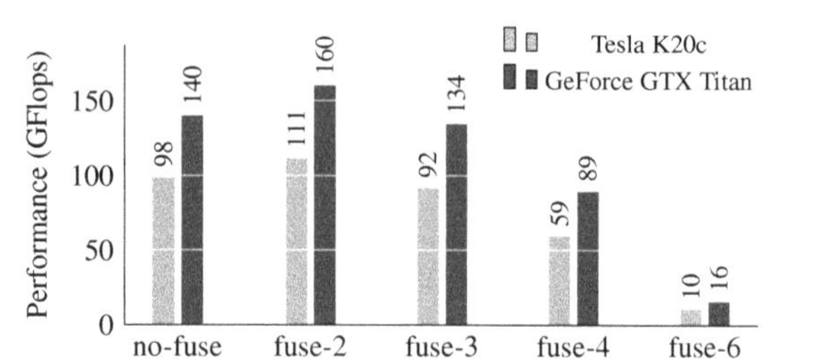

Figure 1: Performance of 12 time steps of a 13-point Jacobi stencil (k=2) for varied degree of fusion

5. CODE GENERATION

The code generation for an input stencil DAG consists of three main steps:

1. Fuse nodes in the DAG using the process described in Sections 3 and 4.
2. Generate a device kernel for each node in the fused DAG to execute the computation represented by the node.
3. Generate a host function to copy input arrays into device memory, launch the kernels generated in Step 2 in a sequence that satisfies dependencies between the fused DAG nodes, and copy the output of the computation back to the host.

Algorithm 3: Device code generation

Input : IN: a node from the post-fusion stencil DAG
Output: D_{gpu}: device function for the node

1 $M_{IN} \leftarrow$ *resource_usage(IN)* ;
2 $D_{gpu} \leftarrow$ *generate_allocated_resources* (M_{IN});
3 **for** *each A in input_arrays (IN)* **do**
4 | D_{gpu}.*append (generate_read_new_plane* (M_{IN}, *A))*;
5 **end**
6 D_{gpu}.*append (generate_stencil_code (IN,* M_{IN}*))*;
7 **for** *each A in (all_arrays (IN) - input_arrays (IN))* **do**
8 | D_{gpu}.*append (generate_rotate_data* (M_{IN}, *A))*;
9 **end**

Algorithm 3 shows the phases involved in the device code generation, and Listing 4 shows the output of our code generator. The output CUDA code can be divided into four distinct parts.

The first part uses the resource map M_{IN} computed in Section 3.3 to allocate GPU resources for different arrays involved in the computation. Function *generate_allocate_resources()* at line 2 declares the required shared memory buffers and registers for arrays *A*, *B*, and *C* at lines 10–12 of Listing 4.

The second part reads a new plane for each input array from global memory into the sliding window. Function *generate_read_new_plane()* at line 4 reads a new plane for the input array A into the shared memory buffer at line 15 of Listing 4.

The third part generates the stencil code for each statement. Function *generate_stencil_code()* at line 6 visits all the accesses in each stencil statement, and replaces it by the assigned GPU resource from M_{IN} (lines 17–28 of Listing 4).

Once the stencil computation is performed, the fourth part slides the window across the arrays cached in shared memory buffers/explicit registers for each statement freeing one resource to read from global memory in the next iteration. Function *generate_rotate_-data()* at line 8 rotates the data for arrays B and C at lines 31–32 of Listing 4, freeing a register for each array in the process.

To write the final accumulated value for the output array C to global memory, a store statement is generated after the last write to C at line 27 of Listing 4. Synchronization barriers are inserted (using *__syncthreads()*) between each part to maintain memory consistency.

Listing 4: Generated CUDA code for DSL of Listing 3

```
1  __global__ void jacobi (float* restrict A,...) {
2    // Determine the block indices
3    int blockdim_i= (int)(blockDim.x);
4    int i0 = (int)(blockIdx.x)*(blockdim_i -4);
5    int i = i0 + (int)(threadIdx.x);
6    int blockdim_j= (int)(blockDim.y);
7    int j0 = (int)(blockIdx.y)*(blockdim_j -4);
8    int j = j0 + (int)(threadIdx.y);
9    // Resource Allocation
10   float __shared__ shA_c0[32][32];
11   float __shared__ shB_m1[32][32];
12   float rB_c0=0, rB_p1=0, rC_m2=0, rC_m1=0, rC_c0=0;
13   for (int k=0; k<=L-1; ++k) {
14     // Fetch new plane
15     shA_c0[j-j0][i-i0] = A[k*M*N + j*N + i];
16     __syncthreads ();
17     if (j >= max (j0+1,1) & ...) {
18       rB_p1 = c * shA_c0[j-j0][i-i0];
19       rB_c0 += stencil (shA_c0);
20       shB_m1[j-j0][i-i0] += b * shA_c0[j-j0][i-i0];
21     }
22     __syncthreads ();
23     if (j >= max (j0+2,1) & ...) {
24       rC_c0 = c * shB_m1[j-j0][i-i0];
25       rC_m1 += stencil (shB_m1);
26       rC_m2 += b * shB_m1[j-j0][i-i0];
27       C[max(k-2,0)*M*N + j*N + i] = rC_m2;
28     }
29     __syncthreads ();
30     // Value rotation
31     shB_m1[j-j0][i-i0] = rB_c0;
32     rB_c0 = rB_p1; rC_m2 = rC_m1; rC_m1 = rC_c0;
33     __syncthreads ();
34   }
35 }
```

Even though we limit the discussion to accumulative statements, our code generator can handle the diagonal access-free stencils as presented in [15, 17, 20] without converting them to accumulations.

6. CASE STUDY AND EVALUATION

In this section we present experimental results comparing performance achieved using other available GPU code generators with the approach described in this paper. We begin with a case study using a component stencil from a DOE mini-application, which we use to illustrate the developed fusion strategy. We follow that by a presentation of experimental results on a set of benchmarks.

6.1 Case Study: Hypterm

We evaluate the impact of applying the fusion heuristics on the hypterm routine of the ExpCNS mini-application from DoE that integrates the Compressible Navier-Stokes (CNS) equations [1]. For the discussion, we set the fusion objective to be minimization of data movement. The hypterm routine reads from a set of input arrays (*cons* and q) to update a set of *flux* arrays. In the stencil DAG of hypterm shown in Figure 2, the intermediate and output nodes (in shades of black) are order-4 stencil operators. There are 15 accumulation statements in the stencil computation, which are labeled in the figure. Different colored edges in Figure 2 represent 1D stencils along different dimensions. The hypterm routine is not time-iterated, and thus efficient data reuse across multiple stencils is crucial for performance. An untiled implementation of hypterm which does not use shared memory achieves only 35.65 GFlops on a Tesla K20c device.

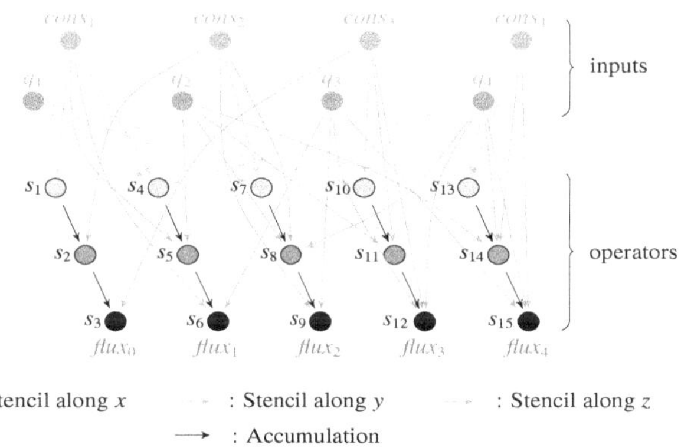

Figure 2: The stencil DAG of hypterm routine. *cons* and q are the input arrays, *flux* is the output array.

The fusion approach is applied to this DAG as follows:

- We begin by noting that s_{12} and s_{15} (s_6 and s_9) apply an order-4 1D stencil along z to three (two) input arrays. The number of registers used for spatial tiling would be $\geq$ 24 ($\geq$ 16), which exceeds M_{reg}. Therefore, these statements with never be fused with any other statements.
- Statements s_{13} and s_{14} accumulate data to the same array, and have two common input arrays. Since their fusion would result in maximum data movement saving among all nodes, the fusion algorithm merges them.
- The next candidates for fusion are clusters $\{s_{10},s_{11}\}$, and $\{s_4,s_5\}$. Both clusters result in a data movement saving of 2. However, the algorithm chooses to fuse s_{10} and s_{11} first, since the resulting node requires fewer total shared memory buffers. Statements s_4 and s_5 are fused in the next step.
- Fusing clusters $\{s_4,s_5\}$ and $\{s_{13},s_{14}\}$ will result in a data movement saving of 3. However, the fusion results in register spills in the generated code, violating the fusibility constraints. Hence this cluster is not fused.
- Statements s_7 and s_8 have a common input, and contribute to the same output. Hence they are fused next.
- Clusters $\{s_4,s_5\}$ and $\{s_7,s_8\}$ are fused next, since fusing them saves on data movement without register spills. Statements s_1 and s_2 are fused as they contribute to the same array.
- Statement s_3 and cluster $\{s_{10}, s_{11}\}$ are fused next, since they have a common input. Cluster s$\{s_1,s_2\}$ and $\{s_{13},s_{14}\}$ are fused to minimize the number of kernel launches.

[1]http://exactcodesign.org/proxy-app-software/

Any further fusion violates the fusibility constraints, since the shared memory usage of the fused cluster would exceed M_{shm}. The final nodes in the optimized DAG are: $\{s_1, s_2, s_{13}, s_{14}\}$, $\{s_3, s_{10}, s_{11}\}$, $\{s_4, s_5, s_7, s_8\}$, s_6, s_9, s_{12}, and s_{14}. As mentioned earlier, statements s_6, s_9, s_{12}, and s_{14} apply an order-4 stencil along the streaming dimension z on two or more input arrays.

Due to the high register pressure with our tiling scheme, we opt for naïve tiling with no use of shared memory or explicit registers for s_{13} and s_{14} in the generated code. The optimized code for the post-fusion DAG achieves 128.98 GFlops on a K20c, a 3.6× speedup over the base unfused version.

Recompilations. If we set the recompilation-bypass size to 1, then we perform nine recompilations to detect any violation of the fusibility constraints – five for clusters of size 2, two for clusters of size 3, and two for clusters of size 4. If the recompilation-bypass size is set to 2, then only four recompilations are needed.

Effect of implicit registers on degree of fusion. Since all the statements in the hypterm stencil are accumulations, a fusion model that does not account for implicit registers will fuse too many statements together. This will create high register pressure in the generated kernel, leading to register spills. In Figure 3, we plot the performance of the generated code for various degrees of fusion. *max-fuse* refers to the version with maximum fusion. It requires a 264 byte stack frame, generating 648 bytes of spill stores and 488 bytes of spill loads. *fuse-8* and *fuse-6* also generate spills. *fuse-8* requires 72 bytes of stack frame (76 bytes spill stores, 92 bytes spill loads), and *fuse-6* requires 16 bytes of stack frame (20 bytes spill stores, 20 bytes spill load). There are no spills generated for *fuse-4* and *fuse-2*. Any advantages from reduction in data movement for a degree of fusion higher than 4 is offset by the increase in global memory traffic from register spills. Since our fusion approach checks for register spills in the fusibility constraints, we generate a code with degree of fusion 4, thereby achieving the highest performance amongst these variants.

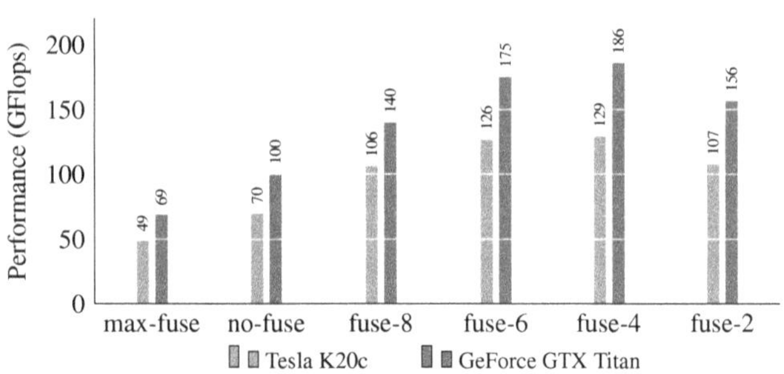

Figure 3: Performance of hypterm for varied degree of fusion

6.2 Experimental Evaluation

We evaluate our framework on a set of benchmarks listed in Table 3, and compare performance against PPCG-0.04 [24], Overtile-0.3.2 [9], and Forma [19]. PPCG and Overtile are open source compilers. All benchmarks use single-precision floating point computations. The code was compiled using NVCC 7.0 with flags '–*use_fast_math Xptxas "-v -dlcm=cg" -maxrregcount=32*'. The objective function was chosen to be minimization of data movement, since the performance of code generated with it was comparable to or better than the variants using other objective functions. The recompilation-bypass size was set to 1.

In each case, the time taken to generate the optimized code is dominated by the time for recompilations. As mentioned earlier, code versions are recompiled because we cannot effectively estimate the impact of fusion on the number of "implicit" registers used by the NVCC compiler. Since the compilation time depends on the host machine on which the code is compiled, instead of reporting absolute time for code generation, we provide information on the number of recompilations needed. The additional time to run the greedy fusion heuristic is negligible compared to the time for the NVCC recompilations. The number of recompiled variants is not excessive because of pruning from violation of any of the resource constraints, and the fact that growth of a fused cluster increases its resource usage. The most complex of the tested stencils was the previously discussed hypterm case study – any topological sort is valid for this stencil DAG, but it required only nine recompilations.

Benchmark	Domain	T	k	Flops	Arrays
Heat	512^3	4	1	15	2
Poisson	512^3	4	1	21	2
Chebyshev	512^3	4	1	39	6
Denoise	500^3	4	2	62	4
MiniGMG	480^3	4	1	27	9
Hypterm	300^3	1	4	358	13
FDTD	300^3	4	1	39	6

Table 3: Characteristics of the 3D benchmarks

Figure 4 presents performance in GFlops, for kernel execution time of the benchmarks from Table 3, on a Tesla K20c and a GeForce GTX Titan device. Figure 5 shows the performance on a GeForce GTX Titan X Maxwell device. For Kepler, the read-only arrays annotated with *__restrict__* keyword can be loaded through the cache used by texture pipeline. To exploit this feature, the input and output arrays were annotated in all the codes except for the baseline PPCG code. PPCG performs default thread coarsening, and the degree of coarsening for the Overtile compiler can be specified as part of the DSL input. Mapping multiple iterations to a thread exposes instruction level parallelism. The performance numbers for Overtile were measured by coarsening the slowest varying dimension by a factor of 2. Our code generator does not support thread coarsening at present. The tile sizes for all codes were tuned to achieve maximum occupancy.

The access offsets in Poisson and Chebyshev make them unresponsive to the optimizations proposed in [15, 17]. We are able to optimize them for storage by associative reordering of operations. For Chebyshev, which reads from four input arrays, time tiling would be impossible if all the input is stored in shared memory. With associative reordering, we are able to offload the storage of some arrays to registers, thereby allowing fusion. Denoise and MiniGMG are multi-statement stencils. Despite the high number of input arrays read, we are able to achieve maximal occupancy by optimizing them for storage. All benchmarks have RAW dependence between stencil statements. For Heat and Poisson, the degree of fusion is limited to 2 by the constraints on shared memory and redundant computations. For MiniGMG, FDTD and Denoise, the constraints on shared memory buffers and explicit registers are violated for fusion degree beyond 2. For Chebyshev, the constraint on explicit registers is violated for a fusion degree beyond 2. For the benchmarks with $T = 4$, we recompile clusters of size 2 only twice to check for a violation of the fusibility constraints.

Since PPCG does classical tiling without utilizing shared memory, the performance of its generated code is not comparable with other code generators. The Overtile compiler could not generate correct code for MiniGMG and Chebyshev. Since hypterm can

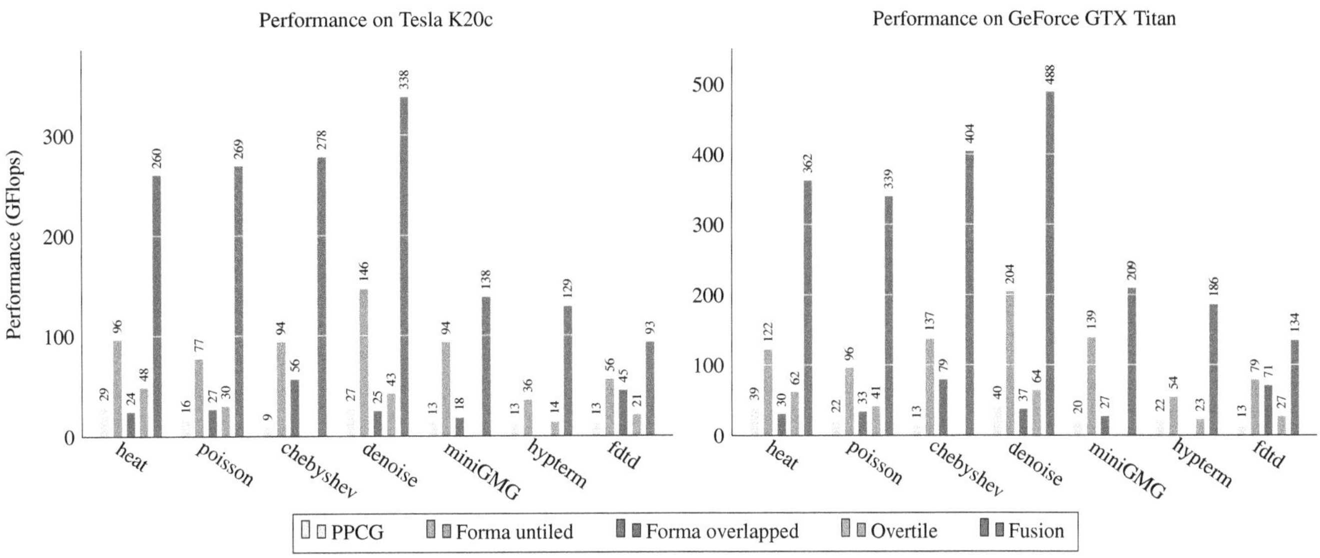

Figure 4: Performance results for 3D benchmarks on Kepler Tesla K20c and GeForce GTX Titan

only be spatially tiled, we do not present the performance numbers for Forma's overlap-tiled code for hypterm. Our optimized auto-generated code achieves 3.6× speedup for hypterm, 2.95× speedup for Chebyshev, and 2.3× speedup for Denoise. The speedup for MiniGMG is only 1.5×, due to the high volume of global transactions to read from a large number of input arrays. FDTD performs global writes and reads for six arrays at each time step. Time tiling reduces global transactions, but increases resource pressure, thereby reducing the achievable occupancy. If the shared memory size increases in future GPU architectures, we would be able to time-tile FDTD without sacrificing occupancy, further improving its performance.

The performance gap between other frameworks and our framework stems from the following factors: (a) we use a fusion heuristic to reduce data movement across stencil operators; (b) we use registers along with shared memory to cache the input data – this not only reduces access latency, but also reduces shared memory pressure, enabling higher occupancy than the other frameworks as the order of the stencil goes up; (c) we leverage associative reordering to transform the computation to a form on which the resource optimizations can be performed – this allows us to optimize a wider range of stencil computations than the other frameworks. As demonstrated by the experimental results, the proposed perspective on fusion and tiling for 3D stencils on GPUs leads to significantly better performance than what is possible with previously developed approaches.

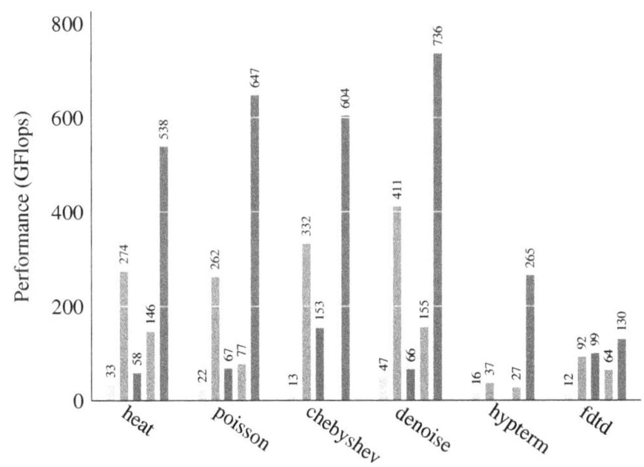

Figure 5: Performance results for 3D benchmarks on Maxwell GeForce GTX Titan X device

7. RELATED WORK

Loop fusion and time tiling for stencil computations have been studied for CPUs. Ahmed et al. [1] present a polyhedral model based approach for synthesizing transformations to enhance data locality in imperfectly-nested loops. Li et al. [14] present a compiler framework for automatic tiling of iterative stencils, with a cost model to minimize cache misses. Mullapudi et al. present PolyMage [16], a domain-specific compiler for image processing pipelines on CPUs. It uses the polyhedral model to develop model-driven transformations for fusion, tiling, and storage optimization for image processing pipelines. However, due to architectural differences, the performance of tiling approaches on CPUs does not necessarily translate well to GPUs, especially for higher-dimensional stencils. High-performance GPU code generation for stencil computations has been a topic of active research [2, 4, 5, 6, 7, 9, 12, 15, 17, 19, 24, 25]. These research efforts can be grouped into four categories.

The first category comprises *automated code generators*, mainly targeting time-iterated stencils [2, 4, 5, 9, 23, 19, 24]. To achieve concurrent execution of tiles with time-tiling, these code generators use some form of non-rectangular tiling, such as overlapped tiling [9, 19, 16], split tiling [23, 5], or hexagonal tiling [4]. PPCG [24] is a polyhedral source-to-source compiler that generates classically time-tiled CUDA code from an annotated sequential program. Patus [2] generates time-tiled code with varying degree of thread coarsening, but without any use of shared memory. Overtile [9] and Forma [19] use shared memory, but do not utilize streaming. The split tile and hexagonal tile approaches of Grosser et al. [4, 5] also do not use streaming; the codes are not publicly available for evaluation. In contrast to our code generator, none of these code generators use fusion across stencil operators to maximize reuse, or streaming to reduce the tile footprint. PolyMage [16] performs fusion across stencils, but does not use streaming and does not address GPU code generation. Pochoir [23] is a stencil compiler that uses a cache-oblivious approach to generate split-tiled code for multi-core CPUs, but does not consider sequences of multiple stencil statements. With prior GPU code generators [2, 4, 5, 9, 19, 24], while good performance was demonstrated on a variety of 2D stencils, very few 3D stencils were evaluated, and performance on any evaluated 3D stencils for large problem sizes was considerably lower than performance achieved with large 2D stencil computations.

The second category of research comprises optimized *hand-tuned implementations* that target specific computations. Micikevicius [15] implemented spatial tiling with registers to alleviate shared memory pressure for a 3D finite difference computation. However, the optimizations in the implementation are limited to cross-stencils with a specific access pattern. Nguyen et al. [17] use the techniques presented in [15] to time-tile a 7-point 3D Jacobi computation that streams through one dimension. Our prior work [20] demonstrated high-performance for many 2D and 3D stencils through manual implementation of overlapped tiling with sliding windows, along with associative reordering for effective use of shared memory and registers.

The third category of research focuses on *auto-tuning* of certain parameters to optimize stencil computations. Datta et al. [3] analyze the performance of a 7-point 3D stencil (as implemented by Nguyen et al. [17]) on an Nvidia GTX280. Kamil et al. [11] develop a code generator and an auto-tuning framework, but their code generator does not utilize shared memory for stencil computations. Zhang and Mueller [27] evaluate a code generator and auto-tuner for 3D stencils on GPU clusters, but do not incorporate time-tiling. For many bandwidth-bound kernels, just spatial tiling is insufficient to achieve high performance. Halide [18] decouples algorithm specification from schedule. Halide schedules can express spatial tiling and sliding-window optimizations. However, the performance depends on either manually writing an efficient schedule, or exploring a vast schedule space with auto-tuning. Instead of auto-tuning, our code generator employs a model-driven approach to choose between fusion configurations.

The fourth category of research addresses the development of *analytical models* for the performance of stencil computations on GPUs. These models are intended for integration into code generators to guide kernel optimizations. Hong and Kim [10] propose an analytical model to predict performance of GPU kernels. However, their model relies on manual gleaning of low-level information about the kernel. Lai et al. [13] analyze a performance upper bound for SGEMM on GPUs, and use register blocking assuming maximum register reuse. Their model only provides performance upper-bounds for compute-bound kernels. Su et al. [22] propose a model that estimates the execution time based on the data traffic between different memory hierarchies. A common limitation of all these models is the precision in prediction, stemming from the complexity of the underlying hardware. Wahib and Maruyama [25] extend the analytical model in [13]. They pose kernel fusion as an optimization problem, and use a code-less performance model to choose a near-optimal fusion configuration amongst other possible variants. The space of feasible solutions is pruned using a search heuristic based on a hybrid grouping genetic algorithm. Gysi et al. [6] also propose a model-driven stencil optimization approach. Like [25], they use a code-less performance model to find the best fusion configuration among *all* valid topological sorts of the stencil DAG. The model has been used to guide kernel fusion in the Stella library [7]. While these works do model the shared memory constraints for kernel fusion, their models cannot accurately account for the register usage of the final kernel generated by NVCC, since the register count is highly influenced by the domain-specific optimizations first performed on the original code. We address this issue by splitting the register usage into two classes, *explicit* and *implicit* registers. While the explicit registers are modeled accurately, the implicit register usage is accounted for by limited compilation of a small number of fused configurations.

It is worth noting that the main focus of this work was not to develop a model that could accurately predict kernel performance for different fusion variants. Instead, our goal was to develop a practically effective model that incorporated fusion, sliding-window overlapped tiling, and associative reordering to enable automated generation of high-performance GPU kernels for 3D stencils. The modeling approach was validated by the performance achieved for many stencil benchmarks. Indeed, if a better model is available that can more accurately predict the performance of the generated CUDA kernels, it can be easily incorporated into the compilation tool-chain.

8. CONCLUSIONS

Several factors are important in enhancing the performance of a 3D stencil computation on a GPU: (a) maximizing use of the processing resources; (b) minimizing global memory accesses; (c) effective use of shared memory and registers; (d) accounting for the computational redundancy introduced by the tiling scheme. We present an automated code generator that manages the allocation of GPU resources, using fusion along with 2D overlapped tiling and streaming through one unpartitioned spatial dimension. A heuristic for fusion choice seeks to optimize the use of shared memory and registers. Experimental results on two GPU devices on a set of resource-intensive benchmarks demonstrate significant performance improvement over other available code generators.

9. ACKNOWLEDGMENTS

We thank the anonymous reviewers for their feedback and constructive comments. This work was supported in part by the National Science Foundation through award ACI-1440749, 1513120, and 1524127, and the Department of Energy through award DE-SC0008844.

10. REFERENCES

[1] N. Ahmed, N. Mateev, and K. Pingali. Synthesizing transformations for locality enhancement of imperfectly-nested loop nests. *Int. J. Parallel Program.*, 29(5):493–544, Oct. 2001.

[2] M. Christen, O. Schenk, and H. Burkhart. PATUS: A code generation and autotuning framework for parallel iterative stencil computations on modern microarchitectures. In *Proceedings of the 2011 IEEE International Parallel & Distributed Processing Symposium*, IPDPS '11, pages 676–687. IEEE Computer Society, 2011.

[3] K. Datta, M. Murphy, V. Volkov, S. Williams, J. Carter, L. Oliker, D. Patterson, J. Shalf, and K. Yelick. Stencil computation optimization and auto-tuning on state-of-the-art multicore architectures. In *Proceedings of the 2008 ACM/IEEE Conference on Supercomputing*, SC '08, pages 4:1–4:12. IEEE Press, 2008.

[4] T. Grosser, A. Cohen, J. Holewinski, P. Sadayappan, and S. Verdoolaege. Hybrid hexagonal/classical tiling for GPUs. In *Proceedings of Annual IEEE/ACM International*

Symposium on Code Generation and Optimization, CGO '14, pages 66:66–66:75. ACM, 2014.

[5] T. Grosser, A. Cohen, P. H. J. Kelly, J. Ramanujam, P. Sadayappan, and S. Verdoolaege. Split tiling for GPUs: Automatic parallelization using trapezoidal tiles. In *Proceedings of the 6th Workshop on General Purpose Processor Using Graphics Processing Units*, GPGPU-6, pages 24–31. ACM, 2013.

[6] T. Gysi, T. Grosser, and T. Hoefler. MODESTO: data-centric analytic optimization of complex stencil programs on heterogeneous architectures. In *Proceedings of the 29th ACM on International Conference on Supercomputing*, ICS '15, pages 177–186. ACM, 2015.

[7] T. Gysi, C. Osuna, O. Fuhrer, M. Bianco, and T. C. Schulthess. STELLA: a domain-specific tool for structured grid methods in weather and climate models. In *Proceedings of the International Conference for High Performance Computing, Networking, Storage and Analysis*, SC '15, pages 41:1–41:12. ACM, 2015.

[8] T. Henretty, R. Veras, F. Franchetti, L.-N. Pouchet, J. Ramanujam, and P. Sadayappan. A stencil compiler for short-vector SIMD architectures. In *Proceedings of the 27th International ACM Conference on International Conference on Supercomputing*, ICS '13, pages 13–24. ACM, 2013.

[9] J. Holewinski, L.-N. Pouchet, and P. Sadayappan. High-performance code generation for stencil computations on GPU architectures. In *Proceedings of the 26th ACM International Conference on Supercomputing*, ICS '12, pages 311–320. ACM, 2012.

[10] S. Hong and H. Kim. An analytical model for a GPU architecture with memory-level and thread-level parallelism awareness. In *Proceedings of the 36th Annual International Symposium on Computer Architecture*, ISCA '09, pages 152–163, New York, NY, USA, 2009. ACM.

[11] S. Kamil, C. Chan, L. Oliker, J. Shalf, and S. Williams. An auto-tuning framework for parallel multicore stencil computations. In *Parallel Distributed Processing (IPDPS), 2010 IEEE International Symposium on*, pages 1–12, April 2010.

[12] S. Krishnamoorthy, M. Baskaran, U. Bondhugula, J. Ramanujam, A. Rountev, and P. Sadayappan. Effective automatic parallelization of stencil computations. In *Proceedings of the 28th ACM SIGPLAN Conference on Programming Language Design and Implementation*, PLDI '07, pages 235–244. ACM, 2007.

[13] J. Lai and A. Seznec. Performance upper bound analysis and optimization of SGEMM on fermi and kepler GPUs. In *Proceedings of the 2013 IEEE/ACM International Symposium on Code Generation and Optimization (CGO)*, CGO '13, pages 1–10, Washington, DC, USA, 2013. IEEE Computer Society.

[14] Z. Li and Y. Song. Automatic tiling of iterative stencil loops. *ACM Trans. Program. Lang. Syst.*, 26(6):975–1028, Nov. 2004.

[15] P. Micikevicius. 3D finite difference computation on GPUs using CUDA. In *Proceedings of 2nd Workshop on General Purpose Processing on Graphics Processing Units*, GPGPU-2, pages 79–84. ACM, 2009.

[16] R. T. Mullapudi, V. Vasista, and U. Bondhugula. Polymage: Automatic optimization for image processing pipelines. In *Proceedings of the Twentieth International Conference on Architectural Support for Programming Languages and Operating Systems*, ASPLOS '15, pages 429–443. ACM, 2015.

[17] A. Nguyen, N. Satish, J. Chhugani, C. Kim, and P. Dubey. 3.5-D blocking optimization for stencil computations on modern CPUs and GPUs. In *Proceedings of the 2010 ACM/IEEE International Conference for High Performance Computing, Networking, Storage and Analysis*, SC '10, pages 1–13. IEEE Computer Society, 2010.

[18] J. Ragan-Kelley, C. Barnes, A. Adams, S. Paris, F. Durand, and S. Amarasinghe. Halide: A language and compiler for optimizing parallelism, locality, and recomputation in image processing pipelines. In *Proceedings of the 34th ACM SIGPLAN Conference on Programming Language Design and Implementation*, PLDI '13, pages 519–530. ACM, 2013.

[19] M. Ravishankar, J. Holewinski, and V. Grover. Forma: A DSL for image processing applications to target GPUs and multi-core CPUs. In *Proceedings of the 8th Workshop on General Purpose Processing Using GPUs*, GPGPU-8, pages 109–120. ACM, 2015.

[20] P. S. Rawat, C. Hong, M. Ravishankar, V. Grover, L.-N. Pouchet, and P. Sadayappan. Effective resource management for enhancing performance of 2D and 3D stencils on GPUs. In *Proceedings of the 9th Annual Workshop on General Purpose Processing Using Graphics Processing Unit*, GPGPU '16, pages 92–102. ACM, 2016.

[21] K. Stock, M. Kong, T. Grosser, L.-N. Pouchet, F. Rastello, J. Ramanujam, and P. Sadayappan. A framework for enhancing data reuse via associative reordering. In *Proceedings of the 35th ACM SIGPLAN Conference on Programming Language Design and Implementation*, PLDI '14, pages 65–76, New York, NY, USA, 2014. ACM.

[22] H. Su, X. Cai, M. Wen, and C. Zhang. An analytical GPU performance model for 3D stencil computations from the angle of data traffic. *J. Supercomput.*, 71(7):2433–2453, July 2015.

[23] Y. Tang, R. A. Chowdhury, B. C. Kuszmaul, C.-K. Luk, and C. E. Leiserson. The pochoir stencil compiler. In *Proceedings of the Twenty-third Annual ACM Symposium on Parallelism in Algorithms and Architectures*, SPAA '11, pages 117–128, New York, NY, USA, 2011. ACM.

[24] S. Verdoolaege, J. C. Juega, A. Cohen, J. I. Gómez, C. Tenllado, and F. Catthoor. Polyhedral parallel code generation for CUDA. *ACM TACO*, 9(4):54:1–54:23, Jan. 2013.

[25] M. Wahib and N. Maruyama. Scalable kernel fusion for memory-bound GPU applications. In *Proceedings of the International Conference for High Performance Computing, Networking, Storage and Analysis*, SC '14, pages 191–202. IEEE Press, 2014.

[26] S. Williams, A. Waterman, and D. Patterson. Roofline: An insightful visual performance model for multicore architectures. *Commun. ACM*, 52(4):65–76, Apr. 2009.

[27] Y. Zhang and F. Mueller. Auto-generation and auto-tuning of 3D stencil codes on GPU clusters. In *Proceedings of the Tenth International Symposium on Code Generation and Optimization*, CGO '12, pages 155–164. ACM, 2012.

Accelerating Linked-list Traversal Through Near-Data Processing

Byungchul Hong†, Gwangsun Kim†, Jung Ho Ahn‡, Yongkee Kwon*, Hongsik Kim*, John Kim†

†KAIST {kaisthong,gskim,jjk12}@kaist.ac.kr

‡Seoul National University gajh@snu.ac.kr

*SK Hynix {yongkee.kwon,hongsik1.kim}@sk.com

ABSTRACT

Recent technology advances in memory system design, along with 3D stacking, have made near-data processing (NDP) more feasible to accelerate different workloads. In this work, we explore near-data processing for a fundamental operation – linked-list traversal (LLT). We propose a new NDP architecture that does not change the existing sequential programming model and does not require any modification to the processor microarchitecture. Instead, we exploit the packetized interface between the core and the memory modules to off-load LLT for NDP. We leverage a system with multiple memory modules (e.g., hybrid memory cube (HMC) modules) interconnected with a memory network and our initial evaluation shows that simply off-loading LLT computation to near-memory can actually *reduce* performance because of the additional off-chip memory network channel traversals. Thus, we first propose NDP-aware data localization to exploit locality – including locality within a single memory module and memory vault – to minimize latency and improve energy efficiency. In order to improve overall throughput and maximize parallelism, we propose batching multiple LLT operations together to amortize the cost of NDP by utilizing the highly parallel execution of NDP processing units and the high bandwidth of 3D stacked DRAM. The combination of NDP-aware data localization and batching can provide significant improvement in performance and energy efficiency compared to host-processing.

Keywords

Near-data processing; Processing-in-memory; Big-memory workload; Linked-list traversal

1. INTRODUCTION

With the recent emergence of 3D memory stacking, 3D stacked memory combined with a logic layer has been proposed to create a hybrid memory cube (HMC) [24]. Micron has developed the first generation HMC [43] and Intel has announced a Xeon Phi system that leverages a variation of the HMC [47]. In this work, we exploit the availability of such memory modules; in particular, the logic layer within an HMC provides the opportunity for offloading computation and near-data processing (NDP) to accelerate different workloads. Linked-list traversal (LLT) is a simple, fundamental operation used to search an element in a linked-list, but conventional CPUs are not efficient in executing LLT because its access patterns are mostly sequential and random [33]. Thus, to achieve efficient execution of linked-list traversal, we explore offloading or near-data processing of the linked-list traversal to the HMC logic layer.

A linked-list is a basic data structure used to store data by chaining multiple elements through pointer chasing. An array data structure has several benefits over the linked-list, including a more compact storage, better performance in retrieving data and better locality. However, an array also has some limitations which include difficulty in adding new elements to the middle of the array and difficulty in storing elements with different sizes. In comparison, linked-list has the opposite properties such as faster update but slower retrieval and is more appropriate for dynamic applications which require frequent updates. To combine the advantages of both data structures, different data structures, such as a linked-list of arrays is used in modern applications. In this work, we evaluate the impact of NDP on different linked-list implementations, including the linked-list of arrays.

Accessing the elements stored in the linked-list requires pointer-chasing and is also referred to as linked-list traversal (LLT). LLT is intrinsically a *sequential* operation because of the data dependency to the next address, and also often accesses *random* addresses. Thus, architectural advances in modern processors (e.g., multiple cache hierarchies, MLP, and prefetching[1]) provide limited performance improvement for LLT. In addition, while the computation for LLT is relatively simple, the main-memory latency is critical to the overall performance.

Emerging big memory applications that use linked-list data structures, such as hash table and adjacency list of graphs, use LLT for data retrieval where LLT represents a significant amount of the total execution time [33]. A breakdown of execution time for different workloads is shown in Figure 1, which are measured on Dell PowerEdge R910 server with Intel Xeon E7540 quad-sockets, and 512GB of

[1]Address correlation between the linked items can be stored in on-chip buffer to help prefetching during the LLT [15]. However, the huge size of linked-lists and random access pattern can limit the benefit of such modern prefetching techniques for big-memory workloads.

PACT '16, September 11-15, 2016, Haifa, Israel

© 2016 ACM. ISBN 978-1-4503-4121-9/16/09...$15.00

DOI: http://dx.doi.org/10.1145/2967938.2967958

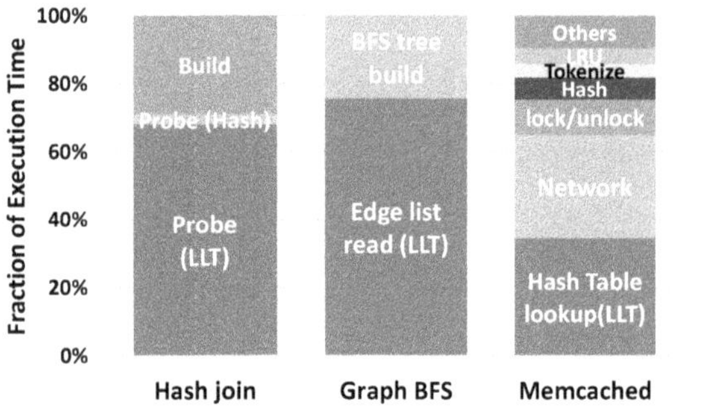

Figure 1: Execution time breakdown of Hash join [8], Graph BFS [39], and Memcached [17] that use LLT.

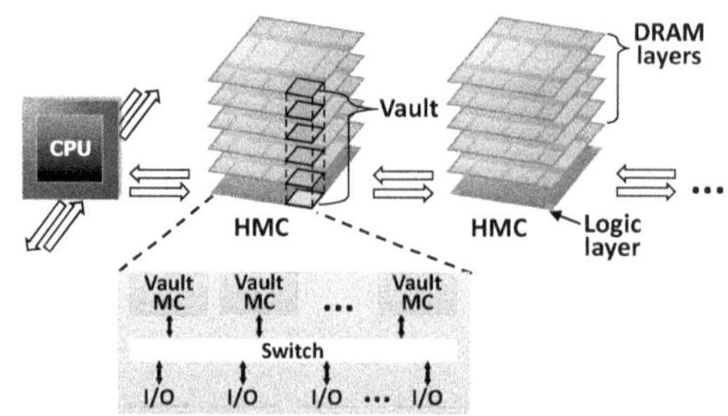

Figure 2: High-level block diagram of hybrid memory cubes (HMCs) and the logic layer, interconnected through memory network.

main memory. Approximately 70-75% of the execution time for Hash join (used by DBMS) [8] and Graph500 BFS [39] and approximately 35% for Memcached [17] is from LLT. In this work, we explore how LLT for these workloads can be accelerated using NDP.

We propose an NDP architecture with multiple memory modules interconnected through a *memory network* [31] to accelerate LLT and exploit the parallelism available across the multiple memory modules. Our approach does not require any modification to the existing sequential programming model and CPU cores. Instead, we exploit the packetized interface between the core and the memory modules to off-load LLT for near-data processing using load/store instructions and simplify the CPU-memory interface. However, we show that simply off-loading LLT does not necessarily improve performance but can actually *decrease* performance because of the additional off-chip channel traversals through the memory network. Thus, we propose NDP-aware data localization to localize data near the NDP execution units to minimize off-chip accesses and reduce LLT latency. In addition, to fully exploit the parallelism available with NDP and improve the LLT throughput, we propose batching of multiple LLT operations within a single packet (and across multiple packets) to improve overall performance and exploit the request-level (or inter-LLT) parallelism.

In particular, the contributions of this work includes the following:

- We propose a near-data processing (NDP) architecture that off-loads linked-list traversal (LLT) to logic near memory using load/store instructions without modifying the existing programming model or core microarchitecture.
- We propose NDP-aware data localization to minimize off-chip accesses and reduce the execution time of LLT.
- We leverage *batching* multiple LLT operations that exploits the inter-LLT parallelism and the parallelism available through the memory network.
- Our evaluation shows that our proposed LLT offloading for NDP can increase performance by 5.9× and energy efficiency by 2.8× compared with host-processing.

2. BACKGROUND AND RELATED WORK

2.1 Hybrid Memory Cube (HMC)

3D integration technology allows the dies fabricated by two or more types of processes to be stacked within a package by TSVs (Through-Silicon Vias). A representative DRAM architecture that exploits the 3D integration technology is HMC (Hybrid Memory Cube) [24], which stacks a logic die and DRAM dies within a package to improve the energy efficiency, bandwidth, and scalability in capacity of main memory systems. Multiple DRAM dies are stacked and divided into vertically aligned partitions that are referred to as *vault* in HMC, as shown in Figure 2. Each vault is connected to the corresponding memory controller located at the logic layer through TSVs. The HMC logic die also has high-speed links through which the memory controllers communicate with other memory modules and the CPU sockets and a switch or an on-chip interconnection network connects these components (the high-speed links and the memory controllers) together. Even with the existence of the links, the controllers, and the interconnect, the logic die has additional area to hold processing elements for acceleration [37, 44]. HMC modules, each becoming a router, can be interconnected together to scale the system and create a memory network [31].

2.2 Linked List

Four different types of linked-list implementation that we consider in this work are shown in Figure 3 and summarized in Table 1. We define an *item* as the data element that is being stored in the linked-list and a *node* as an element that contains the item(s) and a pointer to the next node. The most conventional type of linked-list is shown in Figure 3(a). A single item is stored within each node with a pointer to the next node. Memory efficiency of this type of linked-list can be poor and it also results in a lot of linked-list traversals. However, if an array structure is inappropriate and if neither the size of the items nor the number of items is not known, this data structure can be used. Key-value stores, such as Memcached [17], use this data structure to store various types of data objects.

Figure 3(b) provides a block diagram of linked-list of arrays where each node contains an array of items. Since an array structure is used, the item size needs to be fixed and the items within the node are stored contiguously in memory. In addition, a single pointer is only needed for each array – thus, this implementation reduces the memory requirement and cache locality can be exploited. Hash join [11] is an example that uses this linked-list implementation.

If the total number of items is fixed in addition to the item size, linked-list of arrays can be implemented without a bucket array (Figure 3(c)). Since the pointer reference

Table 1: Different types of linked-list

Type	Item & next ptr.	Item size	# of items	Workloads
1	Unified	Variable	Variable	Memcached [17] LLU [48]
2	Unified	Fixed	Variable	Hash join [11]
3	Unified	Fixed	Fixed	Hash join [8]
4	Separated	-	-	Graph500 [39]

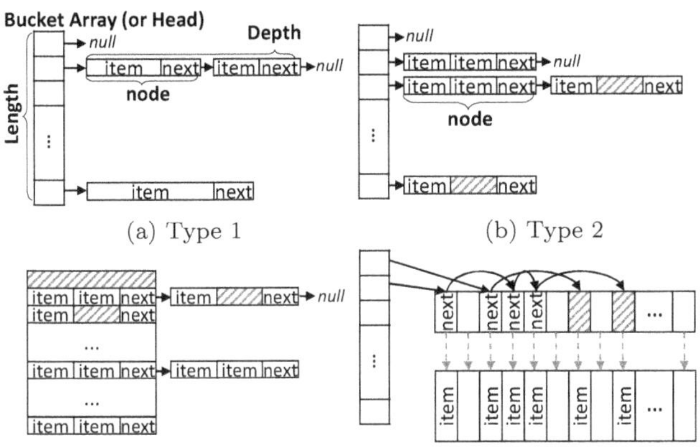

Figure 3: Block diagram of the different linked-list data structures summarized in Table 1.

from the bucket array is removed, reading an item becomes faster; however, unless the index values are uniformly distributed across all of the entries, this approach can waste the memory storage. A different implementation of Hash Join [8] uses this particular data structure type. Linked-list within an array approach is shown in Figure 3(d), where pointers to the next node and items are stored separately. The *List* implementation of Graph500 [39] uses this linked-list type for the adjacency list of graph. While this approach is area-efficient and additional edges can be easily added, significant amount of LLT is required to read the entire adjacency list. In this work, we evaluate our proposed NDP across the different linked-list implementations described in this section.

2.3 Related Work

Near-data processing (NDP) or processing-in-memory (PIM), which tightly integrates functional units with memory units for high performance and energy efficiency, is not new, and has been proposed since the 90s, including FlexRAM [30], IRAM [42], EXECUBE [34], and various smart memory controllers [12, 16, 1]. However, these were not commercialized because DRAM technology did not provide the high performance necessary for the functional units. Recently, NDP has regained interest because of the evolving technology including 3D stacking and big-data applications becoming popular as well as device scaling starting to slow down [6]. As a result, there has been active interest in NDP from the industry and examples include the IBM Active memory cube [41] and the Micron automata processor [14] that can accelerate deep packet inspection and graph analytics. Samsung recently announced a plan to support near data processing of a "search" function in in-memory database [45] by adding FPGA under the stacked DRAM.

NDP with programmable cores: NDC [44] applied NDP to in-memory MapReduce by incorporating energy efficient in-order cores to the logic layer of 3D-stacked memory. Mercury architecture [21] leverages a 3D-stacked memory architecture to improve the physical density and efficiency of key-value store (Memcached) servers. Tesseract [3] accelerates graph workloads by applying processing-in-memory, where in-order core, prefetcher, and message queue are added to each vault, and memory network is used to transfer the data between memory modules. Gao et al. [18] developed an in-memory analytics framework for NDP with a scalable hardware support and run-time system. Kim et al. [32] showed that misses per kilo instructions (MPKI) is one of the most important application characteristics to determine applying near data processing.

NDP with fixed-function/configurable logics: Guo et al. [20] integrated configurable array of hardware logics to an accelerator layer of 3D-stacked memory to accelerate FFT and reshape of data layout while software controls the execution paths of the accelerators. Akin et al. [4] proposed near data processing of data reorganization operations, such as shuffle, pack/unpack, and swap with mathematical framework. Gao et al. [19] proposed heterogeneous reconfigurable logic as near data processing units to increase power and area efficiency. BSSync [35] proposed a hardware support in near memory logic layer to minimize the overhead of atomic operations for machine learning workloads while Nai et al. [40] showed the feasibility of instruction-level offloading for the HMC 2.0 [24] with graph traversal workload.

This work: Our work can be classified as "Fixed-function, Compound PIM operations" based on the taxonomy from Loh et al. [38] as the number of memory accesses is decided by the depth of linked-list. We implement near data processing unit as a fixed-function hardware logic for energy-efficient parallel execution, but with control determined from the off-loading command packet. Compared to prior work on NDP, we provide fine-grained offloading of LLT to NDP through efficient communication interface and exploit the parallelism available through the memory network. Prior work [33] also proposed to accelerate LLT; however, they focused on accelerating LLT for host-processing while this work accelerates LLT with NDP and thus, enables memory access latency to be significantly reduced.

3. NEAR-DATA PROCESSING ARCHITECTURE

Since LLT often has random memory access patterns, on-chip resources in modern CPUs do not necessarily benefit LLT. For example, the probability that the next item of the hash chain in Memcached is read from the CPU on-chip LLC is only 0.56% to 1.2%.[2] Request-level locality (e.g., hot keys) did not increase on-chip cache locality because of the large data set. Thus, we propose to move the execution of LLT closer to the data and reduce LLT latency by minimizing off-chip accesses and improve parallel execution and energy efficiency through dedicated hardware logic or *LLT engine*. The LLT engine that we propose supports all four types of linked-list described earlier in Section 2.2. Throughout this work, we use the term *storage memory* to refer to the memory allocated for the large data set such as a linked-list or a hash table.

[2]Simulation setup used is described in Section 5.2.

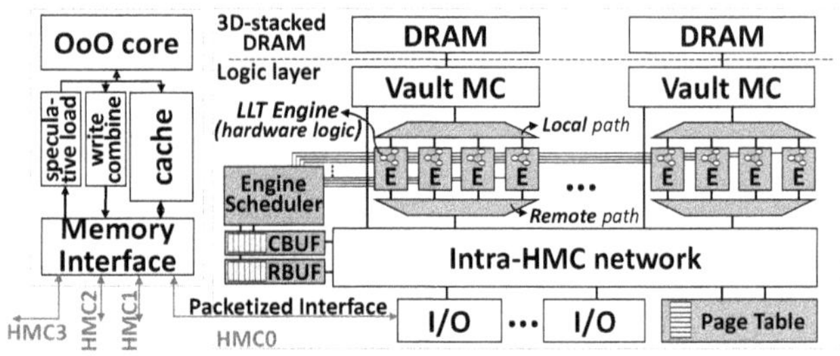

(a) HMC logic layer for near data processing of LLT

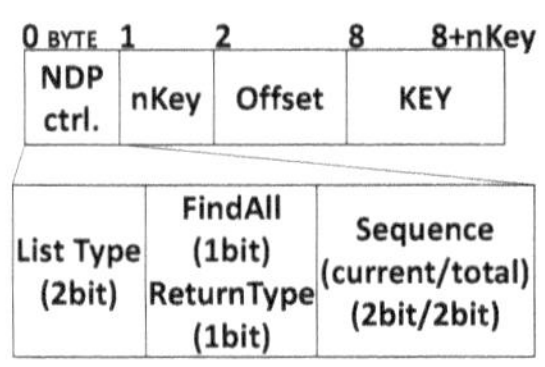

(b) command packet format

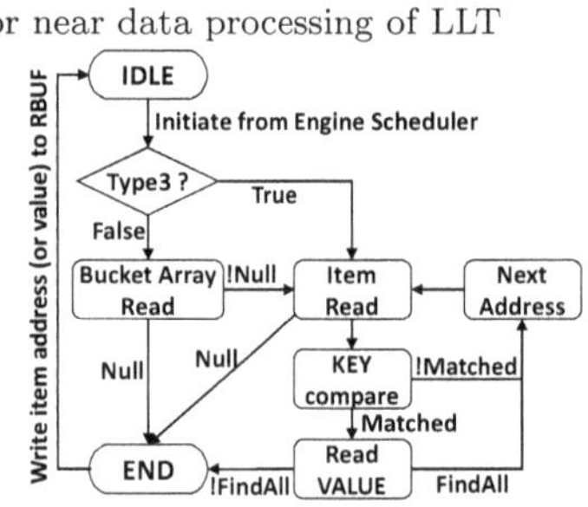

(c) Simplified LLT engine FSM

Figure 4: (a) HMC logic diagram with additional logics for LLT NDP shaded with grey color, (b) offloading command packet format, and (c) simplified finite state machine of the LLT engine.

3.1 NDP Offloading Interface

Without modifying the core architecture, we exploit the packetized interface between the core and the memory modules such that the host CPU communicates with near-data logic through normal load/store instructions. NDP commands/results are communicated through the payload of memory packets. High-level overview of the proposed NDP architecture is shown in Figure 4(a) with the highlighted blocks representing additional logic added to the logic layer, including the command and return buffers (CBUF, RBUF), page table, LLT engines, and LLT engine scheduler. To take advantage of the parallelism with NDP, we assume at least one LLT engine per vault but also later evaluate the impact of increasing the number of LLT engines to further increase parallelism in Section 5.3. To offload LLT operations, the host CPU writes an off-loading command to the command buffer (CBUF) in the target HMC module by transmitting a write packet to the destination memory module. The result or the output of the command is stored in the return buffer (RBUF) and is returned back to the core through a read response packet when host reads the corresponding return buffer. CBUF and RBUF, referred to as *communication* buffers in this work, are divided into 64-Byte entries, same as the memory packet size. Each CBUF entry is mapped to a single RBUF entry, and thus, the result of LLT operation off-loaded to CBUF[n] can be obtained from the RBUF[n], where n is the communication buffer entry ID.

The offloading command packet (Figure 4(b)) consists of control bits (`NDP ctrl`), size of the key (`nKey`), offset of LLT start address from the base address of the storage memory (`Offset`), and the input key to be searched (`Key`). The `Key` represents the identification of an item to be compared when retrieving a data (or the item) from the linked-list. The `Key` can have variable data types such as a variable-length string type in Memcached or a fixed-length integer type in Hash Join. If `Key` is not used during the LLT (e.g., Graph BFS), `nKey` field in the command packet is set to 0 and all of the values in the linked-list are read.

Table 2: Memory type of different memory regions

Region	Memory type	Used for
Storage memory	1GB huge page, Locked, Write-through cache	Linked-lists
Communi -cation	Memory mapped I/O, Uncacheable & write-combine	CBUF/RBUF Page table
Others	4KB page, Write-back cache	Stack, Heap

We assume that packet payload size is fixed to 64B, and if the size of a key is small, multiple offloading commands can be combined into a single command packet through *batching* we describe later in Section 4.2. However, for large keys (e.g., Memcached can have up to 250B size key), the large key is sent across multiple packets. The `sequence` information within the control bits indicates packet ordering, and is used to re-order the packets if they arrive out-of-order. NDP control bits also include information on the linked-list type (`List Type`), and NDP execution control information (`FindAll`, `ReturnType`). `FindAll` determines whether to find all matches in the linked-list or a single first match, and `ReturnType` determines whether to return the address of the value (used for large values) or the value itself.

When an off-loading command is written to CBUF, engine scheduler decodes the command and triggers one of the available LLT engines connected to the target vault that is determined by the `offset` field. LLT engine calculates the start address of the linked-list to be accessed based on the `offset` and the base address[3], and translates it to physical address through the page table (described in Section 3.2). LLT engine then starts pointer-chasing, item format decoding, and key comparison as shown in Figure 4(c), and retrieved results are stored to the return buffer (RBUF). After host CPU writes the off-loading command to CBUF, host CPU reads the corresponding RBUF address by sending a read packet to obtain the NDP result when available. Host usually waits in idle state until the RBUF response arrives as the instructions after LLT may have data dependency on the LLT result and can cause performance degradation. In Section 4.2, we describe how this performance bottleneck can be removed by applying batching.

For safe offloading communication with multiple host CPU threads, it must be guaranteed that multiple threads do not offload to the same entry of the communication buffers. If a fine-grain bucket lock is acquired before LLT operation (e.g., Memcached), the communication buffer entry can be determined based on the bucket lock index and the lock mechanism will protect concurrent access from multiple threads. For workloads that do not acquire the bucket lock, communication buffer is divided by the number of host threads and each thread uses its own entries.

3.2 Address translation and Memory types

In our proposed NDP system, one of the objective is to enable a system that can work with existing CPU architectures with minimal modifications. For LLT, one challenge is address translation since linked-list requires accessing mul-

[3]Static information, such as base address of the storage memory and data structure formats (number of items in a node, byte position of item/next) are written to the configuration registers during initialization phase of workload to minimize the size of the off-loading command.

tiple memory addresses that is not known in advance. The next address stored in the linked-list is a virtual address (VA) since the host CPU builds the linked-list and both NDP and host CPU access the linked-list. The next address can be stored as physical address (PA) to simplify the LLT access, but this would require non-trivial changes to the memory management of the host CPU. As a result, we take advantage of two features that are commonly available in modern systems, huge pages and memory locking, to simplify address translation in our proposed NDP architecture.

LLT engines translate address through the page table that is duplicated within each memory module in the logic layer (Figure 4). To reduce the cost of the duplicated page table, we exploit huge pages to keep the page table size small.[4] For in-memory applications, storage memory is rarely swapped out to the lower-level storage once it is allocated [9]. Therefore, storage memory region can be locked (i.e., `mlock`) to maintain consistent mapping from VA to PA.[5] The page table in near-data logic is managed by the host, and host updates the page table upon the (re)allocation of the storage memory.

Communication buffers use memory mapped I/O and uncacheable region. We assume uncacheable memory similar to the x86 architecture which has a special memory type, called uncacheable speculative write combine (USWC), to enable fast read/write to the uncacheable region [25]. Modern OS and x86 support direct access to memory mapped I/O space in USWC region from the user-level application [25] without OS intervention at run-time. Applications access the communication buffers through load/store instructions, such as `_mm_stream(_load)_si128` in x86 with SIMD registers. If multiple stores to the USWC region have consecutive addresses, they are combined in a write combining buffer until the buffer becomes full or the next store does not have a consecutive address. The write combining buffer sends out multiple stores to memory as a single request packet. In case of read, load instruction (with hint) to the USWC region fills 64 bytes into a speculative load buffer, and subsequent loads to the consecutive addresses are returned from the speculative load buffer. To utilize those architectural optimizations, we change the order of communication buffer accesses as the subsequent accesses have consecutive addresses when sending multiple commands concurrently.

3.3 Cache coherence and memory consistency

Table 2 summarizes the different memory type of each memory region. Storage memory is the only region accessed by NDP, and thus we need to consider cache coherence and memory consistency for this region. Host does both *read* and *write* to the storage memory region, but NDP only does *read* since NDP writes the LLT results to the return buffer and host updates the storage memory with the results if necessary. Memory model should guarantee that the updated data (modified by host) should be visible to NDP units before NDP starts LLT.

To maintain memory consistency, a write-through (WT) cache is used for the storage memory region to ensure that the host writes back the updated data to the main memory without adding hardware cache coherence protocol to NDP. WT cache can cause significant memory traffic, but WT cache in our work is different as only the storage memory uses the write-through policy. In comparison, normal stack/heap regions (which may have high temporal locality) still use write-back (WB) caching. In the workloads that we evaluate, storage memory region is fairly read-intensive as write traffic represents less than 10% of the total memory access – e.g., GET dominant Memcached operations, longer Probe phase than Build phase for Hashjoin/Graph. NDP units can be made as cache coherent devices (or coherent I/O devices [27]) with WB cache for storage memory, and NDP units can send coherent read requests to host. However, this creates significant amount of coherent requests to the host chip, and even with a best case scenario (i.e., data fetched from host on-chip cache), host on-chip cache is not necessarily closer to NDP units compared to the local 3D-stacked memory.

To guarantee the write-back of modified data to main memory before NDP starts LLT, proper synchronization is necessary between the data update and the LLT execution. For Graph search and Hash Join, there is a barrier synchronization between the write phase and read phase that protects the concurrent read/write accesses to the whole storage memory (e.g., Build phase and Probe phase of Hash join). Updated data in write-through region are written-back to main memory at the barrier. For Memcached, concurrent read/write accesses are protected by fine-grain (per bucket) lock – e.g., for two threads (T0, T1) accessing the same bucket,

- T0 : Acquire lock[bucket] => Linked-list update (write by host) => Release lock[bucket]
- T1 : Acquire lock[bucket] => Offloading to NDP => NDP reads linked-list => Release lock[bucket]

Through acquiring the lock that incorporates memory barrier, the memory consistency model is not impacted as offloading cannot precede the lock acquisition in T1. In addition, the updated value by T0 needs to be written back to the memory before NDP reads the linked-list. Thus, the write-back to memory needs to be done on the lock release for the write-through memory region, which is done for the write-combined (WC) and write-through (WT) memory types in x86 [26].

4. NEAR-DATA PROCESSING OF LINKED-LIST TRAVERSAL (LLT)

An example of LLT with host-processing (HSP) and LLT with NDP is shown in Figure 5(a),(b). We assume a star-topology for HSP to minimize diameter while we assume a distributed dragonfly topology [31] for the memory network with NDP. In this example, HSP requires 10 hop count (or network channel traversal) to complete a single LLT with two items shown in the example while NDP requires 14 hop count. As a result, simply off-loading LLT does not necessarily improve LLT performance. In this section, we first describe NDP-aware data localization to increase locality and

[4]Huge-page allocation may have issues if memory is fragmented. However, storage memory is allocated at the application start-up [9] and big memory workloads are usually long running programs (e.g., web server, database), making the huge-page allocation overhead at start-up ignorable.

[5]Since `mlock` does not guarantee consistent mapping to the same physical address if OS migrates physical pages, pages can be pinned (e.g., mm_mpin()) to ensure the consistent mapping. However, to the best of our knowledge, Linux kernels try to avoid migrating huge pages because of its overhead.

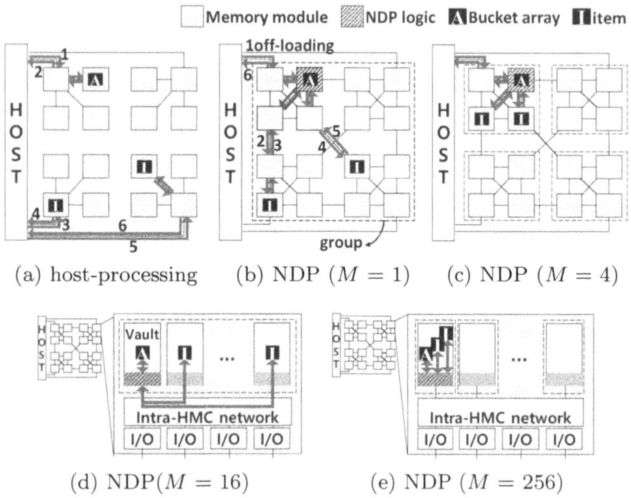

(a) host-processing (b) NDP ($M = 1$) (c) NDP ($M = 4$)

(d) NDP($M = 16$) (e) NDP ($M = 256$)

Figure 5: Data access in host-processing and NDP with different localization degrees.

minimize the memory network hop count. We then propose *batching* multiple LLT operations together to exploit the NDP parallelism available within the logic layer of the memory module.

4.1 NDP-aware data localization

In this section, the number of *memory groups* (M) is defined as the number of main memory partitions and represents the degree of locality in the NDP system. Our baseline NDP for LLT is shown in Figure 5(b) without any localization ($M = 1$). As M increases, the degree of localization increases – for example, with $M = 16$ (and 16 memory modules in Figure 5(d)), the size of a memory group is a single memory module and off-chip memory network traversal is minimized; however, there can be accesses to different vaults within the memory module. If M is further increased to 256 (assuming 16 vaults within each memory module), the locality is further confined to each vault and minimize movement within a memory module as well. While increasing M improves locality, it reduces the amount of memory capacity per memory group and trade-off is discussed later in Section 5.3.

In our proposed NDP system, the unit of off-loading is a single linked-list traversal. For NDP-aware data localization, we store the linked-list to "physically neighboring" memory.[6] To achieve this locality, we modify the application and memory allocation function. We first design a memory manager that allocates *storage memory* that is divided into *partitions* with each partition assigned to one of the memory groups based on the physical address of the partition. In a fine-grain interleaved multi-channel memory system that we assume, the partitioning size should be smaller than the address interleaving granularity ($ITLV$) to make sure each partition is not interleaved across non-neighboring physical memory. We achieve data localization by mapping each memory group to physically neighboring memory (managed by OS and the memory manager) similar to NUMA-aware memory allocation, and by storing a linked-list to a single memory group (managed by application).

[6]Depending on the value of M, the linked-list can be stored in the same memory vault, memory module, or neighboring memory modules.

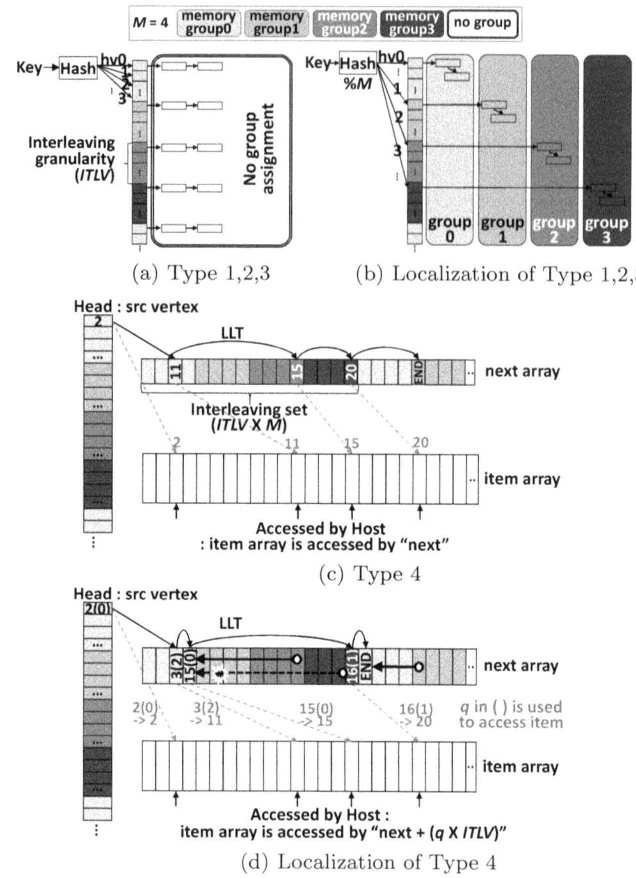

(a) Type 1,2,3 (b) Localization of Type 1,2,3

(c) Type 4

(d) Localization of Type 4

Figure 6: NDP-aware data localization with 4 memory groups for the four different linked-list types.

Figure 6(a,b) show how to localize the linked-list Type 1, 2, and 3. The location of linked-list (i.e., index) is decided by index calculation, such as hashing. Items having hash value (hv) n are normally stored to the nth linked-list as shown in Figure 6(a). However, we change this direct mapping as items having index n are stored to a memory group m using a modulo operation $m = n \ mod \ M$, as shown in Figure 6(b). When application requests memory allocation to store an item, the index value n is given together as a parameter to the memory manager. The memory manager returns a memory address from memory group m, and the item is stored in that particular memory group.

Figure 6(c,d) show how to localize the linked-list Type 4, which stores next pointer and item in different arrays – next array and item array. In Graph500 [39], adjacency list is implemented as a linked-list within the next array, and item array stores the edge information. To localize the linked-list on the next array for NDP, we relocate the location (i.e., index) of the next pointers *within* an interleaving set, which is defined as '$ITLV \times M$'. Next pointer connected to source vertex n, where $n \ mod \ M = m$, is attempted to be relocated to a specific index allocated in the memory group m. For example, when edge x is connected to the source vertex n, where x has an index distance '$q \times ITLV + r$' from the boundary of the interleaving set, x is stored in the next array and next[x] again stores the next connected edge, as shown in Figure 6(c). To localize for NDP, we try to move next[x] to next[x'], where x' has an index distance

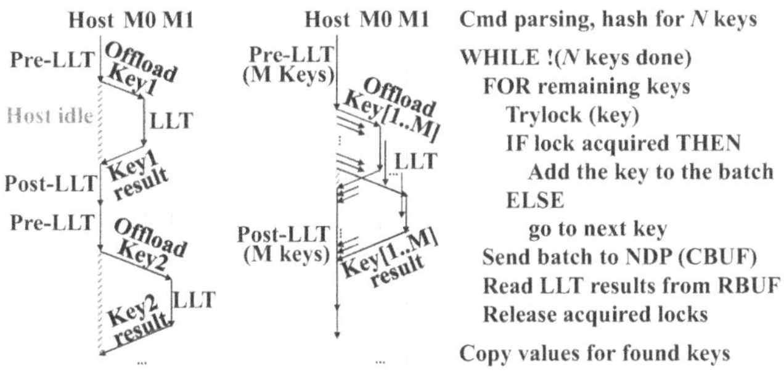

(a) (b) (c)

Figure 7: NDP (a) without batching and (b) with batching, and (c) support for Memcached batching for GET sequence with trylock.

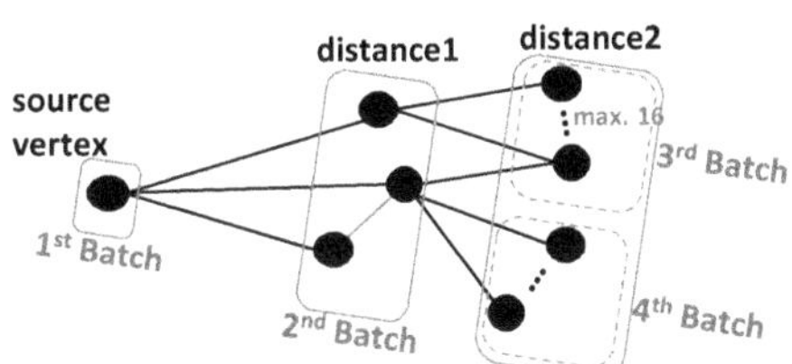

Figure 8: Batching in graph: vertexes connected at the same distance from the source vertex.

'$m \times ITLV + r$' from the boundary of the interleaving set and next[x'] resides in the memory group m. However, item[x] needs to be accessed by the host to get the edge information, and thus the information that can restore the original index x needs to be stored in somewhere. To minimize the required bits to restore the original index, we keep r consistent but only change q in the relocation sequence and q is stored in the MSB of the next pointer.[7] By limiting the range of relocation to inside an interleaving set (i.e., $q < M$), we need $\log_2 M$ bits to store q. Since there are several unused bits in the next pointer (to align the address of array elements with multiple bytes), storing q does not require additional memory capacity.

Relocation can fail or result in a *conflict* if the new index is already occupied by another next pointer that has been relocated. In Figure 6(d), next[15] is attempted to be relocated to next[3], but fails since next[11] is already relocated to next[3]. Note that index 11 and 15 have the same remainder(3) when divided by the $ITLV(4)$. Since conflicts can cause access to remote memory module in NDP, the neighboring memory groups that are mapped physically closer (e.g., remote vaults within the same HMC module when the memory group is a single vault) are used to relocate to minimize off-chip access in LLT. In our experiments with 16 HMC modules and 16 vaults per HMC module, 50.2%/38.8%/11.0% of next pointers are stored to local vault/local HMC/remote HMC modules, respectively.

4.2 Batching multiple LLT operations

While NDP-aware data localization reduces LLT latency (and reduce off-chip memory bandwidth) and improves overall performance compared to host-processing, the parallelism available within NDP is not fully exploited unless the throughput of LLT offloading is increased. As shown in Figure 7(a), the host and NDP work sequentially; however, by exploiting the request-level parallelism (i.e., independent LLTs), overall throughput (and performance) can be significantly improved. Thus, we propose *batching* of multiple or independent LLTs to be off-loaded together to enable highly parallel execution in NDP. Prior work [22] also utilized batching of Memcached GET requests for GPGPU offloading. However, because of the thousands of threads in GPGPUs, the offloading had high overhead as it required batching more than thousands of requests to hide the communication overhead. In comparison, since the overhead for NDP-offloading is relatively low (normal load/store operations to memory modules), tens of requests are sufficient to maximize performance (in our evaluation, the optimal batch size was approximately 32 to 64).

One challenge with batching is to identify the independent LLTs that can be off-loaded together and executed in parallel. Data dependency exists among the accesses within an LLT, but there is usually no dependency among the LLTs (i.e., inter-LLT). For example, probing of a single tuple in Hash join is translated to a single LLT operation, but probing a tuple is independent of probing of other tuples – thus, multiple tuples can be probed in parallel. In Memcached, a GET request initiates a single LLT operation but is independent of other GET requests. In graph search, the neighboring list of multiple vertexes connected at the same distance from the source vertex can be searched independently and in parallel (Figure 8). Based on these parallelism, multiple LLT operations can be offloaded to NDP as a batch (Figure 7(b)). If the key size is small, multiple LLT operations off-loaded to the same memory module can be merged into a single off-loading command packet to further reduce the off-chip accesses (e.g., with 8B keys, 4 LLTs can be sent within a single 64B command packet). Otherwise, the LLT operations within a batch are off-loaded as multiple packets to the memory modules. As we show later in Section 5.3, to fully realize the benefit of batching, multiple LLT engines are needed within each vault of the HMC to maximize the parallelism.

Another challenge of batching is handling lock acquisitions. For the applications acquiring bucket lock before starting an LLT, such as Memcached, batching can result in significant overhead in terms of lock contention. To reduce lock contention with batching, we use *trylock*, or a non-blocking attempt to acquire a lock, as shown in Figure 7(c). To batch multiple keys, trylock is executed once per key and proceeds to the next key even if the lock is not acquired. After trying to obtain the lock for all of the keys remaining in the batch once, only the keys for which bucket locks are acquired are off-loaded to NDP in a batch, and this sequence is iterated for the remaining keys.

5. EVALUATION

5.1 Workloads

The proposed NDP to accelerate LLT is evaluated with the four workloads summarized in Table 3.[8] Except for Memcached, the batch sizes were empirically determined

[7]When host accesses item array, the location (or index) in the item array is decided by 'x' & $MASK + q \times ITLV$'.

[8]In our evaluation, we did not evaluate Type 2 linked-list (Hash Join [11]) since the Hash Join [8] with Type3 was shown to be more optimized for host-processing.

Table 3: Workload description

Workload	Configuration	Batch size
LLU [48]	LLU-d2: Length 32M Depth 2, Item 16B (Value 4B)	64(8)
	LLU-d4: Length 32M Depth 4, Item 16B (Value 4B)	64(4)
Graph500 [39]	R-MAT, 8M vertex, 128M edges Adjacency list: List implement	16(1)
Hash Join [8]	Probe phase of optimized no-partitioning Hash Join. Tables with 16M,128M tuples Key 8B, Payload 8B	64(4)
Memcached [17]	MC(ETC): 16GB hash table Key 16-120B, Value 1B-1MB, Zipf	24(1)
	MC(FIX): 16GB hash table Key 32B, Value 32B, Zipf	24(1)

and the batch sizes with the best performance were used. The number inside the parenthesis represents the maximum number of LLT operations that can be sent together in a single off-loading command packet, which is decided by the size of off-loading command (or return value size), assuming 64B packets.

LLU benchmark [48] is a synthetic workload which consists of only linked-list traversals (LLTs) with parameterized list length and depth. We use LLU benchmark to understand the impact of LLT exclusively with NDP since other workloads have other operations that are executed by the host. We evaluate LLU with two different depths (2 and 4). In LLU benchmark, only offset (i.e., index of the linked-list to be searched) is sent as NDP command (nKey=0) and the values of the linked items are returned to the host as the NDP output.

Hash Join is a join method used by database management systems (DBMS) and consists of two phases. The *Build* phase consists of creating an intermediate hash table based on the smaller table that is being combined. The *Probe* phase consists of hashing and LLT based on each tuple in the larger table. We implement the *Probe* phase with NDP by batching 64 tuples and 4 off-loading commands can be sent in a single command packet with 8B key size. Payloads (or values) of the matched keys are returned as NDP results.

Breadth-first search (BFS) is the main kernel of Graph 500 [39] benchmark and the *list* implementation uses linked-list within an array (Type 4) to implement the adjacency list of the graph. Searching the adjacent vertexes in BFS is composed of LLT within a next pointer array to retrieve the connected edges and then accesses to the item array as shown in Figure 6(c),(d). Traversing the adjacency list array is off-loaded to NDP, and offset of the first entry in the adjacency list array is sent as offset in the off-loading command. The connected next pointers (or the adjacency list of the source vertex) are returned to host as the NDP result, and host accesses to the item array based on the returned next pointers. Batching for graph BFS described in Section 4.2 is used.

Memcached [17] is an in-memory key-value store used as a cache layer in data centers and consists of GET/SET commands. Memcached uses a hash table as a storage memory and uses Type 1 linked-list to store various sizes of items. GET operation is composed of hashing (for indexing) and LLT in the hash table. Offset in the bucket array (decided by hash value) and input key to be searched are sent as

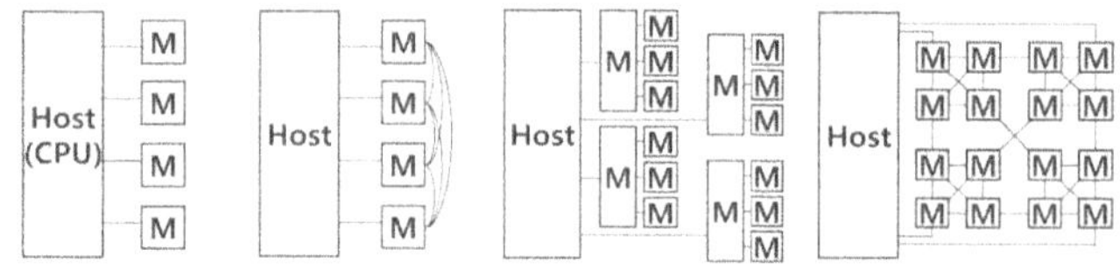

(a) Star (b) FBFLY (c) Star (d) 4 group DFLY

Figure 9: Different topologies with a single host and (a,b) 4 and (c,d) 16 memory modules.

Table 4: Simulator configuration

	Parameter	Configuration
CPU	Core	32 OoO cores @ 3.2GHz Issue width: 4, ROB size: 64
	L1 I/D cache	32KB, 4way, 1cycle latency
	L2 cache	Shared 16MB, 16way, 10cycle
	Cache line size	64B
Memory	HMC org.	8 layers, 16 vaults 16 banks per vault
	HMC capacity	4 GB
	scheduler	FR-FCFS
	DRAM timings	tCK=1.25ns, tWR=12, tCCD=4, tRCD=CL=tRP=11, tRAS=22
Network	Router clock	1.0GHz
	Inter-chip link	16 lanes per direction 12.5 Gbps per lane
	Topology	host-processing: Star NDP: FBFLY, DFLY
	Routing	Minimal

off-loading command, and address of the Value (in case of 'Hit') or Null (in case of 'Miss') is returned as the result from NDP because value size can be larger than available return buffer size. Two different client models (ETC and FIX) [5] are used. Since standard Memcached has limited scalability from global locks, we optimize Memcached by removing all global locks and implementing fine-grain locks [23].[9]

5.2 Methodology

We evaluated the impact of NDP using a detailed cycle-accurate simulator with the configurations summarized in Table 4. To simulate the big-memory workloads with reasonable simulation speed, we used the gem5 [10] simulator but replaced the front end (e.g., the core model) with the trace-based McSimA+ [2] simulator. A cycle-accurate network simulator, Booksim [29], was used to model both the inter-chip network between the CPU and the HMC modules and the intra-chip network within the HMC modules.

We evaluated NDP systems with 4 and 16 memory modules or HMCs – connected to a single multi-core host CPU, and we assumed that each chip has four inter-chip channels. In host-processing, we configured the inter-chip network (or memory network) with Star topology (Figure 9(a),(c)) since only the host accesses the memory modules and no connection between HMC memory modules is needed. For NDP, we configured the memory network as flattened butterfly (FBFLY) for the 4HMC system and 4-way distributed dragonfly (DFLY) topology for the 16HMC system [31] to reduce the NDP traffic latency (Figure 9(b),(d)). Each link or channel is composed of 16 lanes and 12.5 Gbps per lane, and SerDes latency assumed to be 5ns per hop (2.5ns for serialization and 2.5ns for deserialization). For intra-HMC net-

[9]The optimized baseline for host-processing (HSP) used is 7.2× faster than the standard Memcached 1.4.20 version.

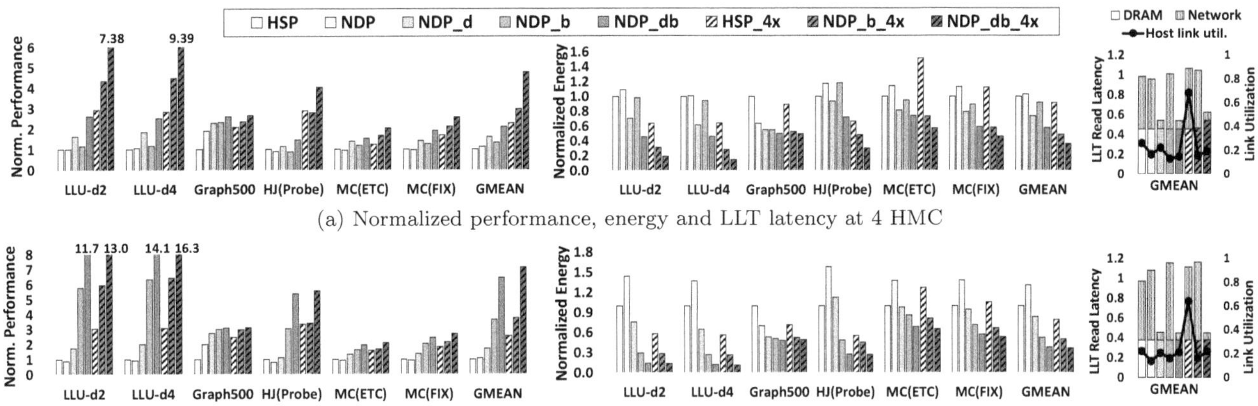

(a) Normalized performance, energy and LLT latency at 4 HMC

(b) Normalized performance, energy and LLT latency at 16 HMC

Figure 10: Normalized performance, energy consumption, average LLT data read latency, and CPU-memory link utilization of host-processing (HSP) and NDP by applying proposed optimizations one by one.

Table 5: Evaluated processing configurations

Abbr.	System configuration
HSP	Baseline host-processing
NDP	Near-data processing with LLT offloading
NDP_d	NDP with data locality
NDP_b	NDP with batching
NDP_db	NDP with data locality and batching
HSP_4×	HSP with 4× processing (i.e., 128 threads)
NDP_b_4×	NDP_b with 4 engines per vault
NDP_db_4×	NDP_db with 4 engines per vault

work, we assumed 5-way concentrated mesh [7], where four vault controllers and a single I/O are connected to a router in each concentration with 1ns router delay and 1ns wire delay for inter-concentration transfer. Each vault within the logic layer has its own memory scheduler, and address map is composed as (Row: Vault: Cube: Column: Layer: Offset). DRAM timing parameters are based on Micron DDR3-1600 1Gbit DRAM specification. The logic layer of HMC (with all additional logics for NDP) is implemented at the Booksim network interface, and NDP logic operates at the same frequency as the network router (1GHz).

For energy estimation, we used McPAT [36] to measure CPU power and CACTI-3DD [13] for 3D stacked DRAM. For link energy, we used the model described in [31], but the per bit energy value is adjusted based on the Micron study [28, 46] – using $4.47pJ/bit$ for real packet and $3.35pJ/bit$ for idle packet. To estimate the power consumption of the additional logics for NDP, CACTI was used for SRAM power and we synthesized RTL and estimated the hardware logic power based on the synthesized area (1.7mW per engine).

5.3 Results

The different configurations under evaluation are summarized in Table 5. The results comparing performance (1/execution time) and energy consumption are shown in Figure 10, with the results normalized to host-processing (`HSP`). Both the `HSP` and `NDP` assumed 32 host threads as the configuration was the most energy-efficient for `HSP`. Except for Graph500, simply offloading LLT (`NDP`) does not result in significant improvement in performance and for some workloads, the performance actually degrades slightly. For the 16-HMC system, the LLT read latency *increases* by 10.7%, as the average hop count between memory modules through memory network (2.1) is larger than the average hop count between the host and memory modules with a host-centric star topology (1.75). Off-loading overhead (offload command building, communication buffer access) also can increase overall LLT execution time, and thus, there is minimal benefit from LLT offloading. Energy consumption also increases in `NDP` from the higher hop-count and the additional static energy consumed in the high-speed interchip links. Among the workloads evaluated, only Graph500 resulted in performance improvement from the baseline offloading (`NDP`). In host-processing, host accesses the next pointer (i.e., edge index) and item (i.e., edge information) sequentially. However, because of the particular linked-list type (i.e., Type 4), we modified the algorithm such that multiple next pointers are retrieved by a single off-loading with NDP, and the host can access multiple items in parallel since the locations are already identified and results in performance improvement.

Impact of data localization: With data localization (`NDP_d` in Figure 10) to each vault ($M = 16$ for 4-HMC systems and $M = 256$ for 16-HMC systems), performance is increased by 63% (72%) for the 4 (16) HMC systems since the LLT read latency is reduced by minimizing the off-chip accesses and intra-HMC network traversals. For LLU synthetic workloads, `NDP_d` improves performance by ∼2× but for other workloads such as Hash Join with small list depth, the performance benefit from localization is limited. As the depth of linked-list decreases, the impact of LLT latency is minimized. Type2 and Type3 linked-lists are better suited for host-processing since multiple items are stored in the contiguous memory (i.e., array), and multiple items can be fetched to host with a single memory access. To increase performance and energy efficiency for these workloads, increasing throughput (parallelism) is necessary and can be achieved through batching. However, note that the benefit of batching is not fully realized without data localization.

Impact of batching: The addition of batching (`NDP_db` in Figure 10) increases overall throughput and provides significant performance improvement especially for larger network size. For the 16-HMC system, `NDP_db` increases performance by 6.7× compared with `NDP_d` for LLU-d2 and by 4.8× for Hash Join. The latency for individual LLT does not change but the overall throughput increases significantly and results in performance improvement. For the small system configuration (4-HMC), the benefit is still limited in NDP_db because of the small number of LLT engines in the overall system. For example, with the 4-HMC system with 16 vaults in each HMC, there is a total of only 64 LLT engines and it is not necessarily sufficient to exploit the parallelism. NDP reduces the host link bandwidth utilization (or CPU-memory data transfer) by moving the computation to near-data logic; batching further reduces host link utilization by sending/receiving multiple NDP commands/results in a single memory packet.

Number of LLT engines: With the parallelism available through the increased number of LLT engines from 1 to 4 (NDP_db_4×), there is an additional 2.3× performance improvement over NDP_db in a 4-HMC system. NDP_db_4× increases the cost slightly at the logic layer but more importantly there is significant energy savings.[10] For the 16-HMC system, the benefit from increased number of LLT engines is smaller (on average 11%) since even with 1 LLT engine per vault, there is already 256 LLT engines in NDP_db and provides sufficient parallelism. The benefit of batching is not fully realized without localization as NDP_b and NDP_b_4× shows the results of using only batching. The impact of localization at higher throughput (NDP_b_4× vs. NDP_db_4×) is slightly reduced compared to the impact at lower throughput (NDP_b vs. NDP_db), but localization still contributes 46% and 37% performance benefits of NDP_db and NDP_db_4×. Overall, Graph500 and Memcached showed smaller overall performance improvement since LLT represented relatively smaller fraction of the overall workload execution time.

To provide a comparison against a prior work with *host-side* LLT acceleration [33], we compare against HSP_4× where we assume 4× acceleration is done on the host, similar to what was proposed by the prior work [33]. Instead of modeling dedicated logic, we assumed additional cores were available and increased the number of CPU threads to 128.[11] As shown in Figure 10, HSP_4× improves performance by 2.3× over the HSP and by 2.1× over the baseline NDP. However, NDP_db_4× exceeds the performance of HSP_4× by 2.1× and 2.8× for the 4-HMC and 16-HMC system since HSP_4× does not reduce the off-chip memory access latency and bandwidth.

Probe phase of Hash Join and LLU benchmark can be parallelized without any synchronizations among the threads. However, the performance scaling of HSP_4× is limited also for LLU and Hash Join. Even though Hash Join has a data structure well suited for host-processing, there is little locality in inter-LLT data accesses because hash function usually decides the address of the linked-list and the addresses are randomly distributed to the giant hash table. Thus, most linked-list traversal creates off-chip accesses, which increases

[10]Our RTL implementation of LLT engine at TSMC 40nm showed 0.0049mm^2 area. Total area of LLT engines with 16 vaults and 4 engines per vault has 0.31mm^2 or 0.31% area of the HMC logic die (assumed 100mm^2), which has negligible area overhead.

[11]Performance of HSP_4× is measured with 128 OoO cores, but power consumption was calculated with 32 OoO cores + 96 in-order cores to mimic the specialized logics added to host side, similar to the prior work [33].

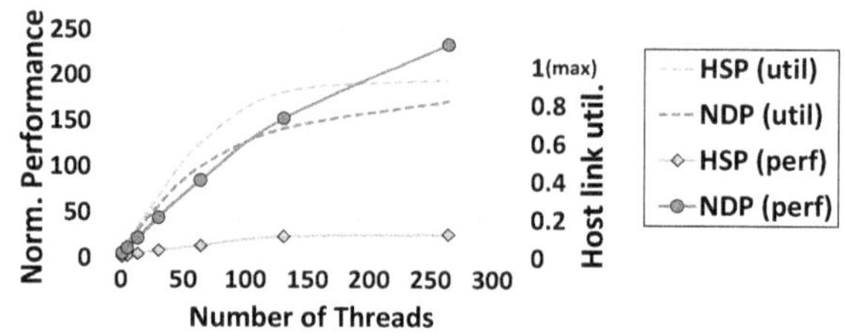

Figure 11: Scalability of HSP and NDP for Hash Join (Probe) workload – Performance normalized to HSP 4 threads.

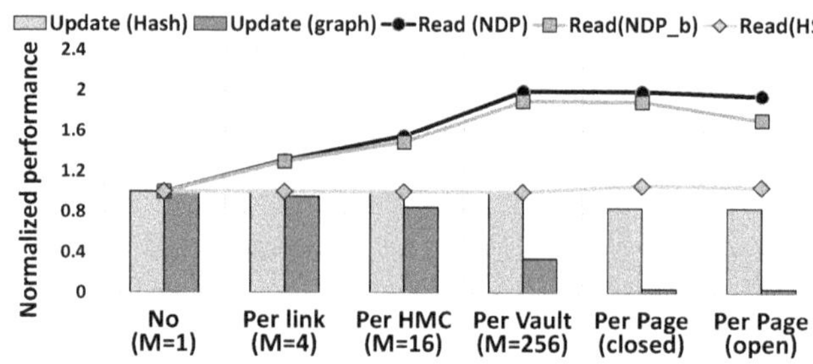

(a) Linked-list read and write performance

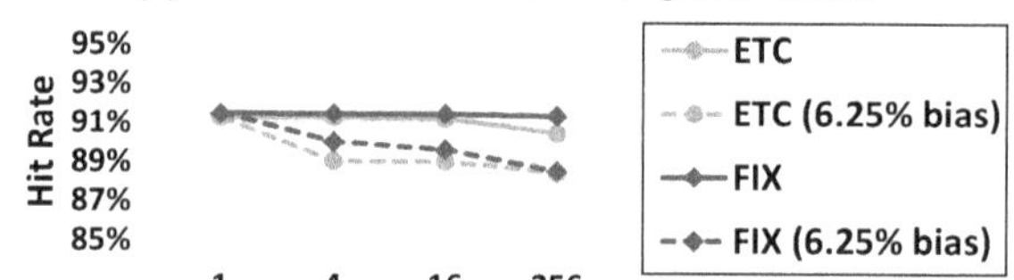

(b) Memcached Hit-rate

Figure 12: Trade-off with different data localization.

bandwidth requirement as the number of processing units increases.

Scalability of HSP and NDP: The scalability of HSP and NDP is shown in Figure 11 as the number of host threads increases, illustrating both performance and host-link bandwidth utilization. In this work, we increase the number of processor cores to scale the number of host threads. As the number of threads increases, the host link bandwidth becomes the bottleneck and beyond 128 threads, the performance of HSP saturates; however, NDP continues to scale up to 256 threads. With NDP, the increase in the number of host threads better exploits the parallelism in NDP while the data localization reduces the memory network bandwidth utilization to improve scalability.

Trade-off with localization: Higher degree of data locality (i.e., higher M) can improve performance but it also decreases the *capacity* per memory group, and update performance can be degraded by the non-uniform utilization of the capacity across the memory groups. Figure 12 shows the trade-off of localization including DRAM page level locality (assumed 2KB page size). Vault controller is configured to closed-page mode except 'per page(open)' configuration. NDP read performance increases as the degree of localization increases by the reduced inter-chip and intra-chip network traversals. With the addition of batching (NDP_b), read performance is still largely affected by the degree of localization, but the impact slightly decreases since the increased processing throughput by batching reduces the sensitivity to the data access latency. Open-page policy with page level

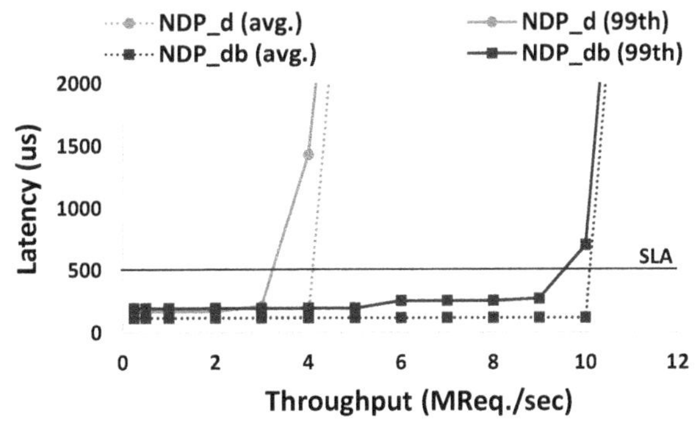

Figure 13: Average and Tail latency of Memcached(FIX) workload.

locality is not translated to page hit in vault controller because of the sequential access pattern of LLT and concurrent accesses to different linked-lists from the multiple processing units. Open-page policy rather increases average DRAM latency by unhidden pre-charge time. NDP-aware localization has minimal impact to the host processing (HSP) read performance, since the capacity of each group is still much larger than on-chip caches except the page level locality and the localization does not result in on-chip cache locality. Page level locality slightly increases host read performance by 4.3%.

With reduced capacity per memory group (larger M), some memory groups become full earlier or conflict occurs more frequently if indexing results are not distributed to all memory groups uniformly, and searching a slot to be stored can take longer execution time. For linked-lists in a hash table, hashing function distributes index values well and the size of vault (256MB) is large enough to amortize the locally skewed distribution. However, linked-list for adjacency list of graph can have severe imbalance in the item distribution because a few vertexes can have much more connected edges. By the severe imbalance in graph, update performance decreases by far from the vault level localization.[12]

For applications such as a key-value store (Memcached), when new elements are added beyond the current memory group size, older elements are dropped *within* each memory group to maintain locality. Smaller capacity per memory group can create more frequent eviction and lower the quality of replacement policy. Thus, item hit rate can decrease with higher degree of localization as shown in Figure 12(b), and biased index distribution can worsen the impact. The degree of localization should be selected properly based on the trade-off of each workload.

Latency sensitive workload: For all workloads except Memcached, completion of the whole LLT operations impacts to the workload completion time, but in Memcached, each LLT operation is mapped to a user request and the latency of each LLT can impact to the latency of the user-level request. Figure 13 shows the average and 99% tail latency of Memcached(FIX). Batching slightly increases the tail latency at low offered throughput. With the proposed trylock scheme, CPU proceeds to next request if lock contention occurs, and the waiting time to acquire the contended lock can be slightly longer, since the lock is released after processing the whole batch. But the tail latency at lower offered throughput is still below the system level agreement (SLA), and the increased throughput enabled by batching gives 2.4× higher request processing throughput under the SLA. Network part is modeled with an assumption to a polling-based light user-level network stack. Client model inserts TCP/IP packets to an outside buffer at a fixed rate (or throughput), and a network model picks the packets from the outside buffer by polling periodically. After parsing the TCP/IP packet, payload (i.e., Memcached commands) is transferred to an inside buffer, the communication buffer between the network model and Memcached.

[12]As described in Section 4.1, relocation sequence checks neighboring memory groups also if conflict occurs at the local memory group. However, if workload has frequent update operation, we can limit the number of trials to small to minimize this update performance degradation.

6. CONCLUSION

In this work, we propose and evaluate near data processing (NDP) of linked-list traversal (LLT). We show how simply offloading LLT for NDP does not necessarily improve performance but can actually degrade energy efficiency because of the additional off-chip channel traversals. As a result, we propose NDP-aware data localization and batching to fully realize the benefits of off-loading to near-memory. NDP-aware data localization minimizes off-chip accesses and reduces LLT latency while batching multiple LLT operations improves overall throughput by exploiting the parallelism available within NDP. We evaluate different big-memory workloads with LLT on our proposed NDP architecture and show up to 5.9× increase in performance and 2.8× reduction in energy compared with baseline host-processing. While this work focused on LLT, the contributions of this work, including exploiting the packetized interface for NDP and using load/store instructions, locality-aware data placement, or batching to maximize throughput, can be possibly extended for other computations that involve significant amount of memory accesses by providing additional hardware logic near the memory.

7. ACKNOWLEDGMENTS

This research was supported in part by the Mid-career Researcher Program (NRF-2013R1A2A2A01069132), in part by the MSIP under the ITRC support program (IITP-2016-H8501-16-1005), and in part by Next-Generation Information Computing Development Program through NRF funded by the Ministry of Science, ICT & Future Planning (2015M3 C4A7065647). This research was also funded by SK Hynix.

8. REFERENCES

[1] J. Ahn *et al.*, "Scatter-add in data parallel architectures," in *HPCA*, 2005, pp. 132–142.

[2] J. Ahn *et al.*, "McSimA+: A manycore simulator with application-level+ simulation and detailed microarchitecture modeling," in *ISPASS*, 2013, pp. 74–85.

[3] J. Ahn *et al.*, "A scalable processing-in-memory accelerator for parallel graph processing," in *ISCA*, 2015, pp. 105–117.

[4] B. Akin *et al.*, "Data reorganization in memory using 3D-stacked DRAM," in *ISCA*, 2015, pp. 131–143.

[5] B. Atikoglu *et al.*, "Workload Analysis of a Large-scale Key-value Store," in *ACM SIGMETRICS*, 2012, pp. 53–64.

[6] R. Balasubramonian *et al.*, "Near-data processing: Insights from a MICRO-46 workshop," *IEEE Micro*, vol. 34, no. 4, pp. 36–42, 2014.
[7] J. Balfour *et al.*, "Design tradeoffs for tiled CMP on-chip networks," in *ICS*, 2006, pp. 187–198.
[8] C. Balkesen *et al.*, "Main-memory hash joins on multi-core CPUs: Tuning to the underlying hardware," in *ICDE*, 2013, pp. 362–373.
[9] A. Basu *et al.*, "Efficient Virtual Memory for Big Memory Servers," in *ISCA*, 2013, pp. 237–248.
[10] N. Binkert *et al.*, "The gem5 simulator," *SIGARCH Comput. Archit. News*, vol. 39, no. 2, pp. 1–7, 2011.
[11] S. Blanas *et al.*, "Design and evaluation of main memory hash join algorithms for multi-core CPUs," in *International Conference on Management of data (SIGMOD)*. ACM, 2011, pp. 37–48.
[12] J. Carter *et al.*, "Impulse: Building a smarter memory controller," in *HPCA*, 1999, pp. 70–79.
[13] K. Chen *et al.*, "CACTI-3DD: Architecture-level modeling for 3D die-stacked DRAM main memory," in *DATE*, 2012, pp. 33–38.
[14] P. Dlugosch *et al.*, "An efficient and scalable semiconductor architecture for parallel automata processing," *IEEE Transactions on Parallel and Distributed Systems*, vol. 25, pp. 3088–3098, 2014.
[15] B. Falsafi *et al.*, "A primer on hardware prefetching," *Synthesis Lectures on Computer Architecture*, vol. 9, no. 1, pp. 1–67, 2014.
[16] Z. Fang *et al.*, "Active memory operations," in *ICS*, 2007, pp. 232–241.
[17] B. Fitzpatrick and A. Vorobey, "Memcached: a distributed memory object caching system," 2011.
[18] M. Gao *et al.*, "Practical Near-Data Processing for In-memory Analytics Frameworks," in *PACT*, 2015, pp. 113–124.
[19] M. Gao *et al.*, "HRL: Efficient and Flexible Reconfigurable Logic for Near-Data Processing," in *HPCA*, 2016, pp. 126–137.
[20] Q. Guo *et al.*, "3d-stacked memory-side acceleration: Accelerator and system design," in *In the Workshop on Near-Data Processing (WoNDP)*, 2014.
[21] A. Gutierrez *et al.*, "Integrated 3D-stacked Server Designs for Increasing Physical Density of Key-value Stores," in *ASPLOS*, 2014, pp. 485–498.
[22] T. H. Hetherington *et al.*, "Characterizing and Evaluating a Key-value Store Application on Heterogeneous CPU-GPU Systems," in *ISPASS*, 2012, pp. 88–98.
[23] B. Hong *et al.*, "Adaptive and Flexible Key-Value Stores Through Soft Data Partitioning," in *ICCD*, 2016.
[24] Hybrid Memory Cube Consortium, "Hybrid Memory Cube Specification 2.0," 2014.
[25] Intel, "Increasing Memory Throughput With Intel Streaming SIMD Extensions 4 (Intel SSE4) Streaming Load," in *White Paper*, 2008.
[26] Intel, "Intel 64 and IA-32 Architectures Software Developer's Manual," 2014.
[27] Intel, "Intel Virtualization Technology for Directed I/O," *Architecture Specification*, 2014.
[28] J. Jeddeloh *et al.*, "Hybrid memory cube new DRAM architecture increases density and performance," in *Symposium on VLSI Technology*, 2012.
[29] N. Jiang *et al.*, "A detailed and flexible cycle-accurate Network-on-Chip simulator," in *ISPASS*, 2013, pp. 86–96.
[30] Y. Kang *et al.*, "FlexRAM: Toward an advanced intelligent memory system," in *ICCD*, 2012, pp. 5–14.
[31] G. Kim *et al.*, "Memory-centric system interconnect design with hybrid memory cubes," in *PACT*, 2013, pp. 145–156.
[32] H. Kim *et al.*, "Understanding Energy Aspects of Processing-near-Memory for HPC Workloads," in *Proceedings of the 2015 International Symposium on Memory Systems*. ACM, 2015, pp. 276–282.
[33] O. Kocberber *et al.*, "Meet the walkers: Accelerating index traversals for in-memory databases," in *MICRO*, 2013, pp. 468–479.
[34] P. M. Kogge, "EXECUBE-A new architecture for scaleable MPPs," in *ICPP*, 1994, pp. 77–84.
[35] J. H. Lee *et al.*, "BSSync: Processing near memory for machine learning workloads with bounded staleness consistency models," in *PACT*, 2015, pp. 241–252.
[36] S. Li *et al.*, "McPAT: an Integrated Power, Area, and Timing Modeling Framework for Multicore and Manycore Architectures," in *MICRO*, 2009, pp. 469–480.
[37] G. H. Loh, "A register-file approach for row buffer caches in die-stacked DRAMs," in *MICRO*, 2011, pp. 351–361.
[38] G. Loh *et al.*, "A processing in memory taxonomy and a case for studying fixed-function pim," in *Workshop on Near-Data Processing (WoNDP)*, 2013.
[39] R. C. Murphy *et al.*, "Introducing to the graph 500," *Cray User's Group (CUG)*, 2010.
[40] L. Nai *et al.*, "Instruction Offloading with HMC 2.0 Standard: A Case Study for Graph Traversals," in *Proceedings of the 2015 International Symposium on Memory Systems*. ACM, 2015, pp. 258–261.
[41] R. Nair *et al.*, "Active Memory Cube: A processing-in-memory architecture for exascale systems," *IBM Journal of Research and Development*, vol. 59, no. 2/3, pp. 17–1, 2015.
[42] D. Patterson *et al.*, "A case for intelligent RAM," *IEEE Micro*, vol. 17, no. 2, pp. 34–44, 1997.
[43] J. T. Pawlowski, "Hybrid Memory Cube (HMC)," in *Hot Chips*, 2011.
[44] S. H. Pugsley *et al.*, "NDC: Analyzing the impact of 3D-stacked memory+ logic devices on MapReduce workloads," in *ISPASS*, 2014, pp. 190–200.
[45] Samsung, "Samsung announces IMDB memory." [Online]. Available: http://www.techeye.net/business/samsung-announces-imdb-memory-with-ndp-hbm-too
[46] G. Sandhu, "DRAM scaling and bandwidth challenges," in *NSF Workshop on Emerging Technologies for Interconnects (WETI)*, 2012.
[47] A. Sodani *et al.*, "Knights Landing: Second-Generation Intel Xeon Phi Product," *IEEE Micro*, vol. 36, no. 2, pp. 34–46, 2016.
[48] C. B. Zilles, "Benchmark health considered harmful," *ACM SIGARCH Computer Architecture News*, vol. 29, no. 3, pp. 4–5, 2001.

Scalable Task Parallelism for NUMA: A Uniform Abstraction for Coordinated Scheduling and Memory Management

Andi Drebes
The University of Manchester
School of Computer Science
Oxford Road
Manchester M13 9PL
United Kingdom
andi.drebes@manchester.ac.uk

Antoniu Pop
The University of Manchester
School of Computer Science
Oxford Road
Manchester M13 9PL
United Kingdom
antoniu.pop@manchester.ac.uk

Karine Heydemann
Sorbonne Universités
UPMC Univ Paris 06
CNRS, UMR 7606, LIP6
4, Place Jussieu
F-75252 Paris Cedex 05, France
karine.heydemann@lip6.fr

Albert Cohen
INRIA and École Normale Supérieure
45 rue d'Ulm
F-75005 Paris
France
albert.cohen@inria.fr

Nathalie Drach
Sorbonne Universités
UPMC Univ Paris 06
CNRS, UMR 7606, LIP6
4, Place Jussieu
F-75252 Paris Cedex 05, France
nathalie.drach-temam@upmc.fr

ABSTRACT

Dynamic task-parallel programming models are popular on shared-memory systems, promising enhanced scalability, load balancing and locality. Yet these promises are undermined by non-uniform memory access (NUMA). We show that using NUMA-aware task and data placement, it is possible to preserve the uniform abstraction of both computing and memory resources for task-parallel programming models while achieving high data locality. Our data placement scheme guarantees that all accesses to task output data target the local memory of the accessing core. The complementary task placement heuristic improves the locality of task input data on a best effort basis. Our algorithms take advantage of data-flow style task parallelism, where the privatization of task data enhances scalability by eliminating false dependences and enabling fine-grained dynamic control over data placement. The algorithms are fully automatic, application-independent, performance-portable across NUMA machines, and adapt to dynamic changes. Placement decisions use information about inter-task data dependences readily available in the run-time system and placement information from the operating system. We achieve 94% of local memory accesses on a 192-core system with 24 NUMA nodes, up to 5× higher performance than NUMA-aware hierarchical work-stealing, and even 5.6× compared to static interleaved allocation. Finally, we show that state-of-the-art dynamic page migration by the operating system cannot catch up with frequent affinity changes between cores and data and thus fails to accelerate task-parallel applications.

PACT '16, September 11-15, 2016, Haifa, Israel

DOI: http://dx.doi.org/10.1145/2967938.2967946

Keywords

Task-parallel programming; NUMA; Scheduling; Memory allocation; Data-flow programming.

1. INTRODUCTION

High-performance systems are composed of hundreds of general-purpose computing units and dozens of memory controllers to satisfy the ever-increasing need for computing power and memory bandwidth. Shared memory programming models with fine-grained concurrency have successfully harnessed the computational resources of such architectures [3, 33, 28, 30, 31, 10, 19, 8, 9, 7, 35]. In these models, the programmer exposes parallelism through the creation of fine-grained units of work, called tasks, and the specification of synchronization that constrains the order of their execution. A run-time system manages the execution of the task-parallel application and acts as an abstraction layer between the program and the underlying hardware and software environment. That is, the run-time is responsible for bookkeeping activities necessary for the correctness of the execution (e.g., the creation and destruction of tasks and their synchronization), interfacing with the operating system for resource management (e.g., allocation of data and meta-data for tasks, scheduling tasks to cores) and efficient exploitation of the hardware.

This concept relieves the programmer from dealing with details of the target platform and thus greatly improves productivity. Yet it leaves issues related to efficient interaction with system software, efficient exploitation of the hardware, and performance portability to the run-time. On today's systems with non-uniform memory access (NUMA), memory latency depends on the distance between the requesting cores and the targeted memory controllers. Efficient resource usage through task scheduling needs to go hand in hand with the optimization of memory accesses through the placement of physical pages. That is, memory accesses must be kept local in order to reduce latency and data must be distributed across memory controllers to avoid contention.

The alternative of abstracting computing resources only and leaving NUMA-specific optimization to the application is far less attractive. The programmer would have to take into account the different characteristics of all target systems (e.g., the number of NUMA nodes, their associated amount of memory and access latencies), to partition application data properly and to place the data explicitly using operating system-specific interfaces. For applications with dynamic, data-dependent behavior, the programmer would also have to provide mechanisms that constantly react to changes throughout the execution as an initial placement with high data locality at the beginning might have to be revised later on. Such changes would have to be coordinated with the run-time system to prevent destructive performance interference, introducing a tight and undesired coupling between the run-time and the application.

On the operating system side, optimizations are compelled to place tasks and data conservatively [13, 24], unless provided with detailed affinity information by the application [5, 6], high-level libraries [26] or domain specific languages [20]. Furthermore, as task-parallel run-times operate in user-space, a separate kernel component would add additional complexity to the solution; this advocates for a user-space approach.

This paper shows that it is possible to efficiently and portably exploit dynamic task parallelism on NUMA machines without exposing programmers to the complexity of these systems, preserving a simple, uniform abstract view for both memory and computations, yet achieving high locality of memory accesses. Our solution exploits the task-parallel dataflow programming style and its transparent privatization of task data. This allows the run-time to determine a task's working set, enabling transparent, fine-grained control over task and data placement.

Based on the properties of task-private data, we propose a dynamic task and data placement algorithm to ensure that input and output data are local and that interacts constructively with work-stealing to provide load-balancing across both cores and memory controllers:

- Our memory allocation mechanism, called *deferred allocation*, avoids making early placement decisions that could later harm performance. In particular, the memory to store task output data is not allocated until the task placement is known. The mechanism hands over this responsibility to the producer task on its local NUMA node. *This scheme guarantees that all accesses to task output data are local.* Control over data placement is obtained through the *privatization* of task output data.
- To enhance the locality of read memory accesses, we build on earlier work [14] and propose *enhanced work-pushing*, a work-sharing mechanism that interacts constructively with deferred allocation. Since the inputs of a task are outputs of another task, the location of input data is determined by deferred allocation when the producer tasks execute. Enhanced work-pushing is a best-effort mechanism that places a task according to these locations before task execution and thus *before* allocating memory for the task's outputs.

This combination of *enhanced work-pushing* and *deferred allocation* is fully automatic, application-independent, portable across NUMA machines and transparently adapts to dynamic changes at run time. The detailed information about the affinities between tasks and data required by these techniques is either readily available or can be obtained automatically in the run-times of task-parallel programming models with inter-task dependences, such as StarSs [30], OpenMP 4 [28], SWAN [33] and OpenStream [31], which allow the programmer to make inter-task data dependences explicit. While specifying the precise task-level data-flow rather than synchronization constraints alone requires more initial work for programmers, this effort is more than offset by the resulting benefits in terms of performance and performance portability.

The paper is organized as follows. Section 2 presents the principles of enhanced work-pushing. For a more complete discussion of our solutions, we propose multiple heuristics taking into account the placement of input data, output data or both. Section 3 introduces deferred allocation, including a brief outline of the technical solutions employed for fine-grained data placement. Sections 4 and 5 present the experimental methodology and results. A comparison with dynamic page migration is presented in Section 6. Section 7 discusses the most closely related work, before we conclude in Section 8.

2. TASK SCHEDULING WITH ENHANCED WORK-PUSHING

Let us start with terminology and hypotheses about the programming and execution models.

2.1 An abstract model for task parallelism

Our solutions are based on shared memory task-parallel programming models with data dependences. Each task is associated with a set of *incoming data dependences* and a set of *outgoing data dependences*, as illustrated by Figure 1. Each dependence is associated with a contiguous region of memory, called *input buffer* and *output buffer* for incoming and outgoing dependences, respectively. The addresses of these buffers are collected in the task's *frame*, akin to the activation frame storing a function's arguments and local variables in the call stack. While the frame is unique and allocated at the task's creation time, its input and output buffers may be placed on different NUMA nodes and allocated later in the life cycle of the task, but no later than the beginning of the execution of the task, reading from input buffers and writing into output buffers. Buffer placement and allocation time have a direct influence on locality and task-data affinity. Since we ought to offer a uniform abstraction of NUMA resources, we assume input and output buffers are managed by the run-time system rather than explicitly allocated by the application. This is the case of programming models such as OpenStream [31] and CnC [8], but not of StarSs [30] and OpenMP 4.0; see Section 7 for further discussion. We say that a task t_c *depends* on another task t_p if t_p has an outgoing dependence associated to a buffer b and if t_c has an incoming dependence associated to b. In this scenario the task t_p is referred to as the *producer* and t_c is the *consumer*.

Although this is not a fundamental requirement in our work, we will assume for simplicity that a task executes from beginning to end without interruption. A task becomes *ready* for execution when all of its dependences have

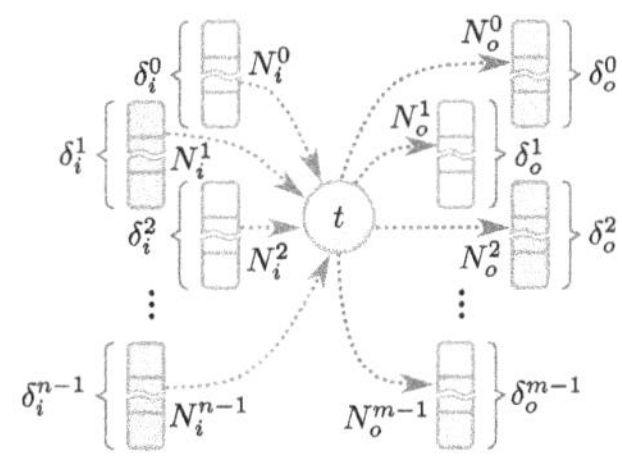

Figure 1: Most general case for a task t: n inputs of size $\delta_i^0, \ldots, \delta_i^{n-1}$, m outputs of size $\delta_o^0, \ldots, \delta_o^{m-1}$, data placed on $n+m$ NUMA nodes $N_i^0, \ldots, N_i^{n-1}, N_o^0, \ldots, N_o^{m-1}$.

been satisfied, i.e., when its producers of input data have completed *and* when its consumers have been created with the addresses of their frames communicated to the task. The *working set* of a task is defined as the union of all memory addresses that are accessed during its execution. Note that the working set does not have to be identical to the union of a task's input and output buffers (e.g., a task may access globally shared data structures). However, since our algorithms require accurate communication volume information, we assume that the bulk of the working set of each task is constituted by its input and output data. This is the case for all of the benchmarks studied in the experimental evaluation.

A *worker* thread is responsible for the execution of tasks on its associated core. Each worker is provided with a queue of tasks ready for execution from which it pops and executes tasks. When the queue is empty, the worker may obtain a task from another one through *work-stealing* [4]. A task is pushed to the queue by the worker that satisfies its last remaining dependence. We say that this worker *activates* the task and becomes its *owner*.

The execution of a task-parallel program starts with a *root task* derived from the main function of a sequential process. New tasks are created dynamically. The part of the program involved in creating new tasks is called the *control program*. If only the root task creates other tasks we speak of a *sequential control program*, otherwise of a *parallel control program*.

2.2 Weaknesses of task parallelism on NUMA systems

Whether memory accesses during the execution of a task target the local memory controller of the executing core or some remote memory controller depends on the placement of the input and output buffers and on the worker executing the task. These affinities are highly dynamic and can depend on many factors, such as:

- the order of task creations by the control program;
- the execution order of producers;
- the duration of each task;
- work-stealing events;
- or resource availability (e.g., available memory per node).

In earlier work [14], we showed that some of these issues can be mitigated by using *work-pushing*. Similar to the abstract model discussed above, the approach assumes that tasks communicate through task-private buffers. However, it also assumes that all input data of a task is stored in a single, contiguous memory region rather than multiple input buffers. As a consequence, the task's input data is entirely located on a single node. This property is used by the work-pushing technique, in which the worker activating a task only becomes its owner if the task's input data is stored on the worker's node. If the input data is located on another node, the task is transferred to a random worker associated to a core on that node. The approach remains limited however: (1) as it assumes that all inputs are located on the same node it is ill-suited for input data located on multiple nodes, and (2) it does not optimize for outgoing dependences.

Below, we first present *enhanced work-pushing*, a generalization of work-pushing, capable of dealing with input data distributed over multiple input buffers potentially placed on different nodes. This technique serves as a basis for the complementary *deferred allocation* technique, presented in the next section, that allows the run-time to improve the placement of output buffers. We introduce three *work-pushing heuristics* that schedule a task according to the placement of its input or output data or both. This complements the study of the effects of work-pushing on data locality. And experimentally in Section 5, it enables us to show the limitations of NUMA-aware scheduling alone, limited to passive reactions to a given data placement.

2.3 Enhanced work-pushing

The names of the three heuristics for enhanced work-pushing are *input-only*, *output-only* and *weighted*. The first two heuristics take into account incoming and outgoing dependences only, respectively. The *weighted* heuristic takes into account all dependences, but associates different weights to incoming and outgoing dependences to honor the fact that read and write accesses usually do not have the same latency.

Algorithm 1 shows how the heuristics above are used by the function *activate*, which is called when a worker w activates a task t (i.e., when the task becomes ready). Lines 1 to 3 define variables u_{in} and u_{out}, indicating which types of dependences should be taken into account according to the heuristic h. The variables used to determine whether the newly activated task needs to be transferred to a remote node are initialized in lines 5 to 8: the *data* array stores the cumulated size of input and output buffers of t for each of the N nodes of the system, D_{in} stands for the incoming dependences of t and D_{out} for its outgoing dependences.

The for loop starting at Line 10 iterates over a list of triples with a set of dependences D_{cur}, a variable u_{cur} indicating whether the set should be taken into account, and a weight w_{cur} associated to each type of dependence. During the first iteration, D_{cur} is identical with D_{in} and during the second iteration identical with D_{out}. For each dependence in D_{cur}, a second loop in Line 12 determines the buffer b used by the dependence, the size s_{b} of the buffer as well as the node n_{b} containing the buffer. The node on which a buffer is placed might be unknown if the buffer has not yet been placed by the operating system, e.g., using the first-touch scheme and the buffer has been allocated but not yet written. If this is the case, its size is added to the total size s_{tot}, but not included into the per-node statistics. Otherwise, the *data* array is updated accordingly by multiplying s_{b} with the weight w_{cur}.

Once the total size and the weighted number of bytes per node have been determined, the procedure checks whether the task should be pushed to a remote node. Tasks whose overall size of dependences is below a threshold are added

Algorithm 1: activate(w, t)

```
 1 if h = input only then (u_in, u_out) ← (true, false)
 2 else if h = output only then (u_in, u_out) ← (false, true)
 3 else if h = weighted then (u_in, u_out) ← (true, true)
 4
 5 data[0, ... N − 1] ← ⟨0, ..., 0⟩
 6 D_in ← in_deps(t)
 7 D_out ← out_deps(t)
 8 s_tot ← 0
 9
10 for (D_cur, u_cur, w_cur) in
     ⟨(D_in, u_in, w_in), (D_out, u_out, w_out)⟩ do
11   if u_cur = true then
12     for d ∈ D_cur do
13       s_b ← size_of(buffer_of(d))
14       n_b ← node_of(buffer_of(d))
15       s_tot ← s_tot + s_b
16       if n_b ≠ unknown then
17         data[n_b] ← data[n_b] + w_cur · s_b
18       end
19     end
20   end
21 end
22
23 if s_tot < threshold then
24   add_to_local_queue(w, t)
25 else
26   n_min ← node_with_min_access_cost(data)
27
28   if n_min ≠ local_node_of_worker(w) then
29     w_dst ← random_worker_on_node(n_min)
30     res ← transfer_task(t, w_dst)
31     if res = failure then
32       add_to_local_queue(w, t)
33     end
34   else
35     add_to_local_queue(w, t)
36   end
37 end
```

to the local queue (Line 24) to avoid cases in which the overhead of a remote push cannot be compensated by the improvement on task execution time. For tasks with larger dependences, the run-time determines the node $n_{\min}$ with the minimal overall access cost (Line 29). The access cost for a node N_i is estimated by summing up the access costs to each node N_j containing at least one of the buffers, which in turn can be estimated by multiplying the average latency between N_i and N_j.[1] If $n_{\min}$ is different from the local node n_{lcl} of the activating worker, the run-time tries to transfer t to a random worker on $n_{\min}$. If this fails, e.g., if the data structure of the targeted worker receiving remotely pushed tasks is full, the task is added to the local queue (Line 32).

2.4 Limitations of enhanced work-pushing

The major limitation of enhanced work-pushing is that, regardless of the heuristic, it can only react passively to a given data placement. This implies that data must already be well-distributed across memory controllers if all tasks should take advantage of this scheduling strategy. For poorly distributed data, e.g., if all data is placed on a single node, a subset of the workers receives a significantly higher amount of tasks than others. Work-stealing redistributes tasks among the remaining workers and thus prevents the system from load imbalance, but cannot improve overall data locality if the initial data distribution was poor. Classical task parallel run-times allocate buffers during task creation [8, 33, 31]; hence data distribution mainly depends on the control program. A sequential control program leads to poorly placed data, while a parallel control program lets work-stealing evenly distribute task creation and buffer allocation. However, writing a parallel control program is already challenging in itself, even for programs with regularly-structured task graphs. Additionally ensuring an equal distribution of data across NUMA nodes through the control program is even more challenging or infeasible, especially for applications with less regularly-structured task graphs (e.g., if the structure of the graph depends on input data). Such optimizations also reject efficient exploitation of NUMA to the programmer and are thus contrary to the idea of abstraction from the hardware by the run-time.

In the following section, we introduce a NUMA-aware allocator that complements the *input only* work-pushing heuristic and that decouples data locality from the control program, leaving efficient exploitation to the run-time.

3. DEFERRED ALLOCATION

NUMA-aware allocation controls the placement of data on specific nodes. Our proposed scheme to make these decisions transparent relies on *per-node memory pools* to control the placement of task buffers.

3.1 Per-node memory pools

Per-node memory pools combine a mechanism for efficient reuse of blocks of memory with the ability to determine on which nodes blocks are placed. Each NUMA node has a memory pool that is composed of k free lists L_0 to L_{k-1}, where L_i contains blocks of size $2^{S_{\min}+i}$ bytes. When a worker allocates a block of size s, it determines the corresponding list L_j with $2^{S_{\min}+j-1} < s \leq 2^{S_{\min}+j}$ and removes the first block of that list. If the list is empty, it allocates a larger chunk of memory from the operating system, removes the first block from the chunk and adds the remaining parts to the free list.

A common allocation strategy of operating systems is first-touch allocation, composed of two steps. The first step referred to as *logical allocation* is triggered by the system call used by the application to request additional memory and only extends the application's address space. The actual *physical allocation* is triggered upon the first write to the memory region and places the corresponding page on the same node as the writing core. Hence, a block that originates from a newly allocated chunk is not necessarily placed on any node.

However, when a block is freed, it has been written by a producer and it is thus safe to assume that the block has been placed through physical allocation. The identifier of the containing node can be obtained through a system call, which enables the run-time to return the block to the correct memory pool. To avoid the overhead of a system call each time a block is freed, information on the NUMA node containing a block is cached in a small meta-data section associated to the block. This memory pooling mechanism provides three fundamental properties for deferred allocation presented below. First, it ensures that allocating a block

[1]We estimated the latencies based on the distance between each pair of nodes reported by the NUMACTL tool provided by LIBNUMA [21].

from a memory pool always returns a block that has not been placed yet or a block that is known to be placed on the node associated to the memory pool. Second, data can be placed on a specific node with very low overhead. Finally, the granularity for data placement is decoupled from the usual page granularity as a block may be sized arbitrarily.

3.2 Principles of deferred allocation

The key idea of deferred allocation is to delay the allocation and thus the placement of each task buffer until the node executing the producer that writes to the buffer is known. This guarantees that accesses to output buffers are always local. The classical approach in run-times for dependent tasks is to allocate input buffers upon the creation of a task [8, 33, 31] or earlier [30]. Instead, we propose to let each input buffer for a consumer task t_c to be allocated by the producer task t_p writing into it, immediately before task t_c starts execution. Since the input buffer of t_c is an output buffer of t_p, the location of input data in t_c is effectively determined by its producer(s). In the following, we use the term *immediate allocation* to distinguish the default allocation scheme in which input buffers are allocated upon creation from deferred allocation.

Figure 2a shows the implications of immediate allocation on data locality for a task t. All input buffers of t are allocated on the node N_c on which the creator of t operates. The same scheme applies to the creators $t^0_{c,o}$ to $t^{m-1}_{c,o}$, causing the input buffers of the tasks t^0_o to t^{m-1}_o to be allocated on nodes N^0_o to N^{m-1}_o, respectively. In the worst case for data locality, t is stolen by a worker operating on neither N_c nor N^0_o to N^{m-1}_o and all memory accesses of t target memory on remote nodes.

When using deferred allocation, the input buffers of t are not allocated before its producers start execution and the output buffers of t are not allocated before t is activated (Figure 2b). When t becomes ready, all of its input buffers have received input data from the producers of t and have been placed on up to n different nodes N^0_i to N^{n-1}_i (Figure 2c). The data locality impact of deferred allocation is illustrated in Figure 2d, showing the placement at the moment when the worker executing t has been determined. Regardless of any possible placement of t, all of its output buffers are placed on the same node as the worker executing the task. Hence, using deferred allocation, write accesses are guaranteed to target local memory. Furthermore, this property is independent from the placement of the creating tasks t_c and $t^0_{c,o}$ to $t^{m-1}_{c,o}$, which effectively decouples data locality from the control program. Even for a sequential control program, data is distributed over the different nodes of the machine according to work-stealing. This way, work-stealing does not only take the role of a mechanism responsible for computational load balancing, but also the role as a mechanism for load balancing across memory controllers.

An important side effect of deferred allocation is a significant reduction of the memory footprint. With a sequential control program, all tasks are created by a single "root" task. This causes a large number of input buffers to be allocated early on, while the actual working set of live buffers might be much smaller. A parallel control program can mitigate the effects of early allocation, e.g., by manually throttling task creation as shown in Figure 3b. However, this requires significant programmer effort and hurts the separation of concerns that led to the delegation of task management to the run-time.

Thanks to deferred allocation, buffers allocated for early tasks can be reused at a later stage. The difference is shown in Figures 3a and 3c. In the first case, all three buffers b_i, b_{i+1} and b_{i+2} are allocated before the dependent tasks t_i to t_{i+3} are executed. In the latter case, the buffer used by t_i and t_{i+1} can be reused as the input buffer of t_{i+3}. Parallel control programs also benefit from deferred allocation as the minimal number of buffers along a path of dependent tasks can be decreased by one (e.g., in Figure 3b only b_i and b_{i+1} are simultaneously live and b_i can be reused for b_{i+2} when using deferred allocation).

3.3 Compatibility with work-pushing

Deferred allocation guarantees local write accesses, but it does not influence the locality of read accesses. By combining deferred allocation with the input-only heuristic of enhanced work-pushing, it is possible to optimize for both read and write accesses.

It is important to note that neither the output-only heuristic nor the weighted heuristic can be used since the output buffers of a task are not determined upon task activation when the work-pushing decision is taken.

4. EXPERIMENTAL SETUP

For the experimental evaluation we implemented enhanced work-pushing and deferred allocation in the run-time system of the OpenStream project [29]. We start with an overview of the software and hardware environment used in our experiments, followed by a presentation of the selected benchmarks.

4.1 Software environment

OpenStream [31] is a task-parallel, data-flow programming model implemented as an extension to OpenMP. Arbitrary dependence patterns can be used to exploit task, pipeline and data parallelism. Each data-flow dependence is semantically equivalent to a communication and synchronization event within an unbounded FIFO queue referred to as a stream. Pragmatically, this is implemented by compiling dependences as accesses to task buffers dynamically allocated at execution time: writes to streams result in writes to the buffers of the tasks consuming the data, while read accesses to streams by consumer tasks are translated to reads from their own, task-private buffers.

We implemented the optimizations presented in this paper into the publicly available run-time of OpenStream [29]. Crucially, we rely on the fact that OpenStream programs are written with programmer annotations explicitly describing the flow of data between tasks. This precise data-flow information is preserved during compilation and made available to the run-time library. We leverage this essential semantic information to determine, at run-time and *before* task execution, how much data is exchanged by any given task.

OpenStream programs are dynamically load-balanced, worker threads use hierarchical work-stealing to acquire and execute tasks whose dependences have been satisfied. If work-pushing is enabled, workers can also receive tasks in a dedicated multi-producer single-consumer queue [14]. Our experiments use one worker thread per core.

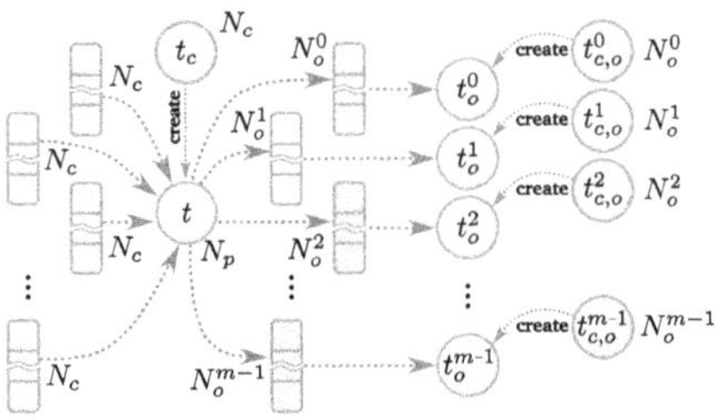

(a) Immediate allocation

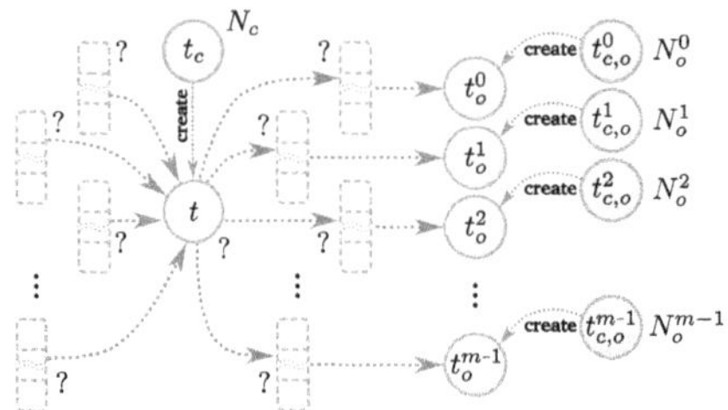

(b) Deferred allocation: after creation of t

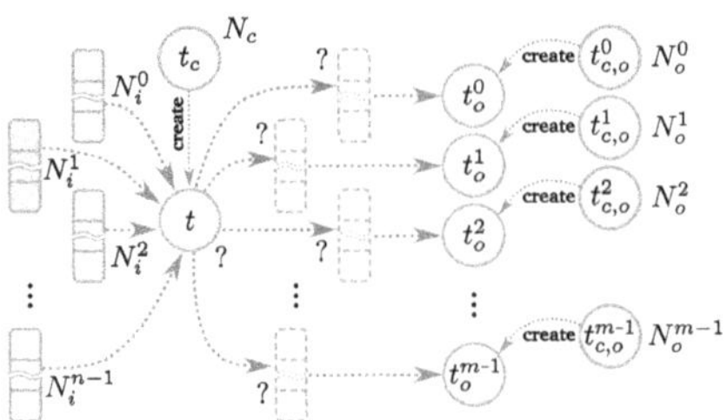

(c) Deferred allocation: activation of t

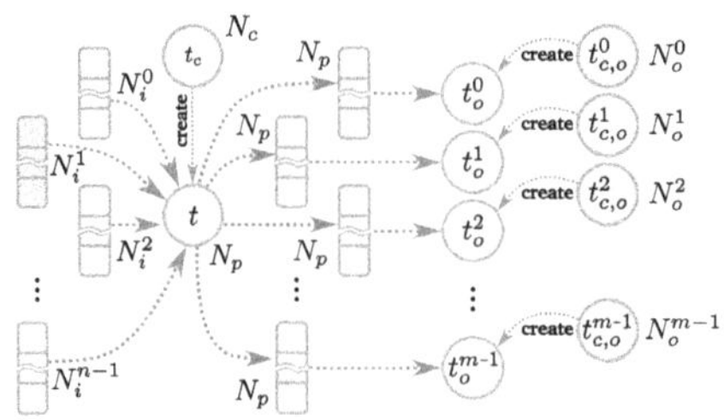

(d) Deferred allocation: final placement

Figure 2: Allocation schemes

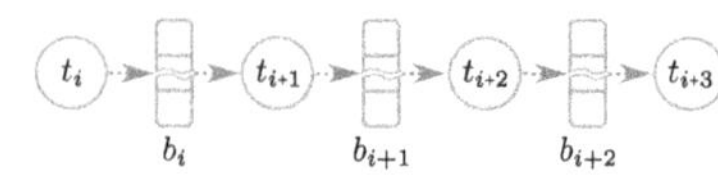

(a) Immediate allocation without buffer reuse

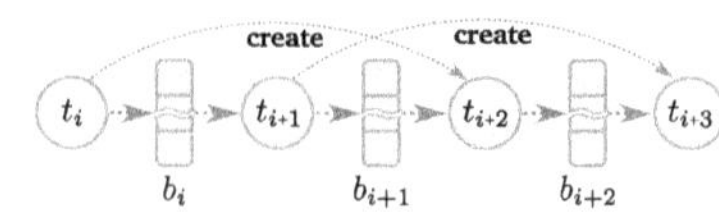

(b) Throttling of task creations

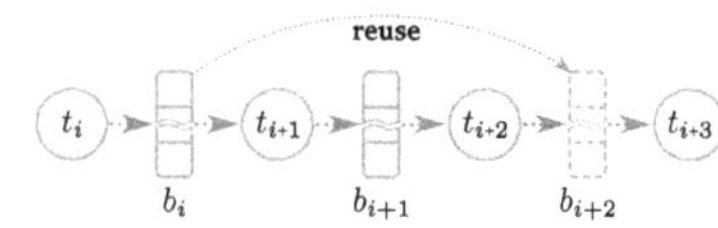

(c) Deferred allocation favoring buffer reuse

Figure 3: Allocation and reuse

4.2 Hardware environment

The experiments were conducted on two many-core systems.

Opteron-64 is a quad-socket system with four AMD Opteron 6282 SE processors running at 2.6GHz, using Scientific Linux 6.2 with kernel 3.10.1. The machine is composed of 4 physical packages, with 2 dies per package, each die containing 8 cores organized in pairs. Each pair shares the first-level instruction cache as well as a 2MiB L2 cache. An L3 cache of 6MiB and the memory controller are shared by the 8 cores on the same die. The 16KiB L1 cache is private to each core. Main memory is 64GiB, equally divided into 8 NUMA domains. For each NUMA node, 4 neighbors are at a distance of 1 hop and 3 neighbors are at 2 hops.

SGI-192 is an SGI UV2000 with 192 cores and 756GiB RAM, distributed over 24 NUMA nodes, and running SUSE Linux Enterprise Server 11 SP3 with kernel 3.0.101-0.46-default. The system is organized in *blades*, each of which contains two Intel Xeon E5-4640 CPUs running at 2.4GHz. Each CPU has 8 cores with direct access to a memory controller. The cache hierarchy consists of 3 levels: a core-private L1 with separate instruction and data cache, each with a capacity of 32KiB; a core-private, unified L2 cache of 256KiB; and a unified L3 cache of 20MiB, shared among all 8 cores of the CPU. *Hyperthreading* was disabled for our experiments. Each blade has a direct connection to a set of other blades and indirect connections to the remaining ones. From a core's perspective, a memory controller can be either local if associated to the same CPU, at 1 hop if on the same blade, at 2 hops if on a different blade that is connected directly to the core's blade or at 3 hops if on a remote blade with an indirect connection.

Latency of memory accesses and NUMA factors.

We used a synthetic benchmark to measure the latency of memory accesses as a function of the distance in hops between a requesting core and the memory controller that satisfies the request. It allocates a buffer on a given node using LIBNUMA, initializes it and measures execution time for a sequence of memory accesses to this buffer from a core on a specific node. Each sequence traverses the whole buffer from beginning to end in steps of 64 bytes, such that each cache line is only accessed once. The buffer size was set to 1GiB to ensure data is evicted from the cache before it is reused and thus to measure only memory accesses that are satisfied by the memory controller and not by the hierarchy of caches.

Tables 1 and 2 indicate the total execution time as a function of the number of hops and the access mode of the synthetic benchmark for both systems. The results show that latency increases with the distance between the requesting core and the targeted memory controller and that writes are significantly slower than reads. The rightmost column of each table shows the access time normalized to accesses targeting local memory. For reads on the Opteron-64 system, these values range from 1.81 for on-package accesses to a memory controller at a distance of one hop to a factor of 4.34 for off-package accesses at a distance of two hops. For writes, these values are lower—1.2 to 2.48—due to the higher latency of local writes. Not surprisingly, the factors for both reads and writes are significantly higher on the larger SGI-192 system (up to 7.48 for reads at three hops). This suggests that locality optimizations will have a higher impact on SGI-192 and that the locality of writes will have the greatest impact.

4.3 Benchmarks

We evaluate the impact of our techniques on nine benchmarks, each of which is available in an optimized sequential implementation and two tuned parallel implementations using OpenStream.

The first parallel implementation uses task-private input and output buffers as described in Section 2.1 and thus enables enhanced work-pushing and deferred allocation. Data from input buffers is only read and never written, while data in output buffers is only written and never read. Hence, tasks cannot perform in-place updates and results are writ-

	Read accesses	Write accesses	Factor R/W
Local	1288.5 ± 1.22ms	2256.9 ± 14.06ms	1.00 / 1.00
1 hop (on-package)	2328.4 ± 0.49ms	2717.6 ± 12.16ms	1.81 / 1.20
1 hop (off-package)	2781.4 ± 0.56ms	3934.6 ± 00.56ms	2.16 / 1.74
2 hops	5601.6 ± 0.57ms	5601.3 ± 00.55ms	4.34 / 2.48

Table 1: Average latency of accesses on Opteron-64

	Read accesses	Write accesses	Factor R/W
Local	934.82 ± 5.74ms	1307.4 ± 2.95ms	1.00 / 1.00
1 hop	4563.1 ± 3.02ms	5282.38 ± 1.56ms	4.88 / 4.04
2 hops	5820.48 ± 2.11ms	6473.38 ± 1.16ms	6.23 / 4.95
3 hops	6991.24 ± 2.71ms	7673.14 ± 0.92ms	7.48 / 5.87

Table 2: Average latency of accesses on SGI-192

ten to a different location than the input data. We refer to this implementation as *DSA* (dynamic single assignment).

The second parallel implementation, which we refer to as *SHM*, uses globally shared data structures and thus does not expose information on memory accesses to the run-time. However, the pages of the data structures are distributed across all NUMA nodes in a round-robin fashion using *interleaved allocation*. We use this implementation to compare our solutions to classical static NUMA-aware optimizations that require only minimal changes to the application. The benchmarks are the following.

- *Jacobi-1d*, *jacobi-2d* and *jacobi-3d* are the usual one-, two- and three-dimensional Jacobi stencils iterating over arrays of double precision floating point elements. At each iteration, the algorithm averages for each matrix element the values of the elements in its Von Neumann neighborhood using the values from the previous iteration.
- *Seidel-1d*, *seidel-2d* and *seidel-3d* employ a similar stencil pattern but use values from the previous and the current iteration for updates.
- *Kmeans* is a data-mining benchmark that partitions a set of n d-dimensional points into k clusters using the K-means clustering algorithm. Each vector is represented by d single precision floating point values.
- *Blur-roberts* applies two successive image filters on double precision floating point elements [22]: a Gaussian *blur filter* on each pixel's Moore neighborhood followed by the *Roberts Cross Operator* for edge detection.
- *Bitonic* implements a bitonic sorting network [1], applied to a sequence of arbitrary 64-bit integers.

Table 3 summarizes the parameters for the different benchmarks and machines. The size of input data was chosen to be significantly higher than the total amount of cache memory and low enough to prevent the system from swapping. This size is identical on both machines, except for *blur-roberts*, whose execution time for images of size $2^{15} \times 2^{15}$ is too short on SGI-192 and which starts swapping for size $2^{16} \times 2^{16}$ on Opteron-64. To amortize the execution of auxiliary tasks at the beginning and the end of execution of the stencils, we set the number of iterations to 60.

The block size has been tuned to minimize the execution time for the parallel implementation with task-private input and output data (DSA) on each machine. To avoid any bias in favor of our optimizations, enhanced work-pushing and deferred allocation have been disabled during this tuning phase. In this configuration, the run-time only relies on optimized *work-stealing* [23] extended with *hierarchical work-stealing* [14] for computational load balancing. We refer to

	Matrix / Vector size	Block size (Opteron-64)	Block size (SGI-192)	Iterations
Jacobi-1d	2^{28}	2^{16}	2^{16}	60
Jacobi-2d	$2^{14} \times 2^{14}$	$2^{10} \times 2^{6}$	$2^{8} \times 2^{8}$	60
Jacobi-3d	$2^{10} \times 2^{9} \times 2^{9}$	$2^{5} \times 2^{6} \times 2^{5}$	$2^{4} \times 2^{6} \times 2^{6}$	60
Seidel-1d	2^{28}	2^{16}	2^{16}	60
Seidel-2d	$2^{14} \times 2^{14}$	$2^{8} \times 2^{8}$	$2^{7} \times 2^{9}$	60
Seidel-3d	$2^{10} \times 2^{9} \times 2^{9}$	$2^{6} \times 2^{5} \times 2^{5}$	$2^{4} \times 2^{8} \times 2^{4}$	60
Blur-roberts	$2^{15} \times 2^{15}$ (Opteron-64) $2^{16} \times 2^{16}$ (SGI-192)	$2^{9} \times 2^{6}$	$2^{10} \times 2^{6}$	-
Bitonic	2^{28}	2^{16}	2^{17}	-
K-means	40.96M pts, 10 dims., 11 clust.	10^{4}	10^{4}	-

Table 3: Benchmark parameters

this *baseline* for our experiments as *DSA-BASE*. Identical parameters for the block size and run-time have been used for the experiments with the shared memory versions of the benchmarks (SHM), which we refer to as *SHM-BASE*.

All benchmarks were compiled using the OpenStream compiler based on GCC 4.7.0. The compilation flags for *blur-roberts* as well as the *jacobi* and *seidel* benchmarks were `-O3 -ffast-math`, while *kmeans* uses `-O3` and *bitonic* uses `-O2`.

The parallel implementations are provided with a parallel control program to prevent sequential task creation from becoming a performance bottleneck. To avoid memory controller contention, the initial and final data are stored in global data structures allocated using interleaved allocation across all NUMA nodes.

Data dependence patterns.

The relevant producer-consumer patterns shown in Figure 4 can be divided into three groups with different implications for our optimizations: *unbalanced dependences* (e.g., one input buffer accounting for more than 90% of the input data) with long dependence paths (*jacobi-1d*, *jacobi-2d*, *jacobi-3d*, *seidel-1d*, *seidel-2d*, *seidel-3d*, *kmeans*), *unbalanced dependences* with short dependence paths (*blur-roberts*) and *balanced dependences* (*bitonic*). The behavior of our heuristics on these patterns is referenced in the experimental evaluation. All of the benchmarks have non-trivial, connected task graphs, i.e., none of the benchmarks represents an embarrassingly parallel workload.

Characterization of memory accesses.

The benchmarks were carefully tuned (block sizes and tiling) to take advantage of caches. However, the effectiveness of the cache hierarchy also depends on the pattern, the frequency and the timing of memory accesses during the execution of a benchmark, leading to more or fewer cache misses for a given block size. Figure 5 shows the cache miss rates at the last level of cache (LLC) on SGI-192 of DSA-BASE, which is a good proxy for the rate of requests to main memory for each benchmark. For all bar graphs in this paper, error bars indicate standard deviation. As the focus of our optimizations is on the locality of memory accesses, we expect a higher impact for benchmarks exhibiting higher LLC miss rates. For this reason, *seidel* and *blur-roberts* are expected to benefit the most from our optimizations, followed by the *jacobi* benchmarks and *bitonic*. *Kmeans* has a very low LLC miss rate and is not expected to show significant improvement.

4.4 Experimental baseline

To demonstrate the effectiveness of our optimizations, our principal point of comparison is DSA-BASE. We validate

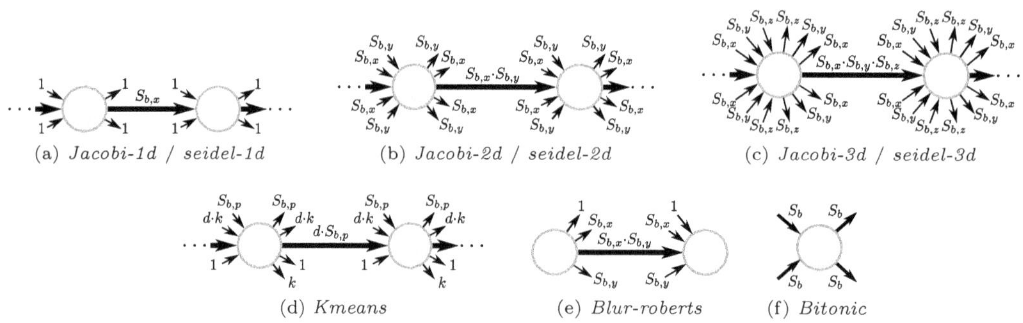

(a) *Jacobi-1d / seidel-1d* (b) *Jacobi-2d / seidel-2d* (c) *Jacobi-3d / seidel-3d*

(d) *Kmeans* (e) *Blur-roberts* (f) *Bitonic*

Figure 4: Main tasks and types of dependences of the benchmarks. The amount of data exchanged between tasks is indicated by the width of arrows. Symbols: $S_{b,x}$, $S_{b,y}$, $S_{b,z}$: number of elements per block in x, y and z direction; $S_{b,p}$: number of points per block, d: number of dimensions, k: number of clusters in *kmeans*; S_b: number of elements per block in *bitonic*.

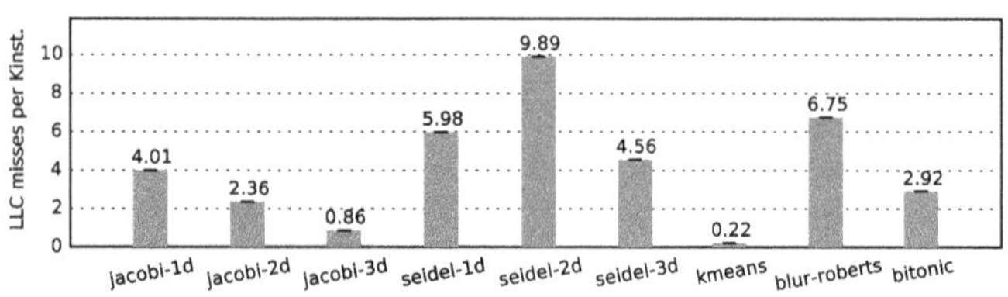

Figure 5: LLC misses per thousand instructions on SGI-192

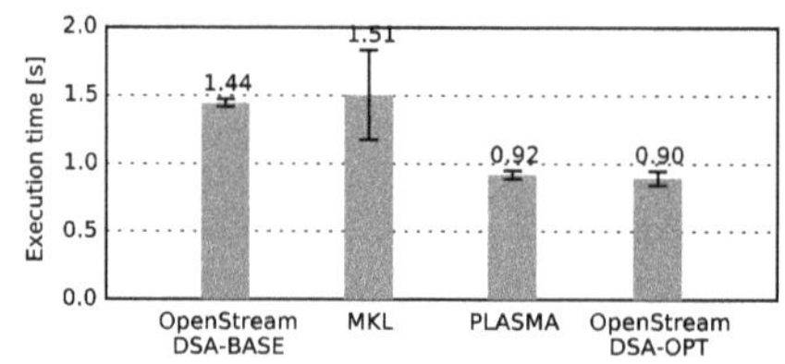

Figure 6: Cholesky factorization on Opteron-64.

the soundness of this baseline by comparing its performance on Cholesky factorization against the two state-of-the-art linear algebra libraries PLASMA/QUARK [35] and Intel's MKL [18]. Figure 6 shows the execution times of Cholesky factorization on a matrix of size 8192×8192 running on the Opteron-64 platform with four configurations: DSA-BASE, Intel MKL, PLASMA and finally optimized OpenStream (DSA-OPT), the latter using our run-time implementing the optimizations presented in this paper. This validates the soundness of our baseline, which achieves similar performance to Intel MKL, while also showcasing the effectiveness of our optimizations, automatically and transparently matching the performance of PLASMA without any change in the benchmark's source code.

5. RESULTS

We now evaluate enhanced work-pushing and deferred allocation, starting with the impact on memory access locality, and following on with the actual performance results.

5.1 Impact on the locality of memory accesses

On the Opteron platform, we use two hardware performance counters to count the requests to node-local memory[2] and to remote nodes,[3] respectively. We consider the locality metric $R^{\mathrm{HW}}_{\mathrm{loc}}$, defined as the ratio of local memory accesses to total memory accesses, shown in Figure 7. We could not provide the corresponding figures for the SGI system due to missing support in the kernel. However, the OpenStream run-time contains precise information on the working set of tasks and on the placement of input buffers, which can be used to provide a second locality metric $R^{\mathrm{RT}}_{\mathrm{loc}}$ that precisely accounts for accesses to data managed by the run-time, i.e., associated to task dependences.

[2] *CPU_IO_REQUESTS_TO_MEMORY_IO:LOCAL_CPU_TO_LOCAL_MEM*

[3] *CPU_IO_REQUESTS_TO_MEMORY_IO:LOCAL_CPU_TO_REMOTE_MEM*

Figure 7 shows the locality of requests to main memory $R^{\mathrm{HW}}_{\mathrm{loc}}$ on Opteron-64. The configurations *input only*, *output only* and *weighted* refer to DSA-BASE combined with the respective enhanced work-pushing heuristic, while *dfa* refers to DSA-BASE combined with deferred allocation, but without enhanced work-pushing. Data locality is consistently improved by our optimizations across all benchmarks. The combination of enhanced work-pushing and deferred allocation (DSA-OPT) is comparable to the output only and weighted heuristics of work-pushing, but yields significantly better results than enhanced work-pushing only for benchmarks with balanced dependences. For all *jacobi* and *seidel* benchmarks as well as *kmeans* the locality was improved above 88% and for *bitonic* above 81%. *Blur-roberts* does not benefit as much from our optimizations as the other benchmarks. As the run-time system only manages the placement of privatized data associated with dependences, short dependence paths, such as in *Blur-roberts*, only allow the run-time to optimize placement for a fraction of the execution. As a result, the overall impact is diluted proportionately. We further note that the input only heuristic of work-pushing—closest to the original heuristic in prior work [14]—does not improve memory locality as much as weighted work-pushing or the combination of deferred allocation with work-pushing. Figure 8 shows $R^{\mathrm{RT}}_{\mathrm{loc}}$ on SGI-192, highlighting the effectiveness of our optimizations on data under the control of the run-time. Not accounting for unmanaged data, we achieve almost perfect locality (up to 99.8%) across all benchmarks, except for *bitonic*, where balanced dependences imply that whenever input data is on multiple nodes, only half of the input data can be accessed locally.

5.2 Impact on performance

Figure 9 shows the speedup achieved over DSA-BASE. The best performance is achieved by combining work-pushing and deferred allocation, with a global maximum of 2.5× on Opteron-64 and 5.0× on SGI-192. Generally, the speedups

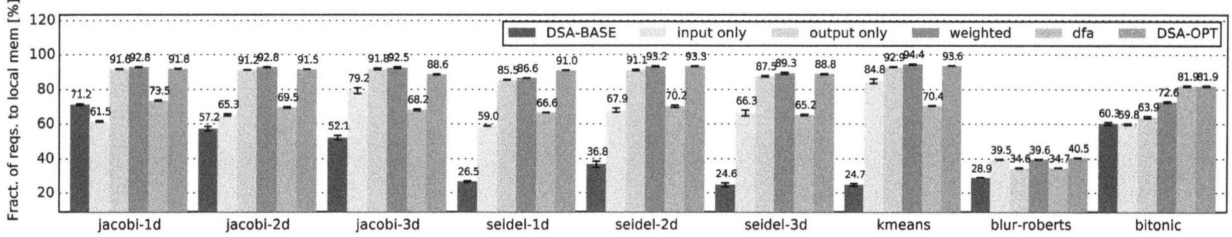

Figure 7: Locality $R_{\mathrm{loc}}^{\mathrm{HW}}$ of requests to main memory on the Opteron-64 system for deferred allocation

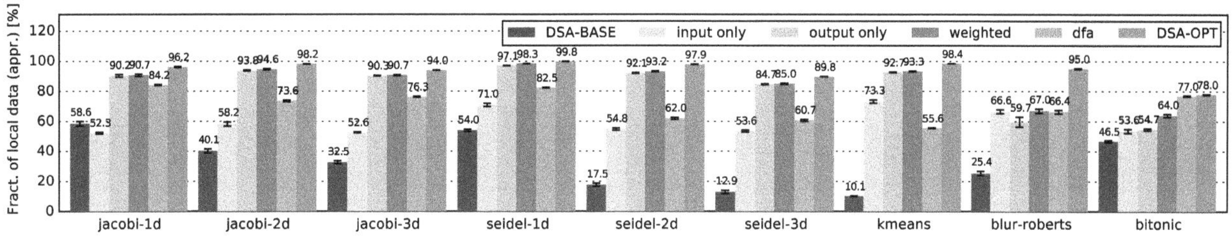

Figure 8: Locality $R_{\mathrm{loc}}^{\mathrm{RT}}$ of data managed by the run-time on SGI-192

are higher on SGI-192, showing that our optimizations have a higher impact on machines with higher penalties for remote accesses. These improvements result from better locality as well as from the memory footprint reduction induced by deferred allocation. Note that the input-only heuristic did not perform well with *jacobi*, highlighting the importance of considering both input and output flows, and of proactively distributing buffers through deferred allocation rather than reactively adapting the schedule only.

5.3 Comparison with interleaved allocation

Figure 10 shows the speedup of the DSA parallel baseline over the implementations using globally shared data structures distributed over all NUMA nodes using interleaved allocation (SHM-BASE). The optimizations achieve up to 3.1× speedup on Opteron-64 and 5.6× on SGI-192. The best performance is systematically obtained by the combined work-pushing and deferred allocation strategy. These results clearly indicate that taking advantage of the dynamic dataflow information provided in modern task-dependent languages allows for more precise control over the placement of data leading to improved performance over static schemes unable to react to dynamic behavior at execution time. In the case of interleaved allocation, the uniform access pattern of the benchmarks evaluated in this work yields good load balancing across memory controllers, but poor data locality.

6. COMPARISON WITH DYNAMIC PAGE MIGRATION

While our study focused on the application and run-time, the reader may wonder how kernel-level optimizations fare in our context. Recent versions of Linux comprise the *balancenuma* patchset [12] for dynamic page migration and a transparent policy migrating pages during the execution of a process based on its memory accesses. The kernel periodically scans the address space of the process and changes the protection flags of the scanned pages such that an access causes an exception. Upon an access to such a page, the exception handler checks whether the page is misplaced with respect to NUMA and migrates it towards the node of the accessing CPU.

We first evaluate the influence of page migration on a synthetic benchmark to determine under which conditions the mechanism is beneficial and show that these conditions do not meet the requirements for task-parallel programs. We then study the impact of dynamic page migration on the SHM parallel baseline with globally shared data (SHM-BASE).

6.1 Parametrization of page migration

For all experiments, we used version 4.3.0 of the Linux Kernel. As the SGI test platform requires specific kernel patches and is shared among many users, we conducted these experiments on Opteron-64 only. The migration mechanism is configured through the procfs pseudo filesystem, as follows:

- Migration can be globally enabled or disabled by setting *numa_balancing* to 1 or 0, respectively.
- The parameter *numa_balancing_scan_delay_ms* indicates the minimum execution time of a process before page migration starts. In our experiments, we have set this value to 0 to enable migration as soon as possible. Page migration during initialization is prevented using appropriate calls to *mbind*, temporarily imposing static placement.
- The minimum / maximum duration between two scans is controlled by *numa_balancing_scan_period_min_ms* / *numa_balancing_scan_period_max_ms*. We have set the minimal period to 0 and the maximum period to 100000 to allow for constant re-evaluation of the mapping.
- How much of the address space is examined in one scan is defined by *numa_balancing_scan_size_mb*. In the experiments, this parameter has been set to 100000 to prevent the system from scanning only a subset of the pages.

In the following evaluation, we calculate the ratio of the median wall clock execution time with dynamic migration (*numa_balancing* set to 1) divided by the median time with-

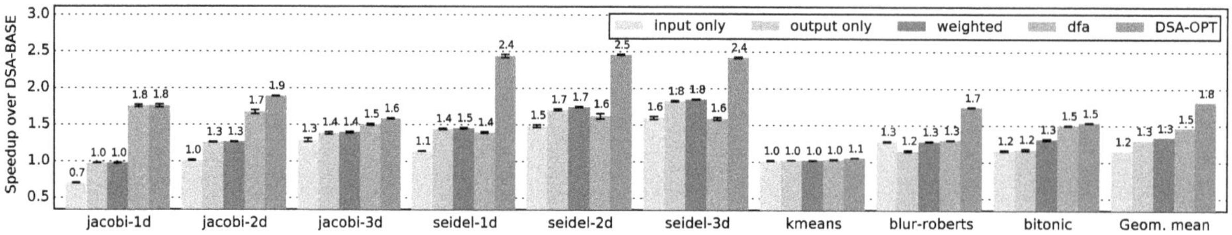

(a) Opteron-64 system

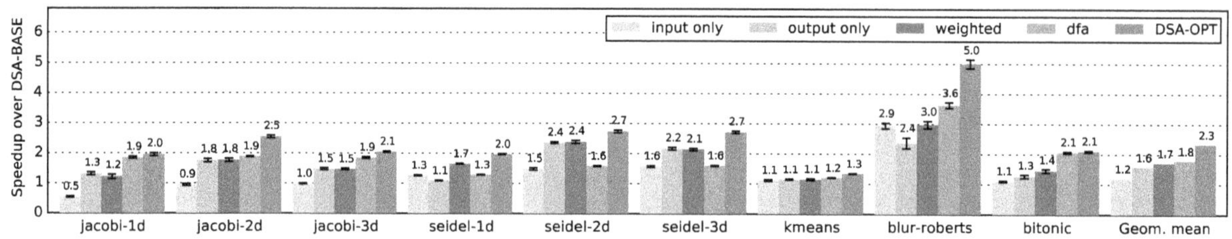

(b) SGI-192 system

Figure 9: Speedup over the parallel baseline DSA-BASE

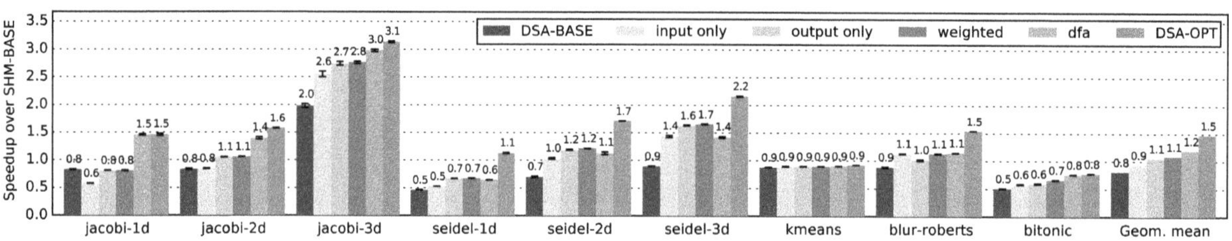

(a) Opteron-64

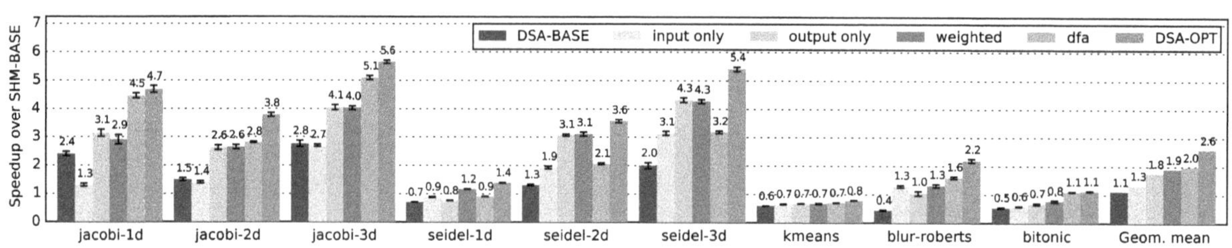

(b) SGI-192

Figure 10: Speedup over the implementations with globally shared data structures and interleaving on all nodes (SHM-BASE)

out migration (*numa_balancing* set to 0) for 10 runs of a synthetic benchmark.

6.2 Evaluation of a synthetic benchmark

The synthetic benchmark has been designed specifically to evaluate the potential of dynamic page migration for scenarios with clear relationships between data and computations and without interference. It is composed of the following steps:

1. Allocate S sets of T 64MiB buffers, distributed in a round-robin fashion on the machine's NUMA node. That is, the i-th buffer of each set is allocated on NUMA node ($i \bmod N$), with N being the total number of NUMA nodes.

2. Create T threads and pin the i-th thread on the i-th core.

3. Assign exactly one buffer of the current set to each thread, with thread i being the owner of the i-th buffer.

4. Synchronize all threads using a barrier and let each thread traverse its buffer I times linearly by adding a constant to the first 8-byte integer of every cache line of the buffer.

5. Change the affinity A times by repeating steps 3 and 4 a total of A times.

6. Synchronize all threads with a barrier and print the time elapsed between the moments in which the first thread passed the first and the last barrier, respectively.

On Opteron-64, the number of 8 cores per NUMA node is equal to the total number of nodes. Thus, the allocation scheme above causes every NUMA node to access every node of the system at the beginning of each affinity change, which allows for load-balancing on the system's memory controllers and thus factors out contention arising from the initial distribution. We have set the total number of affinity changes A to 8.

Figure 11 shows the speedup for a varying number of iterations I before each affinity change. We found that the preferred page size for the buffers has a strong influence on migration overhead. Therefore, we evaluate three configurations: *default* does not impose any specific page size and leaves the choice to the operating system, while *small* and *huge* force the use of 4KiB and 2MiB pages, respectively.

In order to match the performance of the SHM baseline with static placement, at least 12 iterations are necessary for *default* and *huge*. For small pages, at least 70 iterations must be performed. In our benchmarks with task-private input and output buffers, the bulk of the input data of each task is accessed only up to 7 times. The temporal data locality is thus far below these thresholds, which lets us expect that dynamic page migration cannot improve performance.

6.3 Evaluation of OpenStream benchmarks

Let us now study the impact of page migration on the SHM parallel baseline with globally shared data structures. In contrast to task-private buffers, in which each input buffer at each iteration potentially uses a different set of addresses, each block of data of the globally shared data structures is associated to a fixed set of addresses for all iterations with very high temporal locality. As in the previous experiments, we used hierarchical work-stealing, initial interleaved allocation and the parameters for the benchmarks described in Table 3.

Figure 12 shows the speedup of dynamic page migration over the median execution time without migration. For none of the benchmarks does page migration improve performance. In the best case (*jacobi-3d*, *seidel-2d*, *seidel-3d*, *kmeans*, and *blur-roberts*) performance is almost identical with small variations. In many other cases performance degrades substantially (*jacobi-1d*, *jacobi-2d*, *seidel-1d*, and *bitonic*).

The first reason for this degradation is that dynamic page migration is not able to catch up with frequent affinity changes between cores and data. Second, in contrast to task-private buffers, data blocks of the shared data structures do not necessarily represent contiguous portions of the address space and a single huge page might contain data of more than one block, accessed by different cores. In conclusion, page migration only reacts to changes in the task-data affinity while our scheme proactively binds them together and page granularity may also not be appropriate for data placement in task-parallel applications.

7. RELATED WORK

Combined NUMA-aware scheduling and data placement can be split into general methods operating at the thread level—usually implemented in the operating system at page granularity, and task-oriented methods operating at the task level in parallel programming languages—typically in userland.

Starting with userland methods, it is possible to statically place arrays and computations to bring NUMA awareness to OpenMP programs [27, 2, 34, 32] or applications using TBB [26]. Such approaches are well suited to regular data structures and involve target-specific optimizations by the programmer. This is viable in some application areas, but generally not consistent with the performance portability and dynamic concurrency of task-parallel models.

ForestGOMP [5, 6] is an OpenMP run-time with a resource-aware scheduler and a NUMA-aware allocator. It introduces three concepts: grouping of OpenMP threads into bubbles, scheduling of threads and bubbles using a hierarchy of runqueues, and migrating data dynamically upon load balancing. Although the affinity between computations and data remains implicit, ForestGOMP performs best when these affinities are stable over time, and when the locality of unstable affinities can be restored through scheduling without migration. LAWS [11] brings NUMA awareness to Cilk tasks. It specializes into divide-and-conquer algorithms, assuming a one-to-one mapping between task trees and the memory regions accessed during task execution. LAWS puts together a NUMA-aware memory allocator and a task tree partitioning heuristic to steer a three-level work-stealing scheduler, exploiting implicit information on the structure of data accesses and computation. While both ForestGOMP and LAWS show that such information can be exploited to increase locality, their limitations suggest that NUMA awareness is more natural and effective to achieve with the explicit task-data association we consider.

Among dependent task models, one of the most popular is the StarSs project [30], whose OMPSs variant led to dependent tasks in OpenMP 4.0. This model does provide an explicit task-data association. Yet we preferred OpenStream as it facilitates the privatization of data blocks communicated across tasks, and its first-class streams expressing dependences across concurrently created tasks accelerate the creation of complex graphs on large scale NUMA systems. Our analysis of NUMA-aware placement and scheduling and the proposed algorithms would most likely fit other models with similar properties such as CnC [8] or KAAPI [16].

In earlier work [14], we introduced the work-pushing technique for task-parallel application that we extended in this paper. Furthermore, we proposed dependence-aware allocation, a NUMA-aware memory allocation technique that examines inter-task data dependences and speculatively allocates memory for the input data of a task on the node whose cores are likely to execute its producers. However, the techniques presented in this paper achieve better locality and performance since in some cases the prediction might fail and work-stealing might lead to remote write accesses.

Alternatively, one could argue that the operating system should be in charge of providing a NUMA-oblivious abstraction for parallel programs. Operating systems typically follow a first-touch strategy by default, in which a page of physical memory is allocated on the node associated to the core that first writes to the page. A common optimization is to migrate a page dynamically to the node performing the next write access. This strategy, referred to as affinity- or migrate-on-next-touch can be transparent [17] or controlled through system calls [25]. Dashti et al. proposed Carrefour [13], a kernel-level solution whose primary goal is to avoid congestion on memory controllers and interconnects. Carrefour detects affinities between computations and pages dynamically using hardware performance counters. Based on these affinities it combines allocation of pages near the accessing node, interleaved allocation and page replication for read-only data. However, the solution is suited for long-running processes as it uses sampling hardware counters [15]

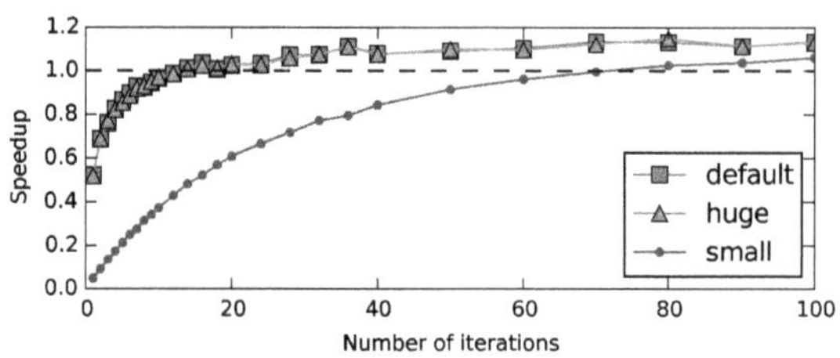

Figure 11: Speedup of page migration (synthetic benchmark)

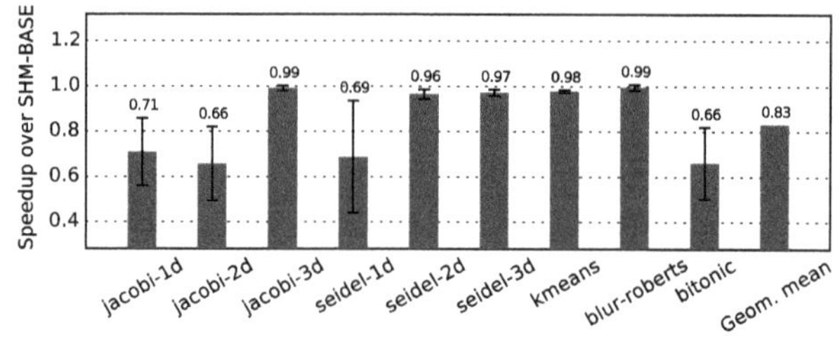

Figure 12: Speedup over static placement (SHM-BASE)

to determine data affinities, requiring high reuse of data for statistical confidence without high overhead [24]. Similar to Carrefour, AsymSched [24]—a combined user-space-kernel solution for data and thread placement—focuses on bandwidth rather than locality, taking into account the asymmetry of interconnects on recent NUMA systems. However, despite a highly efficient migration mechanism, the placement granularity is bound to a page and may not meet the requirements of task-parallel applications.

8. CONCLUSION

We showed that parallel languages with dependent tasks can achieve excellent, scalable performance on large scale NUMA machines without exposing programmers to the complexity of these systems. One key element of the solution is to implement communications through task-private data buffers. This allows for the preservation of a simple, uniform abstract view for both memory and computations, yet achieving high data locality. Inter-task data dependences provide precise information about affinities between tasks and data in the run-time, improving the accuracy of NUMA-aware scheduling. We proposed two complementary techniques to exploit this information and to manage task-private buffers: enhanced work-pushing and deferred allocation. Deferred allocation guarantees that all accesses to task output data are local, while enhanced work-pushing improves the locality of accesses to task input data. By combining hierarchical work-stealing with enhanced work-pushing, we ensure that no processor remains idle, unless no task is ready to execute. Deferred allocation provides an additional level of load-balancing, addressing contention on memory controllers. We showed that our techniques achieve up to 5× speedup over state of the art NUMA-aware solutions, in presence of dynamic task creation and changing dependence patterns. In a comparison with transparent static and dynamic allocation techniques by the operating system, we showed that our solution is up to 5.6× faster than interleaved allocation and that dynamic page migration is unable to cope with the fine-grained concurrency and communication of task-parallel applications.

Acknowledgments

Our work was partly supported by the grants EU FET-HPC ExaNoDe H2020-671578 and UK EPSRC EP/M004880/1. A. Pop is funded by a Royal Academy of Engineering University Research Fellowship.

9. REFERENCES

[1] K. E. Batcher. Sorting networks and their applications. In *Proceedings of the April 30–May 2, 1968, Spring joint Computer Conference*, AFIPS '68 (Spring), pages 307–314, New York, NY, USA, 1968. ACM.

[2] J. Bircsak, P. Craig, R. Crowell, Z. Cvetanovic, J. Harris, C. Nelson, and C. Offner. Extending OpenMP for NUMA machines. In *Supercomputing*. ACM/IEEE, Nov. 2000.

[3] R. D. Blumofe, C. F. Joerg, B. C. Kuszmaul, C. E. Leiserson, K. H. Randall, and Y. Zhou. Cilk: An efficient multithreaded runtime system. In *Proceedings of the 5th ACM SIGPLAN Symposium on Principles and Practice of Parallel Programming*, PPOPP '95, pages 207–216, New York, NY, USA, 1995. ACM.

[4] R. D. Blumofe and C. E. Leiserson. Scheduling multithreaded computations by work stealing. *JACM*, 46(5):720–748, Sept. 1999.

[5] F. Broquedis, O. Aumage, B. Goglin, S. Thibault, P.-A. Wacrenier, and R. Namyst. Structuring the execution of openmp applications for multicore architectures. In *2010 IEEE International Symposium on Parallel & Distributed Processing (IPDPS)*, pages 1–10. IEEE.

[6] F. Broquedis, N. Furmento, B. Goglin, P.-A. Wacrenier, and R. Namyst. ForestGOMP: An efficient OpenMP environment for NUMA architectures. *International Journal of Parallel Programming*, 38(5):418–439, 2010.

[7] F. Broquedis, T. Gautier, and V. Danjean. LIBKOMP, an efficient OpenMP runtime system for both fork-join and data flow paradigms. In *Proceedings of the 8th International Conference on OpenMP in a Heterogeneous World*, IWOMP, pages 102–115, Berlin, Heidelberg, 2012. Springer-Verlag.

[8] Z. Budimlić, M. Burke, V. Cavé, K. Knobe, G. Lowney, R. Newton, J. Palsberg, D. Peixotto, V. Sarkar, F. Schlimbach, and S. Taşirlar. Concurrent collections. *Scientific Programming*, 18:203—217, 2010.

[9] V. Cavé, J. Zhao, J. Shirako, and V. Sarkar. Habanero-Java: The New Adventures of Old X10. In *Proceedings of the 9th International Conference on Principles and Practice of Programming in Java*, PPPJ '11, pages 51–61, New York, NY, USA, 2011. ACM.

[10] P. Charles, C. Grothoff, V. Saraswat, C. Donawa, A. Kielstra, K. Ebcioglu, C. von Praun, and V. Sarkar. X10: An object-oriented approach to non-uniform cluster computing. In *Proceedings of the 20th Annual ACM SIGPLAN Conference on Object-oriented Programming, Systems, Languages,*

and Applications, OOPSLA '05, pages 519–538, New York, NY, USA, 2005. ACM.

[11] Q. Chen, M. Guo, and H. Guan. LAWS: Locality-aware Work-stealing for Multi-socket Multi-core Architectures. In *Proceedings of the 28th ACM International Conference on Supercomputing*, ICS '14, pages 3–12, New York, NY, USA, 2014. ACM.

[12] J. Corbet. NUMA in a hurry, Nov. 2012.

[13] M. Dashti, A. Fedorova, J. Funston, F. Gaud, R. Lachaize, B. Lepers, V. Quema, and M. Roth. Traffic management: A holistic approach to memory placement on NUMA systems. In *Proceedings of the 18th International Conference on Architectural Support for Programming Languages and Operating Systems*, ASPLOS, pages 381–394, New York, NY, USA, 2013. ACM.

[14] A. Drebes, A. Pop, K. Heydemann, A. Cohen, and N. Drach. Topology-Aware and Dependence-Aware Scheduling and Memory Allocation for Task-Parallel Languages. *ACM Transactions on Architecture and Code Optimization*, 11(3):30:1–30:25, Aug. 2014.

[15] P. J. Drongowski. *Instruction-Based Sampling: A New Performance Analysis Technique for AMD Family 10h Processors.* Advanced Micro Devices, November 2007.

[16] T. Gautier, X. Besseron, and L. Pigeon. KAAPI: A thread scheduling runtime system for data flow computations on cluster of multi-processors. In *Proceedings of the 2007 International Workshop on Parallel Symbolic Computation*, pages 15–23. ACM, 2007.

[17] B. Goglin and N. Furmento. Enabling high-performance memory migration for multithreaded applications on linux. In *IEEE International Symposium on Parallel Distributed Processing (IPDPS '09)*, pages 1–9, May 2009.

[18] Intel Corporation. Intel Math Kernel Library. https://software.intel.com/en-us/intel-mkl, accessed 01/2015.

[19] Intel Corporation. Threading Building Blocks. https://www.threadingbuildingblocks.org/, accessed 09/2015.

[20] S. Kaestle, R. Achermann, T. Roscoe, and T. Harris. Shoal: Smart allocation and replication of memory for parallel programs. In *Proceedings of the 2015 Usenix Annual Technical Conference*, USENIX ATC '15, pages 263–276, Berkeley, CA, USA, 2015. USENIX Association.

[21] A. Kleen. A NUMA API for Linux, Apr. 2005.

[22] M. Kong, A. Pop, L.-N. Pouchet, R. Govindarajan, A. Cohen, and P. Sadayappan. Compiler/runtime framework for dynamic dataflow parallelization of tiled programs. *ACM Transactions on Architecture and Code Optimization*, 11(4):61:1–61:30, Jan. 2015.

[23] N. M. Lê, A. Pop, A. Cohen, and F. Z. Nardelli. Correct and efficient work-stealing for weak memory models. In *Proceedings of the 18th ACM SIGPLAN Symposium on Principles and Practice of Parallel Programming*, PPoPP '13, New York, NY, USA, February 2013. ACM.

[24] B. Lepers, V. Quéma, and A. Fedorova. Thread and memory placement on NUMA systems: Asymmetry matters. In *2015 USENIX Annual Technical Conference, USENIX ATC '15, July 8-10, Santa Clara, CA, USA*, pages 277–289, 2015.

[25] H. Löf and S. Holmgren. Affinity-on-next-touch: Increasing the Performance of an Industrial PDE Solver on a cc-NUMA System. In *Proceedings of the 19th Annual International Conference on Supercomputing*, ICS '05, pages 387–392, New York, NY, USA, 2005. ACM.

[26] Z. Majo and T. R. Gross. A library for portable and composable data locality optimizations for numa systems. In *Proceedings of the 20th ACM SIGPLAN Symposium on Principles and Practice of Parallel Programming*, PPoPP 2015, pages 227–238, New York, NY, USA, 2015. ACM.

[27] D. S. Nikolopoulos, E. Artiaga, E. Ayguadé, and J. Labarta. Exploiting memory affinity in openmp through schedule reuse. *SIGARCH Computer Architecture News*, 29(5):49–55, Dec. 2001.

[28] OpenMP Architecture Review Board. *OpenMP Application Program Interface Version 4.0*, July 2013.

[29] http://www.openstream.info.

[30] J. Planas, R. M. Badia, E. Ayguadé, and J. Labarta. Hierarchical task-based programming with StarSs. *International Journal on High Performance Computing Architecture*, 23(3):284–299, 2009.

[31] A. Pop and A. Cohen. OpenStream: Expressiveness and data-flow compilation of OpenMP streaming programs. *ACM Transactions on Architecture and Code Optimization*, 9(4):53:1–53:25, Jan. 2013.

[32] C. Pousa Ribeiro and J.-F. Méhaut. Minas: Memory Affinity Management Framework. Research Report RR-7051, 2009.

[33] P. Pratikakis, H. Vandierendonck, S. Lyberis, and D. S. Nikolopoulos. A programming model for deterministic task parallelism. In *Proceedings of the ACM SIGPLAN Workshop on Memory Systems Performance and Correctness*, MSPC '11, pages 7–12, New York, NY, USA, 2011.

[34] C. P. Ribeiro, J.-F. Mehaut, A. Carissimi, M. Castro, and L. G. Fernandes. Memory affinity for hierarchical shared memory multiprocessors. In *Proceedings of the 21st International Symposium on Computer Architecture and High Performance Computing*, SBAC-PAD, pages 59–66, Washington, DC, USA, 2009. IEEE Computer Society.

[35] A. YarKhan, J. Kurzak, and J. Dongarra. *QUARK Users' Guide - QUeueing And Runtime for Kernels*, 2011. http://ash2.icl.utk.edu/sites/ash2.icl.utk.edu/files/publications/2011/icl-utk-454-2011.pdf, accessed 10/2014.

A Static Cut-off for Task Parallel Programs

Shintaro Iwasaki
Graduate School of Information Science and Technology
The University of Tokyo
Tokyo, Japan
iwasaki@eidos.ic.i.u-tokyo.ac.jp

Kenjiro Taura
Graduate School of Information Science and Technology
The University of Tokyo
Tokyo, Japan
tau@eidos.ic.i.u-tokyo.ac.jp

ABSTRACT

Task parallel models supporting dynamic and hierarchical parallelism are believed to offer a promising direction to achieving higher performance and programmability. Divide-and-conquer is the most frequently used idiom in task parallel models, which decomposes the problem instance into smaller ones until they become "trivial" to solve. However, it incurs a high tasking overhead if a task is created for each subproblem. In order to reduce this overhead, a "cut-off" is commonly used, which eliminates task creations where they are unlikely to be beneficial. The manual cut-off typically enlarges leaf tasks by stopping task creations when a subproblem becomes smaller than a threshold, and possibly transforms the enlarged leaf tasks into specialized versions for solving small instances (e.g., use loops instead of recursive calls); it duplicates the coding work and hinders productivity.

In this paper, we describe a compiler performing an effective cut-off method, called a static cut-off. Roughly speaking, it achieves the effect of manual cut-off, but automatically. The compiler tries to identify a condition in which the recursion stops within a constant number of steps and, when it is the case, eliminates task creations at compile time, which allows further compiler optimizations. Based on the termination condition analysis, two more optimization methods are developed to optimize the resulting leaf tasks in addition to replacing them with function calls; the first is to eliminate those function calls without exponential code growth; the second transforms the resulting leaf task into a loop, which further reduces the overhead and even promotes vectorization.

The evaluation shows that our proposed cut-off optimization obtained significant speedups of a geometric mean of 8.0x compared to the original ones.

Keywords

compilers; performance optimization; task parallelism; cut-off

PACT '16, September 11-15, 2016, Haifa, Israel

DOI: http://dx.doi.org/10.1145/2967938.2967968

1. INTRODUCTION

Task parallel models, which support dynamic creation of fine-grained tasks and their dynamic load balancing, offer a promising prospect for programming processors with an increasing number of cores, as they achieve both productivity and scalability for a range of programs. One notable feature of task parallelism is hierarchical parallelism which is particularly suitable for divide-and-conquer algorithms. A number of parallel systems and libraries including widely-used ones such as Cilk [4], Intel Threading Building Blocks [27], and OpenMP [25] incorporate task parallelism.

While task parallel systems provide good programmability and scalability, naive task parallel divide-and-conquer programs creating tasks until the problems become literally "trivial" to solve suffer from a high runtime overhead of managing tasks. In order to reduce the overhead, it is necessary to enlarge the granularity of tasks by replacing creation of tasks with function calls. This practice is commonly referred to as a "cut-off" and is typically applied manually by the programmer.

Replacing task creations with function calls is often not enough to achieve high absolute performance; the resulting code still has recursive function calls to subproblems, rendering further compiler optimizations difficult to apply. Addressing this problem requires not only removing creation of tasks, but also aggressively optimizing the resulting code. Several studies focusing on an automatic cut-off have been proposed in the literature [3, 6, 34]. Nevertheless, to the best of our knowledge, most of them are *runtime* techniques, deciding whether to create a task or not by observations made at runtime (e.g., the number of tasks and/or processor utilization) and/or a depth from the root. Though the runtime techniques are effective in reducing a task creation overhead in many cases, they reveal limited opportunities for further *compile-time* optimizations. Moreover, runtime techniques have a risk of seriously reducing parallelism by stretching the critical path of computation, as we discuss in Section 5.

To tackle these problems, we propose an effective cut-off technique for divide-and-conquer task parallel programs based on a static analysis of a condition in which the recursion stops within a constant height from leaves. The obtained termination condition is useful not only to generate the cut-off threshold as humans do, but also perform further compile-time optimizations to the programs obtained after eliminating task creations, including inline expansion of function calls and transformations into vectorizable loops. In contrast to the runtime approaches, our static cut-off method has a smaller risk of adversely reducing parallelism,

```
void fib(int n, int* ret){
  if(n < 2){
    *ret = n;
  }else{
    int a, b;
    spawn fib(n-1, &a);
    spawn fib(n-2, &b);
    sync;
    *ret = a + b;
  }
}
```

Figure 1: Original task-parallel Fibonacci

because it guarantees that tasks applied the cut-off are within a constant height from leaves and thus are likely to be small (see Section 3.3). We implemented the algorithms as an optimization pass in LLVM [18].

This paper makes the following contributions:

- We propose a static cut-off technique based on an analysis on a termination condition of recursive task functions. The static cut-off requires no additional cost at runtime and guarantees the adequate parallelism of programs.
- We develop methods for further static optimizations on several types of task parallel programs based on the termination condition analysis, including inline expansion of subproblem calls in a code-bloat-free manner (*code-bloat-free inlining*), and transforming tasks into vectorizable loops (*task loopification*).
- We show the proposed static cut-off technique can be easily combined with runtime cut-off techniques, which are useful as a fallback strategy when none of the static optimizations applies.
- We evaluated performance of the proposal and show a substantial speedup of a geometric mean of 5.0x with the static cut-off, 6.2x with the code-bloat-free inlining, and 21x (up to 220x) with loopification over unoptimized task parallel programs. The performance obtained by the loopification was comparable to, or faster in some cases than the loop-based programs written in OpenMP with GCC and Polly [11].

The rest of this paper is organized as follows. Section 2 presents the overview of our method and the motivation of this research. Section 3 first describes the static analysis of the cut-off condition, and proposes static cut-off transformation composed of three cut-off methods based on the analysis: static task elimination, code-bloat-free inlining, and loopification. Section 4 shows the experimental results of the proposed optimizations. Section 5 discusses related work and Section 6 concludes this paper.

2. OVERVIEW

Before entering into details, this section overviews our cut-off methods using a simple running example. Consider a program in Figure 1, which calculates an nth Fibonacci number.

The original version suffers from a large overhead to create tasks due to its too fine-grained task granularity. A cut-off is a very common method to enlarge the granularity, but making the granularity too large has a risk of reducing parallelism significantly. As is commonly used in a manual cut-off, our compiler applies a cut-off to a function when the call tree rooted from it has a height within a constant

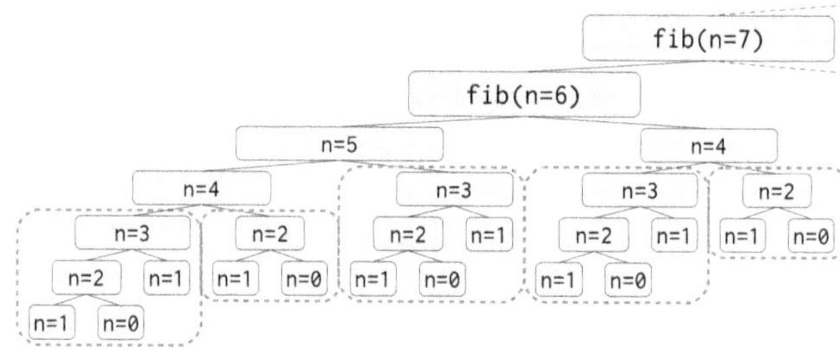

Figure 2: Task tree of fib in Figure 1. Tasks enclosed by a dotted line are the cut-off targets under the 2nd termination condition ($n < 4$).

threshold. With an appropriately chosen threshold, tasks under such conditions will perform a small amount of work, so serializing them will have little impact on the parallelism. Section 3.3 describes how we determine the cut-off threshold. The key of our static analysis is, therefore, to find a condition on function's arguments in which the height of the task tree from leaves to that task is within a constant height H. We call this condition the *Hth termination condition*. In particular, a 0th termination condition is a condition in which a function itself is a leaf and a 1st termination condition a condition in which a function is either a leaf or calls only leaves. Section 3.1 details how to obtain these conditions.

For example, Figure 2 shows cut-off targets (encircled by a dotted line) within a height 2 in the task tree of `fib`. The 2nd termination condition is $n < 4$.

If the compiler successfully identifies the termination condition, it tries to apply one of the transformations presented in Figure 3.

Figure 3a shows the simplest transformation which just replaces task creations with function calls. We call this optimization *static task elimination* (see Section 3.2.1). It reduces a tasking overhead while guaranteeing serialized tasks are small. The overhead still remains high for extremely fine-grained tasks such as `fib` due to the function calls, however.

A traditional method to alleviate function call overheads is inline expansion. It becomes powerful under an Hth termination condition since we can eliminate the innermost recursive calls by inlining H times. However, a usual inlining strategy does not work well in our setting. It is desirable to completely eliminate function calls within a coarsened task (`fib_seq` in Figure 3a), but doing so would increase code size significantly. Typical divide-and-conquer algorithms have multiple recursive call sites, so repeatedly expanding them increases code size exponentially with the depth of inline expansion. To completely inline-expand divide-and-conquer functions without exponential code growth, we develop a method to aggregate the recursive call sites into *a single static call site*. We call the method *code-bloat-free inlining* (see Section 3.2.2). The resulting code after transformation is shown in Figure 3b. Code-bloat-free inlining in general transforms recursive functions into nested loops as deeply nested as the depth of inline expansions.

There are cases in which we can do even better by transforming recursive functions into more natural, flat or shallowly nested loops. A divide-and-conquer vector addition program shown in Figure 3c is such a program which can be represented as a flat loop instead of a deeply nested loop obtained by *code-bloat-free inlining*. Our compiler is able to transform such a function to a flat loop as shown in Fig-

```
void fib(int n, int* ret){
  if(n < 4){
    fib_seq(n, ret);
  }else{
    int a, b;
    spawn fib(n-1, &a);
    spawn fib(n-2, &b);
    sync;
    *ret = a + b;
  }
}
void fib_seq(int n, int* ret){
  if(n < 2){
    *ret = n;
  }else{
    int a, b;
    fib_seq(n-1, &a);
    fib_seq(n-2, &b);
    *ret = a + b;
  }
}
```

(a) Static task elimination

```
void fib_seq(int n, int* ret){
  if(n < 2){
    *ret = n;
  }else{
    int a, b;
    for(int i = 0; i < 2; i++){
      int n2, *ret2;
      switch(i){
      case 0:
        n2=n-1; ret2=&a; break;
      case 1:
        n2=n-2; ret2=&b; break;
      }
      if(n2 < 2)
        *ret2 = n2;
      else
        [...]
    }
    *ret = a + b;
  }
}
```

(b) Code-bloat-free inlining

```
void vecadd(float* a,
            float* b, int n){
  if(n == 1){
    *a += *b;
  }else{
    spawn vecadd(a, b, n/2);
    spawn vecadd(a+n/2, b+n/2,
                 n-n/2);
    sync;
  }
}
```

(c) Task-parallel vector addition

```
void vecadd_seq(float* a,
                float* b, int n){
  for(int i = 0; i < n; i++)
    *(a+i) += *(b+i);
}
```

(d) Loopification

Figure 3: Overview of our methods

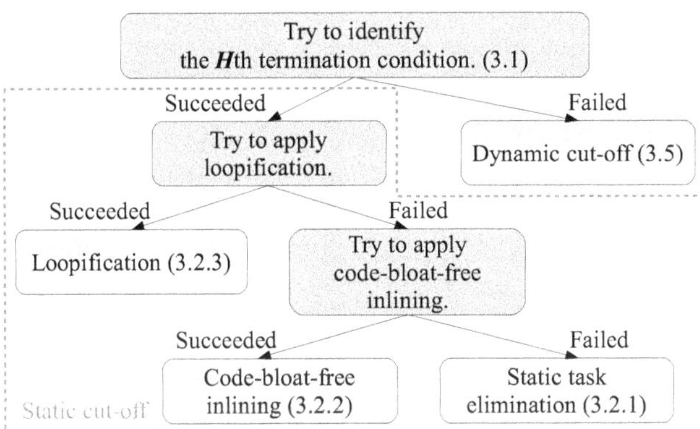

Figure 4: Flow of optimization selection

ure 3d, which then may be vectorized by the backend code generator. We call this optimization *loopification* (see Section 3.2.3). Loopification succeeds typically when the original program is a dense array-based computation such as stencil kernels and dense matrix multiplication. One might argue such loops could have easily been manually written in a parallel loop nest in the first place. We note that, however, the divide-and-conquer version can achieve the effect of cache blocking at all levels [10] with uniform and simple code, whereas loops must be manually and explicitly tiled to enjoy cache blocking. Our goal is to help programmers write cache-friendly parallel programs with high performance.

3. METHOD

This section details the proposed methods. Our compiler first runs an analysis to identify an Hth termination condition for an appropriately chosen threshold H. When the analysis succeeds, a serialized version is generated and the original version is made to call it when the condition is satisfied. For further optimizations, the compiler tries to apply loopification if applicable; otherwise, it attempts code-bloat-free inlining. If the termination condition analysis fails, the compiler applies a dynamic cut-off proposed by Thoman et al. [34] as a fallback strategy. Figure 4 summarizes the flow of the algorithm selection described above.

All of these methods were designed to receive the LLVM intermediate representation (LLVM IR). We believe that these methods can be implemented for any framework based on Static Single Assignment (SSA) form.

3.1 Termination condition analysis

We first show the termination condition analysis, which is essential to applying our static cut-off methods. While it provides useful information for a cut-off, we note that this analysis is applicable to any recursive functions. For a divide-and-conquer task parallel function, its Hth termination condition C_H is a (sufficient) condition on its incoming arguments under which the call tree created by the function call has a height not greater than H.

Based on this definition, a 0th termination condition C_0 is a condition in which it creates no child tasks. We compute C_0 as a condition in which the execution never reaches basic blocks containing self-recursive calls by analyzing the control flow graph and branch conditions of each basic block.

Specifically, let EC_b be a condition in which basic block b may be executed. EC_b can be calculated by solving the following set of equations for all basic blocks ("$\Rightarrow$" means an implication).

$$\bigvee_{p:p\to b} (EC_p \wedge BC_{p\to b}) \quad \Rightarrow \quad EC_b \tag{1}$$

$$EC_{b_{\text{entry}}} \quad = \quad \texttt{true} \tag{2}$$

where b_{entry} is an entry block of the function, $b_1 \to b_2$ denotes a control transfer edge from b_1 to b_2, and $BC_{b_1\to b_2}$ is a condition at the end of b_1 in which the control branches to b_2. Using an SSA representation, they can be obtained by tracing definitions of variables from the branch instruction at the end of b_1.

Given EC_b's, C_0 is calculated as a condition satisfying:

$$C_0 \Rightarrow \bigwedge_{r\in R} \neg EC_{b(r)} \tag{3}$$

where R is the set of self-recursive task creation sites and $b(r)$ the basic block containing $r \in R$. This expression means that C_0 is a condition in which no execution conditions of basic blocks which contain self-recursive task creations are satisfied.

We can then calculate an Hth termination condition re-

```
void nqueens(board b, int row, int col, int* ret){
  put(&b, row, col);
  if(valid(b, row)){
    if(row == N){
      *ret = 1;
    }else{
      int ans[N]; zeroclear(ans, N);
      for(int i = 0; i < N; i++)
        spawn nqueens(b, row+1, i, ans+i);
      sync;
      *ret = sum(ans, N);
    }
  }
}
```

Figure 5: Task parallel N-Queens solver

cursively as follows. The recursion stops within a height H if, for each self-recursive task creation site, either the control never reaches there or its arguments to the recursion satisfy the condition C_{H-1}. Thus, C_H is a condition satisfying:

$$C_H \Rightarrow \bigwedge_{r \in R} (\neg EC_{b(r)} \vee (\text{arguments to } r \text{ satisfying } C_{H-1})) \quad (4)$$

Let us apply the algorithm to our `fib` example in Figure 1. By applying the expression (1), the compiler is able to find, as a 0th termination condition:

$$C_0 \equiv n < 2.$$

Let r_1 and r_2 denote the two self-recursive task creation sites and b_{else} the basic block containing them (the else block in Figure 1). Based on the expression (4), C_1 can be obtained as follows:

$$\begin{aligned} C_1 &\equiv \bigwedge_{r \in \{r_1, r_2\}} (\neg EC_{b_{\text{else}}} \vee (\text{arguments to } r \text{ satisfying } C_0)) \\ &\equiv (\neg EC_{b_{\text{else}}} \vee (\ (n-1) \text{ satisfying } C_0)) \\ &\quad \wedge (\neg EC_{b_{\text{else}}} \vee (\ (n-2) \text{ satisfying } C_0)) \\ &\equiv (n < 2 \vee n - 1 < 2) \wedge (n < 2 \vee n - 2 < 2) \\ &\equiv n < 3. \end{aligned}$$

By continuing this, the Hth termination condition C_H is recursively calculated as $n < 2 + H$.

There are cases when we fail to find a termination condition; it happens when we cannot express the branch condition that appears in the expression (1) in terms of the arguments of the function. Finding the expression for $BC_{p \to b}$ begins with an expression of SSA variables that directly appear in the branch condition; it transitively replaces these variables with their definitions, until the expression involves only the incoming parameters of the function and constants. When we encounter memory references, phi functions, or function calls as a definition along the way, we always overestimate the reachability condition to identify a sufficient termination condition, leading to missing optimization opportunities. If the obtained termination condition is always false, the analysis effectively fails and no static optimizations are applied.

This strategy can detect a useful condition for programs involving a complex control flow. Figure 5 shows an `nqueens` program, which counts solutions for the N-Queens problem; reachability to recursive call sites depends on the return value of a function call `valid(b, row)`, which is unknown. Our analysis assumes the control *may* transfer, from the basic block containing `valid(b, row)`, to the "then" block of the if statement. Our analysis can nevertheless infer a sufficient condition, $N - H \leq \texttt{row} \leq N$, as the Hth termination condition.

3.2 Static cut-off transformations

As shown in Figure 4, when the termination condition analysis succeeds, we choose an appropriate cut-off parameter H (discussed later in Section 3.3) and then try to apply further cut-off optimizations: static task elimination, code-bloat-free inlining, and loopification. We assume the inputs of these transformations are task parallel programs, but they are potentially applicable to non-task self-recursive functions if dependence between multiple recursive calls is properly analyzed.

If the termination condition cannot be obtained, our compiler applies a dynamic cut-off to the task as a fallback.

3.2.1 *Static task elimination*

If the termination condition for a function is successfully obtained, our compiler generates a serialized version in which all task creations are replaced with serial function calls. The transformation always succeeds if the compiler calculates the termination condition successfully. We call this method *static task elimination*, which cuts off tasks and reduces a tasking overhead without a risk of seriously degrading parallelism. Since this naive method alone is insufficient for extremely fine-grained tasks, the compiler tries to apply two further optimizations to the serialized version, which we discuss below.

3.2.2 *Code-bloat-free inlining*

Though static task elimination is effective in reducing the cost of task creation, a serialized function generated by the elimination still confronts a overhead of function calls. Inlining is a well-known remedy; in our setting, inlining is so powerful that applying it H times can even remove all recursive calls derived from tasks in an Hth termination condition. Simply expanding recursive function calls, however, grows code size exponentially when there are multiple recursive call sites, so the simple inline expansion is unlikely to yield the desired result.

Our compiler overcomes this problem by transforming recursive functions so that there is only a single recursive call site prior to inlining. A basic observation is that a divide-and-conquer function often calls itself multiple times in series. In that case, it is usually possible to transform the series of recursive calls into a loop, containing a single recursive call site in its body. If self-recursive calls are made to appear only once, the inlining technique can be safely applied to it repeatedly, increasing the code size linearly, not exponentially.

This method first searches for recursive task creations in the function. If they appear only once, we need no further transformation (e.g., `nqueens` shown in Figure 5); otherwise, it checks if all of them appear in a single basic block. If this is the case, it tries to move other self-recursive calls to the last one in the basic block unless it violates dependence, and replace the last one into a loop calling all of them. This dependence restriction is alleviated by the task semantics that allow execution of spawned tasks to delay to the corresponding `sync`. If all recursive calls cannot be gathered at the same line, it gives up. The transformation is schematically shown in Figure 6a and 6b.

```
A0;
f(a0, b0, ...);
A1;
f(a1, b1, ...);
[...]
AK-1;
f(aK-1,bK-1,...);
AK
```

(a) A basic block containing multiple recursive calls. Each A_i is an arbitrary code sequence without branches.

```
A0;
A1;
[...]
AK-1;
for(int i = 0; i < K; i++){
  a=phi(a0,...,aK-1);
  b=phi(b0,...,bK-1);
  [...]
  f(a,b,...);
}
AK;
```

(b) Prior to inlining recursive calls, recursive call sites are merged into a single call site.

Figure 6: Transformation of code-bloat-free inlining

Once the transformed function has only one static recursive call site, the compiler inlined it H times. Importantly, the innermost loop containing the recursive call can be omitted since it is never executed in the Hth termination condition. This code-bloat-free inlining can therefore completely remove the self-recursive function calls derived from task creations. For example, consider the serialized `fib` function generated by static task elimination with the 1st termination condition shown as `fib_seq` in Figure 3a. It can be converted into a function presented in Figure 7a, and then into a fully inlined version shown in Figure 7b. Note that, in Figure 7b, the innermost loop is removed since it is unreachable in the given termination condition ($n < 3$).

3.2.3 *Loopification*

While code-bloat-free inlining eliminates all recursive calls, the resulting deeply nested loop is not always ideal outcome. Some functions can be converted into more natural (flat or shallowly nested) loops under the cut-off conditions. For example, it is obvious for humans that our `vecadd` example shown in Figure 3c is equivalent to a flat loop shown in Figure 3d. Loopification attempts to recognize just that. The target of loopification is a recursive function whose control flow graph has the following properties, schematically shown in Figure 8.

1. All recursive call sites are in a single basic block. Let us call it *a recursion block* of the function.[1]
2. The recursion block does not contain any side effects of the function besides calling recursions.
3. There are no control flows executing these blocks twice or more in the recursion block (e.g., loop).

We call a part of function including other basic blocks *a leaf function*, which is obtained by substituting a termination condition into the original function. Such a function ultimately performs all its side effects in the leaf function, thus is hopefully equivalent to a loop whose body is the leaf function. Our analysis tries to find such a loop in the following two steps.

[1]The assumption that there is only a single recursion block is mainly for simplifying the exposition and implementation.

```
void fib_seq(int n, int* ret){
  if(n < 2){
    *ret = n;
  }else{
    int a, b;
    for(int i = 0; i < 2; i++){
      int n2, *ret2;
      switch(i){
      case 0:
        n2 = n-1; ret2 = &a; break;
      case 1:
        n2 = n-2; ret2 = &b; break;
      }
      fib_seq(n2, ret2);
    }
    *ret = a + b;
  }
}
```

(a) `fib_seq` which has a single recursive call site.

```
void fib_seq(int n, int* ret){
  if(n < 2){
    *ret = n;
  }else{
    int a, b;
    for(int i = 0; i < 2; i++){
      int n2, *ret2;
      switch(i){
      case 0:
        n2 = n-1; ret2 = &a; break;
      case 1:
        n2 = n-2; ret2 = &b; break;
      }
      // Inline-expand fib_seq(n2, ret2);
      if(n2 < 2){
        *ret2 = n2;
      }else{
        // The innermost loop can be removed
        // in the 1st termination condition.
        //
        //int a2, b2;
        //for(int i2 = 0; i2 < 2; i2++){
        //  int n3, *ret3;
        //  switch(i2){ ... }
        //  fib_seq(n3, ret3);
        //}
        //*ret2 = a2 + b2;
      }
    }
    *ret = a + b;
  }
}
```

(b) Fully inlined `fib_seq` in Figure 7a

Figure 7: Code-bloat-free inlining for `fib` under $n < 3$

1. **Candidate generation:** It selects a few constant values that satisfy the appropriate termination condition and propagates these constants throughout the body of the function, until recursive calls are completely expanded. The resulting code contains a set of leaf functions with arguments. Based on this information, it tries to synthesize a candidate loop.
2. **Induction:** It inductively verifies that the candidate loop is equivalent to the recursive code in an arbitrary termination condition.

We explain the details by following our `vecadd` example showing in Figure 3c. Its leaf function consists of the "then" block containing the assignment `*a += *b;` We write it $L(a, b)$ below.

1. Candidate generation:.

Let us say we have thus far identified the 2nd termination condition, $1 \leq n \leq 4$. By assigning a value satisfying the condition, say 4, to n, and by propagating it, serialized

```
void f(a, b, c, ...){
  if(...){
    // Leaf function.
    L(a, b, c, ...);
  }else{
    // Recursion block.
    ...
    f(a0, b0, c0, ...);
    ...
    f(a1, b1, c1, ...);
    ...
  }
}
```

Figure 8: Loopification target

vecadd (vecadd_seq) becomes:

```
void vecadd_seq(float* a, float* b, int n/*=4*/){
  vecadd_seq(a,   b,   2);
  vecadd_seq(a+2, b+2, 2);
}
```

By traversing recursive functions with constant propagation, it ends up with:

```
  L(a, b);
  L(a+1, b+1);
  L(a+2, b+2);
  L(a+3, b+3);
```

It then observes the set of argument expressions:

$$\{(\mathtt{a},\mathtt{b}),(\mathtt{a}+1,\mathtt{b}+1),(\mathtt{a}+2,\mathtt{b}+2),\ldots,(\mathtt{a}+3,\mathtt{b}+3)\}$$

and tries to express the set by an affine transformation of a rectangle. If it cannot be expressed so, the analysis fails. In this example, it finds:

$$\{(\mathtt{a},\mathtt{b})+i(1,1)\mid i\in[0,4)\}.$$

By assigning a few other values to n and unifying the obtained results, it yields:

$$\{(\mathtt{a},\mathtt{b})+i(1,1)\mid i\in[0,n)\}.$$

The candidate loop thus becomes:

```
  for (i ∈ [0,n))
    L(a + i, b + i);
```

2. Induction:.

Induction phase verifies that the candidate loop is equivalent to the original function by the usual induction.

Base case checks if the generated loop matches the candidate loop in the 0th termination condition.

Induction substitutes the candidate loop for the recursive calls and checks if they can be fused into a single candidate loop.

In our vecadd example, the compiler derives that the base case, under the 0th termination condition $n = 1$, becomes

```
  L(a, b);
```

by propagating $n = 1$ throughout the function body. It is then easy to see this is equivalent to the candidate loop.

For induction, it proves that a recursive block can be translated into the loop if recursive calls can be converted into that loop. We first replace the recursive calls in the recursion block:

```
  vecadd(a,     b,     n/2);
  vecadd(a+n/2, b+n/2, n-n/2);
```

with the candidate loops, obtaining:

```
  for (i ∈ [0,n/2))
    L(a+i,     b+i);
  for (i ∈ [0,n-n/2))
    L(a+n/2+i, b+n/2+i);
```

We can shift the iteration space of the latter loop by n/2, to obtain:

```
  for (i ∈ [0,n/2))
    L(a+i, b+i);
  for (i ∈ [n/2,n))
    L(a+i, b+i);
```

and fuse them into a single loop:

```
  for (i ∈ [0,n))
    L(a+i, b+i);
```

which is equivalent to the candidate. As a general strategy, we try to shift the iteration space of each loop so that its body becomes equivalent to the candidate loop and see if the union of their iteration spaces becomes equivalent to that of the original loop. The order of loops is changed if necessary as long as task parallelism admits reordering.

It is notable that this induction only proves the equivalence in the case where the recursive function terminates, namely in an arbitrary termination condition. Our transformation guarantees that the loopified function is only called in a termination condition which is explicitly introduced by the static cut-off.

In practice, multiple loop candidates are generated for particular tasks because of their arbitrariness of loop nesting order (e.g., a loop with an index i, then a loop with an index j, or vice versa and loop iterations order (ascending or descending)). Either of them calculates the same computation, however the performance is sensitive to the loop representation, especially loop order. The compiler tries to choose one mostly accessing continuous memory in the innermost loop with a smaller number of terms of lower/upper boundaries as possible. Lastly, it attaches metadata conveying dependence information exposed by task parallelism for promoting further loop optimizations including loop vectorization.

3.3 Determining a cut-off height

Determining a height H for the static cut-off is essential to balancing between parallelism of programs and sequential performance; smaller H's allow less effective cut-off, while larger H's might decrease parallelism. Appropriate thresholds are values that mask a task creation overhead; i.e., values that give granularity larger than a constant factor of a task creation overhead. If, for example, we want to keep the tasking overhead lower than 2% of the execution time, we would choose granularity at least 49 times larger than the task creation overhead. Considering that the state-of-the-art runtime systems create a task in roughly a hundred cycles, our compiler estimates the number of cycles of a function under various heights and chooses the minimum height that makes the granularity larger than 5000 cycles. In order to avoid choosing a too small number due to inaccuracy of cycle estimations, we ensure that the chosen height is at least four. For tasks to which loopification is applied, the H effectively determines cache blocking size of the loop in the leaf, so we instead use the largest H whose resulting task is estimated to access at most 256KB of data, a typical L2 cache size, which we experimentally found balances the advantage of cache blocking and straightforward control flows in a loop.

```
void taskWithSizeCheck(arg1,arg2,...){
  if(terminationCondition_{H+H_min}(arg1,arg2,...)){
    // Input is too small.
    taskWithoutCutoff(arg1,arg2,...);
  }else{
    // Input is adequately large.
    taskWithCutoff(arg1,arg2,...);
  }
}
```

Figure 9: Task interface from external calls

To estimate the number of cycles of a function, our current implementation simply sums up the cost of all instructions in the function, obtained by an LLVM's cost function, and then multiplies it by the number of children (or 2 if failed to identify the number) to the power of the cut-off height. There have been several studies on finding an optimal task granularity by autotuning [2] or memory hierarchy-aware task mapping [9], which may improve our rough estimation. In reality, however, as shown in Section 4.4, our experiences so far indicate performance in most programs plateaus with a modest cut-off height (four).

3.4 Guaranteeing a minimum parallelism

Our heuristics to choose the cut-off height tries to ensure the tasking overhead is within a small constant of the execution time. While desirable in most cases, when the height of the whole task tree is smaller or only slightly greater than the cut-off height, it makes more sense to use a smaller cut-off height, even if it is known to have a non-negligible impact on the overhead. To address this issue, we could generate several versions each using a different cut-off height and select an appropriate one when the function is called from outside. We currently adopt a simplified method using only two versions, one that employs a cut-off at the determined height and the other that does not use cut-off at all. We introduce a constant H_{min}, the minimum height from the root up to which tasks are guaranteed to be created. Figure 9 shows the resulting function that serves as an entry from outside the task.

3.5 Dynamic cut-off

A dynamic cut-off is a method which calls functions instead of creating tasks when tasks are estimated to be abundant based on runtime information such as the depth of the task and the number of ready tasks. While we mainly focus on the static cut-off, we also employ a dynamic cut-off technique as an effective fallback method when our static analysis fails.

Our system adopts a state-of-the-art dynamic cut-off technique proposed by Thoman et al. [34], which generates multiple versions and selects one at runtime. They are the original task, ones that unroll recursion a few times, and a completely serialized version (similar to our static task elimination). Since we were unable to implement the "simplification" algorithm [34] in the unrolling step due to lack of details in the paper. We applied inline-expansion and the maximum `-O3` optimization level of LLVM as our best effort.

4. EVALUATION

4.1 Evaluation settings

We implemented the proposed static cut-off algorithms as an optimization pass in LLVM 3.6.0 [18]. All the programs were run on MassiveThreads [22], a lightweight task library employing a child-first random work-stealing scheduler [21]. The task library was modified to implement the dynamic cut-off.

Fifteen benchmarks were prepared to demonstrate the efficacy of our cut-off methods. The benchmarks are as follows:

1) **fib** calculates a 45th Fibonacci number with the naive double recursion.
2) **nqueens** computes all solutions of the N-Queens problem, with $N = 14$. Both of our **fib** and **nqueens** adopt the same task creation patterns in the benchmarks of BOTS [7].
3) **fft** performs a Fast Fourier Transform. The input array has 2^{25} single-precision complex numbers.
4) **sort** is a merge sort with a parallelized merge step [1]. The input is an array of $100M$ single-precision floating-point numbers.
5) **nbody** directly calculates forces between all N to N pairs. The input array consists of $30K$ particles each of which has its mass, position, velocity, and a temporal variable to accumulate the force. Positions, velocities, and forces are 3D vectors.
6) **strassen** multiplies two matrices using the Strassen algorithm. The inputs are two matrices of 1024×1024 single-precision floating-point numbers. Though it is ordinarily written to switch to a normal matrix multiplication by hand when the matrix size gets smaller, this benchmark uses Strassen algorithm all the way until the matrix size becomes 1.
7) **vecadd** is similar to the task shown in Figure 3c, but it adds two float arrays and stores the result into another array. Each array has 10^9 elements.
8) **heat2d** is a stencil computation solving a 2-dimensional thermal diffusion equation on a $30K \times 30K$ mesh.
9) **heat3d** is a 3-dimensional version of **heat2d**, on a $1K \times 1K \times 1K$ mesh.
10) **gaussian** is an image processing kernel that applies a 5×5 Gaussian filter to an array of $30K \times 30K$ single-precision floating-point numbers.
11) **matmul** multiplies two matrices and stores the result into another matrix. All three matrices have 2000×2000 single-precision floating-point numbers.
12) **trimul** multiplies two upper triangular matrices with the size of 2000×2000. It is similar to **matmul**, except that it omits some multiplications with matrices either of which is zero.
13) **treeadd** traverses a binary tree structure and updates values (floating-point numbers) in the leaves. The input is a balanced tree with the height of 30, containing $2^{30} - 1$ elements.
14) **treesum** traverses a binary tree structure and sums up the values (floating-point numbers) in the leaves. The input is a balanced tree with the height of 30 (the same as the input to **treeadd**).
15) **uts** runs Unbalanced Tree Search [24] with the "T1XL" input in the official samples, which generates a geometric tree with 1,635,119,272 elements in total.

Table 1 presents the larger input we used to examine the performance achieved by our proposed methods and those of loop parallel programs shown in Figure 12, which made execution time longer than 0.2 seconds.

Table 1: Data size for an evaluation shown in Figure 12

nbody	$40K \times 40K$	vecadd	$2G$
heat2d	$40K \times 40K$	heat3d	$(1.2K)^3$
gaussian	$40K \times 40K$	matmul	$5K \times 5K$
trimul	$8K \times 8K$		

Table 2: Applicability of cut-off methods ((X/Y) means a method was applied to X out of Y tasks in the benchmark.)

	dynamic	static	cbf	loop
fib	✓	✓	✓	
nqueens	✓	✓	✓	
fft	✓	✓	✓	
sort	✓	(1/2)	(1/2)	
nbody	✓	✓	✓	
strassen	✓	✓	(4/5)	(4/5)
vecadd	✓	✓	✓	✓
heat2d	✓	✓	✓	✓
heat3d	✓	✓	✓	✓
gaussian	✓	✓	✓	✓
matmul	✓	✓	✓	✓
trimul	✓	✓	(1/4)	(1/4)
treeadd	✓			
treesum	✓			
uts	✓			

We wrote the benchmarks in C language, so we first translated them into the LLVM IR with Clang, a frontend C/C++ compiler for LLVM, and then applied our methods to the intermediate representation. Finally, we compiled them into binary programs with the LLVM compiler with optimization flags `-O3 -ffp-contract=fast` and a machine-specifying option. None of them use any manually written cut-off.

Table 2 shows which optimizations were applied to these benchmarks.

We evaluated seven versions of each benchmark:

- **base**: An original version without any optimization.
- **dynamic**: A version with the adaptive multiversioning method presented by Thoman et al. [34]. It contains no optimizations we propose.
- **static**: A version with static task elimination.
- **cbf**: A version with code-bloat-free inlining.
- **loop**: A version with loopification.
- **proposed**: A version automatically selected by the algorithm flow shown in Figure 4; it applies **loop**, **cbf**, and then **static** in this order and selects the first one that succeeds, falling back to **dynamic** when all fail.
- **seq**: A fully serialized version, created by replacing all task creations with function calls.

Some benchmarks have multiple tasks to which applicable optimizations differ. When the transformation specified by the version is inapplicable to the task, the compiler tries to apply **cbf** and then **static**. If both fail, it employs **dynamic**. For example, **sort** has two tasks: a sorting task and a merging task. Whereas code-bloat-free inlining applies to the former for the **cbf** version, neither **cbf** nor **static** to the latter, which is thus optimized by **dynamic**.

The programs were run on a machine running Linux 3.16, which has dual sockets of Intel Xeon E5-2699 v3 (Haswell) processors (36 cores in total). We ran all the benchmarks with `numactl --interleave=all` to balance physical memory across sockets. All results reported are the average of five measurements. Error bars in the charts indicate the 95% confidence intervals.

4.2 Single-threaded performance

We first examine improvement of single-threaded performance, shown in Figure 10. The baseline is a task parallel program with no cut-off (**base**). All programs were parallelized but executed on a single core except for **seq**, which simply serializes all task creations. The degree of improvement depends on applications characteristics (e.g., the size of each leaf calculation and the number of division of the divide-and-conquer strategies), but our optimizations consistently achieved a significant speedup compared to the baseline (**base**). Static task elimination (**static**) achieved from 1.1x to 24.8x speedup (geometric mean of 5.3x), and code-bloat-free inlining (**cbf**) elevated it to 1.1x - 33.5x (geometric mean of 6.6x) where it is applicable. Performance of static task elimination (**static**) was comparable to that of fully serialized ones (**seq**) except **sort** and **strassen**. It presents that it successfully reduced a tasking overhead in most cases.

Loopification (**loop**) further boosted performance, sometimes spectacularly, up to 333x, achieved by removing control flows and by exposing vectorization opportunities to the backend compilers. Though the dynamic cut-off (**dynamic**) has a wider applicability, the achieved speedup was a moderate 0.9x to 5.9x (geometric mean of 2.6x); they were smaller than those of static task elimination (**static**) in all cases except **heat2d**, and those of code-bloat-free inlining (**cbf**) and loopification (**loop**) in all cases where applicable.

Importantly, our proposed optimization (**proposed**) offered the best performance in all cases, showing the effectiveness of the algorithm selection criteria shown in Figure 4.

4.3 Multi-threaded performance

Figure 11 shows the improvement of multi-threaded executions. The same programs we used in the previous experiment were this time executed by 36 threads. The baseline is the parallel performance of the task parallel programs with no cut-off (**base**).

The result was overall similar to the single-threaded one; by using the geometric mean metric, a speedup of 5.0x was achieved by static task elimination (**static**), 6.0x by code-bloat-free inlining (**cbf**), and 21x (up to 220x) by loopification (**loop**), while dynamic cut-off (**dynamic**) yielded a modest 1.8x speedup.

In comparison to the single-threaded performance shown in Figure 10, scalability (speedup from single-threaded execution to multi-threaded execution) tended to be lower in optimized versions than in the base versions, especially in **vecadd** and **heat2d**. It was presumably because they became memory bandwidth-limited after removing task creation overheads.

Finally, for programs naturally expressible in loops, we loop-parallelized them by hand and compared them with task parallel programs optimized by our compiler. We loop-parallelized **nbody**, **vecadd**, **heat2d**, **heat3d**, **gaussian**, **matmul**, and **trimul**. They performed the same calculations with the corresponding task parallel versions, with the only differences in load partitioning and execution order.

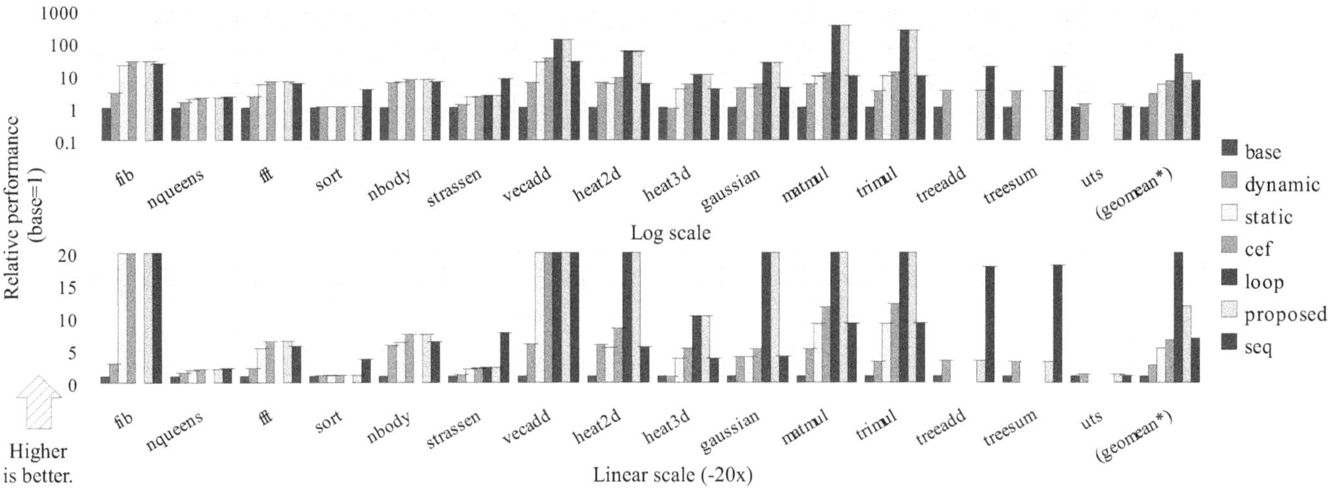

Figure 10: It shows relative single-threaded performance of dynamic cut-off [34] (**dynamic**), static task elimination (**static**), code-bloat-free inlining (**cbf**), loopification (**loop**), our proposal (**proposed**), and a sequential version (**seq**), using the original task parallel program with no cut-off (**base**) as the baseline. The missing results are excluded when we calculate the geometric mean of the overall speedups (**geomean***). Both charts show the same results, different in the scale of y-axis.

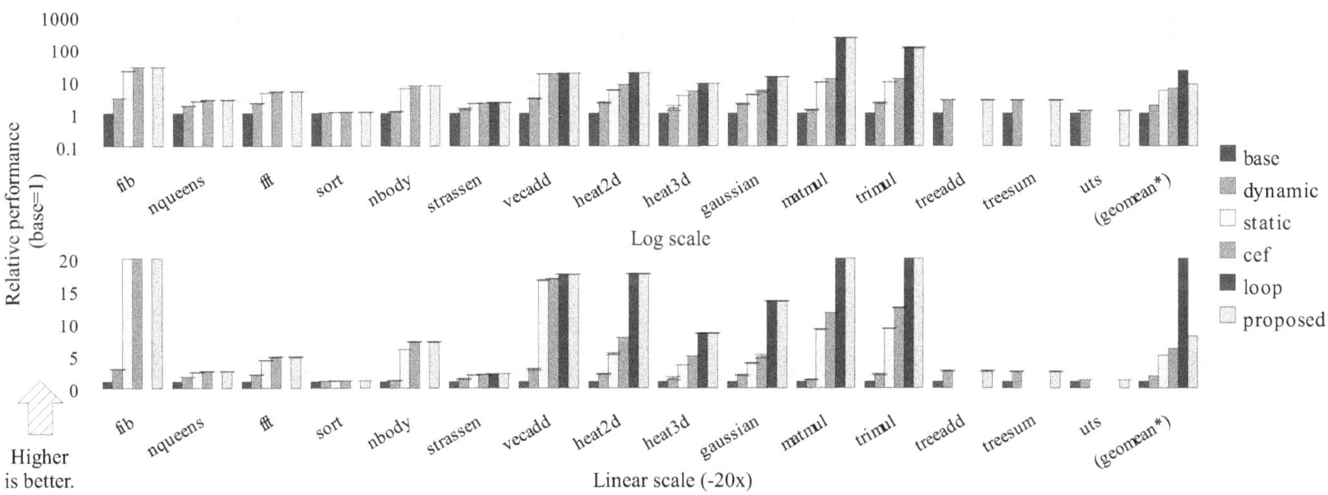

Figure 11: Multi-threaded performance. See Figure 10 for the meaning of labels. The baseline is the original (**base**).

The loop programs were parallelized in two ways: OpenMP with GCC and Polly [11] with LLVM. One was an OpenMP version parallelized by `omp parallel for` pragma. It was compiled by GCC 4.8.4 with `-O3 -ffp-contract=fast` and a machine-specifying option. The other one was automatically parallelized by Polly [11], a locality-optimizer for LLVM based on the polyhedral models with an automatic parallelization feature. The Polly version was compiled by the Clang 3.8.0 with `-O3 -ffp-contract=fast` and the machine-specifying option, and its Polly with `-polly -polly-parallel` and `-polly-vectorizer = stripmine` if it made the program faster. We gave `restrict` keywords appropriately to help automatic parallelization and vectorization in both cases.

Figure 12 shows the relative performance of loop parallel programs, using 36 cores. The baseline is the task parallel version optimized by **proposed** (**task**). **omp** and **polly** are the performance of loop parallel programs optimized by OpenMP with GCC or Polly with Clang. They used default scheduling algorithm and applied no manual locality optimizations such as blocking. We also made **omp_optimized**, a tuned OpenMP program by changing block sizes, scheduling strategies, scheduling parameters (chunk size, etc.), and collapse clauses for nested loops. Since we found that **nbody** and **vecadd** were not parallelized by **polly**, these results missing in the graph are excluded to calculate the geometric mean of speedup (**geomean***). Figure 12 shows the overall performance of **task** was faster than **omp** or **polly**; the geometric mean of **omp**'s relative performance was 0.59x, and that of **polly** was 0.60x. It indicates **task** utilized the cache blocking, especially for **matmul** and **trimul**. However, **omp_optimized** boosted performance significantly to show that of 1.4x; careful manual optimizations (especially blocking) enhanced performance overall. One disadvantage of the divide-and-conquer strategy is that, even if we can choose the best cut-off height, our cache blocking of **task** is not so flexible as to fit the cache size exactly since the problem size is basically evenly divided by the number of recursive calls in a divide-and-conquer strategy.

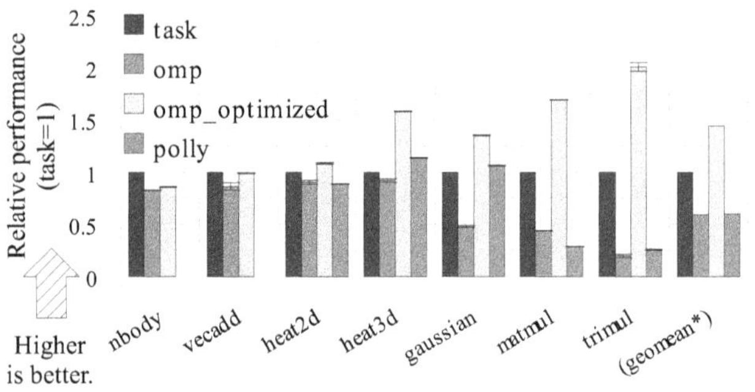

Figure 12: Performance comparison task parallel programs optimized by our methods to loop parallel programs. The baseline is task parallel programs (**task**). **vecadd** and **nbody** are excluded to calculate the (**geomean***) of **polly**

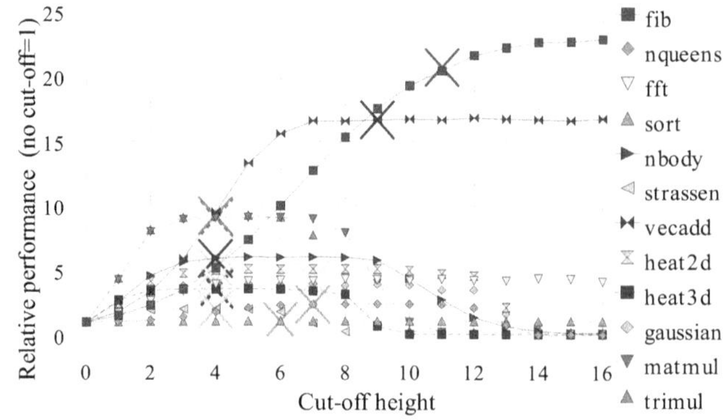

Figure 13: Performance of various cut-off heights. The baseline is task parallel programs with no cut-off (**base**). Crosses denote the heights our compiler automatically selected.

4.4 Cut-off threshold

Figure 13 shows the performance of static task elimination (**static**) using 36 threads, by changing the fixed height parameter H in order to evaluate our current automatic height selection. The baseline is the parallel performance of tasks without cut-off (**base**). Crosses in the figure indicate the heights our compiler automatically selected. Note that some benchmarks (e.g., **fft**) have multiple tasks whose chosen heights are different, thus have multiple crosses. While a few benchmarks had the room for improving performance by larger h (especially for **fib**), the figure overall shows that our algorithm chose good heights that achieved nearly the best performance, without unnecessarily aggressive cut-off heights.

5. RELATED WORK

Automatic cut-off.

Since task granularity is one of the most important factors for the performance of task parallel programs [20], there have been several studies on automating manual cut-off [3, 6, 34]. Duran et al. [6] proposed a heuristic cut-off utilizing the runtime information such as depth of the task and the number of ready tasks. Bi et al. [3] extends their adaptive cut-off to efficiently deal with irregular task parallel programs. Thoman et al. [34] proposed generating multiple versions including inlined versions and fully serialized version, and switching between them based on the similar criteria. These proposals, or runtime-based approaches in general, have advantages of being widely applicable and not requiring substantial compiler development efforts. However, besides the difficulty of applying aggressive optimizations after a cut-off, they have a risk of adversely decreasing parallelism. To see the problem, consider a task creation site:

```
spawn f(x);
```

and say the system decides to serialize it (i.e., not to create a task for it). The decision is made because all or most processors are busy when the execution reaches this statement and they will remain so at least for a while. The true condition that deems this task creation unnecessary is that, however, processors are busy *during the entire span of* $f(x)$, a condition that is difficult to predict at the time of task creation. Were it not the case, an idle processor would lose the opportunity to steal the continuation of $f(x)$, decreasing parallelism.[2] In general, serialization of a task is equivalent to inserting an artificial dependence from the end of the created task to the continuation of the task creation. It may thus lengthen the critical path (the longest dependent chain) of the computation, which determines an achievable speedup [8] and there seems no obvious bounds on the factor it is stretched.

Our static cut-off approach differs from these prior efforts in that we *statically identify small tasks* and specifically target them for cut-off and further aggressive *compile-time* optimizations, such as inlining and loopification.

Optimization of recursive functions.

A number of studies have sought effective techniques to remove recursions, especially in a field of functional programming [5]. Tail call elimination [30] is a well-known technique to transform recursive procedures into jumps (a control flow without stacks). Particularly, it cannot handle most divide-and-conquer algorithms, which perform two or more recursive calls one of which is necessarily not tail-recursive. Tang [32] proposed *complete inlining*, which can be thought of a generalization of tail call elimination. It recognizes, more broadly, recursive calls that can be transformed into a jump. The recursive call does not have to be tail-recursive, yet the technique still cannot handle procedures that perform recursive calls twice or more. In contrast, our approach fully expands such recursions under the condition in which the recursion stops in a certain number of steps.

There have been numerous techniques primarily targeting divide-and-conquer algorithms [13, 29, 31]. Rugina et al. [29] proposed function unrolling and rerolling, which together transform a recursive procedure to another recursive procedure. The success of the transformation relies on "conditional fusions," which essentially require the depths of the two recursions be identical. This condition seems very restrictive; most programs we applied our techniques to do not satisfy it. Herrman and Lengauer [13] have shown transformation of divide-and-conquer Haskell programs to parallel loop nest in C. It assumes Haskell programs written in a specific skeleton (template) and vectorizes them. The vectorizable skeleton essentially assumes that the recursion stops at the same depth everywhere, which seems restrictive for

[2]Here we assume a child-first execution policy [21], but a similar argument holds for help-first policies as well.

practical purposes. An idea of *recursion flattening* proposed by Stitt and Villarrealm [31] is similar to ours, which completely eliminates recursive calls by unrolling. Their algorithm, however, only targets recursive functions whose maximum recursion depth can be determined at compiling time (e.g., constant arguments).

Transformation algorithms translating loops into recursions have been studied previously [15, 35] and some studies [33, 35] aimed at achieving the effect of cache blocking at many different levels [10]. The opposite conversion has also been developed [12, 14, 19], while most of them are targeting functional programming languages and their main purpose is recursion removal. Technical differences are as follows. Harrison's approach [12] cannot convert divide-and-conquer programs. The technique proposed by Himpe [14] preserves an execution order, so the generated loop is less optimal. Liu's method [19] requires a stack for multiple recursive calls in general, or divide-and-conquer algorithms. The target of our loopification, on the other hand, is divide-and-conquer task functions and its resulting code can utilize the cache blocking at all levels.

Vectorization of recursive programs.

Most previous researches on auto-vectorization targeted loops [23] or basic blocks [17]. There have been a few targeting recursive programs. Auto-vectorization on recursive functions written in Haskell has been proposed by Petersen et al. [26], which focuses on a simple recursive function, but a divide-and-conquer function with multiple recursive call sites. Jo et al. [16] have presented an effective auto-vectorization method for programs traversing the same tree many times and it is those multiple traversals to which a vectorization is applied. In a recent work, Ren et al. [28] proposed a general vectorization technique for divide-and-conquer programs, which is very different from ours. In their framework, a compiler assigns multiple tasks created by a single task to different SIMD lanes. This strategy is applied to the root of the task tree, effectively executing subtrees *near the root of the task tree* in different SIMD lanes. In contrast, our compiler tries to convert tasks *near the leaves of the task tree* into loops, which may then be vectorized. Their vectorization technique can be applied to a wider range of programs than our loopification technique. On the other hand, we believe the program generated by our loopification technique still has a number of performance advantages when solely looked at vectorization techniques. It has a simpler control flow and preserves the temporal locality of the original program. Moreover, our loopification straightforwardly co-exists with thread level parallelism.

6. CONCLUSION

This paper proposed an effective static cut-off method for divide-and-conquer task parallel programs and two further optimizations; code-bloat-free inlining and loopification. Our proposed algorithm statically determines a condition in which the recursion reaches near leaves and cut off only those tasks. It then applies either code-bloat-free inlining or loopification of the resulting coarsened tasks. Our static cut-off can be easily combined with the dynamic cut-off, which can widen the applicable range. Compared to the original task parallel programs with no cut-offs, our evaluation shows good performance improvement.

Acknowledgment

We thank the anonymous reviewers for their helpful and constructive comments. This work was in part supported by Grant-in-Aid for Scientific Research (A) 16H01715.

7. REFERENCES

[1] S. G. Akl and N. Santoro. Optimal parallel merging and sorting without memory conflicts. *IEEE Trans. Comput.*, 36(11):1367–1369, Nov. 1987.

[2] J. Ansel, C. Chan, Y. L. Wong, M. Olszewski, Q. Zhao, A. Edelman, and S. Amarasinghe. PetaBricks: A language and compiler for algorithmic choice. In *Proceedings of the 30th ACM SIGPLAN Conference on Programming Language Design and Implementation*, PLDI '09, pages 38–49, Jun. 2009.

[3] J. Bi, X. Liao, Y. Zhang, C. Ye, H. Jin, and L. T. Yang. An adaptive task granularity based scheduling for task-centric parallelism. In *Proceedings of the 2014 IEEE International Conference on High Performance Computing and Communications*, HPCC '14, pages 165–172, Aug. 2014.

[4] R. D. Blumofe, C. F. Joerg, B. C. Kuszmaul, C. E. Leiserson, K. H. Randall, and Y. Zhou. Cilk: An efficient multithreaded runtime system. In *Proceedings of the Fifth ACM SIGPLAN Symposium on Principles and Practice of Parallel Programming*, PPoPP '95, pages 207–216, Jul. 1995.

[5] R. M. Burstall and J. Darlington. A transformation system for developing recursive programs. *J. ACM*, 24(1):44–67, Jan. 1977.

[6] A. Duran, J. Corbalán, and E. Ayguadé. An adaptive cut-off for task parallelism. In *Proceedings of the 2008 ACM/IEEE Conference on Supercomputing*, SC '08, pages 36:1–36:11, Austin, Texas, USA, Nov. 2008.

[7] A. Duran, X. Teruel, R. Ferrer, X. Martorell, and E. Ayguade. Barcelona OpenMP Tasks Suite: A set of benchmarks targeting the exploitation of task parallelism in OpenMP. In *Proceedings of the 2009 International Conference on Parallel Processing*, pages 124–131, Sept. 2009.

[8] D. L. Eager, J. Zahorjan, and E. D. Lozowska. Speedup versus efficiency in parallel systems. *IEEE Trans. Comput.*, 38(3):408–423, Mar. 1989.

[9] K. Fatahalian, D. R. Horn, T. J. Knight, L. Leem, M. Houston, J. Y. Park, M. Erez, M. Ren, A. Aiken, W. J. Dally, and P. Hanrahan. Sequoia: Programming the memory hierarchy. In *Proceedings of the 2006 ACM/IEEE Conference on Supercomputing*, SC '06, Nov. 2006.

[10] M. Frigo, C. E. Leiserson, H. Prokop, and S. Ramachandran. Cache-oblivious algorithms. In *Proceedings of the 40th Annual Symposium on Foundations of Computer Science*, FOCS '99, pages 285–, Oct. 1999.

[11] T. Grosser, H. Zheng, R. Aloor, A. Simbürger, A. Größlinger, and L.-N. Pouchet. Polly - Polyhedral optimization in LLVM. In *Proceedings of the First International Workshop on Polyhedral Compilation Techniques*, IMPACT '11, Apr. 2011.

[12] P. G. Harrison and H. Khoshnevisan. A new approach to recursion removal. *Theoretical Computer Science*, 93(1):91 – 113, 1992.

[13] C. A. Herrmann and C. Lengauer. *Transformation of Divide & Conquer to Nested Parallel Loops*, pages 95–109. PLILP '97. Springer-Verlag, 1997.

[14] S. Himpe, F. Catthoor, and G. Deconinck. Control flow analysis for recursion removal. In *Proceedings of the 7th International Workshop on Software and Compilers for Embedded Systems*, SCOPES '03, pages 101–116. Springer, Sept 2003.

[15] D. Insa and J. Silva. Automatic transformation of iterative loops into recursive methods. *Information and Software Technology*, 58:95 – 109, 2015.

[16] Y. Jo, M. Goldfarb, and M. Kulkarni. Automatic vectorization of tree traversals. In *Proceedings of the 22nd International Conference on Parallel Architectures and Compilation Techniques*, PACT '13, pages 363–374, Sept. 2013.

[17] S. Larsen and S. Amarasinghe. Exploiting superword level parallelism with multimedia instruction sets. In *Proceedings of the ACM SIGPLAN 2000 Conference on Programming Language Design and Implementation*, PLDI '00, pages 145–156, Jun. 2000.

[18] C. Lattner and V. Adve. LLVM: A compilation framework for lifelong program analysis & transformation. In *Proceedings of the International Symposium on Code Generation and Optimization: Feedback-directed and Runtime Optimization*, CGO '04, pages 75–, Mar. 2004.

[19] Y. A. Liu and S. D. Stoller. From recursion to iteration: What are the optimizations? In *Proceedings of the 2000 ACM SIGPLAN Workshop on Partial Evaluation and Semantics-based Program Manipulation*, PEPM '00, pages 73–82, Jan. 2000.

[20] H.-W. Loidl and K. Hammond. On the granularity of divide-and-conquer parallelism. In *Proceedings of the 1995 Glasgow Workshop on Functional Programming*, GWFP '95. Springer-Verlag, Jul. 1995.

[21] E. Mohr, D. A. Kranz, and R. H. Halstead, Jr. Lazy task creation: A technique for increasing the granularity of parallel programs. In *Proceedings of the 1990 ACM Conference on LISP and Functional Programming*, LFP '90, pages 185–197, Jun. 1990.

[22] J. Nakashima and K. Taura. MassiveThreads: A thread library for high productivity languages. In *Concurrent Objects and Beyond*, volume 8665 of *Lecture Notes in Computer Science*, pages 222–238. 2014.

[23] D. Nuzman and A. Zaks. Autovectorization in GCC - two years later. In *Proceedings of the 2006 GCC Developers' Summit*, pages 145–158, Jun. 2006.

[24] S. Olivier, J. Huan, J. Liu, J. Prins, J. Dinan, P. Sadayappan, and C.-W. Tseng. UTS: An unbalanced tree search benchmark. In *Proceedings of the 19th International Conference on Languages and Compilers for Parallel Computing*, LCPC '06, pages 235–250, 2007.

[25] OpenMP Architecture Review Board. OpenMP Application Program Interface Version 3.0, May 2008.

[26] L. Petersen, D. Orchard, and N. Glew. Automatic SIMD vectorization for Haskell. In *Proceedings of the 18th ACM SIGPLAN International Conference on Functional Programming*, ICFP '13, pages 25–36, Sept. 2013.

[27] J. Reinders. *Intel Threading Building Blocks: Outfitting C++ for Multi-Core Processor Parallelism.* O'Reilly Media, 2007.

[28] B. Ren, Y. Jo, S. Krishnamoorthy, K. Agrawal, and M. Kulkarni. Efficient execution of recursive programs on commodity vector hardware. In *Proceedings of the 36th ACM SIGPLAN Conference on Programming Language Design and Implementation*, PLDI '15, pages 509–520, Jun. 2015.

[29] R. Rugina and M. C. Rinard. Recursion unrolling for divide and conquer programs. In *Proceedings of the 13th International Workshop on Languages and Compilers for Parallel Computing-Revised Papers*, LCPC '00, pages 34–48, Aug. 2001.

[30] G. L. Steele, Jr. Debunking the "expensive procedure call"; myth or, procedure call implementations considered harmful or, lambda: The ultimate goto. In *Proceedings of the 1977 Annual Conference*, ACM '77, pages 153–162, Jan. 1977.

[31] G. Stitt and J. Villarreal. Recursion flattening. In *Proceedings of the 18th ACM Great Lakes Symposium on VLSI*, GLSVLSI '08, pages 131–134, May 2008.

[32] P. Tang. Complete inlining of recursive calls: Beyond tail-recursion elimination. In *Proceedings of the 44th Annual Southeast Regional Conference*, ACMSE '44, pages 579–584, Mar. 2006.

[33] Y. Tang, R. A. Chowdhury, B. C. Kuszmaul, C.-K. Luk, and C. E. Leiserson. The Pochoir stencil compiler. In *Proceedings of the 23rd Annual ACM Symposium on Parallelism in Algorithms and Architectures*, SPAA '11, pages 117–128, Jul. 2011.

[34] P. Thoman, H. Jordan, and T. Fahringer. Adaptive granularity control in task parallel programs using multiversioning. In *Proceedings of the 19th International Conference on Parallel Processing*, Euro-Par'13, pages 164–177, Aug. 2013.

[35] Q. Yi, V. Adve, and K. Kennedy. Transforming loops to recursion for multi-level memory hierarchies. In *Proceedings of the ACM SIGPLAN 2000 Conference on Programming Language Design and Implementation*, PLDI '00, pages 169–181, Jun. 2000.

Greater Performance and Better Efficiency: Predicated Execution has shown us the way

Yale N. Patt
The University of Texas at Austin
patt@ece.utexas.edu

Abstract
We have been riding a strong wave of greater and greater performance for decades, to some extent due to the combination of Moore's Law and Dennard scaling. But we are told all this is coming to an end, in part because we cannot continue to double the transistor count on the chip and we cannot run these things at higher and higher frequencies. Much of the silliness promised by multicore is just that, and not the answer. So, what are we to do? It turns out predication gave us the answer more than 30 years ago. Most of us were not paying attention. Today we have no choice. Predication happened because the compiler, the ISA, and the microarchitecture all cooperated so it could happen. That meant breaking the artificial walls in the transformation hierarchy. If we accept this as something we have to do, there are plenty of opportunities (a) for increased performance (attacking latency instead of just multicore bandwidth) and (b) for better energy efficiency. In this talk I hope to point out some of them, and then ask the obvious question: What do we need to do to make this happen?

Author Keywords: higher performance computation; latency; Moore's Law; transformation hierarchy; computer education.

Short Bio
Yale Patt is a teacher at The University of Texas at Austin who enjoys equally teaching the 400 student required freshman course for ECE majors and his advanced graduate course in microarchitecture. He is also the Ernest Cockrell, Jr. Centennial Chair in Engineering. He continues to thrive on regular classroom teaching, supervising the research of six PhD students, and consulting on microarchitecture problems in industry. He earned appropriate degrees from reputable universities and has received more than his share of awards for his research and teaching.

Details can be found on his home page: www.ece.utexas.edu/~patt. He is the co-author with his former PhD student Professor Sanjay Jeram Patel of the University of Illinois, Urbana-Champaign of "Introduction to Computing: from bits and gates to C and beyond," which reflects his motivated bottom-up approach to learning, the correct way to introduce students to computing.

PACT'16, September 11–15, 2016, Haifa, Israel.
ACM ISBN 978-1-4503-4121-9/16/09.
DOI: http://dx.doi.org/10.1145/2967938.2970377

WearCore: A Core for Wearable Workloads

Sanyam Mehta*
Department of Computer Science
University of Illinois at Urbana-Champaign
Urbana, IL USA
sanyam.mehta@gmail.com

Josep Torrellas
Department of Computer Science
University of Illinois at Urbana-Champaign
Urbana, IL USA
torrella@illinois.edu

ABSTRACT

Lately, the industry has recognized immense potential in wearables (particularly, smartwatches) being an attractive alternative/supplement to the smartphone. To this end, there has been recent activity in making the smartwatch 'self-sufficient' i.e. using it to make/receive calls, etc. independently of the phone. This marked shift in the way wearables will be used in future calls for changes in the core microarchitecture of smartwatch processors.

In this work, we first identify ten key target applications for the smartwatch users that the processor must be able to quickly and efficiently execute. We show that seven of these workloads are inherently parallel, and are compute- and data-intensive. We therefore propose to use a multi-core processor with simple out-of-order cores (for compute performance) and augment them with a light-weight software-assisted hardware prefetcher (for memory performance). This simple core with the light-weight prefetcher, called WearCore, is 2.9x more energy-efficient and 2.8x more area-efficient over an in-order core. The improvements are similar with respect to an out-of-order core.

1. INTRODUCTION

Smartwatches, with the potential to perform many of the important functions of smartphones while just being a band on the wrist, are being deemed as the future of consumer electronics. A recent prediction from ABI Research claims that there will be 485 million annual wearable shipments by 2018 [14]; the prediction is backed up by pronounced activity in the industry with Samsung releasing its sixth smartwatch within a span of one year.

Although an attractive supplement/substitute to smartphones on paper, smartwatches have not yet proved to the purpose. The primary reason for this disparity is that smartwatches currently in the market are not 'self-sufficient', i.e. they require to be tethered to a phone (from perhaps the same manufacturer) in close vicinity (via Bluetooth) in order to make/receive calls and be connected to the internet. This greatly limits the utility of a smartwatch since one has to have the phone around always anyway. However, Google and Samsung have overcome this drawback in existing smartwatches, through their latest offerings. Google's latest update to their version of Android Operating System, Android Wear, enables Wi-fi connectivity in the watch that allows it to connect to a distant phone [25]. Samsung, on the other hand, has gone a step further in its latest Gear S smartwatch (that runs Samsung's own Tizen OS) which can house its own SIM card and has built-in 3G connectivity [12], i.e. it can independently make/receive calls, and send/receive messages or mails. Thus, the current trend in industry is towards 'self-sufficient' smartwatches that obviates the need of carrying or being in the vicinity of a smartphone.

While there have been advances in the OS (and 'apps') for the smartwatch, there has been little contribution from computer architects towards the right hardware for the purpose. We identify the following challenges in coming up with that right hardware.

- Firstly, it is important to identify the applications that are critical for smartwatch users. With a significantly different power (and energy) budget, display size and usage scenario from existing smartphones, it is intuitive to expect that a different set of applications will become important to smartwatch users than smartphone users. For example, automatic speech-to-text (and also speech-to-command, as in an Intelligent Personal Assistant like Siri or Google Now) conversion is extremely important in a smartwatch given the extreme difficulty in typing on the watch. Also, this speech-to-text conversion must happen on the device to keep the device functional when not connected to internet. This 'self-sufficiency' is much more important for a smartwatch than a smartphone since the former cannot continue to use the power-expensive 3G service for longer duration.

- With the target applications known, the host processor must be able to efficiently execute them. While energy efficiency has remained critical even in smartphones, it is much more so for the watch for it is constrained to use a much smaller battery and consequently, has a much lower battery life (Samsung's latest watch, Gear S, and phone, Galaxy S6, have battery capacities of 300mAh[1] [10] and 2550mAh [9], respectively). It is therefore imperative to make the right decisions on the type (In-Order(InO), Out-of-Order(OoO), etc.) and number of cores, and also on the specific additional capabilities in the cores so as to meet the Quality of Service (QoS) requirements of critical applications while being as energy-efficient as possible. Currently, the latest smartwatches from the biggest companies display a lot of variety in the type of cores - Samsung, LG and Apple employ a dual-core OoO,

*This author is now with Cray Inc.

[1]The battery life of smartwatches is about an eighth of smartphones. Now, given that a smartwatch will be used less but should last more, we speculate that a power envelope that is a fourth or a sixth of a smartphone seems reasonable for a smartwatch.

PACT '16, September 11-15, 2016, Haifa, Israel
© 2016 ACM. ISBN 978-1-4503-4121-9/16/09...$15.00
DOI: http://dx.doi.org/10.1145/2967938.2967956

a quad-core InO and a single-core OoO processor, respectively. Clearly, the best core for smartwatches is undecided.

In this paper, we make the following contributions,

- We identify ten important applications for smartwatches that the host hardware must accommodate to satisfy the energy-efficiency demands of the consumers. We refer to this set of applications as WearBench throughout the paper. We identify an application as important when it satisfies one or more of the following three criteria, (1) demands a strict QoS, (2) is compute-intensive (and time consuming), and (3) is frequently used. We classify these applications in five categories, (a) speech recognition (speech-to-text and speech-to-command), (b) image processing (image denoising, compression), (c) computer vision (face recognition, image classification), (d) audio playback (mp3), and (e) video rendering (h264 decode). We do not include sensor processing applications in this set since the signals from sensors are efficiently processed in the DSP on the SoC (see Section 3 for more discussion).

- For applications in WearBench, we make the following important observations. (1) 7 out of 10 applications (including applications with a QoS requirement) are parallel and benefit immensely from multiple cores on the chip. (2) These applications are compute and data intensive and not so control intensive. Moreover, 25% of all operations in these applications are SIMD operations on average (and the applications in categories (a), (b) and (c) have fully vectorizable critical loops). As a result, computation in loops finishes very quickly, putting more pressure on the memory. Thus, cache misses become significant. This trend will only become more significant as the industry considers larger vector lengths to speed up applications as in WearBench.

- We make the following decisions based on above observations. (1) We use a quad core CPU as our baseline processor to allow parallel execution. (2) Each of the cores supports only partial out-of-order execution (using a simple scoreboard) that only adds little overhead over in-order cores. (3) In order to prevent stalls on long-latency cache misses, we augment our simple OoO core with a software-assisted hardware prefetcher (SAHP). We call this core as WearCore. Our proposed SAHP is easy to use with the target applications, involves negligible instruction overhead and minimal power/area overhead in the hardware.

- We compare the performance, power and area of WearCore with an OoO and an InO core for applications in WearBench. WearBench proves to be about 2.8x better in terms of area-normalized performance and about 2.9x better in terms of energy-efficiency with respect to both InO and OoO cores.

It is important to note that we do not claim novelty in either WearBench (since we obtain the component applications from other suites) or the choice of core (since scoreboarding for partial out-of-order execution is already known) or the number of cores. Our key contribution is in identifying the advantages and bottlenecks of these choices for the new problem domain of wearables (which we believe has not been explored before), and in our proposal of SAHP to address the last standing limitation in the design of an energy-efficient core for wearables.

The rest of the paper is organized as follows. Section 2 describes each of the ten applications used in WearBench with particular emphasis on the critical speech recognition applications. In Section 3, we discuss why other possible design options were incompatible with WearBench and present our key insights that motivate our specific choices in the design of WearCore. This section also provides an overview of SAHP. The following section details the implementation of SAHP in WearCore. Section 5 describes the microarchitectural details of the different cores used for the purpose of comparison, and also how we use the applications with the microarchitectural simulator used. We present and discuss the results in Section 6; this includes performance comparison, and area and power estimates of the different configurations of cores simulated. We also show the parallel performance achieved by two representative applications in WearBench, and how exploiting parallelism helps them to meet their QoS. Section 7 briefly describes other work related to ours, and we present the conclusion from this work in Section 8.

2. TARGET APPLICATIONS

As mentioned in Section 1, WearBench consists of applications in seven different categories. In this section, we briefly describe those applications and their relevance to a smartwatch.

2.1 Automatic Speech Recognition (ASR)

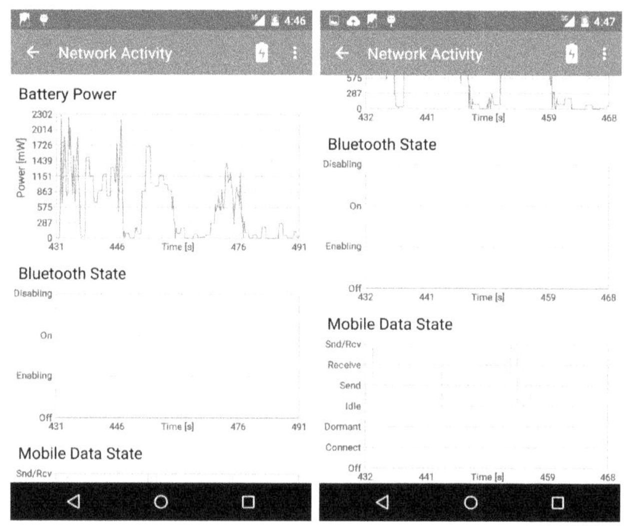

Figure 1: Power profile (left) and mobile data state (right) of Google Nexus3 phone using the Qualcomm Trepn profiler when executing a command through Google Now

This category represents a set of key applications for smartwatch users. The reason for this is that a smartwatch is much more typing-unfriendly than a smartphone due to a tiny screen, and the user has to spend a lot of time to type messages and additionally, rely heavily on automatic correction. This has proved to be very unsatisfactory [13] and therefore future smartwatches will have to rely heavily on automatic speech recognition to (1) convert speech to text to facilitate sending of messages, etc., and (2) convert speech to actions or commands that need to be executed on the watch using an Intelligent Personal Assistant (IPA) like Siri, Google Now, etc. Recently, there has been a lot of interest in offline voice recognition on a smartphone. Google recently developed an accurate, small-footprint, large vocabulary speech recognizer for smartphones that uses state-of-the-art deep neural networks (DNNs) as acoustic models [31]. This enables, typing text or issuing commands using speech even when not connected to the Internet, and also fast response in slower networks. While this is important in the context of a smartwatch too for its self-sufficiency, offline speech recognition is more important from a power/energy perspective on a smartwatch.

Figure 1 shows the power profile and the corresponding change of mobile data state on a phone that is using 3G connection to execute a voice command through the Google's IPA, Google Now. The figure shows that even for a query that is executed and responded to in a few seconds (usually less than 2 seconds), the mobile device has to be in a high power Snd/Rcv state for around 12 seconds, during which it consumes 1200mW of average power and 2300mW peak power as shown in the figure. A DNN-based offline speech recognizer can execute the same query in less than a second at 1000mW peak power (with all 4 cores active) [3], thus being 14.4x more energy efficient.

We choose four applications in this category. All of these applications are also part of the Tonic Suite [27] where the authors use them as representative future server workloads. We adapt those applications for a smartwatch. The first application, *speech-to-text*, uses a speech-to-text decoder adapted from Kaldi [40]. In WearBench, we only consider the DNN scoring that houses the DNN computation and is the most time-consuming portion [31]. This is usually followed by some post-processing. The model used is a standard feed forward neural network with k hidden layers of n_h nodes. Each layer computes a non-linear function of the weighted sum of the outputs of the previous layer. We use the same parameters in our model as in [31], i.e. there are 640 inputs and 2000 outputs. The input chosen is obtained from a few seconds of speech after some pre-processing to obtain its feature vectors. Further, there are (k=6) hidden layers with (n_h=512) nodes each. The DNN computation entails executing the $sgemm$ subroutine from the BLAS library, i.e. matrix multiplication of single-precision floats. Using ARM Streamline performance analyzer [4] on Cortex-A15, we find that multiple $sgemm$ instances together account for 95% of the execution time in DNN scoring. Table 1 shows the size of the largest matrices that are multiplied in different layers of the neural network.

The other three applications are Natural Language Processing (NLP) tasks that gather semantic information from input text. The three applications are, (1) part-of-speech (pos) tagging that assigns a tag to each word of speech (i.e. noun or verb), (2) word chunking (chk) that tags different segments of a sentence as a noun or verb phrase, and (3) name entity recognition (ner) that assigns a label to each word as to whether it is a person or a location; all these three applications are based on Senna [20]. These applications combine with speech-to-text to provide the speech-to-command functionality as needed in an IPA. Using Streamline, we find that the $sgemm$ subroutine within the DNN computation accounts for 68%, 70% and 74% of the execution time, respectively, in the *pos*, *chk* and *ner* applications. Again, the size of the largest matrices that are multiplied in different layers of the neural network is given in Table 1. The input chosen is a vector of 10 words of speech (as can be uttered in around 5 seconds to an IPA) as opposed to a 28-word vector in the Tonic Suite.

Since *sgemm* forms the core of these four applications, we use a very fast implementation of *sgemm*. We make it fast by (1) parallelizing the outermost loop to utilize the multiple cores on the chip, (2) tiling or blocking the matrices as suggested in recent papers [34, 36] that reuses data in both L1 and L2 cache and is also more amenable to prefetching, (3) unrolling the loops and finding the best unroll factors on real hardware, and (4) using ARM neon-vfpv4 SIMD extensions. We use different tile sizes and unroll factors for different sizes of the matrices. For the *sgemm* kernel used in *ASR*, our implementation performs 35% better than that in the OpenBLAS library [8] for ARM Cortex-A15 when tested on real hardware, both for a single-thread and multiple threads.

Category	Application	Layers	Size of matrices
ASR	speech-to-text	6	548x512x512, 548x2000x512
	pos	3	10x300x300
	chk	3	10x300x300
	ner	3	10x300x375
Computer Vision	imc	22	3x4096x4096, 3x4096x9216
	face	7	32x20164x363, 16x3969x2592

Table 1: Configuration of the neural networks used in WearBench applications

2.2 Image Processing

WearBench includes two applications in this category. One of them is the standard JPEG compression (*jpegc*), and the other is image denoising (*denoising*). The latter is particularly relevant to a smartwatch where the camera lens being thinner than that in a smartphone, cannot take sharp images. Thus, image processing applications such as image denoising that attenuate the noise added during image acquisition, can greatly improve the final image quality. *jpegc* involves first reading blocks of 8x8 pixels from the image, and the data in each block undergoes a sequence of operations including discrete cosine transform (DCT) and others. For image denoising, we use a simple and effective algorithm [46] that also involves reading the data in the image into overlapping (or sliding) 16x16 patches of pixels, and then applying DCT followed by inverse-DCT to obtain the denoised image. As in *sgemm*, we unroll the loops in DCT by the best unroll factors found on Cortex-A15, and also vectorize the inner loop.

2.3 Computer Vision

We include two applications in this category that are representative of some forward-looking uses of a smartwatch. The first is the face recognition (*face*). This application is particularly relevant for users as it replaces the task of entering password on the watch (as needed for some of the very important websites as mail, etc.) with a mere glance at the watch asking it to recognize the user's face (see [11] for an example application). This is useful since the user cannot also speak his/her password to sign in, when amidst people. The second application in this category is the image classification (*imc*). This application helps users to organise images taken as reminders, letting them add notes, tags and location data by predicting what the image contains. Both the face recognition and image classification applications are used from the Tonic Suite which contains implementations of these based on Facebook's DeepFace [43] facial recognition network and AlexNet [30], a large scale image classifier. The number of layers and the size of the matrices in the DNN computation within the hidden layers in these two applications is given in Table 1.

2.4 Audio Playback

This is an important category of applications for any smart device. This is particularly relevant for a smartwatch as users are expected to rely heavily on this for music, and it proves to be handy for hearing music when out for a workout, etc. We include a simple mp3 player, mpeg3play [7], in this category. We chose this player particularly because it includes optimizations to improve speed and we find that 14% of all operations executed in the player are vector operations. This application spends most of the execution time in decoding audio frames of an input mp3 file. The decoder source code contains a mix of memory access and arithmetic operations, but the memory footprint of the application is low.

2.5 Video Rendering

This category contains CISCO's open-source implementation of the H264 decoder application. The H264 decoder is used to decode frames from an input video stream and render it on the host. This is useful to allow video streaming on a smartwatch, which would require this capability once equipped with 3G service. Like the mp3 player, most of the execution time is spent on decoding input frames from the stream. Unlike the mp3 player, the memory footprint of the application is larger, and thus efficiently fetching data from memory is critical.

3. MOTIVATION AND KEY INSIGHT

This section presents key insights that lead to our specific design choices and motivates those choices over other possible solutions.

3.1 Why not a DSP for WearBench?

Digital Signal Processors (DSPs) effectively complement CPUs in a mobile SOC by serving as low-power accelerators (with VLIW cores) for audio and video processing. Recently, DSPs have been shown to efficiently handle conditional code and also tolerate (some) memory latency through the use of simultaneous multithreading such as in Qualcomm's Hexagon DSPs [18] that employ three threads in the DSP. It is for these reasons that DSPs are proving effective for processing data from sensors such as in various fitness tracking applications in a smartwatch. However, DSPs do not support multiprocessing in hardware (or software), i.e. a DSP uses only one core since there is not much inherent parallelism in traditional DSP workloads. The DSPs do not support fine-grain parallelism either for similar reasons. As a result, it is not suitable for handling applications in WearBench, most of which have inherent parallelism (coarse- as well as fine-grain). This parallelism must be exploited to minimize the response latency of critical user applications such as speech recognition in order to enhance QoS; the improvement of communication interface in smartwatches such as via speech, etc. has been recently recognized as a key factor governing adoption of this new technology [44].

3.2 Why not an Accelerator?

Since most of the important applications essentially employ a neural network and hence involve a multiplication of matrices (albeit of different sizes for different applications), it appears lucrative to employ an accelerator dedicated to matrix multiplication in a smartwatch. However, there are two drawbacks of this strategy.

1. The design of an accelerator takes long design cycles and requires extensive expertise in hardware design. In the meantime, the algorithms for some of the interesting applications for the smartwatch platform are changing. An example is Google's move from Deep to Recurrent Neural Networks [24] which provide better accuracy in speech recognition. Another example is Samsung's latest introduction of user's hand-gesture recognition for interfacing with the smartwatch. Thus, employing specialization in this emerging domain is risky; we therefore argue that an efficient general-purpose core for this platform will be a win in the long run. Also, the strict area and power constraints of a smartwatch SoC disfavor extensive specialization. That is, it is not feasible to have an H264 unit, an audio decoder, a DNN accelerator and a DSP all on a smartwatch SoC; ARM's NEON SIMD unit is meant to prevent over-specialization.

2. A very recent work [33] presents a way to automatically and efficiently generate accelerators (realized using FPGAs) for various machine learning algorithms. However, the solution is not very effective for neural networks and only achieves a performance improvement of 3x with respect to Cortex-A15 (while it achieves an average improvement of 15x over ten machine learning tasks). This is because the different stages of a neural network cannot be executed in parallel, leading to minimal gains with the accelerator. Furthermore, the opportunity for parallelism within each stage is rather limited as can be observed from the small size of the matrices in one of the dimensions (this dimension corresponds to the outermost loop and is split across parallel units) in many applications in Table 1. The paper also points that the neural network task with 512 inputs and outputs and 256 nodes consumes the maximum resources on the FPGA as compared to any other task; we would need even more resources for WearBench.

3.3 Key Insights

Table 2 compares the number of SIMD instructions and the L1 data cache miss rate (**M**isses **p**er **K**ilo **I**nstructions) for WearBench and BBench [26]. The numbers for WearBench are obtained from the gem5 simulator [15]. We rely on [26] for numbers on data cache miss rate since they obtain them on real hardware. From Section 2 and Table 2, we can make the following important observations.

	SIMD ops (%)	L1 Data Cache Miss Rate (MpKI)
BBench	~0	7
WearBench	25	30

Table 2: Comparison between WearBench and BBench

1. Seven of ten applications in WearBench are inherently parallel and can utilize all the cores on the chip. In some applications such as the automatic speech recognition, it is rather imperative to effectively use all the cores on chip in order to meet the QoS requirement.

2. The average miss rate incurred by WearBench is more than 4x higher than that incurred by BBench. WearBench is clearly more data-intensive than BBench. This pronounced data intensity in WearBench stems from the fact that the applications usually continuously load data (rows of matrices in case of speech recognition and computer vision, frames of audio/video in case of audio/video decoding, etc.) from a lower level of memory and then process that data (for example, multiply-and-accumulate in speech recognition, some signal processing algorithms in image/audio/video processing).

3. On average, 25% of the operations utilize the NEON SIMD unit on the core. In contrast, BBench does not utilize the SIMD unit at all; this is usually attributed to complex control flow within loop bodies in browser source code that makes it hard for the compiler to auto-vectorize loops. The applications in WearBench on the other hand contain loops without complex conditionals and therefore benefit from vectorization. As a result of this vectorization, however, the computation in loops executes very fast. This makes cache miss latency critical to overall application performance.

From the above observations, we make the following conclusions.

1. While future smartwatches must employ multiple cores, the cores must be simple to satisfy the low area and power budget of smartwatches. Clearly, employing multiple out-of-order cores will make it very difficult to meet these requirements. Instead, simpler cores that map well to the target applications and yield comparable performance to the out-of-order cores, will provide the maximum energy efficiency.

2. Given the high data cache miss rate in WearBench, an in-order core that stalls on every miss will not meet the QoS requirements of WearBench. Thus, we propose to use as our

% Samples		Disassembly
In-order	Out-of-order	
		.L40
		...
3.33%	10.34%	**5:** vldr d18, [r2, #-16] 'Vector load'
7.58%	3.45%	**6:** vldr d19, [r2, #-8]
0.91%	-	**7:** add r1, r1, #16 'Integer add'
	-	...
1.82%	8.62%	**10:** vldr d20, [r1, #-16]
5.15%	3.45%	**11:** vldr d21, [r1, #-8]
0.91%	-	**12:** add r0, r0, #16
0.91%	1.72%	**13:** vldr d24, [r5, #-16]
4.24%	13.79%	**14:** vldr d25, [r5, #-8]
		...
1.21%	-	**17:** vfma.f32 q7, q10, q9 'Vector fp multiply-add'
5.76%	-	**18:** vfma.f32 q14, q10, q8
		...
6.36%		**27:** bne .L40 'End of loop'

Figure 2: Disassembly of the innermost loop in the *sgemm* kernel and the time spent in individual instructions within in-order and out-of-order cores, as obtained from the ARM Streamline Performance Analyzer on Odroid-XU3 board with in-order ARM Cortex-A7 and out-of-order ARM Cortex-A15 cores

baseline core, a partial out-of-order core that uses a scoreboard to prevent RAW hazards and allows for few outstanding cache misses. However, since there is no renaming and speculation, the core is much simpler than a full out-of-order core. We further address the area and power concerns by using a smaller L2 cache, and by allowing merely two outstanding data cache misses.

3. The use of scoreboarding alone, however, is not sufficient to achieve performance close to the fully out-of-order core. This can be understood from the assembly shown in Figure 2. Consider the loads in lines 10 and 11 each of which loads a double-word. This data is used (as a quad-word) in the vector floating-point multiply-and-accumulate instruction in line 17. A two-wide instruction issue would imply a three cycle latency between load and use. Thus, unless the data is in the L1 cache (2 cycles in case of Cortex-A7 and Cortex-A15), the core using scoreboard will stall to respect this RAW dependence. The impact of an L1 miss can be seen in Figure 2 where both the cores witness considerable latency for all the loads that are serviced from the L2 cache in the chosen *sgemm* kernel. As a result, we find that using the hardware prefetcher to prefetch the data to L1 still gives a 12% performance gain for an out-of-order core. Clearly, this is much more so for our partial out-of-order baseline core. We thus propose to use a light-weight hardware prefetcher in WearCore to prefetch the data to the L1 cache.

3.4 The Case for a Software-Assisted Hardware Prefetcher

The existing ARM cores provide different prefetching options. The ARMv7-A ISA supports software prefetching through the preload instruction, 'PLD [rn, #offset]' where *rn* is the register carrying the base address and *offset* is the optional offset. Also, the out-of-order core variants employ a powerful hardware streamer prefetcher at the L2 cache that supports large prefetch distances (8 cache lines) and can detect multiple data streams. The in-order variants either do not implement hardware prefetching (as in Cortex-A8) or use a simplistic prefetcher at L1 cache that can track just two data streams (as in Cortex-A7 and A9). However, each of these options proves inadequate for applications in WearBench for the following reasons.

1. Using the preload instruction (PLD) in the innermost loop to prefetch contiguous data accesses worsens the performance by 20% due to the overhead of the PLD instruction itself on the in-order Cortex-A7 core. Thus, software prefetching is unsuitable due to the performance overhead.

2. The simplistic hardware prefetcher (that can track two data streams) at the L1 cache proves insufficient also. This is because the compiler unrolls the loops in many of these applications, and thus exposes multiple data streams (8 in *jpegc*, and 6 in *sgemm* and *denoising*) in the loop body. Also, these cores do not employ a sophisticated hardware prefetcher at L1 since the overhead of the hardware structures needed to track multiple streams in terms of storage, area and power, is large. For example, a 256-entry Global History Buffer (GHB) requires 6KB of storage space, and also consequently area and power overheads since GHB entries need to be updated on every data access.

3. Prefetching the data to the L2 cache using a sophisticated hardware prefetcher is not sufficient either to hide latency when using a partial out-of-order core as above discussed.

Thus, we propose to use a software-assisted hardware prefetcher (SAHP) that combines the advantages of both the software and hardware prefetching and avoids their respective drawbacks. SAHP is triggered by our proposed software prefetch instruction, PLDX, as **PLDX [rn, #nl]**, where *rn* carries the base address as in PLD, and *nl* is the number of cache lines that should be prefetched starting at that address. This has the following advantages.

1. Since it is outside the loop, its contribution to the instruction overhead is negligible.

2. Since the information about what data to prefetch is entirely encapsulated in this instruction, there is no sophisticated hardware needed to track data streams.

3. Once the prefetching is triggered, the hardware assumes complete responsibility to maintain the appropriate prefetch distance such that it hides the latency effectively and also does not cause cache pollution. The latter is important since SAHP prefetches the data all the way to the (smaller) L1 cache for effective latency hiding. Thus, SAHP relieves the user from setting the right prefetch distance, which is known to be difficult to determine.

4. Finally, since the hardware knows well in advance about the number of cache lines that need to be prefetched (possibly across virtual page boundaries), it leverages this information to prefetch across physical pages and thus does not have to stop at physical page boundaries.

It is important to note that the user or the library developer is responsible for the insertion of these prefetch instructions into the code to trigger SAHP. However, the insertion of these instructions is extremely simple for the programmer. In many of the WearBench applications, just a prefetch instruction before a subroutine call or loop body is sufficient since this new prefetch instruction can capture all data needed in the loop body (in the form of the number of the lines to be prefetched that is passed as the second argument in the 'PLDX' instruction) at once. For example, in *denoising*, the three suborutine calls each needed just a single prefetch instruction for the entire subroutine because it contained the one array that was responsible for memory accesses; the number of lines to be prefetched is specified as a function of the image size and is therefore not necessary to be determined at compile time.
We detail the implementation of SAHP in the following section.

Structure	Size	Location	Functionality
prefetch bit	1 bit	Each block in L1 cache	Indicates if this block was prefetched when brought to cache
read bit	1 bit	"	Indicates if this block has been read at least once after being prefetched
mID	4 bits	"	Holds the ID of the MSHR that is servicing the prefetch request responsible for fetching this block to the cache
counter	4 bits	Each MSHR in MSHR file	Contains the count of prefetched blocks that have not yet been read
stop bit	1 bit	"	This bit is set to true when the counter reaches its maximum value of 15, to indicate that this MSHR should stop prefetching further for now
num	16 bits	"	Contains the count of the number of blocks prefetched through this MSHR that have also been read
nblocks	16 bits	"	Contains the number of blocks that remain to be prefetched from the original number of requested blocks in the prefetch request
ID	4 bits	"	Unique ID for this MSHR
Vaddr	20 bits	"	Contains the most significant 20 bits of the virtual address of the block being prefetched

Table 3: Hardware structures added to implement SAHP; SAHP adds an overhead of 6 bits per cache line and 61 bits per MSHR at L1 cache

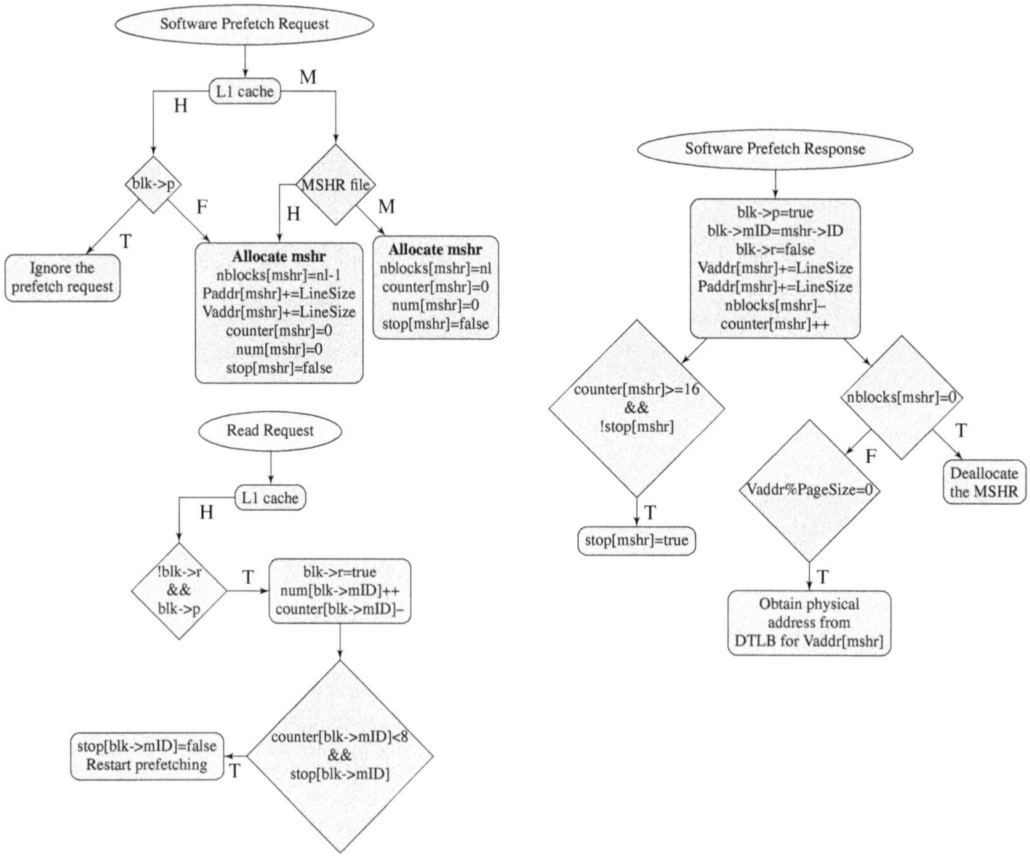

Figure 3: Actions taken at prefetch/read request and response

4. IMPLEMENTATION

Our proposed software-assisted hardware prefetcher (SAHP) is designed to complement our baseline partial out-of-order core for future smartwatches. The core uses scoreboarding for out-of-order execution where we allow a maximum of two outstanding cache misses at any time. That is, if all data is found in the L1 data cache that has a hit latency of 2 cycles, data reads can proceed without stalls. This strategy is similar to Intel's Xeon Phi coprocessor where each thread in the core can issue a load instruction once in two cycles because another load cannot issue unless the data for the first load is returned from the L1 cache (with 2 cycle hit latency). Therefore, like Xeon Phi, our baseline core relies heavily on data having been prefetched to the L1 cache to successfully hide latency.

As mentioned earlier, SAHP is triggered by a software prefetch instruction that specifies the number of cache lines to be prefetched. Once triggered, SAHP prefetches the specified number of lines to the L1 cache through the use of some extra hardware as listed in Table 3. Since SAHP bears the onus to maintain the right prefetch distance, the hardware must provide a mechanism to stop/restart prefetching while the program is executing. This is crucial because in many programs (such as *jpegc* and *denoising* in WearBench), there is intermittent fetch and compute, and the prefetcher could easily run far ahead during the compute phase causing cache pollution if it is not timely stopped.

In SAHP, a single software prefetch instruction instructs the hardware to prefetch all the data needed by a particular data stream. Thus, our 'PLDX' software prefetch instruction remains bound to a single MSHR until all needed cache lines have been prefetched. Each MSHR is therefore equipped with its own counter (and stop bit) to determine when to stop/restart prefetching for its particular stream. This counter is incremented when a prefetch request is responded by the arrival of a requested line in the cache and is decremented upon its first read, i.e. this counter gives the prefetch distance; in SAHP the maximum prefetch distance is 16 cache lines. This counter and other structures needed to implement SAHP come into play at three events during execution: (1) arrival of a prefetch request at L1 cache, (2) arrival of a read request at L1 cache, and (3) when data requested through software prefetch returns to the L1 cache.

The flowcharts in Figure 3 depict how the new hardware structures are updated in SAHP at each of the three events noted above. Upon the arrival of a **Software Prefetch Request**, if the line at the start address is not in the L1 cache or MSHR file, then an MSHR is allocated that would remain bound to the prefetch request until all requested lines (denoted by nl) are prefetched. However, if the line is already present in the cache and was prefetched earlier (indicated by the prefetch bit in the line), then the current prefetch request is ignored since this denotes a possible overlap of prefetch requests (and perhaps a redundant request). If the line has not been prefetched, then the prefetch is initiated, starting at the following cache line.

When the requested line returns (i.e. **Software Prefetch Response**), the prefetch bit in the line is set, and all the structures in the MSHR are updated to initiate prefetch of the following lines. As cache lines are being prefetched continuously for a given stream, three events can happen, (a) all lines are prefetched (i.e. $nblocks$=0) and the MSHR is deallocated, (b) the prefetch distance denoted by $counter$ reaches 15 cache lines, and prefetching for this stream stops, and (c) the stream reaches the page boundary, and the physical address of the next page is retrieved from the DTLB by indexing it via the virtual address of the next page that is being tracked in the MSHR (note that this may also trigger a page walk on a DTLB miss, and SAHP thus also helps to hide this latency of a page walk).

When a prefetched block is read for the first time via a **Read Request**, the counter is decremented and the block is marked as read. If the prefetch distance denoted by $counter$ drops below 8 lines, then the stop bit is reset and prefetching is resumed. Thus, the counter and other structures help to always maintain the prefetch distance for all streams between 8 and 16 cache lines, thus preventing L1 cache pollution and also running sufficiently ahead to hide memory latency. When a read request hits in an MSHR that is servicing a prefetch request to the same cache line and is awaiting response from the lower levels of the memory, the same actions are taken to update the structures.

The num field of an MSHR that is incremented when a prefetched block is read, is indicative of the utility (i.e. how many lines prefetched by this request have been used by the program) of the prefetch request bound to the MSHR. The value of num proves handy when the MSHR Queue is full, and a new request wants an MSHR. In such a case, an MSHR servicing a prefetch request that is currently dormant (i.e. its stop bit is set) and has the lowest value of the num field is deallocated to make way for the new request. This thus helps to prevent a deadlock that may result if all prefetch requests are useless and thus come to a stop, but continue to hold the MSHR. Similarly, if a read request hits an MSHR servicing a prefetch request that is dormant (i.e. prefetch distance or counter is greater than 8; this only happens when the data stream being prefetched is irregular or discontiguous), the counter is reset and prefetching is resumed to prevent a deadlock. Finally, if a prefetch request fetches data that is already present in the L1 cache, the prefetch request is squashed given the likelihood that the request is redundant. This also helps to resolve overlapping prefetch requests.

5. EXPERIMENTAL SETUP

For our evaluation, we use the gem5 simulator [15] to model an in-order core, a full out-of-order core, and our partial out-of-order core (that implements SAHP); all cores run the ARMv7 ISA. In gem5, we simulate an in-order core by using a trimmed down version of the out-of-order core model that allows only one outstanding miss, i.e. the load/store queue has a single entry. We model a partial out-of-order core using the MinorCPU model in gem5. In the following section, we compare the performance and power of these cores armed with different prefetchers. Table 4 details the microarchitectural details of these three cores used in the simulator.

Component	Type of core: in-order	out-of-order	WearCore
Core	2GHz, 2-way superscalar		
Reorder logic	-	Full OoO (renaming + speculation)	Partial OoO (scoreboard)
Prefetcher	-	GHB-based stream prefetcher	SAHP
L1-Icache	32KB, 2-way LRU, 2 MSHRs, 1 cycle		
L1-Dcache	32KB, 4-way LRU, 10 MSHRs, 2 cycles		
L2 Unified	512KB	1024KB	512KB
Cache	8-way LRU, 16 MSHRs, 12 cycles		
DRAM	LPDDR3, 110ns latency [5]		
Execute units	1 int, 1 int/branch, 1 fp/simd, 1 read, 1 write		
Op latency	int: alu=1, mul=3, div=12 float: add/cmp=1, mul=3, div=12 SIMD: floatMultAcc=8, floatDiv=18, others=4 read/write=1		

Table 4: Microarchitectural details of the simulated cores

We test these cores against the ten applications in WearBench discussed in Section 2. For simulation, we identify the most representative portion of the program, i.e. that which is executed again and again during program execution and thus contributes almost entirely to the execution time. For applications that involve DNN/CNN computation (i.e. applications in the category of automatic speech recognition and computer vision), we simulate 2-4 iterations (depending on the problem size) of the outermost loop of the tiled *sgemm* kernel with respective problem sizes. We verify on real hardware that this does not alter the data reuse pattern in either the L1 or L2 cache and is thus representative of the entire kernel execution; the execution time scales linearly with the iterations of outermost loop. For the MP3 playback and H264 decoder applications, we simulate the decoding of each frame of the input audio and video, respectively, since the entire application consists of iterative decoding of all frames in the input. For the image processing applications, we simulate the entire program execution of *denoising* and *jpegc* with input images of sizes 80x80 and 800x600, respectively.

We use the GNU C/C++ Compiler to compile these applications statically for use with the simulator. We use '-funroll-loops -march=armv7 -mtune=cortex-a15 -funsafe-math-optimizations -mfpu= neon-vfpv4' options in the compiler to enable loop unrolling and vectorization wherever possible. In some cases, we manually unroll the loops to get better performance such as in the *sgemm* kernel and also in the subroutine performing forward discrete-cosine transform (DCT) in the denoising application. Finally, we use CACTI 6.5 [32] to obtain our area and power estimates for the 28nm technology node. We obtain dynamic power by calculating the total energy dissipated by the component from the per-access energy values obtained from CACTI, and then dividing it by the time taken to execute the simulated application.

Configuration	Details
InO	The baseline in-order core without any prefetchers. This core is representative of low-power ARM cores used in low-end smartphones and in some smartwatches.
SB	Partial out-of-order execution support through scoreboarding. This core allows two outstanding misses; does not use prefetchers.
O3	This core supports full out-of-order execution using register renaming and speculation. It uses an aggressive hardware prefetcher at L2 cache with a prefetch degree of 8.
SB+SAHP	This is WearCore. It uses scoreboarding and implements our proposed SAHP.
SB+SAHP-L2	Same as above. This core chooses to not have an L2 cache to represent low-power cores or cores in low-power mode.
O3+SAHP	This is an out-of-order core with SAHP, but no hardware prefetchers.

Table 5: Summary of hardware configurations tested

6. RESULTS AND DISCUSSION

Figure 4 compares the performance achieved by different hardware configurations with respect to an in-order core (without hardware prefetching) as baseline. Table 5 summarizes the different configurations; note that although we do not specifically include BIG.little, the BIG OoO core and the little InO core is included separately for comparison. The first ten groups of columns show the performance for each application in WearBench, and the last column shows the geometric mean of performance achieved by each configuration on all applications. In summary, we find that the performance of our proposed core, WearCore (denoted by SB+SAHP in the figure), gets reasonably close to the O3 core - it is 24% slower for WearBench on average. While WearCore incurs the worst performance (42% slower than *O3*) in *denoising*, it is only 12% slower for the critical *speech-to-text* application, which has strict QoS requirements. It is important to observe that *SAHP* adds a crucial 37% performance on top of a core with scoreboarding (denoted by *SB*). When using a partial out-of-order core with SAHP but without an L2 cache (i.e. *SB+SAHP-L2*), the performance degradation is 36% with respect to *O3*. Since the performance degradation is not too drastic (the performance is sometimes even slightly better in cases where there is not much reuse in L2 since we save an L2 lookup every time we go to DRAM), this is also a reasonable alternative that can be useful when the core wants to go to a low-power mode by turning off the L2 cache to conserve battery. Again, the use of SAHP makes this configuration feasible since it can prefetch the data all the way to the L1 cache. Finally, the last bar represents an O3 core with SAHP but no hardware prefetching. This core performs 5% better than *O3* because of prefetching the data to the L1 cache as opposed to the L2 cache. The performance improvement achieved by *O3+SAHP* is as large as 18% for *imc* application, thereby advocating prefetching to the L1 cache. SAHP makes this possible at a low area and power overhead as opposed to a hardware prefetcher, making its incorporation feasible in low-power devices such as a smartwatch.

We next discuss the results for application categories.

Automatic speech recognition and computer vision. The core computation in the six applications that belong to these two categories is the DNN (speech recognition) or CNN (computer vision). Among these six, the *s-to-t*, *imc* and *face* spend most of their time in NN computation (i.e. the *sgemm* kernel), and benefit more from SAHP than *t-to-c*. The reason is that SAHP benefits *sgemm* particularly because of bringing the data to the L1 cache, which is critical given that the computation is entirely SIMDized and completes quickly (thereby stressing memory). This benefit also shows when SAHP is used with *O3*. SAHP, on the other hand, is unable to benefit the computation outside NN in *t-to-c* such as the *viterbi* dynamic programming algorithm to find the most sequence of hidden states, since there are not many accesses to memory. In such cases, *SB* has to stall for every unresolved RAW dependence at the scoreboard. This makes it slower than *O3*. Also, we observe that in *imc*, SAHP adds more performance than in other applications. This is because data gets repeatedly replaced from the L1 cache due to pronounced conflicts arising from the problem size being a multiple of a power of two, and thus prefetching data to L1 boosts the performance more.

Image processing. In *denoising*, the performance gap between WearCore (i.e. *SB+SAHP*) and *O3* is maximum. This is because among all applications, the program spends the maximum fraction of time in compute. The program does read the patches obtained from the input image from the memory (during which SAHP assists), but this is followed by 16x16 DCT and inverse-DCT, where all the data used resides in the L1 cache. In *jpegc* also, the time spent in computation is significant, although SAHP improves performance when the image is read from memory.

Audio playback and video decoding. In *mp3*, SAHP adds a mild 4% improvement over *SB* only. This is because we find that the working set is only around 20KB, and so data is reused from the L1 cache. Also, the program is thus dominated by computation. In *h264dec*, on the other hand, the input frames are larger and processing the frames requires copying them, which yields sufficient opportunities to benefit from prefetching data to L1 cache through SAHP.

6.1 Area and Power Overheads

Component	Organization	Ports	Area (μm^2)	Power (mW)
MSHR file	10 entries x 4 bytes (CAM)	1 r/w 2s	1471	0.144
SAHP overhead in MSHR file (61 bits)	10 entries x 61 bits	1 r/w	1865	0.005
SAHP overhead in Cache (6 bits)	512 blocks x 6 bits	1 r/w	2114	0.034
Input Buffer	16 entries x 4 bytes (CAM)	1 r/w 2s	1471	0.144
Scoreboard	64 entries x 1 byte	1r 1w	2956	0.134
InFlightInstQueue	16 entries x 4 bytes (CAM)	1 r/w 2s	1471	0.144
Store Buffer	8 entries x 4 bytes (CAM)	1 r/w 1s	931	0.01
WearCore			462,279	100.5
Cortex-A15			2,025,000	450

Table 6: Area and power overhead of WearCore over an in-order ARM Cortex-A7 core (Area=450,000μm^2, Power=100mW) when modeled with CACTI6.5 in 28nm. The area and power consumed by ARM Cortex-A15 core is also listed. The numbers do not include the L2 cache.

For the purpose of determining area and power requirements of WearCore, we follow the strategy as adopted in [17] - we use the area and power numbers of a baseline in-order core (ARM Cortex-A7 in our case) as available publicly, and calculate the overhead of the components added over it to implement WearCore. According to ARM [2], the core area and average power consumption of Cortex-A7 are 0.45 mm^2 and 100mW, respectively, in 28nm. WearCore and Cortex-A7 are also compared against the out-of-order ARM Cortex-A15 core, whose area and power consumption are 4-5 times larger than Cortex-A7 [21, 1].

Table 6 lists for each major component in WearCore, the area and average power consumption as calculated using CACTI v6.5 [32] at 28nm. Note that whenever we require to round the size of the structure to the nearest power of 2 in CACTI, we round it to the larger number. The overheads stem from the following causes. (1) In order to support SAHP, WearCore uses a larger MSHR file at the L1 cache as opposed to A7 that only supports two outstanding prefetch requests through the PLD instruction (and one outstanding load). We modeled this component as a CAM. (2) The 61 bits in each MSHR in order to keep track of the prefetch distance in hardware. We model this component as a direct-mapped cache since the corresponding entry is accessed directly either through the *mID* field in a cache block during a cache hit or when the prefetch returns. (3) The 6 bits in the cache. This is modeled as in (2). (4) The input buffer buffers the instructions before the scoreboard determines that it is safe to issue them. We model this as a CAM since loads in this buffer may bypass other instructions thereby requiring an associative lookup. (5) The scoreboard simply tracks the number of in-flight instructions writing to any particular register. It allows a new instruction to issue once there is no in-flight instruction waiting to write to any of the source registers of the new instruction (indicated by a zero count of the source registers in the scoreboard). We model this as a direct-mapped cache since it is indexed by an instruction's source register. (6) The InFlightInstQueue is responsible for in-order commit of all instructions. It stores all instructions that have been issued but have not been completed. (7) The store buffer is used to forward the data to cacheable loads and has 8 entries in our case. In total, the area and power overhead of WearCore is merely 2.7% and 0.5%, respectively, compared to the baseline.

We combine these area and power estimates with the perfor-

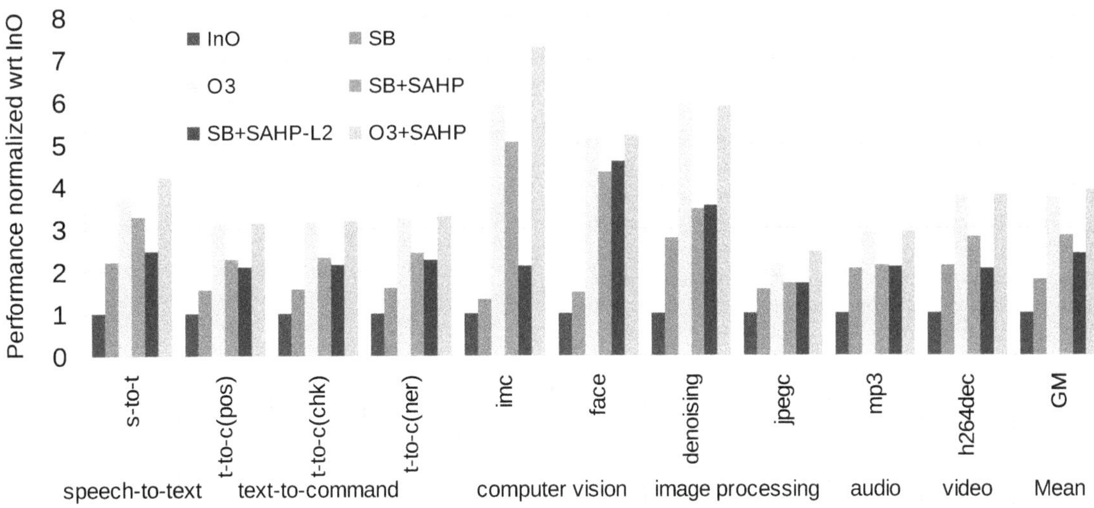

Figure 4: Performance comparison of different cores with their respective prefetchers

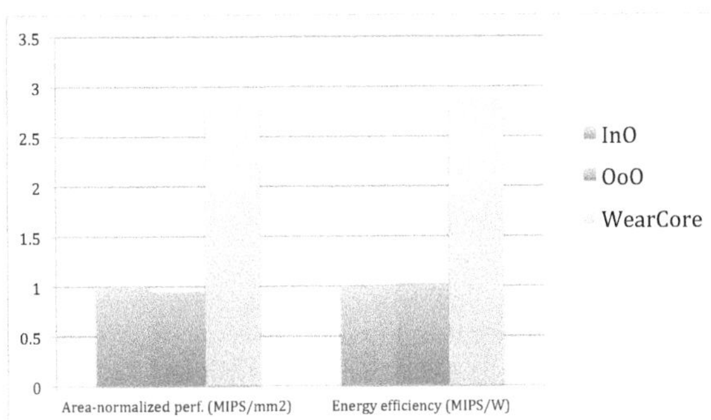

Figure 5: Area-normalized performance and energy-efficiency of WearCore versus an in-order and an out-of-order core

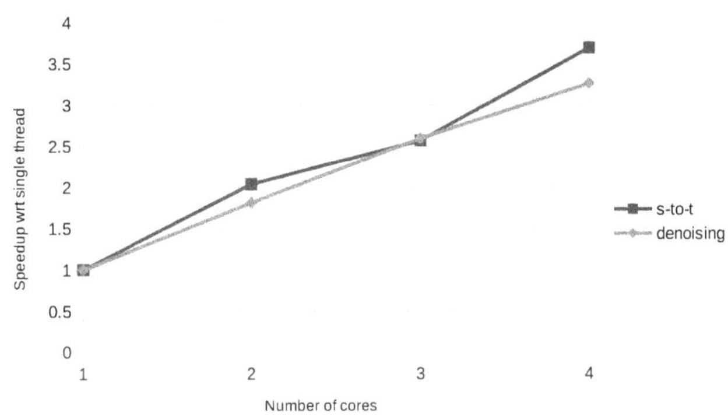

Figure 6: Parallel performance of two WearBench applications; the dip in *s-to-t* at 3-cores is due to load imbalance

mance numbers obtained from gem5. As shown in Figure 5, WearCore achieves an improvement of 2.8x and 2.9x respectively, in terms of area-normalized performance and energy efficiency over an in-order core. On the other hand, the in-order core achieves very similar area-normalized performance and energy efficiency as an out-of-order core. This result is similar to published data [21] about ARM's Cortex-A7 and A15 CPUs. Note that these numbers include the area and power of the L2 cache in each core for better estimates, and that the out-of-order core uses an L2 cache that is double the size of L2 in the in-order core as well as WearCore.

6.2 Parallel Performance

Figure 6 shows the parallel performance achieved by two applications from WearBench, *speech-to-text* and *denoising*. We chose the former as a representative of all six applications that spend the majority of their time in neural network computation and also because this application has strict QoS requirements. The figure shows that these applications scale well with the number of cores, and thus prove the utility of employing multiple cores on the chip. *Speech-to-text* benefits particularly since it can now achieve its target QoS - using four cores, we find that the DNN computation involved in recognizing 5 seconds of speech completes in under 250ms (as opposed to nearly a second on a single core) on WearCore when simulated on gem5 in full-system mode. Also, an 80x80 image can be denoised in 3.5 seconds as opposed to 11.5 seconds.

6.3 Discussion

We thus see that applications in WearBench benefit considerably from WearCore, our proposed core that extends a baseline partial out-of-order core with a software-assisted hardware prefetcher. This proves to be useful in WearBench because of reducing stalls on memory accesses while the computation completes quickly as a result of vectorization. This benefit, however, requires the insertion of our proposed software prefetch instruction in the code by library developers and users. Library developers currently tune their libraries to benefit from the SIMD extensions on the host hardware, such as NEON for ARM. This approach has been tenable for smartphones till now, particularly because of the select applications that run on them. For example, the libraries used in audio and video encode/decode (such as libavcodec) currently provide specific implementations that benefit from the SIMD extensions. This strategy is also adopted by smartphone companies such as Intel, which recently released its chip for smartphones that can perform offline speech recognition in an efficient way by software-hardware co-development [6].

We thus believe that these libraries could similarly include extensions for prefetching in the source code to benefit from SAHP. Although such software prefetch instructions exist in current ARM ISA, but is not beneficial to insert them because of the associated overhead and due to the difficulty in determining where to insert them and what prefetch distance to use. The prefetch instruction in SAHP overcomes both of these limitations, making the task of library developers and users much simpler.

7. RELATED WORK

In the present day, a key goal of computer architects is to extract the maximum energy efficiency from the core. This goal is only getting renewed importance as consumers move from desktop PCs to laptops to smartphones, and now to smartwatches. As architects contend with this goal, they face the well-known tradeoff between performance and power. In order to gain performance, some power-consuming component must be added on the chip. Thus, the ultimate gain in terms of energy-efficiency depends on whether the target applications benefit from the newly added component or not. As we expect the market share of smartwatches to improve, it is important to identify the key target applications and then propose minimal hardware to improve its energy-efficiency.

Workload Characterization. In the recent past, there has been considerable research on identifying key target applications for the smartphone. BBench [26] and MobileBench [39] are representative examples. However, these works have not considered on-device speech recognition or face recognition using DNNs, which are of particular importance to a smartwatch. More recently, Gao et al. [23] show that mobile applications utilize less than 2 cores on average, and thus most mobile processors are overprovisioned with cores with some of them now having as many as eight cores on the chip. We find that having multiple cores of the chip in a smartwatch can be particularly useful for a critical application like *speech-to-text* that has strict quality of service requirement; other applications also make use of multiple cores. We therefore include these workloads in WearBench and propose to have multiple simple cores on chip in a smartwatch. We also show that these applications benefit a lot from the SIMD unit on the core, making for a case to improve memory performance.

In order to improve memory performance, there have been various solutions proposed, mostly hovering around prefetching data to the higher levels of memory hierarchy in order to prevent miss latency.

Software-only solutions to improve energy-efficiency. Software prefetching [16, 37] is a well known technique to hide memory latency. It is for this reason that all existing cores including some of the in-order ARM cores provide support for software prefetching. However, as discussed in Section 3, using software prefetch instructions does not necessarily benefit performance due to the overhead associated with introducing them in the innermost loop. In this work, we use a software prefetch instruction to trigger prefetching, but that instruction appears outside the innermost loop to prevent this overhead.

Software-hardware solutions. Recently, Mehta et al. [35, 22] have proposed coordinated prefetching that relies on coordination between hardware prefetcher and software prefetching. They show that the overhead due to software prefetching can be overcome on Intel's in-order Xeon Phi cores, but they rely on the fact that the vector width is the same as the cache line size. Thus, in that case, there are no redundant prefetch instructions, i.e. there is one prefetch instruction per cache line provided the innermost loop is vectorized. However, the vector width on ARM cores is a fourth of the cache line size and thus redundant prefetches cannot be avoided even when the innermost loop is vectorized. Similarly, the idea of block prefetching where a single prefetch instruction triggers requests to n (usually 4) consecutive lines, suffers from the problem of redundant prefetches; elimination of redundant prefetches via conditional-code/unrolling/short-loops (from strip-mining) prove detrimental to vectorization performance and is thus not used in current production compilers. Other research [29, 41, 28] employs helper threads to predict future load addresses. The authors in [29, 28] use an idle thread (SMT) as the helper thread to prefetch data for another compute thread, whereas Son et al. [41] extend the helper-thread prefetching to work with multiple (many) cores by assigning a customized helper thread to a group of compute threads. However, these solutions are less relevant for smartwatches that do not employ SMT (to keep them simpler) and have many fewer cores than those in current multi- (many-) cores.

Hardware-only solutions. An example in this category is runahead execution [38] where execution does not stop at a cache miss resulting in future data being prefetched to the cache in time. Other examples include designs where the data is precomputed before it is needed [19] and those where the processor resources are freed up for miss-independent instructions [42]. However, these solutions are all proposed for out-of-order cores and require sufficient hardware themselves. These are thus not well suited to low-power devices. Recently, Carlson et al. [17] have proposed the Load Slice Core Microarchitecture that extracts memory hierarchy parallelism (MHP) by enabling memory accesses along with their address-generating instructions to execute while the pipeline is stalled on a long-latency miss. They propose a separate pipeline for independent memory accesses (and their address-generating instructions), and additional hardware that identifies address-generating instructions that lead up to the independent memory accesses. They achieve good energy efficiency by extracting MHP over both in-order and out-of-order cores. While their technique is more general and targeted towards many-core processors, we achieve similar gains for applications in WearBench with simpler hardware, and WearCore is therefore better suited to smartwatches. Another solution in this category that comes close to our work is Guided Region Prefetching (GRP) [45]. In GRP, the compiler provides a hint to the hardware prefetcher about the loop trip count, and the hardware then determines all blocks to be prefetched in a page (region) and dynamically tracks all remaining blocks and the next block to be prefetched in each page. However, since this is done for each stream, and GRP may prefetch arbitrarily ahead on the page (4 KB in its case) for each stream, it starts displacing even the prefetched data before being used in the event of multiple data streams. The key in SAHP, on the other hand, is that the hardware maintains a counter that tracks the current prefetch distance, and the hardware never allows itself to prefetch too far ahead to start displacing useful/prefetched data. GRP also requires re-triggering of the prefetcher (and therefore additional memory accesses) at every new page, while SAHP goes across pages without stopping. Overall, since SAHP requires much less additional hardware, it is more suitable for a smartwatch.

8. CONCLUSION AND FUTURE WORK

In this work, we propose WearCore, a core for efficiently executing smartwatch workloads, that we term WearBench. WearCore is built on the insight that the important workloads for a smartwatch are parallel, and make extensive use of SIMD operations, making it important that the memory requests be serviced quickly for overall good application performance. Thus, building upon a quad-core processor as baseline, WearCore augments it with a light-weight software-assisted hardware prefetcher for reducing the cache misses altogether. This software-assisted hardware prefetcher adds minimal overhead in terms of area and power to the core, but adds a crucial 36% performance on top of the baseline. It is also very easy to use, and does not add instruction overhead either. Experimental results show that WearBench achieves significant improvement in terms of both area and energy efficiency over both an in-order and an out-of-order core.

Acknowledgement This work was supported in part by NSF under grants CCF-1012759 and CCF-1536795.

9. REFERENCES

[1] "Arm cortex-a15," Available at http://www.arm.com/products/processors/cortex-a/cortex-a15.php.

[2] "Arm cortex-a7," Available at http://www.arm.com/products/processors/cortex-a/cortex-a7.php.

[3] "Arm cortex-a9," Available at https://www.arm.com/products/processors/cortex-a/cortex-a9.php.

[4] "Arm streamline performance analyzer," Available at http://ds.arm.com/ds-5/optimize/.

[5] "Cortex a15 dram latency," Available at http://www.7-cpu.com/cpu/Cortex-A15.html.

[6] "Intel voice recognition will blow siri out of the water because it does not use the cloud," Available at http://qz.com/170668/intels-voice-recognition-will-blow-siri-out-of-the-water-because-it-doesnt-use-the-cloud/.

[7] "mpeg3play mp3 music player," Available at http://www.mp3-tech.org/programmer/sources/mpeg3play-0_9_6-src.tgz.

[8] "Openblas - an optimized blas library," Available at http://www.openblas.net/.

[9] "Samsung galaxy s6: Battery life," Available at http://www.trustedreviews.com/samsung-galaxy-s6-review-battery-life-and-charging-page-4.

[10] "Samsung gear s 3g smartwatch: Battery life," Available at http://www.extremetech.com/computing/188828-samsung-unveils-standalone-gear-s-3g-smartwatch-awesome-until-the-battery-runs-out-after-an-hour.

[11] "Logging into twitter and facebook using your face," 2010, Available at http://thenextweb.com/mobile/2010/11/10/brilliant-logging-into-twitter-and-facebook-using-your-face-and-voice-video/.

[12] "Can a smartwatch like the gear s replace your phone?" 2015, Available at http://www.techradar.com/us/news/wearables/can-a-smartwatch-replace-your-phone--1285484.

[13] "The problem of typing on a watch," 2015, Available at http://www.cnet.com/products/samsung-gear-s/.

[14] ABI-Research, "Wearable computing devices, like apple iwatch, will exceed 485 million annual shipments by 2018," 2013, Available at https://www.abiresearch.com/press/wearable-computing-devices-like-apples-iwatch-will/.

[15] N. Binkert, B. Beckmann, G. Black, S. K. Reinhardt, A. Saidi, A. Basu, J. Hestness, D. R. Hower, T. Krishna, S. Sardashti, R. Sen, K. Sewell, M. Shoaib, N. Vaish, M. D. Hill, and D. A. Wood, "The gem5 simulator," *SIGARCH Comput. Archit. News*, vol. 39, no. 2, pp. 1–7, Aug. 2011.

[16] D. Callahan, K. Kennedy, and A. Porterfield, "Software prefetching," in *Proceedings of the Fourth International Conference on Architectural Support for Programming Languages and Operating Systems*, ser. ASPLOS IV. New York, NY, USA: ACM, 1991, pp. 40–52.

[17] T. E. Carlson, W. Heirman, O. Allam, S. Kaxiras, and L. Eeckhout, "The load slice core microarchitecture," in *Proceedings of the 42Nd Annual International Symposium on Computer Architecture*, ser. ISCA '15. New York, NY, USA: ACM, 2015, pp. 272–284.

[18] L. Codrescu, W. Anderson, S. Venkumanhanti, M. Zeng, E. Plondke, C. Koob, A. Ingle, C. Tabony, and R. Maule, "Hexagon dsp: An architecture optimized for mobile multimedia and communications," *IEEE Micro*, vol. 34, no. 2, pp. 34–43, Mar 2014.

[19] J. D. Collins, D. M. Tullsen, H. Wang, and J. P. Shen, "Dynamic speculative precomputation," in *Proceedings of the 34th Annual ACM/IEEE International Symposium on Microarchitecture*, ser. MICRO 34. Washington, DC, USA: IEEE Computer Society, 2001, pp. 306–317.

[20] R. Collobert, J. Weston, L. Bottou, M. Karlen, K. Kavukcuoglu, and P. Kuksa, "Natural language processing (almost) from scratch," *J. Mach. Learn. Res.*, vol. 12, pp. 2493–2537, Nov. 2011.

[21] EE-Times, "How arm's cortex-a7 beats the a15," 2013, Available at http://www.eetimes.com/author.asp?section_id=36&doc_id=1318968.

[22] Z. Fang, S. Mehta, P.-C. Yew, A. Zhai, J. Greensky, G. Beeraka, and B. Zang, "Measuring microarchitectural details of multi- and many-core memory systems through microbenchmarking," *ACM Trans. Archit. Code Optim.*, vol. 11, no. 4, pp. 55:1–55:26, Jan. 2015.

[23] C. Gao, A. Gutierrez, M. Rajan, R. G. Dreslinski, T. Mudge, and C.-J. Wu, "A study of mobile device utilization," *2015 IEEE International Symposium on Performance Analysis of Systems and Software*, 2015.

[24] Google-Research, "Voice search made faster," 2015, Available at http://googleresearch.blogspot.in/2015/09/google-voice-search-faster-and-more.html.

[25] Google-Wear, "Android wear on wi-fi: Using a smartwatch without a phone nearby," 2015, Available at http://www.computerworld.com/article/2919013/android/android-wear-on-wi-fi-using-a-smartwatch-without-a-phone-nearby.html.

[26] A. Gutierrez, R. Dreslinski, T. Wenisch, T. Mudge, A. Saidi, C. Emmons, and N. Paver, "Full-System Analysis and Characterization of Interactive Smartphone Applications," in *the proceedings of the 2011 IEEE International Symposium on Workload Characterization (IISWC)*, Austin, TX, USA, 2011, pp. 81–90.

[27] J. Hauswald, Y. Kang, M. A. Laurenzano, Q. Chen, C. Li, R. Dreslinski, T. Mudge, J. Mars, and L. Tang, "Djinn and tonic: Dnn as a service and its implications for future warehouse scale computers," in *Proceedings of the 42nd Annual International Symposium on Computer Architecture (ISCA)*, ser. ISCA '15. New York, NY, USA: ACM, 2015.

[28] M. Kamruzzaman, S. Swanson, and D. M. Tullsen, "Inter-core prefetching for multicore processors using migrating helper threads," in *Proceedings of the Sixteenth International Conference on Architectural Support for Programming Languages and Operating Systems*, ser. ASPLOS XVI. New York, NY, USA: ACM, 2011, pp. 393–404.

[29] D. Kim and D. Yeung, "Design and evaluation of compiler algorithms for pre-execution," in *Proceedings of the 10th International Conference on Architectural Support for Programming Languages and Operating Systems*, ser. ASPLOS X. New York, NY, USA: ACM, 2002, pp. 159–170.

[30] A. Krizhevsky, I. Sutskever, and G. E. Hinton, "Imagenet classification with deep convolutional neural networks," in *Advances in Neural Information Processing Systems 25*, F. Pereira, C. Burges, L. Bottou, and K. Weinberger, Eds. Curran Associates, Inc., 2012, pp. 1097–1105.

[31] X. Lei, A. Senior, A. Gruenstein, and J. Sorensen, "Accurate and compact large vocabulary speech recognition on mobile devices," in *Proceedings of the 14th Annual Conference of the International Speech Communication Association*, ser. ISCA '13, 2013.

[32] S. Li, K. Chen, J. H. Ahn, J. B. Brockman, and N. P. Jouppi, "Cacti-p: Architecture-level modeling for sram-based structures with advanced leakage reduction techniques," in *Proceedings of the International Conference on*

Computer-Aided Design, ser. ICCAD '11. Piscataway, NJ, USA: IEEE Press, 2011, pp. 694–701.

[33] D. Mahajan, J. Park, E. Amaro, H. Sharma, A. Yazdanbakhsh, J. Kim, and H. Esmaeilzadeh, "Tabla: A unified template-based framework for accelerating statistical machine learning," 2016.

[34] S. Mehta, G. Beeraka, and P.-C. Yew, "Tile size selection revisited," *ACM Trans. Archit. Code Optim.*, vol. 10, no. 4, pp. 35:1–35:27, Dec. 2013.

[35] S. Mehta, Z. Fang, A. Zhai, and P.-C. Yew, "Multi-stage coordinated prefetching for present-day processors," in *Proceedings of the 28th ACM International Conference on Supercomputing*, ser. ICS '14. New York, NY, USA: ACM, 2014, pp. 73–82.

[36] S. Mehta, R. Garg, N. Trivedi, and P.-C. Yew, "Turbotiling: Leveraging prefetching to boost performance of tiled codes," in *Proceedings of the 2016 International Conference on Supercomputing*, ser. ICS '16. New York, NY, USA: ACM, 2016, pp. 38:1–38:12.

[37] T. C. Mowry, M. S. Lam, and A. Gupta, "Design and evaluation of a compiler algorithm for prefetching," in *Proceedings of the Fifth International Conference on Architectural Support for Programming Languages and Operating Systems*, ser. ASPLOS V. New York, NY, USA: ACM, 1992, pp. 62–73.

[38] O. Mutlu, J. Stark, C. Wilkerson, and Y. N. Patt, "Runahead execution: An alternative to very large instruction windows for out-of-order processors," in *Proceedings of the 9th International Symposium on High-Performance Computer Architecture*, ser. HPCA '03, Washington, DC, USA, 2003.

[39] D. Pandiyan, S.-Y. Lee, and C.-J. Wu, "Performance, energy characterizations and architectural implications of an emerging mobile platform benchmark suite - mobilebench," in *Workload Characterization (IISWC), 2013 IEEE International Symposium on*, Sept 2013, pp. 133–142.

[40] D. Povey, A. Ghoshal, G. Boulianne, L. Burget, O. Glembek, N. Goel, M. Hannemann, P. Motlicek, Y. Qian, P. Schwarz, J. Silovsky, G. Stemmer, and K. Vesely, "The kaldi speech recognition toolkit," in *IEEE 2011 Workshop on Automatic Speech Recognition and Understanding*. IEEE Signal Processing Society, 2011.

[41] S. W. Son, M. Kandemir, M. Karakoy, and D. Chakrabarti, "A compiler-directed data prefetching scheme for chip multiprocessors," in *Proceedings of the 14th ACM SIGPLAN Symposium on Principles and Practice of Parallel Programming*, ser. PPoPP '09. New York, NY, USA: ACM, 2009, pp. 209–218. [Online]. Available: http://doi.acm.org/10.1145/1504176.1504208

[42] S. T. Srinivasan, R. Rajwar, H. Akkary, A. Gandhi, and M. Upton, "Continual flow pipelines," in *Proceedings of the 11th International Conference on Architectural Support for Programming Languages and Operating Systems*, ser. ASPLOS XI. New York, NY, USA: ACM, 2004, pp. 107–119.

[43] Y. Taigman, M. Yang, M. Ranzato, and L. Wolf, "Deepface: Closing the gap to human-level performance in face verification," in *Computer Vision and Pattern Recognition (CVPR), 2014 IEEE Conference on*. IEEE, 2014, pp. 1701–1708.

[44] The-Guardian, "Why i have finally taken off the apple watch for the last time," 2016, Available at https://www.theguardian.com/technology/2016/jun/09/apple-watch-smartwatch.

[45] Z. Wang, D. Burger, K. S. McKinley, S. K. Reinhardt, and C. C. Weems, "Guided region prefetching: A cooperative hardware/software approach," in *Proceedings of the 30th Annual International Symposium on Computer Architecture*, ser. ISCA '03. New York, NY, USA: ACM, 2003, pp. 388–398.

[46] G. Yu and G. Sapiro, "Dct image denoising: a simple and effective image denoising algorithm," *Image Processing On Line*, vol. 108, 2011.

Energy Aware Persistence: Reducing Energy Overheads of Memory-based Persistence in NVMs

Sudarsun Kannan
College of Computing,
Georgia Tech
sudarsun@gatech.edu

Moinuddin Qureshi
School of ECE, Georgia Tech
moin@ece.gatech.edu

Ada Gavrilovska
College of Computing,
Georgia Tech
ada@cc.gatech.edu

Karsten Schwan
College of Computing,
Georgia Tech

ABSTRACT

Next generation byte addressable nonvolatile memories (NVMs) such as PCM, Memristor, and 3D X-Point are attractive solutions for mobile and other end-user devices, as they offer memory scalability as well as fast persistent storage. However, NVM's limitations of slow writes and high write energy are magnified for applications that require atomic, consistent, isolated and durable (ACID) persistence. For maintaining ACID persistence guarantees, applications not only need to do extra writes to NVM but also need to execute a significant number of additional CPU instructions for performing NVM writes in a transactional manner. Our analysis shows that maintaining persistence with ACID guarantees increases CPU energy up to 7.3x and NVM energy up to 5.1x compared to a baseline with no ACID guarantees. For computing platforms such as mobile devices, where energy consumption is a critical factor, it is important that the energy cost of persistence is reduced.

To address the energy overheads of persistence with ACID guarantees, we develop novel energy-aware persistence (EAP) principles that identify data durability (logging) as the dominant factor in energy increase. Next, for low energy states, we formulate energy efficient durability techniques that include a mechanism to switch between performance and energy efficient logging modes, support for NVM group commit, and a memory management method that reduces energy by trading capacity via less frequent garbage collection. For critical energy states, we propose a relaxed durability mechanism – ACI-RD – that relaxes data logging without affecting the correctness of an application. Finally, we evaluate EAP's principles with real applications and benchmarks. Our experimental results demonstrate up to 2x reduction in CPU and 2.4x reduction in NVM energy usage compared to the traditional ACID persistence.

1. INTRODUCTION

Industry announcements claim future byte addressable, nonvolatile memory (NVM) technologies like phase change memory (PCM) and 3D Xpoint [1] to have 100x lower access latency compared to that of Flash/SSD devices and to scale to 4-8 times the density of DRAM, without consuming refresh power. The promised outcomes include larger memory capacities [37] at lower energy usage [29] compared to DRAM, coupled with faster persistent data storage and access than Flash/SSD. Given this, current end-user devices such as smartphones, tablets, and laptops with limited DRAM capacity and slow flash storage [27] are an important target for NVM. Particularly attractive are the dual benefits of using NVM for higher memory capacity (volatile heap) and faster data persistence [29, 37, 23].

However, using NVM for persistence requires fail-safe guarantees from application or device failures. For example, when saving a user id (key) and password (value) into a persistent key-value store, a failure after updating the key, but before saving the password can result in an undesired state. To guard against such problems, applications must satisfy atomicity (A), consistency (C), isolation (I), and durability (D), also commonly referred to as ACID. In ACID, 'A' requires either all or none of the operations to complete in a transaction, whereas 'C' requires each update to convert persistent data from one consistent state to another. 'I' ensures concurrent updates are invisible to each other, and is realized through race free mechanisms and synchronization, and finally, 'D' requires that any changes to application data committed before a crash can be recovered, usually achieved by logging the updates.

Prior work has focused mainly on optimizing the performance of persistent storage that satisfies ACID properties by either treating NVM as a fast disk [36, 14, 12] or by using NVM as heap [39, 11, 35], also commonly referred to as memory-based persistence (hereafter simply **memory persistence**). In an NVM-as-a-disk approach, applications rely on the filesystem for ACID guarantees, whereas in memory persistence, applications use persistent allocators to allocate and update heap objects inside a transaction before committing them. The benefits of memory persistence over disk-based persistence has been widely studied for a broad range of applications such as key-value stores, persistent in-memory data structures, object-based storage, NoSQL and SQL database.

When using memory persistence, the correctness of an application is maintained by frequently flushing the application data and the related metadata, whereas durability is achieved by logging them. The metadata refers to information such as the state of a persistent allocator, and the data log headers. Consequently, supporting memory persistence not only increases the energy cost due to increase in NVM accesses but also increases the CPU instructions, hence resulting in a higher CPU energy use. Our analysis shows that memory persistence with ACID guarantees incurs a CPU energy increase of up to 7.3x and NVM energy increases of up to

PACT '16, September 11-15, 2016, Haifa, Israel

DOI: http://dx.doi.org/10.1145/2967938.2967953

5.1x compared to a baseline that does not maintain persistence. For computing platforms (such as mobile devices) where energy consumption is a critical factor, it is important that the energy cost of persistence is reduced.

To address this, we propose **energy-aware persistence** (EAP) as an essential element for deploying NVM in end-user devices. Prior work has sought to reduce the cost of consistent and durable memory persistence [42, 12, 35, 30] using performance-centric solutions. These solutions optimize the transactional component of the memory persistence without considering whether such optimizations address the durability- or correctness-related persistent costs. In contrast, EAP analyzes the energy implications of the correctness and durability software components in detail. Our analysis is the first to identify that durability (logging) costs are the most significant contributor to energy usage in an memory persistence, and to quantitatively demonstrate the significance of both NVM and CPU-related energy costs in the overall energy overheads of supporting persistence. EAP's energy reduction methods are applicable for other non-NVM storage mediums too. EAP leverages these observations to reduce the durability-related energy cost of ACID. The EAP design comprises of two parts, (i) energy efficient durability for low-but-not-critical energy states, and (ii) relaxed durability (ACI-RD) for critically low energy states. We next briefly introduce the key ideas of energy efficient durability and ACI-RD.

Energy efficient durability. Durability methods can be broadly classified into REDO and UNDO logging. In REDO, the application updates are first written to a log, and when the log is full, the log contents are committed to the original data location. This method is also referred to as Write-Ahead Logging (WAL). In contrast, for UNDO, the updates are committed in-place by first taking a backup of the original data. Most state-of-the-art memory persistence designs use WAL because UNDO doubles the required NVM updates in a transaction. However, as we show in Section 3, WAL is performance-efficient but consumes higher energy compared to the UNDO logging. We also show that persistent memory allocation and garbage collection have to be logged, and add a significant CPU and NVM energy cost. To address these issues, we first design energy efficient durability. The energy efficient durability method provides a mechanism to switch automatically between performance-efficient WAL and energy-efficient UNDO logging modes. Further, to reduce the allocation and garbage collection cost, the energy efficient durability reduces frequent allocation and garbage collection, and thereby trades additional NVM capacity use with lower energy cost.

Relaxed durability (ACI-RD). The energy efficient durability method is not sufficient when the energy availability is critical. For such energy critical states, we design ACI-RD, that relaxes the strict application data logging (D of ACID) requirements of a traditional ACID model, without impacting the correctness (ACI) of an application. Although ACI-RD weakens the durability guarantees and increases the application recovery time after a failure, we show that by careful design, energy consumption can be significantly reduced without weakening the correctness property of ACID. Figure 1 provides a high-level timing diagram comparing a traditional ACID vs. our ACI-RD design. In the ACID case, after application execution, both application data, and metadata are ordered, flushed and logged. In contrast, with EAP, when energy is critically low, data durability is relaxed for application data, but not for its metadata, thus maintaining the ACI properties essential for correct operation after a failure.

EAP uses an epoch-based execution model, where the target energy level at the start of each epoch drives the choices of suitable alternatives by dynamically measuring the durability-related energy

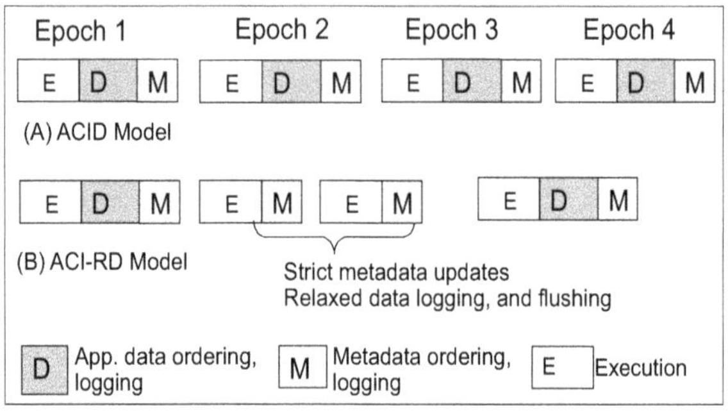

Figure 1: (A) Traditional ACID epoch execution, (B) ACID-RD: Data logging relaxed for critically low energy Epoch 2,3

of each ACID stack component. If the energy budget is low-but-not critical, EAP just uses the efficient durability, but when the energy is critically low, EAP combines the efficient durability methods with ACID-RD by relaxing the durability guarantees.

We implement EAP's software-based efficient durability and ACI-RD methods by extending Intel's NVML [21] open source persistence library. Our evaluations using different memory persistence benchmarks and applications show that EAP's efficient durability for low energy state reduces NVM and CPU energy usage by up to 28% and 41%, respectively. By combining efficient durability with ACI-RD for critical energy states, EAP achieves up to 2.1x and 2.4x CPU and NVM energy reduction, respectively.

In summary, this paper makes the following contributions:

- *Durability cost.* We quantify data durability as the key source of energy bottlenecks for applications with memory persistence with ACID guarantees (Section 3).
- *Energy efficient durability.* To reduce durability-related energy overheads, we propose energy efficient principles that trade off performance and capacity for energy, support flexible logging, and NVM group commit methods when the available budget is low (Section 4).
- *Epoch-based relaxed durability (ACI-RD).* For critically low energy budgets, we design a novel ACI-RD model that relaxes data durability based on the energy usage in each epoch, without affecting application correctness (Section 5).
- *Experimental evaluation.* We evaluate EAP with realistic benchmarks and applications and demonstrate the substantial benefits of EAP (Section 6).

In the rest of the paper, Section 2 discusses the background of the memory-based persistence and the related work, Section 3 analyzes the energy overheads of different memory persistence software components such as cache flush and logging required for providing memory persistence. Section 4 discusses the energy efficient durability principles for low-but-not-critical energy budget. Section 5 describes the ACI-RD design and implementation details for critically low energy budget. Section 6 presents the evaluation methodology, and the energy benefits and implications of the proposed EAP design, followed by the conclusion in Section 7

2. BACKGROUND AND RELATED WORK

Byte-addressable NVMs. NVMs such as PCM are byte-addressable persistent devices expected to be 100x faster (read-write performance) compared to current SSDs [12, 14, 8]. Further, NVM can scale 2x-4x higher density than DRAM [1] as they can store multiple bits per cell with no refresh power, with known limitations imposed by an endurance of a few million writes per cell. These attributes make NVM a suitable candidate for replacing SSDs. Additionally, NVM can be extended as a memory placed in parallel with DRAM, connected via the memory bus. NVMs offer load/store access interface that can potentially avoid POSIX-based block access supported in current storage devices. NVMs' read latency is comparable to DRAM latency, but the write latency is 5x-10x slower due to high SET times [28], and more importantly, the active write energy is 15-40x higher than DRAM [41, 28].

NVM usage models. One usage model is to treat DRAM as a cache for NVM, while also providing a file system interface, such as in [37]. However, with this usage mode, supporting persistence with ACID guarantees can be expensive because the data needs to be flushed and moved to multiple levels (processor cache to DRAM to NVM) before committing it to NVM. Moneta [8], BPFS [12], and PMFS [14] address this by designing a new filesystem for NVM that does not use DRAM as a cache, and provides direct access to NVM. Although the I/O performance improves with these filesystems, the use of the block-based POSIX I/O operations such as *read(), write()* require frequent user-to-kernel transitions.

An alternative usage model is to provide applications with a byte-level access to NVM. This reduces the user-to-kernel transition and the kernel-level filesystem cost. POSIX already provides a byte-level access to a persistent storage device via memory-mapped (*mmap()*) interface. But *mmap()* is coarse grained and inflexible [11, 35, 23, 25], and it does not provide ACID guarantees [14]. Prior research addresses these issues by designing a persistent object store [39, 11, 21] for NVM that provides a byte addressable load-store interface. The object store also provides a persistent memory allocator and transactional persistence support. In EAP, **we use the persistent object store model** and address the energy overheads of persistence.

Durability and consistency. The processor cache can buffer writes and significantly reduce the impact of high NVM write latency. Current OSes and architectures use a write-back cache model in which the cache lines can be evicted in any order. However, for guaranteeing ACID properties in persistent storage, writes to NVM must be ordered for preserving the application correctness [35, 30]. For example, committing the metadata before committing the original data can be dangerous. The prior research uses a write-through cache model [39] with an epoch-based cache eviction [12] supported by memory barriers or introduces a persistent processor cache. Besides the write ordering issues, data durability can be affected due to a power failure that destroys the cached data, resulting in a non-deterministic state. Although applications can flush the cache to reduce non-recoverable failures, for ACID guarantees, other mechanisms such as logging (e.g., UNDO or REDO) are required. However, frequent cache flushes and logging are expensive.

Reducing ACID overheads on performance. Recent research such as [42, 23, 35, 43, 30] have proposed both hardware and software methods to reduce NVM overheads while preserving ACID. They have also considered relaxed consistency models [35, 30] that do not impact application performance. A recent research, persistent hardware transactional memory (PHTM) [7] analyzes the benefits of supporting persistence for the transactional memory hardware when providing strict ACID guarantees. PHTM's hardware extension improves parallelism and transaction performance resulting in application speedup. However, even with the hardware extension, results show up to 5x slowdown for supporting strict ACID guarantees compared to no ACID support. In contrast, EAP aims to reduce the number of CPU instructions, NVM accesses, and energy, by optimizing and relaxing strict ACID guarantees without impacting the correctness of an application. More importantly, EAP does not require hardware changes. We believe its software methods are complementary to the hardware extensions.

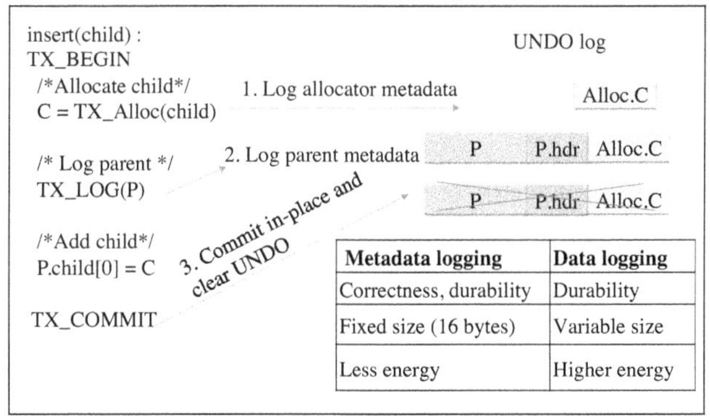

Figure 2: Software NVM memory persistence. The figure shows steps for inserting a child node to a persistent B-tree inside a transaction, including allocator metadata and data logging.

NVM-based memory persistence. Recent research has extensively explored memory persistence for NVMs with ACID guarantees [39, 11]. Support for memory persistence requires application-level changes, and the objects made persistent have to be logged either with a UNDO log or with a write-ahead log (WAL). In contrast, the disk-based persistence used in prior database research [36, 6] log the entire page even when a word in the page changes.

To provide a background of how memory persistence works, Figure 2 shows an example of inserting a new node to a persistent B-tree inside a software transaction. First, a new child node is allocated using the persistent memory allocator and the allocator metadata (Alloc.C) for this child node is logged. Second, before adding the child node to the parent, the parent is backed into an UNDO log. The backup involves first writing the parent node (P) – considered as an application data – to the UNDO log, followed by a header of the application data (P.hdr) – considered as the application metadata. After UNDO logging, the parent pointer to the child node is updated, and when the transaction successfully commits, the UNDO logs (application data and metadata) are cleared. In the event of a failure before a transaction commit, the application metadata (P.hdr) is used to UNDO any data changes and restore the parent (P) to a state before the child node was added, using the UNDO log. The allocator metadata (Alloc.C) is used for the garbage collection of the allocated memory for the child node. Note that the metadata (Alloc.C and P.hdr) is required for correctness of the application and is typically much smaller (16B) than the data, thus requiring much lower energy costs during updates. We target applications which, as in this example, require memory persistence, and we focus on reducing the energy costs associated with providing ACID requirements in memory persistence.

Memory persistence libraries. Prior work has developed memory persistence libraries that include Mnemosyne [39], NV-Heaps [11], NVML [21], and Atlas [9]. Both Mnemosyne and NV-Heaps use transactional memory persistence, and differ in the granularity of logging (word versus object). Atlas, a recent work, differs from prior work by providing semantics for locking-based persistence in contrast to transactional memory persistence. While implementations such as NV-Heaps and Atlas are not openly available, Mnemosyne's legacy user-level Intel STM libraries are no longer functional. Also, Mnemosyne's OS component suffers significant cache overhead [24]. Hence, in this work, we use the NVML library from Intel for its comprehensive memory persistence implementation, SNIA compatibility, and architecture-specific optimizations. Other persistent allocators such as NVMAlloc [31], nvm_malloc [38], and NVMMalloc [40] only provide ACID guarantees for the allocator, but not for the transactional updates important for persistence. We also demonstrate EAP's generic principles for other well-known applications such as SQLite [5], and Snappy compression [16].

Relaxing persistence. To reduce persistence overheads, Pelly et al. [35] propose a consistency model that allows reordering between one or more independent transactions for better concurrency. Reordering is done only for writes to the cache, whereas writes to the NVM from the cache are ordered. This approach constitutes a variation of the epoch-based consistency model that requires hardware and software changes for reordering writes. Y. Lu et al. [30] propose a loose ordering consistency (LOC) protocol for relaxing intra- and inter-transaction ordering. In their approach, the log area is divided into blocks of 64 bytes with one metadata header for seven blocks. Committing log data in block-groups avoids repeated metadata update. After a failure, the consistency is validated using the group-level metadata. LOC assumes the presence of a nonvolatile cache. FIRM [43] improves persistent storage performance by adding intelligence to the memory controller for prioritizing persistent data updates over non-persistent data updates. All of the above proposals require hardware and software modification. A recent software-only solution, NVRAMDB [36], uses NVM as a disk for page-based persistence and proposes performance optimizations specifically for databases. NVRAMDB uses a batched/group commit that first copies the original data to a UNDO rollback/recovery log, then buffers multiple transactions in a DRAM buffer, and finally, it commits all the buffered data to NVM. Although this approach improves the throughput, it does not change the total data logged to NVM. In fact, by buffering transactions in DRAM and then copying to NVM, this solution consumes additional CPU and DRAM energy. In contrast, we propose a group commit update customized for memory persistence that reduces energy use.

EAP versus prior work. EAP differs from the work reviewed above [35, 30, 43, 36] in several ways. (1) EAP identifies and addresses the ACID software components that increase energy. (2) Other than NVM support, EAP does not require additional hardware changes. (3) Prior work principally seeks improvements in application performance, a case in point being the lazy asynchronous, or relaxed atomicity and ordering in [30] and [35]. Using such methods changes when certain actions are taken, but they do not reduce the total CPU instructions or NVM accesses. As a result, prior research does not directly reduce the persistence-related energy consumption. (4) EAP's relaxed durability model is designed for memory persistence where it is important to classify data and metadata for maintaining correctness of the heap and the application state, unlike [35]. Finally, (5) our mechanisms are driven by the current energy availability, with flexibility to switch between the performance and energy efficient modes.

3. DECONSTRUCTING ACID ENERGY COST

To understand the energy costs of memory persistence, we analyze the CPU and NVM energy usage of correctness and durability ACID components. We use the analysis to formulate EAP's energy efficient durability principles and ACI-RD design. All our memory persistence applications use only the NVM [32] as opposed to a DRAM-NVM hybrid model. We report the increase in CPU instructions, NVM writes, and CPU and NVM energy. For NVM energy, we use the PCM energy prediction values as discussed in [28] with a 36x higher active write energy compared to DRAM. Although we use PCM for analysis, EAP's software principles are generic with its main focus toward reducing the necessary parameters such as CPU and NVM use. To validate the benefits of EAP's principles for other competing NVM technologies such as STT-RAM (only 5-10x higher write energy than DRAM), in Section 6, we run the same applications only on DRAM, and measure the full system energy using a power meter.

3.1 Component-level energy analysis

For memory persistence with ACID guarantees, multiple user-level and system-level software components are required. The user-level components include the actual application code, the persistent allocation and garbage collection component, and the transaction component with logging support. System-level components can be a persistent filesystem or persistent memory management mechanisms [11, 23], each maintaining ACID properties for their internal system-level persistent data and metadata structures.

Model. The total energy consumed by a persistent application is the sum of energy used by each of the ACID components that order, flush, fence, and log their states. Our energy-aware optimizations, therefore, address these components and their joint operation. Stated more precisely and focusing on the major contributors of energy consumption – CPU and NVM, the following simple equations denote the total energy used by an application.

$$\left.\begin{aligned} E_{total} &= E_{APP} + E_{datlog} + E_{metalog} + E_{flush} \\ EA = E_{datlog} + E_{metalog} + E_{flush} &= E_{total} - E_{APP} \\ EA &= EA_{CPU} + EA_{NVM} \end{aligned}\right\} \quad (1)$$

E_{APP} denotes energy without ACID, E_{flush} - the energy from cache flush, fence and drain, E_{datlog} - the energy from data logging, $E_{metalog}$ - the energy from metadata logging, and EA - the energy for maintaining ACID guarantees.

NVM emulation and analysis approach. We use an x86 Haswell desktop system running Linux 3.9.4 kernel. The system has a 32KB L1 and 4MB LLC write-back cache, Intel 520 120GB flash memory, and 4GB of DDR3-based DRAM, of which we use 2GB for NVM by mounting the PMFS filesystem [14]. Because byte addressable NVMs such as PCM are not commercially available, to emulate NVM's read and write latency, we inject software delays similar to most of the prior NVM research [39, 11]. Our emulator periodically gets the total load and store cache misses (every 100ms) using the RDTSCP synchronous instruction as a timer with +-20ns accuracy. It uses the delay model proposed by Dulloor et al. [14] to emulate 100ns load and 400ns store latency. For the CPU and NVM energy, we use the RAPL support [18] to first measure the CPU and DRAM energy consumption, and then use the LLC cache misses due to load and store instructions to estimate the NVM energy usage based on the read and write energy values discussed in [28]. In Section 6, we describe the details of our dynamic energy estimation method. We focus our analysis on the fundamental elements necessary for performance and energy such as the increase in CPU instructions and NVM accesses from memory persistence with ACID guarantees. In Section 6, we show that our analysis and solutions are applicable even when the NVM latency and energy cost are same as DRAM.

We extend and optimize the SNIA standard-based [4] NVML library from Intel [21]. NVML already supports transactional object persistence, persistent memory allocations, logging, and persistent barrier. The persistent objects are stored in a large memory-mapped region managed by the PMFS filesystem. NVML provides an API for an UNDO log, as shown in Figure 2, and rolls back failed transactions. We also extend NVML with a support for WAL-based logging. Further, each persistent object has a different virtual address but one unique identifier across application restarts. The unique identifier is used for loading the object from a persistent region.

Applications. Table 1 shows the end-user-centric persistence bench-

Applications	Description	Workload
RB-tree [21]	Red-black trees (cache & memory inefficient)	500K random insert, read, delete operations
B-tree [21]	Persistence-friendly, balance search tree used in databases, software cache etc.	Same as RB-tree
KV-store	Simple key-value store using persistent hashmap	Same as RB-tree
SQLite [5]	Database used extensively in end-user devices	500K operations of SQLite benchmark [15]
Snappy [16]	Fast compression library used in chrome and other Google products. We ported it with memory persistence	1.5GB of image, video, audio, document files
JPEG [3]	Well know image conversion service that we ported with memory-based persistence	40K JPEG images converted to bitmap format

Table 1: Applications.

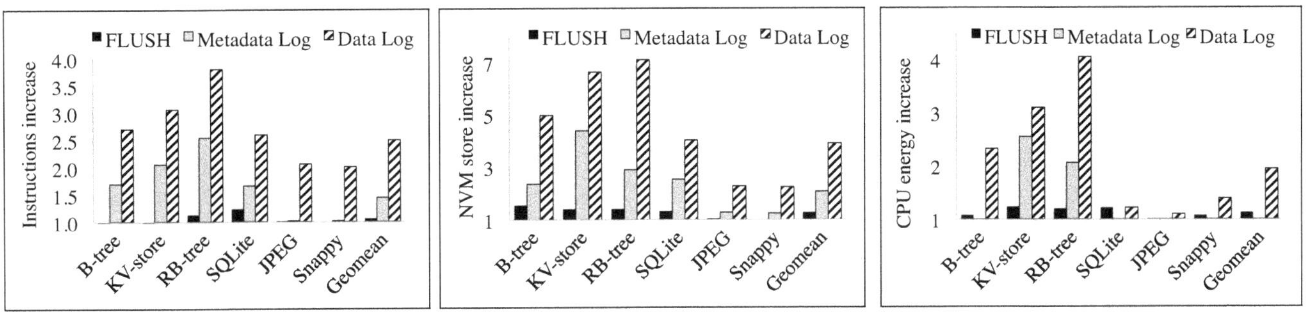

(a) CPU instructions increase. (b) NVM stores increase. (c) CPU energy increase.

Figure 3: ACID cost analysis. Bars show cost of each component. Y-axis shows increase factor relative to No-ACID as the baseline.

marks [30] and applications used in prior studies [30, 23].
(1) B-tree (balance search tree) is a well-known persistence-efficient data structure extensively used in databases, large graph libraries, and also for memory management [21]. B-tree has an O(log n) update or search worst case complexity, and O(n) space complexity. Each B-tree node can have one or many child nodes which reduce the depth of the B-tree. The parent and child nodes can fit inside one cache line reducing the overall cache misses. However, node additions and deletions require re-balancing the tree. Consequently, a memory persistence implementation has to log and commit the changes inside a transaction, and the cost of persistence increases the energy cost significantly.
(2) RB-tree (red-black tree) is extensively used for in-memory data structures inside the OS with an O(log n) insert and O(n) worst-case space complexity. RB-trees are both memory and persistence inefficient because every update to a tree node results in flushing and logging both the parent node and its two child pointers.
(3) A key-value store (KV-store), like those used as a data cache in both end-user and server platforms, is designed using a persistent hashtable. For adding a KV-store entry, first, a hash entry, a key, and its value are allocated using a persistent memory allocator, and the allocations are logged (metadata logging). Next, the data of the key, value and the hash entry pointers are updated and logged. Hence, the persistent KV-store also has a high ACID persistence cost.
(4) The SQLite database is widely used in end-user platforms. It supports both write-ahead logging (WAL), journaling and rollback (referred to as UNDO in this paper). We use the existing in-memory database and logging feature of SQLite with page-based (as opposed to an object-based) persistence to avoid significant code changes to the application.
Finally, we use (5) Google's Snappy object compression library, and (6) JPEG – an image conversion library widely used across different OSes.

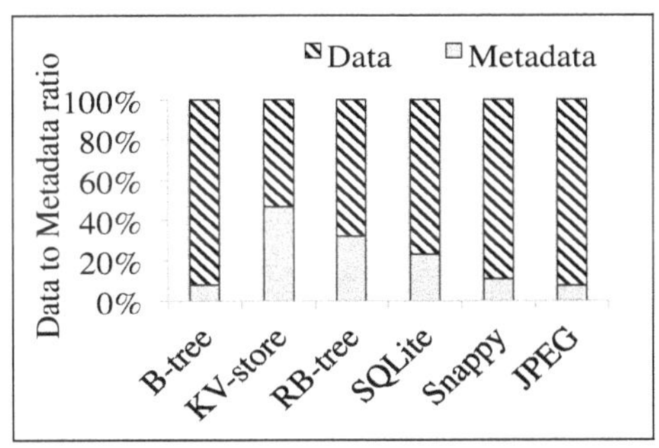

Figure 5: Total data vs. metadata log size ratio.

Analysis. Figures 3.(a)-(c) show the increase in CPU instructions, NVM writes, and CPU energy for applications listed on the x-axis compared to the No-ACID approach that does not offer correctness or durability guarantees. The FLUSH bar refers to persistent barrier cost that includes cache flush and memory ordering (fence and drain operations) instructions [4]. Metadata and Data Log refer to the application and allocator metadata, and data logging cost, respectively.

As the graphs show, supporting ACID for NVM memory persistence increases CPU instructions, NVM accesses, and energy significantly, with durability (metadata and data logging) dominating the cost. The overall CPU energy increases by up to 6.1x for RB-tree of which the data logging alone adds 4.1x overheads. The NVM store increase also shows a similar trend but with even higher overheads. For instance, both RB-tree and KV-store incur 7x more NVM writes. It is important to note that, for KV-store, the metadata to data size ratio is higher compared to all the other application benchmarks as shown in Figure 5. This is primarily due to higher persistent memory allocation and garbage collection cost including the application metadata cost for the reasons we discussed earlier. Therefore, the metadata-related CPU energy and NVM stores in-

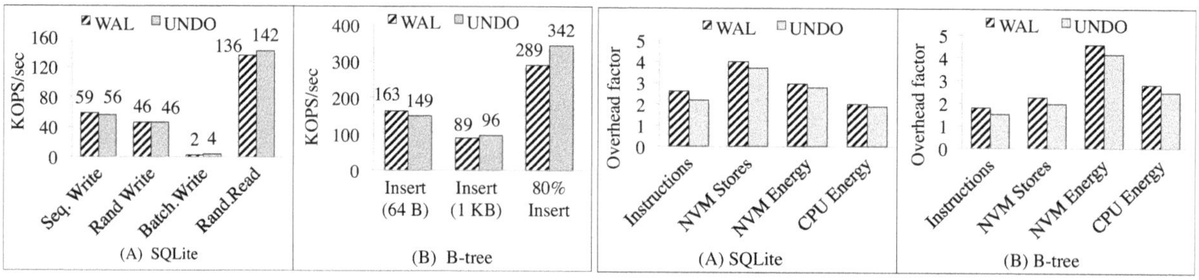

(a) WAL vs. UNDO Kilo operations/second for access patterns.

(b) WAL vs. UNDO Instruction, CPU energy, NVM access. Y-axis is overhead increase factor relative to No-ACID.

Figure 4: WAL vs. UNDO performance and energy comparison.

crease by 2.5x and 3.72x, respectively. Snappy and JPEG have relatively lower metadata logging cost as they process less than 50K files. In contrast, the data logging cost is high mainly from logging large multimedia objects.

3.2 Deciphering durability costs

We next analyze the sources of application data and metadata logging costs. We use the resulting insights to formulate a set of EAP principles for reducing energy usage.

Logging methods. Prior research on NVM memory persistence have used either (1) UNDO (refers to journaling) logging [11] or (2) write-ahead logging (WAL) [39]. Also, to exploit byte addressing capability, the memory persistence research use word or object-based logging unlike page-based logging in disk-based systems. We next discuss the energy implications of such logging methods.

UNDO vs. WAL logging for memory persistence. When using UNDO logging, the original data is backed to a journal (log) in the NVM before modifying the data in-place. After a transaction commits successfully, the log is discarded, or else, if the transaction aborts or if the system fails, the backed up log is used to revert the intermediate updates. Although UNDO requires double writes to NVM for each transaction – first to UNDO journal, and then to actual data address, it allows in-place writes and read-after-writes. In contrast, WAL reduces the double write bottleneck by first appending updates directly to the log, and when the log space runs out, it checkpoints the log contents to the original data location. However, because updates are not in-place, subsequent writes and read-after-writes inside a transaction have to be redirected to a log. To read from the log, WAL maintains an index to locate and fetch the latest version. WAL, therefore, sequentially appends writes, which can improve performance and concurrency for large multi-core systems with write-intensive workloads. However, for read-intensive workloads, access redirections can be expensive in terms of CPU instructions and NVM accesses. Additionally, sequential updates are significantly beneficial for disks, but the gains are limited for NVMs [32, 14]. Redirecting every access to a log can result in significant code changes, eliminating the use of the byte-addressable load-store interface.

As discussed by [32, 14], another drawback of WAL for large data updates is that the fixed size log buffers have to be frequently truncated, and their contents have to be checkpointed to the original data location. Checkpoints require parsing the log records sequentially and copying multiple versions of the same data to the original location. Although the updates are faster with WAL log appends, eventually all log entries should be committed, and hence this does not change the total CPU instructions or NVM access. These issues are relevant for page-based logging mechanisms too [33, 10].

Analysis. We analyze the performance and energy impact of UNDO and WAL logging for the B-tree benchmark that uses NVML's object-based memory persistence, and for SQLite that uses page-based persistence. The system setup and NVM emulation are same as discussed earlier. Figure 4a compares the performance (throughput) of WAL and UNDO for B-tree and SQLite. The y-axis represents thousands of operations per second, and the x-axis shows different access patterns. For small sequential, write-intensive workload as in the case of SQLite and All-insert for B-tree, WAL performs marginally better than UNDO. However, for the read-intensive workload (20% writes, 80% reads) and large data updates for B-tree, the UNDO performance is better, and large SQLite updates show similar trends. Next, regarding the energy use, Figure 4b shows the increase in CPU instructions, NVM writes, and energy for SQLite and B-tree when using WAL and UNDO. The y-axis shows the increase factor compared to the No-ACID (and no logging). The y-axis values are for an entire benchmark (cumulative) run with different access patterns. We observe that, compared to WAL, UNDO logging reduces CPU instructions, NVM writes and energy usage for both B-tree and SQLite. *In short, the performance and energy of logging methods vary based on the workload and implementation. Hence, a mechanism that can switch between energy and performance modes is important.*

Metadata durability cost. Concerning the energy overheads associated with the metadata persistence, the persistent memory allocators' state has to be logged for correctness and durability, which can increase the energy use for applications that frequently allocate and deallocate data structures (e.g., KV-store, B-tree). Our prior research [23] proposes an NVM write-aware allocator that reduces NVM writes by placing complex allocator data structures in DRAM and just maintaining a log of all allocations in the NVM. However, even with this approach, for small and frequent NVM allocations, logging and flushing the allocator state can become expensive, especially when the *metadata/data* ratio increases. As a result, the CPU instructions, NVM accesses, and metadata-related energy cost increase.

4. ENERGY EFFICIENT ACID PRINCIPLES

Based on the insights gained from the analysis of memory persistence ACID overheads, we next formulate a set of energy efficient durability (logging) principles. The principles discussed are the first step towards energy reduction under low-but-not-critical energy budgets for end-user devices. In the next section, we propose a relaxed durability model (ACI-RD) for critically low energy state.

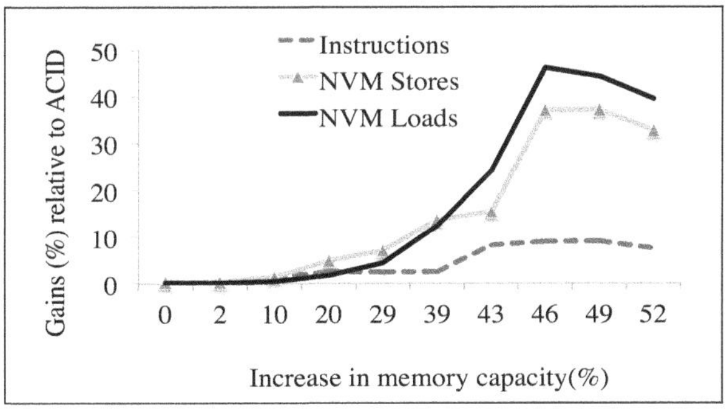

Figure 6: B-tree: y-axis shows the gains relative to ACID by trading memory capacity (x-axis in %).

Instructions	NVM Loads	NVM Stores
11.86%	9.28%	10.68%

Table 2: SQLite gains from trading 35% higher capacity.

4.1 Flexible logging

As discussed in Section 3, although WAL provides marginally higher throughput compared to the UNDO log method for small updates and write-intensive workloads, it increases CPU and NVM energy usage for large and read-intensive workloads.

Key idea. Motivated by these observations, EAP provides a dynamic logging mechanism that transparently switches to an energy-aware logging mode (WAL to UNDO, and vice versa). When energy is not a constraint, applications start with WAL as a default logging mode. At fixed time intervals (epochs), the logging library measures the available energy budget. When energy availability becomes limited, the library switches to UNDO logging. The dynamic switch from WAL to UNDO is initiated only for new transactions because splitting the log for a dirty and uncommitted transaction across WAL and UNDO is suboptimal for logging and recovery. Additionally, all the pending WAL transactions (including nested transactions) are committed before the switch. These restrictions simplify code changes required for SQLite to support EAP's energy-aware methods. We evaluate the additional energy overheads of frequent switching due to small epochs in Section 6.

4.2 Gain energy by trading capacity

We next discuss the principles for reducing persistent memory management energy costs by trading capacity when energy availability is limited.

Reduce allocator work. Modern DRAM and persistent memory allocators strive to provide fast allocation and reduce memory fragmentation. They maintain memory object slabs of different sizes (generally in powers of two), and service request from the slabs. To align requests to the nearest slab, allocators frequently perform complex operations such as merging multiple small objects. When ineffective, they request the OS (via *mmap()* or *break()*) to allocate a batch of pages, and these operations consume significant CPU energy. Requests for a smaller batch result in frequent OS requests, whereas larger batch increases memory fragmentation. The persistent allocator state must also be persisted, which adds to the energy cost. Hence, to reduce energy (and instructions and NVM accesses) usage, EAP's energy efficient durability trades off capacity by using large OS allocations (64MB) only when there is an energy constraint. Consequently, complex merge operations are avoided, reducing CPU work and energy.

Reduce garbage collection overheads. More than the memory allocation, the cost of persistent memory garbage collection is even higher. Most garbage collection methods use a 'mark and sweep' approach (mark, and then delete objects). Prior research have analyzed the performance overheads of DRAM-based garbage collection in end-user devices [34] and server machines [19]. For NVMs, the allocator-related persistence cost is even higher because the allocator has to persist (and log) the allocator state for deletion (*free()*) before requesting the OS to release memory pages using an expensive *munmap()* call. Hence, when the energy is a constraint, EAP delays the garbage collection, and therefore, trades NVM capacity for reduced energy consumption, without affecting the correctness. Garbage collection is delayed only until the system swapping threshold is reached. We modify the persistent memory allocator to mark the objects for deletion but to free them only when the available free NVM capacity is below a threshold. We extend this to the OS-level garbage collection for delaying the release of application heap pages by setting a special one-bit page flag.

Analysis. Figure 6 shows the combined effects of energy efficient allocation and delayed garbage collection. The results show reduced NVM load-store accesses and CPU instructions compared to the memory persistence with traditional ACID approach (y-axis in %). The x-axis indicates the increase in NVM usage as a trade-off for energy. Trading off capacity reduces allocator and garbage collection cost thereby reducing CPU instructions and NVM access. It is important to note that the reduction in NVM accesses is higher compared to the decrease in CPU instructions because recycling objects requires several expensive *memset()*, *memcopy()*, and FLUSH operations. Beyond 45% increase in the capacity, the gains reduce because, after reaching the swap threshold, both the persistent memory allocator and the OS have to release memory aggressively. These actions increase the overall work done by both the allocator and the OS, thereby increasing the total CPU instructions and NVM accesses. Furthermore, a subtle but important reason is that the library allocator maintains all objects as nodes in a B-tree, and their lookup or update time increases as we delay the garbage collection. We observe similar trends for SQLite (see Table 2), but the benefits are lower due to a custom page-management.

4.3 Memory persistence group commit

Transactional updates with persistence barriers can be expensive. Grouping smaller transactions into a larger one, referred to as group commit protocol in databases and filesystems [17] is a well-known technique. NVRAMDB mentioned in Section 2 uses a group commit protocol that buffers updates in DRAM and lazily commits logs and data to NVM [36]. However, NVRAMDB is a performance-centric approach and lacks energy awareness. It increases CPU instructions and accesses to DRAM and NVM by adding a DRAM buffer. Instead, we propose an energy-aware group commit protocol for memory persistence.

Key idea. In a traditional ACID design, a persistence barrier (FLUSH for application data including log [36]) is applied twice, once to the UNDO log before an update, and once to the original data after an in-place update. In contrast, in EAP, we apply barriers only twice in a group of transactions instead of every transaction. The first barrier is used when an object is modified for the first time in a group, and the next barrier when the entire group commits. Also, unlike NVRAMDB [36], our design does not buffer the log updates in DRAM but creates a clean, separate undo log when an object is updated for the first time in a transaction group. For subsequent transactions, logging and in-place updates happen without persistence barriers. Figure 7 shows the pseudocode for inserting a node in B-tree. Before the parent node pointers are updated, an UNDO log is created for every child (update or delete operations). For a

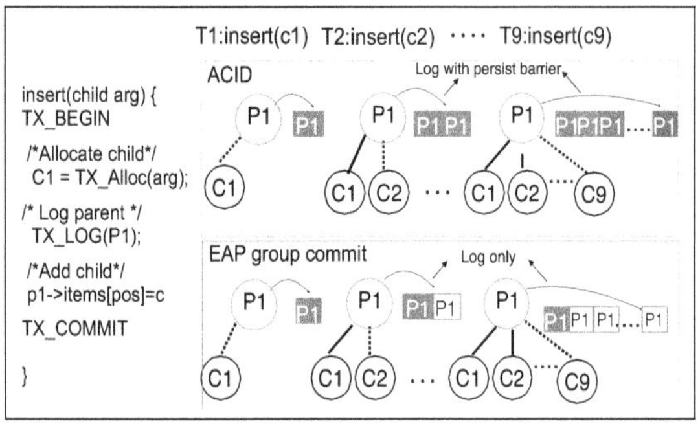

Figure 7: Memory persistence group commit. Circles P, C represent B-tree parent and child nodes. Shaded and non-shaded P1 squares indicate UNDO log with and without persistence barriers, respectively.

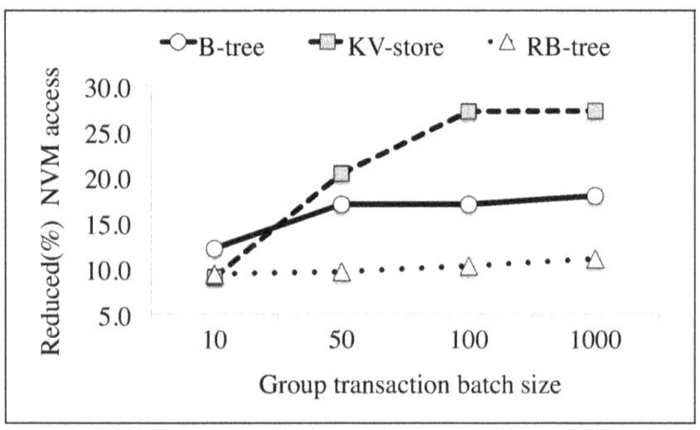

Figure 8: Impact of group commit batch size. Higher object reaccess reduces NVM access.

transaction batch size nine in this example, the persistence barrier for the parent node (P1) is only applied for T1 and T9. If a failure or abort occurs before the group commit, all the updates inside a batch are reverted using the UNDO log. This guarantee of "all or none" is same as the prior group commit approach. We implement this by adding a single bit to the object's allocator metadata and setting the flag first time an object is modified inside a group and resetting the flag when the entire group commits. Figure 8 shows the impact of transaction batch size in the x-axis. Intuitively, the benefits are higher for objects that are repeatedly accessed in the same group. B-tree benefits by reducing the redundant barriers for the parent node when multiple new child nodes are inserted, whereas in the KV-store, repeated barriers for parent hashtable structure is avoided. The energy impact is minimal for RB-tree with fewer reaccess. Hence limiting the group transaction size to increase reaccess per batch is important.

Atomic commits. New persistent memory-specific x86 atomic instructions such as CLWB for cache line write-back without invalidation but ordered store fences, PCOMMIT for non-temporal stores, and CLFLUSHOPT for optimized cache line flush [20] can reduce CPU instruction and NVM access cost by avoiding the need to log values smaller than 64 bytes. This can significantly reduce the metadata logging cost and the data logging cost for small updates.

5. RELAXED DURABILITY – ACI-RD

When the energy budget is critically low, the efficient durability principles discussed in the previous section are not sufficient. In other words, always using a strict ACID approach for end-user devices can substantially drain the battery power preventing an application from running to completion. This impacts the target memory persistence application, as well as other background applications.

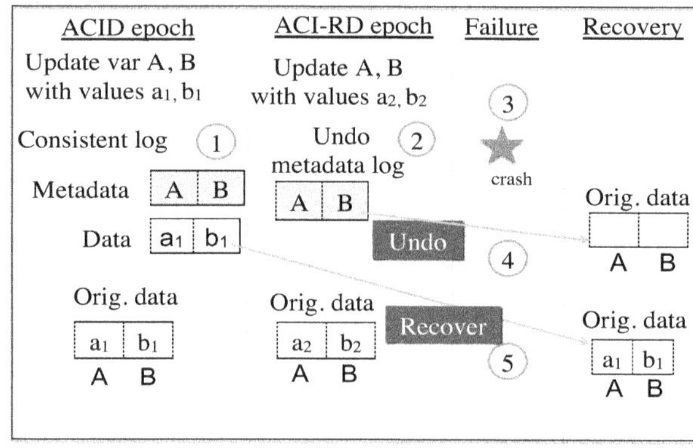

Figure 9: ACI-RD steps. ACI-RD used for critical low energy state.

Key Idea. In memory persistence, all application state, including object data, its metadata (object headers), and library metadata (persistent memory allocator state) is logged to a consistent log. In the group commit approach discussed earlier, the metadata and data logs are written for each transaction, and only persistence barriers are relaxed in a group. For critical energy states, when such optimizations are insufficient, we propose a relaxed durability model – ACI-RD. ACI-RD reduces the frequency of logging by increasing the interval between data logging, but without delaying the application, allocator, and the library metadata logging, critical for the correctness of an application. When ACI-RD is enabled, the metadata is updated to a separate UNDO log used only during ACI-RD. Further, an application can transition from a strict ACID phase to ACI-RD phase, and vice versa, depending on the available energy. We refer to each phase as an 'epoch', corresponding to a fixed time interval during which either an ACID or ACI-RD is used. As discussed in Section 2, prior performance-centric delayed durability methods reduce logging cost by buffering log writes in DRAM and eventually writing them to the NVM. However, they do not reduce the overall CPU instructions, NVM writes and the energy usage. In contrast, EAP, to address critical energy state, writes only the metadata log to UNDO thereby reducing NVM writes, CPU instructions, and energy, without compromising the correctness.

Why to use a separate ACI-RD metadata UNDO log? The use of a separate UNDO log for metadata updates during an ACI-RD epoch is critical for application correctness. In the event of a failure, all metadata updates in the UNDO log are used to revert updates during an ACI-RD epoch, and restore the last checkpoint state where both data and metadata were made durable in a consistent log. Specifically, for memory persistence, the UNDO log contains both application- and library-related metadata and provides information for garbage collection of memory allocated in an ACI-RD epoch. Further, the UNDO log clearly segregates the consistent updates in the ACID epoch from the relaxed updates in the ACI-RD epoch. The separate log avoids the need to parse the entire log sequentially and classify the ACID and ACI-RD updates.

Transition from ACI-RD to ACID. During the transition to ACID, EAP first enables load and store fences, flushes all data updates from the cache lines, followed by all metadata updates, and finally, issues a load and store fence, so as to guarantee that all updates from the previous ACI-RD epoch are complete. This provides the same correctness guarantees as ACID. In-flight errors can exist in both ACID or ACI-RD, and can be avoided if the future hardware provides an acknowledgment upon a successful write [8].

ACID-RD steps. Figure 9 shows the update and recovery steps for two variables A and B, for both ACID and ACI-RD epochs. When

```
for each epoch do
    if energy_save_mode = true then
        /*EAP-ACID (efficient durability)*/
        Switch to undo logging
        Apply EAP batch allocation
        Apply EAP delayed garbage collection
        Apply group commit transactions
        Find ΔTrans_epoch from Equation 3
        if ΔTrans_epoch <= 0 then
            continue;
        end
        if energy_critical = true then
            if commit.size < cacheline.size then
                atomic commit;
            end
            if ΔTrans_epoch > 0 || commit.size > maxsize then
                /* ACI-RD epoch */
                Apply fence
                Update data in-place, FLUSH, drain
                Log metadata to UNDO log
                For transaction commit, return special code
            end
        end
    end
end
```

Algorithm 1: EAP efficient durability and ACI-RD steps.

the variables A and B are updated with values a_1 and b_1 in an ACID epoch with no energy constraints in ①, both data (a_1, b_1), and the metadata (address of A, B, and size of update) are written to a consistent log. When the energy becomes a constraint, in ②, ACI-RD is enabled. In this case, for updates of the variables A and B with values a_2 and b_2 only the metadata (A, B address, and update size) is written to the ACI-RD UNDO log. The data is updated in-place with FLUSH or atomic updates, if applicable. If a failure happens as in ③, first the updates to A and B are reverted using the metadata log as shown in ④, and then the consistent data log is used to restore the previous values a_1 and b_1. The result of this mechanism is a trade-off between durability (D in ACID) and energy, without compromising application correctness.

Intuitively, as the ACI-RD epoch time interval increases, the size of the total data that is not made durable increases. Hence, a failure during the ACI-RD epoch increases restart cost. More formally, as shown in Equation 2, after a failure in the ACI-RD epoch, the restart time (R_{ACI-RD_t}) is approximately the sum of the time to undo all updates in the ACI-RD epoch ($UNDOt$), the time to recover data from the consistent log, and the time to re-execute the 'lost' transactions. The time to recover from a consistent log is equal to the restart time (R_{ACID_t}). The time to re-execute the 'lost' transactions is the product of total relaxed transactions ($N_{Trans_{epoch}}$) and the average per-transaction time ($Trans_t$). $UNDOt$ directly depends on $N_{Trans_{epoch}}$, and average UNDO time per transaction ($UNDO_{Trans_t}$).

$$\left.\begin{aligned} R_{ACI-RD_t} &\approx R_{ACID_t} + UNDO_t + (N_{Trans_{epoch}} * Trans_t) \\ UNDO_t &\approx N_{Trans_{epoch}} * UNDO_{Trans_t} \end{aligned}\right\} \quad (2)$$

$$\left.\begin{aligned} \Delta Trans_{epoch} &= Trans_{epoch_i} - Trans_{epoch_{i-1}} \\ \Delta E_{epoch} &= (E_{epoch_i} - E_{budget})/E_{budget} \end{aligned}\right\} \quad (3)$$

To implement the ACI-RD mechanism, given an energy budget E, the application execution is divided into per-epoch intervals of time t_{msec} with per-epoch energy budget E_{budget}. We assume the value of E_{budget} is known and is equal to the per-epoch energy of the metadata only approach in which only the metadata required for correctness is logged. We estimate this budget by sampling an epoch at runtime [13]. After the end of each epoch, EAP estimates the increase in the epoch's energy usage (ΔE_{epoch}) and the increase in the number of transactions ($\Delta Trans_{epoch}$) relative to the current and previous epoch transactions $Trans_{epoch_i}$ and $Trans_{epoch_{i-1}}$. As discussed in Section 3, the total energy for persistent applications with ACID guarantees is a factor of application execution, data logging, cache flush, and metadata transactions. We use this simple estimation model to avoid the overheads (including energy) of a complicated model.

EAP execution. Algorithm 1 shows EAP's sequence of steps for reducing energy usage. EAP's efficient and relaxed durability are activated only when the energy saving mode is enabled – a feature available in most end-user devices. For low energy budget, EAP applies the energy efficient durability principles described in Section 4 – switching from WAL to UNDO logging, group commit, batched allocation, and relaxed garbage collection – while still maintaining ACID guarantees. We refer to this mode as *EAP-ACID*. In the next epoch, the EAP runtime checks if EAP-ACID is sufficient to meet the per-epoch energy budget, and if not, ACI-RD is activated. These steps are repeated for subsequent epochs until the energy budget is satisfied. Note that unlike checkpointing-recovery protocols with fixed checkpoint interval [26], in a transactional application, the logging frequency depends on the number of transactions executed by the application. EAP uses the energy budget to tailor/relax logging without affecting the application correctness. For ACI-RD epochs, atomic commits can be used for the metadata log, as shown in Algorithm 1. Further, durability for objects larger than a threshold size is relaxed as they consume significantly higher energy.

Application notification and restarts. ACI-RD is a feature of EAP that either a user or a developer can enable. When ACI-RD is enabled for critically low energy budget, our implementation notifies the application about the completion of a transaction with a special return code on commits. If a system with ACI-RD epoch encounters failure, then the application re-executes all ACI-RD transaction for the failed epoch upon restart.

6. EAP EVALUATION

The key goal of our evaluation is to understand the impact of the proposed energy efficient durability (EAP-ACID), relaxed durability (ACI-RD), and the overall benefits of EAP that combine EAP-ACID and ACI-RD. We also analyze the implications of ACI-RD on restart time after a failure, and the overall impact on the system energy.

Methodology. In Section 3, we described our experimental platform details, NVM emulation with software delay, and the use of the RAPL [2] hardware counters to estimate the NVM and the CPU energy. We dynamically query the performance and energy hardware counters every 100ms (minimum frequency to measure energy) to measure the increase in CPU instructions, NVM accesses, and CPU energy. We estimate the NVM energy usage using the load-store cache misses [39, 22]. The latency and energy values are based on a PCM-based NVM [28], but EAP's principles for reducing energy are relevant for other NVM technologies such as STT-RAM. We also validate this by running the applications in a DRAM-based system and measuring the overall system energy using a power meter.

Baselines. We evaluate and compare EAP, a system which combines EAP-ACID and ACI-RD, against four different persistence

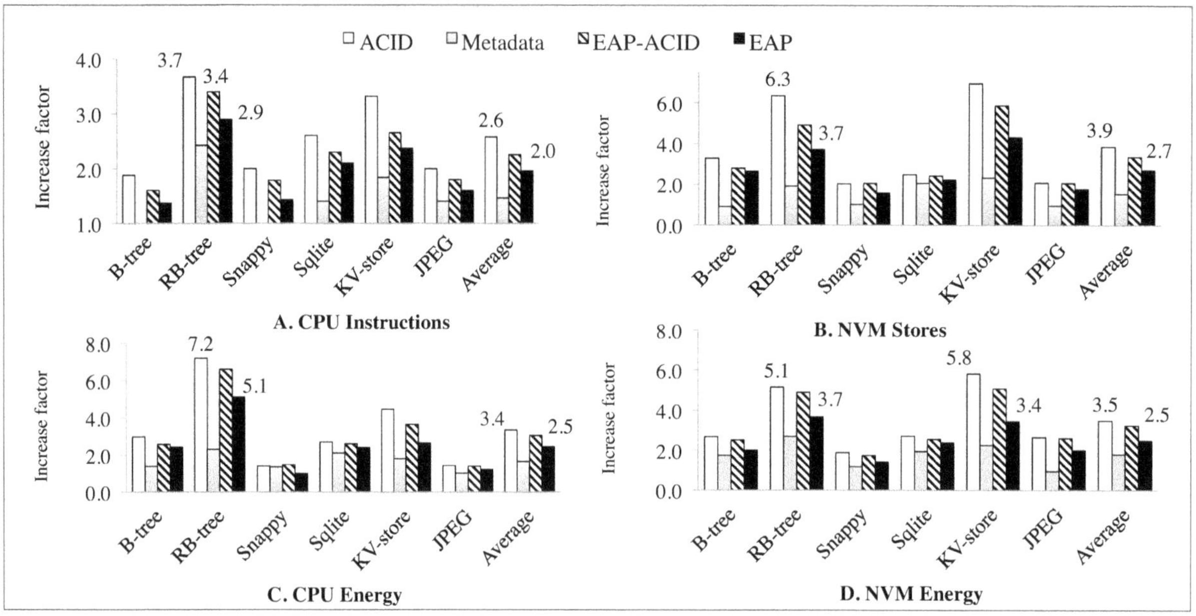

Figure 10: EAP impact on CPU instructions, NVM writes, CPU and NVM energy. Y-axis in the graphs denotes increase factors(x) relative to using only FLUSH. EAP bars include EAP-ACID and ACI-RD.

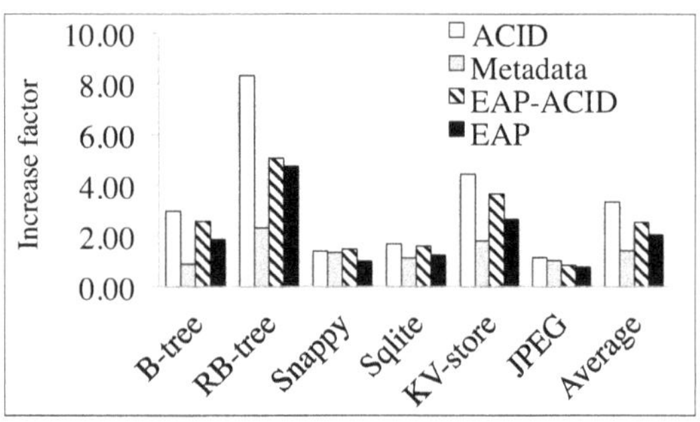

Figure 11: EAP runtime impact.

methods. First, the baseline method – FLUSH – that performs only flush, fence, and orders data in the cache without satisfying durability and correctness. Second, the traditional ACID approach with full data and metadata logging. Third, the Metadata-only method that provides durability only for the allocation and library metadata without the data durability. This method cannot recover any data after a failure and only validates the correctness, and hence, is not useful for most applications. Fourth, the EAP-ACID, which provides efficient durability via flexible logging, energy-aware allocation and garbage collection and the group commit mechanism. Note that unlike EAP, this approach does not relax durability and is applied for low-but-not-critical energy states.

6.1 Reduced energy use with EAP

Figures 10.(A)-(D) analyze the implications of persistence on increase in CPU instructions, NVM writes, CPU energy, and NVM energy, respectively. The y-axis shows the overheads as factor increase relative to the FLUSH approach as a baseline. The experiments use the applications and benchmarks introduced in Section 3. Application runtimes vary between 28 and 64 seconds. In EAP-ACID and EAP, the epoch time is set to 400ms, and we later discuss the epoch interval sensitivity. All the three benchmarks – B-tree, RB-tree, and KV-store – perform insert, find, delete and overwrite operations with 128-byte values.

Analysis. Although B-tree is persistence friendly, ACID increases CPU instructions by 1.9x and NVM accesses by 3.28x compared to the baseline. EAP-ACID with its energy efficient optimization reduces instructions and NVM accesses by 30% and 48% respectively compared to ACID. These benefits are mainly from the memory persistence-based group commit that reduces multiple persistent barriers for the same parent when child nodes are inserted, and from trading capacity by reducing the overhead of garbage collection. In contrast, EAP, by using ACI-RD with 400ms epoch intervals further reduces CPU and NVM energy by 61% and 67%, respectively.

RB-tree is a persistence inefficient data structure and shows the highest the ACID cost. When using only EAP-ACID, the energy reduction gains are minimal (~28% reduction in the CPU energy), most of which are from reducing the garbage collection cost and avoiding redundant log updates using the group commit. In contrast, with EAP, the logging is relaxed for RB-tree updates. Specifically, relaxing a log update for a parent node in the RB-tree avoids the logging cost for two of its child nodes. Consequently, this reduces instructions and NVM access by 80% and 2.6x, respectively. The Metadata-only approach offers higher gains but is less useful. For the KV-store, EAP reduces the high CPU and NVM energy costs of ACID by 2x and 2.5x, respectively. EAP still exhibits high overheads because of the allocator cost. Redesigning the KV-store data structure can reduce such cost.

For Snappy [16], which uses an input workload of 50K files (total 1.5 GB), and file sizes that vary between 10KB-140MB, the metadata logging cost is negligible. However, persisting large files with FLUSH is expensive, and the data logging is even more expensive. EAP relaxes logging for large data updates (see Algorithm 1), which provides considerable improvement. For applications such as Snappy, strict ACID is unnecessary because only files for which compression failed require re-compression. EAP provides a transparent support without depending on the application developer. JPEG image conversion [3] shows similar trends with only 40K transactions but incurs higher number of NVM store accesses because the output files can be larger (up to 30%) adding to

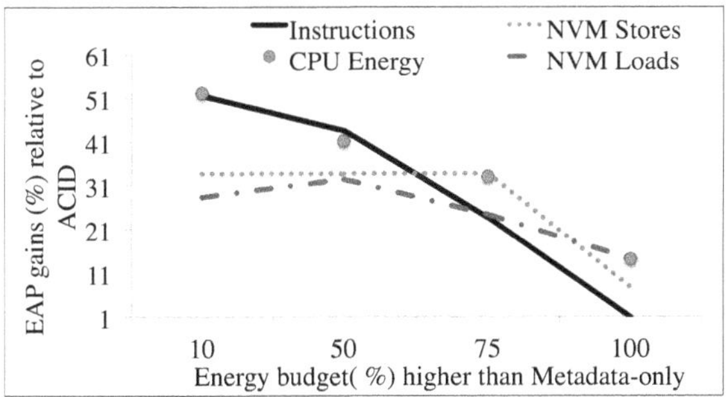

Figure 12: Impact of energy budget.

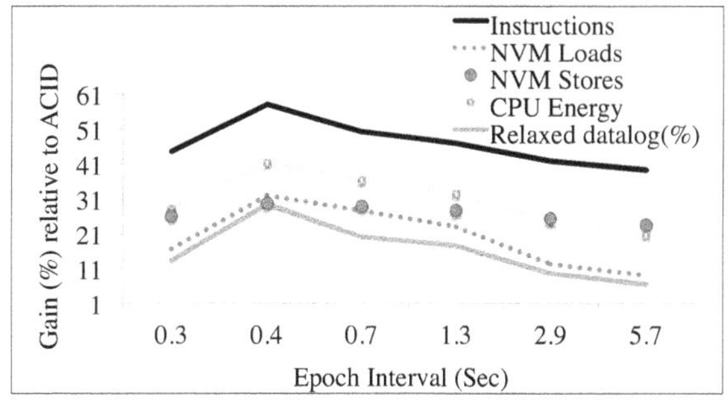

Figure 13: Impact of epoch interval.

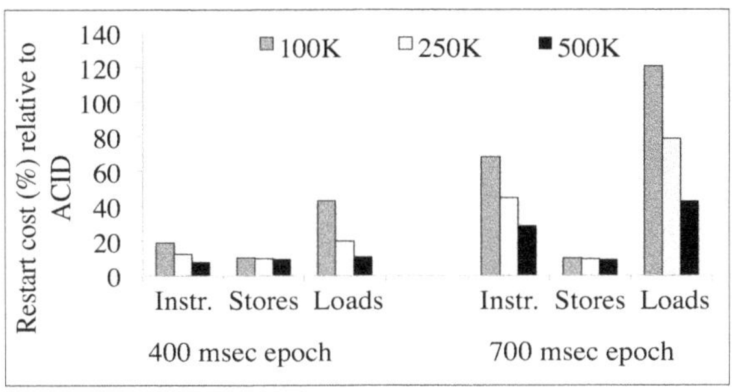

Figure 14: Epoch interval vs. restart cost. Load and stores represent NVM load stores.

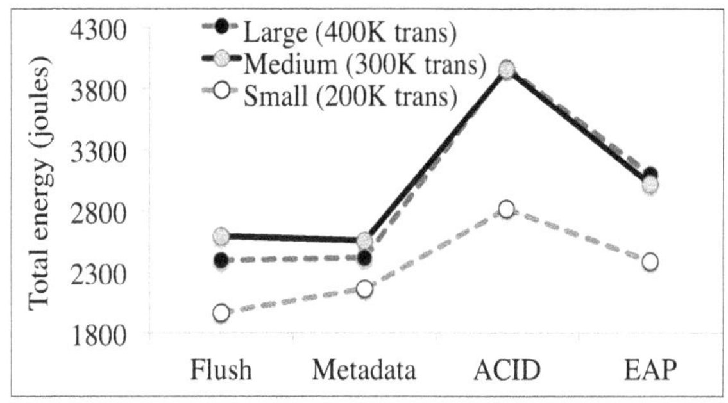

Figure 15: Overall system energy improvements with EAP. Y-axis indicates cumulative energy from running all applications.

the logging cost. With SQLite, EAP-ACID's flexible logging and allocator optimization reduce instructions (16%) and NVM writes (12%), compared to ACID with WAL-based logging. ACI-RD reduces CPU and NVM energy by additional 26-28%. Furthermore, using a page-based persistence limits the gain [33], and redesigning SQLite for memory persistence in the future can improve the benefits. Figure 11 shows the runtime impact of EAP. As shown, EAP, by combining efficient durability with ACI-RD, reduces CPU instructions and NVM writes, thereby improving application runtime. The runtime results show the same trends as the other system parameters.

6.2 EAP parameter sensitivity

We next use the persistence-efficient B-tree benchmark to analyze the sensitivity of the energy gains and the restart cost for EAP, by varying the energy budget and the epoch interval.

Energy budget. Figure 12 shows the impact of the energy budget on the gains that can be achieved with EAP. The x-axis shows the increase (%) in the budget compared to the energy required for the Metadata-only case. The y-axis shows the gains compared to strict ACID. Intuitively, when the budget is high, the number of ACI-RD epochs decreases along with EAP's energy gains. As observed, for 0 to 45% increase in the budget, the CPU instruction and energy reduction gains vary from 56% to 40%, and the NVM accesses vary from 36% to 31%. These results show (1) the significant difference between the ACID and the Metadata-only case, and (2) the need to use both efficient durability (EAP-ACID) and ACI-RD for most epochs when the energy budget is low. When increasing the budget beyond 50%, the number of ACI-RD epochs decreases, and at 90% EAP is turned off to use the strict ACID.

Epoch interval. Figure 13 shows the sensitivity to the epoch interval duration. Note that after each epoch interval, EAP's Algorithm 1 is used to decide if EAP-ACID or ACI-RD should be applied. In addition to the reduction in CPU instructions and NVM accesses, we also show the percentage of the total data log size that is relaxed, compared to the ACID case. We observe the following. First, for B-tree, EAP achieves maximum gains for epoch intervals in the 400-700ms range (10-50K B-tree transactions). Reducing the epoch interval below 400ms or increasing it above one second reduces the EAP's gains. The reduction is because for short execution intervals, the overhead of switching from ACID to EAP or from EAP to ACID dominates the benefits achieved from EAP. The costs include switching to an energy efficient logging mode and EAP's software budget profiling cost, which increase CPU instructions by 10%. When increasing the epoch interval beyond one second, EAP fails to apply ACI-RD when the energy budget exceeds the epoch budget, thus incurring higher data durability cost, as shown in the figure. *These results confirm the high data logging cost, and show that even when relaxing the data logging interval to 400ms, reductions of up to ~60% CPU instructions and ~40% NVM accesses can be achieved with EAP.*

Restart costs. As discussed in Section 5 and Equation 2, the restart cost is dependent on the epoch interval for which data durability is relaxed. For brevity, in Figure 14, we show only the impact of epoch intervals of 400ms and 700ms. The y-axis shows the increase in restart cost compared to strict ACID for 100K, 250K, and 500K transactions. For a 400ms epoch interval with 100K transactions, around 5K transactions are relaxed. For restarts after a failure, the CPU instructions and NVM accesses increase by only 19% and 10%, respectively. For 500K transactions, the CPU instructions and NVM accesses overheads further reduce mainly because the restart cost from loading the UNDO log and other initialization costs amortize. For ACI-RD epoch of 700ms, the additional UNDO operations increase the restart costs. The results show that using an optimal epoch interval (400ms in this case) is important to reduce the increase in restart cost due to ACI-RD.

It is also important to note that the overall duration of a restart is 59x lower than the total application execution time, and the energy benefits of EAP are significantly higher compared to the increase in the restart cost. The results show the sensitivity of EAP's gain towards the epoch interval and energy budget.

6.3 Memory technology independent gains

To validate EAP's principles independent of the NVM technology, we run all applications on DRAM for storage and computation, without emulating PCM-based NVM. We measure the overall system energy consumption by connecting the power source to a power meter. In Figure 15, the y-axis shows the overall energy usage (in joules) when running all applications (B-tree, RB-tree, KW-store, JPEG, and Snappy). The number of total transactions per application is varied (large, medium, and small) by changing the problem or the input data size. The x-axis indicates different persistence methods. For EAP, we use a 400ms epoch interval – the best case in the previous evaluation result. As seen, the overall energy increase from strict ACID memory persistence shows same trends as in the earlier NVM and CPU energy results. For large and medium transactions, ACID increases energy use by 2x compared to the FLUSH only approach. EAP, by combining EAP-ACID and ACI-RD, reduces energy consumption by ~34% compared to the ACID approach. *The results validate EAP's generic energy reduction principles, regardless of the persistent memory technology.*

Summary and Discussion. In summary, EAP, by combining EAP-ACID and ACI-RD provides up to 2.4x reduction in NVM energy and 2.1x reduction in CPU energy for data structures that are not persistence friendly (RB-tree), and up to 64% and 40% CPU and NVM energy gains for persistence-efficient applications (B-tree). Although EAP-ACID is effective for typical systems, for systems with critically low energy budget, ACI-RD may be required to ensure application completion. EAP does not compromise correctness. Support for multi-cache line commits and hardware-based energy profiling can reduce metadata and software energy cost.

7. CONCLUSIONS AND FUTURE WORK

This paper analyzes the energy overheads of persistence, and identifies durability-related costs as the most significant contributor to energy usage. To reduce durability energy costs, we propose energy-aware persistence (EAP). EAP first designs energy-efficient durability principles that under low but not critical energy budgets include flexible logging to trade off a small fraction of performance with energy, delayed garbage collection to trade NVM capacity with energy, and use of an NVM group commit method. For critically low energy conditions, EAP proposes a relaxed durability (ACI-RD) design that reduces energy significantly by relaxing data logging, but without impacting correctness. EAP's evaluation using benchmarks and applications shows a reduction of up to 2.1x in CPU energy and 2.4x in NVM energy, compared to a strict ACID approach. An interesting outcome of this research is that, for reducing persistence cost, it is important to reduce both the CPU and NVM energy. As a future work, we plan to understand the failure modes of end-user devices and to support alternative durability models.

8. ACKNOWLEDGMENT

The authors would like to thank all the anonymous reviewers and our shepherds, Professor Yan Solihin and Professor Larry Rudolph, for their valuable feedback in improving the quality of the paper. We thank the immense contribution of Professor Karsten Schwan whom we will greatly miss. This work was supported in part by the Intel URO program on software for persistent memories, and by C-FAR, one of the six SRC STARnet Centers, sponsored by MARCO and DARPA.

9. REFERENCES

[1] Intel-Micron Memory 3D XPoint. http://intel.ly/1eICR0a.
[2] Intel RAPL driver. http://lwn.net/Articles/545745/.
[3] JPEG library. http://libjpeg.sourceforge.net/.
[4] SNIA specification. http://tinyurl.com/nktmrby.
[5] SQLite. http://www.sqlite.org.
[6] J. Arulraj, A. Pavlo, and S. R. Dulloor. Let's talk about storage & recovery methods for non-volatile memory database systems. In *Proceedings of the 2015 ACM SIGMOD International Conference on Management of Data*, SIGMOD '15, pages 707–722, New York, NY, USA, 2015. ACM.
[7] H. Avni, E. Levy, and A. Mendelson. *Hardware Transactions in Nonvolatile Memory*, pages 617–630. Springer Berlin Heidelberg, Berlin, Heidelberg, 2015.
[8] A. M. Caulfield, A. De, J. Coburn, T. I. Mollow, R. K. Gupta, and S. Swanson. Moneta: A high-performance storage array architecture for next-generation, non-volatile memories. In *MICRO 2010*, pages 385–395.
[9] D. R. Chakrabarti, H.-J. Boehm, and K. Bhandari. Atlas: Leveraging locks for non-volatile memory consistency. In *Proceedings of the 2014 ACM International Conference on Object Oriented Programming Systems Languages & Applications*, OOPSLA '14, pages 433–452, New York, NY, USA, 2014. ACM.
[10] J. Coburn, T. Bunker, M. Schwarz, R. Gupta, and S. Swanson. From aries to mars: Transaction support for next-generation, solid-state drives. In *SOSP 2013*, pages 197–212.
[11] J. Coburn, A. M. Caulfield, A. Akel, L. M. Grupp, R. K. Gupta, R. Jhala, and S. Swanson. Nv-heaps: Making persistent objects fast and safe with next-generation, non-volatile memories. In *ASPLOS, 2011*, pages 105–118.
[12] J. Condit, E. B. Nightingale, C. Frost, E. Ipek, B. Lee, D. Burger, and D. Coetzee. Better i/o through byte-addressable, persistent memory. In *SOSP, 2009*, pages 133–146.
[13] I. Constandache, S. Gaonkar, M. Sayler, R. Choudhury, and L. Cox. Enloc: Energy-efficient localization for mobile phones. In *INFOCOM 2009*, pages 2716–2720, 2009.
[14] S. R. Dulloor, S. Kumar, A. Keshavamurthy, P. Lantz, D. Reddy, R. Sankaran, and J. Jackson. System software for persistent memory. In *EUROSYS, 2014*, pages 15:1–15:15.
[15] Google. LevelDb. http://leveldb.org/.
[16] Google. Snappy Compession. http://tinyurl.com/ku899co.
[17] R. Hagmann. Reimplementing the cedar file system using logging and group commit. In *Proceedings of the Eleventh ACM Symposium on Operating Systems Principles*, SOSP '87, pages 155–162, New York, NY, USA, 1987. ACM.
[18] M. Hähnel, B. Döbel, M. Völp, and H. Härtig. Measuring energy consumption for short code paths using rapl. *SIGMETRICS Perform. Eval. Rev.*, 40(3):13–17, Jan. 2012.
[19] M. Hertz and E. D. Berger. Quantifying the performance of garbage collection vs. explicit memory management. In *OOPSLA, 2015*, pages 313–326.
[20] Intel. Intel Development Manual. http://intel.ly/1CdHj1r.
[21] Intel. Logging library. https://github.com/pmem/nvml.
[22] Intel. PMFS: Persistent memory file system. github.com/linux-pmfs.

[23] S. Kannan, A. Gavrilovska, and K. Schwan. Reducing the cost of persistence for nonvolatile heaps in end user devices. In *HPCA, 2014*, pages 512–523.

[24] S. Kannan, A. Gavrilovska, and K. Schwan. pvm: Persistent virtual memory for efficient capacity scaling and object storage. In *Proceedings of the Eleventh European Conference on Computer Systems*, EuroSys '16, pages 13:1–13:16, New York, NY, USA, 2016. ACM.

[25] S. Kannan, A. Gavrilovska, K. Schwan, and S. Kumar. Nvm heaps for accelerating browser-based applications. In *Proceedings of the 1st Workshop on Interactions of NVM/FLASH with Operating Systems and Workloads*, INFLOW '13, pages 8:1–8:8, New York, NY, USA, 2013. ACM.

[26] S. Kannan, A. Gavrilovska, K. Schwan, and D. Milojicic. Optimizing checkpoints using nvm as virtual memory. In *Parallel Distributed Processing (IPDPS), 2013 IEEE 27th International Symposium on*, pages 29–40, May 2013.

[27] H. Kim, M. Ryu, and U. Ramachandran. What is a good buffer cache replacement scheme for mobile flash storage? *SIGMETRICS Perform. Eval. Rev.*, 40(1):235–246, June 2012.

[28] B. C. Lee, E. Ipek, O. Mutlu, and D. Burger. Architecting phase change memory as a scalable dram alternative. In *ISCA, 2009*, pages 2–13.

[29] R.-S. Liu, D.-Y. Shen, C.-L. Yang, S.-C. Yu, and C.-Y. M. Wang. Nvm duet: Unified working memory and persistent store architecture. In *ASPLOS, 2014*, pages 455–470.

[30] Y. Lu, J. Shu, L. Sun, and O. Mutlu. Loose-ordering consistency for persistent memory. In *ICCD, 2014*, pages 216–223.

[31] I. Moraru, D. G. Andersen, M. Kaminsky, N. Tolia, P. Ranganathan, and N. Binkert. Consistent, durable, and safe memory management for byte-addressable non volatile main memory. In *Proceedings of the First ACM SIGOPS Conference on Timely Results in Operating Systems*, TRIOS '13, pages 1:1–1:17, New York, NY, USA, 2013. ACM.

[32] D. Narayanan and O. Hodson. Whole-system persistence. In *ASPLOS, 2012*, pages 401–410.

[33] G. Oh, S. Kim, S. Lee, and B. Moon. Sqlite optimization with phase change memory for mobile applications. *PVLDB*, 8(12):1454–1465, 2015.

[34] K. Paul and T. K. Kundu. Android on mobile devices: An energy perspective. In *CIT 2010*, pages 2421–2426.

[35] S. Pelley, P. M. Chen, and T. F. Wenisch. Memory persistency. In *ISCA, 2014*, pages 265–276.

[36] S. Pelley, T. F. Wenisch, B. T. Gold, and B. Bridge. Storage management in the nvram era. *Proc. VLDB Endow.*, 7(2):121–132, Oct. 2013.

[37] M. K. Qureshi, V. Srinivasan, and J. A. Rivers. Scalable high performance main memory system using phase-change memory technology. *SIGARCH Comput. Archit. News*, 37(3):24–33, June 2009.

[38] D. Schwalb, T. Berning, M. Faust, M. Dreseler, and H. Plattner. nvm malloc: Memory allocation for nvram. In *VLDB*, 2015.

[39] H. Volos, A. J. Tack, and M. M. Swift. Mnemosyne: Lightweight persistent memory. In *ASPLOS, 2011*, pages 91–104.

[40] C. Wang, S. S. Vazhkudai, X. Ma, F. Meng, Y. Kim, and C. Engelmann. Nvmalloc: Exposing an aggregate ssd store as a memory partition in extreme-scale machines. In *Parallel Distributed Processing Symposium (IPDPS), 2012 IEEE 26th International*, pages 957–968, May 2012.

[41] H. Yoon. Row buffer locality aware caching policies for hybrid memories. In *ICCD, 2012*, pages 337–344.

[42] J. Zhao, S. Li, D. H. Yoon, Y. Xie, and N. P. Jouppi. Kiln: Closing the performance gap between systems with and without persistence support. MICRO-46, pages 421–432, 2013.

[43] J. Zhao, O. Mutlu, and Y. Xie. Firm: Fair and high-performance memory control for persistent memory systems. In *MICRO-47, 2014*, pages 153–165.

Power Tuning HPC Jobs on Power-Constrained Systems

Neha Gholkar[1], Frank Mueller[1], Barry Rountree[2]
[1]North Carolina State University, USA, ngholka@ncsu.edu, mueller@cs.ncsu.edu
[2]Lawrence Livermore National Laboratory, USA, rountree4@llnl.gov

ABSTRACT

As we approach the exascale era, power has become a primary bottleneck. The US Department of Energy has set a power constraint of 20MW on each exascale machine. To be able achieve one exaflop under this constraint, it is necessary that we use power intelligently to maximize performance under a power constraint.

Most production-level parallel applications that run on a supercomputer are tightly-coupled parallel applications. A naïve approach of enforcing a power constraint for a parallel job would be to divide the job's power budget uniformly across all the processors. However, previous work has shown that a power capped job suffers from performance variation of otherwise identical processors leading to overall sub-optimal performance. We propose a 2-level hierarchical variation-aware approach of managing power at machine-level. At the macro level, *PPartition* partitions a machine's power budget across jobs to assign a power budget to each job running on the system such that the machine never exceeds its power budget. At the micro level, *PTune* makes job-centric decisions by taking the performance variation into account. For every moldable job, PTune determines the optimal number of processors, the selection of processors and the distribution of the job's power budget across them, with the goal of maximizing the job's performance under its power budget.

Experiments show that, at the micro level, PTune achieves a performance improvement of up to 29% compared to a naïve approach. PTune does not lead to any performance degradation, yet frees up almost 40% of the processors for the same performance as that of the naïve approach under a hard power bound. At the macro level, PPartition is able to achieve a throughput improvement of 5-35% compared to uniform power distribution.

1. INTRODUCTION

The supercomputing community is headed toward the era of exascale computing, which is slated to begin around 2020. Today's fastest supercomputer, Tianhe-2, consumes 17.8MW to deliver 33.86PFlops [2]. If we were to build an exascale machine with today's technology it would consume up to 350MW of power. A typical power plant generates 1GW of power, which is sufficient to power 700,000 homes [1]. The US DOE has set a power constraint of 20MW per future exascale systems to maintain a feasible electrical power demand. In order to get an exaflop under this constraint, we need at least an order of magnitude improvement in power efficiency with respect to today's systems [5, 7, 19, 31].

PACT '16, September 11-15, 2016, Haifa, Israel
© 2016 ACM. ISBN 978-1-4503-4121-9/16/09...$15.00
DOI: http://dx.doi.org/10.1145/2967938.2967961

Exascale systems are expected to be power-constrained: the size of the machine will be limited by the amount of provisioned power. Existing best practice requires provisioning power based on the theoretical maximum power draw of the machine, despite the fact that only a synthetic workload comes close to this level of power consumption. One of the key contributions in the power-constrained domain is "hardware overprovisioning" [24]. The idea is to provision much less power per node and thus provision more nodes. The benefit is that all of the scarce resource (power) will be used. The drawback is that power must be carefully scheduled within the machine in order to approach optimal performance.

Fig. 1 depicts this foundational idea. Let the hardware overprovisioned system consist of N_{max} processors and let the power budgeted for this system be $P_{m/c}$ Watts. As shown in the figure, with $P_{m/c}$ Watts total system power, only a part of the system (say N_{alloc} where $N_{alloc} < N_{max}$ processors) can be utilized at peak power (collection of nodes in red). Another valid configuration is to utilize the entire system at low power. One of the several other intermediate configurations is to use medium power levels and utilize a portion of the system larger than that at peak power but smaller than that at low power. In each of these configurations, a machine's power budget is uniformly distributed across a varying number of processors, i.e, each processor is allocated approximately $\frac{P_{m/c}}{N_{alloc}}$ Watts of power. This is a naïve approach of enforcing a power budget. Depending on the application's characteristics (memory-, compute-, and communication-boundedness), different applications achieve optimal performance on different configurations. In a nutshell, power procured for a system must be managed as a malleable resource to maximize performance of an overprovisioned system under a power constraint.

To facilitate the selection of different power levels, hardware manufacturers are providing various features like power clamping and on-chip power measurement mechanisms (e.g.,

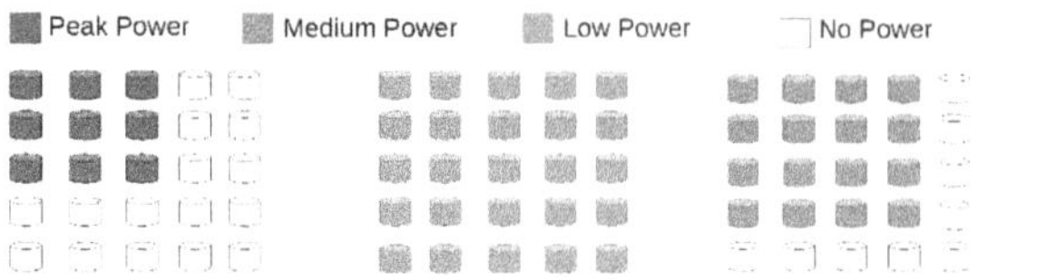

Figure 1: Hardware Overprovisioning under Power Constraint

Intel's Running Average Power Limit or RAPL [20]), as well as component power measurement infrastructures [17, 15]. In this work, we use RAPL to cap and measure the power consumption of the processors, where a processor is a single multi-core chip shipped by Intel.

When processors in the same stock keeping unit (SKU) operate at the same frequency, there is observable variation in power draw [6, 39, 16, 37]. When processors are capped at uniform power, this variation is expressed in terms of performance, i.e., the system is no longer homogeneous [27]. There are many potential root causes of this variation, including, but not limited to, process variation and thermal variation due to ambient machine room temperature.

We observe that these phenomena also translate into variation in the peak power efficiency of the processors. We define *power efficiency* as the performance achieved by a processor per Watt of the power consumed by it. Performance is quantified in terms of number of instructions retired per second (IPS). We make two important observations. First, not all processors are equally power efficient at a fixed power bound. Second, the most efficient processors are most efficient at lower power bounds whereas the least efficient processors are most efficient at higher power bounds. Based on these insights about variation across the system, we propose *power tuning* and *power partitioning* strategies that distribute the power budget non-uniformly across the system to achieve maximum performance irrespective of the cause of variation.

We propose a 2-level hierarchical solution that performs Power Partitioning (PPartition) at macro-level and Power Tuning (PTune) at micro-level to maximize the "science performed per Watt". PPartition aims at improving the throughput of the machine by (re-)partitioning a machine's power budget across jobs while scheduling them. PTune is a variation-aware power manager for moldable jobs whose number of processors can be chosen at dispatch time. For every job, PTune maximizes its performance under its job power budget (assigned by PPartition) by determining the following:

- The optimal selection of a subset of processors from the available ones; and
- the (non-uniform) distribution of the job's power budget across the selected processors.

PTune uses off-line characterization data to make these decisions before the beginning of job execution. PTune achieves a job performance improvement of up to 29% over uniform power. PTune does not lead to any performance degradation, yet frees up 40% of the resources compared to uniform power. PPartition and PTune together improve the throughput of the machine by 5-35% compared to conventional scheduling on an overprovisioned machine.

In this work, we make the following contributions:

- We characterize the performance of contemporary Intel processors with multiple codes at multiple power bounds. Performance variations of up to 30% are observed across these processors. Using this data we conduct a power efficiency study that forms the basis for the work.
- We propose *PTune*, a variation-aware job power tuner that optimizes a job for performance under a strict job power constraint.
- We propose *PPartition*, a variation-aware resource manager that manages a machine's power budget as a resource to maximize the throughput of the machine under a machine-level power constraint.
- We evaluate PTune and PPartition using three of the NAS Parallel benchmark codes [3] and a molecular dynamics proxy application, CoMD [30].

2. MOTIVATION

Research focus has only recently shifted from just performance to minimizing energy usage of supercomputers. Considering the US DOE mandate for a power constraint per exascale site, efforts need to be directed towards using all of the limited amount of power intelligently to maximize performance under this constraint.

As stated previously, uniform power capping is the naïve approach of enforcing a power constraint. In order to understand what happens under such a scheme, we characterized the performance of 600 Ivy Bridge processors on a cluster. We ran three of the NAS Parallel Benchmark (NPB) suite codes [3], viz., Embarrassingly Parallel (EP), Block Tridiagonal solver (BT), Scalar Penta-tridiagonal solver (SP), and CoMD, a molecular dynamics proxy application from the Mantevo suite [30] at several different processor power bounds on all the processors. The processor power bounds were set using RAPL. The results are depicted in Fig. 2. The x-axis represents operating power in Watts while the y-axis represents Instructions Retired per Second (IPS) in billions. A maximum performance of 77, 50, 80, and 60 billions IPS is achieved for CoMD, EP, BT and SP, respectively. The cluster becomes non-uniform under power bounds with performance variations of up to 30% across this cluster for these applications. The potential causes of variability are discussed next but are effectively irrelevant as our proposed methods are agnostic of specific causes. More significantly, our experiments will show that this variability in performance translates into variation in peak *power efficiency* of the processors, which we exploit.

Power Efficiency

Let *power efficiency* be defined as the number of instructions retired per second per Watt of operating power. Fig. 3 represents the power efficiency curves of the processors on the cluster for the same set of codes. The x-axis represents the operating power in Watts and the y-axis represents the power efficiency in billion IPS/W. The rainbow palette represents different processors, where each curve (or each color) in the plots corresponds to a unique processor.

We make the following observations from these experiments:

- The power efficiency of a processor varies with its operating power and is non-monotonic. It is also workload-dependent.

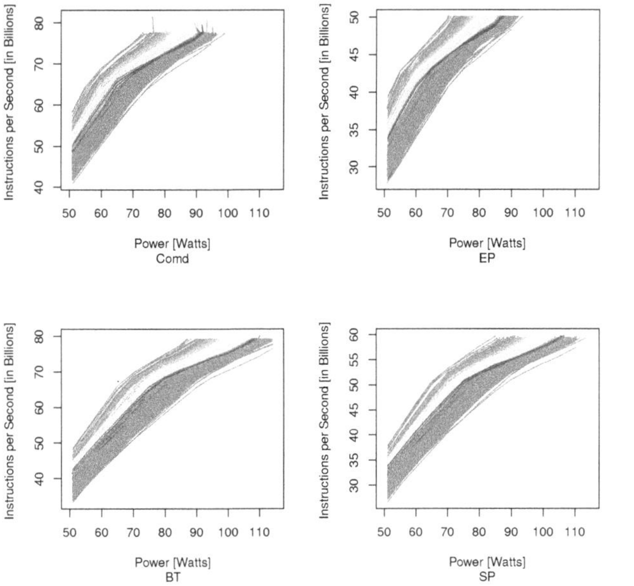

Figure 2: IPS vs. Power for each processor. Each rainbow line represent one processor. Curves in red (bottom) are least efficient, curves in orange (top) are most efficient.

- Peak power efficiency varies across processors.
- Most importantly, efficient processors are most efficient at lower power bounds whereas the inefficient processors are most efficient at higher power bounds. The "peak" of every curve is the point at which the processor achieves the maximum efficiency, i.e., maximum IPS/W. Orange curves (efficient processors) have peaks at lower power compared to the peaks of the red curves (less efficient processors) and the rest lie in between.

Fig. 4 depicts the results of our thermal experiments. The x-axis presents processor IDs (processors are sorted in the order of efficiency). The y-axis presents the measured temperature (triangles) of the processors normalized with respect to the maximum temperature and the unbounded power (crosses) of the processors also normalized with respect to the maximum power. In these experiments, the processors were not capped, and they achieved uniform performance. We observe that the temperature increases as we go from efficient to inefficient processors (left to right), as does the unbounded power. However, not all inefficient processors are hotter than the efficient ones. This shows that thermal variation may be one of the potential causes of variation in efficiency but there are other factors that counter the effect as we do not see a linear trend for temperature (in contrast to the linear trend of unbounded power). We believe that one of the contributing factors is process/manufacturing variation induced at the time of fabrication. In the end, our proposed mechanism is agnostic of the actual cause of variation, it simply exploits the fact that variation (due to whatever reason) exists.

In summary, there exists variation in power efficiency across processors. There is a unique local maximum in every power efficiency curve that occurs at disparate power levels for different processors. Starting from the minimum power, increasing the power assigned to a processor leads to increasing gains in IPS. However, increasing the power

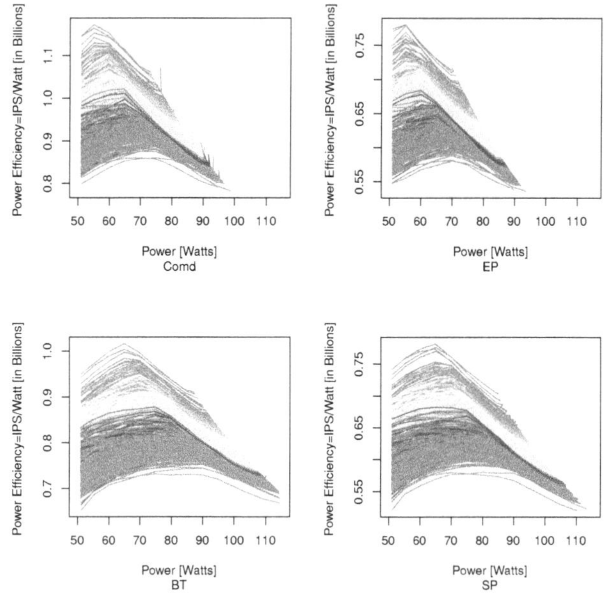

Figure 3: Power Efficiency in IPS/W vs. Operating power. One rainbow line per processor, red curves (bottom) are least, orange ones (top) most efficient.

beyond the peak efficiency point of a processor leads to diminishing returns. Hence, when power is limited, processors should operate at power levels close to their peak efficiency to maximize the overall efficiency of the system. Since the peak efficiency points for efficient processors are at lower power levels than for the inefficient processors, the optimal configuration should select lower power levels for efficient processors and higher power levels for inefficient processors to maximize performance. On the contrary, a naïve / *uniform power* scheme caps all the processors at identical power bounds. Hence, it is sub-optimal.

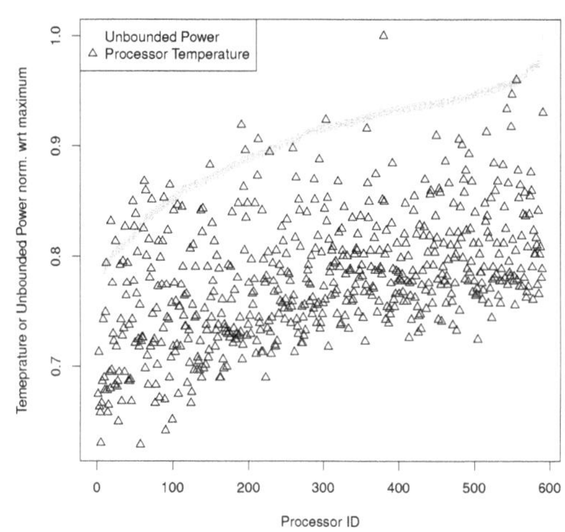

Figure 4: Temperature and unbounded power of processors. Processors are sorted by unbounded power consumption.

An optimal algorithm should aim at leveraging the non-uniformity of the cluster to maximize the performance of a job under its power constraint.

To this end, we propose *PTune*, a power-performance variation-aware power tuner that exactly does this for each job. For every job, given a power budget, it determines the following: (1) the optimal number of processors (say n_{opt});

(2) selection of n_{opt} processors; and (3) the power distribution (say p_k, where $1 \leq k \leq n_{opt}$) across the selected n_{opt} processors.

3. PROBLEM STATEMENT

The problem statement then is as follows: Given a machine level power budget, how should the machine's power be distributed across (a) jobs and (b) tasks within jobs on a given system, where (b) is discussed later. For (a), the process of making these decisions at the macro level of jobs is called *power partitioning*. Each job on the machine receives its own power partition.

We address the following questions:

1. How many partitions do we need at a time? I.e., determine how many jobs should be scheduled at a time.
2. What is the size of each of the power partitions? I.e., determine the power budget assigned to each job.

For (b), at the micro level, given a hard job-level power budget P_{Ji}, we need to determine the optimal number of processors, n_{opt}, with a power distribution (p_1, p_2, ... , $p_{(n_{opt}-1)}$, $p_{n_{opt}}$) such that performance of the job is maximized under its power budget. The constraint on the power distribution is expressed as

$\sum_{k=1}^{n} p_k \leq P_{Ji}; min\_power \leq p_k \leq max\_power_k.$

Here, min_power is the minimum power that needs to be assigned to a processor for reliable performance and max_power_k is the maximum power consumed by the kth processor (uncapped power consumption) for an application. The performance of a job can be quantified in terms of number of instructions retired per second (IPS).[1] For a parallel application on n processors, the effective IPS is the aggregated IPS over n processors ($JobIPS_n$). Hence, the objective function is

$Maximize(JobIPS_n)$.

A processor's IPS is a non-linear function of the power at which it operates. Each processor can be power bounded at several levels using the RAPL capping capabilities, which forces it to operate at various power levels within a fixed range. We know that unbounded power consumption is variable across processors while achieving the same unbounded (peak) performance for a given application. This is depicted in Fig. 5. The x-axis indicates the power at which the processor operates and the y-axis shows the IPS (in billions) of the processor of an application. Each solid curve corresponds to the most efficient processor while the dotted curve correspond to the least efficient processor. The following two observations are made from this data:

1. On a single processor, the performance (IPS) achieved at any fixed power level is different for different workloads.
2. The performance of an application on two different processors at any fixed power level is not the same.

This means that when determining the optimal distribution of power across processors it is necessary to take the processor characteristics and the application characteristics into account. One solution may not fit all applications. The optimal configuration for an application on one set of processors may be different from that on another set of processors because of performance variations under a power cap.

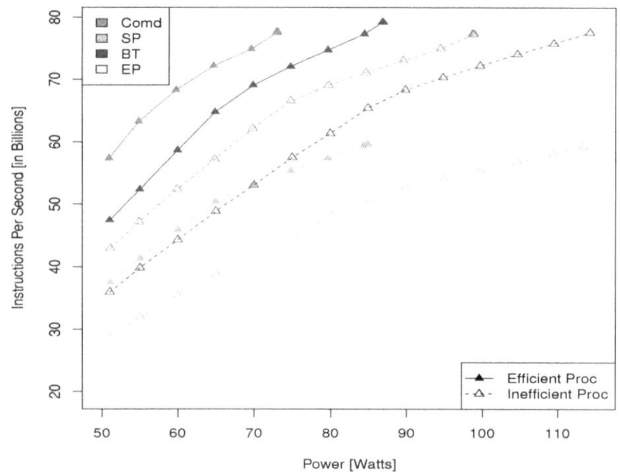

Figure 5: IPS vs. Power for efficient and inefficient processors

4. PROPOSED SOLUTION

We propose a 2-level hierarchical approach of managing power as a resource (see Fig. 6). The parameters of the model are described in Table 1. N_{max}, $P_{m/c}$ and n_{req} are the inputs to the model that we assume. n_{opt} is calculated once for every job at its dispatch time. N_{alloc}, P_{Ji} and p_k are re-calculated every time any job is dispatched. min_power is architecturally defined for every family of processors. Table 2 is populated off-line using the characterization data. We make the assumption that the power consumption of the interconnect is zero, i.e., interconnect power is beyond the scope, and so are task-to-node mapping effects on power. We only consider processor power in this work and assume moldable jobs. DRAM power could not be included due to motherboard limitations at the time of this work. We do not expect the users of the system to predict and request power in their job request. Power decisions are made by our system software (PTune and PPartition). Users may be allowed to influence these decisions by assigning priorities to their jobs.

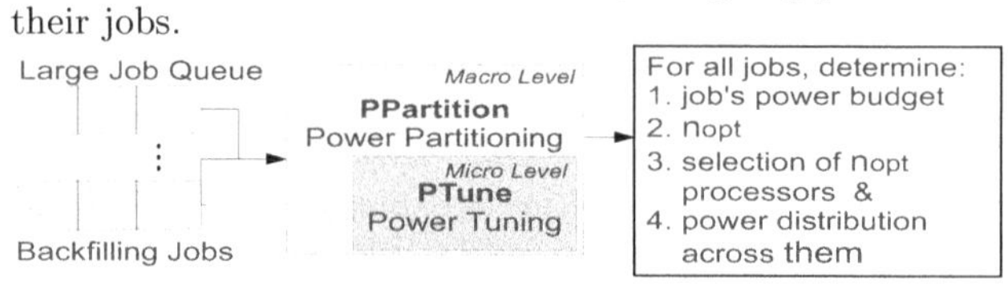

Figure 6: Hierarchical Power Manager

At the macro level, we propose *PPartition*, a technique of partitioning a machine's power budget across jobs while scheduling them. Once a job is dispatched by a conventional scheduler (e.g., slurm or Maui/pbs), PPartition calculates its power budget. If the required power is not available, it steals power from the previously scheduled jobs and provisions this power for the new job. If sufficient power cannot be obtained, PPartition overrides the conventional scheduler's decision based on free resources (nodes) and does not schedule this job until sufficient power is available.

At the micro-level, we propose *PTune*, a power balancing model that determines the distribution of a job's power

[1]The general model holds for other performance metrics as well. We selected IPS here because it closely correlates to power in our experiments.

Table 1: Model Parameters

Parameter	Description	PPartition	PTune
N_{max}	maximum number of processors on a machine	Input	N/A
N_{alloc}	number of processors already allocated to jobs	Output	N/A
$P_{m/c}$	power budget of the machine	Input	N/A
P_{m/c_unused}	unused power budget of the machine	Variable	N/A
n_{req}	number of processors requested by a job	Input	Input
n_{opt}	optimal number of processors for a job	Output	Output
n	number of processors for a job under its power budget	N/A	Variable
P_{Ji}	power budget of the ith job	Output	Input
p_k	power cap of kth processor within a job	N/A	Output
min_power	minimum processor power cap	Input	Input
max_power_j	maximum processor power cap of the jth processors	Input	Input
power-ips table	characterization data Table 2	Input	Input

Table 2: power-ips lookup table (last metric in Tab. 1)

Power Cap[W]	IPS in Billions	Measure Power [W]
60	46.43	59.99
80	64.83	79.88
100	76.33	99.43
120	79.13	104.66

budget (one job at a time) across an optimal selection of processors (among all free resources) to maximize the performance of a job under its power budget.

5. PTUNE

PTune shrinks the job's processor allocation by eliminating the less efficient processors that are expensive in terms of power to maximize the performance of a job under its power budget. Fig. 7 depicts the micro-level power tuner. For each job Ji, a power budget P_{Ji} is calculated at the macro level by PPartition. For every job with this assigned power budget, PTune answers the following questions:

1. How many (n_{opt}) and which processors should a job run on?
2. What should be the power ($p_1, ..., p_{n_{opt}}$) assigned to each of the n_{opt} processors?

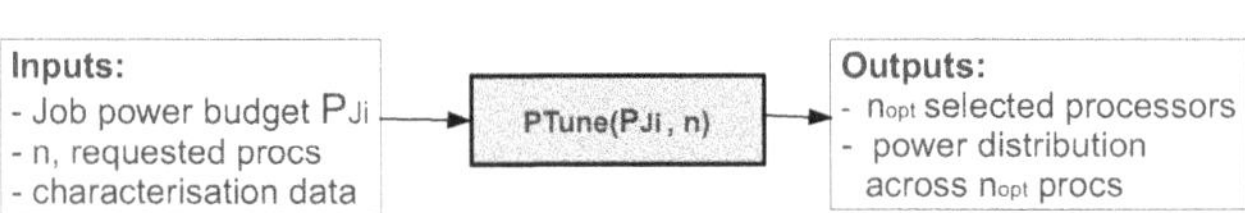

Figure 7: PTune

Let us start by addressing the first question. In order to use a processor, it needs to be assigned at least the minimum power (*min_power*) that is constant across all processors. The upper limit on the processor's power (max_power_k) is variable across processors.

Fig. 8 shows the maximum power consumption of 600 Ivy Bridge processors when they are not power capped. The unbounded performance is uniform across all the processors. The x-axis represents all the processor sorted by power consumption and the y-axis represents the maximum power consumption in Watts. The optimal configuration for maximum performance of a job under a strict power budget consists of the maximum number of most efficient processors (from the left) such that their aggregate power consumption does not exceed the job's power budget.

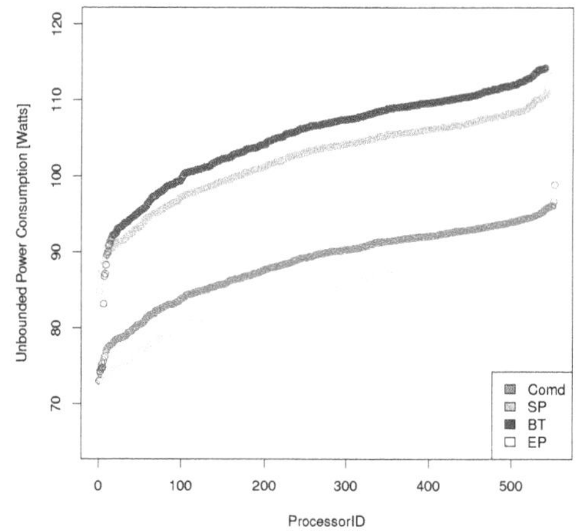

Figure 8: Unbounded power consumption of processors under uniform performance

5.1 Sort the Processors

The first step towards determining the optimal configuration is to sort the available processors by their relative power efficiency. This is equivalent to sorting them by their unbounded power consumption. Let the sorted set of processors be indexed by k.

We divide this distribution of processors into quartiles, viz., Q1, Q2, Q3 and Q4, in the order of efficiency and pick processors from one or more of these quartiles for evaluation purposes.

5.2 Bounds on Number of Processors

The lower bound on n, $n_{\perp}$, can be calculated by determining the maximum number of processors that can be capped at their maximum power, max_power_k, under the power budget. The selection of processors is reformed in the sorted order as described above. $n_{\perp}$ is given by the largest value of n that satisfies the following constraint:

$P_{Ji} \geq \sum_{k=1}^{n} max\_power_k$.

The upper bound on n, $n_{\top}$, represents the maximum number of processors that can be operated at *min_power* under the power budget. The bound $n_{\top}$ is calculated as follows:

$n_{\top} = \frac{P_{Ji}}{min\_power}$.

The processor count, n, is iterated from $n_{\perp}$ to $n_{\top}$, and in each step, the next efficient processor is added to the set of processors. Job-level performance, $JobIPS_n$, is calculated in each iteration by $DistributePower()$ for the power budget P_{Ji} and a given number of processors, n, where $n_{\perp} \leq n \leq n_{\top}$.

The optimal number of processors, i.e., n_{opt}, is the value of n at which a job's IPS is maximized.

$JobIPS_{n_{opt}} = max(JobIPS_{n_{\perp}}, JobIPS_{(n_{\perp}+1)}, ..., JobIPS_{n_{\top}})$.

PTune leads to $n_{opt} \leq n$. Thus, PTune tends to reduce the number of processors required for a moldable job The spare processors are returned back to the global pool of unused resources so that they can be utilized by other jobs.

5.3 Distribute Power: Mathematical Model

DistributePower(), takes three inputs, viz., the number of processors n, the job's power budget, P_{Ji}, and the power distribution across $n-1$ processors determined in the previous iteration. The output of this function is the maximum job IPS that can be achieved under P_{Ji} Watts with n processors. It also calculates the optimal power caps, $(p_1, ..., p_n)$, for n processors, which forms an input for the next iteration. This can be mathematically expressed as follows:

$$DistributePower(n, P_{Ji}, (p_1, ..., p_n)) = DistributePower((n-1), P_{Ji} - p_n, p_1, ..., p_{(n-1)}) + getProcIPS(n, p_n).$$

The function getProcIPS(k,p_k) performs a look-up in Tab. 2 to return the expected performance (IPS) of the kth processor when it is capped at p_k Watts.

5.4 Power Stealing and Shifting

DistributePower() consists of two main steps, viz. Power Stealing and Power Shifting.

Step 1: Power is stolen in discrete quantities (*delta_power*) from the $n-1$ processors to provision power for the nth processor (see Fig. 9). The victim/donor processor is the one that suffers minimum loss in IPS when *delta_power* is stolen from it. If the aggregate stolen power is at least *min_power*, an additional n^{th} processor is added to the processor set.

Step 2: Power is shifted from a donor to a receiver in discrete quantities, *delta_power*, across the n processors. The victim/donor processor is identified in the same way as in step 1. The receiver is the processor that gains maximum IPS on receiving *delta_power*.

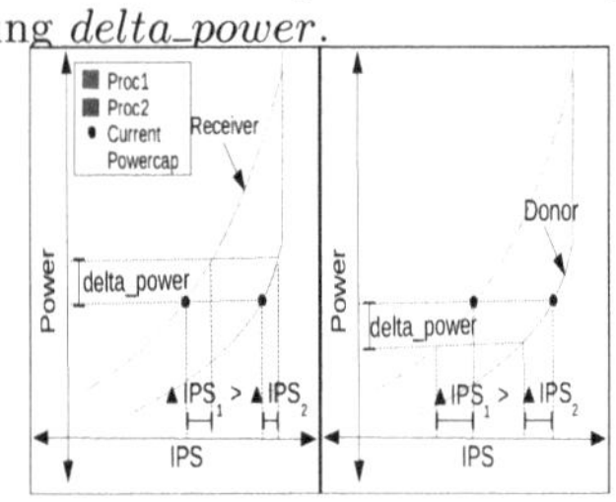

Figure 9: Donor and receiver of discrete power

6. PPARTITION

Fig. 10 depicts the macro-level power partitioning algorithm. The power partitioner co-operates with the conventional scheduler (simulated in R). PPartition receives information on the performance variations across processors. It always chooses the most efficient n_{req} processors of the available processors (or a subset thereof) to schedule a job. The conventional scheduler dispatches a job from the job queue when the requested number of processing resources are available. When job J_i is dispatched, its initial power budget, P_{Ji}, is calculated as follows:

$P_{Ji} \leftarrow P_{m/c} * \frac{n_{req}}{N_{max}}$

If the required power is available, PTune determines the optimal configuration for the job and the job is scheduled. It is important to note that even though the job power budget is proportionate to the number of requested processors, PTune schedules jobs on reduced number of processors. As a result, the machine's power depletes at a faster rate that the processing resources. If the available (unused) power is less than the calculated job power budget, power is stolen from already scheduled jobs. This is called power repartitioning (lower right blue/shaded box in Fig. 10) and detailed next.

Power Repartitioning

The power repartitioning algorithm is shown in Algorithm 1. As all of the machine power budget is already used up by the $N_{allocated}$ processors, a fair power share for the new job is calculated as

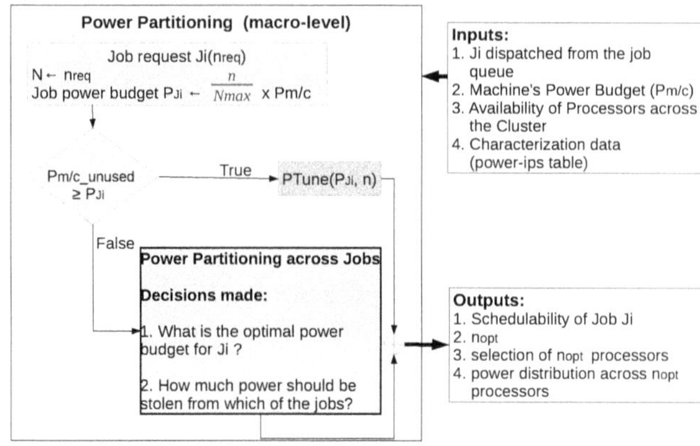

Figure 10: PPartitioning: Repartitioning Power

$P_{Ji} = P_{m/c} * \frac{n}{n+N_{allocated}}$, where n=$n_{req}$.

Algorithm 1 Repartitioning Power For Accommodating the ith job

procedure POWERPARTITIONER(J_i,n_{req})
  $n_{opt} \leftarrow n_{req}$
  do
    $n \leftarrow n_{opt}$
    $P_{Ji} \leftarrow P_{m/c} * \frac{n}{n+N_{allocated}}$ ▷ Recompute P_{Ji} proportional to the portion of busy processors requested
    $n_{opt} \leftarrow PTune(P_{Ji}, n)$ ▷ Recompute n_{opt}
  while $n_{opt} < n$
  ▷ Repartition power across jobs to provision power for the ith job
  for $k \leftarrow 1; k < i; k++$ **do**
    $power\_to\_be\_stolen[k] \leftarrow (P_{Ji} - P_{m/c\_unused}) * \frac{jobpowerbudgets[k]}{\sum jobpowerbudgets}$
    $total\_stolen\_power \leftarrow total\_stolen\_power + ShrinkPartition(power\_to\_be\_stolen[k], k)$
  end for
  if $total\_stolen\_power < P_{Ji}$ **then** ▷ If enough power cannot be stolen, recompute n_{opt}
    $P_{Ji} \leftarrow total\_stolen\_power$
    $n_{opt} \leftarrow PTune(P_{Ji}, n)$
  end if
end procedure

The job is power tuned for the requested n_{req} (assigned to n) processors under P_{Ji} Watts calculated above. PTune gets rid of the unaffordable less efficient processors, if any, leading to $n_{opt} \le n$. We recompute (in the while loop) the proportionate power the new job with n_{opt} processors should have due to power partitioning across all jobs. This new power budget, P_{Ji}, then becomes the base for another PTune, and so on, until the number of processors (monotonically decreasing) for the new job reaches a fixed point (stabilizes) in the while loop. The fixed point guarantees a fair power level (P_{Ji}) relative to other jobs, but we still need to find other jobs to steal just enough power for this job.

In the following for loop, power is stolen from each of the scheduled jobs in a proportionate manner to each other's power budget. This is accomplished by *ShrinkPartition*, which consists of (1) stealing just enough power and (2) power tuning for the remaining power of a job and the same number of processors (since we assume moldable but not malleable applications). Here, we steal as much power as possible while retaining heterogeneous power bounds across a job's processors to respect processor variations and thus ensure a high IPS under lower power budget.

The aggregate stolen power from other jobs is offered to the new job. If the stolen power is less than the fixed power level for the new job, which was P_{Ji}, then the new job needs to be tuned one more time. If the stolen power was sufficient for this last tuning step, the new job is scheduled and the power re-tuning decisions made by ShrinkPartition for the existing ones are enforced. If, however, the stolen power is insufficient (as determined by PTune when the power budget cannot accommodate more than $\frac{n}{2}$ processors), no power is redistributed, i.e., all jobs remain unchanged in their power settings and the new job is deferred until at least another job completes.

7. IMPLEMENTATION

We modified the libmsr [35] library to gather the processor characterization data. We implemented a power-performance profiler using the MPI profiling interface (PMPI) that invoked various subroutines of the libmsr library to assess the power and the performance of MPI applications. We captured several fixed counter values, power consumption, and completion times for each application on all the processors. The processor power consumption was measured using Intel's RAPL interface. This characterization data is made available to PTune and PPartition.

We assume that the jobs are moldable. Our power manager works in co-ordination with the conventional job scheduler. Once a job is dispatched by the conventional scheduler, the power manager (PPartition+PTune) determines its power budget, the selection of processors from those available, and the power distribution (or processor power caps) across them.

We assume a large job queue (> 384 processes) and a backfilling queue (< 48 processes). The conventional job scheduler schedules as many large jobs as it can on the machine before scheduling the backfilling jobs. We assume up to Nmax=550 nodes with 12 cores each (6600 processes). If the power manager decides to schedule the job, power distribution across its processors (and power repartitioning if required) is enforced using RAPL.

8. EXPERIMENTAL SETUP

Experiments were conducted on a 324-node Ivy Bridge cluster. Each node has two 12-core Intel(R) Xeon(R) CPU E5-2695 v2 @ 2.40GHz processors and 128 GB of memory. We used MVAPICH2 version 1.7. The codes were compiled with the Intel compiler version 12.1. The msr-safe kernel module provides direct access to Intel RAPL registers via libmsr [35]. We used the package (PKG) domain of RAPL that provided us the capability of capping power for each of the processors in an experiment. The scheduling environment was simulated in R.

We again used EP, BT, and SP from the NPB suite and CoMD from the Mantevo suite in their pure MPI versions. We exponentially increase the node count for our experiments. The inputs were weakly scaled for different node counts. We report performance in terms of completion time in seconds and power in Watt. The reported numbers are averages across ten runs.

9. RESULTS

Experiments were conducted for single job power tuning and multi-job power partitioning.

Variation under Power Caps: Sorting Required

We now exploit the observed variability in the unbounded power consumption of the processor chips, which translates into variation in performance under a power constraint. This variability may be caused by factors such as manufacturing/process variation (at CMOS/transistor level), ambient machine room temperature in different rack positions (higher/lower to the floor), or others. Yet, our method handles variation irrespective of its causes. Previous work [27] and Section 2 has already established that a cluster is not homogeneous under a power constraint because of such variation. We also observe that scheduling a job on different sets of fixed number of processors under a constant power budget leads to variation in the performance of a parallel job.

We present a selection of configurations to demonstrate this behavior in Figures 11 and 12. The x-axis represents the codes and the number of processors. The y-axis indicates the completion time in seconds. The codes are run on several combinations of processors from one or more quartiles of the processor distribution. The numbers on the top of the bars indicate percentage slowdown with respect to the baseline. The processors are uniformly capped at 51W in this set of experiments, i.e., they maintain a constant job power budget of 8KW, 16KW, and 32KW for 16, 32, and 64 processor experiments, respectively. The baseline for 16 processor experiments (Fig. 11) is the performance on the processors belonging to quartile Q1. For 32 and 64 processors (Fig. 12), the baseline is the performance on the processors belonging to Q1 and Q4 (also see legends). Q1 consists of the most efficient processors whereas Q4 consists of the least efficient processors. We observe a performance slowdown ranging from 2% to 18%. We observe that performance deteriorates as we include less efficient processors (Q2, Q3, Q4) in the mix. Hence, the optimal selection of n_{opt} processors should consist of the most efficient processors from the available ones.

PTune

We evaluate the effectiveness of PTune using the aforementioned codes. In Fig. 13, we present results for three different combinations of processors belonging to different quartiles. There are three data points corresponding to each code.

In the figures, n_{LOWER} (synonymous with $n_{\perp}$) is the maximum number of processors that can operate at maximum power such that their aggregate power does not violate the job level power constraint. This configuration most closely resembles the worst case power provisioning as processors are not power constrained. PTune is the data point corresponding to optimal configuration suggested by the power tuner. Uniform power corresponds to the naïve approach of distributing the job's power budget evenly across all processors in a job. This is the baseline configuration.

Performance

In Fig. 13, the y-axis represents performance (top graph) in terms of wall-clock time (in seconds) and the number of processors recommended by the power manager (bottom graph)

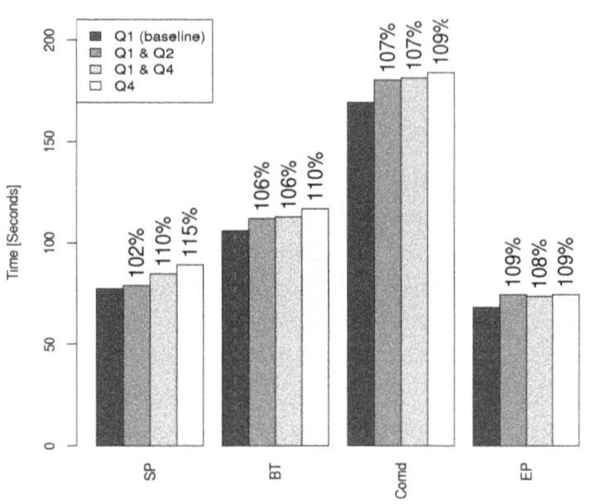

Figure 11: Performance variation on 16 processors

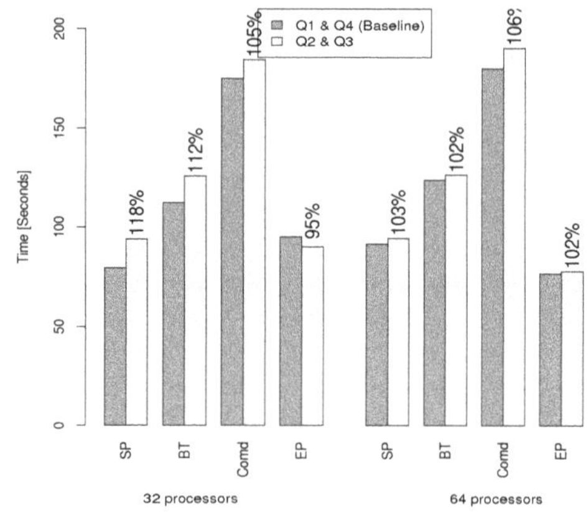

Figure 12: Performance variation on 16 and 32 processors

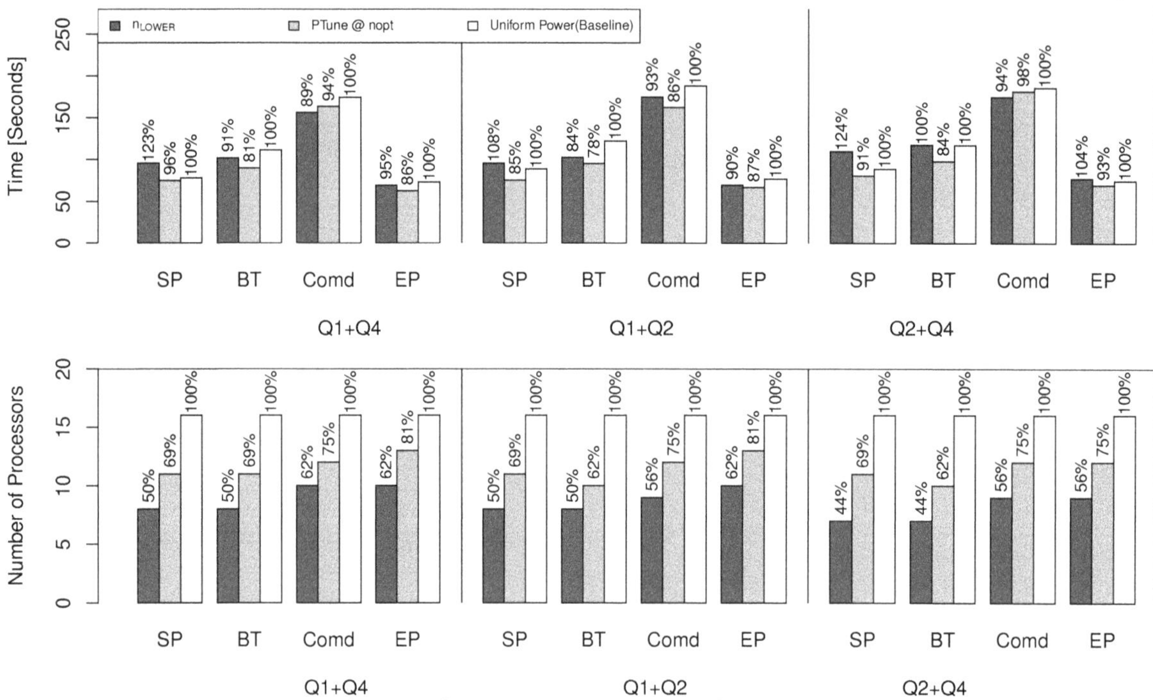

Figure 13: Evaluation of PTune on 16 processors from one or more quartiles

over different codes and quartiles to which the processors belong (x-axis). The numbers on the bars indicate the runtime reduction and utilized number of processors relative to the baseline in percent.

We observe a performance improvement of up to 22%. The gains are dependent on the combination of processors from different quartiles as well as on workload. PTune is able to free up to 38% of the resources while achieving similar or higher performance than the baseline configuration.

Scalability

We evaluate PTune on up to 128 processors. Fig. 14 presents results addressing the scalability of PTune. PTune achieves performance improvements of as much as 29% with a minimum of 1%. More significantly, in case of the minimal performance improvement, PTune frees up 23% of the processors, which subsequently become available to the next scheduled jobs. We observe an error of less than 2% between the total job power consumption (measured via RAPL) of the PTune recommended configurations and the assigned job-level power budget across all experiments.

PPartition

In this section, we perform a macro-level evaluation of our 2-level model. We simulate the conventional scheduler that dispatches jobs from multiple queues, one at a time. Let np be the number of processes. The scheduler handles 3 queues, 1 large job queue ($np \geq 768$ or $n \geq 64$ processors), and two backfill queues ($np \leq 48$ or $n \leq 4$ processors, $48 < np < 768$ or $4 < n < 64$ processors). Larger jobs are scheduled first followed by backfilling jobs to improve the system utilization. We assume $Nmax = 550$ processors. Our job mix consists of 25% jobs from each EP, SP, BT, and CoMD.

We assume a hardware overprovisioned machine with a machine power budget $P_{m/c} = 28KW$. Fig. 15 depicts a scenario in which the job scheduler is oblivious of power management. The machine's power budget is uniformly distributed across all the processors. We call this naïve schedul-

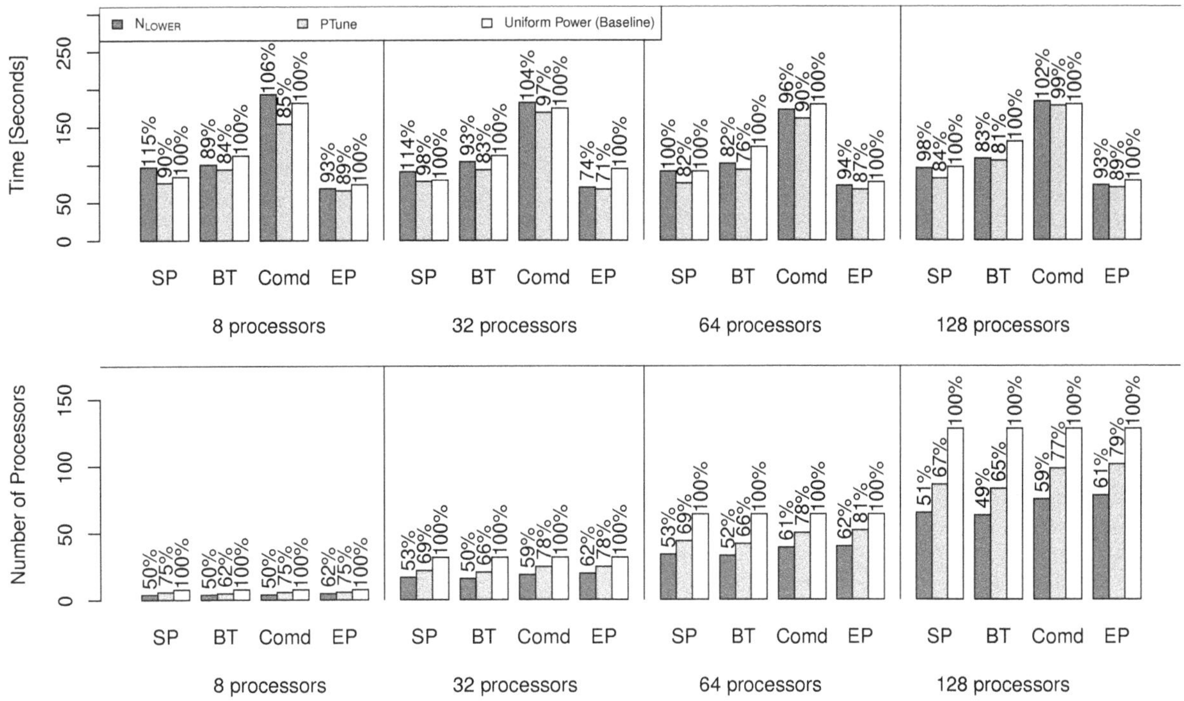

Figure 14: Evaluation of PTune on processors from Q1 and Q4 quartiles

ing. The conventional scheduler schedules jobs as long as the required number of processors are available. Fig. 16 depicts the scenario when our power manager (PTune + PPartition) co-ordinates with the conventional scheduler to make variation-aware power and job scheduling decisions. The x-axes in both the plots represent job identifiers ordered by the time that they are dispatched by the conventional scheduler. We can see that the large 64 processor job is scheduled first followed by the backfilling jobs. The left y-axis denotes job performance in IPS. Each of the red, green and blue curves represents a job's performance as more and more jobs are scheduled over time (moving right along the x-axis).

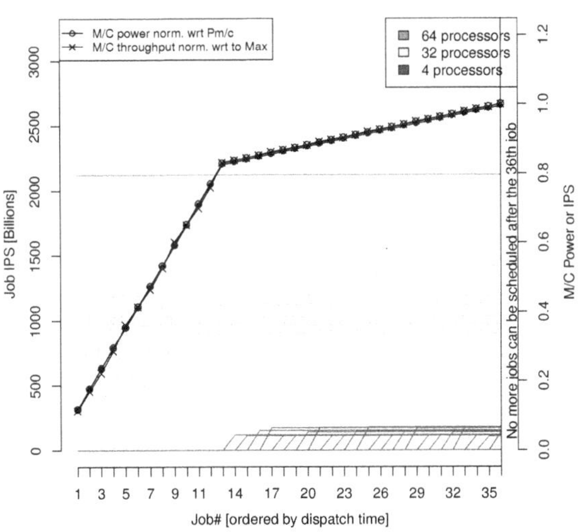

Figure 15: Uniform power distributed across the machine. $P_{m/c} = 28kW$

Our scheduler starts with jobs at high power budget and, hence, high performance. But as more jobs are dispatched, power is stolen from the previously scheduled jobs. This

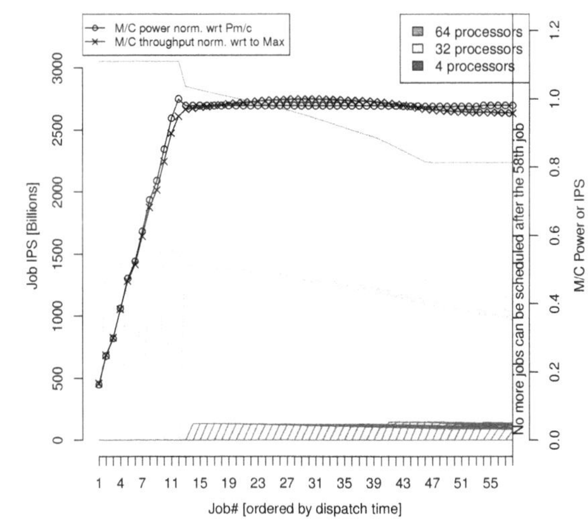

Figure 16: PPartition + PTune. $P_{m/c} = 28kW$.

leads to a drop in their performance. In return, we are able to schedule more jobs at the expense of the performance of already running jobs. In this scenario, our scheme is able to schedule 58 jobs whereas the power-oblivious scheduler is able to schedule only 36 jobs to run at the same time. This is because PTune schedules each job on a reduced number of processors compared to the naïve scheme. The performance of most of the first 36 jobs (that are scheduled under both the schemes) of our approach is at least as good as the naïve one. In addition to these jobs, our power control is able to schedule 22 more backfill jobs that further improve the overall throughput (SysIPS) of the machine (compared to the naïve approach) under the same power constraint.

The right y-axes depict the system's power consumption as a fraction of (normalized to) the overall provisioned system power, $P_{m/c}$, in one line graph (circles) and the system's performance ($SysIPS = \sum JobIPS_i$) normalized to the maximum in the other (crosses). Both graphs track each other closely, but under our power control, the machine power is fully utilized much earlier (after ≈ 10 jobs) whereas 36 jobs are required to reach this level in the naïve case. These initial jobs also achieve higher performance under our scheme (>1500 Billions IPS) than that in the naïve case (900 to 1500 Billion IPS for backfill jobs and 2100 Billion IPS for the large job) before the other jobs are scheduled, and these jobs would thus terminate earlier as they have progressed further under our power control compared to the naïve case. This shows that when there are fewer jobs running on a machine, our power manager is able to direct all machine power to jobs where it is needed to maximize performance under a power constraint unlike the naïve approach.

Fig. 17 presents a comparison of the throughput of our scheme compared to three other naïve schemes. The x-axis denotes the machine's power budget and the y-axis depicts the throughput of the machine (SysIPS) normalized to a maximum throughput at 39KW (left bar per set). Uniform capping schemes assume that an appropriate number of randomly selected processors on the machine are already capped at $P_{m/c}/N_{max}$, 75W (mid-way between minimum power and TDP), and TDP, such that their aggregate power does not exceed the machine's power budget. The rest of the processors in these configurations are not available to the conventional scheduler in the naïve scheme. PTune+PPartition represents our model that makes variation-aware decisions about scheduling jobs across the entire machine under a machine-level power constraint. The percentages on top of bars indicate how much lower the throughput per naïve scheme is compared to our solution. Our model achieves 5-35% higher throughput.

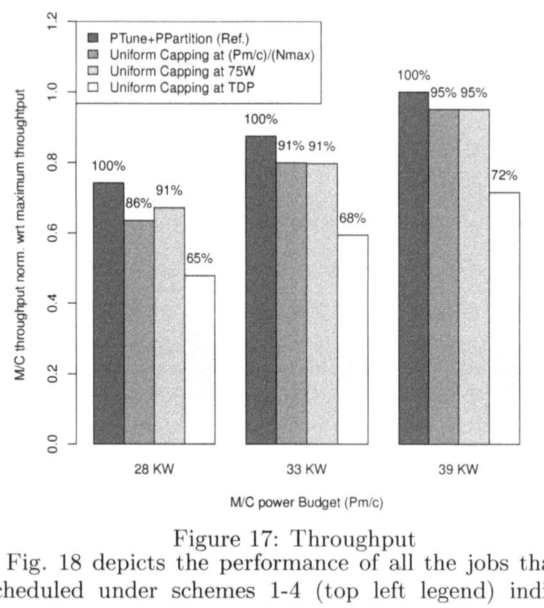

Figure 17: Throughput

Fig. 18 depicts the performance of all the jobs that are scheduled under schemes 1-4 (top left legend) indicated along the x-axis. The y-axis denotes job's performance normalized wrt. to the aggregate job performance (SysIPS) under the respective schemes. We see that our approach (scheme 1) is able to schedule a much larger number of jobs (denser clusters in plot) than the naïve scheduling policy (scheme 2) by trading off performance of some jobs.

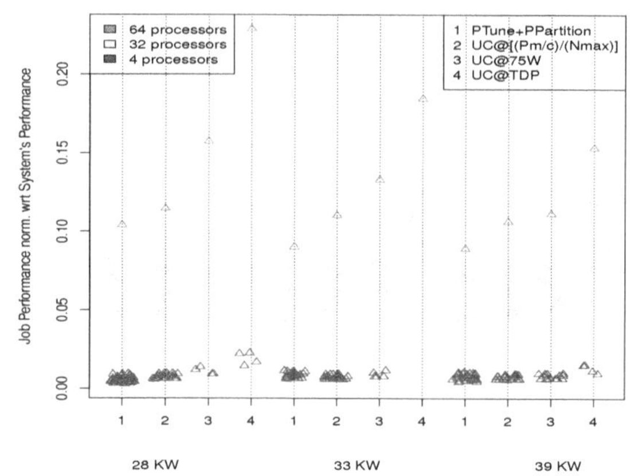

Figure 18: Job performance. A job is represented by a triangle

10. RELATED WORK

Energy has been an important issue in high performance computing (HPC) for over a decade. Supercomputers as old as BlueGene/L have been built with the goal of maximizing power efficiency. Power-scalable clusters that are equipped with voltage and frequency scaling have existed for over a decade that enabled researchers to study the energy problem in HPC. Freeh et al. [14] investigated the energy-time trade off of MPI applications to prove that it is feasible to save energy by scaling the processor down to lower energy levels with or without time penalty depending on the application. Springer et al. [36] proposed a combined approach of performance modeling and performance prediction for minimizing the execution times of MPI applications under energy bounds. They used voltage and frequency scaling on single cores of a small cluster of up to 10 nodes for their experiments. In addition, there is abundant work presenting algorithms that use frequency and voltage scaling mechanisms for energy savings [23, 28, 29, 13, 4]. In contrast, our work uses power capping via the Intel RAPL interface. Totoni et al. [38, 22] presented an ILP-based runtime system that schedules work on a selective *subset* of cores of a single multi-core chip to meet the power or performance constraint. Within-die or core-to-core variation-aware DVFS schemes [37, 16] have been proposed for chip-multiprocessors. These schemes select optimal voltage and frequency set points for each of the cores to achieve improved power to performance ratio for the chip. Our work differs from this work in terms of granularity. We study variation across several processors or chips and not across cores of a single multi-core chip. We manage resources at processor (or chip) level. We use either *all or none* of the cores of the chips/multi-core processors on a machine. Our goal is to improve the performance of a parallel job scheduled on multiple processors under a strict power budget.

System-wide solutions for power constraint systems have been proposed that aim at increasing the throughput of systems by leveraging the idea of *hardware overprovisioning* [12, 24, 32, 33, 11]. Sarood et al. [34] proposed a scheme of determining an optimal number of nodes under strong scaling of applications executing on an overprovisioned system while distributing power between CPU and memory. Etinski et al. [10, 9] proposed the use of dynamic voltage and frequency scaling (DVFS) at the job scheduling-level to save energy and improve overall job performance. Patki et al. [25] proposed power-aware backfilling to improve the throughput of the system. Ellsworth et al. [8] presented a power scheduler that enforced a system-wide power bound by reallocating power across the cluster. Our work differs from all of the above because our approach takes the performance variation across processors of a cluster into account while scheduling and tuning jobs for performance.

Inadomi et al. [18] propose performance optimizations across inhomogeneous processors. It provides a detailed analysis of the phenomenon across multiple clusters and provides a set of simple algorithms for intelligent power balancing. These algorithms, while groundbreaking, suffered from two serious limitations. First, the processor power model assumed that CPU clock frequency increased proportionally with power. While that is a useful simplification, our work here shows that the story is not nearly so simple. Second, the algorithms assumed the ideal number of nodes to use was fixed a priori. In our approach, PPart and PTune jointly determine the ideal number of nodes and the power budget for every job at the time of scheduling. While the result of both of our approaches is a power schedule, we are solving a fundamentally different problem.

Kappiah et al. [21] presented a system that saves energy at the expense of execution time by scaling down the frequencies of the cores when they encounter slack time in an MPI application. Rountree et al. [28] used linear programming to establish a bound on optimal energy savings of an MPI application and presented a runtime algorithm to save energy in HPC applications with negligible delay [29]. Power conservation by means of turning off unwanted nodes is proposed in [26]. In the above presented solutions, authors used one core per node and their goal was to maximize energy savings with minimal impact on the execution time. In contrast to these solutions, we are intolerant to performance degradation. We use multicore processors and our goal is to minimize the completion time as long as we stay within the power budget.

11. SUMMARY

We presented a hierarchical variation-aware machine-wide solution for managing power on a hardware overprovisioned machine. It consists of a macro-level Power Partitioner that makes power and job scheduling decisions and a micro-level Power Tuner that determines the optimal processor selection and their power caps for a job such that its performance is maximized under a power constraint. PTune achieves up to 29% improvement in performance compared to uniform power capping. It does not lead to any performance degradation, yet frees up to 40% of resources compared to uniform power capping. PPartition is able to improve the throughput of the machine by 5-35% compared to naïve scheduling under the same machine power budget.

We established that under a power constraint, the variability in performance transforms into variation in peak power efficiency. We believe that this variation in power efficiency should be one of the primary considerations in the future power management research.

12. ACKNOWLEDGEMENTS

We extend our thanks to Livermore Computing for facilitating Dedicated Access Time on the LLNL cluster. This work was supported in part by NSF grants 1217748, 1058779, 0958311, and by Consortium for Advanced Simulation of Light Water Reactors (CASL). This material is also based upon work supported by the U.S. Department of Energy's Lawrence Livermore National Laboratory. Office of Science, under Award number DE-AC52-07NA27344 and supported by Office of Science, Office of Advanced Scientific Computing Research (LLNL-CONF-656877, LLNL-CONF-698261).

13. REFERENCES

[1] U.s. energy information administration. https://www.eia.gov/electricity/annual/html/epa_04_03.html.

[2] Top 500 list. http://www.top500.org/, June 2002.

[3] D. H. Bailey, E. Barszcz, J. T. Barton, D. S. Browning, R. L. Carter, D. Dagum, R. A. Fatoohi, P. O. Frederickson, T. A. Lasinski, R. S. Schreiber, H. D. Simon, V. Venkatakrishnan, and S. K. Weeratunga. The NAS Parallel Benchmarks. *The International Journal of Supercomputer Applications*, 5(3):63–73, Fall 1991.

[4] P. E. Bailey, A. Marathe, D. K. Lowenthal, B. Rountree, and M. Schulz. Finding the limits of power-constrained application performance. In *Proceedings of the International Conference for High Performance Computing, Networking, Storage and Analysis*, SC '15, pages 79:1–79:12, New York, NY, USA, 2015. ACM.

[5] K. Bergman, S. Borkar, D. Campbell, W. Carlson, W. Dally, M. Denneau, P. Franzon, W. Harrod, J. Hiller, S. Karp, S. Keckler, D. Klein, R. Lucas, M. Richards, A. Scarpelli, S. Scott, A. Snavely, T. Sterling, R. S. Williams, K. Yelick, K. Bergman, S. Borkar, D. Campbell, W. Carlson, W. Dally, M. Denneau, P. Franzon, W. Harrod, J. Hiller, S. Keckler, D. Klein, P. Kogge, R. S. Williams, and K. Yelick. Exascale Computing Study: Technology Challenges in Achieving Exascale Systems. 2008.

[6] S. Borkar, T. Karnik, S. Narendra, J. Tschanz, A. Keshavarzi, and V. De. Parameter variations and impact on circuits and microarchitecture. In *Design Automation Conference, 2003. Proceedings*, pages 338–342, June 2003.

[7] B. Dally. Power and programmability: The challenges of exascale computing. In *Presentation at ASCR Exascale Research PI Meeting*, 2011.

[8] D. A. Ellsworth, A. D. Malony, B. Rountree, and M. Schulz. Pow: System-wide dynamic reallocation of limited power in hpc. In *Proceedings of the 24th International Symposium on High-Performance Parallel and Distributed Computing*, HPDC '15, pages 145–148, New York, NY, USA, 2015. ACM.

[9] M. Etinski, J. Corbalan, J. Labarta, and M. Valero. Optimizing Job Performance Under a Given Power Constraint in HPC Centers. In *Green Computing Conference*, pages 257–267, 2010.

[10] M. Etinski, J. Corbalan, J. Labarta, and M. Valero. Utilization driven power-aware parallel job scheduling. *Computer Science - R&D*, 25(3-4):207–216, 2010.

[11] M. E. Femal and V. Freeh. Boosting data center performance through non-uniform power allocation. In *International Conference on Autonomic Computing*,

pages 250–261, 2005.
[12] M. E. Femal and V. W. Freeh. Safe overprovisioning: using power limits to increase aggregate throughput. In *In International Conference on Power-Aware Computer Systems*, December 2005.
[13] V. Freeh, F. Pan, N. Kappiah, and D. K. Lowenthal. Using multiple energy gears in mpi programs on a power-scalable cluster. In *PPoPP*, pages 164–173, June 2005.
[14] V. Freeh, F. Pan, N. Kappiah, D. K. Lowenthal, and R. Springer. Exploring the energy-time tradeoff in mpi programs on a power-scalable cluster. In *IPDPS*, May 2005.
[15] R. Ge, X. Feng, S. Song, H.-C. Chang, and D. Li. Powerpack: Energy profiling and analysis of high-performance systems and applications. May 2010.
[16] S. Herbert and D. Marculescu. Variation-aware dynamic voltage/frequency scaling. In *High Performance Computer Architecture, 2009. HPCA 2009. IEEE 15th International Symposium on*, pages 301–312, Feb 2009.
[17] J. H. L. III, P. Pokorny, and D. Debonis. Powerinsight - a commodity power measurement capability. In *IGCC'13*, pages 1–6, 2013.
[18] Y. Inadomi, T. Patki, K. Inoue, M. Aoyagi, B. Rountree, M. Schulz, D. Lowenthal, Y. Wada, K. Fukazawa, M. Ueda, M. Kondo, and I. Miyoshi. Analyzing and mitigating the impact of manufacturing variability in power-constrained supercomputing. In *Proceedings of the International Conference for High Performance Computing, Networking, Storage and Analysis*, SC '15, pages 78:1–78:12, New York, NY, USA, 2015. ACM.
[19] InsideHPC. Power Consumption is the Exascale Gorilla in the Room. http://insidehpc.com/2010/12/.
[20] Intel. Intel-64 and IA-32 Architectures Software Developer's Manual, Volumes 3A and 3B: System Programming Guide. 2011.
[21] N. Kappiah, V. Freeh, and D. K. Lowenthal. Just in time dynamic voltage scaling: Exploiting inter-node slack to save energy in mpi programs. In *SC*, Nov 2005.
[22] A. Langer, E. Totoni, U. S. Palekar, and L. V. Kalé. Energy-efficient computing for hpc workloads on heterogeneous manycore chips. In *Proceedings of Programming Models and Applications on Multicores and Manycores*. ACM, 2015.
[23] M. Y. Lim, V. Freeh, and D. K. Lowenthal. Adaptive, transparent frequency and voltage scaling of communication phases in mpi programs. In *SC*, 2006.
[24] T. Patki, D. K. Lowenthal, B. Rountree, M. Schulz, and B. R. de Supinski. Exploring Hardware Overprovisioning in Power-constrained, High Performance Computing. In *International Conference on Supercomputing*, pages 173–182, 2013.
[25] T. Patki, D. K. Lowenthal, A. Sasidharan, M. Maiterth, B. Rountree, M. Schulz, and B. R. de Supinski. Practical Resource Management in Power-Constrained, High Performance Computing. In *HPDC*, 2015.
[26] E. Pinheiro, R. Bianchini, E. V. Carrera, and T. Heath. Load balancing and unbalancing for power and performance in cluster-based systems. In *Workshop on compilers and operating systems for low power*, 2001.
[27] B. Rountree, D. H. Ahn, B. R. de Supinski, D. K. Lowenthal, and M. Schulz. Beyond DVFS: A First Look at Performance under a Hardware-Enforced Power Bound. In *IPDPS Workshops*, pages 947–953. IEEE Computer Society, 2012.
[28] B. Rountree, D. K. Lowenthal, S. Funk, V. Freeh, B. R. de Supinski, and M. Schulz. Bounding energy consumption in large-scale mpi programs. In *SC*, pages 10–16, Nov 2007.
[29] B. Rountree, D. K. Lowenthal, M. Schulz, V. Freeh, and T. Bletsch. Adagio: Making dvs practical for complex hpc applications. In *ICS*, Nov 2009.
[30] Sandia National Laboratory. Mantevo project home page. https://software.sandia.gov/mantevo, June 2011.
[31] V. Sarkar, W. Harrod, and A. Snavely. Software Challenges in Extreme Scale Systems. In *Journal of Physics, Conference Series 012045*, 2009.
[32] O. Sarood. *Optimizing Performance Under Thermal and Power Constraints for HPC Data Centers*. PhD thesis, University of Illinois, Urbana-Champaign, December 2013.
[33] O. Sarood, A. Langer, A. Gupta, and L. V. Kale. Maximizing throughput of overprovisioned hpc data centers under a strict power budget. In *Proceedings of the International Conference on High Performance Computing, Networking, Storage and Analysis*, SC '14, New Orleans, LA, 2014. ACM.
[34] O. Sarood, A. Langer, L. V. Kale, B. Rountree, and B. de Supinski. Optimizing Power Allocation to CPU and Memory Subsystems in Overprovisioned HPC Systems. In *Proceedings of IEEE Cluster 2013*, Indianapolis, IN, USA, September 2013.
[35] K. Shoga, B. Rountree, M. Schulz, and J. Shafer. Whitelisting msrs with msr-safe. In *3rd Workshop on Extreme-Scale Programming Tools at SC*, Nov. 2014. http://www.vi-hps.org/upload/program/espt-sc14/vi-hps-ESPT14-Shoga.pdf.
[36] R. Springer, D. K. Lowenthal, B. Rountree, , and V. Freeh. Minimizing execution time in mpi programs on an energy-constrained,power-scalable cluster. In *PPoPP*, May 2006.
[37] R. Teodorescu and J. Torrellas. Variation-aware application scheduling and power management for chip multiprocessors. In *Computer Architecture, 2008. ISCA '08. 35th International Symposium on*, pages 363–374, June 2008.
[38] E. Totoni, A. Langer, J. Torrellas, and L. Kale. Scheduling for hpc systems with process variation heterogeneity. In *Technical Report YCS-2009-443, Department of Computer Science, University of York*, 2014.
[39] L. Zhang, L. S. Bai, R. P. Dick, L. Shang, and R. Joseph. Process variation characterization of chip-level multiprocessors. In *Design Automation Conference, 2009. DAC '09. 46th ACM/IEEE*, pages

Online Scalability Characterization of Data-Parallel Programs on Many Cores

Younghyun Cho Surim Oh Bernhard Egger

Department of Computer Science and Engineering
Seoul National University, Seoul, Korea
{younghyun, surim, bernhard}@csap.snu.ac.kr

ABSTRACT

We present an accurate online scalability prediction model for data-parallel programs on NUMA many-core systems. Memory contention is considered to be the major limiting factor of program scalability as data parallelism limits the amount of synchronization or data dependencies between parallel work units. Reflecting the architecture of NUMA systems, contention is modeled at the last-level caches of the compute nodes and the memory nodes using a two-level queuing model to estimate the mean service time of the individual memory nodes. Scalability predictions for individual or co-located parallel applications are based solely on data obtained during a short sampling period at runtime; this allows the presented model to be employed in a variety of scenarios. The proposed model has been implemented into an open-source OpenCL and the GNU OpenMP runtime and evaluated on a 64-core AMD system. For a wide variety of parallel workloads and configurations, the evaluations show that the model is able to predict the scalability of data-parallel kernels with high accuracy.

1. INTRODUCTION

With the ongoing consolidation of more and more cores into a single chip, many-core multiprocessor systems are now readily available. While graphics processors have been integrating over a thousand cores for some time now, these days modern general-purpose servers easily integrate a few tens or even hundreds of cores. Machines with such a large number of cores typically comprise multiple physical CPU chips integrated in a multi-socket multi-core non-uniform memory architecture (NUMA) system. At the same time, data-parallel programming models such as OpenCL [20] promising for easy and scalable parallelization have risen in popularity, initially primarily on GPGPUs but recently also on modern general-purpose processors [32, 33, 31]. While in principle data parallel programs scale linearly, architectural realities such as the memory bottleneck limit the scalability as the number of available computing cores increases.

An important problem for runtime systems managing tens or hundreds of cores is allocation of processing cores to parallel applications. The state-of-the-art, static resource reservations or serializing parallel applications and devoting all physical cores to the running application, is not utilizing the computing resources to maximum capacity anymore. To exploit the full potential of the hardware, several parallel applications need to be executed simultaneously. In this context, the main question is how many of the available resources should be allocated to each application in order to achieve maximal system throughput. Scalability prediction models of parallel applications can provide resource managers with the necessary information to make these choices.

Predicting the performance scalability of parallel applications has long been an active topic of HPC research [4, 34, 41, 7, 36, 5, 22]. Sophisticated performance modeling techniques are used to aid application design and performance tuning for HPC systems. Existing techniques for at-runtime many-core management rely on additional efforts before applications are executed such as offline training [25] or machine learning [15, 14] to understand the applications' performance characteristics. If offline information is not available, the standard practice of prior research [27, 9] is to measure an application's throughput by executing it on different resource configurations to obtain information about its scalability. Such techniques not only require additional hardware resources but also a long reconfiguration time. Furthermore, existing techniques can not or only with great difficulty be used to predict the scalability of co-located parallel applications.

In this paper, we propose an accurate, at-runtime performance scalability model for data parallel programs running on commodity NUMA systems. The model is eventually to be employed by the resource scheduler of a runtime system for many-core systems which puts stringent constraints on the tolerable overhead of the model. Furthermore, we target malleable parallel programming models that can change the degree of parallelism during execution of a parallel section. The OpenCL model with work units distributed to worker cores naturally allows adaptation of the number of assigned cores. The standard OpenMP `parallel for` construct with its static even work distribution at the beginning of the loop does not provide malleability within a parallel section. Ways to render OpenMP applications malleable have been proposed [16].

The proposed model does neither require prior analysis, offline profiling, nor modifications of the parallel applications. The model is integrated directly into the parallel runtime, and the performance characteristics of the individ-

PACT '16, September 11 - 15, 2016, Haifa, Israel

ISBN 978-1-4503-4121-9/16/09...$15.00

DOI: http://dx.doi.org/10.1145/2967938.2967960

ual parallel sections are obtained at runtime. The negligible overhead of the brief sampling phase querying hardware performance counters renders the model an ideal candidate to be used in online resource allocation. Furthermore, the model is able to estimate an application's performance scalability in the presence of external workloads competing for the shared resources.

In the data parallel programming model, work units are independent of each other and synchronization only occurs at the end of a parallel section. The main limiting factor of scalability is thus memory contention. Reflecting the architectural design of modern many-core architectures with several cores sharing a last-level cache (LLC), termed `compute node`, and one or more NUMA memory nodes, contention is modeled both at the LLCs of the individual compute nodes and the memory nodes.

Modern NUMA systems by the major vendors for x86 hardware exhibit similar NUMA interconnects with AMD's HyperTransport (HT) and Intel's QuickPath Interconnect (QPI), respectively. Both vendors provide hardware performance counters that allow us to measure relevant NUMA-related performance events. We measure memory accesses per core, misses in the LLCs, and memory requests arriving at the different memory controllers during a brief sampling period initiated when the program enters a parallel section. The throughput of an application in dependence of the number of assigned cores is modeled based on the system-wide workload and memory contention. The presented model consists of a hierarchy of two stacked queuing models to compute contention at the individual memory controllers (MC) and the buses between the last-level caches and the MCs. Scalability predictions are made based hardware performance counters gathered at-runtime during a short sampling period. The model can adapt to different NUMA memory allocation policies and does not require any offline analysis of the data parallel code. This and the negligible overhead of the sampling make the model an ideal candidate for at-runtime resource management and performance tuning.

The model has been implemented into an open-source OpenCL and the GNU OpenMP runtime. OpenCL [20] is an obvious choice as it is one of the most prominent data parallel programming models these days. For OpenMP [10] code we only support the data-parallel `parallel for` loop constructs. The accuracy of the model is validated against measurements on a 64-core AMD multi-socket multi-core NUMA system with various OpenCL and OpenMP kernels. The model is evaluated both by predicting the scalability of standalone applications under different NUMA allocation policies and in co-located parallel applications scenarios. The experimental results show that the model is able to accurately predict the speedup of a data parallel kernel with an error of 6.8% and a coefficient of determination (R^2) of 0.9 for OpenCL and an error of 9.7% and R^2 of 0.88 in OpenMP benchmarks.

The remainder of this paper is organized as follows. Section 2 provides the necessary background on programming models and queuing theory. The scalability prediction model is detailed in Section 3. Sections 4 and 5 describe the implementation on the target architecture for validation and evaluation of the proposed model. Section 6 discusses related work. The paper concludes with Section 7.

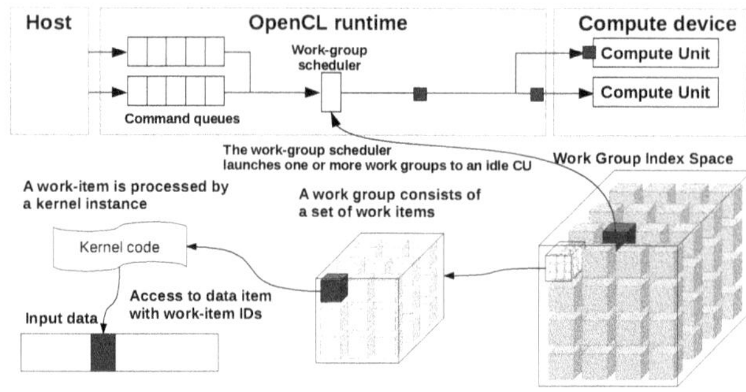

Figure 1: The OpenCL execution model.

2. BACKGROUND

2.1 Data Parallelism in OpenCL

OpenCL [20] is one of the most popular data parallel programming models. An OpenCL application consists of a *host program* and one or several *kernels*. The kernels implement the data-parallel parts of the program while the host program provides initialization and glue between the parallel parts. Via the OpenCL runtime, the host processor dispatches work to the devices, each of which comprises one or more *compute units* (CUs). Each CU is divided into one or several *processing elements* (PEs) within which the computations on a device occur. In OpenCL terminology, a *work-item* refers to the smallest unit in a data decomposition. The minimal execution unit is a *work-group* comprising one or more work-items. All work-items within a work-group are executed concurrently on the PEs of a single CU. Figure 1 shows one possible data composition of a three-dimensional index space into work-groups and work-items.

Following the data parallel model, no synchronization between work-groups is provided. Synchronizations within work-groups and the synchronization of CUs at the end of the entire computation do not invalidate the assumptions of our model since work-groups constitute the smallest execution unit and are executed independently. An OpenCL scheduler can increase or decrease the number of processing CUs while executing a kernel. Performance scalability can thus be a useful indicator for at-runtime resource management and performance tuning for OpenCL programs.

In the context of many-core x86 processors, each processor core constitutes an OpenCL CU. That is, the work-items of a work-group are executed on one core. Most x86 OpenCL runtimes execute work-items serially to avoid the task switching overhead, but concurrent (task switched) execution is also possible. The proposed model is independent of the execution model since the CU is the smallest modeled entity.

2.2 Parallel Loops in OpenMP

OpenMP [10] is widely used for parallel programming on shared-memory systems. Based on the fork-join model, OpenMP provides a variety of functionalities (e.g., synchronization, nested parallelism, etc.) to ease parallel programming. Although OpenMP is not a data parallel programming model per-se, parallel loops in OpenMP executing different parts of the entire workload on assigned cores in parallel exhibit similar properties as data parallel models. In the OpenMP `parallel for` construct, there is no synchro-

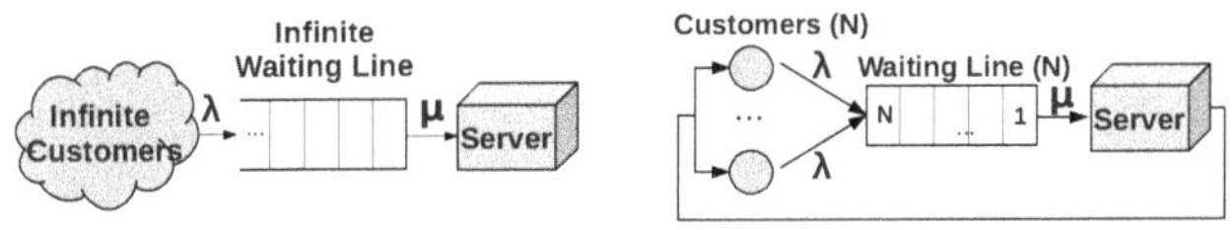

(a) M/M/1 system (b) M/M/1/N/N system

Figure 2: Queuing systems (λ=arrival rate, μ=service rate).

nization or communication between loop iterations except implicit barriers at the end of the parallel loop. Application programmers can annotate the scheduling discipline of the loop and choose between static, dynamic, and guided scheduling. OpenMP parallel loops are not directly malleable with a static work distribution, but predicting the scalability of such loops can be useful if the application is executed more than once. In addition, several researches [16, 8] have presented techniques to render OpenMP programs malleable.

2.3 Queuing Models

Queuing theory is the mathematical study of waiting [35]. For a queuing network, a queuing model can predict the waiting time based on probabilistic methods. Queuing models are widely used for a variety of applications such as telecommunication, market services, or computer systems. In the context of computer systems, queuing models are especially well-suited to model resource contention.

We argue that queuing theory is a good candidate for performance prediction of data-parallel programs for the following reasons. First, there are no data dependencies or synchronization points between the work chunks. Instead, the major bottleneck affecting scalability is contention in the memory system. Second, the individual computing cores processing the chunks of work can be considered independent workers exhibiting similar access patterns to shared resources. These two properties allow us to treat each computing core as a flow-equivalent queuing customer and model memory contention using a queuing model. Employing queuing theory to model memory contention also has the additional benefit of being independent from the NUMA allocation policy as well as allowing us to model the performance of several parallel applications executing simultaneously.

The *M/M/1 model* is one of the simplest and most popular queuing models. An M/M/1 queuing system, illustrated in Figure 2 (a), assumes an infinite number of customers and one single server. The model can estimate the mean service time when input and service rates follow an exponential distribution. For an input rate λ and a service rate μ, $\mu > \lambda$, the expected mean service time is given by Little's Law as

$$r = \frac{1}{\mu - \lambda}$$

With a finite number of customers, the presence of more or fewer cores can have a strong effect on the distribution of arrivals which renders the model ineffective for accurate scalability estimation.

To deal with finite populations, the *M/M/1/N/N model*, also known as the "machine repair problem" can be applied [28, 35]. An M/M/1/N/N queuing system consists of N customers, a waiting line having N entries, and one server as shown in Figure 2 (b). Given an input rate of one customer, λ, and a service rate μ, the mean service time r is given by

$$r = \frac{1}{\mu}\left(\frac{N}{1 - 1/P(0)} - \frac{\mu}{\lambda}\right)$$

where $P(0)$, the probability that no customers request service, is computed as

$$P(0) = \sum_{k=0}^{N} \frac{N!}{(N-k)!}\left(\frac{\lambda}{\mu}\right)^k$$

The M/M/1/N/N model can be used to compute the contention overhead if the access pattern of the customers (the processing cores) to the shared resource (the memory controller) follows an exponential distribution and the access patterns of all involved customers (cores executing the same parallel program) are similar. Tudor *et al.* [39] have shown that parallel workloads in the NAS parallel benchmark [3] implementing the seven dwarfs of HPC [2] do not exhibit bursty memory access patterns unless the workload is small. Data parallel programs typically deal with big amounts of data; we therefore assume that the M/M/1/N/N queuing is adequate for modeling shared memory contention. The results in Section 5 validate this assumption.

3. SCALABILITY PREDICTION MODEL

The presented performance model facilitates the prediction of a data parallel program's scalability in dependence of the allocated number of processor cores. The prediction is based on a two-level M/M/1/N/N model estimating the memory contention at the bus-level as well as at each memory node. The model relies on the properties of data parallel programs, i.e., similar flow, no data dependencies, and no or very little synchronization between processor cores. Every bus from the last-level cache (LLC) of a CPU node to every memory node as well as each memory node are modeled separately. We compute flow-equivalent per-core memory accesses to obtain the contention on buses from the LLC to the memory nodes. Each memory node is treated as a separate queuing server, the customers are the buses arriving from the different LLCs.

We can only claim that the per-core memory access pattern of a data parallel program is stable when all cores behind a shared LLC execute the same kernel. In this paper, our model thus assumes that parallel applications are allocated to cores at the granularity of CPU nodes to avoid sharing of a LLC between several applications. The model parameters are obtained by querying the hardware performance counters during a short sampling period during execution of a parallel program kernel. The model then estimates how the program's performance changes in dependence of a varying number of CPU nodes. The proposed model is able to estimate memory contention and predict scalability of a parallel program in the presence of co-located parallel applications as long as each application is executed on disjoint CPU nodes.

3.1 Mapping NUMA System onto a Queuing System

The majority of all NUMA systems share the architectural characteristics that are important to map the proposed

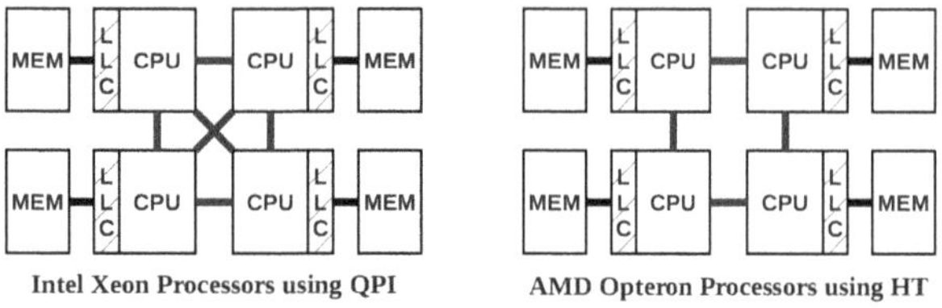

Figure 3: Intel and AMD NUMA systems.

model to a concrete system. CPU cores are grouped into so-called *CPU nodes*. All cores in a CPU node share a common last-level cache (LLC). Each CPU node is connected to its local and several remote memory nodes via a high-speed interconnection network. Figure 3 displays the organization of typical Intel and AMD NUMA systems. The Intel system on the left comprises four CPU chips, each with a local LLC and one memory controller. The CPU chips are connected by a full crossbar network. The AMD system uses a slightly different interconnection network where remote memory accesses can require up to two hops. The interconnection network allows simultaneous accesses from the LLCs to the different memory nodes. That is, the cores behind an LLC can issue memory requests independently and in parallel, but several simultaneous accesses to one memory node may get serialized by the LLC, resulting in a stall of the waiting core(s). Each memory node has a dedicated memory controller which also serializes and processes the incoming requests from the connected compute nodes.

The left hand of Figure 4 illustrates that contention can occur at two different locations: first, on the bus from one of the LLCs to a memory controller. Contention on the bus from one LLC to a given memory node occurs when memory requests by two or more cores behind the same LLC miss and trigger simultaneous requests to the MC that then need to be serialized. Second, at the individual memory controllers themselves. The proposed model reflects this by employing a two-level queuing model to model both bus contention and memory controller contention separately as illustrated on the right-hand side of Figure 4. To model the total contention overhead, we first compute the mean service time observed at each memory controller by using an M/M/1/N/N model. We then add the estimated mean service time of the memory controllers to the bus delay of each memory interconnection bus in an uncongested situation. The bus contention model is then used to compute the mean memory access latency (bus plus memory access latency) based on the measured arrival rates from each core. The following subsection explains the model in detail.

3.2 Scalability Prediction By Contention Modeling

The expected speedup for a number of cores to process a given, specific amount of work is computed as follows. Let W denote the total number of cycles required to complete the given work. In particular, W does not include stall cycles incurred at the two possible contention points. If there is no contention, we can expect linear speedup for a parallel section using N cores and thus divide the total work cycles W by N. Let $C(N)$ be the number of cycles required to serve all memory requests from a core when the core processes a given amount of work with N cores competing for shared

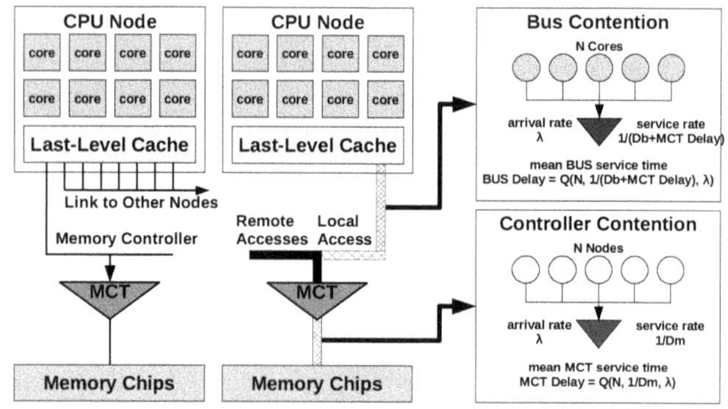

Figure 4: Mapping of NUMA to a queuing system.

Table 1: Model input parameters.

Program-specific parameters	
LLC_m	Per-core LLC miss rate for memory m
BUS_m	Per-core bus access rate for memory m
MCT_m	Per-node memory controller (MCT) access rate for memory m
$D_b[n][m]$	Uncongested bus delay from CPU n to memory m
D_m	Uncongested memory controller delay
Resource allocation	
$N^p = \{n_1^p, n_2^p, ...\}$	Set of reserved CPU nodes for program p
$M = \{m_1, m_2, ...\}$	Set of memory nodes on system
Queuing equation	
$Q(N, \mu, \lambda)$	MM1NN Queuing Equation: N = number of queuing customers, μ = service rate, λ = arrival rate

resources. The speedup is then given by

$$S(N) = \frac{W + C(1)}{W/N + C(N)}$$

To compute $C(N)$, we estimate the mean service time for each individual memory controller. $C(N)$ depends on the number of cores N because of potential contention at the LLCs and the memory nodes. The work per core for N cores (W/N) is multiplied by the average latency to access memory which is the sum of all latencies of requests (mean service request time, R_m) to the different memory controllers, LLC_m. LLC_m denotes the program's per-core miss rate from an LLC to a given memory controller m.

$$C(N) = \frac{W}{N} \cdot \sum_m LLC_m \times R_m$$

The mean service time R_m for memory m is computed by applying the M/M/1/N/N queuing equation as given in Section 2.3. Note that the bus access request rate, denoted BUS_m, differs from LLC_m because the bus access requests include memory write operations, whereas LLC_m only includes (missed) read accesses.

$$R_m = Q(\#\ of\ Cores\ in\ a\ Node, \mu, BUS_m)$$

While all system CPU nodes affect the mean service time of every memory controller, the number of queuing competitors at the bus from an LLC to a memory controller is equal to the number of cores in a CPU node. The mean service rate μ is given by

$$\mu = 1/(Bus\ Delay + Controller\ Delay_m)$$

where *Bus Delay* represents the mean bus delay without any congestion of the nodes allocated to the parallel application and *Controller Delay*$_m$ denotes the memory controller latency of memory m.

We compute *Bus Delay* by taking the program's average delay of each involved processor node to all memory controllers. N^p contains the list of CPU nodes allocated to program p. The computation of the architectural parameters D_b and D_m is explained in Section 4.3.

$$Bus\ Delay = \frac{\sum_{n \in N^p, m \in M}(D_b[n][m] \times Req\ Ratio[m])}{|N^p|}$$

$$Req\ Ratio[m] = \frac{BUS_m}{\sum_{m' \in M} BUS_{m'}}$$

Finally, we compute the mean memory controller delay for each memory node. Unlike the other resources, memory controller contention can be affected by other applications. We thus compute the average per-node arrival rate λ_m for memory m from all running applications. P represents the set of all running programs in the system.

$$Controller\ Delay_m = Q(\sum_{p \in P} |N^p|, 1/D_m, \lambda_m)$$

$$\lambda_m = \frac{\sum_{p \in P}(MCT^p_m \times |N^p|)}{\sum_{p \in P} |N^p|}$$

The required parameters for computing the model are summarized in Table 1. We obtain the three memory access patterns (LLC_m, BUS_m and MCT_m) from an online profiler built into the parallel program execution runtimes.

3.3 Advantages and Limitations of the Model

Here we briefly discuss advantages and limitations of the proposed model. The major advantage of the model is its efficiency and versatility. The model requires only a very short at-runtime profiling phase to collect work cycles and memory access patterns. It is thus possible to employ the model in dynamic resource management to, for example, allocate cores to several running parallel applications such that the overall performance is maximized. The model is versatile because it is orthogonal to how the data is distributed to the system memories in the system and allows us to estimate speedup even in the presence of co-located workloads.

Nevertheless, the current model suffers from a number of limitations. Foremost, the model only predicts performance scalability on node-granularity. This is because the model requires knowledge about the memory access patterns of each processor node. Furthermore, the behavior of execution contexts in an application is only stable when executed on node granularity. We argue that such an allocation is sensible to prevent pollution of the LLC, however, if scalability needs to be estimated on a finer level than processor nodes, it may be necessary to apply other intra-node scalability prediction techniques independently. Second, our model assumes that the workloads exhibit similar memory access patterns independent of the core they are executed on. This condition is satisfied when a workload scheduler distributes the parallel chunks of work to idle cores at runtime without considering data locality. In general, well-known loop scheduling algorithms such as self or guided scheduling do not consider data-locality. However, if the application employs the first-touch NUMA policy and the work-group scheduler considers data locality when distributing the work, the memory access patterns will vary when executed on a different node. We can extend the model to support such a situation by providing additional information to the application runtime; this is part of future work.

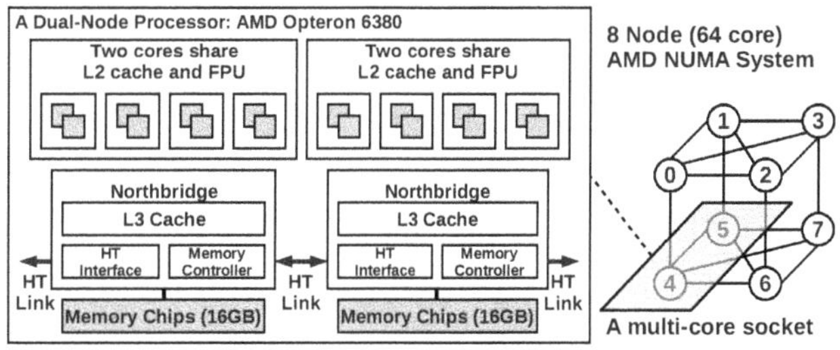

Figure 5: 64-core AMD multi-socket system.

4. MODEL VALIDATION

We validate the proposed model by integrating it into an open-source OpenCL framework and the GNU OpenMP runtime running on an AMD NUMA many-core architecture. This section describes the model's implementation.

4.1 Target NUMA Architecture

The NUMA architecture the proposed model is evaluated on is a 64-core AMD multi-socket NUMA system comprising a total of 8 processor nodes in four physical processor packagings (AMD Opteron 6380 [1]). Each node contains 8 computing cores that share an L3 (last-level) cache and a local memory node. The processor nodes are connected by AMD's hyper-transport with a maximum hop distance of two. Figure 5 shows the organization of the architecture.

4.2 Online Performance Measurement

The at-runtime performance measurement logic and scalability prediction model have been implemented into `SnuCL`, a freely available open-source framework [21] and the GNU OpenMP runtime. The OpenCL runtime profiles each individual OpenCL kernel during a short sampling period at the beginning of a kernel. The OpenMP runtime profiles parallel workloads when a parallel loop is launched.

The following hardware performance counters are measured at runtime (Table 2). On the CPU node, the number of CPU cycles are measured on a per-core basis. LLC miss counts, DRAM requests to the total eight memory nodes, and the local memory node requests are sampled on the north-bridge of each CPU node. While we implement and evaluate our prediction model on an AMD machine, the necessary performance counters are common in modern NUMA

Table 2: Measured performance counters [12].

CPU performance counters	
CPU Cycles PMCx076 - CPU Clocks not Halted	The number of core clocks that the CPU is not in a halted state
NorthBridge performance counters	
L3 Cache Misses NBPMCx4E1 - L3 Cache Misses	The number of L3 cache misses for accesses from each core
DRAM Requests NBPMCx1EO - CPU to DRAM Requests to Target Node	All DRAM reads and writes generated by cores on the local node to the targeted node in the coherent fabric
MCT Requests NBPMCx1F0 - Memory Controller Requests	The total number of read/write request commands sent to the DRAM controller

systems[1]. Since the AMD North-Bridge supports only up to four simultaneous performance measurements [12], several samples are necessary to obtain all values. One sample measures LLC miss counts, MCT requests, and DRAM requests to two of the eight memory nodes, i.e., a total number of four samples are required to measure the DRAM requests to all eight memory nodes. Details on the sampling rate and the number of full samples are given in Section 5.

4.3 Extracting the Model Parameters

To model the scalability of parallel workloads, a total of five application-specific parameters are required (Table 1): three shared-resource access rates (LLC misses, bus requests, and memory controller requests) and the latencies of both bus and memory controller in the uncongested state. The metrics of the shared resources are computed from the sampled performance counters as follows

$$LLC_M = \frac{L3\ Cache\ Misses\ to\ M\ /\ \#\ Cores\ in\ a\ Node}{Work\ Cycles}$$

$$BUS_M = \frac{DRAM\ Requests\ to\ M\ /\ \#\ Cores\ in\ a\ Node}{Work\ Cycles}$$

$$MCT_M = MCT\ Requests\ to\ M\ /\ Work\ Cycles$$

We cannot directly measure the number of L3 cache misses going to a specific node (*L3 Cache Misses to M*); the measured L3 cache misses include accesses to all memories. We compute the value by dividing the measured total number of L3 cache misses by the memory access ratio obtained to a specific memory node M from the DRAM request counters to all memory nodes.

A non-trivial problem is the computation of work cycles on AMD processors. Work cycles refer to the number of CPU cycles required to perform the requested work *excluding* stall cycles caused by memory contention. AMD processors do not support performance counters providing the necessary data[2]. We thus approximate the number of work cycles W as follows. Let T be the total number of cycles required to perform a certain amount of work including contention. Then, T is W plus the stall cycles incurred by LLC cache misses. The average number of LLC stall cycles is obtained by multiplying the number of accesses from the LLC to each of the different memory nodes, denoted L_m, by the service time of each memory controller, R_m. This value is computed by the queuing model (Section 3), which in turn requires the input request rate given by L_m/W.

$$T = W + \sum_m L_m R_m = W + \sum_m L_m Q(L_m/W) \quad (1)$$

In order to solve equation 1 for W, we apply an iterative method to compute an approximated value of W where the initial input (W_0) is set to T. Since $T \geq W$, W_i converges towards the actual number of work cycles. In our implementation, we use the value of the 5th iteration, W_5, to approximate the number of work cycles.

$$W_{i+1} = T - \sum_m L_m Q(L_m/W_i) \quad (2)$$

The model also requires the architecture-specific parameters $D_b[n][m]$ and D_m (Table 1). $D_b[n][m]$ is the latency incurred when accessing memory node m from the LLC of CPU node n in the uncongested state. Accessing a memory node m from a given CPU node n incurs between 0 (local node) and 2 hops (remote nodes) on our target architecture (i.e., D_b only contains three distinct values). D_m, on the other hand, represents the latency of an uncongested memory controller. On the chosen architecture, there are no performance counters to obtain the required values. We perform a regression analysis on the predicted and the measured speedups of all kernels to compute the values for $D_b[n][m]$ and D_m. Once the values are determined, the values are used for every application. Table 3 lists the values for our AMD target architecture.

Table 3: Architecture-specific model parameters.

Parameter	Hops	Latency
D_b	0	3.0
	1	5.5
	2	8.0
D_m	-	12.0

5. EVALUATION

5.1 Experimental Setup

The proposed model is evaluated with two programming models, and a variety of applications and configurations. To make a prediction for 8, 16, 24, 32, 40, 48, 56, and 64-core configurations, the first execution of a kernel/loop is briefly sampled on a given configuration (typically one node, i.e., 8 cores). The baseline is obtained by running the parallel application with a different number of assigned

[1]For example, Intel's Xeon family also provides the performance counters corresponding to each counters on the AMD system: `LONGEST_LAT_CACHE:MISS` for L3 Cache Misses, `DATA_FROM_QPI_TO_NODEx` for DRAM Requests, and `UNC_M_CAS_COUNT:ALL` for MCT Requests [17, 18].

[2]The AMD Opteron architecture provides latency measurement performance counters at the NorthBridge, for example, `CPU Read Command Latency/Requests to Target Nodes` (from NBPMCx1E2 to NPBMCx1E7). However, these counters are not accurate when L3 speculative prefetching is enabled (as is the default) [13].

cores. One sample consists of four sub-samples that extract the different hardware counters as outlined in Section 4.1. We use a sampling frequency of 200 Hz and collect 10 full samples for a prediction, i.e., the entire sampling period takes $4 * 10 * 5ms = 200ms$. We evaluate the model in the following configurations: memory configuration (using 2, 4, and 8 memory nodes), scheduler configuration (static, self, and Li; see next paragraph), and standalone or co-located execution. All experiments were performed three times, and we report the average of the runs.

5.2 Scheduling Policies

The policies for scheduling work units regarding load balancing and dispatch overhead can have a significant effect on the performance scalability of an application.

In the case of OpenCL, scheduling of work-groups is performed by the OpenCL runtime. We test kernels with three scheduling strategies: static scheduling, dynamic (self) scheduling, and guided scheduling. Static scheduling divides and assigns the work-groups of a parallel section equally between the available cores. The dispatch overhead is very small, but the policy may suffer from load imbalances since work-groups are never reassigned. In dynamic scheduling, work-groups are assigned to idle cores at runtime. For the experiments, our dynamic (self) scheduler assigns one work-group at a time. This policy provides good load balancing but suffers from a high dispatch overhead. Guided scheduling assigns several work-groups in one chunk in order to keep the dispatch overhead low yet allow for load balancing. Li's guided scheduling [23], the default in `SnuCL`, assigns $\lceil wg/2N \rceil$ work-groups to an idle core where wg represents the remaining number of work-groups and N the available worker cores. Guided scheduling typically yields the best performance on many-core systems. For OpenMP the programmer can choose between the static, dynamic, and guided scheduling policies by program annotation.

5.3 Target Applications

For the evaluation, we select the kernels of six applications (BT, CG, EP, FT, MG, SP) from SNU-NPB3.3 [30] which provides both OpenCL and OpenMP implementations [29] of the NAS parallel benchmarks [3]. Table 4 lists the characteristics of the target applications.

Our model predicts the scalability of each parallel section individually. The parallel kernels are evaluated with the biggest available input data set. Three classes of kernels are excluded from the evaluation for the following reasons. First, kernels appearing in more than one benchmark application have only been evaluated once. Second, kernels with very short runtimes ($< 0.5sec$) when executed on one CPU node are not considered. Last, we have skipped most of the kernels performing data initialization because their performance either shows linear speedup or saturated performance depending on their memory-boundness. One exception is the `init_ui` kernel with the highest write-intensity of all kernels. We employ the `init_ui` kernel when evaluating the co-located scenario. The selected kernels along with their number of work-groups and work-items are shown in the first three columns of Table 5.

5.4 Evaluation Metrics

The proposed model is evaluated in terms of the accuracy of the predicted scalability. Two metrics, the mean absolute percentage error (MAPE) and the coefficient of determination (R^2), are used to validate our prediction model. MAPE is computed by taking the arithmetic mean of the percentage errors based on the difference between the measured and the predictive value. It is indicated by

$$M = \frac{1}{n}\sum_{k=1}^{n}\left|\frac{a_k - p_k}{a_k}\right|$$

where a_k represents the actual and p_k the predicted value.

The coefficient of determination R^2 indicates the extent to which the speedup can be predicted from the profiled data. R^2 is defined as the square of the correlation between the predicted and the actual speedup.

$$R^2 = 1 - \frac{\sum_{i=1}^{n}(y_i - \hat{y}_i)^2}{\sum_{i=1}^{n}(y_i - \bar{y})^2}$$

Here, n represents the number of data points, y_i the actual and $\hat{y}_i$ the predicted speedup. $\bar{y}$ is the mean value of the observed speedups ($\bar{y} = 1/n \cdot \sum_{i=1}^{n} y_i$). An R^2 value of 1 indicates that the prediction perfectly matches the measured speedup. Values < 0 appear when $\bar{y}$ provides a better fit than the predicted values. The MAPE metric shows how close the prediction is to the actual value, whereas an R^2 value close to one indicates a good match between the predicted scalability trend and the measurement.

Table 4: Target applications.

App	Class (Problem Size)	Description (Workload Characteristics)
BT	D (408×408×408)	Block Tri-diagonal solver (memory intensive; scalable)
CG	D (1500000)	Conjugate Gradient (irregular memory access patterns)
EP	B (2^{30} random number)	Embarrassingly Parallel (CPU intensive)
FT	C (512×512×512)	discrete 3D fast Fourier Transform (all-to-all communication)
MG	D (1024×1024×1024)	Multi-Grid on a sequence of meshes (long and short distance communication)
SP	D (408×408×408)	Scalar Pentra-diagonal solver (memory intensive)

5.5 Scalability Prediction of Standalone OpenCL Kernels

We first analyze the proposed model in the standalone scenario for OpenCL kernels, i.e., except for the program under test, no other (parallel) user programs are running on the server.

Table 5 shows the error (MAPE) and R^2 of each individual kernel for the default system configuration: $200ms$ of sampling using Li's guided scheduling, and memory data allocated to all available eight memory nodes in an interleaving manner. The first three columns list the selected kernels along with their input data settings. The next column labeled `scal.` shows the measured actual speedup of the kernel when running on 8 CPU nodes (64 cores) in relation to the baseline (one CPU node, 8 cores). The last two columns, `err` and R^2, contain the results of predicting the speedup for 64 cores. The average estimation error (geometric mean) and average R^2 (arithmetic mean) across all kernels are shown in the final row of the table.

The results show that, in general, the proposed model accurately predicts scalability with an error of 6.8%. The low

Table 5: Scalability prediction accuracy for the default system configuration.

WGs: # of work-groups, WIs: # of work-items, scal.: scalability

Selected Kernel	WGs	WIs	Prediction		
			scal.	err(%)	R^2
BT.z_solve	406	406	7.21	4.22	0.97
CG.conj_grad_2	640	640	4.52	9.85	0.92
CG.conj_grad_6	640	640	4.04	28.19	0.55
EP.embar	1024	16384	7.71	1.6	1.0
FT.init_ui	2101248	134479872	3.38	19.3	0.53
FT.compute_indexmap	4096	512X512	6.51	2.58	0.95
FT.compute_initial_cond	512	512	7.06	3.59	0.97
FT.cffts1	4096	512X512	4.09	11.47	0.9
FT.cffts2	4096	512X512	5.14	4.34	0.99
FT.cffts3	4096	512X512	5.56	3.48	0.99
SP.exact_rhs2	2842	448X406	4.11	9.64	0.93
SP.exact_rhs3	2842	448X406	5.54	5.19	0.95
SP.exact_rhs4	2842	448X406	5.92	3.77	0.98
SP.compute_rhs1	2856	448X408	5.16	7.55	0.94
SP.compute_rhs2	2856	448X408	4.02	12.45	0.88
SP.compute_rhs3	2842	448X406	4.37	6.2	0.97
SP.compute_rhs4	2842	448X406	6.33	3.64	0.98
SP.compute_rhs5	2842	448X406	7.42	2.18	0.99
SP.z_solve	2842	448X406	4.52	6.93	0.96
SP.tzetar	2842	448X406	4.06	9.52	0.9
MG.kernel_resid	4096	1024X1024	4.13	12.03	0.9
MG.kernel_rprj3	4096	512X512	4.08	25.52	0.6
MG.kernel_interp_1	16384	1024X1024	3.54	11.44	0.86
MG.kernel_psinv	4096	1024X1024	4.22	9.22	0.92
Average			**4.96**	**6.84**	**0.90**

Table 6: Accuracy for different sampling periods.

Kernels having at least 1% differences of MAPE for longer samples.

Kernels	200ms		400ms		Entire run	
	err(%)	R^2	err(%)	R^2	err(%)	R^2
MG.kernel_rprj3	25.52	0.6	19.43	0.78	17.75	0.82

error confirms that the proposed two-level queuing model focusing on congestion in the memory system is adequate to model data-parallel applications. For CPU-intensive kernels such as `BT.z_solve`, `EP.embar`, `FT.compute_indexmap`, and `FT.compute_initial_cond` that rarely access memory and have high scalability, the model predicts speedup within 5% error. Data-intensive (non-trivial) kernels such as `FT.cffts1-3`, `SP.exact_rhs2-4`, `SP.compute_rhs1-5`,`SP.-z_solve` and `SP.tzetar` show an accurate scalability prediction with an error of 2-13%. On the other hand, `CG.conj_grad_6` and `MG.kernel_rprj3` exhibit slightly bigger prediction errors. We suspect that the irregular memory access patterns of `CG` and `MG` are the cause for this behavior. Unlike the regular `BT`, `FT` or `SP` benchmarks, `CG` and `MG` exhibit irregular (or varying) memory access patterns (Table 4). Although guided scheduling can mitigate the influence of irregular memory accesses between work-groups, the scheduler may still fail to distribute memory accesses evenly to the available cores. In these cases, the short default sampling period can cause a larger error because the kernel's memory access patterns cannot be fully captured.

The purpose of the experiments in Table 6 is to determine whether a longer sampling phase than the relatively short 200ms at the beginning of a kernel execution allows for better scalability predictions. We compare the default configuration, 200ms, to sampling 400ms and the entire run. Table 6 displays only the kernels which show at least 1% of differences in terms of MAPE with different sampling periods. We observe that the only kernel that significantly profits from a longer profiling phase is `MG.kernel_rprj3`

Table 7: Scalability prediction accuracy for different work schedulers.

Kernels	Self			Static		
	scal.	err(%)	R^2	scal.	err(%)	R^2
BT.z_solve	7.19	4.21	0.97	7.15	5.14	0.96
CG.conj_grad_2	3.95	24.36	0.7	3.63	31.51	0.11
CG.conj_grad_6	4.14	22.11	0.64	3.87	19.93	0.72
EP.embar	7.63	1.82	0.99	7.97	1.36	1.0
FT.init_ui	0.92	426.77	-1235.12	2.9	26.99	0.54
FT.compute_indexmap	5.84	4.27	0.88	5.2	9.1	0.76
FT.compute_initial_cond	6.76	4.4	0.94	7.17	3.74	0.97
FT.cffts1	6.6	13.89	0.79	2.77	33.81	0.49
FT.cffts2	5.53	4.85	0.97	2.87	34.96	0.44
FT.cffts3	5.83	3.77	0.98	4.15	16.67	0.8
SP.exact_rhs2	4.23	23.34	0.59	4.3	11.32	0.9
SP.exact_rhs3	5.57	6.39	0.93	5.71	7.53	0.92
SP.exact_rhs4	6.05	5.83	0.95	6.28	5.45	0.94
SP.compute_rhs1	2.59	78.38	-9.67	5.91	3.47	0.98
SP.compute_rhs2	5.1	11.75	0.77	4.33	15.78	0.83
SP.compute_rhs3	4.36	6.02	0.97	4.46	6.25	0.97
SP.compute_rhs4	5.84	3.23	0.99	6.29	2.88	0.99
SP.compute_rhs5	6.56	3.01	0.98	7.52	2.04	0.99
SP.z_solve	3.3	44.15	-1.13	4.77	6.97	0.96
SP.tzetar	4.08	8.77	0.91	4.07	9.07	0.9
MG.kernel_resid	3.97	20.77	0.54	1.07	66.14	0.29
MG.kernel_rprj3	3.72	23.92	0.44	1.27	116.85	0.32
MG.kernel_interp_1	3.77	6.19	0.94	2.91	24.07	-0.42
MG.kernel_psinv	3.67	6.38	0.96	3.62	9.55	0.92
Average	**4.54**	**10.47**	**-51.17**	**4.14**	**10.92**	**0.72**

where the accuracy of the prediction increases significantly as the sampling period is prolonged (200ms: 26%, 400ms: 19%, entire-run: 18%). This result confirms that most kernels of the NPB benchmark suite are relatively stable and a sampling period of 200ms is sufficient.

Table 7 shows the results for self- and static scheduling. Self- and static scheduling suffer from scalability issues or load imbalances and thus exhibit higher error rates of 10-12%. For example, `FT.init_ui` and `SP.compute_rhs1` display a very high error (427 and 78%) in Table 7 compared to Li or static scheduling because the central scheduler becomes the bottleneck when delivering work-groups to an increasing number of worker cores. Similarly, `MG.kernel_resid` and `MG.kernel_rprj3` show a high error (66 and 117%) in the static scheduler because of load imbalances caused by the static work distribution as can be seen from the scalability (speedup) values for the different scheduling techniques in Table 5 and Table 7. This is an expected limitation of the proposed model as we assume memory contention to be the only limiting factor and do not account for bottlenecks in the scheduler or imbalanced workloads.

In the next two experiments, the number of available memory nodes are reduced from originally eight to four and two (`Memory-0123` and `Memory-01`, respectively) in order to see how the model performs under increasing memory contention. We observe that the error of the estimation increases as the number of memory nodes decreases. `Memory-01` in particular diverges a lot from the predicted value with an average MAPE of 14.7% and an R^2 of -10.3. With only a small number of available memory nodes, memory-intensive kernels often do not scale at all, i.e., the scalability curve is (almost) flat. Even if the model captures the trend of a kernel's scalability well, modest prediction errors can lead to large percentage errors and negative R^2 values. This is, however, rather a limitation of the evaluation metrics than of the model as the visualization of the predicted versus the actual speedup reveals: the prediction of, for example, `FT.init_ui` on two memory nodes has a percentage error of 42% and

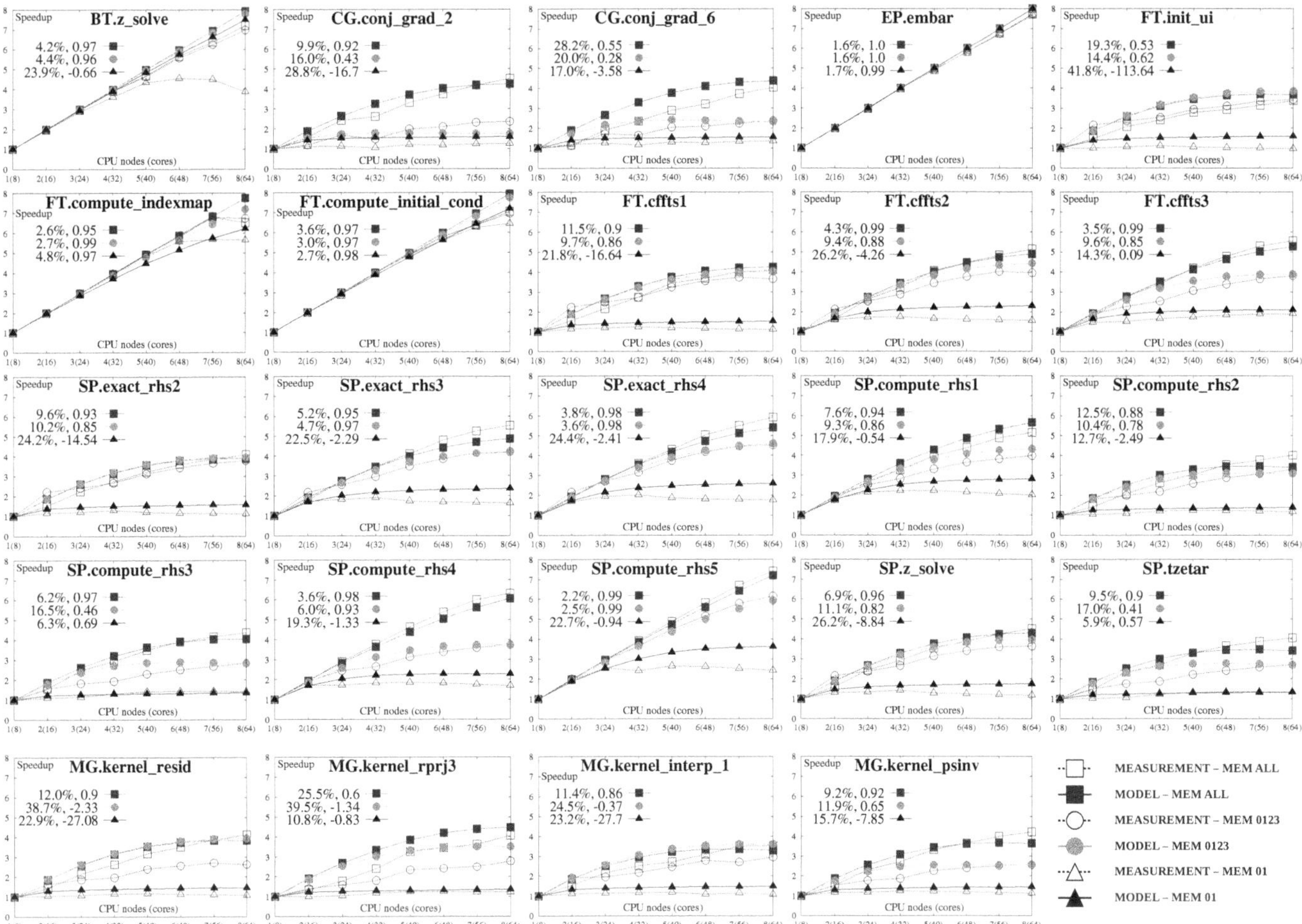

Figure 6: Scalability prediction curves of standalone OpenCL kernels. Each prediction shows MAPE(%) and R^2 values on the graphs.

Table 8: Prediction accuracy for varying memory configurations.

Kernels	Memory 0-3			Memory 0-1		
	scal.	err(%)	R^2	scal.	err(%)	R^2
BT.z_solve	6.99	4.43	0.96	3.87	23.88	-0.66
CG.conj_grad_2	2.36	15.96	0.43	1.27	28.77	-16.7
CG.conj_grad_6	2.37	20.0	0.28	1.35	16.97	-3.58
EP.embar	7.73	1.55	1.0	7.68	1.73	0.99
FT.init_ui	3.43	14.44	0.62	0.97	41.84	-113.64
FT.compute_indexmap	6.74	2.71	0.99	5.65	4.77	0.97
FT.compute_initial_cond	6.96	3.04	0.97	6.45	2.71	0.98
FT.cffts1	3.66	9.75	0.86	1.11	21.81	-16.64
FT.cffts2	3.95	9.39	0.88	1.56	26.2	-4.26
FT.cffts3	3.81	9.57	0.85	1.9	14.35	0.09
SP.exact_rhs2	3.8	10.17	0.85	1.12	24.22	-14.54
SP.exact_rhs3	4.22	4.71	0.97	1.64	22.5	-2.29
SP.exact_rhs4	4.53	3.62	0.98	1.76	24.37	-2.41
SP.compute_rhs1	3.99	9.26	0.86	2.01	17.86	-0.54
SP.compute_rhs2	3.3	10.39	0.78	1.18	12.7	-2.49
SP.compute_rhs3	2.84	16.51	0.46	1.42	6.33	0.69
SP.compute_rhs4	3.73	5.97	0.93	1.69	19.31	-1.33
SP.compute_rhs5	6.15	2.55	0.99	2.43	22.68	-0.94
SP.z_solve	3.64	11.1	0.82	1.18	26.17	-8.84
SP.tzetar	2.71	17.01	0.41	1.34	5.92	0.57
MG.kernel_resid	2.63	38.66	-2.33	1.08	22.93	-27.08
MG.kernel_rprj3	2.78	39.54	-1.34	1.22	10.82	-0.83
MG.kernel_interp_1	2.96	24.5	-0.37	1.07	23.22	-27.7
MG.kernel_psinv	2.56	11.93	0.65	1.13	15.67	-7.85
Average	**3.82**	**9.00**	**0.52**	**1.75**	**14.70**	**-10.33**

an R^2 of -114 even though the model catches the scalability trend well (Figure 6, top-right graph, triangle data series).

Figure 6 visualizes the measured and the predicted speedup for 24 OpenCL kernels and memory allocation policies under Li's guided scheduling and three memory configurations for eight different core configurations ranging from 8 to 64 cores with an increase of 8 cores. Square, round and triangle data series represent the configurations `Memory-ALL`, `Memory-0123`, and `Memory-01`, respectively. The filled shapes show the predicted, and the empty shapes the measured speedup. The predictions are based on sampling the kernel for $200ms$ on one CPU node (8 cores).

As online performance prediction relies solely on performance monitoring at runtime and work-group scheduling has a strong influence on the speedup, the model is not always able to predict the scalability with high accuracy. We observe three special cases in Figure 6. First, the short sampling-based prediction may fail to accurately capture the memory access patterns for irregular applications such as `CG` or `MG`. For some of these kernels a longer sampling period leads to a better prediction (e.g., `MG.kernel_rprj3` in Table 6). Second, our model predicts almost linear speedup for CPU-intensive kernels such as `BT.z_solve`, `FT.compute_indexmap` while the actual speedup can be significantly nonlinear as the number of CPU node increases. The reason

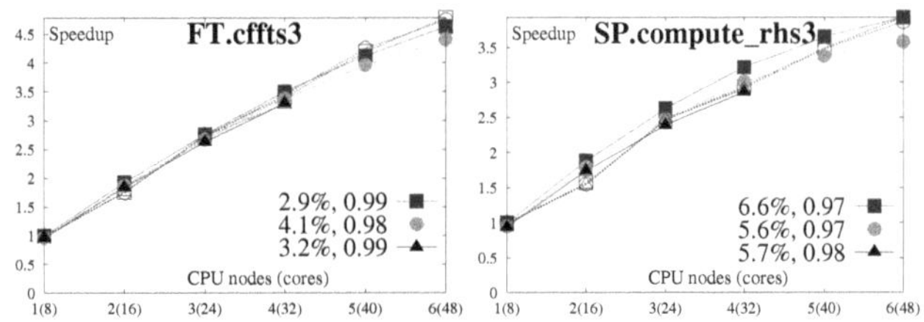

(a) Co-location with a CPU-bound kernel (EP.embar)

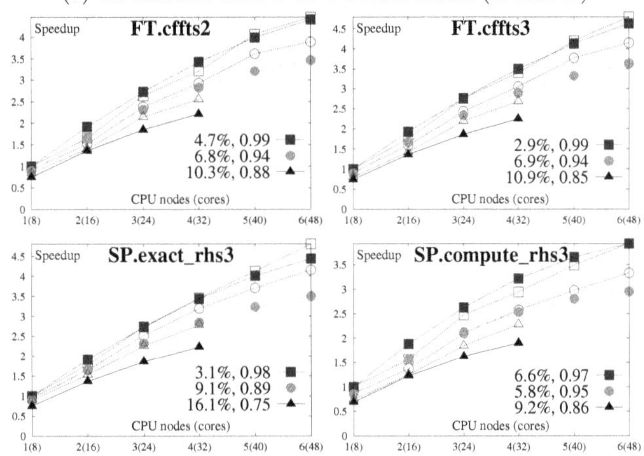

(b) Co-location with a memory-bound kernel (FT.init_ui)

■ standalone execution, ●/▲ co-located workloads executed on 2/4 nodes (16/32 cores), respectively. Empty shapes represent measured, solid shapes predicted values.

Figure 7: Scalability prediction curves of OpenCL kernels with co-located kernels.

is mainly that these kernels have a small number of work groups (Table 5) compared to the number of system cores. In such a case, guided scheduling can fail to distribute the workloads well. In addition, the work-group scheduler overhead plus other operating system tasks executed with the OpenCL kernel can affect its performance when the kernel is executed on all available nodes. Lastly, some measurement have show irregularities such as SP.compute_rhs3 and SP.tzetar where performance remains stable from 24 to 32 but jumps for 40 or more cores. Here, the additional physical processor can mitigate some congestion and the additional remote LLCs can have a positive effect on performance for certain workloads and node counts. Pressure at some memory links can also be alleviated if more nodes are activated. Our model focuses on major contention points and does not capture all memory-related traffic, but the graphs show that, in general, the proposed model captures scalability trends very well for most kernels.

In the standalone scenario, the average error of 6.8% of the scalability prediction for both trivial and non-trivial kernels shows that the proposed model is a viable candidate to accurately estimate both the expected speedup and the scalability trend for a wide variety of kernels despite the very short at-runtime sampling period.

5.6 Scalability Prediction of OpenCL Kernels with Co-located Workloads

We now analyze how the presence of other concurrently running workloads affects the scalability of a kernel. For the experiments, we run one of the following two kernels as an

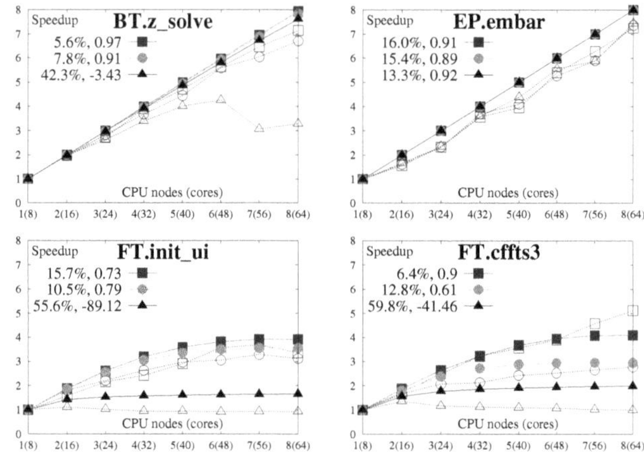

For the legend refer to Figure 6.

Figure 8: Scalability prediction curves of OpenMP parallel loops.

external workload: EP.embar representing a CPU-intensive kernel and FT.init_ui as a representative of a memory-intensive kernel. The co-located workloads are executed in an infinite loop to produce a stable test environment. The kernel under test is then executed on a varying number of CPU nodes. We selected four non-trivial kernels that show good prediction accuracy in the standalone scenario (FT.cffts2/3, SP.exact_rhs3, and SP.compute_rhs3).

Figure 7 visualizes the results. The speedup is normalized to the turnaround time of the target kernel executing standalone on one CPU node. To visualize the performance degradation caused by co-located workloads more clearly, the y axis is scaled to the measured speedup on 6 nodes. As expected, co-location with the CPU-intensive EP.embar does not cause a performance degradation of the kernel under test (Figure 7 (a)). On the other hand, the memory-intensive FT.init_ui causes a visible degradation of performance as shown in Figure 7 (b). The graphs show that the proposed model is able to accurately predict the scalability trend of a single kernel in the presence of co-located parallel applications and can thus be used for dynamic performance tuning or resource management in many-core operating systems.

5.7 Scalability Prediction of OpenMP Parallel Loops

The proposed model can also be applied to OpenMP parallel loops. As for OpenCL, the scalability of a loop is predicted based on a 200ms sampling period at the beginning of a loop. We selected four parallel loops (BT.z_solve, EP.embar, FT.init_ui and FT.cffts3) from SnuNPB for the evaluation (Figure 8). The OpenMP applications implement the same algorithm as their OpenCL counterparts and are tested with the same input data. Compared to the OpenCL scheduler, the OpenMP runtime applies different load balancing and thread management mechanisms which can affect the scalability of the parallel workloads. The OpenMP parallel loops were executed with a static workload distribution. Since our model assumes perfectly balanced workloads, we expect a reduced prediction accuracy for OpenMP loops. For the OpenMP kernels tested, however, the results show that our model still captures the scalability trend well.

6. RELATED WORK

Performance Prediction on HPC Systems.

A number of performance prediction and modeling techniques have been proposed to aid application design and performance tuning for HPC systems. Barnes *et al.* [4] obtain performance data by running an application on different resource configurations and perform multiple linear regressions. Susukita *et al.* [34] predict an application's performance by macro-level simulation tracing the execution flow of the parallel kernels without performing any real computation. Zhai *et al.* [41] use a single node of the target platform for the acquisition of real computation time and predict the performance by observing the computation behavior of the application. Calotoiu *et al.* [7] automatically find asymptotic performance limitations on large-scale machines based on empirical performance modeling and kernel refinements. Bhattacharyya *et al.* [5] generate performance models based on static information refined by performance data obtained during the program's execution. Palm [36] requires source code annotations of certain parameters to ease the generation of an analytic performance model. COMPASS [22], finally, automatically extracts performance parameters from a source-level analysis and predicts the performance on various target platforms from sequential CPU, over GPUs, to heterogeneous systems. In contrast to the techniques above, the presented model can predict the scalability of an application for modern multi-/many-core single- or multi-node NUMA machines. Another distinction is that all of the techniques require offline program analysis, while our model relies solely on performance counters obtained at runtime during a very short sampling period.

Memory Performance on NUMA Systems.

Addressing the issue of shared resource contention on NUMA systems is also an active area of research. Zhuravlev *et al.*, [42], Blagodurov *et al.* [6] and Majo *et al.* [24] focus on scheduling techniques that consider mitigating contention and improving overall system performance through a proper task-to-core mapping. A holistic framework for NUMA resource management is proposed by Dashti *et al.* [11]. These techniques aim to improve system performance with consideration of shared memory contention, but they do not focus on an application's scalability.

Queuing models have been applied for modeling of memory performance [19, 37], but these works are based on simulation. Tudor *et al.* [39, 38] propose analytic models to understand memory contention in multi-threaded programs based on M/M/1 queuing model. In contrast to their work that only accesses memory nodes local to active CPU nodes, the presented model can predict contention for any number of local and remote memory nodes.

A recent work from Wang *et al.* [40] proposes a model that predicts memory bandwidth usage and optimal core allocation of multi-threaded applications on NUMA systems. Integer programming is used to predict the optimal core allocation based on application profiling. Our work is orthogonal to their work as we predict applications' scalability on varying core resources.

Many-core Resource Management.

Moore *et al.* [25] characterize an application's scalability by employing a utility prediction model based on offline training. The model is used to compute the proper number of threads in order to efficiently execute several multi-threaded applications. Grewe *et al.* [15] and Emani *et al.* [14] predict the proper number of threads for an application in the presence of external workloads. The prediction is based on various performance features fed into machine learning models. These researches show that the performance scalability of applications is an important indicator to optimally schedule parallel programs in a many-core environment, but the techniques require offline training obtained.

A number of techniques have been proposed that do not require offline information. Sasaki *et al.* [27] perform scalability based spatial partitioning of multiple multi-threaded applications. To estimate the scalability factors, applications are executed with varying core allocations while measuring the overall throughput. Similarly, Creech *et al.* [9] estimate the scalability of OpenMP parallel sections by creating and concurrently running a serial process executing the same code as the parallel section in order to determine an application's performance scalability. Both techniques estimate the parallel efficiency of a parallel application but require additional resources or additional reconfiguration time. Sasaki *et al.* [26] also perform power and performance optimization with consideration of the scalability of multi-threaded applications by observing per-core CPU utilization as a scalability indicator. In contrast to our work, these approaches do not consider performance degradation caused by shared resource contention or performance inference between multiple applications.

7. CONCLUSION

This paper presents an efficient at-runtime scalability prediction model for data parallel programs running on many-core NUMA systems. The model employs an M/M/1/N/N queuing model to accurately predict contention both at the individual NUMA memory controllers as well as in the buses connecting the last-level caches with the memory controllers. The prediction is made at-runtime based on performance counters obtained during a short $200ms$ sampling period.

The proposed model has been implemented in an open-source OpenCL and the GNU OpenMP runtimes and evaluated on a 64-core NUMA system. Results with a wide variety of parallel kernels and different configurations show that the model, on average, is able to predict the speedup of an OpenCL kernel with an error of only 6.8% in the most common usage scenario. More importantly, the model captures the scalability trend of individual parallel sections which makes it an ideal candidate for online dynamic resource management in a multi-core scheduler.

The model currently does not work well with data-locality-aware schedulers. This issue is part of future work.

Acknowledgments

This work was supported in part by BK21 Plus for Pioneers in Innovative Computing (Dept. of Computer Science and Engineering, SNU) funded by the National Research Foundation (NRF) of Korea (Grant 21A20151113068), the Basic Science Research Program through NRF funded by the Ministry of Science, ICT & Future Planning (Grant NRF-2015K1A3A1A14021288), and by the Promising-Pioneering Researcher Program through Seoul National University in 2015. ICT at Seoul National University provided research facilities for this study.

REFERENCES

[1] AMD. AMD Opteron 6300 Series Processors. http://www.amd.com/en-us/products/server/opteron/6000/6300. [online; accessed March 21, 2016].

[2] K. Asanovic, R. Bodik, B. C. Catanzaro, J. J. Gebis, P. Husbands, K. Keutzer, D. A. Patterson, W. L. Plishker, J. Shalf, S. W. Williams, and K. A. Yelick. The Landscape of Parallel Computing Research: A View from Berkeley. Technical Report UCB/EECS-2006-183, EECS Department, University of California, Berkeley, Dec 2006.

[3] D. H. Bailey, E. Barszcz, J. T. Barton, D. S. Browning, R. L. Carter, L. Dagum, R. A. Fatoohi, P. O. Frederickson, T. A. Lasinski, R. S. Schreiber, et al. The NAS parallel benchmarks. *International Journal of High Performance Computing Applications*, 5(3):63–73, 1991.

[4] B. J. Barnes, B. Rountree, D. K. Lowenthal, J. Reeves, B. De Supinski, and M. Schulz. A regression-based approach to scalability prediction. In *Proceedings of the 22nd annual international conference on Supercomputing*, pages 368–377. ACM, 2008.

[5] A. Bhattacharyya and T. Hoefler. Pemogen: automatic adaptive performance modeling during program runtime. In *Proceedings of the 23rd international conference on Parallel architectures and compilation*, pages 393–404. ACM, 2014.

[6] S. Blagodurov and A. Fedorova. User-level scheduling on NUMA multicore systems under Linux. In *Proc. of Linux Symposium*, 2011.

[7] A. Calotoiu, T. Hoefler, M. Poke, and F. Wolf. Using automated performance modeling to find scalability bugs in complex codes. In *Proceedings of the International Conference on High Performance Computing, Networking, Storage and Analysis*, page 45. ACM, 2013.

[8] A. Collins, T. Harris, M. Cole, and C. Fensch. Lira: Adaptive contention-aware thread placement for parallel runtime systems. In *Proceedings of the 5th International Workshop on Runtime and Operating Systems for Supercomputers*, page 2. ACM, 2015.

[9] T. Creech, A. Kotha, and R. Barua. Efficient multiprogramming for multicores with scaf. In *Proceedings of the 46th Annual IEEE/ACM International Symposium on Microarchitecture*, pages 334–345. ACM, 2013.

[10] L. Dagum and R. Enon. Openmp: an industry standard api for shared-memory programming. *Computational Science & Engineering, IEEE*, 5(1):46–55, 1998.

[11] M. Dashti, A. Fedorova, J. Funston, F. Gaud, R. Lachaize, B. Lepers, V. Quema, and M. Roth. Traffic management: a holistic approach to memory placement on NUMA systems. *ACM SIGPLAN Notices*, 48(4):381–394, 2013.

[12] A. M. Devices. BIOS and kernel developer's guide (BKDG) for AMD family 15h models 00h-0fh processors, 2012.

[13] A. M. Devices. Revision Guide for AMD Family 15h Models 00h-0Fh Processors, 2014.

[14] M. K. Emani, Z. Wang, and M. F. O'Boyle. Smart, adaptive mapping of parallelism in the presence of external workload. In *Code Generation and Optimization (CGO), 2013 IEEE/ACM International Symposium on*, pages 1–10. IEEE, 2013.

[15] D. Grewe, Z. Wang, and M. F. O'Boyle. A workload-aware mapping approach for data-parallel programs. In *Proceedings of the 6th International Conference on High Performance and Embedded Architectures and Compilers*, pages 117–126. ACM, 2011.

[16] T. Harris, M. Maas, and V. J. Marathe. Callisto: co-scheduling parallel runtime systems. In *Proceedings of the Ninth European Conference on Computer Systems*, page 24. ACM, 2014.

[17] Intel. Intel 64 and IA-32 Architectures Software Developer's Manual, 2015.

[18] Intel. Intel Xeon Processor E5 and E7 v3 Family Uncore Performance Monitoring Reference Manual, 2015.

[19] H. Jonkers. Queueing models of parallel applications: the glamis methodology. In *Computer Performance Evaluation Modelling Techniques and Tools*, pages 123–138. Springer, 1994.

[20] Khronos Group. The open standard for parallel programming of heterogeneous systems. https://www.khronos.org/opencl/. [online; accessed March 21, 2016].

[21] J. Kim, S. Seo, J. Lee, J. Nah, G. Jo, and J. Lee. SnuCL: an OpenCL framework for heterogeneous CPU/GPU clusters. In *Proceedings of the 26th ACM international conference on Supercomputing*, pages 341–352. ACM, 2012.

[22] S. Lee, J. S. Meredith, and J. S. Vetter. Compass: A framework for automated performance modeling and prediction. In *Proceedings of the 29th ACM on International Conference on Supercomputing*, pages 405–414. ACM, 2015.

[23] H. Li, S. Tandri, M. Stumm, and K. C. Sevcik. Locality and loop scheduling on NUMA multiprocessors. In *null*, pages 140–147. IEEE, 1993.

[24] Z. Majo and T. R. Gross. Memory management in NUMA multicore systems: trapped between cache contention and interconnect overhead. In *ACM SIGPLAN Notices*, volume 46, pages 11–20. ACM, 2011.

[25] R. W. Moore and B. R. Childers. Using utility prediction models to dynamically choose program thread counts. In *ISPASS*, pages 135–144, 2012.

[26] H. Sasaki, S. Imamura, and K. Inoue. Coordinated power-performance optimization in manycores. In *Proceedings of the 22nd international conference on Parallel architectures and compilation techniques*, pages 51–62. IEEE Press, 2013.

[27] H. Sasaki, T. Tanimoto, K. Inoue, and H. Nakamura. Scalability-based manycore partitioning. In *Proceedings of the 21st international conference on Parallel architectures and compilation techniques*, pages 107–116. ACM, 2012.

[28] A. L. Scherr. *An analysis of time-shared computer systems*, volume 71.

[29] S. Seo, G. Jo, and J. Lee. Performance characterization of the NAS Parallel Benchmarks in OpenCL. In *Workload Characterization (IISWC),*

2011 IEEE International Symposium on, pages 137–148. IEEE, 2011.

[30] S. Seo, J. Kim, G. Jo, J. Lee, J. Nah, and J. Lee. SNU NPB Suite. http://aces.snu.ac.kr/software/snu-npb/, 2011. [online; accessed March 21, 2016].

[31] S. Seo, J. Lee, G. Jo, and J. Lee. Automatic opencl work-group size selection for multicore cpus. In *Parallel Architectures and Compilation Techniques (PACT), 2013 22nd International Conference on*, pages 387–398. IEEE, 2013.

[32] J. Shen, J. Fang, H. Sips, and A. L. Varbanescu. Performance gaps between openmp and opencl for multi-core cpus. In *Parallel Processing Workshops (ICPPW), 2012 41st International Conference on*, pages 116–125. IEEE, 2012.

[33] J. Shen, J. Fang, H. Sips, and A. L. Varbanescu. An application-centric evaluation of opencl on multi-core cpus. *Parallel Computing*, 39(12):834–850, 2013.

[34] R. Susukita, H. Ando, M. Aoyagi, H. Honda, Y. Inadomi, K. Inoue, S. Ishizuki, Y. Kimura, H. Komatsu, M. Kurokawa, et al. Performance prediction of large-scale parallell system and application using macro-level simulation. In *Proceedings of the 2008 ACM/IEEE conference on Supercomputing*, page 20. IEEE Press, 2008.

[35] J. Sztrik. Basic queueing theory. *University of Debrecen: Faculty of Informatics*, 2011.

[36] N. R. Tallent and A. Hoisie. Palm: easing the burden of analytical performance modeling. In *Proceedings of the 28th ACM international conference on Supercomputing*, pages 221–230. ACM, 2014.

[37] T.-F. Tsuei and W. Yamamoto. Queuing simulation model for multiprocessor systems. *Computer*, 36(2):58–64, 2003.

[38] B. M. Tudor and Y. M. Teo. A practical approach for performance analysis of shared-memory programs. In *Parallel & Distributed Processing Symposium (IPDPS), 2011 IEEE International*, pages 652–663. IEEE, 2011.

[39] B. M. Tudor, Y. M. Teo, and S. See. Understanding off-chip memory contention of parallel programs in multicore systems. In *Parallel Processing (ICPP), 2011 International Conference on*, pages 602–611. IEEE, 2011.

[40] W. Wang, J. W. Davidson, and M. L. Soffa. Predicting the memory bandwidth and optimal core allocations for multi-threaded applications on large-scale numa machines. In *2016 IEEE International Symposium on High Performance Computer Architecture (HPCA)*, pages 419–431. IEEE, 2016.

[41] J. Zhai, W. Chen, and W. Zheng. Phantom: predicting performance of parallel applications on large-scale parallel machines using a single node. In *ACM Sigplan Notices*, volume 45, pages 305–314. ACM, 2010.

[42] S. Zhuravlev, S. Blagodurov, and A. Fedorova. Addressing shared resource contention in multicore processors via scheduling. In *ACM SIGARCH Computer Architecture News*, volume 38, pages 129–142. ACM, 2010.

APPENDIX

A. ARTIFACT DESCRIPTION

A.1 Abstract

The software package provided to evaluate the proposed model is composed of several software modules.

- **snucl-model**: the SnuCL framework with an implementation of our online scalability model.
- **gomp-model**: the GNU OpenMP runtime with an implementation of our online scalability model.
- **rte**: a core resource manager (RTE) which manages the core resources for applications (space-sharing). This software is used to execute an application on a specific number of CPU nodes with or without co-located applications.
- **benchmark**: target applications (SNU-NPB) and tools for validating our performance model for both OpenCL and OpenMP applications. The tools include scripts to run the experiments, log analyzers, and plot/table generators.
- **pact16-results**: all experimental results used in the paper are provided here.

All benchmark and visualization tools are written as open-sourced python scripts. The OpenCL and OpenMP runtimes with our online performance model are not open-sourced for now. Instead, we provide pre-compiled binaries of the application runtime libraries.

Our software framework currently runs only on AMD Opteron architectures as it requires access to architecture-specific performance counters. We provide access to our experimental machine, a 64-core AMD server through a guest account. The software package is provided via our private web server. All prerequisites are already installed, on the target architecture. Experiments can be performed immediately without any experimental environment setup.

We also provide detailed installation and benchmark guides in the artifact package. There are two important steps to correctly perform experiments. First, runs requiring access to the hardware performance counters must be executed with super-user privileges. Second, the environment setup as provided in PACT16AE_HOME/env.sh must be maintained. As a consequence, after switching to super-user the environment variables need to be activated (# source env.sh).

A.2 Description

A.2.1 Checklist (artifact meta information)

- **Algorithm**: we present a model for predicting performance scalability. The model is implemented directly into the application runtimes. Performance modeling is performed at runtime and the results are printed when execution of an application ends. It is also possible to model scalability offline by using the collected performance data during application execution. The modeling logic is the same with the online model but scalability predictions can be reproduced efficiently.
- **Program**: we execute SNU-NPB applications. For the experiments we manually adjusted the problem sizes in order to even out the execution time across different benchmarks, but different problem sizes also work.
- **Compilation**: the software modules do not need any special compilers. SnuCL and OpenMP runtimes use gcc/g++, and the benchmark tools require python.
- **Run-time environment**: the software framework runs only on Linux because we use the Linux *perf* interface to query the hardware performance counters.
- **Hardware**: our technique can be applied to other NUMA systems, but the current framework only runs on AMD Opteron NUMA systems.
- **Run-time state**: executing other workloads while collecting performance features of a target applications can negatively affect prediction accuracy.
- **Output**: applications emit log files which include collected performance counter data and predicted speedups values. We analyze the obtained log data to generate graphical outputs.
- **Experiment workflow**: all required experimental steps are explained in a separate file (BENCH) in the software package.
- **Publicly available**? the framework is not publicly available for now.

A.2.2 How delivered

You can download the software package through our private Git server. For the experiments, we also provide a guest account on our evaluated architecture, a 64-core AMD Opteron server. Users requiring access to the software package or the target machine are welcome to contact Younghyun Cho (`younghyun@csap.snu.ac.kr`).

A.2.3 Hardware dependencies

While the performance model is currently only implemented on our target architecture, the technique can be applied to other NUMA systems if such systems support the required performance counters.

A.2.4 Software dependencies

The framework is tested on a Linux operating system (Ubuntu, kernel 3.19). Programs and tools required by our framework (`numactl`, `gnuplot`, and `python` including the `numpy` module) have already been installed in the experimental environment. For more information about software settings and installation please refer to the `INSTALL` file in the software package.

A.2.5 Datasets

While the complete set of experimental results used in the paper is provided in `pact16-results/`, it is also possible to regenerate the same set of experimental data using the provided scripts. The provided data includes raw experimental data, predicted and measured speedups, scalability curve graphs, and table data (Tables 5-8).

In `pact16-results` there are three sub-directories (`10`, `20`, and `full`) in the `plot` directory. The three directories refer to 200ms, 400ms and full execution sampling of a kernel. In addition, in those three directories additional sub-directories labeled `0`, `5`, etc. contain results for different (cache) warm-up periods. The directory `5` contains predictions that ignore the first 5 samples (100ms), and so on. We use 0 warm-up time across all evaluations. We also provide experimental results for different scheduling algorithms (Static, Self, and LI's guided scheduling) where applicable.

For the co-located experiment scenario, there are two sub directories (`embar_1024`, `init_ui_2101248`). The name refers to the co-located workloads. Lastly, the table data for Tables 5-8 is located in the directory `table/`.

Please refer to the BENCH file in the artifact package for more details.

A.3 Installation

While all required programs and tools have already been installed on the target machine, some software modules (GNU OpenMP runtime, SnuCL runtime, target applications) of our experimental framework need to be installed separately for each guest account. The following software modules must be installed:

1. **SnuCL-Model**: pre-compiled binaries for SnuCL runtime are provided. The SnuCL compiler (OpenCL code translation and compilation tools) must be re-installed.
2. **GNU-OpenMP-Model**: for GNU-OpenMP, performance modeling is implemented through dynamic library interpositioning. The required library code is pre-compiled and provided in binary form. Before execution the library needs to be registered in the system library path.
3. **Target applications (SNU-NPB)**: the source code of all application benchmarks is available.
4. **Core resource manager (RTE)**: pre-compiled binaries are provided.

After installation of all required software modules the experiments can be performed. Detailed explanations about the software packaging and the installation steps can be found in the `INSTALL` file in the artifact package.

A.4 Experimental Workflow

Three experiments can be executed with the provided software package.

1. **SnuCL-Model**: scalability prediction of standalone OpenCL kernels.
2. **SnuCL-Model**: scalability prediction of OpenCL kernels with co-located workloads.
3. **OpenMP-Model**: scalability prediction of standalone OpenMP parallel-sections.

Required experimental steps (environmental setup, benchmark scripts, and visualization tools) are explained in the `BENCH` file of the artifact package.

Speculatively Exploiting Cross-Invocation Parallelism

Jialu Huang† Prakash Prabhu† Thomas B. Jablin⊤ Soumyadeep Ghosh

Sotiris Apostolakis Jae W. Lee‡ David I. August

Princeton University {soumyade, august, sa8}@princeton.edu

†Google Inc. {jialuh, prakashp}@google.com

⊤UIUC jablin@illinois.edu

‡Sungkyunkwan University jaewlee@skku.edu

ABSTRACT

Automatic parallelization has shown promise in producing scalable multi-threaded programs for multi-core architectures. Most existing automatic techniques parallelize independent loops and insert global synchronization between loop invocations. For programs with many loop invocations, frequent synchronization often becomes the performance bottleneck. Some techniques exploit cross-invocation parallelism to overcome this problem. Using static analysis, they partition iterations among threads to avoid cross-thread dependences. However, this approach may fail if dependence pattern information is not available at compile time. To address this limitation, this work proposes SpecCross–the first automatic parallelization technique to exploit cross-invocation parallelism using speculation. With speculation, iterations from different loop invocations can execute concurrently, and the program synchronizes only on misspeculation. This allows SpecCross to adapt to dependence patterns that only manifest on particular inputs at runtime. Evaluation on eight programs shows that SpecCross achieves a geomean speedup of 3.43× over parallel execution without cross-invocation parallelization.

Keywords

Automatic parallelization; Barrier speculation; Code optimization

1. INTRODUCTION

Scalable parallel programs are necessary to harness the performance potential of multi-core processors. Automatic parallelization techniques are a promising approach for producing well-performing parallel programs. Most existing automatic parallelization techniques exploit loop level parallelism [1, 11, 28, 36, 38, 39, 40, 42, 48]. These techniques parallelize loops and globally synchronize at the end of each loop invocation. As a result, programs with many loop invocations will experience frequent synchronizations.

For such programs, most existing automatic parallelization techniques do not deliver scalable performance because synchronization forces all threads to wait for the last thread to finish an invocation [30]. At high thread counts, threads spend more time idling at synchronization points than doing useful computation. However, there is an opportunity to improve performance: iterations from different loop invocations can often execute concurrently without violating program semantics. Instead of waiting at synchronization points, threads can execute iterations from subsequent loop invocations. This additional cross-invocation parallelism can improve the processor utilization and help the parallel programs achieve much better scalability.

Prior work has presented some automatic parallelization techniques that exploit cross-invocation parallelism [15, 33, 49, 51]. These techniques respect cross-invocation dependences without inserting coarse-grained global synchronizations such as barriers. Some of these techniques [15, 51] combine several small loops into a single larger loop. This approach side-steps the problem of exploiting cross-invocation parallelism by converting it into cross-iteration parallelism. Other approaches [33, 49] carefully partition the iteration space in each loop invocation so that cross-invocation dependences are never split between threads. However, both types of techniques rely on static analysis, which is inherently conservative. They cannot adapt to runtime dependence patterns manifested by particular inputs. In reality, many statically detected dependences only manifest under specific input conditions. For many programs, these dependences rarely manifest given the most common program inputs. Thus, programs could exploit additional cross-invocation parallelism and achieve greater scalability, if they are adapted to dependence patterns of specific inputs at runtime.

This insight motivates SpecCross, the first automatic parallelization technique designed to aggressively exploit cross-invocation parallelism using high-confidence speculation. SpecCross parallelizes independent loops and replaces the barrier synchronization between two loop invocations with its speculative counterpart. Unlike non-speculative barriers which pessimistically synchronize to enforce dependences, speculative techniques allow threads to execute past barriers without stalling. Speculation allows programs to optimistically execute potentially dependent instructions and later check for misspeculation. If misspeculation occurs, the program recovers using checkpointed non-speculative state. Speculative barriers improve performance by synchronizing only on misspeculation.

SpecCross consists of three components: a parallelizing

PACT '16, September 11-15, 2016, Haifa, Israel

DOI: http://dx.doi.org/10.1145/2967938.2967959

compiler, a profiling library and a runtime library. The parallelizing compiler automatically detects and parallelizes a code region with many loop invocations. The profiling library determines how aggressively to speculate and is the key to achieving high confidence speculation. The runtime library provides support for speculative execution, misspeculation detection, and recovery.

SpecCross uses profiling to find program regions where speculation will be beneficial. Profiling identifies access patterns conducive to barrier speculation. For instance, scanning data access pattern is highly amenable to barrier speculation. In this pattern, when two loop invocations separated by a barrier scan through memory, the last few iterations before the barrier will not interfere with the first few iterations of the loop after the barrier. By determining which regions to speculate, profiling keeps misspeculation rates low.

The SpecCross runtime system allows threads to execute speculatively without synchronization. To support recovery in case of misspeculation, non-speculative program state is checkpointed at regular intervals. Periodically, the speculative threads compute and send signatures encoding summaries of their memory accesses to a checker thread. The checker thread uses these signatures to determine if any cross-thread dependences are violated. If so, the checker thread restores the program to the most recent checkpoint. Restoring a checkpoint allows non-speculative replay.

The contributions of this paper are:

- A novel automatic parallelization technique to exploit cross-invocation parallelism using high-confidence speculation;
- Design and implementation of the first software-only speculative barrier;
- Design and implementation of the first profiler targeting speculative cross-invocation parallelization.

Evaluation over eight benchmark applications shows that SpecCross achieves a geomean speedup of 3.43× over codes without cross-invocation parallelization and 4.59× over the best sequential execution on a 24-core machine.

2. MOTIVATION

2.1 Limitations of Static Analysis-based Parallelization

Figure 1(a) shows a code example before parallelization. In this example, loop `L1` updates array elements in array `A` while loop `L2` reads elements from array `A` and uses those values to update array `B`. The whole process is repeated `STEP` times. Both `L1` and `L2` can be individually parallelized using DOALL [1]. However, dependences between `L1` and `L2` prevent the outer loop from being parallelized.

Ideally, we should only synchronize inner loop iterations that depend on each other, without stalling the execution of independent iterations. If static analysis [33, 49, 53] could prove that each thread accesses a separate section of arrays `A` and `B`, the loops can be naïvely parallelized without any synchronization between two adjacent inner loop invocations. However, since arrays `A` and `B` are accessed in an irregular manner (through index arrays `C` and `D`), static analysis cannot determine the dependence pattern between `L1` and `L2` precisely. As a result, this naïve parallelization may lead to incorrect runtime behavior.

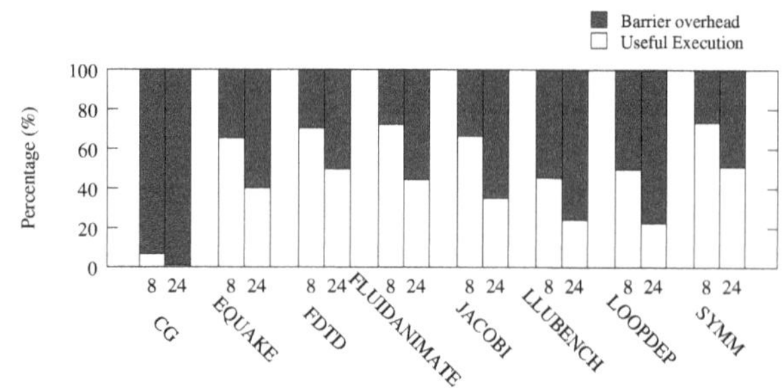

Figure 2: Overhead of barrier synchronizations for programs parallelized with 8 and 24 threads

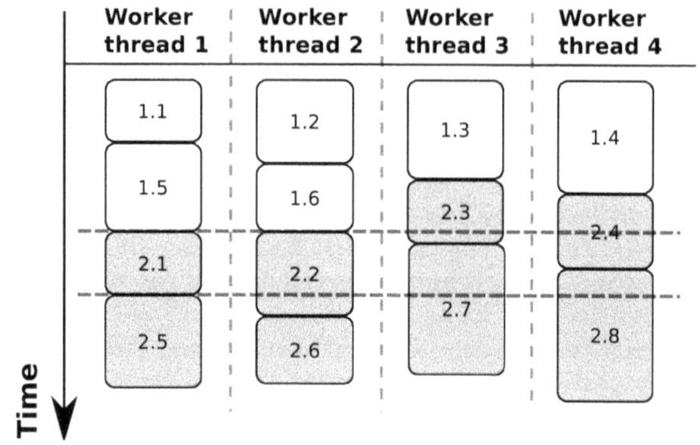

Figure 3: Execution plan for TM-style speculation: each block $A.B$ stands for the B_{th} iteration in the A_{th} loop invocation: iteration 2.1 overlaps with iterations $2.2, 2.3, 2.4, 2.7, 2.8$, thus its memory accesses need to be compared with theirs even though all these iterations come from the same loop invocation and are guaranteed to be independent.

Alternatively, if static analysis could determine a dependence pattern between iterations from two invocations, e.g., iteration `1` from `L2` always depends on iteration `2` from `L1`, then fine-grained synchronization can be used to synchronize only those iterations. But this requires accurate analysis about the dependence pattern, which is in turn, limited by the conservative nature of static analysis. Instead, barrier synchronization is used to globally synchronize all threads (Figure 1(b)). Barrier synchronization conservatively assumes dependences between any pair of iterations from two different loop invocations. All threads are forced to stall at barriers after each parallel invocation, which greatly diminishes effective parallelism. Figure 2 shows the overhead introduced by Pthreads barrier synchronizations on eight programs parallelized with 8 and 24 threads. Barrier overhead refers to the total amount of time threads sit idle waiting for the slowest thread to reach the barrier. For most of these programs, barrier overhead accounts for more than 30% of the parallel execution time and increases with the number of threads. This overhead translates into an Amdahl's Law limit of 3.33× maximum program speedup.

2.2 Speculative Cross-Invocation Parallelization

The conservativeness of barrier synchronization prevents any cross-invocation parallelization and significantly limits performance gain. Alternatively, the optimistic approach unlocks potential opportunities for cross-invocation parallelization. It allows the threads to execute across the invo-

```
sequential_func() {
  for (t = 0; t < STEP; t++) {
L1: for (i = 0; i < M; i++) {
      A[i] = calc_1(B[C[i]]);
    }

L2: for (j = 0; j < M; j++) {
      B[j] = calc_2(A[D[j]]);
    }
  }
}
```

(a) Sequential Program

```
barrier_parallel_func() {
  for (t = 0; t < STEP; t++) {
L1: for (i = TID; i < M; i = i + THREADNUM) {
      A[i] = calc_1(B[C[i]]);
    }
    pthread_barrier_wait(&barrier);
L2: for (j = TID; j < M; j = j + THREADNUM) {
      B[j] = calc_2(A[D[j]]);
    }
    pthread_barrier_wait(&barrier);
  }
}
```

(b) Parallelization with Barrier Synchronization

```
transaction_parallel_func() {
  for (t = 0; t < STEP; t++) {
L1: for (i = TID; i < M; i = i + THREADNUM) {
      TX_begin();
      A[i] = calc_1(B[C[i]]);
      TX_end();
    }

L2: for (j = TID; j < M; j = j + THREADNUM) {
      TX_begin();
      B[j] = calc_2(A[D[j]]);
      TX_end();
    }
  }
}
```

(c) Parallelization with Transactions

Figure 1: Example of parallelizing a program with different techniques

cation boundary under the assumption that the dependences rarely manifest at runtime. Two major optimistic solutions have been proposed in the literature: one relies on transactional memory and the other uses speculative barriers.

Figure 1(c) demonstrates the basic idea of speculative parallelization using transactional memory systems (TM) [21]. In this example, each inner loop iteration is treated as a separate transaction. The commit algorithms proposed in Grace [2] and TCC [19] allow transactions within the same inner loop invocation to commit out of order but guarantee transactions from later invocations should commit after those from earlier ones. However, this approach assumes that every transaction may conflict with another transaction and must be compared against each other for violation detection. It ignores the important fact that for most programs which could benefit from cross-invocation parallelization, all iterations from the same invocation are often guaranteed to be independent at compile time and wrapping them in separate transactions introduces unnecessary runtime checking and commit overhead. For example, in Figure 3, the execution of the first iteration of the second loop invocation (annotated as `2.1`) overlaps with that of iterations `2.2`, `2.3`, `2.4`, `2.7` and `2.8`. Even though they come from the same loop invocation, the TM framework needs to check them for access violations before `2.1` can commit. More coarse-grained transactions can reduce this checking overhead, but they also increase the possibility of misspeculation between two transactions.

Speculative barrier synchronization, on the other hand, preserves the DOALL property of each loop invocation while still allowing threads to execute past the barrier without stalling. Since all existing speculative barrier synchronization techniques [23, 26, 30] require specialized hardware support, we refer to these techniques collectively as hardware-based barrier speculation (HWBS). Compared to execution models supported by TM, HWBS distinguishes speculative and non-speculative threads to avoid unnecessary value buffering and violation checking. Non-speculative worker threads can commit their writes concurrently without waiting. As a result, HWBS is regarded as a better solution for a program pattern where iterations in the same loop invocation are independent and iterations from different invocations may depend on each other.

Despite its effectiveness, HWBS requires specialized hardware to detect misspeculation and recover. Programs parallelized for commodity hardware cannot benefit from it. This limitation motivates us to design and implement the first software-only speculative barrier for SpecCross, which aims at generating scalable parallel programs for commodity multicore machines.

3. SPECCROSS SYSTEM OVERVIEW

SpecCross enables automatic cross-invocation parallelization with software-only speculative barriers. Figure 4 gives an overview of the SpecCross system, which consists of the following three components: parallelizing compiler, runtime library, and profiler. The parallelizing compiler takes a sequential program as input and detects a SpecCross code region as the transformation target (§3.1). A SpecCross code region is often an outermost loop composed of consecutive parallelizable inner loops. The compiler parallelizes each independent inner loop and then inserts SpecCross runtime library function calls to enable speculative cross-invocation parallelization. To avoid high penalty for misspeculation, SpecCross uses a profiler to determine the *speculative range*, which controls how aggressively to speculate (§3.2). Choosing the correct limit for the speculative range keeps misspeculation rates low.

SpecCross's runtime library implements a software-only speculative barrier, which works as a light-weight substitution for HWBS on commodity hardware (§4). This runtime library provides efficient misspeculation detection (§4.1). At runtime, the original process spawns multiple worker threads and a checker thread. All worker threads execute their code sections and periodically send memory access signatures to the checker thread. These signatures approximately summarize all the speculative memory accesses. The checker thread uses these signatures to verify that speculative execution respects all memory dependences.

If the checker thread detects misspeculation, it signals a separate checkpoint process for misspeculation recovery (§4.2). The checkpoint process is periodically forked from the original process. Once recovery is completed by squashing all speculative workers, execution is resumed from the last checkpoint with non-speculative barriers.

3.1 SpecCross Parallelizing Compiler

The SpecCross parallelizing compiler automatically parallelizes the sequential program and applies software-only speculative barriers to enable cross-invocation parallelization. Non-speculative barriers guarantee that all code before a barrier executes before any code after the barrier. Speculative barriers such as the one applied by the SpecCross compiler, violate this synchronization guarantee to achieve higher processor utilization and thus, higher performance.

SpecCross targets a code region whose original parallel performance is limited by frequent global synchronizations.

Often, such a code region is an outermost loop which contains multiple parallelizable inner loops. To locate these code regions, we analyze all hot loops within the sequential program. A hot loop should account for at least 10% of the overall execution time. A hot loop is a candidate for SpecCross if it satisfies three conditions: (1) the outermost loop itself cannot be successfully parallelized by any automatic parallelization technique implemented in the existing parallelizing compiler infrastructure (including DOALL [1], LOCALWRITE [20] and DSWP [34]); (2) each inner loop can be independently parallelized by a non-speculative and non-partition based parallelization technique such as DOALL and LOCALWRITE; and (3) the sequential code between two inner loops can be privatized and duplicated among all worker threads.

After locating the candidate loops, the SpecCross transformation is applied to each of them. The transformation itself consists of two major steps. First, the compiler parallelizes the hot loop by applying DOALL or LOCALWRITE to each inner loop. Second, the compiler inserts SpecCross library function calls in the parallel program to enable barrier speculation. The function calls that comprise the SpecCross runtime library interface are described in §4.3.

3.2 SpecCross Profiler

To determine when speculation is beneficial, SpecCross uses profiling to determine the *speculative range*, which controls how aggressively to speculate (Figure 4). SpecCross assigns each thread an *epoch number* and a *task number*, which are then used to determine the speculative range and also to determine when speculative memory accesses must be checked at runtime.

An *epoch* is defined as the code region between two consecutive barriers, and the *epoch number* counts how many speculative barriers a thread has passed. Non-speculative barriers ensure that all threads have the same epoch number, whereas speculative barriers allow each thread's epoch number to increase independently. When the difference of two threads' epoch numbers is zero, misspeculation is impossible, since nothing is speculated. When the difference is high, misspeculation is more likely, since more intervening memory accesses are speculated. A *task* is the smallest unit of work that can be independently assigned to a thread, and the *task number* counts how many tasks a thread has executed since the last barrier. For many parallel programs, a task is one inner loop iteration. Note that epoch number-task number pairs are not unique across threads as each thread counts epochs and tasks independently.

In profiling mode, all barriers are non-speculative and thus, threads synchronize at every barrier. The profiler compares the memory access signature (summary of memory accesses) of every task to signatures of tasks from earlier epochs. If two tasks conflict, the distance between them is recorded. Note that this dependence distance between tasks refers to the number of intervening inner loop iterations (or *tasks* in our terminology). At the end of the profiling, the smallest dependence distance is set as the speculative range. If the minimum dependence distance is smaller than a threshold value, speculation will not be done. By default, the threshold value is set to be equal to the number of worker threads.

If the dependence distance is large, it means the program has an access pattern suitable for barrier speculation. To reduce the possibility of misspeculation, the minimum dependence distance is passed as an input parameter to the speculation runtime library (§4.3). At runtime, the leading thread stalls if it executes beyond this distance.

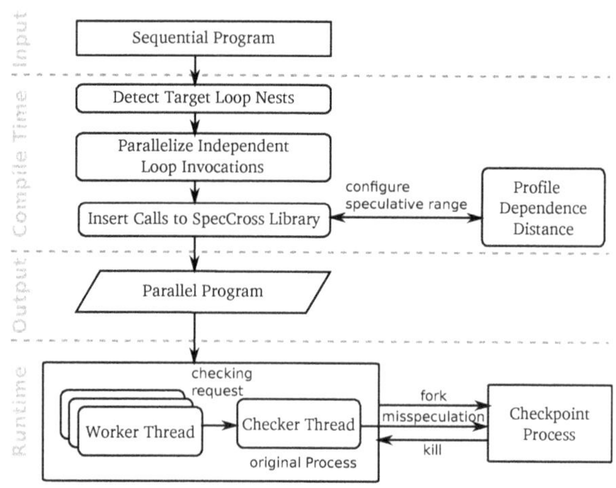

Figure 4: Overview of SpecCross: At compile time, the SpecCross compiler detects code regions composed of consecutive parallel loop invocations, parallelizes the code region and inserts SpecCross library function calls to enable barrier speculation. At runtime, the whole program is first executed speculatively without barriers. Once misspeculation occurs, the checkpoint process is woken up. It kills the original child process and spawns new worker threads. The worker threads will re-execute the misspeculated epochs with non-speculative barriers.

4. SPECCROSS RUNTIME SYSTEM

The runtime system of SpecCross implements a software-only speculative barrier. To maintain the same semantics as non-speculative barriers, speculative barriers check for runtime dependence violations. Upon detecting a violation, the runtime system triggers a misspeculation (§4.1) and rolls back to non-speculative state using the most recent checkpoint (§4.2).

4.1 Misspeculation Detection

Signature-based violation detection. SpecCross uses signature-based violation detection [9, 16, 28, 44, 52] to detect misspeculation. A signature is an approximate summary of memory accesses and provides a customizable tradeoff between signature size and false positive rates. By default, SpecCross defines a thread's signature as the *range of memory addresses speculatively accessed by that thread.* There are two advantages to using this scheme. First, it incurs low runtime overhead, as computing the memory access signature involves keeping the minimum and maximum memory address accessed, instead of logging every speculative memory access. Second, the correctness of this scheme can be proved easily: Threads are deemed independent if the signatures do not overlap.

However, adopting range-based signatures may result in an increase in the number of misspeculations detected by the SpecCross runtime system (*false positives*). To enable users to achieve the right balance between false positives and complexity of checking, SpecCross also provides an API to plug in user-provided signature generation and checking

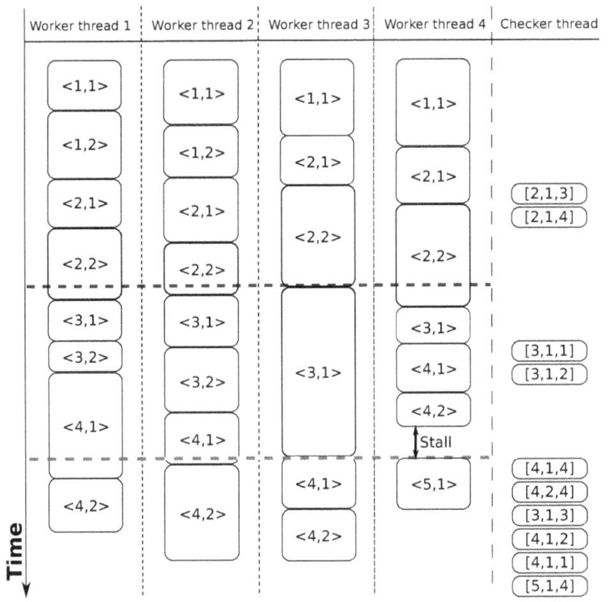

Figure 5: Timing diagram for SpecCross showing epoch and task numbers. Label $<A,B>$: The thread updates its epoch number to A and task number to B when the task starts executing. Label $[A,B,C]$ in the checker thread: Check memory access signature of task with epoch number A, task number B, and executing on worker thread C against the memory access signatures of tasks indicated in Table 1.

Checked tasks	Compared against
[2,1,3]	[1,2,1], [1,2,2]
[2,1,4]	[1,2,1], [1,2,2]
[3,1,1]	[2,2,4]
[3,1,2]	[2,2,4]
[4,1,4]	[3,2,1], [3,1,2], [3,1,3]
[4,2,4]	[3,2,2], [3,1,3]
[3,1,3]	[2,2,1], [2,2,2], [2,2,4]
[4,1,2]	[3,1,3]
[4,1,1]	[3,2,2], [3,1,3]
[5,1,4]	[4,1,1], [4,1,2], [4,1,3]
[5,2,4]	[4,2,1], [4,2,2], [4,2,3]

Table 1: Comparisons of memory access signatures performed by the checker thread for the timeline in Figure 5. Label $[A,B,C]$ refers to thread C executing task number B in epoch number A.

schemes. For instance, range-based signature schemes work well when memory accesses are clustered. For random access patterns, a Bloom filter-based signature can offer lower false positive rates. Our experiments have shown that the simple range-based checking scheme enables effective and efficient misspeculation detection; in fact, there were no false positives in any of the benchmarks evaluated in Section 5.

Violation detection scheme. To determine when the speculative barrier assumptions need to be checked, SpecCross assigns each thread an *epoch number* and a *task number* (defined in §3.2). Worker threads collaborate with the checker thread to detect violations. When a worker thread begins a new task, it updates its own epoch and task numbers and then records the current epoch and task numbers for all the other threads. Next, the worker executes the task itself. During execution, the worker computes the memory access signature for that task by maintaining the minimum and maximum values of memory addresses accessed. Once the task finishes execution, the worker thread saves its signature in a global signature log. On completion of each task, the worker thread sends the following information to the checker thread to enable asynchronous misspeculation detection: (1) the worker thread's current epoch and task numbers, (2) the memory access signature for the task, and (3) the recorded epoch and task numbers of all other threads that were running when the current task began. The checker thread compares the task's memory access signature to all signatures from epochs earlier than the current task's epoch, but at least as recent as the epoch-task number pair recorded when the task began. Signatures from the same epoch are safely ignored as they are not separated by a barrier.

If the checker thread detects misspeculation, it signals a separate checkpoint process for misspeculation recovery (explained in §4.2). By default, SpecCross checkpoints program state once every thousand epochs. Therefore, each worker thread has one thousand entries in the signature log. Worker threads synchronize at the checkpoint and signature log entries can be re-used after checkpointing. Each entry of the signature log contains a pointer to an array used for saving signatures within a single epoch. The size of the array is initialized to store 1024 signatures and is increased dynamically, if the number of tasks exceeds the array size.

Example. Figure 5 is a timing diagram for speculative barrier execution. When worker thread 3 starts task `<3,1>`, the other worker threads are still executing task `<2,2>` in the second epoch. The checker thread must check the access signatures of these three tasks against that of `[3,1,3]` (Table 1). Before task `<3,1>` finishes in worker thread 3, all other threads have already begun the fourth epoch. As a result, the checker thread must check the memory access signatures of task `<4,1>` in threads 1, 2, and 4 and task `<4,2>` in thread 4 against `[3,1,3]` (Table 1).

After sending data to the checker thread, a worker thread may stall to wait for other worker threads if continuing execution would exceed the speculative range. In Figure 5, we assume that the profiler calculates a speculative range limit of two. When thread 4 tries to start task `<5,1>`, tasks `<3,1>`, `<4,1>`, and `<4,2>` have already finished executing in thread 4, whereas thread 3 is still executing task `<3,1>`. Thus, the *dependence distance* between the two threads (defined as the difference in task numbers of the two threads) is three, one more than the limit specified by the profiler. Therefore, thread 4 stalls after executing task `<4,2>`. Note that the example is simplified as in real programs, the speculative range is always at least the number of worker threads and usually much larger.

Overhead of dependence detection. The checker thread forms the actual bottleneck for the dependence detection process. It needs to compare the signature of every task with the signatures of tasks being executed by all other threads at the time when the former task began execution. The checker runs in parallel to the worker threads and can keep up with the worker threads, especially if the number of workers is not high. However, when the worker thread count increases, the checker may not be able to compare signatures fast enough, which would lead to stalls whenever the program reaches a checkpoint. During these stalls, the worker threads wait for the checker to finish all the outstanding signature comparisons to determine if a misspeculation occurred. Once the checker detects no misspeculation, a new checkpoint is then created.

As discussed earlier, the runtime overhead for the worker threads is minimal as the range is defined only by the minimum and maximum address speculatively accessed. While there are potential false positives due to the use of range-based signatures, such false positives were not found in any of the evaluated benchmarks. Further, as the memory accesses of entire tasks are summarized by the range, using range-based signatures also keeps the overhead of checking signatures against each other minimal. The cost of checking is further mitigated by minimizing the number of signature comparisons. Checking is only necessary for two threads separated by a barrier when the two threads execute out-of-order with respect to the non-speculative execution. Thus, signatures from the same epoch are safely ignored as they are not separated by a barrier. Furthermore, if compiler analysis guarantees tasks to be independent, speculative checking is unnecessary and thus, skipped.

Memory consistency issues. There are two subtle memory consistency issues with the checking scheme described above. First, the checking scheme assumes that updates to the epoch and task numbers will be globally visible after all other stores in the previous task. If the memory consistency model allows the architecture to reorder stores, this assumption will be false. In other words, the checking methodology assumes a Total Store Order (TSO) architecture. Modern TSO architectures include: x86, x86-64, SPARC, and the IBM zSeries [27]. For architectures that do not support TSO, such as ARM and POWER, each thread should execute a memory fence before updating the epoch and task numbers. The costs of memory fences may be greater than the costs of speculative barriers when the number of tasks per epoch is high.

Second, the epoch and task numbers must update together atomically. The easiest way to accomplish this is to store these numbers as the high and low bits of a 64-bit word and use an atomic write operation. For x86-64, 64-bit writes are atomic by default, so no special handling is required.

4.2 Checkpointing and Recovery

There are three conditions that trigger misspeculation in SpecCross. First, the checker thread triggers misspeculation if it finds a pair of conflicting signatures. Second, misspeculation occurs if any of the worker threads triggers a segmentation fault. Third, misspeculation can be triggered in response to a pre-defined timeout. Timeouts are necessary, since speculative updates to the shared memory may change the exit condition of a loop and cause infinite execution.

For enabling misspeculation recovery, the worker threads periodically checkpoint their state. Checkpoints act as non-speculative barriers. All worker threads synchronize at the checkpoint, waiting for the checker thread to finish all checking requests before the checkpoint, thereby ensuring the safety of the checkpoint's state. During checkpointing, SpecCross first saves the register state of each thread using the C standard library's `setjmp` function. After the register state is saved, the process forks, duplicating the memory state of the entire process. The newly forked child sleeps until the checker thread detects misspeculation. Upon misspeculation, the child spawns new worker threads and each newly spawned thread executes `longjmp` to inherit the program state of an original thread.

As SpecCross is based on speculating barriers, checkpointing based on epochs is much easier to reason about than checkpointing based on time. Additionally, SpecCross explicitly allocates stacks of worker threads to ensure they are not deallocated by `fork`. This is necessary because the POSIX standard allows processes to deallocate the stacks of associated threads after forking. Explicitly allocating the worker threads' stacks ensures that `longjmp` will restore a valid stack.

Checkpointing Overhead. Our experiments show that recovering from misspeculation requires about one millisecond. The execution time for recovering non-speculative state is dominated by the `kill` and `clone` system calls. The checker thread invokes `kill` to asynchronously terminate misspeculating threads and awaken the checkpoint process. It then invokes `clone` (called internally by `pthread_create`) to create new worker threads. The number of syscalls scales linearly with the number of worker threads, but performance is not affected by either the program's memory footprint or the size of the speculative state.

Checkpointing Frequency. SpecCross's misspeculation recovery mechanism presents a fine tradeoff between the frequency of checkpointing and the overhead of the runtime system. Infrequent checkpointing reduces runtime overhead but increases the cost of misspeculation. SpecCross's profiling library enables very low rates of misspeculation, thus infrequent checkpointing is efficient in practice. By default, SpecCross checkpoints at every thousandth speculative barrier, though it can be re-configured based on program characteristics.

Handling Irreversible Operations. Some epochs contain irreversible operations (for example I/O) which must be executed non-speculatively. Before entering an irreversible epoch, all worker and checker threads synchronize. Just like checkpointing, synchronizing all threads ensures non-speculative execution. After exiting the irreversible region, the program checkpoints. Otherwise, later misspeculation could cause the irreversible region to be repeated.

4.3 Runtime Interface

Table 2 lists the interface functions exposed by SpecCross, along with a description of each function's semantics. Figure 6 shows an instantiation of these functions in a parallel program. In the example, each inner loop invocation is treated as an epoch, and each inner loop iteration as a task. SpecCross provides the same interface functions for both profiling and speculation purposes. As a result, the compiler must only insert the function calls once, for both profiling and speculative execution. Whether to profile or speculate is decided by defining the environment variable `MODE`. The `MODE` value can also be set to `NON-SPECULATIVE`. In non-speculative mode, most interface functions do nothing and speculative barriers are replaced with non-speculative ones. This non-speculative mode is enabled automatically when re-executing the misspeculated epochs after recovering from misspeculation. The following paragraphs describe how the compiler automatically inserts some of these function calls into the program.

A code region between two consecutive `enter_barrier` functions is considered as an epoch. For simplicity, each inner loop invocation is usually treated as an epoch. As a result, the SpecCross compiler inserts `enter_barrier` function calls at the beginning of each inner loop's preheader basic block.

Operation	Description
Functions for Both Profiling and Speculation	
init()	Initialize data structures used for barrier profiling or speculative execution. If in speculation mode, checkpoint the program before beginning the parallel execution.
exit_task(threadID)	Record the signature of the current task in global signature log. Increment the *task number*. If in profiling mode, compare the signature of current task with signatures of tasks belonging to previous epochs and return the minimum dependence distance. If in speculation mode, return value is 0.
spec_access(threadID, callback, addr_list, ...)	Apply callback function to each address in the addr_list to compute the signature.
enter_barrier(threadID, loop_name)	Increment the *epoch number*. If in profiling mode, execute the actual non-speculative barrier operation. If in speculation mode, checkpoint according to the checkpointing frequency.
create_threads(threads, attrs, start_routines, args)	Create worker threads and if in speculation mode, create a checker thread for violation detection.
cleanup()	Wait for worker threads and checker thread to finish. Free data structures allocated for profiling or speculation.
Functions for Speculation Only	
enter_task(threadID, spec_distance)	Collect *epoch number* and *task number* of other worker threads and send them to the checker thread. The parameter spec_distance specifies the speculation distance between two tasks.
send_end_token(threadID)	Send an END_TOKEN to checker thread to inform it of the completion of a worker thread.
sync()	Synchronize all threads before entering the next epoch.
checkpoint()	Checkpoint program state before entering the next epoch.

Table 2: Interface for SPECCROSS runtime library

```
Main thread:

main() {
  init();
  create_threads(threads, attrs, SpecCross_parallel_func, args);
  cleanup();
}

Worker thread:

SpecCross_parallel_func(threadID) {
  for (t = 0; t < STEP; t++) {
    enter_barrier(threadID, "L1");
L1: for (i = threadID; i < M; i = i + THREADNUM) {
      enter_task(threadID, minimum_distance_L1);
      spec_access(threadID, callback, &A[i], &B[C[i]], (char*)0);
      A[i] = do_work(B[C[i]]);
      exit_task(threadID);
    }
    enter_barrier(threadID, "L2");
L2: for (j = threadID; j < M; j = j + THREADNUM) {
      enter_task(threadID, minimum_distance_L2);
      spec_access(threadID, callback, &B[j], &A[D[j]], (char*)0);
      B[j] = do_work(A[D[j]]);
      exit_task(threadID);
    }
  }
  send_end_token(threadID);
}
```

Figure 6: Demonstration of using SPECCROSS runtime library in a parallel program

Function **enter_task** marks the beginning of each task. Since an inner loop iteration is usually treated as a separate task, the SPECCROSS compiler inserts **enter_task** function calls at the beginning of each inner loop's header.

Function **exit_task** marks the end of a task, i.e., it is invoked either before exiting an inner loop invocation or before entering another inner loop iteration. To locate these insertion points, the SPECCROSS compiler checks the terminator instruction of each basic block in an inner loop. If a terminator instruction is an unconditional branch which either exits the loop or branches back to the header of the loop, the compiler inserts an **exit_task** function call right before the terminator instruction. If the terminator instruction is a conditional branch and (1) if one of its targets is a basic block outside the loop and the other is the loop header, the compiler also inserts a call to **exit_task** before the terminator instruction; or (2) if one target is a basic block outside the loop and the other is a basic block within the loop except the loop header, the **exit_task** function is invoked only when the execution exits the loop; or (3) if one target is the header of the loop and the other is some other basic block within the loop, an **exit_task** function is invoked only when the execution branches back to the loop header.

Function **spec_access** is used to calculate the access signature for each task. The compiler inserts calls to this function before each memory operation (store or load) that is involved in a cross-invocation dependence.

Barriers not necessary	Existing techniques not profitable
blackscholes, swaptions (Parsec [4])	mesa, art and ammp (SpecFP [45])
pi, mandelbrot (OMPBench [14])	ferret (Parsec [4])
gemm, doitgen, 2mm (PolyBench [37])	mg (NAS [31])

Table 3: Benchmark programs not suitable for evaluation

5. EVALUATION

The implementation of SPECCROSS parallelization is evaluated on a 24-core shared memory machine. It has four Intel 6-core Xeon X7460 processors running at 2.66 GHz with 24 GB of memory. Its operating system is 64-bit Ubuntu 9.10. All benchmark programs are compiled using clang compiler version 3.0 with -O3.

5.1 Experimental Setup

Twenty programs from six benchmark suites that are parallelizable by SPECCROSS were examined as potential candidates for evaluation, and eight were finally selected. We have taken programs from multiple benchmark suites to demon-

Benchmark	Suite Source	Coverage of Exec. Time	# of tasks	# of epochs	# of checking requests	Minimum Distance	
						train	ref
CG	NAS [31]	12.8	63000	7000	40609	*	*
EQUAKE	SpecFP [45]	98	66000	3000	55181	*	*
FDTD	PolyBench [37]	99	200600	1200	96180	599	799
FLUIDANIMATE	Parsec [4]	99	1379510	1488	295000	54 / *	54 / *
JACOBI	PolyBench [37]	99	99400	1000	67163	497	997
LLUBENCH	LLVMBench [24]	90.5	110000	2000	81965	*	*
LOOPDEP	OMPBench [14]	99	245000	1000	98251	500	800
SYMM	PolyBench [37]	99	500500	2000	369731	*	*

Table 4: Details of benchmark programs. * indicates no access conflicts are detected in profiling.

strate the effectiveness of SpecCross over various application types, which work best with different optimization techniques. Of the twenty candidates, seven programs have a DOALL-able outermost loop and hence do not require barriers. For five programs, existing techniques are not profitable for either outer loop or inner loop parallelization. Table 3 summarizes these rejected programs. The remaining eight programs are chosen because they share two characteristics: their performance dominating loop nests cannot be profitably parallelized by non-speculative automatic parallelization techniques such as DOALL [1], LOCALWRITE [20] or DSWP [34]. Meanwhile, although these loop nests contain parallelizable inner loops, parallelizing them introduces frequent barrier synchronizations limiting overall scalability. These two characteristics are required for SpecCross to have a potential benefit.

Table 4 characterizes these eight programs. We compared two parallel versions of these programs: (a) inner loop parallelization with non-speculative pthread barriers [6]; and (b) outer loop parallelization with SpecCross. The non-speculative technique imposes synchronization on every barrier assuming that there are dependences between any pair of iterations from two different outer loop invocations. Even with a non-pthread barrier method, the performance would not have differed much. The common trait of any such method is that no cross-invocation parallelism is exploited and barrier synchronization is enforced. For performance measurements, the best sequential execution of the parallelized loops is considered the common baseline for both cases.

For most of these programs, the parallelized loops account for more than 90% of the execution time. When parallelizing using SpecCross, each loop iteration is regarded as a separate task. The range-based signature described in §4.1 is used to track the range of memory locations (or array indices) accessed by each task. Each parallel program is first instrumented using the profiling functions provided by SpecCross. The profiling step finds a minimum dependence distance value for use in speculative barrier execution. All benchmark programs have multiple input sets. We chose the training input set for profiling run. Table 4 shows the minimum dependence distance results for the evaluated programs using two different input sets (a training input set for profiling run and another reference input set for performance run). Four of the eight programs had runtime dependences detected by profiling functions while the rest do not. The minimum dependence distance between two inner loops in program FLUIDANIMATE varies a lot. Some of the loops do not cause any runtime access conflicts while others have a very small minimum dependence distance. For the latter case, SpecCross basically serves as a non-speculative barrier. Regarding program JACOBI, the profiler underestimated the speculative range (497 for training input vs. 997 for reference input), resulting in conservative speculation. This reflects in the performance of the benchmark, as shown in Figure 7(e).

5.2 Performance

Figure 7 compares the speedups achieved by the parallelized loops using pthread barriers and SpecCross. It demonstrates the benefits of enabling cross-invocation parallelization. The best sequential execution time of the parallelized loops is considered as the common baseline for both SpecCross and pthread barriers. The original execution with pthread barriers does not scale well beyond a small number of cores. Among the eight programs in barriers, CG performs the worst since each of its epochs only contains nine iterations. With higher thread counts, the overhead caused by barriers increases without any gains in parallelism.

The speculative barrier solution provided by SpecCross enables all programs to scale to higher thread counts when compared to an equivalent execution with pthread barriers. At lower thread counts, pthread barrier implementation for some programs yields better performance than SpecCross. This happens for two reasons: (a) SpecCross requires an extra thread for violation detection. At lower thread counts, one fewer thread is available to do actual work, which is significant when the total number of threads is small; (b) the overhead of barrier synchronization increases with increasing thread counts. As a result, the effectiveness of SpecCross is more pronounced at higher thread counts.

5.3 Overhead Analysis

In our evaluation, the program state is checkpointed once every 1000 epochs. For the eight programs evaluated, profiling results are accurate enough to result in high-confidence speculation and no misspeculation is recorded at runtime. As a result, the operations that contribute to major runtime overheads include computing access signatures, sending checking requests, detecting dependence violation, and checkpointing.

Table 4 shows for each program, the number of tasks executed, the number of epochs, and the number of checking requests for execution with 24 threads. The performance results (Figure 7) indicate that with higher thread counts, the checker thread may become the bottleneck. In particular, the performance of SpecCross scales up to 18 threads and either flattens or decreases after that. The effects of checker thread in limiting performance can be illustrated by considering the example of LLUBENCH. The number of check-

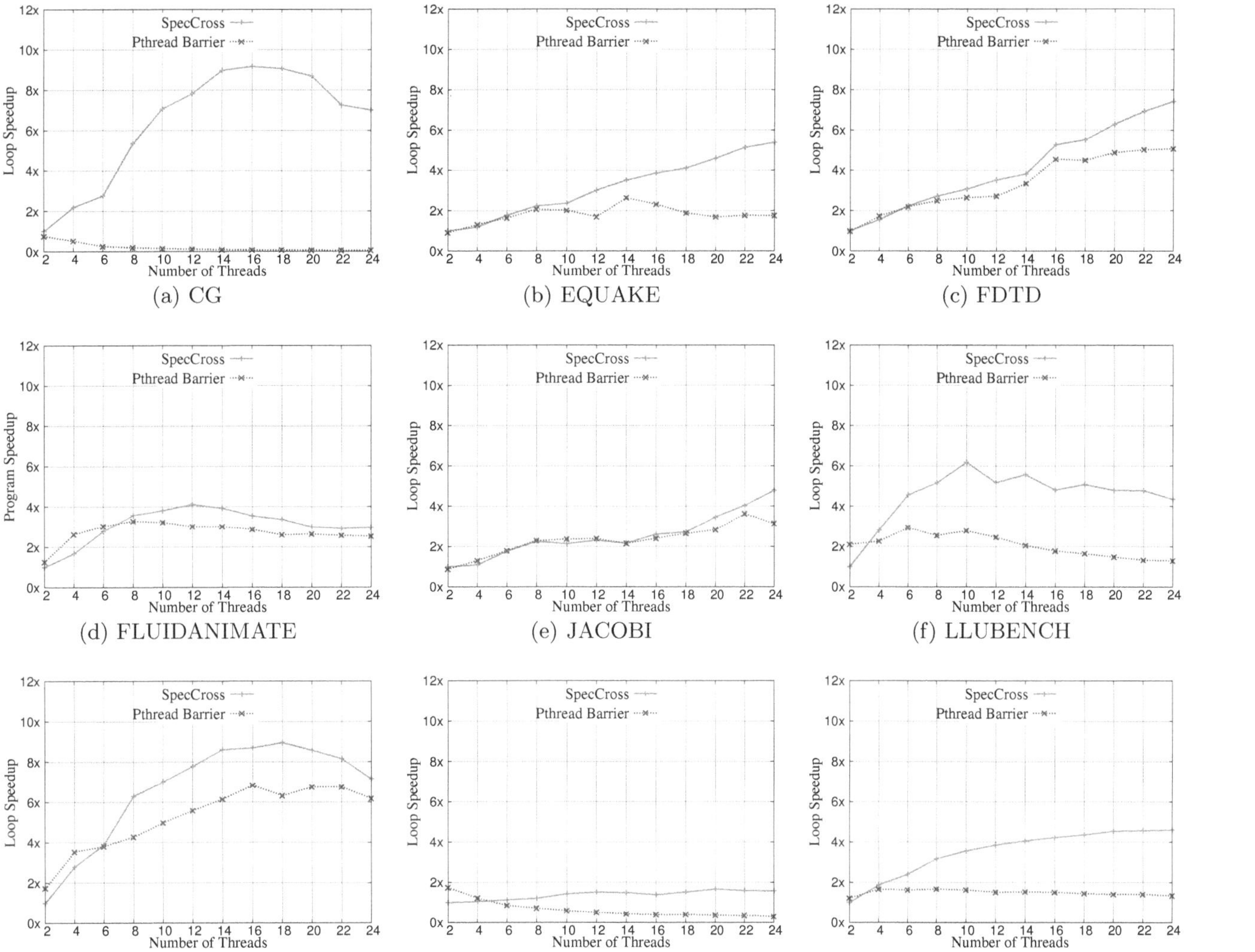

(a) CG (b) EQUAKE (c) FDTD
(d) FLUIDANIMATE (e) JACOBI (f) LLUBENCH
(g) LOOPDEP (h) SYMM (i) GEOMEAN

Figure 7: Performance comparison between code parallelized with or without cross-invocation parallelization.

ing requests for LLUBENCH increases by 3.3× when going from 8 threads to 24 threads, with the resulting performance improvements being minimal. Parallelizing dependence violation detection in the checker thread is one option to solve this problem and is part of future work.

Checkpointing is much more expensive than signature calculation or checking operations and hence is done infrequently. For benchmark programs evaluated, there are fewer than 10 checkpoints, since SPECCROSS by default checkpoints every 1000 epochs. However, frequency of checkpointing can be reconfigured depending on desired performance characteristics. To quantify the impact of checkpointing on performance, Figure 8 shows the geomean speedup results of increasing the number of checkpoints from 2 to 100, for all of the eight benchmark programs. To evaluate the overhead of the whole recovery process, we randomly triggered a misspeculation during the speculative parallel execution. Evaluation results are shown in Figure 8. As can be seen, more checkpoints increases the overhead at runtime, however also reduce the time spent in re-execution once misspeculation happens. Finding an optimal configuration for them is important and will be part of the future work.

The time required by worker threads to compute memory access signatures is another source of overhead for the SPECCROSS system. As mentioned in Section 4.1, the range-based memory access signatures incur a low overhead as it does not need to log every speculative memory access. This is borne out by the 1.04% geomean overhead (for 24 threads) per task in computing these access signatures. The highest overhead was for `CG`, where computing signatures resulted in an average overhead of 6.7% per task. This was because of a relatively large number of speculative memory accesses in every task. On the other hand, for `LLUBENCH` and `EQUAKE`, the number of range computations could be minimized due to compiler analysis, resulting in overheads as low as 0.26% and 0.13% per task.

5.4 Comparison of SpecCross and Previous Work

Figure 9 compares speedups achieved by SPECCROSS and previous work using the same programs [4, 7, 14, 17, 22]. All comparisons were done on our evaluation platform. We have omitted EQUAKE from Figure 9 as it was parallelized by Helix [7] whose source code is not accessible. For all other programs, SPECCROSS achieves better performance.

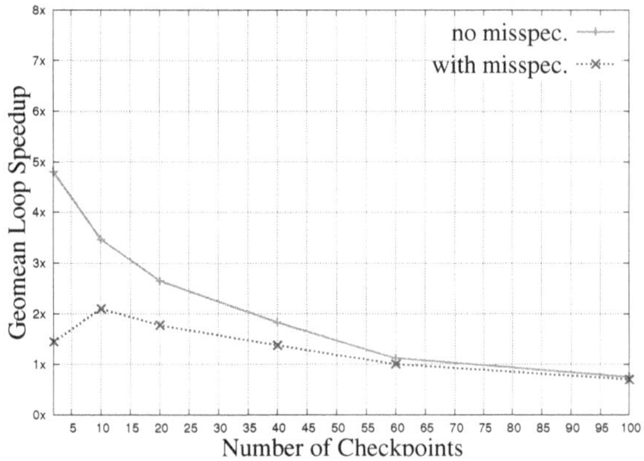

Figure 8: Loop speedup with and without misspeculation for execution with 24 threads: the number of checkpoints varies from 2 to 100. A misspeculation is randomly triggered during the speculative execution. With more checkpoints, overhead in checkpointing increases; however, overhead in re-execution after misspeculation decreases.

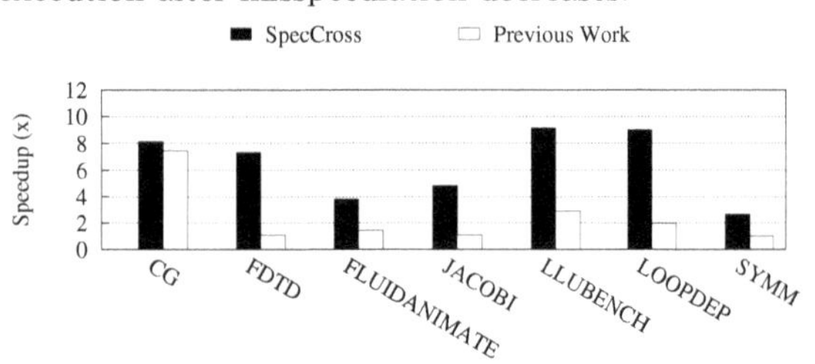

Figure 9: Best performance comparison between SPECCROSS and previous works on the same platform.

Programs `JACOBI`, `FDTD` and `SYMM` were originally designed for Polyhedral optimizations [17]. They can be automatically parallelized by the Polly optimizer in LLVM compiler infrastructure. Polly uses an abstract mathematical representation to analyze the memory access pattern of a program and automatically exploits thread-level and SIMD parallelism. Polly successfully achieves promising speedup for 16 out of 30 Polyhedral benchmark programs. However, it fails to extract enough parallelism from `JACOBI`, `FDTD` or `SYMM` due to the irregular memory access patterns of the outermost loop. SPECCROSS applies DOALL to the inner loops and exploits cross-invocation parallelism using speculative barriers, and therefore achieves much better performance.

`CG` was manually parallelized by DSWP+ technique [22]. DSWP+ performs as a manual equivalence of SPECCROSS parallelization. As shown in the graph, SPECCROSS is able to achieve close performance gain as the manual parallelization.

Both `LOOPDEP` and `FLUIDANMIATE` have a parallel implementation in their benchmark suites. We compare the best performance results of their parallel versions with the best performance achieved by SPECCROSS. Helix automatically parallelized `EQUAKE` and its performance gain was presented in [7]. We compare the best performance reported with that achieved by SPECCROSS. These previous works parallelize the three programs in a similar way: each inner loop within the outermost loop is independently parallelized by DOALL or DOACROSS and non-speculative barrier synchronizations are inserted between inner loops to respect cross-invocation dependences. Those synchronizations limit the scalability of the performance.

We cannot find any existing parallelization result for `LLUBENCH`, so in Figure 9, best performance result of SPECCROSS is compared against the best performance achieved by inner loop DOALL with pthread barrier synchronizations.

6. RELATED WORK

Cross-invocation Parallelization: Existing automatic cross-invocation parallelization techniques all rely on static analysis. Zhao et al. [54] transform an inner DOALL loop to an outer DOALL loop before parallelization in order to avoid barriers between two consecutive parallel loop invocations. Ferrero et al. [15] aggregate small parallel loops into large ones for the same purpose. Tseng et al. [49] apply flow analysis to carefully partition the iteration space so that cross-invocation dependences do not flow across threads. Compared to these techniques, SPECCROSS is not limited by the conservativeness of static analysis, and therefore can adapt to irregular dependence patterns manifested by particular inputs.

Comparison to Other Dynamic Parallelization Systems: Tian et al. [48] proposed Copy-Or-Discard (CoD) execution model for speculative parallelization, which achieves excellent speedup on six benchmarks. CorD's execution model focuses on parallelizing loops, where different iterations of the same loop can be speculatively executed in parallel. By contrast, SPECCROSS aims to exploit cross-invocation parallelism, where tasks from different loop invocations may be speculatively executed in parallel. The other contrast lies in the way the two techniques detect conflicts: CorD uses memory versioning while SPECCROSS uses range-based memory access signatures.

BOP [13] offers a promising method for speculative parallelization by allowing specification of potential for parallel execution of code regions. The specification can be made either via programmer-inserted annotations or by certain profilers. If speculation does not prove profitable, execution time is the same as the sequential execution time. In BOP's execution model, each speculative region is run in a separate process; thus, it incurs extra overhead due to merging of modified pages by different processes (this cost may be partly hidden by copy-on-write mechanisms). By contrast, SPECCROSS speculates barriers which leads to tasks executing in different parallel threads. As a result, speculative accesses once checked, do not require separate copying or merging. Additionally, compared to BOP's page-based monitoring, SPECCROSS monitors only inter-invocation dependences, which may lead to lower checking overheads.

Alternative Synchronizations Fuzzy Barriers [18] specifies a synchronization range rather than a specific synchronization point. However, it also relies on static analysis to identify instructions that can be safely executed while a thread waits for other threads to reach the barrier. Fuzzy barriers cannot reduce the number of barriers; it can only reschedule barriers for more efficient execution.

Some techniques apply speculative barriers between loop invocations to enable cross-invocation parallelization. Nagarajan and Gupta [30] speculatively execute parallel programs past barriers and detect conflicts by re-designing the Itanium processor's *Advanced Load Address Table* (ALAT) hardware. Martínez and Torrellas [26] apply *thread level speculation* [32, 46] to speculatively remove barriers. A speculative synchronization unit (SSU) is designed to detect conflict and recover from misspeculation at runtime.

ECMon [29] exposes cache events to software so that barrier speculation could efficiently detect violations at runtime. These techniques are not limited by complicated dependence patterns; however, they all require special hardware support. By contrast, SpecCross implements a software-based technique which can run on commodity multicore machines.

Ziarek et al. [55] propose language extensions for speculative barriers and formulate safety properties for correct speculation. However, they only apply it to a toy language and provide no concrete implementation or performance results. SpecCross provides the design, implementation and evaluation of a real system that automatically parallelizes programs using speculative barriers.

Transactional Memory Supported Cross-invocation Parallelization: Transactional Memory (TM) [21, 43] was first introduced as a technique providing a way to implement lock-free data structures and operations. The key idea behind TM is to make a sequence of memory reads and writes appear as a single transaction; all intermediate steps are hidden from the rest of the program. A log of all memory accesses is kept during the transaction. If a transaction reads memory that has been altered between the start and end of the transaction, execution of the transaction is restarted. This continues until the transaction is able to complete successfully, and its changes are committed to memory.

Original TM systems do not support cross-invocation speculation since they do not enforce the commit order between transactions from different loop invocations. Grace [2] and TCC [19] extend existing TM systems to support cross-invocation speculation. Grace automatically wraps code between fork and join points into transactions, removing barrier synchronizations at the join points. Each transaction commits according to its order in the sequential version of code. TCC [19] relies on programmers to wrap concurrent tasks into transactions. It requires special hardware support for violation checking and transaction numbering, which ensures the correct commit order of each transaction. As discussed in Section 2, both systems ignore the important fact that a large number of independent tasks do not need to be checked for access violations. Instead, SpecCross is customized for this program pattern, thus it avoids unnecessary overhead in checking and committing. Besides, neither Grace or TCC is an automatic parallelization technique. They are either applied to already parallelized programs or manually inserted as annotations in sequential programs. Instead, SpecCross is an automatic parallelization technique which does not require any manual work.

Load Balancing Techniques: Work stealing techniques, implemented in parallel subsystems like Cilk [5], Intel TBB [41], and X10 [10], balance load amongst parallel threads by allowing one thread to steal work from another thread's work queue. Balancing workloads in turn reduces the impact of barrier synchronization on program performance. However, existing work stealing implementations only allow workers to steal work from the same epoch at any given time. This is because these implementations do not leverage knowledge about program dependences to steal work from multiple epochs (across barriers) at the same time. As a result, programs that have a limited number of tasks in a single epoch (for example, CG in our evaluation) do not benefit from work stealing techniques. In contrast, SpecCross allows tasks from different epochs to overlap and achieve better load balance across epochs. Other load balancing techniques such as guided self-scheduling [35], affinity-based scheduling [25], and trapezoidal scheduling [50] also suffer from the same limitations as the work stealing techniques.

Synchronization via scheduling [3] is a method of load balancing that employs static and dynamic analyses to capture runtime dependences between tasks in a task graph. The task graph is exposed to a scheduler that schedules the tasks onto threads in a way so as to minimize the idling time of each thread. While being able to handle more general dependence patterns than working stealing, this technique still does not overlap tasks from successive executions of the same task graph in parallel.

Multithreaded Program Checkpointing: Several prior techniques implement multithreaded program checkpointing. Dieter et al. [12] propose a user-level checkpointing system for multi-threaded applications. Carothers et al. [8] implement a system call to transparently checkpoint multithreaded applications. SpecCross checkpoints the multithreaded programs for misspeculation recovery. These checkpointing techniques could be merged into the SpecCross framework.

Dependence Distance Analysis: If dependence distance manifests in a regular manner, programs can still be parallelized by assigning dependent tasks to the same worker thread. Dependence distance analysis [47] has been proposed to serve that purpose. Like other static analyses these techniques tend to be conservative and cannot handle irregular dependence patterns. SpecCross takes advantage of profiling information to get a minimum distance and speculates it holds for other input sets to further reduce the misspeculation rate. Since this information comes from profiling, it applies to programs with irregular dependence patterns as well.

7. CONCLUSION

This paper presented SpecCross, the first automatic parallelization technique to aggressively exploit cross-invocation parallelism using high-confidence speculation. Unlike prior techniques which are all limited by conservative static analysis, SpecCross can adapt to irregular dependence patterns determined by input data sets. The SpecCross system consists of three major components: a parallelizing compiler, a runtime library and a profiler. The profiler enables high-confidence speculation, and the runtime library implements a software-only speculative barrier. The parallelizing compiler runs the profiler and automatically transforms a sequential program into a scalable parallel program targeting the runtime library. Evaluation on eight programs demonstrates that SpecCross achieves a geomean speedup of 4.59× over the best sequential execution on a 24-core machine. This demonstrates the effectiveness of SpecCross in realizing well-performing cross-invocation parallelization.

8. ACKNOWLEDGMENTS

We thank the Liberty Research Group for their support and feedback during this work. We also thank Xipeng Shen and the anonymous reviewers for their insightful comments and suggestions. This work is supported by the National Science Foundation (NSF) through Grants OCI-1047879, CCF-1439085, and CNS-0964328. All opinions, findings, conclusions, and recommendations expressed in this paper are those of the Liberty Research Group and do not necessarily reflect the views of the NSF. This work was carried out when the authors were working at Princeton University.

9. REFERENCES

[1] R. Allen and K. Kennedy. *Optimizing Compilers for Modern Architectures: A Dependence-based Approach.* Morgan Kaufmann Publishers Inc., 2002.

[2] E. D. Berger, T. Yang, T. Liu, and G. Novark. Grace: safe multithreaded programming for C/C++. In *OOPSLA*, 2009.

[3] M. J. Best, S. Mottishaw, C. Mustard, M. Roth, A. Fedorova, and A. Brownsword. Synchronization via scheduling: techniques for efficiently managing shared state. In *PLDI*, 2011.

[4] C. Bienia, S. Kumar, J. P. Singh, and K. Li. The PARSEC benchmark suite: characterization and architectural implications. In *PACT*, 2008.

[5] R. D. Blumofe, C. F. Joerg, B. C. Kuszmaul, C. E. Leiserson, K. H. Randall, and Y. Zhou. Cilk: an efficient multithreaded runtime system. In *PPoPP*, 1995.

[6] D. R. Butenhof. *Programming with POSIX threads.* Addison-Wesley Longman Publishing Co., Inc., 1997.

[7] S. Campanoni, T. Jones, G. Holloway, V. J. Reddi, G.-Y. Wei, and D. Brooks. Helix: automatic parallelization of irregular programs for chip multiprocessing. In *CGO*, 2012.

[8] C. D. Carothers and B. K. Szymanski. Checkpointing multithreaded programs. *Dr. Dobbs*, August 2002.

[9] L. Ceze, J. Tuck, J. Torrellas, and C. Cascaval. Bulk disambiguation of speculative threads in multiprocessors. In *ISCA*, 2006.

[10] G. Cong, S. Kodali, S. Krishnamoorthy, D. Lea, V. Saraswat, and T. Wen. Solving large, irregular graph problems using adaptive work-stealing. In *ICPP*, 2008.

[11] R. Cytron. DOACROSS: Beyond vectorization for multiprocessors. In *ICPP*, 1986.

[12] W. R. Dieter and J. E. Lumpp Jr. User-level checkpointing for linuxthreads programs. In *USENIX, FREENIX Track*, 2001.

[13] C. Ding, X. Shen, K. Kelsey, C. Tice, R. Huang, and C. Zhang. Software behavior oriented parallelization. In *PLDI*, 2007.

[14] A. J. Dorta, C. Rodriguez, F. de Sande, and A. Gonzalez-Escribano. The OpenMP source code repository. In *PDP*, 2005.

[15] R. Ferrer, A. Duran, X. Martorell, and E. Ayguadé. Unrolling loops containing task parallelism. In *LCPC*, 2009.

[16] S. Ghosh, Y. Park, and A. Raman. Enabling efficient alias speculation. In *LCTES '15.*

[17] T. C. Grosser. Enabling polyhedral optimizations in llvm. Diploma thesis, Department of Informatics and Mathematics, University of Passau, Germany, April 2011.

[18] R. Gupta. The fuzzy barrier: a mechanism for high speed synchronization of processors. In *ASPLOS*, 1989.

[19] L. Hammond, V. Wong, M. Chen, B. D. Carlstrom, J. D. Davis, B. Hertzberg, M. K. Prabhu, H. Wijaya, C. Kozyrakis, and K. Olukotun. Transactional memory coherence and consistency. In *ISCA*, 2004.

[20] H. Han and C.-W. Tseng. Improving compiler and run-time support for irregular reductions using local writes. In *LCPC*, 1999.

[21] M. Herlihy and J. E. B. Moss. Transactional memory: architectural support for lock-free data structures. In *ISCA*, 1993.

[22] J. Huang, A. Raman, Y. Zhang, T. B. Jablin, T.-H. Hung, and D. I. August. Decoupled Software Pipelining Creates Parallelization Opportunities. In *CGO*, 2010.

[23] K. Z. Ibrahim and G. T. Byrd. On the exploitation of value predication and producer identification to reduce barrier synchronization time. In *IPDPS*, 2001.

[24] LLVM Test Suite Guide. http://llvm.org/docs/TestingGuide.html.

[25] E. P. Markatos and T. J. LeBlanc. Using processor affinity in loop scheduling on shared-memory multiprocessors. In *SC*, 1992.

[26] J. F. Martínez and J. Torrellas. Speculative synchronization: applying thread-level speculation to explicitly parallel applications. In *ASPLOS*, 2002.

[27] P. E. Mckenney. Memory barriers: a hardware view for software hackers, 2009.

[28] M. Mehrara, J. Hao, P.-C. Hsu, and S. Mahlke. Parallelizing sequential applications on commodity hardware using a low-cost software transactional memory. In *PLDI*, 2009.

[29] V. Nagarajan and R. Gupta. ECMon: exposing cache events for monitoring. In *ISCA*, 2009.

[30] V. Nagarajan and R. Gupta. Speculative optimizations for parallel programs on multicores. In *Proceedings of the 22Nd International Conference on Languages and Compilers for Parallel Computing*, LCPC'09, 2010.

[31] NAS Parallel Benchmarks 3. http://www.nas.nasa.gov/Resources/Software/npb.html.

[32] C. E. Oancea and A. Mycroft. Software thread-level speculation: an optimistic library implementation. In *IWMSE*, 2008.

[33] M. F. P. O'Boyle, L. Kervella, and F. Bodin. Synchronization minimization in a SPMD execution model. *J. Parallel Distrib. Comput.*, 29, September 1995.

[34] G. Ottoni, R. Rangan, A. Stoler, and D. I. August. Automatic thread extraction with decoupled software pipelining. In *MICRO*, 2005.

[35] C. D. Polychronopoulos and D. J. Kuck. Guided self-scheduling: a practical scheduling scheme for parallel supercomputers. *IEEE Transactions on Computers*, C-36(12), December 1987.

[36] R. Ponnusamy, J. Saltz, and A. Choudhary. Runtime compilation techniques for data partitioning and communication schedule reuse. In *SC*, 1993.

[37] L.-N. Pouchet. PolyBench: the Polyhedral Benchmark suite. http://www-roc.inria.fr/ pouchet/software/polybench/download.

[38] P. Prabhu, S. Ghosh, Y. Zhang, N. P. Johnson, and D. I. August. Commutative set: A language extension for implicit parallel programming. In *PLDI*, 2011.

[39] L. Rauchwerger, N. M. Amato, and D. A. Padua. A scalable method for run-time loop parallelization.

International Journal of Parallel Programming (IJPP), 26:537–576, 1995.

[40] L. Rauchwerger and D. A. Padua. The LRPD test: Speculative run-time parallelization of loops with privatization and reduction parallelization. *IEEE TPDS*, 1999.

[41] A. Robison, M. Voss, and A. Kukanov. Optimization via reflection on work stealing in TBB. In *IPDPS*, 2008.

[42] J. Saltz, R. Mirchandaney, and R. Crowley. Run-time parallelization and scheduling of loops. *IEEE Transactions on Computers*, 40, 1991.

[43] N. Shavit and D. Touitou. Software transactional memory. In *PODC*, 1995.

[44] M. F. Spear, M. M. Michael, and C. von Praun. RingSTM: scalable transactions with a single atomic instruction. In *SPAA*, 2008.

[45] Standard Performance Evaluation Corporation. http://www.spec.org.

[46] J. G. Steffan, C. Colohan, A. Zhai, and T. C. Mowry. The STAMPede approach to thread-level speculation. *ACM Transactions on Computer Systems*, 2005.

[47] P. Swamy and C. Vipin. Minimum dependence distance tiling of nested loops with non-uniform dependences. In *IPDPS*, 1994.

[48] C. Tian, M. Feng, V. Nagarajan, and R. Gupta. Copy or discard execution model for speculative parallelization on multicores. In *MICRO*, 2008.

[49] C.-W. Tseng. Compiler optimizations for eliminating barrier synchronization. In *PPoPP*, 1995.

[50] T. Tzen and L. Ni. Trapezoid self-scheduling: a practical scheduling scheme for parallel compilers. *IEEE Transactions on Parallel and Distributed Systems*, 4(1), January 1993.

[51] M. J. Wolfe. *Optimizing Compilers for Supercomputers.* PhD thesis, Department of Computer Science, University of Illinois, Urbana, IL, October 1982.

[52] L. Yen, J. Bobba, M. R. Marty, K. E. Moore, H. Volos, M. D. Hill, M. M. Swift, and D. A. Wood. LogTM-SE: decoupling hardware transactional memory from caches. In *HPCA*, 2007.

[53] N. Yonezawa, K. Wada, and T. Aida. Barrier elimination based on access dependency analysis for openmp. In *Parallel and Distributed Processing and Applications.* Springer Berlin / Heidelberg, 2006.

[54] J. Zhao, J. Shirako, V. K. Nandivada, and V. Sarkar. Reducing task creation and termination overhead in explicitly parallel programs. In *PACT*, 2010.

[55] L. Ziarek, S. Jagannathan, M. Fluet, and U. A. Acar. Speculative n-way barriers. In *DAMP*, 2008.

MicroSpec: Speculation-Centric Fine-Grained Parallelization for FSM Computations

Junqiao Qiu, Zhijia Zhao
Department of Computer Science & Engineering
University of California, Riverside
jqiu004@ucr.edu, zhijia@cs.ucr.edu

Bin Ren
Department of Computer Science
The College of William and Mary
bren@wm.edu

ABSTRACT

Finite state machines (FSMs) are basic computation models that play essential roles in many applications. Enabling efficient parallel FSM execution is critical to the performance of these applications. However, they are very challenging to parallelize due to their inherent data dependencies that occur at each step of computations.

Existing efforts on FSM parallelization either explore coarse-grained speculative parallelism or leverage parallel prefix-sum. The former ignores prevalent fine-grained hardware parallelism on modern processors (such as ILP or SIMD parallelism) while the latter limits the benefits of fine-grained parallelism mainly to state enumeration.

This work presents *MicroSpec*, a set of parallelization techniques that, for the first time, expose fine-grained speculative parallelism to FSM computations. Based on a rigorous analysis of three types of parallelism at fine-grained level, *MicroSpec* consists of a list of four fine-grained speculative parallelization approaches along with a speculation-oriented data transformation. Experiments on a large set of real-world FSM benchmarks show that *MicroSpec* achieves substantial performance improvement over the state-of-the-art.

Keywords

Program Parallelization, Finite State Machine, FSM, SIMD, Speculative Parallelization, Vectorization

1. INTRODUCTION

Exposing parallelism is key to computing efficiency and scalability of software applications. Modern microprocessors feature a variety of hardware parallelism from instruction level to on-chip multiprocessors. Effectively leveraging such rich hardware parallelism critically affects the performance.

This work focuses on exposing effective fine-grained parallelism to Finite State Machine (FSM)-based computations, a class of computations that are frequently used in a wide range of applications, including *deep packet inspection* in network intrusion detection system (NIDS) [60, 15, 34, 39],

PACT '16, September 11-15, 2016, Haifa, Israel

DOI: http://dx.doi.org/10.1145/2967938.2967965

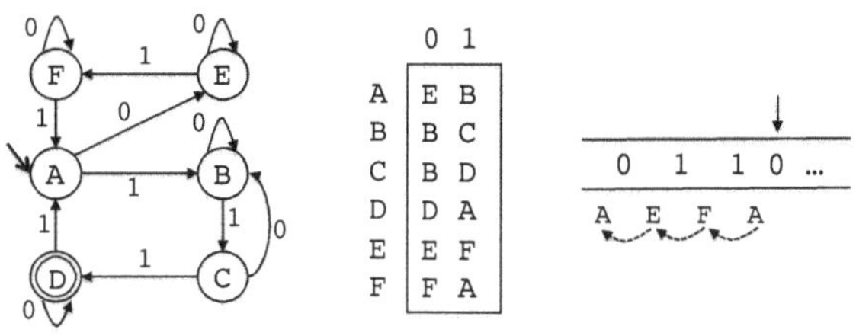

(a) FSM (b) Transition Table (c) Dependences

Figure 1: An FSM Example

motif searching in biological databases (e.g., Genebank and Prosite) [53, 11, 59, 8], *Huffman decoding* in image and video compression [3, 54, 24, 32], *path queries and validation* in semi-structural data stream [44, 9, 19, 58], and *model checking* in software engineering [45, 49, 10, 4], among others.

FSMs are extremely challenging to parallelize, formerly known as "embarrassingly sequential" computations [5]. The challenges lie in the inherent data dependencies among state transitions. Figure 1 shows an example FSM with six states. The valid transitions in an FSM can be represented as a table, called *transition table*. Given an input string, the execution of an FSM starts from a predefined state (called *initial state*). Each time it reads one symbol from the input string. The FSM looks up the transition table based on the current state and the read symbol to find and transition to the next state. The dependence between the current state and next state exists at every transition step. These dependencies form a tight dependence chain, inherently preventing any parallelism from being exposed.

State of The Art. Given their fundamental importance in computing theory and their broad range of real-world applications, recent years have seen growing interests in parallelizing FSM computations, leading to some significant advancements. In general, they fall into two groups based on the types of parallelism that they explore: (1) speculative parallelization [61] and (2) parallel prefix-sum [40] . The former breaks the dependencies by predicting future states. In the cases that some predictions fail, reprocessing might be needed to ensure correctness. In comparison, the latter needs no prediction at all. Instead, it enumerates all the possible states, which always cover the actual one. With either of the two ways, an input string now is allowed to be partitioned into segments and processed in parallel.

Even though they break the barrier of making FSM computations run parallel, none of them has released the full potential of processing power in today's processors. The former relies on sophisticated prediction and only works at thread level; while the latter only exposes fine-grained parallelism to state enumeration – making transitions for each possible state. None of them can further shorten the critical execution path of an individual input segment (see Section 3.2).

To address these concerns, this work introduces two new dimensions of parallelism, *multi-state speculation* and *multi-level speculation*. The former extends the speculation from commonly used single-value prediction to multi-value prediction, while the latter expends the speculative parallelism across different layers of hardware parallelism. Based on a rigorous analysis on parallel prefix-sum and the two new types of parallelism, this work presents *MicroSpec*, a set of speculation-centric parallelization methods that maximize the efficiency of FSM computations by effectively exploiting fine-grained speculative parallelism. Specifically, *MicroSpec* consists of a list of four fine-grained speculation techniques as well as a speculation-oriented data layout optimization. Together, they are able to effectively exploit both Instruction-Level Parallelism (ILP) and Single Instruction Multiple Data (SIMD) parallelism [1].

Our evaluation of *MicroSpec* on a set of 17 FSM benchmarks from four application domains demonstrates its effectiveness in accelerating FSM computations, yielding about 14X speedup on 13 benchmarks, boosting the state-of-the-art by up to a factor of four.

In sum, this work makes the following contributions.

- It proposes two new dimensions to explore the fine-grained parallelism for FSM computations: *multi-state speculation* and *multi-level speculation*, which makes the parallelization design more flexible.
- Through a rigorous analysis on three types of parallelism for fine-grained FSM parallelization, it theoretically reveals the efficiency issue in the state-of-the-art and offers guidelines for the design of efficient FSM parallelization techniques.
- It designs and implements four speculation-centric fine-grained parallelization techniques which, for the first time, enable fine-grained speculative parallelization.
- It evaluates the proposed techniques on a large group of real-world benchmarks, demonstrating significant advancement over the state-of-the-art.

2. BACKGROUND AND PROBLEM

2.1 FSM and Its Dependences

FSMs form the backbone of a variety of applications, ranging from intrusion detection and data decompression to compilation and pattern searching. The core computation of these applications can be formulated as an abstract machine with a finite number of possible states. Transitions are allowed among certain states when satisfying given conditions. FSMs can be deterministic or non-deterministic depending on if a condition can lead to a unique following state. This work focus on deterministic ones for their better efficiency [2].

[1]This work focuses on vectorization on CPUs, but general ideas are applicable to SIMD parallelism on GPUs as well.
[2]Non-deterministic FSM can be converted to deterministic ones through subset construction.

Parallelizing FSM computations are extremely difficult due to their inherent sequential characteristics — dependencies exist between every consecutive state transitions, as illustrated by Figure 1 (c). A natural way to parallelize its execution is to partition the input string into to segments, and let thread process segments concurrently, one segment per thread. However, the starting states are unknown except the first thread (which starts from initial state 'A'). A starting state for a segment is essentially the ending state of the previous segment. These dependencies form a chain structure, preventing any concurrent execution among threads.

Existing work to solve this problem mainly follow two directions: speculative parallelization and parallel prefix-sum. Zhao and others [61] followed the first direction and proposed a coarse-grained speculative parallelization approach to circumvent the dependencies. Instead of speculation, Todd and others [40]'s approach enumerates all the possible cases to leverage classic parallel prefix-sum. They implemented with both coarse-grained and fine-grained parallelism to take advantage of different levels of hardware parallelism. However, each of them has its own limitations. The former is only able to explore coarse-grained thread-level parallelism, leaving widely available fine-grained hardware parallelism (such ILP and SIMD) unused. The latter uses fine-grained hardware parallelism only for enumerating different cases. None of them fully take advantage of the computing power of today's microprocessors.

Hence, the goal of this work is to maximize the parallel efficiency on modern processors by exposing more effective fine-grained parallelism to FSM computations. However, challenges exist at several levels. First, fine-grained parallelism is notoriously more difficult to expose comparing to coarse-grained thread-level parallelism due to the lack of friendly programming models. For example, programming with Intel SSE instruction set requires knowledge about microarchitecture and is more error-prone. Second, different types of parallelism exist for FSM computations, it is non-trivial to find out which ones are more effective at fine-grained levels. Third, fine-grained hardware parallelism varies across different architectures. For example, some microarchitectures may not support `gather` instruction, which is critical for fine-grained FSM parallelization (see Section 4.2).

2.2 Coarse-Grained Speculative Parallelization

As this work mainly follows the first direction – speculation-based parallelization, we briefly summarize its ideas for self-containedness. At high-level, there are four major steps in coarse-grained speculative FSM parallelization. To make it easier to follow, we use Algorithm 1 to illustrate its basic ideas, followed by a step-by-step explanation.

Algorithm 1 Coarse-Grained Speculative Parallelization

Π = coarse_grained_partition(N_{core}); /* Step 1 */
for thread 1 $\cdots$ N_{core} **do**
    $S_{start}(i)$ = predict (suffix of $\Pi(i-1)$); /* Step 2 */
    process($\Pi(i)$, $S_{start}(i)$); /* Step 3 */
thread_join();
for partition 1 $\cdots$ N_{core} **do** /* Step 4 */
    if validate($S_{start}(i)$) == FALSE **then**
        reprocess($\Pi(i)$);

1. **Partitioning.** Given an input string of length L, it first cuts it evenly into N_{core} segments, where N_{core} is the number of available cores.

2. **Predicting Starting States.** For each segment (except the first one), it predicts its starting state with a technique called *lookback*. For segment i, lookback examines the suffix of its prior segment $i-1$ and uses it as conditions to rule out impossible states or states with low chances to be the correct starting state (more details in [61]). Later, a single state is selected as the predicted starting state.
3. **Parallel Execution.** With predicted starting states, it then executes each segment of length $L_{seg} = L/N_{core}$ in parallel. For each individual segment, this execution is the same as a sequential FSM execution.
4. **Validation and Reprocessing.** At last, it validates the correctness of the predicted starting states after the parallel execution. The validation compares the predicted starting state of segment i with the ending state of segment $i-1$, if they are different (i.e., prediction fails), segment i would be reprocessed.

Three things are important to note. First, According to prior results [61], the prediction accuracy highly depends on segment suffix, rather than how far it is away from the input beginning. Second, in Step 4, validations among different segments need to be in sequential order to ensure the correctness; Third, the reprocessing of a segment may stop earlier thanks to the *state convergence* property that widely exists in many FSMs. We elaborate this property using the example in Figure 2.

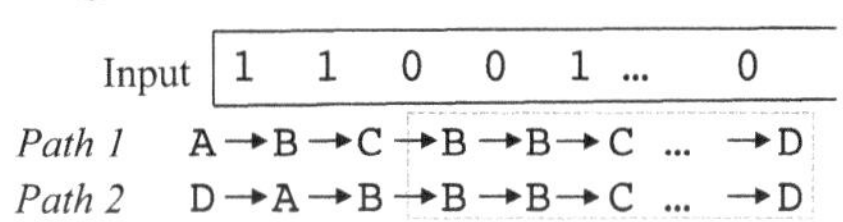

Figure 2: Example of State Convergence.

Consider processing a piece of an input string, starting with two different states A and D. There are two paths of state sequence, each for a different starting state. After processing the first three symbols `110`, both paths get into the same state B. Since then, these two paths would keep producing the same state sequence as they will observe the same symbols. This phenomenon is referred to as *State Convergence* [61, 40].

In the context of reprocessing, as long as the predicted (wrong) state converges with the actual starting state before reaching the end of the segment, the reprocessing can safely stop since the remaining states would be the same as the correct ones. In fact, state convergence is not only useful for speculative FSM parallelization, but also for parallel prefix-sum, where paths from different starting states may also converge and hence maintaining one of them is sufficient. We elaborate the details shortly in Section 3.2.

3. FINE-GRAINED PARALLELISM

Fine-grained parallelism is becoming increasingly prevalent in mainstream microprocessors, in a variety of forms, such as deep pipelining, multi-instruction issue, and SIMD vector units. For example, Intel's recent microarchitectures, `Haswell`, supports Advanced Vector Extensions 2 (AVX2) which features 256-bit vector units that can process 8 integer-typed data in parallel.

Effectively utilizing such fine-grained hardware parallelism is critical to maximizing the efficiency of various applications. In this section, we first discuss three types of parallelism that can be used in fine-grained level, two of which are proposed by this work. Then, we compare their effectiveness with a rigorous analysis, which in turn guides the design of FSM parallelization techniques.

3.1 Three Dimensions

The only fine-grained parallelism that has been seen in prior work comes from *associative parallelism* [35, 40]. We propose two other types of parallelism that are applicable to fine-grained levels, namely, *multi-state speculation* and *multi-level speculation*. We next elaborate each of them. For convenience, we refer to them as P1, P2, and P3.

P1: Parallelism in Associative Operations

Computations with associative operations can be trivially parallelized, such as multiplying a sequence of matrices. In fact, an FSM execution on an input sequence $c_1 c_2 \cdots c_L$ can also be associative. This is achieved by enumerating all the states in the FSM and making transitions for each of them, referred as *prefix-sum parallelism* by Ladner and Fischer [35].

In practice, as described in [40], it first cuts the input into T segments, then it enumerates all the n states for each segment except the first segment (which starts from *initial* state) to start transitions. After a segment has been processed, a mapping between each starting state and its ending state would be available. With the known *initial* state, it finally goes through every resulted mapping in order and selects the correct path. Clearly, it brings in $n-1$ times extra computations, where n is the number of states. It may be beneficial when the available hardware parallelism is more than n. However, with *state convergence* optimization, the extra cost can be dramatically reduced [40] (see Section 2.2).

P2: Parallelism in Multi-State Speculation

Existing work on speculative parallelization of FSMs partition the input based on the number of CPU cores and predict a single starting state for each segment, the one with the highest potential to minimize the misspeculation penalty. A straightforward extension to this approach is *speculating multiple starting states for each segment, instead of one.* The intuition is that the more candidates are used for prediction, the more likely the correct starting state gets covered and the more likely the misspeculation penalty gets reduced. Such extension enables new parallelism as each one of the speculated starting states can start its own path independently. We refer to it as *multi-state speculative parallelism.* The difference between single-state and multi-state speculation is significant because most previous work was based on single-value prediction, such as the BOP system [29].

Essentially, multi-state speculative parallelism provides a tradeoff between single-state speculative parallelization and parallel prefix-sum. It offers more flexibility to deal with FSMs that are hard to speculate and FSMs that are hard to enumerate due to a large number of states.

P3: Parallelism in Multi-Level Speculation

The third way to expose parallelism is further partitioning the N_{core} input segments into $N_{core} * W^{l-1}$ finer-grained segments recursively, assuming that W is the degree of parallelism at fine-grained levels (l is the number of levels). We refer to this type of parallelism as *Multi-Level Speculation.*

Since hardware parallelism is also hierarchical – a CPU has multiple computing cores, each with its own SIMD units

– multi-level speculation offers a natural mapping from software parallelism to hardware parallelism. For example, the first level speculative parallelism can be mapped to coarse-grained thread-level hardware parallelism (i.e., multicores), while the second level can be mapped to fine-grained ILP or SIMD parallelism. Note that such parallelism is not free; it may bring more overhead as it involves more speculation. We will shortly prove that it is still more efficient than the first two types of parallelism when used properly.

3.2 Efficiency Analysis

We next analyze the efficiency of the three types of parallelism theoretically. To facilitate our analysis, we bring two commonly used metrics into the context of FSM execution.

- *Expected Critical Path Length (ECPL).* This is the expected number of state transitions on the longest transition path of an FSM execution.
- *Degree of Parallelism (DoP).* This is the number of processing units that can be effectively used by an FSM execution.

For example, in a sequential execution, an FSM proceeds on a single transition path. Hence, $ECPL(seq) = L$, where L is the input length. As only one processing unit is used for all the transitions, we have $DoP(seq) = 1$.

Since state convergence is used by recent work [61, 40] for its large efficiency boost, we assume that it is applied in our discussion. Without loss of generality, we also assume that the input is partitioned into two segments at a coarse-grained level and the following analysis is on the second segment.

To analyze the effects of state convergence, we introduce two concepts: *convergence length* and *convergence matrix*.

DEFINITION 1. *Given an input string I and two different starting states s_i and s_j. The convergence length between s_i and s_j on I is the least number of transitions for each of them to take in order to transition to the same state, denoted as $L^I(s_i, s_j)$. If by end of I, they end at different states, set $L^I(s_i, s_j) = \infty$.*

Consider the example in Figure 2, we have $L^I(A, D) = 3$. Based on this, we define *convergence matrix* as follows.

DEFINITION 2. *Given an FSM with n states, the convergence matrix over an input I is an $n \times n$ matrix, where each element is the convergence length between states s_i and s_j on input I (i.e., $L^I(s_i, s_j)$), denoted as M_L.*

$$M_L = \begin{bmatrix} L^I(s_1,s_1) & L^I(s_1,s_2) & \dots & L^I(s_1,s_n) \\ L^I(s_2,s_1) & L^I(s_2,s_2) & \dots & L^I(s_2,s_n) \\ \vdots & \vdots & \ddots & \vdots \\ L^I(s_n,s_1) & L^I(s_n,s_2) & \dots & L^I(s_n,s_n) \end{bmatrix} \quad (1)$$

M_L has some properties: (i) It is symmetric as $L^I(s_i, s_j) = L^I(s_j, s_i)$; (ii) $L^I(s_i, s_i) = 0$; (iii) If $L^I(s_i, s_j) = l_1$, $l_1 \leq \|I\|$ and $L^I(s_j, s_k) = l_2$, $l_2 \leq \|I\|$, then $L^I(s_i, s_k) = max\{l_1, l_2\}$, where $\|\cdot\|$ means the length or number of transitions.

Convergence matrix embodies information about how states converge at each step during an FSM execution, it hence can help us reason about the reprocessing cost for P2 and P3.

In P1, each state starts its own transition path (denoted as $Path(s_i)$). Once a path finds that it converges with another path, one of the two paths would be *killed* (stopped), the other one would be kept *live*. Hence, the length of $Path(s_i)$ is the shortest convergence length between s_i and any other states, supposing that s_i converges with at least one of other states. Otherwise, its length would equal to the length of the input. Formally, we have

$$\|Path(s_i)\| = \min\{L^I(s_i, S - \{s_i\}), \|I\|\} \quad (2)$$

where s_i converges with $S - \{s_i\}$ when s_i converges with at least one state from $S - \{s_i\}$. Correspondingly, $L^I(s_i, S - \{s_i\}) = \min\{L^I(s_i, s_j) | s_j \in S - \{s_i\}\}$.

By definition, it is possible that $\|Path(s_i)\| < \|I\|$ for every s_i. To finish the whole input, one of the transition paths $Path(s_i)$, $s_i \in S$, has to continue $\|I\|$ - $\max_{1 \leq i \leq n}\{\|Path(s_i)\|\}$ transitions. Hence, the $ECPL$ of P1 is simply the input length.

LEMMA 1. *Given an input I, the ECPL of P1 is*

$$ECPL(P1) = \|I\| \quad (3)$$

On the other hand, the DoP of P1 may vary as the FSM executes depending on state convergence. Starting from all states S, when the number of live paths at the j-th input symbol, $live(S, j)$, exceeds the number of processing units, PU, the DoP equals to PU; Otherwise, the DoP drops to $live(S, j)$.

$$DoP(P1) = \min\{live(S, j), PU\}, \text{ where } 1 \leq j \leq \|I\| \quad (4)$$

In P2, suppose K states, denoted as S_K, are selected as the prediction. Since the selection does not change the path length of any state, if S_K covers the correct state, then $ECPL$ equals to the input length. Otherwise, it needs to reprocess the input until the correct state converges with one of selected K states. The reprocessing length is

$$\|redo\| = min\{L^I(s_i, s^*) | s_i \in S_K, s^* \text{ is the true state}\} \quad (5)$$

Assuming that the reprocessing in P2 runs sequentially, we have Lemma 2 holds for P2.

LEMMA 2. *Given an input I, the ECPL of P2 is*

$$ECPL(P2) = \|I\| + (1 - P_k) \cdot \|redo\| \quad (6)$$

where P_k is the probability that S_K covers the true state s^*.

Before reprocessing, the DoP of P2 is similar to P1; During reprocessing, the $DoP(P2)$ drops to one.

$$DoP(P2) = \begin{cases} \min\{live(S_k, j), PU\} & 1 \leq j \leq \|I\| \\ 1 & \text{redo} \end{cases} \quad (7)$$

In P3, the input segment is further cut into PU finer-grained chunks, each of them is processed with a predicted starting state $\hat{s}_i$, $1 < i \leq PU$. Suppose the probability of each predicted starting state is $p(\hat{s}_i)$ and the corresponding reprocessing length is $redo(\hat{s}_i)$, then the expected amount of reprocessing is

$$\|\overline{redo}\| = \sum_{i=2}^{PU} (1 - p(\hat{s}_i)) \cdot \|redo(\hat{s}_i)\| \quad (8)$$

Note that the reprocessing of different chunks runs sequentially, since the correctness validation of chunk i depends on the validation of chunk $i - 1$. This is also true at coarse-grained level. Hence, the expected reprocessing length for the whole input should include the reprocessing at both coarse-grained and fine-grained levels, that is, replacing PU in Equation 8 with $PU \cdot (T - 1)$, where T is the number of threads at coarse-grained level.

Putting them together, we have Lemma 3 for P3.

LEMMA 3. *Given an input I, the ECPL of P3 is*

$$ECPL(P3) = \|I\| / PU + \|\overline{redo}\| \quad (9)$$

According to Lemma 3, any misspeculation has the potential to lengthen the critical path, compromising the benefits of speculative parallelization. In the worst case, when all prediction fails, $ECPL(P3)$ would equal to the input length, the same as a sequential execution.

As each processing unit processes a different input chunk, no state convergence would happen. Hence, the DoP of P3 equals to PU before reprocessing and drops to one during reprocessing.

$$DoP(P3) = \begin{cases} PU & 1 \leq j \leq \|I\| \\ 1 & \text{redo} \end{cases} \quad (10)$$

Discussion. Based on the above analysis, we compare the three types of parallelism in terms of both $ECPL$ and DoP.

First, $ECPL$ captures the expected execution length. For P1 and P2, since enumerating all states or a set of states do not shorten the critical path, $ECPL(P1)$ and $ECPL(P2)$ at least equals to the segment length. In comparison, by cutting the segment into finer-grained chunks, $P3$ have the chances to further shorten the critical path length. However, due to the dependence in reprocessing, the $ECPL$ of P3 could be as long as the whole input length, which happens when all prediction fails.

Second, DoP captures the utilization of fine-grained hardware parallelism. $DoP(P1)$ and $DoP(P2)$ start dropping when the number of live paths goes below the number of processing units PU. In another word, some of the processing units become idle. Unfortunately, $DoP(P3)$ cannot guarantee full utilization all the time neither, due to possibility of sequential reprocessing.

Overall, the efficiency of a type of parallelism depends on the properties of FSMs and hardware architecture (e.g., PU). In this work, we choose P3, mainly based on our observation that the reprocessing lengths are usually short thanks to the quick state convergence. This has two positive consequences. First, it ensures that $ECPL(P3)$ is usually much shorter than segment length (see Section 5). Second, it guarantees high hardware utilization by keeping $DoP(P3)$ mostly as high as PU.

4. MICROSPEC

Guided by the analysis in Section 3, we design and implement *MicroSpec*, a library that leverages multi-level speculation to maximize the efficiency of parallel FSM execution on modern processors. We first describes its major techniques, then introduces an optimization to facilitate its use.

4.1 Overview

At high-level, *MicroSpec* consists of four speculation-centric parallelization techniques (denoted as S1 - S4) plus a speculation-oriented data transformation. The parallelization techniques are able to expose fine-grained speculative parallelism to FSM computations while the data transformation automatically re-layouts the input for better locality.

Predicting Starting States. Since starting states prediction is not the focus of this work, we simply choose a relatively straightforward prediction, named *simple lookback*, which has been used by prior work [61, 1]. Basically, it starts from the suffix of a prior segment with a random state, then uses its ending state after processing the suffix as the predicted starting state. More advanced predictions can be ported to *MicroSpec*. However, there will be a tradeoff between accuracy and overhead, which remains to be investigated. In the following, we elaborate these four major techniques and the optimization in details.

4.2 Techniques

In multi-level speculation, each level follows a speculative parallelization scheme that is similar to the one in Algorithm 1. The key differences lie in the implementations. In the following, we consider two cases: two-level speculation and three-level speculation. For the first level, that is, the coarse-grained level, we simply follow the coarse-grained speculative parallelization in Algorithm 1. For the second and third levels, we mainly focus on ILP and SIMD parallelism, both of which are common features owned by modern processors. As the first level is given in Section 2, in the following, we only show the algorithms in the second and third levels. Next, we first present two two-level speculations, followed by two three-level ones.

S1: Speculative SIMD Gather

We first consider SIMD parallelism only for the second-level speculation. Algorithm 2 shows the pseudo-code of this approach. As this approach mainly relies on SIMD operation `gather`, we refer to it as *Speculative Gather*.

Algorithm 2 Speculative SIMD Gather

1: π = fine_grained_partition(W);
2: S = predictInitStates(π);
3: **for** (i=0; $i < L_{seg}/W$, i++) **do**
4: $\quad I$ = readInputVec(i);
5: $\quad F = S \times N_{sym} + I$;
6: $\quad S$ = gather(T, F);
7: **end**

Basically, given an input segment of length L_{seg} from the first-level speculation, speculative gather partitions it based on the SIMD width W (e.g., $W = 8$ for 256-bit integer operations) (Line 1). Then, it predicts the starting states for the W smaller segments with simple lookback (Line 2). Since there are no dependencies among predictions, they can be vectorized with SIMD operations as well.

With the predicted starting states, stored in a vector S, it goes through W smaller segments in parallel with SIMD operations, as shown through Lines 3 to 6 in Algorithm 2. The `readInputVec()` can be implemented either in SIMD operation or a sequence of non-SIMD `read` operations. To find next states, it accesses the transition table T, which is stored in a state-major one-dimensional array. This is finished in two steps. First, it calculates the address of next states and stores them in the offset vector F. Then it leverages a single `gather` operation to load W next states to vector S.

To illustrate the functionality of `gather`, consider the running example. Suppose the SIMD width $W = 8$, current state vector S = [D, C, A, C, F, A, E, B] (i.e., [3, 2, 0, 2, 5, 0, 4, 1]), input vector I = [1, 0, 0, 1, 1, 0, 1, 0], then offset vector $F = S \times 2 + I$ = [7, 6, 0, 5, 11, 0, 9, 2]. The next state vector would be $S = gather(base, F)$ = [A, B, E, D, A, E, F, B].

S2: Speculative Unrolling

Alternatively, we can also consider unrolling for the second-level speculation. Unrolling is one of the major ways to expose ILP. However exposing such low-level parallelism is not straightforward. In fact, by default, due to the tight dependencies across state transitions, unrolling does not provide any benefits. As shown in Figure 3, the performance of after unrolling is almost the same as the default version. This is mainly because the state transition dependencies turn into instruction dependencies, making most unrolled instructions incapable of executing in parallel.

To overcome the above difficulty, we apply the idea of speculation to unrolling, aiming to break the most dependencies among the unrolled instructions. We refer to it as *Speculative Unrolling*, illustrated by Algorithm 3.

Algorithm 3 Speculative Unrolling

π = fine_grained_partition(R);
$s[0 \cdots R-1]$ = predictInitStates(π);
B = L_{seg}/R;
for (i=0; $i < B$, i++) **do**
    c[0] = readInput(i);
    s[0] = T[s[0]][c[0]];
    c[1] = readInput($i + B$);
    s[1] = T[s[1]][c[0]];
    … …
    c[R-1] = readInput($i + B * (R-1)$);
    s[R-1] = T[s[R-1]][c[R-1]];
end

The basic idea of speculative unrolling is as follows. At first, it takes a coarse-grained input segment and partitions it into finer-grained segments according to the unrolling factor, R. Then it predicts the starting state for each fine-grained segment. So far, it is the same as S1, speculative SIMD gather. The difference is in the next. Instead of using some SIMD operations, it unrolls the loop body R times, with a goal to bring in artificial ILPs. Note that, with starting state prediction, the unrolled loop iterations do not have any dependencies, hence, can be executed in parallel and optimized by microprocessors.

A key question in speculative unrolling is the selection of unrolling factor R. If choosing R too high, it takes more risks of bringing in misspeculated segments; If choosing R too low, it may not fully utilize the potential of ILPs in microprocessors. In Section 5, we will examine this with experiments.

Discussion. Note that both of the above approaches rely on speculation to expose fine-grained parallelism. The former exposes SIMD parallelism while the latter exposes ILP. They are essentially orthogonal, hence, might be combined to expose even richer parallelism, the third-level speculative parallelism, pushing the utilization of microprocessor to the extreme. Depending on the order that they are combined, we refer to the combined approaches as *Speculative SIMD Gather+* and *Speculative Unrolling+*, respectively. We elaborate them next, namely, S3 and S4.

S3: Speculative SIMD Gather+

Intuitively, this approach applies speculative unrolling to speculative SIMD gather. This essentially requires more speculation, in particular, $W \times R$ times of speculation for a coarse-grained input segment, where W is the SIMD width and R is the unrolling factor. Algorithm 4 describes this approach. Basically, the loop body in Algorithm 2 is unrolled R times as that in Algorithm 3. Note that the number of loop iterations drops to $L_{seg}/W/R$.

Similarly to speculative unrolling, it also needs to select the loop unrolling factor R. An interesting question is whether

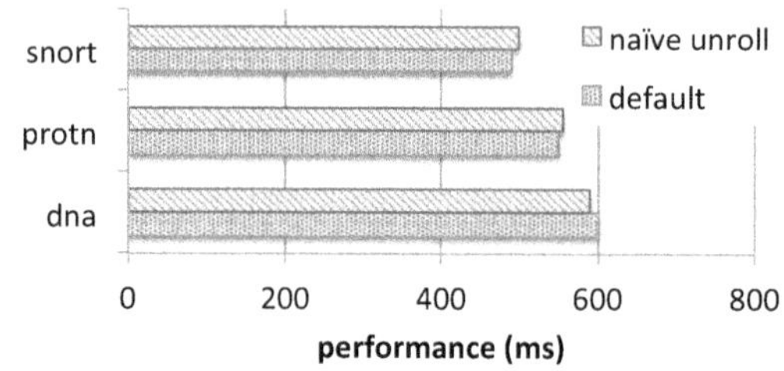

Figure 3: Performance of Naive Unrolling

it has a smaller optimal R comparing to that of speculative unrolling. We show our findings to this question in Section 5.

Algorithm 4 Speculative SIMD Gather+

π = fine_grained_partition($W \times R$);
$S[0 \cdots R-1]$ = predictInitStates(π);
B = $L_{seg}/W/R$;
for (i=0; $i < B$, i++) **do**
    $I[0]$ = readInputVec(i);
    $F[0] = S[0] \times N_{sym} + I[0]$;
    $S[0]$ = gather(T, $F[0]$);
    $I[1]$ = readInputVec($i + B$);
    $F[1] = S[1] \times N_{sym} + I[1]$;
    $S[1]$ = gather(T, $F[1]$);
    … …
    $I[R-1]$ = readInputVec($i + B * (R-1)$);
    $F[R-1] = S[R-1] \times N_{sym} + I[R-1]$;
    $S[R-1]$ = gather(T, $F[R-1]$);
end

S4: Speculative Unrolling+

Different from S3, *speculative unrolling+* first applies speculative unrolling to the second level of speculation, then applies speculative gather to the third level. The pseudo-code of this approach is illustrated as in Algorithm 5. Each for-loop corresponds to the unrolling as in S2. Within each for-loop, a segment is further partitioned into W segments to initiate speculative gather. Similarly to S3, S4 also aims to realize the maximal utilization of the processing power by aggressively increasing the amount of speculation.

In sum, S1 and S2 are based on two-level speculation, while S3 and S4 are based on three-level speculation. The total number of partitions increases from W and R in the former cases to $W \times R$ in the latter cases.

4.3 Optimization

For coarse-grained speculative parallelization, the input is partitioned evenly into coarse-grained segments based on the number of cores. Each thread sequentially accesses its own segment which is stored in a piece of continuous memory (since inputs are arrays). In this case, the locality is ideal. However, when multi-level speculation is used, the accessing pattern is not sequential any more, instead, it becomes stride-based. Even worse, the width of stride is typically large (i.e., the length of a fine-grained segment). This non-coalesced memory accessing pattern could drag the performance benefits down.

To overcome this, we propose a *speculation-oriented data transformation* that re-layouts the data according to the accessing pattern in multi-level speculation scheme to minimize the memory accessing delays. Basically, it transforms

Algorithm 5 Speculative Unrolling+

```
π = fine_grained_partition(W × R);
S[0...R − 1] = predictInitStates(π);
B = L_seg/R ;
for (i=0; i < B/W; i++) do
    I[0] = readInputVec(i);
    F[0] = S[0] × N_sym + I[0];
    S[0] = gather(T, F[0]);
end
for (i=B; i < B + B/W; i++) do
    I[1] = readInputVec(i);
    F[1] = S[1] × N_sym + I[1];
    S[1] = gather(T, F[1]);
end
... ...
for (i=B * (R − 1); i < B * (R − 1) + B/W; i++) do
    I[R − 1] = readInputVec(i);
    F[R − 1] = S[R − 1] × N_sym + I[R − 1];
    S[R − 1] = gather(T, F[R − 1]);
end
```

```
for (i = 0; i < B; i++) /* before transformation */
{  I = (in[i],in[i+B],in[i+2B],in[i+3B]);
   ...
}
```

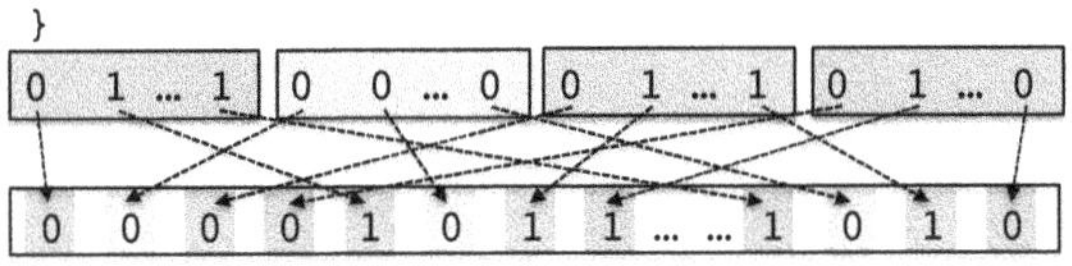


```
for (i = 0; i < Lseg; i = i + W) /* after trans. */
{  I = (in[i],in[i+1],in[i+2],in[i+3]);
   ...
}
W = 4; B = Lseg/W;
```

Figure 4: Spec.-Oriented Data Transformation

the big stride-based accessing to simple sequential accessing. It does this by moving each group of stride-based accessed data next to each other, as shown in Figure 4.

Consider S1, speculative SIMD gather [3]. Suppose the SIMD width $W = 4$, a coarse-grained input segment with length of L_{seg} is further partitioned into four fine-grained segments, each with a length of $B = L_{seg}/W$. To get an input vector I (as in Algorithm 2), the original memory accessing has a stride width of B. After the data transformation, the memory accessing becomes strictly sequential.

Speculation-oriented data transformation can either work offline (pre-layout) or online (on-the-fly re-layout). In many scenarios, the whole dataset is available and stable and different FSMs are executed over the same dataset many times. A typical example is biological sequence analysis, which may search different patterns on the same sequence database multiple times. Though the database may be updated sometimes, it is expected that updating rate is much lower than accessing rate. For scenarios like this, it is reasonable to do offline data transformation as the cost of data transformation will be amortized across different FSM executions.

4.4 Implementation

We prototyped *MicroSpec* as a C library using `Pthread` and Intel's `AVX2` instruction set. The library provides a uniform interface to various FSMs through a set of APIs, which implement both the four speculative parallelization methods and the data transformation. The major arguments to the APIs include the FSM `FSM*` and input `char*`. Other parameters such as the number of threads are automatically configured. In terms of FSM formats, it supports both transition table and `dot` file (a graphical FSM representation). It can also take regular expressions as arguments with the help of some off-the-shelf regular expression processors.

The compilation of *MicroSpec* depends on the use of the APIs. Since S1 does not include any SIMD instructions, it can be compiled even on machines without `AVX2` using standard C compilers, such as GCC or ICC. In comparison, the implementations of S2-S4 use `_mm256_i32gather_epi32` instruction from `AVX2`, hence need to be compiled on recent Intel microarchitectures, such as `Haswell` and its successors. We implement the data transformation in two versions: an API call that can be invoked by S1-S4 at runtime and a standalone tool that runs the transformation offline.

[3]Similar analysis is applicable to other three fine-grained speculation techniques in *MicroSpec*.

5. EVALUATION

In this section, we evaluate the effectiveness of *MicroSpec* using a set of real-world FSM applications that are manually collected from different domains, including *motif searching* in Bioinformatics, *rule matching* in NIDS, and *Huffman decoding* in data decompression, among others.

5.1 Methodology

The evaluation of *MicroSpec* includes all four speculation-based fine-grained parallelization techniques as well as the speculation-oriented data transformation. Table 1 summarizes them and lists their abbreviation used in the evaluation.

Table 1: *MicroSpec* Framework

Techniques in *MicroSpec*	Abbreviation
S1: Speculative SIMD Gather	SpecGather
S2: Speculative Unrolling	SpecUnroll
S3: Speculative SIMD Gather+	SpecGather+
S4: Speculative Unrolling+	SpecUnroll+
Spec.-Oriented Data Trans.	SpecTrans

We compare *MicroSpec* with prior techniques, the coarse-grained speculative parallelization [61] and parallel prefix-sum [40], including both state convergence and range coalescing optimizations. For convenience, we refer to them as *coarseSpec* and *prefixSum*, respectively. Our implementations are based on our best understanding of their papers.

Our major experiments run on a quad-core machine equipped with Intel 2.8GHz Xeon E5-1603 v3 processor with AVX2. The machine runs CentOS Linux 7.2.1511 and has GCC 4.8.5. For comparison, we also tested a machine without AVX2 supports. It is a quad-core machine equipped with Intel 3GHz Xeon CPU E5-1607 v2 processor with SSE 4.2. It runs Ubuntu 14.04.4 LTS and has GCC 4.9.3.

All programs are compiled with "-O3" optimization flag. The timing results reported are the average of 10 repetitive runs with all runtime cost included. We do not report 95% confidence interval of the average when the variation is not significant. In fact, we found that the measurements are usually stable since FSM executions involve a large amount of repetitive but similar computations.

5.2 Benchmarks

The benchmarks are selected to cover a wide range of FSM applications with different levels of complexities. We first

Table 2: **Protein Motifs.** [·] means alternative symbols; 'x' means any symbol; (·) is the number of repetition.

Bench	Description and Regular Expression
protn1	IQ calmodulin-binding motif. `[FILV]Qx(3)[RK]Gx(3)[RK]x(2)[FILVWY]`
protn2	Hemopexin domain signature. `[LIFAT]ILx(2)Wx(2,3)[PE]xVF[LIVMFY][DENQS][STA][AV][LIVMFY]`
protn3	P-type 'Trefoil' domain signature. `[KRH]x(2)Cx[FYPSTV]x(3,4)[ST]x(3)Cx(4)CC[FYWH]`

Table 3: Snort Rules.

<table>
<tr><th>Bench</th><th>Description and Regular Expression</th></tr>
<tr><td>snort1</td><td>(\xff{32})|([0-9A-F]{22})|(Color|Motion)</td></tr>
<tr><td>snort2</td><td>(\xFF\x41)|(Start)|(\/999)</td></tr>
<tr><td>snort3</td><td>(admin|axis2)|(\x3d?\x3d\r\n)|([rs]{4})</td></tr>
<tr><td>snort4</td><td>(\x2F\d{10})|(L\d\d\x00)|(POST\s)</td></tr>
<tr><td>snort5</td><td>(asp\x5C)|(2x\/.*php)|(htr\x5C)</td></tr>
<tr><td>snort6</td><td>snort1 | snort2 | snort3 | snort4 | snort5</td></tr>
</table>

elaborate them by groups, then summarize their statistics.

Biological Sequence Analysis. Pattern searching is a basic way to analyze biological sequences, such as DNA sequences or protein sequences. For example, a DNA motif is a short pattern of nucleic acid, while a protein motif is a pattern of amino acids. Usually, protein patterns are represented as regular expressions. Table 2 lists three protein patterns randomly selected from a widely used protein database PROSITE [13]. For DNA motifs, they are more commonly represented with Hamming distances. In our benchmarks, *dna1* is a DNA motif `ATCGGTCC(8,3)`, which means three of the eight preceding symbols can be different as specified. Similarly, *dna2* and *dna3* are two other DNA motifs `TC-GAGGACCA(10,4)` and `AGGGTAAA(8,1)`, respectively. We converted the above protein and DNA motifs to FSMs using standard regular expression transformation algorithms.

Intrusion Detection Rule Matching. Network Intrusion Detection Systems (NIDSs) use regular expressions (called *signatures*) to detect malicious activities on the internet traffic. Among various NIDSs, Snort [52] is arguably the most widely used open source NIDS. It has a rich body of signatures/rules, most of them have a `pcre` field, where a Perl-compatible regular expression is used to specify the pattern interested.

In our evaluation, we randomly chose a set of 15 PCRE patterns from 15 signatures in Snort version 2.9.8.0 as our benchmarks. They are then randomly put into 5 groups, each with 3 patterns. We created the 6th group by putting all the 15 PCRE patterns together. Each group then is compiled to a single FSM using off-of-shelf PCRE to FSM tools. Table 3 lists the 6 groups with their PCRE patterns. The inputs to the Snort FSMs are network traffic trace collected from a Linux server and a laptop via `tcpdump`.

Mixed FSM benchmarks. This group contains a mixed set of FSM benchmarks, including Huffman decoding, mathematical testing and a couple of searching patterns.

For its optimality, Huffman algorithm has been widely used for encoding and decoding digital data (e.g., text, JPEG and MPEG). During the decoding stage, an FSM is employed to automate the decoding process. Basically, a Huffman decoding FSM contains a set of accept states, each of them corresponding to a code. It runs over an encoded (binary) file. Each time it reaches an accept state, a code is recognized. Note that this work targets the decoding phase, as the encoding phase is embarrassingly parallel [23].

Our Huffman FSM benchmark *huff* is built based on a collection of e-books downloaded from Project Gutenberg (as of Dec 15th, 2015). To make the decoding FSM more applicable, we created a single Huffman tree and a single decoding FSM that are capable of encoding any text files with ASCII symbols and decoding them, respectively. Since extended ASCII contains 256 symbols, there are 256 accept states (i.e., leaf nodes of Huffman tree). Together with 255 non-accept states, *huff* consists of 511 states. The inputs to *huff* are binary files that encode a large collection of e-books.

Mathematical testing benchmarks include *div* and *evenodd*. The former tests if a binary sequence is divisible by seven while the latter tests if a text file of $\{a, b, c, d\}$ satisfies that $|a| + |b|$ is even and $|c| + |d|$ is odd, where $|\cdot|$ means the number of appearances in the file.

We also include two searching patterns that are more challenging to speculate, namely, *commadot* and *likeapple*. Their patterns are $((.+,.+\backslash.)\{4\}|(.+\backslash,)\{4\}|(.+\backslash.)\{4\})\{3\}$ and $(.*l.*i.*k.*e)\{6\} \mid (.*.a.*.p.*.p.*.l.*.e)\{5\}$.

Table 4 summarizes the benchmarks used in our evaluation, including the total number of states, the number of accept states, state visiting frequency range and the state range after range coalescing optimization [40].

Table 4: Summary of FSM Benchmarks.

Bench	#States	#Accept	FRange	CRange
dna1	371	76	0 - 3.6%	133
dna2	2871	583	0 - 2.1%	953
dna3	40	5	0 - 32.9%	15
protn1	69	6	0 - 73.4%	31
protn2	281	14	0 - 24.7%	99
protn3	832	48	0 - 61.9%	509
snort1	86	4	0 - 56.0%	32
snort2	10	1	0 - 99.4%	4
snort3	15	2	0 - 91.3%	5
snort4	19	1	0 - 98.7%	13
snort5	20	3	0 - 91.3%	5
snort6	299	22	0 - 44.7%	72
huff	511	256	0 - 11.3%	255
div	7	1	14.28%	7
evenodd	4	1	25%	4
commadot	130	7	0 - 97.1%	81
likeapple	495	1	0 - 88.3%	494

5.3 Results

Unrolling Factor. Since the selection of the unrolling factor R may affect the performance of *MicroSpec*, we first discuss it. Table 5 shows the execution time of *dna4* on a small testing input using different unrolling factor values. The results answer the question in Section 4.2 – the best R varies across methods, 6 or 8 for *SpecUnroll*, 2 for *SpecGather+* and *SpecUnroll+*. This implies that the ILP for SIMD operations is less effective than the one for non-SIMD operations. Since we found that the best Rs are stable across different benchmarks, we empirically set $R = 8$ for *SpecUnroll* and $R = 2$ for *SpecGather+* and *SpecUnroll+* in the following.

Group A: Motif Searching. Figure 5 shows the perfor-

Table 5: Unrolling Factor Selection

exec. time(ms)	unrolling factor				
method	1	2	4	6	8
SpecUnroll	397.3	199	100.7	73.3	75.6
SpecGather+	145.6	97.6	188	484.1	251.7
SpecUnroll+	147.9	94.6	129.7	299.6	210

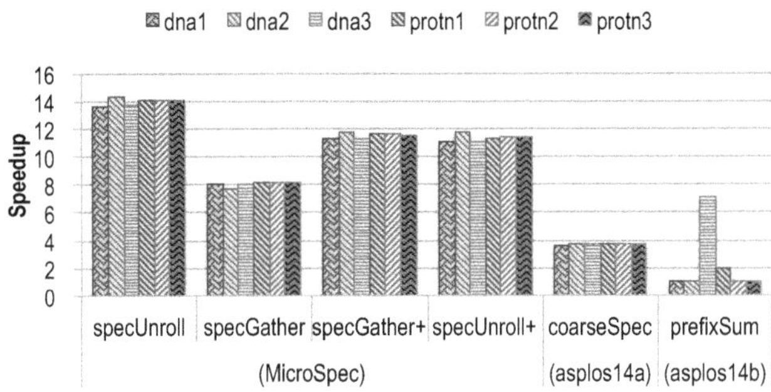

Figure 5: Speedups for Biological Benchmarks

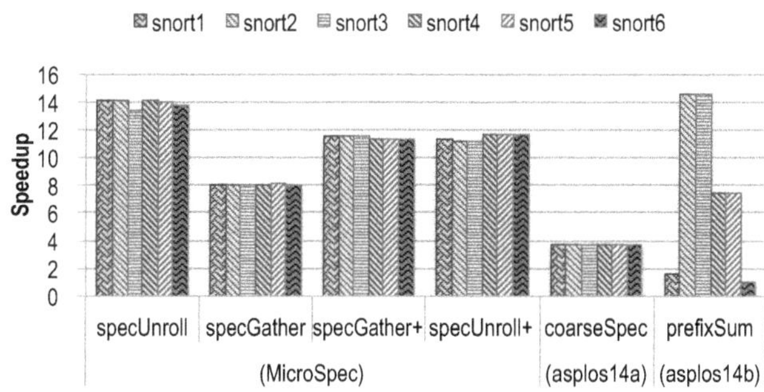

Figure 6: Speedups for Snort Benchmarks

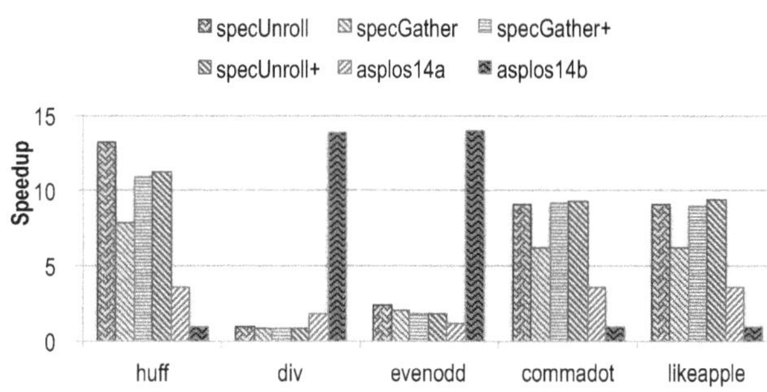

Figure 7: Speedups for Mixed FSM Benchmarks

mance results for *motif searching* benchmark group. Overall, the performance of four speculation-based methods in *MicroSpec* outperform previous two methods substantially, achieving about 14X speedups among all six benchmarks.

More specifically, *specUnroll* yields the best speedups among all tested methods. This implies that even though modern processors come with highly optimized ILP, they can be barely utilized by the default version. *specGather* yields about 8X speedup on average, also exceeding prior methods. It demonstrates the benefits of utilizing **gather** intrinsic from Intel AVX2 for FSM computations. However, on the other hand, it barely reaches around 60% performance of *specUnroll*, which indicates that the limitation of current **gather** compromises the speculation benefits. Methods *specGather+* and *specUnroll+*, yield similar speedups, higher than *specGather* but lower than *specUnroll*.

Note that *prefixSum* yields inconsistent speedups across different benchmarks. The reason is that its performance depends on the properties of FSMs. For FSMs with fast convergence length and less number of states, it tends to perform much better. For example, it gets about 7X speedup on benchmark **dna3**, which has only 40 states. These states converge quickly to a single state within 50 transitions. In comparison *coarseSpec* shows consist but limited speedups due to its unawareness of fine-grained parallelism.

Group B: Snort Rules Matching. Figure 6 shows the performance results for *Snort rules* benchmarks. In general, the results are similar to those in the first group. The main differences come from *prefixSum*, which achieves the best speedups for two benchmarks **snort2** and **snort3**. The reason is that both benchmarks have less than 16 states, smaller than the maximal number of states that a single SIMD shuffle (**_mm_shuffle_epi8**) can handle. This means it only needs a single **shuffle** instruction for each transition. Hence, this shows the optimal speedup of *prefixSum*. Comparing with *specGather*, this also validates that *shuffle* is much more efficient than *gather* on current processors.

Group C: Mixed FSM benchmarks. Figure 7 shows the performance results of the last benchmark group, which are mixed with Huffman decoding (*huff*) and some hard-to-speculate FSM benchmarks *div*, *evenodd*, *commadot*, and *likeapple*. After range coalescing, *huff* has a state range of 255. Though it can be executed by *prefixSum* using a mix of **shuffle** and **blend** operations, it hardly gets any benefits due to the large number of SIMD operations involved. In comparison, the four methods from *MicroSpec* show similar speedups on **huff** as those in the previous two groups.

The other four benchmarks in this group are more difficult to speculate due to their special structures. For *div* and *evenodd*, no states converge no matter what input sequences they are given. In this case, *MicroSpec* either shows limited improvement, about 2X speedup on *evenodd* or even performance degradation, about 10% slowdown on *div*. In comparison, *prefixSum* reaches 1.39X and 14X speedups, respectively, thanks to its speculation-free property and the small number of states in these two benchmarks (7 and 4). The other two benchmarks, *commadot* and *likeapple*, have relatively large number of states, meanwhile most states take long distances to converge (often exceeding 10K transitions). In this situation, *MicroSpec* gets about 8-9X speedup on average. Note that *specUnroll+* and *specGather+* all get similar or better performance than their counterparts, demonstrating the potential of combining SIMD *gather* and with speculation unrolling. In comparison, *prefixSum* could not get any speedups due to a large number of states in these two benchmarks (130 and 495).

Optimization *specTrans*. Table 6 shows the cost of *specTrans* optimization. In fact, the cost is quite comparable to the FSM execution time, about 1/3 of the sequential FSM execution time for input size of 100MB. Hence, it is recommended to used only offline, where the same datasets are reused across different FSM executions, such as different mo-

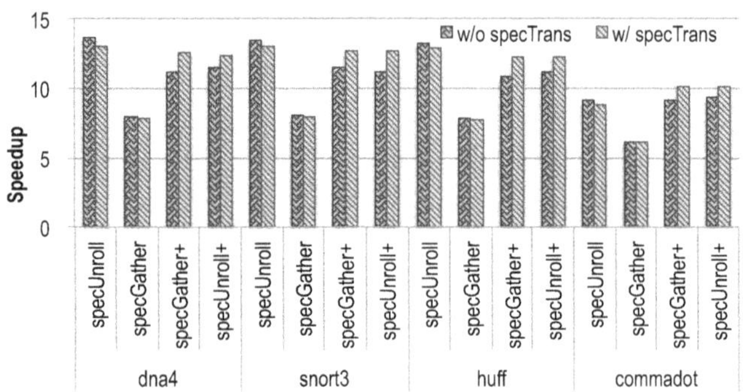

Figure 8: Performance Improvements of *specTrans*

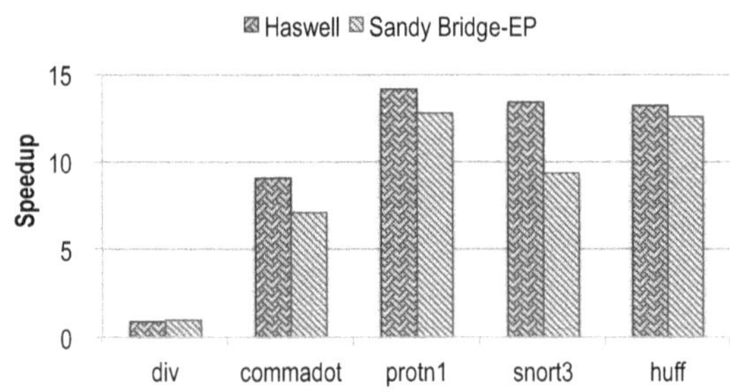

Figure 9: Performance on Different Machines

tif queries to the same DNA or protein sequence database. Figure 8 shows the improvements of *specTrans* optimization. On average, it brings about 8.5% extra speedup.

Table 6: Cost of *specTrans* (ms)

	num. of chunks			
input size	2	4	8	16
10MB	15	13	13	12
100MB	122	105	93	99
1GB	63K	63K	83K	64K

Comparison on Different Architectures. Finally, we also tested *MicroSpec* on an architecture without SIMD gather. In this case, only S2, *specUnroll* is experimented. Figure 9 summarizes the results. `Haswell` has AVX2, which supports an 8-way integer SIMD gather (`_mm256_i32gather_epi32`). In comparison, `Sandy Bridge EP` only comes with an earlier version of instruction set AVX. Overall, the performance on `Sandy Bridge EP` is slightly less than `Haswell`; but both follow a similar pattern. This demonstrates the potential of *MicroSpec* in a larger scope, across different architectures.

6. RELATED WORK

Program parallelization in general has received many efforts from various aspects, including but not limited to language design (e.g. Cilk [17], X10 [7]), hardware support (e.g., TLS [55, 21]) and programming models (e.g., STM [2, 6]). This section focuses the studies that are closed to FSM and speculative parallelization.

FSM and Speculative Parallelization. Traditional ways to parallelize FSM are through parallel prefix-sum or its variations [35]. Todd and others [40] implement this method on machines with vector units with a couple of optimizations. Some other FSM parallelization work focus on a few specific FSM applications, such as browser front-end [27] and JPEG decoder [31]. The basic ideas in these work were later formalized by Zhao and others [61] by introducing a concept called *principled speculation*. Other examples include hot state prediction for FSMs in intrusion detection [38] and speculative parsing [28]. For non-FSM applications, speculative parallelization has been studied for many years, including designing new language constructs [47] and parallelization frameworks [50, 12, 48, 56, 14]. Some of these studies have explored parallelism in irregular programs [33, 20, 46], which provide useful insights for exploiting parallelism in FSM computations, given that FSMs essentially run on an irregular data structure (a graph). They are mainly based on coarse-grained speculative parallelism. Some other prior work have explored bit-parallel fine-grained parallelism for FSMs by converting FSM computations into a sequence of bit operations [41, 36]. In comparison, this work uses both fine-grained and coarse-grained speculative parallelism. Integrating such bit-level parallelism to *MicroSpec* would be an interesting research topic that remains to be studied.

Vectorization and GPU. Vector extensions, such as SSE, have been widely used in many applications such as graphics [25], scientific applications [18], and signal processing [16]. Based on such vector extensions, many efforts have been put into auto-vectorization [42, 43, 57, 22]. However, there are still computations that are difficult to vectorize, due to irregular data structures, heavy branch operations, and noncontinuous memory access. To address these, prior work have vectorized binary tree search [30], tree traversal [26], irregular tree forest and multiple graphs traversal [51], and sparse matrix-vector multiplication [37]. The basic principles of vectorizing irregular applications include both improving the cache performance by careful data layout and resolving the branch operations. FSM parallelization has also been studied on GPU platform in the context of NFAs [62] which naturally run in parallel. Since FSMs are also irregular structure, the results of this work would provide valuable insights to the parallelization of other irregular computations.

7. CONCLUSION

This paper provides a rigorous analysis among three types of parallelism that can be exposed at fine-grained levels for FSM computations. It deepens the understanding to the efficiency of different FSM parallelization schemes. Guided by the analysis, it presents *MicroSpec*, a set of speculation-centric parallelization techniques that expose fine-grained speculative parallelism into FSM computations, along with a data transformation optimization. *MicroSpec* extends the available parallelism in FSM computations to a new level. Experiments show that *MicroSpec* outperforms the state-of-the-art by up to a factor of four, demonstrating the benefits of fine-grained speculative parallelism.

8. ACKNOWLEDGMENTS

We thank all anonymous reviewers for their constructive comments and our paper shepherd Keshav Pingali for his great help with the final version preparation.

9. REFERENCES

[1] Browsing web 3.0 on 3.0 watts: Why browsers will be parallel and implications for education. invited talk at The 3rd Workshop on Software Tools for MultiCore Systems, April, 2008.

[2] M. Abadi, A. Birrell, T. Harris, and M. Isard. Semantics of transactional memory and automatic mutual exclusion. In *Proceedings of ACM Symposium on Principles of Programming Languages*, 2008.

[3] T. Algra. Fast and efficient variable-to-fixed-length coding algorithm. *Electronics Letters*, 28(15):1399–1401, 1992.

[4] R. Alur and M. Yannakakis. Model checking of hierarchical state machines. *ACM Trans. Program. Lang. Syst.*, 23(3):273–303, May 2001.

[5] K. Asanovic, R. Bodik, B. C. Catanzaro, J. J. Gebis, P. Husbands, K. Keutzer, D. A. Patterson, W. L. Plishker, J. Shalf, S. W. Williams, et al. The landscape of parallel computing research: A view from berkeley. Technical report, Technical Report UCB/EECS-2006-183, EECS Department, University of California, Berkeley, 2006.

[6] B. Carlstrom, A. McDonald, H. Chafi, J. Chung, C. Minh, C. Kozyrakis, and K. Olukotun. The atomos transactional programming langauges. In *Proceedings of ACM SIGPLAN Conference on Programming Language Design and Implementation*, 2006.

[7] P. Charles, C. Grothoff, V. Saraswat, C. Donawa, A. Kielstra, K. Ebcioglu, C. von Praun, and V. Sarkar. X10: an object-oriented approach to non-uniform cluster computing. In *OOPSLA*, 2005.

[8] Y. Chen, D. Che, and K. Aberer. On the efficient evaluation of relaxed queries in biological databases. In *Proceedings of the Eleventh International Conference on Information and Knowledge Management*, CIKM '02, pages 227–236, New York, NY, USA, 2002. ACM.

[9] C. Chitic and D. Rosu. On validation of XML streams using finite state machines. In *Proceedings of the Seventh International Workshop on the Web and Databases, WebDB 2004, June 17-18, 2004, Maison de la Chimie, Paris, France, Colocated with ACM SIGMOD/PODS 2004*, pages 85–90, 2004.

[10] A. Cimatti, E. Clarke, E. Giunchiglia, F. Giunchiglia, M. Pistore, M. Roveri, R. Sebastiani, and A. Tacchella. Nusmv 2: An opensource tool for symbolic model checking. In *Computer Aided Verification*, pages 359–364. Springer, 2002.

[11] S. Datta and S. Mukhopadhyay. A grammar inference approach for predicting kinase specific phosphorylation sites. *PLoS ONE*, 10(4):e0122294, 2015.

[12] C. Ding, X. Shen, K. Kelsey, C. Tice, R. Huang, and C. Zhang. Software behavior-oriented parallelization. In *PLDI*, 2007.

[13] L. Falquet, M. Pagni, P. Bucher, N. Hulo, C. J. Sigrist, K. Hofmann, and A. Bairoch. The prosite database, its status in 2002. *Nucleic acids research*, 30(1):235–238, 2002.

[14] M. Feng, R. Gupta, and Y. Hu. Spicec: Scalable parallelism via implicit copying and explicit commit. In *Proceedings of the ACM SIGPLAN Symposium on Principles Practice of Parallel Programming*, 2011.

[15] D. Ficara, S. Giordano, G. Procissi, F. Vitucci, G. Antichi, and A. D. Pietro. An improved DFA for fast regular expression matching. *Computer Communication Review*, 38(5):29–40, 2008.

[16] F. Franchetti and M. Puschel. A SIMD vectorizing compiler for digital signal processing algorithms. In *IPDPS*, pages 7–pp, 2002.

[17] M. Frigo, C. E. Leiserson, and K. H. Randall. The implementation of the Cilk-5 multithreaded language. In *Proceedings of ACM SIGPLAN Conference on Programming Language Design and Implementation*, 1998.

[18] C. García, R. Lario, M. Prieto, L. Piñuel, and F. Tirado. Vectorization of multigrid codes using SIMD ISA extensions. In *IPDPS*, pages 8–pp, 2003.

[19] T. J. Green, G. Miklau, M. Onizuka, and D. Suciu. Processing XML streams with deterministic automata. In *Database Theory - ICDT 2003, 9th International Conference, Siena, Italy, January 8-10, 2003, Proceedings*, pages 173–189, 2003.

[20] M. Herlihy and E. Koskinen. Transactional boosting: A methodology for highly-concurrent transactional objects. In *Proceedings of the 13th ACM SIGPLAN Symposium on Principles and Practice of Parallel Programming*, PPoPP '08, 2008.

[21] M. Herlihy and J. E. Moss. Transactional memory: Architectural support for lock-free data structures. In *Proceedings of the International Symposium on High Performance Computer Architecture (HPCA)*, 1993.

[22] K. Hou, H. Wang, and W.-c. Feng. Aspas: A framework for automatic simdization of parallel sorting on x86-based many-core processors. In *Proceedings of the 29th ACM International Conference on Supercomputing (ICS)*, pages 383–392. ACM, 2015.

[23] P. G. Howard and J. S. Vitte. Parallel lossless image compression using huffman and arithmetic coding. In *Data Compression Conference, 1992. DCC'92.*, pages 299–308. IEEE, 1992.

[24] D. A. Huffman. Notes on information-lossless finite-state automata. *Il Nuovo Cimento (1955-1965)*, 13:397–405, 1959.

[25] N. Ide, M. Hirano, Y. Endo, S. Yoshioka, H. Murakami, A. Kunimatsu, T. Sato, T. Kamei, T. Okada, and M. Suzuoki. 2.44-GFLOPS 300-MHz floating-point vector-processing unit for high-performance 3D graphics computing. volume 35, pages 1025–1033, 2000.

[26] Y. Jo, M. Goldfarb, and M. Kulkarni. Automatic vectorization of tree traversals. In *PACT*, pages 363–374, 2013.

[27] C. Jones, R. Liu, L. Meyerovich, K. Asanovic, and R. Bodik. Parallelizing the web browser. In *HotPar*, 2009.

[28] B. Kaplan. Speculative parsing path. `http://bugzilla.mozilla.org`.

[29] C. Ke, L. Liu, C. Zhang, T. Bai, B. Jacobs, and C. Ding. Safe parallel programming using dynamic dependence hints. In *ACM SIGPLAN Notices*, volume 46, pages 243–258. ACM, 2011.

[30] C. Kim, J. Chhugani, N. Satish, E. Sedlar, A. D. Nguyen, T. Kaldewey, V. W. Lee, S. A. Brandt, and P. Dubey. FAST: fast architecture sensitive tree search on modern CPUs and GPUs. In *ACM SIGMOD*

International Conference on Management of data, pages 339–350, 2010.

[31] S. Klein and Y. Wiseman. Parallel huffman decoding with applications to jpeg files. *Jounal of Computing*, 46(5), 2003.

[32] S. T. Klein and Y. Wiseman. Parallel huffman decoding with applications to JPEG files. *Comput. J.*, 46(5):487–497, 2003.

[33] M. Kulkarni, K. Pingali, B. Walter, G. Ramanarayanan, K. Bala, and L. P. Chew. Optimistic parallelism requires abstractions. In *Proceedings of the 28th ACM SIGPLAN Conference on Programming Language Design and Implementation*, PLDI '07, 2007.

[34] S. Kumar, S. Dharmapurikar, F. Yu, P. Crowley, and J. S. Turner. Algorithms to accelerate multiple regular expressions matching for deep packet inspection. In *Proceedings of the ACM SIGCOMM 2006 Conference on Applications, Technologies, Architectures, and Protocols for Computer Communications, Pisa, Italy, September 11-15, 2006*, pages 339–350, 2006.

[35] R. E. Ladner and M. J. Fischer. Parallel prefix computation. *J. ACM*, 27(4):831–838, Oct. 1980.

[36] D. Lin, N. Medforth, K. S. Herdy, A. Shriraman, and R. Cameron. Parabix: Boosting the efficiency of text processing on commodity processors. In *High Performance Computer Architecture (HPCA), 2012 IEEE 18th International Symposium on*, pages 1–12. IEEE, 2012.

[37] X. Liu, M. Smelyanskiy, E. Chow, and P. Dubey. Efficient sparse matrix-vector multiplication on x86-based many-core processors. In *ACM conference on International conference on supercomputing*, pages 273–282, 2013.

[38] D. Luchaup, R. Smith, C. Estan, and S. Jha. Multi-byte regular expression matching with speculation. In *RAID*, 2009.

[39] S. Misailovic, M. Carbin, S. Achour, Z. Qi, and M. C. Rinard. Chisel: reliability- and accuracy-aware optimization of approximate computational kernels. In *Proceedings of the 2014 ACM International Conference on Object Oriented Programming Systems Languages & Applications, OoarticloOPSLA 2014, part of SPLASH 2014, Portland, OR, USA, October 20-24, 2014*, pages 309–328, 2014.

[40] T. Mytkowicz, M. Musuvathi, and W. Schulte. Data-parallel finite-state machines. In *ASPLOS '14: Proceedings of 19th International Conference on Architecture Support for Programming Languages and Operating Systems*. ACM Press, 2014.

[41] G. Navarro. Nr-grep: a fast and flexible pattern-matching tool. *Software: Practice and Experience*, 31(13):1265–1312, 2001.

[42] D. Nuzman, I. Rosen, and A. Zaks. Auto-vectorization of interleaved data for SIMD. In *PLDI*, volume 41, pages 132–143. ACM, 2006.

[43] D. Nuzman and A. Zaks. Outer-loop vectorization: revisited for short SIMD architectures. In *PACT*, pages 2–11, 2008.

[44] Y. Pan, Y. Zhang, K. Chiu, and W. Lu. Parallel XML parsing using meta-dfas. In *Third International Conference on e-Science and Grid Computing, e-Science 2007, 10-13 December 2007, Bangalore, India*, pages 237–244, 2007.

[45] A. Petrenko. Fault model-driven test derivation from finite state models: Annotated bibliography. In *Modeling and verification of parallel processes*, pages 196–205. Springer, 2001.

[46] K. Pingali, D. Nguyen, M. Kulkarni, M. Burtscher, M. A. Hassaan, R. Kaleem, T.-H. Lee, A. Lenharth, R. Manevich, M. Méndez-Lojo, D. Prountzos, and X. Sui. The tao of parallelism in algorithms. In *Proceedings of the 32Nd ACM SIGPLAN Conference on Programming Language Design and Implementation*, PLDI '11, 2011.

[47] P. Prabhu, G. Ramalingam, and K. Vaswani. Safe programmable speculative parallelism. In *Proceedings of ACM SIGPLAN Conference on Programming Languages Design and Implementation*, 2010.

[48] A. Raman, H. Kim, T. R. Mason, T. B. Jablin, and D. I. August. Speculative parallelization using software multi-threaded transactions. In *Proceedings of the international conference on Architectural support for programming languages and operating systems*, 2010.

[49] R. K. Ranjan, A. Aziz, R. K. Brayton, B. Plessier, and C. Pixley. Efficient bdd algorithms for fsm synthesis and verification. *IWLS95, Lake Tahoe, CA*, 253:254, 1995.

[50] L. Rauchwerger and D. A. Padua. The LRPD test: Speculative run-time parallelization of loops with privatization and reduction parallelization. In *Proceedings of the ACM SIGPLAN'95 Conference on Programming Language Design and Implementation (PLDI), La Jolla, California, USA, June 18-21, 1995*, pages 218–232, 1995.

[51] B. Ren, G. Agrawal, J. R. Larus, T. Mytkowicz, T. Poutanen, and W. Schulte. SIMD parallelization of applications that traverse irregular data structures. In *CGO*, pages 1–10, 2013.

[52] M. Roesch et al. Snort: Lightweight intrusion detection for networks. In *LISA*, volume 99, pages 229–238, 1999.

[53] I. Roy and S. Aluru. Finding motifs in biological sequences using the micron automata processor. In *2014 IEEE 28th International Parallel and Distributed Processing Symposium, Phoenix, AZ, USA, May 19-23, 2014*, pages 415–424, 2014.

[54] P. Shankar, A. Dasgupta, K. Deshmukh, and B. S. Rajan. On viewing block codes as finite automata. *Theoretical Computer Science*, 290(3):1775–1797, 2003.

[55] J. G. Steffan, C. Colohan, A. Zhai, and T. C. Mowry. The STAMPede approach to thread-level speculation. *ACM Transactions on Computer Systems*, 23(3):253–300, 2005.

[56] C. Tian, M. Feng, V. Nagarajan, and R. Gupta. Copy or discard execution model for speculative parallelization on multicores. In *Proceedings of the International Symposium on Microarchitecture*, 2008.

[57] K. Trifunovic, D. Nuzman, A. Cohen, A. Zaks, and I. Rosen. Polyhedral-model guided loop-nest auto-vectorization. In *PACT*, pages 327–337, 2009.

[58] R. van Engelen. Constructing finite state automata for high-performance XML web services. In *Proceedings of*

the International Conference on Internet Computing, IC '04, Volume 2 & Proceedings of the International Symposium on Web Services & Applications, ISWS '04, Las Vegas, Nevada, USA, June 21-24, 2004, pages 975–981, 2004.

[59] Z. G. Wang, J. Elbaz, F. Remacle, R. D. Levine, and I. Willner. All-DNA finite-state automata with finite memory. *Proc. Natl. Acad. Sci. U.S.A.*, 107(51):21996–22001, Dec 2010.

[60] F. Yu, Z. Chen, Y. Diao, T. V. Lakshman, and R. H. Katz. Fast and memory-efficient regular expression matching for deep packet inspection. In *Proceedings of the 2006 ACM/IEEE Symposium on Architecture for Networking and Communications Systems*, pages 93–102, 2006.

[61] Z. Zhao, B. Wu, and X. Shen. Challenging the "embarrassingly sequential": Parallelizing finite state machine-based computations through principled speculation. In *ASPLOS '14: Proceedings of 19th International Conference on Architecture Support for Programming Languages and Operating Systems*. ACM Press, 2014.

[62] Y. Zu, M. Yang, Z. Xu, L. Wang, X. Tian, K. Peng, and Q. Dong. Gpu-based nfa implementation for memory efficient high speed regular expression matching. In *PPoPP '12: Proceedings of the ACM SIGPLAN symposium on Principles and practice of parallel programming*, pages 129–140, 2009.

Hash Map Inlining

Dibakar Gope
gope@wisc.edu

Mikko H. Lipasti
mikko@engr.wisc.edu

Department of Electrical and Computer Engineering
University of Wisconsin - Madison
Madison, WI, USA

ABSTRACT

Scripting languages like Javascript and PHP are widely used to implement application logic for dynamically-generated web pages. Their popularity is due in large part to their flexible syntax and dynamic type system, which enable rapid turnaround time for prototyping, releasing, and updating web site features and capabilities. The most common complex data structure in these languages is the hash map, which is used to store key-value pairs. In many cases, hash maps with a fixed set of keys are used in lieu of explicitly defined classes or structures, as would be common in compiled languages like Java or C++. Unfortunately, the runtime overhead of key lookup and value retrieval is quite high, especially relative to the direct offsets that compiled languages can use to access class members. Furthermore, key lookup and value retrieval incur high microarchitectural costs as well, since the paths they execute contain unpredictable branches and many cache accesses, leading to substantially higher numbers of branch mispredicts and cache misses per access to the hashmap. This paper quantifies these overheads, describes a compiler algorithm that discovers common use cases for hash maps and inlines them so that keys are accessed with direct offsets, and reports measured performance benefits on real hardware. A prototype implementation in the HipHop VM infrastructure shows promising performance benefits for a broad array of hash map-intensive server-side PHP applications, up to 37.6% and averaging 18.81%, improves SPECWeb throughput by 7.71% (banking) and 11.71% (e-commerce).

Keywords

PHP; dynamic languages; JIT compiler; inline caching

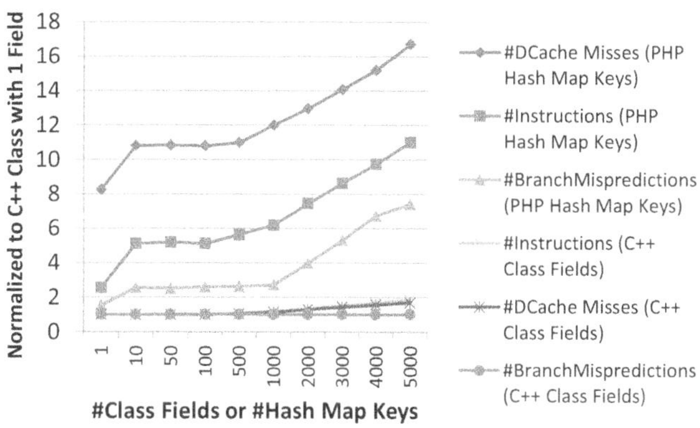

Figure 1: Comparison of branch mispredictions, data cache misses and instructions count between accessing a hash map and a class object (details in evaluation section).

1. INTRODUCTION

In recent years the importance of dynamic scripting languages such as PHP, Python, Ruby and Javascript has grown considerably as they are used for an increasing share of application software. PHP powers many of the most popular web applications such as Facebook and Wikipedia. Despite their considerable increase in popularity, their performance is still the main impediment for developing large applications. Because of their dynamic features, these languages are typically interpreted by virtual machine runtimes. Usually these interpreted implementations are one or two orders of magnitude slower compared to their corresponding implementations in compiled languages [1]. Among general-purpose scripting languages used for server-side web development to access databases and other middleware, PHP is the most commonly used [45, 39], representing 82.1% [9] of all web applications. This has spurred a number of research to improve the performance of PHP scripts through just-in-time(JIT) compilation [15, 21, 24, 35, 45, 11].

Recently the HipHop Virtual Machine(HHVM) [11] PHP JIT compiler from Facebook has shown tremendous gains to close the performance gap with statically-typed languages such as C++. Its basic design of a stack-based bytecode compiled into type-specialized machine code provides large speedups for diverse, real-world PHP applications when compared to an interpreted environment. However, as observed in this work, in a set of popular real-world PHP scripts that power many e-commerce platforms, online news forums, banking servers etc., hash map processing constitutes a large fraction of the overall execution time and failure to optimize accesses to those hash maps by HHVM causes a substantial performance bottleneck. More specifically, server-side PHP scripts will commonly retrieve information from a back-end database management system (DBMS) engine by issuing a SQL query [3], the results of which are communicated to the PHP script as key-value pairs stored in a hash map. The key-value pairs are subsequently processed by application logic in the PHP code to generate dynamic HTML content. Considering the fact that a considerable fraction of the execution time of these scripts are spent on processing such

PACT '16, September 11-15, 2016, Haifa, Israel
© 2016 ACM. ISBN 978-1-4503-4121-9/16/09...$15.00
DOI: http://dx.doi.org/10.1145/2967938.2967949

hash maps (as our results indicate), the cost of populating and accessing these hash maps should be reduced in order to reduce script execution time.

Figure 1 demonstrates the microarchitectural behavior of a microbenchmark that repeatedly updates and accesses a configurable number of key-value pairs stored in a hash map. The bottom three lines illustrate the behavior with accessing class objects with equivalent number of fields. Clearly key lookup and value retrieval from a hash map incur significantly higher number branch mispredictions, cache misses and consequently higher number of instructions.

In this work, we propose *Hash Map Inlining (HMI)* to minimize the overheads associated with populating and accessing key-value pairs stored in hash maps. HMI is a dynamic optimization technique that is triggered whenever runtime profiling indicates that hash maps are being populated and accessed in a *hot*[1] region of the PHP program. HMI dynamically converts a hot hash map into a vector-like data structure that is accessed with fixed, linear offsets for each key value, and specializes the code at each hot access site to use fixed offsets from the HMI base address to update and/or retrieve values corresponding to each key.

Our implementation of HMI is inspired by *inline caching*, an existing approach for specializing code that accesses members (or fields) in dynamically-typed objects. JIT compilers for scripting languages that support dynamic type systems (e.g. Chrome V8 for Javascript [10] and HHVM for PHP [11]) rely on a *shadow class* system to map object field names to offsets for each instance of a dynamic object. With inline caching, code that accesses these fields is specialized to short-circuit expensive offset lookups by including an efficient shadow class type check in the specialized code, followed by a direct offset-based access to the field as long as the type matches the common case. By analogy, HMI treats hash map keys as field names, and specializes direct-offset accesses to the corresponding hash map values while protecting them with a type check similar to the one used for inline caching.

We demonstrate the performance benefits of our implementation of HMI by way of a microbenchmark that repeatedly updates and accesses a configurable number of key-value pairs stored in a hash map. We show that the vast majority of the overhead of hash map accesses can be elided, leading to gains of up to 40 – 45% (with a hash map of 10 or 50 key-value pairs) with our prototype HMI implementation, running on real hardware. The performance gain goes up with bigger hash map sizes.

However, we find that our initial HMI implementation delivers only marginal gains when applied to real-world PHP applications that utilize hash maps to retrieve information from a back-end DBMS. The effectiveness of HMI in these applications is limited for two reasons. First, the hash maps are populated inside SQL runtime libraries written in C code, which are not visible to the HHVM optimizer, effectively preventing HMI from triggering inlining and code specialization. Second, our initial version of HMI can only specialize code for accesses where the hash map keys are specified as literal values at the access site (e.g. myhashmap["literalkey"]), whereas these applications commonly specify the keys as variables (e.g. myhashmap[$myvariablekey]). In theory, flow analysis and constant propagation would reveal that some of the latter cases are in fact constants (literals), but this was not the case for the applications we examined. Instead, we found that the variables at each access site would sequence through a number of different, though predictable, key names at run time.

In order to address these shortcomings, we extended our HMI implementation in two ways. First, we wrote new versions of the SQL runtime library functions used to access DBMS contents: ones that directly utilize inlined hash maps for communicating query results to the PHP scripts. Second, we augmented the HHVM JIT to first check for the necessary set of conditions that trigger correct use of these HMI-friendly functions, and then to specialize any qualifying call sites to call them instead of the original functions. We elaborate on the necessary set of conditions in Section 4 briefly; we can invoke HMI whenever we can guarantee that there is a finite and ordered set of keys that are used to populate the hash map. This condition is trivially satisfied for the SQL runtime library functions we targeted, since the ordered set of keys is determined by the database schema, which is fixed at the time the SQL query is evaluated. In other cases, this condition could also be satisfied based on PHP language semantics. For example, the *foreach* array iterator in PHP iterates over the key-value pairs in the hash map in a fixed order, providing the same guarantee of a finite and ordered set of keys. These two situations allow automatic conversion of hot hash maps into inlined form for these PHP applications, such that subsequent accesses within the PHP code can be efficiently specialized to take full advantage of the inlined hash map structure. Our prototype implementation in HHVM shows performance benefits for a broad array of hash map-intensive PHP scripts, up to 37.6% and averaging 18.81%, improves SPECWeb throughput by 7.71% (banking) and 11.71% (e-commerce).

The remainder of this paper is organized as follows. Section 2 describes how we adapt inline caching, a technique for streamlining access to dynamically-typed objects, to similarly improve the performance of hash maps. Section 3 describes how PHP uses hash maps to interface with SQL databases. Section 4 explains why our initial HMI algorithm fails to work with the SQL interface, and describes how we extend it to capture this opportunity. Section 5 presents details of our modifications to HHVM. Section 6 presents results. Section 7 discusses related work and Section 8 concludes the paper.

[1]A hot region is a region of a program where most time is spent during the program's execution.

2. INLINE CACHING FOR HASH MAPS

2.1 PHP Scripting Language

In PHP variables can hold values from different types during an execution. One prominent feature of PHP is its ability to add new properties to class objects on the fly without having to change the type declaration of the native object. However, the absence of declared types makes it very challenging for the compiler to generate code, as the types of objects depend on the underlying execution of the program. As a result, accessing a given property can not be accomplished using a simple offset access from the start of the object. As shown in Figure 2(a), the two properties *foo* and *bar* can be added to the *MyClass* object at different memory offsets depending on the intervening branch. Thus, in PHP, each property access requires a dictionary lookup to resolve its location in memory.

2.2 Inline Caching for Dynamic Classes

Modern JIT compilers use specialization to mitigate this problem. They essentially depend on the empirical evidence that, at run time, the dynamic type of an object at a given access site tends to stay consistent. The JIT compiler records the most frequently observed dynamic type and specializes accesses for that type. A runtime check ensures that the assumptions used in the generation of specialized code hold at run time. If the check fails, the JIT runtime re-specializes the access for the new type observed. Modern JIT compilers use *shadow classes* to capture different types of a dynamic object. The basic idea is similar to the notion of dynamic

```
        class MyClass {
              ...
        }
        $obj = new MyClass;
        if (...) {
S1              $obj→foo = 10;
        }
S2      $obj→bar = 20;
```
(a)

```
[Inline cache for $obj→bar = 20]

if (obj.shadowclass == B)
  store &Obj [1], 20;
else if (obj.shadowclass == A)
  store &Obj [0], 20;
else
  // jump to JIT runtime/interpreter;
```
(b)

Figure 2: Example PHP code (a) and inline cache to access property *bar* (b).

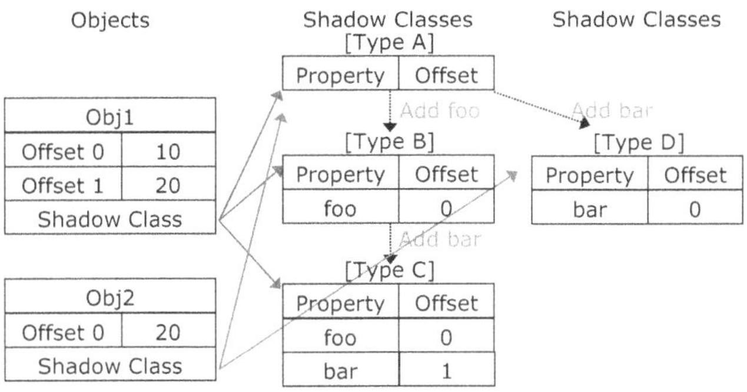

Figure 3: Example of shadow classes.

types in Self [17, 16]. Objects that are created in the same way are grouped in the same shadow class. Each time a new property is added or a previously seen property is introduced in a different order, JIT creates a new shadow class to capture that as a new type of the object.

Figure 3 shows how a JIT compiler creates shadow classes for the code shown in Figure 2(a). When the runtime enters this code section for the first time, JIT creates an empty *MyClass* (not shown in Figure 3) pointing to an empty shadow class type A. Now if a *Not Taken(NT)* branch direction is observed, the runtime adds properties *foo* and *bar* to *Obj1* and creates two more shadow classes B and C of *Obj1* at access site *S1* and *S2* respectively. Shadow classes record the added properties and their offsets. Any future invocation of this code with the branch observing again a *NT* direction will cause the runtime to follow the same shadow class transitions at *S1* and *S2*. Subsequently when a *Taken(T)* branch direction is observed, the runtime will create a new shadow class type D from initially empty type A. So as observed here, access site *S2*'s addition of property *bar* results in an object of either shadow class C or D. This supports the common assumption that at a given site the JIT runtime accesses objects of very few types. Modern JIT compilers use a technique called *inline caching* to exploit this assumption to optimize accesses to properties of objects at a given site. The inline caching mechanism essentially caches the offsets of the property *bar* for the two object types C and D seen before at access site *S2* and specializes the site *S2* as shown in Figure 2(b). Any future invocations of the code, regardless of the intervening branch's behavior, will be able to exploit the cached offsets to map *bar* either to type C or D.

2.3 Adapted to Hash Maps

In this work, we extend this inline caching approach for coping with dynamically-typed objects to also enable specialization of accesses to hash maps. By analogy, our HMI implementation treats hash map keys as property names. Algorithm 1 and 2 describe our initial HMI implementation inspired by inline caching. Note that similar to the inline caching approach, Algorithm 1 and 2 can

Algorithm 1 HMI Populate based on inline caching

Input: Hash Map *h*, *Key*, *Value*, *CallSite PC*

```
if Key.IsStaticLiteral is True then
    if Inline cache found for CallSite PC then
        Perform inlined populate (CallSite PC, Key, Value)
    else if h.IsInlined is True then
        h.SymbolTable.NextKeyOffset++
        Offset ← h.SymbolTable.NextKeyOffset
        h.SymbolTable[Offset] ← (Key, Offset)
        h.Data[Offset] ← Value
        /*Generate inlined populate for CallSite PC*/
        JIT.generateInlineCache(CallSite PC,Key,Offset)
    else if Is CallSite PC Hot then
        h.IsInlined ← True
        h.SymbolTable.NextKeyOffset ← 0
        Offset ← h.SymbolTable.NextKeyOffset
        h.SymbolTable[Offset] ← (Key, Offset)
        h.Data[Offset] ← Value
        /*Generate inlined populate for CallSite PC*/
        JIT.generateInlineCache(CallSite PC,Key,Offset)
    else
        Profile (CallSite PC, Key)
        Regular hash map populate (h, Key, Value)
    end if
else
    /* Key is not a static literal */
    Regular hash map populate (h, Key, Value)
end if
```

only specialize code for accesses where the hash map key is specified as a literal value at the call site. With HMI in Algorithm 1, a call site that has already generated specialized code can perform a direct-offset access to the *Key* as long as the type of the hash map *h* matches with any previously observed types at the site. When it is the first time that the hash map *h* is accessed in a hot region of the PHP program, HMI converts it into a vector-like data structure, adds the *Value* into the first location and records the location information or offset in a table structure, which we call the *Symbol Table*. The symbol table essentially captures the type of a hash map by recording the offsets of inserted keys. Before performing a direct access to a inlined hash map at a call site, the type checking step in HMI finds the appropriate symbol table for the hash map from the set of symbol tables cached previously at the call site. In order to retrieve values from a inlined hash map, Algorithm 2 can look for a key in the generated symbol table of the hash map and specialize the code at that access site to use direct fixed offsets.

In order to investigate the performance impact of our initial HMI implementation, we apply this on a microbenchmark that repeatedly updates and accesses a configurable number of key-value pairs stored in a hash map and observe that the vast majority of the overhead of hash map accesses can be elided. This results in significant performance gains of up to $40-45\%$ with a hash map of 10 and 50 key-value pairs. This benefit primarily comes from the substantial reduction in branch mispredictions, caches misses and overall instructions enabled by direct-offset access from HMI.

However, we observe that our initial HMI implementation delivers marginal or no gains when applied to real-world PHP applications (Table 1) that utilize hash maps to retrieve information from a back-end DBMS. SPECWeb(E-commerce) suite shows marginal benefit of about 1.14% when compared against the unmodified HHVM, whereas the remaining benchmark suites do not deliver any visible performance improvement. Before we investigate the reasons be-

Algorithm 2 HMI Access based on inline caching

```
Input: Hash Map h, Key, CallSite PC
if h.IsInlined is True then
    if Key.IsStaticLiteral is True then
        if Inline cache found for CallSite PC then
            Perform inlined access(CallSite PC, Key)
        else
            Offset ← h.symbolTableLookup(Key)
            /*Generate inlined access for CallSite PC*/
            JIT.generateInlineCache(CallSite PC,Key,Offset)
            return h.Data[Offset]
        end if
    else
        /* Key is not a static literal */
        Regular hash map access (h, Key)
    end if
else
    Regular hash map access (h, Key)
end if
```

```
$q_result = mysql_query("SELECT id, name, initial_price,
max_bid, nb_of_bids, end_date FROM items WHERE
category=$categoryId
AND end_date >= NOW()...");

while ($q_row = mysql_fetch_array($q_result)) {
  $maxBid = $q_row["max_bid"];
  if ($maxBid == 0) $maxBid = $q_row["initial_price"];
  print("<TR><TD><a href=\"/PHP/...itemId=".$q_row["id"].
  "\">".$q_row["name"]."<TD>$maxBid".
  "<TD>".$q_row["nb_of_bids"].
  "<TD>".$q_row["end_date"].
  "<TD><a ...PutBidAuth.php?itemId=".$q_row["id"]...");
}
```

Figure 4: Code snippet of a server-side PHP script.

hind its poor performance with real-world applications, we study the SQL interface in the next section that communicates with back-end DBMS and executes such PHP applications.

3. HASH MAP INTERFACE TO SQL DBMS

When a client makes a HTTP request to a web server, the server usually invokes PHP scripts to serve the request. The PHP scripts in turn formulate the necessary query plans and dispatch those queries to the backend DBMS engine (e.g., SQL or memcached). Once the DBMS engine produces the query result tables, the PHP scripts utilize standard SQL library functions to iterate over the rows in the tables before sending back a response with dynamic HTML contents back to the client. Figure 4 illustrates a example PHP script from a real-word benchmark suite RUBiS [6]; it follows the structure of a typical server-side PHP script as described above.

Note that, retrieving the rows from the query result table *q_result* and mapping their various keys into the *q_row* hash map during the loop iterations in Figure 4 essentially involve repeated interpretation of hash maps. Figure 5 illustrates that a major fraction of the dynamic instructions of server-side PHP scripts (details in Table 1) are spent on populating and accessing hash maps.

Figure 6 excerpts the underlying implementation of the SQL library function mysql_fetch_array(), used in the PHP script in Figure 4 to retrieve rows and populate such hash maps from the query result table. It relies on the loop (starting on line 5) to extract the various keys of a row into the *q_row* hash map. Delving down into the details further, for each and every key, the code sequence

```
Variant mysql_fetch_array (const Resource& mysql_result, ...) {
  .....
1) Array ret; /*Allocate an empty array, resize as per requirement*/
2) MYSQL_ROW mysql_row = mysql_fetch_row(mysql_result);
3) long *mysql_row_lengths=mysql_fetch_lengths(mysql_result);
4)
5) for (mysql_field = mysql_fetch_field(mysql_result), i = 0;
6)      mysql_field;
7)      mysql_field = mysql_fetch_field(mysql_result), i++) {
8)    if (mysql_row[i]) {
9)          data = mysql_makevalue(String(mysql_row[i],
10)         mysql_row_lengths[i],CopyString), mysql_field);
11)   }
12)   ret.set(String(mysql_field->name,CopyString),data);
13)}
14)return ret;
}
```

Figure 6: Implementation of mysql_fetch_array() function.

(from line 5 to line 13) retrieves a value from the row and adds a new (key, value) pair to the hash map (line 12). Close examination of the usage of the populated hash maps inside the while loop of Figure 4 in conjunction with the underlying implementation of mysql_fetch_array() function in populating those hash maps (Figure 6) reveals the following main abstraction overheads.

First, as the mysql_fetch_array() function iterates over the rows in the result table, it allocates a hash map to hold the values associated with the different keys of a row. This introduces a significant number of expensive memory allocations and releases on the critical path. Second, the string key is run through a hashing function to index into an entry of the hash map. The hash computation is followed by a string comparison along a linked list of possible entries to find the appropriate entry for the current key. Finally, the hash maps may need to be resized during runtime in order to accommodate more data. These resizing operations also add a modest overhead, especially when these hash maps are accessed many times during the course of parsing the entire result table. The lookup process also incurs equally high abstraction overheads in hashing and comparison functions when the different keys of the hash maps are retrieved inside the while loop in Figure 4. Analysis using Pin [30] shows that populating such a hash map with 4 keys inside this SQL library function requires about 2,400 instructions. Reading the hash map key inside the while loop of Figure 4 requires about 90 instructions.

In the next section, we investigate the shortcomings with our initial HMI implementation that could deliver only marginal or no gains when applied to real-world PHP applications that utilize hash maps to retrieve information from a back-end DBMS.

4. WHY HMI FAILS FOR DBMS SCRIPTS

4.1 Hidden Library Functions

As described in Section 2, a JIT compiler like HHVM collects profile information at runtime and uses it to specialize a code section written in the scripting language (PHP in this work) of an application. However, SQL library functions, which are implemented in statically-typed languages such as C++, are not visible to the HHVM optimizer. As a result, when hash maps are populated inside the mysql_fetch_array() SQL library function in Figure 6, HMI cannot capture their shape and type. Hence, when these populated hash maps are accessed later in the while loop in Figure 4, HMI cannot anticipate their shape despite staying the same across invocations of this library function. Consequently HMI cannot trigger inlining and code specialization to convert accesses to such DBMS hash maps to simple direct-offset accesses.

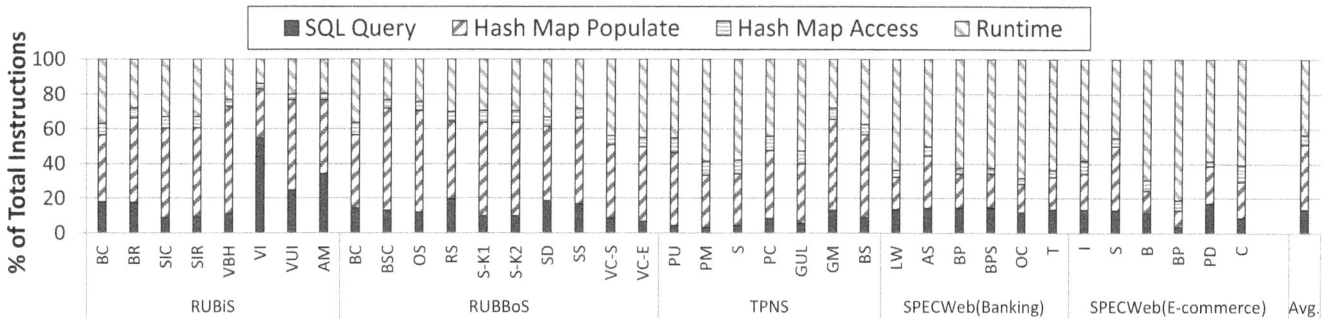

Figure 5: Breakdown of dynamic instructions, measured using Pin [30]. Averaged across scripts in Table 1. Runtime = instructions that execute string operations, regular expressions, and miscellaneous operations.

4.2 Variable Key Names

Even if the SQL library function is described in scripting languages (PHP in this work), due to the reasons detailed below, hash maps populated inside that can not be efficiently inlined using the initial HMI implementation.

Note that, regardless of which control path is followed in the example in Figure 2(a), the name of the properties at the two access sites *S1* and *S2* are static literals. But in case of populating hash maps inside mysql_fetch_array(), as different keys are populated at the same access site (line 12 in Figure 6), the HMI runtime does not observe any static literal keys; instead it ends up observing a variety of keys at that access site. In other words, our initial version of HMI can only specialize code for accesses where the hash map keys are specified as literal values at the access site, such as the key values in our microbenchmark. As a result, when we attempt to apply Algorithm 1 or 2, they fall back on the expensive dictionary lookup.

In order to address this shortcoming, we augment the initial HMI implementation (Algorithm 1 and 2) to handle keys with variable names. However, the HMI runtime now no longer observes a single static literal key when accessing the different keys at the same access site. As a result, populating different keys at the same site requires the HMI implementation to emit code that performs a string comparison to ensure the current string key matching against the key seen before with the current hash map type. Hence, the specialized code will not be able to avoid the expensive string comparison while populating hash maps inside mysql_fetch_array() SQL library function. Figure 7 shows the changes required to the initial HMI implementation to inline populating such hash maps at the same call site inside the SQL library function with all the associated overheads as discussed above. This example assumes the presence of key "x", followed by "y" and so on in the database schema. Note that now in order to specialize the code that inserts keys at the same call site, the HMI implementation needs to include an additional string comparison (highlighted in brown) in addition to the type check in the inlined code.

4.3 High Polymorphism

Figure 7 demonstrates the specialized code that the HMI implementation will emit to inline populating hash maps inside SQL library function at the common call site. However note that, updating a key (for example, key *y*) at the common call site in SQL library function now requires a traversal through a path containing branches for all the other type checks. Hence, populating a key at this site requires performing a linear search for the correct entry in the specialized code that matches the current input types, leading to inefficient execution. A call site that only observes a single type is called *monomorphic*; if it observes multiple types, it is *polymorphic*. The more polymorphic a site becomes in specialized code, the more overhead it adds to the overall execution. Considering the fact that such hash maps inside the SQL library function in our experimental suite typically populate in the range of 6 to 18 keys, the HMI implementation will in turn make the access site highly polymorphic. Although it will avoid the hashing function to index into the hash map while populating keys, the presence of the highly polymorphic access site along with the necessary string comparison to find a cached offset will still accrue substantial overheads. Furthermore, unlike regular PHP code sections, since the SQL library functions are more likely to be called from many places in the application to satisfy various queries, the access site that populates hash maps may end up being highly polymorphic.

However, note that the HMI runtime can avoid the string comparison imposed by variable key names, and can achieve similar benefit to that of inlining accesses to static literal keys, if either of the following conditions are met:

(1) the application (or programmer) ensures a *statically* ordered set of keys being inserted at a call site or

(2) the runtime guarantees a *dynamically* ordered set of keys being inserted at a call site.

In other words, our extended HMI implementation is invoked whenever we can guarantee that the variable at an access site will sequence through a number of different, though predictable, fixed key names at run time. Algorithm 3 describes the algorithm that triggers extended HMI implementation to inline accesses to keys with variable names at a common call site. Note that this condition is trivially satisfied for the SQL runtime library functions we targeted, since the ordered set of keys is determined by the database schema, which is fixed at the time the SQL query is evaluated.

```
Inline cache for ret.set(...) (line 12 in Figure 6)
if (ret is a DBMS hash map &&
    ret.Type == Type_NO_Key) {   /*Type_NO_Key = empty hash map*/

   if (ret.current_key == "x")     /*String comparison to check current key
     return ret[cached_x_offset];   matching against 1st key of schema */
}
else if (ret. Type == Type_K_x) {  /*Type_K_x = hashmap with key "x"*/

   if (ret.current_key == "y")     /*String comparison to check current key
     return ret[cached_y_offset];   matching against 2nd key of schema */
}
...
else if (ret.Type == Type_K_x_y_...)
{...}
...
else {regular hash map access and inline cache update}
```

Figure 7: Required changes to initial HMI implementation.

Algorithm 3 HMI (Handling keys with variable names)

Input: Hash Map *h*, *Key*, *Value*, *CallSite PC*

```
if Key.IsStaticLiteral is True then
    Same as line 2-22 in Algorithm 1
else
    /* Key is not a static literal */
    if Either application can guarantee statically or runtime can
      guarantee dynamically that Key belongs to ordered set of keys
      being inserted at CallSite PC then
        JIT.invokeExtendedHMI (section 5 for SQL)
    else
        /* Regular hash map populate/access */
    end if
end if
```

```
Variant mysql_query (const String& query, ...) {
  .....
  std::vector<StringData *> mysql_key_names;
  for (mysql_field = mysql_fetch_field(mysql_result);
     mysql_field; mysql_field =
     mysql_fetch_field(mysql_result)) {

    /* Collect name of keys */
    mysql_key_names.push_back(makeStaticString
      (String(mysql_field->name, CopyString)));
  }
  /* Generate symbol table at runtime */
  define_MySQL_SymbolTable(mysql_key_names);
}
```

Figure 8: Generate symbol table in mysql_query(*) and expose that to the JIT runtime.

5. EXTENDED HMI FOR SQL

In order to address the shortcomings, we extended our HMI implementation in two ways. First, we wrote new versions of the SQL runtime library functions used to access DBMS contents: ones that directly utilize inlined hash maps for communicating query results to the PHP scripts. Second, we augmented the HHVM JIT to first check for the necessary set of conditions that trigger correct use of these HMI-friendly functions, and then to specialize any qualifying call sites to call them instead of the original functions. In case of SQL library function since the application statically guarantees ordered set of keys being inserted at the call site (line 12 of Figure 6), HMI can redirect the JIT runtime to use symbol table generating version of mysql_query (*step* 1) and vector arrays generating version of mysql_fetch_array thus inlining populating hash maps (*step* 2). Once the symbol table is generated and exposed to the JIT runtime in *step* 1, HMI can use that to inline all future lookups or accesses to hash maps within the PHP script (*step* 3). The following three steps describe this in detail.

(a) Generate symbol table in SQL query function. When a database query is executed, the runtime accesses the associated meta-data about the relation, such as the name of the relation, the number of keys, their names, types, etc. and builds a symbol table that records different keys of the relation and their corresponding offsets. So as shown in the underlying implementation of the SQL query execution function in Figure 8, it is modified to collect information about the keys of the associated database schema at the end of its execution. It thus builds a symbol table, associates that with the current query plan and attaches that to the pool of symbol tables. Note that the keys are mapped to the symbol table in order of their appearance in the query result table. Before defining a new symbol table, the runtime checks if it has already declared a symbol table for the current query plan. If it finds a table with an identical set of keys inserted into it in the same order as that of the current plan in the pool of symbol tables, then it does not create a new symbol table across invocations of the query execution function and returns the old table only. When the database query function subsequently finishes execution, it exposes this populated symbol table to the JIT runtime and returns a pointer to it along with the regular result table. The generated symbol table later is used to inline any subsequent accesses to hash maps populated from the query result table.

(b) Populate vector-like arrays in SQL fetch_array function. When a DBMS engine produces a query result table, mysql_fetch_array() extracts the rows from the table into hash maps. However instead of retrieving rows into hash maps, HMI specializes the mysql_fetch_array() function to map the keys into vector-like arrays. Furthermore, each key is made to update the slot in that array in order of their appearance in the query result table. That way it entirely eliminates the abstraction overheads associated with populating hash maps inside this library function.

Any subsequent accesses to these populated vector-like arrays within the PHP script can then determine the mapping of the keys of the extracted rows into these arrays using the symbol table generated in mysql_query() function above. Thus Extended HMI implementation can inline accesses to such hash maps populated inside the SQL fetch_array() function. This becomes possible since the symbol table map the keys of the relational schema in the mysql_query() function in the same order as the values of different keys from the extracted rows are inserted to form vector-like arrays in mysql_fetch_array() function. HMI essentially decouples hash map accesses from populating vector-like arrays inside the library function. Considering the fact that these hash maps are populated many times during the course of parsing the entire query result table, this decoupling will eliminate the overheads associated with populating those hash maps entirely. Generating a symbol table should add insignificant overhead to a query's execution time.

So as shown in the underlying implementation of mysql_fetch_array() function in Figure 9, the hash map of Figure 6 has been replaced by a vector-like array with size equal to the number of keys in the query relation. As a result, the arrays are no longer required to be resized during runtime in order to accommodate all the keys of the rows and hence they can avoid the resizing and its associated overhead. However, populating any keys not present in the symbol table into vector-like arrays requires falling back to the runtime and using expensive hash map lookups.

(c) Use symbol table to inline accesses to hash maps.
As discussed before, a pointer to the symbol table generated during the execution of a SQL query plan is attached to the vector-like arrays populated from the query result table. As a result, HMI can later use that symbol table to inline accesses to hash maps within the PHP script. It is commonly observed that the shape of hash maps generated inside the mysql_fetch_array() library function tends to be always consistent at a given access site. This holds true for our experimental workloads also. However, if the query plan is designed in such a way that it depends on the schema of the connected database (a database query such as, SELECT * From a Table), then the mysql_query() execution might return symbol tables with different shapes and different sets of keys across invocations. As a result, before performing a inlined access to the hash

```
Variant mysql_fetch_array (const Resource& mysql_result, ...) {
  .....
  /*Allocate vector-like array of size mysql_num_fields()*/
  ret.init_mysql_array (mysql_num_fields(mysql_result));

  for ( mysql_field = mysql_fetch_field(mysql_result), i = 0;
        mysql_field;
        mysql_field = mysql_fetch_field(mysql_result), i++) {
        if (mysql_row[i])
              data = mysql_makevalue(String(mysql_row[i],
              mysql_row_lengths[i],CopyString), mysql_field);
        }
        ret.set(i, data); /*Populate vector-like array locations*/
  }
  return ret;
}
```

Figure 9: Populate vector-like arrays of size mysql_num_fields(*).

Symbol Table

key	offset
id	0
name	1
initial_price	2
max_bid	3
nb_of_bids	4
end_date	5

(a)

```
Inline cache for $q_row["max_bid"]

if (q_row is a DBMS hash map &&
   q_row.symboltable ==
        cached_symboltable)

return q_row[cached_max_bid_offset];

else
  // jump to JIT runtime;
```

(b)

Figure 10: Generated symbol table (a) and inline cache to access key *max_bid* (b).

maps, an access site must check the shape of the symbol table to determine if it has changed from the last time the query was executed. Any change in the shape of the symbol table (set of keys associated with the symbol table or their order of insertion into it) from the last time will necessitate HMI to re-specialize for the new shape and find the offset of the key using the new symbol table.

As a result, while specializing an access site that retrieves values from hash maps populated inside a database library function, HMI first checks the shape of the symbol table attached to the vector-like array. HMI checks if the symbol table matches the cached symbol table seen earlier at this site. If so, the key-value in the hash map can be accessed using a simple cached offset at this site. Figure 10(a) shows the symbol table generated with executing the query in Figure 4 and Figure 10(b) illustrates the specialized code to access the "max_bid" key. Reading "max_bid" from the hash map *row* in Figure 4 is now guarded by the cached symbol table. If it succeeds, "max_bid" is accessed with simple offset-access. However, if the runtime encounters a symbol table it has not seen before, HMI re-specializes the access on the new symbol table observed.

In summary, in case of accessing hash maps with literal keys, traditional inline caching and HMI inline key accesses in the same way as shown in the example of Figure 3. However for accessing hash maps with variable key names as in Figure 4, HHVM will invoke the HMI-friendly version of SQL library functions to populate vector-like arrays instead of hash maps and thus will inline inserting keys to hash maps. The symbol table generated (Figure 10(a)) while executing the SQL library functions will then be used to specialize accesses to keys such as "max_bid" (Figure 10(b)).

5.1 Multiple Call Sites

Since the SQL query function can be called from many call sites in a program to satisfy various queries, HMI must generate different symbol tables to capture various database schemas. When updating a symbol table in the SQL query function, HMI implementation ensures that each query execution points to a distinct symbol table dictated by the program counter of the call site in the bytecode. Note that HMI does not need any extra provisions to handle multiple call sites for the mysql_fetch_array() function. Each of the instantiations of this function receives a distinct symbol table from their corresponding SQL query function, which they attach to the vector-like arrays populated inside them.

5.2 Other DBMS Engines and Languages

There exist popular DBMS engines other than MySQL such as MongoDB [2], Oracle DB [4] etc. They have similar methods for accessing database results. For example, MongoDB uses a collection method (*find()*) in conjunction with cursor methods (*forEach()* or *hasNext()*) (analogous to *mysql_query()* and *mysql_fetch_array()* methods from MySQL) to collect hash maps from database results. Hence these PHP applications accessing MongoDB servers instead will face similar hash map overheads and can benefit from HMI.

In this work we primarily target server-side PHP applications. However server-side workloads developed in any other scripting languages may have similar hash maps with variable key names and thus can benefit from HMI. Creating HMI-friendly versions of DBMS library functions in Figure 8 and 9 introduce minor changes to the HHVM's C++ library. Furthermore we add about 150 lines of code in HHVM to catch opportunity for HMI and generate hash map inlined code. Hence our proposed changes can be easily applied to other DBMS engines and JIT compilers.

5.3 Applying HMI Outside DBMS Queries

HMI is a general technique that can provide significant performance benefit whenever hash maps are accessed repeatedly with a fixed set of key values. To obtain this benefit, the PHP VM must first identify hash map access sites that are suitable, either via straightforward profiling of their key set behavior, or by taking advantage of API semantics (as we describe above). Second, the VM must guarantee that all subsequent access at each access site conform to the same shape, or set of key values. In many cases, this check is rare and/or inexpensive, as outlined above, leading to significant benefit. However, in the most general case, when the set of key values is determined outside the scope of the VM or DBMS interface library (e.g. by reading the key values from an external file, or prompting the user to type them in), the cost of checking the shape of the hash map could equal or even exceed the cost of relying on a standard hash map. Here, the VM should profile the relative frequency of execution of the sites where the hash map shape is set (and the check must be performed) vs. the sites where the hash maps are accessed (where performance benefit is obtained), and should only enable HMI if the former is less frequent than the latter. Such an evaluation is beyond the scope of this paper, as we could not find any workloads where this tradeoff has to be made.

6. EXPERIMENTAL FRAMEWORK AND RESULTS

Our evaluation is divided into three subsections. Section 6.2 presents the impact on performance of benchmark suites with Extended HMI for SQL (Ext_HMI) implementation and compares it against our initial HMI (Init_HMI) (section 2.3) implementation. Section 6.3 investigates the performance bottlenecks in a few benchmark scripts and provides solution to mitigate that. Section 6.4 illustrates the detailed breakdown of execution time of the benchmark scripts.

Table 1: Server-side PHP benchmark suites

Benchmark	Description	Hash map-intensive PHP scripts
RUBiS [6]	An auction site prototype modeled after eBay.com, implements core functionality of an auction site: selling, browsing, bidding for different items.	BrowseCategories(BC), BrowseRegions(BR) SearchItemsByCategory(SIC), SearchItemsByRegion(SIR), ViewBidHistory(VBH), ViewItem(VI), ViewUserInfo(VUI), AboutMe(AM)
RUBBoS [5]	An online news forum benchmark modeled after Slashdot.org, provides essential bulletin board features such as featuring news stories (associated comments) on various topics.	BrowseCategories(BC), BrowseStoriesByCategory(BSC), OlderStories(OS), ReviewStories(RS), Search-keyword1(S-K1), Search-keyword2(S-K2), StoriesOfTheDay(SD), SubmitStory(SS), ViewComment-small/expanded(VC-S/E)
Tiger Php News System [8]	Mimics a typical news site such as displaying news with options for browsing, searching for a specific news etc.	Printnews(User)(PU), Printnews(Moderator)(PM), Search(S), PrintComments(PC), GetUserList(GUL), GetMenu(GM), BrowserStat(BS)
SPECWeb2005 [7] (Banking)	Simulates typical requests to an on-line bank	login_welcome(LW), account_summary(AS), bill_pay(BP), bill_pay_status_output(BPS), order_check(OC), transfer(T)
SPECWeb2005 [7] (E-commerce)	Simulates a web store that sells computer systems; allows users to search, browse, customize, and purchase products.	index(I), search(S), browse(B), browse_productline(BP), productdetail(PD), customize(C)

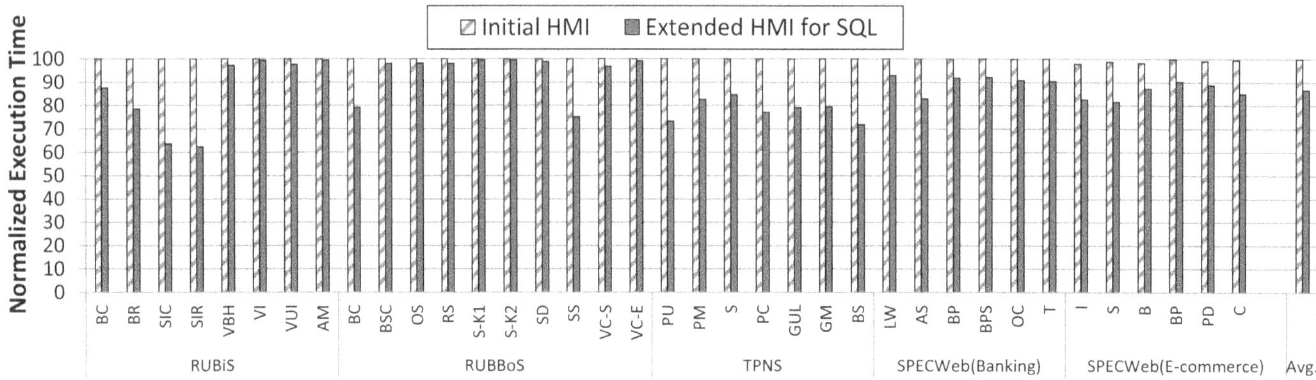

Figure 11: Performance improvement with HMI normalized to unmodified HHVM. Averaged across scripts in Table 1. Ext_HMI improves SPECWeb banking and e-commerce throughput by 7.71% and 11.71% respectively.

6.1 Methodology

We evaluate our enhancements on five real-world server-side PHP benchmark suites (Table 1). We are showing the results for a subset of scripts that spend noticeable time accessing hash maps. The remaining scripts from the different suites spend little or no time accessing hash maps leaving no opportunity for HMI. Note that for the SPECWeb2005 benchmark suite we replace its Besim emulator with an actual SQL server interface in order to account for the overall activity of a PHP script's execution. BeSim emulates a back-end database server that PHP scripts in the SPECWeb2005 suite communicate with to retrieve required database results. We used the latest release of HHVM [11] at the time of this writing with its *Repo.Authoritative* mode turned on for all our evaluations. It activates all the member instruction optimizations present in HHVM. We measure the performance of the benchmarks natively on a 3.6 GHz AMD FX(tm)-8150 eight core machine with 8MB last-level cache, running the 64-bit version of Ubuntu 12.04. The PHP benchmark scripts interact with a MySQL database server installed on the native machine. We used the available test harness to generate client requests. This setup should closely imitate the environment of commercial servers.

6.2 Performance Improvement

Figure 11 shows the improvement in performance with Ext_HMI. Init_HMI brings down the average execution time to only 99.8% of the time obtained with unmodified HHVM, whereas Ext_HMI brings down the execution time to 86.63%. This results in throughput[2] improvement of 7.71% and 11.71% for SPECWeb(Banking) and SPECWeb(E-commerce) suites respectively. *SearchItemsByRegion* script from RUBiS obtains maximum benefit of 37.6% with Ext_HMI implementation. Note that Init_HMI provides marginal benefits for few scripts such as *index*, *search* and *browse* from SPECWeb(E-commerce) suite. The subset of scripts such as *BuyNow, RegisterItem, RegisterUser, StoreBid* etc. from RUBiS, *PostComment,StoreStory* etc. from RUBBoS, *add_payee, change_profile* etc. from SPECWeb(Banking) and *cart, login, shipping* etc. from SPECWeb(E-commerce) suites are omitted since they spend little or no time accessing hash maps. Instead, they spend most of their time executing a database query to retrieve or save a single record; they spend little or no time in PHP scripts, leaving no opportunity for any JIT optimization. Hence, those scripts show no improvements, as expected, so we omit them from our results. However we note that our modifications did not cause overhead either.

Note that several scripts such as *SearchItemsByCategory* from RUBiS, *printnews* from TPNS show substantial improvement with Ext_HMI whereas for scripts like *ViewItem* from RUBiS, *bill_pay* from SPECWeb(Banking) in Figure 11, performance improves modestly. In addition to that, there are a subset of scripts such as *BrowseStoriesByCategory, OlderStories* for which Ext_HMI shows little or no improvement. The reasons behind this uneven improvement in performance will be discussed in the next two subsections.

Note that as the number of fields in class objects changes in Figure 1, the branch and cache MPKI (mispredictions or misses per 1000 instructions) with accessing class objects reduce from 6.84 to 3.72 and from 9.31 to 8.56 respectively. However the branch and cache MPKI with accessing hash maps stays around 4.2 and 16 respectively as the absolute number of mispredictions or misses

[2]Throughput for SPECWeb is measured using an available test harness that generates requests for all the scripts (6 hash map-intensive scripts from Banking and E-commerce each as shown in Figure 11 along with the remaining non-hash map-intensive scripts) from SPECWeb.

```
$result=mysql_query("SELECT story_id, writer FROM comments WHERE ...");

while ($row = mysql_fetch_array($result)) {
  $user_query=mysql_query("SELECT nickname FROM users WHERE
                    id=$row["writer"]);
  ...
}
```

```
$result = mysql_query("SELECT comments.story_id, users.nickname
  FROM comments, users WHERE comments.writer = users.id AND ...");

while ($row = mysql_fetch_array($result)) {
  ...
}
```

Figure 12: Merging nested queries (above) to a single query (bottom).

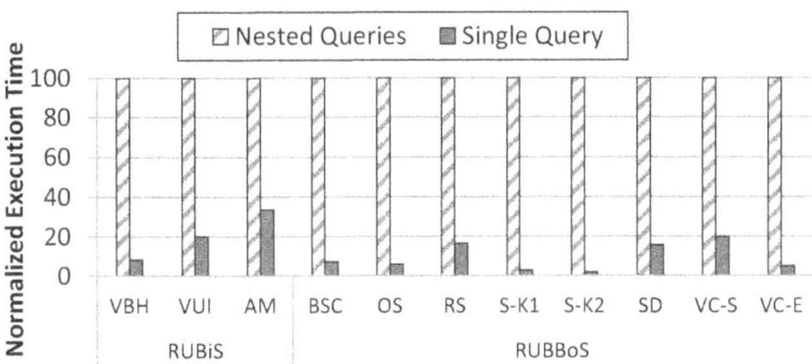

Figure 13: Performance gain with merging nested queries into a single query. Only 11 Scripts have nested queries.

change almost in the same proportion as the number of instructions. As we apply HMI to our workloads in Figure 11, the branch mispredictions and data cache misses in those workloads are reduced to the level of equivalent C++ objects.

6.3 Nested Queries

Careful examination of the subset of scripts such as *BrowseStoriesByCategory, OlderStories* that do not benefit from our Ext_HMI implementation reveals that they contain nested queries in them that require repeated SQL query invocations for each of the rows extracted from the result tables of parent queries. Not surprisingly, these scripts spend most of their execution time within the SQL query execution function, leaving little or no opportunity for dynamic optimization of PHP code. When a database query is invoked, the DBMS engine begins with building hash tables of the *records* before performing any further operations such as scan, join and sort on them. In the case of nested queries, the child query requires building these expensive hash tables for the entire set of database *records* in order to simply look for a single *record* from them, in spite of the fact that the shape of those hash tables stays the same across invocations. This is an unfortunate yet common performance bug in PHP/SQL scripts, and reflects a lack of experience and expertise in SQL on the part of the programmer.

To better evaluate the impact of HMI on code that has already been re-factored to avoid such basic mistakes, we rewrote these scripts to eliminate the unnecessary nested queries by merging the nested queries in them into a single top-level query, as shown in Figure 12. Once the nested queries were merged, these scripts no longer spent virtually all of their time executing redundant SQL, and the performance benefits of the HMI technique were realized for them as well. Figure 13 demonstrates the substantial improvement in execution time due to merging the nested queries for the eleven scripts that contain nested queries. As shown, the unmodified scripts spend most of their time in database query execution.

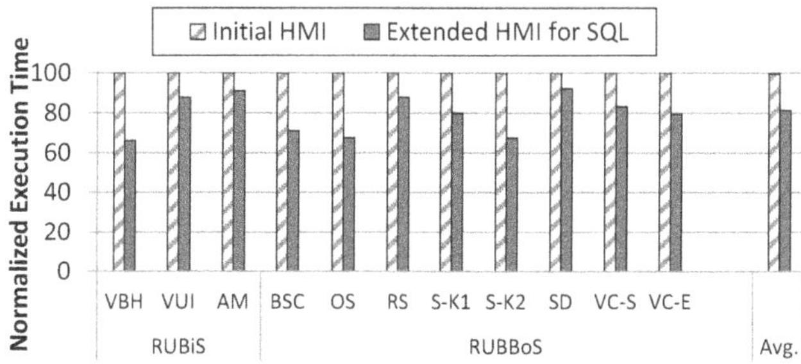

Figure 14: HMI applied to scripts after merging their nested queries. Perf. normalized to unmodified HHVM. Avg. shown considers the improvements to 11 modified scripts from Figure 13 and remaining 26 unmodified scripts with no nested queries from Figure 11 using Ext_HMI.

Merging the nested queries improves their execution time to just $8-10\%$ of their original execution time.

Furthermore, with merging nested queries, scripts such as *BrowseStoriesByCategory, Search-keyword* etc. become amenable to the benefits of Ext_HMI (Figure 14). So with applying Ext_HMI to scripts in Figure 13 after merging their nested queries, the average execution time across all hash map-intensive scripts comes down to 81.18% in Figure 14 from 86.63% obtained before merging nested queries in Figure 11. Note that, $10-12\%$ of the overhead in populating hash maps comes from resizing and consequently only 2.6% performance benefit, instead of the 18.81% shown, can be obtained with initial sizing.

6.4 Breakdown of Execution Time

Figure 15 shows the breakdown of execution time for the benchmark scripts. *mysql_query* represents the time taken in executing the SQL queries. *Hash Map Populate* and *Hash Map Access* denote the times consumed in populating and accessing hash maps in those scripts. We observe that the majority of the improvement in execution time comes from the lower overhead in populating vector-like arrays inside the DBMS library function enabled by our Ext_HMI. This breakdown essentially validates our initial motivation and confirms the fact that hash map processing consumes a significant portion of the overall execution time. Scripts that require retrieval of many rows (and hence populate hash maps many times) from the query result table observe major improvement in execution time. Scripts that are showing only marginal improvement require retrieval of the fewer rows. The *ViewItem* script retrieves only 2 rows and hence does not find any improvement with Ext_HMI. Scripts from the SPECWeb(Banking) suite retrieve few rows (5 rows on average) and hence observe marginal benefit with Ext_HMI. On the other hand, *SearchItemsByCategory* like script pulls out hundreds of rows from the result table and shows a substantial improvement. All the scripts observe expected improvement (5.09% on average from Figure 15) from inlined lookups to the populated hash maps.

7. RELATED WORK

This paper touches on topics across a broad spectrum of computer systems related topics, including, but not limited to: database query optimization, effective data structure selection and type specialization in dynamic languages. We briefly discuss these areas below.

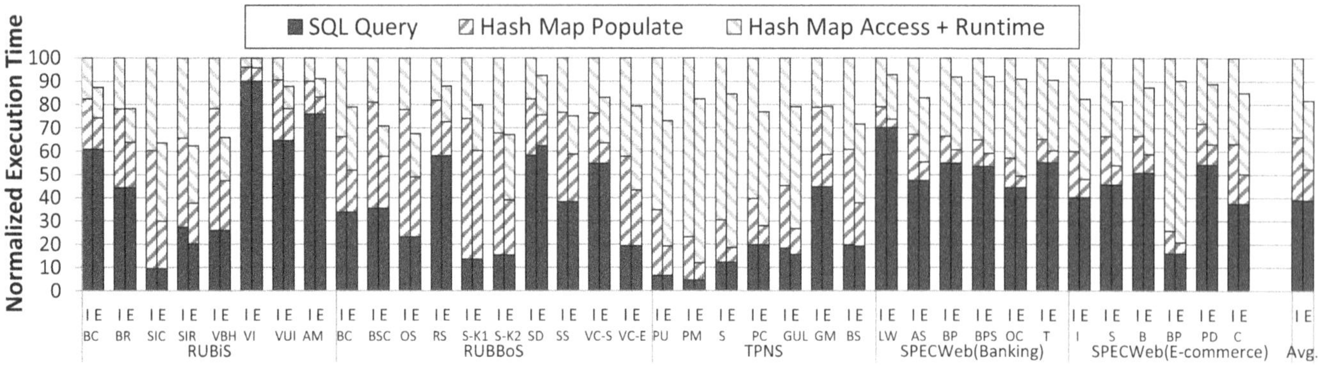

Figure 15: Breakdown of execution time normalized to Init_HMI. *I* and *E* refer to Init_HMI and Ext_HMI implementations respectively. Runtime = time consumed in executing string operations, regular expressions, and miscellaneous operations.

7.1 DBMS-Specific Intra-Operator Optimizations

There has recently been extensive research on how to specialize the code of a query execution by using an approach called Micro-Specialization [42, 44, 43]. In this line of work, the authors propose a framework to encode DBMS-specific intra-operator optimizations, like unrolling loops and removing unnecessary branching conditions by exploiting invariants present during a query execution. Another recent work is the query execution engine of LegoBase [28] that develops a compilation framework to achieve the same. All these works aim to improve database systems by removing unnecessary abstraction overheads during a query execution. Furthermore, there are many works [31, 33, 34, 38] that aim to speed-up query execution by focusing mostly on improving the way data are processed, rather than individual database operators. In contrast our work eliminates the abstraction overheads associated with post-processing the result table of a database query in context of its usage in real-world PHP scripts in a jitted environment. All these software query optimizers and recent works on database hardware accelerators [29, 41] will bring the spotlight on the performance of the post processing phase and the PHP scripts even more in future that our work focuses on.

7.2 Effective Selection of Data Structures

There has been plenty of research [25, 26, 37] in optimizing the usage of data structures in applications written in statically-typed languages. Recent work [25, 26] by Jung et al. proposes a program analysis tool that automatically identifies the data structures used within an application and selects an alternative data structure better suited for the particular application input and the underlying architecture. In contrast to that, our work does not seek to identify optimal data structures for real-world PHP applications.

7.3 Type Specialization in Dynamic Languages

There is a large body of research in type specialization of dynamic scripting languages. SELF [17, 16] and Smalltalk [18] are the early pioneers. They introduced the inline caching and polymorphic inline caching [23] techniques to specialize a code section with any previously observed types and thus optimize access to dynamically typed objects. We have already summarized inline caching and discussed its adaptation to the hash maps in section 2.2 and 2.3. There are many recent research proposals in JavaScript specialization [21, 40, 22, 36, 27, 13]. All these works exploit type inference in conjunction with type feedback in different ways to generate efficient native code. One of the most recent works is [13] by Ahn et al. that examines the way the Chrome V8 compiler defines types, and identifies the key design decisions behind its poor type predictability of class objects in Javascript code from real websites. However all these type specialization techniques do not address the issues with type unpredictability of hash maps in server-side PHP scripts, which our work focuses on.

Note that the adaptation of the well-known inline caching idea to the realm of hash maps is not our primary contribution. Rather the key contribution here is identifying issues with adaptation of polymorphic inline caching to hash maps in real-world applications and providing enhancements to the JIT engine to mitigate those. Furthermore, there are many recent proposals [32, 14, 12] in providing architectural support to optimize the execution of scripting languages. [32, 14] propose microarchitectural changes to avoid the runtime checks associated with jitted execution, whereas [12] improves the energy efficiency of PHP servers by aligning the execution of similar requests together. They are orthogonal to our compiler modifications and their associated benefits.

Note that the well-known perfect hashing or dynamic perfect hashing techniques [20, 19] provide hash functions that can map keys to a hash map with no collisions. Thus they can avoid any potential overhead from traversing a collision chain in case two keys map to the same entry in a hash map. However they cannot avoid the overheads associated with hash map allocation, release, resizing, hash computation etc. which HMI completely eliminates and gets most of the benefit from.

8. CONCLUSION

In this work, we propose Hash Map Inlining to eliminate the overheads associated with accessing hash maps, the most commonly occurring data structure in scripting languages. This work describes compiler enhancements to achieve that for PHP in HHVM compiler. It delivers performance benefits up to 37.6% and averaging 18.81% over a set of hash map-intensive server-side PHP scripts. Furthermore it opens up the opportunity of parallelizing HTML generation within a single request (for example, loops in our workloads) and across multiple client requests as [12] envisions. Thus HMI can improve the efficiency of web servers and in turn can directly influence the throughput of data centers.

9. ACKNOWLEDGMENTS

We thank our anonymous reviewers, Michael Mishkin and shepherd Jennifer Welch for their insightful comments and feedback on the paper. This work was supported in part by NSF grant CCF-1318298.

10. REFERENCES

[1] The computer language benchmarks game, http://shootout.alioth.debian.org/.

[2] Mongodb. https://www.mongodb.org/.

[3] Mysql dbms. https://www.mysql.com/.

[4] Oracle database. https://www.oracle.com/database/index.html.

[5] Rubbos: Bulletin board benchmark. http://jmob.ow2.org/rubbos.html.

[6] Rubis: Rice university bidding system. http://rubis.ow2.org/.

[7] Standard performance evaluation corporation. specweb2005. https://www.spec.org/web2005/.

[8] The tiger php news system benchmark suite. http://sourceforge.net/projects/tpns/.

[9] Usage of server-side programming languages for websites. https://w3techs.com/technologies/overview/programming_language/all.

[10] V8 javascript engine. https://developers.google.com/v8/.

[11] K. Adams, J. Evans, B. Maher, G. Ottoni, A. Paroski, B. Simmers, E. Smith, and O. Yamauchi. The hiphop virtual machine. In *Proceedings of the 2014 ACM International Conference on Object Oriented Programming Systems Languages and Applications*, OOPSLA '14, pages 777–790, New York, NY, USA, 2014.

[12] S. R. Agrawal, V. Pistol, J. Pang, J. Tran, D. Tarjan, and A. R. Lebeck. Rhythm: Harnessing data parallel hardware for server workloads. In *Proceedings of the 19th International Conference on Architectural Support for Programming Languages and Operating Systems*, ASPLOS '14, pages 19–34, New York, NY, USA, 2014.

[13] W. Ahn, J. Choi, T. Shull, M. J. Garzarán, and J. Torrellas. Improving javascript performance by deconstructing the type system. In *Proceedings of the 35th ACM SIGPLAN Conference on Programming Language Design and Implementation*, PLDI '14, pages 496–507, New York, NY, USA, 2014.

[14] O. Anderson, E. Fortuna, L. Ceze, and S. Eggers. Checked load: Architectural support for javascript type-checking on mobile processors. In *Proceedings of the 2011 IEEE 17th International Symposium on High Performance Computer Architecture*, HPCA '11, pages 419–430, Washington, DC, USA, 2011.

[15] P. Biggar, E. de Vries, and D. Gregg. A practical solution for scripting language compilers. In *Proceedings of the 2009 ACM Symposium on Applied Computing*, SAC '09, pages 1916–1923, New York, NY, USA, 2009.

[16] C. Chambers and D. Ungar. Customization: Optimizing compiler technology for self, a dynamically-typed object-oriented programming language. In *Proceedings of the ACM SIGPLAN 1989 Conference on Programming Language Design and Implementation*, PLDI '89, pages 146–160, New York, NY, USA, 1989. ACM.

[17] C. Chambers, D. Ungar, and E. Lee. An efficient implementation of self a dynamically-typed object-oriented language based on prototypes. In *Conference Proceedings on Object-oriented Programming Systems, Languages and Applications*, OOPSLA '89, pages 49–70, New York, NY, USA, 1989.

[18] L. P. Deutsch and A. M. Schiffman. Efficient implementation of the smalltalk-80 system. In *Proceedings of the 11th ACM SIGACT-SIGPLAN Symposium on Principles of Programming Languages*, POPL '84, pages 297–302, New York, NY, USA, 1984. ACM.

[19] M. Dietzfelbinger, A. Karlin, K. Mehlhorn, F. Meyer auf der Heide, H. Rohnert, and R. E. Tarjan. Dynamic perfect hashing: Upper and lower bounds. *SIAM J. Comput.*, 23(4):738–761, Aug. 1994.

[20] M. L. Fredman, J. Komlós, and E. Szemerédi. Storing a sparse table with 0(1) worst case access time. *J. ACM*, 31(3):538–544, June 1984.

[21] A. Gal, B. Eich, M. Shaver, D. Anderson, D. Mandelin, M. R. Haghighat, B. Kaplan, G. Hoare, B. Zbarsky, J. Orendorff, J. Ruderman, E. W. Smith, R. Reitmaier, M. Bebenita, M. Chang, and M. Franz. Trace-based just-in-time type specialization for dynamic languages. In *Proceedings of the 2009 ACM SIGPLAN Conference on Programming Language Design and Implementation*, PLDI '09, pages 465–478, New York, NY, USA, 2009.

[22] B. Hackett and S.-y. Guo. Fast and precise hybrid type inference for javascript. In *Proceedings of the 33rd ACM SIGPLAN Conference on Programming Language Design and Implementation*, PLDI '12, pages 239–250, New York, NY, USA, 2012. ACM.

[23] U. Holzle, C. Chambers, and D. Ungar. Optimizing dynamically-typed object-oriented languages with polymorphic inline caches. In *ECOOP'91 European Conference on Object-Oriented Programming, Geneva, Switzerland, July 15-19, 1991, Proceedings.*

[24] A. Homescu and A. Şuhan. Happyjit: A tracing jit compiler for php. In *Proceedings of the 7th Symposium on Dynamic Languages*, DLS '11, pages 25–36, New York, NY, USA, 2011.

[25] C. Jung and N. Clark. Ddt: Design and evaluation of a dynamic program analysis for optimizing data structure usage. In *Proceedings of the 42Nd Annual IEEE/ACM International Symposium on Microarchitecture*, MICRO 42, pages 56–66, New York, NY, USA, 2009.

[26] C. Jung, S. Rus, B. P. Railing, N. Clark, and S. Pande. Brainy: Effective selection of data structures. In *Proceedings of the 32Nd ACM SIGPLAN Conference on Programming Language Design and Implementation*, PLDI '11, pages 86–97, New York, NY, USA, 2011.

[27] M. N. Kedlaya, J. Roesch, B. Robatmili, M. Reshadi, and B. Hardekopf. Improved type specialization for dynamic scripting languages. In *Proceedings of the 9th Symposium on Dynamic Languages*, DLS '13, pages 37–48, New York, NY, USA, 2013.

[28] Y. Klonatos, C. Koch, T. Rompf, and H. Chafi. Building efficient query engines in a high-level language. *Proc. VLDB Endow.*, 7(10):853–864, June 2014.

[29] O. Kocberber, B. Grot, J. Picorel, B. Falsafi, K. Lim, and P. Ranganathan. Meet the walkers: Accelerating index traversals for in-memory databases. In *Proceedings of the 46th Annual IEEE/ACM International Symposium on Microarchitecture*, MICRO-46, pages 468–479, New York, NY, USA, 2013. ACM.

[30] C.-K. Luk, R. Cohn, R. Muth, H. Patil, A. Klauser, G. Lowney, S. Wallace, V. J. Reddi, and K. Hazelwood. Pin: Building customized program analysis tools with dynamic instrumentation. In *Proceedings of the 2005 ACM SIGPLAN Conference on Programming Language Design and Implementation*, PLDI '05, pages 190–200, New York, NY, USA, 2005. ACM.

[31] S. Manegold, M. L. Kersten, and P. Boncz. Database architecture evolution: Mammals flourished long before dinosaurs became extinct. *Proc. VLDB Endow.*, 2(2):1648–1653, Aug. 2009.

[32] M. Mehrara and S. Mahlke. Dynamically accelerating client-side web applications through decoupled execution. In *Proceedings of the 9th Annual IEEE/ACM International Symposium on Code Generation and Optimization*, CGO '11, pages 74–84, Washington, DC, USA, 2011.

[33] S. Padmanabhan, T. Malkemus, R. C. Agarwal, and A. Jhingran. Block oriented processing of relational database operations in modern computer architectures. In *Proceedings of the 17th International Conference on Data Engineering*, pages 567–574, Washington, DC, USA, 2001. IEEE Computer Society.

[34] V. Raman, G. Swart, L. Qiao, F. Reiss, V. Dialani, D. Kossmann, I. Narang, and R. Sidle. Constant-time query processing. In *Proceedings of the 2008 IEEE 24th International Conference on Data Engineering*, ICDE '08, pages 60–69, Washington, DC, USA, 2008. IEEE Computer Society.

[35] A. Rigo and S. Pedroni. Pypy's approach to virtual machine construction. In *Companion to the 21st ACM SIGPLAN Symposium on Object-oriented Programming Systems, Languages, and Applications*, OOPSLA '06, pages 944–953, New York, NY, USA, 2006.

[36] H. N. Santos, P. Alves, I. Costa, and F. M. Quintao Pereira. Just-in-time value specialization. In *Proceedings of the 2013 IEEE/ACM International Symposium on Code Generation and Optimization (CGO)*, CGO '13, pages 1–11, Washington, DC, USA, 2013. IEEE Computer Society.

[37] O. Shacham, M. Vechev, and E. Yahav. Chameleon: Adaptive selection of collections. In *Proceedings of the 2009 ACM SIGPLAN Conference on Programming Language Design and Implementation*, PLDI '09, pages 408–418, New York, NY, USA, 2009.

[38] J. Sompolski, M. Zukowski, and P. Boncz. Vectorization vs. compilation in query execution. In *Proceedings of the Seventh International Workshop on Data Management on New Hardware*, DaMoN '11, pages 33–40, New York, NY, USA, 2011. ACM.

[39] S. Warner and J. Worley. Specweb2005 in the real world: Using iis and php. In *Proceedings of SPEC Benchmark Workshop*, 2008.

[40] K. Williams, J. McCandless, and D. Gregg. Dynamic interpretation for dynamic scripting languages. In *Proceedings of the 8th Annual IEEE/ACM International Symposium on Code Generation and Optimization*, CGO '10, pages 278–287, New York, NY, USA, 2010.

[41] L. Wu, A. Lottarini, T. K. Paine, M. A. Kim, and K. A. Ross. Q100: The architecture and design of a database processing unit. In *Proceedings of the 19th International Conference on Architectural Support for Programming Languages and Operating Systems*, ASPLOS '14, pages 255–268, New York, NY, USA, 2014. ACM.

[42] R. Zhang, S. Debray, and R. T. Snodgrass. Micro-specialization: Dynamic code specialization of database management systems. In *Proceedings of the Tenth International Symposium on Code Generation and Optimization*, CGO '12, pages 63–73, New York, NY, USA, 2012.

[43] R. Zhang, R. T. Snodgrass, and S. Debray. Application of micro-specialization to query evaluation operators. In *Workshops Proceedings of the 28th International Conference on Data Engineering*, pages 315–321, 2012.

[44] R. Zhang, R. T. Snodgrass, and S. Debray. Micro-specialization in dbmses. In *Proceedings of the 28th International Conference on Data Engineering*, pages 690–701, 2012.

[45] H. Zhao, I. Proctor, M. Yang, X. Qi, M. Williams, Q. Gao, G. Ottoni, A. Paroski, S. MacVicar, J. Evans, and S. Tu. The hiphop compiler for php. In *Proceedings of the ACM International Conference on Object Oriented Programming Systems Languages and Applications*, OOPSLA '12, pages 575–586, New York, NY, USA, 2012.

Sparso: Context-driven Optimizations of Sparse Linear Algebra

Hongbo Rong Jongsoo Park Lingxiang Xiang
Todd A. Anderson Mikhail Smelyanskiy

Parallel Computing Lab, Intel Corporation
{hongbo.rong,jongsoo.park,lingxiang.xiang,todd.a.anderson,mikhail.smelyanskiy}@intel.com

ABSTRACT

The sparse matrix is a key data structure in various domains such as high-performance computing, machine learning, and graph analytics. To maximize performance of sparse matrix operations, it is especially important to optimize across the operations and not just within individual operations. While a straightforward per-operation mapping to library routines misses optimization opportunities, manually optimizing across the boundary of library routines is time-consuming and error-prone, sacrificing productivity.

This paper introduces Sparso, a framework that automates such optimizations, enabling both high performance *and* high productivity. In Sparso, a compiler and sparse linear algebra libraries collaboratively discover and exploit *context*, which we define as the invariant properties of matrices and relationships between them in a program. We present compiler analyses, namely *collective reordering analysis* and *matrix property discovery*, to discover the context. The context discovered from these analyses drives key optimizations across library routines and matrices.

We have implemented Sparso with the Julia language, Intel MKL and SpMP libraries. We evaluate our context-driven optimizations in 6 representative sparse linear algebra algorithms. Compared with a baseline that invokes high-performance libraries without context optimizations, Sparso results in 1.2∼17× (average 5.7×) speedups. Our approach of compiler-library collaboration and context-driven optimizations should be also applicable to other productivity languages such as Matlab, Python, and R.

1. INTRODUCTION

Exploiting sparse connectivity is increasingly important with bigger data, as exemplified by recent work on sparse linear algebra in areas of high-performance computing [18], machine learning [50], and graph analytics [7]. However, harnessing the full potential of modern computing systems for sparse matrix operations poses unique challenges. In dense linear algebra, BLAS and LAPACK interfaces effectively abstract the complexity of highly-optimized library implementations, achieving both performance *and* productivity. In sparse linear algebra, however, a similar approach misses important optimization opportunities that take advantage of the specific sparsity structure of input matrices and whose scope goes beyond individual kernels. We call these optimizations *context-driven optimizations*. Manually applying these optimizations is time-consuming and error-prone even for expert programmers [45] and thus hampers productivity.

See the skeleton code below that is extracted from pre-conditioned conjugate gradient (PCG), a widely used algorithm for solving linear systems.

```
L = ichol(A)          # Incomplete Cholesky factorization
while !converged
    ... = A·p         # Sparse-matrix vector multiplication
    z = L\r           # Forward triangular solver
    z = L^T\z         # Backward triangular solver
    ...
```

A programmer attempting to optimize this code can easily map key operations like sparse-matrix vector multiplication (SpMV, $A\cdot p$) and sparse triangular solver ($L\backslash r$ [1]) to high-performance library routines. However, such a straightforward per-operation mapping is 5.6× slower than code with context-driven optimizations, as will be shown in Section 7.

With the above PCG example, let us briefly introduce context-driven optimizations, which will be detailed later. Sparse triangular solver has data-dependent parallelism [44], so we use the *inspector-executor* approach [39, 49], a context-driven optimization. We *inspect* the input matrix at run-time to arrange triangular solver's computation as a task dependency graph (TDG). Then, we *execute* the tasks in parallel using the TDG. Since the inspection involves non-trivial overhead, we reuse the inspection result to amortize the overhead. However, manually reusing the inspection results adds a burden to programmers; they have to reason about code regions where matrices preserve constant sparsity structures.

Another context-driven optimization, matrix reordering [17, 20, 42, 51], can improve the cache locality of sparse matrix operations. However, this optimization needs to be propagated to other related matrices and vectors. In the PCG code, if we reorder matrix L, we also need to reorder vectors r and z that are used in the same expressions with L. We also need to coordinate among multiple kernels because each may prefer different reordering. For example, in the PCG code, SpMV and triangular solvers may prefer different reordering.

Still, additional context-driven optimizations that will be described in Section 3 are needed for the best performance of PCG. In general, implementing these context-driven optimizations for any application like those in Table 1 needs a considerable amount of effort.

This paper introduces Sparso, a framework that automates context-driven optimizations for sparse matrix applications via

[1] $z = L\backslash r$ is a computation such that $L\cdot z = r$.

PACT '16, September 11-15, 2016, Haifa, Israel

 ISBN 978-1-4503-4121-9/16/09...$15.00
DOI: http://dx.doi.org/10.1145/2967938.2967943

Table 1: Evaluated applications with their brief descriptions, including optimization opportunities

Application	Domain	Description	Source of Matrices	Optimization Opportunities: Exploit Matrix Properties	Optimization Opportunities: Collective Reordering
PCG	Operations research, HPC	A representative of sparse iterative solvers	UF collection [14]	✓	✓
IPM [37]	Operations research	Interior-point method for convex optimization problems	UF collection [14]	✓	
L-BFGS [35]	Machine learning	Optimization algorithm popular for parameter estimation	libSVM [8, 34]	✓	✓
CoSP2 [41]	HPC	Calculate density matrix in electronic structure theory	CoSP2 website [41]	✓	
Adiabatic	HPC	Validate annealing speed of quantum adiabatic simulation		✓	
PageRank [6]	Graph analytics	Rank web pages according to their popularity	UF collection [14]	✓	✓

collaboration between a compiler and libraries. Programmers write straightforward code, and Sparso transparently generates code with context-driven optimizations. The framework centers around the concept of *context*, which we define as the invariant properties of matrices and relationships between them in a code region (like a function or a loop). *Static context* is discovered by compiler analyses, and *run-time context* is discovered by run-time inspections in libraries.

As shown in Figure 1, static context is discovered by key compiler analyses, including *collective reordering analysis* and *matrix property discovery*, whose results are populated in two tables, *reordering control table (RCT)* and *matrix property table (MPT)*, respectively. The tables are shared with a context-sensitive wrapper that is a thin layer around existing libraries like Intel math kernel library (MKL). With the static context in the tables, the wrapper invokes the libraries to inspect matrices, and caches the inspection results back to the tables as run-time context. Sparso generates code such that the run-time context can be reused by subsequent invocations of library routines.

In the PCG code above, the compiler can discover static context like "A is symmetric" and "L has the same sparsity structure as the lower triangular part of A". Such information can be exploited by libraries, as will be described in Section 3. Library routines inspect sparse matrices and generate run-time context like TDG, reordering permutation, and different sparse matrix storage formats.

This paper makes the following contributions:

1. *Sparso framework for context-driven optimizations.* We demonstrate that compiler-library collaboration can effectively automate context-driven optimizations, achieving performance *and* productivity for sparse linear algebra algorithms. Even though inspector-executor and reordering are known ideas, Sparso integrates and automates them to be easily usable by non-expert programmers in productivity languages like Julia [4], Matlab, Python, and R.
2. *Compiler analyses for matrix property discovery and reordering.* We propose a set of dataflow analyses for discovering properties of matrices and relationships among them. We also propose collective reordering, which automates matrix reordering with minimal overhead. The outcome of these analyses drives library optimizations and achieves higher performance.
3. *Performance comparable to manually-optimized implementations.* Compared to a baseline that invokes high-performance library kernels without context, Sparso yields 1.2-17× (average 5.7×) speedups, on a 14-core Intel Haswell Xeon processor. This evaluation is with the 6 representative sparse linear algebra algorithms from various domains shown in Table 1. Sparso's PCG performance corresponds to 67% of the underlying hardware's capabilities and is close to the top results in recent HPCG benchmark lists [18][2]. Performance on other algorithms are also comparable to manually optimized results [41, 46, 54, 55].

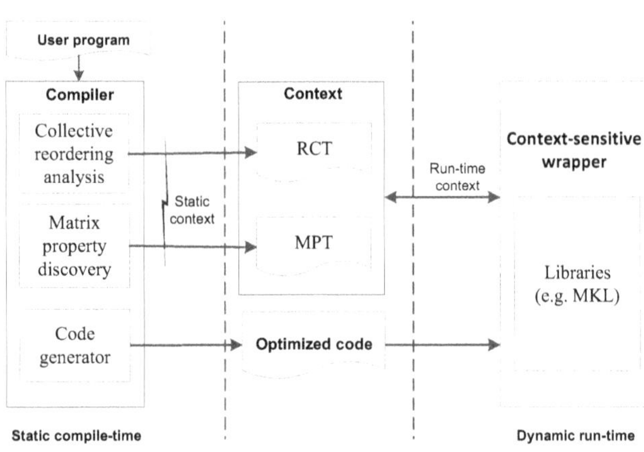

Figure 1: Sparso Work-flow: A compiler discovers static context and generates optimized code. When executed, the optimized code invokes context-sensitive routines in a wrapper interface around existing libraries. Guided by the static context, the wrapper routines generate reusable run-time context, and invoke the best specialized library routines. Both kinds of context are stored in two tables, RCT and MPT.

The rest of this paper is organized as follows: Section 2 defines the notations and reviews preliminaries, which can be skipped by those who are familiar with sparse linear algebra. Section 3 overviews Sparso framework using PCG as an example. Section 4 presents two compiler analyses, matrix property discovery and collective reordering, that derive context-driven optimizations. Section 5 shows examples on how compiler and library can collaboratively optimize sparse linear algebra algorithms by communicating context. Section 6 briefly describes our specific implementation of Sparso framework in Julia, which is used for evaluation presented in Section 7. The readers are encouraged to refer to Appendix B for our open source package on Github (https://github.com/IntelLabs/Sparso.git).

2. SPARSE LINEAR ALGEBRA PRELIMINARIES

In this paper, an *array* refers to either a column vector (denoted as lower-case letters like x) or a matrix (denoted as capital letters like A). We denote scalars as Greek letters like α. In sparse matrices, we store non-zeros only, which are located by *(sparsity) structure* of the matrix [25]. For example, if a matrix is $\begin{bmatrix}1&0&0\\2&4&5\\3&0&0\end{bmatrix}$, its structure can be figuratively shown as $\begin{bmatrix}\bullet&&\\\bullet&\bullet&\bullet\\\bullet&&\end{bmatrix}$. Structures are

[2] HPCG (high-performance conjugate gradient) is a recent benchmark ranking supercomputers by the performance of solving sparse linear systems. The top result was achieved with manually applying various context-driven optimizations that has taken considerable amount of effort [45]. Note that the effort devoted to a high-profile benchmark like HPCG is rarely affordable for general applications, where automation in Sparso is of great value.

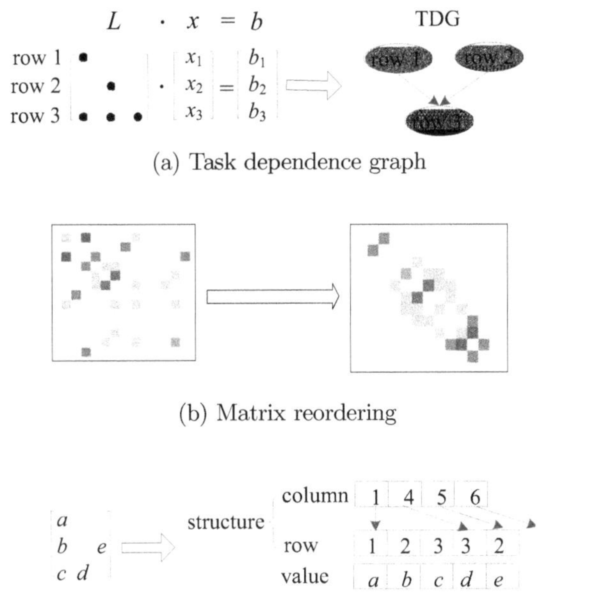

(a) Task dependence graph

(b) Matrix reordering

(c) CSC storage format

Figure 2: Sparse linear algebra preliminaries: TDG, reordering, and storage format

of particular interest because it is often the structure, not the actual values, that determines parallelism and data locality.

For example, Figure 2a shows how structure determines parallelism for the forward triangular solver, which solves $L \cdot x = b$ for the unknown x, where L is lower triangular. Because of the non-zeros' positions, the equations for rows 1 and 2 involve only x_1 and x_2, respectively. Thus, we can solve the two equations in parallel. However, the equation for row 3 involves all unknowns and cannot be solved until the equations of rows 1 and 2 are solved. Therefore, from the structure of matrix L only, we can build a *task dependence graph (TDG)*, as shown to the right of the figure.

Structure also determines data locality. *Matrix reordering* permutes the rows and columns of a sparse matrix to improve locality. Figure 2b shows a matrix before and after being reordered with reverse Cuthill-Mckee (RCM) [11], a well-known reordering algorithm. As illustrated, RCM clusters the non-zeros more closely. In $A \cdot x$ for example, this improves temporal locality of vector x.

A sparse matrix can be stored in various formats. Depending on the sparsity structures of matrices and the computation to perform, one format can outperform the others. Figure 2c shows a common storage format, *compressed sparse columns* (CSC), where non-zeros are stored column by column, along with the corresponding row numbers, and each column has an index pointing to the first non-zero in the column. In CSC, column indices and row numbers collectively represent structure, and, as long as they are constant, inspection results can be often reused. Another common format, *compressed sparse rows* (CSR), is similar to CSC but stores non-zeros row-by-row instead of by columns.

3. OVERVIEW OF SPARSO FRAMEWORK

This section overviews Sparso using PCG as an example. Subsequent sections describe compiler analyses (Section 4) and the compiler-library interface (Section 5) in more detail.

Figure 3a shows a straightforward implementation of PCG, which solves $A \cdot x = b$ for the unknown x. Understanding the details of the code is unnecessary to grasp the optimization opportunities. We can make several observations:

1. *Iterative code structure*: PCG is a typical sparse linear algebra algorithm that repeats key kernels such as SpMV ($A \cdot p$), forward triangular solver ($L \backslash r$), and backward triangular solver ($L^\mathsf{T} \backslash z$) in lines 8-20.
2. *Matrices with constant values and structures*: A and L are never updated, once generated.
3. *Matrices with special structures and relations among them*: Incomplete Cholesky factorization with zero fill-ins (`ichol` in line 1) requires the input A to be symmetric in value, and returns L whose structure is same as the lower triangular part of A.
4. *Storage formats affect performance*: When parallelizing SpMV ($A \cdot p$ in line 10), CSR is preferred to CSC for A to avoid write sharing of the output vector.
5. *Reordering can help performance*: Kernels here can benefit from matrix reordering. For SpMV ($A \cdot p$ in line 10), reordering A improves temporal locality of vector p (recall Figure 2b). Similarly, for the triangular solvers ($z = L \backslash r$ and $z = L^\mathsf{T} \backslash z$ in lines 17 and 18), reordering L reduces false sharing in vector z [45].

Our compiler discovers these facts from the original code shown in Figure 3a, and produces the optimized code shown in Figure 3b. The differences are highlighted in bold face, and new statements are numbered with Roman numerals.

The optimized code in Figure 3b first sets up RCT and MPT (lines I and II). RCT represents the run-time state of collective reordering with a status and a permutation matrix field. MPT has entries for the 3 matrices A, L, and L^T, denoted as MP_A, MP_L, and MP_{L^T}, respectively. Each entry has both static and run-time context. *Static context* includes 4 booleans, `CV` (constant-valued), `CS` (constant-structured), `SV` (symmetric-valued), and `SS` (symmetric-structured). Note that all 3 matrices are constant in value and structure, and A is symmetric in value and structure. Static context also includes two relations, `isLowerOf` and `isUpperOf`, between the matrices' structures. The table shows that the structures of L and L^T are the same as those of the lower and upper triangular parts of A, respectively. *Run-time context* includes a `TDG` and a storage format (`CSR`) field, for this example.

In line 1, the library kernel `ichol` is called with context, MP_A. The kernel may inspect A to build a TDG once (recall Figure 2a) and save the result in MP_A's `TDG` field. This TDG is reused by the triangular solvers in lines 4, 5, 17, and 18: When a triangular solver is invoked, the solver checks MPT, finds that its input matrix's structure is constant and is the lower or upper triangular part of the symmetric matrix A, and thus it can reuse the TDG.

Suppose A is in CSC format, the default format in Julia. In line 10, SpMV may transparently convert A into CSR for more efficient parallelization, and saves the result in MP_A's `CSR` field. Such a conversion happens only once: the next time SpMV is invoked, SpMV can directly access the CSR matrix, because A has not been changed (MP_A`.CV`=true). In fact, in this specific case, the conversion is unnecessary even once, because A is symmetric (MP_A`.SV`=true), which makes A in CSC and CSR identical.

The kernels operating with matrices here may benefit from reordering. However, each may prefer a different permutation. We appoint one kernel as the *decider of reordering*, based on an experiential estimate how much the kernel may benefit from reordering. The kernel that is estimated to benefit most from reordering becomes the decider. Forward triangular solver in line 17 typically has the biggest benefit from reordering, hence it will be chosen as the decider (indicated by the `DECIDER` parameter). When executed, the solver will find a permutation that improves its performance and reorder its inputs L and r, and consequently the output z. Then, the solver will save the permutation, which is represented by a *permutation matrix*, into RCT, and set `RCT.status` to `Init`, indicating that an initial set of arrays have been reordered.

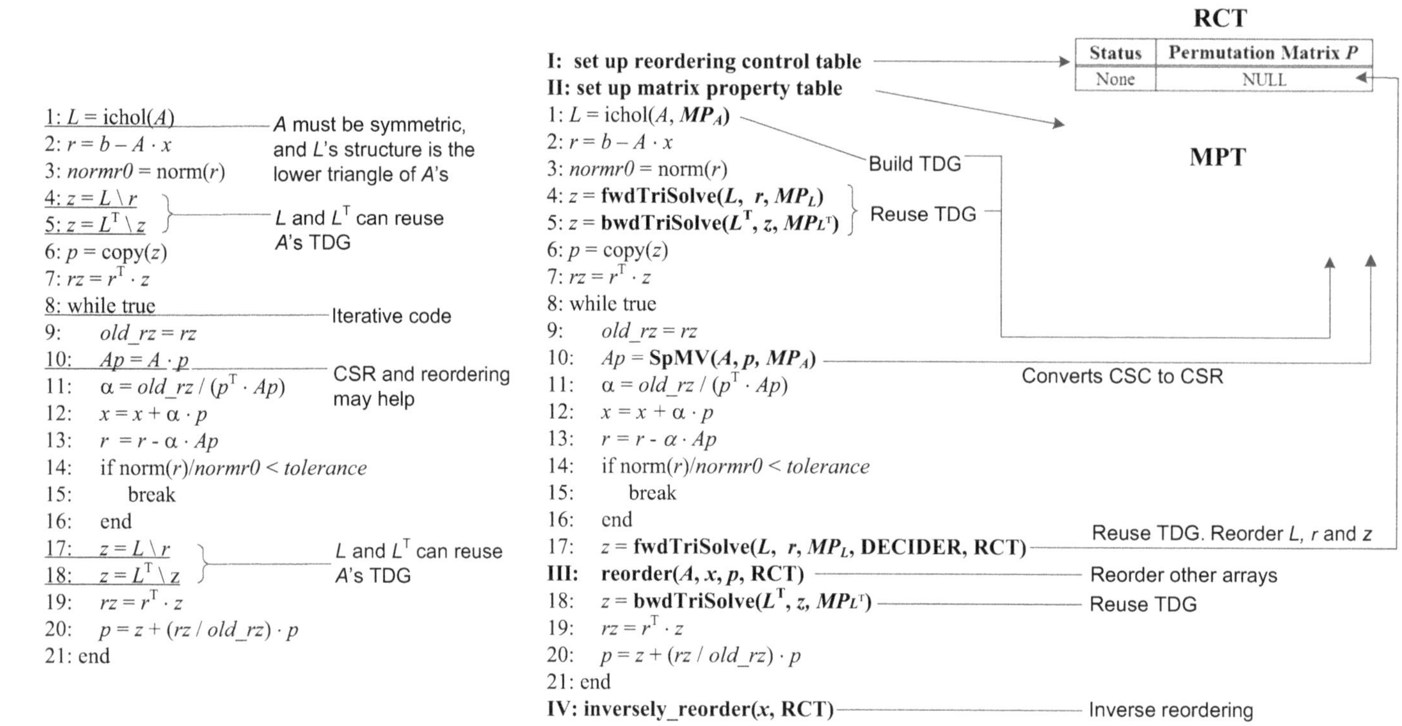

(a) Original PCG code with annotations for optimization opportunities

(b) Optimized code and its execution

Figure 3: An illustration of representative code structure and optimization opportunities in sparse linear algebra algorithms.

After the initial set of arrays have been reordered by the decider, the other arrays that will directly or indirectly take part in a computation with these reordered arrays have to be reordered as well. Here, arrays A, x, and p are related to the already reordered arrays (L,r, and z). Therefore, in line III, `reorder(`A, x, p, `RCT)` is executed. It checks if `RCT.status` equals `Init`, and if so, reorders A, x, and p, and sets `RCT.status` to `Done`, meaning that no more reordering is needed afterwards.

After the loop, live arrays have to be inversely reordered. In our example, x is the only live array to be returned from PCG function. Therefore, in line IV, `inversely_reorder(`x`, RCT)` is executed. It checks if `RCT.status` equals `Done`, and, if so, it inversely reorders x.

Note that we only show the fields of RCT and MPT needed for PCG in Figure 3b. RCT and MPT can have other fields. In general, every permutation matrix can have a field in RCT, and any matrix property can have a field in MPT (e.g., `isDiagonal`, `isTriangular`, etc.), as can be seen later in Sections 4 and 5.

4. COMPILER ANALYSES

We first describe how to discover matrix properties (Section 4.1), and then collective reordering (Section 4.2). The outcome of these compiler analyses is communicated with libraries as will be described in Section 5.

4.1 Matrix Property Discovery

A set of dataflow analyses discover the following matrix properties. First, we analyze the program to identify arrays that are of *constant size, constant value*, and/or *constant structure* in any single run of the program. Note that these compiler analyses do not inspect the actual data of the matrices, which are typically unavailable at compile-time. This distinguishes matrix property discovery from run-time inspection. These analyses extend classical constant propagation algorithm [31, 60], in a way similar to symbolic

Table 2: Example rules for the compiler to derive matrix properties

1. isDiagonal(D) $\rightarrow$ isSymmetric($A{\cdot}D{\cdot}A^{\intercal}$)
2. isSymmetric(A), isSymmetric(B) $\rightarrow$ isSymmetric($\alpha{\cdot}A{+}\beta{\cdot}B$)
3. B=tril(A) $\rightarrow$ isLowerTriangular(B)
4. B=diag(x) $\rightarrow$ isDiagonal(B)
5. B=spones(A) $\rightarrow$ $S_B{=}S_A$, isUnweighted(B)
6. $B{=}\alpha{\cdot}A \rightarrow S_B{=}S_A$
7. isDiagonal(D) $\rightarrow$ $S_{D\cdot A}{=}S_{A\cdot D}{=}S_A$
8. isDiagonal(D) $\rightarrow$ $S_{A\cdot D\cdot B}{=}S_{A\cdot B}$
9. L=ichol(A) $\rightarrow$ isSymmetric(A), isLowerTriangular(L), $S_L{=}S_{\mathrm{lowerTriangleOf}(A)}$

Note:
S_A: structure of A.
isDiagonal(D): D is diagonal.
isUnweighted(B): B is unweighted.
isSymmetric(A): A is symmetric in value (and thus also in structure).
isLowerTriangular(L): L is lower triangular.
lowerTriangleOf(A): the lower triangle of A.
spones(A): a Julia/Matlab operation that creates a sparse matrix with the same structure as that of A, but with 1 in every non-zero position.
tril(A) : a Julia/Matlab operation returning the lower triangle of A.
diag(x) : a Julia/Matlab operation that creates a sparse matrix with the elements of vector x on the main diagonal.

constant propagation [10]. In interior-point method (IPM), for example, based on that A and D have constant structures, we derive that $B{=}A{\cdot}D{\cdot}A^{\intercal}$ also has a constant structure.

Second, we analyze the program for special properties of matrices such as *symmetric value, symmetric structure, triangular structure, diagonal structure, and unweighted*[3], using basic prop-

[3] Unweighted sparse matrices represent unweighted graphs, where we only specify existence of connection, not the weight, between a pair of nodes. All non-zero values are 1, thus we only need to store structures of unweighted matrices, not their values.

erties in linear algebra like the first five rules in Table 2. This approach is similar to Rose's static structural inference [16].

Finally, we analyze the program for relations between the matrices. Example relations are: A and B have the same structure, B is the transpose of A, or L has the same structure as the lower triangular part of A. Rules 5–9 in Table 2 show example rules that we use to discover the relations.

The time complexity of these analyses is $O(EV^2)$, where E is the number of edges in the control flow graph, and V is the number of arrays. This is the same complexity as Kildall's constant propagation algorithm [31], which has been extended symbolically for most of the above analyses.

4.2 Collective Reordering

Reordering and the associated concepts of distributivity and inter-dependence are described in Section 4.2.1. Generating reordering code is then described in Section 4.2.2. Additional supportive details for these topics are contained in the Appendix A.

4.2.1 Reordering, Distributivity, and Inter-dependence

Reordering R is defined as follows:

$$R(A)=P_A\cdot A\cdot Q_A^{\mathsf{T}} \quad (1)$$

$$R(x)=P_x\cdot x \quad (2)$$

$$R(\alpha)=\alpha, \quad (3)$$

where A, x and α represent a matrix, a vector, and a scalar, respectively, as said in Section 2; P_A is a row permutation matrix for A and Q_A is a column permutation matrix for A.

Any permutation matrix P has a useful property:

$$P\cdot P^{\mathsf{T}}=I, \quad \text{the identity matrix.} \quad (4)$$

With this property, the *inverse reordering* can be easily derived[4].

Reordering R is *distributive* over function f if the function's semantics remains the same whether its output is reordered, or its inputs are reordered. That is,

$$R(f(i_1,i_2,...,i_n))=f(R(i_1),R(i_2),...,R(i_n)), \quad (5)$$

where $i_1,i_2,...,i_n$ are the inputs of f.

Reordering is usually distributive over array expressions. For example, it is distributive over SpMV, because

$$R(A\cdot x)=P\cdot(A\cdot x)=(P\cdot A\cdot Q^{\mathsf{T}})\cdot(Q\cdot x)=R(A)\cdot R(x).$$

Similarly, reordering is distributive over $A\cdot B$, $A\pm B$, $A\backslash x$, $x\pm y$, $dot(x,y)$, $\alpha\cdot A$, and $\alpha\cdot x$. A few non-distributive cases are discussed in Appendix A.1.

Inter-dependent arrays are a set of arrays that, if any one of them is reordered, all the others have to be reordered. Suppose A is reordered in expression, $y=A\cdot x$. Since the columns of A are permuted, the corresponding rows of x need to be permuted in the same way, i.e. $Q_A=P_x$. Also, since the rows of A are permuted, the corresponding rows of y need to be permuted in the same way, i.e. $P_A=P_y$. Similarly, if x (or y) is reordered, the columns of A (or rows of A) have to be reordered, respectively. In short, x is inter-dependent with the columns of A, and y is inter-dependent with the rows of A. For arrays inter-dependent with each other, the same permutation matrix is used for reordering. How to identify inter-dependent arrays is described in Appendix A.2.

4.2.2 A Code Generation Scheme with Reordering

The significance of distributivity and inter-dependence is that they enable reordering within an arbitrary piece of code without changing its semantics. Intuitively, if a reordering R is distributive over all the expressions in a region of code, we can insert code before that region to reorder the arrays that are inputs to that code region. Likewise, at the end of the code region, inverse reordering is applied to the arrays that are outputs of the code region and are inter-dependent with the inputs, so as to restore the original semantics of the code.

[4] For example, from Equation 1, we have $P_A^{\mathsf{T}}\cdot R(A)\cdot Q_A=A$. The left side of this equation tells how to recover the original matrix A from a reordered matrix $R(A)$.

THEOREM 4.1 (COLLECTIVE REORDERING). *Given a reordering R, if R is distributive over every expression in an arbitrary piece of code except for array element accesses, then it can be applied to the code in the following way, without changing its semantics:*

Action 1 *At each entry of the code, reorder every array that is live into the code at that entry. Let S be the set of arrays that are inter-dependent with any of these reordered arrays.*

Action 2 *For every element access to an array in S, replace the indices of the access with new indices in the way shown in Appendix A.1.*

Action 3 *At each exit of the code, inversely reorder every array that is in S and is live out of the code.*

For example, in the PCG code in Figure 3a, consider the loop in lines 8–21. Reordering is distributive over every expression in this loop. Usually, the program point right before the loop is regarded as an entry to the loop. However, as we explained in Section 3, considering the fact that there are multiple kernels in the loop that may benefit from reordering, but each might prefer a different reordering, we have to choose one kernel to decide a unique reordering for the loop. Therefore, for the purpose of reordering, the program point right before the decider should be treated as the entry to the loop. When executed, this decider will determine if it is beneficial to perform reordering, and if so, the decider will reorder its input arrays, and consequently, its output array as well. For the other live, unreordered arrays at that entry, the compiler inserts code at the program point after the decider to reorder them explicitly. That accomplishes Action 1.

In this particular example of Figure 3a, we pick the forward triangular solver at line 17, $L\backslash r$ (i.e. `fwdTriSolve`), as the decider of reordering. The loop is viewed to have 1 entry, which is the program point right before the decider (i.e. before line 17), and 1 exit, the program point right after the loop (i.e. after line 21). Since L, r, z, A, x, and p are live at that entry, we need to reorder them there. This is achieved partly by the decider function: L and r are reordered inside the decider function, and z is reordered as a natural consequence of that. After that, A, x, and p are explicitly reordered by a compiler-inserted call to *reorder* (See line III in Figure 3b), a routine in the wrapper interface, as explained before in Section 3. This finishes Action 1. There is no array element access in the loop, and thus Action 2 is unnecessary. For Action 3, since x is an inter-dependent array with the reordered arrays, and is live out at the exit, we inversely reorder it there (See line IV in Figure 3b). A proof of the theorem 4.1 is left to Appendix A.3.

5. COMPILER-LIBRARY INTERACTION

In Sparso, the compiler and libraries interact through context. Context is stored in RCT and MPT, which are shared between the compiler and a wrapper interface around existing libraries such as Intel MKL (recall Figure 1). When the compiler sees a sparse-matrix operation f, it replaces f with a call to its wrapper interface. The compiler passes additional parameters to the wrapper interface for communicating context. The context allows the wrapper to apply various optimizations such as dispatching to a version of f that follows a specialized code path.

Table 3 show examples on how compiler and library can collaboratively optimize sparse linear algebra operations by communicating context. Here, we explain two additional examples in more details:

Example 1. memoizing storage format conversion: Assume that f prefers a certain matrix storage format (e.g., SpMV

Table 3: Examples of matrix properties and relations discovered by the compiler that can be used for optimizing sparse linear algebra operations.

Operation	Matrix properties	Implementation in the wrapper interface of libraries	Applications
	Default	Call SpMV in CSC.	
SpMV $A \cdot x$	isConstantStruct(A)	Convert A to CSR, save it as run-time context. Call SpMV in CSR thereafter.	
(Assume A is in CSC,	isSymmetric(A)	Call SpMV in CSR as if A is in CSR.	PCG, Adiabatic
the default format in Julia)	isUnweighted(A)	Call SpMV optimized for unweighted matrices.	Adiabatic, PageRank
	$B = A^{\intercal}$	Call SpMV in CSR with B.	L-BFGS
	Default	Call inspector-executor pair every time	
fwd/bwdTriSolve(L, x)	isConstantStruct(L)	Save inspection result (a TDG) as run-time context and reuse thereafter.	PCG, IPM
	$S_L = S_{\text{lowerTriangleOf}(A)}$	Reuse the TDG of A, if available.	PCG
	Default	Sparse LU decomposition + triangular solves	
$x = A \backslash b$ (solve $A \cdot x = b$)	isConstantStruct(A)	Save the inspection result of LU decomposition and reuse.	IPM
	isTriangular(A)	Call triangular solve.	PCG
$A = f(...)$ (a function	Default	Allocate space for A every time.	
generating a sparse matrix)	isConstantStruct(A) $\wedge$ hasDedicatedSpace(A)	Allocate space for A, save it as run-time context, and reuse thereafter.	IPM

Note:
isConstantStruct(A): A is constant in structure.
isTriangular(A): A is triangular.
hasDedicatedSpace(A): A has a pre-allocated space for its exclusive use.

prefers CSR to CSC for efficient parallelization). The wrapper function of f can first check if the run-time context in MPT already has a preferred format. If not, the wrapper may convert the input matrix from its current format to the preferred, and memoize the new format in MPT. The compiler also provides context information such as if the matrix has constant structure so that the wrapper function can tell if the conversion overhead can be amortized. Finally, the wrapper invokes an existing library routine for f.

Example 2. collective reordering: Assume that f is chosen by the compiler as the decider of reordering that potentially benefits from reordering. When first called, the wrapper function of f generates a permutation that optimizes the locality for f (e.g., RCM for SpMV and level-set ordering for triangular solvers [44]), reorders the input matrix using the permutation, saves the permutation in RCT as a run-time context, and marks a flag to record that a permutation has been created. Later, Sparso-generated code, `reorder` and `inverse_reorder`, checks the flag and reorders other inter-dependent arrays as in lines III and IV of Figure 3b.

6. A SPARSO IMPLEMENTATION IN JULIA

We have implemented the Sparso framework as a package of Julia, a new scripting language for technical computing [4]. In the current implementation, user specifies which function to optimize. Then, Sparso applies context-driven optimizations only to the loops in the function, as the loops usually dominate the execution time of the function. However, this is a specific implementation choice. In general, our approach can be applied to an arbitrary code region, including both loops and functions.

The compiler analyses in Section 4 are static, thus sometimes it can be difficult or impossible for the compiler to discover certain matrix properties, before actually looking at concrete input matrices at run-time. To address this situation, Sparso allows annotations in a user code. In our experiments with the 6 algorithms in Table 1, user annotations are needed only in a few places, and only 3 kinds of annotations are needed: isSymmetric, isUnweighted, and hasDedicatedSpace. The meaning of the first two annotations has been introduced before in Table 2. The other annotation, hasDedicatedSpace(x), tells the compiler that x has been pre-allocated a space, and that space is not shared with any other variable. Thus, for an expression like $x = f(...)$ inside the loop, the compiler will generate a call to routine f that reuses the allocated space for output in every loop iteration.

7. EVALUATION

We evaluate the performance of Sparso framework on a Haswell generation of Intel Xeon machine, with the details listed in Table 4. The peak memory bandwidth of the machine is measured by the STREAM benchmark [38], which is often the limiting factor of sparse matrix operations' performance due to their low arithmetic intensity [26, 61].

Our experiments use 6 representative sparse linear algebra algorithms listed in Table 1. Not only are these algorithms important in their own right, but also they capture common compute patterns of sparse linear algebra in various domains. We use double precision for floating point numbers. We use various sparse matrices, which is important for evaluating the performance of sparse linear algebra operations, as they heavily depend on specific sparsity structures: e.g., from the University of Florida matrix collection [14], we use all the symmetric positive definite matrices with more than 50 MB for `PCG`, and all the social network and road network matrices with more than 5 MB for `PageRank`.

We test each application with 4 different optimization configurations:

1. `Julia-as-is`: The applications are run in the original Julia, with neither our compiler nor libraries. Note that key linear algebra operations in Julia already call optimized C/Fortran library routines in LAPACK [1] and SuiteSparse [9].
2. `Baseline` (`Call-repl`): We replace all time-consuming linear algebra operations in Julia with calls to Intel MKL [30] and SpMP [43] library routines. Since MKL and SpMP are generally faster than the open source LAPACK and SuiteSparse on the tested machine, we obtain a reasonably high-performance baseline for comparison. Note that `Baseline` runs the library routines already in parallel with OpenMP.
3. `+Matrix-properties`: In addition to `Call-repl`, enable

Table 4: Evaluation Settings

Processor	14-core Xeon E5-2697 v3 @ 2.6 GHz 35MB on-chip L3$
Memory	64 GB DDR with 54 GB/s peak bandwidth
Julia	Version 0.4.6
Libraries	MKL 13.0 SpMP compiled with Intel compiler 15.0.3
Parallelization	OpenMP with options `OMP_NUM_THREADS=14` and `KMP_AFFINITY=granularity=fine,compact,1` (sparse matrix computations generally perform the best with 1 thread per core)

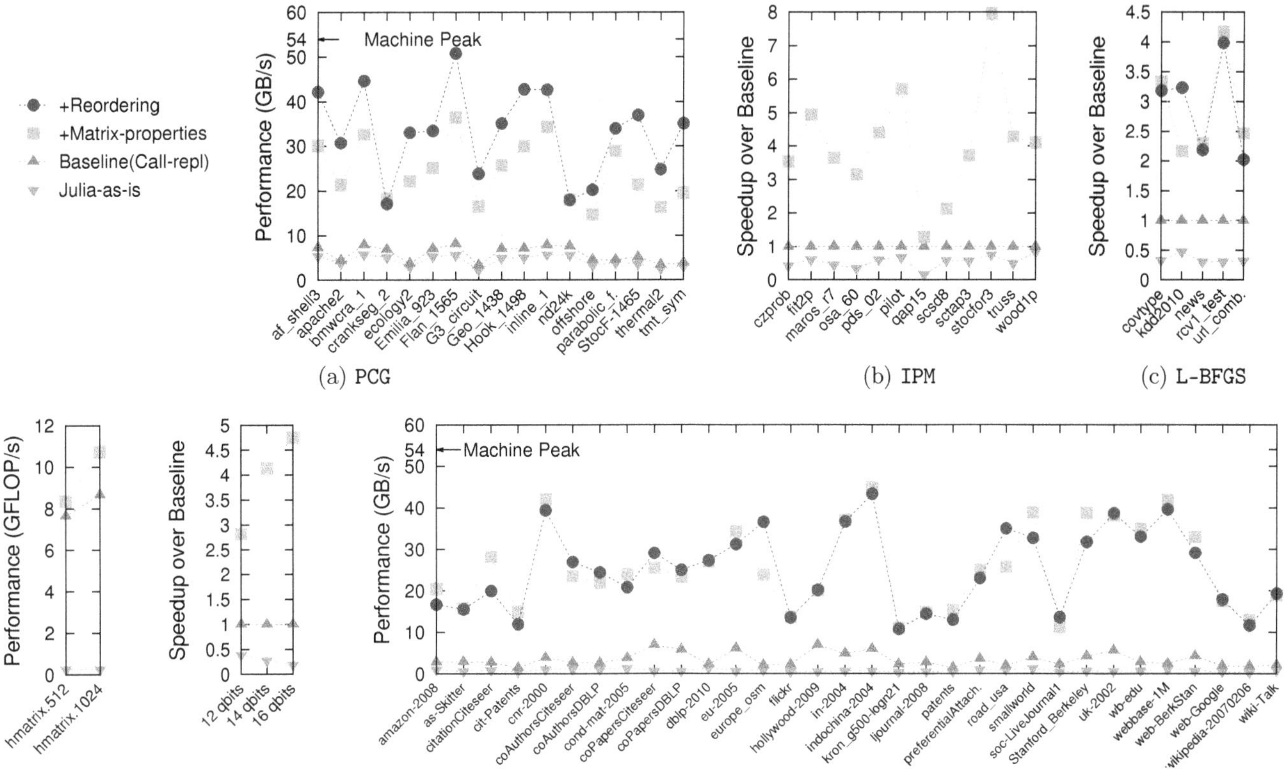

(a) PCG (b) IPM (c) L-BFGS

(d) CoSp2 (e) Adiabatic (f) PageRank

Figure 4: Performance of Sparso with different optimization options.

all the context-driven optimizations *except* collective reordering.

4. `+Reordering`: In addition to `+Matrix-properties`, enable collective reordering as well.

7.1 Overall Performance

Figure 4 shows the performance of the 6 applications with various input matrices. We report the results following a common practice in the high performance computing community. For memory bandwidth-bound applications, including `PCG` (only up to 1 floating-point operation per 6 bytes) and `PageRank` (only up to 1 floating-point operation per 2 bytes), we report performance in GB/s and also compare against the machine peak bandwidth; for the other applications that are neither memory- nor computation-bound, we report GFlop/s when it can be easily computed (`CoSP2`), or otherwise report the relative speedups over `Baseline` (`IPM`, `L_BFGS`, and `Adiabatic`).

With all Sparso optimizations enabled (`+Reordering`), significant speedups are observed for most test cases. The average (harmonic mean) speedups over `Baseline` across all inputs are 5.6×, 3.7×, 2.8×, 1.2×, 3.8×, and 17×, for `PCG`, `IPM`, `L-BFGS`, `CoSp2`, `Adiabatic`, and `PageRank`, respectively.

Noticeably, in `PCG` and `PageRank`, the performance of `+Reordering` often closely approaches the peak capability provided by the evaluated hardware. The performance of `PCG` and `PageRank` is bound by the memory bandwidth, and we utilize on average 67% and 50% of the peak memory bandwidth, respectively. This more-than 50% bandwidth efficiency in sparse matrix computations is hard to achieve even by highly optimized C/C++ implementations, as demonstrated by recent work such as [44, 45].

Comparing `Julia-as-is` and `Baseline`, we observe that *optimized library routines alone, without context information, provide limited speedups.* This result also quantitatively demonstrates the limitation of library-only optimizations for sparse matrix applications — the cost of optimization setup such as matrix inspection cannot be effectively amortized without context information. Even though key routines in `Julia-as-is` and `Baseline` are already parallelized, speedups from parallelization are quite limited. For example, `PCG` and `IPM` obtain only 1.4× and 1.5× speedups by using 14 cores on average, respectively, mainly because the inspection overhead for parallelization is not amortized. On the other hand, with context-driven optimizations, average parallelization speedups over `Julia-as-is` are 7.6× and 5.6×, respectively.

Collective reordering (`+Reordering` vs. `+Matrix-properties`) contributes significant speedups to `PCG`, making it approaching the peak capability of the hardware in several matrices, but exhibits marginal impact in `PageRank`, as some social network matrices used by `PageRank` are already reordered. From the software engineering point of view, Sparso allows programmers to quickly try out reordering without worrying about correctness and restructuring the code.

7.2 Performance of Individual Applications

PCG: Figure 4a shows the performance of `PCG` with incomplete LU with zero fill-ins pre-conditioner until it reaches 10^{-7} relative residual. The evaluated `PCG` implementation is similar to high performance conjugate gradient (HPCG)[5], a recently proposed benchmark for ranking supercomputers [18], and captures characteristics of a wide range of iterative sparse linear solvers

[5]One difference is that our PCG implementation does not use multi-grid method, but key context-driven optimizations are similar.

such as GMRES [53] and AMG [27]. We utilize on average 67% of the machine peak bandwidth, when all optimizations are applied (denoted as `+Reordering`). This corresponds to on average 5.6× higher performance than `Baseline`, and 7.6× higher performance than `Julia-as-is`.

The bulk of speedup comes from exploiting context information. Based on the matrix properties, we apply the following three optimizations: (1) We reuse the result of inspection, a task dependency graph, across the invocations of forward triangular solver. Similar reuse happens for backward triangular solver as well[6]. (2) We dispatch the Julia expression $A \cdot p$ to the SpMV implementation in the SpMP library with A in CSR format, utilizing the property that matrix A is symmetric in value, and thus avoiding unnecessary format conversion (parallel SpMV performs better with CSR than CSC, the default Julia representation). (3) We reorder the matrices and related vectors so that, in the triangular solvers, each thread accesses matrix rows in contiguous manner, reducing false sharing and improving spatial locality.

Relatively small speedups in `Baseline` compared to `Julia-as-is` demonstrates that invoking optimized library kernels without context information is insufficient. For example, even with an efficient parallel sparse triangular solver, the cost of constructing a task dependency graph by inspecting the input matrix every time negates most of parallelization speedups.

IPM: Figure 4b shows the performance of interior-point method for optimizing linear programming problems until it reaches 10^{-7} relative residual. Sparso with context-sensitive optimizations (`+Matrix-properties`) obtains on average 3.7× speedup over `Baseline`, and 5.6× speedup over `Julia-as-is`. In both `Baseline` and `+Matrix-properties`, the SpGEMM used in `IPM` is replaced with a call to an SpGEMM implementation in SpMP library that follows optimizations described in a recent work [46]. The sparse direct solver used in `IPM` is also replaced with a call to MKL PARDISO [30]. In `+Matrix-properties`, the compiler discovers that the output matrix of SpGEMM has a constant structure, which allows reusing the memory allocated for the output matrix. We also reuse the inspection result of the sparse direct solver by exploiting that the input matrices have constant structures. As a result of eliminating most of the redundancies in other parts of `IPM` computation, `+Matrix-properties` spends on average more than 45% of total time in the execution step of MKL sparse direct solver, similar to the manually optimized IPM implementation presented in [55].

L-BFGS: Figure 4c shows the performance of limited-memory Broyden-Fletcher-Goldfarb-Shanno [35], a quasi-Newton optimization method popular for parameter estimation in machine learning, until it reaches 10^{-10} relative residual. `L-BFGS` spends significant time in two SpMV calls: $A^\intercal \cdot x$ and $A \cdot x$. In `+Matrix-properties`, by utilizing the relationship between matrices (i.e. the first call already provides matrix A's transpose in CSC format, which is equivalent to matrix A in CSR format), the second call can be performed directly in CSR without the additional overhead of format conversion.

Compared to `+Matrix-properties`, collective reordering further speeds up `L-BFGS` by about 1.5× with one matrix, and has no significant slowdown with the other matrices. In contrast to `PCG` and `PageRank` where matrices are square, the sparse matrices handled by collective reordering in `L-BFGS` are rectangular: rows correspond to observations and columns correspond to features.

CoSP2: Sparso achieves a 1.1× speedup for `hmatrix.512`, and a 1.2× speedup for the larger `hmatrix.1024` matrix over `Baseline`, which are 31× and 42× speedup over `Julia-as-is`. `CoSP2` spends most of its time in $X \cdot X^\intercal$, an SpGEMM operation. In `Baseline` and `+Matrix-properties`, we replace the SpGEMM operation with an implementation that follows the optimizations described in [46]. `+Matrix-properties` exploits the fact discovered by the compiler that X stays symmetric, thus avoids transposing X. Sparso's 8.4 and 11 GFlop/s CoSP2 performance in double precision is comparable to that of highly optimized SpGEMM implementation in [46] that ranges up to 18 GFlop/s in single precision. Sparso actually outperforms the C implementation from [41] by 1.4 and 1.3× for `hmatrix.512` and `hmatrix.1024`, respectively, due to its more efficient SpGEMM implementation.

Adiabatic: Figure 4e shows the performance of validating annealing speed of adiabatic quantum computation [23] with varying number of qbits. Such validation in classical computation is necessary because adiabatic quantum computation relies on appropriate annealing speed. `Adiabatic` spends a significant fraction of its time in Lanczos algorithm that represents a wide range of iterative eigenvalue solvers and used in other scientific problems such as solving Schrödinger's equation [52]. In `+Matrix-properties`, a matrix is annotated as unweighted, so that we can use an SpMV implementation in the SpMP library specialized for unweighted matrices in CSR. In this version of SpMV, all non-zeros are assumed to be 1, so we skip reading non-zero values, saving memory bandwidth.

PageRank: Figure 4f shows the performance of running 100 iterations of PageRank. The evaluated matrices are mostly social network graphs and a few road network graphs. We realize on average 50% bandwidth efficiency when all optimizations are applied (denoted as `+Reordering`). This corresponds to on average 17× speedup over `Baseline`, and 31× speedup over `Julia-as-is`. Sparso's PageRank performance is also comparable to that of manually optimized implementation reported in [54]. In `+Matrix-properties`, compiler discovers that a matrix is unweighted so that we can use a specialized SpMV in SpMP.

8. RELATED WORK

This section compares Sparso with related work in four categories: sparse linear algebra libraries, frameworks for easier programming of sparse matrix computation, data reordering, and matrix property discovery.

8.1 High-performance Sparse Linear Algebra Libraries

There are many libraries for sparse matrix computations [2, 7, 12, 13, 19, 21, 22, 24, 28, 29, 32, 33, 36, 40, 43, 59]. Basic interfaces provided by these libraries are easy to use but do not allow context-driven optimizations. As an advanced interface, libraries can expose sub-steps of context-driven optimizations for higher performance, but they are not easy to be used by average programmers. For example, a triangular solver can have a 2-step interface with one function for inspection and another for execution as in the latest version of Intel MKL library. However, effectively using such advanced interface requires expertise. This explains why MKL has not provided the inspector-executor interface until very recently [29]. Sparso optimizations enable non-expert programmers to take advantage of such advanced library features without even knowing their existence.

Another example of libraries with such advanced interface is OSKI [59] that can auto-tune sparse matrix kernels, including

[6]As explained in Section 6, the current implementation of the Sparso framework applies `+Matrix-properties` and `+Reordering` to loops only. So for PCG, the current implementation generates optimized code similar to Figure 3b, except that `+Matrix-properties` and `+Reordering` are applied only to the loop between lines 8–21, which contains the forward and backward triangular solver. This still keeps the essence of our approach as well as the performance of the application, as the loop dominates the execution time of PCG.

SpMV and sparse triangular solver. In fact, OSKI can be a good target library of Sparso because it provides various optimization opportunities like matrix storage format selection that can be taken advantage by Sparso. Sparso can complement OSKI by hiding the complexities associated with the additional parameters for auto-tuning and by providing context that spans multiple kernels and matrices.

8.2 Frameworks for Easier Programming of Sparse Matrix Computation

There have been many efforts to alleviate programming burden in sparse matrix computation, automatically or with programmer intervention [3, 5, 17, 47, 48, 56–58]. They often focus on optimizing individual sparse matrix kernels, and cannot optimize across different kernels and different matrices. In more sophisticated approaches, a compiler generates an inspector/executor and hoists the inspector out of a loop [3, 5, 17, 47, 48, 56–58].

In comparison, Sparso reasons about higher level constructs like matrices and vectors, and deduces matrix properties useful for performance optimizations using basic rules of sparse linear algebra (recall Table 2 for example). The matrix properties found are useful contextual information that can be communicated with the libraries, allowing them to follow the path optimized best for the given context (recall Table 3 for example).

8.3 Data Reordering

Given a loop accessing a matrix, either the matrix can be reordered (*data reordering*) or loop iterations can be reordered (*iteration reordering*) to achieve better spatial or temporal locality. This paper focuses on data reordering. In typical linear algebra libraries, data reordering routines find a permutation for a specific kernel invoked with a specific matrix [2, 28, 43]. As in MKL and OSKI, it is often programmers' responsibility to compose with other kernels and propagate the reordering to inter-dependent arrays. Sparso automatically handles these composability issues with collective reordering.

Iteration reordering [17, 57] is a compiler transformation that reorders the iterations of a loop accessing a sparse matrix, so as to improve temporal locality. Compared to data reordering, composability can be a lesser concern because iteration reordering often does not change the data layout that may affect other parts of the program. However, changing the data layout together sometimes results in higher performance due to better spatial locality [45].

8.4 Matrix Property Discovery

The constant size, constant value, and constant structure analyses are extensions of Kildall's classic constant propagation algorithm [31, 60], similar to the static size inference in Falcon [15] and symbolic constant propagation [10].

9. CONCLUSION AND FUTURE WORK

Sparse matrix applications are pervasive, yet difficult to optimize. We present Sparso, a new framework to speed them up by automating experts' manual context-driven optimizations. The key idea is to use context information to drive optimizations across kernels and matrices transparently, providing both performance *and* productivity. Sparso is evaluated with several representative sparse linear algebra algorithms, obtaining performance comparable to the limit bound by machine peak bandwidth for PCG and PageRank, which is hard to achieve even by highly optimized C/C++ implementations. Sparso is open-sourced at https://github.com/IntelLabs/Sparso.git.

We can extend the system to handle contexts that are not constant, but are changing slowly. We can also automate more context-driven optimizations, and port Sparso to other languages like Python and R.

Acknowledgments

We appreciate the valuable feedback of the anonymous reviewers, Jed Brown, Karl Rupp, Brian Lewis, Lindsey Kuper, Michelle Strout, Xipeng Shen, and Jiwon Seo, and the strong support from Tatiana Shpeisman, Christopher Hughes, Gilles Pokam, Rajkishore Barik, Pradeep Dubey, Paul Petersen, Youfeng Wu, and Geoff Lowney.

References

[1] E. Anderson, Z. Bai, C. Bischof, S. Blackford, J. Demmel, J. Dongarra, J. Du Croz, A. Greenbaum, S. Hammarling, A. McKenney, and D. Sorensen. *LAPACK Users' Guide*. Society for Industrial and Applied Mathematics, Philadelphia, PA, third edition, 1999.

[2] S. Balay, W. D. Gropp, L. C. McInnes, and B. F. Smith. Efficient Management of Parallelism in Object Oriented Numerical Software Libraries. In E. Arge, A. M. Bruaset, and H. P. Langtangen, editors, *Modern Software Tools in Scientific Computing*, pages 163–202. Birkhäuser Press, 1997.

[3] S. Benkner. VFC: The Vienna Fortran Compiler. *Scientific Programming*, 7(1):67–81, Jan. 1999.

[4] J. Bezanson, S. Karpinski, V. B. Shah, and A. Edelman. Julia: A Fast Dynamic Language for Technical Computing. *Computing Research Repository*, abs/1209.5145, 2012.

[5] T. Brandes and F. Zimmermann. Adaptor — A Transformation Tool for HPF Programs. In *Programming Environments for Massively Parallel Distributed Systems: Working Conference of the IFIP WG 10.3*, pages 91–96. Birkhäuser Basel, 1994.

[6] S. Brin and L. Page. The Anatomy of a Large-scale Hypertextual Web Search Engine. In *Proceedings of the Seventh International Conference on World Wide Web*, WWW7, pages 107–117. Elsevier Science Publishers B. V., 1998.

[7] A. Buluç and J. R. Gilbert. The Combinatorial BLAS: Design, Implementation, and Applications. *International Journal of High Performance Computing Applications*, 25(4):496–509, Nov. 2011.

[8] C.-C. Chang and C.-J. Lin. LIBSVM: A Library for Support Vector Machines. *ACM Transactions on Intelligent Systems and Technology*, 2(3):27:1–27:27, May 2011.

[9] Y. Chen, T. A. Davis, W. W. Hager, and S. Rajamanickam. Algorithm 887: CHOLMOD, Supernodal Sparse Cholesky Factorization and Update/Downdate. *ACM Transactions on Mathematical Software (TOMS)*, 35(3):22:1–22:14, Oct. 2008.

[10] C. P. Colby. *Semantics-based Program Analysis via Symbolic Composition of Transfer Relations*. PhD thesis, Carnegie Mellon University, 1996. AAI9813822.

[11] E. Cuthill and J. McKee. Reducing the Bandwidth of Sparse Symmetric Matrices. In *Proceedings of the 1969 24th National Conference*, pages 157–172. ACM, 1969.

[12] S. Dalton, N. Bell, L. Olson, and M. Garland. Cusp: Generic Parallel Algorithms for Sparse Matrix and Graph Computations. http://cusplibrary.github.io, 2014. Version 0.5.0.

[13] T. A. Davis. *Direct Methods for Sparse Linear Systems (Fundamentals of Algorithms 2)*. Society for Industrial and Applied Mathematics, 2006.

[14] T. A. Davis and Y. Hu. The University of Florida Sparse Matrix Collection. *ACM Transactions on Mathematical Software (TOMS)*, 38(1):1:1–1:25, Dec. 2011.

[15] L. De Rose and D. Padua. Techniques for the Translation of MATLAB Programs into Fortran 90. *ACM Transactions on Programming Languages and Systems*, 21(2):286–323, Mar. 1999.

[16] L. A. De Rose. *Compiler Techniques for Matlab Programs*. PhD thesis, University of Illinois at Urbana-Champaign, 1996. AAI9712420.

[17] C. Ding and K. Kennedy. Improving Cache Performance in Dynamic Applications Through Data and Computation Reorganization at Run Time. In *Proceedings of the ACM SIGPLAN conference on Programming Language Design and Implementation (PLDI)*, pages 229–241, 1999.

[18] J. Dongarra and M. A. Heroux. Toward a New Metric for Ranking High Performance Computing Systems. Technical Report 4744, Sandia National Laboratories, 2013.

[19] J. Dongarra, A. Lumsdaine, X. Niu, R. Pozo, and K. Remington. LAPACK Working Note 74: A Sparse Matrix Library in C++ for High Performance Architectures. Technical Report CS-94-236, University of Tennessee, 1994.

[20] I. S. Duff. On Algorithms for Obtaining a Maximum Transversal. *ACM Transactions on Mathematical Software (TOMS)*, 7(3):315–330, 1981.

[21] I. S. Duff, M. A. Heroux, and R. Pozo. An Overview of the Sparse Basic Linear Algebra Subprograms: The New Standard from the BLAS Technical Forum. *ACM Transactions on Mathematical Software (TOMS)*, 28(2):239–267, June 2002.

[22] R. D. Falgout, J. E. Jones, and U. M. Yang. Pursuing Scalability for Hypre's Conceptual Interfaces. *ACM Transactions on Mathematical Software (TOMS)*, 31(3):326–350, Sept. 2005.

[23] E. Farhi, J. Goldstone, S. Gutmann, and M. Sipser. Quantum Computation by Adiabatic Evolution. Technical Report MIT-CTP-2936, Massachusetts Institute of Technology, 2000.

[24] S. Filippone and M. Colajanni. PSBLAS: A Library for Parallel Linear Algebra Computation on Sparse Matrices. *ACM Transactions on Mathematical Software (TOMS)*, 26(4):527–550, 2000.

[25] J. R. Gilbert, C. Moler, and R. Schreiber. Sparse Matrices in MATLAB: Design and Implementation. *SIAM Journal on Matrix Analysis and Applications*, 13(1):333–356, 1992.

[26] W. D. Gropp, D. K. Kaushik, D. E. Keyes, and B. F. Smith. Towards Realistic Performance Bounds for Implicit CFD Codes. In *Parallel Computational Fluid Dynamics: towards Teraflops, Optimization, and Novel Formulations*, pages 241–248. Elsevier, 1999.

[27] V. E. Henson and U. M. Yang. BoomerAMG: a Parallel Algebraic Multigrid Solver and Preconditioner. *Applied Numerical Mathematics*, 41:155–177, 2000.

[28] M. A. Heroux, R. A. Bartlett, V. E. Howle, R. J. Hoekstra, J. J. Hu, T. G. Kolda, R. B. Lehoucq, K. R. Long, R. P. Pawlowski, E. T. Phipps, A. G. Salinger, H. K. Thornquist, R. S. Tuminaro, J. M. Willenbring, A. Williams, and K. S. Stanley. An Overview of the Trilinos Project. *ACM Transactions on Mathematical Software (TOMS)*, 31(3):397–423, Sept. 2005.

[29] Intel® . Math Kernel Library Inspector-executor Sparse BLAS Routines. https://software.intel.com/sites/default/files/managed/0a/81/Documentation_inspector_executor_sparse_blas_mkl113b.pdf, 2015.

[30] Intel® . MKL PARDISO - Parallel Direct Sparse Solver Interface. https://software.intel.com/en-us/node/470282, 2015.

[31] G. A. Kildall. A Unified Approach to Global Program Optimization. In *Proceedings of ACM SIGACT-SIGPLAN Symposium on Principles of Programming Languages (POPL)*, pages 194–206, 1973.

[32] A. R. Krommer. Parallel Sparse Matrix Computations in the Industrial Strength PINEAPL Library. In *Proceedings of the 4th International Workshop on Applied Parallel Computing, Large Scale Scientific and Industrial Problems*, pages 281–285. Springer-Verlag, 1998.

[33] X. S. Li. An Overview of SuperLU: Algorithms, Implementation, and User Interface. *ACM Transactions on Mathematical Software (TOMS)*, 31(3):302–325, 2005.

[34] M. Lichman. UCI Machine Learning Repository. http://archive.ics.uci.edu/ml, 2013.

[35] D. C. Liu and J. Nocedal. On the Limited Memory BFGS Method for Large Scale Optimization. *Mathematical Programming*, 45(1), 1989.

[36] A. Lugowski, A. Buluc, J. Gilbert, and S. Reinhardt. Scalable complex graph analysis with the knowledge discovery toolbox. In *Proceedings of the IEEE International Conference on Acoustics, Speech and Signal Processing (ICASSP)*, pages 5345–5348, March 2012.

[37] I. J. Lustig and E. Rothberg. Gigaflops in Linear Programming. *Operations Research Letters*, 18(4):157–165, Feb. 1996.

[38] J. D. McCalpin. Memory Bandwidth and Machine Balance in Current High Performance Computers. *IEEE Computer Society Technical Committee on Computer Architecture (TCCA) Newsletter*, pages 19–25, Dec. 1995.

[39] R. Mirchandaney, J. H. Saltz, R. M. Smith, D. M. Nico, and K. Crowley. Principles of Runtime Support for Parallel Processors. In *Proceedings of the International Conference on Supercomputing (ICS)*, pages 140–152. ACM, 1988.

[40] M. Naumov. Incomplete-LU and Cholesky Preconditioned Iterative Methods Using cuSPARSE and cuBLAS. https://developer.nvidia.com/cusparse.

[41] A. M. Niklasson. Expansion Algorithm for the Density Matrix. *Physical Review B*, 66(15):155115, Oct. 2002.

[42] P. K. S. Norman E. Gibbs, William G. Poole. An Algorithm for Reducing the Bandwidth and Profile of a Sparse Matrix. *SIAM Journal on Numerical Analysis*, 13(2):236–250, 1976.

[43] J. Park. Sparse Matrix Preprocessing Library. https://github.com/IntelLabs/SpMP.

[44] J. Park, M. Smelyanskiy, N. Sundaram, and P. Dubey. Sparsifying Synchronization for High-Performance Shared-Memory Sparse Triangular Solver. In *Proceedings of International Supercomputing Conference (ISC)*, pages 124–140. Springer International Publishing, 2014.

[45] J. Park, M. Smelyanskiy, K. Vaidyanathan, A. Heinecke, D. D. Kalamkar, X. Liu, M. M. A. Patwary, Y. Lu, and P. Dubey. Efficient Shared-memory Implementation of High-performance Conjugate Gradient Benchmark and Its Application to Unstructured Matrices. In *Proceedings of the International Conference for High Performance Computing, Networking, Storage and Analysis (SC)*, pages 945–955, 2014.

[46] M. M. A. Patwary, N. R. Satish, N. Sundaram, J. Park, M. J. Anderson, S. G. Vadlamudi, D. Das, S. G. Pudov, V. O. Pirogov, and P. Dubey. Parallel Efficient Sparse Matrix-Matrix Multiplication on Multicore Platforms. In *Proceedings of International Supercomputing Conference (ISC)*, pages 48–57. Springer International Publishing, 2015.

[47] R. Ponnusamy, J. Saltz, and A. Choudhary. Runtime Compilation Techniques for Data Partitioning and Communication Schedule Reuse. In *Proceedings of the International Conference for High Performance Computing, Networking, Storage and Analysis (SC)*, pages 361–370. ACM, 1993.

[48] W. Pugh and T. Shpeisman. SIPR: A New Framework for Generating Efficient Code for Sparse Matrix Computations. In *Proceedings of the 11th International Workshop on Languages and Compilers for Parallel Computing*, LCPC '98, pages 213–229. Springer-Verlag, 1999.

[49] L. Rauchwerger. Run-time Parallelization: Its Time Has Come. *Parallel Computing - Special issues on languages and compilers for parallel computers*, 24(3-4):527–556, May 1998.

[50] B. Recht, C. Re, S. Wright, and F. Niu. Hogwild: A Lock-Free Approach to Parallelizing Stochastic Gradient Descent. In *Proceedings of Advances in Neural Information Processing Systems (NIPS)*, pages 693–701. Curran Associates, Inc., 2011.

[51] J. K. Reid and J. A. Scott. Reducing the Total Bandwidth of a Sparse Unsymmetric Matrix. *SIAM Journal on Matrix Analysis and Applications*, 28(3):805–821, Aug. 2006.

[52] Y. Saad. *Numerical Method for Large Eigenvalue Problems.* Society for Industrial and Applied Mathematics, 2011.

[53] Y. Saad and M. H. Schultz. GMRES: A Generalized Minimal Residual Algorithm for Solving Nonsymmetric Linear Systems. *SIAM Journal on Scientific and Statistical Computing*, 7(3):856–869, July 1986.

[54] N. Satish, N. Sundaram, M. M. A. Patwary, J. Seo, J. Park, M. A. Hassaan, S. Sengupta, Z. Yin, and P. Dubey. Navigating the Maze of Graph Analytics Frameworks Using Massive Graph Datasets. In *Proceedings of the 2014 ACM SIGMOD International Conference on Management of Data*, SIGMOD '14, pages 979–990. ACM, 2014.

[55] M. Smelyanskiy, V. W. Lee, D. Kim, A. D. Nguyen, and P. Dubey. Scaling Performance of Interior-point Method on Large-scale Chip Multiprocessor System. In *Proceedings of the International Conference for High Performance Computing, Networking, Storage and Analysis (SC)*, pages 22:1–22:11. ACM, 2007.

[56] M. M. Strout, G. Georg, and C. Olschanowsky. Set and Relation Manipulation for the Sparse Polyhedral Framework. In *Proceedings of Languages and Compilers for Parallel Computing: 25th International Workshop, LCPC, Tokyo, Japan, September 11-13, Revised Selected Papers*, pages 61–75. Springer Berlin Heidelberg, 2013.

[57] M. M. Strout, A. LaMielle, L. Carter, J. Ferrante, B. Kreaseck, and C. Olschanowsky. An Approach for Code Generation in the Sparse Polyhedral Framework. Technical Report CS-13-109, Colorado State University, December 2013.

[58] A. Venkat, M. Hall, and M. Strout. Loop and Data Transformations for Sparse Matrix Code. In *Proceedings of the ACM SIGPLAN conference on Programming Language Design and Implementation (PLDI)*, pages 521–532, 2015.

[59] R. Vuduc, J. W. Demmel, and K. A. Yelick. OSKI: A Library of Automatically Tuned Sparse Matrix Kernels. *Journal of Physics: Conference Series*, 16(1):521, 2005.

[60] M. N. Wegman and F. K. Zadeck. Constant Propagation with Conditional Branches. *ACM Transactions on Programming Languages and Systems*, 13(2):181–210, Apr. 1991.

[61] S. Williams, A. Waterman, and D. Patterson. Roofline: An Insightful Visual Performance Model for Multicore Architectures. *Communications of the ACM*, 52(4):65–76, Apr. 2009.

A. APPENDIX

A.1 Distributivity and Inter-dependence

By definition, reordering R is distributive over any function whose inputs and output are all scalars, such as `if(condition)` or `goto(label)`, treating both as accepting a scalar input and returning the same scalar as output. Similar conclusion can be extended to higher-level language constructs like loops (`for`, `while`, etc.).

However, there are functions over which reordering is not distributive:

Case 1. Array element accesses: Reordering changes an array, but not an array index, which is a scalar. An array access $A[i,j]$ or $x[i]$, after A or x being reordered, has to be replaced with $A[i',j']$ or $x[i']$. From Equation 1 and 2, we can derive that i' and j' are such that $P_A[i',i]=1$ and $Q_A[j',j]=1$ for matrix A, and similarly, $P_x[i',i]=1$ for vector x.

Case 2. A function whose inputs are scalars but result is an array: An array creation function whose input is a size is such an example. Reordering the size has no effect, but reordering the output changes the result. Reordering is distributive over the function only when the created array is considered the same with and without reordering, i.e. reordering has

Expression	Inter-dependences	
L=ichol(A)	L_{rows}—A_{rows}	L_{cols}—A_{cols}
$r=b-A\cdot x$	r—b	r—A_{rows}
	b—A_{rows}	A_{cols}—x
$z=L\backslash r$	L_{rows}—r	L_{cols}—z
L^{T}	L_{rows}—$L^{\mathsf{T}}_{\text{cols}}$	L_{cols}—$L^{\mathsf{T}}_{\text{rows}}$
$z=L^{\mathsf{T}}\backslash z$	$L^{\mathsf{T}}_{\text{rows}}$—$z$	$L^{\mathsf{T}}_{\text{cols}}$—$z$
$p=copy(z)$	p—z	
$r^{\mathsf{T}}\cdot z$	r—z	
$Ap=A\cdot p$	Ap—A_{rows}	A_{cols}—p
$p^{\mathsf{T}}\cdot Ap$	p—Ap	
$x=x+\alpha\cdot p$	x—p	
$r=r-\alpha\cdot Ap$	r—Ap	
$p=z+(rz/old\_rz)\cdot p$	p—z	

(a) Inter-dependences for all the expressions.

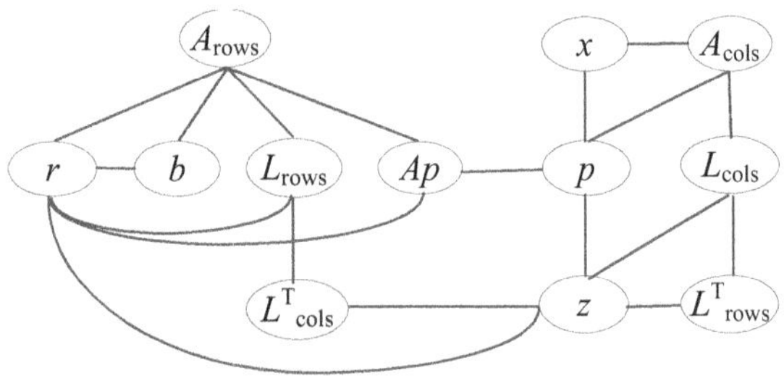

(b) Inter-dependence graph.

Figure 5: Building inter-dependences for the PCG example in Figure 3a.

no impact on the created array. This happens, for example, when the array is initialized to 0 or uninitialized.

By the contraposition of the logic in the case 2 above, we reach the following conclusion:

FACT A.1 (DISTRIBUTIVITY AND INTER-DEPENDENCE). *If reordering is distributive over a function that returns an array, then (1) the function must have at least one input that is an array and is inter-dependent with the returned array, or (2) reordering has no impact on the returned array.*

A.2 Identifying Inter-dependent Arrays

For basic operations, meta-data are required to describe the inter-dependences between their operands. Based on that, any user code can be analyzed for inter-dependent arrays: visit every expression of the code and build up the inter-dependences between the operands.

For example, consider the expression $r=b-A\cdot x$ of PCG code in Figure 3a. With the meta-data of the basic operation $=$, we know r's rows must be permuted in the same way as the rows of the right hand side $b-A\cdot x$. Let us denote the inter-dependence as

$$r \;\text{———}\; (b-A\cdot x)$$

For the same reason, we can find the following inter-dependences:

$$(b-A\cdot x) \;\text{———}\; b$$
$$(b-A\cdot x) \;\text{———}\; (A\cdot x)$$
$$(A\cdot x) \;\text{———}\; A_{\text{rows}}$$
$$A_{\text{cols}} \;\text{———}\; x$$

where A_{rows} and A_{cols} refer to the rows and columns of A, respectively. Since inter-dependence is transitive, we can remove the intermediate expressions like $(b-A\cdot x)$ from the above relations, and get the following inter-dependences between operands:

$$r \;\text{———}\; b$$
$$r \;\text{———}\; A_{\text{rows}}$$
$$b \;\text{———}\; A_{\text{rows}}$$
$$A_{\text{cols}} \;\text{———}\; x$$

Figure 5a shows all the inter-dependences for the PCG example. With them, an *inter-dependence graph* can be built (see Figure 5b), where a vertex represents a vector, a matrix's rows, or a matrix's columns, and an edge represents an inter-dependence between two vertices. All vertices in the same connected component in such a graph are inter-dependent with each other, and thus have the same permutation matrix. For this specific graph, there is only one connected component. Therefore, all vertices have the same permutation matrix. For example, both A_{rows} and A_{cols} are in the component, which means A is reordered by:

$$R(A)=P_A\cdot A\cdot P_A^{\mathsf{T}} \qquad (6)$$

This is exactly how a square matrix is usually reordered, even though our process never assumes A is square.

Note that the concrete content of a permutation matrix like P_A here is not determined by the compiler, but by the decider of reordering (a wrapper routine) at run-time. The compiler only identifies *which* arrays are inter-dependent and thus should be reordered with the same permutation matrix. The decider, when executed at run-time, constructs the concrete permutation matrix, uses the permutation matrix to reorder its input arrays, and memoizes the permutation matrix in RCT. RCT is then used by `reorder()` and `inversely_reorder()` (see Figure 3b) to reorder and inversely reorder other inter-dependent arrays.

Although this example is for PCG, which involves only square matrices, the same process can be applied to any code and rectangular matrices. For example, Sparso automatically reorders rectangular matrices in L-BFGS. The worst case complexity of the process is $O(V^2)$, where V is number of arrays in the user program.

A.3 A Proof of Theorem 4.1

Perform Actions 1 and 2 listed in Theorem 4.1 and prove Action 3 is necessary and sufficient, no matter what path the code has followed in the execution. Note that the code may contain arbitrary conditional branches, and there may be exponential number of possible execution paths.

Assume array Γ is in set S and is live out at an exit. We prove that after Actions 1 and 2, Γ at that exit must equal $R(\Gamma_0)$, where Γ_0 refers to the Γ at the same exit in the original code (with no reordering).

Case 1 Γ has never been defined during the execution of the code. Then, Γ must have been live into the code at the entry that starts the execution, reordered per Action 1.

Case 2 Γ has been defined during the execution, but reordering has no impact on it. Then, it can be considered as reordered.

Case 3 Otherwise, Γ has been defined by an expression $\Gamma = f(\Lambda, ...)$ during the execution, where Λ is an array and is inter-dependent with Γ, per Fact A.1. Apply similar reasoning to Λ. Eventually, we must arrive at either Case 1 or 2. □

B. ARTIFACT DESCRIPTION

B.1 Abstract

The artifact contains the latest version of Sparso on github. It automatically downloads the public data we have used, and produces the results data used for Figure 4.

B.2 Description

1. **Algorithm:** PCG, IPM, L-BFGS, CoSP2, Adiabatic, PageRank
2. **Program:** Julia code
3. **Compilation:** Julia 0.4.6
4. **Transformations:** call replacement, context-sensitive optimizations, and collective reordering
5. **Data set:** Public available matrix market files
6. **Run-time environment:** Ubuntu 16.04 x86-64 desktop
7. **Hardware:** 14-core Xeon E5-2697 v3 @ 2.6 GHz, 35MB on-chip L3, 64 GB DDR

8. **Output:** Execution time, GB/s, and/or GFLOP/s
9. **Experiment workflow:** Install Sparso and related libraries; run the test scripts; observe the results
10. **Publicly available?:** Yes

B.2.1 How delivered

Sparso is an open source package to the Julia language and is hosted with code and build instructions on Github.

B.2.2 Hardware dependencies

A modern x86 machine with more than 10 cores is preferred to run Sparso for performance testing.

B.2.3 Software dependencies

Sparso has been tested on Ubuntu 16.04, although it is a source-level package to Julia and thus is independent of OS and should be runnable on any OS where Julia can run.

Sparso requires MKL and SpMP libraries.

Scripts for validating correctness and performance are provided. For correctness validation, pcregrep is required.

B.2.4 Datasets

A script is provided to automatically download all the datasets that are publically available and in matrix market format. Users are welcome to try other datasets. We currently only support matrix market format files as input.

B.3 Installation

Follow the installation instruction on Sparso's github page (https://github.com/IntelLabs/Sparso.git).

B.4 Experiment workflow

Follow the experiment instruction on Sparso's github page (https://github.com/IntelLabs/Sparso.git). It allows users to validate both correctness and performance.

B.5 Evaluation and expected result

Correctness-wise, a set of tests will be run and should all pass. Log files will be produced, including the original Julia code and the code after being optimized by Sparso.

Performance-wise, expected results include GB/s for PCG and PageRank, execution time for IPM, L-BFGS, and Adiabatic, and GFLOP/s for CoSP2.

B.6 Notes

To know more about Sparso, send feedback, or file issues, please visit our github page (https://github.com/IntelLabs/Sparso.git).

Tardis 2.0: Optimized Time Traveling Coherence for Relaxed Consistency Models

Xiangyao Yu
MIT CSAIL
yxy@mit.edu

Hongzhe Liu
Algonquin Regional High School
liuhenry4428@gmail.com

Ethan Zou
Lexington High School
zouethan20@gmail.com

Srinivas Devadas
MIT CSAIL
devadas@mit.edu

ABSTRACT

Cache coherence scalability is a big challenge in shared memory systems. Traditional protocols do not scale due to the storage and traffic overhead of cache invalidation. Tardis, a recently proposed coherence protocol, removes cache invalidation using logical timestamps and achieves excellent scalability. The original Tardis protocol, however, only supports the Sequential Consistency (SC) memory model, limiting its applicability. Tardis also incurs extra network traffic on some benchmarks due to renew messages, and has suboptimal performance when the program uses spinning to communicate between threads.

In this paper, we address these downsides of Tardis protocol and make it significantly more practical. Specifically, we discuss the architectural, memory system and protocol changes required in order to implement the TSO consistency model on Tardis, and prove that the modified protocol satisfies TSO. We also describe modifications for Partial Store Order (PSO) and Release Consistency (RC). Finally, we propose optimizations for better leasing policies and to handle program spinning. On a set of benchmarks, optimized Tardis improves on a full-map directory protocol in the metrics of performance, storage and network traffic, while being simpler to implement.

1. INTRODUCTION

As the number of cores on a single chip increases, the cache coherence protocol becomes a potential scalability and performance bottleneck. *Snoopy* coherence protocols [1] work well for small-scale systems with a few cores, but do not scale due to the traffic pressure caused by broadcasting messages on the bus. *Directory-based* coherence protocols [2, 3] have better scalability and are widely used in multicore processors today [4, 5]. For future systems with hundreds or even thousands of cores, however, the storage overhead of a full-map directory becomes a serious scalability bottleneck. A number of enhancements to directory coherence protocols have been proposed in the literature [6, 7, 8, 9] to improve scalability. These enhancements typically sacrifice performance and incur extra implementation and verification complexity.

PACT '16, September 11-15, 2016, Haifa, Israel

DOI: http://dx.doi.org/10.1145/2967938.2967942

As an alternative, a recently proposed cache coherence protocol called *Tardis* shows better scalability while maintaining simplicity and high performance [10]. The key insight behind Tardis is that it is sufficient but *unnecessary* to enforce the global memory order in physical time order, which is what traditional coherence protocols do. Instead, Tardis uses a combination of logical timestamps and physical time. In Tardis, a memory write does not invalidate shared copies in other cores' private caches. Instead, the write is immediately performed at a logical timestamp greater than the timestamps of all the shared copies. The new data version can coexist with old versions at the same physical time but is ordered after the old versions in logical time.

Introducing logical timestamps into the coherence protocol brings several salient properties to Tardis. First, Tardis is *scalable*; it has no sharer list and only requires $O(\log N)$ storage per cacheline for an N-core system. It also does not require broadcasting support. Tardis is also *simple*; it uses timestamps to explicitly express the consistency model and is easy to reason about and verify [11]. Different from other protocols, Tardis does not need invalidation and is therefore able to achieve better performance on some benchmarks.

There are three drawbacks of the original Tardis protocol. The first drawback is that it only supports the *sequential consistency* (SC) memory model. While SC is simple and well studied, commercial processors usually implement more relaxed models. Intel x86 [12] and SPARC [13] processors can support *Total Store Order* (TSO); ARM [14] and IBM Power [15] processors implement weaker consistency models. It is difficult for commercial processors to adopt Tardis if the target memory models are not supported.

Another drawback of Tardis is the renew message that is used to extend the logical lease of a shared cacheline in a private cache. These messages incur extra latency and bandwidth overhead. Finally, Tardis uses a timestamp self-increment strategy to avoid livelock. This strategy has suboptimal performance when threads communicate via spinning.

In this paper, we will address these drawbacks of the original Tardis protocol and make it more practical. Specifically, we will discuss the changes to the cores and the memory subsystem in order to implement TSO and other relaxed consistency models on Tardis. A formal proof that our algorithm correctly implements TSO is also given. We also propose new optimization techniques (MESI, livelock detection and lease prediction) to reduce the number of renew messages in Tardis, which improves performance.

Our simulations over a wide range of benchmarks indicate that our optimizations improve the performance and reduce the network traffic of Tardis. Compared to a full-map directory-based coherence protocol at 64 cores, optimized Tardis is able to achieve better performance (1.1% average improvement, up to 9.8%) and lower network traffic (2.9% average reduction, up to 12.4%) at the same time. The improvement increases as the system scales to 256 cores where Tardis improves performance (average 4.7%, upto 36.8%) and reduces the network traffic (average 2.6%, upto 14.6%). While the optimized and baseline Tardis protocols require timestamps in the L1 cache, they are, overall, more space-efficient than full-map directory protocols and simpler to implement.

2. BACKGROUND

In this section, we introduce the key concepts behind the basic Tardis protocol (Section 2.1 and Section 2.2) and the protocol itself (Section 2.3 and Section 2.4). We describe the pros and cons of Tardis vis-à-vis a directory coherence protocol (Section 2.5).

2.1 Physiological Time

Most consistency models define a global order for all memory loads and stores. Traditional cache coherence protocols enforce this global memory order using physical time order. This requires an invalidation mechanism for write-after-read data dependency. Specifically, a write to a shared cacheline has to invalidate all the shared copies of that line because the write must be ordered after all previous reads with respect to physical time. The invalidation mechanism requires either broadcasting support in the network (as in snoopy coherence protocols) or a per cacheline sharer list in the directory (as in directory-based coherence protocols) and is therefore not able to scale to large numbers of cores.

Tardis avoids invalidation by introducing logical timestamps into the cache coherence protocol and enforcing the global memory order in both logical and physical time order. In Tardis, a write does not invalidate shared copies, instead, a new version of the cacheline is created at a later logical time at which point all previous shared copies have expired. This usage of logical time to order data bears some similarity to Lamport clock [16] and the timestamp ordering [17, 18] concept in database concurrency control algorithms.

Specifically, Tardis invented a new concept of time called *physiological time* and enforces the global memory order with respect to it. Using $<_{pt}$ and $<_{ts}$ to represent physical time and logical timestamp order respectively, the physiological time order ($<_{pl}$) is defined by Eq. (1).

$$X <_{pl} Y := X <_{ts} Y \text{ or } (X =_{ts} Y \text{ and } X <_{pt} Y) \qquad (1)$$

An operation X is before Y in physiological time order if X has a smaller timestamp or if they have the same timestamp but X happens earlier in physical time. If two operations happen at the same logical and physical time, then we can use any metric to break the tie (since they do not have a conflict). Physiological time makes it easy to reason about consistency models implemented on Tardis.

2.2 Sequential Consistency (SC)

The original Tardis protocol [10] implements sequential consistency, which requires that *"the result of any execution is the same as if the operations of all processors (cores) were executed in some sequential order, and the operations of each individual processor (core) appear in this sequence in the order specified by its program"* [19].

Sequential consistency can also be defined using the following two axiomatic rules, where X and Y are two memory operations, $<_p$ and $<_m$ are the program and global memory order respectively, and $L(a)$ and $S(a)$ are load and store to address a respectively.

Rule 1: $X <_p Y \Rightarrow X <_m Y$

Rule 2: Value of $L(a)$ = Value of $\text{Max}_{<_m} \{S(a) \mid S(a) <_m L(a)\}$

Rule 1 says that the sequential order should agree with the program order and Rule 2 says that each load should observe the preceding store in the sequential order.

In Tardis, the global memory order ($<_m$) in Rule 1 of SC can be implemented using the physiological time order ($<_{pl}$). Section 2.3 describes in detail how Tardis implements SC.

2.3 Tardis with SC

This section presents the baseline Tardis protocol proposed in [10]. For simplicity, we assume a multicore architecture with a private L1 cache per core and a shared L2 as the Last Level Cache (LLC). We also assume a single-threaded in-order core model where an instruction can be issued only after the previous instruction has finished its execution and committed. In practice, Tardis can be implemented on multi-threaded out-of-order cores as well. The physical time when an instruction commits is its *physical commit time*. Each instruction also has a *logical commit timestamp* indicating the logical time when it commits. For the rest of the paper, the term "timestamp" always indicates logical time. Also, when we say an operation is performed at a certain physical/logical time, we mean the physical/logical commit time of that operation.

2.3.1 Timestamp Management

Although both physical and logical commit time are used for reasoning about Tardis. Physical commit time is not explicitly stored in hardware and thus there is no need to read from CPU clocks. This is an important property which makes Tardis scalable. In Tardis, physical time order is meaningful only for operations that already happen in physical time order, e.g., instructions committed from the same core, or a load observing a preceding store. Orders between other operations are enforced using logical timestamps.

Logical timestamps in Tardis are explicitly stored and managed in hardware. For SC, each thread maintains a program timestamp (*pts*) as the logical commit timestamp of the last operation in the program order. For multithreaded cores, each hardware context maintains its own *pts* in hardware. According to Rule 1 in the definition of SC, the global memory order (i.e., physiological commit time order in Tardis) must agree with the program order. Therefore, the *pts* should monotonically increase with the program order[1].

Each cacheline in Tardis maintains a write timestamp (*wts*) and a read timestamp (*rts*). *wts* is the commit timestamp of the last store and *rts* can be considered the commit timestamp of the last load. Together they mean that the value is valid between *wts* and *rts* in logical time. Without further optimizations, for a cache with (*wts*, *rts*), a load can only be performed at *ts* such that $wts \leq ts \leq rts$, and a store can only be performed at *ts* such that $ts \geq rts + 1$. In terms of logical time, this means that a load always observes the preceding store and only one version of data exists at any timestamp.

2.3.2 Tardis-SC Protocol

We now present the baseline Tardis-SC protocol. For clarity, we first explain how shared caching is implemented in Tardis-SC and then discuss exclusive caching.

Shared Caching

An important concept in Tardis is *timestamp leasing* of a cacheline. In order to load a shared copy into a core's private cache, the core needs to get a lease on the cacheline. Multiple cores can cache the same cacheline in shared state with overlapping leases. But an update can be performed on the cacheline only after all shared leases expire. Leasing in Tardis is implemented with respect to logical but not physical time.

In private caches, the *rts* of a cacheline indicates the end of the lease on the line. A load operation can be performed as long as $pts \leq rts$ and the load updates *pts* to *Max(pts, wts)*. If $pts > rts$,

[1] So for every $X <_p Y$, we have $X \leq_{ts} Y$ and $X <_{pt} Y$ (due to in-order processing) and therefore $X <_{pl} Y$.

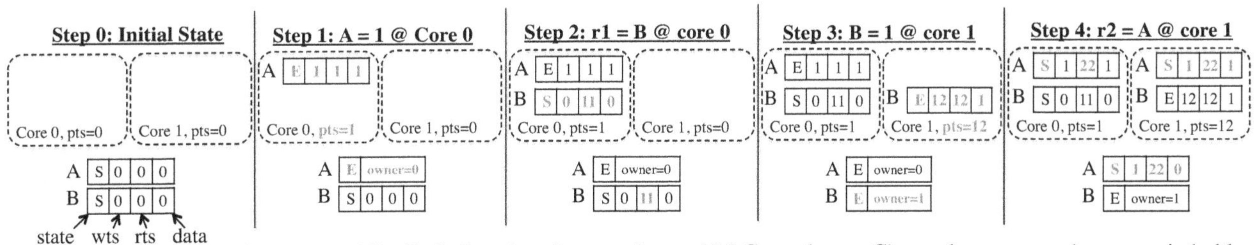

Figure 1: Tardis-SC example ($lease = 10$). Cachelines in private caches and LLC are shown. Changed states at each step are in bold red.

however, the load cannot be directly performed (for example, the line may have been modified in the LLC after *rts* but before *pts* in logical time) and a renew request has to be sent to the LLC to extend the *rts* of the data version. If the version in the LLC is the same as the version in the L1 (i.e., they have the same *wts*), the extension is successful and the extended *rts* is returned. Otherwise, the extension fails and the latest version is returned instead. But regardless, the returned *rts* will be greater than *pts* and the load can now be performed. The baseline Tardis uses speculative loading to hide the latency of renew messages.

In the shared LLC, the *rts* of a cacheline is the maximal *rts* among all the shared copies of the same address, namely, the end of all shared leases. A load or renew request from a core to the LLC may extend the cacheline's *rts* if the requesting core has a sufficiently large *pts*. Specifically, the *rts* is updated to *Max(rts, pts + lease)* for the load request where *lease* is a constant (e.g., *lease* = 10) in the baseline Tardis. The *lease* is chosen to be non-zero so that the line will be valid in the L1 for longer logical time and therefore not be constantly renewed by the core. The data and both *wts* and *rts* are returned to the requesting core in the response.

In Tardis, if a core keeps reading a stale cacheline at a *pts* smaller than the cacheline's *rts*, the core may never observe a later update and livelock may occur. To guarantee that a write is eventually observed by other cores, Tardis forces the *pts* of each core to periodically increase so that a stale version of a cacheline will eventually expire. We return to the subject of livelock in Section 5.2.

Exclusive Caching

Exclusive caching in Tardis is similar to the directory baseline for the most part. For example, a write operation needs to acquire exclusive ownership from the LLC; ownership transfers if a another core writes to the same cacheline; if another core reads the cacheline, the owner downgrades the line to shared state and writes the data back to the LLC. For a write operation at an L1, the newly created version has *new_version.wts = previous_version.rts + 1*.

When a core writes to a cacheline that is shared by one or more cores, however, Tardis has fundamentally different behavior than a traditional cache coherence protocol. When the write request reaches a shared cacheline in the LLC, unlike traditional cache coherence protocols, Tardis does not send invalidations to the sharers. Instead, exclusive ownership can be immediately returned to the requesting core. The core can perform the write at a *wts* greater than the cacheline's current *rts*. Since all the shared copies expire at this *rts*, this current write operation happens at a timestamp greater than all reads to the previous version. Therefore, the write is after those reads in the global memory order. Given the definition of SC (Rule 2 in particular), this behavior is sequentially consistent according to physiological time order.

2.4 Tardis-SC Example

Listing 1: Example Program

```
   initially A = B = 0
[Core 0]           [Core 1]
 A = 1              B = 1
 r1 = B             r2 = A
```

Fig. 1 shows how the dual-thread program in Listing 1 is executed in Tardis-SC. For simplicity, the example executes the four operations one at a time, and executes the operations from core 0 before those from core 1. Initially, both cores' L1s are empty; all cachelines in the LLC are in shared state; and all timestamps are 0.

Step 1: Core 0 stores to address *A*. A store request is sent to the LLC. Since A is in shared state in the LLC, exclusive ownership is immediately returned to core 0. Core 0 performs the store at timestamp $A.rts + 1 = 1$. After the store, core 0's *pts* becomes 1. The new version of *A* has $wts = rts = 1$.

Step 2: Core 0 loads from address *B*. A load request is sent to the LLC with $pts = 1$. *B*'s *rts* in the LLC is extended to $Max(rts, pts + lease) = 11$. The data value and both timestamps are returned to Core 0's L1 cache.

Step 3: Core 1 stores to address *B*. A store request is sent to the LLC. Since *B* is in shared state, exclusive ownership is immediately returned to core 1, which performs the store at timestamp $A.rts + 1 = 12$ and updates the *pts*, *wts* and *rts*. Note that although Core 0 is caching the previous version of *B*, no invalidation is sent for Core 1's store. After the store is performed, there are actually two different versions of *B* coexisting in the core 0's and core 1's L1 caches. However, they are valid at different logical timestamps. Core 0's copy is valid from timestamp 0 to 11, while core 1's copy is valid from timestamp 12. Therefore, sequential consistency is still maintained in physiological time order.

Step 4: Core 1 loads from address *A*. A load request is sent to the LLC. Since Core 0 is the current owner, a message is sent to Core 0 asking for data and *wts*/*rts* writeback. The LLC is updated based on the response and a shared copy is returned to Core 1. Since the *pts* of the load request is 12, the *rts* of all *A*'s cachelines are extended to $pts + lease = 22$.

2.5 Tardis vs. Directory-based Coherence

A key advantage of Tardis compared to a traditional physical time based coherence protocol is the removal of the invalidation mechanism. This simplifies protocol design, reduces storage overhead, and can potentially achieve better performance.

Removing the invalidation mechanism means that the LLC does not notify the sharing cores when a cacheline is modified. So each core should contact the LLC to learn the freshness of a cacheline. This is done through the renew messages (cf. Section 2.3). In a sense, replacing invalidations with renewals is replacing a push-based model with a poll-based model. A poll-based model is usually simpler and more scalable, but may lead to wasted messages. For example, read only data may be constantly renewed due to expiration, but these messages would not exist in an invalidation-based protocol. The latency and bandwidth overhead of the extra renew traffic is the major potential disadvantage of Tardis compared to directory coherence protocols.

Some optimization techniques (e.g., speculative read) have been proposed to hide the latency of renewals [10]. However, the performance and network traffic overhead can still be significant for some benchmarks. We will present our solutions to the renewal problem in Section 5.

3. TARDIS WITH TSO

The original Tardis protocol only supports the sequential consistency (SC) memory model. Although SC is intuitive and precisely defined, it may overly constrain the ordering of memory operations. In practice, this may lead to suboptimal performance. To resolve this disadvantage of SC, relaxed consistency models have been proposed and widely implemented in real systems. Most of these models focus on the relaxation of the program order in SC (Rule 1 in the SC definition). Specifically, the program order of a core may appear out-of-order in the global memory order. The more relaxed a model is, the more flexibility it has to reorder operations, which usually leads to better overall performance.

In this section, we show how Tardis can be generalized to relaxed consistency models. We first use Total Store Order (TSO) as a case study since it has a precise definition and is the most widely adopted. We will present the formal definition of TSO (Section 3.1), the Tardis-TSO protocol (Section 3.2), an example program (Section 3.3) and optimizations (Section 3.4). Finally, we generalize the discussion to other memory models (Section 3.5).

3.1 Formal Definition of TSO

The TSO consistency model relaxed the Store $\rightarrow$ Load constraint in the program order. This allows a load after a store in the program order to be flipped in the global memory order (assuming that the load and the store have no data or control dependency). In an out-of-order processor, this means that an outstanding store does not block the following loads. When a store reaches the head of the *Re-Order Buffer* (ROB), it can retire to the *store buffer* and finish the rest of the store operation there. The loads following the store can therefore commit early before the store is actually done. Since store misses are common in real applications, this relaxation can lead to significant performance improvement.

Similar to SC, the definition of TSO also requires a global order (specified using $<_m$) of all memory instructions. However, the global memory order does not need to follow the program order for Store $\rightarrow$ Load dependency. Specifically, TSO can be defined using the following three rules [20]. The differences between TSO and SC are highlighted in boldface.

Rule 1: $L(a) <_p L(b) \Rightarrow L(a) <_m L(b)$
$L(a) <_p S(b) \Rightarrow L(a) <_m S(b)$
$S(a) <_p S(b) \Rightarrow S(a) <_m S(b)$
~~**S(a) $<_p$ L(b) $\Rightarrow$ S(a) $<_m$ L(b)**~~

Rule 2: Value of $L(a)$ = Value of $\text{Max}_{<m}$ $\{S(a) \mid S(a) <_m L(a)$ **or S(a) $<_p$ L(a)**$\}$

Rule 3: **X $<_p$ FENCE $\Rightarrow$ X $<_m$ FENCE**
FENCE $<_p$ X $\Rightarrow$ FENCE $<_m$ X

In TSO, the program order implies the global memory order only for Load $\rightarrow$ Load, Load $\rightarrow$ Store and Store $\rightarrow$ Store constraints. Since there is no Store $\rightarrow$ Load constraint, a load can bypass the pending store requests and commit earlier (Rule 1). Although the load is after the store in the program order, it is before the store in the global memory order.

In an out-of-order processor, TSO can be implemented using a store buffer which is a FIFO for pending store requests that have retired from ROB. If the address of a load exists in the store buffer, then the value in the store buffer is directly returned; otherwise, the load accesses the memory hierarchy (Rule 2).

TSO uses a *fence* instruction when a Store $\rightarrow$ Load order needs to be enforced (Rule 3). In a processor, a fence flushes the store buffer enforcing that all previous stores have finished so that a later committed load is ordered after stores before the fence in physical time. If all memory operations are also fences, then TSO becomes SC.

3.2 Tardis-TSO Protocol

In this section, we describe how TSO can be implemented on Tardis. Specifically, we discuss the changes to the timestamp management policy as compared to the Tardis SC protocol.

3.2.1 Program Timestamp Management

The original Tardis SC protocol uses a single program timestamp (*pts*) to represent the commit timestamp of an instruction. Since the program order always agrees with the global memory order in SC, *pts* monotonically increases in the program order.

In TSO, however, the program order does not always agree with the global memory order. Following Rule 1 in TSO's definition, a store's timestamp is no less than the timestamps of all preceding loads, stores and fences in the program order. A load's timestamp is no less than the timestamps of all preceding loads and fences, but not necessarily preceding stores. As a result, a single monotonically increasing *pts* is insufficient to represent the ordering constraint.

To express the different constraints for loads and stores respectively, we split the original *pts* into two timestamps. The *store timestamp* (*sts*) represents the commit timestamp of the last store, and the *load timestamp* (*lts*) represents the commit timestamp of the last load. Like *pts*, both *sts* and *lts* are maintained in each core in hardware. According to Rule 1, both should monotonically increase in the program order because of the Load $\rightarrow$ Load and Store $\rightarrow$ Store constraints. Furthermore, the timestamp of a store (*sts*) should be no less than the timestamp of the preceding load (*lts*) because of the Load $\rightarrow$ Store constraint. For a load, however, its *lts* can be smaller than *sts* because there is no Store $\rightarrow$ Load constraint.

A fence can be simply implemented as a synchronization point between *sts* and *lts*. Specifically, a fence sets *lts* = *Max(lts, sts)*. This enforces Rule 3 in TSO because operations after the fence are ordered after operations before the fence in physiological time order (and therefore the global memory order). If each memory operation is also a fence, then the commit timestamp for each operation monotonically increases and the protocol becomes Tardis SC.

In a traditional coherence protocol, the main advantage of TSO over SC is the performance gain due to loads bypassing stores in the store buffer. In Tardis, besides bypassing, TSO can also reduce the number of renewals compared to SC. This is because the *lts*/*sts* in TSO may increase slower compared to the *pts* in SC. As a result, fewer shared cachelines expire.

3.2.2 Data Timestamp Management

The timestamp management logic largely remains the same when the consistency model switches from SC to TSO. However, the timestamp rules for data in the store buffer need some slight changes. For single-threaded cores, timestamp management in the private L1 can also be changed for load requests for potentially better performance.

To load a cacheline in L1 that is not *dirty* (i.e., the data has not been changed by the core since it was cached), the timestamp rule is exactly the same as in SC, i.e., the *lts* should fall within the lease of the cacheline ($wts \leq lts \leq rts$); *lts* jumps to *wts* if *lts* is smaller than *wts* and a renewal is sent if *lts* is greater than *rts*.

For a dirty cacheline in the store buffer or L1 cache, however, the *lts* does not have to be greater than the *wts* of the cacheline. With respect to the global memory order, this means that the load can commit at an *lts* smaller than the commit timestamp of the store

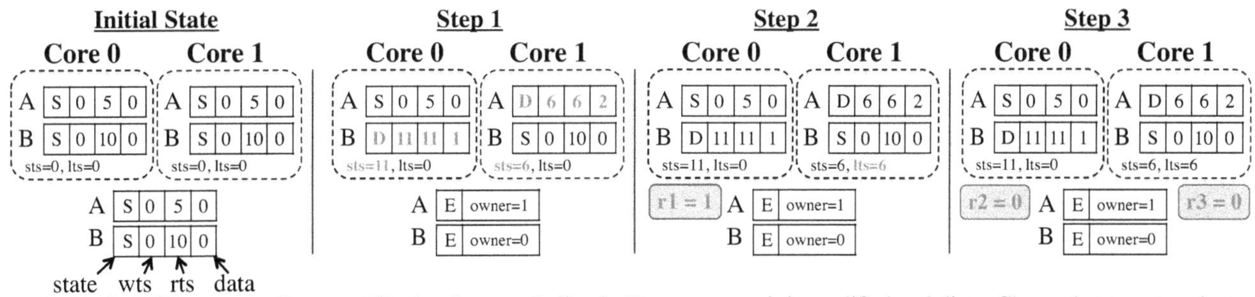

Figure 2: Tardis-TSO example (*lease* = 10). A private cacheline in *D* state means it is modified and dirty. Changed states at each step are highlighted in red.

creating the data (*wts*). This behavior certainly violates SC but it is completely legal in TSO.

According to Rule 2 of TSO, a load should return either the last store in global memory order or the last store in program order, depending on which one has a larger physiological time. Since a dirty cacheline was written by a store from the current core prior to the load, even if the load has a smaller commit timestamp than the store, Rule 2 still holds. A more formal proof of correctness is presented in Section 4.

Unlike in traditional processors, TSO can be implemented with Tardis even on in-order cores that do not have a store buffer. This is because Tardis can figure out the correct memory ordering using logical timestamps as will become clear in the example presented in the next section. We note that our implementation of Tardis TSO still has a store buffer for better performance, but it is not required for functional correctness.

Note that if multiple threads can access the same private cache, then the above optimization for dirty L1 cachelines may not be directly applied in L1 cache (but it is still applied in the store buffer). Because a dirty line might be written by any thread sharing the L1. For these systems, this optimization can be turned off in the L1.

3.3 TSO Example

Listing 2: Example Program

```
[core0]                 [core1]
B = 1                   A = 2
L(B) → r1               FENCE
L(A) → r2               L(B) → r3
```

We use the example program in Listing 2 to demonstrate how timestamps are managed in Tardis TSO. The execution of the program is shown in Fig. 2. For simplicity, we do not model the store buffer and execute one instruction per step for each core.

Initially, both addresses A and B are cached in Shared (S) state in both cores' private caches as well as the shared LLC. *wts* of all lines are 0; *rts* of all lines of address A are 5 and *rts* of all lines of address B are 10.

Step 1: core 0 writes to address B and core 1 writes to address A. Exclusive ownership of A and B are given to core 1 and core 0 respectively, and both stores are performed by jumping ahead in logical time to the end of the lease. After the stores, core 0's *sts* jumps to timestamp 11 and core 1's *sts* jumps to 6, but the *lts* of both cores remain 0.

Step 2: core 0 loads address B. The value of the previous store from core 0 is returned ($r1 = 1$). Since B is in the dirty state, the load does not increase the *lts* (Section 3.2.2). In core 1, a fence instruction is executed which synchronizes the *lts* and *sts* to timestamp 6.

Step 3: core 0 loads address A. Since its *lts* is 0 which falls between the *wts* and *rts* of cacheline A, this is a cache hit and value 0 is returned ($r2 = 0$). In core 1, the load to address B also hits the L1 since its *lts* = 6 falls within B's lease. As a result, the loaded value is also 0 ($r3 = 0$).

Listing 3 shows the physiological commit time for each instruction in Listing 2. It also shows the global memory order using arrows. Physiological time is represented using a logical timestamp and physical time pair (ts, pt) where ts is the commit timestamp and pt is the physical commit time of the instruction. According to the definition, $(ts_1, pt_1) < (ts_2, pt_2)$ if $ts_1 < ts_2$ or ($ts_1 = ts_2$ and $pt_1 < pt_2$).

Listing 3: Physiological commit time and global memory order.

```
[core0]             [core1]
(11, 1) <-.     .-> (6, 1)
           \   /       ↓
(0, 2)      \ /     (6, 2)
   ↓        / \        ↓
(0, 3) ----'   '--- (6, 3)
```

The execution is definitely not sequentially consistent since the program order in core 0 is violated between `B = 1` and `L(B)`. But it obeys all the invariants of TSO. Note that the store buffer is not included in the example since we are modeling in-order cores, but TSO can still be implemented. This feature is not available in traditional physical time based coherence protocols. For this example, adding the store buffer will not change the hardware behavior.

3.4 TSO Optimizations

Many optimization techniques have been proposed in the literature to improve performance of the basic SC/TSO consistency model. Examples include load speculation to hide Load → Load and Store → Load dependency, and store prefetch to enhance Store → Store and Load → Store performance [21]. For TSO, the speculation can go over fences.

Tardis TSO is compatible with these optimizations. In fact, it may be even simpler to support them on Tardis than on traditional coherence protocols since the timestamps can help preserve/check memory order. For example, for load → load relaxation, multiple loads can be speculatively executed in parallel, and the *wts* and *rts* of the loaded cachelines are stored inside the core (e.g., in the ROB). To enforce load → load dependency, the processor only needs to commit instructions with ascending timestamp order (and reissue a load with a new timestamp if necessary). In contrast, a traditional processor needs to snoop on invalidation messages in order to detect a speculation failure. Fence speculation can also be implemented in a similar way using timestamps. In general, Tardis allows all memory operations to be speculatively executed arbitrarily, as long as their commit timestamps obey the consistency model. This flexibility makes it easier to reason about and implement these optimizations.

Table 1: Memory order constraints for different consistency models. L for load, S for store and F for fence. For release consistency, *rel* for release and *acq* for acquire.

Consistency Model	Ordinary Orderings	Synchronization Orderings
SC	L → L, L → S, S → L, S → S	
TSO	L → L, L → S, S → S	S → F, F → L, F → F
PSO	L → L, L → S	S → F, F → S, F → L, F → F
RC		L/S → rel, acq → L/S, rel/acq → rel/acq

3.5 Other Relaxed Consistency Models

Similar to TSO, other memory consistency models (Table 1) can also be supported in Tardis with proper changes to the timestamp rules. Given the relationship between the program order and the global memory order, it is usually straightforward to adapt Tardis for different models. In this section, we briefly discuss Partial Store Order (PSO) and Release Consistency (RC) to illustrate how Tardis can adapt to them with minimal algorithmic change.

3.5.1 Partial Store Order (PSO)

The PSO consistency model [13] relaxes both the Store → Load and the Store → Store orderings. Similar to TSO, we use the *lts* and *sts* to model the program order constraints. In PSO, since Load → Load is enforced but Store → Load is not, which is the same as TSO, the rule for *lts* is also the same as TSO. Namely, *pts* should monotonically increase independently of store timestamps.

The timestamp order for stores, however, does not need to monotonically increase, since Store → Store is relaxed. Therefore, the timestamp of a store (*ts*) only needs to be no less than the *lts* ($ts \geq lts$). And *sts* represents the largest store timestamp so far (instead of the last store timestamp), namely $sts = Max(sts, ts)$.

For a fence instruction, *lts* synchronizes with *sts*, namely $lts = Max(lts, sts)$. The resulting *lts* is the timestamp of the fence.

3.5.2 Release Consistency (RC)

Release consistency [22] relaxes all the program order constraints; furthermore, it also relaxes the ordering constraints for synchronizations. Specifically, an *acquire* guarantees that all the following (but not the previous) operations are ordered after the acquire and a *release* guarantees that all the previous (but not the following) operations are ordered before the release.

In Tardis, we need to maintain timestamps for acquire (*acquire_ts*) and release (*release_ts*) operations, as well as the maximal commit timestamp (*max_ts*) so far. A normal load or store operation (commit timestamp *ts*) can be performed as long as its timestamp is greater than *acquire_ts* ($ts \geq acquire\_ts$); *max_ts* represents the largest commit timestamp as seen by the core so far ($max\_ts = Max(max\_ts, ts)$). At a release instruction, *release_ts* and *max_ts* are synchronized ($release\_ts = Max(release\_ts, max\_ts)$). At an acquire instruction, *acquire_ts* and *release_ts* are synchronized ($acquire\_ts = Max(acquire\_ts, release\_ts)$).

4. PROOF OF CORRECTNESS

In this section, we prove that the algorithm in Section 3.2 correctly implements TSO. We first introduce several definitions and invariants (in the form of lemmas) of the Tardis protocol (Section 4.1). We then use these lemmas to prove that our algorithm implements TSO (Section 4.2).

4.1 Invariants of Tardis protocol

The invariants of Tardis introduced in this section are true regardless of the memory model used by the system. While some of the lemmas come from a proof of Tardis SC ([11]), we restate them in the language of physiological time.

To simplify the discussion, we first introduce the concept of *master* and *snapshot* cachelines.

DEFINITION 1 (MASTER, SNAPSHOT CACHELINE). *A cacheline is a master cacheline if it is in M state in an L1, or in S state in the LLC. A cacheline is a snapshot cacheline if it is in S state in an L1.*

Here are some facts about master and snapshot cachelines:

Fact 1. *For each cacheline with (wts, rts), the data value comes from a previous store that committed at logical time wts.*

In Tardis, the only way to change *wts* of a cacheline is by performing a store to it and the new *wts* after the store always equals the commit timestamp of the store.

Fact 2. *For each address in the system, at most one master cacheline exists but multiple snapshot cachelines may exist.*

This is similar to the single-writer, multiple-reader (SWMR) invariant in traditional coherence protocols. In Tardis, however, multiple snapshot cachelines (i.e., shared L1 cachelines) can coexist with a master cacheline (e.g., exclusive L1 cacheline) at the same physical time.

Fact 3. *A snapshot cacheline is derived by taking a snapshot of data and timestamps of a master cacheline.*

In the protocol, an L1 shared cacheline may be derived from a shared response from the LLC or from downgrading a modified cacheline in an L1. In both cases, it is a snapshot of a master cacheline.

For the proof, we use (ts, pt) to represent the physiological time of an operation, where *ts* and *pt* are the logical and physical commit time of the operation, respectively.

LEMMA 1. *For each address, the wts and rts of the master cachelines never decrease.*

PROOF. *In the basic Tardis protocol, no operation decreases the timestamp of a cacheline. For a master cacheline, its wts/rts can only increase (through writes) or stay the same (through exclusive response to L1 or write back to LLC) but never decrease.* □

LEMMA 2. *For a master cacheline, no store to the address has happened at* (wts', wpt') *such that* $(wts, wpt) < (wts', wpt')$*, where the (wts, wpt) is the physiological commit time of the store that created the data in the cacheline.*

PROOF. *If such a store has ever happened, it would have created a version of master cacheline with write timestamp* $wts' > wts$. *However, Lemma 1 states that the wts of the master cachelines do not decrease. This contradicts the fact that the wts of the cacheline is currently less than* wts'. □

LEMMA 3. *For a snapshot cacheline (with wts and rts) at physical time pt, no store has happened at* (ts, pt') *such that* $(wts, wpt) < (ts, pt') < (rts, pt)$*, where the (wts, wpt) is the physiological commit time of the store that created the data in the cacheline.*

PROOF. *A snapshot cacheline is always copied from a master cacheline. When the snapshot is taken, according to Lemma 2, no store to the address exists at a physiological time after* (wts, wpt). *Since then, according to Tardis rules, a store can only happen at a logical timestamp greater than rts of the cacheline. Therefore, any later store has a greater physiological time than* (rts, ∞). *So no store can exist between* (wts, wpt) *and* (rts, pt). □

4.2 Tardis TSO Proof

We first make the following assumption about a processor implementing TSO.

ASSUMPTION 1. *A TSO processor commits instructions in physical time order if their global memory order has to follow the program order according to Rule 1 and 3 of the TSO definition. Specifically,*

$$L(a) <_p L(b) \Rightarrow L(a) <_{pt} L(b)$$
$$L(a) <_p S(b) \Rightarrow L(a) <_{pt} S(b)$$
$$S(a) <_p S(b) \Rightarrow S(a) <_{pt} S(b)$$
$$X <_p FENCE \Rightarrow X <_{pt} FENCE$$
$$FENCE <_p X \Rightarrow FENCE <_{pt} X$$

This assumption does not require extra hardware changes to existing processors. In fact, processors implementing TSO today already follow this assumption.

THEOREM 1. *The protocol of Section 3.2 implements TSO.*

PROOF. *We will prove that each rule in the definition of TSO is maintained in our protocol.*

Proof for Rule 1. *According to Section 3.2.1, both lts and sts monotonically increase and for a store, its sts is no less than the current lts. In other words,*

$$L(a) <_p L(b) \Rightarrow L(a) \leq_{ts} L(b)$$
$$L(a) <_p S(b) \Rightarrow L(a) \leq_{ts} S(b)$$
$$S(a) <_p S(b) \Rightarrow S(a) \leq_{ts} S(b)$$

Combined with our assumption of a TSO processor (Assumption 1), we have:

$$X \leq_{ts} Y \text{ and } X <_{pt} Y$$
$$\Rightarrow X <_{ts} Y \text{ or } (X =_{ts} Y \text{ and } X <_{pt} Y)$$
$$\Rightarrow X <_{pl} Y$$
$$\Rightarrow X <_m Y$$

which finishes the proof of Rule 1 of TSO.

Proof for Rule 2. *We will prove that for each memory load, the returned value is the one specified by Rule 2 of the TSO definition. According to Fact 1, for each cacheline in Tardis, the data value was created by a store that happened at the cacheline's wts. A load to a cacheline observes the value of this particular store. Assuming that the store committed at physical time wpt, we need to prove that the physiological time of this store, which is (wts, wpt), is greater than all the other stores in the set* $S = S_1 \cup S_2$ *where* $S_1 = \{S(a)|S(a) <_m L(a)\}$ *and* $S_2 = \{S(a)|S(a) <_p L(a)\}$ *and that the observed store is also in this set. Specifically, we consider the following two cases.*

Case 1, load to a shared L1 cacheline. Timestamps of the cacheline are wts and rts. Because $wts \leq lts \leq rts$ *and* $wpt < pt$*, the observed store must be in the set* S_1*. According to Lemma 3, at physical time pt, no store has happened at (wts′, wpt′) such that (wts, wpt) < (wts′, wpt′) < (rts, pt). As a result, the observed store has the largest physiological time in set* S_1*.*

We now prove that all stores in set S_2 *have smaller physiological time than the observed store. This can be proven by contradiction. If such a store has been executed by the current core at (wts′, wpt′) > (wts, wpt), the current core must have owned a master cacheline with wts′ after the store. Since the master cacheline's wts never decreases and a snapshot cacheline is copied from a master cacheline, the current shared cacheline must have wts greater than wts′, contradicting the assumption. So the observed store has the largest physiological time in set* $S_1 \cup S_2$*, proving the invariant.*

Case 2, load to a modified L1 cacheline. In this case, the loaded cacheline is a master cacheline. If the cacheline is not dirty, then $wts \leq lts$*. So the observed store is in* S_1*. If the cacheline is dirty, then the observed store must be before the current load in the program order and is therefore in* S_2*. According to Lemma 2, no store has happened to the address at (wts′, wpt′) > (wts, wpt). So the observed store must have the largest physiological time in set* $S = S_1 \cup S_2$*.*

Proof for Invariant 3. *In Tardis TSO, a fence synchronizes lts and sts. Tardis TSO enforces the following:*

$$X <_p FENCE \Rightarrow X \leq_{ts} FENCE$$
$$X <_p FENCE \Rightarrow X <_{pt} FENCE$$
$$FENCE <_p X \Rightarrow FENCE \leq_{ts} X$$
$$FENCE <_p X \Rightarrow FENCE <_{pt} X$$

Combining these equations and applying the definition of physiological time, we prove the last invariant of TSO. □

5. RENEWAL REDUCTION TECHNIQUES

As discussed in Section 2, a major drawback of the original Tardis protocol is the renewal problem. With load speculation, latency of renew messages can be largely hidden, but network traffic overhead remains. A renew message is unnecessary if the renewed line is unchanged. In this section, we discuss techniques to reduce unnecessary renew messages.

5.1 MESI on Tardis

The original Tardis protocol implements MSI where a read to a private cacheline loads it in S (shared) state in the L1 cache. As the *lts* (or *pts* in SC) increases in a core, these data will expire and be renewed. These renewals are unnecessary since there is no need to maintain coherence for a core's private data.

The MESI protocol can resolve this issue. MESI adds an E (Exclusive) state to MSI. The E state is granted for a request if the cacheline is not shared by other cores. Like a cacheline in M state, an exclusive cacheline in a private cache never expires. If the *lts* is greater than the *rts*, the *rts* of that line can be increased to *lts* with no renewal. This can be done since the line is not shared by other cores, namely, a *master cacheline* according to Definition 1. Therefore, renewal does not happen for private data in MESI.

Different from traditional coherence protocols, Tardis can grant E state to a core even if other cores are still sharing the line. This is similar to granting M state without the need of invalidation. However, for performance reasons, it is still desirable to only grant E state for private data. In Tardis, a cacheline is likely to be not shared if it has just been loaded from DRAM, and if it has just been downgraded from E/M to S state. Therefore, we add an E-bit to each cacheline in the LLC to indicate whether the cacheline is likely to be shared or not. The E-bit is set when the cacheline is loaded from DRAM and also when the cacheline is downgraded to S state. The E-bit is reset when the cacheline becomes cached upon load request. Note that E-bit may be unset even if no core is sharing the line (e.g., all sharers silently evict the line). This does not affect the functional correctness of the implementation.

5.2 Livelock Detection

A disadvantage of Tardis is that propagating a store to other cores may take an arbitrarily long time. This is because the writer does not notify the sharing cores who may not *pull* the latest value if they keep reading the stale version. In the worst case if a core spins on a stale cacheline with a small *lts* (or *pts* in SC), it never sees the latest update and livelock occurs (Listing 4). Although such livelock is not precluded by the consistency model, it should be disallowed by the coherence protocol which requires that every write should eventually propagate to other cores. In practice, this spinning behavior is commonly used for communication in parallel programs.

Listing 4: Threads communicate through spinning

```
[Core 0]                 [Core 1]
//spin (lts = 10)        //store (sts = 20)
while (!done) {          ...
  sleep(1)               done = true
}                        ...
```

5.2.1 Baseline: Periodic Self Increment

The original Tardis protocol solves the livelock problem by self incrementing the *pts* (or *lts* in TSO) periodically to force the logical time in each core to move forward. For a spinning core (e.g., core 0 in Listing 4), the *lts* will increase and eventually become greater than the *rts* of the cacheline being spun on at which point the line expires and the latest value will be loaded.

Frequently self incrementing *lts* causes two performance issues. First, the shared cachelines in the private cache may frequently expire, generating renewals. For programs without spinning, these renewals are unnecessary but incur network traffic and latency. Second, for cachelines that have an *rts* much larger than the current *lts* of the core, it may take a significant amount of time before the *lts* increases to *rts* for the stale line to expire.

5.2.2 Livelock Detector

We make a key observation that a *check* message can be sent to check the freshness of a cacheline even before the cacheline actually expires. Like a renew request, if the latest data is newer than the cached data, the latest cacheline is returned. If the cached data is already the latest version, however, a check response is returned without extending the *rts* of the cacheline in the LLC.

The check request can resolve both drawbacks of the self increment scheme. Since a core does not need to frequently increase its *lts*, the number of renewals can be reduced. Also, a check request can be sent when *lts* is much smaller than *rts*, so a core does not need to wait a long time for the cacheline to expire.

Generally, a check request should be sent when the program seems to livelock as it keeps loading stale cachelines. In practical programs, such a livelock is usually associated with variable spinning, which typically involves a small number of cachelines and is therefore easy to detect in hardware.

Algorithm 1: Livelock Detection Algorithm (called for each read request to a shared L1 cacheline).

```
Input: addr   // memory access address
Return Value: whether to issue check request
Internal State: AHB, thresh_count

if AHB.contains(addr) then
    AHB[addr].access_count ++
    if AHB[addr].access_count == thresh_count then
        AHB[addr].access_count = 0
        return true
    end if
else
    AHB.enqueue(addr)
    AHB[addr].access_count = 0
    return false
end if
```

We designed a small piece of hardware next to each core to detect livelock. It contains an *Address History Buffer* (AHB) and a threshold counter (*thresh_count*). The AHB is a circular buffer keeping track of the most recently loaded addresses. Each entry in AHB contains the address of a memory access, and an *access_count*, which is the number of accesses to the address since it was loaded to AHB. When *access_count* becomes greater than the *thresh_count*, a check request is sent for this address (Algorithm 1). The value of *thresh_count* can be static or dynamic. We chose to use an adaptive threshold counter scheme (Algorithm 2) in order to minimize the number of unnecessary check messages.

Algorithm 2: Adaptive Threshold Counter Algorithm (called for each check response).

```
Input: check_update // whether the checked address has been updated.
Internal State: thresh_count
Constant: min_count, max_count, check_count, check_thresh

if check_update then
    thresh_count = min_count
    check_count = 0
else
    check_count ++
    if check_count == check_thresh and thresh_count < max_count then
        thresh_count = thresh_count × 2
    end if
end if
```

The livelock detection algorithm (Algorithm 1) is executed when reading a shared cacheline. It is not called when accessing cachelines in E or M state since no livelock can occur for those accesses. If the accessed address does not exist in the AHB, a new entry is allocated. Since AHB is a circular buffer, this may evict an old entry from it. We use the LRU replacement policy here but other replacement policies should work equally well. For an AHB hit, the *access_count* is incremented by 1. If the counter saturates (i.e., reaches *thresh_count*), a check request is sent and the *access_count* is reset. All *access_counts* are reset to 0 when the *lts* increases due to a memory access, since this indicates that the core is not livelocking, and thus there is no need to send checks.

The counter *thresh_count* may be updated for each check response (Algorithm 2). If the checked address was updated by another core, then *thresh_count* should decrease to the minimal value, indicating that check requests should be sent more frequently since data seems to be updated frequently. Otherwise, if *check_thresh* number of consecutive check requests returned without data being changed, then *thresh_count* is doubled since it appears unnecessary to send check requests that often. Adaptively determining the value of *thresh_count* can reduce the number of unnecessary check requests if a thread needs to spin for a long time before the data is updated.

Note that the livelock detector can only detect spinning involving loads to less than *M* (the number of entries in AHB) distinct addresses. So in theory, the livelock detector cannot capture all possible livelocks and self incrementing *lts* is still required to guarantee forward progress. For practical programs, however, spinning typically involves a small number of distinct addresses. So the livelock detector is able to capture livelock in the vast majority of programs. We still self increment *lts* periodically but the frequency can be much lower, since most programs' performance does not rely on this mechanism anymore.

5.3 Lease Prediction

During regular operation of Tardis, memory stores are the main reason that the timestamps increase in the system. The amount that an *sts* increases is determined by the lease of the previous data version, because the *sts* of the store must be no less than the cacheline's previous *rts*. Therefore, the lease of each cacheline is important to the timestamp incrementing rate as well as the renew rate. The original Tardis protocol uses a static lease for every shared cacheline. We first show that a static leasing policy may incur unnecessary renewals (Section 5.3.1). We then propose a dynamic leasing policy to mitigate the problem (Section 5.3.2).

5.3.1 Static Lease vs. Dynamic Lease

In the code snippet shown in Listing 5, both cores run the same program. They both load addresses A and B and then store to B. When the cachelines are loaded to L1 caches, they are all reserved with a static lease *L*. When the store to address B is performed, both cores' *sts* jump ahead by at least *L*. At the end of the loop, the FENCE instruction increases *lts* to the value of *sts*.

Listing 5: The case study parallel program

```
[Core 0]                  [Core 1]
 while(B < 10) {          while(B < 10) {
   print A                  print A
   B++                      B++
   FENCE                    FENCE
 }                        }
```

In the next iteration when both cores load A again, the cacheline has expired in the L1 caches. Because the *lts* has already jumped ahead by *L* due to the previous store B and the fence, but the lease on A was also *L*. As a result, in each iteration of the loop, *lts* and *sts* jump ahead by *L* and A is renewed at each core. All these renewals to A are successful, and therefore unnecessary, since A has never been changed. Note that using a larger static *L* does not solve the problem since *lts*/*sts* will jump ahead further and A will still expire.

Our solution to this problem is to use different leases for different addresses. Intuitively, we want to use large leases for read only or read intensive data, and use small leases for write intensive data. In the example in Listing 5, if A has lease 100 and B has lease 10, then each store to B increases the *sts* and *lts* only by 10. So it takes about 10 iterations before A has to be renewed again. The renew rate is mainly a function of the ratio between these two leases; the absolute lease values are not critical.

In a real system, it is non-trivial to decide what data should have a larger or smaller lease. Here, we explore hardware only solutions and design a predictor to decide the lease for each cacheline. It is possible to do this more accurately with software support, such explorations are left for future work.

5.3.2 Lease Predictor

Our lease predictor is based on the observation that cachelines that are frequently renewed are more likely to be read intensive. Therefore, a cacheline should be reserved with a larger lease if it is renewed frequently. The logic to determine the lease value is built into the LLC which has knowledge of all the renewals.

For each renew request from the L1 to the LLC, the last lease (*req_lease*) of the cacheline is also sent to the LLC and is processed by the lease predictor. For an L1 miss, the cacheline has no last lease so the *min_lease* is used. The lease predictor computes a proper lease based on the *req_lease* and the predictor's current internal lease (*cur_lease*). Specifically, the algorithm of our lease predictor is shown in Algorithm 3.

For a write request, the *cur_lease* is updated to the minimal lease value (*min_lease*). Our reasoning is that the write indicates that the cacheline might be write intensive and so assigning a large lease to it may cause unnecessary renewals of other cachelines. For a normal read request, *cur_lease* is used for the requested cacheline. For a renew request, *cur_lease* is compared with the request lease (*req_lease*). If they are different, then *cur_lease* is used for the cacheline. Otherwise, *cur_lease* is doubled since the cacheline

Algorithm 3: Lease Prediction Algorithm (called for each LLC request).

Input
    req_lease *// lease in the request*
    req_type *// WRITE, READ or RENEW*
Return Value: Lease of the returned cacheline.
Internal State: cur_lease

if req_type == WRITE **then**
    cur_lease = min_lease
else if req_type == RENEW **and** req_lease == cur_lease **and** cur_lease < max_lease **then**
    cur_lease = cur_lease × 2
end if
return cur_lease

seems to be renewed multiple times by the same core and is therefore likely to be read intensive. If *cur_lease* already reached the maximal value (*max_lease*), then it should no longer increase.

The initial value of *cur_lease* is the minimal value (*min_lease*). This means that for a cacheline first loaded to the LLC, we always assume it to be write intensive. We made this design decision because incorrectly giving a large lease to a write intensive cacheline is much more harmful than giving a small lease to a read intensive cacheline. If a cacheline with a large lease is written, a large number of cachelines in the core's L1 might expire due to the program timestamp jumping ahead. In contrast, if a read only cacheline is given a small lease, only this cacheline needs to be renewed and other cachelines are not affected.

6. EVALUATIONS

We evaluate the performance of Tardis with relaxed consistency models and the optimizations proposed in Section 5.

6.1 Methodology

6.1.1 System Configuration

We use the Graphite [23] multicore simulator to model the Tardis coherence protocol. Configurations of the hardware, Tardis, and its enhancements are shown in Table 2 and Table 3.

For the baseline Tardis, we implemented all the optimizations in the original Tardis protocol, including speculative reads when a cacheline expires in the L1 cache and not incrementing *sts* for private writes [10]. The static lease always equals 8. And the *lts* self increments by 1 for every 100 memory accesses.

For the livelock detector, the address history buffer (AHB) contains 8 entries by default. The threshold counter can take values ranging from 100 to 800. The threshold counter is doubled if 10 consecutive checks respond that the data has not been changed.

The minimal lease is chosen to be 8 and the maximum lease is 64. There are four possible lease values (i.e., 8, 16, 32, 64) in the system. We chose four lease values because having more values does not significantly affect performance.

6.1.2 Baselines

The following coherence protocols are implemented and evaluated for comparison. Except in Section 6.2, all the configurations use the TSO consistency model and MESI.

Directory: Full-map MESI directory coherence protocol.

Base Tardis: Baseline Tardis [10] where *lts* self increments by 1 for every 100 memory accesses.

Tardis + live: Baseline Tardis with livelock detection. *lts* self increments by 1 for every 1000 memory accesses.

Table 2: System Configuration.

System Configuration	
Number of Cores	N = 64
Core Model	Out-of-order, 128-entry ROB
Memory Subsystem	
Cacheline Size	64 bytes
L1 I Cache	16 KB, 4-way
L1 D Cache	32 KB, 4-way
Shared L2 Cache per Core	256 KB, 8-way
DRAM Bandwidth	8 MCs, 10 GB/s per MC
DRAM Latency	100 ns
2-D Mesh with XY Routing	
Hop Latency	2 cycles (1-router, 1-link)
Flit Width	128 bits

Table 3: Tardis Configuration.

Baseline Tardis	
Static Lease	8
Self Increment Period	100 memory accesses
Livelock Detector	
AHB size	8 entries
Threshold Counter	min 100, max 800
Check Threshold	10
Lease Prediction	
Minimal Lease Value	8
Maximal Lease Value	64

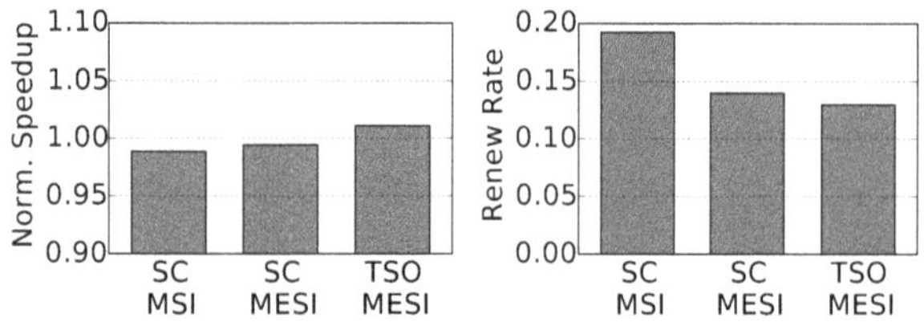

(a) Speedup (b) Renew Rate

Figure 3: MESI and TSO. Average speedup (normalized to directory + MESI + TSO) and renew rate over all benchmarks.

Tardis + live + lease: Tardis with both a livelock detector and lease predictor.

In Tardis, the base-delta timestamp compression scheme [10] was implemented and each timestamp requires 20 bits of storage. This means that each cacheline requires 40 bits in total for *wts* and *rts*, regardless of the number of cores in the system. The full-map directory protocol, in contrast, requires an N-bit sharer list for each cacheline in the LLC for an N-core system. However, note that timestamps are required in the L1 for the baseline and optimized Tardis unlike in the directory protocol.

Our experiments are executed over 22 benchmarks selected from Splash2 [24], PARSEC [25], sparse linear algebra [26] and OLTP database applications [27]. For sparse linear algebra, we evaluated sparse matrix multiplicaion (`SPMV`) and symmetric Gauss-Seidel smoother (`SYMGS`) from the HPCG benchmark suite (Top 500 supercomputer ranking). For OLTP database, we evaluated two benchmarks `YCSB` and `TPCC`. All benchmarks are executed to completion.

6.2 Consistency Models and MESI

Fig. 3 shows the speedup of MESI and TSO on Tardis normalized to the baseline directory coherence protocol with MESI and TSO. All experiments have both livelock detection and lease prediction enabled for a fair comparison. Both MESI and TSO can improve the overall performance of Tardis. On average, using MESI instead of MSI improves the performance of Tardis SC by 0.6%; using TSO instead of SC further improves performance by 1.7%.

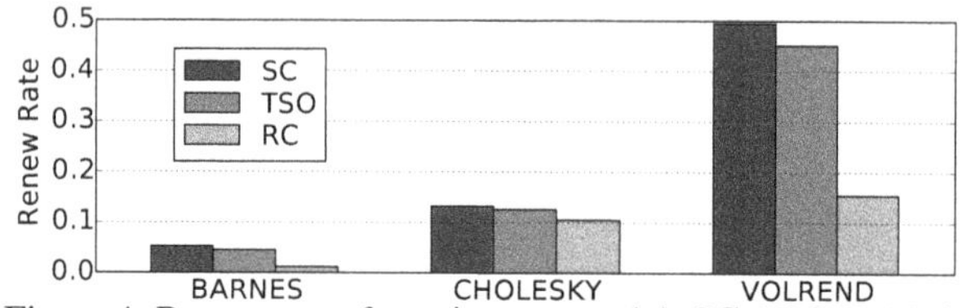

Figure 4: Renew rate of consistency models SC, TSO and RC.

MESI and TSO can also reduce the renew rate of Tardis. We define renew rate as the ratio of the number of renew requests over the total number of LLC accesses. Fig. 3b shows the renew rate reduction of MESI and TSO on Tardis. MESI reduces the number of renew messages since private readonly data is always cached in E state and therefore never renewed. TSO further reduces the renew rate since the *lts* may increase slower than the *pts* in SC (cf. Section 3.2.1) leading to fewer expirations/renewals. MESI and TSO together can reduce the average renew rate from 19.2% to 13.0%.

Although not shown in these figures, TSO can also significantly decrease the rate at which timestamps increase. This is because *lts* can stay behind *sts*. Therefore, *lts* and *sts* may increase slower than how *pts* increases in Tardis SC. On average, the timestamp increment rate in Tardis TSO is 78% of the rate in Tardis SC.

Fig. 4 shows the renew rate of SC, TSO and RC on Tardis with MESI. Due to some issues with running x86 pthread synchronization primitives on RC, we implemented hardware-based synchronization for this experiment and therefore use a separate graph to present the results. For many benchmarks that are *data-race-free*, relaxing the consistency models does not significantly reduce the renew rate. For some other benchmarks (like the ones in Fig. 4), however, more relaxed consistency models lead to significantly fewer renewals.

6.3 Livelock Detector and Lease Predictor

We now evaluate the performance and hardware overhead of the livelock detector and lease predictor of Section 5. All coherence protocols in this section use MESI and TSO.

6.3.1 Performance and Network Traffic

Fig. 5 shows the performance after adding livelock detection and lease prediction compared to the baseline Tardis protocol. All numbers are normalized to the baseline directory protocol.

First, we see that `CHOLESKY` and `SYMGS` on baseline Tardis have much worse performance than the directory protocol. Both benchmarks heavily use spinning to communicate between threads. As a result, it may take a long time for the cacheline spun on to expire. The livelock detector can close the performance gap between Tardis and directory because a spinning core is able to observe the latest data much earlier. `RADIOSITY` also uses spinning. However, the core does other computation between checking the value of the variable. Therefore, our livelock detector cannot capture such spinning behavior and forward progress is enforced through self incrementing *lts*. This leads to suboptimal performance. Completely eliminating such performance degradation requires rewriting the application using synchronization primitives better than spinning. Over the benchmark set, the optimizations improve the performance of Tardis by 7.5% with respect to the baseline Tardis and 1.1% (up to 9.8%) with respect to baseline directory protocol.

Fig. 6 shows the network traffic breakdown for the same four configurations as in Fig. 5. For each experiment, we show *dram traffic*, *common traffic*, *renew traffic* and *invalidation traffic*. *Common traffic* is the traffic in common for both directory coherence

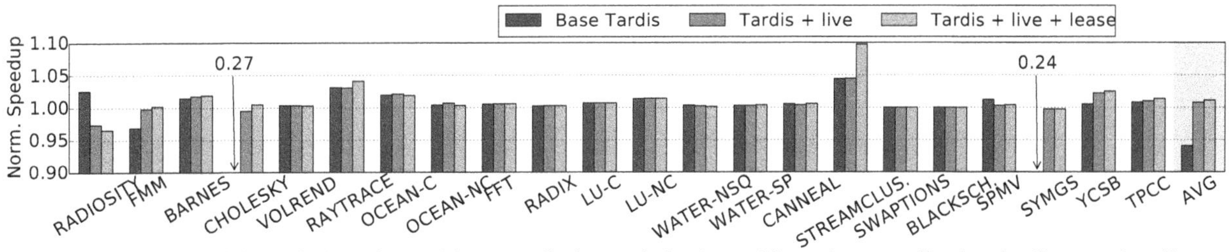

Figure 5: Speedup of livelock detection and lease prediction optimizations. All results normalized to the directory baseline.

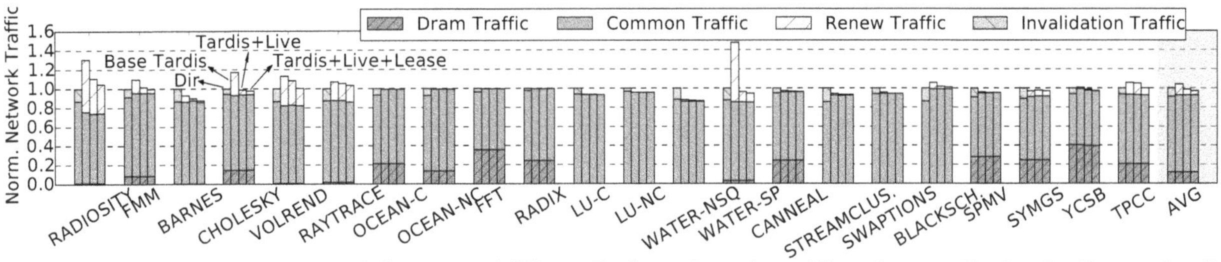

Figure 6: Network Traffic breakdown of directory and different Tardis configurations. All results normalized to the directory baseline.

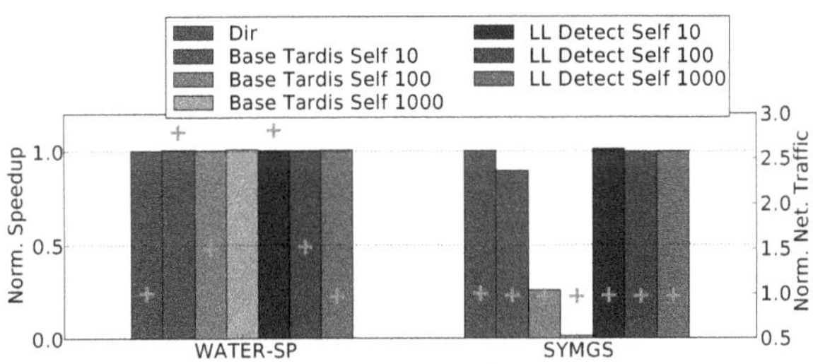

Figure 7: Sweep the *lts* self increment rate.

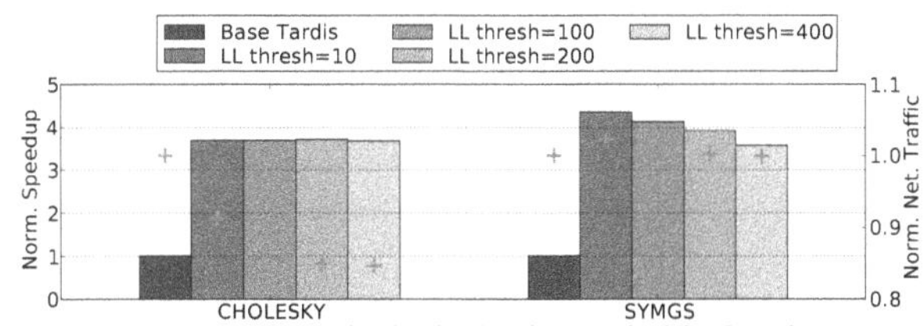

Figure 8: Sweep the livelock check threshold (*thresh_count*).

and Tardis, including shared, exclusive and write back memory requests and responses. *Renew traffic* is specific to Tardis including renew and check requests and responses. *Invalidation Traffic* is specific to the directory-based protocol, including the invalidation requests to shared copies from the directory, as well as the messages sent between L1 and LLC when a shared cacheline is evicted.

Compared to a directory protocol, Tardis is able to remove all the invalidation traffic. However, the renew traffic adds extra overhead. The baseline Tardis configuration incurs a large amount of renew traffic on some benchmarks (e.g., `RADIOSITY`, `CHOLESKY`, `VOLREND` and `WATER-SP`). Some of the renew traffic is due to fast self incrementing *lts* (e.g., `RADIOSITY`, `CHOLESKY` and `WATER-SP`). For these benchmarks, the livelock detection scheme can significantly reduce the self increment rate and therefore reduce the amount of renew traffic. On average, the livelock detection algorithm reduces the total network traffic by 5.4% compared to the baseline Tardis.

For some benchmarks, shared cachelines expire because the *lts* jumps ahead due to a write (e.g., `VOLREND`, `RADIOSITY`) and renew messages are generated. Our lease prediction algorithm is able to reduce these unnecessary renewals by using a larger lease for read intensive cachelines. On top of the livelock detection optimization, lease prediction further reduces the total network traffic by 1.5% on average. With both livelock detection and lease prediction, Tardis can reduce the total network traffic by 2.9% (up to 12.4%) compared to the baseline directory protocol.

Although not shown here, we also evaluated an idealized leasing scheme which is modeled by giving each renew message zero overhead. The idealized scheme has similar performance as the optimized Tardis but eliminates almost all the renewal messages; some renewals are still needed if the data has actually been changed.

6.3.2 Hardware Complexity

The hardware overhead for the livelock detector and lease predictor is generally small. Each livelock detector contains 8 AHB entries and each entry requires an address and a counter. Assuming 48-bit address space and a counter size of 2 bytes, the detector only requires 64 bytes of storage per core.

To implement the lease predictor, we need to store the current lease for each LLC and L1 cacheline. The lease is also transferred for each shared request and response. However, there is no need to store or transfer the whole lease value. Since a lease can only take a small number of possible values (e.g., 4 in our evaluation), we can use a smaller number of bits (e.g., 2 bits) to encode a lease, and the storage overhead is less than 0.4% in the LLC and in each L1.

6.4 Sensitivity Study

6.4.1 Self Increment Rate

Fig. 7 shows the performance and network traffic of Tardis sweeping the self increment period with and without livelock detection. All numbers are normalized to a baseline directory protocol. The `Base Tardis Self 100` is the baseline Tardis configuration and `LL Detect Self 1000` is the default optimized Tardis configuration (`LL Detect` stands for livelock detect).

In `WATER-SP`, changing the self incrementing rate does not affect performance regardless of whether livelock detection is turned on or not. This is because `WATER-SP` does not have spinning and renewals are unnecessary. Having a large self increment period significantly reduces the number of unnecessary renewals as well as the total network traffic.

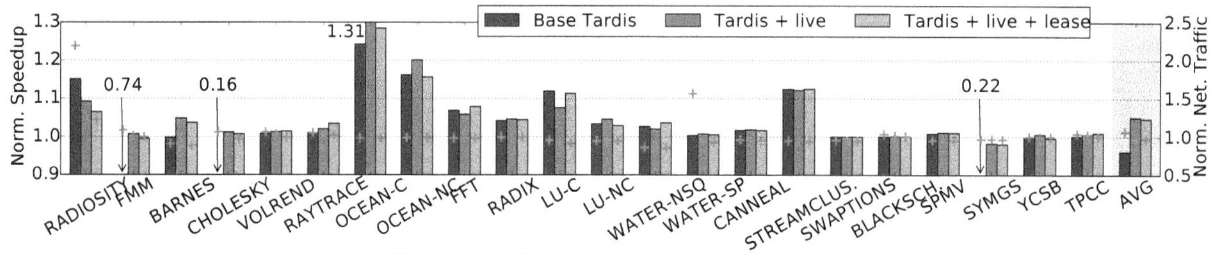

Figure 9: Tardis vs. Directory on 256 cores.

In SYMGS, for Tardis without livelock detection, performance is very sensitive to the self increment period because SYMGS intensively uses spinning to communicate between threads. If self increment is less frequent, a thread waits longer for the stale data to expire and thus performance degrades. With livelock detection, however, check requests are sent when spinning (potential livelock) is detected. Therefore, the latest value of a cacheline spun on can be returned much earlier. Regardless of the self increment period, Tardis with the livelock detector can always match the performance of the baseline directory protocol.

6.4.2 Address History Buffer Size

We swept the number of entries in the address history buffer in a livelock detector for CHOLESKY and SYMGS. According to the results (not shown), as long as the AHB buffer size is no less than 2, performance does not change. This is because in both (and most other) programs, spinning only involves a very small number of distinct memory addresses. CHOLESKY only spins on two addresses and SYMGS only spins on one address. We used a buffer size 8 by default but smaller buffers also work.

There do exist benchmarks where useful work is done during spinning and thus more than 8 distinct addresses are involved (e.g., RADIOSITY). Here, livelock detection is ineffective and correctness is guaranteed by the self incrementing program timestamp.

6.4.3 Livelock Threshold Counter

Fig. 8 shows the performance and network traffic normalized to the baseline Tardis when sweeping the minimal threshold counter (*min_counter* in Algorithm 2) in the livelock detector. The maximal threshold counter is always 8 times of the minimal value. Whenever an address in the AHB has been accessed *thresh_count* times, a check request is sent. With a larger *thresh_count*, checks are sent after spinning for a longer time which may hurt performance. On the other hand, larger *thresh_count* can reduce the total number of check messages and network traffic. In practice, the *thresh_count* should be chosen to balance the tradeoff. We chose 100 as the default threshold counter.

6.4.4 Scalability

Finally, Fig. 9 shows the performance and network traffic (normalized to baseline directory) of all benchmarks running on a 256-core system. Compared to the baseline directory, the optimized Tardis outperforms by 4.7% (upto 36.8%) and reduces the network traffic by 2.6% (upto 14.6%). Although not shown in the graph, we also evaluated Tardis and directory where both schemes consume the same area overhead. Since Tardis requires less area than directory for coherence meta data, it can have a 37% larger LLC. In area normalized evaluation, Tardis can outperform the baseline directory by 6% on average.

Note that at 256 cores, the performance improvement of Tardis is greater than the 64 core case. This indicates that Tardis not only has better scalability in terms of storage as core count increases, it also scales better in terms of performance.

7. RELATED WORK

Memory coherence is an important issue in shared memory systems with private storage in each core or processor. It has been widely studied and implemented in multicore processors [4, 5], multi-socket systems [28, 29] and distributed shared memory systems [30, 31]. Traditional directory or snoopy based coherence protocols enforce the global memory order in a consistency model using physical time order. They need an invalidation mechanism to guarantee correctness, and therefore either require non-scalable storage overhead (e.g., directory-based protocols) or broadcasting in the network (e.g., snoopy-based protocols).

Numerous previous works have tried to improve the scalability of directory coherence protocols [32, 8, 33, 9, 34, 6, 7]. Most of these works focused on better ways to organize the directory structure to improve scalability. Compared to the full-map directory protocol, these optimizations usually hurt performance and increase the design and verification complexity.

Several previous works have proposed to simplify the hardware coherence protocal for relaxed consistency models like release consistency ([35, 36, 37]) or TSO ([38]). Like Tardis, these protocols also do not require the sharer list in the directory. Unlike Tardis, they are based on the self-invalidation mechanism where all shared cachelines in an L1 cache need to be invalidated if the consistency model might be violated. For release consistency self invalidation happens for every synchronization instruction and for TSO it happens for every L1 cache miss.

Among papers along this line of research, TSO-CC [38] is the one most similar to Tardis TSO. However, since TSO-CC is self-invalidation based, it would incur more L1 misses than Tardis for benchmarks with a lot of fences. Another advantage of Tardis over TSO-CC is that Tardis is able to efficiently support any consistency model with minimal hardware reconfiguration. Running a legacy SC program on TSO-CC hardware, however, will end up with sub-optimal performance and efficiency.

8. CONCLUSION

In this paper, several optimization techniques have been applied to Tardis, a very scalable physiological time based cache coherence protocol. Further, more relaxed consistency models such as the Total Store Order (TSO), Partial Store Order (PSO) and Release Consistency (RC) models are now supported in Tardis. On our set of benchmarks, evaluations indicate that optimized Tardis is better than a full-map directory protocol in terms of performance, energy and storage while being simpler.

Acknowledgement: This research was partially supported by MIT PRIMES. We thank Larry Rudolph for helping us improve this paper.

9. REFERENCES

[1] M. S. Papamarcos and J. H. Patel, "A low-overhead coherence solution for multiprocessors with private cache memories," ACM SIGARCH Computer Architecture News, vol. 12, no. 3, pp. 348–354, 1984.

[2] L. M. Censier and P. Feautrier, "A new solution to coherence problems in multicache systems," Computers, IEEE Transactions on, vol. 100, no. 12, pp. 1112–1118, 1978.

[3] C. Tang, "Cache system design in the tightly coupled multiprocessor system," in Proceedings of the June 7-10, 1976, national computer conference and exposition, pp. 749–753, ACM, 1976.

[4] "Tile-gx family of multicore processors." http://www.tilera.com.

[5] Intel, "Intel Xeon Phi Coprocessor System Software Developers Guide," 2014.

[6] J. H. Kelm, M. R. Johnson, S. S. Lumetta, and S. J. Patel, "WAYPOINT: scaling coherence to thousand-core architectures," in Proceedings of the 19th international conference on Parallel architectures and compilation techniques, pp. 99–110, ACM, 2010.

[7] D. Sanchez and C. Kozyrakis, "SCD: A scalable coherence directory with flexible sharer set encoding," in High Performance Computer Architecture (HPCA), 2012 IEEE 18th International Symposium on, pp. 1–12, IEEE, 2012.

[8] G. Kurian, J. Miller, J. Psota, J. Eastep, J. Liu, J. Michel, L. Kimerling, and A. Agarwal, "ATAC: A 1000-Core Cache-Coherent Processor with On-Chip Optical Network," in International Conference on Parallel Architectures and Compilation Techniques, 2010.

[9] Y.-C. Maa, D. K. Pradhan, and D. Thiebaut, "Two economical directory schemes for large-scale cache coherent multiprocessors," ACM SIGARCH Computer Architecture News, vol. 19, no. 5, p. 10, 1991.

[10] X. Yu and S. Devadas, "Tardis: Time traveling coherence algorithm for distributed shared memory," in Parallel Architectures and Compilation Techniques (PACT), 2015 International Conference on, 2015.

[11] X. Yu, M. Vijayaraghavan, and S. Devadas, "A Proof of Correctness for the Tardis Cache Coherence Protocol," CoRR, vol. abs/1505.06459, May 2015.

[12] P. Sewell, S. Sarkar, S. Owens, F. Z. Nardelli, and M. O. Myreen, "x86-tso: a rigorous and usable programmer's model for x86 multiprocessors," Communications of the ACM, vol. 53, no. 7, pp. 89–97, 2010.

[13] D. L. Weaver and T. Germond, "The SPARC Architecture Manual," 1994.

[14] D. Seal, ARM architecture reference manual. Pearson Education, 2001.

[15] S. Mador-Haim, L. Maranget, S. Sarkar, K. Memarian, J. Alglave, S. Owens, R. Alur, M. M. Martin, P. Sewell, and D. Williams, "An axiomatic memory model for power multiprocessors," in Computer Aided Verification, pp. 495–512, Springer, 2012.

[16] L. Lamport, "Time, clocks, and the ordering of events in a distributed system," Communications of the ACM, vol. 21, no. 7, pp. 558–565, 1978.

[17] P. A. Bernstein, D. Shipman, and W. Wong, "Formal aspects of serializability in database concurrency control," IEEE Transactions on Software Engineering, vol. 5, no. 3, pp. 203–216, 1979.

[18] D. P. Reed, Naming and synchronization in a decentralized computer system. PhD thesis, Massachusetts Institute of Technology, 1978.

[19] L. Lamport, "How to make a multiprocessor computer that correctly executes multiprocess programs," Computers, IEEE Transactions on, vol. 100, no. 9, pp. 690–691, 1979.

[20] D. J. Sorin, M. D. Hill, and D. A. Wood, "A primer on memory consistency and cache coherence," Synthesis Lectures on Computer Architecture, vol. 6, no. 3, pp. 1–212, 2011.

[21] K. Gharachorloo, A. Gupta, and J. Hennessy, "Two Techniques to Enhance the Performance of Memory Consistency Models," in In Proceedings of the 1991 International Conference on Parallel Processing, pp. 355–364, 1991.

[22] K. Gharachorloo, D. Lenoski, J. Laudon, P. Gibbons, A. Gupta, and J. Hennessy, Memory consistency and event ordering in scalable shared-memory multiprocessors, vol. 18. ACM, 1990.

[23] J. E. Miller, H. Kasture, G. Kurian, C. Gruenwald, N. Beckmann, C. Celio, J. Eastep, and A. Agarwal, "Graphite: A Distributed Parallel Simulator for Multicores," in International Symposium on High-Performance Computer Architecture, 2010.

[24] S. C. Woo, M. Ohara, E. Torrie, J. P. Singh, and A. Gupta, "The SPLASH-2 Programs: Characterization and Methodological Considerations," in International Symposium on Computer Architecture, 1995.

[25] C. Bienia, Benchmarking Modern Multiprocessors. PhD thesis, Princeton University, January 2011.

[26] J. Dongarra, "Toward a new metric for ranking high performance computing systems," 2013.

[27] X. Yu, G. Bezerra, A. Pavlo, S. Devadas, and M. Stonebraker, "Staring into the Abyss: An Evaluation of Concurrency Control with One Thousand Cores," Proceedings of the VLDB Endowment, vol. 8, no. 3, pp. 209–220, 2014.

[28] D. Ziakas, A. Baum, R. A. Maddox, and R. J. Safranek, "Intel® quickpath interconnect architectural features supporting scalable system architectures," in High Performance Interconnects (HOTI), 2010 IEEE 18th Annual Symposium on, pp. 1–6, IEEE, 2010.

[29] D. Anderson and J. Trodden, Hypertransport system architecture. Addison-Wesley Professional, 2003.

[30] K. Li and P. Hudak, "Memory coherence in shared virtual memory systems," ACM Transactions on Computer Systems (TOCS), vol. 7, no. 4, pp. 321–359, 1989.

[31] P. Keleher, A. L. Cox, S. Dwarkadas, and W. Zwaenepoel, "Treadmarks: Distributed shared memory on standard workstations and operating systems," in USENIX Winter, vol. 1994, 1994.

[32] A. Agarwal, R. Simoni, J. Hennessy, and M. Horowitz, "An evaluation of directory schemes for cache coherence," in 25 years of the international symposia on Computer architecture (selected papers), pp. 353–362, ACM, 1998.

[33] D. Chaiken, C. Fields, K. Kurihara, and A. Agarwal, "Directory-based cache coherence in large-scale multiprocessors," Computer, vol. 23, no. 6, pp. 49–58, 1990.

[34] A. Gupta, W.-D. Weber, and T. Mowry, "Reducing memory and traffic requirements for scalable directory-based cache coherence schemes," in International Conference on Parallel Processing, 1990.

[35] B. Choi, R. Komuravelli, H. Sung, R. Smolinski, N. Honarmand, S. V. Adve, V. S. Adve, N. P. Carter, and C.-T. Chou, "DeNovo: Rethinking the memory hierarchy for disciplined parallelism," in Parallel Architectures and Compilation Techniques (PACT), 2011 International Conference on, pp. 155–166, IEEE, 2011.

[36] A. Ros and S. Kaxiras, "Complexity-effective multicore coherence," in Proceedings of the 21st international conference on Parallel architectures and compilation techniques, pp. 241–252, ACM, 2012.

[37] H. Sung, R. Komuravelli, and S. V. Adve, "DeNovoND: Efficient hardware support for disciplined non-determinism," ACM SIGARCH Computer Architecture News, vol. 41, no. 1, pp. 13–26, 2013.

[38] M. Elver and V. Nagarajan, "TSO-CC: Consistency directed cache coherence for TSO," in International Symposium on High Performance Computer Architecture, pp. 165–176, 2014.

Reducing Cache Coherence Traffic with Hierarchical Directory Cache and NUMA-Aware Runtime Scheduling

Paul Caheny†§ paul.caheny@bsc.es
Marc Casas†§ marc.casas@bsc.es
Miquel Moretó†§ miquel.moreto@bsc.es
Hervé Gloaguen‡ herve.gloaguen@atos.net
Maxime Saintes‡ maxime.saintes@atos.net
Eduard Ayguadé†§ eduard.ayguade@bsc.es
Jesús Labarta†§ jesus.labarta@bsc.es
Mateo Valero†§ mateo.valero@bsc.es

Barcelona Supercomputing Center† Barcelona, Spain
Departament d'Arquitectura de Computadors§ Universitat Politècnica de Catalunya Barcelona, Spain
Bull Atos Technologies‡ Les Clayes-sous-Bois France

ABSTRACT

Cache Coherent NUMA (ccNUMA) architectures are a widespread paradigm due to the benefits they provide for scaling core count and memory capacity. Also, the flat memory address space they offer considerably improves programmability. However, ccNUMA architectures require sophisticated and expensive cache coherence protocols to enforce correctness during parallel executions, which trigger a significant amount of on- and off-chip traffic in the system.

This paper analyses how coherence traffic may be best constrained in a large, real ccNUMA platform through the use of a joint hardware/software approach. For several benchmarks, we study coherence traffic in detail under the influence of an added hierarchical cache layer in the directory protocol combined with runtime managed NUMA-aware scheduling and data allocation techniques to make most efficient use of the added hardware. The effectiveness of this joint approach is demonstrated by speedups of 1.23x to 2.54x and coherence traffic reductions between 44% and 77% in comparison to NUMA-oblivious scheduling and data allocation. Furthermore, we show that the NUMA-aware techniques we employ at the runtime level are crucial to ensure the added hierarchical layer in the directory coherence protocol does not introduce significant coherence traffic to the system.

Keywords

Cache Coherence; NUMA; Task-based programming models

PACT '16, September 11-15, 2016, Haifa, Israel

DOI: http://dx.doi.org/10.1145/2967938.2967962

1. INTRODUCTION

ccNUMA architectures have become a ubiquitous approach in the design of SMP systems that need to scale to large numbers of cores and amounts of memory capacity in pursuit of increased thread level parallelism. ccNUMA architectures provide clear advantages by increasing provision of resources such as capacity, bandwidth and parallelism in the memory hierarchy through physically distributing the cache and memory subsystem while maintaining a logically shared view of memory for the user. Since the cache and memory are both shared and distributed, many memory accesses result in a coherence transaction. Depending on the state of the accessed cache line in the system, such coherence transactions may be costly in terms of number of coherence messages required and latency involved. This coherence traffic travelling through on- and off-chip networks within SMP architectures is responsible for a significant proportion of the system energy consumption [24]. Minimising this data movement by using runtime systems and parallel codes that judiciously manage data locality is therefore crucial for both energy efficiency and performance.

The most common way to program shared memory SMP systems are thread-based programming models like OpenMP [23] or Pthreads [6], which provide basic mechanisms to handle NUMA architectures. The OpenMP 4.0 standard supports tasking and data dependencies. These two features provide the opportunity for a runtime system to automatically handle data locality in a performance optimal NUMA-aware fashion based on knowledge of the NUMA topology of the system, the concrete specification of the data each task requires in the programming model and tracking where the data is allocated within the NUMA regions of the system [10, 28]. Such an approach makes data motion a first class element of the programming model, allowing the runtime system to optimise for energy and performance.

The real impact of NUMA-aware work scheduling mechanisms on the cache coherence traffic that occurs within SMP architectures is not well understood as it may be masked by other factors. For example, to effectively deploy a NUMA-aware work scheduling mechanism over an SMP NUMA system two stipulations are required. (1) Data must be uniformly distributed amongst all the NUMA regions the system is composed of, and, **(2)** work must be scheduled where its requisite data resides. Then, it is not clear what proportion of the observed benefits of a NUMA-aware work scheduling mechanism are due to (1) or (2). In this work we distinguish between the effects of (1) and (2) on both cache coherence traffic and performance.

In this work we directly and in detail characterise cache coherence traffic in a real system with workloads relevant to high performance and data centric computing, relate this traffic to performance and assess the effectiveness of combining runtime managed scheduling and data allocation techniques with hardware approaches designed to minimise such traffic. We use a large SMP architecture, a Bull bullion S [1] server platform, to make our analysis. The bullion S platform utilises a sophisticated ccNUMA architecture composed of sets of 2 sockets grouped into entities called modules. The Bull Coherence Switch (BCS), a proprietary ASIC, manages the inter-module interface and enables scaling up to a maximum configuration of 8 modules (16 sockets of Intel Xeon CPUs) in a single SMP system. The BCS achieves this by providing an extra module level layer in the directory architecture managing coherence among the L3s in the system. The in-memory directory information stored as normal by the Intel architecture tracks directory information for cache lines shared within a module on a per-socket granularity while the directory information tracked in the BCS is at a less granular per-module basis for cache lines which are exported inter-module. The BCS caches module level directory information about cache lines which are transferred between the different modules in the system. This directory information allows the BCS to filter coherence traffic from the system interconnect in certain cases and thus enable scaling to larger coherent systems.

Our work uses the measurement capabilities provided by the BCS to perform a direct fine grain analysis of the coherence traffic within the system. To the best of our knowledge, this paper contains the first study on how a hierarchical directory approach [19] to scaling cache coherence interacts with a runtime managed strategy to promote data locality. Indeed, we show how the extra layer of the coherence hierarchy implemented by the BCS is most fully exploited in combination with runtime managed NUMA-aware regimes for reducing coherence traffic among multiple NUMA regions.

Specifically, these are the main contributions of this paper:

- A complete performance analysis of a large SMP architecture considering three important scientific codes and three regimes of work scheduling and memory allocation: 1) Default (NUMA-oblivious) scheduling and first touch allocation 2) Default (NUMA-oblivious) scheduling and interleaved allocation which uniformly interleaves memory among NUMA regions at page granularity. 3) NUMA-aware runtime managed scheduling and allocation. We see performance improvements up to 2.54x among the benchmarks when utilising the NUMA-aware regime versus the baseline.

- For the three regimes, a detailed measurement of the coherence traffic within the SMP system, broken down into data traffic versus control traffic. We further decompose these traffic types into message classes e.g. data delivered to cache, write backs from cache and the different request and response classes in the control traffic. We see reductions in coherence traffic up to 77% among the benchmarks when utilising the NUMA-aware regime versus the baseline.

- We show that extra layer of the coherence hierarchy implemented by the BCS works optimally when combined with runtime managed NUMA-aware scheduling and data allocation. Such a regime of scheduling and data allocation reduces capacity pressure on the directory cache in the BCS enabling it to make a net reduction in the amount of systemwide snoop related traffic of up to 35%. In contrast, we demonstrate that NUMA-oblivious policies or uneven memory allocations may overwhelm the capacity of the BCS, forcing it to inject extra snoop traffic into the system to maintain its directory state.

This paper is organised as follows: Section 2 details the types and classes of coherence traffic in our analysis. Section 3 describes the architecture of the large SMP system used to make our analysis. Section 4 introduces the programming model and runtime system which supports the three different regimes of work scheduling and data allocation. Section 5 details the three benchmarks used. Section 6 presents the results of our analysis of the performance and coherence traffic. Section 7 discusses related work. Lastly, we conclude the paper in Section 8.

2. CACHE COHERENCE TRAFFIC

While the logically flat view of memory an SMP offers the user is convenient and considerably eases the programming burden, it does require a sophisticated mechanism to enforce coherence between the multiple physically distributed caches and memories in the system.

In order to analyse this mechanism we categorise the coherence traffic it triggers within the SMP into two types, each consisting of different classes of messages. The first type, Data messages, contain user data (cache lines) while the second type, Control messages, are messages that signal activities in the coherence protocol and do not contain user data. For example, a message transferring a cache line from a memory to a cache (or vice versa) belongs to the Data traffic type while asking a certain cache for the status of a cache line or requesting data in a certain state from a memory would be of the Control traffic type.

To understand in greater detail in what nature the software (work scheduling & data allocation regime) techniques and the BCS affect the traffic we further break down the two types of traffic into message classes. An outline of message classes and their role in the coherence protocol follows:

Data Messages: Messages that carry a single cache line payload. If the receiver is a cache the message is of the *DTC (Data To Cache)* class, the sender of such messages may be a memory or another cache. If a memory is the receiver of a Data message, the message falls into the *DWB (Data Write Back)* class, the sender of a DWB message is always a cache.

Control Messages: Messages that carry protocol signalling messages without a data payload. Request messages from a cache to a memory belong to the *HREQ (Home Request)* class. For example such a request could be the cache asking the memory for access to a cache line in a certain state. Depending on the existing state of the cache line in the requesting cache and the state the cache line is requested in, a *HREQ* may be reciprocated by a *DTC* message. *SNP*

Table 1: Coherence protocol message classes

Type	Class	Description
Data	DWB	Data Write Back, message from cache to memory with cache line payload
Data	DTC	Data To Cache, message towards cache with cache line payload
Control	HREQ	Home Request, cache requesting a cache line in a certain state from memory
Control	SNP	Snoop, memory requesting state of cache line or invalidating cache line from cache
Control	HRSP	Home Response, cache providing state of cache line to memory
Control	NDR	Non-Data Response, memory signals transaction completion to cache, data not required

(Snoop) messages are requests from a memory to a cache asking the cache to perform some action, for example to invalidate a cache line or forward it to another cache. Depending on the exact nature of a SNP message it may be reciprocated by a *HRSP (Home Response)* message which is a confirmation sent from a cache to a memory that the action requested by the SNP is completed. An *NDR (Non-Data Response)* message is sent from a memory to a cache to signal the completion of a coherence transaction, where the memory did not need to deliver data to the cache. This could be because, for example, the data was delivered indirectly from another cache to the requesting cache or the requesting cache already had the data but requested to change the state of the cache line.

All these classes, conveniently classified as Data or Control traffic and summarised in Table 1, comprise a total decomposition of the cache coherence traffic at the LLC (Last Level Cache) to memory interface within the SMP and provide an insightful basis upon which to analyse the effectiveness of the three work scheduling and data allocation regimes and the BCS on the coherence traffic.

3. BULLION S ARCHITECTURE

Figure 1 shows a dual module bullion S system. The bullion S platform has the capability to scale to eight modules in its maximum configuration. Each module comprises two Intel Xeon sockets and their local memory connected to a single Bull proprietary ASIC, the BCS.

3.1 Cache Coherence in the bullion S System

The BCS is the glue for connecting multiple modules into a single SMP system. Cache coherence traffic statistics are collected from the BCS during benchmark execution. As all coherence traffic is measured within the BCS, the results we present include only coherence traffic travelling via the BCS (see Figure 1) in each module. Traffic travelling directly between the two CPUs within a single module does not travel via a BCS and is therefore not included. Measurements are recorded at each BCS in the system for both traffic incoming to the BCS (from its two local CPU sockets) and traffic outgoing from the BCS (towards its two local CPU sockets). We term this incoming or outgoing nature of the traffic its directionality. Henceforth, all references to cache refer to the LLC (labelled L3 in Figure 1) of a processor unless otherwise indicated and the coherence traffic observed represents only coherence transactions at the interface of the LLC cache and the system memory (via a BCS). In Figure 1, for the purposes of cache coherence transactions, the system memory is represented by the units labelled MC (Memory Controller).

The BCS is an actor in the cache coherence protocol of the system rather than simply a routing point for inter-module messages. The BCS caches module level directory information about cache lines which have been exported from a memory in its local NUMA regions to caches in other modules. This enables the BCS to act as a proxy for an L3 cache or memory controller in certain inter-module cache transactions, reducing the coherence traffic required in the system.

For example, for SNP and HRSP messages the BCS may filter messages from the system, where it can participate in the coherence transaction in place of a CPU. Therefore, SNP messages may appear as incoming to a BCS in one module without appearing as outgoing in any other module and vice versa for the HRSP messages. In the process of maintaining its own directory information the BCS may also initiate SNP messages to other modules, so CPUs may see SNP messages which originate at a BCS and not at any other processor in the system. Therefore, SNP messages may appear as outgoing from a BCS without having appeared as incoming to any other BCS in the system. When NDR messages are sent by a CPU they may be piggybacked on unused bits in other messages classes as a bandwidth optimisation implemented by the CPUs. To optimise for latency, the BCS does not piggyback NDR messages on other message classes. For these reasons there may be an asymmetry between the incoming and outgoing traffic levels for the SNP, HRSP and NDR message types.

For the HREQ, DTC and DWB message classes, messages recorded as incoming to the BCS in one module will always pass through the inter-module link and appear as outgoing from the BCS in another module and vice versa. This means the amount of traffic for these message classes in the entire system is symmetric in directionality.

By analysing the coherence traffic in the message types and classes defined in Table 1 under the different memory allocation and scheduling regimes it is possible to provide a detailed characterisation of the effect of the different regimes and the BCS on the coherence traffic.

3.2 System Environment & Characteristics

In this work we use an experimental dual module installation of the bullion S platform, running RHEL 6.5 with a Linux kernel version of 2.6.32. Each module is composed of two 15 core Intel *Ivy Bridge EX* E7 8890 v2 processors. Each Intel Xeon socket has a local NUMA region containing 8 GB of system memory made up of two 4 GB DIMMs. This means that of the eight memory channels connected to each socket, two are occupied by DIMMs.

The main memory subsystem may be operated in one of two modes, selectable as a systemwide parameter in the firmware. *Lockstep Mode* provides higher RAS (Reliability, Availability, Service) features than *Performance Mode.* Typically Lockstep Mode can provide around 60% of the memory bandwidth available in performance mode if both modes are configured optimally.

The memory subsystem in the system we use is configured in Lockstep Mode. Therefore the complete system has four sockets and NUMA regions, 32GB of system memory, and a total physical core count of 60. The memory configuration results in each socket having a theoretical maximum memory bandwidth within its local NUMA region of 10.6 GB/s

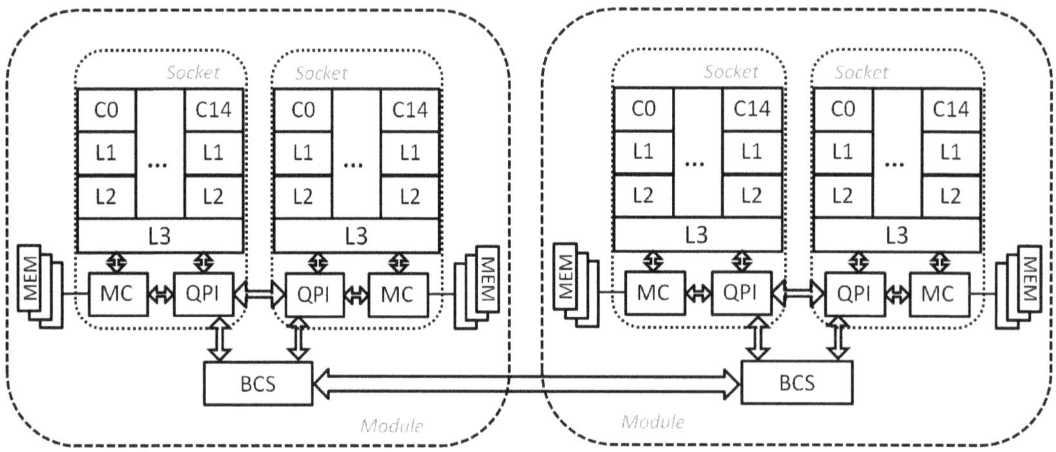

Figure 1: Logical view of a dual module bullion S system

Table 2

(a) NUMA distances

Region	0	1	2	3
0	10	15	40	40
1	15	10	40	40
2	40	40	10	15
3	40	40	15	10

(b) Latencies (ns)

0	1	2	3
115.4	178.5	407.5	404.5
183.2	109.9	400	398
419.6	401.9	109.9	173.4
415.5	401.8	173.7	110.6

Table 3: Bandwidth for the different NUMA distances in the system with the STREAM Triad benchmark (GB/s)

Region	0	1	2	3
0	5.39	4.15	4.12	**4.92**
1	4.14	5.40	4.12	**4.92**
2	4.11	4.12	5.40	**4.96**
3	4.09	4.12	4.15	**6.86**

Information regarding the NUMA topology of a system is typically available from the firmware via the OS. The `numactl -hardware` command may be used to display the information the OS provides to the runtime regarding NUMA distances. As denoted in Tables 2 and 3 by the three different colours, the system has three levels of NUMA distance. A coherence message may travel within the local NUMA region (green), to the single 'near' remote NUMA region, i.e. the other NUMA region in the local module (yellow), or to one of two 'far' remote NUMA regions, i.e. the NUMA regions in the remote module (red). Table 2a shows the three classes of NUMA distance in the system. Besides the NUMA distances provided by the firmware we measure the real latencies and memory bandwidths available across the different NUMA distances in the system. We use Intel's Memory Latency Checker (MLC) [29] to measure the latencies and the STREAM benchmark [20] to measure the memory bandwidths. The latencies in the system (Table 2b) follow the same pattern and similar ratios to the NUMA distances in Table 2a. On average there is a 58% latency penalty in accessing memory in the neighbouring NUMA region in the same module in comparison to accessing memory in the local NUMA region. There is a further latency penalty of 129% to access data in either of the NUMA regions in the other module (or a 264% penalty for inter-module access compared to local NUMA region access).

Table 3 shows the memory bandwidths measured in the system for the STREAM Triad benchmark. These results use all the threads available on a single socket (15) to saturate the bandwidth to the memory of a given NUMA region. The memory bandwidth values measured follow the same pattern seen in Tables 2a and 2b, with a small aberration, the values in bold (column 3 of Table 3) are higher than the figures for the other NUMA distances in the same class (i.e. of the same colour in the table). This is due to dual rank DIMMs being installed in NUMA region 3 and single rank DIMMs elsewhere in the system.

4. MEMORY ALLOCATION AND SCHEDULING

In this work we use a task-based data-flow programming model, an approach supported by OpenMP 4.0. In this model the execution of a parallel program is structured as a set of tasks with dependences among them. The programmer identifies tasks by annotating serial code with directives. Data-flow is represented by clauses in the directives which specify what data is used by a task (called input dependencies) and produced by each task (called output dependencies). The runtime manages parallel execution of the tasks, relieving the programmer from explicitly synchronising and scheduling tasks and thus promoting programmability.

We use the OmpSs [11] task-based data-flow programming model to experiment with a diverse set of memory allocation and scheduling regimes. The OmpSs programming model supports task constructs in a very similar way to OpenMP 4.0. The task-based data-flow programming model supported by both OpenMP 4.0 and OmpSs provide the potential to implement NUMA-aware scheduling in the runtime system. The OmpSs runtime system, called Nanos++ [3], already supports NUMA-aware scheduling in the release we use, version 0.9a.

The default (NUMA-oblivious) OmpSs runtime scheduler maintains one global queue of ready tasks for the entire SMP system. Tasks are scheduled among cores without considering where their data dependencies reside. In contrast, the NUMA-aware OmpSs scheduler maintains one ready queue per NUMA region within the SMP system. Tasks are enqueued in the NUMA region in which the largest proportion of their data dependencies reside. The runtime system accomplishes this through bookkeeping of data location [5]. When data is first tied to a physical memory location (at the time of the data's initialisation) within an OmpSs task the runtime system records which NUMA region the data is physically located in. When scheduling subsequent tasks the runtime system examines the data dependencies of each task to calculate which NUMA region contains the largest proportion of each task's data dependencies. Each task is then added to the ready queue of the NUMA region which has the largest amount of data required by the task.

We use three regimes of task scheduling and memory allocation to analyse the impact of NUMA-aware scheduling on the coherence traffic classes defined in Section 2.

4.1 Scheduling & Memory Allocation Regimes

The OmpSs features described above allow us to define several execution regimes of task scheduling and memory allocation. In all cases where we use less than the maximum number of cores in the system the cores in use are uniformly distributed among the four NUMA regions of the system.

__D__efault scheduling & __F__irst __T__ouch allocation (__DFT__): Tasks are scheduled in a NUMA oblivious fashion among all available cores in the system, ensuring load is balanced. Data is allocated in the NUMA region of the core where the allocation happens to execute, via the Linux first touch memory allocation policy. In a worst case scenario, all data may happen to be allocated in a single NUMA region, leaving others entirely unused. Tasks using the allocated data are scheduled among the available cores without any consideration for where their requisite data resides.

__D__efault scheduling & __I__nterleaved allocation (__DI__): Tasks are scheduled in a NUMA-oblivious fashion, as in DFT, ensuring load is balanced. Nevertheless, all data allocations are uniformly distributed among all the NUMA regions in the system. This is achieved with the Linux NUMA interleaved memory allocation policy which distributes allocated memory among all NUMA regions at a page granularity, regardless of what core the allocation runs on. Data is guaranteed to be uniformly distributed among all NUMA regions in the system (at page granularity). However, tasks using allocated data run without any consideration for where their data dependencies reside.

__N__UMA-__A__ware scheduling & __F__irst __T__ouch allocation (__NAFT__): Tasks are scheduled in a NUMA-aware fashion. The application's memory allocating code is encapsulated in tasks by the programmer. The runtime system automatically recognises tasks which allocate data and schedules them in a uniformly distributed arrangement among the NUMA regions. Each task which allocates data allocates all its data locally in the NUMA region it runs in via the Linux first touch memory allocation policy. Memory is therefore guaranteed to be uniformly distributed among all NUMA regions in the system (at a per-task allocation granularity, determined by the programmer). Tasks using the allocated data are scheduled on cores in the NUMA region where the majority of their data dependencies reside. Uniquely under NAFT, it is possible load imbalance may occur due to the NUMA-aware scheduling. In this case the runtime system handles it via work-stealing. Load imbalance was negligible in all our experiments.

A regime utilising NUMA-aware scheduling & interleaved allocation is not a valid combination. This is because, in order to create data locality, the NUMA-aware scheduler depends on each task allocating data to do so in its local NUMA region only, via first touch.

5. BENCHMARKS

We chose three benchmarks for use in our evaluations, representative of important problems in both high performance and data centric computing, with significantly different data access patterns. One is from the PARSEC benchmark suite [4] and two are based on linear algebra problems [2].

PARSEC Streamcluster This benchmark from the PARSEC suite is based on the online clustering problem. This problem organises large volumes of continuously produced streaming data in real-time with applications in areas such as network intrusion detection, data mining and pattern recognition. The benchmark is dominated by a streaming read data access pattern and is adapted to a task-based implementation in the OmpSs programming model. This benchmark runs using the native input data set as specified by the PARSEC documentation and is executed on a varying number of cores (16 to 32) distributed evenly across the four sockets in the system.

Cholesky This benchmark uses a modern tile-based algorithm for the Cholesky factorisation problem in linear algebra which exposes fine grained parallelism and is implemented in the task-based OmpSs programming model.

Symmetric Matrix Inversion (SMI) This benchmark is a larger linear algebra problem which inverts a symmetric matrix in three stages. It also follows a tile-based algorithm thus exposing fine grained parallelism. It is implemented in the task-based OmpSs programming model.

Both linear algebra benchmarks exhibit a complex data access pattern comprising a mix of reads and writes and are run across different core counts (16 to 32) with threads distributed evenly across the four sockets in the system. In all cases, the size (N) of the NxN matrix we use in both linear algebra benchmarks is 20480. At this value of N, in all cases, the benchmark's performance has reached the maximum attainable (in GFLOP/s) and is no longer increasing with larger values of N. We experimented with different tile sizes for both linear algebra benchmarks and found a tile size of 512 to give the best performance in all cases and this is the tile size used for all the linear algebra results we present. All performance and coherence traffic measurements are repeated three times and the mean value reported.

6. RESULTS AND ANALYSIS

6.1 Introduction

In this section we present a detailed analysis of the coherence traffic generated by running the benchmarks presented in Section 5 on different numbers of cores on the bullion S system. We present results for the benchmarks under the three regimes detailed in Section 4.1 : DFT, DI and NAFT. First, in Section 6.2 we present a decomposition of the coherence traffic into the two Data message classes (DWB and DTC) plus aggregate Control traffic (which comprises

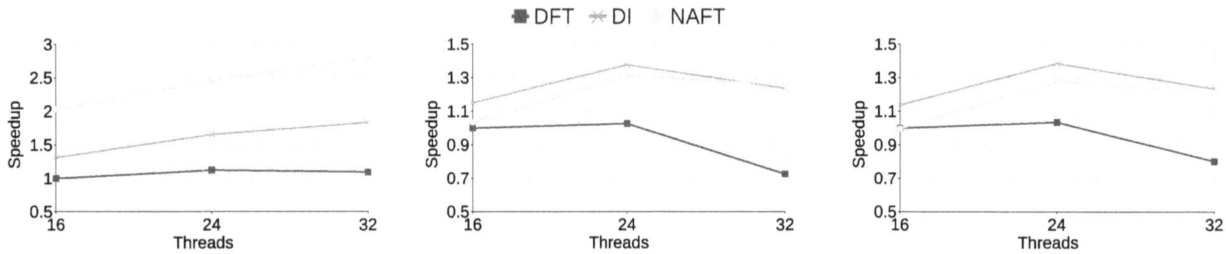

(a) Streamcluster (b) Cholesky (c) SMI

Figure 2: Speedup DFT, DI, NAFT regimes under increasing thread count

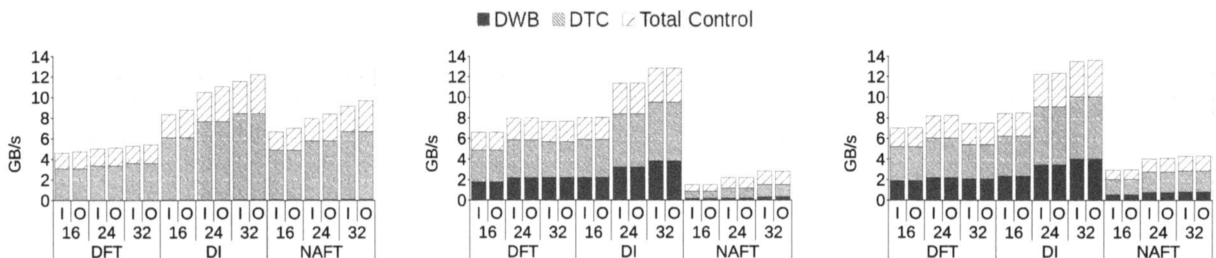

(a) Streamcluster (b) Cholesky (c) SMI

Figure 3: Coherence Bandwidth: DWB, DTC and Control traffic

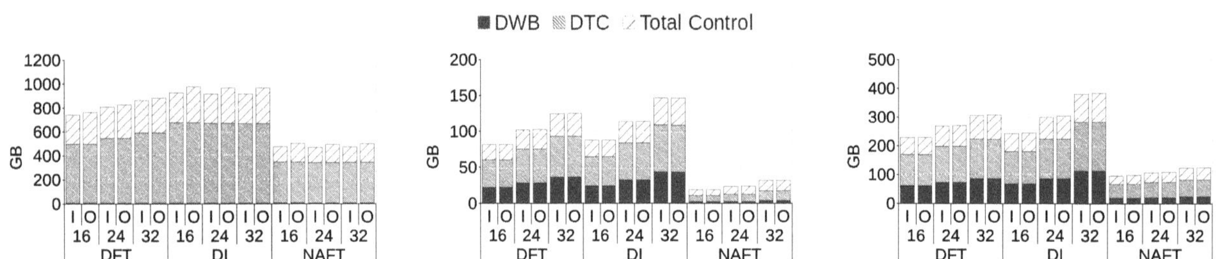

(a) Streamcluster (b) Cholesky (c) SMI

Figure 4: Coherence Movement: DWB, DTC and Control traffic

SNP, HRSP, HREQ and NDR). Secondly, in Section 6.3 we present a detailed breakdown of the Control traffic type into its individual message classes. Thirdly, in Section 6.4 we focus on the interplay between the three software based regimes for task scheduling and memory allocation and the two level directory hierarchy managing coherence among the L3s in the system.

For each benchmark, thread count and execution regime, we present the coherence traffic profile in two views, both measured at the BCS (see Section 3.1 for the site of measurement and precisely which coherence traffic we measure): **(1)** the bandwidth utilised by coherence traffic during benchmark execution, called **Coherence Bandwidth**, and **(2)** the total coherence traffic data moved over the entire course of the benchmark execution, called **Coherence Movement**. The coherence bandwidth and coherence movement views are related via the execution time as coherence bandwidth is the coherence movement per second of execution time. All Figures show the systemwide (i.e. both modules aggregated) coherence traffic. The traffic's directionality (see Section 3.1) is labelled as I and O in all figures for incoming and outgoing traffic respectively. In order to clearly distinguish between the two, we always refer to the bandwidth to memory in the system as memory bandwidth and the bandwidth of coherence traffic travelling between modules and measured at the BCS as coherence bandwidth.

To place the coherence traffic analysis that follows in a performance context Figure 2 shows the speedup for each benchmark and regime combination at varying thread counts on the bullion S system. These speedup figures use the DFT regime at a thread count of 16 as the baseline (equal to 1 in Figure 2) and are discussed in Section 6.2.

It is important to note that in a ccNUMA architecture the bandwidth to memory is also distributed among the NUMA regions of the system. If the number of NUMA regions in a system is R and a workload allocates memory in only $K < R$ NUMA regions the maximum availability of memory bandwidth will be K/R times the systemwide maximum possible. Similarly the system contains two BCS, one in each module. Each BCS implements a module level directory which caches directory information for cache lines exported from that module to L3s in a remote module. If a workload allocates memory in only 1 module, only half of the systemwide BCS resources are utilised.

Table 4: Speedup and reduction in coherence movement at best performing thread count: Streamcluster (32 threads), Cholesky (24 threads) and SMI (24 threads).

(a) NAFT regime in comparison to DFT regime

Benchmark	Speedup	DWB	DTC	Control	Total
Streamcluster	2.54x	12%	42%	50%	44%
Cholesky	1.28x	91%	78%	60%	77%
SMI	1.23x	71%	58%	52%	60%

(b) NAFT regime in comparison to DI regime

Benchmark	Speedup	DWB	DTC	Control	Total
Streamcluster	1.52x	12%	49%	48%	48%
Cholesky	0.95x	92%	80%	63%	79%
SMI	0.92x	75%	62%	57%	64%

6.2 DWB, DTC and Control Coherence Traffic

Figures 3 and 4 show the measured traffic in coherence bandwidth and coherence movement views respectively, broken down into the two Data message classes, DWB and DTC, and the Control message type which comprises HREQ, SNP, HRSP and NDR. In all cases the Data message classes are symmetric in directionality. This symmetry reflects the fact that messages belonging to these classes originate at either a CPU cache or local memory within one module and travel through the inter-module interconnect (via first the local and then the remote BCS) to their respective memory or cache destination in the other module. Therefore these messages always appear as both incoming to the BCS in one module and outgoing from the BCS in the other module.

6.2.1 *Streamcluster*

The Streamcluster results show markedly different performance (Figure 2a) among the three scheduling and memory allocation regimes as the number of threads employed increases. The NAFT regime performs best at all thread counts. Using the DFT regime at 16 threads as a baseline, the best performance measured is with the NAFT regime at 32 threads, where it performs at 2.78x the performance baseline compared to 1.09x and 1.83x the performance baseline for the DFT and DI regimes respectively at 32 threads.

Figure 3a shows that for Streamcluster both the DI and NAFT regimes utilise more coherence bandwidth than the DFT regime at all thread counts. This happens because, as trace analysis shows, under the DFT regime all the data allocated by the benchmark is located in NUMA region 0 and the other NUMA regions remain unused. In contrast, under the DI and NAFT regimes data is allocated uniformly (see Section 4.1) among all four NUMA regions. Thus under the DFT regime the memory bandwidth is limited to that of the single NUMA region the benchmark's data is allocated in (i.e. 1/4 of the systemwide memory bandwidth).

The coherence bandwidth utilised by Streamcluster increases with thread count at varying rates under the DI and NAFT regimes (Figure 3a). The increase is not very significant in the case of the DFT regime due to the previously mentioned bottleneck caused by all memory being allocated in a single NUMA region. Despite the NAFT scheduler utilising more coherence bandwidth than the DFT scheduler, Figure 4a shows that it causes significantly less coherence movement, and therefore consumes less energy, than the DFT regime over the course of the benchmark.

The traffic results of the three regimes allow us to decouple the performance limiting factors of the Streamcluster benchmark when run under the DFT regime.

First, since the DI regime uniformly spreads the memory allocation among all four NUMA regions, the single NUMA region utilisation bottleneck of the DFT regime is eliminated, allowing the Streamcluster benchmark to use the full systemwide memory bandwidth. At 32 threads the DFT and DI regimes have a similar level of aggregate (Incoming + Outgoing) coherence movement in the system at 1751 GB and 1884 GB respectively. However, the DI regime moves its coherence data at a substantially higher aggregate (Incoming + Outgoing) coherence bandwidth through the two BCS in the system, reaching 23.8 GB/s of aggregate coherence bandwidth. In comparison, the DFT regime utilises only 10.7 GB/s of aggregate coherence bandwidth.

Under the NAFT regime, as well as utilising the full systemwide memory bandwidth due to a uniform allocation of memory among the NUMA regions, the coherence movement (and thus energy use) is significantly reduced in comparison to both DI and DFT regimes due to the higher data locality achieved by the NUMA-aware task scheduling.

We can also see from Figure 4a that the Streamcluster Data coherence movement is almost entirely made up of the DTC message class with a negligible amount of DWB traffic present. DWB traffic makes up less than 3% of the Data coherence movement across all regimes and thread counts. This reflects the characteristics of the Streamcluster benchmark which has a streaming read pattern of memory access with little data being written. The large proportion of the traffic made up of DTC messages represent cache lines being delivered from the memory of one NUMA region to the LLC cache of a socket in the other module for reading, via the inter-module link. The Control message type makes up between 26% and 35% of total coherence movement and is analysed in more detail in Sections 6.3 and 6.4.

6.2.2 *Linear Algebra benchmarks*

The mix of both DWB and DTC message classes in the Data coherence movement of both linear algebra benchmarks demonstrates the more complex memory access patterns involved in these benchmarks compared to the Streamcluster benchmark. The DWB message class represents modified cache lines being written back from the LLC of one socket to memory in the cache line's home NUMA region in a remote module. Under the DFT and DI regimes, DWB traffic makes up between 26% and 30% of Data coherence movement for both Cholesky and the more complex SMI benchmark. Under the NAFT regime, DWB traffic as a percentage of total Data coherence traffic falls to 11% and 19% respectively for Cholesky and SMI. This demonstrates that the NAFT regime is particularly effective in reducing the amount of inter-module DWB traffic. The Control message type makes up between 25% and 27% of total coherence movement under the DFT and DI regimes for both linear algebra benchmarks. This figure rise to between 30% and 46% of the reduced total coherence movement under the NAFT regime. The Control message type is analysed in greater detail in Sections 6.3 and 6.4.

For both Cholesky (Figures 3b and 4b) and SMI (Figures 3c and 4c) we can see that the NAFT regime is utilising less

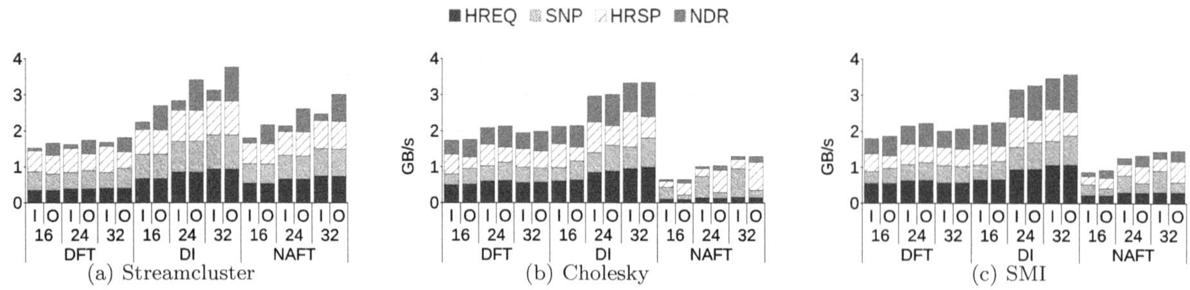

(a) Streamcluster (b) Cholesky (c) SMI

Figure 5: Coherence Bandwidth: Control traffic by message class

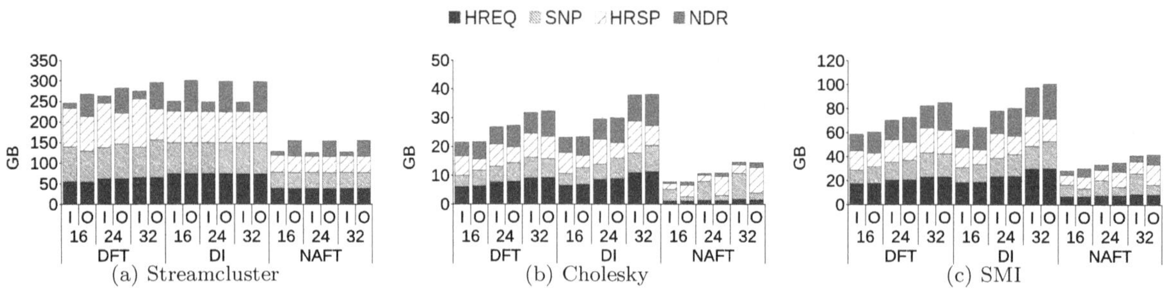

(a) Streamcluster (b) Cholesky (c) SMI

Figure 6: Coherence Movement: Control traffic by message class

coherence bandwidth and causes significantly less coherence movement than either the DFT or DI regimes. This shows that the NUMA-aware scheduling employed by the NAFT regime achieves a strong co-location of tasks and their requisite data within each of the individual NUMA regions of the system.

In terms of performance, in both Cholesky (Figure 2b) and SMI (Figure 2c) the DFT regime shows almost no scaling moving from 16 to 24 threads. This is due to a large majority of the required memory being allocated in only the first and second NUMA regions (both in the same module), with very little of the required memory allocated in the third and fourth NUMA regions of the system. So, in the case of the DFT regime only close to 2/4 of the systemwide memory bandwidth is used. Both the DI and NAFT regimes utilise the full systemwide memory resources available and scale better than the DFT regime. However, performance deteriorates moving from 24 to 32 threads for both the DI and NAFT regimes, due to contention among the increasing number of threads for the same limited (detailed in Section 3.2) memory bandwidth in the system.

Figures 3b and 3c show that under the DI regime Cholesky reaches 22.7 GB/s at 24 threads and 25.7 GB/s at 32 threads of aggregate coherence bandwidth while the corresponding figures for SMI are 24.6 GB/s at 24 threads and 27.2 GB/s at 32 threads. Under the NAFT regime, coherence bandwidth does not reach above 8.6 GB/s at any thread count for Cholesky or SMI. In this case hardware counter analysis shows that IPC per thread is decreasing as thread count is increasing. As can be seen from the low levels of inter-module coherence traffic under the NAFT regime in Figures 3b and 3c most coherence traffic is localised within each of the individual NUMA regions. The performance bottleneck for all regimes exists within the memory subsystem (memory controller, bandwidth to DRAM) within each separate NUMA region and not in the inter-module link routed via the BCS. Were the inter-module link via the BCS to become the performance bottleneck (if, for example, greater memory bandwidth were available or there were more modules in the system) then the NAFT regime would, in addition to reducing coherence traffic and energy cost, enable better scaling of performance than DFT or DI due to its much lower coherence bandwidth and coherence movement requirements.

6.2.3 *Summary*

In the coherence movement view (Figure 4) for all benchmarks, at all thread counts, the DI regime requires the largest coherence movement closely followed by the DFT regime. The NAFT regime enables a significant reduction in coherence movement in comparison to the other two regimes, the magnitude of which depends on the benchmark and thread count. The reductions in coherence movement by the NAFT regime in comparison to the DFT regime at the best performing thread count for each benchmark are listed in Table 4a. The NAFT regime reduces the total coherence movement by 44%, 77% and 60% respectively for the Streamcluster, Cholesky and SMI benchmarks in comparison to the the DFT regime. Table 4b summarises the differences between the DI and NAFT regimes.

It is important to note for both linear algebra benchmarks in Table 4b that even though the NAFT regime does not outperform the DI regime in the system we use, it does significantly reduce coherence movement (by 48%, 79% and 64% for Streamcluster, Cholesky and SMI respectively) which has substantial implications for energy efficiency. In both linear algebra benchmarks under the DI and NAFT regimes the computation is limited by the memory resources in the experimental bullion S system installation we used rather than by the inter-module coherence traffic. In an installation of this system with a larger memory configuration or in a lager

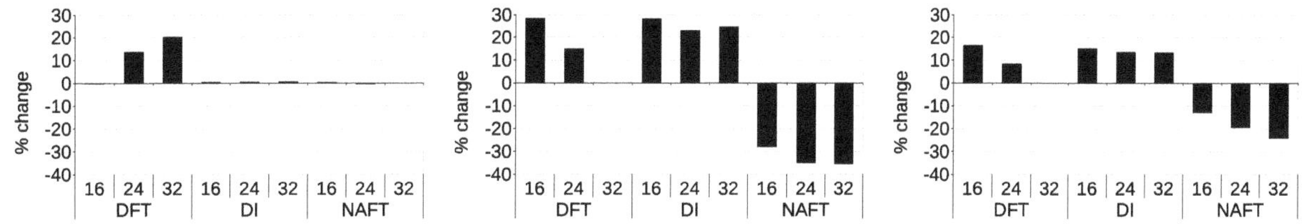

(a) Streamcluster (b) Cholesky (c) SMI

Figure 7: SNP/HRSP coherence movement only, net change due to BCS

(> 2 modules) bullion S system the coherence bandwidth generated would become a more important factor in performance where the substantial reduction in coherence movement realised by the NAFT regime would enable greater scaling than both the DFT and DI regimes.

6.3 Control Coherence Traffic Decomposition

Figures 5 and 6 show the coherence bandwidth and coherence movement for all three benchmarks for the Control coherence traffic only, now decomposed into the individual Control message classes HREQ, SNP, HRSP and NDR.

In the Control message classes we see a symmetry between the incoming and outgoing traffic for the HREQ message class, as was also evident for the Data message classes (DWB and DTC). Each HREQ message originates at a cache within one module and travels through the inter-module interconnect (via first the local and then the remote BCS) to its respective memory destination in the other module. Therefore, in the two module system we use, HREQ messages always appear as incoming traffic to the BCS in their source module and as outgoing traffic from the BCS in their destination module.

For the remaining Control type messages (SNP, HRSP and NDR) this symmetry between incoming and outgoing traffic does not necessarily hold, as explained in Section 3. Figures 6b and 6c show the asymmetry in directionality of the SNP and HRSP traffic is most pronounced under the NAFT regime for both linear algebra benchmarks. These asymmetries represent cases where the action of the BCS in the coherence protocol is having a significant impact on the SNP and reciprocal HRSP coherence movement and we investigate this behaviour further in Section 6.4. The best performing thread count for both linear algebra benchmarks is 24 threads. With Cholesky at 24 threads the total outgoing SNP traffic in the system is only 26% of the total incoming SNP traffic. For the more complex SMI linear algebra problem, the total outgoing SNP traffic in the system is 56% of the total incoming SNP traffic. The asymmetry visible across the benchmarks for the NDR traffic is due to the CPU (but not the BCS) in some cases piggybacking the NDR message on top of unused bits in other message classes as a bandwidth optimisation.

We also note a significant difference in the ratio of the count (not coherence bandwidth or coherence movement) of correlated HREQ and DTC messages between the Streamcluster benchmark and both linear algebra benchmarks. In the Streamcluster benchmark across all thread counts and regimes, there is never more than a 4% deviation from a 1:1 ratio for the message counts of HREQ:DTC. This is evidence of the streaming read nature of Streamcluster where HREQ messages ask for a cache line in a read state and do not ask to further change the state of the cache line before evicting it. This results in a 1:1 call and response between HREQ and DTC. For the Cholesky and SMI benchmarks, which have a more complex memory access pattern including write accesses and shared data among threads, the same HREQ:DTC ratio varies from 1:0.63 up to 1:0.91 depending on the regime and thread count. This is explained by the observation that in some cases cache lines will be first requested read-only (1:1 HREQ:DTC ratio) and subsequently upgraded to modified for writing. In the upgrade case, a HREQ is required to ask to upgrade the state of the cache line. However, as the cache already has a valid copy of the data, no DTC is required.

6.4 Impact of NUMA-Aware Scheduling on Effectiveness of BCS

The BCS may affect the amount of SNP/HRSP traffic in two ways: **(1)** Filter SNP/HRSP transactions out of the system where it can participate in a transaction in place of a CPU, reducing SNP/HRSP traffic. **(2)** Add SNP/HRSP transactions in the process of maintaining its own directory state. The directory cache maintained by the BCS is inclusive of all cache lines exported from its local module to L3 caches in any remote module, and L3 caches may silently evict cache lines. In order to maintain inclusivity, if the directory cache in the BCS is under capacity pressure due to a high volume of cache lines being exported from the module (poor data locality) and needs to evict an existing directory entry in order to allocate a new one, this eviction from the directory cache in the BCS requires the cache line be evicted from the remote L3 caching it, requiring a BCS initiated evicting SNP/HRSP transaction.

The actual SNP and HRSP coherence movement measured in the system (which includes the impact of the BCS in the protocol) is made up of the sum of the incoming SNP, outgoing SNP, incoming HRSP and outgoing HRSP traffic featured in Figure 6.

We measure how effectively the BCS affects the number of SNP/HRSP transactions in the system by comparing the SNP/HRSP transactions initiated by the CPUs with the total system SNP/HRSP transactions in the system. CPU initiated SNP/HRSP transactions include only incoming SNPs (which originate at CPUs) and outgoing HRSPs (response to the incoming SNPs). If the BCS did not exist in the system all the incoming SNPs measured would have appeared as outgoing SNPs in the opposite module and all the outgoing HRSPs would have appeared as incoming HRSPs in the opposite module. Therefore we double the (incoming SNP + outgoing HRSP) traffic to extrapolate what the total traffic in both modules would have been without the intervention of the BCS in the coherence protocol.

Figure 7 presents the net change in coherence movement for the SNP/HRSP message classes in isolation, due to the actions of the BCS. It shows the BCS can produce a net reduction in SNP/HRSP traffic under the NAFT regime for both linear algebra benchmarks resulting in reductions of between 13% and 35%. Due to the high data locality produced by the NAFT regime, the directory cache in the BCS can filter more SNP/HRSP traffic from the system than any amount it introduces in maintaining its directory. Under the other regimes with poorer data locality (DFT, DI) where we see an increase in SNP/HRSP traffic (up to 29%) the BCS is aiding scalability by creating an extra (less granular) hierarchical level of coherence tracking to the system, at the cost of the added SNP traffic to maintain its directory state.

These figures show the high data locality of the software based NAFT regime exploits the function of the BCS to best effect. Under the NAFT regime the BCS achieves a net reduction of the SNP/HRSP coherence movement in two of the three benchmarks, and in all cases the NAFT regime uses the BCS more effectively than the DFT or DI regimes.

7. RELATED WORK

Intel's recent Xeon CPUs use the Intel Quick Path Interconnect (QPI) [16] specification to connect Caches and Memories. The Coherence Protocol utilised by QPI is the MESIF protocol which is an extension of the well known MESI protocol [25, p. 362]. The microarchitectural details of Intel's MESIF protocol remain unpublished, however Molka and Hackenberg et al. gave insight [21] [13] into such details via sophisticated synthetic benchmarking. Molka et al's work differs from ours in that it presents aggregated total memory bandwidth and latency figures utilising synthetic benchmarks whereas we characterise the traffic and memory bandwidth utilised by real world benchmarks at the level of individual coherence protocol message types.

There has been much recent work on simplifying cache coherency systems to make them perform or scale better or be more energy efficient. Choi et al. [9] proposed restraining the shared memory programming model to enable improvements in power, performance, simplicity and verifiability in the coherency system. Manivannan et al. [18] [17] showed how the runtime and coherency system could co-operate to provide performance benefits for particular data access and sharing patterns in task-based programming models. Hammond et al. [14] proposed changing the memory consistency model to a transactional model which allows for a less complex coherency system. All these papers utilised a simulation based approach to evaluate the impact of their designs on coherence whereas in our work we characterise directly the impact of a runtime managed approach to reducing coherence traffic in a real system.

Regarding NUMA-aware data distribution and scheduling Al-Omairy et al. [2] measured the performance benefits of NUMA-aware scheduling for both the Cholesky and Symmetric Matrix Inversion algorithms versus the best state of the art implementations that are widely used in modern production environments. Muddukrishna et al. also investigated [22] the performance impacts of NUMA-aware scheduling and data distribution for multiple real world benchmarks. Our work differs from both these as it directly and in detail quantifies the effect of the NUMA-aware scheduling on coherence traffic and data motion within the system, rather than performance. Other recent work such as the Runnemede [7], SARC [26] and Runtime Aware Architecture [27] [8] proposals follow a hardware/software co-design approach to relaxing hardware provided cache coherency and moving responsibility for dynamically managing disjoint memory spaces to software.

To the best of our knowledge our work is the first to study the effects of NUMA-aware scheduling and data allocation in combination with hierarchical directory coherence on cache coherence traffic.

8. CONCLUSIONS

ccNUMA architectures continue to dominate the SMP design space and are likely to grow in prevalence and complexity alongside the trend towards higher core counts and memory capacity requirements in SMP designs. These developments bring challenges for both computer architecture and software alike. In the architecture design space the nature of the coherence traffic required to implement the ccNUMA design is an important factor in balancing the demands of energy efficiency and performance in the design.

In this work we characterise the coherence traffic within a modern large SMP design at the granularity of individual classes of coherence traffic using three important scientific benchmarks. We show the balance between the different types of coherence traffic, Data and Control traffic, and further break down these types into individual message classes. We present evidence for the ability of the BCS to mitigate the cost of coherence traffic with increasing system scale.

We show that NUMA-aware policies improve the efficacy of the BCS. This combined hardware-software solution achieves significant reductions in coherence movement which in turn has implications for energy savings. We show evidence that the NAFT regime combined with the BCS is able to reduce the coherence movement in all cases, with reductions ranging from 44% to 77%. Other NUMA-oblivious regimes combined with the BCS do not show such synergistic potential, which is indeed an important conclusion to take into account in the way future computing infrastructures and system software stacks are designed [15, 7, 12, 27].

Acknowledgements

This work has been supported by the Spanish Government (Severo Ochoa grants SEV2015-0493), by the Spanish Ministry of Science and Innovation (contracts TIN2015-65316-P), by the Generalitat de Catalunya (contracts 2014-SGR-1051 and 2014-SGR-1272), by the RoMoL ERC Advanced Grant (GA 321253) and the European HiPEAC Network of Excellence. The Mont-Blanc project receives funding from the EU's Seventh Framework Programme (FP7/2007-2013) under grant agreement n° 610402 and from the EU's H2020 Framework Programme (H2020/2014-2020) under grant agreement n° 671697. M. Moretó has been partially supported by the Ministry of Economy and Competitiveness under Juan de la Cierva postdoctoral fellowship number JCI-2012-15047. M. Casas is supported by the Secretary for Universities and Research of the Ministry of Economy and Knowledge of the Government of Catalonia and the Cofund programme of the Marie Curie Actions of the 7th R&D Framework Programme of the European Union (Contract 2013 BP_B 00243).

9. REFERENCES

[1] Data center optimization with bullion. 2015.

[2] R. Al-Omairy, G. Miranda, H. Ltaief, R. Badia, X. Martorell, J. Labarta, and D. Keyes. Dense matrix computations on NUMA architectures with distance-aware work stealing. *Supercomputing Frontiers and Innovations*, 2(1), 2015.

[3] J. Balart, A. Duran, M. González, X. Martorell, E. Ayguadé, and J. Labarta. Nanos mercurium: a research compiler for openmp. In *European Workshop on OpenMP*, EWOMP '04, pages 103–109, 2004.

[4] C. Bienia, S. Kumar, J. P. Singh, and K. Li. The parsec benchmark suite: Characterization and architectural implications. In *Proceedings of the 17th International Conference on Parallel Architectures and Compilation Techniques*, PACT '08, pages 72–81. ACM, 2008.

[5] J. Bueno, X. Martorell, R. M. Badia, E. Ayguadé, and J. Labarta. Implementing ompss support for regions of data in architectures with multiple address spaces. In *Proceedings of the 27th International Conference on Supercomputing*, ICS '13, pages 359–368. ACM, 2013.

[6] D. R. Butenhof. *Programming with POSIX Threads.* Addison-Wesley Longman Publishing Co., Inc., Boston, MA, USA, 1997.

[7] N. Carter, A. Agrawal, S. Borkar, R. Cledat, H. David, D. Dunning, J. Fryman, I. Ganev, R. Golliver, R. Knauerhase, R. Lethin, B. Meister, A. Mishra, W. Pinfold, J. Teller, J. Torrellas, N. Vasilache, G. Venkatesh, and J. Xu. Runnemede: An architecture for ubiquitous high-performance computing. In *Proceedings of the 19th International Symposium on High Performance Computer Architecture*, HPCA '13, pages 198–209. IEEE Computer Society, 2013.

[8] M. Casas, M. Moretó, L. Alvarez, E. Castillo, D. Chasapis, T. Hayes, L. Jaulmes, O. Palomar, O. S. Unsal, A. Cristal, E. Ayguadé, J. Labarta, and M. Valero. Runtime-aware architectures. In *Proceedings of the 21st International Conference on Parallel and Distributed Computing*, Euro-Par '15, pages 16–27. Springer Berlin Heidelberg, 2015.

[9] B. Choi, R. Komuravelli, H. Sung, R. Smolinski, N. Honarmand, S. Adve, V. Adve, N. Carter, and C. Chou. Denovo: Rethinking the memory hierarchy for disciplined parallelism. In *Proceedings of the 20th International Conference on Parallel Architectures and Compilation Techniques*, pages 155–166. IEEE Computer Society, 2011.

[10] A. Drebes, K. Heydemann, N. Drach, A. Pop, and A. Cohen. Topology-aware and dependence-aware scheduling and memory allocation for task-parallel languages. *ACM Trans. Archit. Code Optim.*, 11(3):30:1–30:25, 2014.

[11] A. Duran, E. Ayguadé, R. Badia, J. Labarta, L. Martinell, X. Martorell, and J. Planas. Ompss: A proposal for programming heterogeneous multi-core architectures. *Parallel Process. Lett.*, 21:173–193, 2011.

[12] Y. Durand, P. Carpenter, S. Adami, A. Bilas, D. Dutoit, A. Farcy, G. Gaydadjiev, J. Goodacre, M. Katevenis, M. Marazakis, E. Matus, I. Mavroidis, and J. Thomson. EUROSERVER: Energy Efficient Node for European Micro-Servers. In *17th Euromicro Conference on Digital System Design*, DSD '14. IEEE Computer Society, 2014.

[13] D. Hackenberg, D. Molka, and W. E. Nagel. Comparing cache architectures and coherency protocols on x86-64 multicore smp systems. In *Proceedings of the International Symposium on Microarchitecture*, MICRO 42, pages 413–422. IEEE Computer Society, 2009.

[14] L. Hammond, V. Wong, M. Chen, B. D. Carlstrom, J. D. Davis, B. Hertzberg, M. K. Prabhu, H. Wijaya, C. Kozyrakis, and K. Olukotun. Transactional memory coherence and consistency. In *Proceedings of the 31st International Symposium on Computer Architecture*, ISCA '04, pages 102–113. IEEE Computer Society, 2004.

[15] J. H. Kelm, D. R. Johnson, M. R. Johnson, N. C. Crago, W. Tuohy, A. Mahesri, S. S. Lumetta, M. I. Frank, and S. J. Patel. Rigel: An architecture and scalable programming interface for a 1000-core accelerator. In *Proceedings of the 36th Annual International Symposium on Computer Architecture*, ISCA '09, pages 140–151. ACM, 2009.

[16] R. Maddox, G. Singh, and R. Safranek. *Weaving high performance multiprocessor fabric: architectural insights into the Intel QuickPath Interconnect.* Intel Press, 2009.

[17] M. Manivannan, A. Negi, and P. StenstrÃűm. Efficient forwarding of producer-consumer data in task-based programs. In *Proceedings of the 42nd International Conference on Parallel Processing*, ICPP '13, pages 517–522. IEEE Computer Society, 2013.

[18] M. Manivannan and P. Stenstrom. Runtime-guided cache coherence optimizations in multi-core architectures. In *Proceedings of the 28th International Parallel and Distributed Processing Symposium*, IPDPS '14, pages 625–636. IEEE Computer Society, 2014.

[19] M. M. K. Martin, M. D. Hill, and D. J. Sorin. Why on-chip cache coherence is here to stay. *Commun. ACM*, 55(7):78–89, 2012.

[20] J. McCalpin. Memory bandwidth and machine balance in current high performance computers. *IEEE Computer Society Technical Committee on Computer Architecture (TCCA) Newsletter*, pages 19–25, December 1995.

[21] D. Molka, D. Hackenberg, R. Schone, and M. S. Muller. Memory performance and cache coherency effects on an intel nehalem multiprocessor system. In *18th International Conference on Parallel Architectures and Compilation Techniques*, PACT '09, pages 261–270. IEEE Computer Society, 2009.

[22] A. Muddukrishna, P. A. Jonsson, V. Vlassov, and M. Brorsson. Locality-aware task scheduling and data distribution on numa systems. In *Proceedings of the 9th International Workshop on OpenMP*, IWOMP '13, pages 156–170. Springer Berlin Heidelberg, 2013.

[23] OpenMP: Application program interface, version 4.0. 2013.

[24] A. Patel and K. Ghose. Energy-efficient MESI cache coherence with pro-active snoop filtering for multicore microprocessors. In *Proceedings of the International*

Symposium on Low Power Electronics and Design, ISPLED '08, pages 247–252. ACM, 2008.

[25] D. Patterson and J. Hennessy. *Computer Architecture: A Quantitative Approach.* Morgan Kaufmann Publishers Inc., San Francisco, CA, USA, 1990.

[26] A. Ramirez, F. Cabarcas, B. Juurlink, A. M, F. Sanchez, A. Azevedo, C. Meenderinck, C. Ciobanu, S. Isaza, and G. Gaydadjiev. The SARC architecture. *IEEE Micro*, 30(5):16–29, 2010.

[27] M. Valero, M. Moretó, M. Casas, E. Ayguadé, and J. Labarta. Runtime-aware architectures: A first approach. *Supercomputing frontiers and innovations*, 1(1), 2014.

[28] R. Vidal, M. Casas, M. Moretó, D. Chasapis, R. Ferrer, X. Martorell, E. Ayguadé, J. Labarta, and M. Valero. Evaluating the impact of OpenMP 4.0 extensions on relevant parallel workloads. In *Proceedings of the 11th International Workshop on OpenMP*, IWOMP '15, pages 60–72. Springer International Publishing, 2015.

[29] V. Viswanathan, K. Kumar, and T. Willhalm. Intel memory latency checker v2, 2013.

Characterizing and Optimizing the Performance of Multithreaded Programs Under Interference

Yong Zhao Jia Rao
The University of Texas at Arlington
yong.zhao@mavs.uta.edu
jia.rao@uta.edu

Qing Yi
The University of Colorado Colorado Springs
qyi@uccs.edu

ABSTRACT

As virtualization becomes ubiquitous in datacenters, there is a growing interest in characterizing application performance in multi-tenant environments to improve datacenter resource management. The performance of parallel programs is notoriously difficult to reason about in virtualized environments. Although performance degradations caused by virtualization and interferences have been extensively studied, there still lacks a comprehensive understanding why parallel programs have unpredictable slowdowns when co-located with different types of workloads.

This paper presents a systematic and quantitative study of multithreaded performance under interference. We design synthetic workloads to emulate different types of interference and study the behavior of parallel programs under such interferences. We find that unpredictable performance is the result of complex interplays between the design of the program, the memory hierarchy of the host system, and the CPU scheduling at the hypervisor. To understand the intricate relationships between multiple factors, we decompose parallel runtime into compute, synchronization and steal time, and use the runtime breakdown to measure program progress and identify execution inefficiency under interference. Based on these findings, we develop an online approach to predicting performance slowdown without requiring parallel programs to be completed, and devise two scheduling optimizations at the hypervisor to reduce slowdowns. Experimental results with Xen and representative parallel workloads show that the online performance prediction achieves on average less than 4.5% error and the optimizations reduce runtime slowdown by as much as 38% compared to stock Xen.

Keywords: Virtual Machine Scheduling; Multicore Systems; Parallel Performance modeling and Optimization

1. INTRODUCTION

Cloud computing, powered by warehouse-scale datacenters, provides users with abundant parallelism and potentially unlimited scalability. While the cloud is believed to be an ideal platform for hosting parallel applications, its nature of multi-user sharing and resource over-commitment makes parallel performance often quite disappointing and unpredictable. Although many studies [11, 16, 23, 29, 32, 33] have identified the excessive synchronization delays due to multi-tenant interferences as the culprit, there lacks a full understanding of the quantitative relationship between changes in synchronization and the overall performance loss. As performance modeling plays a fundamental role in designing traditional parallel systems, a systematic and quantitative study of parallel performance under cloud interferences would help improve the resource and power management in datacenters. Most importantly, predicting parallel performance allows users to evaluate the outcome of their cloud lease without completing long-running applications and select cloud services wisely to meet their expectations.

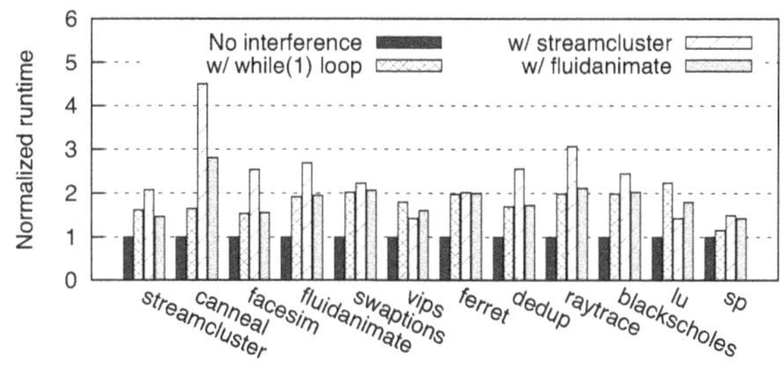

Figure 1: The runtime slowdown of parallel workloads under different interference scenarios.

However, parallel performance is notoriously difficult to reason about in a shared cloud environment. Memory locality and resource contentions on the CPU function units, shared cache and memory bandwidth could all affect the speed of individual threads. Moreover, the performance of parallel programs as a whole also depends critically on the cooperation of multiple threads. Contentions on CPU time cause the well-known lock-holder preemption (LHP) problem [32], in which threads holding important locks are prematurely de-scheduled, leading to exceedingly long synchronizations and out-of-sync executions at multiple threads. The major challenges in modeling parallel performance are twofold: 1) individual threads have varying slowdowns when co-located with different interferences; 2) the quantitative relationship between slowdowns at individual threads and the overall slowdown remains unclear.

To demonstrate the severity of performance degradation and its unpredictability in multi-tenant clouds, Figure 1 shows the slowdown of various parallel programs under dif-

PACT '16, September 11-15, 2016, Haifa, Israel
© 2016 ACM. ISBN 978-1-4503-4121-9/16/09...$15.00
DOI: http://dx.doi.org/10.1145/2967938.2967939

ferent interference scenarios. The parallel workloads include programs from the PARSEC [31] and NASA parallel benchmarks (NPB) [2] with different synchronization methods (i.e., busy-waiting and blocking), varying task granularities, and different work assignment policies (i.e., static and dynamic/work-stealing assignments). The interferences contain a synthetic workload that only competes for CPU cycles (i.e., `while(1)` loop) and two real workloads from the PARSEC benchmarks. Both the parallel workloads and the interferences run with 4 threads (see Section 3.1 for detailed settings). From the figure, we can see that performance slowdowns vary substantially across different workloads, even under the same type of interference. For example, the synthetic loop incurred more than 100% slowdown to *lu* while it merely slowed *sp* by 13%. More interestingly, slowdowns become more unpredictable when the background interference changes. For example, while *facesim* suffers a 165% slowdown with *streamcluster*, its degradation with *fluidanimate* is only 53%. In contrast, some workloads suffer more severe slowdowns under *fluidanimate* compared to that under *streamcluster*, e.g., *lu* and *vips*. The difference in memory contentiousness of the interfering workloads alone can not explain the varying slowdowns. The unpredictability is the result of complex interplays between the designs of the program, the memory hierarchy of the host machine, and the underlying CPU scheduling at the hypervisor. Understanding how these factors interact with each other is crucial to fully understanding parallel performance in the cloud.

In this paper, we aim to uncover the mystery of parallel performance under interference. Our methodology is to study parallel performance in controlled experiments so that individual factors can be examined separately. To this end, we design a set of synthetic workloads to emulate different types of interference. The synthetic workloads include `while(1)` loops with *persistent*, *periodic* and *intermittent* interference patterns and configurable CPU demands. To further pinpoint the source of unpredictability, we design a profiling tool, `vProfile`, to derive a detailed breakdown of parallel runtime, and to report important scheduling and hardware statistics. With the help of fine-grained profiling, we have the following findings: 1) the slowdown of individual threads depends on the amount of CPU allocated to the thread, which is largely affected by the synchronization granularity of the program in a shared environment; 2) while interference is believed to slow down individual threads due to contentions on shared resources, it can constructively accelerate threads in memory-bound applications due to the alleviation of intra-program contentions; 3) Uncoordinated scheduling of co-running parallel programs causes out-of-sync execution between multiple threads, leading to further performance degradation.

Based on these findings, we develop an online approach to predicting the performance of parallel programs under interference. Our online prediction first profiles parallel execution under interference for a short period of time and compares the completed *useful* work during sampling with that in a dedicated environment during the same length of period. The difference in completed useful work is used to predict the overall slowdown. We define useful work as the necessary computation needed by a thread assuming an ideal memory system with zero latency and perfect synchronization with no spinning and blocking cost. Specifically, we determine useful work by removing cycles that are stolen by other tenants, perform spinning or context switching (i.e., sleep and wakeup), and are spent in the memory hierarchy from the profiling sample. Experimental results show that, for regular parallel programs in which individual threads are assigned the same amount of work and perform iterated computations, the online approach achieves on average less than 4.5% errors in predicting the overall slowdown.

We also devise two scheduling optimizations at the hypervisor to reduce slowdowns. To avoid premature preemptions, we propose *delayed preemption* (DP) to interleave the computations of the parallel program and background interferences. We further make DP adaptive to the varying synchronization granularities for different programs. Experimental results show that DP improves the performance of PARSEC benchmarks by up to 23%. Another optimization motivated by our analysis is *differential scheduling* (DS), which purposely avoids co-scheduling of parallel threads by having different time slices on multiple CPUs. Results show that this simple technique outperforms stock Xen by as much as 38% in NPB benchmarks.

The rest of the paper is organized as follows. Section 2 introduces the design of vProfile and the synthetic interferences. Section 3 provides an analysis of parallel performance under interference. Section 4 and 5 present an approach for online performance prediction and two hypervisor-level optimizations motivated by the analysis, respectively. Section 6 discusses limitations and future work. Section 7 discusses related work and Section 8 concludes this paper.

2. PROFILING THE PERFORMANCE OF MULTITHREADED PROGRAMS

The key to understanding parallel performance under interference is to identify the sources of slowdown. A breakdown of parallel runtime from experiments in a controlled environment would help pinpoint the culprit and inspire possible remedies. In general, parallel runtime consists of compute time and idle time. Traditionally, idle time due to load imbalance and synchronization is considered the major source of parallel overhead as no progress can be made during idle time. In a virtualized environment, guest operating systems (OSes) schedule application threads onto virtual CPUs (vCPUs) and multiple vCPUs from different virtual machines (VMs) can share the same physical CPU (pCPU). Steal time is the time a vCPU waits to run on a pCPU while the hypervisor is servicing another vCPU. A large steal time indicates severe contentions on the CPU allocation. Therefore, we decompose parallel runtime into *compute*, *synchronization* and *steal* time to study the causes of slowdown. We design `vProfile` to report the breakdown of parallel runtime and record important scheduling statistics in the hypervisor. vProfile provides two hypercalls [1]: `vprofile_start` and `vprofile_stop` to mark the start and end of a profiling period.

2.1 Decomposing Parallel Runtime

During profiling, vProfile tracks per-vCPU state changes in the hypervisor. Xen defines four vCPUs states, i.e., `running`, `runnable`, `blocked`, and `offline`. Steal time can be accounted using time spent in the runnable state, which counts the time a vCPU is ready to run but fails to ac-

[1] We describe the design of vProfile in a Xen environment. Other hypervisors can be easily modified to support vProfile.

quire the pCPU. The accounting of synchronization time depends on the synchronization methods used by the parallel program. For blocking synchronization, such as `mutex` and `semaphore`, synchronization time is simply the time a vCPU stays in the blocked state.

Accounting synchronization time is more challenging for programs using busy-waiting synchronization (e.g., spinlocks) as vCPUs are always in the running state. There is existing work detecting spinning by instrumenting guest OS kernels [33], tracking user-kernel mode switches [32], and monitoring hardware performance events [5, 25]. We use the lightweight spin detection proposed in [25] to break the time in the running state into compute and synchronization (or spinning) time. As spin loops usually contain only a few instructions and are executed repeatedly, spinning vCPUs show high branch per instruction and low branch miss prediction rates compared to sibling vCPUs that are performing regular computation. We add a new `spinning` state to Xen and place a vCPU to such a state when spinning is detected. Synchronization time is then the time a vCPU stays in the spinning state.

2.2 Recording Performance Events

The breakdown of execution time alone is not sufficient to identify the causes of slowdown. For example, an increase of synchronization could be due to long latencies at a few synchronization points or prolonged wait time at many places. Detailed execution statistics can help find the root cause and develop approaches to mitigate slowdowns. vProfile reports per-vCPU statistics of the scheduling and hardware performance events listed in Table 1. Events `YIELD` and `PREEMPT` shed light on the contentions between co-located VMs while `IDLE` reflects the overall utilization of the pCPU as well as the efficiency of the scheduler. Performance statistics from hardware counters can trace the low-level program behaviors under interference and reveal the complex interactions between the program and the hardware. vProfile can be configured to track various hardware statistics, including cycles spent in the offcore memory system (`OFFCORE_STALL`), LLC misses per thousand instructions (`MPKI`), and other events related to cache coherence traffic between private L2 caches.

Event	Description
YIELD	Voluntary yield to other vCPUs due to idling
PREEMPT	Involuntary preemption by the scheduler
IDLE	The time the pCPU in the idle state
HARDWARE_STAT	Statistics from hardware performance counters

Table 1: vProfile performance events.

2.3 Enabling Dedicated Mode

vProfile enables online performance prediction by temporarily throttling co-located workloads to estimate their reference performance. It provides a short period of dedicated execution to emulate the performance on a dedicated machine. We assume that the sampling should cover a number of major iterations of the parallel program and contain sufficient information for performance prediction. The dedicated mode can be enabled multiple times once program phase change is detected. vProfile can integrate existing phase change detection techniques.

vProfile exports a new hypercall `sys_enable_dedicated` to the VM hosting the parallel application. Upon receiving the hypercall, the hypervisor takes vCPUs other than the calling VM's vCPUs off pCPUs' run queues and places them into the `offline` mode. The hypervisor freezes vCPUs of co-running VMs for a pre-defined period (e.g., 300 scheduling epochs). To minimize the impact of the dedicated mode on regular scheduling, we disable CPU time accounting (i.e., credit debiting in Xen's credit scheduler) during dedicated mode. As such, fair CPU allocation is not affected when normal execution is resumed.

2.4 Synthetic Interference

Synthetic workloads should slow down individual threads to faithfully reflect contentions on CPU time and shared resources, such as the last-level cache (LLC) and memory bandwidth. It should also be able to emulate the complex patterns of real workloads that simultaneously interfere with multiple threads. To this end, we design the synthetic workloads as simple CPU loops consisting of interleaved busy and idle intervals. The busy-to-idle ratio, which is configurable, determines the intensity of the interference. While the synthetic interference only contends for CPU cycles, it can emulate contentions on shared hardware resources because a decrease in allocated CPU time is equivalent to an increase in memory access cost for the parallel applications under test. We create the following three types of interference to study the complex interplay between the parallel program, the memory hierarchy and the underlying CPU scheduling:

- *Persistent* interference comprises of simple `while(1)` loops demanding 100% of CPU time. It emulates the CPU demand of long-running sequential jobs or parallel applications with busy-waiting synchronization. Due to its simplicity, it is scheduled by hypervisors at predictable time points and does not incur preemptions to the parallel threads.
- *Periodic* interference demands CPU at regular intervals or otherwise stays idle. The ratio of the CPU burst and the idle period determines the level of contention (i.e., CPU demand). Periodic interference has fixed burst-to-idle ratio and fixed length of computation at each interval. It emulates regular parallel applications that have predictable computations and synchronizations. Periodic interference is more complex than persistent interference as it sleeps and wakes up periodically, leading to preemptions of parallel threads.
- *Intermittent* interference demands CPU at irregular intervals. The ratio of CPU burst and sleep remains unchanged, but the length of computation changes randomly. It emulates multi-programmed workloads with independent (random) demands from individual threads or parallel applications with irregular CPU demands. Compared to periodic interference, whose computation and idling are predictable, intermittent interference has unpredictable demands. This helps to study the behavior of parallel programs when their execution is out-of-sync.

We use the method of differential analysis [18, 20] to compare the execution profiles of parallel programs under different types of interference. The low-level metrics that are highly correlated to the overall performance are examined to identify the causes of performance slowdown. We set the CPU demand of periodic and intermittent interference to 50% of the pCPU. The periodic interference performs 10ms

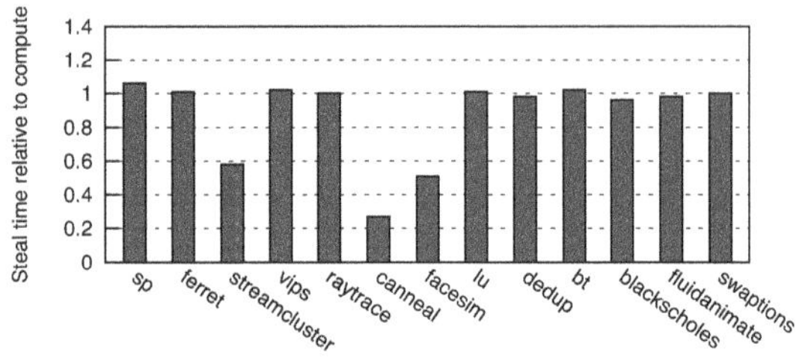

Figure 2: Varying resilience to interference.

computation and stays idle for 10ms. In contrast, the computation in intermittent interference varies randomly from 1ms to 40ms with the idle period changing accordingly to generate the 50% CPU demand. We use single-threaded interferences to study the slowdown of individual threads and the multi-threaded version to evaluate the efficiency of multiple parallel threads.

3. UNDERSTANDING PARALLEL PERFORMANCE

In this section, we use the statistics reported by vProfile to explain the mystery of parallel performance under interferences. We found that programs show different levels of resilience to interferences, leading to varying CPU allocations to the parallel program (Section 3.2). Interference may accelerate program execution by reducing the compute time needed in normal execution (Section 3.3). Finally, the overall performance is determined by the complex interplay between multiple factors (Section 3.4).

3.1 Experimental Setup

We ran shared-memory multi-threaded programs on an Intel multicore machine with three types of interference. The host machine has a NUMA architecture with 16GB memory and two Intel Xeon E5620 2.40GHz 4-core processors. Each core in the processor has a private 256KB L2 cache and shares a 12MB L3 cache. Hyperthreading was disabled for all experiments. To isolate program performance from other factors, e.g., memory locality, we created the VM hosting the parallel programs in one memory node and pinned vCPUs of the VM to the processor affiliated with the node. Thus, all memory accesses were local and parallel threads shared the same last-level cache. We configured the VM running parallel programs with 4GB memory and 4 vCPUs, each pinned to a separate core in the same memory node. The background interfering VM had an identical configuration with all its vCPUs pinned to the same set of cores. Note that pinning vCPUs to pCPUs is to obtain reproducible results. We observed on average 55% performance slowdown and 15% variation when CPU affinity was turned off. We assigned equal weights to both VMs.

We implemented vProfile in Xen 4.0.2 and modified Linux guest kernel 2.6.32 to use the profiling hypercalls. We selected the benchmarks in PARSEC 2.1 and the NAS Parallel Benchmark suite. The PARSEC benchmarks were compiled with *gcc-pthreads* and blocking synchronizations. We used the OpenMP version of the NPB benchmarks and set the environment variable `OMP_WAIT_POLICY` to active to use busy-waiting synchronization. All benchmarks were configured with 4 threads. We set vProfile to report performance statistics for the entire execution after programs complete.

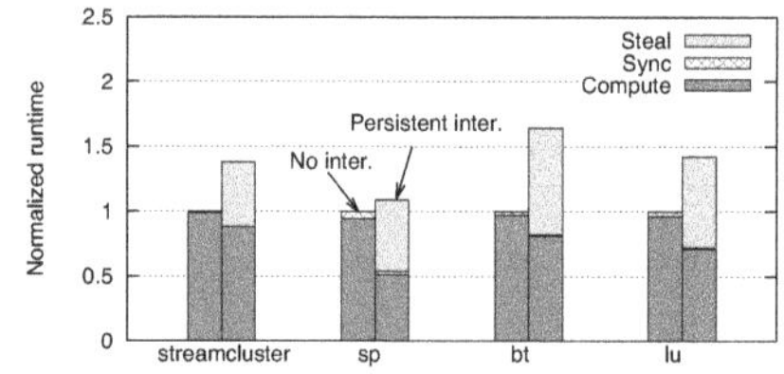

Figure 3: Interference reduces compute time.

3.2 Varying Resilience to Interference

First, we study the slowdown at individual threads due to contentions on the CPU time. We placed a single-threaded persistent interference with one parallel thread and measured how much time was stolen (i.e., steal time) from the thread by the persistent interference. In this simple scenario, the thread co-located with the persistent loop would be the slowest thread in the parallel program, thereby deciding the overall performance. Figure 2 shows the steal time of various benchmarks relative to their compute time under the 1-loop persistent interference. Intuitively, the ratio of steal and compute time should be 1 if CPU is fairly allocated to the parallel program and the interference. However, Figure 2 suggests that some programs (i.e., *canneal*, *streamcluster* and *facesim*) be more resilient to interference and were stolen less time. An examination of program code revealed these benchmarks have fine-grained synchronizations and block frequently at synchronizing barriers. Zhou *et al.*, also showed that deliberately designed attacks can obtain excessive CPU allocations by exploiting the accounting vulnerabilities in Xen [37]. Harris *et al.* found the CPU time that each job receives can be drastically different and hard to control when multiple jobs run together [13]. In our experiments, the varying CPU allocation is due to the prioritization of latency-sensitive workloads in Xen.

Xen's credit scheduler considers vCPUs that wake up from sleep as latency-sensitive and assigns them a higher priority (i.e., the *boost* priority). Such vCPUs will preempt the current running vCPUs. Although the prioritization mechanism in theory benefits any programs that block, the granularity of synchronization plays an important role in gaining more CPU allocations. Xen implements a coarse-grained CPU scheduler which checks if the current running vCPU should be de-scheduled every 30ms (i.e., the default time slice). Whenever a vCPU is prioritized, it gains a full time slice unless voluntarily giving up the CPU, e.g., blocking due to synchronization. Thus, programs with fine-grained synchronization, e.g., those with computation less than 30ms between synchronization, are never forcibly de-scheduled by Xen due to the expiration of time slices, thereby being resilient to CPU contention. This issue is not specific to Xen and has also been observed in KVM [3].

As parallel programs have varying CPU allocations in response to interference, it is important to monitor *steal* time to determine the slowdowns at individual threads. However, the resilience to interference alone does not explain the unexpected marginal slowdown of *sp* in Figure 1, though it suffers significant steal in Figure 2. We uncover the reasons in the next subsection.

3.3 Varying Compute Time under Interference

In addition to the varying steal time, we find another factor that affects the slowdown at individual threads – the

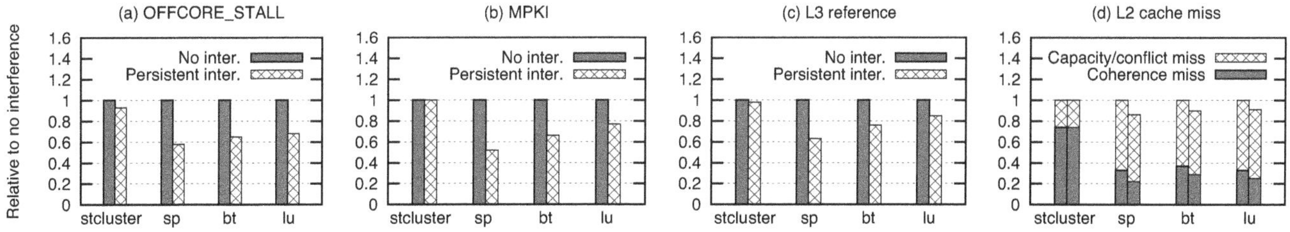

Figure 4: Interference alleviates intra-program contentions.

cost to access the memory hierarchy can change due to interference, leading to varying compute time. Figure 3 shows the runtime breakdown for programs that have unexpected slowdowns. These programs are expected to have slowdowns as much as their stolen time. The figure suggests that the computations needed to complete these programs decrease under the 1-loop persistent interference. The compute times for *streamcluster*, *sp*, *bt*, and *lu* in the complete program execution drop by 12%, 49%, 19%, and 29%, respectively.

To find the reasons for the reduced compute time, we show the statistics of hardware performance counters in dedicated execution and execution with 1 persistent interference in Figure 4 (a) - (d). The figures only show the statistics of the thread with interference and data is normalized to the no interference case (left bar in each group). `OFFCORE_STALL` refers to the cycles spent in the offcore memory subsystem on Intel processors. It measures the overall cost of accessing LLC and DRAM. `MPKI` measures LLC misses per thousand instructions. Figure 4 (a) suggests that these programs had fewer `OFFCORE` stalls under interference because on average there were fewer threads running simultaneously, thereby incurring less contention on the memory hierarchy. Figure 4 (b) shows that `MPKI` also drops under interference. Since the straggling thread progressed slower than sibling threads, it spent little time spinning and its instruction count decreased. A drop in the overall `MPKI` then indicates a significant drop in the number of LLC misses. Intuitively, the total LLC footprint of the parallel threads should remain unchanged, thus the LLC miss rate should not change.

We find that interference changes the way parallel applications interact with the memory hierarchy. Figure 4 (c) shows that the reduction in LLC misses was mainly due to fewer LLC references. For example, the number of LLC references for *streamcluster*, *sp*, *bt*, *lu* drop by 2%, 37%, 24%, 15%, respectively. Since LLC (L3 in our testbed) reference is the result of L2 misses, we further draw the breakdown of L2 misses in Figure 4 (d) to pinpoint the culprits of reduced L3 reference. Figure 4 (d) only shows demand data and instruction misses. Prefetching misses are excluded from the figure. We used L2 events `DEMAND.I_STATE` and `RFO.I_STATE` to count *coherence* misses and the remaining misses were *capacity* or *conflict* misses. The data shown in Figure 4 (c) and (d) is normalized to the no interference case.

From Figure 4 (d), we can see that the change in L2 coherence miss contributes most to the overall L2 miss reduction. A study of program source code reveals that most coherence misses are caused by *false sharing* between threads. The out-of-sync execution of parallel threads due to interference can constructively alleviate the contention on shared cache lines. Threads with different progression will see fewer cache line invalidations from sibling cores. Interference not only reduces the inter-core cache coherence traffic but also avoids some unnecessary L3 references. For example, miss on an unmodified L2 cacheline can be serviced by forwarding the line from a sibling core without sending requests to the L3 cache. This effectively reduces the number of capacity/conflict misses on the L3 cache. An exception is *streamcluster* whose change in compute time is mostly attributed to prefetching misses.

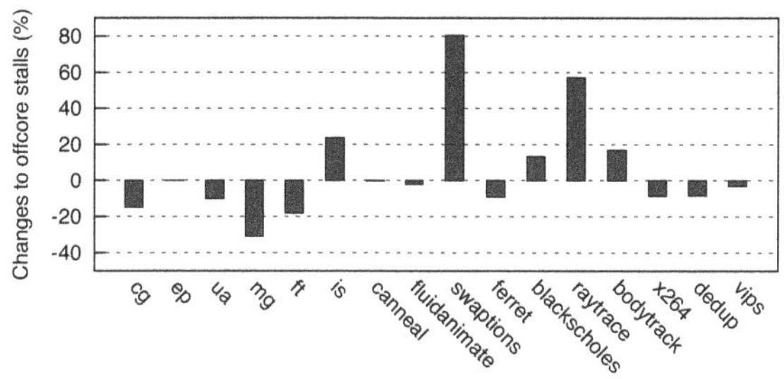

Figure 5: Interference changes memory access time.

Next, we show that most programs in the NBP and PARSEC benchmarks have varying memory cost under interference. Figure 5 shows the changes in `OFFCORE_STALL` under interference relative to the no interference case for the benchmarks not shown in Figure 4. Negative values suggest reductions in memory cost and vice versa. As we can see, the cost to access memory varies wildly from -30.9% to 80.2%, with most programs susceptible to such changes. If the compute time comprises mostly memory access time (i.e., memory-bound), the changes in memory cost due to interference could greatly affect the overall performance. While the increase in memory access time can be attributed to the loss of locality, e.g., threads dynamically stealing work from straggling threads in *raytrace* and *bodytrack*, the reduction in memory cost due to the mitigation of intra-program contentions can be exploited to improve datacenter efficiency. We carefully co-located *sp* with four intermittent interferences, with 5%, 8%, 10%, 15% CPU demands, respectively. The setting is to create out-of-sync execution at parallel threads to mitigate the false sharing between them.

	No inter.	w/ inter.
CPU %	400%	363% (**-9.2%**)
Runtime	1004s	914s (+**9.0%**)

Table 2: Better *sp* performance with less resources.

Table 2 shows that *sp* achieved 9.0% better performance with 9.2% less allocated resource. This case study **suggests** a group of symbiotic datacenter workloads, in which seemingly destructive competitions help constructively mitigate intra-program contentions on shared resources.

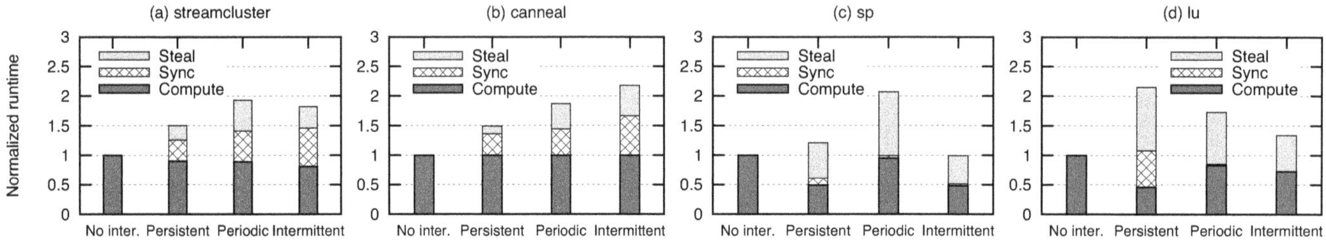

Figure 6: Program performance under different types of interference (4-loop).

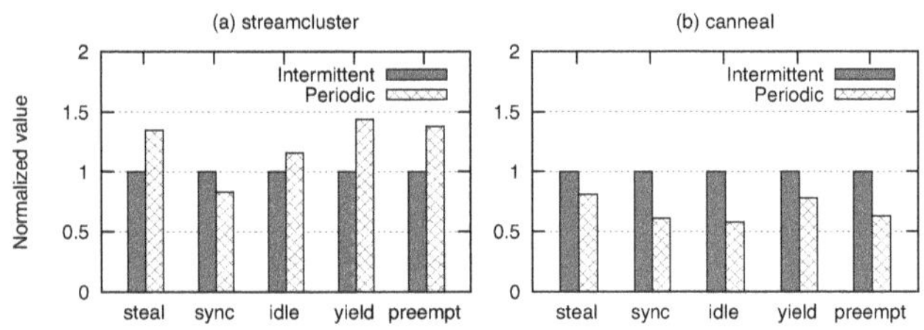

Figure 7: Low-level metrics under interference.

3.4 Complex Interactions with the Scheduler

Performance is even harder to characterize if all threads of the parallel program are affected by interference. In the simple one persistent interference scenario, program resilience to CPU contention or the change in compute time plays a major role in performance. In contrast, when all vCPUs have interference, the overall performance is a function of compute, sync, and steal time. Figure 6 shows the performance of parallel programs under different types of 4-loop interference, i.e., *persistent*, *periodic*, and *intermittent*. As shown in Figure 6(a) and (b), both *streamcluster* and *canneal* achieved the best performance under persistent interference but suffered under the other two. However, these two benchmarks behaved differently under periodic and intermittent interferences. While *streamcluster* had the largest slowdown under the periodic interference, *canneal* suffered most under the intermittent interference. Such uncertainty is due to the complex interactions among the parallel program, the interference, and the scheduler. For example, as discussed in Section 3.2, steal time is affected by the granularity of synchronization. A drop in compute time will decrease steal time but lead to increased sync time. The overall slowdown is determined by the interplays between these factors.

Figure 7(a) and (b) show the low-level performance metrics of *streamcluster* and *canneal* when co-running with periodic and intermittent interferences, respectively. The figures summarize the statistics for all vCPUs in the parallel VM. We find that low-level metrics shed light on the unpredictability of high-level performance. Except sync time, all other low-level metrics are highly correlated with the overall slowdown. Among these metrics, *idle* time is the key to understanding the performance difference. `Idle` refers to the time neither the parallel program nor the interference was running. A longer idle time indicates a larger overlap between parallel program's computation and the CPU burst of the interfering loop. This results in more severe contentions on the pCPU. From the figure, we can see that longer idle time always leads to more preemptions of the parallel program and more yields, which is the sign of vCPU blocking due to imbalanced execution. The **implications** from these observations are that reducing the number of preemptions would help improve performance under interference and the system idle time is a good indicator of scheduling efficiency.

For programs with busy-waiting synchronization, such as NPB benchmarks *sp* and *lu*, both spin (or sync) time and compute time are counted as the CPU consumption of the parallel VM. Since steal time depends on the CPU usage of the VM, the performance of *sp* and *lu* is determined by their combined spin and compute time. Figure 6 (c) and (d) show the runtime breakdown of *sp* and *lu*, respectively. We make three key observations. First, co-running with intermittent interference achieved the best performance among the three interference scenarios. Second, persistent interference caused longer spin time than the other two. Third, periodic interference did not significantly increase sync time. These observations provide valuable insight into the complex interplays between busy-waiting workloads and interference.

The asynchrony in scheduling multiple vCPUs contributed most to the reduction of compute time under persistent and intermittent interferences. When co-locating the parallel program with persistent interference, individual vCPUs are likely scheduled in an uncoordinated manner on multiple pCPUs and the asynchrony remains until the completion of the parallel program because the scheduling rhythm (i.e., switching vCPUs at time slice expirations) on multiple pCPUs will not change for compute-bound workloads (i.e., spinning workload and persistent interference). However, the constant asynchrony continuously incurs exceeding spinning at faster vCPUs and eventually degrades overall performance. The randomness in intermittent interference also creates asynchrony on multiple vCPUs and helps reduce memory access cost. Contrary to persistent interference, it does not cause long spin time and neither does the periodic interference. The frequent switching between computation and idling (i.e., 10ms in periodic and 1-30ms in intermittent interferences) in these two interferences forces the hypervisor to perform scheduling at a much finer granularity compared to the default 30ms time slice in Xen. There have been studies using small time slices to improve the performance of virtualized IO [1, 34]. In our case, the fine-grained scheduling helps stop spinning vCPUs in a timely manner, which not only reduces the overall sync time but also saves the precious CPU time for useful work in the parallel program. Our analysis motivates a possible **optimization** at the hypervisor to improve the performance of busy-waiting workloads: *differentiating scheduling on multiprocessors.*

4. ONLINE PERFORMANCE PREDICTION

In this section, we present an approach for online performance prediction based on the breakdown of parallel runtime. The idea is to sample parallel execution under interference and compare the execution profile with that in an interference-free environment. The key is to compare the amount of *useful* work completed in the two profiles and infer the slowdown from the difference in the speed of program progression. *We define useful work as the necessary work needed to complete the parallel job assuming an ideal memory system with zero latency and perfect load balancing.* As we have shown, the cost of accessing memory and performing synchronization can vary under interference, leading to dynamic computations required to complete parallel programs. In a machine with an ideal memory system, computation is performed in the CPU front-end which is an invariant in the presence of interference or unpredictable thread scheduling. With perfect load balancing, the time spent in synchronization, i.e., spinning or performing context switches, is almost zero. Thus, the compute time in such an ideal platform is only determined by compilation and the dynamic instruction scheduling on individual CPUs. As these two factors are not affected by interference, the ideal compute time is a **reliable metric** to measure program progress.

To measure useful work, or the compute time on an ideal platform, we remove the time spent in the memory hierarchy, synchronization, and the time stolen by other users, from the total time. Specifically, we calculate useful work t_{ideal} in a sampling period as follows:

$$t_{ideal} = t_{total} - t_{steal} - t_{sync} - t_{mem},$$

where t_{steal} measures the resilience of the program to interference and is reported directly by vProfile. We use the time spent on Intel's offcore memory subsystem (i.e., OFF-CORE_STALL) to approximate t_{mem}. For programs with busy-waiting synchronization, t_{sync} refers to the spinning time recorded by vProfile. For programs with blocking synchronization, t_{sync} includes the time in the blocked state and the time performing vCPU context switches. While the blocked time is already included in the execution profile, we infer the cost of context switching by comparing the cycles spent by different threads in the same parallel program. Specifically, after removing t_{steal} and t_{mem} from the total time, we compare the remaining time of individual threads and attribute the difference to the varying numbers of context switches performed by them, assuming that each thread has been assigned an equal amount of work. As such, we calculate the per context switch cost (in CPU cycles) and multiply the number of vCPU blocking to derive t_{sync}.

The online sampling profiles parallel execution in two steps. First, it enables the *dedicated mode* to collect statistics for an interference free execution. The dedicated mode sampling is then followed by a normal sampling with interference turned on. The length of the sampling can be tuned to produce the best accuracy. We empirically set the sampling length to 30 seconds. vProfile reports the runtime breakdown of all vCPUs in the VM under the two execution modes, respectively. The overall slowdown is then calculated as $\frac{t'_{ideal}}{t_{ideal}}$, where t'_{ideal} and t_{ideal} are the amount of useful work done by all threads in the parallel program during the dedicated mode and under interference, respectively.

Figure 8 shows the accuracy of the proposed online prediction compared with two representative prediction approaches based on misses per thousand instructions (MPKI) and cycles per instruction (CPI). We employed the same sampling-based method to predict the overall program slowdown using

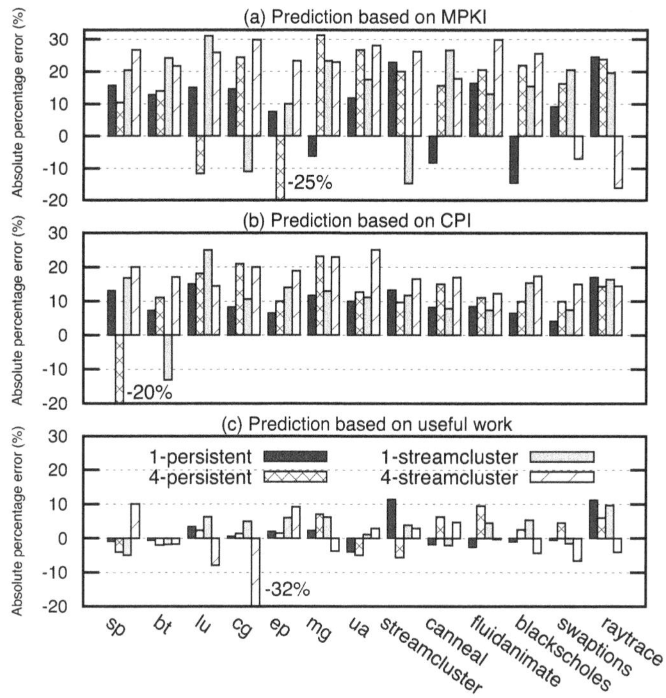

Figure 8: The accuracy of performance prediction.

these two metrics. For example, the slowdown is predicted as $\frac{CPI}{CPI'}$ when using CPI to measure program progress under interference and under the dedicated mode. We used the synthetic workload and the real *streamcluster* workload as the interferences, respectively. For each type of interference, we evaluated the prediction with both the single-threaded (i.e., *1-persistent* and *1-stcluster*) and the multi-threaded (i.e., *4-persistent* and *4-stcluster*) interferences. With the synthetic persistent interference, which has predictable CPU demands and almost zero memory footprint, we test how well the prediction deals with the uncertainties due to parallel programs' varying resilience and memory accessing cost in response to interference. Then, we evaluate how accurate the prediction would be with real workload *streamcluster* that has varying CPU demands and contends on shared memory resources.

As shown in Figure 8 (a) and (b), MPKI and CPI-based predictions incurred significant prediction errors with on average 20.3% and 15.2% mean absolute percentage errors (MAPE), respectively, across all workloads. The inaccuracies were due to the misrepresentation of parallel performance by these two metrics. As shown in Figure 5, memory access cost can either increase or decrease under interference but the overall performance is determined by multiple factors. Thus, memory-related metrics alone, e.g., MPKI, fail to accurately predict performance slowdown. CPI is a effective metric to predict the performance of serial programs as it measures the cost to execute instructions, assuming that the number of instructions needed to complete a program is constant. However, this assumption does not hold in parallel programs. The number of instructions executed by individual threads is variable due to the spinning and blocking performed by threads. For example, it is possible that a spinning thread making no execution progress can have a decreasing CPI because waiting on spinlocks does not cause any memory accesses and has a low CPI. Therefore, CPI

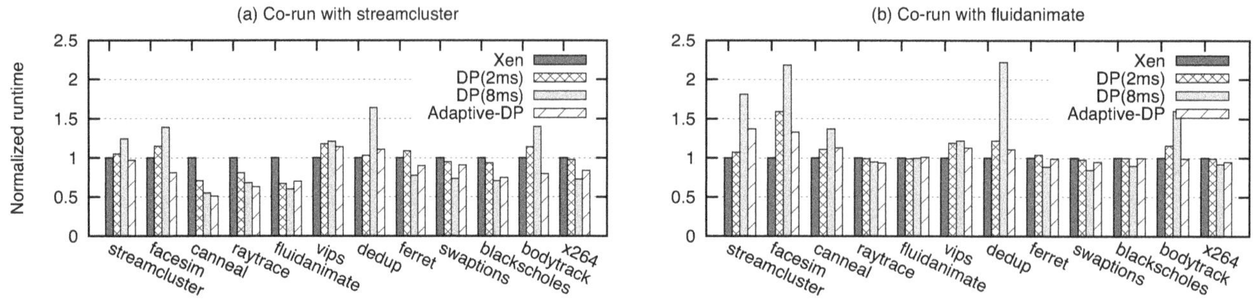

Figure 9: Performance of PARSEC benchmarks under *delayed preemption* (DP).

alone does not capture synchronization in parallel programs and is not accurate in predicting the overall performance.

In contrast, as shown in Figure 8 (c), the performance predictions based on the useful work were accurate with an average MAPE of 4.5% across all workloads. In general, predictions with the synthetic interference are more accurate than that with *streamcluster* and predictions with single-threaded interference tend to incur less error. Except for *cg*, all predictions caused less than 10% errors even for *raytrace*, which implements dynamic work assignment at the user level to improve load balancing. While dynamic work assignment at the application level mitigates interference by assigning less work to straggling threads, it presents challenges to online performance prediction as the work done by individual threads does not reflect the overall progress. Our online prediction addressed this issue by counting useful work on all threads to measure program progress as a whole and achieved less than 10% prediction error for *raytrace*.

Sources of inaccuracy The accuracy of the prediction relies on one assumption: the sampling is representative of the overall parallel execution. This assumption do not always hold, leading to inaccurate predictions. For example, some applications, e.g., *cg*, have quite dynamic memory footprint at different execution stages. The dynamism can affect the effectiveness of the sampling-based prediction, especially when the interference is also dynamic. As shown in Figure 8, the prediction incurred 32% error on *cg* under the 4-thread *streamcluster* interference. As discussed in Section 3.2, the CPU allocation to *streamcluster* depends on its synchronization granularity. As *cg*'s memory demand changed, *streamcluster* had varying computation between synchronizations, thereby affecting the CPU allocation to *cg*. Thus, predictions based on one execution sample can be inaccurate.

5. OPTIMIZATIONS

Our analysis in Section 3 found that involuntary preemptions are especially detrimental to performance and randomness in CPU scheduling help mitigate intra-program contentions on shared resources. Inspired by these findings, we developed two simple optimizations, *delayed preemption* and *differential scheduling*, at the hypervisor to improve parallel performance under interference. Results show that the two optimizations derived from our analysis with the synthetic workloads are effective in reducing performance slowdowns when real parallel applications are co-located.

5.1 Delayed Preemption

Harmful preemptions happen when parallel programs co-locate with periodic or intermittent interference. The frequent wakeups of interfering vCPUs can cause longer steal time and synchronization time in the parallel VM. While preemptions due to the expiration of CPU time quantum are necessary for fair allocation, the boosted wakeups are needed for minimizing latencies of interactive or IO workloads. In a contended environment, such premature preemptions may cause cascading performance degradations in parallel programs. Figure 7 suggests that even CPU is heavily contended, there still exists idle time in which both parallel threads and the interfering loops are in blocked (or sleep) state. When these vCPUs wake up, preemptions between the two competing sides cause ping-pong scheduling. To address this issue, we propose *delayed preemption* (DP) to overlap computations with blocking/sleeping, and to minimize premature preemptions.

Inspired by the design of hybrid synchronization, which uses a spin-then-block approach to attain a balance between low latency and wasting CPU time, our approach temporarily delays a wakeup vCPUs for a short period of time in the hope that current running vCPU would voluntarily yield CPU due to waiting for synchronization. Our implementation in Xen is quite simple and the change only consists of 50 lines of code. We added a single shot timer to the pCPU that has a waking vCPU. If the current running vCPU voluntarily yields CPU, the timer is stopped. Otherwise, the expiration of the timer forces a call to the `schedule` function in Xen to preempt the current vCPU. However, the selection of the delayed period is challenging as different applications attain the best performance with different delays.

Figure 9 shows the performance of PARSEC benchmarks due to stock Xen and DP. We co-located PARSEC benchmarks with two background workloads. *streamcluster* has fine-grained synchronizations at the granularity of 20-30ms while *fluidanimate* has coarse-grained synchronizations every 6 seconds. Benchmarks in Figure 9(a) suffer involuntary preemptions caused by the background *streamcluster* and the background *fluidanimate* in Figure 9(b) is the victim of premature preemptions. In general, the optimal delay setting varies across benchmarks. As shown in Figure 9(a), short delay (i.e., DP(2ms)) is more desirable for *streamcluster*, *facesim*, *dedup*, and *bodytrack*, while long delay (i.e., DP(8ms)) worked best for other workloads. Similarly, workloads also have their respective preferences of delay in Figure 9(b).

To meet applications' diverse needs of preemption delay, we make DP adaptive (i.e., *adaptive-DP*). As discussed in Section 3, the *idle* time on pCPUs is a key indicator of the efficiency of parallel scheduling. For PARSEC benchmarks, vCPUs become idle/blocked when synchronizing with sib-

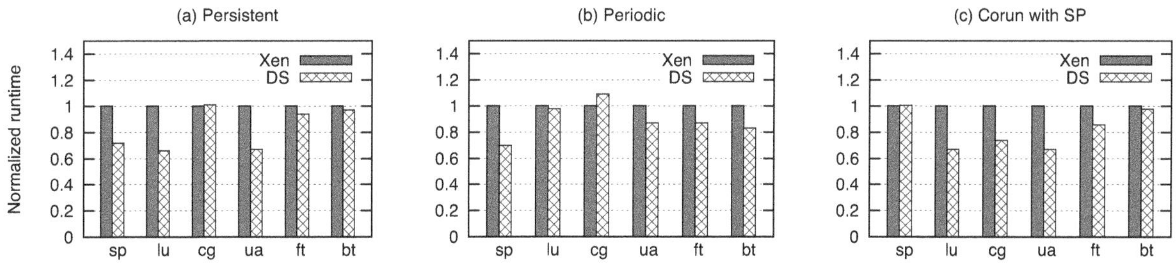

Figure 10: Performance of NPB benchmarks under *differential scheduling* (DS).

ling vCPUs. Interference could slowdown sibling vCPUs and prolong the idle period. In multiprocessor scheduling, uncooperative preemptions could leave CPU time on pCPUs unused when vCPUs from competing workloads are all blocked by synchronization. The objective of adaptive-DP is to dynamically adjust the preemption delays for co-running parallel workloads so that the overall preemptions and the idle time on pCPUs are minimized. We decompose runtime into *compute* and *idle* time and the latter includes *sync* and *steal* time. We adaptively change the preemption delay for a vCPU until its compute time approximates its expected fair share in a shared environment. If all vCPUs from co-running applications attain their fair share, the idle time would be dominated by the steal time, thereby minimizing the sync time and preemptions. Specifically, the preemption delay is updated as follows:

$$lag = \frac{t_{comp} - t_{fair}}{t_{comp} + t_{idle}}, \quad (1)$$

$$delay = delay + lag \times (delay + \texttt{MICROSECS(10)}), \quad (2)$$

where t_{fair} and t_{comp} refer to the ideal fair allocation of CPU time and the actual attained compute time, respectively. The preemption *delay* is updated according to the *lag* relative to the ideal fair CPU allocation. A positive lag increases the delay a vCPU waits to preempt the current running vCPU, giving other applications more time to execute. `MICROSECS(10)` is to ensure no-zero changes in case delay becomes zero.

As shown in Figure 9 (a) and (b), *adaptive-DP* automatically determines the optimal delay for different applications. When co-running with fine-grained *streamcluster* (Figure 9 (a)), adaptive-DP outperformed both DP (2ms) and DP (8ms) for applications with fine-grained synchronizations, e.g., *streamcluster*, *facesim*, and *canneal*. Adaptive-DP effectively identified better delay values for such workloads compared to the manually determined 2ms and 8ms delays. For coarse-grained workloads, such as *swaptions*, *blackscholes*, and *x264*, adaptive-DP struck a balance between the foreground and background workloads and achieved performance in-between the manually tuned delays. When co-running with *fluidanimate* (Figure 9 (b)), adaptive-DP had similar performance to stock Xen as Xen with zero preemption delays always prioritized the foreground workloads with fine-grained synchronization. We calculated the geometric mean of the slowdowns of the foreground and background workloads relative to their performance in dedicated systems. The background workloads were repeated until all foreground workload completed. Adaptive-DP outperformed Xen by 12% in the overall slowdown, indicating more efficient scheduling in a shared environment.

5.2 Differential Scheduling

Differential Scheduling (DS) is also motivated by our observations in Section 3. We found that the randomness in intermittent interference helps alleviate the contention on shared memory resources, which significantly reduces the required computation. The irregularity in CPU demand and sleep intervals forces the CPU scheduling on multiprocessors to proceed at different paces. This effectively leads to different lengths of time slice at different CPUs because the intermittent loops yield CPU at irregular intervals. The result is not only the release of pressure placed by the concurrent vCPUs to the memory hierarchy but also a reduction of wasted spinning time due to fine-grained scheduling.

To emulate the benefits brought by co-running with intermittent interference, we purposely make the schedulers on multiple CPUs have different time quantum. Xen uses a master timer for each pCPU to generate periodic timer interrupt to force a call to the `schedule` function. The default timeout (i.e., the time slice) is 30ms. In DS, the interval of the timer is randomly generated. Each time Xen sets the timeout for the next timer interrupt, it picks a random interval based on the readings of the Time Stamp Counter (tsc) register. Given the micro-second resolution (approximately 2430 cycles on our platform) of hardware timers, the last two digits of the tsc readings are likely device noises and are a good source of randomness. We set the time quantum on individual pCPUs to the range of 10ms to 30ms to enable fine-grained scheduling.

Figure 10 shows the performance of NPB benchmarks due to stock Xen and DS. Since DS already adds randomness into vCPU scheduling, we present the performance of DS when NPB benchmarks ran with persistent, periodic interferences (excluding the intermittent interference), and the real workload *sp*. The selection of *sp* is due to its memory contentiousness to co-running programs. Figure 10 (a) suggests that with persistent interference, DS was only effective in optimizing memory-bound programs, such as *sp*, *lu*, and *ua*. On average, DS outperformed Xen by 32% in these workloads. For CPU-bound program, e.g., *cg*, DS neither significantly degraded or improved performance. For periodic interference (shown in Figure 10 (b)), DS outperformed Xen in all benchmarks except *cg*. DS does not help mitigate memory contentions as *cg* is primarily CPU-bound and hurts performance because differential time slices slow down the tightly coupled phases in *cg*.

Interestingly, DS was able to outperform Xen even for compute-bound benchmarks, e.g., *cg* (as shown in Figure 10 (c)) when the background workload was memory-bound *sp*. The alleviation of memory pressure from the background *sp* helped improve the performance of foreground workloads.

However, the inability of DS to improve foreground *sp* performance in Figure 10 (c) suggests that DS work best for workloads with complementary memory access patterns. Another advantage of DS is that the randomness in scheduling significantly reduces runtime variations across runs, with an average variation of 0.5%.

6. DISCUSSIONS AND FUTURE WORK

Enable per-thread runtime breakdown Currently, vProfile can only report runtime breakdown at per-vCPU level for parallel applications that have a one-to-one mapping from user-level threads to vCPUs. There exist many parallel workloads with more threads than vCPUs. Examples include web servers and workloads implementing worker pools, such as *dedup*, *ferret* and *vips*. Enabling per-thread runtime breakdown would help further pinpoint the source of slowdown but require tracing thread switches in the guest OS.
Extend prediction to more sophisticated workloads The online prediction currently focuses on multithreaded parallel programs on shared memory systems. Predicting parallel performance on distributed memory systems present significant challenges. Much effort is needed to devise a lightweight and accurate sampling approach on multiple machines. Further, our prediction treats the useful work on any threads equally. For more sophisticated programs, especially those having strong dependencies between threads, e.g., *dedup* and *ferret* with pipeline parallelism, the prediction should be based on the useful work of the most critical thread.
Identify symbiotic workloads Experimental results show that DP and DS are effective for blocking-based workloads (e.g., PARSEC benchmarks) and workloads with complementary memory demands, respectively. However, no one size fits all. DS can hurt the performance of CPU-bound and tightly bounded workloads, and DP is ineffective for applications with busy-waiting synchronization. Identifying symbiotic workloads that either have complementary resource demands or can be managed under similar schemes would help improve resource utilizations and reduce energy consumptions in datacenters.

7. RELATED WORK

Performance interference has been well studied in literature. Most work focused on contentions on shared resources, such as last-level caches [4, 6, 10, 12, 14], memory controllers [10, 21], and hardware prefetchers [17], between sequential programs or multi-programmed/threaded workloads. There are also recent work measuring the interference in datacenters [8, 9, 15, 19, 22, 30, 35, 36]. These studies either assume space sharing between workloads [7, 24, 27, 28], use cycles per instruction (CPI) as a proxy of performance [8, 9, 35, 36] or use offline profiling to estimate the contentiousness of co-runners [19, 22]. These approaches can not be easily extended to manage performance interference of parallel applications. First, techniques addressing single-thread resource contentions do not necessarily optimize the execution of parallel programs as parallel performance is a function of single-thread computing and synchronizations. Second, widely used metrics such as CPI are not reliable in measuring performance in parallel programs because CPI can be either inflated or deflated due to synchronizations. Third, parallel applications are usually long-running jobs. Offline profiling is prohibitively expensive in production systems. In this work, we measure the amount of useful work completed to predict slowdown in an online manner.

There are also existing studies addressing the overhead of running parallel program in virtualized environments. Our optimizations are closely related to these works. Common issues include lock-holder preemption (LHP) [32], CPU stacking [29], and expensive traps to the hypervisor [11, 26]. Co-scheduling [23, 29] aims to schedule cooperative threads synchronously to avoid the LHP issue. However, our findings in this work show that *differential scheduling* may be more desirable for memory-bound programs. *Delayed preemption* shares the similar idea with demand-based coordinated scheduling [16] to temporarily delay the preemption of important threads. The scheduler in [16] delays the preemption of vCPUs that initiate wakeup IPIs to avoid LHP. Our purpose is to interleave the computations between parallel programs and interference to avoid future harmful preemptions. Ding et. al., found that consolidating multiple threads onto one vCPU to avoid blocking leads to significant performance boost in KVM [11]. Contrary to their findings, our experiments show that programs with fine-grained synchronization are more resilient to persistent interference in a Xen environment. The contradiction can be attributed to the different designs of Linux CFS scheduler and Xen's credit scheduler.

8. CONCLUSIONS

This paper presents a systematic study of parallel performance under interference. We find that the speed of individual threads under interference is determined by their varying resilience to interferences and the computation required to complete the parallel program can change vastly under interference due to alleviated intra-program contentions. Further, the overall performance is the result of the complex interplays between these factors. Avoiding harmful vCPU preemptions or maintaining asynchrony between vCPUs helps reduce slowdown under interference for different kinds of workloads. Inspired by these findings, we develop an accurate online approach for predicting slowdowns under interference without requiring completing the parallel program, and devise two scheduling optimizations at the hypervisor to improve performance.

9. ACKNOWLEDGEMENTS

We are grateful to the anonymous reviewers for their constructive comments. This research was supported in part by the U.S. National Science Foundation under grants CNS-1320122, CCF-1261584 and CCF-1261811.

10. REFERENCES

[1] J. Ahn, C. H. Park, and J. Huh. Micro-sliced virtual processors to hide the effect of discontinuous cpu availability for consolidated systems. In *Proc of MICRO*, 2014.

[2] D. H. Bailey, E. Barszcz, J. T. Barton, D. S. Browning, R. L. Carter, L. Dagum, R. A. Fatoohi, P. O. Frederickson, T. A. Lasinski, R. S. Schreiber, H. D. Simon, V. Venkatakrishnan, and S. K. Weeratunga. The nas parallel benchmarks summary and preliminary results. In *Proc. of SC*, 1991.

[3] K. based virtual machine. http://www.linux-kvm.org/.

[4] S. Blagodurov, S. Zhuravlev, and A. Fedorova. Contention-aware scheduling on multicore systems. *ACM Trans. Comput. Syst.*, 28(4), 2010.

[5] K. Chakraborty, P. M. Wells, and G. S. Sohi. Supporting overcommitted virtual machines through hardware spin detection. *IEEE Trans. Parallel Distrib. Syst.*, 23(2), 2012.

[6] D. Chandra, F. Guo, S. Kim, and Y. Solihin. Predicting inter-thread cache contention on a chip multi-processor architecture. In *Proc. of HPCA*, 2005.

[7] T. Creech, A. Kotha, and R. Barua. Efficient multiprogramming for multicores with scaf. In *Proc. of MICRO-46*, 2013.

[8] C. Delimitrou and C. Kozyrakis. Paragon: Qos-aware scheduling for heterogeneous datacenters. In *Proc. of ASPLOS*, 2013.

[9] C. Delimitrou and C. Kozyrakis. Quasar: Resource-efficient and qos-aware cluster management. In *Proc. of ASPLOS*, 2014.

[10] T. Dey, W. Wang, J. W. Davidson, and M. L. Soffa. Characterizing multi-threaded applications based on shared-resource contention. In *Proc. of ISPASS*, 2011.

[11] X. Ding, P. B. Gibbons, M. A. Kozuch, and J. Shan. Gleaner: Mitigating the blocked-waiter wakeup problem for virtualized multicore applications. In *Proc. of USENIX ATC*, 2014.

[12] F. Guo and Y. Solihin. A framework for providing quality of service in chip multi-processors. In *Proc. of MICRO*, 2007.

[13] T. Harris, M. Mass, and V. J. Marathe. Callisto: Co-scheduling parallel runtime systems. In *Proc. of EuroSys*, 2014.

[14] R. Iyer, L. Zhao, F. Guo, R. Illikkal, S. Makineni, D. Newell, Y. Solihin, L. Hsu, and S. Reinhardt. Qos policy and architecture for cache/memory in cmp platforms. In *Proc. of SIGMETRICS*, 2007.

[15] M. Kambadur, T. Moseley, R. Hank, and M. A. Kim. Measuring interference between live datacenter applications. In *Proc. of SC*, 2012.

[16] H. Kim, S. Kim, J. Jeong, J. Lee, and S. Maeng. Demand-based coordinated scheduling for smp vms. In *Proc. of ASPLOS*, 2013.

[17] F. Liu and Y. Solihin. Studying the impact of hardware prefetching and bandwidth partitioning in chip-multiprocessors. In *Proc. of SIGMETRICS*, 2011.

[18] X. Liu and B. Wu. Scaanalyzer: A tool to identify memory scalability bottlenecks in parallel programs. In *Proc. of SC*, 2015.

[19] J. Mars, L. Tang, R. Hundt, K. Skadron, and M. L. Soffa. Bubble-up: Increasing utilization in modern warehouse scale computers via sensible co-locations. In *Proc. of MICRO*, 2011.

[20] P. E. McKenney. Differential profiling. *Software - Practice and Experience*, 29(3), 1999.

[21] O. Mutlu and T. Moscibroda. Stall-time fair memory access scheduling for chip multiprocessors. In *Proc. of MICRO*, 2007.

[22] D. Novaković, N. Vasić, S. Novaković, D. Kostić, and R. Bianchini. Deepdive: Transparently identifying and managing performance interference in virtualized environments. In *Proc. of USENIX ATC*, 2013.

[23] J. Ousterhout. Scheduling techniques for concurrent systems.

[24] A. Raman, A. Zaks, J. W. Lee, and D. I. August. Parcae: A system for flexible parallel execution. In *Proc. of PLDI*, 2012.

[25] J. Rao and X. Zhou. Towards fair and efficient smp virtual machine scheduling. In *Proc. of PPoPP*, 2014.

[26] X. Song, H. Chen, and B. Zang. Characterizing the performance and scalability of many-core applications on virtualized platforms. Technical Report FDUPPITR-2010-002, Parallel Processing Institute, Fudan University, 2010.

[27] S. Sridharan, G. Gupta, and G. S. Sohi. Holistic run-time parallelism management for time and energy efficiency. In *Proc. of ICS*, 2013.

[28] S. Sridharan, G. Gupta, and G. S. Sohi. Adaptive, efficient, parallel execution of parallel programs. In *Proc. of PLDI*, 2014.

[29] O. Sukwong and H. S. Kim. Is co-scheduling too expensive for smp vms? In *Proc. of EuroSys*, 2011.

[30] L. Tang, J. Mars, W. Wang, T. Dey, and M. L. Soffa. Reqos: Reactive static/dynamic compilation for qos in warehouse scale computers. In *Proc. of ASPLOS*, 2013.

[31] The PARSEC benchmarks. http://parsec.cs.princeton.edu/.

[32] V. Uhlig, J. LeVasseur, E. Skoglund, and U. Dannowski. Towards scalable multiprocessor virtual machines. In *Proc. of VM*, 2004.

[33] C. Weng, Q. Liu, L. Yu, and M. Li. Dynamic adaptive scheduling for virtual machines. In *Proc. of HPDC*, 2011.

[34] C. Xu, S. Gamage, P. N. Rao, A. Kangarlou, R. R. Kompella, and D. Xu. vslicer: Latency-aware virtual machine scheduling via differentiated-frequency cpu slicing. In *Proc. of HPDC*, 2012.

[35] H. Yang, A. Breslow, J. Mars, and L. Tang. Bubble-flux: Precise online qos management for increased utilization in warehouse scale computers. In *Proc. of ISCA*, 2013.

[36] X. Zhang, E. Tune, R. Hagmann, R. Jnagal, V. Gokhale, and J. Wilkes. Cpi2: Cpu performance isolation for shared compute clusters. In *Proc. of EuroSys*, 2013.

[37] F. Zhou, M. Goel, P. Desnoyers, and R. Sundaram. Scheduler vulnerabilities and coordinated attacks in cloud computing. *J. Comput. Secur.*, 2013.

Optimizing Indirect Memory References with `milk`

Vladimir Kiriansky
MIT CSAIL
vlk@csail.mit.edu

Yunming Zhang
MIT CSAIL
yunming@csail.mit.edu

Saman Amarasinghe
MIT CSAIL
saman@csail.mit.edu

ABSTRACT

Modern applications such as graph and data analytics, when operating on real world data, have working sets much larger than cache capacity and are bottlenecked by DRAM. To make matters worse, DRAM bandwidth is increasing much slower than per CPU core count, while DRAM latency has been virtually stagnant. Parallel applications that are bound by memory bandwidth fail to scale, while applications bound by memory latency draw a small fraction of much-needed bandwidth. While expert programmers may be able to tune important applications by hand through heroic effort, traditional compiler cache optimizations have not been sufficiently aggressive to overcome the growing DRAM gap.

In this paper, we introduce **milk** — a C/C++ language extension that allows programmers to annotate memory-bound loops concisely. Using optimized intermediate data structures, random indirect memory references are transformed into batches of efficient sequential DRAM accesses. A simple semantic model enhances programmer productivity for efficient parallelization with OpenMP.

We evaluate the MILK compiler on parallel implementations of traditional graph applications, demonstrating performance gains of up to 3×.

1. INTRODUCTION

Memory bottlenecks limit the performance of many modern applications such as in-memory databases, key-value stores, graph analytics, and machine learning. These applications process large volumes of in-memory data since DRAM capacity is keeping pace with Moore's Law. Indirect memory references in large working sets, however, cannot be captured by hardware caches. Out-of-order execution CPUs also cannot hide the high latency of random DRAM accesses, and most cycles are wasted on stalls. Compiler cache optimizations also cannot statically capture locality in irregular memory accesses even when loop-level locality exists.

Any execution order is often acceptable, yet performance dramatically depends on the access pattern. The following read-modify-write loop is typical in many domains, e.g., graph analysis, image processing, and query planning:

```
#pragma omp parallel for
for(int i=0; i<N; i++)
  #pragma omp atomic
  count[d[i]]++;
```

On contiguous DRAM-resident inputs this loop achieves 18% of peak DRAM bandwidth of Intel Haswell CPUs; if inputs are always sorted we can optimize to remove atomics and reach 54% of peak bandwidth. On uniform random inputs, however, this loop's effective bandwidth is only 2%.

For this loop on random inputs, the MILK compiler achieves 4× end-to-end speedup. Our compiler transformations dynamically partition the index values in `d` to capture all available locality in accesses to `count`. Each partition accesses a subset of memory that fits in cache. In addition, synchronization is eliminated since threads process disjoint partitions. Just adding **milk** clauses to the OpenMP directives enables these optimizations.

To achieve high performance and low overhead, MILK's *DRAM-conscious Clustering* transforms loops into three logical phases: Collection, Distribution, and Delivery. In Collection, dynamically generated indices of indirect accesses (e.g., simply `d[i]` above) are first collected in cache local buffers. In Distribution, indices are written to DRAM resident partitions using efficient sequential DRAM access. In Delivery, each partition's deferred updates are read from DRAM and processed, along with dependent statements.

These three logical phases are similar to inspector-executor style optimizations [18, 32, 40]; in MILK, however, to eliminate materialization of partitions and conserve DRAM bandwidth, the phases are fused and run as coroutines. Prior research either focused on expensive preprocessing that resulted in net performance gain only when amortized over many loop executions, or explored simple inspection for correspondingly modest gains. In contrast, our transformations are well optimized to pay off within a single execution — as required in real applications that use iterative algorithms with dynamically changing working sets or values.

The Milk execution model is a relaxed extension of the bulk-synchronous parallel (BSP) model [50], in which communicating processors work on local memory during a *superstep* before exchanging data at a global barrier. Milk virtual processors access randomly only one DRAM-resident cache line per superstep, in addition to sequential memory or cache-resident data. All indirect references are deferred to the next superstep. A Milk superstep may encompass loop nests that include billions of deferred references. Ref-

PACT '16 September 11–15, 2016, Haifa, Israel

ACM ISBN 978-1-4503-4121-9/16/09…$15.00
DOI: http://dx.doi.org/10.1145/2967938.2967948

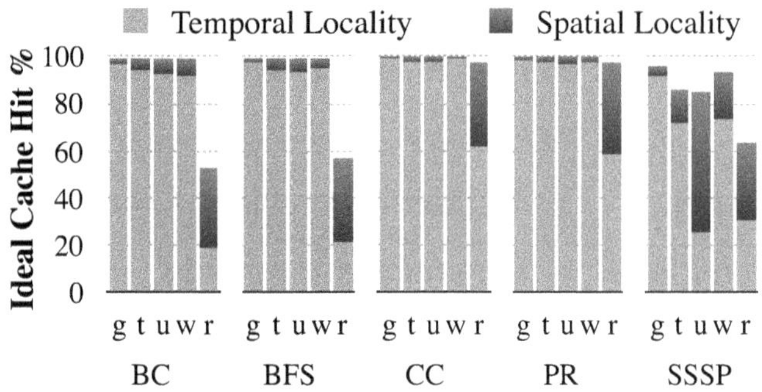

Figure 1: Temporal and spatial locality on an infinite cache with 64-byte lines of indirect memory references per superstep of **B**etweenness **C**entrality, **B**readth-**F**irst **S**earch, **C**onnected **C**omponents, **P**age**R**ank, and **S**ingle-**S**ource **S**hortest **P**aths. Synthetic graphs with V=128M vertices and avg. degree d=16: power law Graph500 (**g**) and uniform (**u**); and real-world graphs: US roads V=24M, d=2.4 (**r**); Twitter V=62M, d=24 (**t**); weblinks V=51M, d=39 (**w**).

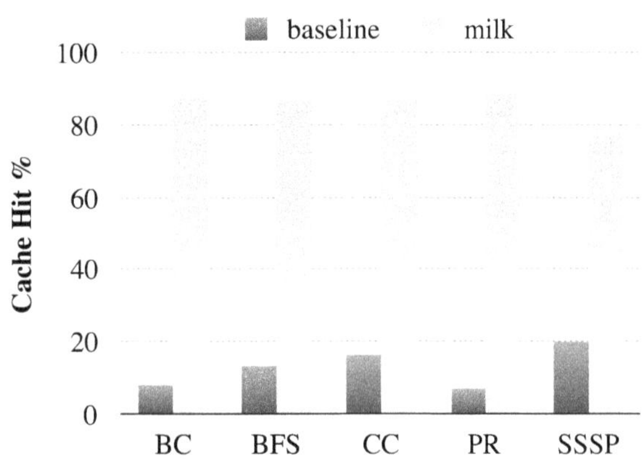

Figure 2: Cache hit rates of demand reads on 256 KB L2, 8 MB shared L3 [2], for V=32M, d=16(uniform).

erences targeting the same cache line are grouped to maximize locality, and are processed by a single virtual processor to eliminate synchronization. This abstract programming model is similar to MapReduce [16] with discrete phases of *Map* and *Reduce* for processing references to distinct memory locations. Milk programs, however, allow programmers to continue thinking in terms of individual references and to maintain traditional serial or OpenMP syntax, usually without semantic change.

We investigate the total locality available in applications, compare to locality captured by hardware, and show MILK's effectiveness. To find an upper bound on locality within a Milk superstep, we use an ideal cache model. An ideal cache would not incur cache capacity or cache conflict misses, or true or false sharing coherence misses on a multiprocessor system. The only memory demands should be compulsory cache misses and output write-backs. (We assume all data is written to memory between supersteps, therefore reuses across supersteps are counted as compulsory misses.)

Since compulsory cache misses, temporal locality, and spatial locality are program- and data-dependent, we instrumented the indirect memory references of commonly used [11, 36,43,47] graph applications with state-of-the-art implementations in the Graph Algorithm Platform Benchmark Suite (GAPBS) [10]. The GAPBS datasets include public samples of real graphs (*Twitter*, *USA road*, and *web crawl*), and synthetic graphs (*uniform* and *power law* [13,21]) to compare sensitivity to graph degree distributions and diameters. We describe the applications in more detail in Section 6, where we also show their handwritten in OpenMP critical loops.

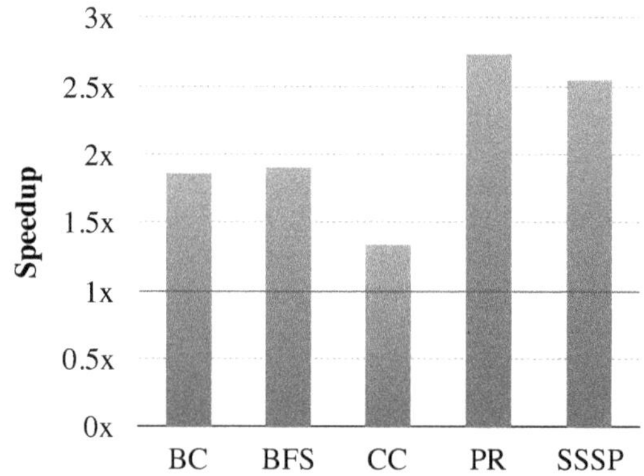

Figure 3: MILK overall speedup. 8MB L3, V=32M, d=16(u).

Figure 1 shows that, on an ideal cache, the total locality within a superstep is close to 100% for most graphs and applications, and above 50% for all. Temporal locality on an infinite cache (i.e., reuse of the same address) captures more than 90% of accesses for high-degree low-diameter graphs. However, for the road graph and for SSSP, harnessing spatial locality (i.e., capturing reuse of 64-byte cache lines) is important. Unlike hit rates on the ideal infinite cache, the cache hit rates observed on real hardware are much lower, and most cycles are wasted on memory stalls.

Figure 2 shows the low cache hit rates of real hardware are improved by 4× with MILK. On a synthetic graph with 32 M vertices, most applications have greater than 128 MB total working sets, and little locality is captured by the 8 MB shared L3 cache and 256 KB L2 per core on a Haswell CPU [2]. To isolate indirect memory reads during full program execution, we use hardware performance counters that track non-prefetch demand reads that hit L2 or L3 caches. In the baseline 80–90% of all L1 misses require a DRAM access, while with MILK they are served by L2 and L3 caches. Figure 3 shows that these improved hit rates translate to end-to-end speedups, ranging from 1.3× to 2.7×.

The rest of this paper is organized as follows: In Section 2, we explore memory system complexities and opportunities in more detail. We introduce the Milk programming model and MILK compiler and runtime library design in Section 3, **milk** syntax and semantic extensions in Section 4, and implementation details of MILK optimizations in Section 5. We demonstrate Milk expressiveness on parallel graph applications in Section 6, and we evaluate performance in Section 7. Section 8 surveys related work and Section 9 concludes.

2. BACKGROUND

We now examine the organization of DRAM to show why random memory references are often 10–20× slower than sequential memory accesses. We also explain why hardware approaches for hiding long latency penalties are ineffective.

2.1 DRAM Organization

The memory hierarchy is optimized for sequential accesses, often at the expense of random accesses, at all levels: DRAM chip, DRAM channel, memory controllers, and caches.

Sequential DRAM reads benefit from spatial locality in DRAM chip *rows*. Before a DRAM read or write can occur, a DRAM row – typically 8–16KB of data – must be destructively loaded (*activated*) into an internal buffer for its contents to be accessed. Consecutive read or write requests to the same row are limited only by DRAM channel bandwidth, thus sequential accesses take advantage of spatial locality in row accesses. In contrast, random accesses must find independent request streams to hide the high latency of a row cycle of different banks (*DRAM page misses*), or worse the additional latency of accessing rows of the same bank (*DRAM page conflicts*).

Hardware memory controllers reorder requests to minimize page misses, and other high-latency request sequences to minimize bus turnarounds and read-to-write transitions. But requests can be rescheduled only within a short window of visibility, e.g., 48 cache lines per memory channel [38] shared among cores. Requests are equally urgent from hardware perspective, and cannot be reordered outside of this window.

DRAM interfaces are also optimized for sequential accesses. Modern CPUs transfer blocks of at least 64 bytes from DRAM. Double Data Rate (DDR) DRAM interfaces transfer data on both rising and falling edges of a clock signal: e.g., a DDR3-1600 [24] chip operating at 800 MHz delivers a theoretical bandwidth of 12.8 GB/s. Current generation CPUs use DDR3/DDR4 interfaces with burst transfers of 4 cycles (mandatory for DDR4), leading to a 64-byte minimum transfer for a 64-bit DRAM. Even though larger transfers would improve DRAM power, reliability, and peak performance, this size coincides with current cache line sizes.

Sequential memory accesses benefit significantly from large cache lines, as they have good spatial locality and can use all of the data within each line. By contrast, random memory accesses use only a small portion of the memory bandwidth consumed. In many applications with irregular memory accesses, each DRAM access uses only 4–8 bytes out of cache lines transferred – 64 bytes transferred for reads, and 128 bytes for writes (a cache-line read and write-back) – netting 3–6% effective bandwidth.

Applications that are stalling on memory but do not saturate the memory bandwidth are bound by memory latency. Random DRAM device latency has been practically stagnant at ~50 ns for the last decade [41, 42]. A DRAM request at peak bandwidth has 100× worse latency than an L1 cache lookup, and in the time it takes to wait for memory, a SIMD superscalar core can execute ~5,000 64-bit operations.

2.2 CPU Request Reordering

CPU out-of-order execution allows multiple long delay memory accesses to be handled but only up to the limits of small hardware structures. By Little's Law, memory throughput is the ratio of outstanding memory requests over DRAM latency. The visible effect of either low memory level parallelism or high DRAM latency is underutilized memory bandwidth. Such "latency bound" programs perform well in-cache, and may have no explicit data dependencies, but become serialized on large inputs.

Hardware prefetchers for sequential accesses increase memory level parallelism with more outstanding DRAM requests. Therefore, sequential reads and writes achieve higher DRAM bandwidth than random accesses. Current hardware has no prefetchers for random requests.

Current CPUs can handle 10 demand requests per core (Line Fill Buffers between L1 and L2) [1, 11] as long as all requests fit within the out-of-order execution window. The effective Memory Level Parallelism (MLP) is most constrained by the capacity limits of resources released in FIFO order, e.g., reorder buffer, or load and store buffers. A loop body with a large number of instructions per memory load may reduce the effective parallelism, e.g., a 192 *micro-op* entry reorder buffer (ROB) must fit all micro-ops since the first outstanding non-retired instruction. Branch misprediction, especially of hard to predict branches that depend on indirect memory accesses further reduce the effective ROB size. Finally, atomic operations drain store buffers [44] and reduce Instruction Level Parallelism (ILP). While hardware mechanisms, including memory controllers and out-of-order schedulers, can reorder only a limited window of tens of operations, MILK efficiently orchestrates billions of accesses.

3. DESIGN

Given the inefficiency of random DRAM references and the limitations of hardware latency-hiding mechanisms, in order to harvest locality beyond hardware capabilities, the MILK compiler uses a software based approach to plan all memory accesses. To use the MILK compiler, programs must fit the Milk execution model and have **milk**[1] annotations.

MILK achieves significant performance improvement by reordering the memory accesses for improved cache locality. The reordered memory references maximize temporal locality by partitioning all indirect references to the same memory location within the cache capacity. The planned accesses also improve spatial locality by grouping indirect references to neighboring memory locations. Furthermore, MILK avoids true sharing, false sharing, and expensive synchronization overheads by ensuring only one core writes to each cache line.

However, naively reorganizing indirect references can add non-trivial overhead. MILK keeps all additional bandwidth low by using only efficient sequential DRAM references. Although data transformations require an investment of additional CPU cycles and sequential DRAM bandwidth, we show how to minimize these overheads with *DRAM-conscious Clustering*.

In order for the MILK compiler to perform the optimization automatically, users must annotate indirect accesses in parallel OpenMP loops with a **milk** clause, which is sufficient for simple loops like Figure 4a. Explicit **milk** directives can select indirect references that should be deferred, along with their context (see line 12 in Figure 4b). Optional *combiner* functions allow programmers to summarize the combined effects of updates targeting the same address. Section 4 describes **milk**'s syntax in more detail.

The Milk execution model is similar to MapReduce [16]. We do not offer a *Map* interface, however, since efficient iteration over in-memory data structures can use domain-specific knowledge (e.g., incoming vs. outgoing neighbor traversal in graph processing, 2-D loop nests for image pro-

[1] Milk's **milk** is an homage to Cilk's **cilk** [19].

```
01 void f(int a[], int ind[], int x) {
02 #pragma omp parallel for milk
03 for(int i=0; i<n; i++)
04     a[ind[i]] = x;
05 }
```

(a) Implicit Indirect References with **milk**.

```
06 void g(float a[], int ind[],
07        float b[]) {
08 #pragma omp parallel for milk
09   for(int i=0; i<n; i++) {
10      float value = b[i];
11      int index = ind[i];
12 #pragma milk pack(value:+) tag(index)
13 #pragma omp atomic if(!milk)
14      a[index] += value;
15   }
16 }
```

(b) Explicit Indirect References with **milk**.

```
17 .milk.outlined.f(int _tag,
18                  Context *c) {
19   c->a[_tag] = c->x;
20 }
21 .milk.outlined.g(int index,
22                  float value,
23                  Context *c) {
24     c->a[index] += value;
25 }
```

(c) Outlined functions for *Delivery*.

```
26 void f(int a[], int ind[], int x) {
27   _Milk_containers c;
28   #pragma omp parallel
29   {
30     #pragma omp for nowait
31     for(int i=0; i<n; i++)
32       _Milk_collect(ind[i], &c);
33     _Milk_distribute(&c);
34     _Milk_deliver(&c, Context(a, x),
35                   .milk.outlined.f);
36   }
37 }
38 void g(float a[], int ind[],
39        float b[]) {
40   _Milk_containers c;
41   #pragma omp parallel
42   {
43     #pragma omp for nowait
44     for(int i=0; i<n; i++)
45       _Milk_collect(&c, ind[i], b[i]);
46     _Milk_distribute(&c, SumCombine);
47     _Milk_deliver(&c, Context(a),
48                   .milk.outlined.g,
49                   SumCombine);
50   }
51 }
```

(d) Logical transformation overview.

Figure 4: DRAM-conscious Clustering transformation.

cessing, 3-D loop nests in physical simulations, etc.). Leaving the outer loop structure to programmers allows further algorithm-specific optimizations, such as use of bit vectors, Bloom filters, priority queues, etc. Further knowledge about power-law data distributions can be used to maximize load balance in parallel loop nests, or to identify accesses that are likely to be cached. Domain-specific frameworks that apply user-supplied *Map* functions over the input can be built on top of our **milk** primitives.

3.1 Collection, Distribution, and Delivery

In the *Collection* and *Distribution* phases, MILK plans memory accesses by grouping references into cache-sized partitions. In the *Delivery* phase, the reordered memory references and deferred dependencies are applied. These phases are a generalization of cache partitioning [45] used in heavily optimized database hash-join [5,8,26,30,45,49,51], with additional DRAM optimizations shown in Section 5.2.

Figure 4d shows a logical overview of the DRAM-conscious Clustering transformation to Collection, Distribution, and Delivery phases. The transformation for line 4 in `f()` shows how a tag index is collected, while the more complex case of line 14 in `g()` also includes a payload value, and a combiner function.

During Collection, indirect reference expressions are evaluated as *tags*, e.g., `ind[i]` on lines 4 and 11. If additional per-reference state is needed, it is also collected with *pack* as a payload; an optional *combiner* enables coalescing of payloads targeting the same tag (e.g., line 12). Tag and pack variables can be initialized with any dynamically evaluated expression and can have side effects (e.g., queue iterators can consume items), since they are written to temporary buffers.

During Distribution, tags are partitioned into clusters such that maximum cache line and DRAM page locality can be achieved for accesses during Delivery. Depending on the range of tag values, if too many partitions would be needed, multiple Distribution passes are required. Each additional Distribution pass uses only sequential transfers to DRAM.

During Delivery, an outlined program slice from the original code is executed using a dynamically constructed context valid for each Delivery thread. Milk captured statements allow arbitrary C++ expressions and function calls, e.g., arbitrary containers can be accessed during Delivery. Figure 4c shows the outlined functions created to capture the deferred execution of lines 4 and 14, respectively, on lines 19 and 24.

Distribution phases are always fused with the previous or next processing stage: the first Distribution pass is fused with Collection, and the final Distribution pass is fused with Delivery. The three distinct phases shown as functions are coroutines, i.e., Collection receives one element at a time to pass to Distribution, and early Delivery can be triggered at any time if memory for temporary buffers is exhausted. Unlike inspector/executor-style [40] preprocessing, the three phases are distinct only logically, and different threads and different tags may be in different phases at the same time.

3.2 Performance Model

A simple model predicts MILK DRAM bandwidth savings as a high order estimate of performance on bandwidth-bound applications. Let us take a workload that makes m random read-modify-writes to n distinct location, e.g., processing a graph with n vertices and m edges. Assume n is

	Original	MILK		
		Collection	Distribution	Delivery
L2		$8m$		$128m$
DRAM	$128m$		$8m$	$8m+8n$

Table 1: MILK reduction of DRAM bandwidth in bytes, for m random references to n locations.

much larger than the cache size, and that updated values, indices, and payloads are 4 bytes. If $n \ll m$, the MILK version uses 8× less bandwidth than the original.

Table 1 summarizes the bandwidth required by the transformed workload and overheads of Milk phases. Original references read and write back a random cache-line on each update. The transformed updates are within L2 caches and use DRAM bandwidth only for compulsory cache-fill and write-back of accessed cache lines. When spatial locality is high, as seen earlier in Figure 1, these use $2n \cdot 4B$. Collection arranges tag and pack records in L1/L2 caches, and Distribution and Delivery write and read DRAM sequentially.

3.3 Milk Correctness Conditions

All BSP-model [50] applications are correct under Milk, as are some non-BSP programs allowed under the more relaxed Milk execution model. Correctness proofs of BSP algorithms hold for Milk execution. The only difference is the number of virtual processors, i.e., tens of threads vs. millions of cache lines. Loops in which read and write sets do not overlap will not change behavior when split in Milk supersteps. For non-BSP programs, a loop *may* read results produced within the same step. Programs that produce externally deterministic [12] output but vary intermediate results (e.g., Connected Components in Figure 9a) may incur more per-iteration work or a lower convergence rate with Milk but will be correct.

Programs with read/write dependencies, which produce non-deterministic outputs under OpenMP, have to be validated or modified for Milk. Domain knowledge may allow divergence from sequential semantics, e.g., in traditional bank check processing all checking account debits are processed or bounced first, and only then any account credits are applied. Splitting a loop into separate parallel loops to break dependence chains allows the alternative sequential execution, OpenMP, and Milk to all agree on the output.

4. MILK SYNTAX AND SEMANTICS

The MILK compiler allows programmers to use the Milk execution model for C/C++ programs with OpenMP extensions and loop annotations. Adding a **milk** clause to a loop directive is often sufficient to enable optimizations. To achieve further optimization control, programmers can select which references in a loop should be deferred by adding a **milk** directive and its clauses. A `tag` clause selects the destination, while `pack` clauses specify the values necessary for deferred dependent statements. The `if` clause allows programmers to express dynamic knowledge about data distribution by deferring only references that are unlikely to be cached. Additional language and library features support safe avoidance of synchronization, deterministic performance, and deterministic outputs with minimal overhead. Table 2 summarizes the clauses of the `pragma` **milk** directive and extended OpenMP directives.

Directive	Clause	Section
milk	`if`	4.1.1
milk	`pack(`v`[:all])`	4.1.3
milk	`pack(`v`:+|*|min|max|any)`	4.1.4
milk	`pack(`v`:first|last)`	4.1.4, 4.4
milk	`tag(`i`)`	4.1.2
`atomic`	`if`	4.3
`for`	**milk**	4.1
`ordered`	**milk**	4.4

Table 2: **milk** OpenMP extensions.

```
01 void BFS_Depth(Graph &g, int current,
02                int depths[]) {
03 #pragma omp parallel for milk
04   for (Node u=0; u<g.num_nodes(); u++)
05     if (depths[u] == current)
06       for (Node v : g.out_neigh(u))
07 #pragma milk
08         if(depths[v] == -1)
09           depths[v] = current + 1;
10 }
```

Figure 5: Breadth-First Search (BFS) with **milk**.

4.1 `milk` Directive and Clause

milk directives within a **milk** loop afford fine-level control when Collecting indirect accesses. This use is similar to the OpenMP `ordered` loop clause and the identically named directive used in the loop body; we borrow the same nesting and binding rules [3]. Figure 5 illustrates this annotation syntax for a Breadth-First-Search traversal (BFS), which produces a vector of depths from the source node. Sequential access on line 5 can be processed directly, but random accesses on lines 8–9 are deferred with **milk**.

4.1.1 `if` Filters

MILK optimizations are effective only when locality exists within a superstep, but is beyond the reach of hardware caches. When programmers can cheaply determine effectiveness, they can provide such a hint as a superstep property, or as a dynamic property of each indirect reference. A loop can be marked for execution without deferral if programmers can determine that the optimization will be ineffective because the range of accesses is small, there are too few requests, or if little locality is expected. For example, a `parallel for` can be marked with OpenMP 4.5 `if:` syntax, e.g.: `#pragma omp milk for if(milk: numV<cacheSize)`.

Individual **milk** directives can be tagged with an `if` clause when domain-specific knowledge can cheaply determine that a specific address is likely in cache. For example, in graph algorithm implementations where graph nodes are ordered by degree, the high-degree nodes that are in cache can be skipped, e.g.: `#pragma milk if(v>hot)`.

4.1.2 `tag` Clause

The `tag` clause can make explicit the definition of the index variable used in the following statement or block, as seen in Figure 4b. The clause takes as an argument the identifier of a variable that programmers should define to use the smallest possible type for supported inputs. An explicit tag is also required when using user-defined collections that do not use the subscript operator `[]`.

4.1.3 pack *Clause*

The pack clause explicitly specifies data needed for correct continuation execution. It takes a list of variables that must be carried as a different payload for every tag. Programmers should minimize the number of variables whenever it is possible to evaluate expressions early (e.g., lines 47 and 98 on Figures 8b and 9c).

Reducing the size of pack variables also directly reduces overhead. The performance of traditional indirect reference-bound kernels is a function of the number of cache lines touched regardless of the amount of data. The costs are identical whether 1 bit or 2 doubles are written: a random DRAM read, and a random DRAM writeback upon cache eviction. Reducing precision is ineffective traditionally if the reduced working set is still larger than cache. MILK transformations, however, are bandwidth bound. Thus, the smallest type for the expected range should be used for pack variables. Floating point variables can be cast to lower precision types, e.g., users can explore the non-standard bfloat16 communication type from TensorFlow [4], which is simply a 16-bit bitcast of float.

4.1.4 pack *Combiners*

For each packed variable, a combiner function can be specified, e.g., pack(u:min), pack(value:+), etc., which may be used to combine pack payloads before Delivery. When a combiner is used, programmers must ensure the program is correct, whether all, one, or a subset of all items is delivered. Valid combiners can be defined for all applications we study in Section 6.

Combiners are optional, as their performance advantage depends on the data distribution and access density for each partition. For uniform distributions, for example, early evaluation of combiners will not discover temporal locality to match tags. Combiners evaluated immediately before executing the continuation allow faster processing of all updates targeting a given tag. While not saving bandwidth, late combiner execution enables deterministic outputs, e.g., with min/max combiners.

The default binary operations supported include the standard OpenMP reductions, e.g., +, *, min. When OpenMP 4.0 user defined reductions [3] are supported by clang, we will also allow similar syntax for user defined combiner expressions. While OpenMP reduction clauses for scalars (or short dense arrays in OpenMP 4.5) use unit value initializers (e.g., 0, 1, INT_MAX), the explicit initialization incurs significant overhead on large and sparsely accessed data. Therefore, Milk combiners are assigned or copy/move constructed only on first access.

Additional pre-defined pack combiner identifiers include all, any, first, and last. Specifying all explicitly documents that each value must be delivered without a combiner. When any value can be used in any order, any marks that duplicate pack values can be dropped. Alternatively, first and last select one pack value in the respective order it would be collected in serial execution.

4.2 Elision Version Semantics

Same-source programs can be compiled in several versions – traditional serial, OpenMP parallel, and Milk (serial or parallel) – dispatched depending on input size. Eliding Milk annotations produces valid serial programs. Milk programs without atomics are succinct and easier to reason about

```
CountDegrees(vector<Edge>& edges) {
    vector<Node> degrees(n, 0);
#pragma omp parallel for milk
    for (Edge e : edges) {
#pragma omp atomic if(!milk)
        degrees[e.u] += 1;
        if (!directed)
#pragma omp atomic if(!milk)
            degrees[e.v] += 1;
    }
}
```

Figure 6: CountDegrees with multiple atomic updates.

than OpenMP parallel programs. Parallel non-Milk programs, however, may be desired for efficient execution on small cache-resident inputs. When correctness of parallel non-Milk versions requires additional synchronization, integration with OpenMP allows correct and efficient execution.

4.3 Atomic Accesses

When unnecessary for **milk** loops, synchronization can be eliminated by marking omp atomic if(!milk). This OpenMP syntax extension allows an if clause in atomic.

All threads updating data concurrently must be in the same **milk** loop. As a safe default, we preserve the behaviour of unmodified omp atomic directives to use atomics, in case they were intended for synchronization with other thread teams, or with external threads via shared memory. During Delivery, atomic operations operate on cache resident data and are executed by a single thread. Such atomics are faster than DRAM resident or contended cache data with expensive cache-to-cache transfers. However, atomics still drain store buffers and destroy instruction and memory parallelism, incurring 3× overhead. When possible, unnecessary atomics should be eliminated.

Milk safely allows either only reads or only writes to the same array. Mixing reads and writes, or atomic capture clauses may change non-BSP program semantics. Currently, loops with internal producer-consumer dependencies should be transformed manually to unidirectional accesses per array per loop to ensure program semantics does not change. Deferring an atomic update can be treated as a write and requires no semantic change.

Read-modify-write update operations that do not peek into results can issue in parallel. For example, the CountDegrees kernel – used for building a graph in GAPBS – shown in Figure 6 can access two edges with an atomic update.

4.4 Deterministic and Ordered Extensions

Adding an ordered clause ensures deterministic outputs by restricting **milk** processing order. This improves programmer productivity and enables new application use cases, e.g., database replication and fault tolerance. Milk processing can give deterministic execution guarantees very efficiently: there are very few thread synchronization points during Distribution, while the cost of enforcing deterministic order is amortized across thousands of individual memory references. The main concern in deterministic execution is that it exacerbates load imbalance during a Collection work-sharing loop, therefore programmers have to explicitly mark these after addressing load imbalance.

5. COMPILER AND RUNTIME LIBRARY

The MILK compiler and runtime library are implemented within the LLVM [27] framework, as Abstract Syntax Tree (AST) transformations in Clang and code generation of LLVM IR. Collection and Delivery phases are implemented as AST lowering phases emitting specializations of the Distribution container library. Table 3 summarizes additional programmer-facing intrinsics.

5.1 Dynamically Constructed Closure

Milk Delivery's indirect memory references are logically separate continuations, but we dynamically construct the full context using four classes of data: a static context shared among all continuations for each deferred block, a tag to construct address references to one or more arrays, an optional payload carried with each tag, and optional thread-local variables.

While similar to C++ lambda expressions, continuations need to allow access to out-of-scope variables across different threads. Compared to `delegate` closures in distributed systems [34], we minimize per-item overhead by optimizing for space and capturing only unique values across iterations. Explicit uses of `tag` and `pack` define the only variables that are unique per tag and packaged as payloads. All variables other than globals used in a continuation must be captured in a shared context.

5.1.1 Shared Context

To minimize space overhead, we use a single closure to capture the original block and all variable references necessary for execution during Delivery of continuations.

Variables that are independent of the iteration variable are simply captured by reference only once for all iterations, e.g., the array base and value in `{m[ind[i]] += val;}` can capture `m` and `val` as long as they are not aliased. If `m` may change, however, programmers should either add `pack(m)`, or recompute `m` in the continuation.

Loop-private variables cannot be passed by reference for Delivery; if programmers can hoist them out of the loop, they are automatically stored in the shared context. Otherwise, variables need to be either explicitly passed by value with `pack`, or recomputed.

5.1.2 Tags

Each block must have a single implicit or explicit `tag`, but multiple references based on the same tag can access different arrays, vectors, or C++ objects with overloaded `operator[]`, e.g., `if (a[v]) b[v]++`. Therefore, tags stored in Collection are indices, not pointers.

5.1.3 Pack payloads

Initialization of variables in `pack` clauses is evaluated during Collection. Variables are not added automatically to `pack` clauses; any non-packed variable reference that is not in the shared context results in a compile-time error. Currently, programmers have to decide whether an expression should be evaluated during Collection, Delivery, or in both.

Evaluation during Collection is best for expressions that make sequential accesses, or can be `pack`ed as a compact payload, e.g.: `bool b = (a[i]>1); Pack(b){...}`. (The `Pack` macro expands to `_Pragma("milk pack")`).

Evaluation during Delivery is favorable when indices are smaller than values and refer to cache-resident data, or expressions have larger size, e.g.:
`Pack(i) {double ai=a[i], r = 1.0/i; ...}`.

Evaluation on both sides trades memory bandwidth for arithmetic unit cycles; programmers must explicitly recompute any shadowed variables, e.g.:
`double d = f*f; Pack(f) {double d = f*f; ...}`.

Intrinsic	Section and Use
`milk_collect_thread_num`	5.1.4 Collecting thread ID
`milk_deliver_thread_num`	5.1.4 Delivering thread ID
`milk_set_max_memory`	5.2.2 Maximum memory
`milk_set_strict_bsp`	5.2.2 Superstep splitting
`milk_touch`	5.2.2 Working set estimate

Table 3: MILK API summary.[2]

5.1.4 Thread-Local Variables

Thread-local variable expressions may be expected to be exclusive to their owner, but are now accessed in both Collection and possibly different Delivery threads. Thread-local variables here refers both to OpenMP `threadprivate` global variables and to indirection via CPUID, thread ID (TID), or `omp_get_thread_num`.

TID references in left-hand expressions in continuations are usually intended to use variables of Delivery threads. A common use for thread-local variables is to implement reductions manually, e.g., lines 32 and 103 in Section 6. The alias `milk_deliver_thread_num` explicitly documents the intent that `omp_get_thread_num` should use Delivery thread local variables. When user-defined reductions [3] are explicitly declared, thread-local references use Delivery threads.

TID references in right-hand expressions may have to be evaluated in the Collect threads. For `const` references, the intrinsic `milk_collect_thread_num` should replace TID references. This helps reduce payload size as many requests share the same source TID value. Thread-local variables cannot be passed by non-`const` reference to continuations, as multiple Delivery threads may update the same item. To guarantee correct execution without atomics, expressions can be evaluated and packed during Collection, e.g., to generate unique ID's in a pre-allocated per thread range: `{m[ind[i]] = state[TID].id++;}`.

5.2 Milk Containers and Distribution

Milk Distribution fuses a nested multi-pass radix partitioning optimized for all levels of the memory hierarchy from registers to DRAM. Distribution is a generalization of cache partitioned join [45], and TLB-aware radix join [30], adjusted for the capacity and access costs of modern hardware memory hierarchy with additional optimizations for maximizing DRAM bandwidth. Naively appending to a per-partition buffer in DRAM would require $2 \cdot 64$B random updates, and negate any cache partitioning benefits. The internal Distribution coalesces updates in full cache lines using a container library specialized for transportation of different sized tags and payloads. As illustrated in Figure 7, for each partition there is a *jug* and/or a *pail*, and a list of *tubs*. These append-only two-dimensional structures are logically simple, but they require careful choice of widths (i.e., number of elements), heights (i.e., fan-out), address placement and access patterns.

A *jug* is an L1-cache-resident container, optimized for fast writes with low register pressure. Branch misprediction im-

[2]MILK's API reference is at milk-lang.org/api.html

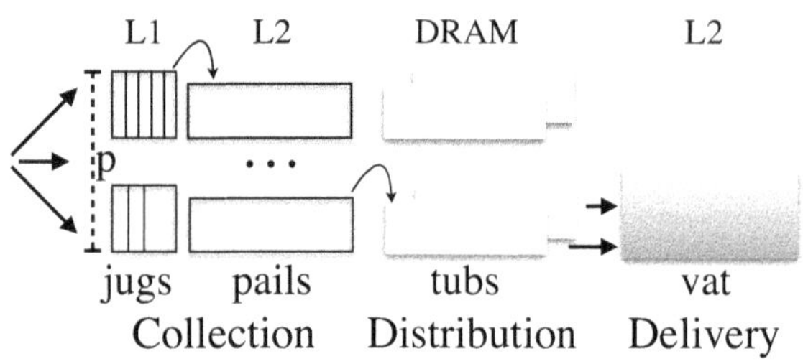

Figure 7: Containers for DRAM-conscious clustering.

pact on jug overflow can be reduced with wider jugs, but that increases total L1 cache occupancy, thus typical widths are 32–512 bytes. A full jug is emptied into one or two *pails*.

A *pail* is an L2-cache-resident container primarily designed to build full cache lines with streaming stores to the next stage. Pails are optimized for cache capacity, and further optimized to avoid cache associativity conflicts. Additionally, when appending to a pail unused bits can be trimmed, e.g., when partitioning into 256 pails with a bit mask, only the remaining 24-bits need to be stored. When compiled for Haswell, streaming and partition indexing can take advantage respectively of 256-bit Advanced Vector Extensions (AVX2) instructions and Bit Manipulation Instructions (BMI).

A *tub* is a large DRAM-resident container used for multipass processing. When full or finalized, tubs are linked into thread-local lists and eventually added to global lists. Tubs are tagged with the creating thread-ID if access to thread-local variables is needed in a captured continuation. TLB reach and fan-out constrain the maximum size of a single tub. All active tubs for each thread are TLB-reachable, achieved at the cost of additional memory fragmentation.

A *vat* is a random access cache-resident container for mixing *tubs* targeting a fixed output subset. Depending on the expected spatial or temporal locality different variants are selected. The simplest vat handles the case of expected high spatial locality with dense range updates, e.g., when every cache line is used and the full content of each cache line is overwritten. Other specializations handle low density or low coverage cases, e.g., sparse cache-line writes when few cache lines within a range are modified, or when partial cache line content is either preserved or can be overwritten.

Milk containers are by default emptied in Last-In First-Out (LIFO) order to maximize cache locality. LIFO order is acceptable, when the sequential consistency of a `parallel for` is acceptable. Even if deterministic, this order does not match serial program semantics when that may be desirable, e.g., for `a[ind[i]] = i` to observe the last write. If `ordered` processing is requested, containers are emptied in First-In First-Out (FIFO) order, and a Milk program can match the output of a serial program.

5.2.1 *Container Sizing to Hardware*

For a desired cache level and a given cache budget, the total number of partitions (i.e., height) has priority over pail width. The height and the range of valid indices determine the number of partitioning passes, e.g., we can partition using 9-bit partitioning at every pass with height 512, while height 256 uses 8-bit partitioning that may require an additional pass to partition the full input.

Wider pails improve DRAM row hits on writes to tubs, as these are otherwise random cache-line writes. Pails width, however, is limited by cache capacity, including the need to fit cache resident additional application data and code during Collection.

Tubs are limited by memory capacity. Memory management is a simple linked list of chunks. Tub layout is guided by low-level optimization opportunities: the TLB entries are a per-core resource, thus the threads on a core fit all their active tubs within TLB reach; the DRAM banks are a global resource, thus the active tubs are interleaved across all threads on a socket to maximize DRAM open page hits.

5.2.2 *Container Sizing for Applications*

The maximum memory that can be allocated for temporary space during Distribution is the most important attribute, set with `milk_set_max_memory`. If memory limits are reached this will force compaction and/or BSP superstep splitting. Applications targeting Milk-only execution can eschew double-buffering and disallow superstep splitting with `milk_set_strict_bsp`.

Tuning hints that limit the container sizes are expressed from the perspective of the user program, i.e., L1, L2, L3 cache sizes and TLB entries that should be reserved for cache resident data and code that are not managed by Milk. Container implementation details do not need to be exposed to users. When optimal cache-resident size cannot be inferred, tuning hints (i.e., bytes touched per `tag`) control the number of partitions and fan-out. External library footprint can be summarized with the `milk_touch` intrinsic, e.g., a call to a function that touches 3 floats on average for the expected data distribution can be accompanied by a call to `milk_touch(3*sizeof(float))`.

6. APPLICATIONS

To demonstrate the applicability and performance improvements provided by MILK, we use the five fundamental graph applications from the GAP Benchmark Suite [10, 11] building on the high performance OpenMP reference implementations.

In Figure 8 and Figure 9, we show the concise **milk** implementations of the inner loops of the kernels. These are also valid serial programs without **milk**, but parallel variants need additional compare-and-swap (CAS) logic as noted on lines 16, 31, and 102, e.g., line 102 replaces ten lines of a compare-and-swap loop in the reference implementation. Thread-local data structures are accessed using the delivery thread's ID, therefore the TID macro on lines 17, 32, and 103 is simply `omp_get_thread_num`.

Betweenness Centrality (BC). BC is an important graph algorithm that analyzes the relative importance of nodes based on the number of shortest paths going through each, e.g., to identify critical nodes in power grids, terrorist communication networks, or HIV/AIDS propagation [15,28]. BC is also an integral building block for many state-of-the-art community detection algorithms [35].

The forward- and backward- step kernels of BC are shown in Figure 8b. The continuation block line 28 defers random access to the neighbors of u, and `packs` the number of paths to be added. An optional sum combiner can accumulate the contributions along all incoming edges of v. For backward propagation line 50, we use a similar floating point combiner for each contribution.

```
Graph<Node> g;
Queue<Node> queue;    // global
Queue<Node>* lqueue; // per-thread

vector<Node> parent;
long outedges;
void BFS_TopDown(int depth) {
#pragma omp parallel for milk \
            reduction(+ : outedges)
  for (Node u : queue)
    for (Node v : g.out_neigh(u))
#pragma milk pack(u : min) tag(v)
    {
        Node curr = parent[v];
        if (curr < 0) {
          parent[v] = u;  // CAS
          lqueue[TID].push_back(v);
          outedges += -curr;
        }
    }
}
```

(a) Breadth-First Search with **milk**

```
vector<Node> paths, depths;
void Brandes_Forward(int depth) {
#pragma omp parallel for milk
  for (Node u : queue) {
    Node pathsU = paths[u];
    for (Node v : g.out_neigh(u))
#pragma milk pack(pathsU : +) tag(v)
      {
        if (depths[v] == -1) {
          depths[v] = depth;  // CAS
          lqueue[TID].push_back(v);
        }
        if (depths[v] == depth)
#pragma omp atomic if(!milk)
          paths[v] += pathsU;
      }
  }
}
vector<Queue<Node>::iterator> wave;
vector<float> deltas;
void Brandes_Reverse(int d) {
#pragma omp parallel for milk
  for (auto it = wave[d-1];
            it < wave[d]; it++) {
    Node v = *it;
    float contribV = (1 + deltas[v]) /
                      paths[v];
    for (Node u : g.in_neigh(v)) {
#pragma milk pack(contribV : +) tag(u)
      if (depths[u] == d - 1)
#pragma omp atomic if(!milk)
        deltas[u] += paths[u] * contribV;
    }
  }
}
```

(b) Betweenness Centrality with **milk**

Figure 8: Modified BFS-traversal kernels from GAPBS [10]

```
vector<Node> comp;
bool change;

void ShiloachVishkin_Step1() {
#pragma omp parallel for milk
  for (Node u = 0; u < g.num_nodes(); u++) {
    Node compU = comp[u];
    for (Node v : g.out_neigh(u))
#pragma milk pack(compU : min) tag(v)
      if ((compU < comp[v]) &&
          (comp[v] == comp[comp[v]])) {
        comp[comp[v]] = compU;
        change = true;
      }
  }
}
```

(a) Connected Components with **milk**

```
vector<float> contrib, new_rank;

void PageRank_Push() {
#pragma omp parallel for milk
  for (Node u=0; u < g.num_nodes(); u++) {
    float contribU = contrib[u];
    for (Node v : g.out_neigh(u))
#pragma milk pack(contribU : +) tag(v)
#pragma omp atomic if(!milk)
      new_rank[v] += contribU;
  }
}
```

(b) Page Rank with **milk**

```
WeightedGraph<Node> wg;
vector<Weight> dist;

Weight delta;
vector<Node> frontier;
vector<vector<Node>>* lbins; // per-thread

void DeltaStep_Relax(int bin) {
#pragma omp parallel for milk
  for (Node u : frontier) {
    if (dist[u] < delta * bin)
      continue;
    for (WEdge e : wg.out_neigh(u)) {
      Weight newDist = dist[u] + e.weight;
      Node v = e.dest;
#pragma milk pack(newDist : min) tag(v)
      if (dist[v] > newDist) {
        dist[v] = newDist; // CAS
        lbins[TID][newDist/delta].push_back(v);
      }
    }
  }
```

(c) Single Source Shortest Path with **milk**

Figure 9: Modified kernels from GAPBS [10]

Breadth-First Search (BFS). BFS traversal is an important component of larger graph kernels, such as BC. BFS is also used in path analytics on unweighted graphs. Figure 8a shows a **milk** version of TopDown, which tracks the parent of each vertex. Unlike the traversal in BC above, or the variant in Figure 5 which tracks only depths of each vertex, this variant tracks parents for validation. Therefore, source vertex id is `pack`ed along each visited edge, while a `min` combiner ensures deterministic results. Adaptive optimizations in state of the art implementations [9] also depend on a sum reduction of the outdegrees of all vertices added to the BFS frontier.

Connected Components (CC). CC is critical for understanding structural properties of a graph. It finds connected components in a large graph by propagating the same label to all vertices in the same connected component.

Our baseline implements Shiloach-Vishkin's algorithm [46] with optimizations [7]. The **milk** implementation of CC is shown in Figure 9a. While the output of CC is deterministic, traditional implementations have non-deterministic performance, i.e., the number of iterations is dependent on race resolution of line 68, and results in 20% run-to-run variation. While the BSP model does not allow a synchronous step to observe updates within the same step, Milk allows updates during Delivery, e.g., `comp[v]` references can still observe simultaneous updates by other neighbors. A `min` combiner allows deterministic performance.

PageRank (PR). PageRank is an iterative algorithm for determining influence within a graph, initially used to sort web search results [37]. The PageRank-Delta variant [29] more efficiently propagates updates from vertices that receive large deltas between iterations. The commonly benchmarked in prior work, however, traditional algorithm propagates till convergence contributions from all vertices in every iteration as shown in Figure 9b.

Single-Source Shortest Paths (SSSP). For weighted graphs, SSSP computes the distance from a start vertex to all reachable vertices, e.g., travel distance or travel time on a road network. Δ-stepping [31] is among the few parallel SSSP variants that outperform a well-optimized serial Dijkstra algorithm. Figure 9c shows Δ-stepping with **milk**.

According to the benchmark specifications all non-pointer data types are 32-bit, therefore all `tag` keys are 32-bit integers, and `pack` values are 32-bit integer or floating point numbers. We do not modify the precision of floating point numbers in `pack` types or combiner accumulators.

7. EVALUATION

We compare the performance of MILK on top of `clang` 3.7 to an OpenMP baseline, on the graph applications from GAPBS [10, 11] v0.8 using the modified kernels shown in Section 6 with **milk** extensions. We report end-to-end performance gains while exploring the effects of varying numbers of vertices and edges, as well as sensitivity to available temporary memory.

7.1 System Characterization

Table 4 summarizes the characteristics of the evaluated platform which has high memory bandwidth per core, as well as low latency. We measured achievable read and streaming write bandwidths using all cores to be >90% of 6.5 GB/s per-core DRAM theoretical bandwidth. Idle and loaded latencies are measured using MLC [33]. We cross-checked with `perf` that these measurements match the average L1 miss latency of 452 cycles on DRAM-bound references, e.g., PageRank on uniform graphs, which sustains Memory Level Parallelism (MLP) of 8 outstanding L1 misses.

Cores	Cache		TLB	
	L2	L3 Shared	Entries	Reach
4	256 KB	8 MB	1024	2 GB
Core	**DRAM Bandwidth**			**Latency**
Frequency	Peak	*Read*	*Write*	*Read*
4.2 GHz	26 GB/s	*92 %*	*98 %*	*58–130* ns

Table 4: System specifications [2] and *measurements*.

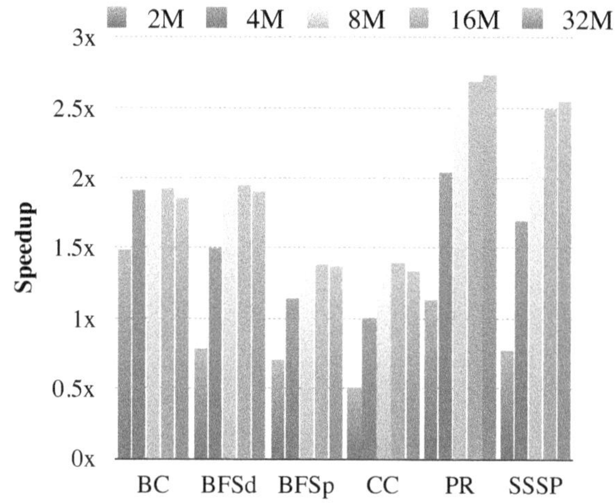

Figure 10: Overall speedup with MILK on random graphs with 2—32 million vertices, *d*=16(uniform), 8 MB L3.

The Haswell microarchitecture has much improved TLB reach compared to previous generations: each core can reach up to a 2 GB working set with low TLB overhead. For larger working sets, 2 MB page table entries are cache resident, and a TLB miss does not access DRAM.

7.2 Speedup

We show end-to-end speedups, ranging from 1.4× on CC and 2× for BFS, to 2.7× on PR, and analyze MILK's performance on synthesized random graphs with variable working set size and temporal and spatial locality.

Figure 10 shows speedups when vertices range from V=2^{21} to V=2^{25}, with an average degree of 16 in uniform degree distribution (i.e., Uniform⟨21..25⟩). We show two BFS variants – BFSd from Graph500 [21] (in Figure 5), as well as BFSp from GAPBS (Figure 8a). The two variants help compare effects of payload size: the BFSd variant has no payload as it only tracks the constant per superstep depth of each vertex, while the BFSp variant uses more bandwidth as it needs to `pack` the parent ID. On CC, MILK per-iteration speedup is stable, however, CC is sensitive to vertex labeling and race resolution. These effects result in non-deterministic iteration count and per-iteration time, the former may vary by up to 20% in the baseline. All other applications have under 2% noise between runs.

Figure 10 also shows the characteristic transition from L3 to DRAM-bound references with a corresponding increase in MILK speedups. The randomly accessed data per vertex varies for the different benchmarks, e.g., either 1 or 3 random

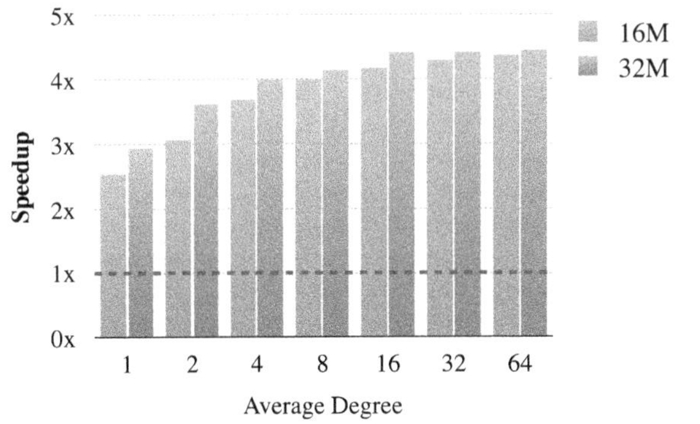

Figure 11: MILK Speedup on Histogram, counting degree of 16M or 32M vertices with 16M–2B edges.

references to 32-bit values in BC, vs. a single 32-bit value in the other benchmarks. At $V = 2M$ the total working set is already larger than cache size for BC, while for the other applications requests are mostly served by the L3 cache. Once the working set size more than doubles the cache capacity, very little locality is captured by hardware caches and the baseline random accesses run at DRAM latency, while MILK's access time per indirect reference remains constant.

In Figure 11, we compare performance while varying vertex degrees to show sufficient spatial locality can be exploited even at a low average degree. We use the Count-Degree (Histogram) kernel of Graph500, shown in Figure 6, which is used to construct a graph data structure from a list of edges in graph applications, and is critical in other applications [25]. Figure 11 shows speedups on Histogram in uniform distributions with average degrees from 1 to 64. Low degree graphs have lower temporal and spatial locality, and only 2.5× speedup. When the average degree is larger than 16, however, all vertices have an incident edge, and spatial locality reaches 100%, i.e., all words accessed per cache line are useful. At degree 16 and higher, we gain 4.2×–4.4×.

Most real-world web and social graphs have much higher degrees than 16, even within subgraphs of graphs partitioned across distributed systems. Characterization of actual social network graphs [6, 14] shows that Twitter's ∼300 million users have ∼200 followers on average, and Facebook's ∼1.5 billion users have 290 friends on average.

Real-world graphs also exhibit better cache hit rates than synthetic uniformly random graphs, due to power law structure, and to a lesser extent due to graph community structure. While current hardware caches are able to capture some locality in power law graphs [11], the actual social and web graphs are orders of magnitude larger than public datasets. We tested on 8 MB L3 cache size in order to simulate the effects of larger graphs while preserving the graph structure. On Twitter(V=62M, d=24) we observe 20–50% L3 hits, and only 5–20% L2 hits.

We evaluated performance while varying the size of synthetic power law graphs – R-MAT [13] used for Graph500 benchmarks as a proxy for real-world graph structure. On RMAT25 (V=32M,d=16) CountDegree achieves 3.2× speedup. Spatial locality is lower here since half of the generated vertices have degree 0, while the hottest vertices are cache-resident, e.g., the top 3% of vertices have 80% of the edges. Although the majority of edges are incident on hot vertices, processing hot vertex edges is faster than handling indirect

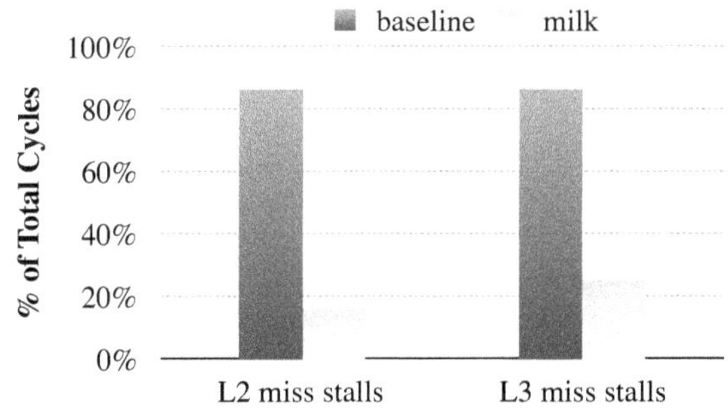

Figure 12: Stall cycle reduction with MILK on PR, V=32M, 256 KB L2, 8 MB L3.

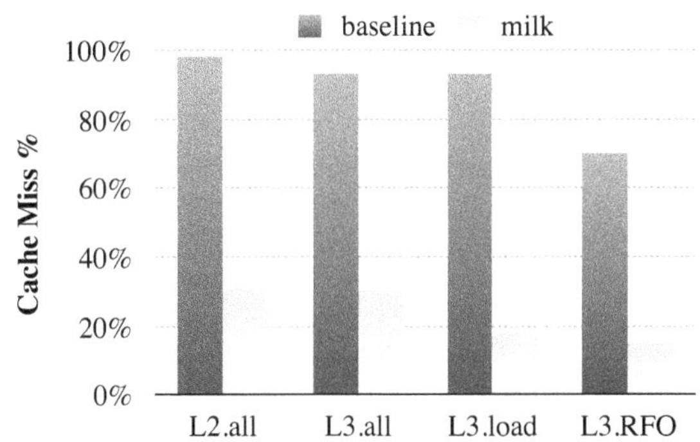

Figure 13: Cache miss rate reduction with MILK on PR, V=32M, 256 KB L2, 8 MB L3. L3 miss rates show all references (including prefetches), non-prefetch loads, and non-prefetch store Requests For Ownership (RFOs).

references that miss caches. Speedups on RMAT25 are comparable to speedups on smaller size uniform graphs; e.g., BC goes from 1.9× speedup on Uniform25 to 1.3× on RMAT25, and SSSP goes from 2.5× to 2.2×.

Filtering accesses to hot references is necessary for effective use of both hardware caches and Milk. In graphs, hot references to high-degree vertices are easy to identify as described in Section 4.1.1.

7.3 Performance Analysis

Cache miss rates and cycles stalled metrics based on hardware performance counters indicate that MILK effectively converts random DRAM references into cache hits.

Figure 12 shows that effective blocking at L2-cache sized partitions dramatically reduces cycles stalled on L2 and L3 misses. While a Haswell core can execute 4 μops per cycle at ideal ILP, these measurements show cycles with complete execution stalls while there is a pending cache miss, i.e., waiting on L3 or DRAM.

Figure 13 further breaks down L3 misses by access type – indirect memory references appear as demand loads and stores, while most sequential accesses are prefetched. With MILK, demand accesses are no longer a major contributor to cache misses, and most misses are on sequential requests.

7.4 Space Overhead

MILK's maximum space overhead is proportional to the number of references per superstep, but even within a fraction of the maximum space, applications with ample spatial

Kernel	Overhead % Resident	pack Type	Tag + Pack Bytes
BC	104 %	int/float	8
BFS_Depth	58 %	—	4
BFS_Parent	113 %	int	8
CC	176 %	int	8
PR	184 %	float	8
SSSP	4 %	int	8

Table 5: Maximum memory overhead of MILK. Measured as maximum resident size over baseline for V=$32M$. `tag` clauses, and where needed `pack`, use 32-bit variables.

locality attain good performance. For example, at only 12% memory overhead PageRank maintains > 2.7× speedup. For graph applications, the number of indirect references is a function of the number of active edges accessed during each iteration. Most algorithms make a different number of indirect references during each iteration: few edges are processed in BC/BFS, very few in SSSP, and only CC and PR always touch all edges. If less memory than the maximum required is available, a superstep will have to be forcefully divided, and may not be able to capture all available locality. Superstep splitting has minimal performance impact when temporal locality is high, e.g., as shown in Figure 11 where splitting is required on graphs with degree 64.

Table 5 shows the maximum additional memory required on the evaluated kernels without memory limits, compression, filters, or combiners. Baseline memory consumption varies based on the graph representation and other algorithm overheads, e.g., unweighted graph plus 1 bit per edge for BC vs. a weighted graph plus additional 4 bytes per edge for SSSP. MILK memory consumption is primarily a function of the number of indirect references per superstep, multiplied by the size of the `pack` and `tag` variables. For example, BC forward traversal carries an `int`, and backward traversal – a `float`. Small additional overhead is added by bookkeeping and internal fragmentation in Milk containers.

8. RELATED WORK

Milk's distribution phases are most similar to the heavily optimized table join operations in relational databases. The two best join methods are to sort both database relations, or to build a hash table with tuples of one relation and then probe the hash table for each tuple of the other relation. Increasing data sizes and perennial hardware changes have fueled continuous innovation: Shatdal et al. [45] demonstrated hash join with cache partitioning, further improved to consider TLB impact [30], and to optimize for SIMD, NUMA, non-temporal write optimizations, software buffering, etc [5,8,26,49,51]. Our runtime library data structures and compiler generated code are designed for modern microarchitectures (e.g., on Haswell TLB overhead is less critical), and focus on avoiding increasingly important DRAM contention and turnaround delays. Milk's compiler support for indirect expressions is more general than database join, and we are the first to use similar techniques to accelerate graph applications.

Graph processing is an important application that we have shown significantly benefits from Milk optimizations. Graph applications expose irregular access patterns that render traditional compiler optimizations ineffective [39]. Creating efficient shared memory graph frameworks [36, 47] has received considerable research attention, but overheads and abstraction mismatch lead to significant slowdown compared to hand-optimized code [43]. Milk allows optimized by hand iterators and algorithm-specific data structures to use familiar and concise indirect array accesses.

The inspector/executor [40] family of two-phase optimizations inspect indirect references before an alternative execution. The original optimization [40] rearranged the base array A in `A[ind[i]]` not the index, as it targeted better scheduling for message passing machines. Follow-up research explored two main directions: either very cheap per-step index array analysis (like determining bounding box (min/max) for MPI and NUMA boundary exchanges [48]), or very expensive data reorganizations to be applied as preprocessing steps. Coalescing references targeting different cores to reduce MPI messaging overhead is explored for the HPCC RandomAccess benchmark [20]. The workload is similar to Histogram of degree 4 (Figure 11) but disallows BSP semantics. Since the benchmark allows at most tens of requests per core to be reordered, short coalescing buffers are needed, yet cache resident buffers can discover very little locality in DRAM-sized working sets. In shared-memory settings, sharding memory and coalescing requests to owning cores eliminate atomics at the cost of message-passing overhead. Inexpensive methods, however, do not improve the performance of DRAM indirect references.

Expensive locality reorganization methods have not been able to amortize costs within a single iteration, and they are limited to applications that repeatedly process the same references, e.g., rearranging the index array [17,32] and remapping all arrays in a loop, or graph partitioning [22, 23] or cheaper reorderings with lower benefits (e.g., space filling curves). Recent inspector/executor work [18] traded lower cache hit rate for improvement of DRAM row buffer hits for 14% net gains. Milk achieves up to 4× gains on static reference loops, and pays off in one iteration to also allow dynamic references.

9. CONCLUSION

We introduced the **milk** C/C++ language extension in order to capture programmer's intention when making indirect memory references, while the compiler and runtime system choose the most efficient access order. As demonstrated, the annotations can easily be added across a suite of popular graph applications and when compiled with MILK enable performance gains of up to 3×.

We believe the right level of abstraction to enable high-performance applications for graph analytics, machine learning, or in-memory databases is not necessarily a domain specific framework, nor an optimized collection of algorithms — i.e., hash vs. sort join, nor a data structure — i.e., bit vector vs. hash table. Instead, best performance and flexibility are enabled by the most broadly relied upon low-level primitive — the indirect memory reference — and just adding **milk**.

Acknowledgments

We thank our anonymous reviewers and our shepherd Bronis de Supinski for their helpful probing questions and their specific suggestions for improving our presentation. This research is based upon work supported by NSF grant CCF-1533753, and DOE awards DE-SC008923 and DE-SC014204.

10. REFERENCES

[1] Intel 64 and IA-32 Architectures Optimization Reference Manual. http://www.intel.com/content/www/us/en/architecture-and-technology/64-ia-32-architectures-optimization-manual.html.

[2] Intel Core i7-4790K Processor (8M Cache, up to 4.40 GHz). http://ark.intel.com/products/80807/Intel-Core-i7-4790K-Processor-8M-Cache-up-to-4_40-GHz.

[3] OpenMP Application Program Interface 4.0. http://openmp.org/wp/openmp-specifications/, 2013.

[4] M. Abadi, A. Agarwal, P. Barham, E. Brevdo, Z. Chen, C. Citro, G. S. Corrado, A. Davis, J. Dean, M. Devin, S. Ghemawat, I. Goodfellow, A. Harp, G. Irving, M. Isard, Y. Jia, R. Jozefowicz, L. Kaiser, M. Kudlur, J. Levenberg, D. Mané, R. Monga, S. Moore, D. Murray, C. Olah, M. Schuster, J. Shlens, B. Steiner, I. Sutskever, K. Talwar, P. Tucker, V. Vanhoucke, V. Vasudevan, F. Viégas, O. Vinyals, P. Warden, M. Wattenberg, M. Wicke, Y. Yu, and X. Zheng. TensorFlow: Large-scale machine learning on heterogeneous systems, 2015. Available at tensorflow.org.

[5] M.-C. Albutiu, A. Kemper, and T. Neumann. Massively parallel sort-merge joins in main memory multi-core database systems. *Proc. VLDB Endow.*, 5(10):1064–1075, June 2012.

[6] L. Backstrom, P. Boldi, M. Rosa, J. Ugander, and S. Vigna. Four degrees of separation. In *Proceedings of the 4th Annual ACM Web Science Conference*, WebSci '12, pages 33–42, New York, NY, USA, 2012. ACM.

[7] D. A. Bader, G. Cong, and J. Feo. On the architectural requirements for efficient execution of graph algorithms. In *Parallel Processing, 2005. ICPP 2005. International Conference on*, pages 547–556, June 2005.

[8] C. Balkesen, J. Teubner, G. Alonso, and M. T. Özsu. Main-memory hash joins on modern processor architectures. *IEEE Trans. Knowl. Data Eng.*, 27(7):1754–1766, 2015.

[9] S. Beamer, K. Asanović, and D. Patterson. Direction-optimizing breadth-first search. In *Proceedings of the International Conference on High Performance Computing, Networking, Storage and Analysis*, SC '12, pages 12:1–12:10, Los Alamitos, CA, USA, 2012. IEEE Computer Society Press.

[10] S. Beamer, K. Asanović, and D. A. Patterson. The GAP benchmark suite. *CoRR*, abs/1508.03619, 2015.

[11] S. Beamer, K. Asanović, and D. A. Patterson. Locality exists in graph processing: Workload characterization on an Ivy Bridge server. In *2015 IEEE International Symposium on Workload Characterization, IISWC 2015, Atlanta, GA, USA, October 4-6, 2015*, pages 56–65, 2015.

[12] G. E. Blelloch, J. T. Fineman, P. B. Gibbons, and J. Shun. Internally deterministic parallel algorithms can be fast. In *Proceedings of the 17th ACM SIGPLAN Symposium on Principles and Practice of Parallel Programming, PPOPP 2012, New Orleans, LA, USA, February 25-29, 2012*, pages 181–192, 2012.

[13] D. Chakrabarti, Y. Zhan, and C. Faloutsos. R-MAT: A recursive model for graph mining. In *Proceedings of the Fourth SIAM International Conference on Data Mining, Lake Buena Vista, Florida, USA, April 22-24, 2004*, pages 442–446, 2004.

[14] A. Ching, S. Edunov, M. Kabiljo, D. Logothetis, and S. Muthukrishnan. One trillion edges: Graph processing at Facebook-scale. *Proceedings of the VLDB Endowment*, 8(12):1804–1815, 2015.

[15] T. Coffman, S. Greenblatt, and S. Marcus. Graph-based technologies for intelligence analysis. *Commun. ACM*, 47(3):45–47, Mar. 2004.

[16] J. Dean and S. Ghemawat. MapReduce: Simplified data processing on large clusters. In *Proceedings of the 6th Conference on Symposium on Opearting Systems Design & Implementation - Volume 6*, OSDI'04, pages 10–10, Berkeley, CA, USA, 2004. USENIX Association.

[17] C. Ding and K. Kennedy. Improving cache performance in dynamic applications through data and computation reorganization at run time. In *ACM SIGPLAN Notices*, volume 34, pages 229–241. ACM, 1999.

[18] W. Ding, M. Kandemir, D. Guttman, A. Jog, C. R. Das, and P. Yedlapalli. Trading cache hit rate for memory performance. In *Proceedings of the 23rd International Conference on Parallel Architectures and Compilation*, PACT '14, pages 357–368, New York, NY, USA, 2014. ACM.

[19] M. Frigo, C. E. Leiserson, and K. H. Randall. The implementation of the Cilk-5 multithreaded language. In *Proceedings of the ACM SIGPLAN 1998 Conference on Programming Language Design and Implementation*, PLDI '98, pages 212–223, New York, NY, USA, 1998. ACM.

[20] R. Garg and Y. Sabharwal. Optimizing the HPCC RandomAccess benchmark on Blue Gene/L supercomputer. In *Proceedings of the Joint International Conference on Measurement and Modeling of Computer Systems*, SIGMETRICS '06/Performance '06, pages 369–370, New York, NY, USA, 2006. ACM.

[21] Graph500. Graph 500 benchmark. http://www.graph500.org/specifications.

[22] H. Han and C.-W. Tseng. Improving compiler and run-time support for irregular reductions using local writes. In *Languages and Compilers for Parallel Computing*, pages 181–196. Springer, 1998.

[23] H. Han and C.-W. Tseng. Exploiting locality for irregular scientific codes. *IEEE Transactions on Parallel and Distributed Systems*, 17(7):606–618, July 2006.

[24] JEDEC. DDR3 SDRAM Standard. http://www.jedec.org/standards-documents/docs/jesd-79-3d.

[25] W. Jung, J. Park, and J. Lee. Versatile and scalable parallel histogram construction. In *Proceedings of the 23rd International Conference on Parallel Architectures and Compilation*, PACT '14, pages 127–138, New York, NY, USA, 2014. ACM.

[26] C. Kim, T. Kaldewey, V. W. Lee, E. Sedlar, A. D. Nguyen, N. Satish, J. Chhugani, A. Di Blas, and P. Dubey. Sort vs. hash revisited: Fast join implementation on modern multi-core CPUs. *Proc. VLDB Endow.*, 2(2):1378–1389, Aug. 2009.

[27] C. Lattner and V. Adve. LLVM: A compilation framework for lifelong program analysis and transformation. CGO '04, San Jose, CA, USA, Mar 2004.

[28] F. Liljeros, C. R. Edling, L. A. N. Amaral, H. E. Stanley, and Y. Åberg. The web of human sexual contacts. *Nature*, 411(6840):907–908, 2001.

[29] Y. Low, D. Bickson, J. Gonzalez, C. Guestrin, A. Kyrola, and J. M. Hellerstein. Distributed GraphLab: A framework for machine learning and data mining in the cloud. *Proc. VLDB Endow.*, 5(8):716–727, Apr. 2012.

[30] S. Manegold, P. Boncz, and M. Kersten. Optimizing main-memory join on modern hardware. *IEEE Trans. on Knowl. and Data Eng.*, 14(4):709–730, July 2002.

[31] U. Meyer and P. Sanders. Δ-stepping: A parallelizable shortest path algorithm. *J. Algorithms*, 49(1):114–152, Oct. 2003.

[32] N. Mitchell, L. Carter, and J. Ferrante. Localizing non-affine array references. In *Parallel Architectures and Compilation Techniques, 1999. Proceedings. 1999 International Conference on*, pages 192–202. IEEE, 1999.

[33] MLC. Intel Memory Latency Checker v3.0. https://software.intel.com/en-us/articles/intelr-memory-latency-checker.

[34] J. Nelson, B. Holt, B. Myers, P. Briggs, L. Ceze, S. Kahan, and M. Oskin. Latency-tolerant software distributed shared memory. In *Proceedings of the 2015 USENIX Conference on Usenix Annual Technical Conference*, USENIX ATC '15, pages 291–305, Berkeley, CA, USA, 2015. USENIX Association.

[35] M. E. J. Newman. Detecting community structure in networks. *The European Physical Journal B - Condensed Matter and Complex Systems*, 38(2):321–330, 2004.

[36] D. Nguyen, A. Lenharth, and K. Pingali. A lightweight infrastructure for graph analytics. In *Proceedings of the Twenty-Fourth ACM Symposium on Operating Systems Principles*, SOSP '13, pages 456–471, New York, NY, USA, 2013. ACM.

[37] L. Page, S. Brin, R. Motwani, and T. Winograd. The PageRank citation ranking: Bringing order to the web. Technical Report 1999-66, Stanford InfoLab, November 1999.

[38] I. Papazian, S. Kottapalli, J. Baxter, J. Chamberlain, G. Vedaraman, and B. Morris. Ivy Bridge server: A converged design. *Micro, IEEE*, 35(2):16–25, Mar 2015.

[39] K. Pingali, D. Nguyen, M. Kulkarni, M. Burtscher, M. A. Hassaan, R. Kaleem, T.-H. Lee, A. Lenharth, R. Manevich, M. Méndez-Lojo, D. Prountzos, and X. Sui. The tao of parallelism in algorithms. In *Proceedings of the 32nd ACM SIGPLAN Conference on Programming Language Design and Implementation*, PLDI '11, pages 12–25, New York, NY, USA, 2011. ACM.

[40] J. Saltz, K. Crowley, R. Michandaney, and H. Berryman. Run-time scheduling and execution of loops on message passing machines. *Journal of Parallel and Distributed Computing*, 8(4):303–312, 1990.

[41] Samsung. DDR3L SDRAM 240pin Registered DIMM M393B2G70BH0 datasheet:. http://www.samsung.com/global/business/semiconductor/file/product/ds_ddr3_4gb_b-die_based_1_35v_rdimm_rev16-5.pdf, 2012.

[42] Samsung. DDR4 SDRAM 288pin Registered DIMM M393A2G40DB1 datasheet. http://www.samsung.com/semiconductor/global/file/product/DS_8GB_DDR4_4Gb_D_die_RegisteredDIMM_Rev15.pdf, 2015.

[43] N. Satish, N. Sundaram, M. M. A. Patwary, J. Seo, J. Park, M. A. Hassaan, S. Sengupta, Z. Yin, and P. Dubey. Navigating the maze of graph analytics frameworks using massive graph datasets. In *Proceedings of the 2014 ACM SIGMOD International Conference on Management of Data*, SIGMOD '14, pages 979–990, New York, NY, USA, 2014. ACM.

[44] H. Schweizer, M. Besta, and T. Hoefler. Evaluating the cost of atomic operations on modern architectures. San Francisco, CA, 2015. Parallel Architectures and Compilation Techniques (PACT'15).

[45] A. Shatdal, C. Kant, and J. F. Naughton. Cache conscious algorithms for relational query processing. In *Proceedings of the 20th International Conference on Very Large Data Bases*, VLDB '94, pages 510–521, San Francisco, CA, USA, 1994. Morgan Kaufmann Publishers Inc.

[46] Y. Shiloach and U. Vishkin. An O(log n) parallel connectivity algorithm. *Journal of Algorithms*, 3(1), 1982.

[47] J. Shun and G. E. Blelloch. Ligra: A lightweight graph processing framework for shared memory. In *Proceedings of the 18th ACM SIGPLAN Symposium on Principles and Practice of Parallel Programming*, PPoPP '13, pages 135–146, New York, NY, USA, 2013. ACM.

[48] J. Su and K. Yelick. Automatic support for irregular computations in a high-level language. In *Proceedings of the 19th IEEE International Parallel and Distributed Processing Symposium (IPDPS'05) - Papers - Volume 01*, IPDPS '05, Washington, DC, USA, 2005. IEEE Computer Society.

[49] J. Teubner, G. Alonso, C. Balkesen, and M. T. Ozsu. Main-memory hash joins on multi-core CPUs: Tuning to the underlying hardware. In *Proceedings of the 2013 IEEE International Conference on Data Engineering*, ICDE '13, pages 362–373, Washington, DC, USA, 2013. IEEE Computer Society.

[50] L. G. Valiant. A bridging model for parallel computation. *Commun. ACM*, 33(8):103–111, Aug. 1990.

[51] J. Wassenberg and P. Sanders. Engineering a multi-core radix sort. In *Proceedings of the 17th International Conference on Parallel Processing - Volume Part II*, Euro-Par'11, pages 160–169, Berlin, Heidelberg, 2011. Springer-Verlag.

Scaling Data Analytics with Moore's Law

Kunle Olukotun
Pervasive Parallelism Laboratory
Stanford University

Abstract

Analyzing the volume, variety and velocity of big data requires the use of modern heterogeneous computing platforms composed of multicores with SIMD execution units, GPUs, clusters, FPGAs and in the future new reconfigurable architectures. However, programming in this environment is extremely challenging due to the need to use multiple low-level programming models and then combine them together in ad-hoc ways. Furthermore, many data analytics algorithms do not take full advantage of modern hardware capabilities. To optimize big data applications both for modern hardware and for modern programmers needs algorithms specialized for modern hardware and a high-level programming model that executes efficiently on heterogeneous parallel hardware. In this talk, I will describe the Delite DSL framework, which uses nested parallel patterns encapsulated in domain specific languages (DSLs). I will describe how a nested parallel pattern based programming model can be used to develop new data analytics algorithms that are optimized for architectures as diverse as multicore/NUMA, clusters, GPUs, FPGAs and a new reconfigurable architecture called Plasticine.

Author Keywords: Data Analytics, Heterogeneous architectures, Domain Specific Programming Languages, Reconfigurable Architectures.

Short Bio

Kunle Olukotun is the Cadence Design Systems Professor in the School of Engineering and Professor of Electrical Engineering and Computer Science at Stanford University.

Olukotun is well known as a pioneer in multicore processor design and the leader of the Stanford Hydra chip mutlipocessor (CMP) research project. Olukotun founded Afara Websystems to develop high-throughput, low-power multicore processors for server systems. The Afara multicore processor, called Niagara, was acquired by Sun Microsystems. Niagara derived processors now power all Oracle SPARC-based servers. Olukotun currently directs the Stanford Pervasive Parallelism Lab (PPL), which seeks to proliferate the use of heterogeneous parallelism in all application areas using Domain Specific Languages (DSLs). Olukotun is an ACM Fellow and IEEE Fellow.

PACT'16, September 11–15, 2016, Haifa, Israel.
ACM ISBN 978-1-4503-4121-9/16/09.
DOI: http://dx.doi.org/10.1145/2967938.2970375

Bridging the Semantic Gaps of GPU Acceleration for Scale-out CNN-based Big Data Processing: Think Big, See Small

*Mingcong Song[1], *Yang Hu[1], Yunlong Xu[2], Chao Li[3], Huixiang Chen[1], Jingling Yuan[4], Tao Li[1]
[1]Department of Electrical and Computer Engineering, University of Florida, Gainesville, USA
[2]School of Electronic and Information Engineering, Xi'an Jiaotong University, Xi'an, China
[3]Department of Computer Science and Engineering, Shanghai Jiao Tong University, Shanghai, China
[4]Wuhan University of Technology, Wuhan, China
{songmingcong, huyang.ece, stanley.chen}@ufl.edu, xjtu.ylxu@stu.xjtu.edu.cn, lichao@cs.sjtu.edu.cn, yjl@whut.edu.cn, taoli@ece.ufl.edu

ABSTRACT

Convolutional Neural Networks (CNNs) have substantially advanced the state-of-the-art accuracies of object recognition, which is the core function of a myriad of modern multimedia processing techniques such as image/video processing, speech recognition, and natural language processing. GPU-based accelerators gained increasing attention because a large amount of highly parallel neurons in CNN naturally matches the GPU computation pattern. In this work, we perform comprehensive experiments to investigate the performance bottlenecks and overheads of current GPU acceleration platform for scale-out CNN-based big data processing.

In our characterization, we observe two significant semantic gaps: framework gap that lies between CNN-based data processing workflow and data processing manner in distributed framework; and the standalone gap that lies between the uneven computation loads at different CNN layers and fixed computing capacity provisioning of current GPU acceleration library. To bridge these gaps, we propose *D³NN*, a Distributed, Decoupled, and Dynamically tuned GPU acceleration framework for modern CNN architectures. In particular, *D³NN* features a novel analytical model that enables accurate time estimation of GPU accelerated CNN processing with only 5-10% error. Our evaluation results show the throughput of standalone processing node using *D³NN* gains up to 3.7X performance improvement over current standalone GPU acceleration platform. Our CNN-oriented GPU acceleration library with built-in dynamic batching scheme achieves up to 1.5X performance improvement over the non-batching scheme and outperforms the state-of-the-art deep learning library by up to 28% (performance mode) ~ 67% (memory-efficient mode).

Keywords: GPU; Deep Learning; Distributed System; Big Data.

1. INTRODUCTION

Recent years have seen massive research efforts on developing deep neural networks (DNNs). Among these DNNs, the Convolutional Neural Networks (CNNs) [24, 36, 38] are the most popular subsets. Typically, the CNN is comprised of one or more fully connected layers and multiple convolutional layers. The most appealing feature of CNN is that it has far fewer parameters than fully connected DNNs, which makes CNNs easier to train and more practical [12]. Today, CNNs have been extensively adopted [1, 14, 22, 23, 34, 41, 46] and have substantially advanced the state-of-the-art accuracies of object recognition, which is the core function for image/ speech/ language processing applications.

Due to the inefficiency of general-purpose processors when processing CNN workloads, researchers perceive the opportunities to tap into CNN accelerators. Various accelerators based on FPGA [44], GPU [15] and ASIC [3] have been proposed recently to improve the performance of CNN workloads. Among these approaches, GPU-based accelerators gained increasing attention since a large amount of highly parallel neurons in CNN naturally matches the GPU computation pattern. Furthermore, the proliferation of commodity GPU deployment (bare metal and virtualized) in cloud data centers [2, 37] provides a mature and ready-to-use platform for cloud-based CNN acceleration. DjiNN [15] makes the first attempt to explore commodity GPU-based CNN accelerator server platform and provides beneficial implication to future warehouse-scale computer design. However, the enormous amount of data that generated in current IT big-names' warehouse-scale computers present significant challenges for scale-out CNN-based big data processing [18, 26, 47]. For example, more than 350 million photos are being posted to Facebook per day [13, 25] and 100 hours of video are being uploaded to YouTube per minute [42], such daunting amount of data arrival remarkably embarrasses the throughput of traditional standalone CNN accelerators.

Rather than pushing the limit of standalone CNN accelerators, we instead explore a complementary opportunity to benefit scale out CNN-based big data processing that leverages state-of-the-art heterogeneous CNN acceleration techniques such as commodity GPGPU and widely used distributed computing frameworks such as Hadoop. In this paper, we perform comprehensive experiments to investigate the performance bottlenecks and overheads of current GPU acceleration platform for scale-out CNN-based big data processing. We study three most representative networks: AlexNet [24], GoogLeNet [38] and VGGNet [36]. As many fine-tuned convolutional neural networks are designed based on these representative networks and share the same network architecture, we expect the observations hold valid to their derivatives.

We find significant challenges are associated with GPU acceleration support for scale-out CNN-based big data processing.

PACT '16, September 11-15, 2016, Haifa, Israel
© 2016 ACM. ISBN 978-1-4503-4121-9/16/09…$15.00
DOI: http://dx.doi.org/10.1145/2967938.2967944
*Authors with equal contribution

Table 1. CNNs

CNN Architecture	Fine-tuned Models
AlexNet	FCN-AlexNet, SOS-AlexNet, Places205-AlexNet, Hybrid-CNN, R-CNN, CaffeNet
GoogLeNet	Places205-GoogLeNet, GoogLeNet_cars
VGGNet	FCN-Xs, SOS-VGG16, ParseNet

First, we observe a framework semantic gap that lies between CNN-based data processing workflow and data processing manner in current distributed framework. Specifically, the lack of accurate processing time estimation approach for heterogeneous GPU acceleration nodes presents as an obstacle to provide agile proactive load balance for a distributed CNN acceleration framework, which could result in significant waste of valuable computing resource that provided by the state-of-the-art heterogeneous CNN acceleration hardware.

To bridge this semantic gap, we explore the opportunity to benefit from leveraging GPU acceleration library by looking into more details of standalone CNN acceleration platform implementation. We surprisingly observe another standalone semantic gap that lies between the uneven computing loads at different CNN layers and fixed computing capacity provisioning of current GPU acceleration libraries. Specifically, the uneven GPU resource utilization pattern caused by the lack of awareness of per CNN layer computing load poses significant challenges for achieving optimal GPU utilization. This unpredictable GPU utilization also impacts the performance and restricts the possibility to accurately estimate the CNN acceleration processing time.

Motivated by our characterization observations, we propose *D³NN*, a Distributed, Decoupled, and Dynamically tuned GPU acceleration framework. *D³NN* features a distributed data processing framework, a CNN-oriented GPU acceleration library, and a novel analytical model that bridges the semantic gaps in modern scale-out CNN-based big data processing platform.

D³NN incorporates a CNN-oriented GPU acceleration library that dynamically tunes the batch size of input data at each CNN layer to bridge the standalone semantic gap by waxing mismatch of uneven computing loads at different CNN layers and fixed computing capacity provisioning of current GPU acceleration library. Based on our GPU acceleration library, we also propose an analytical model that bridges the semantic gap to provide accurate processing time estimation approach for heterogeneous GPU acceleration nodes and accurate multi-process number determination method. The distributed data processing framework employs a Producer-Consumer scheme to decouple the CNN data preparation process and CNN data processing process at each slave node, and a semaphore-based data synchronization scheme to bridge the framework semantic gap by matching the distributed data processing manner to CNN-based data processing workflow.

Note that due to the similarity of convolutional neural network architectures, *D³NN* is applicable to any newly developed CNN. Our evaluation results show the throughput of standalone processing node using *D³NN* gains up to 3.7X performance improvement over current standalone GPU acceleration platform. Our CNN-oriented GPU acceleration library with built-in dynamic batching scheme achieves up to 1.5X performance improvement over the non-batching scheme and outperforms the state-of-the-art deep learning library (cuDNN) [5] by 28% (performance mode) ~ 67% (memory-efficient mode). More importantly, as a hierarchical CNN acceleration solution, the decoupled architecture we proposed could also apply to other state-of-the-art works, such as multi-GPU servers [15] and ASIC-based CNN accelerators [3, 4].

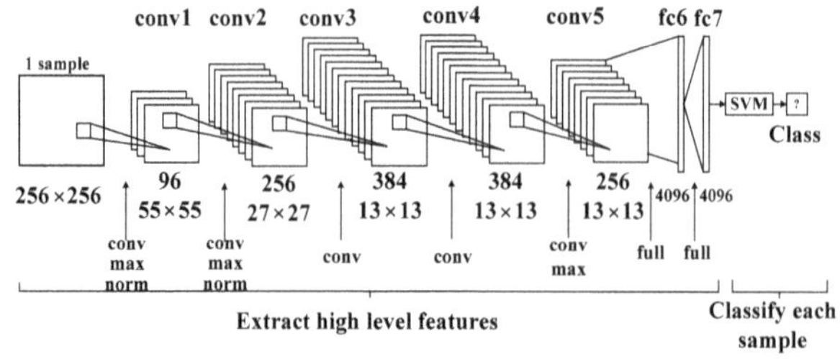

Figure 1. A representative CNN architecture - AlexNet

2. BACKGROUND

CNN: CNN can tackle various multimedia processing applications such as car classification [41], pedestrian classification [34], scene recognition [46], salient object subtilizing [45], object detection [14], video analysis [22] and image captioning [21]. In this study, our characterizations and optimizations mainly focus on three representative CNNs: AlexNet, GoogLeNet, and VGGNet. AlexNet, the ILSVRC [33] 2012 winner model, is the first study that popularized CNN in computer vision. It could be fine-tuned on other databases to implement richer functions. In recent years, deeper and more complicated convolutional networks have been developed to achieve better accuracy. To reflect the latest research on CNNs in our design, we also characterize two latest ILSVRC winners, GoogLeNet and VGGNet. Most fine-tuned CNN models are designed based on them, as shown in Table 1. Although parameters in these fine-tuned CNN models have to be re-trained using new training dataset, their architectures remain the same and the CNN performance will not change drastically.

We introduce essential preliminaries of CNN using AlexNet as an example, shown in Figure 1. It consists of five convolutional layers, three max-pooling layers, and two classifier layers. The convolutional layers perform dot products between the filters and local regions of the input image [6]. These operations dominate the execution time of CNN computation. The convolutional operations in a convolutional layer benefit from the optimized matrix multiplication libraries, such as cuBLAS [7].

We demonstrate a typical matrix multiplication based convolutional operation in Figure 2. In step ①, an operation called im2col [6] stretches out the local regions in the input image (D) into column-major matrix (D_m). Similarly, in step ② the weights of the CONV layer (F) are stretched out into filter matrix (F_m). Then the original convolutional operation could be lowered into a matrix multiplication ($F_m \times D_m$) in step ③. In Figure 2, the filter matrix F_m has dimensions $N_f \times S_f^2 N_c$, while the data matrix D_m has dimensions $S_f^2 N_c \times W_o H_o$. The output matrix O_m has dimensions $N_f \times W_o H_o$. Therefore, we can calculate the number of float point operations in a convolutional layer through the number of multiply-accumulate operations of $F_m \times D_m$:

$$\text{Conv}_{flops} = 2N_f \times S_f^2 N_c \times W_o H_o \quad \text{(Eq1)},$$

where a single multiply-accumulate operation counts as 2 flops. The Convflops is usually used to measure the computational intensity in a convolutional layer.

GPU: A GPU has multiple streaming multiprocessors (SMs). The SM is the main SIMD processing engine and has several

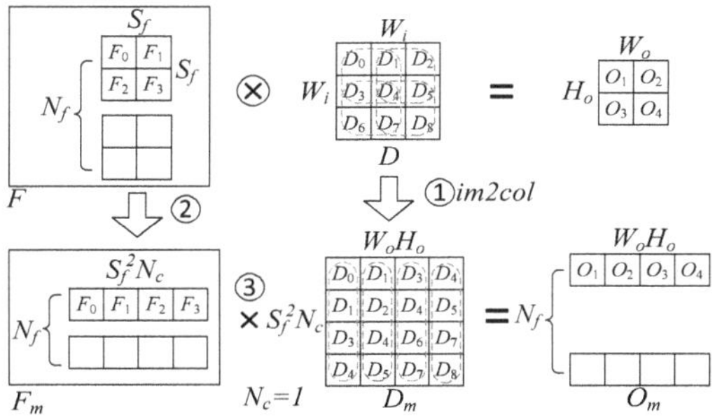

Figure 2. Convolutional operation in a CNN layer

functional blocks, such as integer/floating point ALUs, load/store units, special functional blocks. Execution of general-purpose programs on heterogeneous GPU/CPU architectures is realized by various application programming interfaces (API) such as CUDA [30], and OpenCL [32]. Using these APIs a programmer can launch thousands of threads onto GPU device from the host CPU. Multiple threads (called a warp) execute simultaneously on an SM following the same instruction multiple data (SIMD) paradigm. Several warps form a thread block (TB) that are executed on the same SM; TBs group together to form a grid that executes a GPU kernel.

During the execution of a GPU kernel, the work distributor checks whether the required resources of a TB can be satisfied by one of the SMs. These resources include the shared memory, the number of registers, and the maximum number of warps concurrently active on an SM. If all these resources requirements are satisfied by an SM, one TB will be dispatched onto it. GPUs hide memory latency through fast context switch among active warps; thus sufficient numbers of active warps should be maintained on an SM. Occupancy [8], which is the ratio of the number of active warps per SM to the maximum number of active warps, is an important metric in determining how effectively the hardware is used. Theoretical occupancy is the upper limit for occupancy imposed by the kernel launch configuration and the capabilities of the GPU, while achieved occupancy is the actual measured occupancy of the running kernel. The achieved occupancy is usually less than the theoretical occupancy mainly due to (1) limited problem size, and (2) unbalanced workload within and/or across TBs.

Hadoop: Hadoop [39] is a most widely used framework for distributed processing of large data sets across a cluster of computers. Hadoop was inspired by Google's MapReduce [10], a software framework in which an application is broken down into numerous small map/reduce tasks. Any of these tasks can be run on any node in the cluster. Hadoop includes a Distributed File System (HDFS), which is usually mounted on each slave node and provide data storage service for MapReduce.

3. CHARACTERIZATION AND IMPLICATION

To understand how to design optimized GPU acceleration system for CNN applications, we perform an in-depth, hierarchical characterization of the performance of existing computing framework and GPU acceleration library for CNN to identify inefficiencies and bottlenecks. Compared to previous work that largely focuses on performance characterization of GPU computation [15], our comprehensive characterization shed light on some ignored realities. We first describe our experimental setup in Section 3.1. In Section 3.2, we explore the bottlenecks that constitute framework semantic gap. In Section 3.3, we delve into standalone CNN processing platform to explore the limitations of current GPU-accelerated implementation for CNN, which result in the standalone semantic gap. We summarize the root causes of these inefficiencies in Section 3.4.

Table 2. Platform configurations

Item	Value
GPU Type	Nvidia Tesla K20c
GPU Core Config	2496 CUDA cores, 706 MHz
GPU Resources/Core	Max. 2048 Threads (64 Warps, 32 Threads/Warp), 48KB Shared Memory, 65536 Registers
GPU Memory	5120MB Global Memory, 2600MHz Memory Clock Rate, 320-bit Memory Bus Width
CPU Type	Intel Xeon E5530
CPU Core Config	8 Cores, 2.4GHz

3.1 Experimental Setup and Methodology

We characterize AlexNet, GoogLeNet, and VGGNet on Nvidia's Tesla K20c GPU, which is deployed at DELL PowerEdge R710 server. The detailed parameters are listed in Table 2. The Nvidia driver version is 340.32 and CUDA version is 6.5. We gather GPU runtime information using Nvidia Visual Profiler [31]. We use 8 slave nodes and 1 master node in our distributed framework characterization. The CNN models are trained by Caffe [20], an open-source deep learning framework widely used in both academia and industry. We also use Caffe to implement our CNN networks. The test data is from ILSVRC2012 (157.3GB) [11]. We scale up the above data sets appropriately with increased number of computing nodes.

We develop a state-of-the-art heterogeneous MapReduce framework that enables CPU to cooperate with GPU to do big data processing. We make heavy modifications to Hadoop framework so that it is capable of running multimedia workloads using GPU. Note that although we choose Hadoop in our current implementation, our proposed design and optimization can be integrated with other popular distributed computing frameworks such as Spark [43].

In this paper we define GPU temporal utilization as the proportion of GPU-involved runtime in the whole CNN runtime and GPU spatial utilization as GPU hardware resource utilization.

3.2 Framework Semantic Gap

3.2.1 Distributed Framework Overheads

We set out to analyze the nontransparencies in CNN workflow for distributed framework that cause the overheads in an inefficient integration of distributed CNN acceleration platform.

In a typical CNN-based application, the processing workflow consists of three stages: neural network initialization, data pre-processing and data processing. In our baseline implementation, each Hadoop map task is associated with a CNN processing process. While due to Hadoop job consists of a large amount of independent map tasks with short lifecycle, naïvely associating the whole deep learning process with map task incurs several overheads. We elaborate these overheads that are illustrated in Figure 3.

Repeated Network Initialization: Each map task will initialize the neural network. Since the network initialization is really time- and resource- consuming, this causes a large amount of

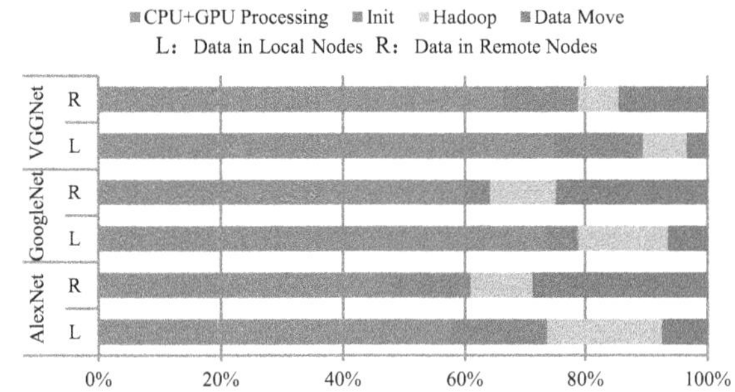

Figure 3. Overheads of distributed framework

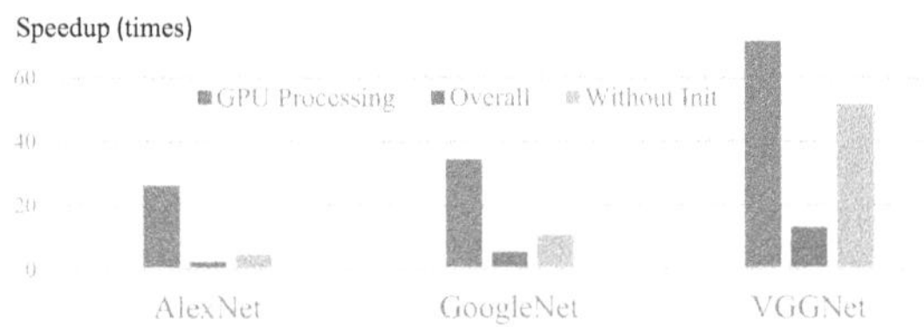

Figure 4. GPU speedup over CPU

unnecessary repeated network initialization time. These are depicted as *Init* in Figure 3.

GPU Calling Procedure: The launch of GPU processing in Hadoop also introduces overhead. The GPU processing program is invoked by the following steps [39]. First, task-tracker sends task requests to jobtracker using heart beat. Then, the jobtracker assigns certain tasks to the tasktracker based on the information of heart beat. After receiving commands from the jobtracker, tasktracker launches a child JVM to run the map task. Finally, the map task calls CUDA program via JNI [17] to start the processing. The calling procedure contributes to the overhead of *Hadoop* in Figure 3.

Hadoop Load Balance: When running multimedia workloads, the heterogeneity of nodes aggravates the cluster performance. This is because the Hadoop scheduler will execute load shedding by moving data from low-performance nodes to high-performance nodes to balance the overall application execution time, while the data processing stage will be blocked until the data preparation fetches data from remote nodes. Such waiting time is a great waste of computing resource. Figure 3 illustrates the impact of the *data movements* on the overall performance of a Hadoop cluster. We observe that fetching data remotely costs up to 29% application runtime. Under the distributed framework, the performance of CNN-based application could be expressed as:

$$T_{distribute} = T_{standalone} + t_{data\,move} + t_{ds} + t_{init} \text{ (Eq2)},$$

where $t_{date\,move}$ indicates the time spent on the data transfer to local disk, t_{ds} is the overhead of distributed framework and t_{init} is the overhead of repeated network initialization. The equation shows that more non-GPU related operations are introduced in the distributed framework, which leads to a low GPU temporal utilization.

Implication: Due to the inefficiency of the framework the non-computation related overheads account for up to 51% overall runtime, as shown in Figure 3. These overheads are mostly introduced due to the whole CNN process is associated with a map task. The task mapping mechanism in conventional distributed framework should be optimized for CNN based data processing flow. In addition, the modern heterogeneous distributed framework calls for efficient load balance to avoid wastes of GPU resource. An analytical model based processing time estimation for processing node would greatly optimize the task dispatch among heterogeneous processing nodes with various processing capacities and reduce the data movement among nodes. This motivates us to delve into lower standalone processing node level to explore the opportunity to achieve this goal.

3.3 Standalone Semantic Gap

To bridge the framework semantic gap, we opt to trap into the details of standalone CNN acceleration platform implementation to identify overheads and opportunities to provide insights for implementing predictive and efficient GPU-accelerated CNN processing.

3.3.1 GPU Temporal Inefficiency

We begin with a simple image recognition benchmark on three typical CNN networks to identify where the speedup bottlenecks locate at the standalone level. To maximize the system throughput, we set the input data as a batch of 64 images from ImageNet. We report the speedup of computation part, overall task with/without counting in network initialization stage in Figure 4. We observe that although GPU efficiently accelerates the computation (average 44X), the overall speedups are still very low (average 7X). Even if the network initialization time is not counted in, there is still much room for further optimization (average 60%). We then investigate the time distribution of overall tasks across all three networks and find that the GPU computation accounts for less than 20% of the task execution duration, while the most of the application runtime is consumed by network initialization (loading parameters from storage) and CPU processing (image data pre-processing). Therefore, the CNN application runtime on a standalone system could be described as (without counting in network initialization):

$$T_{standalone} = t_{cpu} + t_{memcpy} + t_{gpu} \text{ (Eq3)},$$

where t_{cpu} is the time of CPU pre-processing, t_{memcpy} indicates the time cost of copying parameters from CPU to GPU, and t_{gpu} is the GPU processing time. In the Eq3, the non-GPU related operations dominate the performance of CNN-based applications and GPU is idle during the most of the application execution time. Therefore, the low GPU temporal utilization leads to low overall speedup. We name this bottleneck as GPU temporal inefficiency.

Implication: Our investigation suggests that current CNN service framework requires higher computation proportion to reach desirable throughput. This could be achieved by shrinking the network initialization time and increasing the number of input batched image package in the entire CNN execution workflow.

3.3.2 Multiple Processes Contention

The multi-process technique has been introduced to improve the low data throughput. For example, Nvidia's Multi-Process Service (MPS) [29] is developed to allow multiple kernels running concurrently on shared GPU resource pool. However, our investigation suggests that current task-level parallelism solution is not optimal for deep learning applications [19, 28]. First, CNN based applications are memory-intensive. Running multiple GPU processes may exhaust GPU memory. We characterize the memory consumption by varying the batch size of input data. Figure 6 demonstrates that a single process of VGGNet could consume around 5GB GPU memory when the batch size is 64. In

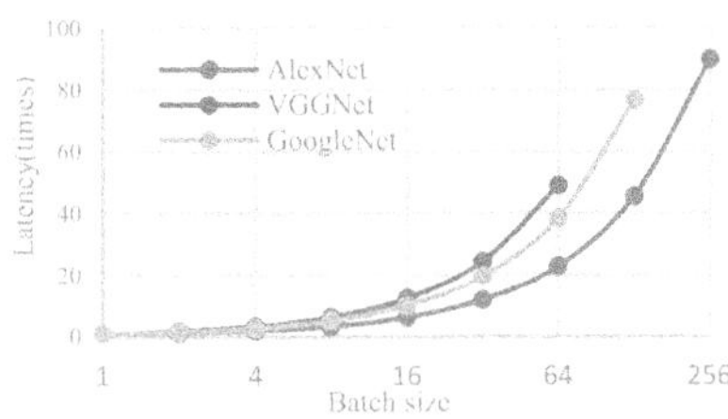

Figure 5. Batch size vs. latency

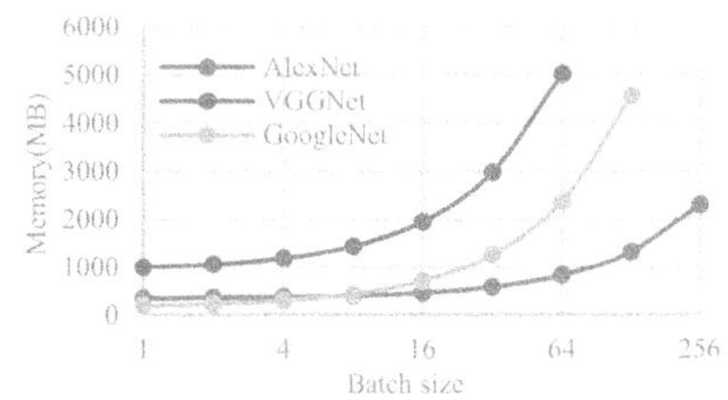

Figure 6. Memory usage

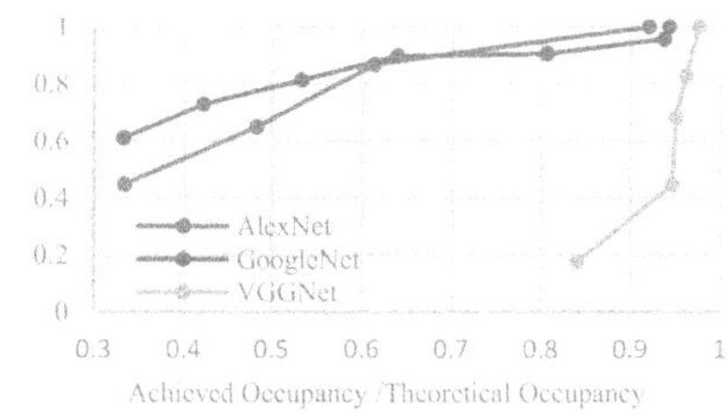

Figure 7. CDF of Achiv/Theo occupancy

Table 4. The critical kernels

Application	Kernel		Percent	Block Size	Registers /Thread	Shared Memory/Block	Warps Limit	Theoretical Occupancy
AlexNet	MM1	sgemm_sm35_ldg_nn_64×16×64×16×16	72.5%	[16, 16, 1]	71	8.27KB	24	37.5%
GoogLeNet	MM1	sgemm_sm35_ldg_nn_64×16×64×16×16	66.3%	[16, 16, 1]	71	8.27KB	24	37.5%
VGGNet	MM1	sgemm_sm35_ldg_nn_64×16×64×16×16	20.4%	[16, 16, 1]	71	8.27KB	24	37.5%
	MM2	sgemm_sm35_ldg_nn_128×8×128×16×16	37.3%	[16, 16, 1]	127	8.145KB	16	25%
	MM3	sgemm_sm35_ldg_nn_64×16×128×8×32	21.2%	[8, 32, 1]	115	12.27KB	16	25%

this case, three processes, even with MPS-enabled, could easily run out of state-of-the-art GPU memory (e.g. 12GB per K80).

Moreover, the interference and resource contention could severely degrade the performance of multiple processes. Table 3 presents the computation throughput (CT: images/s) of one GPU process, two GPU processes, and two GPU processes with MPS-enabled. We can observe that the throughput of two processes is much lower than the theoretical throughput (2X). Even with the MPS-enabled, the multi-process only gain limited improvement. Here we use a metric, *Kif*, expressed as Eq4, to quantify the degree of interference. The larger *Kif* is, the more interference among multiple processes. The optimal value of *Kif* is 0, which means no resource contention.

$$K_{if} = \frac{CT_{single-process} \times \text{the number of processes}}{CT_{multi-process}} - 1 \quad \text{(Eq4)}.$$

To identify the reasons of interference, we begin by investigating the GPU critical kernels of CNNs using Nvidia Visual Profiler. We define the critical kernels as the most time-consuming kernels within an application. We gather their information and corresponding micro-architectural characteristics and summarize the results in Table 4. The kernels of Matrix Multiplication (MM) account for more than 66 percent of execution time across three CNNs. For Nvidia Tesla K-Series GPUs, the matrix multiplications are conducted by the kernel of Single-precision General Matrix Multiply (SGEMM) from cuBLAS [7]. However, the MM kernel is register-intensive. Due to the demanding register request for each thread each SM is limited to simultaneously execute 24 warps in AlexNet and GoogLeNet, and 16 warps in VGGNet. The limited warps indicate limited available computing resource. The limited available computing resource shared with multiple processes leads to contentions among concurrent executing kernels.

Implication: While the notion of employing the multi-process technique to improve the throughput appears appealing, our results indicate that current multi-process solution lacks proper memory and interference management. The number of concurrently running process in multi-process implementation should also be considered judiciously. Running too few processes may lead to waste of GPU resource. While over employing processes could incur severe GPU resource contention, even memory overcommit. Though a profiled based method is helpful to determine the number of processes, this is impractical in distributed cluster-based implementation due to the diversity of CNN workloads and a large number of slave nodes. An analytical model based criterion would greatly improve the efficiency.

3.3.3 Inefficiency of GPU Acceleration Library

Table 3. Throughput and K_{if}

	2 P	2 P in MPS	1P	K_{if}	K_{if} in MPS
AlexNet	348	436	289	0.7	0.3
GoogLeNet	125	156	116	0.8	0.5
VGGNet	43	49	42	1.0	0.7

Our previous characterization implications motivate an analytical model to provide accurate performance estimation for distributed framework and process number selection in multi-process technique. In this section, we explore the computation patterns of CNN workloads and GPU acceleration library to find the answer.

Bottlenecks: We start by characterizing the convolution layers in CNN workloads. To better quantify the performance of CNN convolutional layers, we define throughput efficiency, *tpE*, which indicates the GPU computational efficiency of each layer, as:

$$tpE = \frac{Throughput}{GPU\ Peak\ Throughput} \quad \text{(Eq5)}.$$

Since the throughput of each convolutional layer could be calculated by dividing the number of executed floating point (FP) instructions by the GPU time, Eq5 can be expressed as:

$$tpE = \frac{\text{Conv}_{flops}}{GPU\ time \times GPU\ Peak\ Throughput} \quad \text{(Eq6)}.$$

We examine the GPU computational efficiency of the three networks at each layer using *tpE* and the results are shown in Figure 8. We observe that the *tpE* in most of the convolutional layers is less than 60%. In AlexNet, none of the layers has a *tpE* greater than 40%. The poor *tpE* indicates the inefficiency of current GPU computational operations for CNN applications.

Root Causes: To identify the root causes of the inefficiency of GPU computational operations, we calculate the amount of computation of each layer based on Eq1. As shown in Figure 9, most layers have a small amount of computation. The low amount of computation leads to GPU resource under-utilization (i.e. low GPU spatial utilization), which results in low occupancy in kernel level. We further characterize the ratio of achieved occupancy and theoretical occupancy, which quantifies the GPU resource utilization. The results are presented as Cumulative Distribution Function (CDF) in Figure 7. Each point represents the kernels

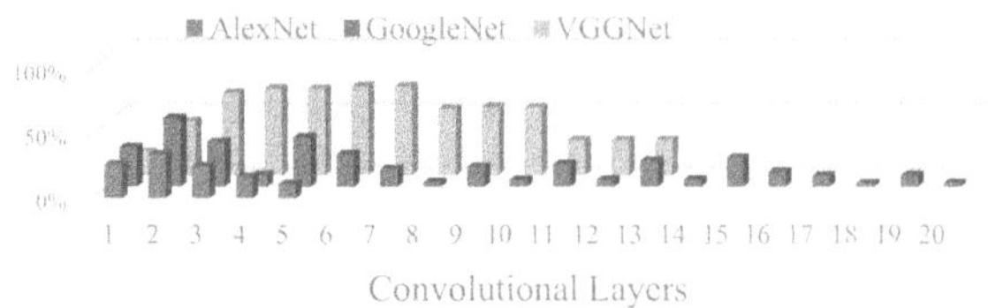

Figure 8. Throughput efficiency for each CONV layer

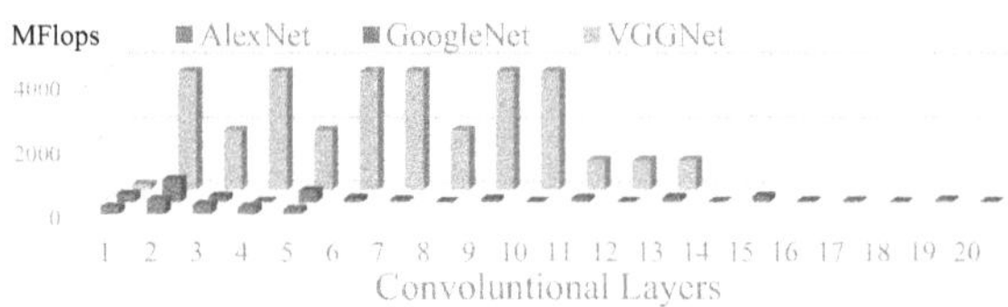

Figure 9. Varying computations of convolutional layers

with the same GPU resource utilization in a network. For example, 60% of the kernels have GPU resource utilization below 50% (GPU spatial inefficiency) in AlexNet and GoogLeNet. This leads to the low *tpE* value in Figure 8.

Intuitively, batching multiple images/frames into a larger frame at each layer is usually adopted to improve the amount of computation in CNNs. However, due to the uneven computation amount at each CNN layers, using fixed batch size for all layers is not desirable. We conduct an experiment to compare the non-batching method with batching method based on cuBLAS. As shown in Figure 10, we observe that for those layers with ideal *tpE* (>60%), batching method does not help to further improve computational efficiency, while significantly increases the latency. Figures 5 and 6 illustrate the variation in latency and memory with the change of batch size. Without caution, the batching method will consume more memory and increase latency.

Implication: Due to the non-uniform computation amount across convolutional layers, we need to design a balanced scheme to improve *tpE* with less latency and memory usage. With the improved *tpE*, the resource utilization of GPU hardware could be pushed to near limit. This also could benefit the building of a performance estimation analytical model, because the throughputs of most convolutional layers are proportional to the GPU peak performance under this situation.

3.4 Summary

To sum, the inefficiencies of CNN-based applications stem from the GPU temporal inefficiency in framework level and the GPU spatial inefficiency in architecture level. The large number of non-GPU involved operations in Eq2 leads to GPU temporal inefficiency, which results in unsatisfactory speedup. At the architecture level, the small computation throughput of convolutional layers results in low GPU spatial inefficiency. These observations point us towards a hierarchical design that waxes the GPU resource supply-demand mismatches at the architecture level and eliminates distributed overheads at the framework level.

4. OVERCOMING BOTTLENECKS: BUILDING HIGH THROUGHPUT GPU ACCELERATION FRAMEWORK

Motivated by our characterization experiences, we present D^3NN, a Distributed, Decoupled, and Dynamically-tuned GPU

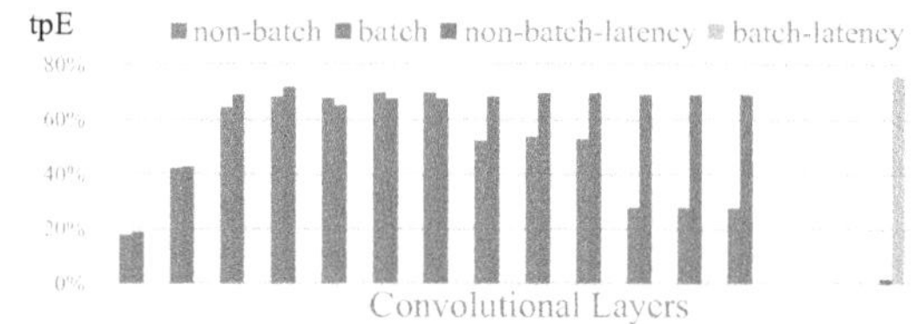

Figure 10. Non-batch vs batch in VGGNet

acceleration framework for modern CNN network architectures. D^3NN features three novel designs.

1. A CNN oriented GPU acceleration library that **dynamically** selects the optimal batch size of input data for each CNN layer.
2. An analytical model that enables accurate GPU processing time estimation in standalone GPU processing node. The analytical model provides insights for a load balance free distributed framework design and profiling-free multi-process technique.
3. A distributed data processing framework that **decouples** the CPU based data preparation and GPU-based data processing in CNN applications.
4. A contention mitigation scheme that alleviates the GPU resource contention caused by task-level parallelism.

4.1 Dynamic Batch Size Tuning Scheme

We first bridge the performance gaps among convolutional layers by designing a dynamic batching GPU acceleration library. We then design an analytical model that is able to accurately estimate GPU processing time.

In section 3 we show that using fixed batch size for all CNN layers may not be beneficial. Given the uneven computation amount at different CNN layers, two questions should be answered. First, *when should we apply the batching method?* Second, *how to select the best batch size if the batching method is adopted?*

Using batching or not, it highly depends on the GPU resource supply and demand at each CNN layer. We define a metric, *cpRatio*, to reflect the proportion of demanded resource to available resource at given CNN layer:

$$cpRatio = \frac{GridSize}{maxBlocks} \quad \text{(Eq7)},$$

The maximum number of blocks (maxBlocks) is defined in Eq8, which is mainly determined by the registers per thread (i.e. r in Eq8) and total number of registers per SM:

$$\text{maxBlocks} = \left\lfloor \frac{Total\ Registers\ per\ SM}{r * BlockSize} \right\rfloor \times num\ of\ SM \quad \text{(Eq8)}.$$

The GridSize (the number of blocks of MM kernel in a given layer) is defined in Eq9. Since in the matrix multiplication based convolution, MM kernel divides the result matrix into sub-matrices, with each sub-matrix mapped to a block.

$$\text{GridSize} = \left\lceil \frac{Result\ Matrix\ Size_{each\ layer}}{Sub-matrix\ Size_{MM\ kernel}} \right\rceil \quad \text{(Eq9)}.$$

We use *cpRatio* to indicate whether the batching method is adopted: If measured *cpRatio* is bigger than 1, then all available GPU resource (blocks) is consumed by CNN kernel. Therefore the batching method is not necessary for this layer. As shown in Figure 11, in CNN layers whose *cpRatios* are bigger than 1, the non-batching method performs better. The batching method in the last six layers achieves better performance than non-batching, where the measured *cpRatios* are all less than 1.

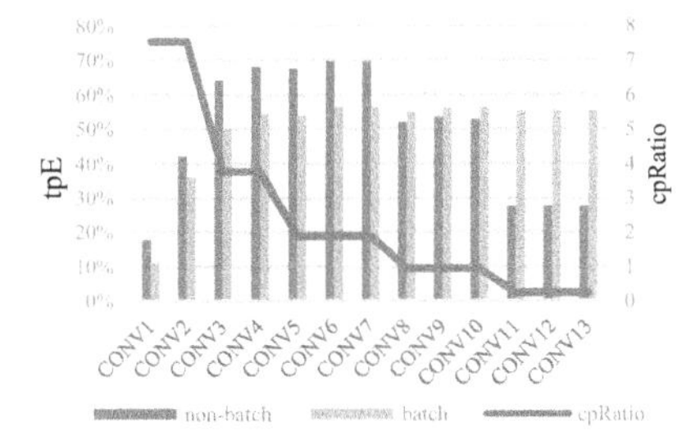

Figure 11. Effectiveness of batching method in VGGNet

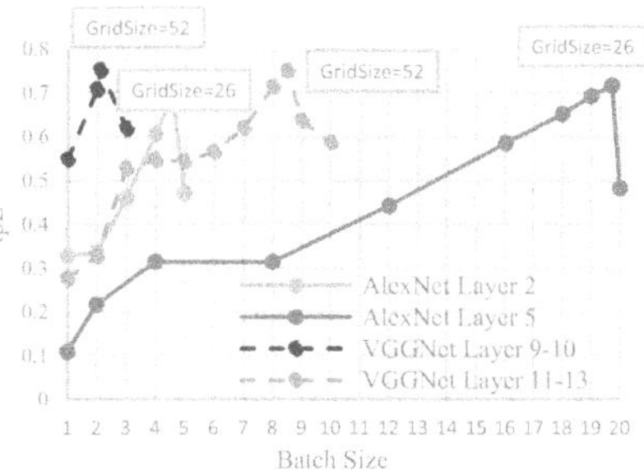

Figure 12. Performance variation

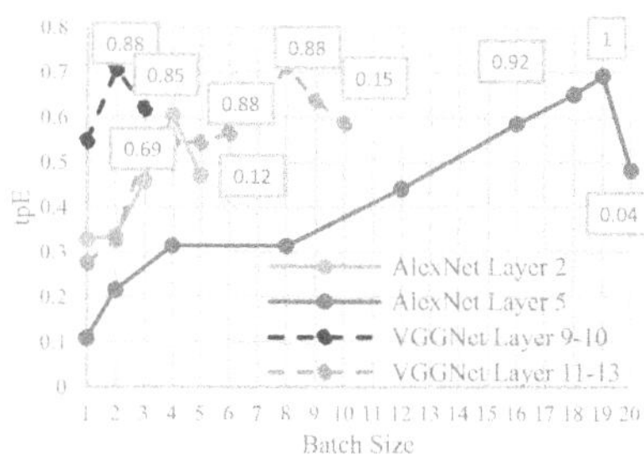

Figure 13. ***Util*** **in different batch sizes**

To identify the optimal batch size, we first exhaustedly characterize convolutional layers' performance using different batch sizes in Figure 12. We can observe the performance of CNN layers do not increase monotonically with the increasing of batch size. At the peak, its kernel's GridSize is a multiple of maxBlocks (26 for K20c), which means GPU MM kernel will achieve the best performance when it fully utilizes GPU resource. The performance of each CNN layer reaches the peak only if the value of GridSize is integer multiples of the maxBlocks. This implies the *cpRatio* is desired to be chosen as an integer to avoid performance degradation. We design a metric *Util* to indicate whether the batch size is optimal.

$$\text{Util} = \begin{cases} BcpRatio & if \quad BcpRatio > 0 \\ 1 & if \quad BcpRatio = 0 \end{cases} \text{(Eq10)},$$

where: $\text{BcpRatio} = \text{cpRatio} \bmod 1$. Figure 13 validates this policy: the point with the maximum value of *Util* always indicates the best batch size at given CNN layer. For example, the optimal batch size for AlexNet Layer No.2 is 4, where the value of *Util* is the maximum 0.88.

Based on our dynamic batching method, we design analytical models to estimate the CNN computing time and memory copy time swiftly. Since the dynamic batching method could boost the throughput of most of the convolutional layers to the maximum throughput, we can estimate the runtime of each convolutional layer based on its maximum throughput:

$$t_{CONVi} = \frac{Batch\ Size \times CONV_{flops}}{maxFLOPS \times Util} \text{ (Eq11)},$$

and then estimate the GPU computing time as:

$$t_{gpu} = \frac{\sum_{i=1}^{N} t_{CONVi}}{\delta} \text{ (Eq12)},$$

where δ is the ratio of convolutional layers in CNN. The memory copy time can be described as:

$$t_{memcpy} = \frac{\text{InputSize} + \text{ParameterSize}}{Throughput_{PCIE}} \text{ (Eq13)},$$

where InputSize is the size of pre-processed images and ParameterSize is the size of CNN parameters (mainly composed of parameters of fully connected layers).

$$\text{ParameterSize} = \sum_{i=1}^{N} N_{f_i} \times S_{f_i}^2 \times N_{c_i} \text{ (Eq14)}.$$

4.2 Distributed and Decoupled Framework

D³NN exploits three novel mechanisms for the efficient data processing in the distributed data processing framework: (1) Producer-Consumer scheme that decouples the data preparation and data processing at each slave node to hide the data preparation latency; (2) Semaphore-based data synchronization scheme that ensures the maximum single node throughput; and (3) Analytical model-based resource allocation that maximizes resource utilization.

Comments: *M* consumers work on a slave node and the depth of semaphore is *N*, which means *N* consumers can access GPU simultaneously

```
sem_data = 1     //access data pool atomically
sem_GPU = N      //N consumers share a GPU, N <= M
sem_prod = 2M    //prepare 2 data for each consumer
sem_cons = 0     //consumer will be waked-up by producer
```

Figure 14. Semaphores initialization

```
down → sem_prod
  copy data from HDFS to data pool
  down → sem_data
    make data available to consumers
  up → sem_data
up → sem_cons          //wake up a consumer
```

Figure 15. Producer workflow

```
create CNN and do the initial work
while(1) {
   down → sem_cons
     down → sem_data
       select a data from data pool
     up → sem_data
     load and pre-proceesing by CPU
     down → sem_GPU
       GPU do processing
     up → sem_GPU
   up → sem_prod  //notify producer to prepare next data
   pid = fork() //fork a new thread to upload result to HDFS
   if(pid ==0)
     child thread upload result to HDFS
}
```

Figure 16. Consumer workflow

Producer-Consumer scheme: The overall architecture of *D³NN* distributed framework is shown in Figure 17. Compared to baseline system in Section 3.2, we re-organize the task execution flow at slave node by separating the deep learning based multimedia process into data preparation process and data processing process. We employ a data preparation engine (Producer) and a data processing engine (Consumer), which run simultaneously on each slave node. The data preparation engine consists of map tasks, which act as data preparation processes and are responsible for downloading data from distributed storage to local disk. The data processing engine consists of data processing

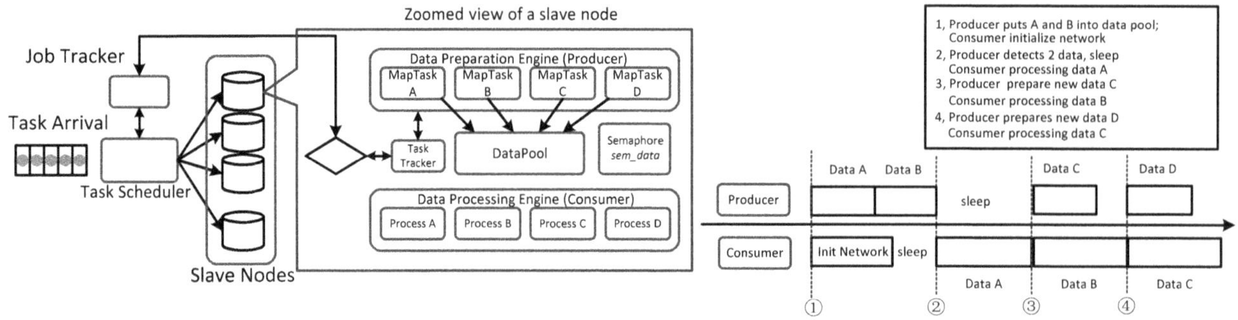

Figure 17. An overview of D³NN workflow

processes, which are in charge of data processing and network initialization. We employ a data pool to buffer the data produced by data preparation engine, which is a critical region for the producers and consumers to access data atomically.

Semaphore-based data synchronization scheme: We design a synchronization mechanism using a semaphore to coordinate the data preparation (Producer) and data processing (Consumer) in Figures 14-16. First, the producer starts to put data into data pool. At the same time, the consumer completes initial work and enters the sleep state to wait for *sem_consumer*. Once the producer completes a task of data preparation, it will trigger the consumer to process the incoming data. When the consumer is processing current data, the producer continues to prepare the next data for it. If there are more than 2M available data in data pool, the producer will enter the sleep state until the consumer completes a task of data processing and increases *sem_producer*. In this way, the consumer will keep pace with the producer.

A typical workflow of data preparation engine and data processing engine is presented in Figure 17. By running data preparation task and data processing task in parallel with different phases, the data processing time is well overlapped with data preparation time. Since the consumer services are never terminated, the network initialization only needs to be executed once, thereby eliminating considerable overheads. Therefore, the gaps resulted from distributed framework has been bridged and the distributed processing time is mainly dominated by the time of standalone CNN processing. Now Eq2 can be rewritten as:

$$T_{distribute} = T_{standalone} = t_{cpu} + t_{gpu} + t_{memcpy} \quad \text{(Eq15)}.$$

An analytical model based resource allocation: As mentioned in our motivations, the analytical model plays a critical role to bridge the semantic gap in scale-out CNN based big data processing platform. We leverage our analytical model to estimate the processing capacity of each computing node in distributed framework. This helps us to avoid great overheads on passive load balance among heterogeneous cluster, and always keeps the high utilization of heterogeneous hardware.

The analytical model could also guide us to select optimal process number in multi-processing technique with the lowest contention. Based on the analytical model, we can estimate the current GPU temporal utilization as:

$$gpuUtil = \frac{t_{gpu}+t_{memcpy}}{T_{standalone}} \quad \text{(Eq16)}.$$

Therefore, the optimal process number equals to *1/gpuUtil*. And this could boost GPU utilization to nearly 100%. We will further discuss this interference management scheme.

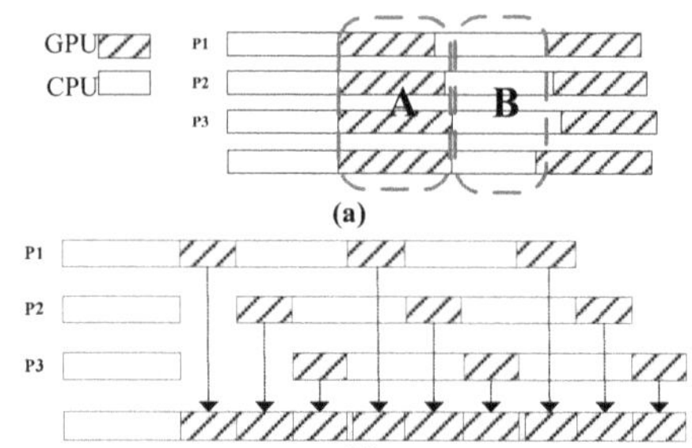

Figure 18. Contention management scheme

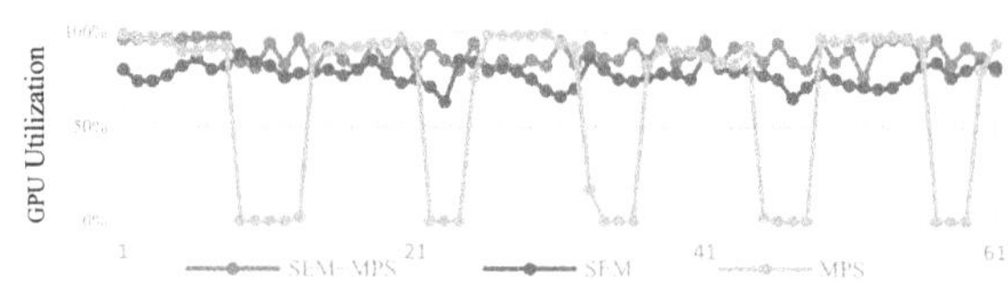

Figure 19. Real measurement of GPU utilization

4.3 Multi-Processing Contention Mitigation

As discussed in Section 3.3.2, the task-level parallelism of CNN based processes will cause intensive interference. In region A of Figure 18(a), all processes contend for GPU resource almost simultaneously, thus leading to interference and GPU memory over-committing. However, the GPU utilization decreases to zero in region B, as all processes are in their data preprocessing stage executed by CPU. This imbalance of GPU usage inevitably causes low GPU utilization. We also show the measurement of GPU utilization statistics with MPS-enabled in Figure 19. We observe a noticeable intermittent pattern in GPU utilization.

We propose a contention mitigation scheme to handle task-level parallelism bottlenecks. As shown in Figure 18(b), our contention management scheme pipelines the GPU processing tasks to avoid GPU resource contention, thus improves GPU utilization. Since K_{if} is high among CNN based applications, running too many processes does not help improve the data processing throughput. The contention mitigation scheme first calculates the optimal number of processes (*1/gpuUtil*) using Eq16. It then provides an access mechanism based on semaphore primitive. For contention-intensive applications (e.g. VGGNet), the initial value of the semaphore is 1, so that only one process can access the GPU resource at a time. After this process completes GPU processing and releases the semaphore, another process immediately acquires the semaphore and accesses GPU resource. In this way, the contention could be avoided and GPU remains busy as shown in *SEM+MPS* of Figure 19.

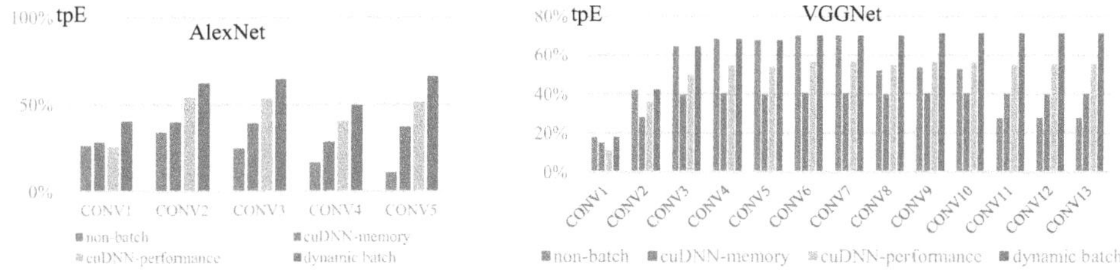

Figure 20. The comparison of throughput efficiency among CONV layers

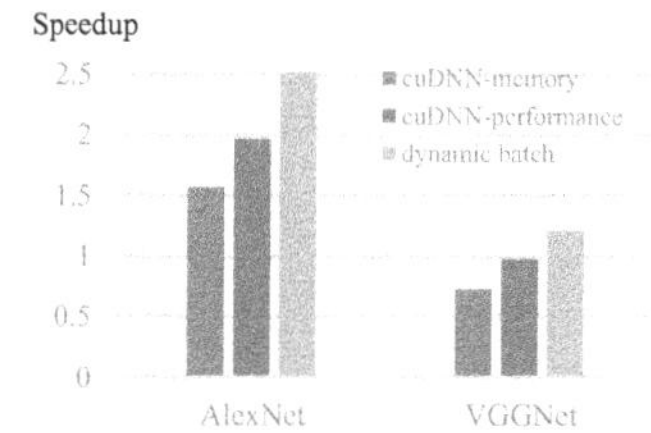

Figure 21. Speedup over non-batch

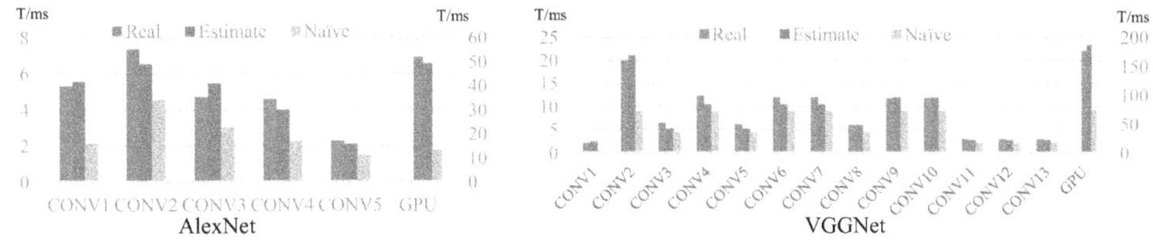

Figure 22. Evaluate the accuracy of analytical model

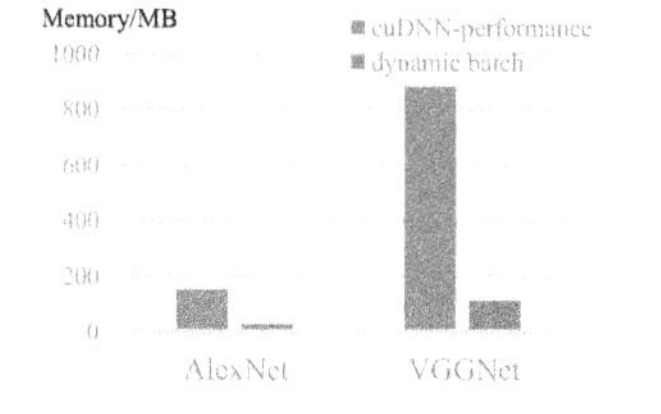

Figure 23. Memory usage

Note that the decoupled architecture is not simply designed for distributed cluster. This design also applies to a single node design with single GPU or multiple GPUs. This is because the GPU idle time is inevitable in single node design with CPU pre-processing. Worse, the current multi-process scheme for GPU incurs severe interference because of the GPU resource contention.

5. EVALUATION

5.1 Architecture Level Evaluation

We evaluate our dynamic supply-demand optimization scheme on two typical CNNs (AlexNet and VGGNet). In our dynamic method, matrix multiplication is based on cuBLAS and the stretching out the local regions into column vectors is implemented by the kernel im2col. Table 5 illustrates the batch size of each layer calculated using Eq10. Note that we avoid choosing the batch size as prime number (though it may be optimal) at each layer, because a big prime number causes a huge overall batch size. Here the overall batch size for a CNN is the least common multiple of batch size in each layer. Since different layers have different batch size, each layer needs to run $\frac{\text{overall batch size}}{\text{batch size of this layer}}$ times to perform an overall processing.

We compare our dynamic batch method with the non-batch method and batch method used in cuDNN, which is a state-of-the-art DNN library developed by NVIDIA [19]. The cuDNN now allows control over the balance between performance and memory footprint using different algorithms [9]. We include these two policies in our comparison. One is IMPLICIT_GEMM, which uses no extra working space and is memory-efficient. The other is GEMM and it is the fastest approach. Under the same overall batch size, we report the throughput efficiency (*tpE*) of the non-batch method, cuDNN (with memory-efficient and performance-preferred policies) and our dynamic batching method at each layer in Figure 20. Experimental results (Figure 21) show that our dynamic batching scheme can achieve up to 1.5X performance improvement compared with the one without batching. Our method even outperforms the state-of-the-art deep learning library (cuDNN) by up to 67% (memory-efficient policy) and 28% (performance-preferred policy). Moreover, as shown in Figure 23, our method consumes less GPU memory than cuDNN with performance-preferred policy. To summary, our analysis suggests that dynamic batching is an effective method to tackle the imbalance among multiple layers for CNNs with less latency and memory usage.

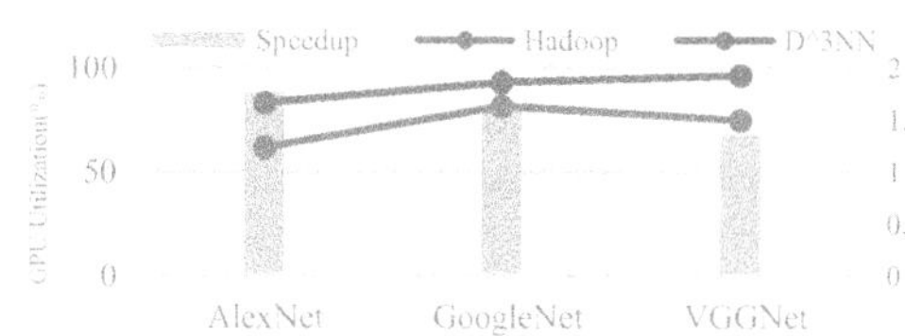

Figure 24. Hadoop vs D^3NN

Since the analytical model plays a critical role to bridge the semantic gaps in scale-out CNN based big data processing platform, we continue to evaluate the accuracy of our analytical model. Here we leverage the analytical model to calculate the runtime then use it to compare with real runtime and a naive method. Figure 22 depicts the runtime comparisons of the per-convolutional layer and total GPU. By dividing the number of floating point operations at each layer by peak performance of specific GPU, the naïve method only obtains 27-40% accuracy. Our results show that we can predict the performance of CNN with only 5-10% error.

5.2 System Level Evaluation

We evaluate the effectiveness of D^3NN in terms of system performance and load balance.

Performance: We evaluate the performance improvement of D^3NN under the three CNNs. We first report the GPU utilization and application speedup in Figure 24. We observe that D^3NN outperforms our baseline significantly in GPU utilization (average 30% improvement) and runtime (average 1.5X speedup). We then evaluate the impact of the decoupled implementation on single node throughput. The results are shown in Table 6. Mode *Overall* denotes the overall image processing throughput on the standalone platform. Mode *No-Init* denotes the throughput without counting in the network initialization. Mode *Proc-only* denotes the throughput of data processing stage on a standalone platform, while excluding the data pre-processing and network initialization. Mode D denotes the throughput of a single slave node in D^3NN. We calculate the throughputs in Modes *Overall*, *No-Init* and *Proc-only* by leveraging the built-in tool in our processing program. The throughput in Mode D is calculated through the task statistics

Table 5. The recommend batch size for each layer

	AlexNet		VGGNet	
CONV Layers	**cpRatio**	**Batch size**	**cpRatio**	**Batch size**
1	1.82	None	7.54	None
2	0.22	4	7.54	None
3	0.15	18	3.77	None
4	0.08	9	3.77	None
5	0.05	18	1.89	None
6	X	X	1.89	None
7	X	X	1.89	None
8, 9, 10	X	X	0.94	2
11, 12, 13	X	X	0.24	8

Table 6. The comparison of throughputs (images/s)

Slave	**K20c**			
Mode	**Standalone**			**Single Node**
	Overall	**No-Init**	**Proc-only**	**D**
AlexNet	39	75	289	350
GoogLeNet	43	59	116	125
VGGNet	18	31	42	43

from Hadoop. Our results shows: (1) the throughput of D gains remarkable improvement (up to 7.9X) compared to the throughput of Overall and even has 3.7X speedup over the throughput of *No-Init*, which justifies our decoupling optimization. (2) The throughput of D outperforms the throughput of *Proc-only*, which implies that the GPU has been fully utilized.

Load balance: We further evaluate the effectiveness of D^3NN's load balance capability. In this experimental setup, we deploy D^3NN on a cluster with three different GPU computing nodes (Titan X, K20c, and M2050), and compare the performance of D^3NN with the scheme of equally allocating tasks to each node (*Equal* in short). In D^3NN, the tasks are allocated based on the ratio of their performance derived from our analytical model. The ratio of load balance is calculated by the number of completed tasks for each node divided by the node's processing capability, which is the real processing throughput profiled at standalone mode. The results are shown in Table 7. We can see that the ratios of D3NN are close to 1, which means D^3NN has a superior load balance capability. For the Equal scheme, since the total running time of the cluster is determined by the slowest node (M2050), the runtime will be up to 2.6X more than D^3NN.

6. RELATED WORK

Deep Learning: Sirius [16] is an open end-to-end intelligent personal assistant based on DNN services. The DjiNN [15] further brings the community the characterization of GPU acceleration server system running DNN services and provides insights into designing future warehouse-scale computer architectures for DNN services. Our work distinguishes itself from DjiNN in four aspects: (1) We perform comprehensive characterizations of GPU acceleration platform instead of computation scope and explore the root causes of low system throughput; (2) We disclose the inefficiency of multi-process technique and propose semaphore-based optimization; (3) We propose dynamic batching scheme and an analytical model for CNN based GPU processing. (4) We present a decoupled distributed framework to facilitate the GPU acceleration at scale.

Several recent projects [3, 4, 12, 27, 44] begin to use FPGAs and ASICs as the accelerators to achieve high performance at low energy. Most of them are on-going efforts and could not be flexibly deployed and programmed at large-scale. Recently, Nvidia released its deep learning library (cuDNN) [5] based on

Table 7. Evaluation of load balance

Task Allocation		**Titan X**	**K20c**	**M2050**
AlexNet	Equal	0.51	0.94	2.62
	D^3NN	0.96	0.98	1.00
GoogLeNet	Equal	0.48	0.94	2.58
	D^3NN	0.93	0.95	1.00
VGGNet	Equal	0.54	1.06	2.66
	D^3NN	0.93	0.95	1.00

batching method. However, it does not consider using dynamic batching to tackle the compute-intensive CNN, such as VGGNet.

GPU Task Execution: Sethia et al. [35] proposed Equalizer, a low overhead hardware runtime system that dynamically adapts the resource to the needs of running kernel. When a GPU kernel is running, Equalizer could adjust the number of concurrent thread blocks based on the runtime profiling information. Equalize will not improve the performance of CNN with small batch size because of its underutilization of GPU resource. To fully utilize GPU resource, our proposed techniques determine the GridSize of kernel based on the problem size of each CNN layer before the kernel is executed. Therefore, Equalizer could be incorporated into our proposed schemes to further ensure that GPU resources match the requirement of the executing kernels. Similar to our work, Xu et al. [40] also proposed optimization for task execution in CPU-GPU heterogeneous systems to improve the utilization of GPU resources. However, their optimization objective is maximizing the schedulability of real-time tasks (i.e., the amount of work of real-time tasks that can be accomplished before deadlines), while our objective is maximizing the throughput of the whole CPU-GPU system.

7. CONCLUSION

This work presents the first in-depth empirical study on characterizing the performance of GPU acceleration system for CNN applications. Our characterization results demonstrate two significant semantic gaps: framework gap and standalone gap. Framework gap indicates the mismatch between CNN-based data processing workflow and data processing manner in current distributed framework. The uneven computing loads at different CNN layers and fixed computing capacity provisioning of current GPU acceleration library results in the standalone gap. Motivated by our characterization findings, we propose D^3NN, a Distributed, Decoupled, and Dynamically tuned GPU acceleration framework for modern CNN architectures. More importantly, D^3NN features a novel analytical model that enables accurate time estimation of GPU accelerated CNN processing with only 5-10% error. Our evaluation results show the throughput of standalone processing node using D^3NN gains up to 3.7X performance improvement over current GPU acceleration platform.

8. ACKNOWLEDGMENTS

This work is supported in part by NSF grants 1527535, 1423090, 1320100, 1117261, 0937869, 0916384, 0845721(CAREER), 0834288, 0811611, 0720476, by SRC grants 2008-HJ-1798, 2007-RJ-1651G, by Microsoft Research Trustworthy Computing, Safe and Scalable Multi-core Computing Awards, and by three IBM Faculty Awards. Jingling Yuan is supported by NSFC grant 61303029.

9. REFERENCES

[1] Abdel-Hamid, O., Mohamed, A., Jiang, H., Deng, L., Penn, G. and Yu, D. 2014. Convolutional neural networks for speech recognition. IEEE/ACM Transactions on audio, speech, and language processing. 22, 10 (2014), 1533–1545.

[2] Amazon G2 instance: http://docs.aws.amazon.com/AWSEC2/latest/UserGuide/using_cluster_co mputing.html.

[3] Chen, T., Du, Z., Sun, N., Wang, J., Wu, C., Chen, Y. and Temam, O. 2014. DianNao: A Small-Footprint High-Throughput Accelerator for Ubiquitous Machine-Learning. Proceedings of the 19th International Conference on Architectural Support for Programming Languages and Operating Systems (2014), 269–284.

[4] Chen, Y., Luo, T., Liu, S., Zhang, S., He, L., Wang, J., Li, L., Chen, T., Xu, Z. and Sun, N. 2014. DaDianNao: A Machine-Learning Supercomputer. Proceedings of the 47th Annual IEEE/ACM International Symposium on Microarchitecture (2014), 609–622.

[5] Chetlur, S., Woolley, C., Vandermersch, P., Cohen, J., Tran, J., Catanzaro, B. and Shelhamer, E. 2014. cuDNN: Efficient Primitives for Deep Learning. arXiv preprint arXiv:1410.0759. (Oct. 2014).

[6] CS231n: Convolutional Neural Networks for Visual Recognition: http://cs231n.github.io/convolutional-networks/.

[7] cuBLAS: https://developer.nvidia.com/cuBLAS.

[8] CUDA Profiler User's Guide: docs.nvidia.com/cuda/profiler-users-guide/.

[9] cuDNN v2: Higher Performance for Deep Learning on GPUs: http://devblogs.nvidia.com/parallelforall/cudnn-v2-higher-performance-deep-learning-gpus/.

[10] Dean, J. and Ghemawat, S. 2008. MapReduce : Simplified Data Processing on Large Clusters. Communications of the ACM. 51, 1 (2008), 1–13.

[11] Deng, J., Dong, W., Socher, R., Li, L.-J., Li, K. and Fei-Fei, L. 2009. ImageNet: A large-scale hierarchical image database. Proc. IEEE Conf. on Computer Vision and Pattern Recognition (CVPR). (2009), 1097–1105.

[12] Du, Z., Fasthuber, R., Chen, T., Ienne, P., Li, L., Luo, T., Feng, X., Chen, Y. and Temam, O. 2015. ShiDianNao: Shifting Vision Processing Closer to the Sensor. Proceedings of the 42nd Annual International Symposium on Computer Architecture (2015), 92–104.

[13] Facebook, Ericsson and Qualcomm 2013. A focus on efficiency.

[14] Girshick, R., Donahue, J., Darrell, T., Berkeley, U.C. and Malik, J. 2014. Rich feature hierarchies for accurate object detection and semantic segmentation. Proc. IEEE Conf. on Computer Vision and Pattern Recognition (CVPR). (2014), 580–587.

[15] Hauswald, J., Kang, Y., Laurenzano, M.A., Chen, Q., Li, C., Dreslinski, R., Mudge, T., Mars, J. and Tang, L. 2015. Djinn and Tonic: DNN as a Service and Its Implications for Future Warehouse Scale Computers. Proceedings of the 42Nd Annual International Symposium on Computer Architecture (2015), 27–40.

[16] Hauswald, J., Laurenzano, M.A., Zhang, Y., Li, C., Rovinski, A., Khurana, A., Dreslinski, R.G., Mudge, T., Petrucci, V., Tang, L. and Mars, J. 2015. Sirius: An Open End-to-End Voice and Vision Personal Assistant and Its Implications for Future Warehouse Scale Computers. Proceedings of the Twentieth International Conference on Architectural Support for Programming Languages and Operating Systems (2015), 223–238.

[17] He, W., Cui, H., Lu, B., Zhao, J., Li, S., Xue, J. and Feng, X. 2015. Hadoop+: Modeling and Evaluating the Heterogeneity for MapReduce Applications in Heterogeneous Clusters. Proceedings of the 29th ACM on International Conference on Supercomputing (2015), 143–153.

[18] Hu, Y., Li, C., Liu, L. and Li, T. 2016. HOPE: Enabling Efficient Service Orchestration in Software-Defined Data Centers. Proceedings of the 2016 International Conference on Supercomputing (2016), 10:1–10:12.

[19] Hu, Y., Song, M., Chen, H. and Li, T. 2016. Towards Efficient Server Architecture for Virtualized Network Function Deployment: Implications and Implementations. Proceedings of the 49th Annual IEEE/ACM International Symposium on Microarchitecture (2016).

[20] Jia, Y., Shelhamer, E., Donahue, J., Karayev, S., Long, J., Girshick, R., Guadarrama, S., Darrell, T. and Eecs, U.C.B. 2014. Caffe : Convolutional Architecture for Fast Feature Embedding. Proceedings of the 22Nd ACM International Conference on Multimedia. (2014), 675–678.

[21] Karpathy, A. and Fei-Fei, L. 2015. Deep visual-semantic alignments for generating image descriptions. Proc. IEEE Conf. on Computer Vision and Pattern Recognition (CVPR). (2015), 3128–3137.

[22] Karpathy, A. and Leung, T. 2014. Large-scale Video Classification with Convolutional Neural Networks. Proc. IEEE Conf. on Computer Vision and Pattern Recognition (CVPR) (2014), 1725–1732.

[23] Kim, Y. 2014. Convolutional neural networks for sentence classification. Proceedings of the 2014 Conference on Empirical Methods in Natural Language Processing (EMNLP). (2014), 1746–1751.

[24] Krizhevsky, A., Sutskever, I. and Hinton, G.E. 2012. ImageNet Classification with Deep Convolutional Neural Networks. Advances In Neural Information Processing Systems. (2012), 1097–1105.

[25] Li, C., Hu, Y., Liu, L., Gu, J., Song, M., Liang, X., Yuan, J. and Li, T. 2015. Towards Sustainable In-situ Server Systems in the Big Data Era. Proceedings of the 42nd Annual International Symposium on Computer Architecture (2015), 14–26.

[26] Li, C., Hu, Y., Zhou, R., Liu, M., Liu, L., Yuan, J. and Li, T. 2013. Enabling Datacenter Servers to Scale out Economically and Sustainably. Proceedings of the 46th Annual IEEE/ACM International Symposium on Microarchitecture (2013), 322–333.

[27] Liu, D., Chen, T., Liu, S., Zhou, J., Zhou, S., Teman, O., Feng, X., Zhou, X. and Chen, Y. 2015. Pudiannao: A polyvalent machine learning accelerator. Proceedings of the Twentieth International Conference on Architectural Support for Programming Languages and Operating Systems (2015), 369–381.

[28] Liu, L., Cui, Z., Xing, M., Bao, Y., Chen, M. and Wu, C. 2012. A software memory partition approach for eliminating bank-level interference in multicore systems. Proceedings of the 21st international conference on Parallel architectures and compilation techniques (2012), 367–376.

[29] MULTI-PROCESS SERVICE: https://docs.nvidia.com/deploy/pdf/CUDA_Multi_Process_Service_Overview.pdf.

[30] NVIDIA CUDA Programming Guide: http://docs.nvidia.com/cuda/pdf/CUDA_C_Programming_Guide.pdf.

[31] NVIDIA Visual Profiler: https://developer.nvidia.com/nvidia-visual-profiler.

[32] OpenCL: http://www.khronos.org/opencl/.

[33] Russakovsky, O., Deng, J., Su, H., Krause, J., Satheesh, S., Ma, S., Huang, Z., Karpathy, A., Khosla, A., Bernstein, M., Berg, A.C. and Fei-Fei, L. 2015. ImageNet Large Scale Visual Recognition Challenge. International Journal of Computer Vision. 115, 3 (Sep. 2015), 211–252.

[34] Sermanet, P., Kavukcuoglu, K., Chintala, S. and Lecun, Y. 2013. Pedestrian detection with unsupervised multi-stage feature learning. Proc. IEEE Conf. on Computer Vision and Pattern Recognition (CVPR) (2013), 3626–3633.

[35] Sethia, A. and Mahlke, S. 2014. Equalizer: Dynamic Tuning of GPU Resources for Efficient Execution. Proceedings of the 47th Annual IEEE/ACM International Symposium on Microarchitecture (2014), 647–658.

[36] Simonyan, K. and Zisserman, A. 2014. Very Deep Convolutional Networks for Large-Scale Image Recognition. CoRR. abs/1409.1, (2014).

[37] SoftLayer offers Nvidia's most powerful GPU as-a-service: http://www.datacenterdynamics.com/app-cloud/softlayer-offers-nvidias-most-powerful-gpu-as-a-service/94407.fullarticle.

[38] Szegedy, C., Liu, W., Jia, Y., Sermanet, P., Reed, S., Anguelov, D., Erhan, D., Vanhoucke, V. and Rabinovich, A. 2015. Going deeper with convolutions. Proc. IEEE Conf. on Computer Vision and Pattern Recognition (CVPR). (2015), 1–9.

[39] White, T. 2012. Hadoop: The definitive guide. " O'Reilly Media, Inc."

[40] Xu, Y., Wang, R., Li, T., Song, M., Gao, L., Luan, Z. and Qian, D. 2016. Scheduling Tasks with Mixed Timing Constraints in GPU-Powered Real-Time Systems. Proceedings of the 2016 International Conference on Supercomputing (2016), 30:1–30:13.

[41] Yang, L., Luo, P., Loy, C.C. and Tang, X. 2015. A Large-Scale Car Dataset for Fine-Grained Categorization and Verification. Proc. IEEE Conf. on Computer Vision and Pattern Recognition (CVPR) (2015), 3973–3981.

[42] Youtube press statistics: http://youtube.com/yt/press/statistics.html.

[43] Zaharia, M., Chowdhury, M., Das, T. and Dave, A. 2012. Resilient distributed datasets: A fault-tolerant abstraction for in-memory cluster computing. Proceedings of the 9th USENIX Conference on Networked Systems Design and Implementation. (2012).

[44] Zhang, C., Li, P., Sun, G., Guan, Y., Xiao, B. and Cong, J. 2015. Optimizing FPGA-based Accelerator Design for Deep Convolutional Neural Networks. Proceedings of the 2015 ACM/SIGDA International Symposium on Field-Programmable Gate Arrays (2015), 161–170.

[45] Zhang, J., Sameki, M., Ma, S., Price, B., Mech, R., Shen, X., Betke, M., Sclaroff, S. and Lin, Z. 2015. Salient object subitizing. Proc. IEEE Conf. on Computer Vision and Pattern Recognition (CVPR) (2015), 4045–4054.

[46] Zhou, B. and Lapedriza, A. and Xiao, J. and Torralba, A. and Oliva, A. 2014. Learning Deep Features for Scene Recognition using Places Database. Advances In Neural Information Processing Systems (2014).

[47] Zhou, R., Chen, H. and Li, T. 2015. Towards Lightweight and Swift Storage Resource Management in Big Data Cloud Era. Proceedings of the 29th ACM on International Conference on Supercomputing (2015), 133–142.

A DSL Compiler for Accelerating Image Processing Pipelines on FPGAs

Nitin Chugh
International Institute of Information Technology
Hyderabad 500032 India
nitin.ch@research.iiit.ac.in

Vinay Vasista
Dept of CSA
Indian Institute of Science
Bengaluru 560012 India
vinay.vasista@csa.iisc.ernet.in

Suresh Purini
International Institute of Information Technology
Hyderabad 500032 India
suresh.purini@iiit.ac.in

Uday Bondhugula
Dept of CSA
Indian Institute of Science
Bengaluru 560012 India
uday@csa.iisc.ernet.in

ABSTRACT

This paper describes an automatic approach to accelerate image processing pipelines using FPGAs. An image processing pipeline can be viewed as a graph of interconnected stages that processes images successively. Each stage typically performs a point-wise, stencil, or other more complex operations on image pixels. Recent efforts have led to the development of domain-specific languages (DSL) and optimization frameworks for image processing pipelines. In this paper, we develop an approach to map image processing pipelines expressed in the PolyMage DSL to efficient parallel FPGA designs. Our approach exploits reuse and available memory bandwidth (or chip resources) maximally. When compared to Darkroom, a state-of-the-art approach to compile high-level DSL to FPGAs, our approach (a) leads to designs that deliver significantly higher throughput, and (b) supports a greater variety of filters. Furthermore, the designs we generate obtain an improvement even over pre-optimized FPGA implementations provided by vendor libraries for some of the benchmarks.

1. INTRODUCTION

An image processing pipeline can be viewed as a directed acyclic graph, where each node performs simple processing on image pixels; the edges of the graph represent producer-consumer relationships between the nodes. Each node is referred to as a *stage* or a *filter* and typically involves the application of a point-wise, stencil, or other more complex operations on image pixels. Examples of domains that employ such pipelines include computational photography, embedded vision, and medical imaging. High performance and acceleration is highly desirable either due to the volume of data, the requirement to provide a response in real time, or the growing complexity of algorithms compounded with high resolutions and frame rates.

The advantages offered by Field-Programmable Gate Arrays (FPGAs) in comparison to general-purpose microprocessors are well-known, and so are the programmability issues surrounding them [3]. The difficulty of programming FPGAs has restricted FPGA technology to small and specialized segments. High-level Synthesis (HLS) through C-based languages [6, 27, 37, 25, 13, 24], OpenCL/CUDA-based ones [26, 28], high-level language frameworks [2, 15], and model-based frameworks like NI LabVIEW [10] and MATLAB HDL coder [21] are various efforts that improve FPGA programmability. A comprehensive survey of all these approaches can be found in [3]. In the last decade, HLS suites [6] have significantly advanced and have made it easier for programmers to use a C/C++ like high-level interface to program FPGAs instead of hardware description languages (VHDL or Verilog). Nearly all EDA vendors now provide suites supporting HLS — examples of these include Xilinx Vivado, Cadence C-to-silicon compiler, Synopsys Synphony C compiler, and Mentor Graphics Catapult C.

Domain-specific languages (DSLs) provide a high-level language interface suitable to a domain, to improve programmability as well as deliver performance for both general-purpose processors as well as accelerators like GPUs and FPGAs. In the context of compiling for FPGAs, HLS programming interfaces are an interesting level of abstraction to target, for DSL compilers and code generators. The approach we take in this paper is that of adding support for FPGA compilation in a DSL compiler by targeting the input interface of a HLS suite. There have been several recent efforts on building domain-specific languages and compilers for image processing pipelines [32, 16, 33, 23]. Darkroom [15] is a language embedded in Terra for describing image processing pipelines. Although Darkroom's approach extracts maximum reuse, it does not exploit degrees of data parallelism that could lead to a higher or maximal utilization of memory bandwidth or chip resources, as the case may be. Extracting data parallelism while allowing reuse of data between stages of the pipeline poses unique challenges, and we address these.

In this paper, we present an FPGA backend for PolyMage [30,

PACT '16, September 11–15, 2016, Haifa, Israel.

DOI: http://dx.doi.org/10.1145/2967938.2967969

23], a DSL for image processing pipelines, and study the potential for acceleration of image processing pipelines using FPGAs. Our approach first starts by exploiting the pipeline structure evident from the directed graph of image processing stages; it then replicates processing elements to exploit data parallelism in the filters until (a) either all of the memory bandwidth is utilized or (b) FPGA slices or other on-chip resources are exhausted. Irrespective of whether the kernel is compute-bound or memory bandwidth bound, we obtain designs with near-peak throughput in this manner. We take in PolyMage DSL as input and express our design in C++ code that serves as input to the Xilinx Vivado HLS compiler.

Our transformation and optimization approach is tailored to the domain of image processing pipelines considered, in particular, sequences of stencil-like operations on images. We will see that our transformations cannot be realized as a composition of traditional loop transformations – the latter have been considered by several existing FPGA compiler and HLS approaches [13, 12, 24, 11, 36, 5, 1, 31]. Thus, our DSL-based approach provides a level of abstraction much higher than that provided by generic HLS efforts, and automates a specialized optimization strategy.

The rest of this paper is organized as follows. Section 2 presents necessary background on image processing pipelines, FPGAs, and PolyMage. Section 3 and 4 describe our approach in detail. Related work is discussed in Section 6 and conclusions are presented in Section 7.

Figure 1: DAG representation of the Unsharp Mask pipeline. **Image credit:** Input image by Finlay Cox [38] (C) Copyright 2016 used under CC BY-SA 3.0 [8]; the output image is its sharpened form and is licensed under CC BY-SA 3.0 by Nitin Chugh.

2. BACKGROUND ON POLYMAGE

PolyMage is a domain-specific language (DSL) and compiler for automatic optimization of image processing pipelines. It supports optimization of pipelines where the filters are either point-wise, stencil, upsampling or downsampling operations. Other data-dependent operations and reductions are also supported but optimizations (fusion and tiling) are limited in the presence of such filters (to program parts that do not comprise such filters). PolyMage DSL is embedded in Python, i.e., it is an internal DSL. Optimized OpenMP C++ code can be generated for shared-memory parallel systems, typically, a multi-socket system with general-purpose multicore processors.

The PolyMage language is functional – each function corresponds to a stage in the pipeline. Functions in PolyMage (with the exception of reductions) are data parallel and apply on the entire set associated with the variables in the function's domain; the variables have corresponding intervals specified when defining the function. For brevity, we do not describe constructs that are not relevant to the remaining content of this paper. More detail can be found in [23]. Compiler transformation and code generation happens when the Python code is executed; the generated OpenMP/C++ code is compiled on-the-fly, and the compiled code can be used subsequently in the Python program or offline as an optimized routine.

PolyMage DSL code for an image processing algorithm, unsharp mask, is shown in Listing 1. Unsharp mask is an image sharpening technique, very commonly used in digital image processing systems. In signal processing context we can visualize unsharp mask as a filter that amplifies the high-frequency components of an input signal. The algorithm is expressed as a composition of four pipelined stages. The first two stages performs a Gaussian blur of the original input image along the x and the y directions subsequently. These stages are written using the PolyMage's `Stencil` construct. This construct takes as input, the point around which the stencil should be applied, a global weight for stencil output, and a stencil kernel with its weights specified using a list of lists. The third stage of unsharp mask computes a weighted sum of the resultant blur and outputs a sharpened image. The final stage chooses pixels, to be written to the output, between the original and the sharpened image, which is done in PolyMage using the `Select` construct. Sharpened pixels are chosen, upon the difference between the original and its blur image crossing a threshold value.

3. MAPPING TO PIPELINES ON FPGAS

This section describes our approach and primary contribution in detail. We describe our technique to map image processing pipelines to parallel implementations on the FPGA. We also show how we add this support into PolyMage's DSL compiler. A brief overview of our framework is given in Figure 2.

3.1 Parallelism and Reuse

Image processing pipelines exhibit several forms of parallelism that can be extracted on FPGAs. They can be classified into four categories. Most importantly, there exists *data parallelism* due to the application of the same operator on all the pixels of an image. This data parallelism can be exploited in a fine-grained manner or a coarse-grained manner. We discuss this choice a little later. Secondly, there exists parallelism that can be obtained by pipelining through the different stages or filters of the pipeline. We choose to extract this *inter-stage pipelined parallelism* in a fine-grained manner, which is clearly the right granularity for FPGAs. Thirdly, a filter that works on color images has to be applied to each of the channels of an image (three in case of RGB). This can be done in a completely parallel fashion if the filter computation at a point

```
# Params
R = Parameter(Int, "R")
C = Parameter(Int, "C")
thresh = Parameter(Float, "thresh")
weight = Parameter(Float, "weight")

# Vars
x = Variable(Int, "x")
y = Variable(Int, "y")
c = Variable(Int, "c")

# Input Image
img = Image(Float, "input", [3, R+4, C+4])

# Intervals
cr = Interval(Int, 0, 2, 1)
xrow = Interval(Int, 2, R+1, 1)
xcol = Interval(Int, 0, C+3, 1)
yrow = Interval(Int, 2, R+1, 1)
ycol = Interval(Int, 2, C+1, 1)

# Pipeline
blurx = Function([c, x, y], [cr, xrow, xcol],
                 Float, "blurx")
blurx.defn = [ Stencil(img(c, x, y), 1.0/16,
                       [[1], [4], [6], [4], [1]]) ]

blury = Function([c, x, y], [cr, yrow, ycol],
                 Float, "blury")
blury.defn = [ Stencil(blurx(c, x, y), 1.0/16,
                       [[1, 4, 6, 4, 1]]) ]

sharpen = Function([c, x, y], [cr, yrow, ycol],
                   Float, "sharpen")
sharpen.defn = [ img(c, x, y) * ( 1 + weight ) \
               + blury(c, x, y) * ( -weight ) ]

masked = Function([c, x, y], [cr, yrow, ycol],
                  Float, "mask")
absv = Abs((img(c, x, y) - blury(c, x, y)))
masked.defn = [ Select(Condition(absv, '<',thresh),
                       img(c, x, y),
                       sharpen(c, x, y) ) ]
```

Listing 1: PolyMage DSL code for Unsharp Mask

is performed independently for each of the individual channels, and extracting this *channel-level parallelism* is straightforward. Fourth, the single operator applied to produce an output pixel at any intermediate stage involves many computations (for example, a 3x3 convolution) and this computation exhibits a limited amount of parallelism. We leave this lower-level operator-level parallelism for the HLS synthesis tool to exploit – by guiding it via directives that we explain later in this section. Thus, our main challenge here is to exploit inter-stage pipelined parallelism and data parallelism efficiently. These two forms of parallelism also involve reuse of data. With data parallelism, input data is reused (for example, due to convolution widths), and producer-consumer reuse exists for inter-stage parallelism. We say that the exploited reuse is *maximal* if all uses of a produced value happen without the value being stored and reloaded from memory, i.e., input data is read and output data is written out while all intermediate data is produced and consumed on-chip. Due to limited off-chip bandwidth available to an FPGA, it is important to exploit reuse on the chip.

3.2 Dependences

User code written in PolyMage is translated into a directed acyclic graph (DAG) wherein each node corresponds to a stage of the pipeline and the edges represent the dependences

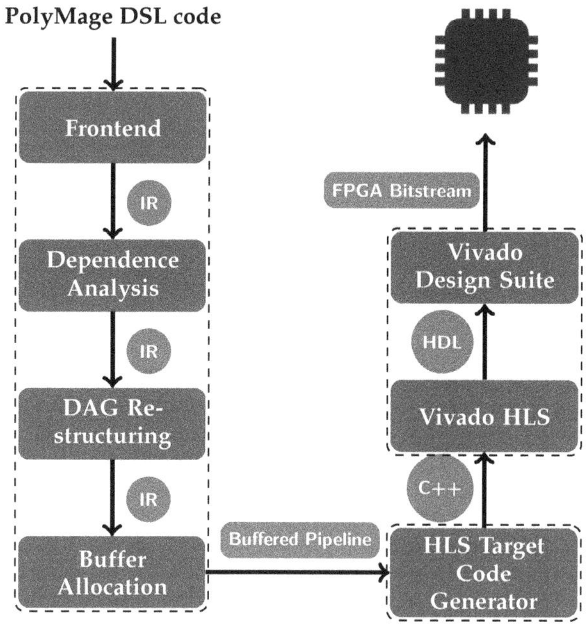

Figure 2: PolyMage high-level compilation for FPGAs

between the stages. Figure 1 shows the DAG associated with the Unsharp Mask program. The stage *img* is an idempotent operation which provides the input image to the subsequent consumer stages such as *blurx, sharpen* and *mask*. We associate with each edge of the DAG, a set of integral vectors similar to the traditional dependence vectors used in compiler analysis, but with a different notion. For example, the distance vector set associated with the edge $(blurx, blury)$ is $\{(0,0,i) | -2 \le i \le 2\}$ indicating that the computation of $blury(c,x,y)$ depends on the values $\{blurx(c,x,y+i) | -2 \le i \le 2\}$. Similarly, the distance vector set annotating the edge $(blury, sharpen)$ contains only one vector, $(0,0,0)$, as *sharpen* is a point-wise computation.

3.3 Structuring the Pipeline in Hardware

The pipeline compiler uses the DAG representation to topologically sort all the stages. Each stage of the pipeline is translated in to an equivalent C++ code using a *k*-way nested loop where *k* is the number of dimensions of the domain on which the corresponding stage acts. A *stream* or a *queue* is associated with every edge of the DAG. The stage at the source of an edge enqueues its output on to the associated stream, from which the destination stage dequeues during its computation. The dequeue and enqueue operations associated with a stream s are similar to $s.read()$ and $s.write()$ method calls. Such a streaming approach has two key advantages. Firstly, a stage need not wait for the completion of its predecessor stages. It can start computing an array location as soon as all the required inputs are available in its input streams. It thus follows the *data flow* model of computation. The second advantage is that the size of the intermediate buffer linking a producer and a consumer stage will be a function of the stencil structure as opposed to the total image size. For example, if the consumer stage is a point operation, the size of the intermediate buffer would be just a constant. Overall, when the entire C++ code generated by the hardware compiler is fed to a high-level synthesis compiler with appropriate direc-

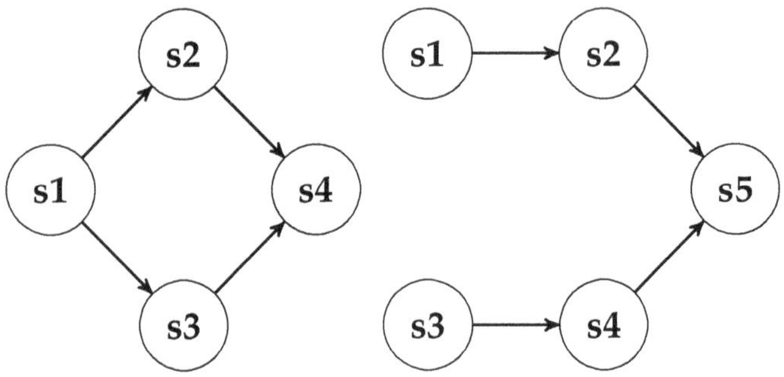

(a) (b)

Figure 3: DAGs representing non-linear pipelines

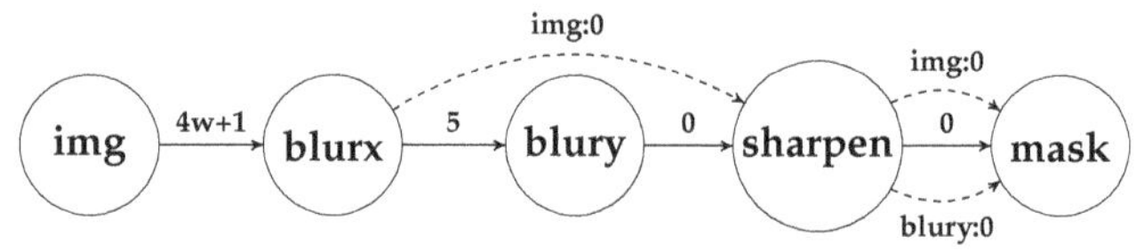

(a) DAG with initial buffer estimates

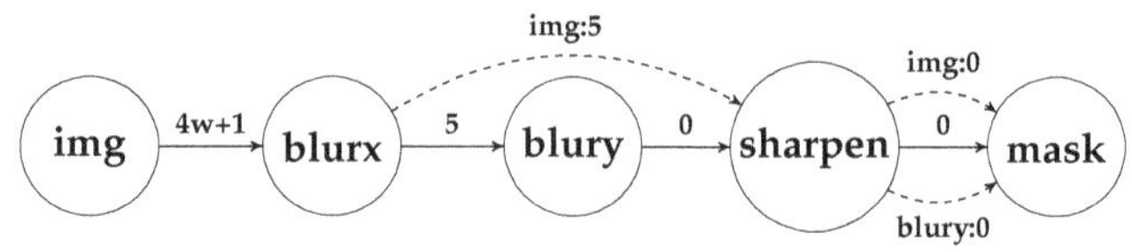

(b) DAG with final buffer requirements

Figure 4: DAG representing the auto-generated hardware pipeline. An edge label gives the buffer name and size. The source node of an edge gives the default buffer name.

tives, we get a pipelined hardware design where each stage of the pipeline corresponds to a node in the DAG.

Based on the above discussion, we observe that if a stage has k different successors, say $s_1, \cdots, s_k$, it has to write output on all k output streams. Such multiple write operations in a stage could become a bottleneck in the pipeline. We circumvent this problem by forwarding the data from a producer to a consumer via intermediate consumers, using them as relays. For example, in the Unsharp Mask program (Figure 1), the output of stage *blury* is consumed by stages *sharpen* and *mask*. Instead of *blury* creating two output streams, it just writes to one output stream that is read by the first consumer *sharpen*, which in turn forwards it to *mask*. Figure 4 shows how data from a producer stage is forwarded to a consumer stage in the Unsharp Mask program. The solid arrows indicate regular write operations whereas dashed arrows indicate data relay operations. For example, the dashed arrow between *sharpen* and *mask* with label *blury* indicates that *sharpen* is forwarding *blury* to *mask*.

Without loss of generality, assume that the consumer stages $s_1, \cdots, s_k$ occur in that order in the topologically sorted listing of the DAG stages. Then the data reaches the stage s_i through a sequence of $i-1$ stream copy operations going through the stages s_1 to s_{i-1}. This reduces the *write* load on the stage s from k to 1 by distributing it across all its consumers. Finally, since data is forwarded in a pipelined fashion, stage i can maintain a steady-state computation except for the initial idle cycles when it waits for the first set of required input data. This approach is an improvement over the Darkroom [15] technique wherein the data generated by a stage has to pass through all the intermediate stages in the linearized pipeline before it reaches a consumer stage. This leads to unnecessary increase in the line buffer size requirements which we avoid.

Non-linear Pipeline Structure.

As mentioned earlier, our framework follows a dataflow model of computation, wherein a stage can perform a computation as soon as the required input data is available. It even supports non-linear pipelines, as opposed to Darkroom [15] where the pipeline is completely linearized. So, given a DAG such as in Figure 3b, the stages s_1 and s_2 can perform their computations independent of the stages s_3 and s_4, and vice-versa. Between the stages s_1 and s_2 (s_3 and s_4), there will be pipelined parallelism. However, for the DAG in Figure 3a, although the stages s_2 and s_3 can execute in parallel, we introduce a false dependency between them to reduce the write load on the stage s_1. However, depending on the available memory bandwidth, such false dependences can be avoided. Our compiler framework allows for such design space exploration with ease.

3.4 Line Buffer Allocation

Each stage maintains a line buffer corresponding to each incoming input stream. Hence, if a stage has k input streams, it maintains k line buffers. The size of a line buffer depends on the stencil structure and the structure of the DAG. We compute the minimum size required for each line buffer in two steps.

In the first step, we use the distance vector set associated with an edge to estimate the line buffer size. Let $\vec{d} = \vec{d_u} - \vec{d_l}$ where $\vec{d_l}$ and $\vec{d_u}$ are the lexicographically smallest and largest distance vectors respectively. Assuming a two dimensional case, for the sake of simplicity, let $\vec{d} = (d_1, d_2)$. Then, the line buffer size is determined as $wd_1 + d_2 + 1$, where w is the image width. For example, in the case of *blury*, the size of the line buffer is five as its distance vector set is $\{(0,0,i) | -2 \leq i \leq 2\}$. Similarly in the case of *blurx*, the size of the line buffer is $4w+1$, where w is the image width, as the distance vector set is $\{(0,i,0) | -2 \leq i \leq 2\}$. Figure 4a shows the DAG representation of the Unsharp Mask program where the edges are annotated with the corresponding line buffer size estimates. These estimates define a lower bound on the buffer requirements, since for each dependence, we considered the producer and consumer stage in isolation from the rest of the DAG. For example in Figure 4a, the *sharpen* stage cannot start its computation until it gets data from the *blury* stage and the relayed *img* data from the *blurx* stage. The *blury* stage starts producing data only once its line buffer is full with the output of *blurx*; *img* data is however relayed to the *sharpen* stage without any delay. Hence, we need a minimum buffer size of five associated with the edge going from *blurx* to *sharpen*, to store *img* data until the first output of *blury* is available. In the second step, to find the exact buffer estimates, we increase the line buffer size between two stages by computing the longest path between them in the DAG wherein each edge has been annotated with the line buffer size estimates from the first step. Figure 4b shows the DAG for the Unsharp Mask program with revised line buffer size requirements.

A stage reads data from an input stream and moves it to the corresponding line buffer. Once all line buffers are full,

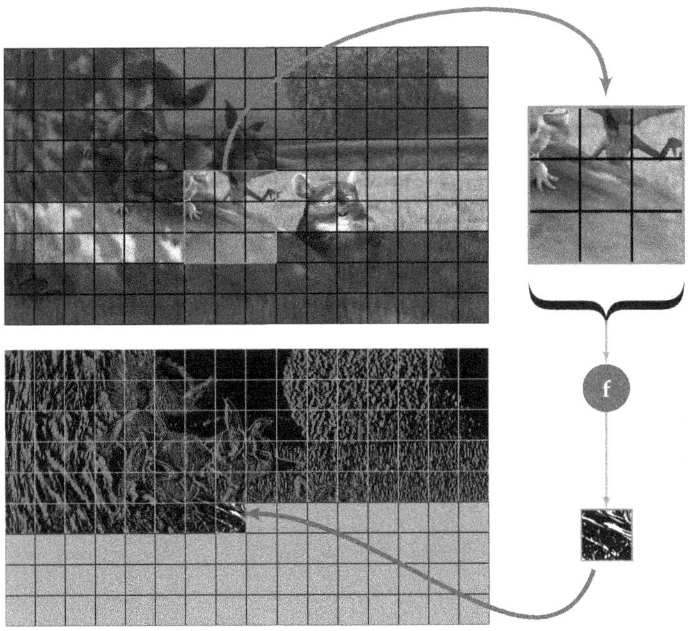

Figure 5: Input is read from a stream into a line buffer stored in BRAM. The current stencil window is stored in the shift registers. The output of the stage is enqueued into stream which feeds the next stage of the pipeline. Each image cell here conceptually represents an image pixel, the highlighted cells – the pixels in a line buffer. The window pixels are read by the stencil function **f**, a `Sobel` operator, to compute an output pixel. **Image credit:** The input image is a derivative of a still from the Big Buck Bunny movie (C) Copyright 2008 by Blender Foundation [4] used under the CC BY 3.0 license [7].

the stage can start computation and output data in a steady-state fashion. All line buffers are incrementally updated with data from respective input streams in each clock cycle. The amount of incremental update is a small constant depending on the stencil structure and size. For example, in *blurx* and *blury*, we perform five copy operations per incremental update. The line buffers are allocated memory in the FPGA block RAM (BRAM). Furthermore, the data points required for the current computation is moved from the line buffer to a window buffer by incrementally copying one column for every new pixel read into the line buffer. The memory for the window buffer is allocated on the shift registers. Figure 5 illustrates this approach for a single stage. If the memory requirement of a line buffer is small, such as in the case of the $(blurx, blury)$ edge, memory is allocated on the shift registers itself instead of BRAM.

3.4.1 *Discussion on Line Buffer Allocation and Scheduling*

Consider the DAG in Figure 6 wherein the label l_{ij} on an edge (s_i, s_j) indicates the minimum data required by the destination stage s_j from the corresponding source stage s_i. If the throughput of each stage is one pixel per clock cycle, then the stage s_5 can start its computation from clock cycle $w + 1$.

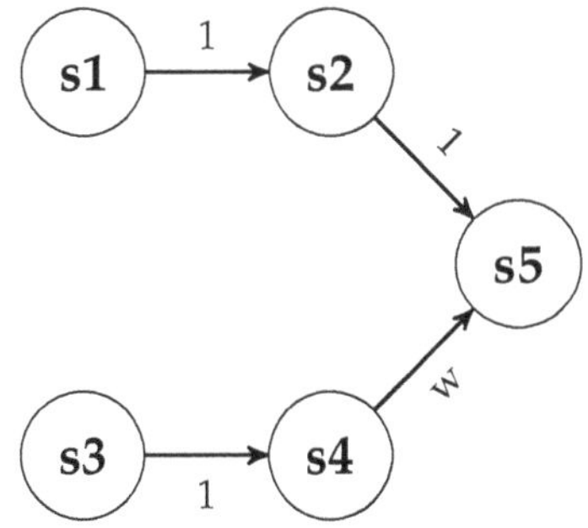

Figure 6: DAG illustrating issues in line buffer allocation

Meanwhile, the pixels generated by stage s_2 have to be accumulated on its output line buffer, and hence its size has to be at least w. We can avoid this extra line buffer usage by scheduling stage s_1 to start its computation in clock cycle $w - 1$.

This observation can be generalized to obtain a polynomial time algorithm to compute the line buffer sizes on all the DAG edges such that the sum total of memory allocated to all of them is minimized. This is accomplished by delaying the clock cycle at which each stage of the DAG starts computing by as much as possible without affecting the critical path. Let S be the set of source vertices (stages) whose in-degree is zero, and S' be the set of sink vertices whose out-degree is zero. Let e_s be the earliest clock cycle by which a stage s can start execution without violating dependences, i.e., by clock cycle e_s the entire required input data is available to stage s. Then $e_s = 0$ for all $s \in S$. For every other stage s in the DAG, $e_s = max_{p \in Pred(s)} (e_p + l_{ps})$ where $Pred(s)$ consists of all the stages whose output is consumed by stage s. We can compute all e_s values by making a *forward pass* on the stages of the DAG in the topologically sorted order. Then we make a *backward pass* on the DAG in reverse topological order to determine e'_s, which gives the last clock cycle to which the computation in stage s can be delayed without affecting the critical path leading to any of the sink nodes. For every $s \in S'$, $e'_s = e_s$. For every other stage s in the DAG, $e'_s = min_{p \in Succ(s)} (e'_p - l_{sp})$ where $Succ(s)$ consists of all stages which consume the output generated by stage s.

From the above discussion, we notice that the initial computational cycle of any stage can be shifted to any value in the range $[e_s, e'_s]$. If a stage s is in the critical path of any output sink stage, then $e_s = e'_s$ in that case. If we schedule the initial computation of each stage s in cycle e'_s, then the required line buffer size associated with a DAG edge (q, r) is $e'_r - e'_q$. In Figure 6, $e'_{s5} = w + 1$ and $e'_{s2} = w$, and hence the required size of the line buffer on the associated edge is one. Finally, if two source stages consume the same input image and their initial cycle shifts are different, then we either need more memory bandwidth to read the same input again or store it in an on-chip memory resource such as a line buffer for reuse. In the latter case, where we use a line buffer to store the input image for reuse, the savings obtained in other parts of the DAG pipeline structure gets consumed here. For example, in Figure 6, if both s_1 and s_3 are reading the same input image, we need to add a line buffer of size $w - 2$ before the stage s_1, in which the streamed input image pixels can be stored. This offsets the line buffer savings we obtained by shifting the initial computation cycle of stage s_2 to cycle w.

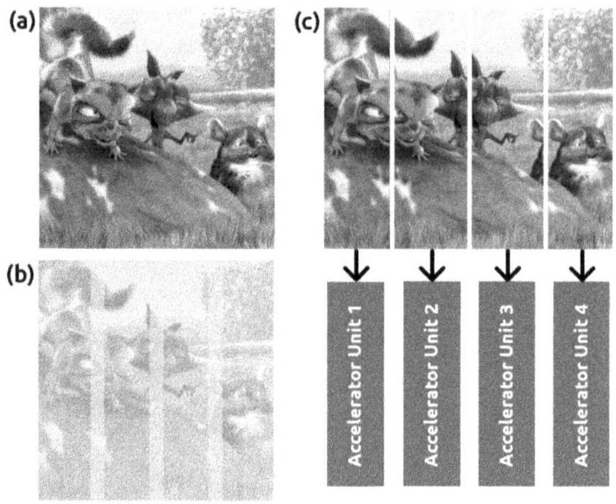

Figure 7: Partitioning computation in an overlapped manner. **Image credit:** This image is a derivative of a still from the Big Buck Bunny movie (C) Copyright 2008 by Blender Foundation [4] used under the CC BY 3.0 license [7].

3.5 Coarse-Grained Data Parallelism with Fusion

The approach described so far to generate FPGA implementations can only process one pixel per clock cycle and does not make use of available data parallelism. For example, each pixel output from the *blurx* stage can be computed in parallel from the input image instead of in a streaming/sequential fashion. High-speed serial transceiver technology or PCI-ex DMA provides FPGAs with communication interfaces capable of operating at high data rates and deliver multiple pixels per clock cycle as an aggregated bit vector, which we will refer to as a *data beat* in the rest of this section.

In order to further improve overall pixel throughput, we split the image vertically into partitions, where each vertical partition is fed into its corresponding streaming accelerator. Thus, pixels from different partitions are processed in parallel. The performance gain is thus limited only by either the external off-chip memory bandwidth or available on-chip resources.

Next, we avoid communication between accelerator units while processing boundary pixels using a realization of an existing technique for general-purpose parallelization called *overlapped tiling* [20]. This is shown in Figure 7. The vertical slices of the image being processed overlap at their boundaries, i.e., it is not a disjoint partitioning. Such an overlap is necessary to avoid communication when convolutions or stencil type filters are involved. The width of the overlap at the boundaries depends on the size of the convolution or the width of the stencil applied. The idea of performing redundant computation at the boundaries to avoid communication or cache misses has been used in several code generation approaches for CPUs and GPUs including [17, 39, 32, 23].

The architecture of the parallel implementation can be broken into multiple stages as shown in Figure 8. The first stage of the implementation is a *distributor* that assigns incoming data beats to buffer queues. From the buffer queues, data is consumed by *unpack units*, which extract pixels from data beats and forward them to accelerators. Usually, only a subset of pixels inside the data beat are required in the overlap region. Thus, the unpack units must extract only those pixels that belong to the iteration domain of the accelerators and contribute to the computation, rest are discarded. After processing, the output of the accelerators is packed into data beats by *pack units* and gathered by a *collector* in the same order as provided by the distributor. In effect, the data rate at the input and output will ideally match the combined processing rate of the accelerators. If an accelerator's throughput is q pixels per clock cycle and there are p such accelerator replicas, then we pack pq pixels per data beat to sustain the maximal pixel throughput under the constraints. For ideal load balancing, the input is ordered in a way such that it alternates between the pixels required by each accelerator, i.e., in the first data beat, pixels from the first image stripe are sent; in the second one, pixels from the second image slice, and so on.

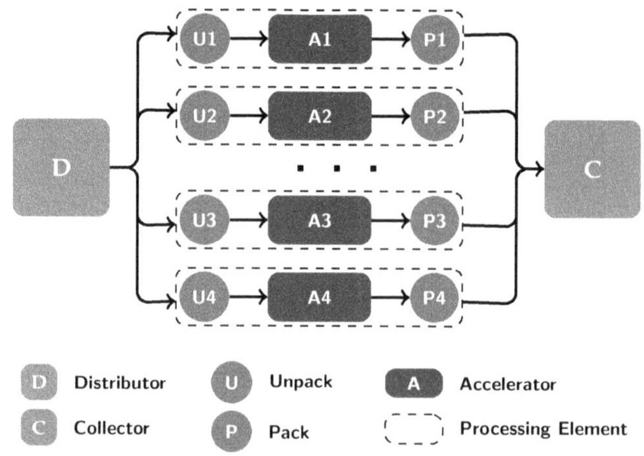

Figure 8: Architecture for parallel computation of image slices

Upsampling and downsampling operations are handled without any special additional techniques. If a scaled access with a scale factor of k or $1/k$ (k being an integer) is observed, instead of performing the calculation every iteration, it is performed every k iterations (or k operations are performed in 1 iteration when the scale factor is $1/k$).

4. OPTIMIZATIONS FOR HLS TARGET

In this section, we describe additional steps necessary to use a HLS software as a target.

4.1 Vivado Synthesis Directives

A central element of Vivado HLS is the synthesis directives, which allow us to specify how an input design is to be parallelized and optimized. These directives can be placed directly in the code as pragmas or written in a script file that is applied during synthesis. The few major directives that we use are for pipelining the innermost loops, array partitioning of the buffers, and specifying depth of FIFOs that interconnect the streaming pipeline stages. The other important directive we use is the DATAFLOW directive which specifies to the Vivado HLS compiler that the loops and functions can be processed as soon as their input is made available, and to not execute them sequentially. Our DSL compiler automatically annotates code with the appropriate directives as part of the code generation process.

4.2 Using Arbitrary Data Types

Software programmers often tend to use standard primitive data types like int, float for variables like loop counters and pixel data. For image processing applications, we rarely need the entire width of these types. Using more bits than required results in excessive resource utilization and can also degrade the maximum achievable clock frequency. Hence, we use arbitrary precision data types provided by Vivado HLS to ensure that our design always uses the optimal representation for variables — this reduces resource consumption and helps achieve shorter critical paths.

4.3 Transforming Kernels

A kernel in image processing is a matrix that on convolution with an image can achieve various effects like blurring, edge-detection, etc. This convolution in effect is a sum of products of the similarly positioned elements in the two matrices. In many cases, the floating point kernel coefficients can be given an integral representation and all arithmetic can be carried out in the integral domain reducing the number of required DSP units on an FPGA. The integral representation can be translated back to floating point representation in the last stage of computation.

If user-provided mask coefficients have fractional parts, our framework automatically transforms them into integers. This transformation is only applied if each coefficient can be scaled to a natural number when multiplied by a normalization factor N, where N is the inverse of the smallest coefficient (ensuring that the smallest coefficient is scaled to one). If the scaled coefficients are not natural numbers, they are rounded to the nearest natural number. Only if the rounding error is less than a certain threshold for all scaled coefficients, this optimization is applied; else the kernel transform is skipped to avoid inaccurate results.

4.4 Restructured HLS Code

We now show how our code generator restructures the code making it amenable for the HLS compiler to generate an efficient hardware design in Verilog/VHDL. We will also point out as to why writing such code by hand is non-trivial and tedious. We use the Unsharp Mask program from the Listing 1 as the running example here.

A standard way of implementing filters in hardware is through the use of a line buffer or a window buffer depending on the requirement. Assuming the input image is serialized in a row major order, pixel by pixel, the Gaussian blur along the horizontal direction just needs a sliding window buffer, as only the pixels equal to the size of the stencil are needed to be kept in memory at any point in time to perform the computation. The corresponding window buffer declaration with the variable name `blury_blurx_Wbuffer` can be obtained in the generated source code from the Listing 2. We use a line buffer when applying Gaussian blur along the vertical direction, as that requires us to store four lines of the input image. Ideally this needs a line buffer that can store pixels equal to $4 * image\_width + 1$. For ease of understanding, we declare a 2-d array for the line buffer with variable name and dimensions as `blurx_input_Lbuffer[5][MAX_C]` (refer Listing 2).

4.5 Discussion

Listing 2 shows the auto-generated C++ code from the Polymage Unsharp Mask program source. This is only a partial listing due to space constraints. The code for every pipeline

```
void pipeline_unsharp_mask(int_t R, int_t C, int_t
    thresh, int_t weight, hls::stream<int_t> &input,
    hls::stream<int_t> &mask)
{

 /* Stage 1 - Gaussian Blur Vertical */
 const int_t _ct0 = 3;
 const int_t _ct1 = (R+4);
 const int_t _ct2 = (C+4);
 hls::stream<data_t> blurx_out_stream("blurx_out_strm
     ");
 hls::stream<data_t> input_sharpen_stream("
     input_sharpen_strm");
 data_t blurx_input_LBuffer[5][MAX_C];;
 const int_t blurx_input_Coeff[5] = {1,4,6,4,1};
 const data_t blurx_input_N = 0.0625;
 for (int_t _ci0=0; _ci0<=(_ct0-1); _ci0=(_ci0+1)) {
  for (int_t _ci1=0; _ci1<=(_ct1-1); _ci1=(_ci1+1)) {
   for (int_t _ci2=0; _ci2<=(_ct2-1); _ci2=(_ci2+1))
       {
    data_t input_in_val = input.read();
    data_t out_val = 0;
    for (int_t i=0;i<5;i++) {
     data_t vwin_val=i<4?blurx_input_LBuffer[i][_ci2
         ]:input_in_val;
     out_val += vwin_val*blurx_input_Coeff[i];
     if (i>0) blurx_input_LBuffer[i-1][_ci2]=vwin_val
         ;
    }
    out_val*=blurx_input_N;
    if (_ci1>=4){
         if (_ci2>=2 && _ci2<=_ct2-2)
          input_sharpen_stream.write(
               blurx_input_LBuffer[2][_ci2]);
     blurx_out_stream.write(out_val);
    }
   }
  }
 }

 /* Stage 2 - Gaussian Blur Horizontal */
 const int_t _ct3=3;
 const int_t _ct4=R;
 const int_t _ct5=(C+4);
 hls::stream<data_t> blury_out_stream("blury_out_strm
     ");
 data_t blury_blurx_WBuffer[5];
 const int_t blury_blurx_Coeff[5] = {1,4,6,4,1};
 const data_t blury_blurx_N = 0.0625;
 for (int_t _ci3=0; _ci3<=(_ct3-1); _ci3=(_ci3+1)) {
  for (int_t _ci4=0; _ci4<=(_ct4-1); _ci4=(_ci4+1)) {
   for (int_t _ci5=0; _ci5<=(_ct5-1); _ci5=(_ci5+1))
       {
    data_t blurx_in_val=blurx_out_stream.read();
    data_t out_val=0;
    for (int_t i=0;i<5;i++){
     blury_blurx_WBuffer[i] = (i<(5-1))?
          blury_blurx_WBuffer[i+1]:blurx_in_val;
     out_val += blury_blurx_WBuffer[i]*
          blury_blurx_Coeff[i];
    }
    out_val*=blury_blurx_N;
    if (_ci5>=4) blury_out_stream.write(out_val);
   }
  }
 }

 /* Stage 3 - Sharpening */
 ...

 /* Stage 4 - Masking */
 ...
```

Listing 2: Auto-generated restructured HLS code for Unsharp Mask

stage consists of a set of data structure declarations and a nested loop that does the actual computation. In this implementation, we see that each pipeline stage, either consumes the input image or the outputs of the previous stages. Before providing this code to the HLS tool to generate a hardware implementation, we annotate the code with certain directives: two of the most important directives are *dataflow* and *pipeline*. The dataflow directive ensures that each stage is scheduled as soon as its required inputs are available, which gives us the desired parallel processing of different stages in a pipelined manner. The *pipeline* directive is used to further parallelize each stage internally — this exploits the operator-level parallelism mentioned in Section 3.1.

An important point is to ensure that for each stream, the number of pixels written are exactly the same as number of pixels read. For this the iteration domain for each stage is matched to the unified output domains of all its input stages. Also, it is necessary to ensure that the set of pixels written by the producer stage into a stream belong to the same location as expected by the consumer stage reading that stream. This becomes a non-trivial task, since these pixels are not array-indexed, but a flowing stream of data and there has to exist a lock-step synchronization between the producer and consumer stages to ensure correctness of the generated HLS code. For the example in Listing 2, we see that the iteration domain of stage 2 is [3,R,C+4] which is the output filtered domain of its input stage (Stage 1). Furthermore, when Stage 1 replicates the input stream for Stage 3, it is bounded by if conditionals to match the image domain that Stage 3 processes.

In this implementation, once all pipeline buffers are filled, a throughput of one data output per clock cycle can be achieved, which is optimal by manual design. Furthermore, if we treat this pipeline as a single accelerator unit of the parallel architecture in Figure 8, we can achieve a throughput of multiple data output per clock cycle. We will see in the next section that the upper bound on the number of PEs will be decided by the amount of memory bandwidth available, i.e., we run out of memory bandwidth before we hit the limit for any type of on-chip resource.

5. EXPERIMENTAL EVALUATION

To evaluate the effectiveness of our approach, we consider several standard image processing algorithms. Although these algorithms are well-known, they can vary in their implementations. Hence, we provide below a brief overview of the benchmarks used for evaluation.

5.1 Benchmarks

We briefly describe each of the benchmarks evaluated below. Versions of these benchmarks in C (both naive and optimized by PolyMage) are publicly available [29]. The number of stages in the DAGs representing the respective pipelines of these benchmarks are provided in Table 1 along with the number of lines of code required to express them in PolyMage DSL.

Unsharp Mask (USM) algorithm is actually used to sharpen an image. This is done by computing a weighted sum of the image and its blur at pixels where both differ significantly in intensity.

Harris Corner Detection (HC), first introduced by Harris and Stephens, consists of a complex image processing pipeline comprising local and point operators. The algorithm uses the Sobel operator to compute image gradients, Gaussian blur for smoothing, and computes a corner response map. This map is later used to pick corner points using a threshold.

Table 1: Benchmarks: number of stages in pipeline and lines of code in PolyMage DSL

Benchmark	Stages	LOC
HC	11	43
USM	4	16
OF	15	75
DUS	4	50

Optical Flow (OF) is the distribution of apparent velocities of objects in an image. Our implementation uses the Horn-Schunck method [19] to iteratively solve for the estimates of optical flow from one image to another, assuming that it is smooth over the entire image. This benchmark involves a total of 15 stages in the pipeline, out of which the last five stages are run for four iterations.

Downsampling and Upsampling (DUS): The original image is sampled down to half the original resolution along both the dimensions. The smaller image thus obtained is interpolated to get back an approximation of the original.

5.2 Experimental Setup

The FPGA results were obtained using the Xilinx Vivado Design Suite version 2015.2 for a Xilinx Virtex-7 690T FPGA. The code for the algorithm specification was synthesized using Vivado HLS, and Post Place and Route (PPnR) characteristics were obtained using the Vivado Design Suite 2015.2. For the evaluation, we used 24-bit floating point data types, where 12 bits are used to store the fractional part and the remaining 12 bits for the integral part. Images used are color images (3-channel RGB) of size 1920 x 1080, except for Harris corner detection, which takes a grayscale image as input. The throughput and latency results reported in this section are obtained by post place and route simulations using the Xilinx Vivado tool.

5.3 Performance Analysis

Table 2 shows resource usage of the generated designs on a Virtex-7 FPGA. Results with one and four PEs are shown to demonstrate scalability with more PEs. In Table 3, the reported designs have processing elements that are 3-way parallel in addition — to compute on all three channels of an image concurrently. On the other hand, designs of Table 2 are for grayscale images or a single channel. Note that several image processing algorithms (like HC) operate on grayscale input. The results also show the amount of external I/O bandwidth needed. Assuming a 16-lane PCI-express 3.0 interface, the peak theoretical bandwidth available is 15.76 GB/s ($16 * 985$ MB/s). If we use a sustainable bandwidth estimate of 9.9 GB/s (measured using NVIDIA CUDA's bandwidth test sample), we observe that the amount of bandwidth that can be sustained in each direction is four times the bandwidth required for the listed designs (in Table 2), i.e., 16 PEs can be accommodated for each of the designs reported. Similarly, for the designs in Table 3, five PEs can be accommodated. We also note that these designs utilize a small fraction of the resources of a modern FPGA such as Virtex-7 690T (cf. Table 2 last column). Hence, the entire off-chip band-

Table 2: Post place and route results comparing resource requirements and throughput achieved when using a single PE and when using 4 PEs, where each PE processes a single channel

Benchmark	Clock period (nanoseconds)		Latency (milliseconds)		Slices		LUT		BRAM		DSP		Throughput (MPixels/s)		Bandwidth (MB/s)		Virtex-7 690T slices used
	1 PE	4 PEs	1 PE	4 PEs	1 PE	4 PEs	1 PE	4 PEs	1 PE	4 PEs	1 PE	4 PEs	1 PE	4 PEs	1 PE	4 PEs	for 4 PEs
USM	2.990	3.643	18.6	5.85	352	2,500	751	6,883	4	16	0	0	115	357	345	1071	2.30%
HC	2.880	3.429	5.95	1.83	1,161	5,422	1,902	11,314	22	56	21	60	351	1133	351	1133	5.00%
OF	3.208	3.827	19.9	6.09	1,923	8,386	3,928	19,922	46	60	28	112	108	345	324	1035	7.74%
DUS	3.047	3.446	19.0	5.39	401	2,352	811	6,115	12	20	0	0	115	386	345	1158	2.17%

Table 3: Post place and route results comparing resource requirements and throughput achieved when using a single PE, and when using 2 PEs, where each PE processes 3 channels in parallel; throughput is in MegaPixels/sec

Benchmark	Clock period (ns)		Latency (ms)		Slices		LUT		FF		BRAM		DSP		Throughput	
	1 PE	2 PEs	1 PE	2 PEs	1 PE	2 PEs	1 PE	2 PEs	1 PE	2 PEs	1 PE	2 PEs	1 PE	2 PEs	1 PE	2 PEs
USM	3.127	3.182	6.48	3.32	1,279	2,431	2,794	6,342	3,266	6,268	12	24	0	0	323	627
OF	3.135	3.27	6.48	3.41	6,036	13,023	12,128	28,022	18,747	44,440	162	180	93	186	320	620
DUS	2.855	3.126	5.92	3.36	1,277	2,572	2,681	6,177	3,970	7,860	36	42	0	0	352	620

Table 4: Comparison with Xilinx's OpenCV library for Vivado HLS

Benchmark	Xilinx OpenCV		PolyMage-FPGA (1 PE)		Speedup
	Latency (ms)	LUTs	Latency (ms)	LUTs	
HC	8.67	2,180	5.95	1,902	1.45×
USM	10.23	10,936	6.48	2,794	1.59×

Table 5: Estimated performance (execution time) on a Xilinx Virtex-7 690T FPGA (with PCIex 3.0 connectivity) and comparison with an optimized and tuned reference implementation on a 16-core (2-socket) Intel Xeon E5-2680 (SandyBridge)

Benchmark	PolyMage-CPU-naive		PolyMage-CPU-opt		PolyMage-FPGA	Estimated speedup over
	1 core	16 cores	1 core	16 cores	(16 PEs on Virtex-7 690T)	PolyMage-CPU-opt
HC	35.25 ms	6.97 ms	15.39 ms	1.51 ms	0.53 ms	2.85×
USM	36.92 ms	11.0 ms	19.12 ms	1.72 ms	1.62 ms	1.06×
OF	303.6 ms	162.9 ms	186.8 ms	38.96 ms	2.50 ms	15.60×
DUS	16.07 ms	3.54 ms	16.23 ms	1.47 ms	1.40 ms	1.05×

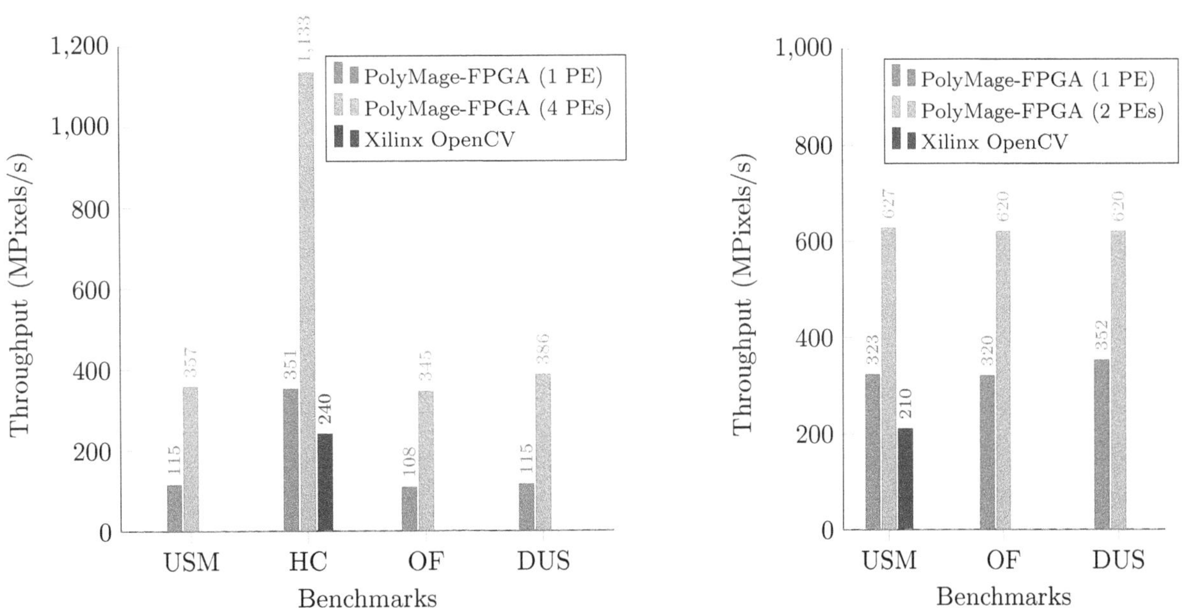

(a) single channel (b) three channels

Figure 9: Throughput obtained with various FPGA designs (in million pixels/s)

width is saturated before all on-chip FPGA resources can be utilized, i.e., the designs are bandwidth-bound.

5.4 Comparison with Xilinx OpenCV Library

We also compare with Xilinx's OpenCV library for Vivado HLS. The Xilinx OpenCV library is expected to have manually optimized and tuned FPGA implementations of commonly used image processing functions, and it thus serves as an optimized reference implementation for FPGAs. We were able to perform this comparison for Harris Corner Detection and Unsharp Mask – for the former, the library include a routine, while for the latter, we had to write it by composing simpler routines from the library. Table 4 shows the comparison of the designs; we use the single PE version of PolyMage-FPGA to provide a level comparison with respect to chip resources used. We observe that designs generated by us even outperform such pre-optimized library routines; these routines are also known to optimize across stencils kernels in the pipeline. Without access to the sources and the underlying implementation details, we are unable to comment on the reasons for the better performance.

5.5 Comparison with Multicore CPUs

In order to place the performance of these FPGA designs in relation to general-purpose multicores, we compare with highly optimized and tuned codes generated by PolyMage for general-purpose multicore systems. This comparison is shown in Table 5. PolyMage generated code for the CPU was compiled using Intel C/C++ compiler 15.0 with flags "-O3 -xHost", and executed on a dual socket 16-core Intel Xeon E5-2680 2.70 GHz (Intel SandyBridge-based) server. Note that the performance reported is the execution time per image in a steady-state mode where input and output are continuously being streamed in and out respectively. A trend that we observe is that the acceleration with FPGAs is higher for benchmarks with deeper pipelines — this is as expected. Significant acceleration is obtained for Harris corner and Optical flow benchmarks.

5.6 Summary

Figure 9 compares throughput obtained by various FPGA implementations expressed in millions of pixels processed per second. The results demonstrate the effectiveness of our approach. Although a direct experimental comparison with the approaches of Darkroom [15] or HIPAcc [16] is not possible, both of these approaches do not extract coarse-grained data parallelism that we do through multiple PEs; hence, we expect the performance obtained by Darkroom and HIPAcc to be of the order of our single PE case. A comparative discussion is provided in Section 6.

6. RELATED WORK

Halide [32], Darkroom [15], PolyMage [23], Forma [33], and HIPAcc [22, 16] are recent DSL compilation efforts aimed to improve productivity and simultaneously deliver high performance. While the Halide DSL uses a scheduling language that allows a programmer to obtain high performance code in a semi-automatic manner, Forma and PolyMage attempt to arrive at schedules completely automatically although using very different transformation strategies. None of these approaches consider targeting FPGAs. HIPAcc [16] focuses on programmability and the ability to target accelerators (GPUs and Xeon Phi), and provides relatively little detail on transformations that enhance reuse and parallelism. Although our approach provides a mapping and code generation strategy for FPGAs for PolyMage, the developed techniques are equally applicable to the other image processing DSLs. FPGA backends have been developed for Darkroom [15] and HIPAcc that we will compare with below.

Darkroom [15] is a recent effort on compiling image processing pipelines to FPGAs. The Darkroom compiler directly maps programs written in the Darkroom language into line-buffered pipelines with all intermediate data stored on chip. Although this approach extracts maximal reuse, it does not exploit degrees of data parallelism, either in a fine-grained or coarse-grained manner. Whenever a larger amount of external memory bandwidth is available via PCI-express or another interconnect, exploiting such additional parallelism will also lead to a greater utilization of available chip resources (slices and block RAM). For the experimental results reported by Hegarty et al.[15], although the designs therein were memory bandwidth bound, had much higher bandwidth been available, not all of it would have been utilized. In addition, Darkroom currently only supports compositions of pointwise and stencil type filters. In addition to these, our approach is able to deal with multiscale computations as well. The FPGA backend support for HIPAcc [34] targets a C-based HLS like ours, but has the same limitations that we mentioned for Darkroom above.

There have been several HLS approaches that are able to apply high-level compiler transformations including loop transformations such as loop fusion, tiling, unrolling, and pipelining to aid HLS. The key optimization that drives the domain-specific approach presented in this paper is that of overlapped tiling of multiple fused stages by performing redundant computation at the boundaries. The idea of performing redundant computation at the boundaries to avoid communication or cache misses, or to aid local buffering has been used in several automatic code generation approaches including [17, 39, 32, 23] for CPUs or GPUs. Such an optimization cannot be realized as a composition of loop fusion and other traditional loop transformations performed by existing FPGA compiler approaches like ROCCC [13], StreamC [12], SA-C [24] and many others [35, 9, 36, 5, 1, 31]. The redundant computation introduced at the boundaries is necessary to break the dependence between two adjacent tiles, achieving both coarse-grained parallelization and locality after fusion. In addition, memory for the tiles need to be re-allocated for overlapped tiling – it is tedious to analyze or perform such a transformation starting from C code or any other languages where memory / memory allocation has not been abstracted away from the programmer. PolyMage input leaves memory allocation completely to the compiler – one of our motivations behind using a DSL. Without the overlapped tiling, the fused loops for a sequence of stencils would be sequential, and coarse-grained data parallelism cannot be exploited.

There are more generic compiler-based approaches to address problems associated with design space exploration and mapping to FPGAs or accelerators with similar resource constraints [9, 35, 11, 36, 5, 1, 31]. Alias et al. [1] address generation of off-chip communication code to maximize reuse on the FPGA and hide communication costs by pipelining. Their approach primarily deals with precise determination of communication sets (to maximize on-chip reuse), once a loop tiling and other polyhedral transformations have been applied for a coarse-grained mapping. Pouchet et al. [31] developed a design space exploration approach by leveraging polyhedral loop transformations – effectively studying the impact of loop transformations on factors such as communication volume and on-chip memory utilization, and thus reuse. In contrast to all of these works that are more generic, our approach is domain-specific and customized not just to the computation patterns in context but to the particular parallelization strategy employed. For example, a standard loop tiling does not involve redundant computation while our mapping approach does exploit it to provide a better mapping for parallelism, locality, and simplified on-chip scratchpad access. A domain-specific approach thus simplifies the mapping choice and code generation, as is usually the case with other efforts on high-performance DSL compilation.

NI LabView [10] and MATLAB HDL coder [21] are frameworks that provide a high-level design language with an interactive environment to target FPGAs, besides other architectures. Several OpenCL-based and CUDA-based HLS frameworks [26, 28] exist to compile explicitly parallel languages to VHDL/Verilog. Although all of these HLS frameworks aim to improve programmability, we found C-based HLS tools that provided dataflow style primitives to be the right abstraction for our DSL code generator to target. Although C is used as input by such HLS tools, we have been able to easily realize dataflow style designs (as opposed to Von Neumann style architectures) by using the right constructs and directives (in this case provided by Xilinx Vivado) through our DSL approach.

There has been work on compiling high-level streaming languages or streaming applications to streaming hardware designs on FPGAs [18, 14]. The space of optimization and design choices is different from that involved in image processing since streams are one-dimensional while image processing pipelines involve parallelism and reuse along typically two dimensions.

7. CONCLUSIONS

We described a domain-specific high-level synthesis (HLS) approach to accelerate image processing pipelines using FPGAs. Our approach is implemented in the compiler for the PolyMage domain-specific language and uses existing vendor HLS as its target. Our mapping technique exploits all available reuse and maximal parallelism under the constraints of available off-chip memory bandwidth and chip resources. When compared to other state-of-the-art approaches to map image processing pipelines to FPGAs, our approach (a) leads to designs that deliver significantly higher throughput, and (b) supports a greater variety of image processing filters than the state-of-the-art. Furthermore, our designs perform even faster (by a factor of 1.5× on average) than corresponding pre-optimized FPGA implementations from vendor-supplied libraries.

Acknowledgments

We would like to thank Google for an unrestricted research gift under the Google Faculty Research Awards program in 2015.

8. REFERENCES

[1] C. Alias, A. Darte, and A. Plesco. Optimizing remote accesses for offloaded kernels: application to high-level synthesis for FPGA. In *International workshop on Polyhedral Compilation Techniques (IMPACT)*, 2012.

[2] J. Auerbach, D. F. Bacon, I. Burcea, P. Cheng, S. J. Fink, R. Rabbah, and S. Shukla. A compiler and runtime for heterogeneous computing. In *Design Automation Conference*, pages 271–276, 2012.

[3] D. F. Bacon, R. M. Rabbah, and S. Shukla. FPGA programming for the masses. *Commun. ACM*, 56(4):56–63, 2013.

[4] Blender Foundation. Big Buck Bunny, 2008. The movie. http://www.bigbuckbunny.org/ License: CC BY 3.0 https://creativecommons.org/licenses/by/3.0/.

[5] U. Bondhugula, J. Ramanujam, and P. Sadayappan. Automatic mapping of nested loops to FPGAs. In *ACM SIGPLAN PPoPP*, Mar. 2007.

[6] J. M. Cardoso and D. P. C. *Compilation Techniques for Reconfigurable Architectures*. Springer US, 2009.

[7] Creative Commons Attribution 3.0 license (CC BY 3.0). https://creativecommons.org/licenses/by/3.0/.

[8] Creative Commons Attribution-ShareAlike 3.0 license (CC BY-SA 3.0). https://creativecommons.org/licenses/by-sa/3.0/.

[9] A. Darte, R. Schreiber, B. R. Rau, and F. Vivien. A Constructive Solution to the Juggling Problem in Processor Array Synthesis. In *IPDPS*, pages 815–822, 2000.

[10] C. Dase, J. Falcon, and B. MacCleery. Motorcycle control prototyping using an FPGA-based embedded control system. *Control Systems, IEEE*, 26(5):17–21, 2006.

[11] P. C. Diniz, M. W. Hall, J. Park, B. So, and H. Ziegler. Bridging the Gap between Compilation and Synthesis in the DEFACTO System. In *LCPC*, pages 52–70, 2001.

[12] M. B. Gokhale, J. M. Stone, J. Arnold, and M. Kalinowski. Stream-oriented FPGA computing in the Streams-C high level language. In *IEEE symposium on Field-Programmable Custom Computing Machines*, pages 49–56, 2000.

[13] Z. Guo, W. Najjar, and B. Buyukkurt. Efficient hardware code generation for FPGAs. *ACM Trans. Archit. Code Optim.*, 5(1):6:1–6:26, May 2008.

[14] A. Hagiescu, W.-F. Wong, D. Bacon, and R. Rabbah. A computing origami: Folding streams in FPGAs. In *ACM/IEEE Design Automation Conference*, pages 282–287, 2009.

[15] J. Hegarty, J. Brunhaver, Z. DeVito, J. Ragan-Kelley, N. Cohen, S. Bell, A. Vasilyev, M. Horowitz, and P. Hanrahan. Darkroom: Compiling high-level image processing code into hardware pipelines. *ACM Trans. Graph.*, 33(4):144:1–144:11, 2014.

[16] The Heterogeneous Image Processing Acceleration Framework. http://hipacc-lang.org/.

[17] J. Holewinski, L.-N. Pouchet, and P. Sadayappan. High-performance code generation for stencil computations on GPU architectures. In *International conference on Supercomputing*, pages 311–320, 2012.

[18] A. Hormati, M. Kudlur, S. Mahlke, D. Bacon, and R. Rabbah. Optimus: Efficient realization of streaming applications on FPGAs. In *2008 International Conference*

on Compilers, Architectures and Synthesis for Embedded Systems (CASES), pages 41–50, 2008.

[19] B. K. P. Horn and B. G. Schunck. Determining optical flow. *Artif. Intell.*, 17(1-3):185–203, 1981.

[20] S. Krishnamoorthy, M. Baskaran, U. Bondhugula, J. Ramanujam, A. Rountev, and P. Sadayappan. Effective Automatic Parallelization of Stencil Computations. In *ACM SIGPLAN conference on Programming Languages Design and Implementation*, 2007.

[21] MATLAB HDL Coder. The MathWorks Inc. http://in.mathworks.com/products/hdl-coder//.

[22] R. Membarth, O. Reiche, F. Hannig, J. Teich, M. Körner, and W. Eckert. Hipacc: A domain-specific language and compiler for image processing. *IEEE Trans. Parallel Distrib. Syst.*, 27(1):210–224, 2016.

[23] R. T. Mullapudi, V. Vasista, and U. Bondhugula. Polymage: Automatic optimization for image processing pipelines. In *International Conference on Architectural Support for Programming Languages and Operating Systems (ASPLOS)*, pages 429–443, 2015.

[24] W. A. Najjar, W. Böhm, B. A. Draper, J. Hammes, R. Rinker, J. R. Beveridge, M. Chawathe, and C. Ross. High-level language abstraction for reconfigurable computing. *Computer*, 36(8):63–69, Aug. 2003.

[25] R. S. Nikhil and Arvind. What is bluespec? *SIGDA Newsl.*, 39(1):1–1, Jan. 2009.

[26] M. Owaida, N. Bellas, K. Daloukas, and C. Antonopoulos. Synthesis of platform architectures from OpenCL programs. In *IEEE Field-Programmable Custom Computing Machines (FCCM)*, pages 186–193, May 2011.

[27] P. R. Panda. Systemc: A modeling platform supporting multiple design abstractions. In *14th International symposium on Systems Synthesis*, pages 75–80, 2001.

[28] A. Papakonstantinou, K. Gururaj, J. A. Stratton, D. Chen, J. Cong, and W. W. Hwu. Efficient compilation of CUDA kernels for high-performance computing on FPGAs. *ACM Trans. Embedded Comput. Syst.*, 13(2):25, 2013.

[29] PolyMage benchmarks, 2015. https://github.com/bondhugula/polymage-benchmarks.

[30] PolyMage: A DSL and compiler for automatic optimization of image processing pipelines, 2015. http://mcl.csa.iisc.ernet.in/polymage.html.

[31] L. Pouchet, P. Zhang, P. Sadayappan, and J. Cong. Polyhedral-based data reuse optimization for configurable computing. In *ACM/SIGDA International symposium on FPGAs*, pages 29–38, 2013.

[32] J. Ragan-Kelley, C. Barnes, A. Adams, S. Paris, F. Durand, and S. Amarasinghe. Halide: a language and compiler for optimizing parallelism, locality, and recomputation in image processing pipelines. In *ACM SIGPLAN conference on Programming Languages Design and Implementation*, pages 519–530, 2013.

[33] M. Ravishankar, J. Holewinski, and V. Grover. Forma: A dsl for image processing applications to target gpus and multi-core cpus. In *8th Workshop on General Purpose Processing Using GPUs*, pages 109–120, 2015.

[34] O. Reiche, M. Schmid, F. Hannig, R. Membarth, and J. Teich. Code generation from a domain-specific language for C-based HLS of hardware accelerators. In *2014 International Conference on Hardware/Software Codesign and System Synthesis*, pages 17:1–17:10, 2014.

[35] R. Schreiber, S. Aditya, S. Mahlke, V. Kathail, B. R. Rau, D. Cronquist, and M. Sivaraman. PICO-NPA: High-Level synthesis of non-programmable hardware accelerators. *J. VLSI Signal Process. Syst.*, 31(2):127–142, 2002.

[36] B. So, M. W. Hall, and P. C. Diniz. A compiler approach to fast hardware design space exploration in FPGA-based systems. In *ACM SIGPLAN conference on Programming Languages Design and Implementation*, pages 165–176, 2002.

[37] C. B. Spear. *SystemVerilog for Verification: A Guide to Learning the Testbench Language Features*. Springer, 2nd edition, 2010.

[38] Adult tortoise, 2016. Finlay Cox. http://www.pasthorizonspr.com/wp-content/uploads/2016/02/tortoise.jpg License: CC BY-SA 3.0 https://creativecommons.org/licenses/by-sa/3.0/.

[39] X. Zhou, J.-P. Giacalone, M. J. Garzarán, R. H. Kuhn, Y. Ni, and D. Padua. Hierarchical overlapped tiling. In *International symposium on Code Generation and Optimization*, pages 207–218, 2012.

Automatically Exploiting Implicit Pipeline Parallelism from Multiple Dependent Kernels for GPUs

Gwangsun Kim, Jiyun Jeong, John Kim
KAIST
{gskim, cjy9037, jjk12}@kaist.ac.kr

Mark Stephenson
NVIDIA
mstephenson@nvidia.com

ABSTRACT

Execution of GPGPU workloads consists of different stages including data I/O on the CPU, memory copy between the CPU and GPU, and kernel execution. While GPU can remain idle during I/O and memory copy, prior work has shown that overlapping data movement (I/O and memory copies) with kernel execution can improve performance. However, when there are multiple dependent kernels, the execution of the kernels is serialized and the benefit of overlapping data movement can be limited. In order to improve the performance of workloads that have multiple dependent kernels, we propose to automatically overlap the execution of kernels by exploiting implicit pipeline parallelism. We first propose *Coarse-grained Reference Counting-based Scoreboarding (CRCS)* to guarantee correctness during overlapped execution of multiple kernels. However, CRCS alone does not necessarily improve overall performance if the thread blocks (or CTAs) are scheduled sequentially. Thus, we propose an alternative CTA scheduler – *Pipeline Parallelism-aware CTA Scheduler (PPCS)* that takes available pipeline parallelism into account in CTA scheduling to maximize pipeline parallelism and improve overall performance. Our evaluation results show that the proposed mechanisms can improve performance by up to 67% (33% on average). To the best of our knowledge, this is one of the first work that enables overlapped execution of multiple *dependent* kernels without any kernel modification or explicitly expressing dependency by the programmer.

Keywords

GPGPU; Pipeline parallelism; Overlapping Kernels; Thread Block Scheduling

1. INTRODUCTION

GPUs have been widely used in various domains to accelerate data-parallel workloads. While significant research effort has been made to improve the performance and efficiency of GPUs, relatively little research has been done to reduce the overhead of non-kernel portions of GPGPU workloads. The overhead mainly consists of two different components – accessing I/O devices (e.g., HDD, SSD, or network card), and memory copy between host and device memory. The time spent on accessing I/O devices to initialize input data or storing results can significantly outweigh the memory copy overhead since I/O devices provide much lower bandwidth than the PCIe bus (for discrete GPUs) or on-chip bus (for integrated GPUs). Even the state-of-the-art SSD has ~3.2× lower bandwidth than PCIe 3.0 x16 (and 16-40× lower than NVLink).[1] Thus, in a typical usage scenario, where input data are read from HDD or SSD to host memory and then copied to device memory, the time for I/O device access will surpass the time for memory copy. Furthermore, integrated GPUs with unified main memory for CPU and GPU [23] can eliminate the memory copy overhead and make the I/O overhead even more significant. The I/O overhead can be mitigated by overlapping the kernel execution with I/O device access. GPUfs [30] and GPUnet [21] enable file and network access within a kernel, respectively, and HSA (Heterogeneous System Architecture) [23] can also provide similar functionality.

However, prior work [30, 21] results in little improvement for many workloads that have multiple kernels with inter-kernel dependencies – 20 out of 30 workloads from the Rodinia [10] and Parboil [34] benchmark suites combined have such characteristics. Under the current bulk-synchronous programming model, implicit synchronization barriers exist between dependent kernels to prevent data hazards and guarantee correct execution. As a result, while execution of the first kernel can be overlapped with input file access (or I/O), the subsequent kernels cannot start execution until the first kernel is finished due to possible dependency. If there are many kernels, only the first kernel can be overlapped with the I/O device access, resulting in minimal overall performance improvement.

Overlapping multiple kernels with I/O device access and appropriately leveraging pipeline parallelism that exists between the dependent kernels can result in a significant improvement in performance. However, currently available manual optimization methods to leverage pipeline parallelism among kernels pose a significant challenge. While optimizing a workload with a *single* kernel to achieve such an overlap can be relatively straightforward by using CUDA

[1]The sequential read bandwidth of Intel SSD DC P3608 series [1] is up to 5 GB/s whereas the bandwidth of PCIe 3.0 x16 is 15.75 GB/s. The NVLink can provide approximately 80 to 200 GB/s of bandwidth between CPU and GPU [13].

PACT '16, September 11-15, 2016, Haifa, Israel
© 2016 ACM. ISBN 978-1-4503-4121-9/16/09...$15.00
DOI: http://dx.doi.org/10.1145/2967938.2967952

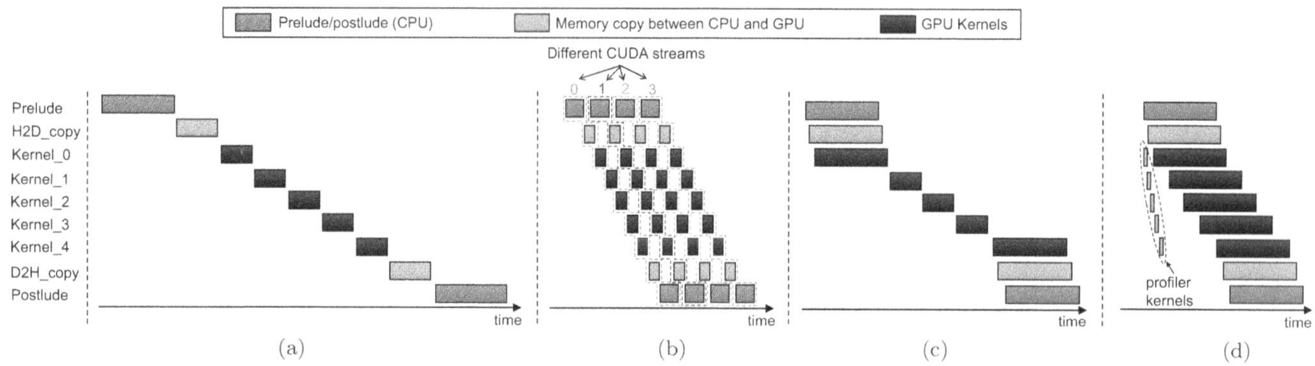

Figure 1: Timeline diagram of (a) baseline execution with no optimization, (b) manually optimized workload execution with dependency tracking by the programmer, (c) execution with the state-of-the-art approaches, and (d) our proposed approach (CRCS and PPCS) combined with the existing approaches.

streams [32, 28], for workloads with *multiple* dependent kernels, splitting each kernel into separate kernels can drastically increase the complexity of the dynamic dependency tracking that needs to be done by the programmer. With multiple streams, there can be *intra*-stream and *inter*-stream dependencies for complex workloads, but the CUDA runtime only checks intra-stream dependencies. Thus, the programmer has to manually manage the *inter*-stream dependencies, which requires a significant programmer effort. Task-parallel languages [33] have been proposed as an alternative to better exploit the high parallelism in GPUs, but they still require additional programmer effort. Although they provide high-level APIs to aid synchronization and communication between tasks, dependency information still needs to be *explicitly* expressed by the programmer. On the other hand, enabling *implicit* pipeline parallelism for CUDA and OpenCL, which are currently the de facto standard for GPU computing, can achieve high performance without degrading programmability.

In this work, we propose a novel, hardware-software-based approach to automatically exploit implicit pipeline parallelism from multiple dependent kernels of GPGPU workloads without any kernel modification by the programmer. Since our approach moves dynamic dependency tracking into hardware, the programmer does not have to manage dependencies nor modify existing CUDA or OpenCL kernels. By combining our mechanisms with existing approaches that overlap a kernel with I/O access (e.g., GPUfs [30] or GPUnet [21]), the multiple dependent kernels can be overlapped with I/O device access, resulting in a significant overall speedup.

In order to avoid data hazards while overlapping dependent kernels, we propose a lightweight, profiler-assisted dependency tracking mechanism on the GPU. The profiler is automatically generated at compile time as a kernel from the original kernel code by a source-to-source translator and executed on the GPU. The profiler uses a sampling method [20] to determine the bounds of the memory addresses accessed by each thread block or CTA (Cooperative Thread Array) within each kernel with minimal overhead. The profiler kernel is executed before the main kernel begins and stores the access range information in the GPU's *reference count table*, which is used during runtime to properly issue instructions while guaranteeing correct execution.

Due to a large number of threads (and CTAs) in modern GPUs, it is infeasible to keep all of the profiled dependency information in the GPU. Thus, we propose *Coarse-grained Reference Counting-based Scoreboarding (CRCS)* that only requires keeping reference counters for each kernel in the reference count table. It is coarse-grained as dependency tracking is done in CTA granularity (compared to thread granularity) and per page (instead of per word). CRCS is also based on reference counting, rather than keeping exhaustive dependency information.

However, even with CRCS, the performance improvement can be limited if pipeline parallelism is not properly considered in scheduling CTAs across multiple kernels. Thus, we propose a *Pipeline Parallelism-aware CTA Scheduler (PPCS)* that takes into account the amount of available data for each kernel and determines how many SMs (Streaming Multiprocessors) will be assigned for each kernel. We show how our mechanisms significantly reduce overall runtime by overlapping multiple kernels with I/O access. To summarize, the contributions of this work include the following:

- We propose novel mechanisms to automatically exploit implicit pipeline parallelism that exists between multiple dependent kernels for GPGPU workloads without any programmer effort to modify the kernel.
- In order to automatically track dependencies between a large number of CTAs from different kernels at low cost, we propose Coarse-grained Reference Counting-based Scoreboarding (CRCS) that guarantees correct execution while overlapping multiple *dependent* kernels with other stages.
- Since the baseline FIFO scheduler does not take data availability into account when scheduling CTAs from multiple kernels, we propose a Pipeline Parallelism-aware CTA Scheduler (PPCS) that considers data availability to further improve performance.
- We show that while prior work to overlap I/O access with kernel execution alone results in limited improvement for workloads with multiple kernels, by combining our proposed CRCS and PPCS with I/O access overlap, significant speedup can be achieved up to 67% (33% on average).

2. BACKGROUND / MOTIVATION

2.1 GPGPU Pipeline Parallelism

GPGPU workloads typically consist of several different stages executed serially. Figure 1(a) illustrates an example timeline of a GPGPU workload that consists of five kernels (`Kernel_0` to `Kernel_4`) that have dependencies – the result of the first kernel is input to the second kernel, which in turn generates input to the third kernel, and so on. Before the kernels can start execution, input data need to be initialized by the CPU (e.g., read input data from disk) and we refer to this stage as a *prelude*. The input data also needs to be copied from CPU memory to GPU memory (`H2D_copy`). After the kernels finish execution, the results are copied back to the CPU memory (`D2H_copy`). The CPU thread then post-processes or writes the final result to an I/O device which we refer to as a *postlude* stage.

For workloads with a non-negligible prelude and postlude, there is an opportunity to overlap them with other stages. GPUs have much higher throughput compared to the PCIe and I/O devices, and a significant amount of computation can be done on the GPU while the prelude is being executed. For example, NVIDIA Tesla K40 GPU has a peak throughput of 4.79 Tflops (for single-precision) and with 4 bytes for each single-precision floating number, the peak throughput amounts to 17.2 TB/s, which is multiple orders of magnitude higher than the peak throughput of the state-of-the-art SSD [1]. Even with memory-bound workloads, Tesla K40 has a peak memory bandwidth of 288 GB/s which is two orders of magnitude higher than the peak SSD throughput.

Thus, if input data needs to be processed through multiple kernels, overlapping them with prelude can potentially provide significantly higher performance than overlapping a single kernel only. Figure 2 shows the execution time breakdown of two workloads measured on an NVIDIA Tesla M2050. For each workload, we varied the input data size to evaluate its impact on the prelude and postlude stages. While the overall execution time increases with a larger input data size, the execution time is normalized to illustrate the ratio of the different stages. While the portion of the kernel can either vary or remain constant as the input problem is varied depending on the complexity of the kernel computation, the ratio of time spent on prelude and postlude can be as high as approximately 86%. Prior work on the Rodinia benchmark [10] has also shown that a significant portion of overall execution time can be spent on the I/O overhead.[2] Properly overlapping kernel execution with I/O device access can potentially reduce the overall runtime considerably, but given the large number of kernels (denoted by N_k in Figure 2), only overlapping the first and the last kernel with I/O device access can have a very small impact overall.

2.2 Exploiting Pipeline Parallelism in GPU Computing

In a baseline system (Figure 1(a)), all stages are serialized and result in poor performance and system resource underutilization – the GPU stays idle during prelude, memory copy, and postlude stages, and conversely, the CPU remains idle during data transfer and kernel execution.

However, by overlapping different stages, the overall system resource utilization can be increased, resulting in runtime reduction. Overlapped execution can be realized by manual optimization (Figure 1(b)) through CUDA stream and asynchronous memory copy API [32, 28] to exploit pipeline parallelism *explicitly*. For very simple workloads, this can be easily done since there would be only *intra*-stream dependencies. However, in general, such optimizations become very complicated due to *inter*-stream dependencies. For example, there can be data shared by multiple split-kernels or the output data may need to be merged across outputs from multiple split-kernels. With manual optimization, the dependencies have to be dynamically managed during runtime by the programmer or the workload algorithm needs to be modified such that the kernel can be split into independent, smaller kernels. Figure 3 shows an example of an iterative 1D stencil computation implemented as multiple dependent kernels. It highlights the data dependencies in calculating the jth and kth elements at the ith iteration. Manual optimization with N_s streams results in N_sN_i kernels, where N_i is the number of total iterations. Across each iteration, there can be N_s^2 possible dependencies, resulting in a total of $N_iN_s^2$ possible dependencies. The dependency tracking will be further complicated as the input and output array are swapped across each iteration, especially with 2D or 3D data. Prior work [30, 21, 23] overlaps the execution of a kernel with prelude or postlude by enabling I/O device access within a kernel as shown in Figure 1(c). However, dependent kernels are still serialized and limit the overall performance.

In this work, we propose to overlap execution of the kernels by automatically tracking dependency between CTAs across kernels. By combining our approach with existing approaches, as shown in Figure 1(d), all of the different stages in a GPGPU workload can be overlapped and the overall utilization of CPU, GPU, and I/O devices can be maximized. In addition, our approach exploits pipeline parallelism *implicitly* as we do not require a programmer to express dependency or parallelism available in a workload.

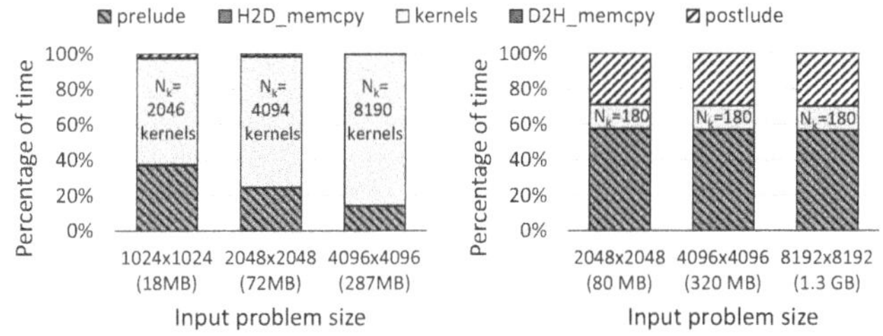

(a) Gaussian (b) Hotspot

Figure 2: Runtime breakdown on an NVIDIA Tesla M2050 of (a) Gaussian and (b) Hotspot workloads as input problem size is varied. N_k denotes the number of kernels launched.

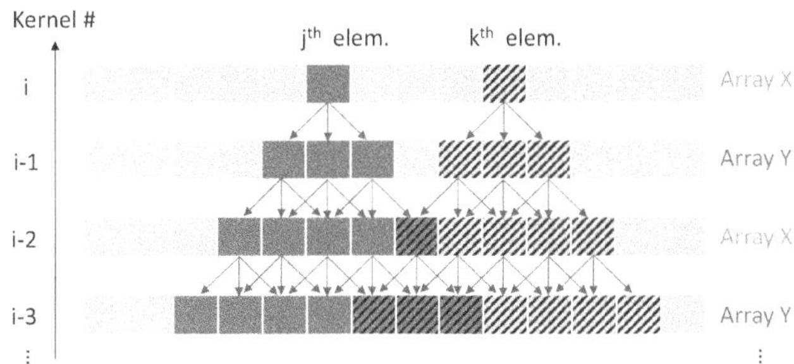

Figure 3: Example of an iterative 1D stencil computation. An arrow between cells denote dependency.

[2]This overhead is not to be confused with memory copy overhead between host and device. Running a workload on a CPU instead of a GPU can remove memory copy overhead but not the I/O overhead.

```
//Input data initialization (Prelude)
ReadFromFiles(host_A, host_B, file_A, file_B);

//Input data transfer (host-to-device)
MemcpyAsync(A, host_A, size, MemcpyH2D);
MemcpyAsync(B, host_B, size, MemcpyH2D);

//Kernel launch
VecAdd <<<gridDim, blkDim>>>(A, B, C, N);
VecAdd <<<gridDim, blkDim>>>(C, A, D, N);

//Output data transfer (device-to-host)
MemcpyAsync(host_D, D, size, MemcpyD2H);

//Wait until all tasks are finished
DeviceSynchronize();

//Writing output data to a file (Postlude)
WriteToFile(host_D, file_D);
```

(a)

```
 1: //Instantiate an OverlappedExec object
 2: OverlappedExec (
 3:   [=]() {
 4:     //Input data initialization (Prelude)
 5:     ReadFromFiles(host_A, host_B, file_A, file_B);},
 6:   [=]() {
 7:     //Input data transfer (host-to-device)
 8:     MemcpyAsync(A, host_A, size, MemcpyH2DOverlap);
 9:     MemcpyAsync(B, host_B, size, MemcpyH2DOverlap);},
10:   [=]() {
11:     //Kernel launch
12:     VecAdd <<<gridDim, blkDim>>>(A, B, C, N);
13:     VecAdd <<<gridDim, blkDim>>>(C, A, D, N);},
14:   [=]() {
15:     //Output data transfer (device-to-host)
16:     MemcpyAsync(host_D, D, size, MemcpyD2HOverlap);},
17:   [=]() {
18:     //Writing output data to a file (Postlude)
19:     WriteToFile(host_D, file_D);}
20: ).run(); //Start overlapped execution
```

(b)

Figure 4: (a) Baseline host thread code example for VectorAdd with two kernels with dependencies and (b) the host thread code for overlapping non-kernel stages.

3. OVERLAPPING NON-KERNEL STAGES WITH KERNEL EXECUTION

While our main contribution is the mechanism for overlapping execution of multiple kernels, it can be effective when non-kernel stages (i.e., prelude, memory copy, and postlude) are overlapped with the kernel. Prior work, such as HSA [23], GPUfs [30], and GPUnet [21], can be used for the overlapping. In this work, without any loss of generality, we assume a simple host model that is presented in this section. This model can be considered as an example implementation of overlapping non-kernel stages with the kernel and is orthogonal to our main contribution described in Section 4.

3.1 Host Thread Code Modification

In order to overlap a kernel the non-kernel stages, kernel execution needs to be initiated before the prelude and memory copy begins,[3] and a separate host thread for postlude needs to be created. The reordering and thread creation is transparently done by the host model's library, but we assume the programmer expresses what needs to be done at each stage.

In the original host code, the prelude comes first and then H2D copy, kernel launch, D2H copy, and postlude follow as shown in Figure 4(a).[4] A modified example code that uses the `OverlappedExec` class provided by the library is shown in Figure 4(b). The code uses lambda functions supported by standard C++11 and recent CUDA to express each stage's task in a simple way. An `OverlappedExec` object is instantiated by providing five lambda functions to the constructor in the order of prelude, H2D copy, kernel, D2H copy, and postlude. For memory copy API calls, `MemcpyH2DOverlap` or `MemcpyD2HOverlap` was given as the type of operation. Then the different tasks start execution when the `run` method is called for the object (line 20). The library first initiates the D2H and H2D memory copy functions to set up DAT entries and the CPU and GPU page tables (Section 3.2). Then, the kernel is launched and another host thread is created to execute the postlude function.[5] Finally, the prelude is started and the execution of different stages will be overlapped. The `run` method is a blocking function and will return after all tasks are finished, but the library can also provide a non-blocking version as well. This approach is not necessarily optimal and is only one of many possible approaches. The goal of this section is to present a reasonable, programmer-friendly approach to express different stages of GPGPU workloads.

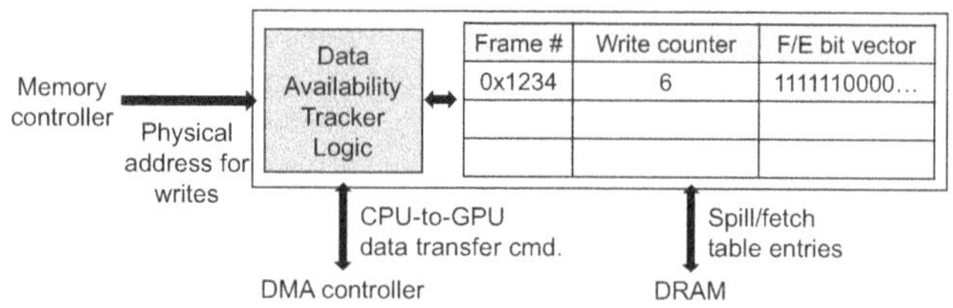

Figure 5: Data availability tracker in CPU for prior work's host model.

3.2 Overlapping Data Transfer with CPU/GPU Execution

In the host model that we assume, the CPU needs to automatically transfer input data to device memory as they become available. The *Data Availability Tracker (DAT)* shown in Figure 5 is placed near the memory controller and is responsible for detecting data availability and initiating data transfer. When the overlapped H2D copy API is called (line 8-9 in Figure 4(b)), an entry is created at DAT for each page in host memory through OS. For correct operation, the corresponding host pages need to be page locked or pinned to avoid changing the mapping between pages and frames. Each entry consists of a frame number, a *write counter*, and a *F/E bit vector*. The write counter signifies the number of words initialized and the F/E bit vector indicates which words are initialized. The write counter is initialized to zero, and as words are written to the frame, the F/E bit vector is checked for the corresponding offset in the frame, and if it toggles to 1, the counter is incremented. If there are multiple writes to the same memory address, the F/E bit will stay at 1 and the write counter will be only incremented for the first write. The write counter will reach the size of a page when its corresponding F/E bit vector is all 1, which

[3]Otherwise, the opportunity to overlap the kernel with the prelude and memory copy will be lost.

[4]The kernel code is shown in Figure 7.

[5]If there are shared data between the prelude and postlude, the programmer is responsible for ensuring mutual exclusion between them or choosing not to overlap either of them.

indicates that all words in the page are ready. Then, H2D transfer is issued through DMA and the entry is destroyed. Similar to page tables, the DAT entries are stored in DRAM, but recently used entries are cached on-chip. If the on-chip entries are insufficient, an LRU entry is evicted to DRAM and fetched back as needed. The GPU page table has a *ready bit* that indicates whether the page has been transferred from the CPU and this bit will be set after DMA transfer is done. Until the ready bit is set, memory requests from GPU threads will not be serviced as the data are not available.

This approach can support different types of data sources during the prelude such as a file, network, or host thread computation. However, one limitation is that it assumes all words in the input array will be initialized by the CPU at least once. This is not the case if the input data from an I/O source is partially pre-processed before being copied to the GPU. In that case, since the DAT is not aware of when each page is initialized, the memory copy cannot be automatically done. In such a case, the original data can be first written to a temporary memory region, pre-processed, and written to the final host memory region from which data will be transferred to the GPU. Alternatively, the programmer can still avoid such a modification by choosing not to overlap some part of the pre-processing with kernel execution.

For some workloads, the input data initialization sequence during the prelude can affect the portion of prelude that can be actually overlapped with kernel execution. If the GPU threads access multiple input arrays of similar sizes, it is desirable to interleave the initialization of the arrays during the prelude. For example, if there are two arrays A and B, a chunk of array A is initialized, a chunk of array B is initialized, and then other chunks of array A and B are initialized, and so on. However, even with an arbitrary initialization order, most workloads can still effectively overlap prelude with other stages as we shown in Section 5. Another common pattern in GPU workloads is having a small data structure shared by all threads to perform computation on a large data structure (e.g., image filtering). In that case, it is desirable to initialize the small input data first, and then start initializing the large data such that the small shared data quickly become available to all threads.

In the baseline, non-overlapped execution, the postlude on the CPU can only begin after the final kernel's output data are transferred to host memory. In order to overlap postlude with other stages, our library creates a separate host thread for postlude before the prelude begins. However, the postlude thread should be allowed to access data only after the page is transferred to host memory. This can be done by clearing the valid bits in the CPU page table for D2H copy range at first, and setting the valid bits after the pages are transferred from the GPU. When the host accesses a page that is not ready, a page fault occurs and the thread is blocked by the OS handler until the page is transferred and becomes ready.

4. OVERLAPPING MULTIPLE DEPENDENT KERNELS

This section describes our proposed approach to exploit implicit pipeline parallelism from multiple kernels with software and hardware support. To provide correct overlapped execution, dynamic dependency tracking is performed by CRCS (Section 4.1) on the GPU with support from GPU MMU. It requires a source-to-source translator at compile time to generate profiler code that analyzes the memory access range (Section 4.2). To further improve performance, we propose PPCS (Section 4.4) that takes into account available parallelism while scheduling CTAs from multiple kernels.

4.1 Coarse-grained Reference Counting-based Scoreboarding

Warp schedulers in GPUs use scoreboarding hardware to check data availability and determine which warp to schedule [2]. In order to guarantee correct execution while overlapping different stages in this work, the availability of a page needs to be checked by the scheduler. In addition, for overlapped execution of multiple dependent kernels, the scheduler needs to check if dependencies between threads from the different kernels can cause data hazards in determining the eligibility of each warp instruction. In particular, global memory accesses should occur in program order except for orderings between reads, and the warp scheduler should not allow memory accesses to the same location that can cause RAW, WAR, or WAW hazards. However, identifying and keeping data dependency information for each CTA at a word granularity is not feasible due to the large number of CTAs – e.g., $\approx 9.22 \times 10^{18}$ CTAs per kernel – for recent GPUs[2]. Even at a page granularity, the number of pages that a CTA can access is only bound by the size of the virtual address space and keeping such information is also not feasible. Thus, we employ a per-page, CTA-wise *reference counting* to minimize the overhead of tracking dependencies between CTAs across kernels. Reference counting is commonly used for garbage collector based resource management [12]. Based on the technique and CTA-granularity dependency tracking, we propose *Coarse-grained Reference Counting-based Scoreboarding (CRCS)* that augments existing scoreboarding hardware in warp schedulers.

CRCS requires a memory access range *pre*-profiler (Section 4.2) that analyzes how many CTAs in each kernel access each page and records the information in a *reference count table* shown in Figure 6, which resides in the GPU DRAM. Each table entry consists of a kernel ID, and write and read CTA reference counts that indicate how many CTAs in the kernel *might* read from or write to the page. The number of accesses to the page by a CTA does not impact the reference count as it only signifies if a CTA will ever access the page. The reference count is conservative[6] and some of the CTAs that have incremented the counter may not actually access the page. However, if all the reference counts of pages incremented for a CTA are properly decremented when the CTA finishes, the dependencies between kernels can be correctly tracked. It is important to note that false dependencies only impact performance, but do not affect the correctness of our approach.

Each GPU page table entry keeps a pointer to its corresponding reference count table and holds *owner kernel ID*, and remaining read and write reference counts by current owner kernel. We define owner kernel of a page as the oldest kernel that has unfinished CTAs that have one or more dependencies to the particular page. All threads in the owner kernel can safely access the owned page without causing any

[6]For each CTA, the profiler increments the reference count for all pages within the analyzed low and high bounds for each array.

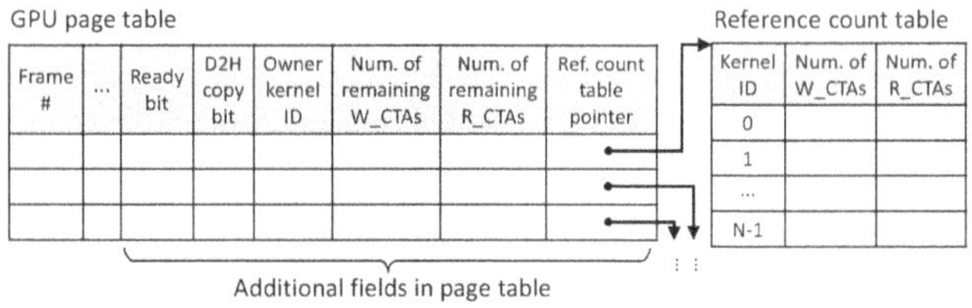

Figure 6: GPU page table with reference counters for Coarse-grained Reference Counting-based Scoreboarding (CRCS).

hazard. In the beginning, the first kernel that appears in the reference count table is designated as the owner of the page and the remaining read and write CTA counters are initialized with the reference counts stored in the reference count table for the kernel. When a warp accesses global memory, scoreboard logic checks if the kernel owns the pages to determine the warp's eligibility. After the instruction is decoded and all accessed memory addresses are known, the scoreboard accesses the SM's TLB [36] and compares the owner of each accessed page with current kernel ID (stored in a per-SM register). The instruction can be issued only if all accessed pages are owned by the kernel; otherwise, the warp stalls.

During execution, when a CTA is finished, the remaining reference counters of the pages accessed by the CTA are decremented. However, the challenge is that the accessed page range for this CTA obtained by the pre-profiler (Figure 7(b)) is not kept in the GPU memory to minimize overhead. Thus, we append a *post*-profiler code to the kernel (line 5-22 in Figure 7(c)) to execute it at the end of the kernel for this CTA. This can be done with low overhead since the profiler code only has few instructions. For all the pages in the range, the reference counters corresponding to the type of accesses (read-only, write-only, or read-and-write) are decremented. If both read and write reference counters reach zero, it indicates that the page will not be accessed by the current owner kernel any longer. Thus, the owner kernel ID and the counters (number of remaining W_CTAs/R_CTAs) are updated with that of the next kernel by looking up the reference count table of the page. When the kernel owner is updated, the MMU notifies other SMs of the change such that the next kernel's warps can be executed on other SMs. If the current kernel is the last kernel that accesses the page, depending on the mechanism used for overlapping memory copy and the CPU thread, device-to-host memory copy and postlude execution will be done. For the example approach described in Section 3, if the D2H bit in the page table is true, the MMU notifies the DMA engine to transfer the page to the host for the postlude thread.

CRCS is used only for global memory and is not needed for private local memory or other read-only memory such as texture and constant memory. For an irregular kernel, the profiler detects irregularity (Section 4.2) and CRCS only overlaps the current oldest, unfinished kernel with the prelude by looking up the page's ready bit. Other kernels fall back to the baseline, non-overlapped execution.

4.2 Profiler Code Generation

4.2.1 Sampling Method

While it is possible to statically classify the memory access pattern of a kernel into different categories (e.g., regular/irregular or contiguous/discontiguous) detailed dependency information between CTAs and pages can be dependent on runtime arguments and only available at runtime. Thus, we profile the data dependencies of each kernel at runtime before kernel execution. Our profiler collects dependency information at the granularity of a CTA. In order to identify the pages accessed by each CTA, we leverage the sampling-based memory access range analysis proposed by Kim et al. [20]. Figure 7(a,b) shows examples of an original kernel and a corresponding pre-profiler that will be executed before the main kernel, respectively. This method only requires sampling the memory addresses accessed by threads at the *corners* of the CTA (i.e., thread index for each dimension of the CTA is either 0 or $N_d - 1$, where N_d is the size of the CTA in dimension d) to obtain the lower and upper bounds of access range for an array. Specifically, among the memory addresses calculated for sampling, the lowest and highest addresses give the lower and upper bounds, respectively, for the particular array. If an array is accessed multiple times with different index functions (e.g., to perform a calculation with multiple neighboring data elements

```
_global_ void VecAdd (float* A, float* B, float* C, int N){
idx = blockDim.x * blockIdx.x + threadIdx.x;
if (idx < N)
   C[idx] = A[idx] + B[idx];
}
```

(a)

```
_global_ void VecAdd_profiler (float* A, float* B,
                          float* C, int N, dim3 origBlkDim){

sampleLow = origBlkDim.x * blockIdx.x + 0;
sampleHigh = origBlkDim.x * blockIdx.x + origBlkDim.x - 1;

C_low = C + min (sampleLow, sampleHigh);
C_high = C + max (sampleLow, sampleHigh);
SetRange (C, C_low, C_high, FLAG_W);

A_low = A + min (sampleLow, sampleHigh);
A_high = A + max (sampleLow, sampleHigh);
SetRange (A, A_low, A_high, FLAG_R);

// ... Similar code for array B ...
}
```

(b)

```
0: _global_ void VecAdd (float* A, float* B, float* C, int N){
1: idx = blockDim.x * blockIdx.x + threadIdx.x;
2: if (idx < N)
3:    C[idx] = A[idx] + B[idx];
4:
5: //Wait until all threads from this CTA finishes
6: __syncthreads();
7:
8: // Only one thread needs to execute this for each CTA
9: if (threadIdx.x == 0) {
10:     sampleLow = blockDim.x * blockIdx.x + 0;
11:     sampleHihg = blockDim.x * blockIdx.x + blockDim.x - 1;
12:
13:     C_low = C + min (sampleLow, sampleHigh);
14:     C_high = C + max (sampleLow, sampleHigh);
15:     ReleaseRange (C, C_low, C_high, FLAG_W);
16:
17:     A_low = A + min (sampleLow, sampleHigh);
18:     A_high = A + max (sampleLow, sampleHigh);
19:     ReleaseRange (A, A_low, A_high, FLAG_R);
20:
21:     // ... Similar code for array B ...
22: }
23: }
```

(c)

Figure 7: VectorAdd workload code example with (a) original kernel, (b) pre-profiler code, and (c) kernel with post-profiler code generated by a source-to-source translator appended.

as shown in Figure 3), all of the accesses are taken into account in obtaining the bounds.

The prior work [20] specified the conditions to use the sampling method. As one condition is that the array index is an affine function of CTA ID and thread ID, it cannot be used for irregular memory access patterns (e.g., an array referenced by an index read from another array). In that case, since the exact memory access range cannot be determined before kernel execution, we assume that the kernel can access the entire memory address space. If the kernel includes an indirect memory reference, the profiler does not perform sampling and simply marks the kernel as irregular and passes the information to the GPU for scoreboarding (Section 4.1).

Another condition is that the array reference is not contained in a conditional or branch statement. However, since such a statement frequently appears in many workloads, we release the condition by performing sampling for both cases of a conditional statement to make it usable for such workloads. Since this can only increase the detected memory access range, it still gives the correct range bound while it is more conservative and can result in false dependencies in some cases.

4.2.2 Pre-profiler

We execute the profiler on the GPU since we use the memory access range on the GPU. At compile time, our source-to-source translator takes the original kernel code and generates a pre-profiler kernel.[7] The pre-profiler is launched with the same grid dimensions as the original kernel, but each CTA requires only one thread to calculate the CTA's memory access range bounds. Thus, the profiler kernel takes the original kernel's CTA block dimension as an argument in addition to all arguments to the original kernel (line 0-1 in Figure 7(b)). For each array access in the original kernel, access range bounds are calculated and the `SetRange` function is called once for each array. It takes the starting address of the array, low and high bounds of access to the particular array, and access type (either read-only, write-only, or read-and-write). The function increments the count in the reference count table (Figure 6) for the given access type for all pages within the memory range. If the calculated bounds exceed the region allocated for the array by the CUDA memory allocation API call, the function ignores the out-of-bound region. The dependency information collected by the profiler will be used by our scoreboard mechanism (Section 4.1) to correctly execute the main kernel.

4.2.3 Post-profiler

After each CTA in the main kernel is finished, the remaining reference counters need to be decremented based on the pre-profiled dependency. However, the dependency information is not kept in memory to avoid the high overhead. Thus, we re-compute the dependency information for each CTA after it is finished to minimize overhead. This update is done by a *post*-profiler that is appended to the original kernel by the source-to-source translator. Figure 7(c) shows a modified kernel with appended code to release accessed memory region by decrementing the remaining reference counters (Section 4.1). The same bound calculation as in the pre-profiler is performed but instead of `SetRange`, the `ReleaseRange` function is called, which decrements the remaining reference counters in the *page table entry* for all pages within the bounds. However, since the bound calculation is conservative, the bound can include pages that are never accessed by the CTA and currently owned by an earlier kernel. In that case, the counter in the *reference count table* is decremented instead. Since the main kernel can have many threads in a CTA unlike the pre-profiler that spawns only one thread per CTA, a conditional statement (line 9 in Figure 7(c)) is added to only execute it with a single thread for each CTA. A synchronization statement (line 6 in Figure 7(c)) is also added to wait for all other threads in the CTA to finish execution. Since the pre- and post-profilers perform the same computation, they both obtain the exactly same memory access range and will not result in incorrect execution (e.g., a kernel indefinitely waiting due to false dependencies). In addition, as `SetRange` and `ReleaseRange` are called within a GPU kernel, we assume they can access the GPU page table and update the counters (e.g., through a special instruction).

4.2.4 Implementation and Overhead

Our library will setup a modified version of CUPTI [5] library to automatically launch the pre-profiler kernels through GPU driver support before main kernels are executed. The pre- and post-profilers have minimal overhead as they only involve simple calculations and do not require any memory access except for updating the reference count table. In our evaluation, the pre-profilers represented only 0.85% of the runtime on average (up to 2.7%) for CRCS with FIFO scheduling. To reduce the overhead of the pre-profiler, the profiler kernel can be concurrently executed with any other kernels except for its corresponding main kernel, which can start execution after its pre-profiler.

4.3 Cache Coherence

Current GPUs provide L1 and L2 caches, but they do not employ cache coherence. In particular, a write to the global memory by an SM does not invalidate other SMs' L1 cache lines and it is allowed for an L1 cache to hold a stale copy. The L1 cache is not flushed when a new CTA from the same kernel is issued to an SM and the programmer is responsible for appropriately handling possible stale L1 accesses across CTAs if it affects the program's correctness. However, the stale data access should not occur across kernels when multiple dependent kernels are overlapped. Thus, an SM has to flush its L1 cache when all CTAs running in an SM are finished such that the next kernel's CTAs that will be scheduled on the SM can fetch the most recent data from L2 (or DRAM) instead of accessing possibly stale data in the local L1 fetched by an earlier kernel.

To guarantee correct execution, CTA scheduling also has to be carefully done such that CTAs from different kernels are not executed in an SM at the same time. Thus, scheduling CTAs from the next kernel has to be delayed until all CTAs executing the current kernel on the current SM are finished. Due to this requirement, the maximum number of kernels that can be simultaneously executed needs to be less than or equal to the total number of SMs.

[7]The prior work [20] describes the implementation of the sampling method that uses well-known compiler techniques such as program slicing, forward substitution, and constant propagation. We implemented the method in a similar way aside from how conditional and branch statements are handled as described in this section.

4.4 Pipeline Parallelism-aware CTA Scheduler

Even with CRCS, if a baseline FIFO CTA scheduler is used where older kernel's CTAs are always prioritized regardless of data availability, GPU utilization cannot be maximized. Thus, our proposed scheduler takes data availability into account to improve pipeline parallelism and performance. With the baseline (non-overlapped execution of kernels), kernels are serially executed one at a time as shown in Figure 8(a) which we refer to as a FIFO (First-In-First-Out) CTA scheduler. In this example, we assume that the execution order is prelude, kernel 0-3, and then postlude, and the CTA $\#N$ is dependent on page $\#N$ from its prior stage (e.g., CTA 0 in kernel 0 is dependent on page 0 initialized in the prelude, CTA 0 in kernel 1 is dependent on page 0 processed by CTA 0 in kernel 0, and so on). With the baseline, a later kernel cannot start execution until all CTAs from its preceding kernel finished execution and the synchronization barrier at the end of the kernel is reached, even if there are idle SMs.

Figure 8(b) shows how FIFO scheduler works for overlapped execution. The CTAs from the first kernel are scheduled on SMs in the beginning (before t_0), but they cannot start execution until the required pages become ready in the GPU. In addition, there is an overlap of kernels as some CTAs from the second kernel (Kernel 1) are scheduled while some CTAs from the first kernel are still executing (e.g., during $t_6 - t_8$). However, the SMs remain idle for a long time since the CTAs are dependent on unavailable data (e.g., CTA 4 during $t_1 - t_4$ that is dependent on page 4). Furthermore, for most of the prelude ($t_0 - t_6$), all kernels except for the first are not executed even though there are available data for later kernels. For example, at t_1, the CTA 0 from kernel 0 finishes execution and the data for CTA 0 in kernel 1 become available, but the CTA is only scheduled at t_6.

In order to better exploit parallelism with overlapped kernel execution, we propose Pipeline Parallelism-aware CTA Scheduler (PPCS). Since accurately tracking dependencies for each individual CTA is not feasible due to a large number of CTAs possible, we propose a *best-effort* scheduler that can be effective for workloads with regular access patterns while the optimal scheduling decision is not guaranteed to minimize complexity. We first define an *SM share* of a kernel as the portion of SMs that the kernel is scheduled on. Similarly, *page share* of a kernel is defined as the portion of the pages owned by the kernel out of all *available* pages (i.e., pages that are initialized by the prelude and transferred).

The intuition behind PPCS is that parallelism can be maximized when CTAs across multiple kernels are scheduled such that the SM share of each kernel matches the page share of each kernel. At first, CTAs from the first kernel are scheduled at all SMs in a round-robin manner (i.e., first n CTAs on SM 0, the next n CTAs on SM 1, etc., where n is the maximum number of CTAs that can be scheduled on SM). Next scheduling does not occur until an SM becomes completely idle (i.e., all CTAs executing in that particular SM are finished). This is because our cache coherence policy (Section 4.3) prevents CTAs from different kernels being executed on the same SM simultaneously. Although it is still possible to schedule CTAs from the *same* kernel on the same SM, such scheduling can prevent fully exploiting pipeline parallelism since other kernels cannot be scheduled. For example, the SM can stay idle for a long time if the currently scheduled CTAs are waiting for the

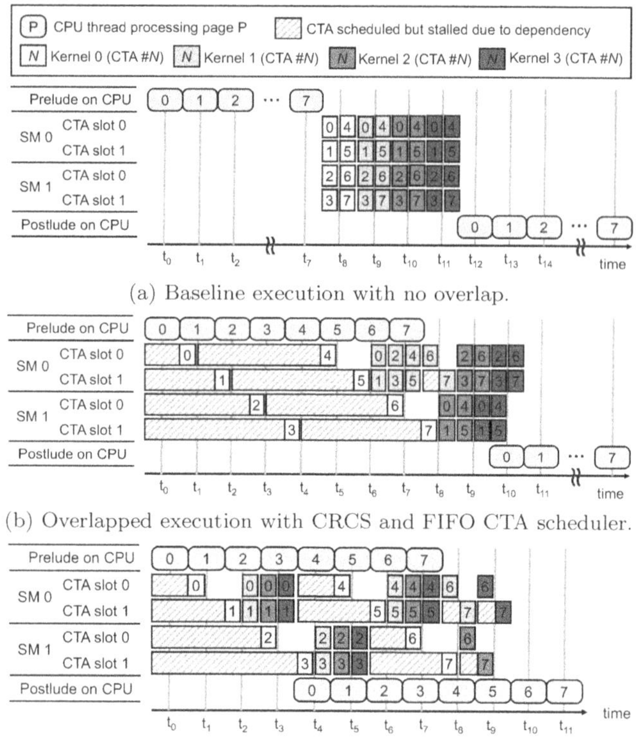

(a) Baseline execution with no overlap.

(b) Overlapped execution with CRCS and FIFO CTA scheduler.

(c) Overlapped execution with CRCS and PPCS.

Figure 8: Example timeline diagrams of different CTA schedulers with dependent kernels. For simplicity, the data transfer between host and device is not shown.

data that will be initialized at a later time by the prelude. Thus, scheduling is done when an SM becomes completely idle. The scheduler computes the SM share and page share of each kernel and chooses the kernel that has the maximum value of ($page\_share - SM\_share$). Then, CTAs from the chosen kernel are scheduled on the idle SM. PPCS can be implemented with $O(n_k)$ complexity, where n_k is the total number of kernels, by maintaining a sorted list of kernels with respect to the ($page\_share - SM\_share$) difference and performing incremental sorting whenever a page's owner is changed, an SM becomes idle, or another kernel is scheduled.

An example scheduling by PPCS is shown in Figure 8(c). At t_1, SM 0 becomes partially idle, but since there is a CTA still executing on the SM, no other CTA is scheduled on the SM. At t_2, SM 0 becomes completely idle and as kernel 0 decrements reference counters for page 0 and 1, kernel 1 becomes the owner of the pages. At this point, since only page 0 and 1 are available, the page share is 0.0 for kernel 0, and 1.0 for kernel 1. In addition, as no CTA is scheduled on SM 0 and kernel 0's CTAs are scheduled on SM 1, the SM share is 0.5 for kernel 0 and 0.0 for kernel 1. The difference ($page\_share - SM\_share$) is $0.0 - 0.5 = -0.5$ for kernel 0 and $1.0 - 0.0 = 1.0$ for kernel 1. Thus, kernel 1 has a greater difference and CTAs from kernel 1 are scheduled on SM 0. As the SMs become idle, CTAs from subsequent kernels are scheduled and pipelined execution of kernels as well as postlude (for pages processed by the last kernel) is achieved. As a result, the total runtime can be significantly reduced.

However, as PPCS is conservative (i.e., it waits until an SM becomes idle before scheduling another set of CTAs) it can perform worse than the FIFO scheduler when all data are available to the GPU. Thus, we only use PPCS while prelude is still in progress and switch to the baseline FIFO CTA scheduler when prelude is finished[8] and all data becomes available to the GPU. For our evaluated workloads, if PPCS was used past the end of prelude, the performance was almost the same as switching to FIFO, but if imbalance between CTAs exists, continuing to use PPCS can degrade performance. The imbalance between CTAs can occur when the CTAs have a different amount of computation to perform. With PPCS, if the CTAs running on the same SM finish at different time, the SM's resources freed up by a short CTA will remain idle until the other CTAs on the SM are finished. When there is only a single kernel in the workload, we use the baseline FIFO CTA scheduler.

5. EVALUATION

5.1 Methodology

We used GPGPU-sim version 3.0.1 [7] to model the proposed approach with parameters given in Table 1 that results in similar peak performance as NVIDIA Kepler GK110 [2]. For prelude and postlude, we employ a simple model and assume that the data is initialized by reading files from a solid-state drive (SSD) at 500 MB/s [1] to host memory and the postlude writes the output to a file at another SSD with the same bandwidth. We assumed the PCIe bandwidth of 15.75 GB/s in each direction (Gen 3.0 x16) and the PCIe bus is fully utilized during memory copy. We assume 4KB page for both the CPU and GPU. We used clang, a front-end for LLVM compiler [25], to implement our source-to-source translator that receives kernel code as input and generates the profiler code. The runtime is measured from the beginning of the prelude to the end of the postlude. We used workloads with multiple kernels from NVIDIA CUDA SDK examples [4], Parboil [34], Rodinia [10], PolyBench [15], and CUDA example code [19] listed in Table 2. Some workloads were not included because of the limitation of our simulation infrastructure. The evaluated workloads have diverse characteristics in runtime ratios of different stages and we also present a sensitivity study result with varying ratio of kernel execution time. We modified the host code of the workloads to read input from file(s), instead of generating random input in the CPU. For workloads that require multiple input data arrays, we assumed that the initialization of the arrays is interleaved (i.e., one page at a time for each array in turn) but we also provide a result with an adversarial, randomized initialization.

5.2 Performance Improvement

Figure 9 shows the speedup of different execution models compared to that of baseline, non-overlapped execution. In addition to the proposed mechanisms, we present the speedup from completely eliminating the memory copy while other stages are not overlapped. This represents the performance bound of integrated GPUs and full/empty bit approach [27], which only addresses the memory copy overhead. We also show the performance bound of the state-of-the-art that only overlaps a single kernel with other stages

[8]The detection of the end of prelude can be done in different ways depending on how prelude is overlapped with a kernel. For our host model assumed in Section 3, it can be detected when the prelude lambda function (e.g., line 3-5 in Figure 4(b)) is finished.

Table 1: GPGPU-sim configuration.

Parameter	Value
SM	64 SMs, 1024 threads/SM, 8 CTAs/SM 32768 registers/SM, SIMD width: 32
SM/ICNT/L2/MC freq.	700/700/924/1600 (MHz)
Shared memory	16 KB
L1 instruction cache	4 KB/SM, 4-way, 128 B line
L1 data cache	32 KB/SM, 4-way. 128 B line
L2 cache	1.5 MB, 8-way, 128 B line
Memory controller	6 MCs, FR-FCFS
DRAM	tRP=12, tCCD=2, tRCD=12, tCL=12 tWR=12, tRAS=28, 16 banks

Table 2: Evaluated workloads.

Abbr.	# of kernels	Input problem size	Description
3MM	3	$256\times256\times3$	3 matrix multiplication [15]
STN	50	$128\times128\times32$	3D stencil operation [34]
HSP	10	512×512	Hotspot [10]
BFS	16	16K nodes	Breadth-first search [10]
LPC	10	256×256	2D laplace equation [19]
CONV	6	512×512	Separable conv. filter [4]
PATH	20	$100\text{K}\times100\times5$	Path Finder [10]

while kernels cannot be overlapped. This model assumes that the first and last kernel are completely overlapped with prelude and postlude, and zero memory copy overhead, which may not be possible to realize.

Our proposed mechanisms provided more significant speedups than the bound of prior approaches. While the state-of-the-art was bounded by 11% speedup, combining CRCS with PPCS resulted in an overall speedup of 33% (up to 67%). PPCS resulted in up to 40% (14% overall) higher performance compared to the FIFO scheduler by more efficiently scheduling CTAs from multiple kernels based on data availability. Figure 10 compares the progress of each kernel in `HSP` during runtime for FIFO scheduler and PPCS. Each curve represents how many CTAs in each kernel have finished execution by the time given in x-axis. The vertical dashed line at the center indicates the time the prelude is finished. With FIFO scheduler, all kernels except for the first one were not well overlapped with the prelude and resulted in a relatively small speedup of 10%. On the contrary, PPCS executed most of all kernels even before the prelude is finished, and resulted in a significant speedup of 50% by better exploiting pipeline parallelism. Similarly, for `LPC` and `CONV`, CRCS with FIFO scheduler resulted in 20% and 10% speedup, and PPCS further improved performance to 39% and 51%, respectively. For `PATH`, as 95% of the total runtime was spent on the prelude in the baseline (Figure 11), even though other stages were well overlapped with the prelude, the total runtime was reduced by only 4% regardless of CTA scheduler. For `BFS`, due to the nature of the breadth-first-search algorithm, its first few steps (or kernels) typically only access a small part of the graph. Thus, some kernels were finished even before the prelude was done, resulting in a 25.4% speedup for single-kernel overlap. CRCS with FIFO or PPCS resulted in the same performance since the profiler cannot analyze the memory access range due to the irregular access pattern, and the kernels are serialized. We focused on workloads with regular accesses and `BFS` is the only irregular workload we evaluated. `STN` is an adversarial workload for PPCS as the profiler cannot accurately capture the kernel's memory access pattern and becomes too conservative. In the kernels, threads access the input array multiple times with a stride in a loop. Thus, all pages be-

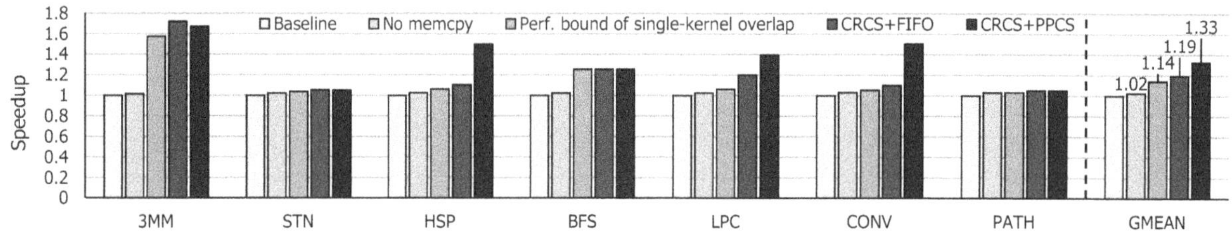

Figure 9: Speedup with different overlapped execution mechanisms compared to the baseline with no overlap.

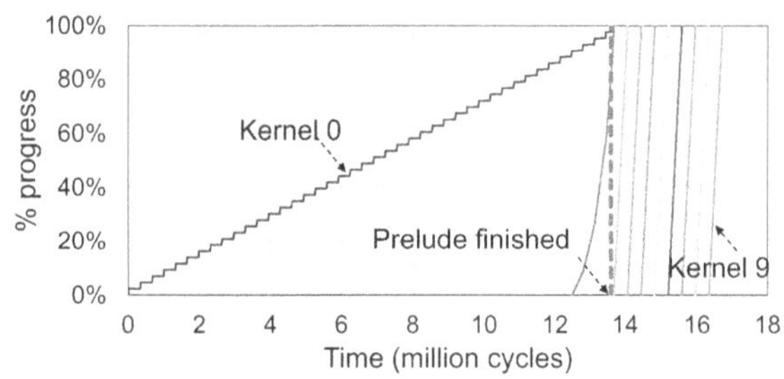

(a) Overlapped execution with CRCS + FIFO scheduler.

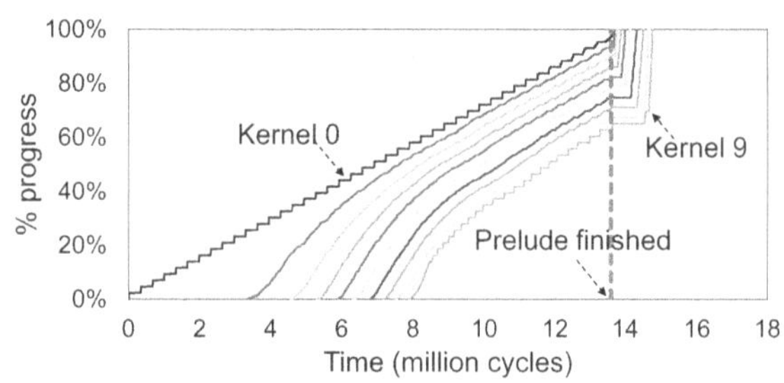

(b) Overlapped execution with CRCS + PPCS.

Figure 10: Curves showing progress of kernels in HSP workload. Each curve corresponds to a kernel.

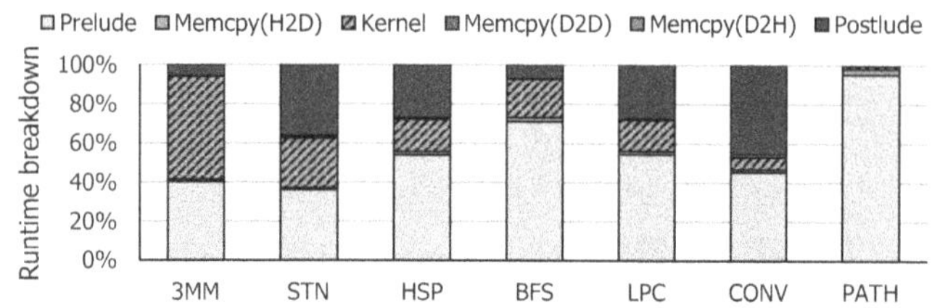

Figure 11: Runtime breakdown of the workloads.

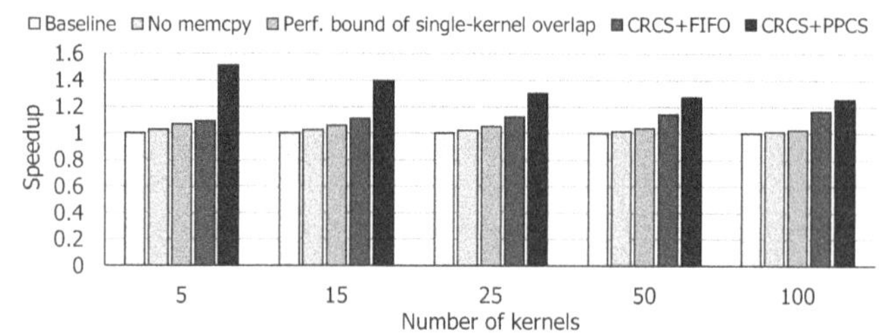

Figure 12: Speedup of HSP as the number of iterations (kernels) is varied.

tween the first and the last stride accessed were included in the access range bounds by the profiler, resulting in false dependencies that prevented PPCS from exploiting pipeline parallelism that exists. This issue can be resolved by better expressing memory access pattern [9] with compiler support, but such compiler optimization is beyond the scope of this paper.

While PPCS resulted in higher or similar performance as FIFO scheduler for most workloads, it degraded performance for 3MM. In this workload, a matrix multiplication kernel is launched three times to compute $E = A \times B, F = C \times D, G = E \times F$. As the first kernel generated the matrix E, PPCS began scheduling the third kernel as well as the second kernel since the third kernel's input data (i.e., matrix E) became partially available. However, the third kernel cannot perform any computation until the matrix F is generated by the second kernel. Thus, some SMs were left idle and resulted in lower performance than CRCS with FIFO scheduler. Nonetheless, the two schedulers resulted in only 5% difference in speedup and the PPCS resulted in 67% speedup over baseline.

Except for 3MM which has only three kernels, there was little potential improvement from the prior state-of-the-art as only one or two kernels can be overlapped with other stages. As shown in Figure 11, the portion of runtime spent on memory copy or the first and last kernel is very small. Pipeline parallelism can be more effectively exploited if multiple dependent kernels can be overlapped.

5.3 Sensitivity Study

The fraction of the total runtime for the different stages can impact the potential improvement from overlapped execution. The maximum performance benefit can be obtained if the different stages take a similar portion of total runtime, but if there is a significant imbalance in the portion of different stages during runtime, the performance improvement decreases. Thus, as a sensitivity study, we varied the number of iterations in HSP from 5 to 100 while keeping other parameters constant and compared how performance improvement is varied in Figure 12. All numbers are normalized to that of the baseline, non-overlapped execution. With 5 and 100 kernels, the kernels took 9.0% and 66% of total runtime, respectively, with the baseline. With 5 kernels, the kernels and postlude were well overlapped with the prelude by PPCS, resulting in a 51% speedup, whereas the performance of single-kernel overlap was bound by a 7% speedup. With 100 kernels, the performance improvement was reduced as the fraction of the prelude is reduced and thus, the opportunity to overlap it with kernels is also decreased. However, PPCS still resulted in a 26% speedup, while the performance of single-kernel overlap was bound by only 2% speedup. PPCS provided better performance than FIFO scheduler by properly scheduling CTAs from the kernels that had available data.

To study the sensitivity of performance to the order of input data initialization (Section 3.2), we randomly initialized the input data during the prelude while initializing the arrays one by one. Performance improvement for CONV, LPC, and HSP was reduced but still resulted in 8%, 20%, and 38%

speedups over the baseline, respectively. For other workloads, the impact of initialization order was very small and the performance was very similar (within 2%).

5.4 Hardware Cost

The CRCS needs a single ready bit for each instruction buffer entry. To support the modified GPU page table structure, assuming that 128-entry TLB [36] keeps a ready bit, D2H copy bit, owner kernel ID (10 bits to support overlapping 1024 kernels), two 10-bit remaining reference counters, and a 32-bit pointer to the reference count table in each entry, the overhead is 1KB per SM. Additional hardware required to support PPCS includes 26 bits of storage per kernel (10-bit kernel ID, 5 and 11 bits to keep the number of SMs scheduled and pages owned, respectively), resulting in 3.25KB overhead for the entire GPU, assuming 1024 kernels. Assuming the baseline GPU has 32KB L1 data cache, 32KB shared memory, 48 KB read-only cache for each of 64 SMs, and 1.5MB L2 cache, the CRCS, and PPCS only results in 0.77% storage overhead for the entire GPU.

6. RELATED WORK

While several prior works addressed the overhead of non-kernel stages, they were limited to only overlapping them with a single kernel. They can be combined with our mechanisms to overlap multiple kernels to further improve performance.

6.1 Memory Copy Overhead

Gregg and Hazelwood [16] showed that memory copy overhead can be large in GPGPU workloads and the speedup by GPU reduces if the overhead is properly considered. Prior work focused on reducing memory copy overhead, but did not enable overlapped execution of multiple dependent kernels. ADSM [14] and DyManD [18] provide automatic memory management between CPU and GPU and overlap memory copy with prelude and postlude. GPUdmm [22] uses the device memory as a cache of host memory and their hardware-based dynamic GPU memory management can overlap data transfer with the kernel execution. COMP [31] proposed several compiler optimizations for Intel Xeon Phi coprocessor that can overlap data transfer with the kernel but is not directly applicable to GPUs. Dymaxion [11] proposes memory remapping and overlapping it with data transfer to hide its overhead. NVIDIA Unified Memory (UM) [17] removes GPU memory allocation and memory copy code by automatically performing them to improve programmability, but can result in performance degradation for many workloads [24]. Zheng et al. [36] proposed several optimization techniques to improve the performance of UM. Integrated GPUs can share the same physical memory with the CPU, and thus, remove the need for memory copy between them [3]. However, discrete GPUs provide much higher performance and still require memory copy.

6.2 Prelude and Postlude Overhead

GPUfs [30] and GPUnet [21] enable file and network access within a kernel, respectively, but the kernel needs to be rewritten to use their API. GPUdrive [29] proposed optimized SSD array and software stack to improve I/O performance. HSA [23]-based integrated GPUs can handle page faults from the GPU core, and thus, I/O device access and memory copy can occur within a kernel. Current HSA only supports integrated GPUs and it is unclear how HSA will support discrete GPUs in the future. GPGPU spatial multitasking [6] is proposed to address the underutilization of GPU resources by simultaneously executing multiple workloads. However, it does not necessarily address the resource underutilization due to I/O overhead since the I/O access from different workloads can occur simultaneously. In addition, it does not improve the runtime of each workload.

6.3 Exploiting Pipeline Parallelism from Kernels

There are task-parallel languages designed to exploit pipeline parallelism [35, 8, 33], but the programmer has to *explicitly* express the dependencies and programmability is degraded. On the contrary, our approach *implicitly* leverages pipeline parallelism and is based on CUDA and OpenCL, which are currently the de facto standard. While NVIDIA GPUs [2] can simultaneously execute multiple kernels through Concurrent Kernel Execution (CKE), it is limited to *independent* kernels; dependent kernels still have to be executed one at a time with an implicit synchronization barrier at the end of each kernel.

Lustig and Martonosi [27] addressed memory copy overhead with fine-grained full/empty-bit based synchronization to overlap data transfer with kernel execution. For some workloads where multiple kernels do not write to the same memory location, their approach can overlap the kernels. However, most iterative algorithms such as stencil shown in Figure 3 require multiple kernels to repeatedly update memory data in the same region and cannot be parallelized by their approach. In general, overlapping kernels requires properly preventing read-after-write (RAW), write-after-read (WAR), and write-after-write (WAW) hazards. To the best of our knowledge, no prior work supports data hazard prevention between dependent kernels while overlapping them. Alternative CTA scheduling [26] has been proposed to improve overall performance but prior CTA scheduling does not consider the impact of overlapping the data movement with the kernel execution.

7. CONCLUSION

In this work, we proposed a hardware-software approach to overlap multiple dependent kernels without the programmer modifying the kernel. The Coarse-grained Reference Counting-based Scoreboarding (CRCS) was proposed to guarantee correct execution while overlapping multiple dependent kernels. In addition, Pipeline Parallelism-aware CTA Scheduler (PPCS) was proposed to improve performance from dependent kernel overlapping by taking into account the amount of data available for the different kernels. Our evaluation results show that combining our approach with existing mechanisms to overlap kernels with non-kernel stages can provide a speedup of up to 67%.

Acknowledgements

We would like to thank the anonymous reviewers for their insightful comments. This research was supported in part by the Mid-career Researcher Program (NRF-2013R1A2A2A01 069132), in part by the MSIP under the ITRC support program (IITP-2016-H8501-16-1005), and in part by Next-Generation Information Computing Development Program through NRF funded by the Ministry of Science, ICT & Future Planning (2015M3C4A7065647).

8. REFERENCES

[1] Intel Solid-State Drive DC P3608 Series Product Specification. Intel.

[2] NVIDIA's Next Generation CUDA Compute Architecture: Kepler GK110.

[3] APU 101: All about amd fusion accelerated processing units. AMD White Paper, 2011.

[4] CUDA C/C++ SDK code samples. NVIDIA, 2011.

[5] CUPTI User's Guide. NVIDIA, 2015.

[6] J. T. Adriaens, K. Compton, N. S. Kim, and M. J. Schulte. The case for gpgpu spatial multitasking. In *Proceedings of HPCA'12*, pages 1–12.

[7] A. Bakhoda, G. Yuan, W. Fung, H. Wong, and T. Aamodt. Analyzing CUDA workloads using a detailed GPU simulator. In *Proceedings of ISPASS'09*, pages 163–174.

[8] M. E. Belviranli, C.-H. Chou, L. N. Bhuyan, and R. Gupta. A paradigm shift in gp-gpu computing: Task based execution of applications with dynamic data dependencies. In *Proceedings of DIDC'14*, pages 29–34.

[9] J. Cabezas, L. Vilanova, I. Gelado, T. B. Jablin, N. Navarro, and W.-m. W. Hwu. Automatic parallelization of kernels in shared-memory multi-gpu nodes. In *Proceedings of ICS'15*, pages 3–13.

[10] S. Che, M. Boyer, J. Meng, D. Tarjan, J. Sheaffer, S.-H. Lee, and K. Skadron. Rodinia: A benchmark suite for heterogeneous computing. In *Proceedings of IISWC'09*, pages 44–54.

[11] S. Che, J. Sheaffer, and K. Skadron. Dymaxion: Optimizing memory access patterns for heterogeneous systems. In *Proceedings of SC'11*, pages 13:1–13:11.

[12] G. E. Collins. A method for overlapping and erasure of lists. *Commun. ACM*, 3(12):655–657, Dec. 1960.

[13] D. Foley. NVLink, Pascal and Stacked Memory: Feeding the Appetite for Big Data, http://devblogs.nvidia.com/parallelforall/nvlink-pascal-stacked-memory-feeding-appetite-big-data.

[14] I. Gelado, J. E. Stone, J. Cabezas, S. Patel, N. Navarro, and W.-m. W. Hwu. An asymmetric distributed shared memory model for heterogeneous parallel systems. In *Proceedings of ASPLOS'10*, pages 347–358.

[15] S. Grauer-Gray, L. Xu, R. Searles, S. Ayalasomayajula, and J. Cavazos. Auto-tuning a high-level language targeted to gpu codes. In *Proceedings of InPar'12*, pages 1–10.

[16] C. Gregg and K. Hazelwood. Where is the data? why you cannot debate cpu vs. gpu performance without the answer. In *Proceedings of ISPASS'11*, pages 134–144.

[17] M. Harris. Unified memory in cuda 6.0. NVIDIA GPU Technology Theater, SC'13.

[18] T. B. Jablin, J. A. Jablin, P. Prabhu, F. Liu, and D. I. August. Dynamically managed data for cpu-gpu architectures. In *Proceedings of CGO'12*, pages 165–174.

[19] A. Joshi. Accelerating various c++ applications using cuda. http://joshiscorner.com/files/src/blog/laplace-cuda-code.html.

[20] J. Kim, H. Kim, J. H. Lee, and J. Lee. Achieving a single compute device image in OpenCL for multiple GPUs. In *Proceedings of PPoPP'11*, pages 277–288.

[21] S. Kim, S. Huh, X. Zhang, Y. Hu, A. Wated, E. Witchel, and M. Silberstein. Gpunet: Networking abstractions for gpu programs. In *Proceedings of OSDI'14*, pages 201–216.

[22] Y. Kim, J. Lee, J.-E. Jo, and J. Kim. GPUdmm: A high-performance and memory-oblivious gpu architecture using dynamic memory management. In *Proceedings of HPCA'14*, pages 546–557.

[23] G. Kyriazis. Heterogeneous system architecture: A technical review. AMD, 2012.

[24] R. Landaverde, T. Zhang, A. K. Coskun, and M. Herbordt. An investigation of unified memory access performance in cuda. In *Proceedings of HPEC'14*, pages 1–6.

[25] C. Lattner and V. Adve. Llvm: A compilation framework for lifelong program analysis & transformation. In *Proceedings of CGO'04*, pages 75–.

[26] M. Lee, S. Song, J. Moon, J. Kim, W. Seo, Y. Cho, and S. Ryu. Improving gpgpu resource utilization through alternative thread block scheduling. In *Proceedings of HPCA'14*, pages 260–271.

[27] D. Lustig and M. Martonosi. Reducing gpu offload latency via fine-grained cpu-gpu synchronization. In *Proceedings of HPCA'13*, pages 354–365.

[28] S. Rennich. CUDA C/C++ Streams and Concurrency. GPU Technology Conference, 2011.

[29] M. Shihab, K. Taht, and M. Jung. Gpudrive: Reconsidering storage accesses for gpu acceleration. In *Proceedings of ASBD'14*.

[30] M. Silberstein, B. Ford, I. Keidar, and E. Witchel. Gpufs: Integrating a file system with gpus. In *Proceedings of ASPLOS'13*, pages 485–498.

[31] L. Song, M. Feng, N. Ravi, Y. Yang, and S. Chakradhar. Comp: Compiler optimizations for manycore processors. In *Proceedings of MICRO'14*, pages 659–671.

[32] J. Stam. Maximizing GPU Efficiency in Extreme Throughput Applications. GPU Technology Conference, 2009.

[33] M. Steinberger, M. Kenzel, P. Boechat, B. Kerbl, M. Dokter, and D. Schmalstieg. Whippletree: Task-based scheduling of dynamic workloads on the gpu. *ACM Trans. Graph.*, 33(6):228:1–228:11, Nov. 2014.

[34] J. Stratton, C. Rodrigues, I. Sung, N. Obeid, L. Chang, N. Anssari, G. Liu, and W. Hwu. Parboil: A Revised Benchmark Suite for Scientific and Commercial Throughput Computing. *Center for Reliable and High-Performance Computing*, 2012.

[35] J. Sugerman, K. Fatahalian, S. Boulos, K. Akeley, and P. Hanrahan. Gramps: A programming model for graphics pipelines. *ACM Trans. Graph.*, 28(1):4:1–4:11, Feb. 2009.

[36] T. Zheng, D. Nellans, A. Zulfiqar, M. Stephenson, and S. W. Keckler. Towards High Performance Paged Memory for GPUs. In *Proceedings of HPCA'16*, pages 345–357.

CAF: Core to Core Communication Acceleration Framework

Yipeng Wang[1], Ren Wang[2], Andrew Herdrich[2], James Tsai[2], and Yan Solihin[1]

[1]ECE, North Carolina State University
{ywang50, solihin}@ncsu.edu

[2]Intel Corporation
{ren.wang, andrew.j.herdrich, james.tsai}@intel.com

ABSTRACT

As the number of cores in a multicore system increases, core-to-core (C2C) communication is increasingly limiting the performance scaling of workloads that share data frequently. The traditional way cores communicate is by using shared memory space between them. However, shared memory communication fundamentally involves coherence invalidations and cache misses, which cause large performance overheads and incur a high amount of network traffic. Many important workloads incur significant C2C communication and are affected significantly by the costs, including pipelined packet processing which is widely used in software-based networking solutions. In these workloads, threads run on different cores and pass packets from one core to another for different stages of processing using software queues.

In this paper, we analyze the behavior and overheads of software queue management. Based on this analysis, we propose a novel C2C Communication Acceleration Framework (CAF) to optimize C2C communication. CAF offloads substantial communication burdens from cores and memory to a designated, efficient hardware device we refer to as Queue Management Device (QMD) attached to the Network on Chip. CAF combines hardware and software optimizations to effectively reduce the queue-induced communication overheads and improve the overall system performance by up to $2-12\times$ over traditional software queue implementations.

Keywords

Hardware queue; multicore communication; hardware accelerator

1. INTRODUCTION

New trends in network design and architecture, including Software Defined Networking (SDN) and Network Function Virtualization (NFV), are leading to rapid development of software-based packet processing on general purpose servers, which often requires high speed communication among multiple cores with packets passing through different processing stages [2]. Other workloads, such as job distributors and in-memory map-reduce algorithms used in machine learning [32] also involve frequent core-to-core (C2C) communication. Our study shows that C2C communication becomes a critical performance bottleneck in contemporary chip multi-processors (CMPs) for such workloads. The bottleneck can be attributed to the increasing number of processing elements (e.g., cores, accelerators, etc.) on a chip, that run workloads with cooperating threads that require multiple cores to exchange data frequently. In a typical CMP, the software queue structure is an important and commonly-used construct to realize C2C communication. However, software queues incur substantial performance overheads in modern data centers running SDN and NFV workloads, where significant core resources are dedicated for dequeue and enqueue operations to exchange data between cores. There is a clear demand for a more efficient communication method on the general purpose platforms.

To point out an example, Algorithm 1 shows a simplified pseudo code of a dequeue operation for a single-producer single-consumer queue. The algorithm is derived from a widely used software queue implementation, and has been optimized using a lock-free design (to avoid synchronization), batching (to amortize queue management overheads), and localizing global variables (to reduce coherence-related communication). Generally, each queue object has an array and four bookkeeping variables. The array represents the queue structure itself, which is shown as the variable *ring*. It contains pointers pointing to the actual data content. The four bookkeeping variables are producer head, producer tail, consumer head, and consumer tail respectively. A consumer thread will read and write the consumer head and tail, while only reading the producer tail. A producer thread will read and write the producer head and tail, while only reading the consumer tail. While optimized, the algorithm still suffers from significant performance overheads and scalability bottlenecks.

One source of overheads and bottleneck come from the communication triggered by the coherence protocol. The code involves multiple memory accesses, and each memory access may cause

Algorithm 1 SW queue dequeue function.

```
procedure DEQUEUE(dataArray, bulkSize)
    localHead = consumerHead;
    availEntries = producerTail − localHead;
    if availEntries < bulkSize then
        return ERROR;
    consumerHead+ = bulkSize;
    index = localHead;
    for i ← 0, bulkSize − 1 do
        dataArray[i] = ring[index];
        next(index);
    consumerTail = consumerHead;
    return OK;
```


PACT '16, September 11-15, 2016, Haifa, Israel

DOI: http://dx.doi.org/10.1145/2967938.2967954

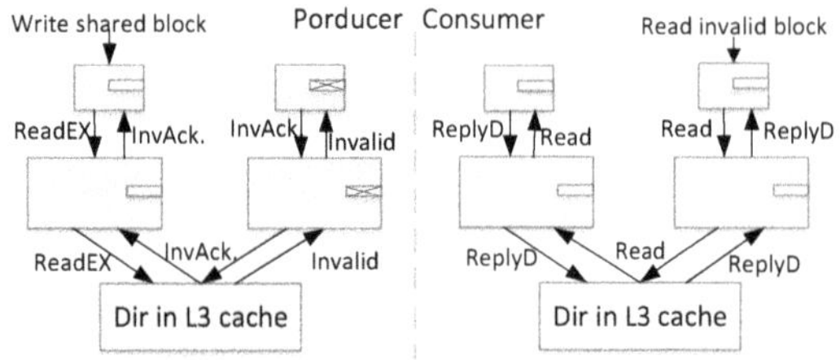

Figure 1: Illustrating the coherence-related communication overheads.

coherence-related communication. For example, when the consumer reads out of the *ring* array, the entries are likely still residing in the producer core's private L1 or L2 cache; in which case, coherence is triggered to forward the data to the target core, which could cost more than one hundred cycles. Thread contention will introduce even more overheads. In a more complex situation involving multiple consumers and multiple producers (code not shown), bookkeeping variables and data pointers are written and read by multiple threads. For example, in the dequeue algorithm, the *consumerHead* is read at line 2 but updated at line 6. In the multi-consumer situation, if this code section is not properly protected with critical section, one thread may use a stale *consumerHead* and update it with a wrong value. In the lock-free queue algorithms, dedicated instructions like compare and swap (CAS) are used to commit or retry the critical section. The critical section code is not scalable with more threads.

We refer to the cost of manipulating queue entries and bookkeeping variables (and to ensure thread-safety) as *control plane overhead*. To alleviate the control plane overhead, the algorithm employs bulk-processing, i.e., the application enqueues or dequeues a batched set, or a "bulk size" of data items each time to amortize the maintenance overhead. While this approach improves throughput through overhead amortization, it comes with a costly trade-off: higher and more unpredictable delays/jitters, due to each thread waiting for the bulk completion. Consequently, many real applications prefer the smallest bulk size that achieves a target throughput.

Another type of overhead inherent in C2C communication is what we call as *data plane overhead*. Data plane overhead is not explicitly shown in the pseudo code but becomes evident when the dequeued items are actually consumed. In common packet processing applications, the queue itself is merely an array of pointers pointing to actual data items, and the data items are the payload of the network packets that are passed from one processing stage to the next. The overhead for a core to access the data items that are pointed by the queue entries is referred as the data plane overhead. The data plane overhead may be large because the payload of a packet may be large, and the data items usually reside in another core's private cache. Figure 1 shows the communication overhead of a consumer reading an block residing in the producer's private cache, and a producer writing a shared block. Coherence flow is triggered to forward or invalidate the cache blocks from another core's local cache. The round-trip communication is very costly compared to accessing data directly from one core's local cache or the shared last level cache (LLC).

In this paper, we propose the C2C **Communication Acceleration Framework** (CAF) as a co-optimized software and hardware solution to improve C2C queue-based communications. CAF includes a new hardware structure called the *queue management device* (QMD). QMD is a device that is attached to the Network on Chip (NoC) of a CMP and acts as an accelerator for various queue management functionalities. A core can request services from the QMD through the Instruction Set Architecture (ISA), i.e. executing special enqueue and dequeue instructions. QMD achieves several significant benefits. First, it makes queue operations fast. Instead of executing hundreds of instructions at the core to manage a software queue, a core can execute an enqueue or dequeue instruction, with QMD handling the rest. Consequently, QMD frees up the core to work on more useful jobs. Second, QMD can handle multiple producers and consumers without requiring locks or synchronizations. Third, QMD removes most coherence-related communication incurred in software queue implementations, both in the control plane and in the data plane. The last two benefits increase the scalability ceiling vs. software queues. Furthermore, the scalability ceiling of QMD can be further lifted by making QMD distributed. Our results show up to $2-12\times$ throughput improvement compared to a fully optimized software queue structure. Finally, QMD can provide new functionalities. By using credit-based management system that controls the traffic flow for each thread, QMD can support Quality of Service (QoS). We also extend the functionality of QMD to accelerate more universal C2C communication applications, such as for job distributor.

The rest of the paper is organized as follows. Section 2 discusses related works. Section 3 describes the design specifics of CAF. Section 4 evaluates the proposal and Section 5 discusses some extensions to the basic design of CAF. Section 6 concludes the work.

2. RELATED WORK

Prior techniques in queue-based C2C communication in general fall into two categories: software and hardware approaches. For software approaches, numerous software queue algorithms have been proposed since decades ago until recently [18, 21, 10, 26, 34, 12, 33]. Those algorithms try to improve the scalability and throughput of the software queue by optimizing memory allocation or reducing thread contention. Meanwhile, one widely used queue algorithm in data centers for packet processing on a general processor is the Intel's DPDK [2] library. The queue algorithm from DPDK is well optimized for x86 systems and implements various optimizations, such as bulk processing. However, even a well-optimized software algorithm still requires substantial core resources to maintain the queue data structure and cannot avoid the costly thread contention. Packet processing workloads running in modern data centers still require significant core resources to be dedicated for pure dequeue and enqueue operations. Our proposed CAF offloads all queue maintenance work from the core to a dedicated hardware engine.

For hardware approaches, there are studies focusing on hardware-accelerated task queues [17, 20, 31], which reduce software overheads in task scheduling and load balancing. They are very different from CAF according to their hardware design and use cases. However, we will show that CAF can be used for task scheduling as well with an extra load balancing module. The most related work to ours is HAQu [22]. Like CAF, HAQu proposes hardware acceleration for queue operations. Although sharing the same purpose, CAF is fundamentally different from HAQu in several ways. HAQu maintains the queue information in the core, whereas CAF maintains the queue information in a NoC-attached device. In HQAu, cores spend many cycles to bookkeep queue information, and queue items still reside in cache, triggering memory access and coherence overheads. In contrast, QMD is attached to the NoC; this relieves the core and cache hierarchy from bookkeeping and keeping coherence. Furthermore, HAQu does not support multi-producer multi-consumer communication, because each core has its own local copy of the queue's head and tail. Extending

HAQu to support multi-producer multi-consumer requires keeping these heads and tails coherent across cores, which incurs a problematic new coherence problem. In contrast, CAF centralizes the queue structures, hence it does not incur new coherence issues between cores. CAF keeps modifications to the core minimum (adding new instructions). CAF allows multi-producer and multi-consumer queue communications, which is a critical support for packet processing.

In industry, Freescale designs a set of hardware components called DPAA [1] on a system-on-chip (SoC) to accelerate C2C communication. The detailed design and performance specification of DPAA is unknown to the public. However, to our best knowledge, the hardware queue manager of DPAA is not closely integrated with the core architecture. The potential latency is longer and the complexity of communication steps between the core and the queue manager is much higher than our proposed hardware design.

3. SYSTEM ARCHITECTURE AND DESIGN

The basic idea of the proposed Communication Acceleration Framework (CAF) is to offload the queue-related communication maintenance from the core to an efficient device. CAF consists of two major parts: 1) the Queue Management Device (QMD), which is attached to the NoC and works like an accelerator core to perform various queue management functionalities; and 2) three new instructions added to the ISA to accelerate dequeue, enqueue, and data movement operations. We will first discuss the new instructions, then discuss QMD design.

3.1 New Instructions

CAF adds three new instructions to the ISA:

- `enqueue reg, qid_reg`, where `reg` is a 64-bit operand containing the data to enqueue, and `qid_reg` is the concatenation of queue ID, priority, or other operation flags. The flags can be used to specify various operation modes. The QMD can decode the request by using simple masks.
- `dequeue reg, qid_reg`, where `reg` is the destination register to hold the value returned by QMD. `qid_reg` contains the queue ID, priority, and other operation flags.
- `prepush mem`, where `mem` specifies memory block that will be invalidated in the local cache and pushed to the shared last level cache.

enqueue and *prepush* are used for C2C communication through the QMD. They differ slightly from store instructions. As store-like instructions, the new instructions execute non-speculatively and go through the store buffer. When the instructions arrive at the head of the reorder buffer (ROB), if their operands are ready, they can be retired. Retired *enqueue* and *dequeue* instructions are held in the store buffer until they get responses from the QMD. After getting responses, they are regarded as completed and can be removed from the store buffer. In contrast to regular stores, dequeue uses the writeback stage to write data to the destination registers. In addition, enqueue and dequeue do not access memory so they do not incur page faults.

prepush request behaves like the inverse of a *prefetch* request, hence the name. Instead of fetching a cache block from a lower level cache to the upper level caches, *prepush* will push a cache block to the shared cache and invalidate the copy in its private caches. *prepush* is similar to stores and updates from literature [3, 30], speculative push [29], or forwarding write [16], pushing stores [27], however *prepush* is non-binding and because it only pushes data block to the shared cache, it reuses the writeback path of the cache hierarchy. Basic *prepush* is similar to early write back [19], but applied only to private caches.

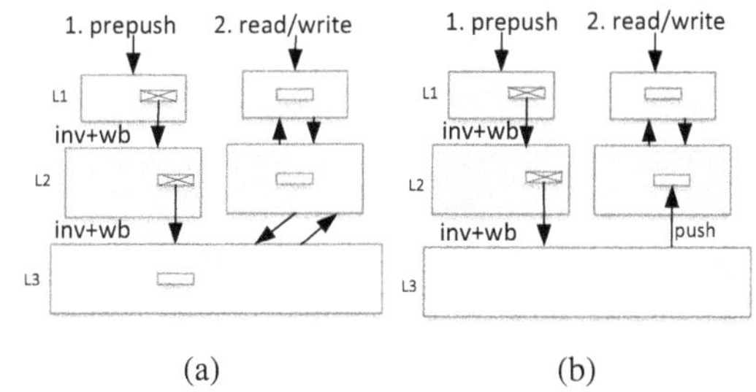

Figure 2: Two prepush schemes: basic (a) and advanced (b).

After *prepush*, another core that reads or writes to the pushed block can read it from shared cache instead of triggering coherence-based data forwarding or invalidation requests, saving a large number of cycles and NoC bandwidth. The process is illustrated in Figure 2(a). An alternative way to implement *prepush* is to push the cache block directly to the target core's local cache as shown in Figure 2(b). This will be discussed more in Section 5. We implement *prepush* as non-speculative. Similar with a store instruction, *prepush* also goes through store buffer.

To illustrate the use of the new instructions, consider network applications where producers and consumers rely on these enqueue or dequeue to communicate the pointers to the network packets. *prepush* can be used to reduce the data plane overhead incurred during queue-based communication. After the pointer of a packet is enqueued, the producer core can prepush the content of the packet to the shared cache so that the consumer core can get data from the shared cache and avoid expensive coherence and data forwarding.

Memory ordering. We assume a system implementing relaxed consistency model which relaxes load-to-store ordering (e.g. Intel IA-32 and SPARC total store order (TSO)). This is also the consistency model assumed by gem5 [4] simulator, which we used for our simulation. Generally speaking, the x86-TSO ordering principles include: a) a store is not reordered with respect to other stores; b) a store is not reordered with older loads; c) a load may be reordered with older stores to different locations. With our new instructions, additional ordering principles should be followed: a) a dequeue request is not reordered with other dequeue requests and an enqueue request is not reordered with other enqueue requests if they access the same queue; b) an enqueue request is not reordered with older stores; c) a store can be reordered with a *prepush* if the prepushed cache block address is different from that of the store.

Queue requests from a thread (or core) for a particular queue must arrive at the QMD in the program order. One way to achieve this is to use an ordered NoC, i.e. using routing that guarantees ordered message delivery such as deterministic single-path routing. It is also possible to use non-ordered NoC with an additional mechanism (e.g. scratch buffering resource and packet reordering based on sequence numbers) to restore the message order. At the processor pipeline, queue requests are not reordered with earlier stores. For example, if the program first stores data to a memory location, then the latter enqueue must happen after the earlier store is completed. As a result, the enqueued address always points to the updated data. Similarly, *prepush* is not reordered with an older store to the same block address so that the pushed block will have the latest value. Additional ordering between queue instructions and others can be enforced by using memory fence instructions.

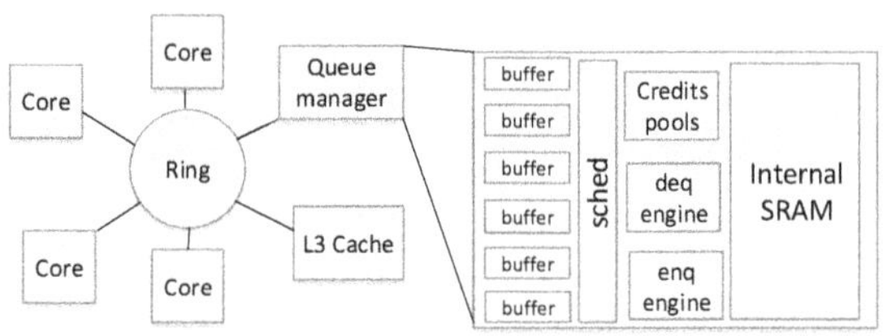

Figure 3: Queue management device architecture.

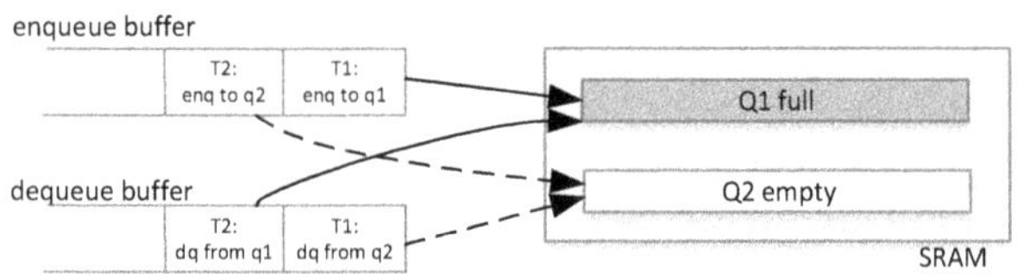

Figure 4: Illustration of a possible deadlock situation.

3.2 Queue Management Device

As shown in Figure 3, QMD is attached to the NoC. The figure shows a ring as an example but other NoC topologies are possible. When an application wants to use a queue, it makes a system call to request a queue to be allocated. The OS checks QMD for available hardware resources. If the allocation succeeds, the OS returns a queue ID to the application. Otherwise, an error message is returned. The application also makes a system call to deallocate a queue.

After queue allocation, the application can start using the queue. Enqueue and dequeue requests sent out by a core will be routed to the QMD. After each successful enqueue or dequeue operation, QMD sends a response back to the core. We describe QMD's hardware components in detail as below.

1. *Request buffers.* Every enqueue and dequeue request will be put into one of the request buffers. These buffers hold incoming requests temporarily until the QMD is able to serve them. In a basic design, enqueue requests go to one buffer and dequeue requests go to another. In a more advanced design, to enable fine-grained Quality of Service (QoS), we can associate each buffer with a priority. With *n* priorities, there are *n* enqueue buffers and *n* dequeue buffers.

2. *Scheduler.* The scheduler is responsible for removing requests from the buffers and send them to the enqueue or dequeue engine. In each cycle, a buffer is selected, and then the scheduler removes the request from the head of the selected buffer. The buffer selection can be accomplished using various policies, such as Round Robin (RR) or Weighted Round Robin (WRR). With WRR, the scheduler consider priorities of buffers into account. After scheduling, the enqueue or dequeue engine reads from or writes to the internal SRAM where the queue is managed. If the queue is full (for an enqueue), the request tries again in the next cycle. Similarly, if the queue is empty (for an dequeue), the request tries again in the next cycle. One caveat with this scheme is that one thread's requests may potentially block another thread's requests in the same buffer, thus a deadlock can occur as illustrated in Figure 4. In the figure, thread T1's enqueue request blocks thread T2's enqueue request while T1's dequeue request can only be performed after T2's requests is completed. To address this, one option is to have a dedicated set of buffers for each core. Alternatively, we can have a single set of virtual buffers for each core, but physically all the cores share a set of physical buffers. A simple arbitration (e.g. round-robin) between virtual buffers is sufficient.

3. *Queue storage.* The internal SRAM supports a configurable number and size of queues. In our configuration, each queue entry is 8 bytes, equal to the size of a pointer in x86-64. Thus, a 16KB SRAM can support one big queue with 2K entries or 16 smaller queues each with 128 entries. QMD maintains internal registers for the head and tail of each queue, which will be updated after processing a queue request. After successfully completing a queue request, a response is sent out to the response port, which is then routed back to the core that sent out the request.

4. *Credit management module.* In the basic mode, QMD operates without credit management. In this mode, queues behave as blocking when empty or full so that threads can keep sending requests until the cores stall. However, non-blocking behavior may be preferred in some cases. In this scenario, the credit management feature is used to inform the program how many resources in the QMD can be used by each thread. The number of credits given to a producer corresponds to the number of empty entries in the target queue. A thread should obtain credits before sending any enqueue or dequeue requests. Each thread may be granted different numbers of credits to control their traffic. We will discuss the credit management in Section 3.5.

5. *Interrupt.* QMD can send interrupts to cores. This is required to avoid the situation that when one thread crashes, the corresponding threads that is working on the same queue might be frozen. At the software side, a guarding thread may be used to inform QMD to send out an interrupt whenever necessary. The core receiving the interrupt drains all the incomplete queue requests. A timer in the QMD may be used to determine a time out when QMD may have blocked some cores. For example, if no request is successfully fulfilled for a long time from one buffer, QMD may drop requests in the buffer and send out an interrupt to the corresponding core.

6. *Others.* Other modules can be integrated with QMD to provide additional features such as data reducing and job distribution. The additional modules can be used and configured by enqueue/dequeue instructions with special flags or bit masks as the second operands. In Section 3.5, we will discuss several possible additional modules.

3.3 Power and Area Overhead

We use analytical power and area modeling tools to estimate the power and area overheads of QMD. We use both CACTI [36] and ORION [15] together to model the QMD. CACTI estimates power and area of the internal SRAM, and ORION estimates the power and area of the buffers, the scheduler, and the crossbar in the QMD. We leave out special modules such as the credit manager and the load balancer since they are optional. For a 45 nm technical node, we model a 32KB SRAM with 8 byte block size, and 2 routers (one for enqueue and one for dequeue) each with 3 buffers and a round robin scheduler. Our modeling tool shows 0.04 watts for the routers and 0.09 watts for the internal SRAM at full load. For the total area, the routers consume $0.03mm^2$ and the SRAM requires $0.71mm^2$, which means that the area cost is on a par with a core's first level cache.

3.4 Distributed QMD

Although QMD can offload a huge amount of work from core and memory, saving power, bandwidth, CPU cycles, etc, it still has limited hardware resources to handle all the requests. Like any shared hardware component, large amount of requests may saturate QMD. Fortunately, the QMD can easily be scaled by distributing it. One can have several QMDs on the network with each as a complete functional QMD as in the centralized design. Each QMD will contain numbers of physical queues in its internal SRAM just like in the centralized QMD. Each queue of the QMDs will have its unique queue ID for thread to access. The number of QMDs is determined by the area and power budget during the chip design process. We will discuss more on this topic in the evaluation and extension sections.

3.5 Advanced Features

The basic QMD design can accelerate simple queue operations. Some advanced features can help QMD do work that might be costly or impossible to be done in software. In this section, we discuss examples of advanced features that can be added to the QMD.

Credit based flow control. The first feature is *thread level credit based flow control*. Sometimes, programmers may want to control the throughput of certain threads due to power, priority, or fairness concerns. Thread-level flow control is not easy to implement in software but can be added to the QMD credit management module. With credit management, a thread must reserve credits before sending out a request. The credits represent the resources allocated to a thread. If a thread sends more requests than the number of credits it has obtained, QMD will drop the extra requests silently. Software is responsible for recording credits it has obtained or consumed. For implementation, the dequeue instruction with a special flag is used to obtain credits for a certain queue. Although this mode adds additional credit reservation and bookkeeping overheads, it has certain benefits: a) it is useful for programs requiring non-blocking behavior, b) misbehaved threads cannot take over all the resources of QMD and starve other threads, and c) the credit mechanism enables another level of flow control among all threads, i.e., by giving a different number of credits to each individual thread, the speed of a thread can be controlled precisely. Thus, the maximum service time for each thread can be guaranteed.

The credit management module is designed to maintain multiple credit pools for each queue, including local and global credit pools, in its internal hardware registers. A thread can only obtain credits from its own local credit pool. There is also a global credit pool which maintains credits that have not been distributed to the local credit pools yet. In other words, the local credit pool represents the amount of resources a thread can use, while the global credit pool indicates the resources QMD holds. When a producer or consumer thread requests credits, it can only request from its local credit pool. The local credit pool will reduce the number of credits from its pool accordingly. In our current design, we let the local credit pool give out all its credits to any credit obtaining request to maximize throughput. When the enqueue or dequeue takes place in QMD, the global credit pool will be replenished first. For example, an item that is enqueued will increase the global dequeue credits by one. Then, QMD decides how credits will be distributed from the global credit pool to local credit pools. Different credit distribution policies can be used. For example, a WRR policy distributes credits to local credit pools in a weighted round robin fashion based on predefined thread priority. Under such a policy, no matter how fast or slow one thread is, the ratio of the maximum amount of service time for each thread is fixed. The credit distribution and replenishment are handled by hardware, so no software overheads are incurred.

Load balancer. Besides pipelined packet processing, another common use of queue is for distributing jobs (tasks) to different worker threads [17, 5, 31, 20]. The goal of a job distributor is to keep all cores busy. There are several ways to achieve this. One way to implement this is to have a single job queue. All workers draw jobs from this queue. After completing a job, a worker

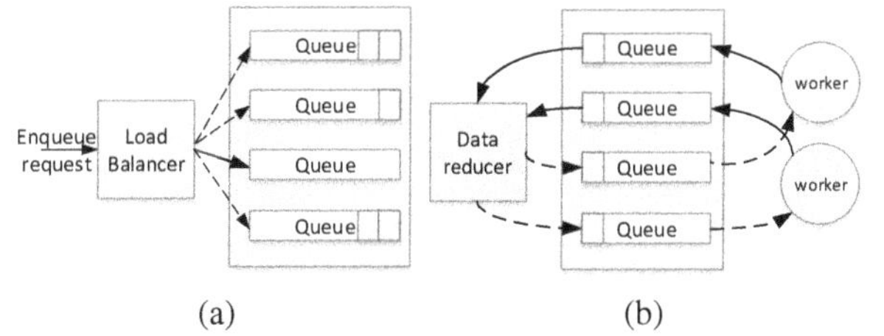

Figure 5: Illustration of load balancer (a) and data reducer (b).

thread will dequeue another job. This keeps all workers busy at all time. However, using a single job queue means the jobs are not distinguishable. If certain jobs can only be handled by certain workers, a different scheme is needed. A single queue also suffers from scalability issue even though queue operations are processed by hardware. So, an alternative method is to allocate one queue to each worker thread. Special jobs can be enqueued to the queues for specific threads. Multiple queues also makes it more scalable with a large number of threads. However, the job producer needs to do load balancing in software. Without the knowledge of the status of each queue, it is difficult for the producer thread to distribute jobs to different queues optimally. To solve this issue, QMD could include a load balancer to help balance the requests for different queues. Figure 5(a) shows the concept of this component. In the load balancing mode, queue requests will be automatically distributed to different queues. For example, the load balancer will search for the queue with the smallest number of items and send the next enqueue request to it. With this feature, programmer can create a job distributor quickly without much software complexity. A configuration step needs to be performed to set up the distribution mapping.

Data reducer. If power and area budget allows, a more aggressive feature is to build a data processing unit into the QMD. For example, a data reducer is designed to help with in-memory Map Reduce [8, 7, 14] applications. Map Reduce is a popular programming model for parallel computing such as machine learning algorithms. In the Map Reduce model on a CMP, a master core is responsible for assigning (mapping) data to different workers. After the workers complete computation, the master collects the results from each worker and reduce them. In a large class of machine learning algorithms, the training procedure consists of a loop of a Map Reduce process [32]. The loop is iterated until the parameters converge. Thus, the machine learning algorithms may incur a lot of inter-core communications, especially with a high core count. Usually, the reducing function is simple and can be directly handled by hardware accelerators. Using a general purpose core to handle the task is wasteful. QMD would be a good accelerator for such task. Figure 5(b) shows a data reducer engine built into the QMD to act as the master core. Each worker enqueues the map results to the QMD and retrieve new data from the QMD for the next round of calculation.

Other features for QMD are possible but beyond the scope of this paper. We will evaluate certain advanced features and show QMD's effectiveness in the evaluation section.

4. EVALUATION

4.1 Modeling Details

We use the detailed mode of a full-system cycle-accurate simulator based on gem5 [4] to model CAF. We added the three new instructions into the x86-64 ISA and all their pipeline stages and memory behaviors are modeled at the cycle-accurate level. We use gem5 classic cache model but tune access latencies to approximate

Table 1: Baseline configuration.

Core	16 cores, each 2GHz, x86-64 ISA, 8-wide out-of-order superscalar Num. of entries: IQ:64 LQ:72 SQ:64
Cache	Non-inclusive property, MOESI protocol 64B block size, LRU replacement policy Private L1-D: 32KB, 8-way, 4-cycle latency Private L2: 256KB, 8-way, 10-cycle latency Shared L3: 24MB, 24-way, 45-cycle latency
QMD	50ns SRAM access latency, fully pipelined, 1GHz
DRAM	Single channel 8GB DDR3

the behavior of an Intel directory-based multi-core processor. We attach a centralized QMD to a dedicated interconnect which directly connects to each core. We use 50 CPU cycles as the round trip time between cores and the QMD, which is larger than the measured round trip time to the L3 cache on a real platform. Buffers and schedulers are modeled at the cycle-accurate level so that contention of requests at QMD is properly accounted for. The enqueue and dequeue engines take 50 ns to access its internal SRAM, which is rather conservative compared to access time of a cache. To make the simulation time manageable, we limit our detailed simulation to a system with 16 cores connected to a shared bus. We also simulate a 64-core distributed QMD design connected to a 2D mesh. Table 1 shows the baseline architecture configuration we use for detailed simulation throughout the evaluation section.

4.2 Queue Application Results

We wrote micro-benchmarks to evaluate the performance of CAF against a state-of-the-art software queue algorithm from the DPDK [2] library, which is widely used in today's data centers for packet processing workloads. A simplified version of the algorithm is shown in Algorithm 1. Other popular software queue algorithms in research literatures are more or less variants of this algorithm and are not promising better performance, especially on an x86 system. The algorithm also uses bulk processing to amortize queue maintenance overhead, but as we mentioned in Section 1, real applications always prefer small or no bulk. Therefore we use bulk size up to 8 in most of our experiments. Furthermore, going from a bulk size of 8 to 32, the software throughput improves by only 40%, due to diminishing returns.

The queue algorithm was modified minimally to run in our simulation environment [1]. We also compare CAF with HAQu in the single-producer single-consumer case since HAQu does not support concurrent queues. To see the raw performance improvement for different applications, we use the basic operating mode of QMD without advanced credit management mechanism. We tested the credit management in Section 4.5.

1. **Pure QMD dequeue speedup test:** We use a micro-benchmark to test the speedup of pure dequeue operations of the QMD. We pre-populated the queue structures and then used multiple threads to dequeue all the items. After each dequeue, the items are discarded by the consumer, thus the test does not incur any data plane overhead. We fixed the number of total items and increase the number of threads. We used a bulk size of 8 to amortize the control plane overhead of the software implementation. We recorded the time until the queue became empty, i.e. the execution time of the slowest thread, normalized to the software queue's 2-thread case,

[1] We use gem5's magic instructions to protect critical code section in the multi-producer multi-consumer queue case, due to gem5's lack of support for modeling x86's atomic instruction, at the time we conducted the research. The magic instruction is expected to be faster than an atomic instruction.

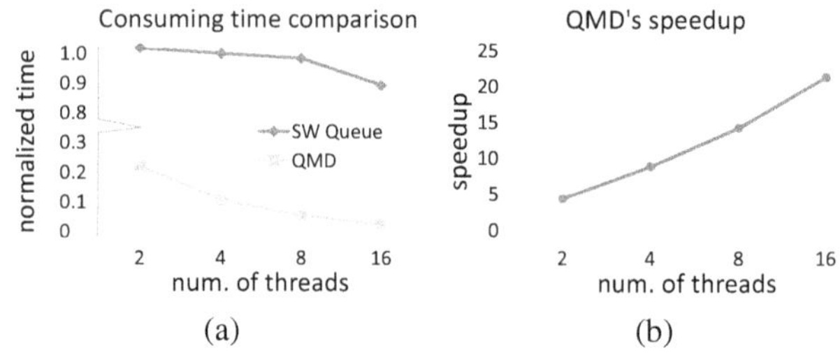

Figure 6: Normalized execution time of CAF vs. software queue (a), and CAF speedup over software queue (b).

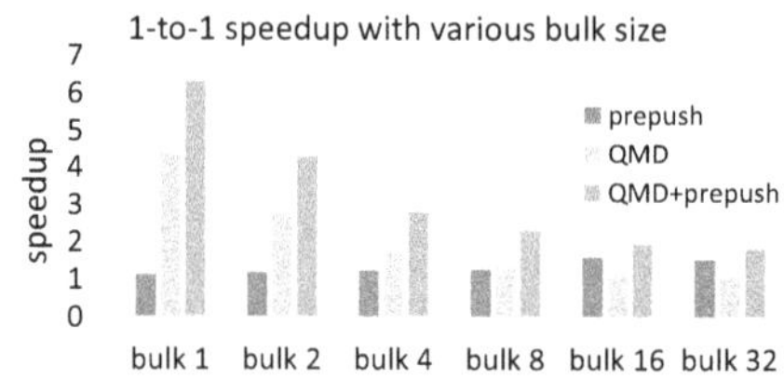

Figure 7: Speedup of CAF for a single-producer single-consumer workload.

and show the results in Figure 6(a). By measuring the execution time of the slowest thread (until the queue becomes empty), the speedup we measure is also throughput speedup. For the rest of the paper, we measure throughput speedup in a similar fashion. We may guess that the execution time will be inversely proportional to the number of threads as more threads will consume the queue faster. However, the software queue execution time only decreases by about 10% going from 2 to 16 threads. This is due to the contention caused by multiple threads accessing the global variables. On the other hand, CAF's execution time decreases by about 80%, or a speedup factor of 5×. This is because the software-related contention is eliminated when queue operations are offloaded to the hardware. For comparison, Figure 6(b) shows the speedup of CAF relative to software queue on equal numbers of threads, with varying number of threads. Confirming the previous observation, the speedup increases as the number of threads increases, reaching as high as 20× speedup in the 16-thread case.

2. **One-to-One communication:** In order to consider a more realistic workload that includes data plane overheads, we first created a benchmark to represent a single-consumer single-producer use case. In this packet processing benchmark, a memory pool is managed in a queue from which the producer can allocate new packets. After the packets are allocated, the pointer to the packet is inserted into another queue waiting for the consumer to dequeue. The consumer dequeues the pointers and fetches the pointed packets to perform a simple arithmetic operation. Afterwards, the memory space used by the packets is returned to the memory pool. This use case represents basic packet processing applications. In the software queue implementation, we enable bulk processing with various bulk sizes to amortize the control plane overhead. In the CAF implementation, we use QMD for queue management and also issue *prepush* following each enqueue request. Figure 7 shows the speedup of CAF compared to the software queue implementation with various bulk sizes. The figure shows QMD's speedup (representing control plane speedup) and the *prepush*'s speedup (representing data plane speedup) separately. The results show that as the bulk size increases, the control plane speedup becomes less significant as it is increasingly amortized by the larger bulk size. When

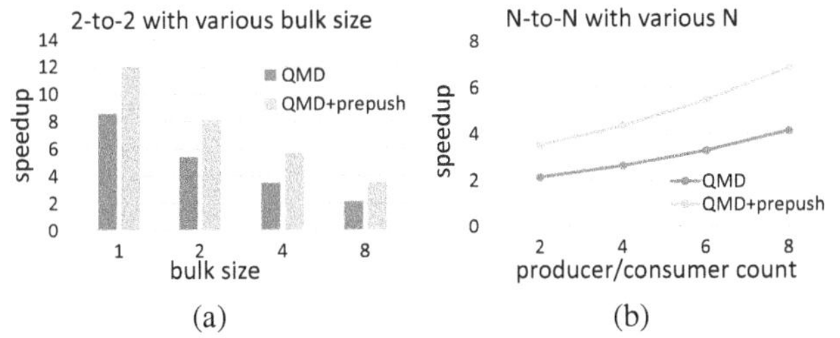

Figure 8: The N-to-N benchmark workload's speedup with CAF with various bulk sizes (a), and with increasing numbers of threads (b).

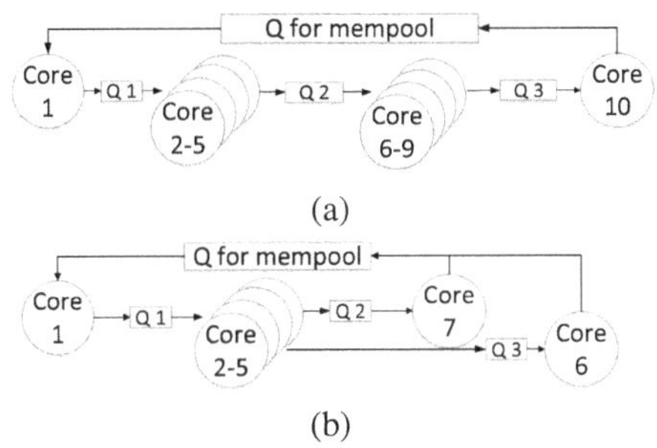

Figure 9: Pipelined/clustered hybrid application (a), and firewall application (b).

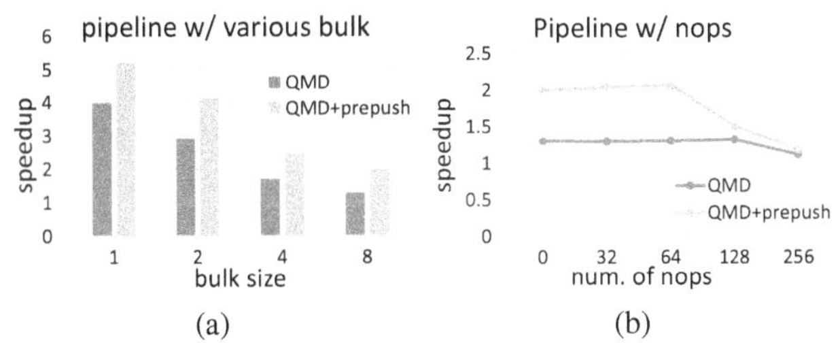

Figure 10: For the pipeline benchmark, the speedup of CAF with various bulk sizes (a), and the speedup with various nops inserted (b).

the software queue does not use bulk, CAF achieves more than 6× speedup. This means that CAF is very effective for more real-time applications such as telecommunication applications which prefer no bulk. With a bulk size larger than 8, CAF still achieves about 2× speedup, however a smaller bulk is preferred in real applications since a larger bulk may lead to a longer latency where critical packets may be delayed for a long time waiting for the composition of a large block of packets.

3. **N-to-N communication:** This is similar to the single-producer single-consumer case, but with multiple producers and consumers. First, we used two producers and two consumers but vary the bulk size from 1 to 8. Figure 8(a) shows that the speedup is up to 12×. Then we fixed the bulk size at 8 and varied the number of producers and consumers. The speedup results are shown in Figure 8(b). Due to the high overhead of global variable contention in software queues, CAF achieves about 7× speedup in the case of 8 producers and 8 consumers. QMD-only also achieves about 4× speedup. This again shows that CAF is especially helpful in the multi-producer multi-consumer case, and it scales better than software queue.

4. **Hybrid packet processing: pipeline of interconnected clusters.** Figure 9(a) shows a more complex packet processing scenario, with two clusters of threads working at different pipeline stages. The job is thus pipelined and distributed to different cores to maximize throughput. As noted in [9], this is a common packet processing scheme on general purpose x86 platforms. Figure 10(a) shows the speedup with various bulk sizes. CAF shows up to 5× speedup when we use small bulk sizes. Then we fix the bulk size at 8 and insert *nops* in each worker thread to mimic different amounts of packet processing work. The results are shown in Figure 10(b). We can see that when the workload is light, CAF can achieve 2× speedup. When the amount of work is large, the benefit of CAF diminishes. This is because the packet processing work itself eventually becomes the bottleneck of the benchmark and CAF is not designed to accelerate the core's execution speed. However, in a largely distributed application, the amount of work for each core is expected to be relatively light.

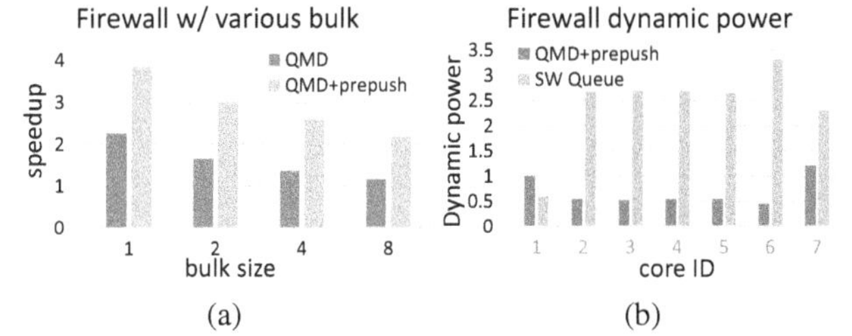

Figure 12: Performance evaluation of the firewall application on CAF with various bulk sizes (a), and the per core dynamic power consumption (b).

5. **Firewall packet filtering:** In this benchmark, we emulate the behavior of a firewall when processing incoming network traffic. The application scheme is shown in Figure 9(b). Core 2 to core 5 are responsible for filtering the packets based on firewall policies. Any suspicious packet is rerouted to core 6 for further analysis or bookkeeping, and then dropped. Normal packets are passed to core 7. To mimic real use cases, each packet occupies a 2KB memory buffer, with the first three 64-byte blocks in the 2KB buffer representing the packet header. The packet header will be passed from core-to-core for examination. In our experiments, on average every 8 packets, core 1 sends out a "suspicious" packet with one of the header locations set to a special value. One can regard the value as an IP address or a port number. The workers (core 2 to core 5) check this value to see if it is suspicious. Similar to the previous test cases, core 6 and core 7 return the used memory buffers back to the memory pool when packets are dropped by core 6 or consumed by core 7.

Figure 12(a) shows the speedup. We vary the bulk size from 1 to 8 and find up to 4× speedup. To further show the benefit of CAF, we fix the bulk size as 8 and collect power and cache performance statistics. We use McPAT [24] to model the dynamic power consumption of each core. Figure 12(b) shows the dynamic power consumption and Figure 11 shows each core's detailed performance data including dynamic instruction count, data cache access count, data forwarding count, and data invalidation count. Since a core could be stalled instead of spin waiting for available queue resources when queue is blocking, dynamic instruction count and data cache access count are significantly reduced by using CAF, halving the dynamic power of the whole processor. Also, CAF helps eliminate a large amount of coherence-based communication overhead including both data forwarding and data invalidation, which means considerable NoC bandwidth and power could also be saved.

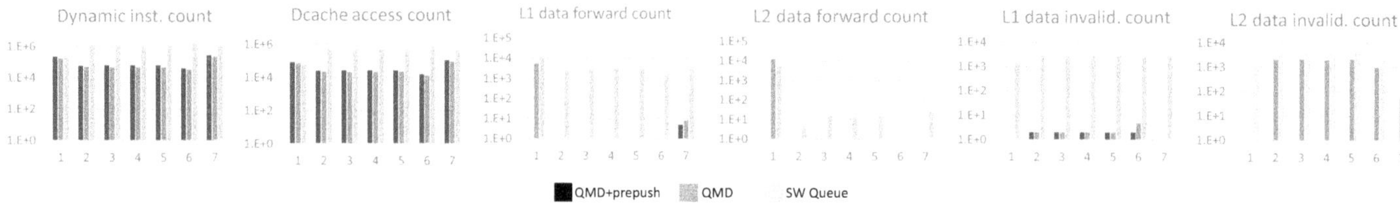

Figure 11: Comparison of QMD (with and without prepush) against the software queue implementation using various statistics. The x axis shows the core ID corresponding to Figure 9 (b). The y axis is shown in logarithmic scale.

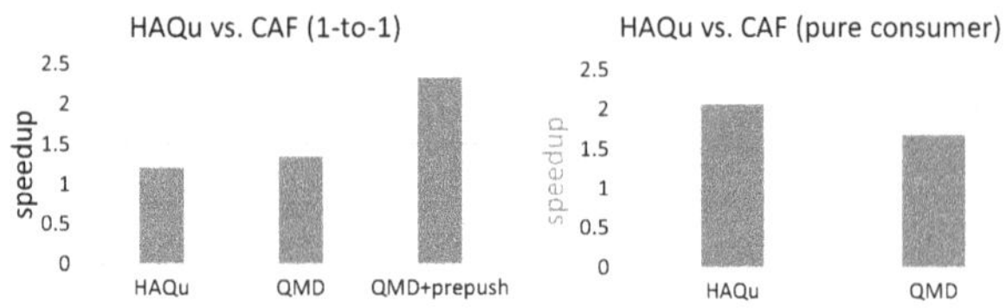

(a) (b)

Figure 13: Comparing HAQu and CAF throughput on the single-producer single-consumer benchmark evaluation (a) and pure consumer benchmark (b).

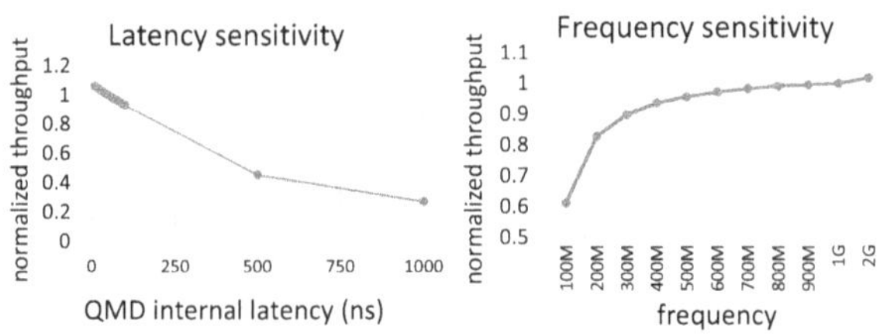

(a) (b)

Figure 14: Throughput with various latencies (a), and with various clock frequencies (b).

6. **Comparison with HAQu:** HAQu [22] is a state-of-the-art hardware queue acceleration approach, but it does not support the multi-producer multi-consumer applications or any advanced QMD features. Thus, we only compared our design with HAQu for the single-producer single-consumer benchmark. Figure 13 shows the comparison of CAF and HAQu. Fundamentally, HAQu does not eliminate any overhead associated with accessing the queue heads and tails. In other words, heads and tails are still stored and managed in shared memory. Thus, in the single-producer single-consumer case in which the heads and tails of the queue are updated frequently, HAQu performs worse than QMD (1.2× vs. 1.35×). However, HAQu does not have the latency overhead to access the queue content given that the queue information is kept in the core. Dequeue requests in HAQu only require the overhead of a regular cache access. In the pure consumer test, there are no frequent updates to the heads and tails, therefore the HAQu performs better than the QMD (2.1× vs. 1.7×). However, the pure consuming benchmark is less realistic. Also, since HAQu does not support multi-producer multi-consumer cases and requires substantial modifications to cores, CAF is a more appealing solution for general purpose platforms.

4.3 Sensitivity Study

For sensitivity study, we vary the latency, i.e. time for the enqueue or dequeue engine in QMD to access its internal SRAM,

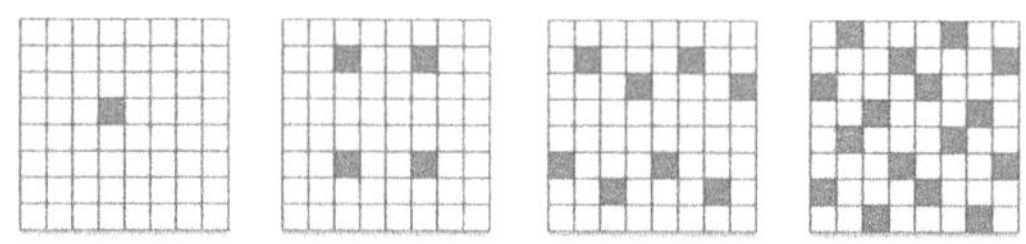

Figure 15: A possible placement of 1, 4, 8, and 16 QMDs on a 64-core mesh.

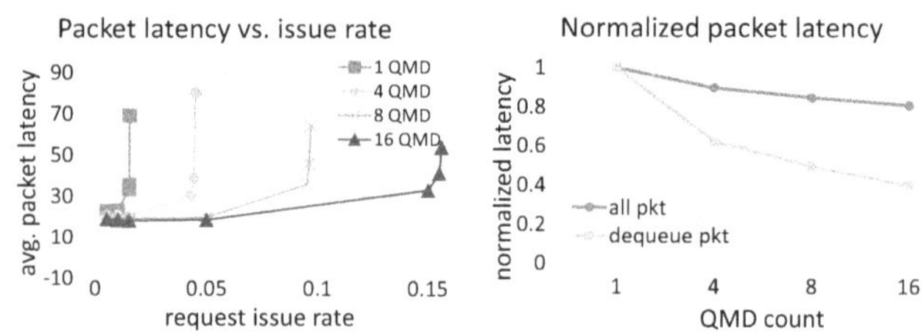

(a) (b)

Figure 16: The average packet latency with various issue rates (a), and the average latency comparison for all packets and dequeue-only packets (b).

from 10 ns to 1 ms, while keeping the clock frequency at 1GHz. Then, we change the frequency from 100MHz to 2GHz, while keeping the latency at 50 ns. We use the single-producer single-consumer benchmark as our test case. Figure 14(a) shows the throughput changes by changing the internal latency and Figure 14(b) shows the throughput changes by changing the frequency. For the latency sensitivity results, the throughput changes almost linearly when the internal latency is less than 500 ns. There is about 10% difference between 100 ns and 10 ns latency. The number is not large because multiple dequeues and enqueues can be in-flight simultaneously, which amortize the latency for each request. For the frequency sensitivity results, we see that beyond 500MHz, the throughput does not increase much, but from 300MHz to 100MHz, there is a big drop. This is because frequency determines how fast the QMD can pick up requests from the buffers. Only when buffers are stressed, increasing frequency will improve the system's throughput.

4.4 Distributed QMD

As we mentioned in Section 3.4, a centralized QMD may be saturated by a large amount of requests, which will affect its performance. The result in Figure 14 also shows the effect: when QMD's speed decreases by 10 times from 1GHz (similar to a requests rate increaseing by 10 times at 1GHz), the performance decreases by 40%. To solve this problem, we introduce the distributed QMD design. One can regard our previous 16-core evaluation as part of a larger system with distributed QMDs.

To evaluate the benefit of distributed QMDs over a centralized

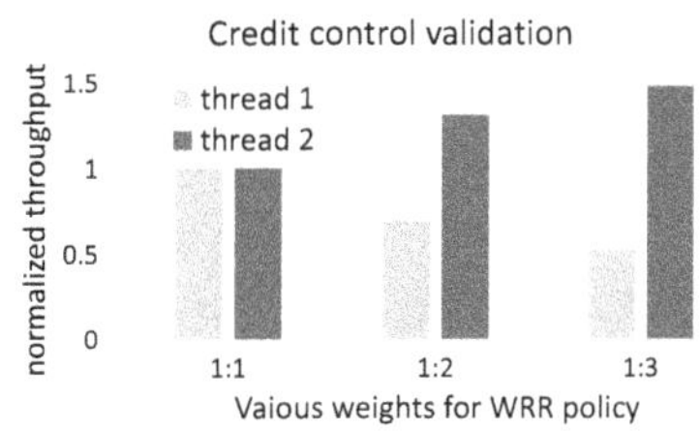

Figure 17: Throughput of two threads with a weighted round robin policy.

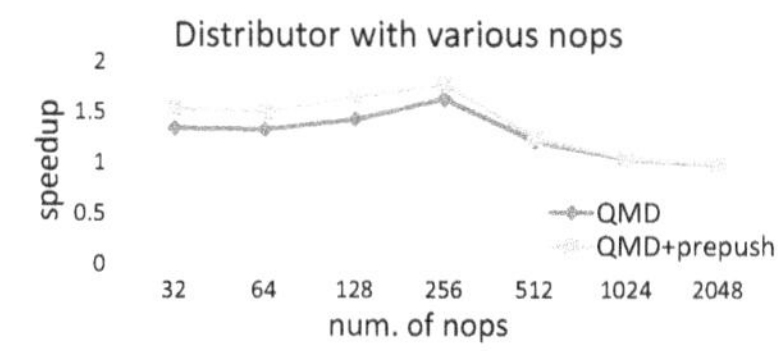

Figure 18: CAF speedup for the distributor application.

QMD, we model a 64-core system based on the BookSim [13] simulator. Each core is connected to a router in a 8×8 mesh. We model each core to issue enqueue and dequeue requests to the QMDs with certain issue rates. We let the number of enqueue to be equal to the number of dequeue requests and assume a policy that the physical queues used are always located close to the consumer cores. In other words, enqueue could be issued to any QMD, but all the dequeues will be issued to the nearest QMD. We assume this policy because dequeue instructions usually stay in the critical path of an application. We use 1, 4, 8, and 16 QMDs placed as shown in Figure 15. For 8 and 16 QMDs, the placement is optimized for the minimum hop distance according to [37]. We vary the average issue rate of each core and collect the average packet latency. Figure 16(a) shows the average packet latency against the issue rate with different numbers of QMDs. When the latency increases dramatically, it means the QMD cannot finish processing each request fast enough so that the network is saturated. By using 16 QMDs, the system can support more than $10\times$ higher requests issue rate and achieve lower packet latency, meanwhile sustain the throughput of each thread. Figure 16(b) shows the average packet latency of all packets and dequeue-only packets for different numbers of QMDs. We found that the dequeue spend 60% less time on the network scaled to include 16 QMDs.

These results show that if there is no high volume of queue requests, a centralized QMD would be enough, although hop distance could be high for certain cores. Meanwhile, a high volume of queue access requests could saturate the network and in turn affect the performance. In future many-core CMP systems, a distributed QMD design may be necessary.

4.5 Advanced Features

1. **Evaluation of credit management system:** The credit management system enables *thread-level flow control* and non-blocking behavior as discussed in Section 3.5, although an extra credit obtaining step is needed. To test the effectiveness of the flow control, we run a test with two producers and one consumer working on the same queue. Each producer sends out a credit obtaining request first. According to the credits it obtains, it will then issue a matching number of enqueue requests. After credits are consumed, it will request for credits again. We set the credit control system to implement a weighted round robin policy for distributing the credits to the local credit pools according to their weights. Other policies are also possible. Figure 17 shows the normalized throughput of the 2 producer threads. By setting the weights to be 1:1, 1:2, and 1:3, the throughputs of the two threads are changed accordingly. Note that there is no good way to control traffic in software unless using expensive synchronizations and communications.

2. **Distributor application:** By including a queue balancer, we can use the QMD to work as a job distributor as we discussed in 3.5. To show how fast that QMD can optimally distribute jobs to different workers, we first implement a software solution in which the producer loops around worker threads to distribute jobs to the idle ones. To avoid unnecessary overhead, each worker thread only has one shared variable with the producer to store one incoming job. When one worker finishes its job, it will mark itself as idle, so that the producer will find and put a new job in its shared variable. Without maintaining queues, this software distributor is simple and fast. We will compare the throughput with our QMD implementation.

With QMD, we set up a specific queue for each worker. In the load balancing mode, the load balancer module automatically distributes jobs to the worker with the least jobs waiting. To compare the results, we use four workers and insert different numbers of *nop*s to the workers to mimic different amounts of workload. Figure 18 shows the speedup of QMD against the software implementation. For these tests, we see up to $1.8\times$ speedup. Notice that we do not even use queues for buffering packets in the software implementation. If queue management and queue status check overhead is involved, the speedup of CAF may be even higher.

3. **Machine learning algorithm:** As discussed in Section 3.5, we may add a data processing engine into QMD to accelerate applications with Map Reduce programming model. To show the benefit, we use stochastic gradient descent (SGD) to solve logistic regression (LR) [6, 28] algorithm which is a typical method used in classification and language processing. Although we only test a single algorithm, many other machine learning algorithms could be abstracted into a similar form [35]. The algorithm we are using is:

$\theta_j := \theta_j + \varepsilon \sum_{i=1}^{m} (y^i - h_\theta(x^i)) x_j^i$

In this equation, θ is the vector of the parameters (or weights). ε is the step size. y^i is the corresponding label for data vector $\vec{x^i}$. h is the hypothesis function. In each iteration, a new θ will be calculated and used for the next iteration. With Map Reduce, each worker works on a part of the data vectors. The master core sums the results from each worker and updates θ. In the software implementation, we synchronize the workers and the master at the end of each iteration so that they proceed in lock-step. In the QMD implementation, we let each worker enqueue its result to the QMD. We add a data reducing engine into QMD to do a reducing (summation) of all the enqueued data. The engine is also responsible for copying the reduced data back to each queue. Then the workers will dequeue the new data and proceed to the next iteration. For the implementation, we consider one cycle for the data reducer to read one item, one cycle for an arithmetic operation, and one cycle to store the data back. We input a set of vectors each having 13 attributes from the Statlog (Heart) Data Set [25]. We change the number of workers and the number of input vectors handled by each worker for evaluating the benefit.

Figure 19 shows that QMD achieves 15% speedup when worker count is as large as 16, and each worker only works on a small subset of the data (one row of the input matrix). This is because the communication overhead will take a larger portion of the overall overhead in this case. Meanwhile, if the communication overhead does not dominate, the benefit is small. We believe QMD has the

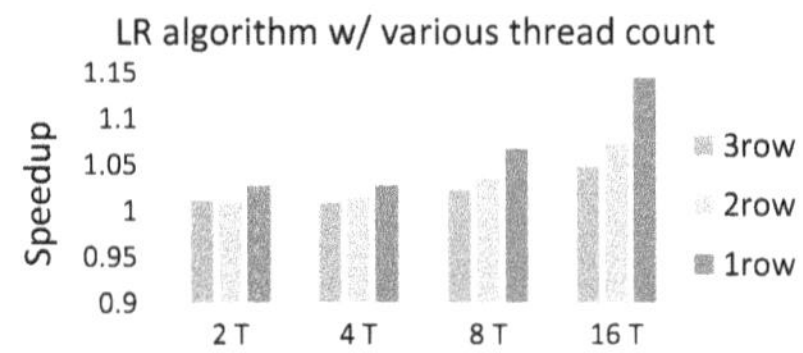

Figure 19: Throughput of the Map Reduce application.

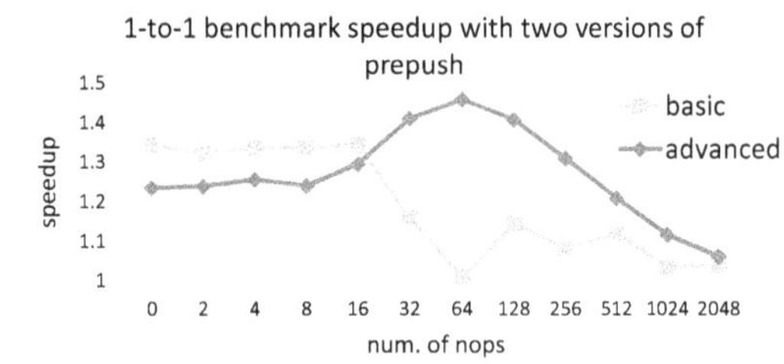

Figure 20: The speedup comparison between basic and advanced *prepush* implementation.

potential to benefit machine learning applications in future many-core system with a large number of processing elements.

5. EXTENSIONS

We already discussed the general scheme and advanced features of CAF. In this section, we will discuss some possible extensions to the current design and provide some preliminary results. These extensions include a more advanced *prepush* implementation, queue protection, and queue virtualization.

5.1 Advanced Prepush

In Section 3.1, we introduced the *prepush* instruction with a basic implementation of pushing data into the shared LLC. A more advanced implementation of *prepush* is to push the data directly into the destination core's private caches (illustrated in Figure 2(b)). New store or update instructions proposed by [27, 16, 23, 3, 11, 30] have a similar behavior. One choice we made is to push data to the private L2 cache of the destination core instead of the private L1 cache, in order to avoid unnecessary pollution to small L1 cache. One major concern of this mechanism is how to recognize the core to push the data to. In this discussion, we will assume a simple approach which allows the programmer or compiler to specify the destination core, and we set up core-affinity for the threads. Compared to the previous *prepush*, the new *prepush* instruction now takes the destination core ID as another operand.

We implemented the advanced *prepush* and evaluated it with the single-producer single-consumer benchmark as our test case. In this benchmark, the producer is initially slower than the consumer, so we add *nop*s to the consumer thread to change the relative speed of the producer and the consumer. Figure 20 shows that when the producer is relatively slow, the advanced *prepush* does not benefit more than the basic *prepush*. This is because the new *prepush* only speeds up the consumer, however in this case the producer is the bottleneck. Also, since the advanced *prepush* needs to read the core ID and wait for the data to be pushed to another core, it slows down the producer. As we add more *nop*s to the consumer, the advanced *prepush* begins to show larger benefits. The benefit is from the cycles saved by the consumer to access private L2 cache instead of the shared LLC. Although there is an advantage with the advanced *prepush*, issues such as core ID determination and cache pollution need to be carefully addressed. Furthermore, the advanced *prepush* also complicates the hardware design and the coherence protocol, whereas the basic *prepush* utilizes the write back path of the cache hierarchy.

5.2 Queue Protection and Queue ID Virtualization

In complex general-purpose systems, multiple processes may co-execute and access queues concurrently. Previously, we assume there are no misbehaving processes so that we do not need to protect the queues used by one process from another process. With this assumption, a software queue allocation mechanism may be enough to distribute hardware queue resources to multiple processes. However, without proper protection, one misbehaving process may starve another process or steal items from a queue that does not belong to it. To enforce process isolation and enable queue protection, a hardware component is necessary to monitor all the enqueue and dequeue requests, which we refer to as queue ID management unit (QIMU). Queue ID ranges and permissions can be set up in QIMU for regulating the queue usage for each process.

Another benefit of introducing QIMU is that we can use it for run-time queue ID translation which provides queue ID virtualization support. With queue ID virtualization, the physical queue being used can be migrated from one QMD to another dynamically without being discovered by the user level program. After migration, the OS just needs to re-map the logical queue to the new physical queue. Dynamic queue migration enables the optimization opportunities of packet latency, NoC traffic, and QMD workload balance. For example, when a thread migrates from one core to another, the physical queue it uses should also migrate to the new core's nearest QMD. Analogous to a memory management unit (MMU), one issue of using QIMU for translation is that translating each queue request is costly. To solve this issue, a queue translation lookaside buffer (QTLB) is needed. Operations for TLB also apply to QTLB. Each queue access request will look up QTLB for virtual queue ID to physical queue ID mapping. If the translation is found, the access will be translated directly. Otherwise, the mapping in memory will be looked up and brought into the QTLB. Like a TLB, context switch requires flushing the QTLB.

6. CONCLUSION AND FUTURE WORK

In this paper, we have proposed and evaluated a core-to-core Communication Acceleration Framework (CAF) to significantly reduce software queue communication overhead and improve overall system performance. We proposed new instructions to accelerate control and data plane communication, and new hardware component to accelerate control plane communication. Our gem5 based simulation model shows up to $2-12\times$ speedup in test cases representing real usage patterns compared to an optimized software queue algorithm. We also show that CAF can support various advanced features to extend its usage to more universal applications like job distributor and machine learning algorithms.

7. ACKNOWLEDGMENT

Much of the work was done when Yipeng Wang was a research intern at Intel Labs and in collaboration with his Ph.D. advisor Yan Solihin. We would like to thank the anonymous reviewers for their helpful feedback.

8. REFERENCES

[1] QorIQ DPAA Primer for Software Architecture. Technical report, Freescale Semiconductor Inc, 2012.

[2] Data Plane Development Kit: Programmer's Guide. Technical report, Intel Corp, 2015.

[3] W. Berke. A cache technique for synchronization variables in highly parallel, shared memory systems. In *Courant Institute of Mathematical Sciences*, 1988.

[4] N. Binkert, B. Beckmann, G. Black, S. K. Reinhardt, A. Saidi, A. Basu, J. Hestness, D. R. Hower, T. Krishna, S. Sardashti, R. Sen, K. Sewell, M. Shoaib, N. Vaish, M. D. Hill, and D. A. Wood. The gem5 simulator. *SIGARCH Computer Architecture News*, 39(2), 2011.

[5] R. D. Blumofe, C. F. Joerg, B. C. Kuszmaul, C. E. Leiserson, K. H. Randall, and Y. Zhou. Cilk: An efficient multithreaded runtime system. In *Proceedings of the Fifth ACM SIGPLAN Symposium on Principles and Practice of Parallel Programming*, 1995.

[6] L. Bottou. Large-scale machine learning with stochastic gradient descent. In *Proceedings of the 19th International Conference on Computational Statistics*, Paris, France, August 2010. Springer.

[7] R. Chen, H. Chen, and B. Zang. Tiled-mapreduce: Optimizing resource usages of data-parallel applications on multicore with tiling. In *Proceedings of the 19th International Conference on Parallel Architectures and Compilation Techniques*, 2010.

[8] J. Dean and S. Ghemawat. Mapreduce: Simplified data processing on large clusters. In *Proceedings of the 6th Conference on Symposium on Opearting Systems Design & Implementation*, 2004.

[9] C. F. Dumitrescu. Design Patterns for Packet Processing Applications on Multi-core Intel Architecture Processors . Technical report, Intel Corp., 2008.

[10] J. Giacomoni, T. Moseley, and M. Vachharajani. Fastforward for efficient pipeline parallelism: A cache-optimized concurrent lock-free queue. In *Proceedings of the 13th Symposium on Principles and Practice of Parallel Programming*, 2008.

[11] J. R. Goodman, M. K. Vernon, and P. J. Woest. Efficient synchronization primitives for large-scale cache-coherent multiprocessors. In *Proceedings of the Third International Conference on Architectural Support for Programming Languages and Operating Systems*, 1989.

[12] A. Haas, M. Lippautz, T. A. Henzinger, H. Payer, A. Sokolova, C. M. Kirsch, and A. Sezgin. Distributed queues in shared memory: Multicore performance and scalability through quantitative relaxation. In *Proceedings of the ACM International Conference on Computing Frontiers*, 2013.

[13] N. Jiang, D. Becker, G. Michelogiannakis, J. Balfour, B. Towles, D. Shaw, J. Kim, and W. Dally. A detailed and flexible cycle-accurate network-on-chip simulator. In *Proceedings of the International Symposium on Performance Analysis of Systems and Software*, April 2013.

[14] W. Jiang, V. Ravi, and G. Agrawal. A map-reduce system with an alternate api for multi-core environments. In *Proceedings of the 10th IEEE/ACM International Conference on Cluster, Cloud and Grid Computing(CCGrid)*, 2010.

[15] A. Kahng, B. Li, L.-S. Peh, and K. Samadi. Orion 2.0: A fast and accurate noc power and area model for early-stage design space exploration. In *Design, Automation Test in Europe Conference Exhibition*, April 2009.

[16] D. A. Koufaty, X. Chen, D. Poulsen, and J. Torrellas. Data forwarding in scalable shared-memory multiprocessors. *IEEE Transactions on Parallel and Distributed Systems*, 7(12), Dec 1996.

[17] S. Kumar, C. J. Hughes, and A. Nguyen. Carbon: Architectural support for fine-grained parallelism on chip multiprocessors. In *Proceedings of the 34th Annual International Symposium on Computer Architecture*, 2007.

[18] L. Lamport. Specifying concurrent program modules. *ACM Trans. Program. Lang. Syst.*, 5(2), Apr. 1983.

[19] H.-H. S. Lee, G. S. Tyson, and M. K. Farrens. Eager writeback - a technique for improving bandwidth utilization. In *Proceedings of the 33rd Annual ACM/IEEE International Symposium on Microarchitecture*, 2000.

[20] J. Lee, C. Nicopoulos, H. G. Lee, S. Panth, S. K. Lim, and J. Kim. Isonet: Hardware-based job queue management for many-core architectures. *IEEE Transactions on Very Large Scale Integration (VLSI) Systems*, 21(6), June 2013.

[21] P. Lee, T. Bu, and G. Chandranmenon. A lock-free, cache-efficient multi-core synchronization mechanism for line-rate network traffic monitoring. In *Proceedings of International Symposium on Parallel Distributed Processing*, 2010.

[22] S. Lee, D. Tiwari, Y. Solihin, and J. Tuck. Haqu: Hardware-accelerated queueing for fine-grained threading on a chip multiprocessor. In *Proceedings of 17th International Symposium on High Performance Computer Architecture*, 2011.

[23] D. Lenoski, J. Laudon, K. Gharachorloo, W.-D. Weber, A. Gupta, J. Hennessy, M. Horowitz, and M. Lam. The stanford dash multiprocessor. *Computer*, 25(3), 1992.

[24] S. Li, J. H. Ahn, R. Strong, J. Brockman, D. Tullsen, and N. Jouppi. Mcpat: An integrated power, area, and timing modeling framework for multicore and manycore architectures. In *Proceedings of the 42nd International Symposium on Microarchitecture*, Dec 2009.

[25] M. Lichman. UCI machine learning repository, 2013.

[26] M. M. Michael and M. L. Scott. Simple, fast, and practical non-blocking and blocking concurrent queue algorithms. In *Proceedings of the Fifteenth Annual ACM Symposium on Principles of Distributed Computing*, 1996.

[27] J. Park, R. M. Yoo, D. S. Khudia, C. J. Hughes, and D. Kim. Location-aware cache management for many-core processors with deep cache hierarchy. In *Proceedings of the International Conference on High Performance Computing, Networking, Storage and Analysis*, 2013.

[28] D. Pregibon. Logistic regression diagnostics. *The Annals of Statistics*, 9(4), 1981.

[29] R. Rajwar, A. Kägi, and J. R. Goodman. Inferential queueing and speculative push for reducing critical communication latencies. In *Proceedings of the 17th Annual International Conference on Supercomputing*, 2003.

[30] E. Rosti, E. Smirni, T. D. Wagner, A. W. Apon, and L. W. Dowdy. The ksr1: Experimentation and modeling of poststore. In *Proceedings of the 1993 ACM SIGMETRICS Conference on Measurement and Modeling of Computer Systems*, 1993.

[31] D. Sanchez, R. M. Yoo, and C. Kozyrakis. Flexible architectural support for fine-grain scheduling. In

Proceedings of the Fifteenth Edition of ASPLOS on Architectural Support for Programming Languages and Operating Systems, 2010.

[32] B. Schölkopf, J. Platt, and T. Hofmann. Map-reduce for machine learning on multicore. In *Proceedings of Conference of Advances in Neural Information Processing Systems*, 2007.

[33] T. R. Scogland and W.-c. Feng. Design and evaluation of scalable concurrent queues for many-core architectures. In *Proceedings of the 6th ACM/SPEC International Conference on Performance Engineering*, 2015.

[34] P. Tsigas and Y. Zhang. A simple, fast and scalable non-blocking concurrent fifo queue for shared memory multiprocessor systems. In *Proceedings of the Thirteenth Annual ACM Symposium on Parallel Algorithms and Architectures*, 2001.

[35] J. Wei, W. Dai, A. Qiao, Q. Ho, H. Cui, G. R. Ganger, P. B. Gibbons, G. A. Gibson, and E. P. Xing. Managed communication and consistency for fast data-parallel iterative analytics. In *Proceedings of the Sixth ACM Symposium on Cloud Computing*, 2015.

[36] S. Wilton and N. Jouppi. Cacti: an enhanced cache access and cycle time model. *IEEE Journal of Solid-State Circuits*, 31(5), May 1996.

[37] T. Xu, P. Liljeberg, and H. Tenhunen. Optimal memory controller placement for chip multiprocessor. In *Proceedings of the 9th International Conference on Hardware/Software Codesign and System Synthesis*, Oct 2011.

Vectorization of Multibyte Floating Point Data Formats

Andrew Anderson
Lero, Trinity College Dublin
aanderso@cs.tcd.ie

David Gregg
Lero, Trinity College Dublin
dgregg@cs.tcd.ie

ABSTRACT

We propose a scheme for reduced-precision representation of floating point data on a continuum between IEEE-754 floating point types. Our scheme enables the use of lower precision formats for a reduction in storage space requirements and data transfer volume. We describe how our scheme can be accelerated using existing hardware vector units on a general-purpose processor (GPP). Exploiting native vector hardware allows us to support reduced precision floating point with low overhead. We demonstrate that supporting reduced precision in the compiler as opposed to using a library approach can yield a low overhead solution for GPPs.

CCS Concepts

•Computer systems organization → Single instruction, multiple data; •Software and its engineering → *Software performance;* Data types and structures; **•Theory of computation →** *Vector / streaming algorithms;*

Keywords

Approximate Computing; Floating Point; Multiple Precision; SIMD; Vector Architecture

1. MOTIVATION

It has long been recognized that different applications and algorithms need different amounts of floating point precision to achieve accurate results [3, 13, 16]. For example, 64-bit double precision floating point is often needed for scientific applications, whereas 32-bit single precision is sufficient for most graphics and computer vision applications.

Modern GPUs and embedded processors increasingly support 16-bit floating point for applications that are highly tolerant of approximation such as speech recognition [6].

In some contexts it is possible to customize the level of precision precisely to the application. For example, field-programmable gate arrays (FPGAs) can be used to implement customized floating point with bit-level control over the size of the mantissa and exponent [5, 16].

More recently, Schkufza et al. [14] have shown how super-optimization can be used to generate iterative floating point algorithms that guarantee a given level of accuracy. For example, an exponential function may return a 64-bit floating point value in which at least the first, say, 40 bits of the mantissa are guaranteed to be accurate.

A problem with customizing floating point precision on general-purpose processors (GPPs) is that most support only two standard types: IEEE-754 single precision (or `binary32`) and double precision (`binary64`). If an operation needs more precision than `binary32` and less than `binary64`, the developer has no choice but to use `binary64`.

In this paper we propose a compiler-based mechanism for supporting several non-standard *multibyte* floating point memory formats, such as 24-, 40-, or 48-bit floating point. By *multibyte* we mean that these formats differ in length from standard IEEE-754 formats by multiples of 8 bits.

By using these types, a developer can reduce the precision of floating point data in memory, resulting in reduced storage requirements for their data.

An increasingly important factor in the design of computing systems is energy consumption. In embedded computing systems the energy consumed by data movement can be much greater than the energy used to perform arithmetic [4].

According to Gustafson [7], a typical 64-bit multiply-add operation costs around 200pJ, while reading 64 bits from cache costs 800pJ and a 64-bit main memory read costs 12000pJ. Reducing the amount of data movement is therefore essential to reducing energy consumed by an application, and in particular, reducing the number of costly last-level cache misses.

Customizing precision of floating point data to the needs of the application is one way to reduce data movement. It is straightforward to implement a C/C++ data type representing, for example, 24-bit floating point values (Figure 1).

However, we have found that the performance of such code can be extraordinarily poor when operating on arrays of data. We therefore propose a technique to generate vectorized code that performs a number of adjacent reads or writes together, along with the required packing or unpacking.

Contributions

- We present a practical representation of multibyte floating point values that can easily be converted to and from the next largest natively-supported type.

PACT '16, September 11-15, 2016, Haifa, Israel

DOI: http://dx.doi.org/10.1145/2967938.2967966

- We propose a compiler vectorization scheme for packing and unpacking our floating point types, enabling their use in vectorized floating point computations.

- We demonstrate experimentally that our techniques provide a low-overhead way to support customized floating point types on general-purpose processors.

2. CUSTOMIZING FLOATING POINT

The IEEE-754 2008 standard [17] defines a number of finite binary representations of real numbers at different resolutions (16, 32, and 64 bits, among others). Each format encodes floating-point values using three binary integers: *sign*, *exponent*, and *mantissa*, which specify a point on the real number line following a general formula:

$$v = (-1)^s \times (1 + \sum_{i=1}^{M}(m_i 2^{-i})) \times 2^{e-bias}$$

v is the real number obtained by the evaluation of the formula for a floating-point value with sign s, mantissa m of length M bits, and exponent e. The value *bias* is an integer constant which differs for each format. Different formats (`binary32`, `binary64`, etc.) use different numbers of bits for the exponent and mantissa components.

The exponent determines a power of two by which the rest of the number is multiplied, while the mantissa represents a fractional quantity in the interval $[1, 2)$ obtained by summing successively smaller powers of two, starting from 2^{-1} and continuing up to the length of the mantissa. If the ith mantissa bit is set, the corresponding power of two is present in the sum. For normalized numbers (those with a nonzero exponent), the leading 1 is not explicitly stored in the mantissa, but is implied.

The structure of the IEEE-754 binary encoding means that a change in an exponent bit strongly influences the resulting value, while a change in a mantissa bit has less influence. Furthermore, a change in any bit of the mantissa has exponentially greater effect on the resulting value than a change in the next-least-significant bit.

These observations lead naturally to a scheme for representing values at precisions between those specified by the IEEE-754 standard: varying the number of low-order mantissa bits. Previous proposals based around this concept have typically made use of either customized floating point hardware support via FPGA [5] or high-level data reorganization in massively parallel systems [9].

In this paper, we demonstrate how reduced precision floating point representations can be used on general-purpose processors without requiring any special hardware support.

The rest of our paper is organized as follows: first, in Section 3, we discuss our scheme for representing floating point numbers with reduced precision in memory, and a straightforward implementation of the scheme in scalar code using a library of datatypes implementing different memory representations of floating point numbers with different precision.

Next, in Section 4, we discuss aspects of contemporary GPP architecture which confound the straightforward library approach, and propose a vectorized, compiler-accelerated approach. Section 5 discusses *rounding*, an important aspect of implementing floating point. Section 6 presents an experimental evaluation of both library and compiler-accelerated schemes on a recent general-purpose processor. Section 7 discusses related work, and Section 8 concludes.

3. REDUCED PRECISION ON GPPS

It is possible to *emulate* floating point operations in software using integer instructions. However, each floating point operation requires many integer instructions so emulation is slow.

In particular, the IEEE-754 standard has several special values and ranges such as not-a-number (NaN), positive and negative zero, infinities, and sub-normal numbers, each of which adds to the complexity of software emulation [15].

Modern processors provide hardware floating point units which dramatically reduce the time and energy required for floating point computations. However, these units normally support just two floating point types, typically `binary32` (`float`) and `binary64` (`double`).

3.1 Our Approach

We propose a set of non-standard **fl**oating point multib**yte** types that we refer to as *flytes*. Rather than emulating computation on *flytes* in software, we convert them to/from the next largest natively supported type. Thus, a 24-bit *flyte* (`flyte24`) is converted to `binary32` before computation, and the `binary32` result is converted back to `flyte24` afterwards.

We need to solve two problems: (1) efficiently loading and storing non-standard data sizes, such as 24-bit data, where there is no hardware support for such operations, and (2) quickly converting between built-in floating point types and our non-standard types.

In general, converting between floating point formats has many special cases. In particular, converting between formats with different-sized exponents may cause numbers to overflow to infinity or underflow to/from sub-normal numbers. Dealing correctly with these cases in software is complicated and slow.

Our solution to the problem is that in all our *flyte* types, the size of the exponent is equal to the size of the exponent of the **next largest built-in type**. For example, in our `flyte16` and `flyte24` types, the exponent has eight bits, just like `binary32`. This dramatically reduces the complexity of conversions.

Efficiently supporting non-standard floating point types using this approach creates two types of problems. The first is supporting the loading, storing, and conversion of reduced precision types with acceptably low overhead. This is the topic of the majority of this paper.

The second type of problem is that performing computation in one floating point type and storing values in a less precise type introduces issues, such as double-rounding, that complicate numerical analysis. We make every effort to be clear about this latter group of problems but in most cases we do not have comprehensive solutions. Double rounding in particular is a topic of extensive study, and we refer the reader to the work of Boldo and Melquiond [2] for an in-depth discussion.

Our techniques are aimed squarely at problems where some approximation is acceptable and the developer has a good understanding of exactly how much precision is required. Our main contribution is to show *how* to implement multibyte floating point formats efficiently; the question of *whether* to use them in any particular algorithm depends on the numerical properties of the algorithm.

3.2 Simple Scalar Code Approach

Figure 1 shows a simple implementation of the `flyte24` type in C++. It relies on the *bit field* facility in C/C++ to specify that the `num` field contains a 24-bit integer. It also uses the GCC `packed` attribute to indicate to the compiler that arrays of the type should be packed to exactly 24 bits, rather than padded to 32 bits. Figure 1 also shows a routine for converting from `flyte24` to `float` (i.e. `binary32`). The 24-bit pattern stored in the `flyte24` variable is scaled to 32 bits and padded with zeros. The resulting 32-bit pattern is returned as a `float`.

```
class flyte24 {
private:
  unsigned num:24;
public:
  operator float() {
    u32 temp = num << 8;
    return(cast_u32_to_f32(temp));
  };
  ...
} __attribute__((packed));
```

Figure 1: Simple implementation of `flyte24` in C++

The code that is sketched in Fig. 1 can be used to implement programs with arrays of `flyte24` values, but it is very slow. Figure 6a shows a comparison of the execution time of several BLAS kernels using `flyte24` and other `flyte` and IEEE-754 types.

The order of magnitude difference in execution time is the result of (1) the cost of converting between `flyte24` and `binary32` before and after each computation; and (2) the cost of loading and storing individual 24-bit values.

In particular, storing data to successive elements of packed `flyte24` arrays can result in sequences of overlapping 3-byte aligned stores. Load/store hardware in GPPs is not designed to deal with such operations, which results in extraordinarily slow execution.

Table 1 summarizes our proposed set of *multibyte* formats for floating-point values which preserve the sign and exponent fields of the corresponding IEEE-754 representations.

Table 1: *flyte* storage formats for IEEE-754 types.

		flyte layout (bits)		
IEEE-754 type	*flyte* format	Sign	Exp.	Mant.
`binary32`	16-bit	1	8	7
`binary32`	24-bit	1	8	15
`binary32`	32-bit	1	8	23
`binary64`	40-bit	1	11	28
`binary64`	48-bit	1	11	36
`binary64`	56-bit	1	11	44
`binary64`	64-bit	1	11	52

4. ACCESS IN REDUCED PRECISION

Reading and writing reduced precision representations might be expected to incur a significant performance penalty due to the overheads outlined in Section 3.2. Particular concerns are (1) the overhead of conversion between data formats, in addition to (2) the overheads of memory access to arrays of datatypes that may have non–power-of-two byte width, where memory movements may be overlapping and misaligned. Although these overheads are encountered both when reading and when writing reduced-precision representations, there are important differences between the two cases.

4.1 Reading In Reduced Precision

Modern instruction set architectures typically have native support for data movement using types with power-of-two byte widths – usually 1, 2, 4, and 8 bytes. Since our *flyte* types differ in width from standard IEEE-754 types by multiples of 8 bits, this means we can always fetch a *flyte* with a single read using a wider native type (e.g. a 4-byte read for a `flyte24`).

Since we propose to store *flyte*s packed consecutively in arrays without padding, the majority of such accesses will be misaligned. Specifically, a consecutive *flyte* array access will only be aligned to the next largest native type once every $lcm(\texttt{native}_{bits}, \texttt{flyte}_{bits})/\texttt{flyte}_{bits}$ array elements.

Unaligned access can cause extra cache misses versus aligned access due to the possibility that the accessed item spans a cache line boundary. The strategy of using overlapping accesses at the next largest native type allows us to utilize the vectorization approach of Anderson et al. [1]. (Section 4.3) for our vector memory accesses. Also, the conversion process when reading *flytes* is relatively simple, requiring only that the read data be shifted and padded with zero bits.

4.2 Writing In Reduced Precision

Writing data to a reduced-precision format is more complex than reading, both in terms of the memory movement (since memory locations are modified), and due to the fact that when writing, the number format narrows, and precision is lost.

Loss of precision is a natural consequence of working with floating point numbers. The precise result of a floating point computation can be a real number which cannot be exactly encoded in a finite representation (for example, it might require infinitely many digits). In these cases, loss of precision is necessary to make the result representable.

The IEEE-754 standard specifies several methods which are used to *round* numbers to a nearby representable value. One straightforward way to perform rounding is to simply truncate extra digits (i.e. bits, in a binary representation). This is the standard round-to-zero rounding mode [17]. Other rounding modes are specified by the IEEE-754 standard, including round-to-nearest-even and round-to-infinity (positive or negative).

4.3 Vectorized Reading and Writing

We propose a compiler-based approach which can greatly reduce the overhead of operating on *flyte* arrays using automatic vectorization. Our approach uses vector instructions to load, convert, and store *flytes*. We generate vectorized code to load a number of *flyte* values at once, and unpack those values in parallel to the next largest IEEE type using vector shuffle and blend instructions. We use vectorization not only to amortize the cost of converting each element (as it does for other operations), but also to help overcome penalties associated with `flyte` types' unnaturally aligned memory accesses.

By restricting the size of a *flyte* to be a multiple of 8 bits, we ensure that widely available fast byte-level vector reorganization instructions can be used. Finally, when computation is complete, we again use vector instructions to convert back to *flyte* types. This may involve a rounding step when reducing the precision of a standard IEEE-754 format to a *flyte* type, followed by packing the data in vector registers before the results are written to memory.

Vectorized loading and storing of packed data elements that do not correspond to any native machine type presents additional challenges over scalar memory movement. Since vector lengths on modern GPPs are usually a power-of-two bytes, vectorized access to *flyte* arrays often leads to the splitting of data elements across vector memory operations, where the leading bytes of an element are accessed by one operation, and the trailing bytes by the next. Figure 2 displays one such scenario: storing in **flyte24** format computational results produced in **binary32**.

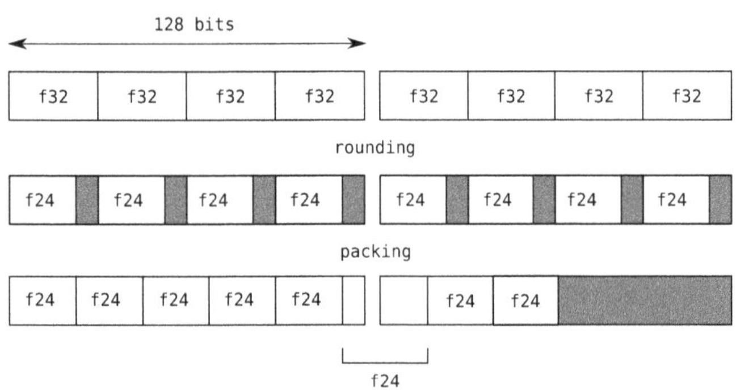

Figure 2: Layout of data in 128-bit (16-byte) vector registers. (top) before format conversion, (center) after rounding to the desired size, and (bottom) the desired layout in memory. Note that the desired memory layout requires data elements to straddle the boundary between vector registers.

While vectorized reading is not significantly more complicated than scalar reading, vectorized writing has additional issues. A straightforward approach to vectorized writing of unpadded *flyte* data could pack as many consecutive *flyte* elements in a vector register as would fit, and perform a store with the trailing unused byte positions predicated off.

Subsequent stores, if there are more than one, could overlap prior stores in these unused positions, so that the data is consecutive in memory. Due to the structure of load/store hardware in GPPs, this approach is likely to be extremely inefficient.

Our vectorized approach to storing values in reduced precision format works by packing all the rounded data elements to be stored consecutively in a set of vector registers, which are mapped to a set of consecutive, **non-overlapping** vector memory movements (shown in Figure 2).

We use a two-phase permute and blend approach. Vector permute instructions are initially used to compact the rounded data in each register into memory order, and align the contents of some registers so that the leading data element in each register is located at the position of the first unused byte in the previous register. Next, the compacted vector registers are combined together using vector blend instructions until a number of fully packed vector registers result.

The resulting registers can be stored without overlap, and data elements are correctly split across register boundaries. If the data written cannot be packed perfectly into full vector registers, some vector stores may be partial stores with some additional implementation concerns. These are described in detail in the vectorization approach of Anderson et al. [1].

4.4 Controlling Format Conversion

Programming language designers have three conflicting goals when deciding the rules for evaluating floating point expressions. Evaluating expressions at higher precision may result in more accurate answers, which suggests that higher precision should be used if it is available.

On the other hand, programmers like to get bit-exact identical results from their program regardless of which compiler is used, which suggests that the language should strictly define the precise precision and each floating point operation.

The IEEE-754 standard stipulates [17, §11] that conforming languages *should* support reproducible programming, and defines circumstances when programs should have numerically identical results across compliant platforms. Finally, giving the compiler the freedom to choose precision may result in more efficient code.

Controlling exactly when format conversion occurs is an important part of using non-standard formats such as our *flytes*. Languages such as C99 [8] provides features aimed at providing consistency in the output of the same program on different platforms.

In particular, the programmer can choose to specify the rules determining the precision of intermediate values in expressions using the `FLT_EVAL_METHOD` facility.

The programmer can also use the pragma directive `STDC FP_CONTRACT` to enable or disable *contraction* – atomic evaluation of floating point expressions which can use higher precision and omit rounding errors implied by the source code and `FLT_EVAL_METHOD` [8, §6.5]. Both facilities modify behaviour at the expression level.

For example, the programmer can choose to have all subexpressions within an expression tree evaluated at the exact width of the widest operand to each operator (by setting `FLT_EVAL_METHOD = 0`).

Such strict constraints on the types of all intermediate floating point values can result in very poor performance for *flytes*. For example, **flyte24** is stored in memory as a 24-bit value, but we must convert it to **binary32** before performing any operations. In a larger expression of **flyte24** values, the generated code is likely to be much faster if all intermediate values can be kept in **binary32** rather than being converted down to **flyte24** after every operation.

C99 also provides a feature that allows floating point operations to be performed at a higher precision than the source values or result: *contraction* of floating point expressions, which is controlled by the standard pragma directive `FP_CONTRACT`. In all our experiments, `FP_CONTRACT` is on.

One problem not addressed by C99's floating point support is the issue of using higher precision values across *statements*. C99 requires that the value stored in a variable must be convered to the type of that variable at the point where it is written to storage.

We propose a type qualifier `AT_LEAST` which is used to tag a floating point type informing the compiler that it is free to use a higher precision to store results of that type, rather than converting strictly to the precision of the storage type.

This allows the use of higher-precision types in code like that in Figure 3 where accumulation into a variable would otherwise result in many lossy conversions.

```
flyte24 sum(flyte24 * a, int size)
{
  AT_LEAST flyte24 sum = 0.0;
  for(int i = 0; i < size; i++) {
    sum = sum + a[i];
    /*
       without AT_LEAST, C99 will truncate
       sum here in every loop iteration
     */
  }
  return sum;
}
```

Figure 3: Example of the use of the `AT_LEAST` qualifier to allow accumulation in a higher precision than the input/output.

The code in Figure 3 shows the variable `sum` of type `AT_LEAST flyte24` which the compiler can represent as any floating point type with at least the precision of a `flyte24`. In general, the next largest native type is a good choice for a use of the `AT_LEAST` qualifier.

5. ROUNDING

When numbers represented in IEEE-754 floating point format are used in computations (such as addition and subtraction), the natural result of computation is often a real number which is not exactly representable in the finite representation. In these cases, the standard specifies a way to round these numbers to a nearby representable value.

Computations on *flytes* are performed using the next largest standard floating point size. After each operation, the built-in floating point type performs its own rounding. However, a question arises when we convert from IEEE floating point types to *flytes*: should we round again during conversion?

Double rounding is discussed in considerable depth by Boldo and Melquiond [2], and we do not reproduce their arguments here. Note that our aim in this paper is simply to demonstrate that a low-overhead implementation of customized floating point types is feasible on general purpose processors.

Any compiler framework which might implement our proposed scheme should take the necessary steps to ensure that the transformations applied to convert between floating point representations are correct; in the remainder of this section, we describe some low-overhead mechanisms which can be used to implement them.

5.1 Round-towards-zero

The simplest approach is to round by truncating the lower matissa bits, an option which is known as *round-towards-zero* in IEEE 754. Rounding towards zero is simple to implement, but IEEE floating point has a number of special cases that we must treat correctly.

In IEEE-754 a NaN value has an exponent consisting entirely of ones, and a mantissa value that is non-zero. If the non-zero part of the mantissa is in the lower bits, truncating those bits may cause the entire mantissa to have a zero value. This would change the value from NaN to a value with all ones in the exponent and zero matissa, which represents infinity in IEEE-754.

However, there are two types of NaNs: signalling NaNs, which cause a floating point exception, and quiet NaNs which indicate an invalid value with causing an exception. In IEEE-754 binary floating point formats, quiet NaNs are distinguished from signalling NaNs by the value of the *most significant bit* of the mantissa, which is preserved by truncation of up to $M - 1$ bits.

In IEEE-754, a subnormal number has a zero exponent, and the mantissa represents a very small fixed-point number. Truncating the final bits of a sub-normal number may cause its value to change to zero. This is correct behaviour, since the non-zero part of the number is too small to represent in our smaller *flyte* type, and zero is the closest representable value.

5.2 Round-to-nearest

Round-towards-zero is simple to implement, but it can result in large errors. For example, if round-towards-zero were applied in decimal, the number 9.9 would be rounded to 9, rather than 10. The maximum error can be reduced by rounding to the nearest representable number rather than simply truncating.

A special case is where the number to be rounded is exactly between two values. To break the tie, IEEE-754 specifies that exact ties should be rounded to the nearest even number.

Figure 4 shows a 32-bit floating point number being rounded to our 24-bit representation using round-to-nearest, where exact ties between two values are rounded to the nearest even value.

Rounding to nearest even is expressed in terms of the relationship between three bits (Guard, Round and Sticky) around the point where the number is rounded. There are no hardware instructions in conventional processors for rounding floating point values to *flytes*, and we must therefore round in software.

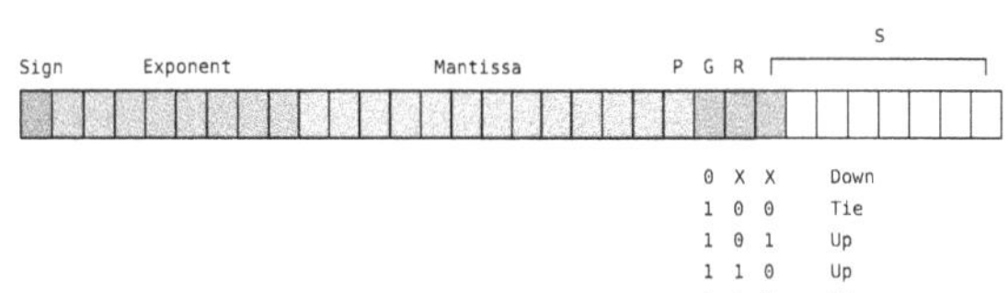

Figure 4: Rounding to nearest even. Marked bit positions correspond to **G**uard, **R**ound, and **S**ticky bits. To avoid overflow into the exponent when rounding to nearest even in software, the pre-guard bit (**P**) must also be inspected.

In the most straightforward case, rounding to nearest even simply involves computing the nearest representable number. An easy way to do this is shown in Figure 5.
The code in Figure 5 adds half of a unit of least precision (ULP) in the new smaller format to the value in the existing larger format.

As long is the number to be rounded is not exactly between two representable values in the new format, this will result in correct round-to-nearest-even. Implementing precise round-to-nearest-even requires checking for this tied special case, and rounding accordingly. In addition, there are

```
flyte24 round_to_nearest(float num)
{
  u32 temp = cast_f32_to_u32(num);
  // round by adding 0.5 ULP
  temp = temp + 128;
  // truncate last eight bits
  temp = temp >> 8;
  return cast_u32_to_flyte24(temp);
}
```

Figure 5: Heuristically rounding to nearest even by adding half of a unit of least precision (ULP).

numerous special cases which must be checked to correctly implement IEEE-754 mandated behaviour.

5.3 Treatment of Special Values

The IEEE-754 floating point standard has special values and ranges as previously outlined in Section 2. Rounding interacts in different ways with these values and ranges, and behaviour which may be appropriate for some scenarios may not be for others.

The application programmer must make a choice of rounding approach based on the information available. We describe the behaviour of each of our proposed rounding approaches here with respect to IEEE-754 special values and ranges.

5.3.1 Normalized numbers

When a normalized number is being rounded, an infinity occurs when the rounded value is so large that the exponent is all ones after rounding (overflow). This is a natural consequence of conversion from a larger to a smaller finite representation.

However, when a normalized number is so small that its exponent is all zeros after rounding (underflow), it does not get rounded directly to zero, but instead to a subnormal number.

Underflow is *gradual*, and a number will underflow to zero only when it is so small that both exponent and mantissa are all zeros after rounding. Normalized numbers may therefore naturally be rounded to several different classes of value.

Very large positive or negative numbers may go to infinity when rounded, and very small numbers may become subnormal. This behaviour conforms to IEEE-754 semantics.

5.3.2 Subnormal numbers

Subnormal numbers are distinguished by a zero exponent, and lack the implied leading 1 in their mantissa. They represent numbers very close to zero. The expected behaviour of format conversion for subnormal numbers is slightly complicated due to the issues of overflow and underflow.

The closest value in the target representation for a very large subnormal number may be a very small normalized number (overflow), while the closest value for a very small subnormal number may be zero (underflow).

For subnormal numbers, rounding may validly cause the class of the value to change, either by underflow to zero, or by overflow to a small normalized number.

5.3.3 Infinities

Positive and negative infinities are encoded with an exponent which is all 1s and a zero mantissa. There are only two values in this class, which are distinguished from each other by their sign. The expected behaviour of format conversion for infinities is a correctly signed infinity in the target format.

5.3.4 NaN values

NaN values represent the result of expressions of *indeterminate form*, which cannot be computed, such as $\infty - \infty$. The expected behaviour of format conversion of a NaN value is a NaN value in the target format. However, NaN is not a singular value, but a value *range*. NaN values occupy a range of bit patterns distinguished by an exponent which is all ones and any nonzero value in the mantissa.

Since the mantissa is truncated by conversion to a shorter format, some NaN values cannot be represented after down-conversion, and indeed truncation may cause the non-zero part of the mantissa to be lost entirely.

However, as described in section 5.1, IEEE-754 non signalling (or *quiet*) NaNs always have a 1 in the *most significant bit* of their mantissa. Thus, although the exact mantissa value of a NaN may change after truncation, a quiet NaN cannot become a non-NaN value through truncation.

Signalling NaNs are different: the non-zero bits of a signalling NaN's mantissa may be entirely in the lower bits. A signalling NaN may be corrupted to become an infinity value by truncation. Thus, signalling NaNs should not be used with *flyte* values, unless the signal handler is modified to place a non-zero value in the higher-order bits of the NaN.

When using our add-half-an-ULP heuristic, a further problem can arise with non-signalling NaNs. If the mantissa value of the non-signalling NaN is the maximum representable value after truncation, then adding even half an ULP will cause an overflow from the mantissa to the exponent, and potentially into the sign bit, if the exponent is all ones.

Our slowest and most correct round-to-nearest mode checks for this case, and corrects the value if necessary. Our fast heuristic round to nearest approach (Figure 5) does not. However, despite extensive testing we have never seen a case where the floating point unit creates such a pathological NaN value as the result of arithmetic.

6. EXPERIMENTAL EVALUATION

We benchmarked the performance of our proposed scalar code implementation from Section 3.2 and vectorized implementation from Section 4.3. Experiments were run on 64-bit Linux with a 4.2 series kernel, using a machine with 16GB of RAM and an Intel Core i5-3450 (Ivy Bridge) processor.

We followed Intel's guidelines for benchmarking short programs on this architecture [12]. Figures 6 and 7 present the results of benchmarking. In our experiments, we use rounding towards zero, `FP_CONTRACT` is on, and variables which are used to accumulate are declared as `AT_LEAST` the target precision.

Problem size in experimental figures refers to the number of elements in arrays in BLAS operations - for vector-vector operationss (BLAS Level 1) this is the number of elements in a vector, while for operations involving matrices (BLAS Level 2 and 3) this is the number of elements in a row or column of a square matrix, so that the total number of data elements is the square of the problem size.

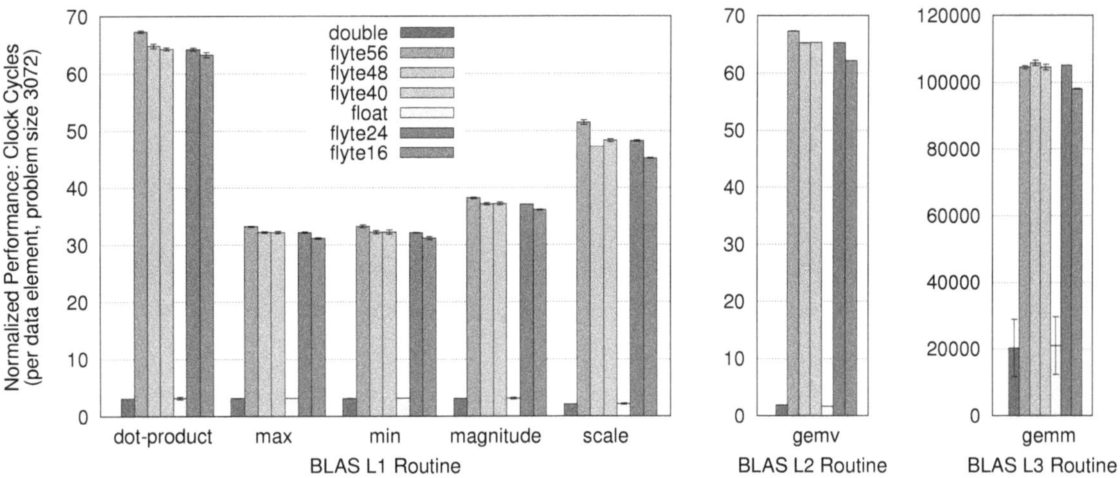

(a) Scalar code (Approach shown in Figure 1)

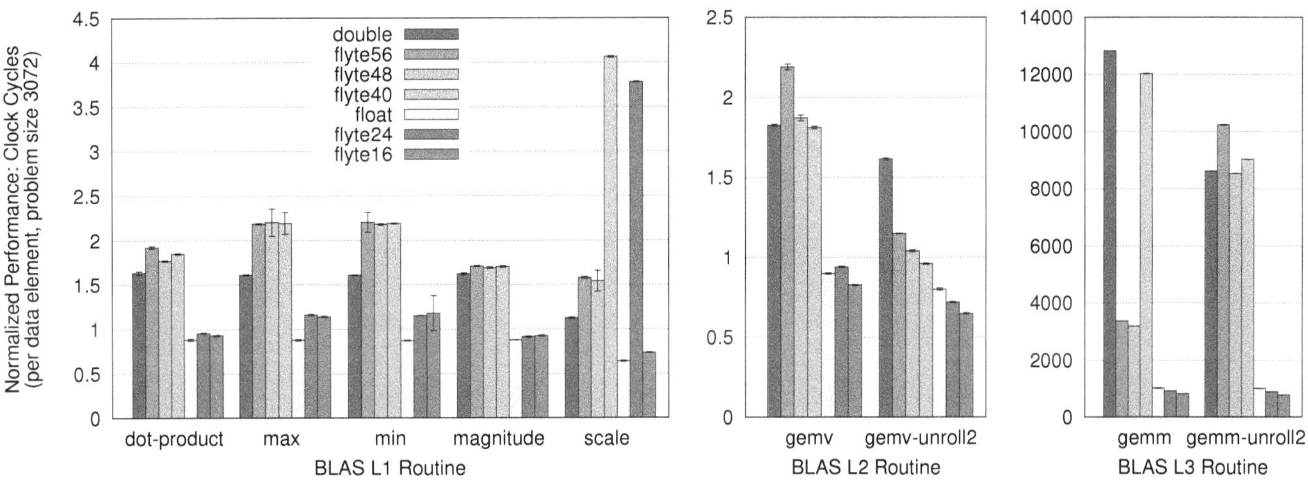

(b) 128-bit SSE code (Approach shown in Figure 2)

Figure 6: Variation of performance with precision of memory representation across a number of BLAS kernels. Performance displayed as normalized execution time (cycles per data element) – **lower is better**. Overhead versus native types can be read as the difference between any `flyte` type and the next largest native type.

6.1 Overheads: SIMD vs Non-SIMD

The large overhead of scalar access in Figure 6a is due to the design mismatch between our non-standard use-case and the typical structure of a GPP scalar datapath, discussed in more detail in Section 3.2. The GPP datapath is ill equipped to handle simultaneous misaligned accesses to data stored in packed non–power-of-two multibyte formats.

In contrast, our compiler-based vectorized approach (Figure 6b) marshalls and unmarshalls this data into consecutive, non-overlapping power-of-two length accesses which are the best-case for performance using the (SSE) vector datapath.

Overheads in the scalar implementation are in the mid to high tens of cycles per accessed element, while in the vectorized implementation, overheads versus native IEEE-754 types are on the order of a single cycle per data element. In computationally heavy programs like `magnitude` this overhead is effectively hidden by instruction-level parallelism (Figure 6b).

The relatively high overhead of `flyte40` and `flyte24` in the `scale` benchmark in Figure 6b is due to two factors: the alignment of the accesses is odd (5 and 3 bytes, respectively) meaning that data must be shuffled *between* vectors, rather than simply within vectors, as with other types. Furthermore, the benchmark performs an *in-place* update of the data, where reads and writes overlap, which reduces the available instruction-level parallelism.

However, the overhead is still on the order of 3 cycles per data element in the worst case, which may be perfectly acceptable in many scenarios in return for a 37.5% reduction in memory traffic. Indeed, as can be seen from our results in Figure 7a, `flyte40` is only marginally slower overall considering BLAS Level 1 programs, and significantly reduces second-last and last-level cache misses for BLAS Level 2 and Level 3 programs.

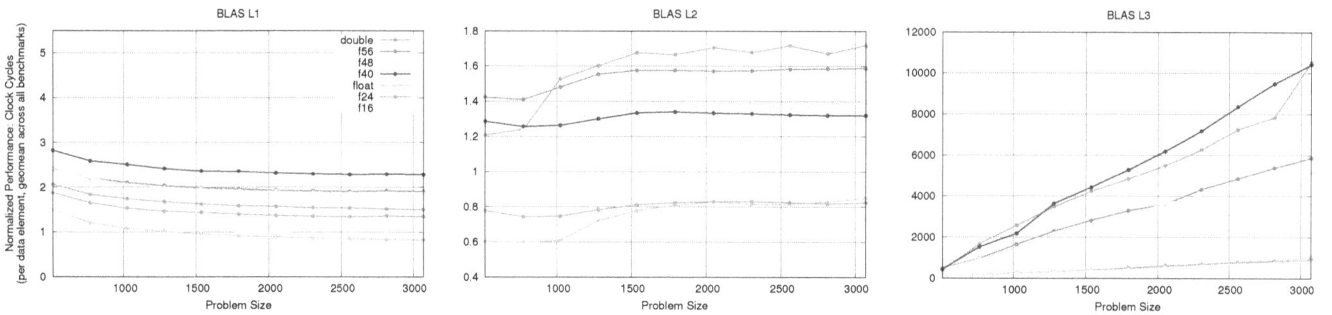

(a) Normalized variation in absolute performance (clock cycles per element processed) at each BLAS level as problem size increases. **Lower is better**.

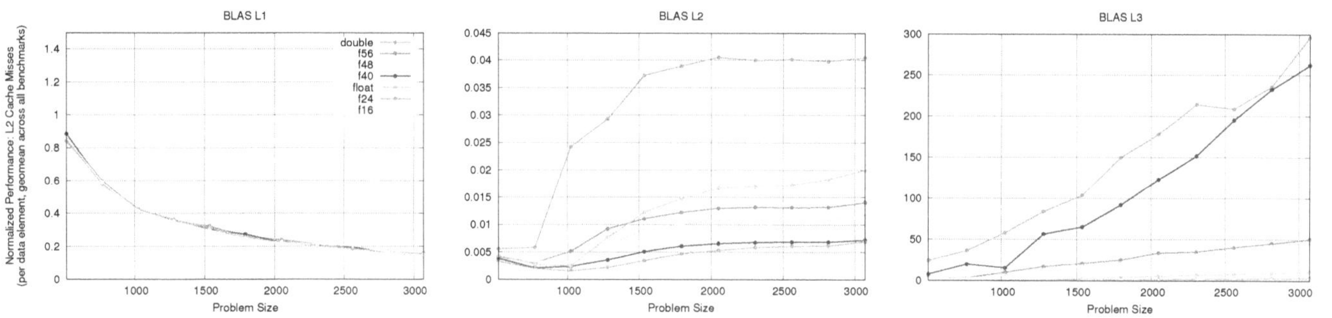

(b) Normalized variation in second-last level cache misses as problem size increases (misses per element processed). **Lower is better**.

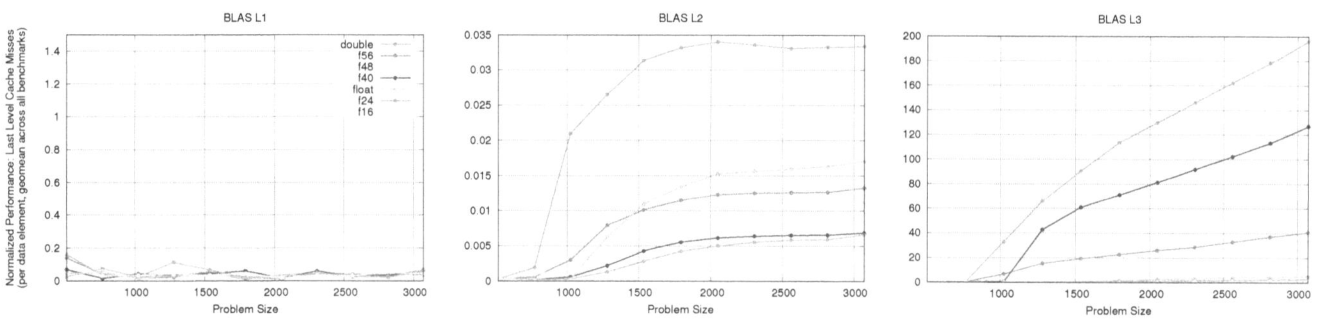

(c) Normalized variation in last-level cache misses as problem size increases (misses per element processed). **Lower is better**.

Figure 7: Summary of absolute performance (cycles per processed element) and cache behaviour (cache misses at L2 and L3) for our vectorized BLAS benchmark programs as problem size increases. Performance for each BLAS level is measured as the geometric mean performance across all the programs in that level. The programs in each BLAS level are shown in Figure 6b.

6.2 Effect of Unrolling Loops

The benchmark `gemv-unroll2` in Figure 6b is the BLAS Level 2 `GEMV` kernel unrolled twice to increase the amount of data movement per vectorized loop iteration. In this benchmark, data transfer accounts for a large portion of total execution time.

The benchmark demonstrates that a win-win is possible: the choice of a reduced-precision memory representation can actually *increase* overall performance versus the next largest IEEE-754 type, while also reducing memory requirements, even on a general purpose processor without special hardware support for non-standard floating point.

The benchmark `gemm-unroll2` in Figure 6b is the BLAS Level 3 `GEMM` kernel unrolled twice to increase the amount of data movement per vectorized loop iteration.

In effect, unrolling is equivalent to a simple 1-dimensional loop tiling with tile size $2 \times \texttt{VF}$ where `VF` is the vectorization factor. In this benchmark, data transfer accounts for a large portion of total execution time.

However, unlike `GEMV`, `GEMM` exhibits a slowdown when unrolled. We inspected the performance data and found that the number of last level cache misses was significantly elevated when `GEMM` was unrolled.

In this case, unrolling simply introduces too much data movement in the inner loop. It is likely that less naïve tilings could mitigate this effect, however, we aim only to show the effect of using reduced precision types.

6.3 Effect on Cache Behaviour

The primary effect of using shorter data representations is seen in the behaviour of the second-last and last-level caches. Using a shorter data representation means that each individual memory operation (i.e. cache line read or write from DRAM) stores or retrieves a larger proportion of data elements, resulting in fewer cache misses overall. Reducing the number of last-level cache misses in particular has a large effect on performance, and on energy efficiency [7].

6.3.1 BLAS Level 1

Figure 7 displays a summary of the absolute performance (cycles per data element) as well as the second-last and last-level cache behaviour for our benchmark programs. As in Figure 6, the programs are divided into three categories, one for each BLAS level.

For BLAS level 1 programs, we see that the variation in absolute performance remains small as problem size increases. BLAS level 1 programs are mostly compute-bound, so using smaller types does not significantly affect performance.

Figures 7b and 7c show that, for BLAS Level 1, there is very little difference in the number of second-last and last-level cache misses from using shorter types.

6.3.2 BLAS Level 2

For BLAS level 2 programs, we see that initially there is little variation in performance at small problem sizes. However, as the problem size increases, the effect of using smaller types becomes apparent. For BLAS Level 2 programs, we see a large variation in performance once the problem size exceeds the capacity of the L1 cache.

In Figure 7a, we see that for BLAS Level 2 programs, `float` and `double` initially outperform their reduced-precision representations, but once the problem size grows large enough, the situation is reversed.

Moreover, smaller representations outperform larger ones, in general. At the largest problem size in experiments, `GEMV` on `flyte40` outperforms `GEMV` on `double` by 23.5% (Figure 7a, center graph).

Figures 7b and 7c display the large reduction in second-last and last-level cache misses for BLAS Level 2 programs. In some cases, the reduction is as many as $6\times$ fewer last-level cache misses (compare `flyte40` and `double` in Figure 7c, center graph).

6.3.3 BLAS Level 3

For BLAS Level 3, we again see that using smaller types results in many fewer second-last and last-level cache misses, although the reduction is less pronounced for `flyte40`. 5-byte accesses are frequently split across cache lines, causing two misses, which offsets the reduction in misses from simply transferring less data overall.

However, we again see that performance closely tracks cache behaviour - our straightforward implementation of `GEMM` is heavily memory-bound, so this is not surprising. Overall, we see a significant reduction in cache misses for smaller types: as many as $4.5\times$ fewer last-level cache misses comparing `flyte56` and `double` (Figure 7c, rightmost graph).

7. RELATED WORK

Much prior work discusses reduced precision floating point [3, 10,13]. Jenkins et al. [9] evaluate a reduced-precision scheme using GPPs in an extreme-scale computing context. They do not utilize SIMD, address only reads, and convert in a pre-pass.

Many approaches use FPGAs or otherwise customized hardware; notably Tong et al. [16], who propose customizing ALUs to support short-mantissa representations. More recently, De Dinechin et al. [5] also propose custom hardware to support reduced precision. Ou et al. accelerate mixed-precision floating point using a vector processor with a customized datapath [11].

Our approach, since it targets GPPs, is necessarily less flexible than FPGA/custom hardware based approaches. However, it is precisely because GPPs are so widely deployed that reduced precision support on GPPs is attractive.

Prior work on loading only portions of floating point numbers by Jenkins et al. [9] does not perform an explicit rounding step, but directly truncates values. They perform a byte-level transpose on a matrix of floating point numbers stored in memory, chopping off some number of trailing bytes of each number.

This conversion approach is semantically equivalent to rounding to zero. Jenkins et al. evaluate the error introduced by rounding to zero and find it acceptable for their purposes.

In contrast, using our proposed techniques, the rounding step in Figure 2 can be implemented in any way which is suitable for the needs of the application, including rounding towards zero, rounding to nearest even, or rounding to odd as proposed by Boldo and Melquiond [2].

8. CONCLUSION

In this paper, we propose *flytes*; a scheme representing floating-point data in memory at precisions along a continuum between IEEE-754 types, converting to and from standard IEEE-754 types to perform computations.

We propose a method for converting between IEEE-754 floating point and *flytes*, and show how it can be accelerated using vectorization on general purpose processors, without requiring special hardware support.

Our proposed technique handles both reads and writes, and supports reduced precision floating point memory representations with very low overhead.

Our investigation shows that reducing the precision of floating point data in memory, and using SIMD operations as the basis of a compiler-accelerated scheme for performing conversions presents a low-overhead path to supporting customized floating point on commodity general purpose processors.

Acknowledgements

We would like to thank Ayal Zaks for many helpful comments on an initial draft of this paper. We would also like to thank the reviewers of PACT 2016 for their close attention which helped us greatly in improving the presentation.

This work was supported by Science Foundation Ireland grant 12/IA/1381, and also by Science Foundation Ireland grant 10/CE/I1855 to Lero — the Irish Software Research Centre (www.lero.ie).

9. REFERENCES

[1] A. Anderson, A. Malik, and D. Gregg. Automatic vectorization of interleaved data revisited. *ACM Transactions on Architecture and Code Optimization (TACO)*, 12(4):50, 2015.

[2] S. Boldo and G. Melquiond. When double rounding is odd. In *17th IMACS World Congress*, page 11, 2004.

[3] A. Buttari, J. Dongarra, J. Kurzak, J. Langou, J. Langou, P. Luszczek, and S. Tomov. Exploiting mixed precision floating point hardware in scientific computations. In *High Performance Computing Workshop*, 2006.

[4] W. J. Dally, J. Balfour, D. Black-Shaffer, J. Chen, R. C. Harting, V. Parikh, J. Park, and D. Sheffield. Efficient embedded computing. *IEEE Computer*, (7), 2008.

[5] F. De Dinechin, C. Klein, and B. Pasca. Generating high-performance custom floating-point pipelines. In *International Conference on Field Programmable Logic and Applications*. IEEE, 2009.

[6] P. R. Dixon, T. Oonishi, and S. Furui. Fast acoustic computations using graphics processors. In *International Conference on Acoustics, Speech and Signal Processing*. IEEE, 2009.

[7] J. Gustafson. Exascale: Power, cooling, reliability, and future arithmetic. *HPC User Forum Seattle*, September 2010.

[8] B. S. Institution. *The C standard: incorporating Technical Corrigendum 1 : BS ISO/IEC 9899/1999.* John Wiley, 2003.

[9] J. Jenkins, E. R. Schendel, S. Lakshminarasimhan, D. Boyuka, T. Rogers, S. Ethier, R. Ross, S. Klasky, N. F. Samatova, et al. Byte-precision level of detail processing for variable precision analytics. In *International Conference for High Performance Computing, Networking, Storage and Analysis (SC)*. IEEE, 2012.

[10] M. O. Lam, J. K. Hollingsworth, B. R. de Supinski, and M. P. LeGendre. Automatically adapting programs for mixed-precision floating-point computation. In *International Conference on Supercomputing*. ACM, 2013.

[11] A. Ou, K. Asanovic, and V. Stojanovic. Mixed precision vector processors. *Technical Report No. UCB/EECS-2015-265*, 2015.

[12] G. Paoloni. How to benchmark code execution times on Intel IA-32 and IA-64 instruction set architectures. *Intel Corporation*, 2010.

[13] C. Rubio-González, C. Nguyen, H. D. Nguyen, J. Demmel, W. Kahan, K. Sen, D. H. Bailey, C. Iancu, and D. Hough. Precimonious: Tuning assistant for floating-point precision. In *International Conference on High Performance Computing, Networking, Storage and Analysis (SC)*. ACM, 2013.

[14] E. Schkufza, R. Sharma, and A. Aiken. Stochastic optimization of floating-point programs with tunable precision. *ACM SIGPLAN Notices*, 49(6), 2014.

[15] N. Sidwell and J. Myers. Improving software floating point support. *Proceedings of GCC DeveloperâĂŹs Summit*, 2006.

[16] J. Y. F. Tong, D. Nagle, R. Rutenbar, et al. Reducing power by optimizing the necessary precision/range of floating-point arithmetic. *IEEE Transactions on Very Large Scale Integration Systems*, 8(3), 2000.

[17] D. Zuras, M. Cowlishaw, A. Aiken, M. Applegate, D. Bailey, S. Bass, D. Bhandarkar, M. Bhat, D. Bindel, S. Boldo, et al. IEEE Standard for Floating-point Arithmetic. *IEEE Std 754-2008*, 2008.

Rinnegan: Efficient Resource Use in Heterogeneous Architectures

Sankaralingam Panneerselvam
University of Wisconsin-Madison
sankarp@cs.wisc.edu

Michael Swift
University of Wisconsin-Madison
swift@cs.wisc.edu

ABSTRACT

Current processors provide a variety of different processing units to improve performance and power efficiency. For example, ARM's big.LITTLE, AMD's APUs, and Oracle's M7 provide heterogeneous processors, on-die GPUs, and on-die accelerators. However, the performance experienced by programs using these processing units can vary widely due to contention from multiprogramming, thermal constraints and other issues. In these systems, the decision of where to execute a task must consider not only execution time of the task, but also current system conditions.

We built Rinnegan, a Linux kernel extension and runtime library, to perform scheduling and handle task placement in heterogeneous systems. The Rinnegan kernel extension monitors and reports the utilization of all processing units to applications, which then makes placement decisions at user level. The Rinnegan runtime provides a performance model to predict the speedup and overhead of offloading a task. With this model and the current utilization of processing units, the runtime can select the task placement that best achieves an application's performance goals, such as low latency, high throughput, or real-time deadlines. When integrated with StarPU, a runtime system for heterogeneous architectures, Rinnegan improves StarPU by performing 1.5-2x better than its native scheduling policies in a shared heterogeneous environment.

1. INTRODUCTION

Systems with heterogeneous processors and a variety of accelerators are becoming common as a solution to the power wall [27, 65]. Intel and AMD place CPUs and GPUs on the same chip [4, 32]. ARM's big.LITTLE architecture [5] includes processors with different microarchitectures on the same die. IBM's canceled WireSpeed processor [20] and Oracle's M7 [43] have accelerators for specific tasks like XML parsing, compression, encryption, and query processing.

In addition to static heterogeneity from different processing units, systems exhibit dynamic heterogeneity as the performance observed by programs can vary over time. Contention for accelerators [25, 56] alters the performance benefits for programs. With more mature programming models [12, 48, 49], more programs will try to leverage specialized processing units and compete for access to them. Virtualization can also lead to contention, as processing units may by shared not just by multiple programs but also by multiple guest operating systems [25]. Furthermore, the data copy and dispatching overhead can greatly diminish performance benefits offered by certain accelerators [59].

In this environment, applications that decide statically where to run code may perform poorly by waiting for a specific processing unit while there are idle resources in the system. For example, an encryption program that offloads work to the GPU may wait if the GPU is used by other programs while there are idle CPUs available. Ideally, applications would select the processing unit offering the performance, considering both the speedup it offers as well as the overhead of moving data, dispatching a task, waiting time for the unit to be available, and the application's share of the unit's time. With modern programming languages that can generate code for multiple targets, such as OpenCL [49], a programmer should be able to write the code once and let the system decide where it should execute.

However, in today's systems, it is difficult for applications to predict the utilization they can achieve on a processing unit: OS kernels generally do not tell applications how much CPU time or how many threads they can use. GPUs and other accelerator are often treated as external devices, and may lack any support for fairly sharing them between applications. It may be up to the device driver for an accelerator to make scheduling decisions, which may not be coordinated with CPU scheduling. While there have been research systems such as PTask and others [25, 41, 56] that perform scheduling for tasks on a single processing unit, they are unable to select between multiple possible units for a task. Conversely, application runtimes for heterogeneous systems can run a task on different processing units [6, 39], but support only static heterogeneity, where the performance of a processing unit does not vary over time.

The goal of our work is to efficiently execute programs on dynamically heterogeneous systems. To that end, we built *Rinnegan*, a system that (1) provides system-level scheduling support for non-CPU processing units such as GPUs and (2) extends heterogeneous runtimes with kernel support to make informed placement decisions. Rinnegan separates resource management, which is performed by the kernel and can enforce global share or priority policies, from task placement decisions, which are performed by the application runtime.

PACT '16, September 11-15, 2016, Haifa, Israel

DOI: http://dx.doi.org/10.1145/2967938.2967964

To support high-quality placement decisions, Rinnegan provides information to applications about their expected utilization of a processing unit: how much time they will receive, and with what delay. This allows an application runtime to make an informed decision about whether to use an accelerator; under contention, it may be better to run the task immediately on the CPU rather than waiting for a small share of the accelerator.

However, without control over how processing units are used, Rinnegan cannot accurately predict the utilization an application will receive: another application could monopolize a processing unit. Rinnegan therefore enforces a scheduling discipline on all processing units. For the CPU, this is already performed by the Linux kernel scheduler. For other processing units such as GPUs, Rinnegan adds an agent that can selectively delay or reorder tasks from different application to achieve desired policies, such as priorities, or proportional sharing.

Complementing this kernel support, Rinnegan provides a runtime library that automatically makes task placement decisions for applications. Rinnegan builds a performance model for the system that incorporates the time to transfer data to a processing unit (e.g., data copy to GPU memory) and the overhead of dispatching a task. For each of an application's tasks, Rinnegan builds a simple model predicting its runtime on each type of processing unit. At runtime, Rinnegan combines the utilization information from the OS with this model to predict how an application task will perform on each processing unit and selects the best place for it to execute.

A key advantage of Rinnegan's architecture is that it easily supports applications with different goals: the decision of what is "best" is determined different for each application, so some may choose highest throughput for batch tasks, while others may choose a processing unit that offers the lowest latency or best energy efficiency. Rinnegan also supports adaptable applications that can vary the behavior based on available resources; for example, by reducing fidelity or accuracy under heavy contention. In such cases, Rinnegan can call back into the application notifying it when performance goals are not met or when there are idle resources, allowing it to adapt its behavior.

An interesting benefit of Rinnegan's approach is that applications that achieve the best speedup on a processing unit will naturally use more of it. Applications that receive only a marginal speedup tend to prefer less contended resources, leaving only those that benefit greatly. As a result, even with fully decentralized placement decisions made indirectly by each applications, total system performance is high.

While useful as a stand-alone runtime, Rinnegan is best suited as an execution platform for heterogeneous programming systems. For example, we modified StarPU [6], which distributes tasks among heterogeneous processing units but is not aware of contention, to use Rinnegan. Unmodified StarPU applications, when run with Rinnegan, automatically make placement decision based on system conditions.

The Rinnegan approach advances over past heterogeneous schedulers and runtimes in the following ways. First, the fastest accelerator unit for a stand-alone application may always not be best when multiple programs compete for that accelerator. Runtimes assuming static heterogeneity, or systems that select a processing unit at compile time cannot adapt at runtime. Rinnegan shows that by exposing system state information, such as waiting time for accelerators, placement decisions can be made dynamically. Second, self-placement of tasks enables applications to optimize for different metrics (e.g., throughput for servers, deadlines for media applications, and resource usage for cloud applications). Rinnegan allows application to specify their own scheduling goals, rather than relying on a system-wide policy. Finally, the operating system performs scheduling for compute units to provide fairness between applications. Rinnegan separates scheduling and task placement, which helps achieve soft isolation among applications and simplifies the OS kernel by offloading the job of task placement to applications.

We performed an extensive set of experiments with GPUs and emulated heterogeneous CPUs on a variety of workloads. Rinnegan outperforms native StarPU by 1.5-2x when multiple applications contend for resources. We also show that the performance of the Rinnegan's decentralized design, in which each application makes their own placement decisions, is comparable to an idealized centralized scheduler with global view of the system. We also show that Rinnegan provides performance isolation among applications and enables applications to achieve application-specific performance goals.

2. DESIGN

We designed Rinnegan as a decentralized architecture separating *resource management* (how much access a process gets to a resource), from *task placement* (where tasks run) decisions as shown in Figure 1. The former is left to the OS kernel, which is responsible for isolation among applications, while the latter is pushed closer to applications. To support high-quality placement, the OS publishes information allowing an application to accurately predict its expected performance on all processing units in the system.

Compared to prior systems that perform both resource management and task placement in the kernel [25, 56, 57], this architecture offers several benefits:

- Application frameworks for heterogeneous systems already perform task placement, so this design fits well into existing systems.
- Applications can easily specify their own performance goals or modify their behavior in response to contention, as the placement policy is tightly coupled to the application.
- Performing placement in applications avoid adding complexity to the OS kernel and makes the Rinnegan more easily portable to other operating systems.

Terminology. (i) We use the words *application* and *program* interchangeably. (ii) The term *processing units* refers to all compute units including CPUs, GPUs, and accelerators. (iii) A *task* in Rinnegan refers to a coarse-grained functional block such as a parallel kernel or a function, such as encrypting a block of data, that executes independently and to completion. (iv) We use the term *scheduling* to mean selecting the next task to execute on a processing unit, and for deciding how long that task may run. We use *placement* to mean selecting the processing unit for a task.

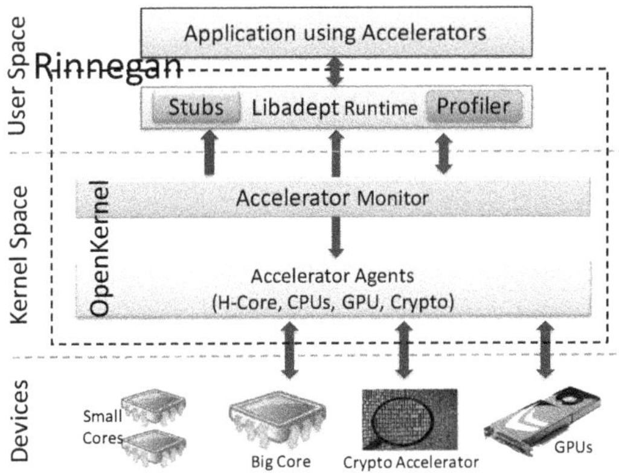

Figure 1: Rinnegan architecture

2.1 Platform Requirements

We designed Rinnegan to target heterogeneous systems with multiprogrammed workloads such as desktops and laptops, mobile devices [21], and shared clusters [34].

Heterogeneous. Rinnegan target architectures that provide heterogeneous processing units in the form of discrete or on-chip accelerators, and both single-ISA and multi-ISA heterogeneous processors. Target systems include unified CPU/GPU chip, such as AMD's APUs [4], systems with discrete GPUs, or with on-chip accelerator devices [20, 64].

Multiprogrammed. Without multiprogramming, a single application can take complete control of the hardware and thus assume the heterogeneity is static and predictable. In contrast, multiprogramming leads to contention and variable performance as applications come and go.

2.2 Resource Management

Rinnegan promotes shared resources like accelerators as first-class entities through its resource management support in the kernel. The major responsibilities of the kernel layer in Rinnegan are resource allocation, enforcing isolation and exposing usage information about processing units. We call this kernel component the *OpenKernel* because of the transparency it provides to applications. The OpenKernel consists of *Accelerator Agents* which act as resource managers and the *Accelerator monitor*, which publishes usage information from agents.

Accelerator agents. In order to support a wide variety of devices with different characteristics, Rinnegan attaches an agent to each unique type of processing unit, such as CPUs, GPUs, and each type of accelerator. Agents perform two key tasks. First, agents act as the scheduler for a type of processing unit and enforce global policy about how much and when each process can use a processing unit. Second, agents gather utilization information about processing units.

Agents implement scheduling policies by controlling when tasks are dispatched to processing units; by delaying tasks from one application, a unit can be used by others. This allow agents to implement global scheduling policies. For example, agents can use shares to provide proportional-share scheduling that is consistent across all processing units, which can provide performance isolation and also guarantee performance for critical applications. Alternatively, shares can also be allocated separately for each unit for finer-grained control. Maximum shares for an application is set by the administrator.

Agents gather and share usage information about the processing units they manage. The agent tracks information needed to predict performance, such as utilization by every application, average size of tasks, and number of applications. This information is provided by the agents to the accelerator monitor (described next) which then publishes it to applications.

Accelerator monitor. The accelerator monitor is a kernel service that publishes usage information from various agents. Some information, such as total utilization of a processing unit, is published globally to all applications. Other information, such as an application's expected share of a unit, is specific to a process; the monitor calculates and shares this information separately with each process. The per-application information reflects the priority, share, or scheduling guarantees of an application. For example, processing units that have been reserved for exclusive use by one application will show up as busy for all other applications.

2.3 Task Placement

Rinnegan follows other runtimes for heterogeneous architectures [6,12,46,49] and employs a task-based programming interface. The programmer or compiler generates task implementations for multiple processing units (not necessary for single-ISA systems). There are several runtimes [12, 49], research systems [17,37] and initiatives like HSAIL [30] that allow code to be written once and then compiled into binaries optimized for different compute devices. For more varied architectures, such as fixed-function accelerators, a programmer may have to code multiple implementations.

The user-mode runtime layer of Rinnegan is contained in the *libadept* library and provides three key services. First, the runtime builds a performance model for every program task on each processing unit, which allows it to predict performance. Second, it provides a simple interface for placing tasks on the best available processing unit. Finally, it allows applications to specify performance goals that guide the placement decision.

Performance model. The runtime builds a model to predict the performance of program tasks on different processing units. Rinnegan measures basic system performance, such as the overhead to dispatch a task and to copy data to processing units that lack coherent memory. For each application, the runtime measures the performance of an application's tasks on different processing units; this allows it to calculate processing time per unit data from the task execution time and the amount of data operated on. These measurements form a model of uncontended (stand alone) performance that can be used to calculate turnaround time of a task on any processing unit in the system, including dispatch overhead, data copying, and actual execution. The stand-alone performance from the model is later combined with utilization information from the accelerator monitor to predict the expected turnaround time even in the presence of contention.

Accelerator stubs. Rinnegan abstracts different processing units into a single procedural interface, so application developers reason about invoking a task but not *where* the task should run. Applications invoke a *stub* interface to launch a task. The overall launch process involves two stages: (a) choosing the right processing unit (b) dispatching task to the chosen unit. The stub considers a processing unit for task offload only if an implementation of the task for that processing unit is available. Stubs use information from the

OpenKernel and the performance model from the profiler to predict the performance of the task on (runnable) processing units. The processing unit that yields the best performance is chosen based on these predictions, and the task is offloaded to that unit by the stub. The second stage deals with the actual dispatch of the task. The Rinnegan runtime contains dispatch and data transfer routines specific to an agent (and thus specific to a processing unit). The stub handles transferring data to the unit if necessary (e.g., it lacks coherent memory and the data is not already at the unit) and then dispatching the task using these routines.

Rinnegan applications can specify performance goals to libadept, which are used by the stub in selecting the best placement for a task. For example, an application may specify maximum throughput, indicating it is willing to wait for an accelerator that provides a high speedup, while others may seek minimum latency and prefer a lower performing CPU that is available immediately.

Optimizer. For tasks that have specific performance targets, such as a desired long-term throughput, Rinnegan provides an *optimizer* that ensures these goals are met. The optimizer is part of the runtime and runs as a thread within the application. It monitors application performance by invoking a *tracker* function provided by the application, which returns the current performance of the application. If performance is below the desired level, the optimizer can either request more resources from the OS (e.g., increase priority or share), or invoke a callback registered by the application to reduce the amount of work (trade-off quality of the results for performance) so performance is acceptable. For example, a compression application may decrease compression to sustain a throughput when insufficient CPU is available. The optimizer can also detect that performance is above what is desired, and again either invoke the OS to release resources or notify the application that it can do more work.

3. IMPLEMENTATION

We implemented Rinnegan as an extension to the Linux 3.4.4 kernel. The code consists of accelerator agents for CPU and GPU, the accelerator monitor, and the libadept shared library linked to user-mode applications. The OpenKernel and the libadept runtime consists of around 2000 and 3400 lines of code respectively. In this section we describe the implementation of Rinnegan, beginning with how agents schedule tasks and then discuss about user-mode task placement.

3.1 Accelerator Agents

We implemented accelerator agents for GPUs and single-ISA heterogeneous CPUs (with standard and fast cores). These agents enforce a scheduling policy by delaying requests, and pass processor usage information to the accelerator monitor. Table 1 shows the statistics generated by the agents. Rinnegan does not yet handle directly accessible accelerators, but disengaged schedulers [41] can be extended to implement the agent functionality for such devices.

GPU agent. The GPU agent manages any GPUs present. As GPU drivers are usually closed binaries that we cannot extend with agent functionality, we therefore implement the GPU agent functionality in a separate kernel-mode component that receives scheduling information (policy, priorities/shares) from an administrator and enforces scheduling policy. The libadept runtime invokes the GPU agent before offloading tasks, which can stall tasks to enforce the scheduling policy. To track device usage (e.g., task size), libadept passes task execution time to the agent after it completes.

Table 1: Details published by agents. (# - Number of)

Agent	Details Published	Visibility
CPU	# active threads at each priority level	Global
	Schedule time ratio for each priority	Global
	# standard cores per application	Private
GPU	Current utilization by an application	Private
	Maximum share allowed for an application	Private
	Average task size	Global
	# active applications	Global
	Runqueue status of each priority queue	Global

The agent calculates GPU utilization by each application from the information passed by the runtime. As short-lived processes do not accumulate much utilization (e.g., *current utilization* is zero), agents also report the average task size on each GPU and the number of applications using the device. We implement three different policies in the agent: *FIFO*, *Priority-based* and *Share-based*.

The FIFO policy is the default policy in GPU drivers and exposes a simple FIFO queue for scheduling tasks from different applications. However, this policy cannot enforce performance isolation if tasks have different execution times: a long task can monopolize the device because current GPU drivers only support context switching at the granularity of an application kernel (i.e., task).

The *Priority-based* policy prevents monopolization by reordering requests to allow higher-priority applications to run before lower-priority ones. However, without preemption support that is not supported in current GPUs, low latency cannot be guaranteed if a long task is running.

The default policy in Rinnegan is *Share-based*. This policy provides soft performance isolation by guaranteeing execution time to each application. The share distribution is maintained by Rinnegan over coarse time scales on the order of hundreds of milliseconds. This is due to the lack of preemption support in GPUs, wherein long-running tasks with low shares can temporarily exceed their share distribution. This policy defines three application classes: CUSTOM, NORMAL and BACKGROUND. In the CUSTOM class, designed for applications with strict performance requirements, applications reserve an absolute share of one or more GPUs, and the total shares on a device cannot exceed 100. Possession of 50 shares on a GPU guarantees the application a minimum of 50% time on the device. The shares unused by the CUSTOM class are given to applications in the NORMAL class, where the remaining shares are distributed proportionally among applications according to the shares they possess. Finally, BACKGROUND applications use the GPUs only when applications of the other two classes are not using the device. To implement this policy, the agent monitors the utilization by each process, and throttles applications using more than their share. Thus, after executing a long task, an application will be blocked from running more tasks to let other applications use the GPU.

CPU agent. The CPU agent supports two classes of CPU cores, *standard* and *fast*, under the assumption that parallel code runs best by having as many cores as possible, while mostly sequential code prefers one or a few fast cores. Rather than providing a new scheduler, the agent uses Linux's native CFS scheduler [13], which already provides priorities and shares. The CPU agent publishes usage information including the number of threads and fraction of time given to threads at each priority level. This information allows the monitor to predict how much CPU time a thread will get on each class of cores. The share based policies (described above) for strong performance guarantees can be implemented by dynamically mapping the amount of shares to a `nice priority` value. This leverages the fact that every priority level has a time slice ratio over other levels.

Additionally, for standard cores, the agent provides hints on the number of standard cores a program can use exclusively, similar to scheduler activations. The calculation is based on a min-funding [67] policy: all cores are allocated to applications based on their priority or share, and unused cores are redistributed. For example, a single-threaded application can use only a single core and other cores it *could use* are instead given to parallel applications. This enables parallel applications to avoid time shares cores in most cases.

Accelerator monitor. The accelerator monitor aggregates information from all agents and publishes it to applications. While Linux already publishes CPU utilization information under `/proc`, we need a higher-performance mechanism given the frequency of access. The monitor shares two pages of data with application using Rinnegan, which have read-only access to the pages. The *global data page* is mapped in all Rinnegan processes and has information about the whole system, such as the average task size on a GPU. The *private page* has process-specific information, such as its maximum allowed utilization (e.g., what fraction of the time it can expect) for each processing unit.

Agents invoke the monitor with the visibility of information, an identifier for the information, and a new value (e.g., <public, GPU average task size, 40 ms>). Agents calculate utilization information at periodic intervals of 10ms, which they immediately push to the monitor. All information calculated by the agents are moving averages. We currently do not synchronize access between the monitor and applications. However, the data is entirely scalar values used as scheduling hints, so races are benign.

3.2 libadept Adaptive Runtime

Every Rinnegan application links to libadept, which consists of the performance model, stubs, and the optimizer.

Performance model. The runtime builds and maintains a performance model for each of the application's tasks. The profiler predicts the task execution time by the amount of data processed by the task; we assume that task execution time is proportional to the amount of data processed, which is true for many applications. For applications where this is not the case, a more sophisticated performance model should be used; we experienced this with the *Sphyraena* workload (Table 4) that executes SQL select queries. The execution time is dependent on the selectivity of the operators which our model did not consider. Rinnegan also allow individual applications to provide their own performance model. During task dispatch, libadept invokes the application to get the predicted task performance on different processing units, which it then combines with information from the monitor. This allows the flexibility of using a custom performance model for every application, such as more mature models [24, 36, 42].

During application startup, we execute an initial set of offloaded tasks from the application on all processing units, similar to Qilin [38]. This generates a set of parameters—the processing time per unit data—that are later used to predict execution time. The model is saved for use across program invocations. For short-lived applications, the developer can request that the model be generated incrementally over multiple invocations of the program, rather than as one step the first time the program runs. A program with a fewer number of tasks is considered short-lived and the profiling stage should not adversely impact such applications.

With this initial data, the performance model generates predictions for task execution time. libadept continuously monitors the accuracy of predictions; if it is off by more than 25% for more than 10 predictions, libadept recalibrates the model by running tasks on different processing units to generate a new set of measurement for the model. Rinnegan does not expect the model prediction to be 100% accurate and accommodates some error in prediction. The amount of error that can be handled depends on the speedup ratio between processing units. More details on the impact of errors in performance model is analyzed in Section 4.6.

libadept runs a generic profiling task during system startup to measure system performance, such as the latency and bandwidth of copying data to/from a GPU and latency of dispatching tasks. For processing units with coherent memory, such as CPUs, the performance model assumes no copy is required. The current implementation of libadept does not account for the contention in I/O bus. This is approximated by a fixed overhead for transfers in addition to the per-byte cost.

Accelerator stubs. Rinnegan stubs are implemented as a single `Accelerate` function that can launch any task on any processing unit. Applications register a task by providing a set of implementations (one per processing unit type). They then invoke `Accelerate` with the task object and its parameters. The `Accelerate` function invokes the performance model to determine where to run the task, moves data to the selected processing unit if necessary, and launches the task on the unit. While we use OpenCL [49] to generate implementations for CPU and GPU, they can also be hand written for better performance

`Accelerate` invokes the performance model to predict the task execution time, and then computes the expected turnaround time as follows:

$$Latency = Overhead + Data\ Copy + (Predicted\ Task\ Execution * (100 / Utilization))$$

The term utilization comes from the agent and is the fraction of time the process can expect to receive on the processing unit. It captures both expected wait time, as wait time is inversely proportional to utilization, as well as its share.

The stub dispatches tasks to a GPU by informing the GPU agent about the start of the tasks, managing any data movement if required and finally invoking the OpenCL or CUDA runtime to submit the task to the kernel driver. For processing units with coherent memory, no movement is required. For those without coherence, such as discrete GPUs, stubs explicitly migrate data to and from the GPU's memory when necessary.

To dispatch tasks onto CPU cores, libadept starts worker threads affinitized to each core in each CPU class (e.g., standard and fast) during program startup. At runtime, it adds tasks to workqueues serviced by the desired worker threads.

The `Accelerate` function also takes a flag to indi-

Table 2: System configurations

Name	System Configuration	Accelerators
asym_config	12 cores in 2 Intel Xeon X5650 chips, 12 GB RAM	2 fast cores–one per socket–at 62.5% duty cycle Remaining 10 cores at 37.5% duty cycle
simd_config	12 cores in 2 Intel Xeon X5650 chips, 12 GB RAM	*GPU-Bulky* (GPU-B): NVIDIA GeForce 670 with 2 GB GDDR5 RAM *GPU-Wimpy* (GPU-W): NVIDIA GeForce 650 with 512 MB GDDR5 RAM

cate whether the task should run synchronously or asynchronously. Asynchronous tasks return an event handle that can be used to wait for their completion. The tasks are queued to an internal scheduler that maintains a central queue. Tasks are processed (the prediction process) in-order from the central queue and then pushed onto processing unit-specific task queues. The application must enforce any data dependencies between tasks. Task execution may not happen immediately upon queuing to the central queue. The internal scheduler keeps the length of the processing unit specific queues low to maintain predictor accuracy by avoiding a long latency between selecting a unit and executing a task.

Optimizer. Rinnegan enables applications to target different performance goals, such as throughput guarantees or minimum execution time (best performance). The optimizer expects two inputs: the performance goal (e.g., 100 MB/Sec or 10 Frames/Sec) and, a tracker function that measures and returns current application performance. The optimizer, part of the libadept runtime, spawns a thread that periodically (every 500ms) invokes the tracker function. The tracker function is to be implemented by every application and it is registered as a callback with the runtime during application start-up. The function is responsible for returning the current application performance (same performance metric — throughput or latency — as that of the target performance) on invocation. Applications without a performance goal always seek maximum performance (minimum execution time) and the optimizer does not run in this case.

The optimizer operates in three phases when the tracker function indicates that an application is not meeting its goal. Each phase is carried out only when the preceding phase fails to improve performance to meet the target. First, the optimizer tries to spread tasks across more processing units. Applications can thus offload multiple (asynchronous) tasks at once to different units. This is not the default behavior, because the libadept tries to minimize resource cost by ensuring performance on minimum resources. Second, for applications with appropriate privileges, it invokes the operating system to increase priority for desired processing units. This phase targets the application to be in CUSTOM class share-based scheduler, and is important if applications need to meet strict performance goals (e.g., throughput or soft real-time). If the second phase does not succeed, for example if the application lacks the privilege to increase its share or all the shares are already allocated, the optimizer notifies the application via a registered callback function (different from the tracker function). The application uses this callback function, which provides achieved performance, to modify its workload. For example, a game could reduce its frame rate or resolution. Upon availability of more resources (when other applications exit), the application automatically gets additional resources since the shares are proportional.

When an application performs above its goal or the optimizer observes that an application is not using its maximum utilization, it performs the same phases in reverse. This allows the application to modify its workload to increase its workload. e.g., frame rate, or to release resources to the OS by relinquishing its shares.

```
    TaskGPU(      *args) {/* Task logic on GPU */}
    TaskCPU(      *args) {/* Task logic on CPU */}
   main() {
  Task *tasks[10];
     (     i = 0; i < 10; i++) {
    tasks[i] = IntializeAcceleratorTask(SIMD,
         TaskGPU, TaskCPU, args);
    Accelerate(task[i], ASYNC);
  }
     (     i = 0; i < 10; i++)  {
    WaitForTask(tasks[i]);
  }
}
```

Listing 1: Program using libadept

Data movement. When launching tasks, the stub may need to migrate the task's data to the selected GPU if it lacks coherent access to memory. Moving a task back and forth between processing units can hurt due to excess data copies. This can occur when a task is at the break-even point between two processing units, so a small change in utilization can push the task to switch processors. It can also occur when there are rapid changes in the utilization of a unit and predictions of performance are inaccurate.

Rinnegan implements mechanisms to avoid both causes of task migration. For tasks near the break-even point, Rinnegan dampens movement with a *speedup threshold*: tasks only migrate if the expected speedup is high enough to quickly amortize the cost of data movement. Thus, small performance improvements that require expensive copies are avoided. In addition, for subsequent task offloads, stubs make an aggregate decision that determines where to dispatch the next group of tasks, rather than making the dispatch decision for each task before switching to the new unit. In this *task aggregation*, group size grows with the data movement overhead.

Stability. Rapid changes in utilization can occur when multiple applications simultaneously make an offload decision: they may all run tasks on the same processing unit, leading to poor performance and then all migrate away from the unit. This *ping-pong problem* is common to distributed control systems, such as in routing [35]. Rinnegan takes a two-step approach to resolve the ping-pong problem. First, libadept detects when the predicted runtime is different than the actual runtime. This indicates that the utilization obtained from the monitor was wrong. Second, libadept temporarily uses the *actual* turnaround time of the last task instead of predicted turnaround time. Thus, the first applications to use the unit runs quickly and observe high performance, while those arriving later experience queuing delay from congestion and hence lower performance. Applications with higher delays will tend to choose a different processing unit, while those with less delay stay put.

Table 3: GPU application characteristics. Speedups are relative to the CPU alone, and size is relative to *AES*.

Applications	Task Size Ratio	Task Speedup Ratio	
		GPU-B	GPU-W
AES	1	32	22
LBM	3.33	1.4	0.5
DXT	5.6	16	4.5
lavaMD	20	27	7.5
Grep	33	10	3.3
Histogram	83	12	4

Programmer effort. Rinnegan exposes new interfaces for programmers. We created a simple task-based programming model to help prototype a complete system from programming model to system software. Though writing a program using the new interfaces can be done without much effort as shown in Listing 1, it still requires program modifications for the new interface. To avoid this extra work, we integrated the libadept runtime with the StarPU [6] heterogeneous runtime system. libadept is used as an execution platform; we invoke `Accelerate` from StarPU's dispatch function. However, we did not need to make any changes to the StarPU's interfaces meant for application development. It already incorporates a profiling stage, that we use for Rinnegan' performance model. Thus programs already written for the StarPU model can leverage the Rinnegan's dynamic task placement without any code changes.

4. EVALUATION

We address four major questions in our evaluation: (a) How beneficial is adaptation in a shared environment? (b) Can Rinnegan satisfy application-specific performance goals? (c) Can Rinnegan isolate applications from each other? (d) How well a decentralized scheduler performs? We also evaluate the overhead and accuracy of individual components of Rinnegan.

The experiments in this section focus on understanding the behavior of Rinnegan when applications of different characteristics (speedup, size of the task, long running/short lived) are run together. We evaluate the performance of Rinnegan against other systems such as StarPU and c-sched (a centralized system we wrote to be similar to an Oracle) and also with different scheduling policies. The primary goal is to show how Rinnegan handles resource contention, which can occur in real systems.

4.1 Experimental Methods

Table 2 lists the configurations used in our experiments. We disable Turbo Boost and hyperthreading to avoid performance variability.

Platform. We emulate an asymmetric CPU (*asym_config*) using Intel's clock-modulation feature [31] (in our platforms DVFS cannot be used for a single core) to slow down all cores but the *fast* cores. Similar mechanisms have been used in past research to emulate asymmetric processors [3]. We wanted a single infrastructure with different forms of heterogeneity (asymmetric cores and several accelerators). So, we chose to emulate the asymmetry rather than using a separate real hardware such as big.LITTLE processors [5]. Though none of our experiments make use of both forms of heterogeneity, we believe this infrastructure will serve best for the extension of this work. We emulate powerful cores by setting ten cores to run at 62.5% duty cycle and the remaining two at 37.5%. So, the speedup of fast core is 1.6x over slow core [5]. Where noted, we run some applications at 100% to emulate applications-specific speedups. The *simd_config* configuration comprises two GPUs of different performance and 12 CPU cores. Applications access these processing units through OpenCL, which uses the NVIDIA OpenCL SDK for GPUs and Intel OpenCL SDK for CPUs.

Table 4: Workloads

Name	Description
Blackscholes [9]	Mathematical model for a financial market
Dedup [9]	Deduplication
Pbzip [51]	file compression
AES [1]	AES-128-ECB mode encryption, OpenCL
LBM [63]	Fluid dynamics simulation, OpenCL
DXT [47]	Image Compression, OpenCL
lavaMD [14]	Particle simulation, OpenCL
Grep [60]	Search for a string in a set of files, OpenCL and OMP for CPU
Histogram [60]	Finding the frequency of dictionary words in a list of files, OpenCL and OMP for CPU
Sphyraena [7]	Select queries on a sqlite database, CUDA
EncFS [56]	FUSE based encrypted file system, CUDA
Truecrack [66]	Password cracker, CUDA
x264 [40]	Video Encoder, OpenCL

The GPU workloads are run simultaneously for all experiments performed on *simd_config*. We run workloads continuously, and present the relative throughput (tasks/second) for applications on the system under test compared to running all the applications on GPU-B. For a few experiments, those shown in Figure 3 and Figure 5, we allow some applications to finish in order to show how the system reconfigures.. The application properties are shown in Table 3.

Workloads. We run the workloads listed in Table 4 in a multi-programmed environment to create contention for hardware resources. We select workloads with specific characteristics, such as tasks suitable for fast cores and varying task sizes to demonstrate Rinnegan's capabilities and to exercise different forms of heterogeneity.

Dedup, *Pbzip* and *Blackscholes* are parallel applications with tasks that can benefit from running on powerful CPU cores. We use six workloads for GPUs, described in Table 4. These workloads demonstrate the effect of task size and implementation style. For OpenCL programs, we compile to both GPU and CPU code. The same set of applications was also ported on to StarPU runtime. For CUDA programs, we use a separate implementation for the CPU. Table 3 shows the speedup for these applications when running on GPUs and their average task sizes (relative execution time). The speedup shown is relative to using all 12 CPUs at full performance. We report the average of five runs and variation was below 2% unless stated explicitly.

4.2 Adaptation

A major benefit of Rinnegan compared to existing heterogeneous runtimes is its ability to use application-specific performance models to select the best placement for a task, but at the same time dynamically adapting to runtime conditions. We evaluate how well applications adapt to a set of common contention scenarios.

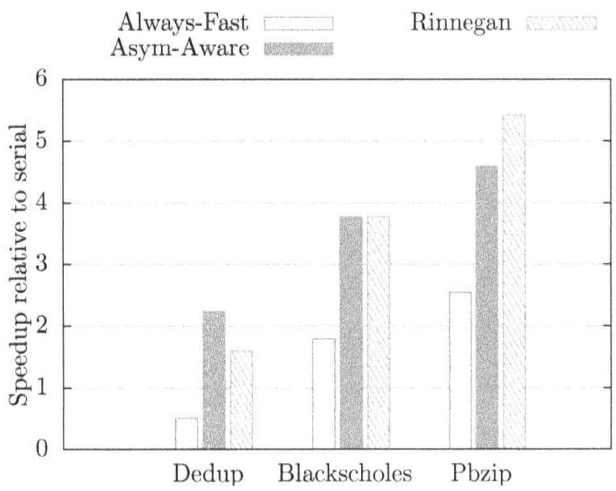

Figure 2: Contention for fast cores.

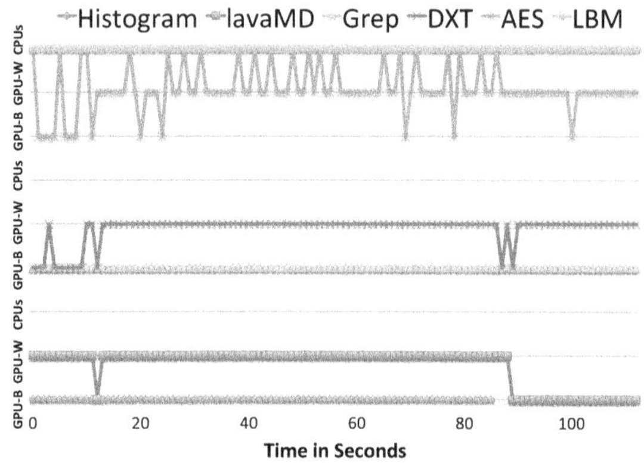

Figure 3: Rinnegan task placement with FIFO policy.

Contention for fast cores. Rinnegan allows applications to accelerate important code regions on a small number of fast cores. We run multiple parallel applications concurrently that have tasks suitable for a fast CPU: the compression phase in *Dedup* and *Pbzip*, and the financial calculation in *Blackscholes*. The speedup of fast core over regular core is 1.6x. Using *asym_config*, we compare three configurations: (a) *Always-Fast* is a compile-time static policy that always runs all tasks on the fast cores, (b) *Asym-Aware* is similar to Global Task Scheduling (GTS [33]) in which it modifies the Linux scheduler to execute tasks on normal cores but migrate them to a powerful core if it becomes idle, and (c) *Rinnegan*, where the stub decides where to run tasks based on speedup achievable. To demonstrate the ability of Rinnegan to prioritize fast cores for applications with better speedup, we made *Pbzip* receive a speedup of 2.65x on the faster cores. This speedup boost was applied for all three configurations. This was done by modifying the scheduler to increase the duty cycle to 100% only when *Pbzip* runs on the faster core.

Figure 2 shows performance normalized to serial versions of the applications running on a regular core. The overall performance of Rinnegan and *Asym-Aware* is comparable though both configurations perform differently on *Dedup* and *Pbzip*. Rinnegan runs the application with the best speedup, *Pbzip*, on the fast cores, which gives that application an 18% speedup compared to *Asym-Aware*. The *Asym-Aware* greedily schedules task on faster cores as they become available without any regard to their speedup. Rinnegan trades-off the performance of other applications for the high speedup application *Pbzip*. The *Always-Fast* performs poorly because it under-utilizes the regular CPU cores while waiting for the fast CPUs. Overall, the system throughput is 3% higher in Rinnegan than *Asym-Aware*.

Contention for accelerators. A key goal of Rinnegan is to manage contention for shared accelerators. In current systems, applications cannot choose between processing units and thus must wait for the contended accelerator. Rinnegan, though, allows applications to use other processing units *if* they are faster than waiting. As a result, applications with large benefit from an accelerator tend to use it preferentially, while applications with lesser benefit will migrate their work to other processing units. Task size also plays a role with the FIFO policy: large tasks dominate the usage on bulky GPU. We ran all the OpenCL GPU workloads concurrently on *simd_config* using the FIFO policy.

In the *Native* system, all applications offload tasks to GPU-B, which leaves GPU-W and the CPUs idle. In contrast, Rinnegan achieves 1.8x better performance because it makes use of GPU-W and the CPU to run tasks as well. To explain these results, Figure 3 plots the processing unit used by each applications from a run where we launch all apps at the same time. *LBM* uses the CPU only exclusively because it gets low performance on the GPUs. In contrast, *Histogram* and *Grep* always uses GPU-B, because of their relatively larger tasks. This causes long delays for other applications, and hence *lavaMD* and *DXT* move to GPU-W. When *Histogram* completes, *lavaMD* switches to GPU-B and shares the device with *Grep*. On the other hand, *AES* switches execution between CPU and GPUs since the amount of data to encrypt varies with every task offloaded by the program. For smaller data, *AES* runs on the CPU to avoid costly data copies. The three column stacks labeled *FIFO* in Figure 6 shows the percentage of time each application gets on different processing units. The native stack at the left shows the default behavior where all tasks are offloaded to GPU-B.

Rinnegan as an execution engine. We integrated Rinnegan as the execution engine for StarPU, a runtime for heterogeneous architectures, to analyze the impact of contention awareness in the runtime. We rewrote all six GPU workloads to run on the StarPU runtime. We compare three different configurations for this experiment. We use two of StarPU's native policies [6, 62]: *DMDA* (deque model data aware) offloads task to the best performing processing unit taking into account the previously queued tasks from the local application and *Eager* employs a task stealing approach where worker threads of any processing unit can run a task as long as the implementation for that unit is available. The third configuration is StarPU with Rinnegan, where task offload decisions are made by Rinnegan based on input from OpenKernel. Rinnegan makes StarPU aware of other applications in the system.

The *DMDA* policy is representative of application runtimes [6, 55] for heterogeneous architectures where tasks are offloaded to the processing unit that performs best for that application (inclusive of all tasks from an application) in isolation. As a result, DMDA always offloads tasks to GPU-B for our workloads since it offers highest speedup. Since the task placement decisions consider only individual task performance but not contention at accelerators (due to other applications), DMDA's performance suffers by not utilizing the lower performing processing units such as GPU-W and CPUs when GPU-B is busy.

The eager policy, similar to runtimes such as Cilk [10] and others [58], employ a task stealing approach for task distribution in heterogeneous architectures. With this policy, the

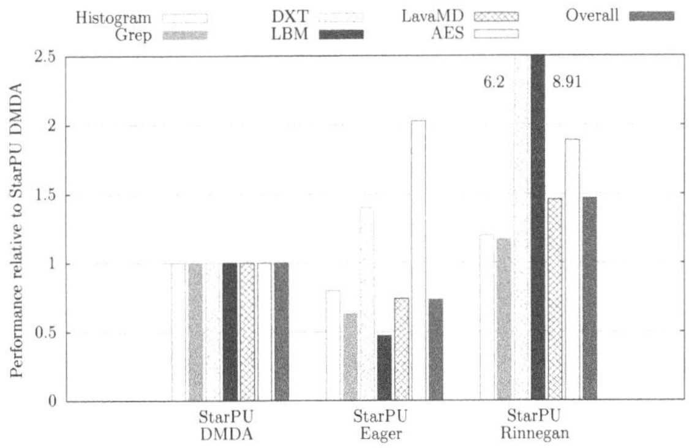

Figure 4: Throughput of StarPU-based systems.

Table 5: Stand-alone performance of CUDA workloads. W/S - Words/s; Q/S - Queries/s; F/S - Frames/s

	Truecrack	Sphyraena	EncFS (read)	x264
GPU-B	320 W/S	38 Q/S	340 MB/S	15 F/S
GPU-W	230 W/S	13 Q/S	190 MB/S	-
CPU	15 W/S	0.2 Q/S	13 MB/S	-

StarPU runtime for each application spawns worker threads for every compute unit in the system (12 workers for every CPU, 2 workers for each GPU). Every worker thread pulls task from the task pool when they are free without any regard to task speedup on that processing unit. As a result, when the GPU is temporarily busy, CPU worker threads pull many tasks that could have run at higher speedup on a GPU. Thus, the eager policy provides the lowest performance of the configurations.

We show the individual applications throughput and the overall system throughput relative to StarPU DMDA in Figure 4. Rinnegan is able to utilize the less-loaded processing units and thus provide better throughput than other policies. As a result, the overall system throughput of StarPU+Rinnegan is 2x and 1.5x better than native policies of StarPU (Eager and DMDA) respectively.

4.3 Application-Specific Goals

The libadept library allows applications to set their own performance goals through an optimizer that guides offload decisions. We demonstrate Rinnegan's ability to support application-specific performance goals by running the CUDA applications—*x264*, *Sphyraena*, and *EncFS*—with their own goals in CUSTOM class and *Truecrack* in BACKGRND class. Native performance of application is shown in Table 5. The goals for each application are:

x264	15 Frames/Sec, can degrade quality for performance.
EncFS	275MB/Sec on sequential reads.
Sphyraena	20 Queries/Sec. minimum
Truecrack	Background: use GPU only when unused.

Of these applications, *x264* can adapt by reducing fidelity and *Sphyraena* uses asynchronous tasks and can spread its work across multiple processing units.

We started the applications in their respective classes where libadept assigns default shares to applications (15 shares on GPU-B each for applications in CUSTOM class and no shares assigned for BACKGRND class applications). We let libadept request shares automatically from agents after the initial assignment. We expect Rinnegan to automatically adapt—find the right set of processing units, or adjust shares, or callback to applications to alter configurations to adjust performance—without any manual intervention. The adaptation of the system is shown in form of a time graph in Figure 5. We start *x264*, *Sphyraena* and *Truecrack* at time zero, and *EncFS* at time 60. When applications finish, we do not restart them so as to release resources for other applications' use.

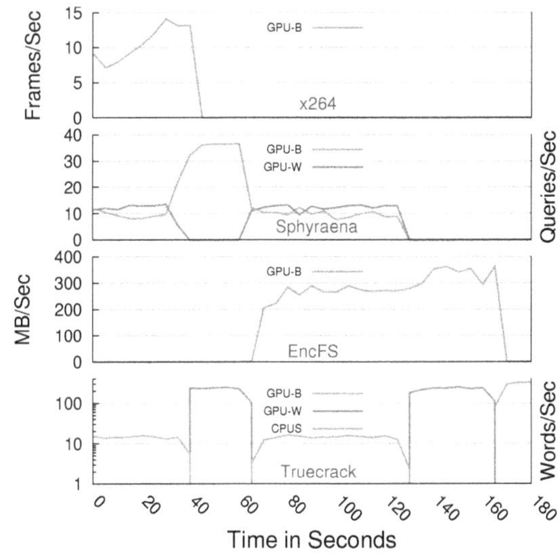

Figure 5: CUDA workload adaptation.

As the application runs, the optimizer detects the lag in performance and attempts to use multiple GPUs. *x264*, as a synchronous application, cannot leverage multiple GPUs. However, *Sphyraena* spreads its tasks across both GPU-B and GPU-W. *x264* receives around 80 shares on GPU-B and *Sphyraena* gets 20 on GPU-B and 100 shares (all) on GPU-W. Around 5th second, the runtime (through optimizer) notifies applications to reduce fidelity to improve performance. *x264* adapts by reducing quality and is able to reach 13 FPS. *Truecrack*, being a background application, runs on CPU since the accelerators (GPUs) are occupied.

When x264 completes, *Sphyraena* receives the whole GPU-B and achieves its goal of more than 20 queries/sec, and *Truecrack* adapts by moving to GPU-W, which greatly increases its throughput. We start *EncFS* at 60 seconds and the optimizer adjusts the shares such that both applications achieve their goals by giving 80 shares of GPU-B to *EncFS*, and remaining of GPU-B and the whole GPU-W were given to *Sphyraena*. Truecrack is forced to move to the CPUs at this point, as both GPUs are totally saturated. Only when *Sphyraena* completes around 120 seconds does *Truecrack* move to GPU-W, and then to GPU-B when *EncFS* completes at 160 seconds. These results demonstrate how applications adapt to the changing use of the system, as well as how the optimizer allows applications to achieve their goals by spreading the work, increasing the share of a processing unit, or reducing the workload.

4.4 Preserving Isolation

Rinnegan only does placement in user-mode and leaves scheduling and policy enforcement in the kernel to protect against poorly behaved applications. To demonstrate Rinnegan's ability to isolate the performance of different applications, we allotted CUSTOM shares on GPU-B in the ratio of 25:25:25:10:10:5 to *Histogram*, *Grep*, *DXT*, *lavaMD*, *LBM*

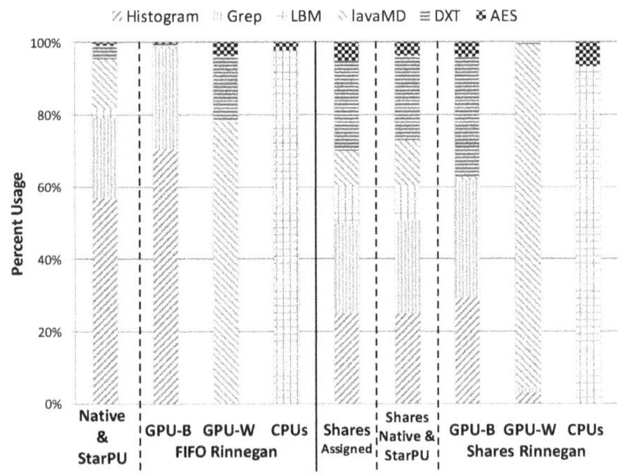

Figure 6: Percentage of time spent on different devices with various policies. Native & StarPU and Shares Native & StarPU columns uses only GPU-B. Shares Assigned column is input.

and *AES*. Such a share ratio was used to show that (a) applications with large tasks (*Histogram*) can be constrained, (b) small tasks (*LBM*) can receive guaranteed share, and (c) isolation is achieved even in the presence of varied task sizes.

Rinnegan applications. The three stacks on the right labeled *Shares Rinnegan* in Figure 6 show the portion of each processing unit used by each application. *Histogram* gets major portion of GPU-B because of its large task sizes in FIFO-based policy. With share-based scheduling, *Histogram*, *Grep* and *DXT* evenly share GPU-B, while *lava-MD* uses GPU-W since it yields better performance than the guaranteed 10 shares on GPU-B. We observe that three applications (*Histogram*, *Grep* and *DXT*) receive more than their assigned 25% on GPU-B (30% each) because other applications decided to offload tasks on GPU-W or CPUs. So, these three active applications enjoy equal share on GPU-B. Also, applications with lower shares of GPU-B, such as *lavaMD* and *LBM*, offload tasks to GPU-W and CPUs respectively since the performance is better than on their 10% of GPU-B.

StarPU applications. We also show how Rinnegan can isolate applications that are not using Rinnegan by running StarPU version of our GPU workloads. However, we modified the workloads to notify the agents about their task execution time. The leftmost stack in Figure 6 shows the utilization received by each application with StarPU's native uses DMDA policy that runs all tasks on GPU-B. The *Shares native & starpu* column in the center-right shows the performance when share-based policy is enforced by the Rinnegan GPU agent: the resulting utilization almost exactly tracks the shares assigned. These results show both that native Linux and StarPU alone cannot or do not enforce performance isolation, while Rinnegan can provide isolation even for applications not actively using it for task placement. We note that without GPU driver support, Rinnegan relies on applications to call into the agent to know start and completion time of the task, and not all applications may do this. However, this functionality can be enforced either through GPU driver modifications or disengaged scheduling [41].

4.5 Decentralized vs. Centralized

Task placement in Rinnegan is decentralized: individual applications make placement decisions based on the state

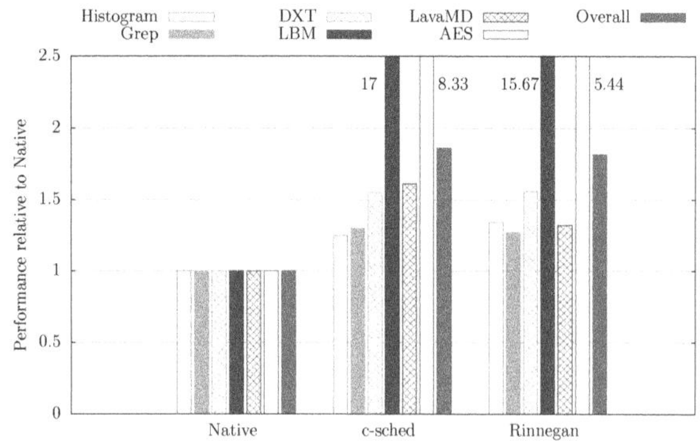

Figure 7: Centralized vs. Decentralized systems.

information exposed by the monitor. However, the information can be stale due to the delay between when it is generated and when applications place a task based on the information. In contrast, task placement in a centralized architecture is performed by a single central entity for all applications. It has global knowledge of all tasks dispatched so far and can make accurate decisions for future tasks. We compare the behavior of Rinnegan against a centralized system to understand how much performance is lost due to a decentralized architecture.

Centralized scheduler. We built a simple centralized scheduler, *c-sched*, that behaves similarly to PTask [56] or Pegasus [25] but without the complexity and kernel modifications of those systems. libadept maintains task queues per processing unit for each application to track all dispatched tasks from that application. With c-sched, these queues are made global by implementing them on a shared page accessible by all applications, so the per-applications task queues becomes system-wide task queues. This enables c-sched to have a global view of the system and to predict the wait time for every processing unit accurately. Thus the c-sched scheduler is aware of tasks from all applications and can make perfect task placement decisions. However, it requires applications to be cooperative and can be easily gamed by providing erroneous speedup values.

Contention results. Using the same six GPU applications as used in previous experiments with the FIFO policy, we compare the individual applications and the total system throughput of c-sched against Rinnegan. We also consider a native system that offloads task to GPU-B, the highest speedup processing unit. The results, shown as the c-sched and Rinnegan bars in Figure 7, demonstrate that despite being decentralized Rinnegan still performed within 2.5% of a perfect centralized scheduler. Rinnegan performs close to the optimal scheduler is less prone to gaming and supports application-level adaptation, which is difficult in a centralized system. To achieve adaption, application-specific constraints and adaptation techniques would have to be conveyed to the centralized service, making it more complex.

Short-lived applications. Task placement for short-lived applications is hard without the global knowledge of the system since the utilization information can fluctuate. We generated such applications that start, run a small task for 0.5 – 2ms and then exit. We generated small tasks with varying inputs for *AES* and *DXT* workloads. We ran an experiment running multiple such applications periodically to test the overall throughput of the system in terms of tasks processed per second. The c-sched system should provide the best performance since it has a global knowledge of the system. The performance of Rinnegan is only 3.5% lower than c-sched whereas the native system that offloads all tasks to GPU-B is 20% slower than c-sched. Rinnegan performs well even without global knowledge of all workloads by using the average task size and average number of applications metrics rather than utilization information.

4.6 Overhead and Accuracy

We separately measured the overhead of Rinnegan's mechanisms and the accuracy of its profiler.

Overheads. The primary overhead in Rinnegan comes from stubs, which must decide where to dispatch tasks. The overhead of stubs ranged between $1\mu s$ when choosing between fast and regular CPU cores to $2\mu s$ for selecting among different GPUs. Aggregation can reduce this by changing the dispatch decision less often.

Task profiler accuracy. We measure the difference between the task profiler's predicted run time and the actual task latency including the wait time. Across all our experiments, the prediction error is between 8–16%. The error came from two sources. First, Rinnegan predicts that task size is a linear function of input data size, which is not true for all applications (e.g., *Sphyraena*). Second, we found that the data copy latency to the GPU varied due to contention for the PCIe bus.

To understand the importance of accurate performance predictions, we built an analysis tool to observe the impact of profiler error on task placement. For applications with 10x speedup, when the error rate increases from 5–100% the probability of making an incorrect decision increases by only 0.5%–5%. For the same range of error with applications getting only a 2x speedup, the error probability varies from 2.3%–25%. This shows that error in profiler prediction does not impact placement for tasks with better speedups.

Reducing data movement. Rinnegan reduces the amount of data movement by limiting the frequency with which tasks move between processing units with task aggregation and the speedup threshold. To measure the benefit of Rinnegan's mechanisms for limiting data movement, we disabled the mechanisms and randomly varied *LBM*'s maximum utilization for GPU-B between 65–75%. Its preference flips between GPU-B and the CPUs and performance suffers as a result. Compared to a system without the threshold and aggregation mechanisms, the speedup threshold improves performance by 5%, and task aggregation improves performance by an additional 60%.

Ping-pong problem. We also investigated the impact of the ping-pong problem by comparing Rinnegan against our c-sched centralized scheduler. Because it has global knowledge of the utilization of all processing units, c-sched does not have the ping-pong problem. For the contention experiments described in Section 4.2, we compared the task movements of Rinnegan to c-sched. We found that both systems had similar amounts of task movement. Because of varied task size, applications saw different processing unit utilization and hence made different scheduling decisions. To force a ping-pong problem, we ran five copies of the same *Grep* workload, which offloaded tasks of the same size. Rinnegan's ping-pong avoidance mechanism helped in stabilizing task placement sooner, resulting in the same task throughput same as the c-sched. Without the mechanism, the system took 8-10 task offloads to stabilize, as compared to 2-3 with ping-pong prevention.

5. RELATED WORK

Runtimes for heterogeneous architectures. Many systems provide runtime layers to aid applications in using heterogeneous units (e.g., StarPU [6], OmpSs [18, 53–55], Merge [37], Harmony [17], Lithe [50]). Rinnegan shares the goal of automatically selecting where to run a task based on predicted performance on different compute units. Unlike these runtimes, Rinnegan supports multi-programmed systems where there may be contention for processing units by exposing system-wide resource usage to applications. Runtimes for databases help in task scheduling on heterogeneous architectures [11, 26]. However, they assume the system resources are not shared with other applications.

Other systems abstract the presence of heterogeneous processing units. For example, PTask [56] provide an abstraction for GPU programming that aids in scheduling and data movement. Rinnegan differs by exposing multiple types of processing units, not just GPUs, and by exposing usage to applications to self-select a place to execute. In contrast, PTask manages allocation and scheduling in the kernel.

Some runtimes [55, 58] employ task-stealing for better utilization of all compute units in the system. Sbîrlea et. al in their runtime [58] perform stealing without regard to the speedup of the stealer destination over the task's current placement whereas the OmpSs runtime [55] does not consider the contention caused by other applications. As a result, the stolen task might perform worse at the destination compute unit. Rinnegan employs a task steering approach in contrast to the stealing approach in which tasks are dispatched to an appropriate processing unit based on its standalone performance and also the current load at the processing unit.

Resource scheduling. Many past systems provide resource management for heterogeneous systems (e.g., PTask [56], Barrelfish [8], Helios [44], Pegasus [25]). In contrast to these systems, where the OS transparently handles scheduling and resource allocation, Rinnegan cooperatively involve the participation of applications. It exposes processing unit utilization via the accelerator monitor to allow applications to predict where to run their code, instead of making the choice for the application.

Other systems provide contention-aware scheduling (Grand central dispatch [22], Scheduler activations [2]), where applications or the system can adjust the degree of parallelism. Rinnegan enables a similar outcome, but over longer time scales. Unlike scheduler activations, Rinnegan does not notify applications during change in resource allocation, but allows applications to monitor their utilization. Baymax [15] offers QoS guarantees for critical applications in a shared heterogeneous environment. Unlike Rinnegan, it employs a centralized architecture and focuses on tail latency as the key metric.

Adaptive Systems. Rinnegan is inspired by many previous works in the area of adaptive systems. Odyssey [45] was built as an adaptation platform for mobile systems. Rinnegan employs a similar architecture for shared heterogeneous systems and uses alternate processing units as a mode of adaptation. Application heartbeats [29] tunes applications according to available resources, but does not address heterogeneous platforms nor provide kernel-level scheduling control over non-CPU processing units. Similar adaptive techniques have been employed in databases [23] where new interfaces between OS and databases are designed for better performance. Varuna [61] tackles a similar problem but targets only parallel programs. Performance is improved by dynamically adapting the parallelism in the applications based on the runtime conditions. However, the system runs strictly at user level and does not offer isolation across applications due to the lack of resource management.

Multi Level Scheduling. Many systems [16, 19, 28, 52] distribute resource management across two levels. The first system layer is responsible for resource allocation to ensure isolation among applications. The second layer lies within every application, which decide for themselves how to manage these allocated resources. These systems are generally designed for homogeneous platforms and are concerned with the number/duration of CPUs available but not the type. In most heterogeneous systems, though, applications or runtimes decide where to run their tasks (based on type of processing unit) but are oblivious to the shared environment. Rinnegan integrates the two designs — resource allocation by system layer and task placement by applications — by allowing the system to manage resources and also enable applications to make informed task placement decisions aware of contention.

6. CONCLUSION

Heterogeneity in various forms will be prevalent in future architectures. Rinnegan exposes available heterogeneity with the OpenKernel along with the system state information, and uses libadept to conceal the complexity from application programmers. The kernel retains control over resource management but provides application-level code with the flexibility to execute wherever is best for the application. The decentralized design employed by Rinnegan performs well and at the same time does not require extensive changes to the kernel. As future work, we plan to explore how to better handle power-limited heterogeneous systems.

Acknowledgements

This work is supported in part by National Science Foundation (NSF) grants CNS-1302260, CNS-1117280 and CCF-1533885. We would like to thank our shepherd and the anonymous reviewers for their invaluable feedback. Swift has a significant financial interest in Microsoft.

7. REFERENCES

[1] "Advanced Encryption Standard (AES)," http://www.csrc.nist.gov/publications/fips/fips197/fips-197.pdf, 2001.

[2] T. E. Anderson, B. N. Bershad, E. D. Lazowska, and H. M. Levy, "Scheduler Activations: Effective Kernel Support for the User-level Management of Parallelism," in *Proceedings of the Thirteenth ACM Symposium on Operating Systems Principles*, ser. SOSP '91. New York, NY, USA: ACM, 1991, pp. 95–109.

[3] M. Annavaram, E. Grochowski, and J. Shen, "Mitigating Amdahl's Law Through EPI Throttling," in *Proceedings of the 32Nd Annual International Symposium on Computer Architecture*, ser. ISCA '05. Washington, DC, USA: IEEE Computer Society, 2005, pp. 298–309. [Online]. Available: http://dx.doi.org/10.1109/ISCA.2005.36

[4] "AMD A-Series Desktop APUs," http://www.amd.com/us/products/desktop/processors/a-series/Pages/nextgenapu.aspx.

[5] ARM Limited, "big.LITTLE Technology: The Future of Mobile," www.arm.com/files/pdf/big_LITTLE_Technology_the_Futue_of_Mobile.pdf.

[6] C. Augonnet, S. Thibault, R. Namyst, and P.-A. Wacrenier, "StarPU: A Unified Platform for Task Scheduling on Heterogeneous Multicore Architectures," in *Proceedings of the 15th International Euro-Par Conference*, ser. Lecture Notes in Computer Science, vol. 5704. Delft, The Netherlands: Springer, Aug. 2009, pp. 863–874.

[7] P. Bakkum and K. Skadron, "Accelerating SQL Database Operations on a GPU with CUDA," in *Proceedings of the 3rd Workshop on General-Purpose Computation on Graphics Processing Units*, ser. GPGPU '10, 2010, pp. 94–103.

[8] A. Baumann, P. Barham, P.-E. Dagand, T. Harris, R. Isaacs, S. Peter, T. Roscoe, A. Schüpbach, and A. Singhania, "The Multikernel: A New OS Architecture for Scalable Multicore Systems," in *Proceedings of the ACM SIGOPS 22Nd Symposium on Operating Systems Principles*, ser. SOSP '09. New York, NY, USA: ACM, 2009, pp. 29–44. [Online]. Available: http://doi.acm.org/10.1145/1629575.1629579

[9] C. Bienia and K. Li, "PARSEC 2.0: A New Benchmark Suite for Chip-Multiprocessors," in *Proc. 5th Workshop on Modeling, Benchmarking and Simulation*, June 2009.

[10] R. D. Blumofe, C. F. Joerg, B. C. Kuszmaul, C. E. Leiserson, K. H. Randall, and Y. Zhou, "Cilk: an efficient multithreaded runtime system," in *Proc. of the 12th ACM SIGPLAN Symp. on Principles and Practice of Parallel Programming (PPOPP)*, Aug. 1995, pp. 207–216.

[11] S. Breß and G. Saake, "Why It is Time for a HyPE: A Hybrid Query Processing Engine for Efficient GPU Coprocessing in DBMS," *Proc. VLDB Endow.*, vol. 6, no. 12.

[12] "C++ AMP : Language and Programming Model," http://download.microsoft.com/download/4/0/E/40EA02D8-23A7-4BD2-AD3A-0BFFFB640F28/CppAMPLanguageAndProgrammingModel.pdf.

[13] "CFS Scheduler," https://www.kernel.org/doc/Documentation/scheduler/sched-design-CFS.txt.

[14] S. Che, M. Boyer, J. Meng, D. Tarjan, J. Sheaffer, S.-H. Lee, and K. Skadron, "Rodinia: A benchmark suite for heterogeneous computing," in *Workload Characterization, 2009. IISWC 2009. IEEE International Symposium on*, 2009, pp. 44–54.

[15] Q. Chen, H. Yang, J. Mars, and L. Tang, "Baymax: Qos awareness and increased utilization for non-preemptive accelerators in warehouse scale computers," pp. 681–696, 2016.

[16] J. A. Colmenares, G. Eads, S. Hofmeyr, S. Bird, M. Moretó, D. Chou, B. Gluzman, E. Roman, D. B. Bartolini, N. Mor, K. Asanović, and J. D. Kubiatowicz, "Tessellation: Refactoring the os around

explicit resource containers with continuous adaptation," in *Design Automation Conference (DAC), 2013 50th ACM/EDAC/IEEE*, May 2013, pp. 1–10.

[17] G. F. Diamos and S. Yalamanchili, "Harmony: An Execution Model and Runtime for Heterogeneous Many Core Systems," in *Proceedings of the 17th International Symposium on High Performance Distributed Computing*, ser. HPDC '08. New York, NY, USA: ACM, 2008, pp. 197–200. [Online]. Available: http://doi.acm.org/10.1145/1383422.1383447

[18] A. Duran, E. Ayguadé, R. M. Badia, J. Labarta, L. Martinell, X. Martorell, and J. Planas, "OmpSs: a Proposal for Programming Heterogeneous Multi-Core Architectures," *Parallel Processing Letters*, vol. 21, no. 02, pp. 173–193, 2011.

[19] D. R. Engler, M. F. Kaashoek, and J. O'Toole, Jr., "Exokernel: An Operating System Architecture for Application-level Resource Management," in *Proceedings of the Fifteenth ACM Symposium on Operating Systems Principles*, ser. SOSP '95, 1995, pp. 251–266.

[20] H. Franke, J. Xenidis, C. Basso, B. M. Bass, S. S. Woodward, J. D. Brown, and C. L. Johnson, "Introduction to the wire-speed processor and architecture," *IBM Journal of Research and Development*, vol. 54, no. 1, pp. 3:1 –3:11, january-february 2010.

[21] A. Frumusanu, "The Samsung Exynos 7420 Deep Dive - Inside A Modern 14nm SoC," http://www.anandtech.com/show/9330/exynos-7420-deep-dive/2.

[22] "Grand Central Dispatch," http://developer.apple.com/library/ios/#documentation/Performance/Reference/GCD_libdispatch_Ref/Reference/reference.html.

[23] J. Giceva, T.-i. Salomie, A. Schupbach, G. Alonso, and T. Roscoe, "COD: Database / Operating System Co-Design," in *Conference on Innovative Data Systems Research (CIDR)*, 2013.

[24] D. Grewe and M. F. P. O'Boyle, "A Static Task Partitioning Approach for Heterogeneous Systems Using OpenCL," in *Proceedings of the 20th International Conference on Compiler Construction: Part of the Joint European Conferences on Theory and Practice of Software*, ser. CC'11/ETAPS'11. Berlin, Heidelberg: Springer-Verlag, 2011, pp. 286–305.

[25] V. Gupta, K. Schwan, N. Tolia, V. Talwar, and P. Ranganathan, "Pegasus: coordinated scheduling for virtualized accelerator-based systems," in *Proceedings of the 2011 USENIX conference on USENIX annual technical conference*, 2011, pp. 3–3.

[26] M. Heimel, M. Saecker, H. Pirk, S. Manegold, and V. Markl, "Hardware-oblivious Parallelism for In-memory Column-stores," *Proc. VLDB Endow.*

[27] M. D. Hill and M. R. Marty, "Amdahl's Law in the Multicore Era," *IEEE Computer*, pp. 33–38, Jul. 2008.

[28] B. Hindman, A. Konwinski, M. Zaharia, A. Ghodsi, A. D. Joseph, R. Katz, S. Shenker, and I. Stoica, "Mesos: A Platform for Fine-grained Resource Sharing in the Data Center," in *Proceedings of the 8th USENIX Conference on Networked Systems Design and Implementation*, ser. NSDI'11. Berkeley, CA, USA: USENIX Association, 2011, pp. 295–308.

[29] H. Hoffmann, S. Sidiroglou, M. Carbin, S. Misailovic, A. Agarwal, and M. Rinard, "Dynamic Knobs for Responsive Power-aware Computing," in *Proceedings of the Sixteenth International Conference on Architectural Support for Programming Languages and Operating Systems*, ser. ASPLOS XVI. New York, NY, USA: ACM, 2011, pp. 199–212.

[30] "HSA Intermediate Language," https://hsafoundation.app.box.com/s/m6mrsjv8b7r50kqeyyal, May 2013.

[31] Intel Corporation, "Thermal Protection And Monitoring Features: A Software Perspective," http://www.intel.com/cd/ids/developer/asmo-na/eng/downloads/54118.htm, 2005.

[32] "Intel Sandy Bridge," http://software.intel.com/en-us/blogs/2011/01/13/a-look-at-sandy-bridge-integrating-graphics-into-the-cpu.

[33] B. Jeff, "big.LITTLE Technology Moves Towards Fully Heterogeneous Global Task Scheduling," http://www.arm.com/files/pdf/big_LITTLE_technology_moves_towards_fully_heterogeneous_Global_Task_Scheduling.pdf, Nov. 2013.

[34] S. Kanev, J. P. Darago, K. Hazelwood, P. Ranganathan, T. Moseley, G.-Y. Wei, and D. Brooks, "Profiling a Warehouse-scale Computer," in *Proceedings of the 42Nd Annual International Symposium on Computer Architecture*, ser. ISCA '15, 2015, pp. 158–169.

[35] A. Khanna and J. Zinky, "The Revised ARPANET Routing Metric," in *Symposium Proceedings on Communications Architectures &Amp; Protocols*, ser. SIGCOMM '89. New York, NY, USA: ACM, 1989, pp. 45–56. [Online]. Available: http://doi.acm.org/10.1145/75246.75252

[36] K. Kofler, I. Grasso, B. Cosenza, and T. Fahringer, "An Automatic Input-sensitive Approach for Heterogeneous Task Partitioning," in *Proceedings of the 27th International ACM Conference on International Conference on Supercomputing*, ser. ICS '13, 2013.

[37] M. D. Linderman, J. D. Collins, H. Wang, and T. H. Meng, "Merge: A Programming Model for Heterogeneous Multi-core Systems," in *Proceedings of the 13th International Conference on Architectural Support for Programming Languages and Operating Systems*, ser. ASPLOS XIII. New York, NY, USA: ACM, 2008, pp. 287–296.

[38] C.-K. Luk, S. Hong, and H. Kim, "Qilin: Exploiting Parallelism on Heterogeneous Multiprocessors with Adaptive Mapping," in *Proceedings of the 42Nd Annual IEEE/ACM International Symposium on Microarchitecture*, ser. MICRO 42, 2009.

[39] "Qualcomm MARE: Enabling Applications for Heterogeneous Mobile Devices," https://developer.qualcomm.com/downloads/whitepaper-qualcomm-mare-enabling-applications-heterogeneous-mobile-devices, Apr. 2014.

[40] E. Marth and G. Marcus, "Parallelization of the x264 encoder using OpenCL," http://li5.ziti.uni-heidelberg.de/x264gpu/.

[41] K. Menychtas, K. Shen, and M. L. Scott, "Disengaged Scheduling for Fair, Protected Access to Fast Computational Accelerators," in *Proceedings of the 19th International Conference on Architectural Support for Programming Languages and Operating Systems*, ser. ASPLOS '14. New York, NY, USA: ACM, 2014, pp. 301–316.

[42] N. Mishra, H. Zhang, J. D. Lafferty, and H. Hoffmann, "A Probabilistic Graphical Model-based Approach for Minimizing Energy Under Performance Constraints," in *Proceedings of the Twentieth International Conference on Architectural Support for Programming Languages and Operating Systems*, ser. ASPLOS '15, 2015, pp. 267–281.

[43] T. P. Morgan, "Oracle Cranks Up The Cores To 32 With Sparc M7 Chip," http://www.enterprisetech.com/2014/08/13/oracle-cranks-cores-32-sparc-m7-chip/, Aug. 2014, enterpriseTech.

[44] E. B. Nightingale, O. Hodson, R. McIlroy, C. Hawblitzel, and G. Hunt, "Helios: Heterogeneous Multiprocessing with Satellite Kernels," in *Proceedings of the ACM SIGOPS 22Nd Symposium on Operating Systems Principles*, ser. SOSP '09. New York, NY, USA: ACM, 2009, pp. 221–234.

[45] B. D. Noble, M. Satyanarayanan, D. Narayanan, J. E. Tilton, J. Flinn, and K. R. Walker, "Agile Application-aware Adaptation for Mobility," in *Proceedings of the Sixteenth ACM Symposium on Operating Systems Principles*, ser. SOSP '97, 1997.

[46] NVidia, Inc., "CUDA Toolkit 4.1," http://www.developer.nvidia.com/cuda-toolkit-41, 2011.

[47] "NVIDIA OpenCL SDK," http://developer.download.nvidia.com/compute/cuda/3_0/sdk/website/OpenCL/website/samples.html.

[48] "The OpenACC Application Program Interface," http://www.openacc-standard.org/.

[49] "OpenCL - The open standard for parallel programming of heterogeneous systems," http://download.microsoft.com/download/4/0/E/40EA02D8-23A7-4BD2-AD3A-0BFFFB640F28/CppAMPLanguageAndProgrammingModel.pdf.

[50] H. Pan, B. Hindman, and K. Asanović, "Composing Parallel Software Efficiently with Lithe," in *Proceedings of the 31st ACM SIGPLAN Conference on Programming Language Design and Implementation*, ser. PLDI '10. New York, NY, USA: ACM, 2010, pp. 376–387.

[51] "Parallel Implementation of bzip2," http://compression.ca/pbzip2/.

[52] S. Peter, A. Schüpbach, P. Barham, A. Baumann, R. Isaacs, T. Harris, and T. Roscoe, "Design Principles for End-to-end Multicore Schedulers," in *Proceedings of the 2Nd USENIX Conference on Hot Topics in Parallelism*, ser. HotPar'10, 2010, pp. 10–10.

[53] J. Planas, R. M. Badia, E. AyguadÃľ, and J. Labarta, "Self-Adaptive OmpSs Tasks in Heterogeneous Environments," in *Parallel Distributed Processing (IPDPS), 2013 IEEE 27th International Symposium on*, May 2013, pp. 138–149.

[54] J. Planas, R. M. Badia, E. Ayguade, and J. Labarta, "AMA: Asynchronous Management of Accelerators for Task-based Programming Models," *Procedia Computer Science*, vol. 51, pp. 130–139, 2015.

[55] J. Planas, R. M. Badia, E. Ayguadé, and J. Labarta, "SSMART: Smart Scheduling of Multi-architecture Tasks on Heterogeneous Systems," in *Proceedings of the Second Workshop on Accelerator Programming Using Directives*, ser. WACCPD '15. New York, NY, USA: ACM, 2015, pp. 1:1–1:11.

[56] C. J. Rossbach, J. Currey, M. Silberstein, B. Ray, and E. Witchel, "PTask: Operating System Abstractions To Manage GPUs as Compute Devices," in *Proceedings of the Twenty-Third ACM Symposium on Operating Systems Principles*, 2011, pp. 233–248.

[57] J. C. Saez, M. Prieto, A. Fedorova, and S. Blagodurov, "A Comprehensive Scheduler for Asymmetric Multicore Systems," in *Proceedings of the 5th European Conference on Computer Systems*, ser. EuroSys '10. New York, NY, USA: ACM, 2010, pp. 139–152.

[58] A. Sbîrlea, Y. Zou, Z. Budimlíc, J. Cong, and V. Sarkar, "Mapping a Data-flow Programming Model Onto Heterogeneous Platforms," in *Proceedings of the 13th ACM SIGPLAN/SIGBED International Conference on Languages, Compilers, Tools and Theory for Embedded Systems*, ser. LCTES '12. New York, NY, USA: ACM, 2012, pp. 61–70.

[59] M. Shoaib Bin Altaf and D. Wood, "LogCA: A Performance Model for Hardware Accelerators," *Computer Architecture Letters*, vol. PP, no. 99, pp. 1–1, 2014.

[60] M. Silberstein, B. Ford, I. Keidar, and E. Witchel, "GPUfs: integrating a file system with GPUs," in *Proc. 18th ASPLOS*, 2013, pp. 485–498.

[61] S. Sridharan, G. Gupta, and G. S. Sohi, "Adaptive, Efficient, Parallel Execution of Parallel Programs," in *Proceedings of the 35th ACM SIGPLAN Conference on Programming Language Design and Implementation*, ser. PLDI '14, 2014, pp. 169–180.

[62] "StarPU Task Scheduling Policy," http://starpu.gforge.inria.fr/doc/html/Scheduling.html.

[63] J. Stratton, C. Rodrigues, I. Sung, N. Obeid, L. Chang, N. Anssari, G. Liu, and W. Hwu, "Parboil: A Revised Benchmark Suite for Scientific and Commercial Throughput Computing," *Center for Reliable and High-Performance Computing*, 2012.

[64] N. Sun and C.-C. Lin, "Using the Cryptographic Accelerators in the UltraSparc T1 and T2 Processors," http://www.oracle.com/technetwork/server-storage/archive/a11-014-crypto-accelerators-439765.pdf, Nov. 2007.

[65] M. B. Taylor, "Is dark silicon useful?: harnessing the four horsemen of the coming dark silicon apocalypse," ser. DAC '12.

[66] "Truecrack," https://code.google.com/p/truecrack/.

[67] C. A. Waldspurger and W. E. Weihl, "An Object-oriented Framework for Modular Resource Management," in *Proceedings of the 5th International Workshop on Object Orientation in Operating Systems (IWOOOS '96)*, ser. IWOOOS '96, 1996.

Auto-tuning Spark Big Data Workloads on POWER8: Prediction-Based Dynamic SMT Threading

Zhen Jia
Institute of Computing Technology, Chinese Academy of Sciences
University of Chinese Academy of Sciences
jiazhen@ict.ac.cn

Chao Xue
IBM Research-China
xuechao@cn.ibm.com

Guancheng Chen
IBM Research-China
chenguancheng@gmail.com

Jianfeng Zhan*
Institute of Computing Technology, Chinese Academy of Sciences
University of Chinese Academy of Sciences
zhanjianfeng@ict.ac.cn

Lixin Zhang
Institute of Computing Technology, Chinese Academy of Sciences
zhanglixin@ict.ac.cn

Yonghua Lin
IBM Research-China
linyh@cn.ibm.com

Peter Hofstee
IBM Research-Austin
hofstee@us.ibm.com

ABSTRACT

Much research work devotes to tuning big data analytics in modern data centers, since even a small percentage of performance improvement immediately translates to huge cost savings because of the large scale. Simultaneous multithreading (SMT) receives great interest from data center communities, as it has the potential to boost performance of big data analytics by increasing the processor resources utilization. For example, the emerging processor architectures like POWER8 support up to 8-way multithreading. However, as different big data workloads have disparate architectural characteristics, how to identify the most efficient SMT configuration to achieve the best performance is challenging in terms of both complex application behaviors and processor architectures.

In this paper, we specifically focus on auto-tuning SMT configuration for Spark-based big data workloads on POWER8. However, our methodology could be generalized and extended to other programming software stacks and other architectures. We propose a prediction-based dynamic SMT threading (PBDST) framework to adjust the thread count in SMT cores on POWER8 processors by using versatile machine learning algorithms. Its innovation lies in adopting online SMT configuration predictions derived from micro-architecture level profiling, to regulate the thread counts that could achieve nearly optimal performance. Moreover it is implemented at Spark software stack layer and transparent to user applications. After evaluating a large set of machine learning algorithms, we choose the most efficient ones to perform online predictions. The experimental results demonstrate that our approach can achieve up to 56.3% performance improvement and an average performance gain of 16.2% in comparison with the default configuration—the maximum SMT configuration—SMT8 on our system.

*Jianfeng Zhan is the corresponding author.

PACT '16, September 11-15, 2016, Haifa, Israel

DOI: http://dx.doi.org/10.1145/2967938.2967957

Keywords

Dynamic SMT tuning; POWER8; Spark big data

1. INTRODUCTION

Society is experiencing a dramatic growth in the amount of data. The volume of data created worldwide has been growing over 50% per year [5]. IDC projects that about one quarter of the world's data have potential value, but found that by 2012 only 3% had been tagged, and only 0.5% had been analyzed [23]. Those situations lead to the emergence of big data analytics applications, which own the capabilities of manipulating, analyzing, and achieving business value from the large scale of data.

At the software layer, many large-scale data analytics frameworks are being proposed to facilitate and accelerate the development of big data analytics applications, such as Hadoop [46], Spark [47], Flink [1] etc. At the hardware layer, besides the development of VLSI, architecture techniques are enhanced to cater the need of high performance. One of the architectural techniques widely used in modern processors to improve the overall performance is Simultaneous Multithreading (SMT), which has been introduced to

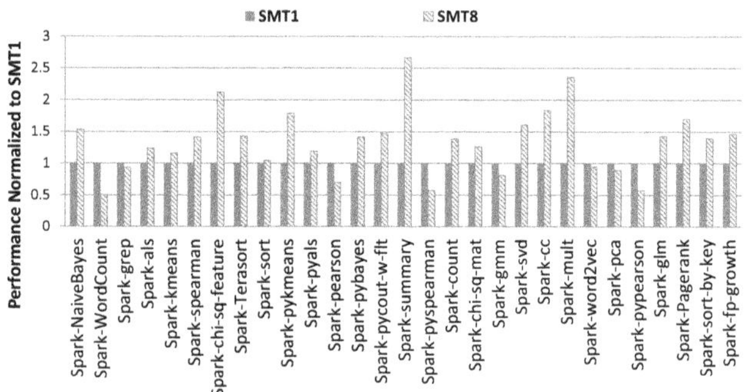

Figure 1: Performance gaps between SMT1 and SMT8 on a POWER8 system.

modern processor designs for over a decade [43] and has been adopted in most of current generations of microprocessors.

In SMT processors, most resources are shared competitively among hardware threads, such as execution units, data and instruction caches, address translation units, branch prediction resources etc. The application performance could be improved because of the increased pipeline utilization. However, saturating the SMT threads in each core can not always achieve the best performance, since resource contentions caused by SMT may degrade performance as many previous studies shown [22, 33, 38]. Figure 1 shows the normalized performance of the 29 Spark applications we investigate in this paper. SMT has a significant performance impact on those applications. Some applications prefer to lower level SMTs (e.g., Spark-WordCount); some prefer to higher ones (e.g., Spark-NaiveBayes). There are also workloads whose performance is not very sensitive to the SMT thread number. Due to the large performance gap between the best SMT configuration (thread counts in SMT cores) and the worst one, it is of great importance to identify the optimal SMT configuration, which not only achieves performance improvements but also reduces the energy consumption(less active threads need less power supply). However it is not a trivial issue to find the best configuration without exhaustive experiments.

This paper proposes a novel, user-application transparent framework (shown in Figure 3) for online SMT configuration adaptation so as to accelerate big data analytics. We integrate the framework into the Spark software stack. Due to the unavailability of multi-node POWER8 systems, we evaluate its performance on a single-node one with the pseudo-distributed mode. The POWER8 processor supports up to 8-way multithreading (referred to SMT8) [40]. In comparison with the default configuration, our method achieves up to 56.3% performance improvement and an average performance gain of 16.2%. Specifically, our contributions are summarized below.

- We present an online SMT configuration prediction approach on the basis of dynamically collected and analyzed task profiles of stages in big data analytics. The profiles are collected by accessing hardware performance counters. And we use machine learning algorithms to predict the optimal or near-optimal SMT configurations (i.e., thread counts in each SMT core).
- We build a comprehensive framework, called PBDST (Prediction-Based Dynamic SMT Threading), for automatic SMT configuration tuning of big data analytics applications. It is transparent to application programmers and consists of a hardware performance event profiler, an on-the-fly predictor using the feedback from the profiler, and the necessary thread number adaptation mechanisms.
- We leverage a large set of machine learning algorithms to predict the optimal SMT configurations. After a comprehensive evaluation, we find that the K-nearest neighbor algorithm and logistic regression algorithm usually achieve near-optimal predictions statically with average prediction accuracies of 93.2% and 95.9%, respectively.
- We deploy and evaluate our PBDST framework on Spark applications running on a POWER8 based system. The experimental results demonstrate that our auto-tuning approach has the capability of improving performance of Spark applications. The PBDST framework can attain up to 56.3% performance improvement and an average performance gain of 16.2% in comparison with the default configuration—the maximum SMT configuration on our POWER8 system—SMT8. And for most of applications, it can achieve performance very close to the best static case, which can only be acquired post facto after exhaustive tests.

2. BACKGROUND

2.1 POWER8 Processor

The POWER8 [40] provides many new features compared with its predecessor (i.e., POWER7+) [41]. It doubled the hardware thread parallelism and supports up to 8-way multithreading. The eight hardware threads in POWER8 processor are split into two thread-sets: the even thread-set (T0, T2, T4, and T6) and the odd thread-set (T1, T3, T5, and T7). Each thread-set occupies half the issue queue entries and half the execution pipelines. The POWER8 processor improves thread-switch time and removes thread placement restrictions. That is to say, any software thread can be run on any thread-set.

The POWER8 system maintains a measurement of system load in terms of the number of running or runnable software-threads, and provides features to adapt hardware-thread strength to meet workload requirements. For instance, the core will be transitioned to SMT1 (single thread) mode if only one hardware thread is busy, regardless of the position of the hardware thread. When the second hardware thread begins running work, the core is in SMT2 mode. There may be an imbalance in the number of active threads per thread-set, either after an SMT-mode change, or as threads are disabled. The POWER8 processor provides the capability of rebalancing the thread distribution across the thread-set automatically. Thread(s) will be moved across the thread-set boundary automatically to keep the threads in balance to achieve higher throughput.

2.2 Spark Software Stack

Spark [47] is a fast and general emerging engine for big data processing. The basic idea of Spark is keeping the working set of data in the memory. The proposed abstraction Resilient Distributed Dataset (RDD) provides a restricted form of shared memory, based on coarse grained transformations rather than fine-grained updates to shared state so as to achieve fault tolerance efficiently.

To use Spark, developers need to write a driver program that connects to a cluster of workers. The driver defines one

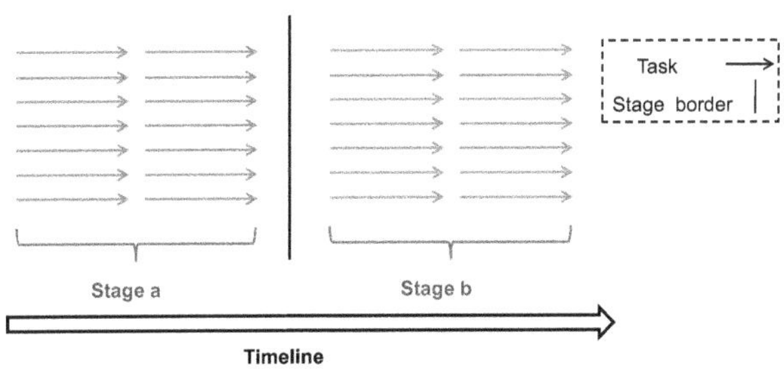

Figure 2: Spark job execution procedure.

or more RDDs and invokes actions on them. Each action in the diver program will trigger a Spark job. Each Spark job consists of several stages. Task is the unit of computations in each stage as shown in Figure 2. Each partition of a RDD is processed by one task. So the number of tasks in one stage equals to the number of RDD partitions. The tasks in the same stage execute the same code but process different data partitions. And each task will occupy one hardware thread. So if the number of data partitions in a stage is greater than the number of available hardware threads, there will be several rounds of tasks in the stage.

3. AUTO SMT TUNING

For a SMT processor, more active threads mean more sharing in processor pipelines and better processor resources utilization, which may achieve performance improvements. However more active threads also can cause resource contentions, e.g., more cache misses, which may degrade application performance. Modern processors provide hardware performance counters, by accessing which we can obtain micro-architecture level profiles and use them as the potential indicators that help guide the optimization of *SMT configuration*. In this paper, we refer to the number of active threads in each SMT core as the *SMT configuration*. However, it is difficult to reason about the exact relationship between those profiles and the proper SMT configurations. For instance, a high cache miss rate may be an indicator that the number of threads should be increased so as to alleviate the pipeline stalls caused by cache misses. On the other hand, when more threads are activated, the risk, which application performance is decreased due to cache or other processor resource contentions, is increased. And the relationship between those indicators and the SMT configurations is closely related to application behaviors. In addition, the processor also plays an important role. Different processor own diverse architectures and performance models, so the relationship derived on one kind of processors may do not fit to others. The difficulty in establishing a relationship between application profiles and SMT configurations motivates us to explore machine learning approaches.

In this section we propose a framework, called PBDST (Prediction-Based Dynamic SMT Threading), to automatically optimize the SMT configuration through machine learning algorithms. The goal of PBDST is to dynamically predict the optimal or near-optimal SMT configuration in each stage of a big data analytics application, so as to achieve better performance. In order to achieve this goal, PBDST adopts a two-phase (offline training phase and online prediction phase) method to perform predictions automatically, which is depicted in Figure 3. After establishing the prediction models, the PBDST will be triggered by hooks in the big data analytics software stack (i.e., Spark software stack in this paper) and the optimal SMT configuration will be predicted and applied to the application.

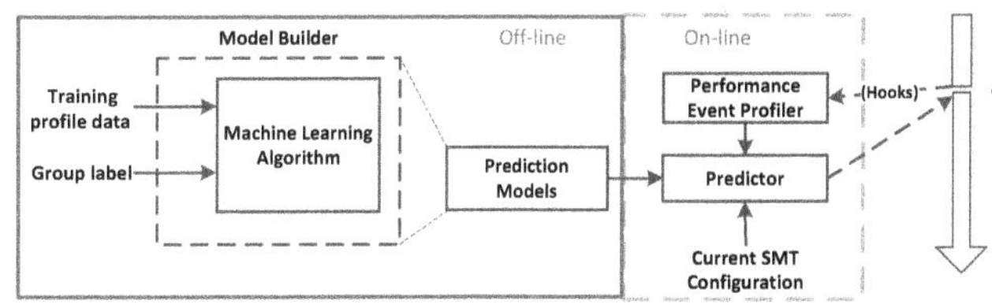

Figure 3: The PBDST framework.

3.1 Offline Training

The purpose of the offline training phase is to build prediction models, which will be used in the online prediction phase. Given the training application set, each application should be executed under varying SMT configurations and the micro-architecture level statistics will be collected. After all SMT configurations are traversed, the best SMT configuration that achieves the best performance will be recorded. Different SMT configurations will affect application behaviors from the perspective of micro-architecture level. For instance, even for the same application, running at SMT8 and SMT2 can achieve totally different thread IPCs (Instructions per Cycle) and cache miss rates. So in the offline training phase, we will train one model for each SMT configuration. For each model, a two-item training dataset is used: *the training profile data* and *the group label. The training profile data* is a matrix and each row is the micro-architecture level statistics of one training application. Those statistics are obtained from hardware performance counters and normalized by the running instructions of the application. *The group label* is an array, which records the best SMT configurations for the training applications. With the training dataset, a prediction model for one certain SMT configuration will be established by applying a specific machine learning algorithm.

3.2 Online Prediction

In the online prediction phase, the PBDST predictor predicts the optimal SMT configuration by using profiles collected from live execution of applications. The hardware performance event profiler starts collecting the micro architecture level statistics when a big data analytics application moves to a new stage. At the end of the sampling period, the collected profiles (i.e., the micro architecture level statistics) are used by PBDST predictor to predict the optimal SMT configuration for the upcoming tasks of the stage. The PBDST framework stops the sampling and performs the prediction when the first round of tasks are finished. The rational behind this is that the tasks in the same stage execute the same code but process different data as illustrated in Section 2.2. So we can use the first round of tasks' micro-architecture level profiles to predict the optimal SMT configuration for the upcoming tasks in the same stage.

As mentioned in offline training phase (Section 3.1), we construct one prediction model for each SMT configuration. Even though those models are homogeneous (trained by the same algorithm), *the training profile data* (micro-architecture level statistics collected at a certain SMT configuration) used to train models are diverse. As a consequence, the same live profiles feeding to different models will lead to different results (i.e., the optimal SMT configurations). So for each prediction, the PBDST framework will select the corresponding prediction model (M) according to the current SMT configuration (s), and perform predictions by using the collected profile (P) as the input. The predicted optimal SMT configuration is $M_s(P)$.

4. IMPLEMENTATION

In this paper, the IBM POWER8 processor is used as the vehicle to study our PBDST framework for it supports a wide range of SMT threads. For the big data analytics software stack, we choose Spark [47] in this paper, since it is gaining wide industry attention in big data field due to its superior performance, simple interfaces, and a rich library for analysis and calculation.

There are two necessary assumptions for implementing the PBDST framework. First, it depends on the underlying software stack's capability of adjusting the thread count used to process tasks online. We modify the Spark software stack to achieve this capability, which will be illustrated in this section. Second, the running time of a stage in an application should be longer than the sampling period.

4.1 Hardware Performance Event Selection

POWER8 provides more than one thousand hardware performance events for measurement. It is impractical and unnecessary to monitor all those events. The performance events that are irrelevant to SMT configurations should be excluded for they may cause a negative impact on the accuracy of the machine learning models. On the other hand, there are only several hardware performance counters in each core, which limits the number of performance events that monitored concurrently. Even though the time multiplexing technique is used when the number of performance events is greater than the available hardware performance counters, the precision of sampled data is affected. We carefully select 11 performance events, which can accurately measure the effects of SMT configurations. They are RUN_INST_CMPL, RUN_CYC, L1_ICACHE_MISS, LD_MISS_L1, ST_MISS_L1, DATA_FROM_L3, LLC_ST_MISS, BR_MPRED_CMPL, IERAT_RELOAD, LSU_DERAT_MISS, and DATA_ALL_FROM_MEMORY. All those performance events reflect the performance of the specific processor resources that are shared by all available threads, so they are directly affected by the SMT configurations. At the same time, they are not specific to the POWER8 processors, and similar events can be found on the other architectures. Several advanced performance events of POWER8 processors may also achieve good performance, such as the events that describe the POWER8CPI stack. However, they are too specific to POWER8 architecture. We prefer to use more generalized events so that our framework can be also applicable to other platforms. In order to collect profiles of those performance events, Perf [2], a profiling tool for Linux 2.6+ based system, is used to configure and access the hardware performance counters.

4.2 Machine Learning Algorithms

We employ diverse predictors by implementing a large set of machine learning algorithms in our PBDST framework, including K-nearest neighbor (KNN), logistic regression (LogR), support vector machines (SVM), adaptive boosting (Adaboost), Naive Bayes (NB), decision tree (DT), locally weighted linear regression (LWLR) and linear regression (LiR). Actually, our predictor model is a classifier, who takes an input vector x and assigns it to one of K discrete classes C_k where $k = 1, ..., K$. In our scenario, the vector x is the micro-architectural data, and class C is a specific SMT configuration. In the KNN model [4], Euclidean distances between the live application performance statistics and the training application ones are calculated. The K nearest training applications' best SMT configurations are selected and the optimal one is chosen with the principle of plurality. Logistic regression (LogR) [18] and Support vector machines (SVM) [36] are usually referred to as linear models for classification, which have the formula: $y = f(w^T x)$. Where x is the input vector; w is the weight parameter; T is the transposition factor; f is the link function, y is the output class. Then the loss function $L(y, f(w^T x))$ is defined and is minimized in order to calculate the weights. For LogR, $f(x) = 1/(1 + exp(-w^T x))$ and $L(w) = log(1 + exp(-yw^T x))$; while in SVM, $f(x) = w^T x$ and $L(w) = max(0, 1 - yw^T x)$. In LogR a set of regression coefficient is searched by stochastic gradient descent method, which can update the classifier incrementally. In the SVM model, both the linear kernel and the radial basis kernel function are evaluated respectively. Due to the relatively good result and rapidity of the linear kernel, we use it as the kernel function for SVM model in our framework, since the prediction speed will greatly affect the performance of the dynamic SMT configuration adjustment. The probability model, i.e., the Naive Bayes model [25], seeks the maximal likelihood of the probability of class given by the input vector. In the Naive Bayes model, quantization is required because the micro-architectural metrics are numeric of continuous value. The magnitude of minimal quantized interval is 10^{-5}. The Laplace smoothing is involved to eliminate the case of probability of zero for Naive Bayes model. Also, we implement a decision tree model, which has been used in the previous work [50, 35]. The decision tree model is not a probability model, it does not need data normalization and standardization, and hence it is very suitable for boosting method. In the decision tree model, classification and regression tree (CART) [7] with Gini index is evaluated to build decision trees in order to perform the divide-and-conquer strategy. In the adaptive boosting model (Adaboost) [15], a weakly learning model, which is called decision stump, is used to build a strongly learnable model. The weights of every sample in the training application statistics are iterated with error classified probability. We set the maximal number of iterations to be 30. Furthermore, we also try the linear regression (LiR) model, which has been verified by Curtis-Maury et al. [10, 9]. In the linear regression model [34], we refer to the idea of logistic regression except for the rule of estimating the coefficient, which is based on the minimization of square error of testing data and training data. The locally weighted linear regression model (LWLR) [17] is also implemented in our framework. We assign different weights to different training points according to the distances between the testing points. And a Gaussian kernel is chosen

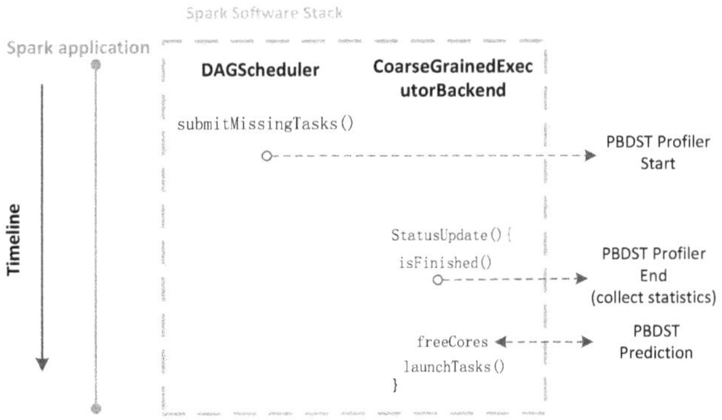

Figure 4: PBDST hooks and their triggers.

to evaluate the weights. Finally, we extend LogR, SVM and AdaBoost to multiple classifiers [21], and normalize the micro-architectural statistics to get rid of the numeric imbalance effect because of their heterogeneous nature.

4.3 Integration with Spark Software Stack

We integrate the PBDST framework into Apache Spark software stack (version 1.3.0 in our implementation). The Spark software stack is integrated with several hooks that trigger PBDST functionality. Applications do not need to change since we keep all modifications confined to the Spark runtime system. Spark applications can simply submit jobs to the PBDST-enabled Spark runtime system. An overview of the hooks that implement the PBDST framework, including their main functionality and how they are integrated into Spark software stack, are illustrated in Figure 4.

Inside the Spark software stack, the *DAGScheduler* implements stage-oriented scheduling. It computes a DAG (Directed Acyclic Graph) of stages for each job, keeps track of which RDDs and stage outputs are materialized, and finds a minimal schedule to run the job. It then submits *stages* as *TaskSets* by invoking the *submitMissingTasks* function. We add a call to *Profiler*'s begin hook in the function. The *CoarseGrainedSchedulerBackend* is a scheduler backend that holds onto each executor for the duration of the Spark job. It receives *StatusUpdate* messages through Akka, updates executor information and launches new tasks if there is a task finished. We add a call to *Profiler*'s end hook in the *CoarseGrainedSchedulerBackend* when it receives a *StatusUpdate* message from a finished task. Before *CoarseGrainedSchedulerBackend* launches new tasks, the PBDST's prediction hook will be invoked and the machine learning algorithm will determine the optimal SMT configuration for the upcoming tasks in the stage. The variable of *freeCores* will be modified according to the optimal SMT configuration so as to drive the Spark software stack to adjust the number of software threads.

4.3.1 Per-stage Tuning

The PBDST framework tunes the SMT configurations for Spark applications at the granularity of stage. Here we would like to illustrate how to automatically tune the number of threads in each core (i.e., SMT configuration) for each stage by invoking the hooks we mentioned above.

Algorithm 1 shows the algorithm used in the *DAGScheduler* to trigger the PBDST hooks. The algorithm is executed when a new stage is submitted. It takes three parameters, the current SMT configuration (i.e., the thread count in each core), the number of cores used for Spark applications, and the *TaskSet* information. Before starting the PBDST profiler to configure hardware performance counters, two conditions should be satisfied. The first condition is that no stage is in running state with a profiler instance. If there is one stage running at present and the PBDST profiler has been started, starting a new profiler instance will introduce extra overhead and impact the accuracy of the micro-architecture level statistics that will be collected. This is because two profiler instances, which access the same set of hardware performance counters, will interfere with each other. The second condition is that the number of tasks in the stage is greater than the number of total available hardware threads (i.e., the number of cores multiplied by the number of threads in each core). In our PBDST framework, we profile the first round of tasks in each stage, and predict the optimal SMT configuration for the upcoming tasks in the stage. The number of the tasks that are initiated when the stage is submitted, equals to the number of total available hardware threads in the system. If the task number of the stage is less than the available hardware threads, the stage will be finished after the first round task executions and the prediction result is useless since the stage is already finished when the prediction is performed. So only both of the conditions are met, the *DAGScheduler* will trigger the PBDST hook and the profiler starts configuring and accessing hardware performance counters. Otherwise, the PBDST hook will not be triggered.

Algorithm 1 Algorithm used to trigger the PBDST hooks in *DAGScheduler*

Input: Variables:
Current SMT configurations: $CurSMT$;
The number of cores: $cores$;
The TaskSet information: $taskSet$;

if $submitTaskSet()$ **then**
  if $noStageIsRuningWithProfiler()$ **then**
    if $taskSet.size > CurSMT * cores$ **then**
      $PBDST.profiler.start()$;
    end if
  end if
end if

Algorithm 2 shows the algorithm used to trigger PBDST hooks in the *CoarseGrainedSchedulerBackend* for our PBDST-enabled Spark software stack implementation. The algorithm is executed when a task is finished. It takes four parameters, the current SMT configuration (i.e., current thread count in each core), the task state (i.e, running or finished), current stage ID and the last stage ID in which the algorithm is executed previously. When a task is finished, the PBDST framework will compare the last stage ID with the current stage ID. If they are the same, the prediction of the optimal SMT configuration for this stage has been triggered before. Otherwise the PBDST will update the value of variable *lastStageId* and perform the prediction. However if the PBDST profiler is not running at present for some reasons, the PBDST prediction will also not be triggered. This situation happens because of the following two cases: first, errors occur in the PBSDT profiler; second, the stage does not satisfy with the conditions that profiler starts, for

Algorithm 2 Algorithm used to trigger the PBDST hooks in *CoarseGrainedSchedulerBackend*

```
Input: Variables:
    Current SMT configurations: CurSMT;
    Task state: state;
    Current Stage Id: curStageId;
    Last Stage Id: lastStageId;
if isFinished(state) then
  if lastStageId != curStageId then
    lastStageId = curStageId
    if profilerIsRuning() then
      PBDST.profiler.stop();
      predictSMT = PBDST.prediction(CurSMT);
      if predictSMT != CurSMT then
        for excutor in excutorMap do
          executor.freeCores.updating(predictSMT);
        end for
      end if
    end if
  end if
end if
```

example, the number of tasks in the stage is less than the total available hardware threads (line 3 in Algorithm 1). The PBSDT prediction hook will be invoked with the parameter of current SMT configuration as the input, which is used to choose the correct prediction model. After this procedure, the predicted SMT configuration is obtained and the PBSDT framework will update the *freeCores* variable for each *executor* according to the prediction result if the predicted SMT configuration and the current one are not the same.

4.3.2 Small Stage Prediction

Some Spark workloads may have several small stages in the whole lifetime, which may be finished in hundreds of milliseconds. Small stages may be caused by the following cases: 1). limited number of tasks, for instance, only two rounds of tasks are finished in the stage; 2). a fast processing speed for each task; 3). both 1) and 2). For our POWER8 system, which owns powerful cores and up to 192 hardware threads, the small stages are more likely to appear. For a small stage, because of the penalty of profiles collecting, SMT configuration predicting and adjusting, the performance gains brought by SMT configuration adjustment may be very limited especially for a small stage with limited number of tasks. So for the small stages, we do not perform prediction nor adjust SMT configuration. In our implementations, we separate large-stage case from small-stage according to the first round of tasks' runtime. If the runtime is less than 2 seconds [1], we classify the whole stage into small-stage case.

4.3.3 Prediction Scheme

In our PBSDT framework, SMT configuration predictions and adjustments are performed at a stage granularity. So each stage of a Spark application is analyzed independently and executed with its own locally optimal SMT configuration. Since applications may have behaviors that varies across stages, using locally optimized SMT configurations may improve the overall performance compared to using a single SMT configuration with the whole lifetime. However, using locally optimal SMT configuration for each stage may introduce performance penalty. The penalty can stem from frequently thread-switching, rebalancing the thread distribution across thread-set [41] and predicting. And if the Spark applications do not have varied behaviors across stages, only performing prediction once is enough. For this case, multiple predictions will occupy computing resources but will not obtain performance gains.

For the above concerns, we propose two prediction schemes for Spark applications. The first scheme performs multiple predictions, and each stage uses its locally optimal SMT configuration. The second scheme simply predicts the best SMT configuration in the first stage and keeps it unchanged in all stages, regardless of their locally optimal SMT configurations.

[1]The number is a heuristic number, which depends on the number of rounds in each stage. We observe that most of our applications have 2 to 5 rounds of tasks within each stage, so we choose 2-second as the threshold.

Table 1: Spark applications used in our experiments.

	No.	Name	Source
Training Set	1	Spark-als	Spark-perf
	2	Spark-kmeans	Spark-perf
	3	Spark-spearman	Spark-perf
	4	Spark-chi-sq-feature	Spark-perf
	5	Spark-NaiveBayes	BigDataBench
	6	Spark-terasort	BigDataBench
	7	Spark-grep	BigDataBench
	8	Spark-sort	BigDataBench
	9	Spark-pykmeans	Spark-perf
	10	Spark-pyals	Spark-perf
	11	Spark-pearson	Spark-perf
	12	Spark-pybayes	Spark-perf
	13	Spark-pycout-w-fltr	Spark-perf
	14	Spark-summary-statistics	Spark-perf
	15	Spark-pyspearman	Spark-perf
	16	Spark-count	Spark-perf
	17	Spark-chi-sq-mat:	Spark-perf
	18	Spark-gmm	Spark-perf
	19	Spark-svd	Spark-perf
	20	Spark-WordCount	BigDataBench
Testing Set	21	Spark-ConnectedComponent	BigDataBench
	22	Spark-block-matrix-mult	Spark-perf
	23	Spark-word2vec	Spark-perf
	24	Spark-pca	Spark-perf
	25	Spark-pypearson	Spark-perf
	26	Spark-glm	Spark-perf
	27	Spark-PageRank	BigDataBench
	28	Spark-int-sory-by-key	Spark-perf
	29	Spark-fp-growth	Spark-perf

4.4 Discussions

Our prediction-based SMT threading approach is not particularly designed for Spark. It is also applied to other big data software stacks by adjusting the number of tasks executing in parallel. For example, we need to tune the number of map and reduce slots by inserting hooks in Hadoop1 TaskTracker. Our method is also applied to Flink—another emerging big data software stack by adding hooks to adjust the slot number of TaskManager. The framework is also suitable to other SMT platforms. What we need to do is choose appropriate performance events on different platforms and training new prediction models on those.

The framework is also suitable to other SMT platforms. The only things need to do is using other set of performance events according to the platforms used and training new prediction models.

5. EVALUATION

In this section, we first state our experiment environment (Section 5.1). And then we examine the effects of our diverse predictor implementations so as to find the efficient ones (Section 5.2). At last, we use the efficient predictors with different prediction schemes to auto-adjust SMT configurations for the Spark applications dynamically (Section 5.3).

5.1 Experiment Setup

5.1.1 Application Selection

In order to evaluate our Prediction-Based Dynamic SMT Threading (PBDST) framework, we choose 29 Spark based applications from BigDataBench [45] and Spark-perf [3], both of which provide the representative Spark based data analytics workloads with diverse algorithms. Table 1 presents the 29 workloads [2].

5.1.2 System Configuration

In order to run those Spark applications, we deploy a Spark cluster in the pseudo-distributed mode on a IBM POWER S822L (8247-22L) server with the POWER8 processors. The S822L server includes four sockets and each socket has six out-of-order cores with speculative pipelines. Each core supports up to 8-way multithreading. Table 2 lists important configurations of the server.

The operation system we use is Ubuntu 15.04 and the Linux kernel version is 3.19.0. The version of Spark software stack is 1.3.0. We use HDFS (Hadoop Distributed File System) provided by Hadoop version 1.2.1 to store the input and output data. The Java version in our system is 1.7.0 and we use the IBM J9 as the Java runtime environment implementation.

5.1.3 Prediction Model Building

We split the 29 workloads into two sets, which are shown in Table 1. We select 20 applications randomly as the training set, whose workload characteristics are used to train prediction models. And the remaining 9 applications form the testing set, which will be used to evaluate our PBDST approach. In order to obtain the prediction models, we run all 20 applications in the training set (Table 1) with different SMT configurations, from one thread per core to eight threads per core. For each workload, we collect the micro-architecture level statistics during the whole lifetime. Following the method illustrated in Section 3.1, we build 8 prediction models for each predictor.

5.2 Prediction Effect

In this subsection, we evaluate the effects of different predictors (machine learning algorithms) implemented in Section 4.2. We run each application in the testing set with

[2]Those workloads share Pagerank, K-means, Connected Component, PCA and TeraSort benchmarks with Spark-Bench [30].

Table 2: Details of POWER8 system configurations.

CPU Type	IBM POWER8
# Total Cores	24 @ 3.02 GHz
# Maximum threads per core	8
# Sockets	2
Architecture	ppc64le
Byte Order	Little Endian
Cache Line	128B
L1 Data Cache	64KB
L1 Instruction Cache	32KB
L2 Cache (unified)	512 KB per core
L3 Cache (unified)	8 MB per core
# Memory controllers	4
Memory	256 GB
Pagesize	64 K
Memory bandwidth	192 GB/s per socket
Disk	4 * 1 TB

different SMT configurations (from 1 thread per core to 8 threads per core), and collect the whole lifetime statistics and running time. With the 9 testing workload statistics, we use the prediction models built in Section 5.1.3 to predict the optimal or near-optimal SMT configuration for each of them.

Since there are SMT configurations that own running time very close to the optimal one for certain applications, here, we use the performance difference to indicate the prediction error, which is calculated by using Equation 1. The $Time_{predict}$ is the application execution time using the predicted SMT configuration, and the $Time_{optimal}$ is the minimum application execution time with the optimal SMT configuration.

$$Prediction\ Error = \frac{Time_{predicted} - Time_{optimal}}{Time_{optimal}} \quad (1)$$

Figure 5 shows the average prediction errors of different predictors implemented in this paper when we perform predictions with different SMT configurations. The X-axis gives the predictor names represented by the machine learning algorithm names. The Y-axis shows the average prediction errors of the nine testing applications. The subgraphs from (a) to (h) indicate the SMT configurations we used when we collect micro-architecture level statistics and perform predictions.

We can find that different predictors have different effects. The prediction errors are varied among different SMT configurations. For the decision tree (DT) predictor that is proposed [50] and [35], the effects are not stable among different SMT configurations. For some SMT configurations, it can achieve very low prediction errors, for instance, 2%when prediction is performed at five threads per core. While for some other SMT configurations, the decision tree owns high prediction errors, for instance, a 17.5% prediction error is observed with 7 threads per core. The linear regression (LiR) model that is used in [9] and [10], seems to be the worst predictor among all machine learning algorithms. It achieves pretty high prediction errors for most of the SMT configurations. Among all machine learning algorithms, the logistic regression (LogR) and the K-nearest neighbor (KNN) are more stable and achieve better performance than the other

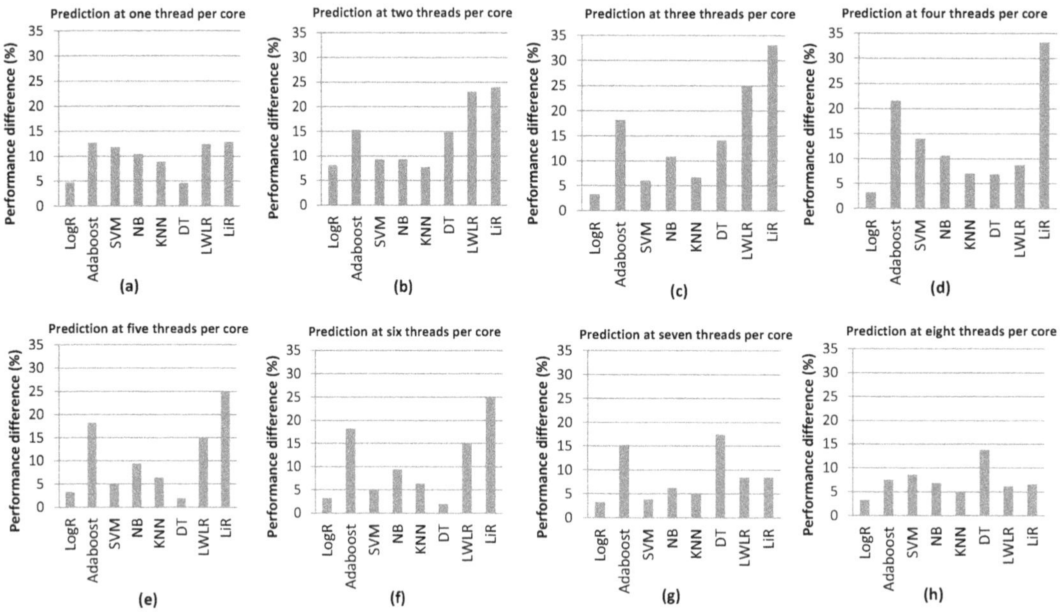

Figure 5: The average static prediction errors of different predictors with diverse SMT configurations.

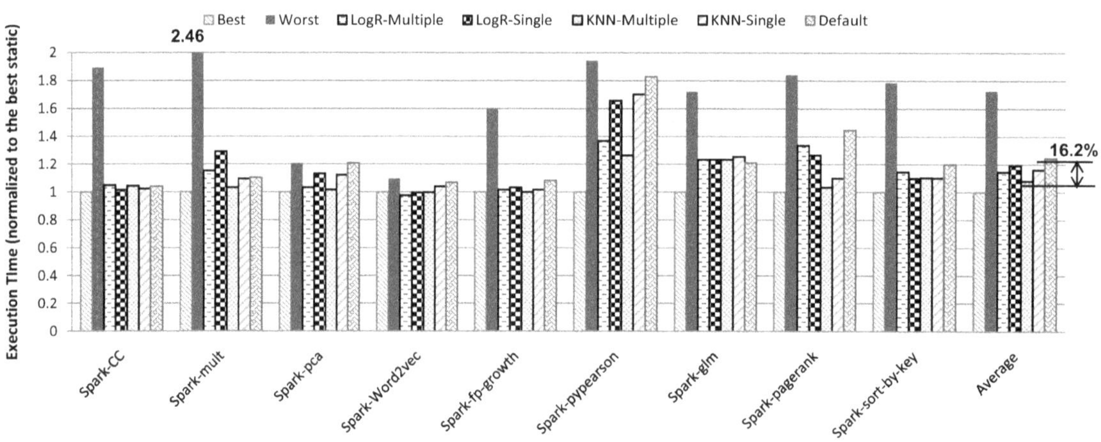

Figure 6: Effects of using different machine learning algorithms when perform automatic predictions.

machine learning algorithms. The prediction errors of both of them are always below 10% for all SMT configurations, 4.1% and 6.8% on the average.

The algorithms (i.e., decision tree and linear regression), which are much efficient in the previous work, do not perform well in our cases because of different application domains and architectures. As mentioned in Section 3, the prediction model is relevant to the architecture. We target a state-of-the-art processor (i.e., POWER8) whose architecture and performance model are totally different from the processors used in the previous work. More important, the POWER8 processor supports up to 8-way multithreading. The interaction between threads and hardware and inter-thread interference are more complicated in SMT8 processors than in SMT2 or SMT4 processors. And we investigate the emerging big data analytics applications, which own distinct micro-architectural characteristics that place them in a different class from traditional scientific calculation applications [24, 14]. The distinguished application domain and architecture directly affect the decisions. For instance, the work in [10] always prefers to disable the SMT technology for the OpenMP applications running on Intel Xeon MP processors. However, our work shows that SMT8 can achieve a significant performance improvement for the Spark applications as presented in Figure 1. From a perspective of machine learning algorithm, we further explain why some predictors, including the predictors used in previous work, do not achieve good performance as below:

From the perspective of machine learning algorithm, we can explain why some predictors, including the predictors used in previous work, do not achieve good performance as below:

1. The distribution of prediction errors is more like Bernoulli distribution than Gaussian distribution, so logistic regression (LogR) is more efficient than linear regression (LiR) and locally weighted linear regression (LWLR) [18].

2. Some SMT configurations own very close execution time for certain Spark workloads. So for the decision tree (DT) predictor, some models confront an over-fitting problem [37], which affects the prediction accuracy and makes it unstable among SMT configurations.
3. For the diverse behaviors of the Spark applications, some monitored micro-architectural statistics of corresponding applications may deviate significantly from other applications. So some deviation-sensitive algorithms like adaptive boosting (Adaboost) do not achieve high prediction accuracy [17].

5.3 Automatic Prediction

For the logistic regression (LogR) and the K-nearest neighbor (KNN) own lower prediction errors than other machine learning algorithms as evaluated in Section 5.2, we apply both of them to our automatic dynamic predictions. Figure 6 shows the normalized execution time of the best (fastest) static configuration, the worst (slowest) static configuration, the default SMT configuration (i.e., SMT8) and our PBDST-enabled ones for each Spark application in the testing set. In this figure, all the execution time is normalized by the per-application best static case. The best static case means that a Spark application executes with the single SMT configuration for whole lifetime, which achieves the shortest running time. And the best static case can be derived only post facto after exhaustive tests. In our PBDST implementation, we also consider different prediction schemes, just as we discussed in Section 4.3.3: performing prediction only once and applying the single optimal SMT configuration of the first stage to upcoming stages of an application; or performing multiple predictions and using the locally optimal SMT configuration for each stage. So in the figure, the performance of different prediction schemes is also shown.

We can find that no matter with single prediction scheme or multiple prediction scheme, the PBDST-enabled applications always consume much less time than the worst configurations. The PBDST-enabled applications also outperform the default configuration (i.e., SMT8) in most cases. For the multiple prediction scheme, the execution time of many PBDST-enabled applications is very close to the best static configurations. When comparing the effects of logistic regression (LogR) predictor with that of the K-nearest neighbor (KNN) predictor, we can find that the KNN algorithm performs better than LogR algorithm in most cases, which indicates the K-nearest neighbor is more suitable to perform the automatic dynamic predictions.

When we investigate the performance of different prediction schemes, we can find that the multiple prediction scheme owns less execution time than the single one nearly for all situations, which indicates that Spark applications have varies behaviors across stages and the multiple prediction scheme is preferred. For Spark-CC and Spark-fpgrowth, both prediction schemes have similar execution time. This is because that for those two applications, the predicted optimal SMT configurations do not change among stages. For Spark-CC, the performance of the default configuration is very close to that of the best static configuration, which indicates that the default configuration (i.e., SMT8) is the near-optimal one.

From the figure we can conclude that the PBDST framework can achieve an automatic dynamic SMT configuration tuning with comparable performance. The bars in the rightmost of Figure 6 show the average normalized execution time of the nine applications. When compared with the default SMT configuration (i.e., SMT8), our PBDST framework can achieve average performance improvements ranging from 5.2% to 16.2% for different predictors with different prediction schemes. Specifically, for the KNN predictor with multiple prediction scheme, it can achieve performance better than default configuration nearly for all Spark applications and owns an average performance improvement of 16.2% over the default one. Spark-pypearson achieves 56.3% performance gain in comparison with the default SMT configuration. At the same time, for most of Spark applications the KNN predictor with multiple prediction scheme obtains performance very close to the best static cases (Figure 6), which can be acquired only post facto after exhaustive experimentation. KNN algorithm is reasonable to acquire good performance. From the perspective of algorithm, KNN can always perform pretty well in most situations at the cost of high space complexity [18]. However, when compared with the data scale that big data analytics process, the impact of the space complexity of KNN is relatively small.

There are several factors that may affect the PBDST framework's efficiency and decrease the performance improvements in our experiments. We explain as follows:

1. Prediction accuracy. It is unpractical to construct a predictor that has 100% prediction accuracy. For a multiple-stages application, if a wrong prediction is performed in one stage, it will offset the performance improvements brought in in other stages through much more accurate accurate predictions.
2. Sampling period delay. Our PBDST framework has a sampling period, which characterizes the first round of tasks and then gives the optimal SMT configuration for the rest of the stage. So there is a delay between a stage running and applying the optimal SMT configuration. When a new stage is submitted to execute, the Spark software stack will use the previous stage's optimal SMT configuration. If the previous stage's optimal SMT configuration is the worst one for the current stage unfortunately, the performance will be greatly reduced, since there is a huge performance gap between the best SMT configuration and the worst one (up to 2.46 times in Figure 6). In addition, if there is limited number of tasks in a stage, the sampling period (the first round of tasks) will finish most of tasks. For this case, it will not have lots of performance improvements even the optimal SMT configuration is predicted correctly.
3. Hardware penalty. When we change the SMT configuration, the processor may perform thread switching and rebalancing, which will consume additional time.
4. Prediction penalty. The PBDST framework will collect micro-architectural statistics and perform predictions for each stage of the Spark applications. The collection and prediction will introduce some penalties since the extra prediction code is executed.

Here we would like to roughly analyze the performance impacts of those 4 factors. In this analysis, we take KNN as an example. KNN achieves the best performance in an automatic prediction (i.e., 16.2% performance improvements). Meanwhile, it also owns an average prediction error [3] of

[3]The metric is defined by Equation 1, which measures the performance difference between the optimal SMT configuration and the predicted one.

6.8%. In an ideal situation, if we can increase the prediction accuracy, we can have up to 8.5% ($\frac{1+16.2\%}{1-6.8\%}$) more performance improvement. For most of our Spark workloads, each stage has 2 to 5 rounds of tasks, so the sampling period takes up 20% to 50% of the total runtime. So if we can reduce the sampling time, we may achieve up to 6.2% ($\frac{1+16.2\%-50\%}{50\%} \times 1-(1+16.2\%)$) extra performance improvement. The last two factors (i.e., hardware penalty and prediction penalty) have trivial impacts with respect to the first two factors. Thread-switching and rebalancing are performed by processors automatically and are transparent to applications. Accessing hardware performance counters also has little overhead since most of the mechanisms are implemented at the hardware level. The prediction process will be finished in several hundreds of hundreds microseconds.

6. RELATED WORK

Simultaneous Multithreading (SMT) has long been researched and remains an active research topic for it has a great potential to increase performance of the whole system. Using workload characteristics to direct program and system optimization has become a frequently-used method for architecture research communities. To the best of our knowledge, our work is the first to use workload characteristics to guide automatic dynamic SMT configuration tuning for big data analytics by means of machine learning technologies.

Substantial previous research has been performed on symbiotic SMT job scheduling on SMT systems. Moseley et al. [35] and Snavely et al. [42] present methods to predict IPC values and use the IPC to derive decisions for co-scheduling. Settle et al. [39] build a job scheduler with customized hardware performance counters to create a fine-grained view of micro-architect level profiles. De Vusyt et al. [12] use a sampling phase to evaluate the performance interference due to co-locations. Eyerman et al. [13] adopt a probabilistic model to co-schedule applications without sampling. Zhang et al. [49] present a methodology that enables precise performance interference prediction on SMT processors. All those studies are designed to find high performing co-schedules from running applications. They do not try to optimize the thread counts in each SMT core for multi-task big data analytics applications.

Several researchers have investigated the concurrency throttling or loop scheduling for parallel applications. Zhang et al. [48, 50] propose several OpenMP loop schedulers based on empirical search and decision tree to select the number of threads and scheduling policy. Jung and Lee et al. [26, 27] use a feedback based compiler preprocessor to determine the optimal number of threads for each parallel loop in OpenMP applications. They build an execution time estimation model to direct the tuning. Curtis-Maury et al. [9, 10] illustrate an execution method using instantaneous prediction to find the optimum thread count for OpenMP applications. They perform linear regression to construct the prediction model. Heirman et al. [20] propose ClusteR-aware Undersubscribed Scheduling of Threads (CRUST) mechanism, which dynamically reduce the number of application threads so as to match application's working size and off-chip bandwidth. The CRUST is also implemented in the OpenMP runtime. They also extend CRUST to incorporate the effects of simultaneous multithreading and evaluate it on Intel Xeon Phi [19]. Creech et al. [8] present the Scheduling and Allocation with Feedback (SCAF) system, which makes thread allocation decisions based on observed efficiency for OpenMP applications. Li et al. [28] present runtime search algorithms to find locally optimal power-efficient processor count and DVFS level. Curtis-Maury et al. [11] perform a synergistic tuning of DVFS and core count by using a model build with linear regression. Vega et al. [44] propose a coordinated power management algorithm to actuate DVFS and core-folding so as to achieve power-performance efficiencies. Even though those work shares similar objectives, our work differs from them in several key aspects. First, different application domains. All of those research aims at optimizing performance or power-efficiency for traditional parallel applications, most of which are OpenMP applications. Our work towards the emerging big data analytics workloads, which are more complicated and own different characteristics from those traditional applications. The mechanisms implemented in the OpenMP runtime are difficult to be used in big data analytics software stacks. Second, different processor architectures. Our approach is implemented on a state-of-the-art processor, which supports 8 SMT threads. Most of the previous work performs on two SMT threads processors, and only work in [19] is evaluated on four SMT threads co-processors. The interaction between threads and hardware and inter-thread interference are more complicated in SMT8 processors than in SMT2 or SMT4 ones, which increase the difficulty of performing such a prediction. Third, different solutions. Just as we illustrated and analyzed in Section 5.2, the solutions (decision tree and linear regression) used by previous work are not very efficient in our scenario both because of different application domains and processor architectures. And the search method has the overhead of multiple times profiling, which is reduced via prediction in our work. Moreover, some studies [9, 10, 6] are energy-efficiency oriented, ours is toward performance only at present. Our approach may increase the energy-efficiency for we reduce the execution time, which is proportional to energy consumption in some degree. However we do not perform measurements due to lacking of the corresponding device (i.e., power meter).

There are also some studies try to understand the workload behaviors on SMT processors. Huang et al. [22] and Mathis et al. [33] examine the characterizations of traditional applications running on Intel Hyper-Threading supported processor and IBM SMT supported POWER5 processor, respectively. Ruan et al. [38] perform macroscopic analysis as well as micro-architectural measurements to understand the origins of the performance bottlenecks for SMT processors on network servers. Those work gives implications but does not attempt optimizations. Funston et al. [16] describe an SMT-selection metric that predicts the change in application performance with different SMT levels. However, the metric is not applicable for our POWER8 processor for two reasons. The first one is that the metric is calculated based on an assumption that the instruction mix can reflect how instructions fill the available function units. While, for the POWER8 processor, a single function unit can execute multiple kinds of instructions. For instance, the load-store execution unit also has the capability of executing fixed-point operations apart from load and store instructions [40]. The second one is that it will be less accurate with the increase of core count and thread number as author mentioned. So for our POWER8 system (24 cores and up to 192 threads), it will incur lots of mis-predictions.

Machine learning algorithms are used by some researchers to optimize their systems from different perspectives, dynamically or statically. Lo et al. [32] use machine-learning technique to manage Turbo Mode dynamically. Liao et al. [31] and Li et al. [29] propose machine learning-based static and dynamic prefetch optimizations respectively. The SMT technology is different from those technologies that are transparent to upper-level applications. For SMT, in order to take the advantages of the dynamic thread count adjusting, the applications should increase or decrease the number of threads accordingly. Our approach presents a framework to manage SMT configurations dynamically and integrate it into Spark software stack, which makes it transparent to Spark user applications.

7. CONCLUSION

Selecting the best thread count for SMT cores is an important optimization problem for big data analytics applications. In response we design and implement an automatic online SMT configuration tuning framework in which profiles from hardware performance counters are collected and analyzed dynamically, so as to predict the optimal or near-optimal SMT configurations. Our evaluations on a POWER8 system show that with the PBDST framework the Spark applications can achieve up to 56.3% performance improvements and an average performance improvement of 16.2% over the default SMT configuration—the maximum SMT configuration—SMT8. And for most of Spark applications, the PBDST framework can obtain performance very close to the best static case, which can be derived only post facto after exhaustive tests.

8. ACKNOWLEDGMENTS

We are very grateful to anonymous reviewers and our shepherd, Dr. Miquel Moreto.

9. REFERENCES

[1] Apache Flink. https://flink.apache.org/index.html.

[2] Performance counters for linux. https://perf.wiki.kernel.org/index.php.

[3] Spark Performance Tests. In *Webpage: https://github.com/databricks/spark-perf*.

[4] D. W. Aha, D. Kibler, and M. K. Albert. Instance-based learning algorithms. *Machine learning*, 6(1):37–66, 1991.

[5] BAE Detica. The big data refinery: Distilling intelligence from big data. White Paper, https://www.baesystemsdetica.com/uploads/resources/Big_Data_Refinery_Whitepaper_single_pages_19.06.12.pdf, July 2012.

[6] R. Bertran, M. Gonzalez, X. Martorell, N. Navarro, and E. Ayguade. Decomposable and responsive power models for multicore processors using performance counters. In *Proceedings of the 24th ACM International Conference on Supercomputing*, pages 147–158. ACM, 2010.

[7] L. Breiman, J. Friedman, C. J. Stone, and R. A. Olshen. *Classification and regression trees*. CRC press, 1984.

[8] T. Creech, A. Kotha, and R. Barua. Efficient multiprogramming for multicores with scaf. In *Proceedings of the 46th Annual IEEE/ACM International Symposium on Microarchitecture*, pages 334–345. ACM, 2013.

[9] M. Curtis-Maury, F. Blagojevic, C. D. Antonopoulos, and D. S. Nikolopoulos. Prediction-based power-performance adaptation of multithreaded scientific codes. *IPDPS*, 19(10):1396–1410, 2008.

[10] M. Curtis-Maury, J. Dzierwa, C. D. Antonopoulos, and D. S. Nikolopoulos. Online power-performance adaptation of multithreaded programs using hardware event-based prediction. In *Proceedings of the 20th annual international conference on Supercomputing*, pages 157–166. ACM, 2006.

[11] M. Curtis-Maury, A. Shah, F. Blagojevic, et al. Prediction models for multi-dimensional power-performance optimization on many cores. In *Proceedings of the 17th international conference on Parallel architectures and compilation techniques*, pages 250–259. ACM, 2008.

[12] M. De Vuyst, R. Kumar, and D. M. Tullsen. Exploiting unbalanced thread scheduling for energy and performance on a cmp of smt processors. In *20th International Parallel and Distributed Processing Symposium*, pages 10–pp. IEEE, 2006.

[13] S. Eyerman and L. Eeckhout. Probabilistic job symbiosis modeling for smt processor scheduling. *ACM Sigplan Notices*, 45(3):91–102, 2010.

[14] M. Ferdman, A. Adileh, O. Kocberber, et al. Clearing the clouds. In *Architectural Support for Programming Languages and Operating Systems (ASPLOS)*, 2012.

[15] Y. Freund, R. Schapire, and N. Abe. A short introduction to boosting. *Journal-Japanese Society For Artificial Intelligence*, 14(771-780):1612, 1999.

[16] J. R. Funston, K. El Maghraoui, J. Jann, et al. An smt-selection metric to improve multithreaded applications' performance. In *Parallel & Distributed Processing Symposium (IPDPS), 2012 IEEE 26th International*, pages 1388–1399. IEEE, 2012.

[17] P. Harrington. *Machine learning in action*. Manning, 2012.

[18] T. Hastie, R. Tibshirani, J. Friedman, and J. Franklin. The elements of statistical learning: data mining, inference and prediction. *The Mathematical Intelligencer*, 27(2):83–85, 2005.

[19] W. Heirman, T. E. Carlson, K. Van Craeynest, et al. Automatic smt threading for openmp applications on the intel xeon phi co-processor. In *Proceedings of the 4th International Workshop on Runtime and Operating Systems for Supercomputers*. ACM, 2014.

[20] W. Heirman, T. E. Carlson, K. Van Craeynest, et al. Undersubscribed threading on clustered cache architectures. In *IEEE 20th International Symposium on High Performance Computer Architecture*, pages 678–689. IEEE, 2014.

[21] C.-W. Hsu and C.-J. Lin. A comparison of methods for multiclass support vector machines. *Neural Networks, IEEE Transactions on*, 13(2):415–425, 2002.

[22] W. Huang, J. Lin, Z. Zhang, and J. M. Chang. Performance characterization of java applications on smt processors. In *IEEE International Symposium on Performance Analysis of Systems and Software*, pages 102–111. IEEE, 2005.

[23] IDC. The digital universe in 2020: A universe of opportunities and challenges. http://www.emc.com/leadership/digital-universe/iview/executive-summary-a-universe-of.htm, 2012.

[24] Z. Jia, L. Wang, J. Zhan, L. Zhang, and C. Luo. Characterizing data analysis workloads in data centers. In *IEEE International Symposium on Workload Characterization*, pages 66–76. IEEE, 2013.

[25] G. H. John and P. Langley. Estimating continuous distributions in bayesian classifiers. In *Proceedings of the Eleventh conference on Uncertainty in artificial intelligence*, pages 338–345. Morgan Kaufmann Publishers Inc., 1995.

[26] C. Jung, D. Lim, J. Lee, and S. Han. Adaptive execution techniques for smt multiprocessor architectures. In *Proceedings of the tenth ACM SIGPLAN symposium on Principles and practice of parallel programming*, pages 236–246. ACM, 2005.

[27] J. Lee, J.-H. Park, H. Kim, C. Jung, D. Lim, and S. Han. Adaptive execution techniques of parallel programs for multiprocessors. *Journal of Parallel and Distributed Computing*, 70(5):467–480, 2010.

[28] J. Li and J. F. Martinez. Dynamic power-performance adaptation of parallel computation on chip multiprocessors. In *The Twelfth International Symposium on High-Performance Computer Architecture*, pages 77–87. IEEE, 2006.

[29] M. Li, G. Chen, Q. Wang, et al. Pater: A hardware prefetching automatic tuner on ibm power8 processor. *IEEE Computer Architecture Letters.*

[30] M. Li, J. Tan, Y. Wang, et al. Sparkbench: a comprehensive benchmarking suite for in memory data analytic platform spark. In *Proceedings of the 12th ACM International Conference on Computing Frontiers*, page 53. ACM, 2015.

[31] S.-w. Liao, T.-H. Hung, D. Nguyen, et al. Machine learning-based prefetch optimization for data center applications. In *Proceedings of the Conference on High Performance Computing Networking, Storage and Analysis*, page 56. ACM, 2009.

[32] D. Lo and C. Kozyrakis. Dynamic management of turbomode in modern multi-core chips. In *High Performance Computer Architecture (HPCA), 2014 IEEE 20th International Symposium on*, pages 603–613. IEEE, 2014.

[33] H. M. Mathis, A. E. Mericas, J. D. McCalpin, et al. Characterization of simultaneous multithreading (smt) efficiency in power5. *IBM Journal of Research and Development*, 49(4.5):555–564, 2005.

[34] D. C. Montgomery, E. A. Peck, and G. G. Vining. *Introduction to linear regression analysis*, volume 821. John Wiley & Sons, 2012.

[35] T. Moseley, J. L. Kihm, D. A. Connors, and D. Grunwald. Methods for modeling resource contention on simultaneous multithreading processors. In *2005 International Conference on Computer Design*, pages 373–380. IEEE.

[36] J. C. Platt. Using analytic qp and sparseness to speed training of support vector machines. *Advances in neural information processing systems*, pages 557–563, 1999.

[37] J. R. Quinlan. Induction of decision trees. *Machine learning*, 1(1):81–106, 1986.

[38] Y. Ruan, V. S. Pai, E. Nahum, and J. M. Tracey. Evaluating the impact of simultaneous multithreading on network servers using real hardware. In *ACM SIGMETRICS Performance Evaluation Review*, volume 33, pages 315–326. ACM, 2005.

[39] A. Settle, J. Kihm, A. Janiszewski, and D. Connors. Architectural support for enhanced smt job scheduling. In *Proceedings of the 13th International Conference on Parallel Architectures and Compilation Techniques*, pages 63–73. IEEE Computer Society, 2004.

[40] B. Sinharoy, J. A. V. Norstrand, R. J. Eickemeyer, et al. Ibm power8 processor core microarchitecture. *IBM Journal of Research and Development*, 59(1):2:1–2:21, Jan 2015.

[41] B. Sinharoy, R. Swanberg, N. Nayar, et al. Advanced features in ibm power8 systems. *IBM Journal of Research and Development*, 59(1):1:1–1:18, Jan 2015.

[42] A. Snavely and D. M. Tullsen. Symbiotic job scheduling for a simultaneous mutlithreading processor. In *International Conference on Architecture Support for Programming Languages and Operating Systems.*, pages 234–244. ACM, 2000.

[43] D. M. Tullsen, S. J. Eggers, J. S. Emer, et al. Exploiting choice: Instruction fetch and issue on an implementable simultaneous multithreading processor. In *ACM SIGARCH Computer Architecture News*, volume 24, pages 191–202. ACM, 1996.

[44] A. Vega, A. Buyuktosunoglu, H. Hanson, P. Bose, and S. Ramani. Crank it up or dial it down: coordinated multiprocessor frequency and folding control. In *Proceedings of the 46th Annual IEEE/ACM International Symposium on Microarchitecture*, pages 210–221. ACM, 2013.

[45] L. Wang, J. Zhan, C. Luo, et al. Bigdatabench: a big data benchmark suite from internet services. In *20th International Symposium on High Performance Computer Architecture*, pages 488–499. IEEE, 2014.

[46] T. White. *Hadoop: The Definitive Guide.* O'Reilly Media, 2009.

[47] M. Zaharia, M. Chowdhury, et al. Resilient distributed datasets: A fault-tolerant abstraction for in-memory cluster computing. In *USENIX Conference on Networked Systems Design and Implementation*, 2012.

[48] Y. Zhang, M. Burcea, V. Cheng, et al. An adaptive openmp loop scheduler for hyperthreaded smps. In *International Conference on Parallel and Distributed Systems*, pages 256–263, 2004.

[49] Y. Zhang, M. A. Laurenzano, J. Mars, and L. Tang. Smite: Precise qos prediction on real-system smt processors to improve utilization in warehouse scale computers. In *the 47th Annual IEEE/ACM International Symposium on Microarchitecture*, pages 406–418, 2014.

[50] Y. Zhang, M. Voss, and E. Rogers. Runtime empirical selection of loop schedulers on hyperthreaded smps. In *19th IEEE International Parallel and Distributed Processing Symposium*, pages 44b–44b, 2005.

APPENDIX

A. ARTIFACT DESCRIPTION

A.1 Abstract

The artifact contains our Prediction-Based Dynamic SMT Threading (PBDST) framework as well as the prediction models trained for POWER8 platforms. It can support the runtime results in Figure 6 of our PACT'2016 paper ***Auto-tuning Spark Big DataWorkloads on POWER8: Prediction-Based Dynamic SMT Threading****. To validate the results, deploy the framework and check the benchmark runtime.*

A.2 Description

A.2.1 Check-list (artifact meta information)

- **Program: BigDataBench and Spark-perf**
- **Compilation: sbt 2.10; python 2.7+; Java 1.7**
- **Data set: generated by corresponding benchmark suite**
- **Run-time environment: Ubuntu 15.04 with Linux Perf and numactl tool**
- **Hardware: IBM POWER8 Little Endian processors**
- **Run-time state: SMT8 mode**
- **Execution: root user or users that can execute sudo without password**
- **Output: runtime**
- **Experiment workflow: Deploy the PBDST framework and corresponding software stacks; run benchmarks; record the runtime; compare the benchmark runtime**
- **Publicly available?: Yes**

A.2.2 How delivered

We have uploaded our PBDST framework code and corresponding documents on Github:

https://github.com/jiazhentim/PACT2016.

The benchmark suites we use in the paper are also open source projects, which can be found by following links:

BigDataBench home page:

http://prof.ict.ac.cn/BigDat-aBench.

We upload the BigDataBench user manual and the benchmarks to our Github repository.

Spark-perf home page:

https://github.com/databricks/spark-perf.

A.2.3 Hardware dependencies

The PBDST framework can be applied to other SMT processors, however it only supports IBM POWER8 currently. So IBM POWER8 processors are required.

A.2.4 Software dependencies

Java version 1.7; Hadoop version 1.2.1; Spark version 1.3.0. Python 2.7+ and the corresponding packages, i.e., numpy, match, pickle, operator, sys and os.

A.2.5 Datasets

All datasets can be generated by corresponding benchmark suites. Users can find the data generation method in the user menu or can run the workloads directly. The generation parameter used in our paper for the Spark-ConnectedComponent is 25. The generation parameter used in our paper for the Spark-PageRank is 27.

A.3 Installation

The PBDST framework is released as a patch. Users need to apply the patch to the Spark software stack and put the files we provide in corresponding directories. More details can be found on our Github repository (mentioned in Section A.2.2). Following the deploying instruction (Deployment.txt) users can deploy our PBDST framework correctly.

A.4 Experiment workflow

For the single prediction scheme can not outperform the multiple prediction one, we only provide the multiple prediction scheme for users. We provide the commands of executing the 9 workloads used in Section 5.3 of our paper. After deploying those benchmarks and generating corresponding datasets according to our previous descriptions, users can adopt the commands in *command.txt* of our Github repository to drive the 9 workloads.

Before performing the experiments, users should make sure there is no other workload running and there is no other Spark or Hadoop daemon running. The "pkill java" command can kill all java processes including Hadoop and Spark daemons.

Before starting Spark, users should make sure that the Hadoop is started. We use HDFS (Hadoop distributed filesystem) to store the input datasets for some workloads.

A.4.1 Hadoop related commands

Under the home directory of Hadoop, users can start or stop Hadoop by using the following commands.

Start Hadoop:

#bin/start-all.sh

Stop Hadoop:

#bin/stop-all.sh to stop it.

If Hadoop is started, users will find the following daemons when executing jps:

#jps

JobTracker

TaskTracker

NameNode

DataNode

SecondaryNameNode

A.4.2 Spark related commands

Under the home directory of Spark, users can start or stop Spark by using the following commands.

Start Spark:

#sbin/start-all.sh

Stop Spark:

#sbin/stop-all.sh

A.5 Evaluation and expected result

To evaluate the performance of the PBDST framework, users need to run those workloads on POWER8 platform in default SMT mode (i.e., SMT8) with unmodified Spark software stack (i.e., without PBDST framework) and with PBDST based Spark. It is suggested to run each workloads several times and use the average runtime to perform comparison. The workloads running with PBDST framework are expected to consume less time than the counterparts that use unmodified Spark software stack. There should be similar phenomena like Figure 6 in our paper.

A.6 Experiment customization

Users can use different prediction algorithms to train the models and perform predictions.

The PBDST framework can also be used on other SMT platforms. If so, users need to change the PMU events and train different models.

Since the PBDST framework is user-application transparent, it can support any Spark based application.

A.7 Notes

We provide the prediction models, which are trained for our POWER8 system, for the artifact evaluation, since it may cost several weeks to reproduce our training procedure, which is too expensive for the artifact evaluation. However, it is suggested to train the models by users themselves. Since even though the same kind of processor is used, the details of software and hardware configurations may also be different, which will affect the accuracy of predictions.

EXCITE-VM: Extending the Virtual Memory System to Support Snapshot Isolation Transactions

Heiner Litz
Stanford University
353 Serra Mall
Stanford, CA, 94305
heiner.litz@stanford.edu

Benjamin Braun
Stanford University
353 Serra Mall
Stanford, CA, 94305
bbraun@stanford.edu

David Cheriton
Stanford University
353 Serra Mall
Stanford, CA, 94305
cheriton@cs.stanford.edu

ABSTRACT

Multi-core programming remains a major software development and maintenance challenge because of data races, deadlock, non-deterministic failures and complex performance issues. In this paper, we describe EXCITE-VM, a system that provides snapshot isolation transactions on shared memory to facilitate programming and to improve the performance of parallel applications. With snapshots, an application thread is not exposed to the committed changes of other threads until it receives the updates by explicitly creating a new snapshot. Snapshot isolation enables low overhead lockless read operations and improves fault tolerance by isolating each thread from the transient, uncommitted writes of other threads. This paper describes how EXCITE-VM implements snapshot isolation transactions efficiently by manipulating virtual memory mappings and using a novel copy-on-read mechanism with a customized page cache. Compared to conventional software transactional memory systems, EXCITE-VM provides up to 2.2x performance improvement for the STAMP benchmark suite and up to 1000x speedup for a modified benchmark having long running read-only transactions. Furthermore, EXCITE-VM achieves a 2x performance improvement on a Memcached benchmark and the Yahoo Cloud Server Benchmarks. Finally, EXCITE-VM improves fault tolerance and offers features such as low-overhead concurrent audit and analysis.

1 Introduction

Developing and maintaining a multi-threaded application is a challenge. Developers need to ensure that all shared mutable data items are protected by suitable synchronization, including library routines invoked by the application. This synchronization is hard to get right and when not, leads to difficult-to-diagnose problems such as data races, memory corruption and deadlock. Even when executing correctly, a multi-threaded application can have inscrutable performance, given the complex dynamic interaction between locks that can be occurring. For example, consider a graph application in which threads concurrently modify nodes while some threads analyze shared data to generate a summary. The analysis may have uncertain execution time and an uncertain effect on the rest of the application because of the conflicts between the read locks it needs to acquire and the write locks being requested and held by other threads.

In this paper, we present Elastic Snapshot-Isolation Transaction Extensions in Virtual Memory (EXCITE-VM), a system that enables snapshot isolation semantics to address the issues of multi-core programming. With our system, threads can operate on consistent snapshots of shared memory, enabling safe and protected access, avoiding data races and memory corruption. With snapshot isolation (SI) [6], shared memory does not appear to change for a given thread until it explicitly creates a new snapshot of shared memory. This enables consistent reads to shared memory in the presence of concurrent writes by other threads, reducing synchronization overheads. To continue with the graph example above, with SI, threads can checkout a consistent snapshot of the graph for analysis, while update threads can modify the graph concurrently without competing for locks or executing synchronization code. Snapshots provide further utility such as lock-less global stats generation, and concurrent garbage collection.

Besides improving parallel application development, EXCITE-VM improves fault tolerance by enabling application threads to terminate, for example due to a division by zero exception and subsequently restart without restarting the whole application because none of its writes are visible to other threads until committed. Finally, snapshots address the challenge of creating checkpoints of parallel application state while enabling concurrent writes to shared memory enabling fault tolerance and durability. A thread can simply checkout a snapshot and persist it to non-volatile storage without interfering with other application threads. EXCITE-VM, hence, allows applications to achieve persistence and durability similarly to what is provided by a traditional database without incurring the overheads and code modifications required by the latter.

Having motivated the utility of snapshots, the challenge is to achieve acceptable performance, given the overhead of creating a memory snapshot. To address this concern, EXCITE-VM introduces a novel technique for manipulating virtual memory mappings depending on the snapshot. We propose a new copy-on-read approach supported by an efficient page caching scheme to minimize the cost of generating snapshots. Combining these techniques, EXCITE-VM outperforms conventional STMs on the STAMP [31] benchmark

PACT '16, September 11 - 15, 2016, Haifa, Israel

ISBN 978-1-4503-4121-9/16/09...$15.00

DOI: http://dx.doi.org/10.1145/2967938.2967955

suite by up to 2.2x, and up to 1000x on modified benchmarks having long read-only transactions. Furthermore, EXCITE-VM provides up to 2x the performance of Libitm in Memcached and the Yahoo Cloud Server Benchmark.

2 Snapshot Generation

This section discusses existing software approaches to generate snapshots, their shortcomings and how EXCITE-VM improves over them.

2.1 Snapshots in Transactional Memory

SI-STM [40] is a Java based transactional memory system that maintains multiple versions of all shared data objects to reduce transaction abort rates. Whenever referencing an object, a separate data structure is queried which maintains the references to the individual versions. The implementation of SI-STM offers three disadvantages. First, each object dereference necessitates an additional level of indirection, second, conflict validation is performed on the granularity of objects which performs poorly for large objects and third, it requires the application developer to modify every object or class description that needs to be snapshottable.

We observe that to implement the required indirection layer, we can leverage the *virtual to physical address translation* mechanism. Utilizing hardware resources such as the translation lookaside buffer (TLB) and the page walk engine, threads obtain direct access to snapshots without incurring the overhead of an additional indirection layer. Accessing static objects incurs zero overhead while incorporating changes for multiple objects can be batched on a per 4KB page basis. EXCITE-VM also does not require programmers to modify their objects as snapshots are maintained transparently on a page based granularity.

2.2 VM Based Thread Synchronization

DThreads [28] and Conversion [29] are two systems that leverage virtual memory and per-thread page tables for synchronization purposes. The two approaches follow a computation model in which all threads start off with the same consistent state, then diverge into per-thread states by intercepting writes, i.e. Copy-on-Write (CoW), and finally form the next globally consistent state by merging all writes. DThreads and Conversion require additional synchronization logic such as locking, as both only support a last committer wins policy in which multiple writes to the same data item do not conflict but merely overwrite each other. Like Conversion, EXCITE-VM uses a threading model where each thread has its own virtual-to-physical address mapping representing a snapshot. However, EXCITE-VM differs from both DThreads and Conversion in multiple ways. First, EXCITE-VM logs committed changes, allowing threads to efficiently update their snapshots without synchronization overhead. Second, EXCITE-VM supports transactional semantics including an efficient conflict detection scheme and retry capability. Third, EXCITE-VM introduces a novel Copy-on-Read (CoR) mechanism that uses page caching to address the shortcomings of CoW and pure CoR.

Copy-on-Write (CoW) techniques as proposed in prior work [28, 29] have leveraged CoW for isolating threads by applying writes only to thread local memory, effectively hiding them from other threads. To implement this technique, pages are mapped read-only such that every write leads to a trap into the page fault handler which can then map a thread local page, copying the original state of the read only page. Under CoW, reads are served directly from the snapshot with no added overhead.

To enable snapshots via CoW, each thread must update its entire per-thread page table to the committed state at the start of each transaction. Unfortunately, this incurs the cost of invalidating TLB entries to keep the page table consistent. Furthermore, the thread must modify its page table for each modified page, even if it does not access that page in the subsequent transaction. These factors, on top of the page fault cost for writes, make CoW perform poorly, especially for short transactions.

Copy-on-Read (CoR) avoids the high upfront costs of CoW for creating snapshots. In CoR, instead of synchronizing page tables during the start of a transaction, snapshots are generated on the fly whenever a page is read or written. In either case, a page fault occurs and the handler maps in a thread local page which can be read or written to. Though CoR avoids unnecessarily updating pages that are not accessed, it has its costs. First, the first read or write to a page in each transaction will incur an expensive page fault. Second, during commit, all pages that have been accessed within the prior transaction need to be removed from the page table and the corresponding TLB entries invalidated.

While it seems promising to leverage address translation as the indirection layer for implementing snapshots, both CoW and CoR techniques introduce high overheads. EXCITE-VM implements CoR, but avoids its overheads using a page cache that holds onto mapped-in pages over the duration of multiple transactions.

3 EXCITE-VM Architecture

EXCITE-VM leverages the virtual-to-physical address translation mechanism of contemporary processors to enable efficient snapshotting of shared memory state in parallel applications. In order to allow multiple threads to access snapshots at different points in time, each thread in EXCITE-VM has its own page table, and hence, its own virtual-to-physical address mapping. Whenever a thread starts a transaction it acquires a snapshot of the current state of shared memory, generated on the fly via CoR. As a result, in EXCITE-VM, the existence of a set of pages representing the most recent consistent state of shared memory is not required. Instead, every thread maintains only a subset of the shared memory state (the pages it has faulted in) corresponding to a particular version or snapshot. To re-generate a snapshot for a particular page when processing a CoR fault, EXCITE-VM maintains a *global write log*. The global write log represents the central data structure of EXCITE-VM as it contains the history of all writes ever performed on shared memory, similarly as in a log-structured file system [41]. By scanning the log and applying the appropriate writes, any version of any page that existed in shared memory in the past can be re-generated. Once a page is re-generated, it is stored in thread local memory and mapped into the thread's address space so that the subsequent reads and writes to that page incur no overhead. Unfortunately, the cost of re-generating a page for a particular snapshot scales with the length of the log and an unbounded log will eventually consume too much main memory capacity. EXCITE-VM addresses this issue with checkpoints.

3.1 Checkpoints

A checkpoint represents the state of shared memory at a particular point in time EXCITE-VM uses designated checkpointing threads to create checkpoints lazily by periodically applying the write log to the prior checkpoint. After a log entry has been incorporated into the new checkpoint, and after all active threads' snapshots are more recent, the log entry can be either deleted or moved to high capacity, non-volatile storage enabling queries of historical main memory state. Checkpoints bound the cost of re-generating a snapshot to the number of log entries that exist between the last checkpoint and the snapshot to be re-generated. Even with checkpointing, frequent page faulting represents a prohibitive overhead. EXCITE-VM addresses this issue with the *page cache*.

3.2 Page Cache

The page cache is a software cache that buffers memory pages over the duration of multiple transactions. Instead of clearing the faulted-in pages after each transaction, pages remain in the cache so they are available for the next transaction without incurring another page fault. To incorporate the writes of remote threads, the page cache needs to be updated whenever a thread takes a new snapshot by traversing the global log entries that have been committed between the last snapshot of the thread and the current state of memory. While this represents a cost, it is significantly lower as the overhead incurred by the CoW approach which needs to update the entire shared memory state. Furthermore, keeping pages in the cache avoids resetting the access and protection bits of the page table entry reducing TLB flushes. The use of the page cache reduces the number of page faults significantly compared to pure CoR, particularly for applications with high spatial locality in terms of the shared memory pages they frequently access. Sizing the page cache correctly and applying a good replacement policy is important for achieving high performance. A too large page cache that mostly contains unused pages increases update costs and consumes memory, while a too small page cache triggers too many page fault. We study the effect of different cache sizes in Section 6.2.2.

3.3 Transactional Memory Extensions

While providing an efficient snapshotting capability is useful on its own as outlined in Section 1, EXCITE-VM supports snapshot isolation transactional memory (SI-TM) semantics to make snapshots readily accessible by programmers. Snapshots enable to buffer writes without making them visible to other threads providing efficient isolation between threads. As a consequence, the only mechanisms required to support SI-TM are a conflict detection scheme and the ability to rollback transactional state. In SI-TM, reads are always consistent even in the presence of writes and, as a result, SI transactions are only required to abort on write-write conflicts. To guarantee forward progress and to enable batching of the validation overhead into a single operation, EXCITE-VM implements lazy conflict detection. Transactional writes are buffered in a tentative log entry that is only committed to the global log after successful validation. While most other STMs introduce significant overheads to track transactional reads and writes including atomic operations and memory barriers, EXCITE-VM imposes no cost for reads and introduces minimal instrumentation overheads for writes. Validation itself is performed by comparing a transaction's writeset against the log entries that have been committed concurrently by other threads. In case of a conflict, the transaction is aborted by undoing all local writes, dropping the write log entry and by re-executing the transaction.

3.4 Example Transaction Sequence

Figure 1 shows the steps in an EXCITE-VM transaction. The shared global log is shown on the left, whereas per-thread structures, including the timestamp of the current snapshot, the write log of the current transaction, the page cache and its referenced physical pages, and the per-thread page table, are shown on the right. The log contains an entry for each write which indicates the address of the write as well as the delta between the previous and the written value. A page table entry contains the physical address a virtual address is mapped to and whether said page is present or write enabled.

3.4.1 Transaction Begin:

Figure 1a shows how the active thread creates a snapshot at ts=7 by reading the global timestamp counter. As the page cache is outdated (at ts=5) it is updated by applying the writes of log 6 and log 7. The write to address v8 committed at ts=7 hits the page cache and is hence applied to the corresponding cached page.

3.4.2 Transactional Writes:

Figure 1b shows the active thread performing a transactional write to shared memory at address v2. As the page containing v2 is unmapped, a page fault is triggered which allocates a new physical page, then walks the page table to install the new mapping and subsequently inserts the entry into the page cache. The newly created page is now initialized with the content of the checkpoint page (CoR) which is currently at version 3. This page copy is performed using a lockless procedure described further in Section 4.3. The thread then traverses the global log to determine writes (v2 is contained in log 4, 5 and 6) and applies them to the new page. Furthermore, the write is inserted into the write log of the current transaction. Following this, the thread performs a write operation to address v8 that hits the page cache. Handling this write does not require any action besides inserting it into the write log. Note that write logging is performed via the transactional instrumentation logic and not via the page fault mechanism.

3.4.3 Commit:

Figure 1c presents the commit processing of a transaction including validation of the write set against other committed writes. In the example, a remote thread has committed the write log entry (ts=8). As a result, the local thread needs to validate its writes against log 8. As the writesets do not overlap, validation is successful. The transaction obtains a commit timestamp (ts=9) and appends its write log entry to the shared global log. Lastly, infrequently used page cache entries are evicted by clearing the entry from the page cache, unmapping the page in the page table, flushing the hardware TLB and freeing the physical memory page.

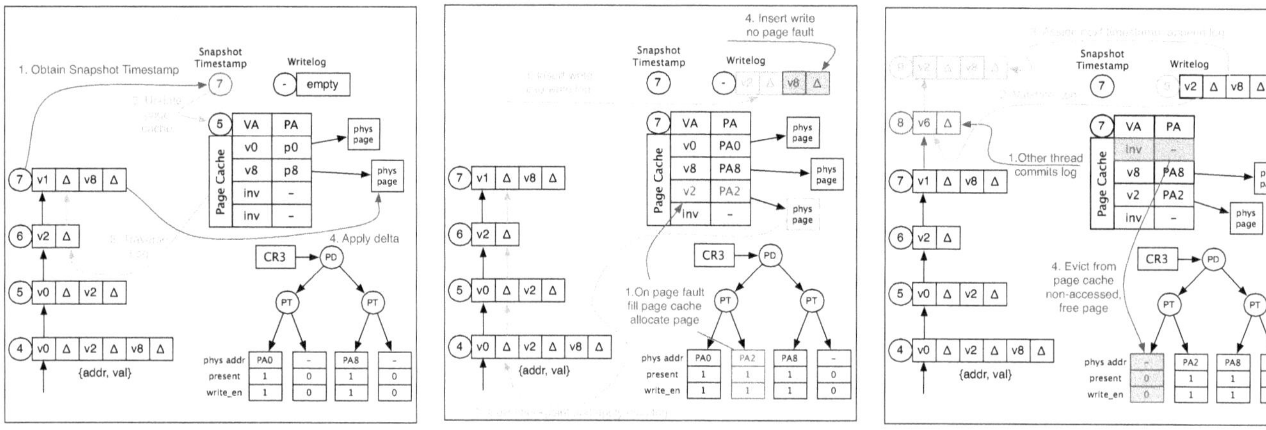

(a) Transaction Begin (b) Transactional Writes (c) Transaction Commit

Figure 1: Example Transaction Sequence

4 Implementation

This section describes the implementation of EXCITE-VM, particularly Copy-on-Read, global log management and page caching.

4.1 Copy-on-Read

In order to implement Copy-on-Read, EXCITE-VM must map in the desired version of a page for a thread running transactions whenever a page fault occurs. Instead of modifying the page fault handler in the Linux kernel, we leverage Dune [5], a system that offers safe user-level access to privileged CPU features like page table management. Dune utilizes the virtualization hardware of modern microprocessors to provide virtual machine-like capabilities to basic processes. Dune processes gain access to virtualized hardware, such as a second page table layer for manipulating virtual address mappings, but are still isolated from the host operating system and hence are not more privileged than a usual process. We opted for Dune over a kernel based implementation due to performance advantages as well as development and stability reasons. Managing page tables in a user level library avoids a large part of the kernel specific complexity and reduces context switching overheads, so in particular, Dune reduces the cost of a trap from 2821 cycles to 587 [5]. Dune also facilitated the development process as a crash occurring in a Dune page fault handler does not lead to a kernel panic but instead only exits the Dune process.

An EXCITE-VM thread prepares itself to perform transactions by entering Dune mode and by copying the page table of its caller, similarly to what occurs during a call to `fork()`. During transaction processing, the per thread page table is modified to provide the desired snapshot view of the shared segment to the thread. Process switching is potentially expensive compared to thread switching. To address this issue, we utilize process context IDs (PCIDs) avoiding flushing the TLB when switching between page tables.

The entire CoR logic is implemented within a custom page fault handler which is registered via Dune. When a transaction is started on a thread for the very first time, the presence and write enable bit for all pages is cleared. As a result, the first access to shared memory traps into the EXCITE-VM page fault handler which in return creates a local copy of the page matching the contents of that page in the transaction's snapshot and maps this page with writable permissions into the thread's page hierarchy. Outside of a transaction, we map an empty page table into the thread's page hierarchy for the shared segment. Hence, accesses to the shared segment outside of a transaction will fail, revealing a bug in the application.

4.2 Page Cache

The page cache is implemented as a software cache of configurable size and holds frequently accessed pages which optimistically get updated to a snapshot version during transaction begin. The page cache supports the following simple replacement policy. Every *Scan* transactions, where *Scan* is a configurable parameter, all pages within the page cache whose access bit is cleared are evicted from the cache. Then, the access bit of all remaining pages is cleared and the corresponding TLB entries are flushed. Whenever the page is accessed again by application software, the hardware automatically sets the accessed bit. By configuring *Scan*, an EXCITE-VM user determines the frequency of cache evictions and the resulting memory consumption.

4.3 Global Log

The global log maintains all writes that have been applied to shared memory in chronological order. There exists one global log per application instance running on EXCITE-VM. It is a shared data structure accessed by application threads to re-generate snapshots as well as to perform conflict detection. To avoid being a concurrency bottleneck, the global log is implemented as a doubly linked list supporting lockless reads. New log entries are only appended to the end using an atomic operation. Log entries are removed only by the checkpointing thread and only if they are guaranteed to be older than the oldest snapshot that is currently in use by any thread. The only race condition that exists in this mechanism is between the checkpointing thread and a page faulting thread. If the checkpointing thread updates a particular page while an application thread tries to fault in said page, a race condition might occur. To avoid this issue, readers implement the sequence lock mechanism [8] enabling concurrent checkpointing and page faulting without obtaining locks. In particular, the checkpointing thread modifies a shared page by setting its version number to dirty, then applies the updates and then increments the version number of the page. The readers on the other hand, check the page version number before and after copying the page and if the two versions are not identical, retries the sequence. The entries of the shared log are identified by a version number which is the unique timestamp assigned to this entry during commit. The writeset tracks writes on a quad-word granularity, whereas each entry is defined by its address and a 64 bit delta value which can be added to roll a version forward (redo) or subtracted to roll a version backwards (undo).

The size of the writeset influences both the snapshot generation and the transaction validation cost. Hence, to reduce the size of the writeset, EXCITE-VM supports a stream optimization which stores writes to consecutive addresses using a base address plus length notation. As a result, frequent operations such as memcpy and memset generate only a single entry within the writeset at the only expense of an additional branch instruction during write logging.

4.4 Libitm Integration

EXCITE-VM exposes transactions to programmers through GCC's libitm [17, 2]. Libitm defines a new keyword, `transaction_atomic{}`, which is used by the programmer to declare transactions. Libitm automatically instruments reads and writes and exposes those to library developers via a modular, internal API. We added SI-TM as a new algorithm to libitm by providing support for three main APIs. To implement `transaction_begin()` a thread reads out the global 64 bit timestamp counter setting the snapshot for this transaction. Before entering the transaction, the thread needs to update its page cache, which is performed by traversing the global log, starting from the snapshot the page cache is currently at (the snapshot of the last transaction). For each write, it queries the page cache and if existent updates the corresponding page. The `transaction_write()` API is called whenever a shared memory location is written and it is handled by buffering the address and value of the write, forming a new log entry. The most costly operation is `transaction_commit()` as it requires to validate the write set against all other committed transactions that overlap in time.

4.5 Commit processing

We support a set of techniques to reduce the validation cost. First, to provide scalability, commit processing is performed by all threads in parallel. By allowing lockless reads, the global log can be accessed by all committers concurrently. Nevertheless, to avoid races between concurrent committers, validation and appending a new log entry needs to be performed atomically. Therefore, committers determine the newest log entry before validation and then recheck for the newest log after validation. If another thread committed a new log in between, then the committer needs to validate against this log as well. This guarantees that a committer always sees all other commit logs even those that are appended during validation. Second, the bloomfilter signature which is contained in each commit log entry is utilized to perform hierarchical validation to cut short the validation sequence in case of no conflict. For example, if the intersection of the bloomfilter of two transactions is empty, there exists no write-write conflict between the two transactions and fine grain word based validation can be skipped. By maintaining the bloomfilters on a page based granularity all writes to a page set the identical filter bits which keeps the filter sparse and avoids false positives. In case no conflict exists between two transactions, this allows to validate all writes within a page using a single operation. Third, supporting streams (a sequence of writes to consecutive addresses) reduces the cost of validating a sequence of writes to a single base-bound check. Fourth, by applying techniques such as loop unrolling, prefetching and vectorization using AVX-256 instructions, EXCITE-VM is capable of checking up to four addresses in parallel.

4.6 Lines of code

EXCITE-VM has been programmed in C/C++ and contains 6330 lines of code, not including blank lines and comments. The GCC patch to enable EXCITE-VM as a new TM algorithm for libitm is 233 lines of code. The dune library adds another 5,898 lines although we utilize only a subset of its components. As a comparison, Linux's virtual memory system (mm) contains 62,877 lines of code as of version 3.13.0.

5 EXCITE-VM Guarantees

We now discuss the guarantees EXCITE-VM provides in terms of fault tolerance, security and consistency.

5.1 Fault Tolerance

EXCITE-VM improves fault tolerance and robustness over conventional multi-threaded systems by tolerating certain programming errors. As threads maintain local copies of the pages that are written during a transaction, uncommitted writes are never visible to other threads. Hence, in case a thread terminates due to a runtime error, the shared state remains unaffected. We assume that the EXCITE-VM system itself does not suffer from runtime errors as it can only protect against runtime errors of the application. The EXCITE-VM commit logic, however, does perform address checking of the write log. So in case a thread tries to commit a writelog that modifies locations outside of shared memory, the log is rejected to avoid segmentation violations induced by EXCITE-VM code. EXCITE-VM provides the means of removing a failed thread from the system, the option of spawning a new thread as well as enabling the other threads to continue operation. Nevertheless, to support fault tolerance in a meaningful way application awareness is required. In particular, the application must be able to tolerate the information loss of the failing thread. For applications that partition the work among threads during startup this might be difficult, whereas for real time server applications that continuously process client requests using multiple threads, it is feasible. For example, Memcached (See Section 5.5) can be extended such that on a thread failure only the in-flight request is lost but that the application can continue to run and accept request subsequently. In summary, EXCITE-VM provides the necessary facilities to considerably improve the robustness of a shared memory system.

5.2 Security

As mentioned in Section 4.1, each thread in EXCITE-VM uses Dune to access virtualized hardware, but these threads still have only the usual privileges and protections. Since each thread in EXCITE-VM has its own virtual-to-physical mapping, threads cannot access each others page caches and hence observe uncommitted writes. To prevent malicious threads gaining access to the transaction processing code and to virtual memory management instructions (which would jeopardize the guarantees above,) application code should be executed in as user, i.e. Dune ring 3, while EXCITE-VM needs to run in non-root, Dune ring 0. As a result, transaction begin and transaction commit operation need to be performed via system calls requiring a ring change which adds an overhead of 587 cycles in case of Dune [5]. Note that write instrumentation can be solely performed in user space as long as EXCITE-VM checks the validity of the write log (e.g. for buffer overflows) during commit.

5.3 Consistency

EXCITE-VM implements the SI isolation level [6], which guarantees consistent reads but permits the write-skew anomaly. A write-skew anomaly may occur when two concurrent transactions update separate variables (so no write-write conflict) but together causing a constraint to be violated. For example, consider the constraint: $a < b + c$. One transaction may modify b while a concurrent transactions modifies c. Though the constraint is satisfied in both thread's snapshots, the constraint may be violated after merging both writes into a new shared state. A write skew can only arise if there is a dependency cycle between reads and writes across two or more concurrent transactions. Such a cycle can be broken by *promoting* a read to be treated as part of the write set, thereby causing a write-write conflict and aborting the second transaction. Prior research [16, 14, 27] presented techniques to detect and remove write skew automatically which we adopt for our system. In particular, EXCITE-VM supports read promotion to avoid write skew anomalies. In our experience, this approach leads to significantly fewer aborts than forcing complete serializability of transactions while reliably preventing anomalies. The performance overhead introduced by read promotion is negligible [27].

In applications where strict serializability is required, programmers can apply locks for synchronization and utilize snapshots for fault tolerance and consistent reads. For example, LevelDB, a fast key-value storage library written by Google follows such a hybrid model by supporting atomic PUT and GET operations while also offering read-only snapshots. Finally, in future work we will support SSI-TM [36] which avoids write-skew by detecting dependency cycles at runtime.

6 Evaluation

We evaluate EXCITE-VM by comparing it to three baselines including SI-STM, Libitm and single global lock. *SI-STM* is a C/C++ re-implementation of Riegel's Java based system [40]. *Libitm* represents the default TM algorithm of GCC/Libitm which utilizes ownership records to guarantee consistency in the case of concurrent shared memory accesses and which is similar in function to TL2 [15]. We also compare to the single *Global Lock* implementation included in Libitm, which is not expected to scale well but which should provide lowest instrumentation overheads. We do not compare against hardware TM implementations such as Intel TSX due to the following reasons. Firstly, at the time of writing this paper no Intel Haswell with more than four cores was available to us and secondly a STAMP comparison between HTM and a TL2 STM has been performed before in [50] which the interested reader can consult for comparison.

We perform our measurements using different software applications, including Microbenchmarks, the STAMP application suite [43], Memcached and the Yahoo Cloud Server Benchmark. To support EXCITE-VM we had to modify the applications moderately by replacing malloc calls for shared data to a version that calls into the EXCITE-VM system. We also had to move all globally defined shared variables onto the heap[1]. From the STAMP suite, we have successfully ported Genome, Kmeans, Labyrinth, Vacation, SSCA2 and Intruder as well as all datastructures. Yada does not work correctly with TMs that deploy lazy conflict detection [43], Bayes we omitted due to the non-deterministic behavior of the application leading to inconsistent results [43]. Porting the applications required a certain understanding of the code at least to the degree of determining shared memory data structures. Porting the applications took us one day per application in average with only few lines of code modified.

We disable two features of EXCITE-VM for these performance comparisons, the first being the mapping of a dummy page table outside of a transaction to catch out-of-transaction accesses (see Section 4.1) and the second being that commit processing is performed in user mode Dune ring 3 (see Section 5.2). These features provide bug-checking and security, but none of the systems we compare against provide either feature. All applications were compiled with GCC 5.0. We run our experiments on an 8-core Intel Xeon CPU E5-2670 running at 2.6 GHz with 20 MBytes of cache running Ubuntu Linux 14.4.

6.1 Microbenchmarks

To compare EXCITE-VM against SI-STM we use two micro benchmarks both taken from the original SI-STM paper. By leveraging the virtual memory system, EXCITE-VM reduces the instrumentation overheads of reads and as a result, outperforms SI-STM by up to 5.9x as shown in Figure 2. The list benchmark evaluates concurrent lookup, insert and delete operations to a linked list initialized with 250 elements. We run 1, 2, 4 and 8 thread configurations and varying the ratio of read-only (lookup) and read-write (insert and delete) operations. This is a read-heavy benchmark as even when using a workload of 100% write transactions each insert and delete operation must partially traverse the list. EXCITE-VM scales well on this benchmark and outperforms the other systems at any write percentage, and by 5.9x under a read-only workload. The bank benchmark is a write-heavy benchmark involving a sequential array of account objects where write transactions transfer money from one account to another and read-all transactions sum up the value of all accounts. We show results from the benchmark

[1]EXCITE-VM currently does not support shared data to reside in the global data/bss segment, however, we plan to add this in a future revision

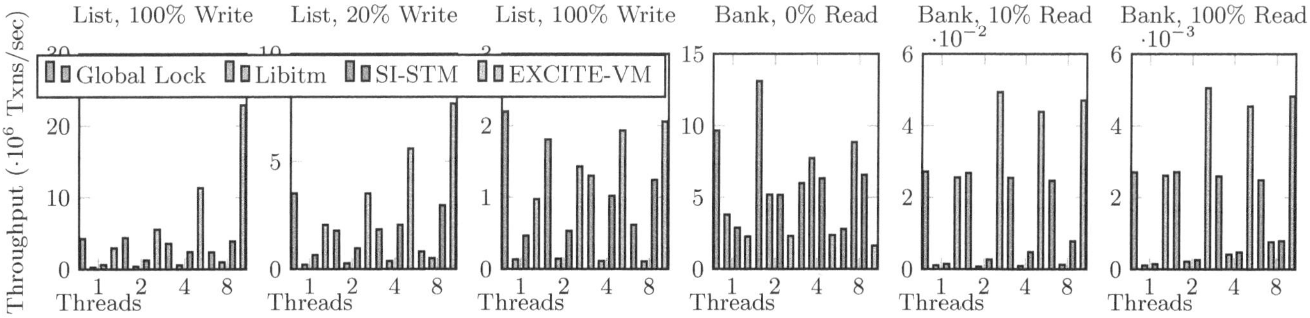

Figure 2: Microbenchmarks

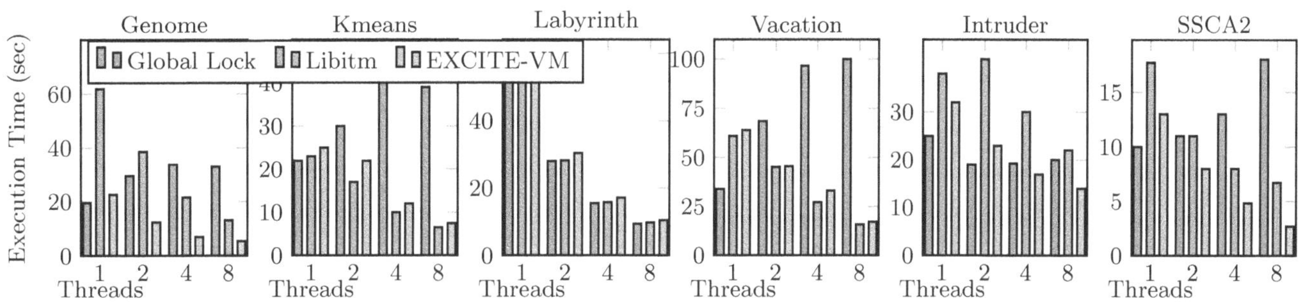

Figure 3: STAMP Execution Time

using 1 million accounts, each a 64-bit integer. When executing 8 threads on a workload of entirely write transactions, EXCITE-VM is 5.5x slower than the highest performing system, Libitm. This is due to the comparably higher cost of writes in EXCITE-VM. However, when read-all transactions are included, EXCITE-VM reaches the bandwidth of the shared last level cache with as few as 2 threads and achieves 6.8x higher throughput than SI-STM or Libitm.

6.2 Applications

6.2.1 *STAMP*

We evaluate EXCITE-VM using the STAMP benchmark suite and observe up to 2.2x performance improvements over all of the other tested approaches. To evaluate STAMP, we utilized the default configuration parameters with the high contention option. Figure 3 shows the execution time of the STAMP applications on EXCITE-VM. The Genome benchmark is very read intensive, which causes Libitm to spend more than 50% of its execution time on read instrumentation costs as reported by `perf`. In contrast, EXCITE-VM has almost no read overheads and matches the performance of the global lock implementation on a single thread while also scaling well to eight threads. Libitm also scales well EXCITE-VM, however, it is 3x slower for any thread configuration. Kmeans is a write heavy application and, as a result, EXCITE-VM shows a slightly higher single thread overhead than either the global lock or Libitm on this benchmark. Both EXCITE-VM and Libitm scale comparably well. Labyrinth only spends a small amount of time in transactions, furthermore, most of the work can be executed completely parallel without any kind of synchronization. As a result all three systems show good scalability and low overheads. Vacation offers a mixed load of both update-heavy and read-heavy transactions. Hence, EXCITE-VM offers comparable performance to Libitm due to outperforming Libitm on read-heavy transactions but having higher overhead on update-heavy transactions. Both Libitm and EXCITE-VM exhibit good scalability and outperform the global lock. Intruder performs significant number of byte reads which are instrumented on the per access level and which lead to high instrumentation overheads for Libitm. Hence, on this benchmark EXCITE-VM shaves 30% off the runtime of the other tested systems at 8 threads. Read instrumentation for this benchmark under EXCITE-VM shows up as a 10% overhead in `perf`, although this instrumentation is unnecessary for EXCITE-VM and is implemented as an empty virtual function call solely to match the Libitm API. GCC currently does not support link time optimization in combination with transactional memory which would be required to completely remove this overhead. Finally, in SSCA2, EXCITE-VM shows good scalability and, at 8 threads, shows a 2.2x performance improvement over all other tested systems. We do not compare against SI-STM as it cannot run STAMP due to being an object based TM implementation. Neither the original authors nor us have been able to evaluate SI-STM in complex benchmarks due to this limitation.

6.2.2 *Memory Overhead*

EXCITE-VM introduces potential memory overheads due to the per thread page cache, the per thread page table and the global log. The page tables approximately have a size of 1/512 the of the physical memory in use and in experiments their size has been below 1% of the total memory consumption. The global log size is determined by the oldest live transaction. For the applications we evaluated, the global log has introduced less than 1% memory overheads. The

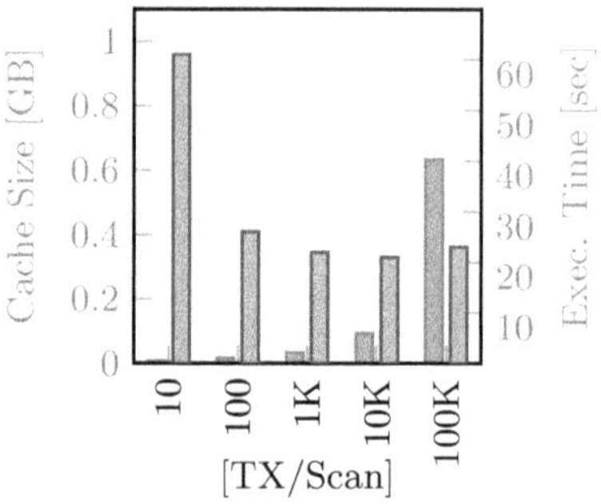

Figure 4: Pagecache 1 Thread

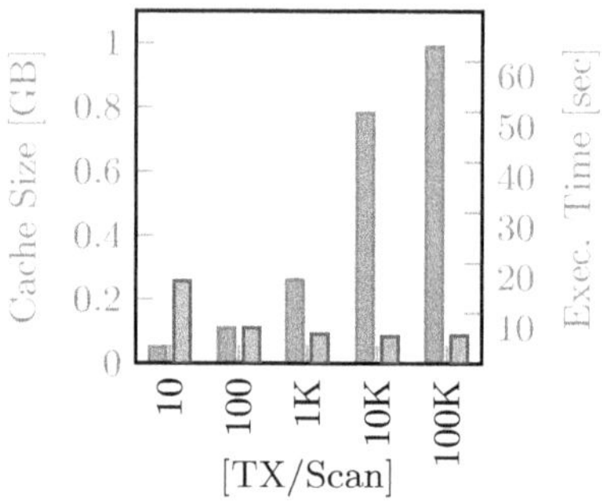

Figure 5: Pagecache 8 Threads

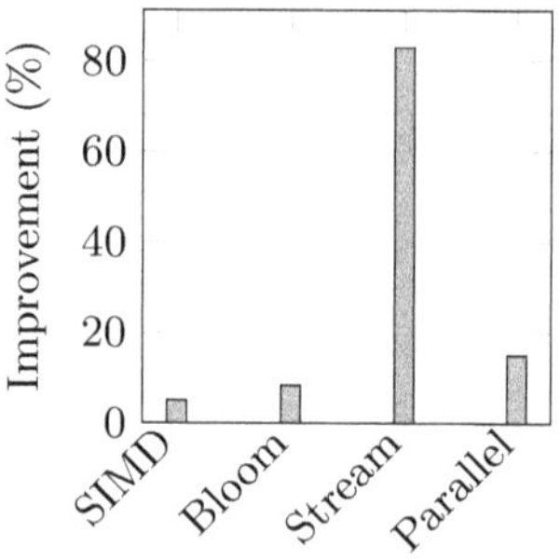

Figure 6: Optimization Techniques

log size can be further bound by generating intermediate checkpoints. To evaluate the memory overhead of the page cache, we studied the effect of different eviction scan periods when running the STAMP application suite to understand the page cache trade-off between memory and performance. A shorter scan period tends to reduce the size of the page cache. Figure 4 and Figure 5 shows Genome at 1 and respectively 8 threads with the ratio of transactions per scan varying between 100 and 100,000, showing the effect on both cache size and execution time. To put the cache size into perspective, note that Genome itself has a memory footprint of 300 MB. For 1 thread and a TX/Scan ratio of 100 the page cache is 8 MB and hence represents an overhead of less than 3%. However, for 8 threads and a 100,000 TX/Scan ratio the cache grows to over 900 MB representing an overhead of 300%. Our current system employs a default TX/Scan ratio of 10,000 which provides close to optimal performance with a memory overhead of 1.9x for 8 threads. This ratio has been proven adequate for the other evaluated applications as well.

Interestingly, the cache size does not necessarily grow linearly in the number of threads, e.g. in Figures 4 and 5 the cache size for 8 threads in the 100,000 case is much less than 8x that for 1 thread. This is because the application partitions some of its state into per-thread working sets, causing some pages to associate with a single thread's page cache. We observed that increasing the scan ratio past 100,000 TX/Scan reduced performance for this experiment, due to the inflicted cost of updating cached pages that are not subsequently accessed. An analysis of the page cache contents revealed that many of the pages in the caches are duplicates, suggesting that further optimizations, such as page sharing and deduplication could improve performance [23, 30]. Genome was representative of results obtained for the other STAMP benchmarks, hence we omit the other applications for brevity.

6.2.3 *Impact of Optimization Techniques*

The implementation Section discusses thread optimization techniques that improve the performance of EXCITE-VM. We provide the average performance improvement for the STAMP applications running at 8 threads. In particular, we discuss four optimizations: vectorization, bloomfilters, streams and parallel commit.

First, vectorization (SIMD) capabilities of Intel processors both improve validation, by comparing multiple elements of a write set in parallel, as well as log traversal and application, again by applying multiple writes with a single instruction. SIMD is implemented by extracting inner loops into function bodies adhering to the form required by GCC and then enabling auto vectorization. In cases where GCC was unable to auto-vectorize we apply inline assembly. Figure 6 shows a 4% improvement on end-to-end performance for SIMD for Genome (the other STAMP applications behave similar) for eight threads.

Second, we evaluate the 64 bit bloomfilter that is maintained for each write log entry, which allows checking for non-intersection of two write sets with a single operation. By avoiding costly entry-by-entry comparison of writesets in the usual case, bloomfilters reduce validation overhead leading to a 7% improvement as shown in Figure 6.

Third, we evaluate the effect of streams. Streams enable to store a set of writes to consecutive addresses, as emitted by memcpy and memset, as a single pair of start address and length. This optimization reduces the average writeset size and as a result reduces validation cost leading to a mean speedup of 90% or almost 2x.

Finally, we evaluate the effect of performing commits in parallel when executing 8 threads. In the baseline, EXCITE-VM threads obtain a commit lock to perform validation and to append their log entry. In the optimized approach, threads iterate over the log in parallel for validation. Validation and appending a log is still performed atomically, however, if another thread commits a new log concurrently it is sufficient to validate against this new log entry instead of restarting the entire validation process. Parallel commit delivers an improvement of 15%.

6.2.4 *Online Analytical Processing*

STAMP's Vacation simulates an online transaction processing (OLTP) workload on a large database. Due to the database size, conflicts are rare and both libitm and EXCITE-VM scale equally well. Besides performing OLTP, database operators are generally interested in analyzing their data. For this purpose, we added an online analytical processing (OLAP) workload to Vacation. Concurrent with 7 OLTP threads we execute a single OLAP thread, which chooses one table at random and performs on it range scans of different size to compute an aggregation. The OLAP workload is read-only and requires a consistent view of the database, respectively no concurrent conflicting writes to the same data items can be tolerated. We measure the effect of the OLAP thread on the execution time of the OLTP threads as well as the analysis performance that can be achieved con-

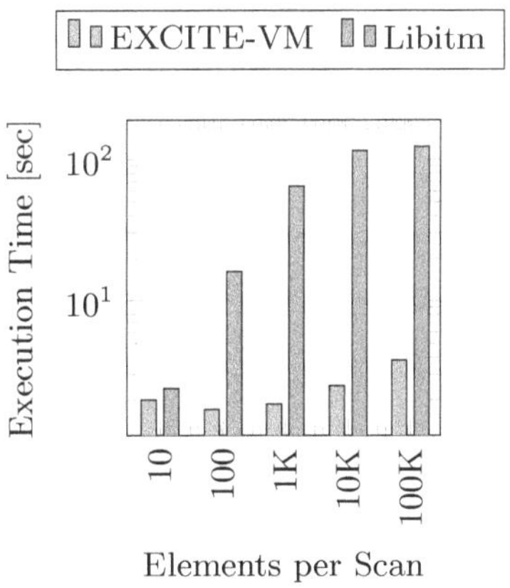

Figure 7: Vacation OLTP

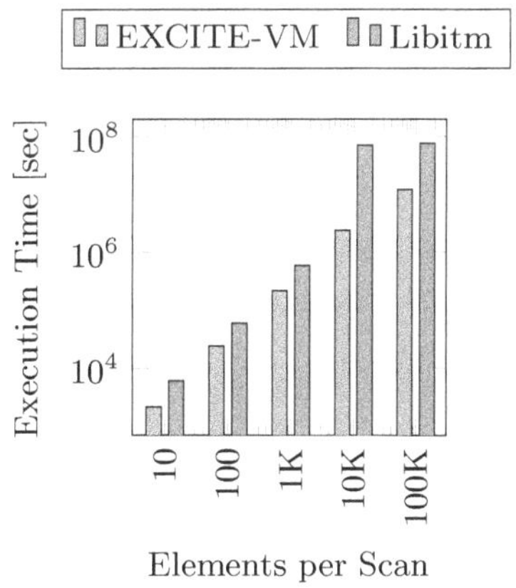

Figure 8: Vacation OLAP

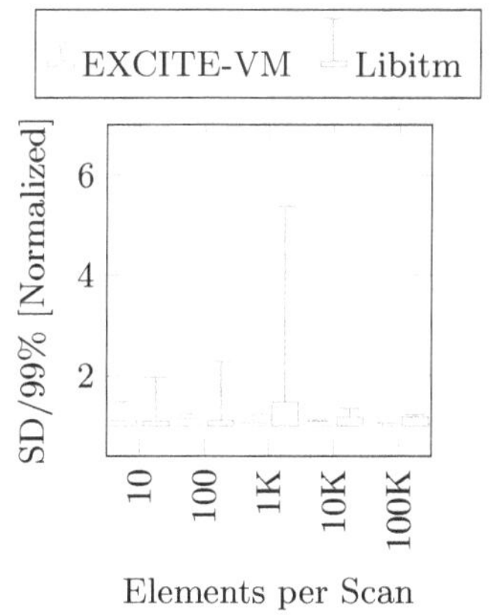

Figure 9: Predictability

currently. Figure 7 shows the effect of the OLAP thread on OLTP performance. As it can be seen, the performance of EXCITE-VM remains relatively stable while Libitm execution time increases by 1000x for long range scans of 100k elements. Even when running a single OLTP thread, the slow down for Libitm is at the same order of magnitude, effectively rendering the OLAP workload impossible to support on Libitm due to conflicting memory accesses. EXCITE-VM only introduces a 1.9x slowdown for the 100k range scan mainly due to cache effects. Profiling revealed that for the 100k scans abort rates of OLTP transactions are unaffected by the OLAP thread, however, the last level cache miss rate increases, presumably long range scans trash the L3 cache. Figure 8 shows the average execution time of an OLAP transaction. Libitm shows a 3x increase in execution time for OLAP over EXCITE-VM for all scan sizes (note the log scale). As it can be seen, Libitm's slowdown of OLTP performance (1000x) is significantly higher than the slowdown for OLAP (3x). The reason, therefore, is that Libitm switches to serial mode after a phase of high contention and as long running OLAP transactions have the same priority to obtain the serial lock, the effect on the OLTP transactions is more significant.

EXCITE-VM gives predictable performance, which is important for applications such as user-facing databases that need to meet service level objectives (SLOs). Figure 9 shows the standard deviation (SD) and maximum 99th percentile (99%) duration of OLAP transactions. For both Libitm and EXCITE-VM SD and 99% increases to a maximum for the 1000 element scans. For even larger scans variability decreases due to the sheer duration of the transactions. Nevertheless, EXCITE-VM significantly outperforms Libitm by up to a factor of 1.4x for SD and 4.3x for the 99 percentile.

6.2.5 *Elastic Memcached*

We now evaluate Memcached, a popular key-value cache, that was transactionalized to run on Libitm by Ruan et al. [44]. We ported this code to EXCITE-VM, by allocating shared data structures and several global variables on the EXCITE-VM heap. To evaluate the performance we execute the Memcached server with 1 to 8 threads and apply memslap as a load generator using the following parameters: `-concurrency=8 -execute-number=416667 -s localhost:11211 -binary`. Figure 10 shows execution time for Memcached for both Libitm and EXCITE-VM. The two systems show similar performance, while EXCITE-VM shows better scalability for 8 threads.

Furthermore, to demonstrate the fault tolerance capabilities of EXCITE-VM, we built a modified version of Memcached by introducing programmer bugs that trigger a segmentation fault at different locations at an arbitrary randomized point in time. We then ran Memcached 1000 times in this configuration with only the affected thread died in each execution without affecting other server threads and without corrupting the shared state. Memslap detects a timeout in this case for the outstanding request and then continues its operation. This shows the improved fault tolerance provided by EXCITE-VM. We plan to extend Memcached with a functionality that detects failing threads and, in this case, elastically spawns a new thread. As a result failing threads should have a minimal impact on performance.

6.2.6 *Yahoo Cloud Server Benchmark*

Yahoo Cloud Server Benchmark (YCSB) [12] represents a benchmark suite to test webscale key-value store implementations. It can be used to test scale-up as well as scale-out systems, whereas we focus on scale-up. YCSB defines six workloads which model realistic applications by setting put, get and scan parameters accordingly. For brevity we select only two workloads: Workload A which is an update heavy workload stressing the write performance as well as workload E which executes short range scan operations. We ported YCSB to C++ and perform measurements against the Libitm baseline. Figure 11 and Figure 12 shows the results for the two workloads. In workload A, EXCITE-VM achieves 700,000 operations per second while providing full transactional semantics, e.g. we support multiple atomic put/get operations as a single transaction. Both systems scale well, however, EXCITE-VM shows a slightly higher overhead leading to a slowdown of 5% over Libitm. This workload represent a worst case scenario for EXCITE-VM due to many updates and yet EXCITE-VM shows only modest degradation in performance. Workload E on the other hand performs scans for which EXCITE-VM shows reduced instrumentation overhead and linearly scaling up to eight threads. In particular it shows 2.2x performance increase over Libitm for eight threads.

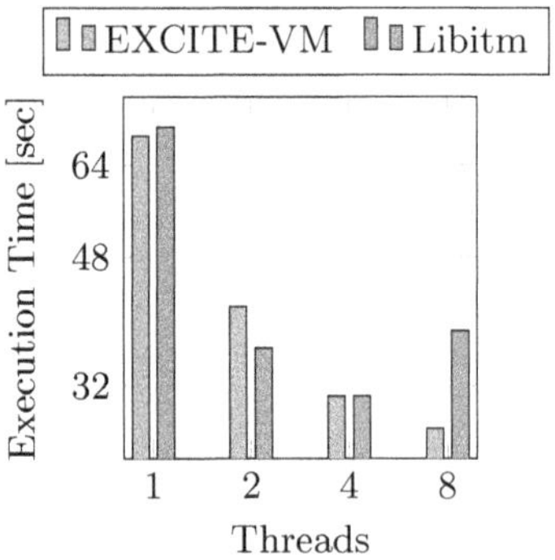

Figure 10: Memcached

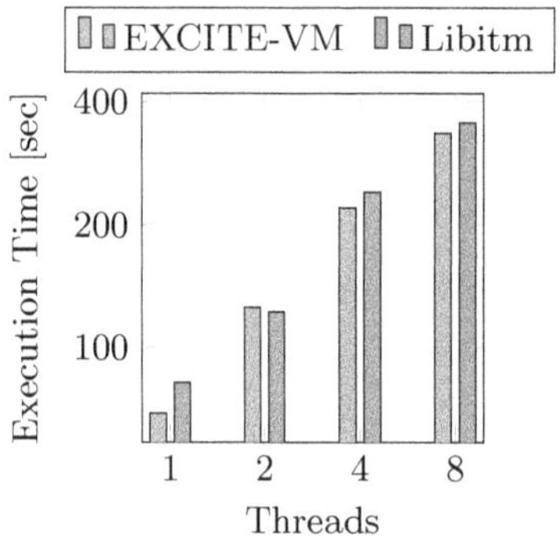

Figure 11: YCSB-A

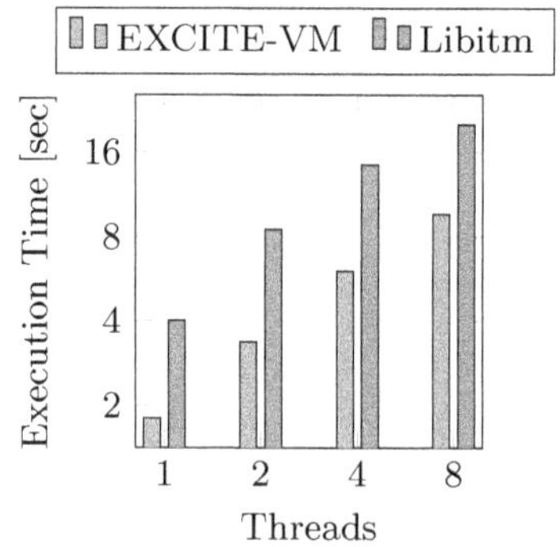

Figure 12: YCSB-E

7 Related Work

Snapshots are supported by HyPer [24] utilizing Linux's fork mechanism to instantiate in-memory database snapshots for read-only transactions. Forking the page table on on each transaction begin is significantly more expensive than creating an updated snapshot with EXCITE-VM. Moreover, there is no mechanism to merge modified snapshots atomically into committed state, as provided in EXCITE-VM. All major databases, PostgreSQL [32], MySQL [34], HANA [47] and OracleDB [22] support snapshot isolation transactions. However, incorporating a database into an application introduces overheads and requires significant changes to the data model. Particularly, instead of relying on standard data structures, as provided for example by the STL, all data needs to be stored in tables. EXCITE-VM, on the other hand, adds these capabilities with low overhead, while avoiding changes to the data model.

SpiceC [18] is a parallel programming technique that enforces isolation between threads by generating thread local copies of shared data on each access. Instrumenting every read operation introduces significant overheads (as in SI-STM), which EXCITE-VM avoids by means of the virtual memory system. Doppler [35] utilizes thread local copies to reduce contention on frequently accessed data structures. In contrast to EXCITE-VM, it is restricted to commutative operations. Burckhardt proposes to program with revisions and isolation types [9] leveraging a fork-join task model to exploit concurrency. Changing a conventional lock-based programming model into a task model requires significant changes whereas EXCITE-VM requires minor modifications. Furthermore, the technique does not support speculation and, as a result, requires the programmer to define a merge function for each data type to handle write-write conflicts, whereas, EXCITE-VM leverages transactions.

There exists a large body of research on *Transactional Memory* [21, 46, 37, 19, 15, 33, 25, 13, 45, 7, 49, 20]. More relevant to our work is unbounded page-based transactional memory (PTM) [10] which leverages the virtual memory system to support transactions overflowing the cache and to avoid aborts due to context switches and exceptions. In contrast to EXCITE-VM, PTM requires hardware modifications and does not provide snapshots. Similarly, SI-TM, [26] which provides the same guarantees as our system, requires hardware modifications of the memory system. Riegel proposes lazy snapshots [39] to provide consistent reads addressing the linearly growing validation overhead, however, the system does not support snapshot isolation semantics.

Memory protection hardware has been proposed to address the privatization problem and to achieve strict atomicity between transactional and non-transactional data accesses [1]. In contrast to our system, which also provides strict atomicity, the work neither addresses fault tolerance nor provides SI. Memory protection techniques are also utilized to enable the concurrent execution of an STM and a bounded hardware to form an efficient Hybrid TM system [4]. Furthermore, virtualization techniques have been previously utilized by TM systems to achieve unbounded transactions [38] and fully virtualized transactions [11]. Similar techniques have been implemented on the operating system level to achieve virtualization [48] and to manage transactional memory as in TxLinux [42]. In distributed systems, Microsoft's CORFU project [3] shares similarities with EXCITE-VM.

8 Conclusions

EXCITE-VM provides a new concurrent programming model supporting snapshot isolation transactions on shared memory. It delivers high performance by enabling threads to directly access shared memory while providing the synchronization-free application programming model provided by inter-process messaging. EXCITE-VM also provides the ability to have individual threads fail and restart without restarting the entire application. Our evaluation shows that this approach achieves performance which is equal, and in most cases superior to, the alternative approaches, especially when applications have a significant number of read-only transactions. In particular, we have shown that for applications leveraging long read-only transactions, EXCITE-VM can be 1000x faster than a conventional TM solution. EXCITE-VM also delivers performance predictability, as read-only transactions never abort or block in the presence of update transactions.

Several implementation techniques are critical to achieving this performance, including the page cache, periodic checkpointing, parallel lazy commit, vectorization, bloom-filters and CoR snapshotting. We also showed that periodically creating a checkpoint for use by read-only transactions reduces the cost of these transactions while allowing the log to be pruned periodically. A natural extension for EXCITE-VM is to provide durability by persisting the log and modified pages to stable storage as part of checkpointing. Another is to allow distributed transactions by distributing the log and the commit operation over the network.

9 References

[1] M. Abadi, T. Harris, and M. Mehrara. Transactional memory with strong atomicity using off-the-shelf memory protection hardware. In *ACM Sigplan Notices*, pages 185–196. ACM, 2009.

[2] A.-R. Adl-Tabatabai, T. Shpeisman, and J. Gottschlich. Draft specification of transactional language constructs for c++, 2009.

[3] M. Balakrishnan, D. Malkhi, T. Wobber, M. Wu, V. Prabhakaran, M. Wei, J. D. Davis, S. Rao, T. Zou, and A. Zuck. Tango: Distributed data structures over a shared log. In *Proceedings of the Twenty-Fourth ACM Symposium on Operating Systems Principles*, pages 325–340. ACM, 2013.

[4] L. Baugh, N. Neelakantam, and C. Zilles. Using hardware memory protection to build a high-performance, strongly-atomic hybrid transactional memory. *ACM SIGARCH Computer Architecture News*, 36(3):115–126, 2008.

[5] A. Belay, A. Bittau, A. Mashtizadeh, D. Terei, D. Mazières, and C. Kozyrakis. Dune: Safe user-level access to privileged cpu features. In *Proceedings of the 10th USENIX Conference on Operating Systems Design and Implementation*, OSDI'12, pages 335–348, Berkeley, CA, USA, 2012. USENIX Association.

[6] H. Berenson, P. Bernstein, J. Gray, J. Melton, E. O'Neil, and P. O'Neil. A critique of ansi sql isolation levels. *ACM SIGMOD Record*, 1995.

[7] J. Bobba, K. Moore, H. Volos, L. Yen, M. Hill, M. Swift, and D. Wood. Performance pathologies in hardware transactional memory. In *ACM SIGARCH Computer Architecture News*. ACM, 2007.

[8] H.-J. Boehm. Can seqlocks get along with programming language memory models? In *Proceedings of the 2012 ACM SIGPLAN Workshop on Memory Systems Performance and Correctness*, pages 12–20. ACM, 2012.

[9] S. Burckhardt, A. Baldassin, and D. Leijen. Concurrent programming with revisions and isolation types. In *ACM Sigplan Notices*, pages 691–707. ACM, 2010.

[10] W. Chuang, S. Narayanasamy, G. Venkatesh, J. Sampson, M. Van Biesbrouck, G. Pokam, B. Calder, and O. Colavin. Unbounded page-based transactional memory. In *ACM Sigplan Notices*. ACM, 2006.

[11] J. Chung, C. C. Minh, A. McDonald, T. Skare, H. Chafi, B. D. Carlstrom, C. Kozyrakis, and K. Olukotun. Tradeoffs in transactional memory virtualization. In *ACM SIGARCH Computer Architecture News*, pages 371–381. ACM, 2006.

[12] B. F. Cooper, A. Silberstein, E. Tam, R. Ramakrishnan, and R. Sears. Benchmarking cloud serving systems with ycsb. In *Proceedings of the 1st ACM symposium on Cloud computing*, pages 143–154. ACM, 2010.

[13] P. Damron, A. Fedorova, Y. Lev, V. Luchangco, M. Moir, and D. Nussbaum. Hybrid transactional memory. In *ACM Sigplan Notices*. ACM, 2006.

[14] R. Dias, J. Lourenço, and N. Preguiça. Efficient and correct transactional memory programs combining snapshot isolation and static analysis. In *Proceedings of the 3rd USENIX conference on Hot topics in parallelism (HotPar'11), HotPar*, volume 11, 2011.

[15] D. Dice, O. Shalev, and N. Shavit. Transactional locking ii. In *Proceedings of the 20th international conference on Distributed Computing*, DISC'06, pages 194–208, Berlin, Heidelberg, 2006. Springer-Verlag.

[16] A. Fekete, D. Liarokapis, E. O'Neil, P. O'Neil, and D. Shasha. Making snapshot isolation serializable. *ACM Trans. Database Syst.*, 30(2):492–528, 2005.

[17] P. Felber, C. Fetzer, U. Müller, T. Riegel, M. Süßkraut, and H. Sturzrehm. Transactifying applications using an open compiler framework. *TRANSACT, August*, pages 4–6, 2007.

[18] M. Feng, R. Gupta, and Y. Hu. Spicec: scalable parallelism via implicit copying and explicit commit. In *ACM SIGPLAN Notices*, pages 69–80. ACM, 2011.

[19] L. Hammond, V. Wong, M. Chen, B. D. Carlstrom, J. D. Davis, B. Hertzberg, M. K. Prabhu, H. Wijaya, C. Kozyrakis, and K. Olukotun. Transactional memory coherence and consistency. In *Proceedings of the 31st annual international symposium on Computer architecture*, ISCA '04, pages 102–, Washington, DC, USA, 2004. IEEE Computer Society.

[20] T. Harris, J. Larus, and R. Rajwar. Transactional memory. *Synthesis Lectures on Computer Architecture*, 5(1):1–263, 2010.

[21] M. Herlihy and J. E. B. Moss. Transactional memory: architectural support for lock-free data structures. In *Proceedings of the 20th annual international symposium on computer architecture*, ISCA '93, pages 289–300, New York, NY, USA, 1993. ACM.

[22] K. Jacobs, R. Bamford, G. Doherty, K. Haas, M. Holt, F. Putzolu, and B. Quigley. Concurrency control, transaction isolation and serializability in sql92 and oracle7. *Oracle White Paper, Part*, 1995.

[23] K. Jin and E. L. Miller. The effectiveness of deduplication on virtual machine disk images. In *Proceedings of SYSTOR 2009: The Israeli Experimental Systems Conference*, page 7. ACM, 2009.

[24] A. Kemper and T. Neumann. Hyper: A hybrid oltp&olap main memory database system based on virtual memory snapshots. In *IEEE 27th International Conference on Data Engineering (ICDE),*, 2011.

[25] S. Kumar, M. Chu, C. J. Hughes, P. Kundu, and A. Nguyen. Hybrid transactional memory. In *Proceedings of the eleventh ACM SIGPLAN symposium on Principles and practice of parallel programming*, pages 209–220. ACM, 2006.

[26] H. Litz, D. Cheriton, A. Firoozshahian, O. Azizi, and J. P. Stevenson. Si-tm: reducing transactional memory abort rates through snapshot isolation. In *Proceedings of the 19th international conference on Architectural support for programming languages and operating systems (ASPLOS-19)*, pages 383–398. ACM, 2014.

[27] H. Litz, R. J. Dias, and D. R. Cheriton. Efficient correction of anomalies in snapshot isolation transactions. *ACM Transactions on Architecture and Code Optimization (TACO)*, 11(4):65, 2015.

[28] T. Liu, C. Curtsinger, and E. D. Berger. Dthreads: efficient deterministic multithreading. In *Proceedings of the Twenty-Third ACM Symposium on Operating Systems Principles*, pages 327–336. ACM, 2011.

[29] T. Merrifield and J. Eriksson. Conversion: multi-version concurrency control for main memory segments. In *Proceedings of the 8th ACM European Conference on Computer Systems*, pages 127–139. ACM, 2013.

[30] D. T. Meyer and W. J. Bolosky. A study of practical deduplication. *ACM Transactions on Storage (TOS)*, 7(4):14, 2012.

[31] C. Minh, J. Chung, C. Kozyrakis, and K. Olukotun. Stamp: Stanford transactional applications for multi-processing. In *Workload Characterization, 2008. IISWC 2008. IEEE International Symposium on.* IEEE, 2008.

[32] B. Momjian. *PostgreSQL: introduction and concepts*, volume 192. Addison-Wesley New York, 2001.

[33] K. Moore, J. Bobba, M. Moravan, M. Hill, and D. Wood. Logtm: Log-based transactional memory. In *Proceedings of the 12th International Symposium on High-Performance Computer Architecture (HPCA-12).* Austin: IEEE Computer Society, 2006.

[34] A. MySQL. *MySQL Administrator_s Guide and Language Reference.* Sams Publishing, 2006.

[35] N. Narula, C. Cutler, E. Kohler, and R. Morris. Phase reconciliation for contended in-memory transactions. In *Proceedings of the 11th USENIX conference on Operating Systems Design and Implementation*, pages 511–524. USENIX Association, 2014.

[36] D. Ports and K. Grittner. Serializable snapshot isolation in postgresql. *Proceedings of the VLDB Endowment*, 2012.

[37] R. Rajwar and J. Goodman. Speculative lock elision: Enabling highly concurrent multithreaded execution. In *Proceedings of the 34th annual ACM/IEEE international symposium on Microarchitecture*, pages 294–305. IEEE Computer Society, 2001.

[38] R. Rajwar, M. Herlihy, and K. Lai. Virtualizing transactional memory. In *Computer Architecture, 2005. ISCA'05. Proceedings. 32nd International Symposium on.* IEEE, 2005.

[39] T. Riegel, P. Felber, and C. Fetzer. A lazy snapshot algorithm with eager validation. In *Distributed Computing*, pages 284–298. Springer, 2006.

[40] T. Riegel, C. Fetzer, and P. Felber. Snapshot isolation for software transactional memory. In *TRANSACT06*, volume 298, 2006.

[41] M. Rosenblum and J. K. Ousterhout. The design and implementation of a log-structured file system. *ACM Transactions on Computer Systems (TOCS)*, 10(1):26–52, 1992.

[42] C. J. Rossbach, O. S. Hofmann, D. E. Porter, H. E. Ramadan, B. Aditya, and E. Witchel. Txlinux: Using and managing hardware transactional memory in an operating system. In *ACM SIGOPS Operating Systems Review*, pages 87–102. ACM, 2007.

[43] W. Ruan, Y. Liu, and M. Spear. Stamp need not be considered harmful. In *Ninth ACM SIGPLAN Workshop on Transactional Computing*, 2014.

[44] W. Ruan, T. Vyas, Y. Liu, and M. Spear. Transactionalizing legacy code: An experience report using gcc and memcached. *SIGPLAN Not.*, 2014.

[45] B. Saha, A. Adl-Tabatabai, and Q. Jacobson. Architectural support for software transactional memory. In *Microarchitecture, 2006. MICRO-39. 39th Annual IEEE/ACM International Symposium on.* IEEE, 2006.

[46] N. Shavit and D. Touitou. Software transactional memory. *Distributed Computing*, pages 99–116, 1997.

[47] V. Sikka, F. Färber, W. Lehner, S. K. Cha, T. Peh, and C. Bornhövd. Efficient transaction processing in sap hana database: the end of a column store myth. In *Proceedings of the 2012 ACM SIGMOD International Conference on Management of Data*, pages 731–742. ACM, 2012.

[48] M. M. Swift, H. Volos, N. Goyal, L. Yen, M. D. Hill, and D. A. Wood. Os support for virtualizing hardware transactional memory. In *Procs. of the 3rd ACM SIGPLAN Workshop on Transactional Computing*, 2008.

[49] L. Yen, J. Bobba, M. R. Marty, K. E. Moore, H. Volos, M. D. Hill, M. M. Swift, and D. A. Wood. Logtm-se: Decoupling hardware transactional memory from caches. In *High Performance Computer Architecture, 2007. HPCA 2007. IEEE 13th International Symposium on*, pages 261–272. IEEE, 2007.

[50] R. M. Yoo, C. J. Hughes, K. Lai, and R. Rajwar. Performance evaluation of intel transactional synchronization extensions for high-performance computing. In *Proceedings of SC13: International Conference for High Performance Computing, Networking, Storage and Analysis*, SC '13, 2013.

POSTER: Fly-Over: A Light-Weight Distributed Power-Gating Mechanism for Energy-Efficient Networks-on-Chip

Rahul Boyapati, Jiayi Huang, Ningyuan Wang*, Kyung Hoon Kim, Ki Hwan Yum, Eun Jung Kim
Department of Computer Science and Engineering
Texas A&M University *Google Inc.
{rahulboyapati,jyhuang,khkim,yum,ejkim}@cse.tamu.edu nywang@google.com

ABSTRACT

Reducing static NoC power consumption is becoming critical for energy-efficient computing as technology scales down since NoCs are devouring a large fraction of the on-chip power budget. We propose *Fly-Over (FLOV)*, a light-weight distributed mechanism for power-gating routers. With simple modifications to the baseline router architecture, FLOV links are facilitated over power-gated routers. A Handshake protocol that allows seamless router power-gating in addition to a dynamic routing algorithm, that provides best-effort minimal path without the necessity for global network information, maintain normal NoC functionality. We evaluate our schemes using synthetic workloads as well as real workloads from PARSEC 2.1 benchmark suite. The results show that FLOV can achieve on average 19.2% latency reduction and 15.9% total energy savings.

1. INTRODUCTION

Static power consumption of the on-chip circuitry is increasing at an alarming rate with the scaling down of feature sizes and chip operating voltages towards near-threshold levels. Power-gating, cutting off supply current to idle chip components, is an effective circuit-level technique that can be used to mitigate the worsening impact of on-chip static power consumption. Router Parking (RP) [2] power-gates routers whose attached cores are power-gated, but requires a centralized fabric manager for network reconfiguration, which creates a huge synchronization overhead, and the whole network has to stall until the reconfiguration is completed.

We propose Fly-Over (FLOV), a light-weight distributed power-gating mechanism that eliminates the need for centralized control to power-gate routers. FLOV tries to power-gate routers as soon as the attached cores are powered down by the OS, in a distributed manner. Since such a distributed power-gating mechanism may create interconnect partitions without communication paths, FLOV links in power-gated routers are provided to enable incoming packets to travel straight through for network connectivity. Specifically, FLOV comprises of the FLOV router microarchitecture, handshake protocol, and a partition-based dynamic routing algorithm.

PACT '16 September 11-15, 2016, Haifa, Israel

ACM ISBN 978-1-4503-4121-9/16/09.
DOI: http://dx.doi.org/10.1145/2967938.2974058

2. FLOV MECHANISM

In this section we explain the three major components of the FLOV mechanism, namely, the router microarchitecture, handshake protocol and the dynamic routing algorithm.

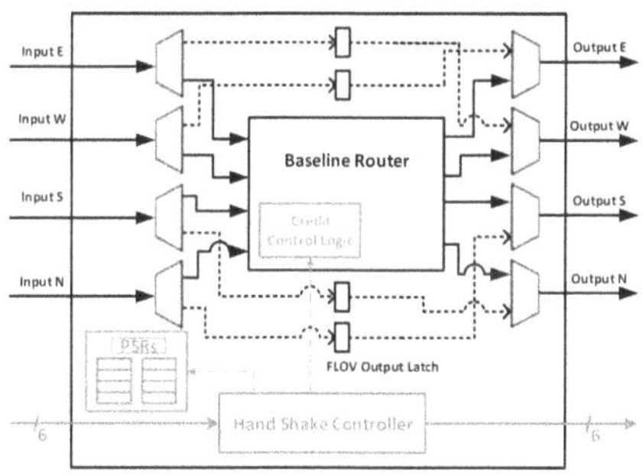

Figure 1: FLOV Router Architecture.

2.1 FLOV Router Architecture

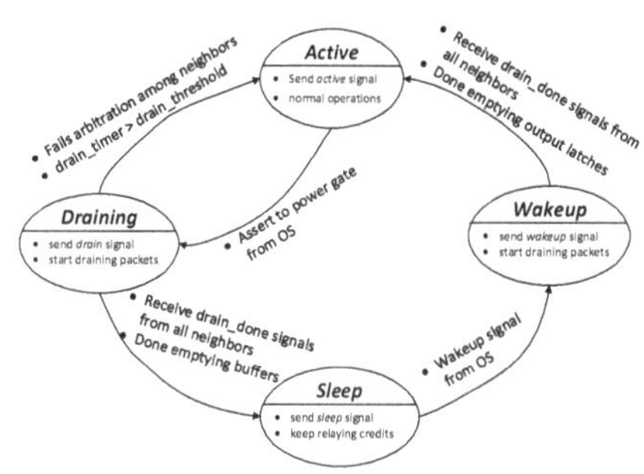

Figure 2: Router Power State Transition Diagram.

As shown in Figure 1, the FLOV router architecture has multiplexers and demultiplexers added to input/output links, in addition to a latch in each direction. When a FLOV router is powered-on, it functions like the baseline 3-stage virtual-channel router, and the muxes/demuxes are set to 0 as well as the latches are power-gated. When the router is power-gated, all the components of the baseline router are power-gated and the muxes/demuxes are set to 1 to activate the FLOV links.

2.2 HandShake Protocol

The HandShake Control logic (HSC) block shown in Figure 1 connects to all the neighboring routers and implements the hand-

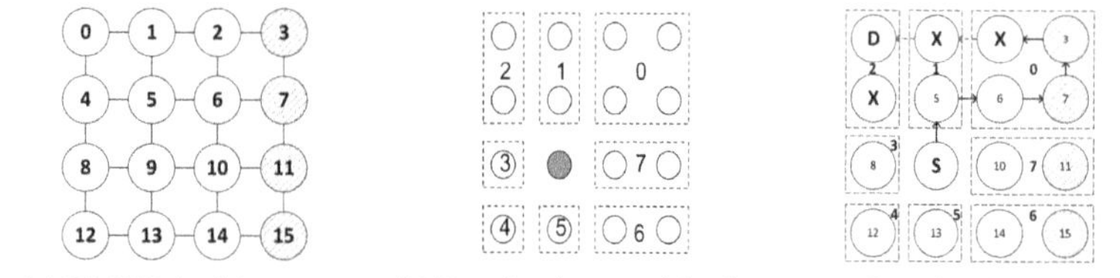

(a) FLOV Architecture. (b) Destination partitioning. (c) Routing Example.

Figure 3: FLOV Architecture, Destination partitioning, Routing Algorithm Example.

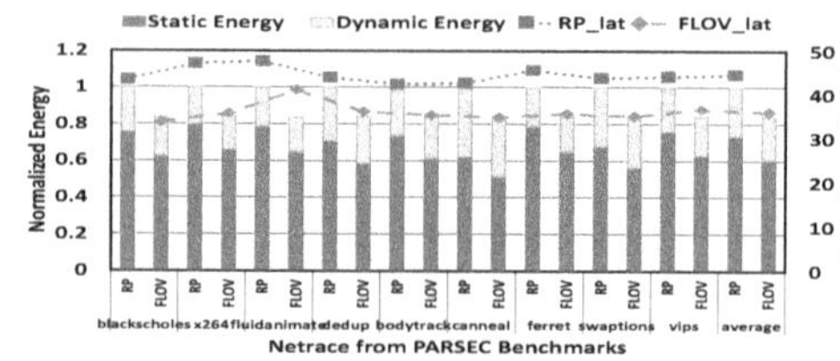

Figure 4: Normalized Energy Consumption and Network Latency.

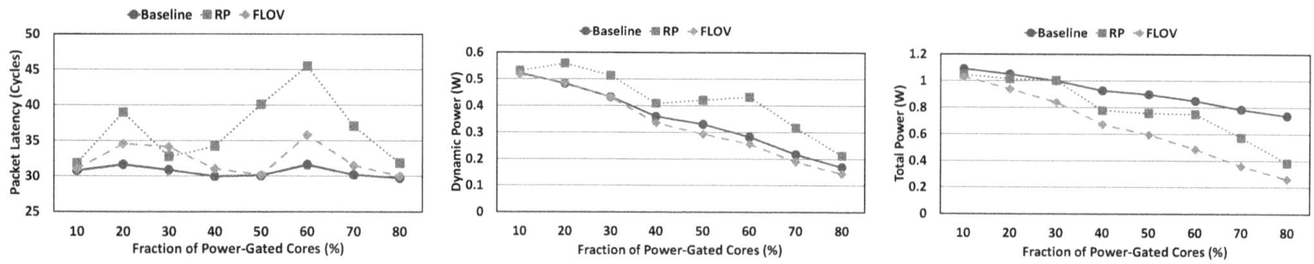

(a) Average Latency (b) Dynamic Power Consumption (c) Total Power Consumption

Figure 5: Latency, Dynamic and Total Power Comparison for Injection Rate 0.08 flits/node/cycle with Uniform Random Traffic.

shake protocol between logical adjacent routers required before power-gating a router.

The state transition diagram in Figure 2 depicts the power states a router can be in. The router initially goes into *Draining* from *Active* when it wants to be power-gated, once the attached core is power-gated. The router immediately sends a drain signal to its neighbors and starts to drain the packets residing in its input buffers. Routers that want to drain at the same time but fail to win arbitration with their neighbors come back into *Active*. Once all the router's neighbors finish any intermittent transmissions destined to it and the packet draining is finished, the router can go into *Sleep*. In the *Sleep* state the router sends a sleep signal to all its neighbors after turning off the baseline router operation and starting the FLOV operation. The router starts relaying credits between its powered-on neighbors using the Credit Control Logic(CCL). A router goes to *Wakeup* from *Sleep* when its attached core is powered on.

2.3 Dynamic Routing Algorithm

Figure 3(a) shows a (4×4) 2D mesh network with the proposed FLOV routers. The pattern-shaded routers (3, 7, 11, and 15) are connected to memory controller (MC) nodes that should be never power-gated. We propose a partitioned-based dynamic routing algorithm based on YX routing. Each router divides the network into partitions as shown in Figure 3(b). The routing decision is made based on two variables, the partition which the destination falls into and the power states of neighboring routers.

In the example show in figure 3(c), the packet is rerouted through the last column since routers 1 and 0 are power-gated. The main idea behind the algorithm is that in the worst case the packets are directed to the EAST direction so we can guarantee that the packet will be able to make a turn toward the destination in the always powered-on edge router of the corresponding row.

3. EXPERIMENTAL EVALUATION

In this section we evaluate the FLOV mechanism by comparing the power consumption and NoC latency with Router Parking [2]. We use a cycle-accurate network simulator, BookSim [1], that models all the router pipeline stages and link latencies. The simulation testbed is an 8×8 2D mesh network, with 4 VCs (6-flit depth) in each input channel and a packet size of 4 flits. We simulate a 2 GHz clock frequency with 32nm technology.

Figure 5 shows the performance and power consumption of the different mechanisms as the percentage of power-gated cores in increased. As shown in Figure 5 (a), FLOV performs better than RP since the RP mechanism always reroutes packets through powered-on routers and links connecting them leading to increased path length whereas FLOV uses the FLOV links to achieve near minimal path. We observe from Figures 5 (b) and (c) that the total and dynamic power consumption of FLOV is less that RP. The dynamic power consumption of FLOV is smaller since in RP when reruotes happen, every hop in the elongated traversal path will execute the total router pipeline whereas with FLOV we can use low cost FLOV links even with detour. As shown in Figure 4 for PARSEC network traces evaluation, FLOV achives 19.2% lower latency than RP and reduce total energy by 15.9% on average when 29 out of 64 cores are off.

4. CONCLUSIONS

We proposed Fly-Over (FLOV), a light-weight distributed router power-gating mechanism for NoCs. FLOV power-gates routers attached to powered-down cores without global network information, but still ensures network connectivity. Performance evaluations using synthetic and real workloads show that FLOV not only achieves better NoC power savings due to power-gating more routers but avoids aggregated traffic rerouting in the network unlike Router Parking.

5. REFERENCES

[1] N. Jiang, D. U. Becker, G. Michelogiannakis, J. Balfour, B. Towles, D. E. Shaw, J.-H. Kim, and W. J. Dally. A Detailed and Flexible Cycle-Accurate Network-on-Chip Simulator. In *International Symposium on Performance Analysis of Systems and Software (ISPASS)*, pages 86–96. IEEE, 2013.

[2] A. Samih, R. Wang, A. Krishna, C. Maciocco, C. Tai, and Y. Solihin. Energy-Efficient Interconnect via Router Parking. In *International Symposium on High Performance Computer Architecture (HPCA)*, pages 508–519. IEEE, 2013.

POSTER: Exploiting Asymmetric Multi-Core Processors with Flexible System Sofware

Kallia Chronaki[*‡], Miquel Moretó[*‡], Marc Casas[*], Alejandro Rico[+],
Rosa M. Badia[*†], Eduard Ayguadé[*‡], Jesus Labarta[*‡] and Mateo Valero[*]
[*]Barcelona Supercomputing Center, Barcelona, Spain
[‡]Universitat Politècnica de Catalunya - BarcelonaTech, Barcelona, Spain [+]ARM, Austin, Texas
[†]Research Institute (IIIA) - Spanish National Research Council (CSIC), Barcelona, Spain

ABSTRACT

Energy efficiency has become the main challenge for high performance computing (HPC). The use of mobile asymmetric multi-core architectures to build future multi-core systems is an approach towards energy savings while keeping high performance. However, it is not known yet whether such systems are ready to handle parallel applications.

This paper fills this gap by evaluating emerging parallel applications on an asymmetric multi-core. We make use of the PARSEC benchmark suite and a processor that implements the ARM big.LITTLE architecture. We conclude that these applications are not mature enough to run on such systems, as they suffer from load imbalance.

Furthermore, we explore the behaviour of dynamic scheduling solutions on either the Operating System (OS) or the runtime level. Comparing these approaches shows us that the most efficient scheduling takes place in the runtime level, influencing the future research towards such solutions.

1 Introduction

Energy efficiency has become the main challenge for future parallel computing designs [14], motivating prolific research to face the *Power Wall*. An interesting approach towards energy efficiency is the use of asymmetric multi-core architectures [2,17] with different types of cores targeting different performance and power optimization points. Such systems have been successfully deployed in the mobile domain, where simple in-order cores (*little*) have been combined with aggressive out-of-order cores (*big*) to build these systems.

Many researchers are pushing towards building future parallel systems with asymmetric multi-cores [9,10,12,13,23] and even mobile chips [20]. However, it is unclear if current parallel applications will benefit from these asymmetric platforms. Load balancing and scheduling are two of the main challenges in utilizing such heterogeneous platforms, as the programmer has to consider them from the very beginning to obtain an efficient parallelization.

PACT '16 September 11-15, 2016, Haifa, Israel

ACM ISBN 978-1-4503-4121-9/16/09.
DOI: http://dx.doi.org/10.1145/2967938.2976038

In this work we evaluate the suitability of modern asymmetric multi-core platforms for highly parallel applications. First, we demonstrate that out-of-the-box parallel applications do not run efficiently on asymmetric multi-cores as the asymmetry of the system leads to load imbalance.

When load-balancing techniques are not included in the original application, we evaluate alternative solutions that, without relying on the programmer, can leverage the opportunities that asymmetric systems offer. These solutions consist of dynamic schedulers on either the OS or on the runtime system level. We use a state of the art dynamic OS scheduler that is aware of the asymmetry of the platform. Another approach is the use of a runtime system that is responsible to schedule the workload to the appropriate idle cores dynamically. This is done with the use of a modern task-based programming model that allows the specification of inter-task dependences and lets the runtime system to track dependences between tasks. We compare and analyse the outcome of this evaluation in terms of performance, power and energy.

Although there has been remarkable research on asymmetric systems, we consider that their experimental evaluation is limited compared to our work. First, there are many works that base their evaluation on a simulated or emulated environment [1, 2, 11–13, 15–17, 19, 21–23, 25, 26], in contrast to our real asymmetric system. Furthermore, many works use either random task dependency graph generators or scientific kernels instead of real scientific applications [5,7,22,24]. Finally, many of the existing works do not present power and energy results [5,11,17,22,25,26].

2 The ARM big.LITTLE Architecture

The ARM big.LITTLE [6,10] is a modern asymmetric multi-core architecture that has been successfully deployed in the mobile market. In this work, we make use of one of the commercially available development boards featuring a big.LITTLE architecture: the Hardkernel Odroid-XU3 development board. The Odroid-XU3 includes an 8-core Samsung Exynos 5422 chip with four ARM Cortex-A15 (big) cores and four Cortex-A7 (little) cores. For the remainder of the paper, we refer to Cortex-A15 cores as *big* and to Cortex-A7 cores as *little*.

Scheduling a set of processes on an asymmetric multi-core system is more challenging than the traditional process scheduling on symmetric multi-cores. An efficient OS scheduler has to take into account the different characteristics of the core types of the system. The ARM big.LITTLE systems provide three mainstream OS schedulers: *cluster*

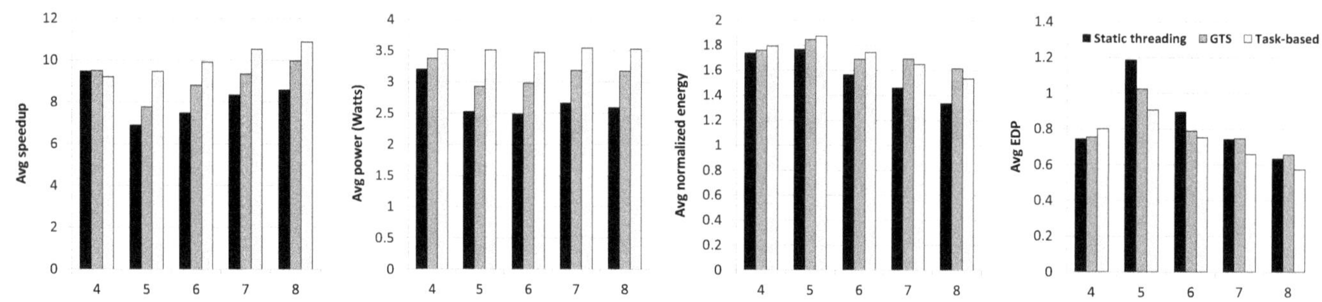

Figure 1: Average results when running on 4 to 8 cores with 4 of them big. Speedup is over 1 little core, static threading on 4 little cores is the baseline of energy consumption and EDP

switching [6], *in-kernel switch* [18] and *global task scheduling* (GTS) [6]. GTS allows running applications on all cores in the asymmetric multi-core and is considered as the most sophisticated scheduler. In GTS, all cores are available and visible to the OS scheduler, and this scheduler is aware of the characteristics and each core type. GTS tracks the CPU utilization of each process and dynamically schedules high CPU utilization processes to big cores and low CPU utilization processes to little cores. As a result, cores are active according to the characteristics of the running processes.

3 Evaluation

The experiments of this work are performed on the Hardkernel Odroid XU3 described in Section 2. In these experiments, we set the big cores to run at 1.6GHz and the little cores at 800MHz through the `cpufreq` driver.

We measure the performance, power and energy of the original PARSEC codes [3] together with a task-based implementation of nine benchmarks[1] of the suite [4]. For space purposes we only show the average results among these benchmarks. The original codes make use of the **pthreads** library for all the selected benchmarks, while the task-based implementation is done using the OmpSs programming model [8]. The OmpSs applications follow the same parallelization strategy implemented with OpenMP 4.0 task annotations.

In the search of the optimal solution, we compare three different scenarios of parallel execution when transferring the scheduling responsibility to different levels of the software stack: *(a) Static Threading:* the scheduling responsibility is on the application level. *(b) OS Scheduling (GTS):* the OS is responsible for performing the scheduling. Specifically we use the GTS provided by ARM described in Section 2. *(c) Task-based:* the runtime system is responsible for the dynamic scheduling.

Figure 1 shows the average results among the evaluated benchmarks. We refer to the system configurations as $B+L$ where B is the number of big cores and L is the number of little cores. The speedup chart of Figure 1 shows that the *Static threading* approach does not benefit from adding little cores to the system. In fact, this approach brings an average 15% slowdown when adding four little cores (configuration `4+4`). This is a result of the static thread scheduling; the same amount of work is assigned to each core, so when the big cores finish the execution of their part, they become idle and under-utilized. GTS achieves a limited speedup of 5% with the addition of four little cores to the `4+0` configuration. The addition of a single little core brings a 22% slowdown (from `4+0` to `4+1`) and requires three additional little cores to reach the performance of the symmetric configuration (configuration `4+3`). Finally, the *Task-based* approach always benefits from the extra computational power as the runtime automatically deals with load imbalance. Performance improvements keep growing with the additional little cores, reaching an average improvement of 16% over the symmetric configuration when 4 extra cores are added.

The power chart of Figure 1 shows oppositional benefits among the three approaches. We can see that *Static threading* and *GTS* benefit from asymmetry, effectively reducing average power consumption. *Static threading* reduces power consumption when moving from the `4+0` to the `4+4` system by 23% while *GTS* does so by 6.2%. On the other hand, the *task-based* approach keeps the big cores busy for most of the time so it maintains the average power nearly constant. By keeping the power stable, the energy consumption of the task-based approach shown in the third chart of Figure 1 is minimized since it only depends on the execution time.

To see the impact on both performance and energy efficiency we plot the average energy delay product (EDP) on the rightmost chart of Figure 1. In this chart the lower values are the better. We observe that the *task-based* approach is the one that has the best performance-energy combination for the asymmetric configurations since it maintains the lowest EDP for all cases. *Static threading* manages to reduce the average EDP by 7% while *GTS* and *task based* approaches do so by 10% and 37% respectively.

4 Conclusions

In this paper we examine the maturity of asymmetric multicore systems to support emerging parallel applications, showing results for performance, power, energy and EDP. Through our comparison of the three scheduling approaches, we conclude that the task-based approach is the optimal solution to dynamically balance the load among the asymmetric resources. Contrarily to the static and OS scheduling approaches, the task-based approach constantly improves performance as asymmetry is increasing. Moreover, relying on the runtime system for the efficient scheduling keeps power static which results in energy savings. Finally, according to the EDP results, the conclusion is that the task-based approach offers the optimal performance and energy trade-off for asymmetric systems.

[1]The benchmarks used are: blackscholes, bodytrack, canneal, dedup, facesim, ferret, fluidanimate, streamcluster and swaptions.

5 References

[1] A. Agarwal and P. Kumar. Economical Duplication Based Task Scheduling for Heterogeneous and Homogeneous Computing Systems. In *IACC*, 2009.

[2] S. Balakrishnan, R. Rajwar, M. Upton, and K. K. Lai. The impact of performance asymmetry in emerging multicore architectures. In *ISCA*, pages 506–517, 2005.

[3] C. Bienia. *Benchmarking Modern Multiprocessors*. PhD thesis, Princeton University, January 2011.

[4] D. Chasapis, M. Casas, M. Moreto, R. Vidal, E. Ayguade, J. Labarta, and M. Valero. PARSECSs: Evaluating the Impact of Task Parallelism in the PARSEC Benchmark Suite. *Trans. Archit. Code Optim.*, 2015.

[5] K. Chronaki, A. Rico, R. M. Badia, E. Ayguadé, J. Labarta, and M. Valero. Criticality-aware dynamic task scheduling for heterogeneous architectures. In *ICS*, pages 329–338, 2015.

[6] H. Chung, M. Kang, and H.-D. Cho. Heterogeneous Multi-Processing Solution of Exynos 5 Octa with ARM big.LITTLE Technology. Technical report, Samsung Electronics Co., Ltd., 2013.

[7] M. Daoud and N. Kharma. Efficient Compile-Time Task Scheduling for Heterogeneous Distributed Computing Systems. In *ICPADS*, 2006.

[8] A. Duran, E. Ayguadé, R. M. Badia, J. Labarta, L. Martinell, X. Martorell, and J. Planas. Ompss: a Proposal for Programming Heterogeneous Multi-Core Architectures. *Parallel Processing Letters*, 21, 2011.

[9] A. Fedorova, J. C. Saez, D. Shelepov, and M. Prieto. Maximizing Power Efficiency with Asymmetric Multicore Systems. *Communications of the ACM*, 52(12), 2009.

[10] P. Greenhalgh. big.LITTLE Processing with ARM Cortex-A15 & Cortex-A7. *ARM White Paper*, 2011.

[11] M. A. Iverson, F. Özgüner, and G. J. Follen. Parallelizing Existing Applications in a Distributed Heterogeneous Environment. In *HCW*, 1995.

[12] J. A. Joao, M. A. Suleman, O. Mutlu, and Y. N. Patt. Bottleneck identification and scheduling in multithreaded applications. In *ASPLOS*, pages 223–234, 2012.

[13] J. A. Joao, M. A. Suleman, O. Mutlu, and Y. N. Patt. Utility-based acceleration of multithreaded applications on asymmetric CMPs. In *ISCA*, pages 154–165, 2013.

[14] P. Kogge, K. Bergman, S. Borkar, D. Campbell, W. Carson, W. Dally, M. Denneau, P. Franzon, W. Harrod, K. Hill, and Others. Exascale Computing Study: Technology Challenges in Achieving Exascale Systems. Technical report, University of Notre Dame, CSE Dept., 2008.

[15] D. Koufaty, D. Reddy, and S. Hahn. Bias scheduling in heterogeneous multi-core architectures. In *EuroSys*, pages 125–138, 2010.

[16] R. Kumar, K. I. Farkas, N. P. Jouppi, P. Ranganathan, and D. M. Tullsen. Single-isa heterogeneous multi-core architectures: The potential for processor power reduction. In *MICRO*, pages 81–92, 2003.

[17] R. Kumar, D. M. Tullsen, P. Ranganathan, N. P. Jouppi, and K. I. Farkas. Single-isa heterogeneous multi-core architectures for multithreaded workload performance. In *ISCA*, pages 64–75, 2004.

[18] Mathieu Poirier. In Kernel Switcher: A solution to support ARM's new big.LITTLE technology. Embedded Linux Conference 2013, 2013.

[19] T. Y. Morad, U. C. Weiser, A. Kolodny, M. Valero, and E. Ayguade. Performance, power efficiency and scalability of asymmetric cluster chip multiprocessors. *IEEE Comput. Archit. Lett.*, 5(1):4–17, Jan. 2006.

[20] N. Rajovic, P. M. Carpenter, I. Gelado, N. Puzovic, A. Ramirez, and M. Valero. Supercomputing with Commodity CPUs: Are Mobile SoCs Ready for HPC? In *SC*, 2013.

[21] R. Rodrigues, A. Annamalai, I. Koren, and S. Kundu. Scalable thread scheduling in asymmetric multicores for power efficiency. In *SBAC-PAD*, pages 59–66, 2012.

[22] G. Sih and E. Lee. A Compile-Time Scheduling Heuristic for Interconnection-Constrained Heterogeneous Processor Architectures. *IEEE Trans. Parallel Distrib. Syst.*, 4(2), 1993.

[23] M. A. Suleman, O. Mutlu, M. K. Qureshi, and Y. N. Patt. Accelerating critical section execution with asymmetric multi-core architectures. In *ASPLOS*, pages 253–264, 2009.

[24] H. Topcuoglu, S. Hariri, and M.-Y. Wu. Performance-Effective and Low-Complexity Task Scheduling for Heterogeneous Computing. *IEEE Trans. Parallel Distrib. Syst.*, 13(3), 2002.

[25] K. Van Craeynest, S. Akram, W. Heirman, A. Jaleel, and L. Eeckhout. Fairness-aware Scheduling on single-ISA Heterogeneous Multi-cores. In *PACT*, 2013.

[26] K. Van Craeynest, A. Jaleel, L. Eeckhout, P. Narvaez, and J. Emer. Scheduling heterogeneous multi-cores through performance impact estimation (pie). In *ISCA*, pages 213–224, 2012.

Acknowledgments

This work has been supported by the Spanish Government (SEV2015-0493), by the Spanish Ministry of Science and Innovation (contracts TIN2015-65316-P), by Generalitat de Catalunya (contracts 2014-SGR-1051 and 2014-SGR-1272), by the RoMoL ERC Advanced Grant (GA 321253) and the European HiPEAC Network of Excellence. The Mont-Blanc project receives funding from the EU's Seventh Framework Programme (FP7/2007-2013) under grant agreement number 610402 and from the EU's H2020 Framework Programme (H2020/2014-2020) under grant agreement number 671697. M. Moretó has been partially supported by the Ministry of Economy and Competitiveness under Juan de la Cierva postdoctoral fellowship number JCI-2012-15047. M. Casas is supported by the Secretary for Universities and Research of the Ministry of Economy and Knowledge of the Government of Catalonia and the Cofund programme of the Marie Curie Actions of the 7th R&D Framework Programme of the European Union (Contract 2013 BP_B 00243).

Poster: Easy PRAM-based High-performance Parallel Programming with ICE *

Fady Ghanim[1] Rajeev Barua[1] Uzi Vishkin[1,2]

[1]Electrical and Computer Engineering Department
[2]University of Maryland Institute for Advanced Computer Studies (UMIACS)
University of Maryland
College Park, MD, 20742, USA
{fghanim,barua,vishkin}@umd.edu

ABSTRACT

Large performance growth for processors requires exploitation of hardware parallelism, which, itself, requires parallelism in software. In spite of massive efforts, automatic parallelization of serial programs has had limited success mostly for regular programs with affine accesses, but not for many applications including irregular ones. It appears that the bare minimum that the programmer needs to spell out is which operations can be executed in parallel. However, parallel programming today requires so much more. The programmer is expected to partition a task into subtasks (often threads) so as to meet multiple constraints and objectives, involving data and computation partitioning, locality, synchronization, race conditions, limiting and hiding communication latencies. It is no wonder that this makes parallel programming hard, drastically reducing programmer's productivity and performance gains hence reducing adoption by programmers and their employers.

Suppose, however, that the effort of the programmer is reduced to merely stating operations that can be executed in parallel, the 'work-depth' bare minimum abstraction developed for PRAM (the lead theory of parallel algorithms). What performance penalty should this incur? Perhaps surprisingly, the upshot of our work is that this can be done with no performance penalty relative to hand-optimized multi-threaded code.

CCS Concepts

•Theory of computation → Parallel algorithms;•Computing methodologies → Parallel algorithms; Parallel programming languages;•Computer systems organization → *Parallel architectures;*

Keywords

Parallel Programming Languages; ease of programming; ICE; Parallel Algorithms; PRAM

1. INTRODUCTION

Parallel programming for performance is hard. But, can parallel programming languages alone mitigate that? While languages can help, we believe that the answer lies in the whole ecosystem they represent: the underlying algorithmic theory (or lack thereof) they are based on, and whether parallel hardware can support irregular applications. What is needed is a well-integrated ecosystem of (i) an easy-to-program programming model, backed by (ii) a solid algorithmic theory tailored to (iii) a hardware architecture capable of exploiting parallelism in irregular programs, and supported by (iv) an efficient compiler that make them work in concert. While relying on a published platform, our work contributes: new programming model and compiler, and experimental evaluation of the compiler efficiency. In this work we use a new programming model called Immediate Concurrent Execution (ICE).

The Algorithm Theory. ICE is grounded in the Parallel Random Access Machine/Model (PRAM) algorithmic theory. Developed in the 1980s and early 1990s, PRAM is the parallel equivalent of the standard Random Access Machines serial algorithmic theory. PRAM is very rich and feature diverse in algorithms and techniques, and is very simple to use. The lead PRAM abstraction known as work-depth (WD) defines ICE. WD prescribes a sequence of time steps, each containing a set of operations to be executed concurrently within unit time. The ICE computation model abstracts away opportunities for using local memories, and minimizing communication or synchronization, work distribution and scheduling making it much easier to specify PRAM parallel algorithms. PRAM/ICE is a desirable choice for parallel programmers due to its expressiveness, brevity, and its aforementioned properties.

The Programming Language. The ICE programming model transcribes PRAM algorithms as-is. ICE extends the C language by the keyword `pardo`(imported from PRAM) for specifying lock-step parallelism. In a lock-step parallel program, each statement in a parallel loop executes exactly in the same cycle across all iterations. **Example.** Figure 1(b) provides ICE code for the basic PRAM list ranking algorithm, defined in 1(a). In every iteration of the serial while loop the `pardo` instruction guides that for every element i whose successor $S(i)$ is not yet the last element: (i) its weight is updated to the distance to the successor of its current successor; and (ii) this successor of successor is first read (for all elements) and only later stored as the new successor; namely, the right hand side of all concurrent instructions is executed prior to to the left hand side of any of these instructions.

The System Platform. We test case our programming model using the explicit multi-threaded (XMT) platform developed at the University of Maryland (UMD) [1] (not to be confused with the CRAY XMT). XMT was designed with irregular programs such as those found in PRAM algorithms in mind, which allows it to attain excellent performance for such programs. This made it an ideal platform for testing our work. The XMT architecture is programmed through a multi-threaded programming language called XMTC, which is a modest extension to the C language. XMTC uses `spawn` to express concurrent threads.

*A detailed technical report of this work is available at http://drum.lib.umd.edu

PACT '16 September 11-15, 2016, Haifa, Israel

ACM ISBN 978-1-4503-4121-9/16/09.

DOI: http://dx.doi.org/10.1145/2967938.2974053

Problem:

Given a linked list with n elements, find for every elements its distance from the last element.

Input:

- *Array S(1...n)*: S(*i*) contains the index of the successor of element I. The successor of the last element is the element itself.
- W(1...n): W(*i*) contains the weight of element *i*. Initially *W(i)=0 for the last element in the list and W(i)=1 for all other elements.*

Output

- *S(i) is the index of the last element of the list.*
- *W(i) is the distance of element i from this last element.*

(a) Problem specification

```
pardo (unsigned i = 0; n-1;1) {
    while (S[i] != S[S[i]]) {
        W[i] = W[i] + W[S[i]];
        S[i] = S[S[i]];
    }
}
```

(b) ICE program

```
psBaseReg flag; // number of threads that require
                   another loop iteration
void pointer_jump(int S[n], int W[n], int n) {
    int W_tmp[n];
    int S_tmp[n];
    do {
        spawn(0, n-1) {
            if (S[$] != S[S[$]]) {
                W_tmp[$] = W[$] + W[S[$]];
                S_tmp[$] = S[S[$]];
            } else {
                W_tmp[$] = W[$];
                S_tmp[$] = S[$];
            }
        }
        flag = 0;
        spawn(0, n-1) {
            if (S_tmp[$] != S_tmp[S_tmp[$]]) {
                int i = 1;
                ps(i, flag);
                W[$] = W_tmp[$] + W_tmp[S_tmp[$]];
                S[$] = S_tmp[S_tmp[$]];
            } else {
                W[$] = W_tmp[$];
                S[$] = S_tmp[$];
            }
        }
    } while (flag != 0);
}
```

(c) XMTC program

Figure 1: Pointer jumping Algorithm.

The ICE Lock-step assumption created a serious implementation challenge. Due to a variety of technology constraints (such as hierarchical memory and power), the quest for parallel scalability is mainly through multi-threading in hardware. Hence, for scaling practically all parallel programming languages use multi-threading, where a thread proceeds at its own pace until the next synchronization point. The XMT system platform is also multi-threaded and cannot efficiently implement the tight synchrony dictated by the lock-step assumption. This meant that our same-cycle lock-step assumption had to be enforced by the compiler translating ICE to XMTC. See Section 2. Contrasting the ICE code in Figure 1(b) and the hand-optimized XMTC code in Figure 1(c) can help appreciate: (i) the challenge in providing effective translation, (ii) the simplicity of programming in ICE over XMTC, (iii) the difference in code size, and (iv) the implied relative ease in producing the ICE code.

Our main accomplishment in this new work is that the translation does not incur, on average, any performance penalty over hand-optimized multi-threaded programming in XMTC. See Section 3. Consequently, ICE is the first language that can transcribe PRAM algorithms and automatically translates them into effective threaded programs. Combined with prior XMT work, this establishes feasibility of reducing the main (work-depth) abstraction of parallel algorithmic theory to practice, arguably a major result.

2. TRANSLATION

In this work we translate programs written in ICE to the XMTC high level language. Parallel regions in ICE are expressed using the `pardo` keyword as seen in Figure 1(b). During translation barriers are introduced into parallel sections to maintain the correctness of the lock-step ICE program. Threads advance unpredictably at their own pace, which may result in executing memory reads and writes in a different order than originally intended. Barriers will ensure that the lock-step pacing is maintained. During translation, we split a pardo block into multiple spawn blocks. Splitting occurs at points where a barrier was added.

Splitting a pardo into multiple spawns and using memory to communicate information between spawns degrades performance, due to overhead. This is exacerbated when the number of splits is high. Hence it is crucial to avoid splitting whenever possible, and to mitigate the effects of the unavoidable splits. To minimize the number of splits needed, we rearrange memory accesses within a pardo region into clusters. Each cluster represents a spawn block. These clusters consist of a group of memory accesses that have no dependencies between them across different parallel contexts.

```
M: set of all memory accesses
CL_i = {m ∈ M : m is a member of cluster i}
NM = {m ∈ M : m is not a member of any cluster}

For an m ∈ NM:
L_m = {m_L ∈ M : loop carried dependence between m_L and m}
F_m = {m_F ∈ M : m is Data flow dependent on m_F }
C_m = {m_C ∈ M : m is control dependent on value of m_C }.
NL_m = L_m ∩ NM
NF_m = F_m ∩ NM
NC_m = C_m ∩ NM

Define Procedure ConflictsWith ( m, CL ) :
    if NL_m ≠ Φ then
        return true
    if L_m ∩ CL ≠ Φ then
        return true
    for m_F ∈ NF_m do
        if ConflictsWith (m_F , CL ) then
            return true
    for m_C ∈ NC_m do
        if ConflictsWith (m_C , CL ) then
            return true
    return false

Define Procedure cluster:
    Def: integer i = 0
    While (NM ≠ Φ) do
        define new cluster CL_i
        for m ∈ NM do
            if ConflictsWith (m, CL_i) then
                skip m
            else
                Add m to CL_i
        i = i + 1
```

Figure 2: The clustering algorithm.

When a pardo region is first split into multiple spawns, often there are more splits than necessary. By rearranging and grouping independent memory accesses into same spawn block we keep only the necessary splits. This is performed through a list scheduling scheme we call clustering. Figure 2 shows the algorithm used.

3. RESULTS

In this section we present the results of our experiments comparing the performance of ICE and hand-optimized XMTC. We developed a suite of 11 benchmarks based on common PRAM algorithms. For each benchmark, a pseudo-code was written, then based on that pseudo-code we implemented two versions: an XMTC version that is manually optimized for best performance, and the ICE version. The results are summarized in figure 3.

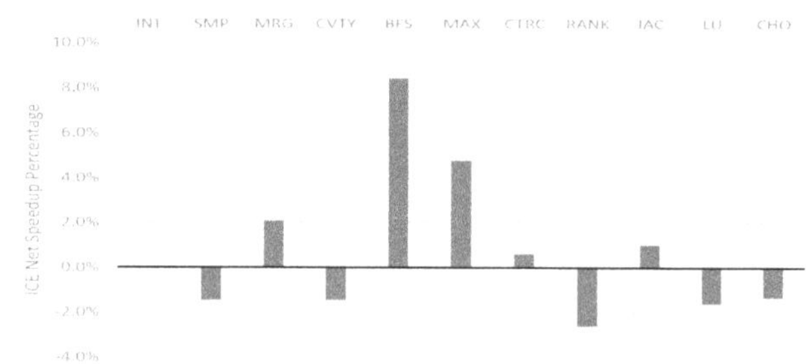

Figure 3: ICE Net speedup normalized to optimized XMTC

As we see in figure 3, ICE code achieves comparable performance to hand-optimized XMTC code, in spite of the latter taking considerably greater programming effort. ICE has a 0.76% speedup on average, with maximum slowdown of 2.5% when compared to the performance of optimized XMTC. We also notice that for some benchmarks, ICE has achieved a speed up when compared to hand-optimized XMTC. However, we do not claim in this work that ICE can provide speed ups over XMTC.

4. ACKNOWLEDGMENTS

Partial support by NSF award 1161857 is gratefully acknowledged.

References

[1] U. Vishkin, "Using simple abstraction to guide the reinvention of computing for parallelism," *CACM*, vol. 54,1, pp. 75–85, 2011.

POSTER: Fault-tolerant Execution on COTS Multi-core Processors with Hardware Transactional Memory Support

Florian Haas, Sebastian Weis, and Theo Ungerer
Department of Computer Science
University of Augsburg, Germany
{haas,weis,ungerer}@informatik.uni-augsburg.de

Gilles Pokam, Youfeng Wu
Intel Corporation, Santa Clara
{gilles.a.pokam,youfeng.wu}@intel.com

ABSTRACT

Software-based fault-tolerance mechanisms can increase the reliability of multi-core CPUs while being cheaper and more flexible than hardware solutions like lockstep architectures. However, checkpoint creation, error detection and correction entail high performance overhead if implemented in software. We propose a software/hardware hybrid approach, which leverages Intel's hardware transactional memory (TSX) to support implicit checkpoint creation and fast rollback. Hardware enhancements are proposed and evaluated, leading to a resulting performance overhead of 19 % on average.

1. INTRODUCTION & RELATED WORK

Intel introduced the *Transactional Synchronization Extensions* (TSX) as part of the Haswell instruction set architecture [2]. TSX uses the L1 cache to hold back transactional data, which have not yet committed. Its implicit rollback mechanism can be utilized for fault tolerance to recover from detected errors. Loosely coupled lockstep architectures like [4] support multi-core processors, but complex changes to the hardware are required. A similar, but software-only approach is PLR [3]. An approach which leverages transactional memory for error correction was proposed in [1].

This paper presents an evaluation for the Intel Haswell architecture and with respect for proposed hardware enhancements. The instrumentation mechanisms provide an increased code coverage with less performance overhead than other approaches. Combining the flexibility of software-based redundant execution with existing hardware transactional memory allows efficient checkpointing and rollback for fault-tolerant execution of individual applications.

2. ERROR DETECTION & RECOVERY

The main principle of our approach is to execute each user process redundantly and to instrument signature-based comparison on function level. The loosely coupled execution of both processes allows error detection. With the encapsulation of blocks in transactions, error recovery is realized. The instrumentation is done on the binary and the process duplication takes place at runtime. Thus, the executed code of both processes is almost identical.

Comparison of both processes is done on the level of function-based blocks. For an efficient comparison, we create signatures of these blocks which then are exchanged from one process to its duplicate. Fig. 1 shows a schematic of the redundant execution and block-based comparison. A process is duplicated at a user-defined entry point function call. All code within this function is executed redundantly (step 1). Binary instrumentation divides this code into blocks, which are aligned at function boundaries (step 2). Signatures of these blocks are calculated in each process and transferred from the leading process to the trailing process through a shared-memory FIFO queue (step 3). Only the trailing process instruments transaction begin and end instructions around each block. Before committing the transaction, the locally calculated signature and the leading process' signature are compared. In case of a detected error, the transaction is explicitly aborted, leading to a restart at the beginning of the block. To ensure a correct state of the leading process, it is killed by means of the operating system and a `fork` creates a new leading process. The program execution then continues at the beginning of the previously faulty block.

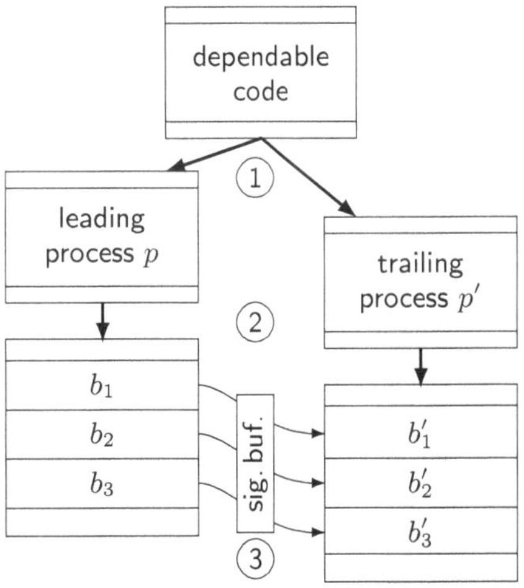

Figure 1: Instrumentation on function-based blocks b_n and redundant execution in processes p and p'.

PACT '16 September 11-15, 2016, Haifa, Israel

ACM ISBN 978-1-4503-4121-9/16/09.
DOI: http://dx.doi.org/10.1145/2967938.2974051

3. HARDWARE ENHANCEMENTS

We propose hardware enhancements for the Intel Haswell micro-architecture, which could further improve our approach in terms of code coverage and performance. The potential impact of these enhancements is investigated by emulation:

Signature Generation.

Since the most relevant bottleneck is the signature generation, our approach benefits from hardware signature generation. A possible hardware extension may calculate the signature implicitly, by issuing a hash calculation on every read from a register and on every write to a register or to memory. The signature can be stored in a dedicated register, which can be reset and read by the software.

Hardware Queue.

Further improvement is possible by supporting signature exchange in hardware. This requires a mechanism to send data uni-directional between individual cores, additionally with buffering to form a FIFO queue. It is sufficient to connect pairs of cores, a queue between every single core is not required. The assignment of processes to cores is handled by the software library.

Transactional Memory.

Enhancements to TSX can also increase the performance of our approach. Increased robustness of TSX lowers the overhead related to aborting transactions. In our approach, transactions should not abort in the error-free case, since conflicts do not occur. Robust transactions which survive events like cache-overflows, interrupts and system calls allow a guaranteed transactional execution, resulting in a better coverage and less overhead for instrumented programs. Furthermore, the communication between transactions will always lead to conflicts between both processes, and thus prohibits parallel transactional execution of both redundant processes. With escape actions, signatures can be exchanged during the commit phase. The transaction will only be allowed to commit if the signatures match. Otherwise, both transactions roll back and try again. This reduces overhead of error-correction.

4. EVALUATION

Fault-tolerant execution of instrumented benchmarks leads to varying amount of runtime overhead. The code coverage for all selected benchmarks is 92.5 % on average. To determine the sources of the overhead, parts of the instrumentation have been measured individually. Results are shown in Fig. 2. One source of overhead is the transaction instructions, which wrap

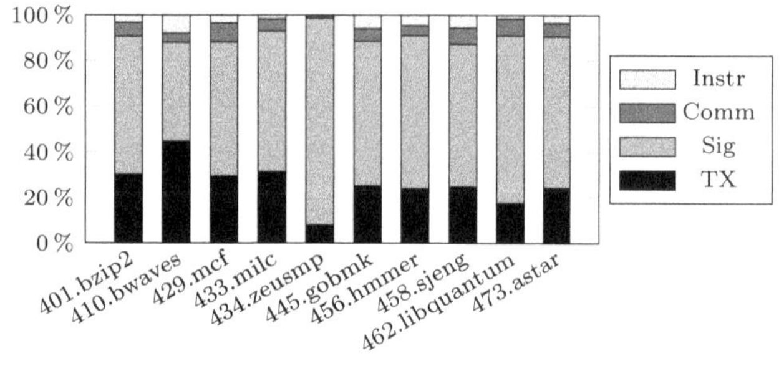

Figure 2: Performance overhead arising from transaction instructions, signature generation and exchange, and binary instrumentation.

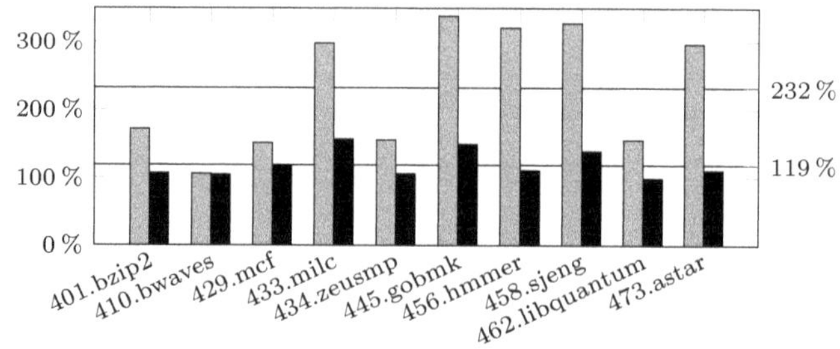

Figure 3: Runtime of instrumented benchmarks compared to original execution. Average overhead is 132 % (gray bars). The black bars show the performance with hardware optimizations (19 % overhead on average).

the dependable blocks in the trailing process. Since TSX does not guarantee a non-conflicting transaction to commit eventually, random aborts may occur. Within Fig. 2, the fraction of the performance overhead related to transactional memory instructions is shown in the black bars at the bottom. The overhead of individual, per-block generation of signatures depends on the size of the blocks and on the number of blocks. The impact of signature generation can be seen in the third gray bar from top in Fig. 2. The execution time overhead related to signature exchange through the FIFO queue is shown in the second gray bars from the top in Fig. 2. Remaining overhead is due to additional instructions inserted during instrumentation. The gray bars on top in Fig. 2 represent the instrumentation overhead, which is 3.95 % on average.

The gray bars in Fig. 3 show the relative execution time of the fault-tolerant execution compared to the original benchmark execution. On the Haswell Core i7, the redundant execution on two cores takes more than twice the time for some benchmarks, and 132 % on average. The emulation of hardware support for signature generation and exchange leads to significantly improved performance. The overhead of our approach could be decreased to reach a relative performance overhead of 19 % on average (see black bars in Fig. 3). The overhead can be further reduced with enhancements to TSX, e. g. escape actions or guaranteed transactional execution. This also increases the overall applicability.

5. REFERENCES

[1] F. Haas, S. Weis, S. Metzlaff, and T. Ungerer. Exploiting Intel TSX for Fault-Tolerant Execution in Safety-Critical Systems. In *Proceedings of the International Symposium on Defect and Fault Tolerance in VLSI and Nanotechnology Systems (DFT)*, pages 197–202, 2014.

[2] P. Hammarlund, A. J. Martinez, A. A. Bajwa, D. L. Hill, E. Hallnor, et al. Haswell: The Fourth-Generation Intel Core Processor. *IEEE Micro*, 34(2):6–20, 2014.

[3] A. Shye, J. Blomstedt, T. Moseley, V. J. Reddi, and D. A. Connors. PLR: A Software Approach to Transient Fault Tolerance for Multicore Architectures. *IEEE Transactions on Dependable and Secure Computing (TDSC)*, 6(2):135–148, 2009.

[4] J. C. Smolens, B. T. Gold, B. Falsafi, and J. C. Hoe. Reunion: Complexity-Effective Multicore Redundancy. In *Proceedings of the International Symposium on Microarchitecture (MICRO)*, pages 223–234, 2006.

POSTER - Collective Dynamic Parallelism for Directive Based GPU Programming Languages and Compilers

Guray Ozen
Barcelona Supercomputing Center, Universitat Politecnica de Catalunya
Barcelona, Spain
guray.ozen@bsc.es

Eduard Ayguade
Barcelona Supercomputing Center, Universitat Politecnica de Catalunya
Barcelona, Spain
eduard.ayguade@bsc.es

Jesus Labarta
Barcelona Supercomputing Center, Universitat Politecnica de Catalunya
Barcelona, Spain
jesus.labarta@bsc.es

ABSTRACT

Early programs for GPU (Graphics Processing Units) acceleration were based on a flat, bulk parallel programming model, in which programs had to perform a sequence of kernel launches from the host CPU. In the latest releases of these devices, dynamic (or nested) parallelism is supported, making possible to launch kernels from threads running on the device, without host intervention. Unfortunately, the overhead of launching kernels from the device is higher compared to launching from the host CPU, making the exploitation of dynamic parallelism unprofitable.

This paper proposes and evaluates the basic idea behind a user-directed code transformation technique, named collective dynamic parallelism, that targets the effective exploitation of nested parallelism in modern GPUs. The technique dynamically packs dynamic parallelism kernel invocations and postpones their execution until a bunch of them are available. We show that for sparse matrix vector multiplication, CollectiveDP outperforms well optimized libraries, making GPU useful when matrices are highly irregular.

1. INTRODUCTION AND MOTIVATION

Graphics Processing Units (GPU) have become an essential component in high-performance computing) architectures to address the computational and energy-efficiency requirements of a broad range of applications. Early GPU programs were based on a flat, bulk parallel programming model, in which programs had to perform a sequence of kernel launches, each kernel trying to expose enough data parallelism to efficiently use the available resources in the GPU. In order to give support to more irregular codes (e.g. graph algorithms with irregular data access patterns and unpredictable control flows), the latest GPU released architectures include Dynamic Parallelism (DP). DP makes it possible to launch kernels from threads running on the device, without intervention of the threads running on the host processor.

Unfortunately, the overhead of launching kernels from the device is much higher compared to launching from the host. Recent studies [2, 3] show that DP introduces a noticeable overhead during kernel launch, precluding in most cases the exploitation of nested parallelism to improve application performance. In order to mitigate this overhead, this paper proposes Collective Dynamic Parallelism (CollectiveDP), a code transformation technique for directive-based programming model in order to efficiently exploit the potential performance of nested parallelism.

OpenMP and OpenACC are the two most widely used directive-based GPU programming languages. The latest version of OpenACC supports nested parallel regions to target DP in recent Nvidia GPUs; however OpenMP standard does not support yet. A recent study [1] proposed the semantics for nested teams regions in OpenMP and gave an implementation based on the use of DP. Figure 1 shows a simple example to illustrate the support for directive nesting in these two approaches.

```
/* Nested parallelism in OpenACC */
#pragma acc parallel loop
for (int i = 0; i < N-1; ++i) {
  #pragma acc parallel loop
  for (int j = arr[i] ; j < arr[i+1] ; ++j)
      // BB.Process
}

/* Nested parallelism in extended OpenMP */
#pragma omp target
#pragma omp teams distribute parallel for
for (int i = 0; i < N-1; ++i) {
  #pragma omp teams distribute parallel for
  for (int j = arr[i] ; j < arr[i+1] ; ++j)
      // BB.Process
}
```

Figure 1: Simple example with nested regions in OpenACC and extended OpenMP [1].

2. CODE TRANSFORMATION

In DP a parent kernel can instantiate the execution of child kernels. Instead of directly launching the execution of these child kernels, *CollectiveDP* dynamically bundles kernel instantiations made by the parent kernel and postpones their execution until a sufficiently large number of them is available, mitigating the excessive overhead introduced by DP. To do that, *CollectiveDP* saves in a buffer the necessary context (variables) of the parent kernel in order to execute the child kernel instantiation a posteriori. Finally, when all threads executing the parent kernel finish, *CollectiveDP* launches the execution of a single kernel, named *Next-Level*

PACT '16 September 11-15, 2016, Haifa, Israel

ACM ISBN 978-1-4503-4121-9/16/09.
DOI: http://dx.doi.org/10.1145/2967938.2974056

parallel Kernel (NLK), to actually execute the finer-grained invocations in parallel. Hence, *CollectiveDP* is able to thoroughly minimize kernel launching count and making nested parallelism usable, providing the right granularity for irregular applications.

Figure 2 shows the skeleton of the transformed code implementing the basic *CollectiveDP* idea. After initializing the data structures necessary to support *CollectiveDP* in `BB.CollectiveDP.Init` (line 2), the parent kernel may iterate several times (lines 5–6) depending on the size of the problem `N`. Later, each thread executing the parent kernel decides (conditional statement in line 8, checking if enough iterations need to be executed) whether to immediately execute the loop (lines 11–14) or to save the context for postponed execution of the loop as a child kernel (line 9). Finally, in `BB.CollectiveDP.HandleCases` (line 16) all postponed kernel invocations are executed through a single *NLK* dispatch (line 19). The thread responsible for launching *NLK* can be either the master of warp or the master of CTA (two implementations named -CTA and -WARP).

```
1 __global__ macc_collectivedp(..., MT* buffer) {
2   BB.CollectiveDP.Init
3   int tid = threadIdx+blockIdx.x * blockDim.x;
4   int numThreads = grimdDim.x * blockDim.x;
5   for (int u = tid; u < N;
6            u += numThreads) {
7     BB.BeforeProcess
8     if (tc > threshold)
9       BB.CollectiveDP.Save
10    else {
11      for(int p = ptrs[u];
12          p < ptrs[u+1]; p++)
13            BB.Process
14      BB.AfterProcess
15    }
16    BB.CollectiveDP.HandleCases
17    if(macc_master() && buff_counter) {
18      int BS = get_optimal_thread();
19      macc_NLK<<<buff_counter,BS>>>(...);
20} } }
```

Figure 2: Code transformation skeleton for the exemple in Figure 1.

Figure 3 shows the skeleton for the *NLK* kernel that processes the contexts that were saved in a buffer (`buffer`) for postponed kernel executions. First, *NLK* pops a context of the parent thread according to its block identifier; after that it simply executes the code in the original kernel with the context popped from the buffer in parallel. In this example, the context only contains the value of `u` in Figure 2.

```
__global__ void macc_NLK(..., MT *buffer) {
  int u = buffer[blockIdx.x].macc_u;
  for(int p = ptrs[u] + threadIdx.x ;
      p < ptrs[u + 1]; p += blockDim.x)
        BB.Process
  BB.AfterProcess
}
```

Figure 3: NLK generated by the compiler

3. EVALUATION

Experiments are done on compute nodes equipped with a CPU Intel(R) Core(TM) i7-4820K, 64GB of main memory, executing 64-bit Debian OS and a Nvidia Tesla Titan-X GPU with 3072 CUDA cores, compute capability 5.2 and 12GB of device memory.

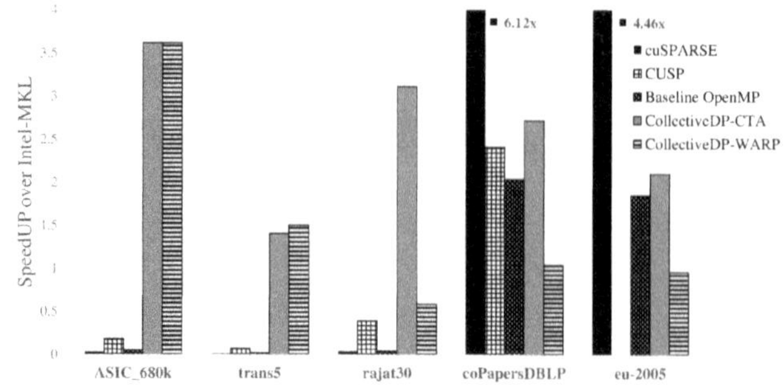

Figure 4: Speed–up for SpMV over Intel MKL library on the host.

We selected sparse matrix vector multiplication (SpMV `y = Ax`), one of the most used kernels in HPC. We compared *CollectiveDP* with state-of-the-art libraries: Nvidia cuSPARSE and CUSP. Figure 4 presents the speed–ups, relative to Intel MKL library (11.2 using Intel OpenMP) executed on the host, that are obtained with the different *CollectiveDP* approaches. For highly irregular input matrices (on the left) *CollectiveDP* speeds up up to 3.61x, 1.6x and 3.16x; for the other two less irregular matrices it achieves maximum speed-up of 2.7x and 2.1x.

4. CONCLUSION

This paper proposes and evaluates a code transformation technique, *CollectiveDP* to effectively support nested parallelism in GPUs, mainly tailored to compilers for user-directed accelerator programming models such as OpenACC or OpenMP. *CollectiveDP* dynamically packs kernel invocations and postpones their execution until a bunch of them are available. Performance is evaluated using different input matrices for a sparse matrix vector multiplication kernel.

5. ACKNOWLEDGMENTS

This work is partially supported by the IBM/BSC Deep Learning Center Initiative, by the Spanish Government (Severo Ochoa program SEV-2015-0493), by the Spanish Ministry of Science and Technology (TIN2015-65316-P project) and by the Generalitat de Catalunya (contract 2014-SGR-1051).

References

[1] G. Ozen, E. Ayguadé, and J. Labarta. Exploring dynamic parallelism in openmp. In *Proceedings of the Second Workshop on Accelerator Programming using Directives, WACCPD 2015, Austin, Texas, USA, November 15, 2015*, pages 5:1–5:8, 2015.

[2] J. Wang and S. Yalamanchili. Characterization and analysis of dynamic parallelism in unstructured GPU applications. In *2014 IEEE International Symposium on Workload Characterization, IISWC 2014, Raleigh, NC, USA, October 26-28, 2014*, pages 51–60, 2014.

[3] Y. Yang and H. Zhou. CUDA-NP: realizing nested thread-level parallelism in GPGPU applications. In *ACM SIGPLAN Symposium on Principles and Practice of Parallel Programming, PPoPP '14, Orlando, FL, USA, February 15-19, 2014*, pages 93–106, 2014.

POSTER – Firestorm: Operating Systems for Power-Constrained Architectures

Sankaralingam Panneerselvam
University of Wisconsin-Madison
sankarp@cs.wisc.edu

Michael Swift
University of Wisconsin-Madison
swift@cs.wisc.edu

Hardware Trends. Moore's law paved the way for doubling the transistors in the same chip area with every generation. However, with the end of Dennard's scaling, voltage and hence the power draw of transistors is no longer dropping proportionally to size. As a result, modern processors cannot use all parts of the processor simultaneously without exceeding the power limit. This manifests as an increasing proportion of *dark silicon* [4]. In other words, the compute capacity of current and future processors is and will be over-provisioned with respect to the available power.

Power limits are influenced by different factors such as the capacity of power distribution infrastructure, battery supply limits, and the thermal capacity of the system. Power limits in datacenters can arise from underprovisioning power distribution units relative to peak power draw. Energy limits are also dictated by the limited capacity of batteries. However, in many systems, the primary limit comes not from the ability to acquire power, but instead from the ability to dissipate power as *heat* once it has been used.

Thermal limits are dictated by the physical properties of the processor materials and also comfort of the user.Thus, power is limited to prevent processor chips from overheating, which can lead to thermal breakdown. As a result, the maximum performance of a system is limited by its *cooling capacity*, which determines its ability to dissipate heat. Cooling capacity varies across the computing landscape, from servers with external chilled air to desktops with large fans to laptops to fan-less mobile devices.

Current Support. Processors support mechanisms to enforce both power and temperature limits. For example, recent Intel processors provide Running Average Power Limit (RAPL) counters to enforce a power limit on the entire processor [1]. In software, power capping services, such as the Linux power capping framework uses these limits to control power usage. Processor vendors define Thermal Design Power (TDP) metric for every processor model to guide the requirements of the cooling system needed to dissipate power. Most processors have a safeguard mechanism that throttles the processor by reducing the frequency or duty cycle (fraction of cycles where work happens) on reaching a critical temperature. In software, the thermal daemon [11] tries to achieve system-wide goals, such as maximum performance by increasing cooling before throttling the processors.

PACT '16 September 11-15, 2016, Haifa, Israel

ACM ISBN 978-1-4503-4121-9/16/09.
DOI: http://dx.doi.org/10.1145/2967938.2975607

Challenges. The drawback with current hardware and software mechanisms that enforce power and thermal limits are that *they only offer system-wide guarantees but are ignorant of individual application needs and priorities.* This raises following challenges in a shared environment.

Power distribution: When power is limited, current systems throttle all applications equally. However, this approach ignores users' scheduling priorities: power should be distributed among applications based on their importance, so that high-priority applications can use more power to run faster, while low-priority applications have their power reduced and bear most of the performance lost.

Thermal interference: An application that makes heavy use of a processor can trigger temperature throttling that reduces CPU frequency or duty cycle. This can affect all cores, and hence all running applications. As a result, a low priority or malicious application can trigger throttling that reduces the performance of high-priority applications.

Performance Boosting: Applications may be able to temporarily overclock the core to achieve extra performance if they run for short enough periods such that throttling does not get triggered. This is often called computational sprinting [9]. Turbo Boost [6] is similar but more conservative. The challenge is to ensure sufficient thermal headroom to run without overheating by not allowing other applications to exhaust the thermal capacity of the processor.

Firestorm. Just as the OS actively manages resources such as CPU and memory, we argue that operating systems should treat power and thermal capacity as primary resources in the system. Towards this goal, we built Firestorm, an extension to Linux that adds power and thermal awareness. Firestorm introduces new abstractions to enable resource management over power and thermal capacity. It presents new interfaces for applications to gather power and thermal resources, and allow application-specific use of power and thermal capacity for guaranteed performance. Finally, it employs new policies to balance the varied performance requirements of different applications. The overall architecture of Firestorm is shown in Figure 1.

Power as a Resource. Firestorm focuses on power-limited architectures where all compute units cannot be used at maximum performance within the power budget. Firestorm enforces control over the total power consumed by processing

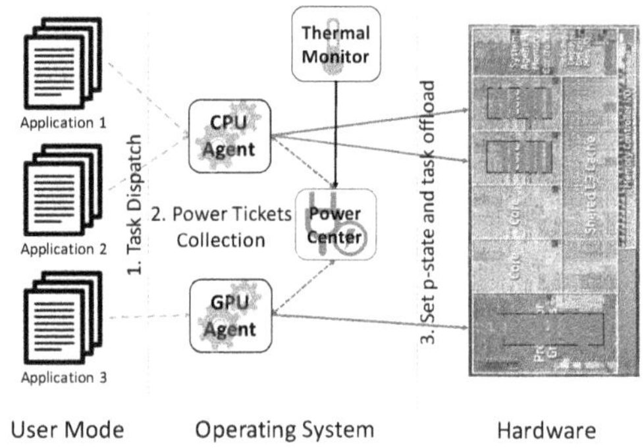

Figure 1: Control flow in Firestorm

units as well as the power consumed by individual applications to enable application guarantees and at the same time avoid interference across applications.

Firestorm abstracts the notion of power in the form of *power tickets* to quantify power as a resource in the system. A power ticket represents the ability to use power: for example, a ticket represents the ability to use one hundredth of a watt. All tickets in the system are managed by a *power center* that can enforce a power limit by controlling the total number of tickets available to the system.

Firestorm requires all applications to gather power before executing their tasks on any compute unit (e.g., CPU or GPU). This is enforced through agents that act as resources managers for each type of compute unit. Any use of a compute unit by an application has to go through the corresponding agent. The agent predicts the power requirement of a task using a compute-unit-specific power model and tries to acquire the required power tickets from the power center. Firestorm employs a pay-before-use model, to ensure the performance of an application is proportional to the power received and also to stay within power limits.

The center employs a proportional share policy to distribute power, which distributes power tickets to applications based on the shares assigned to them. The policy also help isolate applications from each other by ensuring applications to receive their shares irrespective of other applications in the system. Firestorm also support preemption of power tickets when application shares change or a new application enters the system. The share allocation is automatically readjusted by the proportional share policy.

Heat as a Resource. Firestorm takes initial steps toward introducing thermal awareness into operating systems. It avoids or minimizes thermal interference caused by low-priority applications and also allows applications to reserve thermal capacity to ensure guaranteed performance. The above are made possible by promoting thermal capacity as a primary resource in the system.

Firestorm incorporates a *thermal monitor* to avoid thermal interference and reserve thermal capacity. The monitor tracks the processor temperature and take necessary actions based on the policy it employs. The *selective throttling* policy help isolate applications from thermal interference caused by background or low priority applications. When the processor is nearing the critical temperature (temperature beyond which processors can breakdown), power given to low priority applications is reduced. The monitor notifies the power center to reduce the number of power tickets issued to those applications. Performance of important applications is preserved at the cost of low priority applications.

In order to support the thermal requirements of high-priority programs, Firestorm introduces a new *thermal conserve* policy that allows applications to reserve thermal capacity (i.e., keep the processor cooler) needed during execution. Thus, the system does not allow other applications to raise the temperature too high and thus exhaust the thermal capacity. Firestorm incorporates a system-specific thermal model to predict the thermal capacity needed based on the work to be performed by an application.

Firestorm abstracts the thermal capacity of the system in terms of the processor chip temperature. The difference between the current chip temperature and the critical temperature is the available thermal capacity of the system. To make it usable, the system offers a thermal model to predict the amount of time required for the chip temperature to rise from a start temperature to an end temperature. The model is based on the amount of work done by the processor which is the power consumption of the compute units.

Processors from Intel [6], AMD [2] and Samsung [3] boost single core performance only when sufficient thermal headroom is available (neighboring cores are in idle state). In order to provide the benefits of boosted frequency to important applications, Firestorm extends Chameleon's [8] execution object abstraction to aggregate thermal headroom from multiple cores to be used by fewer cores. This is done by creating execution object over multiple cores where few cores are forced to an idle state and the resultant power savings is used to boost the performance of the active cores.

Contributions. Firestorm actively allocates power to applications, reserves thermal capacity for high-priority applications and enable software control over the use of turbo boost like techniques. It also provide interfaces required for a system to interact with a power and a thermal model for making power management decisions, and present simple power and thermal models that are fast and simple enough to deploy practically.

Results. Through experiments we show that Firestorm is able to assign more power to applications with higher shares and prevent interference from lower priority programs. Firestorm also balances the performance of multiple applications under a power budget compared to the native Linux RAPL mechanism that prefers parallel programs over sequential programs. In a case where thermal interference from background application costs performance, Firestorm allows high-priority tasks to run at full speed, as compared to 19% slower under native Linux, while background tasks in Firestorm run 28% slower to reduce heat production.

Prior Work. The prior works can be classified under the theme of improving performance (e.g., [7]) or energy efficiency (e.g., [10]), and minimizing interference within a power or thermal limit (e.g., [5]). These works differ from ours in that they assume a homogeneous set of application performance goals, while our work deliberately targets systems that run a mix of soft real time, best effort, and background tasks. Also, power available and thermal capacity are dependent on each other, where one without another does not guarantee performance. Power without thermal capacity results in overheating and thermal capacity without power results in low performance due to insufficient power to run processor at a higher speed. Our system takes a holistic view on both power and thermal capacity by allowing applications to co-allocate them for better performance.

1. REFERENCES

[1] "Intel® 64 and IA-32 Architectures Software Developer Manuals," http://www.intel.com/content/www/us/en/processors/architectures-software-developer-manuals.html, December 2015.

[2] AMD Corporation, "AMD Turbo Core Technology."

[3] Andrei Frumusanu, "Early Exynos 8890 Impressions And Full Specifications," http://www.anandtech.com/show/10075/early-exynos-8890-impressions.

[4] H. Esmaeilzadeh, E. Blem, R. S. Amant, K. Sankaralingam, and D. Burger, "Dark Silicon and the End of Multicore Scaling," in *Proc. ISCA*, Jun. 2011.

[5] M. Gomaa, M. D. Powell, and T. N. Vijaykumar, "Heat-and-run: Leveraging smt and cmp to manage power density through the operating system," in *Proceedings of the 11th International Conference on Architectural Support for Programming Languages and Operating Systems*, ser. ASPLOS XI, 2004, pp. 260–270.

[6] Intel Corporation, "Intel Turbo Boost Technology 2.0," http://www.intel.com/content/www/us/en/architecture-and-technology/turbo-boost/turbo-boost-technology.html.

[7] J. Li and J. F. Martinez, "Dynamic power-performance adaptation of parallel computation on chip multiprocessors," in *High-Performance Computer Architecture, 2006. The Twelfth International Symposium on*, Feb 2006, pp. 77–87.

[8] S. Panneerselvam and M. M. Swift, "Chameleon: operating system support for dynamic processors," in *Proceedings of the seventeenth international conference on Architectural Support for Programming Languages and Operating Systems*, ser. ASPLOS '12, 2012, pp. 99–110.

[9] A. Raghavan, Y. Luo, A. Chandawalla, M. Papaefthymiou, K. P. Pipe, T. F. Wenisch, and M. M. K. Martin, "Computational sprinting," in *Proc. 18th HPCA*. Washington, DC, USA: IEEE Computer Society, 2012, pp. 1–12.

[10] T. Somu Muthukaruppan, A. Pathania, and T. Mitra, "Price theory based power management for heterogeneous multi-cores," in *Proceedings of the 19th International Conference on Architectural Support for Programming Languages and Operating Systems*, ser. ASPLOS '14, 2014, pp. 161–176.

[11] "Linux Thermal Daemon," https://01.org/linux-thermal-daemon.

POSTER: ξ-TAO: A Cache-centric Execution Model and Runtime for Deep Parallel Multicore Topologies

Miquel Pericàs
Chalmers University of Technology, SE-412 96 Göteborg, Sweden
miquelp@chalmers.se

1. INTRODUCTION

Computational task DAGs are executed on parallel computers by a task scheduling algorithm. Intelligent scheduling is critical for achieving high parallelism, low overheads and reduced communication. A key technique for load balancing task DAGs is work stealing (WS), which Blumofe et al. popularized for fork-join computations [2]. In scenarios of high parallel slackness, WS's distributed nature allows it to scale to a large number of cores with low overhead [4]. However, the space of a WS computation grows proportionally to the number of cores. Targeting a lower bound, Blelloch et al. proposed the parallel-depth-first (PDF) scheduler [1]. PDF schedules tasks by following the depth-first (serial) order of computation and has space requirements closer to the serial execution. PDF has been shown to provide constructive cache sharing in modern multicore architectures [3]. However, implementing PDF requires a centralized scheduler which limits scalability. Targeting NUMA architectures, Olivier et al. proposed to load balance multiple PDF schedulers via WS [8]. While enabling scalability to larger systems, such approach still suffers from centralized scheduling of fine-grained parallelism [9]. Furthermore, for applications in which the amount of parallelism varies greatly, a fixed hierarchy of PDF queues is not enough.

NUMA architectures pose an additional challenge for WS and PDF. These schedulers were developed in a context in which the total work per computation could be assumed constant. However, modern multicores and manycores are increasingly bound by shared cache capacity and memory bandwidth, potentially leading to work time inflation (WTI) [7]. To adapt to the complexities of modern NUMA systems it is important to optimize cache use and reduce pressure on the memory bandwidth. However, most runtimes implement greedy scheduling algorithms which attempt to keep cores busy. This can easily lead to memory bandwidth saturation and inefficient cache use. Thread-centric execution models are ill-equipped for managing resources in modern NUMA systems with shared caches. Instead, what is called for is a cache-centric execution model.

PACT '16 September 11-15, 2016, Haifa, Israel

ACM ISBN 978-1-4503-4121-9/16/09.
DOI: http://dx.doi.org/10.1145/2967938.2974052

2. THE ξ-TAO EXECUTION MODEL

Our goal is to develop a distributed scheduler similar to work-stealing with the constructive cache sharing provided by PDF-like schedules. Furthermore, in the event of cache and bandwidth saturation, we want the scheduler to avoid scheduling tasks beyond the capacity of individual processors. We call this *cache-centric* scheduling.

PDF exposes parallelism on the depth-first traversal of the task DAG. In order to feed a large number of cores, finer-grained tasks need to be generated, similar to strong scaling. However, parallelism is usually organized in patterns [5]. Even in dynamically generated task graphs subsets of the depth-first traversal can frequently be identified offline. We leverage this observation to overcome the costly discovery and scheduling of fine-grained parallelism. Instead of traditional single-threaded tasks, we propose to organize applications based on pre-built task groups with internal data sharing. These task groups become the basic scheduling units of the application's dynamic task graph. This procedure can be viewed as a form of coarsening in which depth-first partitions of the task graph are encapsulated into multithreaded computations.

This poster presents an execution model called ξ-TAO ("XiTAO" in Latin script) and a supporting runtime called `GO:TAO` which implement this idea. In ξ-TAO the vertices of the computational DAG (called the TAO-DAG) are *generalized* tasks known as Task Assembly Objects (TAO). A TAO is a scheduling unit containing a task graph, a scheduling policy and a resource requirement. The internal task graph consists of single-threaded tasks that are either independent or synchronized by explicit dependencies. Each TAO can attach its own scheduler. When there are no dependencies, as is often the case in loops, a *static* policy allows ξ-TAO to partition the work among the cores with negligible overhead, similar to OpenMP's `omp for schedule(static)`. If dependencies exist, a *dynamic* scheduler that tracks task readiness is appropriate. Finally, the *resource requirement* specifies how many cores the TAO needs for execution. At the source level, a TAO sees only *virtual* cores. The virtual cores are assigned physical core numbers during the mapping process. Once assigned, TAO mappings are irrevocable. This scheme has two benefits: First, since cores are hardwired to cache memories, by selecting a number of cores we implicitly specify at which level of the memory hierarchy reuse and sharing should happen. Second, since a TAO holds the resources during its execution, this scheme can be used to avoid interfering tasks from executing on idle cores that share the same cache or memory access. Finally, a TAO

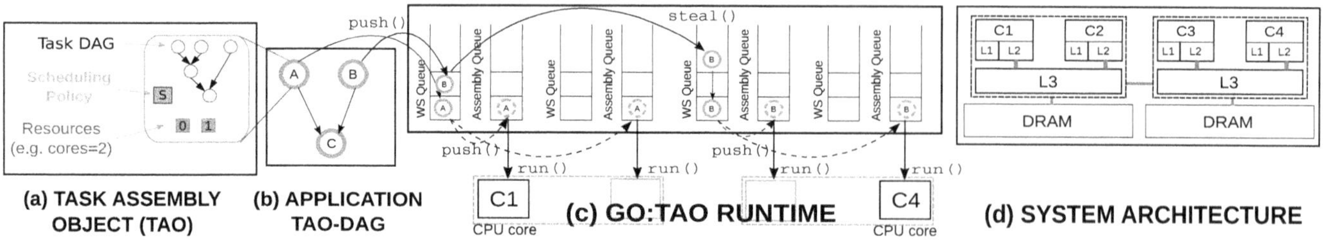

Figure 1: A TAO (a) is composed of a task graph, a scheduler and a resource requirement. The application is a general DAG of TAOs (b). The `GO:TAO` runtime (c) pushes ready TAOs from the TAO-DAG into distributed `WS` queues with support for load balancing via work stealing. TAOs are mapped to the system topology (d) by pushing them into a set of distributed, FIFO-ordered Assembly Queues (one per core). Finally, the cores asynchronously fetch TAO references and jointly start working on the TAO objects.

can also contain a virtual topology location which indicates to which NUMA node or cache a specific TAO should be scheduled. This is akin to the problem of topological mapping in MPI, and can be used to improve TAO locality with respect to caches and DRAM.

The architecture of ξ-TAO enables many desirable properties in scheduling:

1. *Distributed work queues.* Distributed per-core work-stealing queues can be used. This allows TAOs to be scheduled in parallel with low overhead.
2. *Coarse-grained stealing.* Restricting work stealing to TAOs avoids expensive steals of fine-grained work units.
3. *Locality-aware scheduling.* Several techniques can be used to improve locality. First, TAOs can be dynamically mapped to cores sharing particular levels of caches, enabling constructive cache sharing. Second, by executing consumer tasks on the same caches as their parents temporal reuse can be achieved. Third, the TAO-DAG expresses inter-TAO locality that can be exploited by a depth-first traversal of the TAO-DAG. And fourth, *topological mapping* enables the exploitation of reuses across distant TAO objects.
4. *Cache-centric scheduling*: Individual TAOs can dynamically set their resource requirements to map different levels of caches, processor interconnect links and memory controllers. By avoiding idle cores to run computations when cache capacity and memory bandwidth resources are already exhausted, the resources of the system can be managed more efficiently.
5. *Hierarchical scheduling*: Since TAOs attach a local scheduler, they can optimize their own execution. Unconventional schedulers beyond *static* or *dynamic* are transparently supported.

We have implemented these concepts in a compact runtime written in C++11 called `GO:TAO`. `GO:TAO` implements a distributed scheduler which manages TAOs via work stealing queues and maps individual objects to locality domains of the system topology. Figure 1 shows the concept of task assemblies and summarizes how `GO:TAO` operates.

3. RESULTS

We have analyzed the ξ-TAO model and runtime with three benchmarks: a parallel hybrid quicksort/mergesort, a 2D Jacobi stencil, and the Unbalanced Tree Search (UTS) benchmark. We run ξ-TAO implementations of these benchmarks on a Dell PowerEdge R815 server with four AMD Opteron 6348 processors, totalling 8 NUMA nodes and 48 cores. Figure 2 shows the scalability of UTS+ξ-TAO compared to thread-centric runtimes based on work stealing (MassiveThreads [6], Intel TBB) and hierarchical WS+PDF (Qthreads [10]). UTS was implemented in ξ-TAO by grouping sibling nodes into a TAO and attaching a static scheduler. UTS has a very small working set, hence the best performance is achieved when each TAO is mapped to a single core (ξ-TAO-w1). The combination of tight reuse, pre-built task groups and static scheduling results in high scalability for UTS+ξ-TAO. Unlike UTS, the parallel sorting and 2D Jacobi benchmarks are memory intensive benchmarks. By selecting assemblies of width *two* (i.e., *core-width* of the L2 caches) and *six* (i.e., *core-width* of the L3 cache) ξ-TAO is able to outperform competing approaches thanks to better management of available memory bandwidth and shared cache capacity.

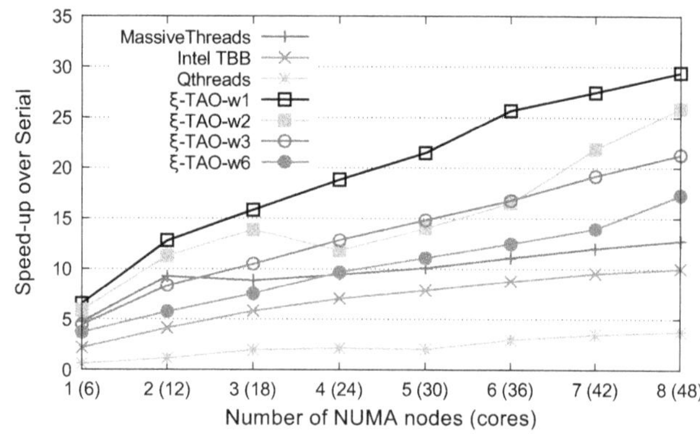

Figure 2: UTS+ξ-TAO scalability for different TAO core-widths (-wx) compared to WS and PDF+WS runtimes

Acknowledgments

This work has been supported in part by the Swedish Foundation for Strategic Research (SSF) under the SCHEME project (RIT10-0033).

4. REFERENCES

[1] G. E. Blelloch, P. B. Gibbons, and Y. Matias. Provably efficient scheduling for languages with fine-grained parallelism. *Journal of the ACM*, 46(2):281–321, Mar. 1999.

[2] R. D. Blumofe and C. E. Leiserson. Scheduling multithreaded computations by work stealing. *Journal of the ACM*, 46(5):720–748, Sept. 1999.

[3] S. Chen, P. B. Gibbons, M. Kozuch, V. Liaskovitis, A. Ailamaki, G. E. Blelloch, B. Falsafi, L. Fix, N. Hardavellas, T. C. Mowry, and C. Wilkerson. Scheduling Threads for Constructive Cache Sharing on CMPs. 2007.

[4] M. Frigo, C. E. Leiserson, and K. H. Randall. The Implementation of the Cilk-5 Multithreaded Language. In *Proceedings of SIGPLAN 1998*, June 1998.

[5] T. Mattson, B. Sanders, and B. Massingill. *Patterns for Parallel Programming*. Addison-Wesley Professional, first edition, 2004.

[6] J. Nakashima and K. Taura. Massivethreads: A thread library for high productivity languages. 8665:222–238, 2014.

[7] S. L. Olivier, B. R. de Supinski, M. Schulz, and J. F. Prins. Characterizing and mitigating work time inflation in task parallel programs. In *Proceedings of SC12*, SC12, Nov. 2012.

[8] S. L. Olivier, A. K. Porterfield, K. B. Wheeler, M. Spiegel, and J. F. Prins. Openmp task scheduling strategies for multicore numa systems. *International Journal of High Performance Computing Applications*, 26(2):110–124, May 2012.

[9] M. Pericàs, A. Amer, K. Taura, and S. Matsuoka. Analysis of data reuse in task-parallel runtimes. *High Performance Computing Systems. Performance Modeling, Benchmarking and Simulation: 4th International Workshop, PMBS 2013, Denver, CO, USA, November 18, 2013. Revised Selected Papers*, pages 73–87, 2014.

[10] K. Wheeler, R. Murphy, and D. Thain. Qthreads: An api for programming with millions of lightweight threads. In *Proceedings of MTAAP '08*, 2008.

POSTER: Efficient Self-Invalidation/Self-Downgrade for Critical Sections with Relaxed Semantics

Alberto Ros
Universidad de Murcia
aros@ditec.um.es

Carl Leonardsson
Uppsala Universitet
carl.leonardsson@it.uu.se

Christos Sakalis
Uppsala Universitet
chrissakalis@gmail.com

Stefanos Kaxiras
Uppsala Universitet
stefanos.kaxiras@it.uu.se

ABSTRACT

Cache coherence protocols based on self-invalidation allow simpler hardware implementation compared to traditional write-invalidation protocols, by relying on data-race-free semantics and applying self-invalidation and self-downgrade on synchronization points. This work examines how self-invalidation and self-downgrade are performed in relation to atomicity and ordering and shows that they do not need to be applied conservatively, as so far implemented. Our key observation is that, often, critical sections which are not ordered in time, are intended to provide only atomicity but not thread synchronization.

Keywords

Cache coherence; memory consistency; self-invalidation; critical sections; atomicity

1. INTRODUCTION

Recently, a number of proposals aim to simplify coherence by relying on data-race-free (DRF) semantics and on self invalidation to eliminate invalidation traffic and the need to track readers at the directory [5, 2, 3, 6]. With the addition of self-downgrade, the directory can be eliminated [6] and virtual cache coherence becomes feasible at low cost, without reverse translation [4].

In these coherence protocols, writes to memory are not explicitly signaled to sharers, and the written value will be visible to the sharers when they self-invalidate their local copy. Most of these proposals offer sequential consistency for data-race-free (SC for DRF) programs [1]. Data-race-free semantics require that conflicting accesses (e.g., a read and a write to the same address from different cores) must be separated by synchronization. Self-invalidation is therefore initiated on synchronization. Unfortunately, exposing all synchronization to the hardware, causes indiscriminate self-invalidation on lock, barrier, and wait constructs.

PACT '16 September 11-15, 2016, Haifa, Israel

ACM ISBN 978-1-4503-4121-9/16/09.
DOI: http://dx.doi.org/10.1145/2967938.2974050

We show that self-invalidation does not need to be applied conservatively. Our key observation is that `lock` / `unlock` synchronization (i.e., ensuring atomic execution of a critical section) is often *not* intended to constitute DRF synchronization for its *surrounding code.* The execution of such critical sections is therefore unordered in time and cannot successfully separate conflicting accesses that straddle critical sections. This indicates that self-invalidation in a critical section should be restricted only to the data accessed inside it, and should not affect any data accessed prior to its execution. Using similar reasoning, only data modified between the lock and unlock operations should be made globally visible when exiting the critical section; not necessarily data that were modified prior to the critical section.

2. ORDERING VERSUS ATOMICITY

Ordering. Some synchronization primitives, such as barriers or signal/wait, are clearly intended to establish order between memory accesses from different threads. The expectation is then that all data written before a synchronization in thread 1 become visible in thread 2 after its corresponding synchronization. Thread 2 is then disallowed from using its stale data found in its cache. Symmetrically, in the case of barriers, any data written by thread 2 after the synchronization will not yet be visible to thread 1 before its synchronization. Such synchronization primitives establish happens-before order between memory accesses, and are often used to accomplish data race freedom [1].

Atomicity. On the other hand, some other synchronization primitives do not inherently establish order. A common example is the critical section shown in Figure 1. Assume that we are only interested in performing an atomic read and write of the global variable `count`, but not in enforcing any order between other memory accesses. Assume now that we access data *unrelated* to the critical sections. For example, we access the same variable `x` before and after a critical section in thread 1. Should `x` be self-invalidated when entering the critical section (acquire semantics)? The answer is *no.* The reason is that the lock is intended to provide atomicity for the increment of `count`. It is not intended to provide any ordering for `x` or between thread 1 and thread 2. Therefore self-invalidating `x` is unnecessary, and would hurt performance since it will cause a cache miss when re-accessing `x` after exiting the critical section.

However, it is also possible to write code that detects the order in which different critical sections execute. A typical

Thread 1	Thread 2

`lock(l);`
`  count += my_count;`
`unlock(l);`
	`lock(l);`
	`  count += my_count;`
	`unlock(l);`

Figure 1: Critical sections used for atomicity.

Thread 1	Thread 2

`x = 1;`
`lock(l);`
`  flag++;`
`unlock(l);`
	`lock(l);`
	`  local = flag;`
	`unlock(l);`
	`if (local)`
	`  print(x);`

Figure 2: Critical sections used for ordering.

example is shown in Figure 2. Here the variable `flag` is used to detect the order in which the critical sections execute. The variable `x` is only read by thread 2 when the detected execution order guarantees that the load is not in a data race with the store to `x` by thread 1. Hence, the code in Figure 2 is data race free despite having conflicting accesses to `x` located outside of any critical section.

3. PROPOSAL

We propose new synchronization primitives for locks: Forward Self-Invalidation (FSI) and Forward Self-Downgrade (FSD). In a critical section, the accesses between `lock` and `unlock` are always self-invalidated/downgraded. However, the programmer can specify if the accesses outside the critical section should be also self-invalidated or self-downgraded, depending on the semantics of the critical section: pure atomicity (Figure 1) or thread-ordering (Figure 2). Hence, our new primitives allow for applications to be optimized by preventing self-invalidation/downgrade of variables surrounding critical sections for the case when the locks only provide atomicity. When the programmer needs to take care of accesses surrounding thread-ordering critical sections, conservative self-invalidation/downgrade is employed.

Forward Self-Invalidation (FSI). From the time of its activation, e.g., on a lock operation, FSI invalidates each cache line that is accessed, exactly once (on its first access). The invalidated cache lines immediately cause misses and need to be re-fetched and cached again. FSI continues until its deactivation, e.g., upon the next unlock operation. The FSI implementation is simple: we use an additional *access* bit per cache line that is set when entering FSI. Accessing a cache line with the FSI bit set, invalidates the cache line and resets the bit. Ending FSI, all the FSI bits are reset.

Forward Self-Downgrade (FSD). When exiting a critical section, only the data written inside it need to be made globally visible. An efficient implementation of FSD is based on write-throughs via a coalescing write buffer that delays write throughs for a small period of time [6]. Our implementation uses a *write* bit per write-buffer entry that is reset when entering FSD. Writing to a cache line sets its *write* bit. Ending FSD, all the entries in the write buffer with the *write* bit set are self-downgraded, and their corresponding *write* bits are reset.

4. RESULTS

Our proposal is evaluated for an extensive set of benchmarks from Splash3 and PARSEC, where locks have been modified appropriately to take advantage of FSI and FSD where possible. Our evaluation using the GEMS simulator for 64-core multiprocessors show that our techniques significantly limit penalties occurring in synchronization-intensive benchmarks. Results report significant improvements over a traditional directory-based coherence protocol (17.1% in execution time and 33.9% in energy consumption) and also over state-of-the-art VIPS-M coherence protocol [6] that employs Callbacks [7] for efficient spin-waiting (7.6% in execution time and 9.1% in energy consumption).

5. CONCLUSIONS

We found that self-invalidation and self-downgrade, that conventionally affect what happened in the past, can be substantially improved if we turn them forward in time. This is possible for critical sections that do not ascertain thread-order without changing program semantics. This way, important performance and energy improvements are obtained over traditional and state-of-the-art self-invalidation cache coherence protocols.

6. ACKNOWLEDGMENTS

This work has been jointly supported by the "Fundación Séneca – Agencia de Ciencia y Tecnología de la Región de Murcia" under the project "Jóvenes Líderes en Investigación" 18956/JLI/13, the Spanish MINECO, as well as European Commission FEDER funds, under grant TIN2015-66972-C5-3-R, the Linnaeus center of excellence UPMARC, Uppsala Programming for Multicore Architectures Research Center, and the Swedish VR (grant no. 621-2012-5332).

7. REFERENCES

[1] S. V. Adve and M. D. Hill. Weak ordering – a new definition. In *17th Int'l Symp. on Computer Architecture (ISCA)*, pages 2–14, June 1990.

[2] T. J. Ashby, P. Díaz, and M. Cintra. Software-based cache coherence with hardware-assisted selective self-invalidations using bloom filters. *IEEE Transactions on Computers (TC)*, 60(4):472–483, Apr. 2011.

[3] B. Choi, R. Komuravelli, H. Sung, R. Smolinski, N. Honarmand, S. V. Adve, V. S. Adve, N. P. Carter, and C.-T. Chou. DeNovo: Rethinking the memory hierarchy for disciplined parallelism. In *20th Int'l Conf. on Parallel Architectures and Compilation Techniques (PACT)*, pages 155–166, Oct. 2011.

[4] S. Kaxiras and A. Ros. A new perspective for efficient virtual-cache coherence. In *40th Int'l Symp. on Computer Architecture (ISCA)*, pages 535–547, June 2013.

[5] A. R. Lebeck and D. A. Wood. Dynamic self-invalidation: Reducing coherence overhead in shared-memory multiprocessors. In *22nd Int'l Symp. on Computer Architecture (ISCA)*, pages 48–59, June 1995.

[6] A. Ros and S. Kaxiras. Complexity-effective multicore coherence. In *21st Int'l Conf. on Parallel Architectures and Compilation Techniques (PACT)*, pages 241–252, Sept. 2012.

[7] A. Ros and S. Kaxiras. Callback: Efficient synchronization without invalidation with a directory just for spin-waiting. In *42nd Int'l Symp. on Computer Architecture (ISCA)*, pages 427–438, June 2015.

POSTER: SILC-FM: Subblocked InterLeaved Cache-Like Flat Memory Organization

Jee Ho Ryoo
Department of Electrical and Computer Engineering
The University of Texas at Austin
Austin, TX
jr45842@utexas.edu

Mitesh R. Meswani
AMD Research
Austin, TX
mitesh.meswani@amd.com

Reena Panda, Lizy K. John
Department of Electrical and Computer Engineering
The University of Texas at Austin
Austin, TX
reena.panda@utexas.edu, ljohn@ece.utexas.edu

ABSTRACT

In this paper, we present a flat address space organization called SILC-FM that allows subblocks from two pages to coexist in an interleaved fashion in die-stacked DRAM. Data movement at subblocked granularity consumes less bandwidth compared to migrating the entire large block and prevents fetching useless subblocks that may never get accessed. SILC-FM can get more spatial locality hits than CAMEO and PoM due to page-level operation and interleaving blocks respectively. The interleaved subblock placement improves performance by 55% on average over a static placement scheme without data migration. We also selectively lock hot blocks to prevent them from being involved in the hardware swapping operations. Additional features such as locking, associativity and bandwidth balancing improve performance by 11%, 8%, and 8% respectively, resulting in a total of 82% performance improvement over no migration static placement scheme. Compared to the best state-of-the-art scheme, SILC-FM gets performance improvement of 36%.

1. INTRODUCTION

Die-stacked DRAM is an emerging technology that offers much higher bandwidth than the conventional DDR technology [8, 11, 12, 21]. Over the years, the capacity of available die-stacked DRAM modules has increased steadily from a few hundred megabytes to a few gigabytes, so exposing the die-stacked DRAM capacity for application usage can make an impact for capacity constrained applications [3]. Researchers focus on ways to manage tags (metadata) efficiently by managing data at different cacheline sizes to reduce the metadata storage overheads, while at the same time, they try to perform selective cacheline fetching from the off-chip DRAM to reduce off-chip bandwidth usage [4, 5, 6, 7, 13, 14, 15, 17, 19, 22, 24, 25].

In this work, we present SILC-FM, Subblocked InterLeaved Cache-Like Flat Memory Organzation, which fully utilizes the die-stacked DRAM capacity while intelligently placing hot pages in die-stacked DRAM. The subblock level data movement reduces the bandwidth usage compared to PoM [23] and prevents fetching data that may not get utilized much. However, SILC-FM fetches a higher number of small size blocks at a time, resulting in more spatial locality hits compared to CAMEO [3]. In effect, SILC-FM gets benefits of both CAMEO and PoM. Furthermore, SILC-FM allows interleaving between die-stacked and off-chip DRAM hot blocks, so subblocks from both die-stacked and off-chip DRAM can coexist together in a die-stacked DRAM page. Our scheme is a hardware data management scheme that is robust to common problems associated with hardware data management such as thrashing and conflicts since SILC-FM can exclude and lock hot pages from being involved in data migration operations. Our associative structure also protects those pages that are not locked and are actively participating in hardware data migrations from being frequently swapped out of die-stacked DRAM. In addition, we maximize the memory bandwidth by utilizing both die-stacked memory bandwidth and off-chip memory bandwidth. We achieve this by moving only a certain subset of memory traffic to off-chip memory rather than servicing all memory requests from die-stacked DRAM. Thus, we further improve performance by utilizing the sum of both die-stacked and off-chip DRAM bandwidth.

2. SILC-FM MEMORY ARCHITECTURE

In this section, we will explain details of the SILC-FM architecture. The SILC-FM scheme uses Near Memory (NM) as OS visible space while internally operating with subblock based mechanisms. Each block contains four subblocks and the mapping is direct-mapped. This implies that multiple subblocks from only one large block (from the same set) in Far Memory (FM) can swap into corresponding subblocks in NM at any one point of time. The migration between two pages within the same set occurs at subblock granularity. This is bandwidth efficient as only 64B worth of data is migrated, yet managing the remap table at a large block granularity reduces the remap table overheads. The subblock tracking is done using a bit vector per NM block where indi-

PACT '16 September 11-15, 2016, Haifa, Israel

ACM ISBN 978-1-4503-4121-9/16/09.
DOI: http://dx.doi.org/10.1145/2967938.2974060

Processor	Values
Number of Cores (Freq)	8 (3.2GHz)
Width	4 wide out-of-order
Caches	**Values**
L1 I-Cache (private)	64 KB, 2 way, 4 cycles
L1 D-Cache (private)	16 KB, 4 way, 4 cycles
L2 Cache (shared)	8 MB, 16 way, 11 cycles
HBM	**Values**
Bus Frequency	800 MHz (DDR 1.6 GHz)
Bus Width	128 bits
Channels	8
Ranks	1 Rank per Channel
Banks	8 Banks per Rank
Row Buffer Size	8KB (open-page policy)
tCAS-tRCD-tRP-tRAS	7-7-7-28 (memory cycles)
DDR3	**Values**
Bus Frequency	800 MHz (DDR 1.6 GHz)
Bus Width	64 bits
Channels	4
Ranks	1 Rank per Channel
Banks	8 Banks per Rank
Row Buffer Size	8KB (open-page policy)
tCAS-tRCD-tRP-tRAS	11-11-11-44 (memory cycles)

Table 1: Experimental Parameters

vidual bits validate the corresponding subblock's residency in NM. When a block is swapped out of NM, the history of bit vectors is stored in a small SRAM structure called a bit vector table. Multiple subblocks are fetched using this bit vector when a block is swapped in again. This exploits spatial locality as previously used subblocks are swapped at the same time, so any subsequent request to either of the subblocks results in a subblock serviced from NM. Since this scheme does not swap any other undesirable subblocks, it is more bandwidth efficient than large block based schemes, which have to swap every subblock within a large block.

An index to access a page is calculated using the modulo operator in order to access the remap entry and data in NM. Also along with LLC access, the PC and the request address are used to access the predictor. The request is sent to NM using the calculated index and predicted way. If the lock bit and the remap field is set and matched, the NM data is fetched. In case of a remap mismatch, the request address is checked whether it falls under the NM address space. If so, the bit vector is checked to determine the location of the requested subblock (If resident in NM, the bit has to be 0). The prediction can skip the previously mentioned metadata fetching steps. If the block address does not fall under NM space, then the remap entry update and subblock swap from FM are initiated. The subblock is swapped to available ways within the set. A similar operation occurs for a remap mismatch. If the request was made to one of locked blocks, the remap entry is checked. If it matches, then the corresponding subblock is fetched from NM. If not, then the subblock is swapped from FM to NM blocks other than this locked block. For every swap from FM operation, the access rate is checked. If it is beyond a threshold, then the swap from FM bypasses NM and becomes a fetch from FM without any metadata update. In the case of the way prediction misspeculation, the remap entry check takes longer as four remap entries are checked in serial.

3. EXPERIMENTAL SETUP

To evaluate the SILC-FM scheme, we use a Pin-based Sniper simulator [2]. We also use a detailed memory simulator, Ramulator [16]. For NM memory, we use HBM generation 2 technology and derived timing parameters from 235A [11, 12] along with other publicly available sources [1, 8, 9, 21]. DDR3 technology is used as FM memory with latency parameters derived from JEDEC and vendor datasheet [10, 20]. Simulation parameters are shown in Table 1. We compare our scheme against other three other die-stacked DRAM designs: Random Static Placement (Rand), HMA [18], CAMEO (CAM). Random uses the entire NM and FM as OS visible address space and maps pages randomly. Thus, this scheme does not consider different bandwidth/latency characteristics of NM and FM, and rather, treats them the same.

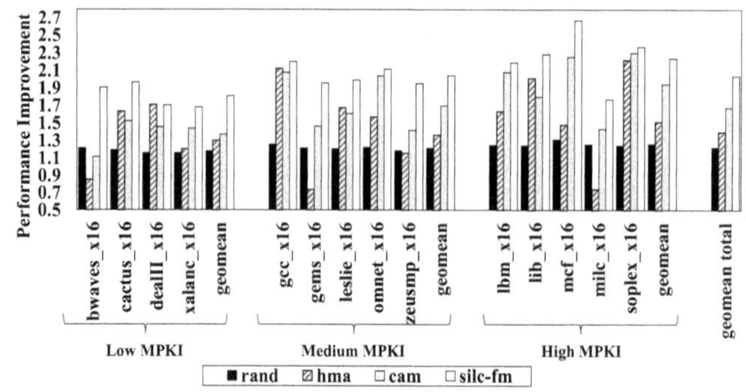

Figure 1: Performance Comparison with Other Schemes

4. EVALUATION

Figure 1 shows the performance improvement of our proposed scheme against other schemes. Unless otherwise specified, we use the baseline as the system without NM. First, the Random scheme does not see much significant performance improvement. The placement is done randomly without considering NM and FM characteristics, so pages are statically allocated. The SILC-FM scheme effectively removes conflicts by offering associativity and locked blocks. Unlike HMA, the blocks are locked in NM as soon as the access count reaches the threshold. This makes the hot block capturing ability of our scheme to respond much quickly to changes in the hot working set. The associativity reduces conflicts among those pages that are not locked yet. This additional performance gain makes SILC-FM achieve higher performance than the state-of-the-art scheme, CAMEO. Furthermore, the bypassing feature makes certain workloads such as milc extract performance opportunities by using FM bandwidth, which would have been idle in other schemes due to its high access rate.

5. CONCLUSION

Prior approaches focused on using block or epoch based schemes, but adopting either one will benefit only a subset of different workloads. In this paper, we have presented an associative locking memory architecture called SILC-FM that locks hot pages in NM and intelligently remaps FM subblocks into NM. In the end, SILC-FM is able to achieve on average 36% performance improvement over state-of-the-art die-stacked DRAM architecture. In conclusion, SILC-FM is a novel memory architecture that takes the advantage of the large NM capacity by holding as many hot data as possible in NM.

6. ACKNOWLEDGEMENT

This work was supported in part by National Science Foundation grants 1337393 and 1117895 and AMD. Any opinions, findings, conclusions or recommendations expressed in this material are those of the authors and do not necessarily reflect the views of sponsors.

7. REFERENCES

[1] AMD Working With Hynix For Development of High-Bandwidth 3D Stacked Memory. 2013.

[2] T. E. Carlson, W. Heirman, and L. Eeckhout. Sniper: Exploring the Level of Abstraction for Scalable and Accurate Parallel Multi-core Simulation. In *Proceedings of 2011 International Conference for High Performance Computing, Networking, Storage and Analysis*, SC '11, 2011.

[3] C. Chou, A. Jaleel, and M. K. Qureshi. CAMEO: A Two-Level Memory Organization with Capacity of Main Memory and Flexibility of Hardware-Managed Cache. In *Proceedings of the 47th Annual IEEE/ACM International Symposium on Microarchitecture*, MICRO-47, 2014.

[4] M. El-Nacouzi, I. Atta, M. Papadopoulou, J. Zebchuk, N. E. Jerger, and A. Moshovos. A dual grain hit-miss detector for large Die-Stacked DRAM caches. In *Design, Automation Test in Europe Conference Exhibition (DATE), 2013*, pages 89–92, 2013.

[5] S. Franey and M. Lipasti. Tag tables. In *High Performance Computer Architecture (HPCA), 2015 IEEE 21st International Symposium on*, 2015.

[6] N. Gulur, M. Mehendale, R. Manikantan, and R. Govindarajan. Bi-Modal DRAM Cache: Improving Hit Rate, Hit Latency and Bandwidth. In *Microarchitecture (MICRO), 2014 47th Annual IEEE/ACM International Symposium on*, 2014.

[7] F. Hameed, L. Bauer, and J. Henkel. Simultaneously Optimizing DRAM Cache Hit Latency and Miss Rate via Novel Set Mapping Policies. In *Proceedings of the 2013 International Conference on Compilers, Architectures and Synthesis for Embedded Systems*, CASES '13, 2013.

[8] HMC Consortium. HMC Specification 1.0. 2012.

[9] M. T. Inc. HMC Generation 2. 2013.

[10] JEDEC. DDR SDRAM (JESD79-3C). 2008.

[11] JEDEC. High Bandwidth Memory (HBM) DRAM (JESD235), 2013.

[12] JEDEC. High Bandwidth Memory (HBM) DRAM Gen 2 (JESD235A). 2016.

[13] D. Jevdjic, G. Loh, C. Kaynak, and B. Falsafi. Unison Cache: A Scalable and Effective Die-Stacked DRAM Cache. In *Microarchitecture (MICRO), 2014 47th Annual IEEE/ACM International Symposium on*, 2014.

[14] D. Jevdjic, S. Volos, and B. Falsafi. Die-stacked DRAM Caches for Servers: Hit Ratio, Latency, or Bandwidth? Have It All with Footprint Cache. In *Proceedings of the 40th Annual International Symposium on Computer Architecture*, ISCA '13, 2013.

[15] X. Jiang, N. Madan, L. Zhao, M. Upton, R. Iyer, S. Makineni, D. Newell, Y. Solihin, and R. Balasubramonian. CHOP: Integrating DRAM Caches for CMP Server Platforms. *IEEE Micro*, 31(1), 2011.

[16] Y. Kim, W. Yang, and O. Mutlu. Ramulator: A Fast and Extensible DRAM Simulator. *Computer Architecture Letters*, PP(99):1–1, 2015.

[17] G. Loh and M. D. Hill. Supporting Very Large DRAM Caches with Compound-Access Scheduling and MissMap. *IEEE Micro*, 32(3), May 2012.

[18] M. Meswani, S. Blagodurov, D. Roberts, J. Slice, M. Ignatowski, and G. Loh. Heterogeneous memory architectures: A HW/SW approach for mixing die-stacked and off-package memories. In *High Performance Computer Architecture (HPCA), 2015 IEEE 21st International Symposium on*, 2015.

[19] J. Meza, J. Chang, H. Yoon, O. Mutlu, and P. Ranganathan. Enabling Efficient and Scalable Hybrid Memories Using Fine-Granularity DRAM Cache Management. *Computer Architecture Letters*, 11(2):61–64, July 2012.

[20] Micron Technology Inc. TN-46-03 Calculating Memory System Power for DDR. 2001.

[21] J. T. Pawlowski. Hybrid Memory Cube (HMC). In *Proceedings of 23rd Hot Chips*, 2011.

[22] M. K. Qureshi and G. H. Loh. Fundamental Latency Trade-off in Architecting DRAM Caches: Outperforming Impractical SRAM-Tags with a Simple and Practical Design. In *Proceedings of the 2012 45th Annual IEEE/ACM International Symposium on Microarchitecture*, MICRO-45, 2012.

[23] J. Sim, A. R. Alameldeen, Z. Chishti, C. Wilkerson, and H. Kim. Transparent Hardware Management of Stacked DRAM as Part of Memory. In *Proceedings of the 2014 47th Annual IEEE/ACM International Symposium on Microarchitecture*, MICRO-47, 2014.

[24] J. Sim, G. H. Loh, H. Kim, M. O'Connor, and M. Thottethodi. A Mostly-Clean DRAM Cache for Effective Hit Speculation and Self-Balancing Dispatch. In *Proceedings of the 2012 45th Annual IEEE/ACM International Symposium on Microarchitecture*, MICRO-45, 2012.

[25] L. Zhao, R. Iyer, R. Illikkal, and D. Newell. Exploring DRAM cache architectures for CMP server platforms. In *Computer Design, 2007. ICCD 2007. 25th International Conference on*, pages 55–62, 2007.

Hybrid Data Dependence Analysis for Loop Transformations

Diogo Sampaio
Institut National de Recherche en Informatique
diogo.nunes-sampaio@inria.fr

Alain Ketterlin
Institut National de Recherche en Informatique
alain-ketterlin@inria.fr

Louis-Noël Pouchet
The Ohio State University
pouchet@cse.ohio-state.edu

Fabrice Rastello
Institut National de Recherche en Informatique
fabrice.rastello@inria.fr

Keywords

Compilers; Polyhedral Transformation; Code Versioning

1. INTRODUCTION

Loop optimizations span from vectorization, scalar promotion, loop invariant code motion, software pipelining to loop fusion, skewing, tiling [6, Ch.9] and loop parallelization. These transformations are essential in the quest for automated high-performance code generation.

Determining the validity of loop transformations at compile time requires analyzing all possible data dependences that may exist at run-time, i.e., all may-dependences. One fundamental issue faced by loop optimizers relates to the precision of alias and dependence information. Static alias and dependence analysis has been extensively studied [3], but many factors make the problem extremely tough.

We provide theoretical and practical foundations to *safely* apply aggressive loop transformations on programs with polynomial data access relations. We do so by inverting how the may-dependence problem is usually attacked. Instead of providing alias information to the optimizer such that it can filter invalid transformations, we request that it performs a transformation believed to reduce the execution time and we generate a fast and precise test to validate, at run-time, if the optimization can be taken.

2. OPTIMIZING FRAMEWORK

We have implemented a framework to *safely* apply complex polyhedral transformations, including thread level parallelization, in any loop with polynomial memory accesses over the loop induction variables. We achieve that, by code versioning the transformed region, guarded by a low-overhead run-time test that is sufficient to validate the transformed code use. The steps of our framework are the following:

1) Loop transformation: Decide on a loop transformation, either by applying a polyhedral optimizer, such as (Pluto [2] / pocc [1]), on a simplified program with appropriate (potentially incorrect) assumptions, or by using profiling data, or by any other means.

2) Generate test: Given a (sequence of) loop transformation(s) that forms the optimized program, and the original application, our framework builds sufficient conditions to validate the transformation, regarding data dependences.

3) Quantifier Elimination: The generated test is composed by sets of inequalities, where each set describes the space where a dependence is not preserved in the optimized schedule. Each quantifier in the system represents a loop induction variable, such that a loop is needed at run-time to explore all it's possible values. Eliminating a quantifier removes the need for this loop, providing a massive gain in the run-time check speed. To handle multivariate-polynomials our quantifier elimination extends the *Fourier-Motzkin Elimination* (FME) method using Schweighofer's et. al [4] algorithm to determine expressions signs and to eliminate redundant constraints.

4) Code versioning: At this stage we combine the original and optimized loops into a if-then-else region controlled by our simplified test. At run-time, if the test fails it means no dependences are broken for the given input and the optimized version of the loop is taken, otherwise, the original one. We emphasize that, different from speculative run-time frameworks[5], we always produce a loop-less test that is hoisted outside the optimized loop region.

3. EXPERIMENTS

To demonstrate the soundness of our system we altered PolyBench/C 4.1 [1] to contain linearized matrices, and we apply the same transformations done by PLuTo to achieve speedups over the original code. To further test the capacity of our quantifier eliminator we wrote a symmetric Floyd-Warshall (FW) algorithm, with access to a linearized triangular matrix and analyze each outermost loop separately. We compare execution times of the original code, optimized code and versioned code. We acknowledge that this methodology holds no assurances that the compiler is

PACT '16 September 11-15, 2016, Haifa, Israel

ACM ISBN 978-1-4503-4121-9/16/09.
DOI: http://dx.doi.org/10.1145/2967938.2974059

Application	Quant. Systems	Quant. Terms	Simpl. Systems	Simpl. Terms	Taken	Original (s)	Pluto (s)	Hybrid (s)	Opts
2mm	189	3101	25	178	Original	5.7171	2.5394	5.7159	fips
3mm	128	2014	59	369	Optimized	12.3388	0.8827	0.8813	fFip
atax	23	257	9	36	Optimized	0.0086	0.0037	0.0038	fipt
bicg	34	399	12	47	Optimized	0.0134	0.0037	0.0037	Fip
cholesky	28	408	1	1	Optimized	2.1342	2.1300	2.1240	f
covariance	42	577	7	28	Optimized	12.6110	0.2911	0.2896	Fp
doitgen	6	142	4	20	Optimized	0.7748	0.1323	0.1283	Fp
fdtd-2d	5083	91455	-	-	Original	2.5852	1.1275	2.5818	fipst
gemm	24	422	12	74	Optimized	0.5669	0.1869	0.1873	Fip
gemver	88	1149	7	13	Original	0.0441	0.0079	0.0440	fip
gesummv	40	437	19	58	Optimized	0.0058	0.0016	0.0016	Fp
heat-3d	9744	254488	-	-	Original	2.5983	2.4720	2.6071	fps
jacobi-2d	1712	32428	-	-	Original	2.2792	0.7953	2.2755	fpst
lu	22	376	1	1	Optimized	12.9030	7.2813	7.2663	fpst
mvt	63	819	10	28	Optimized	0.0408	0.0095	0.0095	fp
seidel-2d	1440	30744	1	2	Original	21.5708	5.4186	21.5736	ps
symm	26	411	35	252	Optimized	7.9743	1.3752	1.3278	F
syr2k	37	679	18	84	Optimized	22.6612	0.4959	0.4996	ip
syrk	8	422	29	251	Optimized	1.8875	0.4831	0.4828	Fip
trisolv	48	527	3	9	Optimized	0.0032	0.0015	0.0015	pt
FW-t-1	360	7041	1	1	Optimized	23.8913	14.1972	14.1891	ps

Table 1: *Quant./Simpl. systems:* The number of conjunctions that form the quantified/simplified test. *Quant./Simpli. Terms:* Total number of constraints of the quantified/simplified test. *Taken:* If the executed version was the original or optimized. *Original / Pluto / Hybrid:* Average execution time of each version. *Opts:* Applied transformations: fusion, Fission, loop interchange, thread parallelism, skewing, tilling.

capable to apply the same optimizations over the three distinct applications.

Using PolyBench large dataset we observe that the run-time overhead of the generated tests are negligible compared to the execution time of the guarded regions. Our results are summarized in table 1.

Even when complex transformations are applied, our quantifier eliminator always generates tests with run-time complexity of $O(1)$ that is sufficient to secure it's use, where the original tests have a complexity equals to the complexity of the optimized code squared. The three applications where the simplified tests are too conservative, *2mm*, *gemver* and *seidel-2d*, are due the fact that we did not extensively detect permutable reductions. The applications with missing simplified test information, our quantifier eliminator did not manage to join simplified systems into a single one, in a time limit of 1h.

Performance improvements: We emphasize that our purpose is not to find the best transformations, but instead to demonstrate the potential impact of complex polyhedral transformations applied *safely* after a complete may-alias and validity run-time check. Transformed programs have been built by PLuTo, using tiling, multidimensional fusion, skewing and automatic parallelization. Our framework takes care of handling the dependence validation using linearized arrays everywhere, this include a compact representation for FW where no existing polyhedral technique, including over-approximation, can generate a parallel-skewed optimization due to the purely polynomial access. With our proposed scheme, powerful polyhedral transformations can be seamlessly applied to programs with polynomial array access functions, potentially leading to high gains.

4. FUTURE WORK

To further expand the usefulness of our framework we work in using trace analyses to guide the optimizer in choosing what are desirable transformations to be done and being able to optimize programs with polynomial memory access expressions, totally automating the transformation process.

5. REFERENCES

[1] PoCC, the Polyhedral Compiler Collection, version 1.3. http://pocc.sourceforge.net.

[2] U. Bondhugula, A. Hartono, J. Ramanujam, and P. Sadayappan. Pluto: A practical and fully automatic polyhedral program optimization system. In *Proceedings of the ACM SIGPLAN 2008 Conference on Programming Language Design and Implementation (PLDI 08), Tucson, AZ (June 2008)*. Citeseer, 2008.

[3] M. Hind. Pointer analysis: haven't we solved this problem yet? In *Proceedings of the 2001 ACM SIGPLAN-SIGSOFT workshop on Program analysis for software tools and engineering*, pages 54–61. ACM, 2001.

[4] M. Schweighofer. An algorithmic approach to schmüdgen's positivstellensatz. *Journal of Pure and Applied Algebra*, 166(3):307 – 319, 2002.

[5] A. Sukumaran-Rajam, J. Martinez Caamaño, W. Wolff, A. Jimborean, and P. Clauss. Speculative program parallelization with scalable and decentralized runtime verification. In *Runtime Verification*, volume 8734 of *Lecture Notes in Computer Science*, pages 124–139. Springer International Publishing, 2014.

[6] M. Wolfe. *High Performance Compilers for Parallel Computing*. Adison-Wesley, 1st edition, 1996.

POSTER: An Optimization of Dataflow Architectures for Scientific Applications

Xiaowei Shen[1,2] Xiaochun Ye[1] Xu Tan[1,2]
Da Wang[1] Zhimin Zhang[1] Dongrui Fan[1] Zhimin Tang[1]
[1]SKL of Computer Architecture, Institute of Computing Technology, Chinese Academy of Sciences
[2]University of Chinese Academy of Sciences
Beijing, China
shenxiaowei@ict.ac.cn

ABSTRACT

Dataflow computing is proved to be promising in high-performance computing. However, traditional dataflow architectures are general-purpose and not efficient enough when dealing with typical scientific applications due to low utilization of function units. In this paper, we propose an optimization of dataflow architectures for scientific applications. The optimization introduces a request for operands mechanism and a topology-based instruction mapping algorithm to improve the efficiency of dataflow architectures. Experimental results show that the request for operands optimization achieves a 4.6% average performance improvement over the traditional dataflow architectures and the TBIM algorithm achieves a 2.28x and a 1.98x average performance improvement over SPDI and SPS algorithm respectively.

CCS Concepts

• **Computer systems organization→Architectures→Other architectures→Data flow architectures**

Keywords

Request for operands; topology-based instruction mapping; dataflow computing; high-performance computing.

1. INTRODUCTION

Dataflow computing is proved to be promising in high-performance computing [1]. Dataflow computing exploits the parallelism of programs and reduces the accesses to shared storages. Data are transferred from instructions to instructions directly and instructions can be fired (executed) as soon as the operands are prepared in dataflow processors. In scientific applications, the data are very regular and each data block is processed with the same operations. Scientific applications focus on data, which is the same as dataflow computing. The same operations on different data blocks can be represented by a dataflow graph. After data flow through the dataflow graph, the results are produced. Dataflow is very suitable for scientific applications. However, traditional dataflow processors such as TRIPS [2] are designed for general-purpose, which cannot achieve high performance on scientific applications. The utilization of processing elements in traditional dataflow processors is low because instructions are waiting for their operands.

Based on the blocking and parallelism features of scientific applications, in this paper, we propose an optimization of dataflow architectures for scientific applications. The optimization introduces a RFO (request for operands) mechanism and a topology-based dataflow instruction mapping algorithm for scientific applications.

2. OPTIMIZATION OF DATAFLOW ARCHITECTURE

In scientific applications, the problem data space is usually divided into many blocks. Operations on different blocks are the same so different data blocks are processed with the same dataflow graph. The instructions in the dataflow graph are mapped into the PE array and data blocks streams into the array.

To achieving high performance, a request for operands (RFO) mechanism is introduced in dataflow architectures for scientific applications. In the mechanism, an instruction can only send its result to the consumers after its consumers have requested for it. After an instruction was fired, the instruction sends messages to its producer instructions to request for its new operands. If the producer instructions have already prepared their results, they can send the results to the consumer instructions directly. If not, the producers will wait for their operands. After the operands arrived, the producers fire the ready instructions and send their results to the consumers. With the request for operands mechanism, there is only one datum existing in the path from the producer to the consumer. Only after the operand has been consumed, the producer can send another operand to the router. Operands in the router will never been blocked by PEs because every operand in the routers has an available buffer in their consumers.

In the dataflow architectures with request for operands mechanism, instruction mapping algorithms should focus on three rules: load-balance, parallelism and communication latency. To achieve high performance and to reduce the requirement for on-chip network bandwidth, a topology-based instruction mapping (TBIM) algorithm is proposed as Figure 2. TBIM algorithm maps the instructions into the array of processing elements focusing on load-balance and augments the algorithm with parallelism and communication latency.

PACT'16, September 11–15, 2016, Haifa, Israel.
ACM 978-1-4503-4121-9/16/09.
http://dx.doi.org/10.1145/2967938.2974054

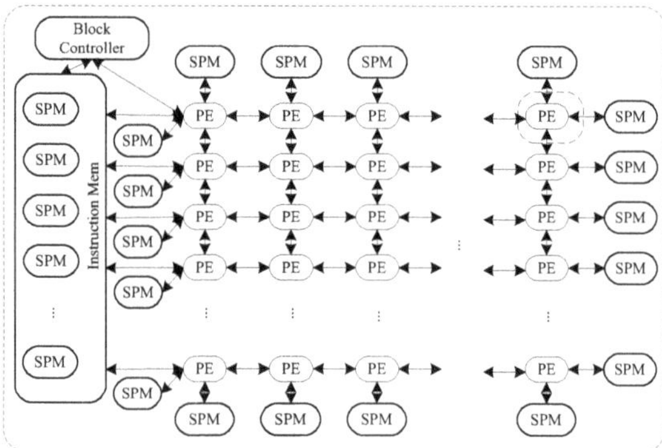

Figure 1 Architecture of a dataflow accelerator

Input: *G* – dataflow graph, *A* - array of PEs
Output: *M* – a mapping *G* -> *A*

```
(L, NL) = divideByLoop(G)
if L not null
    {FL, IL} = divideByInstType(L)
end if
if NL not null
    {FNL, INL} = divideByInstType(NL)
end if
for each set s in {FL, IL, FNL, INL}
  if s not null
     SC = groupByTopo(s, A, M)
     PEC = clusterByPE(SC, A, M)
     for each cluster c in PEC
        M += clusterMap(c, A, M)
     end for
   end if
end for
```

Figure 2 The TBIM algorithm

For each set, there are three steps: grouping by topology, clustering by PE and cluster mapping. Firstly, based on the parallelism of scientific applications, instructions in the set are grouped to many groups. Secondly, based on the topology of groups and the topology of the PE array, the groups are clustered to several clusters. Finally, the clusters are mapped to the PE array by the cluster mapping function.

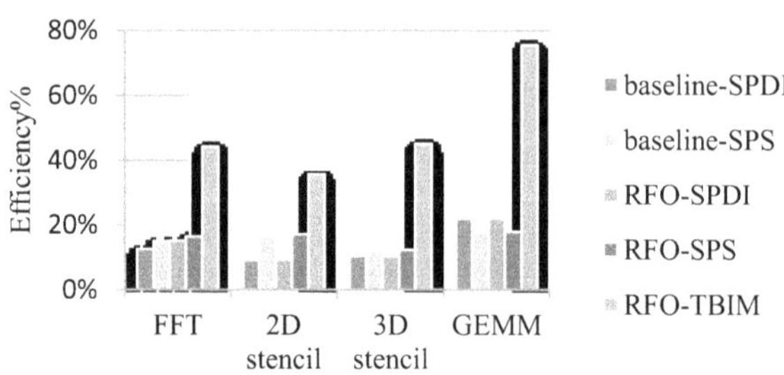

Figure 3 Efficiencies of applications on different architectures with different mapping algorithms with 4 mesh networks

3. EVALUATION AND RESULTS

We evaluate the request for operand mechanism and the TBIM algorithm in a dataflow processor simulator implemented based on a simulator framework SimICT [3]. The proposed RFO mechanism can't achieve good efficiency with 4 networks but can improve the efficiency of dataflow architectures with 8 networks by 4.6% in average. The proposed TBIM instruction mapping algorithm improves the efficiency of dataflow architectures with 4 networks by 2.28x and 1.98x when compared with SPDI [4] and SPS [5] respectively.

4. CONCLUSIONS

Traditional dataflow architectures like TRIPS are not efficient enough in typical scientific applications such as stencil and FFT due to their low utilization of PEs. In the execution of traditional dataflow processors, a new block is allocated only after the finish of an active block. Only few blocks in flight result in much idle time of PEs.

Based on the blocking and parallelism features of scientific applications, in this paper, we propose an optimization of dataflow architectures for scientific applications. The optimization introduces a RFO mechanism and a topology-based dataflow instruction mapping algorithm for scientific applications.

We evaluate the performance of the proposed RFO mechanism via a dataflow processor simulator. The experimental results show that the RFO mechanism improves the efficiency of floating point function units in dataflow architectures by 4.6% in average on typical scientific applications. TBIM improves the efficiency of dataflow architectures by 2.28x and 1.98x when compared with SPDI and SPS respectively.

5. ACKNOWLEDGMENTS

This work is in part supported by the 863 Program of China under grant No. 2015AA01A301, the National Major Project of China under grant No. 2013ZX0102-8001-001-001 and the National Natural Science Foundation of China under grant No. 61332009 and No. 61521092.

6. REFERENCES

[1] H. Fu, L. Gan, R. G. Clapp, H. Ruan, O. Pell, O. Mencer, M. Flynn, X. Huang and G. Yang. Scaling reverse time migration performance through reconfigurable dataflow engines. *IEEE Micro*, 34(1): 30-40, 2014.

[2] D. Burger, S. W. Keckler, K. S. McKinley, M. Dahlin, L. K. John, C. Lin, C. R. Moore, J. Burrill, R. G. McDonald, W. Yoder and the TRIPS Team. Scaling to the end of silicon with EDGE architectures. *IEEE Computer,* 37(7): 44-55, 2004.

[3] X. Ye, D. Fan, N. Sun, S. Tang, M. Zhang and H. Zhang. SimICT: A fast and flexible framework for performance and power evaluation of large-scale architecture. In *Proceedings of the IEEE International Symposium on Low Power Electronics and Design*, pages 273-278, 2013.

[4] R. Nagarajan, S. K. Kushwaha, D. Burger, K. S. McKinley, C. Lin and S. W. Keckler. Static placement, dynamic issue (SPDI) scheduling for EDGE architectures. In *Proceedings of the 13th International Conference on Parallel Achitecture and Compilation Techniques*, pages 74-84, 2004.

[5] K. E. Coons, X. Chen, S. K. Kushwaha, D. Burger and K. S. McKinley. A spatial path scheduling algorithm for EDGE architectures. In *Proceedings of the 12th International Conference on Architectural Support for Programming Languages and Operating Systems*, pages 129-140, 2006.

POSTER – hVISC: A Portable Abstraction for Heterogeneous Parallel Systems

Prakalp Srivastava
University of Illinois at Urbana-Champaign
psrivas2@illinois.edu

Maria Kotsifakou
University of Illinois at Urbana-Champaign
kotsifa2@illinois.edu

Matthew D. Sinclair
University of Illinois at Urbana-Champaign
mdsincl2@illinois.edu

Rakesh Komuravelli
Qualcomm Technologies Inc.
rakesh.komuravelli@qti.qualcomm.com

Vikram Adve
University of Illinois at Urbana-Champaign
vadve@illinois.edu

Sarita Adve
University of Illinois at Urbana-Champaign
sadve@illinois.edu

ABSTRACT

Programming heterogeneous parallel systems can be extremely complex because a single system may include multiple different parallelism models, instruction sets, and memory hierarchies, and different systems use *different combinations* of these features. We propose a carefully designed parallel abstraction of heterogeneous hardware – *a hierarchical dataflow graph with shared memory and vector instructions* – that is able to capture the parallelism in a wide range of popular parallel hardware. We use this abstraction, which we call *hVISC*, to define a Virtual Instruction Set Architecture (ISA) that aims to address both functional portability and performance portability across heterogeneous systems. *hVISC* is more general than existing virtual instruction sets such as PTX, HSAIL and SPIR, e.g., it can capture both streaming parallelism and general dataflow parallelism.

1. MOTIVATION

Programming heterogeneous systems is extremely challenging because of the diversity of the underlying hardware components. *Developers* must be able to develop portable algorithms and reason about their performance and scalability; write efficient, yet portable source-level programs; and tune program performance for a range of different hardware.

At a fundamental level, these challenges arise from the diversity in hardware parallelism models, memory architectures, and hardware instruction sets. A promising approach to address these challenges is to develop *a parallel model that captures these diversities* and thus can be mapped down to a wide range of different parallel hardware. In particular, a suitable unified set of abstractions can enable parallel algorithm development, parallel language design, compiler optimizations and code generation for parallel programs, performance tuning, and both source and object code portability.

PACT '16 September 11-15, 2016, Haifa, Israel

ACM ISBN 978-1-4503-4121-9/16/09.
DOI: http://dx.doi.org/10.1145/2967938.2976039

2. PARALLEL ABSTRACTION DESIGN

In this work, we propose a parallel abstraction we call *hVISC* that abstracts away differences between parallelism models in hardware. In *hVISC*, a program is represented as a hierarchical dataflow graph. The nodes represent computations and may use shared memory and vector instructions. The edges capture explicit data transfers between nodes, while ordinary load and store instructions can be used to perform implicit communication via shared memory.

For example, Figure 1 shows an *hVISC* example of a Laplacian estimate computation for a greyscale image. The computation is represented by three dataflow nodes – `Dilation Filter`, `Erosion Filter` and `Linear Combination` – connected by edges. The code for the `Linear Combination` filter is shown, and includes load and store instructions accessing shared memory as well as explicit vector instructions with a parametric vector length [6].

A single static dataflow node or edge in a graph may represent multiple *dynamic instances* of the node or edge. The instances of a node are required to be independent of each other, i.e., can be executed fully in parallel. This succinctly captures fine-grain data parallelism, which can be targeted to a range of parallel hardware efficiently. Moreover, dataflow graphs in *hVISC* can be hierarchical: each node in a graph may itself contain a full-fledged dataflow graph (called parent and child graph respectively). In Figure 1, `Dilation Filter`, `Erosion Filter` and `Linear Combination` are child graphs to parent `Laplacian Estimate` graph. Typically, the top-level graph captures parallelism and explicit data transfers across major compute units in a heterogeneous system, while lower-level dataflow graphs capture fine-grain parallelism within individual compute kernels, which can be mapped to a GPU, vector hardware or a multicore host processor. The graph hierarchy is also an effective way to capture tiling of computations, useful in exploiting cache hierarchy or GPU scratchpad memory.

Finally, a dataflow graph edge may be either a one-time data transfer edge or a "streaming" edge that executes repeatedly. Streaming edges enable pipelined parallelism on long input streams to be expressed naturally and translated effectively to a wide range of hardware. In Figure 1, the node `Laplacian Estimate` is one stage in an image processing pipeline and the dashed arrows for I, I_d, I_e and L show streaming edges representing streams of images.

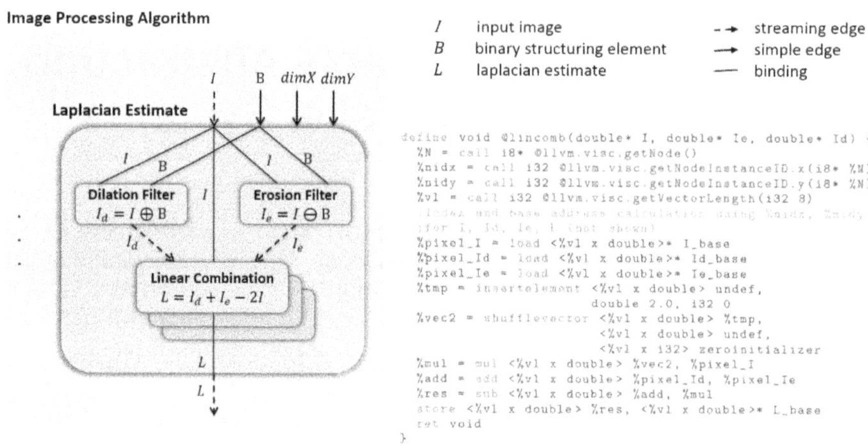

Figure 1: Non-linear Laplacian computation in *hVISC*

In this work, we use *hVISC* to define a *virtual instruction set* (ISA) that is an extension of the LLVM virtual instruction set [4]. *hVISC* can be used to ship programs as "virtual object code," and each DF node in a program can be translated to different hardware compute units either at install-time or run-time. This is similar to PTX [5], HSAIL [1] and SPIR [3]. However, *hVISC* provides more powerful and general abstractions for parallelism, such as (regular or irregular) dataflow graphs or pipelined, streaming codes (in addition to the SIMT and short-vector SIMD parallelism targeted by HSAIL or SPIR), which can be used to represent a much wider range of parallel programs.

3. COMPILER INFRASTRUCTURE

We have designed and implemented "back-end" code generators from *hVISC* to three different classes of parallel hardware: GPUs (using NVIDIA's PTX), vector SIMD (Intel's AVX), and multicore CPUs (using Posix threads). We believe *hVISC* can also support other kinds of hardware well, e.g., FPGAs, but code generation for such targets is left to future work. We have also implemented an efficient run-time system that supports data transfers between compute units, buffering for streaming edges, and optimizations to avoid redundant transfers by tracking the "last location" for data objects identified via shared memory pointers.

4. EVALUATION

Figure 2 shows that *hVISC* achieves performance close to or on par with *hand-coded* performance on both GPU and vector platforms. We use the *same hVISC* code for seven applications from the Parboil [7] benchmark suite, and compare them against the best performing OpenCL implementation of each one in the Parboil suite *on its respective target*, compiled using nVidia's proprietary OpenCL compiler or the Intel OpenCL compiler [2] respectively. *hVISC* achieves performance near that of hand-tuned OpenCL for all benchmarks except bfs, where the overhead is 20% due to lack of support for global barriers In the vector case, the performance of *hVISC* is within 7% in the worst case.

Figure 3 shows that *hVISC* can (a) capture pipelined, streaming computations effectively; and (b) is flexible enough to allow a wide range of pipeline mapping configurations with different performance characteristics from a

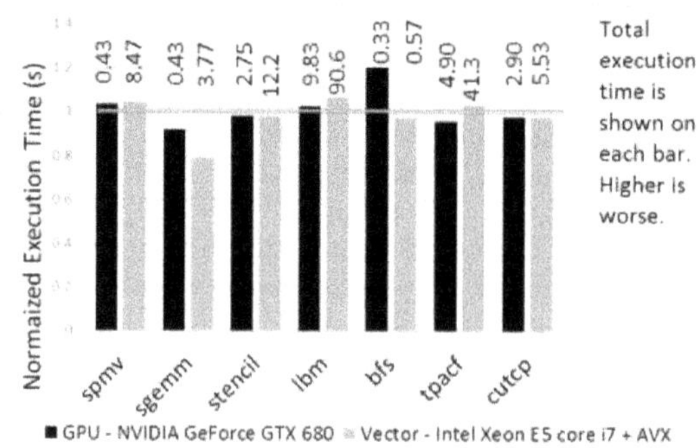

Figure 2: GPU and Vector Experiments

single code. We use Edge Detection in grey scale images, a six-stage image processing pipeline; we can map each stage to one of three targets (GPU, vector or a CPU thread), allowing a total of $3^6 = 729$ different configurations, all generated from a single *hVISC* code. The graph shows seven of the configurations, and illustrates the dramatic differences in performance that can result from different mappings. This flexibility of *hVISC* enables a (future) run-time scheduler to choose configurations based on properties of the code, available hardware resources, and energy constraints.

5. ACKNOWLEDGEMENTS

This work was supported in part by the National Science Foundation (grant number CCF 13-02641), and by C-FAR, SRC STARnet Center sponsored by MARCO and DARPA.

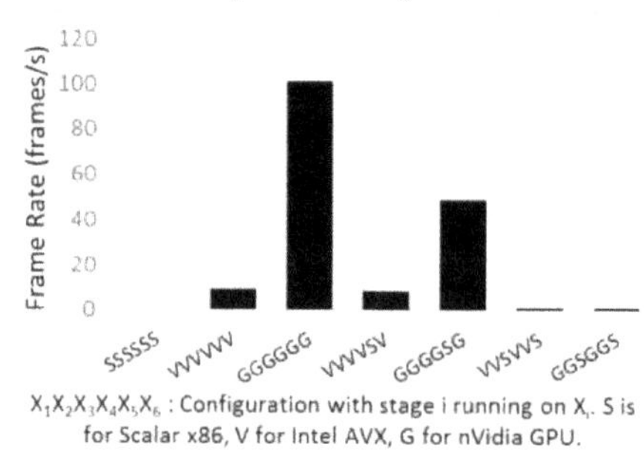

Figure 3: Frame rates of different configurations through single *hVISC* object code.

6. REFERENCES

[1] HSAIL. http://www.hsafoundation.com/standards/. Accessed: August 1, 2016.

[2] Intel. https://software.intel.com/en-us/intel-opencl. Accessed: August 1, 2016.

[3] Khronos Group. SPIR 1.0 Specification for OpenCL. http://www.khronos.org/registry/cl/specs/spir_spec-1.0-provisional.pdf.

[4] C. Lattner and V. Adve. LLVM: A compilation framework for lifelong program analysis and transformation. In *Proc. Conf. on Code Generation and Optimization*, pages 75–88, San Jose, CA, USA, Mar 2004.

[5] Nvidia Compute. PTX: Parallel thread execution isa version 2.3. http://developer.download.nvidia.com/compute/DevZone/docs/html/C/doc/ptx_isa_2.3.pdf, 2011.

[6] P. Srivastava, M. Kotsifakou, M. Sinclair, R. Komuravelli, V. Adve, and S. Adve. hVISC: A portable abstraction for heterogeneous parallel systems. Technical report, Department of Computer Science, University of Illinois at Urbana-Champaign, 2016.

[7] J. A. Stratton, C. Rodrigues, I.-J. Sung, N. Obeid, L.-W. Chang, N. Anssari, G. D. Liu, and W.-M. W. Hwu. Parboil: A revised benchmark suite for scientific and commercial throughput computing. *Center for Reliable and High-Performance Computing*, 2012.

POSTER: An Integrated Vector-Scalar Design on an In-order ARM Core

Milan Stanic
Barcelona Supercomputing Center
Barcelona, Spain
milan.stanic@bsc.es

Oscar Palomar
University of Manchester
Manchester, UK
oscar.palomar@manchester.ac.uk

Timothy Hayes
Barcelona Supercomputing Center
Barcelona, Spain
timothy.hayes@bsc.es

Ivan Ratkovic
Barcelona Supercomputing Center
Barcelona, Spain
ivan.ratkovic@bsc.es

Osman Unsal
Barcelona Supercomputing Center
Barcelona, Spain
osman.unsal@bsc.es

Adrian Cristal *
Barcelona Supercomputing Center
Barcelona, Spain
adrian.cristal@bsc.es

Mateo Valero †
Barcelona Supercomputing Center
Barcelona, Spain
mateo.valero@bsc.es

ABSTRACT

In the low-end mobile processor market, power, energy and area budgets are significantly lower than in other markets (e.g. servers or high-end mobile markets). It has been shown that vector processors are a highly energy-efficient way to increase performance; however adding support for them incurs area and power overheads that would not be acceptable for low-end mobile processors. In this work, we propose an integrated vector-scalar design for the ARM architecture that mostly reuses scalar hardware to support the execution of vector instructions. The key element of the design is our proposed block-based model of execution that groups vector computational instructions together to execute them in a coordinated manner.

CCS Concepts

•Computer systems organization → Single instruction, multiple data;

*He is also affiliated with Universitat Politècnica de Catalunya and CSIC - Artificial Intelligence Research Institute (IIIA)

†He is also affiliated with Universitat Politècnica de Catalunya

PACT '16, September 11–15, 2016, Haifa, Israel.

ACM ISBN 978-1-4503-4121-9/16/09..

DOI: http://dx.doi.org/10.1145/2967938.2974057

Keywords

vector processors; low-power; energy efficiency; mobile

1. INTRODUCTION

Vector processors [1] are energy efficient architectures that yield high performance whenever there is enough data-level parallelism (DLP) [7]. Besides the long and successful history of vector processors in supercomputers, vector units have been proposed in microprocessor design [6, 4, 2]. Recent research on vector processors shows that they can be a good match even for applications from domains such as column-store databases [5]. Although vector processors are energy efficient, they still have too high power and area overheads for low-end mobile processors. This is mostly due to their highly restrictive power and area budget.

This paper contributes a method to increase the performance of the low-power low-end embedded systems in an energy-efficient way. The energy efficiency is attained by modifying a scalar core to execute vector instructions on the existing infrastructure. In particular, we propose an integrated vector-scalar design that combines scalar and vector processing mostly using existing resources of an energy-efficient scalar processor (in our evaluation environment it is based on the ARM Cortex A7). In addition to a design that uses a conventional vector execution model, we also contribute a novel block-based model of execution for vector computational instructions.

2. INTEGRATED DESIGN

As a baseline, we use a scalar core based on the highly energy-efficient ARM Cortex-A7. It is an in-order processor that implements the ARM v7 architecture with an 8-stage pipeline (non-highlighted gray blocks in Figure 1).

In our proposed integrated vector-scalar design, we attempt to maximize the reuse of resources already present

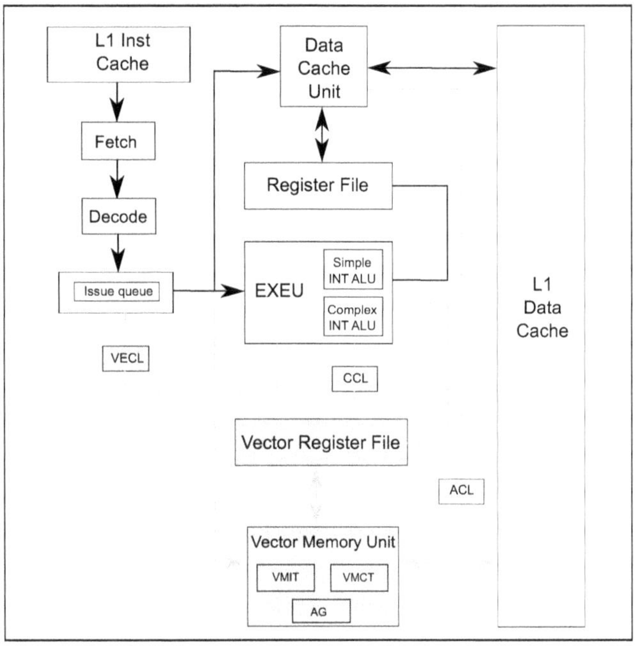

Figure 1: Block diagram of the integrated design.

in the baseline scalar core (white blocks in Figure 1) while adding support for vector instructions. While the front-end of the pipeline is the same (fetch and decode[1] stages), in the back-end we added two structures to support the execution of vector instructions on the scalar core: a vector register file, and a vector memory unit (blue blocks in Figure 1). There is also additional logic that controls the execution of vector instructions.

2.1 Vector Computational Instructions

For executing the vector computational instructions on the existing scalar FUs, we study two alternatives: 1) the One-By-One model of execution (*OBO*), in essence the classic vector execution model, in which a vector instruction is executed to completion once it starts execution in a functional unit, i.e. for all the operations of the vector; and 2) a novel execution model called Block-Based Execution (*BBE*). In this model, for a block of consecutive vector computational instructions, first all operations on the first element of the vectors are executed, then the operations of the second element, and so on.

2.1.1 Block-Based Execution

In order to support this model of execution, we added simple control logic and a small table that keeps the information of the instructions of the block. In the design presented in this paper, the blocks of vector computational instructions are formed dynamically in a very simple way: once a computational vector instruction is ready for execution, the control logic examines the next instruction in the issue queue and adds it to the block if it is a vector computational instruction. This process stops when the next instruction in the issue queue is of another type (a scalar or vector memory instruction) or the block table is full.

[1]With the obvious exception of the decode logic, which needs to be extended to support the new vector instructions.

3. INITIAL EVALUATION

We have extended the gem5 simulator [3] and McPAT [8] to evaluate our integrated design. We used eight kernels from various benchmarks and vectorized them. The results show that our integrated design reduces energy over the scalar baseline for most of the kernels with a small area overhead (only 4.7% when using a vector register with 32 elements). We report up to 5x energy reduction for our block-based execution model over the scalar baseline. Additionally, we found that the block-based execution model provides better results (up to 26% of energy saving) than a conventional vector unit with dedicated units. The area overhead of adding the conventional vector unit with a floating-point unit is significant, around 44% with vector registers of 32 elements. Regarding performance gains, we report more than a 6x speed-up compared to the scalar baseline. Moreover, our block-based execution model is up to 1.4x faster than the conventional vector unit for floating-point kernels.

4. CONCLUSION

Power dissipation, energy consumption and area are critical concerns in processor design, especially for embedded systems in the low-end market. In this paper, we propose an integrated vector-scalar design. The integrated design allows for execution of vector computational instructions mostly reusing resources of an ARM in-order core. We implement two models to execute vector computational instructions: one-by-one and block-based execution models. Initial evaluation shows substantial savings.

5. ACKNOWLEDGMENTS

The research leading to these results has received funding from the RoMoL ERC Advanced Grant GA no 321253 and is supported in part by the European Union (FEDER funds) under contract TIN2015-65316-P. This research has been also supported the Agency for Management of University and Research Grants (AGAUR - FI-DGR 2014).

6. REFERENCES

[1] K. Asanovic. *Vector Microprocessors.* PhD thesis, University of California, Berkeley, May, 1998.

[2] C. F. Batten. *Simplified vector-thread architectures for flexible and efficient data-parallel accelerators.* PhD thesis, Cambridge, MA, USA, 2010.

[3] Binkert et al. The gem5 simulator. *SIGARCH Comput. Archit. News*, 39(2):1–7, aug 2011.

[4] R. Espasa et al. Tarantula: A vector extension to the alpha architecture. ISCA '02, pages 281–292, 2002.

[5] T. Hayes et al. Vector extensions for decision support dbms acceleration. In *MICRO 45*, pages 166–176, 2012.

[6] C. Kozyrakis and D. Patterson. Overcoming the limitations of conventional vector processors. In *ISCA '03*, pages 399–409, 2003.

[7] Y. Lee et al. Exploring the tradeoffs between programmability and efficiency in data-parallel accelerators. ISCA '11, pages 129–140, 2011.

[8] S. Li et al. Mcpat: An integrated power, area, and timing modeling framework for multicore and manycore architectures. In *MICRO 42*, pages 469–480, Dec 2009.

POSTER: Pagoda: A Runtime System to Maximize GPU Utilization in Data Parallel Tasks with Limited Parallelism

Tsung Tai Yeh, Amit Sabne, Putt Sakdhnagool, Rudolf Eigenmann, Timothy G. Rogers
Department of Electrical and Computer Engineering
Purdue University
{yeh14, asabne, psakdhna, eigenman, timrogers}@purdue.edu

ABSTRACT

Massively multithreaded GPUs achieve high throughput by running thousands of threads in parallel. To fully utilize the hardware, contemporary workloads spawn work to the GPU in bulk by launching large tasks, where each task is a kernel that contains thousands of threads that occupy the entire GPU.

GPUs face severe underutilization and their performance benefits vanish if the tasks are narrow, i.e., they contain less than 512 threads. Latency-sensitive applications in network, signal, and image processing that generate a large number of tasks with relatively small inputs are examples of such limited parallelism. Recognizing the issue, CUDA now allows 32 simultaneous tasks on GPUs; however, that still leaves significant room for underutilization.

This paper presents Pagoda, a runtime system that virtualizes GPU resources, using an OS-like daemon kernel called MasterKernel. Tasks are spawned from the CPU onto Pagoda as they become available, and are scheduled by the MasterKernel at the warp granularity. This level of control enables the GPU to keep scheduling and executing tasks as long as free warps are found, dramatically reducing underutilization. Experimental results on real hardware demonstrate that Pagoda achieves a geometric mean speedup of 2.44x over PThreads running on a 20-core CPU, 1.43x over CUDA-HyperQ, and 1.33x over GeMTC, the state-of-the-art runtime GPU task scheduling system.

CCS Concepts

•Software and its engineering → Runtime environments;

Keywords

GPU scheduling; many task computing

1. INTRODUCTION

GPGPU computing has demonstrated an ability to accelerate applications that have a high degree of parallelism, where iterations of large parallel loops are executed on the GPU. These applications see significant performance benefits since they can fully utilize the GPU's hardware resources by launching enough concurrent threads.

The GPU's performance benefits start to vanish as the degree of parallelism lessens. Conventionally, large parallel loops are offloaded to the GPU, while retaining the execution of smaller ones on the CPU. The main thesis of this paper is that despite having a smaller degree of parallelism, applications can benefit from using the GPU, provided that the involved task (or CUDA kernel) count is sufficiently high. Each such task, called a *narrow task*, has limited parallelism (< 512 data parallel threads in practice). Narrow tasks emerge in a number of scenarios. One set of such applications comprises latency-driven, real-time workloads. E.g. online sensors that generate small inputs, resulting in tasks with low parallelism; however, many such tasks are generated in quick succession and require immediate processing. These workloads have been characterized as having mixed task and data parallelism [4]. Secondly, irregular applications can exhibit narrow tasks. These applications often contain varying amounts of computation among different threads, and/or among loop iterations. To reduce load imbalance, these applications are often represented using many tasks with low degrees of parallelism [3]. Irregular workloads may also arise in multi-programmed environments. Different applications with low degrees of parallelism can be co-executed on a node to exploit all the computing resources. Each of these applications may launch one or more tasks of different computation sizes, resulting in narrow tasks.

GPU underutilization is the key reason why narrow tasks are conventionally executed on the CPU. This paper presents Pagoda, a runtime system that highly improves GPU utilization in the presence of narrow tasks. Pagoda introduces novel elements of a massively parallel OS to flexibly and efficiently virtualize and dynamically schedule GPU core resources at the warp granularity, enabling hundreds of tasks to execute concurrently.

2. PAGODA RUNTIME SYSTEM DESIGN

Pagoda is a CPU/GPU system that overrides the traditional CUDA kernel launching API. Pagoda's CPU component handles the spawning and mapping of tasks to different streaming multiprocessors (SMX), while a dameon-like MasterKernel is launched to override CUDA's default threadblock scheduler with Pagoda's software scheduler. Pagoda tracks the many tasks it is capable of running in a novel data structure called the TaskTable (shown in Figure 2),

PACT '16 September 11-15, 2016, Haifa, Israel

ACM ISBN 978-1-4503-4121-9/16/09.
DOI: http://dx.doi.org/10.1145/2967938.2974055

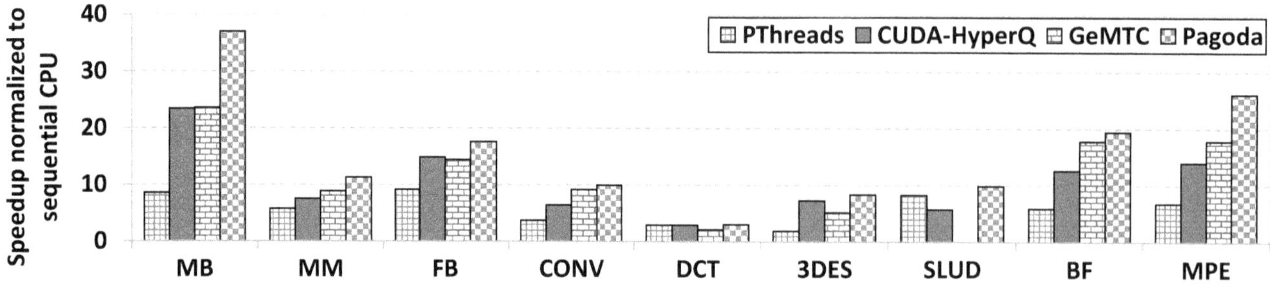

Figure 1: ***Overall Performance Comparison:*** *The number of tasks in each benchmark is constant (32K), except SLUD, which contains 273K tasks. Each GPU task uses 128 threads. The measurement of execution time contains both data copy and compute times. Pagoda significantly outperforms CUDA-HyperQ(1.43x), 20-core PThreads(2.44x), and GeMTC(1.33x), owing to the higher utilization. GeMTC sees high overheads when task execution times are low, such as in DCT and 3DES.*

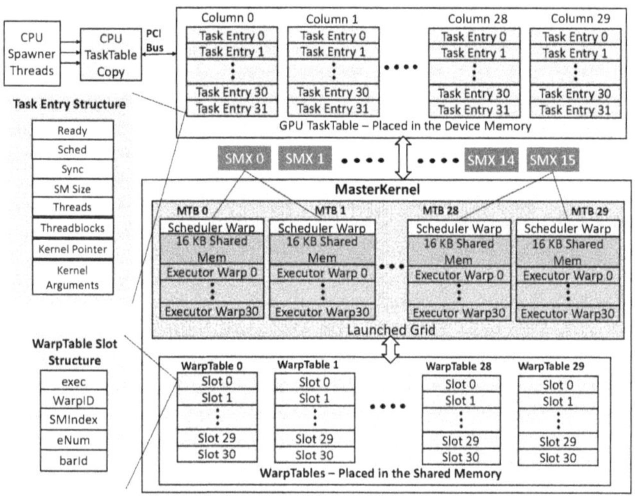

Figure 2: ***The MasterKernel Composition in the NVIDIA Tesla K40 GPU:*** *The 30 MasterKernel threadblocks (MTBs) have 1024 threads and 16 KB shared memory each. TaskTable is mirrored on both the CPU and GPU. Each entry of the task and warp table contains multiple flags to record states of scheduling. Two columns of warp table correspond to one SMX.*

which is stored in both CPU and GPU memory. The distributed Task:Table features a lazy copy mechanism that enables efficient task launching and scheduling. Since Pagoda overrides CUDA's default threadblock scheduler, it supports the native CUDA runtime model by implementing an efficient shared memory allocator in software and by managing named barriers to emulate the behaviour of __syncthreads.

3. EVALUATION

Figure 1 plots the performance of Pagoda and several other solutions. The GPU implemenations use an NVIDIA Tesla K40, while the PThreads and sequential implementations use two hyper-threaded 10 core Intel Xeon CPUs. Figure 1 shows that Pagoda obtains higher performance than other runtime schemes, namely, PThreads on the CPU, and CUDA-HyperQ [2] and GeMTC [1] on the GPU. The speedup is calculated over the entire execution time, i.e, it measures both compute and data copy times. The benefit is attributed to the high utilization achieved by Pagoda. The GeMTC versions do not use shared memory, since GeMTC has no support for it. We could not implement SLUD in GeMTC; GeMTC needs the number of tasks to be predefined, which is not the case in SLUD. SLUD represents an interesting case where HyperQ is slower than PThreads, but Pagoda is faster. Speedup achieved by all GPU schemes is low in DCT since the application is data copy bound. We tried OpenMP data parallelism, OS-based task scheduling, Python-based thread pooling, and PThreads-based task-level parallelism on the CPU to run narrow tasks. PThreads obtained the best results, which we include in Figure 1.

4. CONCLUSION

Pagoda is a GPU runtime system that overcomes underutilization in the presence of narrow tasks. Pagoda virtualizes GPU resources via MasterKernel, a persistently executing daemon on the GPU. Pagoda launches tasks on the GPU as long as some free warps are available. Unlike previous work, Pagoda supports all functionality of the native CUDA model. A key distinction in Pagoda is the task spawning and scheduling mechanism. Pagoda's novel TaskTable, which is shared between the CPU and GPU reduces handshaking during the spawning process to greatly reduce overhead.Pagoda achieves concurrent task scheduling, and overlaps task spawning, scheduling, and execution through pipelining. The experimental evaluation showed that Pagoda achieves geometric mean speedups of 1.43x over CUDA-HyperQ, 1.33x over GeMTC, and 2.44x over 20-core CPU Pthreads. The evaluation also showed that Pagoda can outperform static fusion schemes by 2.31x, and achieves much lower latency per task.

5. REFERENCES

[1] S. J. Krieder, J. M. Wozniak, T. Armstrong, M. Wilde, D. S. Katz, B. Grimmer, I. T. Foster, and I. Raicu. Design and evaluation of the gemtc framework for gpu-enabled many-task computing. In *Proceedings of the 23rd International Symposium on High-performance Parallel and Distributed Computing*, HPDC '14, pages 153–164, New York, NY, USA, 2014. ACM.

[2] NVIDIA. Hyper-Q Example. [Online]. Available: http://docs.nvidia.com/cuda/samples/6_Advanced/simpleHyperQ/doc/HyperQ.pdf, 2012. (accessed March. 5, 2016).

[3] K. Ousterhout, A. Panda, J. Rosen, S. Venkataraman, R. Xin, S. Ratnasamy, S. Shenker, and I. Stoica. The case for tiny tasks in compute clusters. In *Presented as part of the 14th Workshop on Hot Topics in Operating Systems*, Berkeley, CA, 2013. USENIX.

[4] J. Subhlok and G. Vondran. Optimal use of mixed task and data parallelism for pipelined computations. *J. Parallel Distrib. Comput.*, 60(3):297–319, 2000.

Student Research Poster: Slack-Aware Shared Bandwidth Management in GPUs

Saumay Dublish
University of Edinburgh
saumay.dublish@ed.ac.uk

ABSTRACT

Due to lack of sufficient compute threads in memory-intensive applications, GPUs often exhaust all the active warps and therefore, the memory latencies get exposed and appear in the critical path. In such a scenario, the shared on-chip and off-chip memory bandwidth appear more performance critical to cores with few or no active warps, in contrast to cores with sufficient active warps.

In this work, we use the slack of memory responses as a metric to identify the criticality of shared bandwidth to different cores. Consequently, we propose a slack-aware DRAM scheduling policy to prioritize requests from cores with negative slack, ahead of row-buffer hits. We also propose a request throttling mechanism to reduce the shared bandwidth demand of cores that have enough active warps to sustain execution. The above techniques help in reducing the memory latencies that appear in the critical path by increasing the memory latencies that can be hidden by multithreading.

Keywords

GPU; Memory Management; Bandwidth Bottleneck

1. INTRODUCTION

GPUs employ heavy multithreading to overlap the high latency memory operations with concurrent execution. When a *warp* executing on an SIMT core encounters a long latency memory operation, it is de-scheduled and deemed inactive, and a new warp is scheduled from a pool of active warps. In memory-intensive applications, cores often exhaust all the active warps thereby exposing the latency of memory operations. In such a scenario, the shared on-chip and off-chip memory bandwidth appear more performance critical to cores with few or no active warps, in contrast to cores with sufficient active warps. Therefore, when such disparate cores are present during the same epoch of execution, the criticality of the available memory bandwidth varies for different cores. In the existing policy, however, the pending memory request tries to acquire a fraction of the shared memory bandwidth as soon as it is conceived, while being oblivious to the relative criticality of the shared bandwidth across other cores.

In addition, memory latencies in memory-intensive applications often exceed the normal memory latencies by a factor of 2-3×. This is because each core employs a *greedy* policy to acquire the shared bandwidth in order to maximize its own bandwidth utilization, thereby excessively depleting the shared bandwidth and causing congestion. It is analogous to the *Tragedy of the Commons*, a problem in economics where a strategy best for an individual in using an unregulated common resource may not yield the most optimal outcome for the group.

In summary, the existing policy of allocating shared on-chip and off-chip memory bandwidth presents two major shortcomings– ❶ allocating bandwidth to cores without regard to their criticality, and ❷ excessive depletion of available bandwidth leading to congestion and therefore high memory latencies.

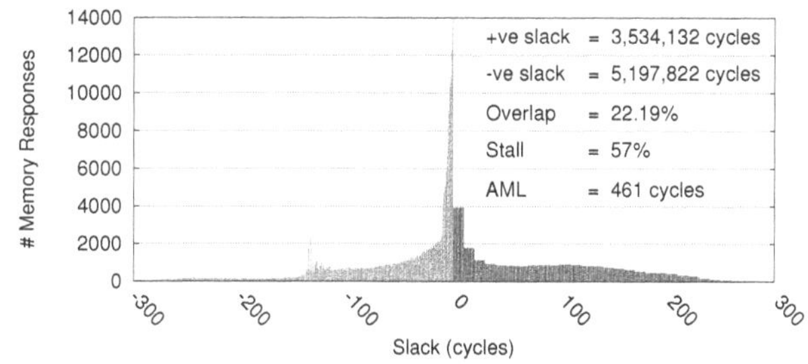

Figure 1: Slack distribution for dwt2D

2. SHARED BANDWIDTH MANAGEMENT

To measure the difference in criticality of shared memory bandwidth on different cores, we record the *slack* in utilizing a cache line that is newly fetched from the lower levels of the memory. We refer to the slack as positive if the memory response arrives sooner than it is required to prevent the core from stalling, and negative if the memory response arrives after the core has stalled. Therefore, positive slack is proportional to the number of active warps on a core whereas negative slack is equal to the cycles for which the core has been stalled since the last issue cycle. In Figure 1, we analyze *dwt2D*, a representative memory-intensive benchmark,

PACT '16 September 11-15, 2016, Haifa, Israel

ACM ISBN 978-1-4503-4121-9/16/09.
DOI: http://dx.doi.org/10.1145/2967938.2971470

and record the slack for each memory response that arrives at the cores. For our experiments, we model a Fermi-like architecture on GPGPU-Sim. We observe that despite high negative slack (also indicated by high stall cycle percentage of 57%), there is a considerable positive slack as well. We also detect the presence of positive and negative slack across different cores, coinciding in the *same epoch of execution*, where the epoch length is 100 cycles. We observe that in such epochs, on average 22.19% of the total negative slack overlaps with positive slack. It indicates that there exists an opportunity to prioritize memory requests from cores that are scarce in active warps (*poor cores*) over cores that have sufficient active warps (*rich cores*). It can lead to a reduction in stall cycles of poor cores without impacting the performance of rich cores. In addition, high average memory latency (AML) of 461 cycles, in contrast to the normal off-chip memory latency of 220 cycles, indicates high level of congestion in the memory system. Therefore, regulating the shared bandwidth allocation also presents an opportunity to reduce the severity of congestion.

To this end, we propose the following two techniques to address the shortcomings discussed above.

❶ *Slack-aware DRAM scheduling.* In epochs where cores with disparity in slack are detected, the proposed scheduler prioritizes requests from cores with negative slack, ahead of row-buffer hits. Therefore, it reduces the memory latencies that lie in the critical path (reducing negative slack) at the cost of increasing the latencies that can still be hidden by multithreading (reducing positive slack). Among cores with varying negative slack, we prioritize cores that are stalled for the longest durations as they have more accumulated pending hits on outstanding memory requests from other warps, allowing more warps to resume execution upon receiving memory response.

❷ *Request throttling.* While the above DRAM scheduling policy regulates the off-chip bandwidth allocation, the congestion in the on-chip memory hierarchy plays an important role in leading to high memory latencies. Therefore, in the proposed scheme, we throttle the rate of sending requests to the shared level for cores that contain high number of active warps, resulting in reduced congestion in the memory system without penalizing performance. In other words, lower the slack of a core, higher the bandwidth allocated to the core.

With the above techniques, preliminary results for *dwt2D* suggest a 7% reduction in negative slack and a 5% reduction in AML.

3. RELATED WORK

Jog *et al.* [2] proposed a DRAM scheduling policy based on core criticality, focusing solely on off-chip bandwidth management. In contrast, we propose a comprehensive policy for regulating on-chip bandwidth (via request throttling) and off-chip bandwidth (via slack-aware scheduling). In addition, they consider a metric that accords equal priority to all stalled cores. On the other hand, we assign different priorities to the stalled cores based on the *slack* metric, to benefit from the accumulated pending hits on outstanding memory requests.

Ebrahimi *et al.* [1] proposed source-throttling in the realm of CMPs with the objective of improving fairness in utilizing shared resources by different applications running on different cores. Similarly, other works have employed fairness oriented schemes to prevent starvation of applications in a co-scheduled environment. For instance, Mutlu *et al.* [3] proposed batch scheduling to prevent starvation of non-memory-intensive application over a memory-intensive application when both applications are scheduled together. In contrast, our work presents a memory management policy for threads *within the same application*, running on different cores in a GPU during different phases of execution.

4. REFERENCES

[1] E. Ebrahimi, C. J. Lee, O. Mutlu, and Y. N. Patt. Fairness via Source Throttling: A Configurable and High-performance Fairness Substrate for Multi-core Memory Systems. In *Proceedings of the Fifteenth Edition of ASPLOS on Architectural Support for Programming Languages and Operating Systems*, ASPLOS XV, pages 335–346, New York, NY, USA, 2010. ACM.

[2] A. Jog, O. Kayiran, A. Pattnaik, M. T. Kandemir, O. Mutlu, R. Iyer, and C. R. Das. Exploiting core criticality for enhanced GPU performance. In *Proceedings of the 2016 ACM SIGMETRICS International Conference on Measurement and Modeling of Computer Science, Antibes Juan-Les-Pins, France, June 14-18, 2016*, pages 351–363, 2016.

[3] O. Mutlu and T. Moscibroda. Parallelism-Aware Batch Scheduling: Enhancing Both Performance and Fairness of Shared DRAM Systems. In *Proceedings of the 35th Annual International Symposium on Computer Architecture*, ISCA '08, pages 63–74, Washington, DC, USA, 2008. IEEE Computer Society.

Student Research Poster - From Processing-in-Memory to Processing-in-Storage

Roman Kaplan
Technion – Israel Institute of Technology
Haifa, Israel
sromanks@tx.technion.ac.il

ABSTRACT

In Most contemporary high performance computers are based on von Neumann architecture. It is widely recognized that such architecture suffers from CPU-memory bottleneck. The problem affects both performance and power efficiency of multicore and manycore architectures. With continuation of CPU scaling (driven by Moore's law and parallelization), the von Neumann bottleneck problem will become even more acute.

Another major factor affecting today's high performance computing is the slowdown in scaling of traditional charge-based memories such as DRAM and NAND Flash. In response, many novel nano-devices and materials are under investigation to create an alternative to charge-based memory, namely *resistive memory*. Such alternatives include memristors, RRAM, PCM, 3D Xpoint, STT-MRAM and others. These technologies have a wide range of potential applications beyond memory, including solid state disks, digital computing, neuromorphic computing, etc.

New approaches for processing-in-memory (PiM) have been suggested. One promising technology is 3D stacking, which integrates separate logic and DRAM layers with high-bandwidth, low-energy through-silicon vias. Leveraging 3D stacking technology, researchers have proposed near-DRAM acceleration architectures that integrate accelerator logic and custom 3D DRAM devices. They focus on either accelerator architecture, where the memory system is separate from the host processor's main memory system or the integration of accelerators and DRAM.

The amounts of data gathered by companies and institutions keeps increasing exponentially (IoT serves as the most recent contributor), with it the difficulty to process big-data datasets. Numerous studies have established that the main performance and energy bottlenecks in case of big-data processing is transferring the data from storage to memory. Therefore moving the bulk of processing from CPU to main memory has a limited benefit and will not provide the orders of magnitude improvement in energy and performance required to handle the challenges of big-data.

In my research, I am studying a new technology and approach – *Processing-in-Storage* (*PrinS*). Resistive technologies have shown high-density, high-endurance and low-energy. Such features might provide the conditions for a peta-scale storage device, where each cell has both storage and processing capabilities.

There are numerous research directions in studying the approach, to list a few: building peripheral circuitry to support multiple types of computations, maintaining low latency for data access, providing high-throughput processing, ease of programmability, etc.

My first two works showed different types of applications for PrinS. The first (*Deduplication in Resistive CAM based SSD,* in press) showed how data deduplication will benefit from the in-storage approach. Data deduplication is a technique for storing only a single copy of each data block in a storage appliance. In today's storage appliances, large key-value data structures are required for managing the single-copy condition. Conventional implementations of deduplication require a dedicated computer within the storage appliance. In case of PrinS, Content Addressable Memory (CAM) capabilities are possible by comparing the entire stored data with a specific key. I showed that most of the data structures for managing deduplication are no longer required with PrinS, in addition to a an improvement of I/O performance and energy consumption.

My second work (*an in-storage implementation of Smith-Waterman in Resistive CAM*) focused on a different application for PrinS - DNA local sequence alignment, a well-known and computationally intensive problem in bioinformatics. The Smith-Waterman algorithm (S-W) is the most efficient algorithm to provide an optimal solution for the problem. It is based on dynamic programming and requires to calculate a scoring matrix which of size $O(n^2)$, resulting in execution with quadratic time complexity. Many works on accelerating the algorithm exist. In recent years, the most widely-used accelerator for the task is GPGPU. A recent work by Sandes et al. examined the execution of human vs. chimpanzee chromosomes (up to 250 Million base-pairs in length) on a 128-node cluster with a total of 384 GPUs. In my work, I have showed a PrinS implementation for S-W and simulated its execution time. The results showed that in-storage execution of S-W can improve performance by 3.4x and orders of magnitude in energy compared to the 384 GPU implementation.

The future direction I will pursue is to suggest a comprehensive design for a peta-scale PrinS device. It will include a complete architectural description, in-module details, cell-level SPICE simulations, self-developed cycle-accurate simulator and demonstration of applications. The application will include a deep learning neural net with complete benchmark execution. Additional machine learning algorithms, such as KNN and PCA will also be examined. The goal is to compare state-of-the-art performance and energy consumption of the mentioned algorithm to a PrinS peta-scale device.

PACT '16, September 11-15, 2016, Haifa, Israel
ACM 978-1-4503-4121-9/16/09.
http://dx.doi.org/10.1145/2967938.2971463

Student Research Poster: Network Controller Emulation on a Sidecore for Unmodified Virtual Machines

Arthur Kiyanovski
Technion, Israel Institute of Technology
arthurk@cs.technion.ac.il

ABSTRACT

Paravirtual I/O devices are known to outperform emulated I/O devices but this performance improvement comes with two major drawbacks: Guest machine owners must install hypervisor-specific device drivers every time they switch hypervisors, and these device drivers must be implemented by the hypervisor providers for all major operating systems. Emulated devices do not suffer from these drawbacks because their drivers are implemented by the manufacturers of the bare-metal devices, and come preinstalled.

We used optimizations from the virtio-net paravirtual network device combined with a sidecore to improve emulation of the E1000 network device in the QEMU hypervisor. Initial results show that the performance gap between emulated and paravirtual I/O devices is smaller than was previously thought. The small performance difference between paravirtual and emulated devices, along with the aforementioned advantages of the latter, makes emulation a natural choice when flexibility takes precedence over performance.

1. VIRTIO-NET BASED OPTIMIZATIONS

We found four reasons why E1000 emulation is slower than virtio-net: 1. It breaks down the TCP segments into MTU sized frames. 2. It calculates the TCP checksum for each segment. 3. It copies the data from the guest to the host before sending it. 4. It handles interrupt coalescing poorly for throughput scenarios.

Virtio-net avoids the first two problems by leaving segment breakdown and checksum calculation to the hardware of the bare-metal network device, which performs both tasks much more quickly. Virtio-net doesn't perform copying since the buffers will not change until they are handled by the device. Finally, in throughput scenarios, virtio-net raises interrupts at a considerably lower rate than E1000 emulation, reducing the overhead caused by interrupts.

We used the aforementioned characteristics of virtio-net to solve these four problems in the emulated E1000, increasing throughput significantly. In a setup of guest-to-host transmission, while forcing maximum size (64KB) TCP segments in the guest, we reduced the throughput gap between virtio-net and the E1000 emulation from 14.3X to 1.3X, when assigning a single core to run the guest machine.

PACT '16 September 11-15, 2016, Haifa, Israel

ACM ISBN 978-1-4503-4121-9/16/09.

DOI: http://dx.doi.org/10.1145/2967938.2971469

2. E1000 WITH A SIDECORE

Whenever a device is virtualized using the trap and emulate paradigm, exits are a significant slowdown factor. An exit is the context switch between the guest and host machine, which happens when the guest machine tries to perform an instruction that needs to be emulated by the hypervisor. Paravirtual devices are designed to minimize the number of exits. This is in contrast to emulated devices, whose design is dictated by the specifications of the device they emulate. Emulated devices thus suffer more from the overhead caused by exits. In the E1000 emulation, most exits occur when the device driver writes to E1000's registers.

The sidecore paradigm is known to reduce the number of exits. It was first introduced by Kumar *et al.* [3] and later employed in several other works [1, 2], but has never been used before with a full-fledged emulated I/O device.

When using the sidecore paradigm, the device registers are mapped to the memory so that when the registers are written to, exits no longer occur. A polling thread is run on a dedicated core, polls the control registers of the device and emulates the necessary behavior whenever a register's value is changed.

We used a sidecore on the registers that control the transmission of frames. Combining this with the virtio-net based optimizations, we reduced the throughput gap between virtio-net and the E1000 emulation from 18.2X to 1.06X when using the same setup as before, only this time assigning 2 cores to run the guest machine.

3. REFERENCES

[1] N. Amit, M. Ben-Yehuda, D. Tsafrir, and A. Schuster. vIOMMU: Efficient IOMMU Emulation. In *USENIX Annual Technical Conference (ATC)*, 2011.

[2] N. Har'El, A. Gordon, A. Landau, M. Ben-Yehuda, A. Traeger, and L. Razya. Efficient and Scalable Paravirtual I/O System. In *USENIX Annual Technical Conference (ATC)*, 2013.

[3] S. Kumar, H. Raj, and K. Schwan. Re-architecting VMMs for Multicore Systems: The Sidecore Approach. In *Workshop on Interaction between Operating Systems & Computer Architecture (WIOSCA)*, 2007.

Student Research Poster: A Low Complexity Cache Sharing Mechanism to Address System Fairness*

Vicent Selfa, Julio Sahuquillo, Salvador Petit and María E. Gómez
Dept. of Computer Engineering
Universitat Politècnica de València
viselol@disca.upv.es

1. INTRODUCTION

Shared caches have become, *de facto*, the common design choice in current multi-cores, ranging from embedded devices to high-performance processors. In these systems, requests from multiple applications compete for the cache resources, degrading to different extents their *progress*, quantified as the performance of individual applications compared to isolated execution. The difference between the progresses of the running applications yields the system to unpredictable behavior and causes a *fairness* problem. This problem can be addressed by carefully partitioning cache resources among the contending applications, but to be effective, a partitioning approach needs to estimate the per-application progress.

This work proposes Fair-Progress Cache Partitioning (FPCP), a low-overhead cache partitioning approach which addresses fairness by distributing cache resources among applications depending on their progress. To estimate progress, we have implemented two state-of-the-art performance models, ASM [3] and PTCA [1], which estimate, at runtime, the performance a given application would have if executed in isolation.

2. THE FPCP PARTITIONING APPROACH

FPCP implements a tree-based algorithm, so the applications running on the processor are subdivided recursively until the subsets have only two applications, building a binary tree. Figure 1 shows, as an example, the resulting tree for 8 applications sharing a cache in an 8-core processor. Each leaf node contains the number of ways assigned to an application as well as its progress.

Each non-leaf node, on the other hand, stores i) the total number of ways assigned to its children and ii) the minimum progress between its children. To ease the understanding of the example, we use dashed lines to indicate the least-progressing child node.

Each Level i in the tree except Level 0 has an associated number of intervals I_i (i indicates the level depth). Every I_i intervals, for each node in the i level, the minimum progress between its children in the $i-1$ level is determined and stored in the node. Then, there are three possible cases: 1) The node has the same number of ways than its children combined. When this occurs, the most progressing

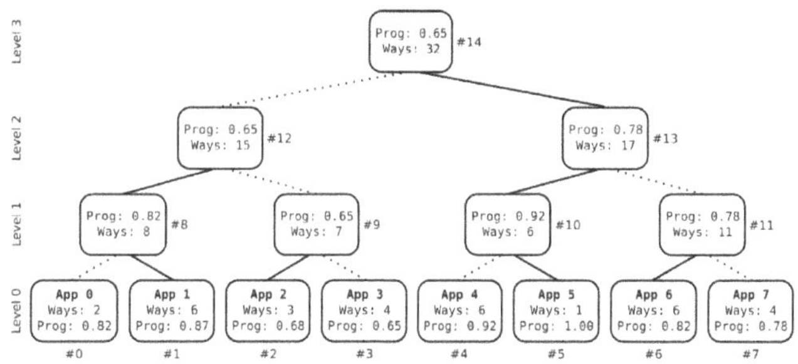

Figure 1: Logical binary tree structure.

child relinquishes a cache way (provided it has more than one) in favor of the least progressing child. 2) The node has more ways assigned than its children. In this case, no child has its ways reduced, but the least progressing node gains a way. 3) The node has less ways assigned than its children. If this happens, then no child receives a way, and a way is subtracted from the most progressing child, if possible, or its brother, if not.

FPCP has been evaluated and compared against a baseline without partitioning and two state-of-the-art cache partitioning approaches UCP [2] and ASM-Cache [3] over 175 4-application workloads and 100 8-application workloads.

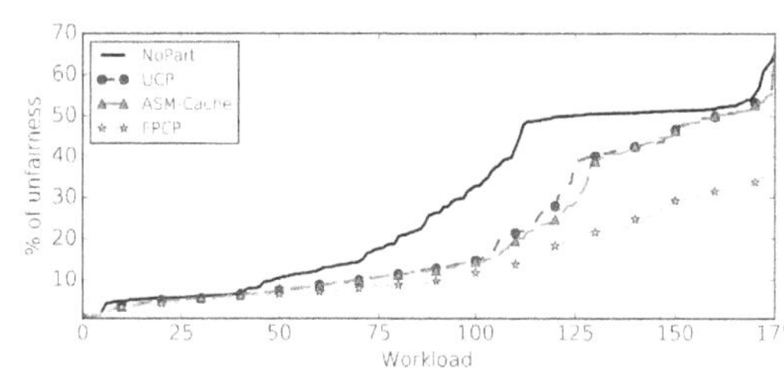

Figure 2: Unfairness results.

Requiring less hardware complexity than any other existing proposal, FPCP reduces unfairness by 48%, on average, for the 4-application workloads (see Figure 2), and by 28%, on average, for the 8-application workloads. Moreover, fairness results are achieved without damaging the performance, with FPCP achieving similar performance results to the best performing approach.

3. REFERENCES

[1] K. Du Bois, S. Eyerman, and L. Eeckhout. Per-thread cycle accounting in multicore processors. *ACM Trans. Archit. Code Optim.*, 9(4):29:1–29:22, 2013.

[2] M. Qureshi and Y. Patt. Utility-based cache partitioning: A low-overhead, high-performance, runtime mechanism to partition shared caches. In *MICRO*, pages 423–432, 2006.

[3] L. Subramanian, V. Seshadri, A. Ghosh, S. Khan, and O. Mutlu. The application slowdown model: Quantifying and controlling the impact of inter-application interference at shared caches and main memory. In *MICRO*, pages 62–75, 2015.

*Work supported by MINECO with Plan E funds under Grant TIN2015-66972-C5-1-R and Grant TIN2014-62246-EXP, and by the Valencian Government under Grant AICO/2016/059.

PACT '16 September 11-15, 2016, Haifa, Israel

ACM ISBN 978-1-4503-4121-9/16/09.
DOI: http://dx.doi.org/10.1145/2967938.2971464

Student Research Poster: A Scalable General Purpose System for Large-Scale Graph Processing

Jiawen Sun*
Supervisors: Hans Vandierendonck and Dimitrios S. Nikolopoulos
Queen's University Belfast, University Road, Belfast,UK BT7 1LR
jsun03@qub.ac.uk

1 Introduction

Graph analytics is an important and computationally demanding class of data analytics. It is essential to balance scalability, ease-of-use and high performance in large scale graph analytics. As such, it is necessary to hide the complexity of parallelism, data distribution and memory locality behind an abstract interface [2].

Our aim is to build a scalable graph analytics framework that does not demand significant parallel programming experience based on NUMA-awareness. The realization of such a system faces two key problems: (i) how to develop a scale-free parallel programming framework that scales efficiently across NUMA domains; (ii) how to efficiently apply graph partitioning in order to create separate and largely independent work items that can be distributed among threads.

2 Graph Processing Model

We address the scalability issue through extending parallel programming models using numa-aware for parallelism. In the task dataflow model all data touched by a task is explicitly annotated, along with read/write side effects. This allows the runtime to schedule tasks during execution while respecting dataflow dependencies [4].

We build on Swan [4], a Cilk extension that supports dataflow with NUMA-awareness. This allows executing the Ligra graph analytics system [3] unmodified in shared memory. Ligra optimizes the graph traversal method depending on whether the frontier, the set of currently active vertices, is densely populated or sparsely populated. If densely populated, it scans over all vertices to locate active vertices in either a *backward* or a *forward* traversal [3]. If sparsely populated, it performs direct access to the active vertices in *forward* mode.

3 Graph Partitioning

We extend Ligra [3] to partition graphs using the same strategy as GraphChi [1] and Polymer [5]. This partitions the set of edges and *replicates* vertices across partitions.

Partitioning introduces a significant number of vertices with zero in- or out-degree. We extend the graph representation by adding to each vertex the index of the next vertex

PACT '16, September 11–15, 2016, Haifa, Israel.

ACM ISBN 978-1-4503-4121-9/16/09.
DOI: http://dx.doi.org/10.1145/2967938.2971465

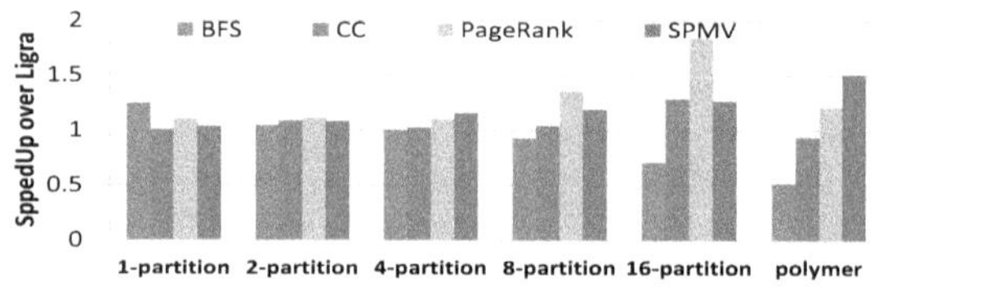

Figure 1: Speed-up over Ligra for twitter graph (96 threads). N-partition is our optimized partitioning method, No-NUMA-Optimization, polymer uses 4-partition, twitter graph.

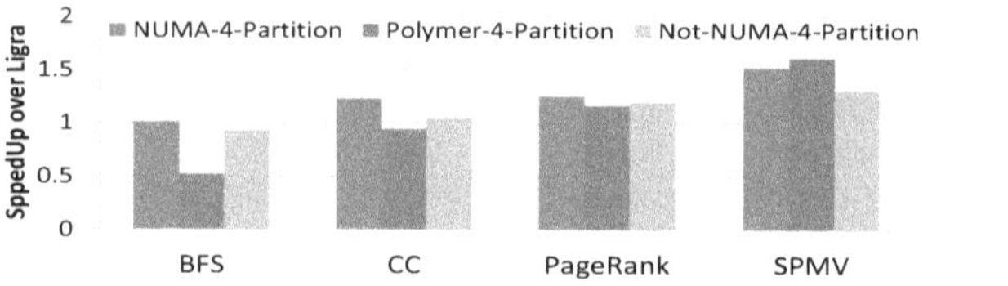

Figure 2: NUMA optimization of 4-partition across 4 NUMA node machine (96 threads), twitter graph

with non-zero degree. This allows us to skip ahead during graph traversal and improves performance by 11.5% on average. We furthermore optimize the calculation of the frontier. We adapt the traversal routines to operate on either sparse or dense frontiers to avoid conversion of the frontier.

Preliminary results are on a quad-socket 2.6GHz Intel Xeon E7-4860 processor,totaling 96 cores. They show that partitioning increases instruction count for *dense backward*, which affects BFS and CC. While Polymer performs worse on CC compared to Ligra, our optimization improves performance over Ligra. The partitioning furthermore improves locality during the *dense forward*, which explains improved performance for PageRank and SPMV (Figure 1, 2). After NUMA-aware scheduling, we could get better performance.

In future work we will further investigate graph partitioning to improve performance and refine the scale-free programming model.

4 References

[1] A. Kyrola, G. E. Blelloch, and C. Guestrin. GraphChi: Large-scale graph computation on just a PC. In *OSDI*, 2012.

[2] G. Malewicz *et al.* Pregel: a system for large-scale graph processing. In *SIGMOD*, 2010.

[3] J. Shun and G. E. Blelloch. Ligra: a lightweight graph processing framework for shared memory. In *PPoPP*, 2013.

[4] H. Vandierendonck, G. Tzenakis, and D. S. Nikolopoulos. A unified scheduler for recursive and task dataflow parallelism. In *PACT*, 2011.

[5] K. Zhang, R. Chen, and H. Chen. NUMA-aware graph-structured analytics. In *PPoPP*, 2015.

Student Research Poster: Compiling Boolean Circuits to Non-deterministic Branching Programs to be Implemented by Light Switching Circuits.

Tartakovsky Vladislav
Haifa University

1. INTRODUCTION

The MOS transistor technology is well studied and found in billions of devices, however, there are several problems which force us to search for an alternative:

- The major problem- we almost reached the limits of current technology. Transistors are already being fabricated in atomic scale and soon we will be unable to make them any smaller.
- Each transistor device has switching and propagation delays since it is essentially a composition of resistors an capacitors.
- Current digital devices use CMOS based Boolean circuits (BCs) where one transistor in gate I triggers the transistors of the next gate in the BC and the calculation speed is limited by BC's depth.

We propose to bypass the depth limitations of BCs by replacing them with optical non-deterministic branching programs (NBPs) which are basically networks of switching elements. In NBPs the computation is carried out as follows:

1. Based on input values all the switches of the NBP are reconfigured in one parallel step;
2. A signal is propagated through the NBP and its exit locations determine the result of the computation.

We propose to overcome technological limitations of CMOS by using optical ring resonators (ORR) [4], as switching device for NBPs.

This approach is very promising, since optical switch devices don't have any propagation delay, the signal is propagated with the speed of light (in silicon). Optic device fabrication is already exists in industry. It is rather cheap and uses the same methods as CMOS device fabrication.
Other quantum effect based technologies can be used to combine NBPs in current CMOS VLSI chips to reduce power and computation latencies. For example : Ballistic Deflection Transistors (BDT) [1] and Mechanical Mirrors(MEM) [3].

We propose a design process for these mixed NBPs + BCs chips that is based on high-level synthesis from C/C++-code to silicon layout where the main component is a compiler that efficiently transforms BCs to NBPs without incurring large size blowup of the resulting NBPs. Note that theoretically had BCs of size n could be converted to NBPs of size $poly(n)$ then the polynomial hierarchy would collapse to NC and all sequential polynomial computations could be implemented with parallel log-depth circuits. Indeed, all restricted formats of NBPs that have been proposed, suffers from large size blowup[2] when converted from BCs.

Using NBPs we developed an heuristic algorithm, which builds NBP from one node, iteratively growing it up. The algorithm does the optimizations inside each iteration on relatively small graphs, preventing size blowup.

The current system composed of: LLVM-compiler, conversion of byte-code to algebraic circuits (ACs), synthesizing AC to BC and the BC to NBP algorithm. Preliminary results already show that this system achieves high conversion ratio where not only there is no size blowup but the resulting NBPs are smaller than their origin BCs. Additional unit for SPICE simulation of the resulting NBP circuits using one of the above three technologies will be developed to complement the proof for feasibility and the expected gain of the proposed process.

PACT '16 September 11-15, 2016, Haifa, Israel

ACM ISBN 978-1-4503-4121-9/16/09.
DOI: http://dx.doi.org/10.1145/2967938.2971468

2. REFERENCES

[1] Q. Diduck, M. Margala, and M. J. Feldman. A terahertz transistor based on geometrical deflection of ballistic current. In *2006 IEEE MTT-S International Microwave Symposium Digest*, pages 345–347. IEEE, 2006.
[2] C. Meinel and T. Theobald. *Algorithms and Data Structures in VLSI Design: OBDD-foundations and applications*. Springer Science & Business Media, 2012.
[3] M. J. Moghimi, K. N. Chattergoon, C. R. Wilson, and D. L. Dickensheets. High speed focus control mems mirror with controlled air damping for vital microscopy. *Journal of Microelectromechanical Systems*, 22(4):938–948, 2013.
[4] Y. H. Wen, O. Kuzucu, T. Hou, M. Lipson, and A. L. Gaeta. All-optical switching of a single resonance in silicon ring resonators. *Optics letters*, 36(8):1413–1415.

Student Research Poster: Software Out-of-Order Execution for In-Order Architectures

Kim-Anh Tran
Department of Information Technology
Uppsala University
kim-anh.tran@it.uu.se

ABSTRACT

Processor cores are divided into two categories: fast and power-hungry out-of-order processors, and efficient, but slower in-order processors. To achieve high performance with low-energy budgets, this proposal aims to deliver out-of-order processing by software (SWOOP) on in-order architectures.

Problem: A primary cause for slowdown in in-order processors is last-level cache misses (caused by difficult to predict data-dependent loads), resulting in cores stalling.

Solution: As loads are non-blocking operations, independent instructions are scheduled to run before the loads return. We execute critical load instructions earlier in the program for a three-fold benefit: increasing memory and instruction level parallelism, and hiding memory latency.

Related work: Some instruction scheduling policies attempt to hide memory latency, but scheduling is confined by basic block limits and register pressure. Software pipelining [3] is restricted by dependencies between instructions and decoupled access-execute (DAE) [1] suffers from address re-computation. Unlike EPIC [2] (evolved from VLIW), SWOOP does not require hardware support for predicated execution, speculative loads and their verification, delayed exception handling, memory disambiguation etc.

Keywords

Software Out-of-Order Execution; Energy; Compiler

1. THE SWOOP COMPILER

Contribution: (1) *Overcoming dependent loads.* SWOOP detects dependent load chains and splits them up into multiple access phases, enabling independent instructions to be scheduled in-between. (2) *Handling of unknown memory dependencies.* May-aliasing loads are turned into safe prefetches. (3) *Balancing of latency and register pressure.* SWOOP selectively turns safe loads to prefetches to control register pressure. We transform the code using LLVM in a way similar to DAE. Figure 1 shows the transformation and execution. SWOOP (1) hoists critical loads, (2) creates multiple access phases to maximize separation, (3) turns may-aliasing loads to prefetches to overcome unknown dependencies, and (4) inserts a *ckmiss* instruction. On a cache miss in an access phase, the ckmiss will trigger a branch to the next iteration's access phase. We introduce a register remapping technique to ensure that execute phases consume registers of their respective access phases. Figure 2 shows the normalized speedup of memory-bound benchmarks (SPEC 2006CPU, CIGAR, NAS) evaluated with the Sniper Simulator. We compare an in-order core (InO~Cortex-A7), the SWOOP core (InO with register remapping) and an out-of-order core (OoO~Cortex-A15), and achieve an average improvement of 34% in runtime and a reduction by 23% in energy consumption (not shown) over the InO.

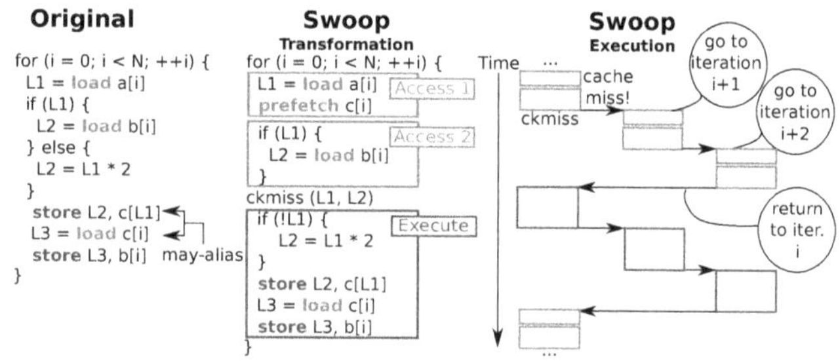

Figure 1: SWOOP Transformation.

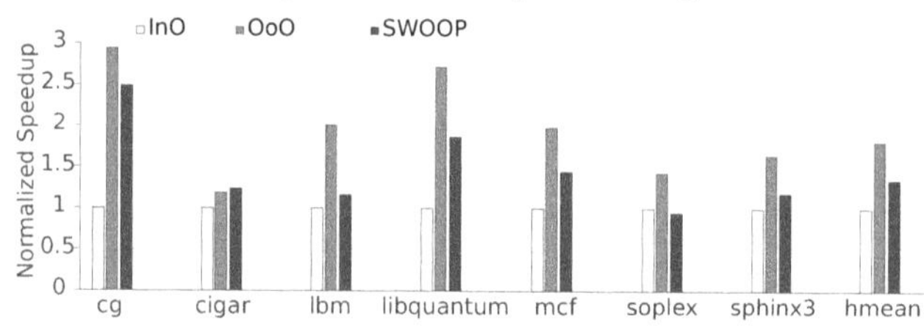

Figure 2: Normalized speed up.

2. ACKNOWLEDGMENTS

I would like to thank my advisors Alexandra Jimborean and Stefanos Kaxiras for their guidance and support.

3. REFERENCES

[1] A. Jimborean et al. Fix the code. don't tweak the hardware: A new compiler approach to voltage-frequency scaling. In *CGO*, 2014.

[2] J. L. Hennessy and D. A. Patterson. *Computer Architecture: A Quantitative Approach, Appendix H.* Morgan Kaufmann Publishers Inc., 2011.

[3] M. Lam. Software pipelining: An effective scheduling technique for VLIW machines. In *PLDI*, 1988.

PACT '16 September 11-15, 2016, Haifa, Israel

ACM ISBN 978-1-4503-4121-9/16/09.

DOI: http://dx.doi.org/10.1145/2967938.2971466

Author Index

www.ingramcontent.com/pod-product-compliance
Ingram Content Group UK Ltd.
Pitfield, Milton Keynes, MK11 3LW, UK
UKHW051413290926
15471UKWH00009B/1581

9 781450 346788